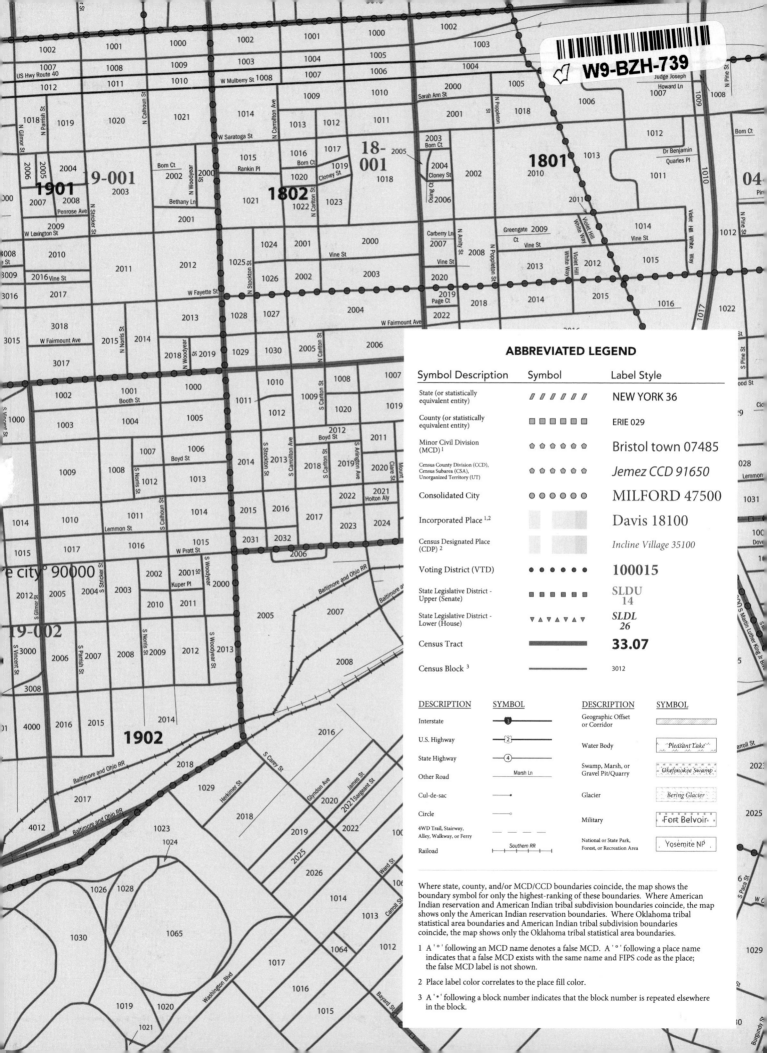

ABBREVIATED LEGEND

Symbol Description	Symbol	Label Style
State (or statistically equivalent entity)	/ / / / / /	NEW YORK 36
County (or statistically equivalent entity)	▢ ▢ ▢ ▢ ▢ ▢	ERIE 029
Minor Civil Division (MCD) [1]	⬠ ⬠ ⬠ ⬠ ⬠	Bristol town 07485
Census County Division (CCD), Census Subarea (CSA), Unorganized Territory (UT)	⬠ ⬠ ⬠ ⬠ ⬠	*Jemez CCD 91650*
Consolidated City	⚬ ⚬ ⚬ ⚬ ⚬ ⚬	MILFORD 47500
Incorporated Place [1,2]		Davis 18100
Census Designated Place (CDP) [2]		*Incline Village 35100*
Voting District (VTD)	● ● ● ● ● ●	**100015**
State Legislative District - Upper (Senate)	▪ ▪ ▪ ▪ ▪ ▪	SLDU 14
State Legislative District - Lower (House)	▽ ▲ ▽ ▲ ▽ ▲ ▽	*SLDL 26*
Census Tract	▬▬▬▬▬	**33.07**
Census Block [3]	─────	3012

DESCRIPTION	SYMBOL	DESCRIPTION	SYMBOL
Interstate	—③—	Geographic Offset or Corridor	
U.S. Highway	—②—	Water Body	*Pleasant Lake*
State Highway	—④—	Swamp, Marsh, or Gravel Pit/Quarry	*Okefenokee Swamp*
Other Road	Marsh Ln		
Cul-de-sac	•———•	Glacier	*Bering Glacier*
Circle	•———○	Military	Fort Belvoir
4WD Trail, Stairway, Alley, Walkway, or Ferry	– – – –	National or State Park, Forest, or Recreation Area	Yosemite NP
Raiload	Southern RR		

Where state, county, and/or MCD/CCD boundaries coincide, the map shows the boundary symbol for only the highest-ranking of these boundaries. Where American Indian reservation and American Indian tribal subdivision boundaries coincide, the map shows only the American Indian reservation boundaries. Where Oklahoma tribal statistical area boundaries and American Indian tribal subdivision boundaries coincide, the map shows only the Oklahoma tribal statistical area boundaries.

1 A '°' following an MCD name denotes a false MCD. A '°' following a place name indicates that a false MCD exists with the same name and FIPS code as the place; the false MCD label is not shown.

2 Place label color correlates to the place fill color.

3 A '*' following a block number indicates that the block number is repeated elsewhere in the block.

ENCYCLOPEDIA OF THE
U.S. CENSUS

ENCYCLOPEDIA OF THE
U.S. CENSUS

From the Constitution to the American Community Survey

SECOND EDITION

Editors
Margo J. Anderson,
Constance F. Citro,
and Joseph J. Salvo

Los Angeles | London | New Delhi
Singapore | Washington DC

Los Angeles | London | New Delhi
Singapore | Washington DC

For information:

CQ Press
An Imprint of SAGE Publications, Inc.
2455 Teller Road
Thousand Oaks, California 91320
E-mail: order@sagepub.com

SAGE Publications Ltd.
1 Oliver's Yard
55 City Road
London, EC1Y 1SP
United Kingdom

SAGE Publications India Pvt. Ltd.
B 1/I 1 Mohan Cooperative Industrial Area
Mathura Road, New Delhi 110 044
India

SAGE Publications Asia-Pacific Pte. Ltd.
33 Pekin Street #02-01
Far East Square
Singapore 048763

Development Editor: John Martino
Production Editor: Elizabeth Kline
Copy Editors :   Janine Stanley-Dunham and Paula Fleming
Typesetter: C&M Digitals (P), Ltd.
Proofreader: Kate Stern
Indexer: Enid Zafran
Cover Designer: Naylor Designs, Inc.
Marketing Manager: Ben Krasney

Printed in the United States of America

Library of Congress Cataloging-in-Publication Data

Encyclopedia of the U.S. Census : from the constitution to the American community survey / Margo J. Anderson, Citro, Constance F., Salvo, Joseph J. — 2nd ed.

p. cm.
title: Encyclopedia of the United States census Includes bibliographical references and index.

ISBN 978-1-60871-025-6 (alk. paper)

1. United States—Census—Encyclopedias. I. Anderson, Margo J., Citro, Constance F., Salvo, Joseph J.

HA37.U55E53 2013
304.6072′3—dc23   2011036339

This book is printed on acid-free paper.

12 13 14 15 16 10 9 8 7 6 5 4 3 2 1

ABOUT THE EDITORS

Margo J. Anderson is professor of history & urban studies at the University of Wisconsin–Milwaukee. She specializes in American social, urban, and women's history and has research interests in urban history, the history of the social sciences, and the development of statistical data systems, particularly the census. She is the author of *The American Census: A Social History* (1988) and coauthor, with Stephen E. Fienberg, of *Who Counts? The Politics of Census-Taking in Contemporary America* (revised edition, 2001). Most recently she coedited, with Victor Greene, *Perspectives on Milwaukee's Past (2009)*. She served as president of the Social Science History Association in 2006, is a fellow of the American Statistical Association, and has served as chair of the History Department and of the Executive Committee of the Faculty at the University of Wisconsin–Milwaukee. She holds MA and PhD degrees in history from Rutgers University.

Constance F. Citro is director of the Committee on National Statistics (CNSTAT) at the National Academy of Sciences/National Research Council, an independent nonprofit organization that advises the nation in accordance with its 1863 congressional charter. Prior to becoming director in 2004, she was a senior program officer with CNSTAT for 20 years and, before that, an American Statistical Association/National Science Foundation research fellow at the Bureau of the Census, a vice president of Mathematica Policy Research Inc., and a vice president of Data Use and Access Laboratories (DUALabs). For CNSTAT, she served as study director for numerous panels, including the Panel on Estimates of Poverty for Small Geographic Areas, the Panel on Poverty and Family Assistance, the Panel to Evaluate the Survey of Income and Program Participation, and the Panel on Decennial Census Methodology. Her research has focused on the quality and accessibility of large, complex microdata files and analysis related to income and poverty measurement. She is a fellow of the American Statistical Association, an elected member of the International Statistical Institute, and a past president of the Association of Public Data Users. She received MA and PhD degrees in political science from Yale University.

Joseph J. Salvo is director of the Population Division at the New York City Department of City Planning. He began his career as a demographer/statistician at the U.S. Bureau of the Census. He is a former president of the Association of Public Data Users; is on the Board of Trustees of the Center for Migration Studies; and has been a member of the Commerce Secretary's 2000 Census Advisory Committee, the Census Bureau Scientific Advisory Committee, and the Population Association of America's Committee on Population Statistics. Salvo has served on several National Research Council panels, including the Panel on Future Census Methods, Panel on the Functionality and Usability of the American Community Survey, and Panel on Group Quarters in the American Community Survey; he also chaired a special Working Group on the 2000 Census Local Update of Census Addresses (LUCA) program. His recent research includes various studies on the evaluation and use of the American Community Survey and the demography of immigration. He is a recipient of the Sloan Public Service Award from the Fund for the City of New York and is a fellow of the American Statistical Association. He holds MA and PhD degrees in sociology from Fordham University.

ACKNOWLEDGMENTS

Many people contributed to the success of this revised and updated encyclopedia. More than ninety distinguished editors and contributors appear as authors or revisers of entries for this edition. In addition, many others made the success of the volume possible, including our editors at CQ Press. Doug Goldenberg-Hart conceived of a volume that would update and expand the 2000 edition. Joan Gossett and Elizabeth Kline managed the final production of the volume and the myriad details of design and composition that result in an elegant book. Copy editors Janine Stanley-Dunham and Paula L. Fleming produced the professional text. Naylor Design produced our new cover design; intern Margaret Palmer helped with file formatting. Throughout, John Martino worked tirelessly with the editorial board to make the vision a reality and provided the administrative support necessary for a large project with many writers.

The project could not have been accomplished without the help and support of officials and experts at the U.S. Census Bureau. Several current and former bureau staffers wrote for the encyclopedia, and many others provided reference support and good words for the project. Particular thanks for the second edition go to Thomas Mesenbourg, Laura Schebler, Victor Romero, and Michael Morgan and, from the first edition, Carolee Bush, Susan Miskura, Jorge del Pinal, Roderick Harrison, David Pemberton, Paula Schneider, and Stephanie Shipp. Desmond Barlow of AP Images went the extra mile to identify the two images from the previous edition.

CONTENTS

⁓

INTRODUCTION

The first edition of the *Encyclopedia of the U.S. Census* (published in 2000) provided for the first time a comprehensive, one-volume work that offered ready reference information on the U.S. decennial census. It described the concepts, politics, and history of the decennial census while also offering clear, accessible information on current census methods and results. In short, the encyclopedia has supplied authoritative, concise, and accurate answers to questions about census taking in the United States, past and present.

Nevertheless, the time has come for a second edition, and not simply to incorporate the results of the 2000 and 2010 censuses. Since 2000, the decennial census long-form sample, which was the source of social and economic data for geographic areas and population groups in the United States from 1960 to 2000, has been replaced by the continuous American Community Survey (ACS). The second edition covers this sea change in official demographic data collection with a new special section on the American Community Survey, which appears at the beginning of the entries. Other entries are also updated to incorporate this development. In addition, a host of new and updated entries capture the continued conceptual, methodological, and technical changes that affected the design and execution of the 2010 census. The new edition therefore is an up-to-date as well as historical look at the U.S census, including census results as of spring 2011. It is also available in a searchable digital format by subscription at http://library.cqpress.com/.

The essays in this volume, organized alphabetically, identify the principal techniques, terms, processes, issues, and concepts of census taking. The underlying logic of the volume is based on the logic of census taking in the United States. We include essays on the mechanics of the census: the procedures for preparing the questionnaire, printing and mailing the forms, retrieving the information from American households, processing the data, and disseminating data products to users. We discuss the data produced from the census: the demographic results, how to get access to the information, and who makes use of the data. Other essays discuss the decennial census in the context of public policy, including its origins in the federal Constitution as a mechanism for apportioning seats in the House of Representatives. We include short articles that provide a snapshot of the nation at each of the decennial censuses from 1790 to the present. And we address census controversies, both historical and current, including the legal controversies surrounding census taking; the apportionment of Congress; the privacy of census information; and the propriety and usefulness of particular questions on such sensitive issues as income, race, and family status.

The encyclopedia includes some 140 signed articles by prominent scholars, professionals, and other census experts. The articles have been written to be accessible to students, scholars, and general readers, and the book is structured in such a way as to facilitate retrieval of information. Accompanying each article are cross-references to related articles and a brief bibliography that suggests further reading. A detailed index guides readers to the information they need.

In addition to the articles, the encyclopedia includes a wide assortment of maps, tables, and figures. A sixteen-page photo gallery documents the history of census taking in America. The appendix contains useful tabular data and other supplementary materials, such as the budget for taking the census; a list of Census Bureau directors; examples of census and ACS forms and questions; a center-of-population map and U.S. population totals from each census taken since 1790; information on the apportionment of Congress, including apportionment methods and formulas among other reference materials.

Census taking may be one of the most routine and ordinary functions of the federal government, yet it is little understood. It is also one of the oldest activities of the federal government, dating, like postal service and tax collection, to the birth of the republic in 1789. But unlike these other venerable government activities, the census has historically been infrequent, arriving on the public scene only once a decade and then receding from public consciousness between counts. The separation of social and economic content from the data used strictly for reapportionment and redistricting, however, has produced a paradigm shift, altering the once-in-a-decade time stamp that has been the familiar hallmark of the census This volume is designed to help readers understand this shift by providing what they need to know about the census, from the earliest to the most recent enumeration, including advances that have been recently incorporated, and by providing a glimpse into what may lie ahead for the American census.

Definitions: What Is a Census?

A census is a count of the population of a country as of a fixed date. National governments conduct censuses to determine how many people live in different areas of the country; to assess whether the population is growing, stable, or declining in the country as a whole and in particular parts of the country; and to describe the characteristics of the population in terms of age, sex, ethnic background, marital status, income, and other variables. Generally, governments collect the information by sending a questionnaire in the mail or an interviewer to every household or residential address in the country. The questionnaire asks the head of the household or a responsible adult in the household (the respondent) to list all of the people who live at the address as of a particular date and to answer a series of questions about each of them. The respondent or the interviewer is then responsible for sending the answers back to the government agency, which in turn tabulates or aggregates the answers for the country overall and for political subdivisions such as states or provinces, cities, counties, or other civil divisions. The agency usually reports the results to the public a few months or years after the census; the results are considered "news" and are reported by the media.

Because censuses aim to count the entire population of a country, they are very expensive and elaborate administrative operations and thus are conducted relatively infrequently, generally at five- or ten-year intervals. Between censuses, governments estimate the size and characteristics of the population by extrapolating the trends identified in the census into the future, by estimating the population from other data systems such as vital statistics or tax records, or by conducting periodic sample surveys. Researchers also can use representative probability samples to collect information from a small portion of the population; these can be conducted frequently, even monthly. In the United States, the Current Population Survey of about 60,000 households is conducted and reports monthly, and the American Community Survey reports results yearly. (See *American Community Survey*; *Federal household surveys*.) To provide more frequent updates of population characteristics for small geographic areas and to streamline the decennial census, the U.S. Census Bureau has turned to the continuous ACS to collect many types of data traditionally collected in the census.

National governments also conduct other types of censuses, particularly of economic activity such as agriculture, manufacturing, or business. Such censuses collect information on the number and characteristics of farms, businesses, or manufacturing firms. In the past the U.S. Census Bureau conducted such censuses at the same time as the population census. Today the economic censuses are generally conducted on a different schedule from the population census. (See *Agricultural censuses; Censuses in other countries; Economic censuses*.)

The American Experience

Censuses have been taken since ancient times. Emperors and kings used them to assess the strength of their realms. These early censuses were conducted sporadically and generally served to measure the tax or military capacity of a particular area. Unlike modern censuses, they tended to count only adult men, men liable for military service, or tithables (people liable

to pay taxes). The modern census of all persons dates from the seventeenth and eighteenth centuries, when the colonial powers of western Europe sought to determine the success of their overseas colonies. (See *Colonial censuses*.)

The U.S. decennial census was mandated by the 1787 federal Constitution as a mechanism for determining the political representation for each state in the House of Representatives. Article I of the Constitution created Congress (the House of Representatives and the Senate) and defined its membership and capacities. Paragraph three of section 2 described the method of constituting the House:

> Representatives and direct Taxes shall be apportioned among the several States which may be included within this Union, according to their respective numbers, which shall be determined by adding to the whole Number of free Persons, including those bound to Service for a Term of Years, and excluding Indians not taxed, three-fifths of all other Persons. The actual Enumeration shall be made within three Years after the first Meeting of the Congress of the United States, and within every subsequent Term of ten Years, in such Manner as they shall by Law direct.

Section 9 of Article I included the only other mention of the census in the Constitution: "No capitation, or other direct, Tax shall be laid, unless in Proportion to the Census or Enumeration herein before directed to be taken." The language of Article I provided the solution to one of the fundamental political controversies of the American revolutionary era: how to allocate representation in legislative assemblies. Before the American Revolution, the colonists had protested their lack of representation in the British Parliament. They had also objected to the existence of rotten boroughs—legislative districts with few or no people living in them. A legislator from such a district cast the same single vote as a representative from a city with thousands of people.

After declaring their independence in 1776, the newly united thirteen colonies struggled over the problem of equitably distributing the burdens and resources of the national government among large and small states. In the Continental Congress and under the Articles of Confederation during the 1770s and 1780s, states voted as units, regardless of their wealth or population. The larger states opposed this system, which was one element of government that they sought to reform in the 1787 Constitution.

The framers of the Constitution resolved the dispute between large and small states by allocating representation in the House according to population and in the Senate by state. In the Senate each state, regardless of size, would have two members. Since the framers also intended for "direct taxes" to be allocated among the states according to population, the large states would gain greater House representation but would pay higher taxes to the federal government. The strength of each state in the Electoral College to select the president and vice president would be determined by summing its Senate and House members. Finally, the framers were well aware that populations—and especially the American population—grew and shifted over time and that no legislative apportionment could be permanent.

The census and apportionment mechanisms of the federal Constitution were crucial pieces of the Great Compromise among the large and small states that made a new national government possible. The United States became the first nation in the world to take a regular population census and to use it to apportion legislative seats. Since then, the decennial census and reapportionment, like regular elections, have facilitated the always difficult process of transferring political power among various elements of the population.

The issue of allocating representation based on population was complicated further by the institution of racial slavery and the relationships between the Euro-American majority and American Indians. At the time of the Revolution, about 20 percent of the American population was enslaved. If population were the apportionment measure, should the southern states be granted political representation for the slave population? Should the slaves be considered "property" for purposes of tax assessments? Northern states were already beginning to abolish the institution of slavery and were wary of writing any support for the system into the Constitution. Southerners insisted that the slaves be counted as part of the population. The framers decided to base both representation and direct taxes on population. The rather clumsy solution to the slavery dilemma was the Three-fifths compromise. Slaves would be counted in the census but would be "discounted" to 60 percent of a free person when calculating the state population totals for apportionment.

At the time of the American Revolution, Indian tribes were considered sovereign powers. The Constitution gave Congress the power to "regulate Commerce . . . with the Indian Tribes" and created the category of "Indians not taxed," that is, American Indians who lived within the boundaries of the United States but did not owe taxes to the United States since they maintained allegiance to their tribe. "Indians not taxed" thus became the one population group within U.S. territory specifically excluded from enumeration in the decennial census. Thus, until passage of the Fourteenth Amendment in 1868, the census recognized three civil statuses: free, slave, and nontaxed Indian. The amendment, which granted full civil and political rights to the former slaves, retained the exemption from enumeration for nontaxed Indians. The exemption for American Indians was finally ended in 1924 with the passage of the Indian Citizenship Act. (See *American Indians and Alaska Natives*.)

Since the purpose of the census was to distribute House seats among the states, Congress mandated that the census count the population by geographic area so that it could allocate political representation. The states, too, began to use census data to allocate representation to particular geographic areas in state and local legislative bodies.

Implementing the System

The censuses from 1790 to 1840 were simple counts of the people in each household or family. Congress instructed the U.S. marshals to appoint assistants, who in turn were supposed to contact each household head to find out how many people in particular age, race, and sex categories lived in the household. The assistant totaled the household counts and transmitted them to the U.S. marshal, who in turn totaled the assistants' counts and transmitted them to Washington, D.C. The secretary of state and a clerk or two added the numbers obtained from all U.S. marshals and submitted them to Congress. No bureaucracy existed to check the coverage or accuracy of the enumeration. Neither the federal government nor the marshals were required to map their local areas. Congress required that the census workers take an oath that they had faithfully counted everyone; returns were posted in a public place so that people could check them. The major concern of government officials in those early years of the census was that the returns be collected at all. In the sparsely settled nation, it took about a year to conduct the census, and Congress routinely had to legislate extra time for the marshals to collect the information.

Despite these difficulties, by the early nineteenth century the census had developed a successful record. The population was counted, and Congress was reapportioned. Congress experimented with direct-tax measures based on the census in the late 1790s and again during the War of 1812. It found, however, that the tariff was a more efficient source of federal revenue and thus let this provision of the Constitution fall into disuse. The country at the time was overwhelmingly agricultural and rural. The U.S. population was also growing rapidly—at the rate of 30 to 35 percent a decade. In a society where the prime issues were integrating new states into the Union and accounting for growth based on the settlement of western land, the census proved to be an effective mechanism by which to allocate and reallocate political power each decade.

Today we know what nineteenth-century Americans were just beginning to realize: the United States has one of the most heterogeneous and flourishing populations in the history of the world. From a mere 3.9 million rural residents spread along the East Coast in 1790, the population has grown to more than 300 million spread from coast to coast. Until the early twentieth century the nation was predominantly rural; now it is overwhelmingly urban. Racially and ethnically the population was and is diverse, though the character of that diversity has changed throughout the country's history. That the American political system has absorbed the shocks of these demographic and economic changes is remarkable.

The census has been one of the chief mechanisms for absorbing the shocks because it guarantees that geographic areas receive political representation in proportion to their population. Over time states with populations that grew relative to the rest of the nation received relatively more representation in Congress. Those with stable or declining populations lost representation. By 1820 several of the original thirteen states began to lose seats in the House. By the outbreak of the Civil War, in 1861, the original thirteen states no longer held a majority of House seats.

Once Americans had acquired several decades of experience with census taking, they began to ask questions about technical issues of counting the population and the meaning of rapid population growth. Almanacs began to publish census figures for local areas. Local boosters in western states used these figures to encourage further settlement. On the downside, political leaders from parts of the country that were not growing as fast as others began to realize that slower relative population growth meant their political power would erode after the next reapportionment.

Over time, states that thought of themselves as "losing" in the population growth game began to object to a system that rewarded growth so relentlessly and began to scrutinize the underlying census results. Although their objections never disrupted the functioning of the census, at several points in the past two centuries the decennial census and reapportionment process brought into sharp relief other political controversies. The first major controversy arose during the Civil War era and reflected the growing conflict between North and South over the future of slavery and control of the national government. The second occurred in the 1920s, as the rural areas of the country refused to relinquish control of legislative bodies to the new urban majority. The third began with the Supreme Court decisions of the 1960s mandating the one-person, one-vote rule for legislative apportionment. That controversy continued to 2000. As the census was politicized, it lost its major original function as a mechanism to defuse the contentiousness surrounding the allocation of political power among the constituent elements of the population. And in all three eras—the 1860s, the 1920s, and the 1960s—the controversies surrounding the census led to technical and administrative reforms of the census taking process, which in turn has provided Americans with ever greater amounts of information about their society.

Demographic Challenges and the Engine of Census Innovation

Western population growth did not pose a dangerous challenge to American governmental stability because there was a general consensus that western expansion was a good thing. However, other shifts in population were more problematic. By the 1820s it was clear that the southern population was not growing as fast as the northern. Each census and reapportionment therefore weakened southern power in the House and hence made control of the Senate and the presidency that much more important. The growing demographic imbalance between North and South also drew increasing attention to the census process. The first major effort to reform the census took place in the same session of Congress that debated the Compromise of 1850. (See *Decennial censuses: 1850 census.*) Congress created the post of census superintendent and authorized a large, temporary office in the Interior Department to tally and publish the census. Congress required that each person in the country have a separate line on the census form. In other words, the individual rather than the household became the unit of analysis. Also, many new questions were added to the census schedule.

Further changes were made during the Civil War years. The southern states began to secede after Abraham Lincoln's election in November 1860, as the 1860 census was completed and reports of the continuing decline of the relative strength of the southern population were appearing in the press. As southerners looked to the future, they saw that they would face more losses in the House. The relentless, recurring process of census taking and reapportionment exacerbated the sectional crisis. Northerners endorsed the census and apportionment process because they worked to the North's political advantage. As Lincoln and the Republicans took over the government, they were unconcerned that the simple constitutional mechanism of awarding power in accordance with population did not take account of the dislocation faced by regions that lost in the race of relative growth.

Northern Republicans realized that the census and reapportionment would work to their political *dis*advantage after the Civil War and Reconstruction. The Thirteenth Amendment to the Constitution, which abolished slavery, also implicitly ended the Three-fifths compromise. (The Fourteenth Amendment would abolish the three-fifths formula explicitly.) With its demise, the southern states would gain a windfall of increased representation in Congress. However, since few policymakers expected the freed slaves to be able to vote initially, they realized that a disfranchised free black population would strengthen the white-led southern states and permit the Democrats to come dangerously close to gaining control of the presidency as early as 1868.

The logic of population counting and apportionment, therefore, was one of the major forces driving Congress to extend further political and civil rights to the freedmen. The Fourteenth Amendment extended citizenship, due process, and equal protection of the laws to all "persons born or naturalized in the United States." It also contained a provision—never enforced—to reduce the representation of a state that disfranchised any portion of its male citizenry. The ambiguity of that sanction led to passage of the Fifteenth Amendment, which declared that the right to vote "shall not be abridged by the United States or by any State on account of race, color, or previous condition of servitude."

In the years after the Civil War, the American population continued to grow and spread rapidly, by world standards, but never again would it achieve a national growth rate of 30 percent a decade. By 1890 the census superintendent announced the closing of the frontier. At the same time, the census takers documented rapid urban growth. Cities had replaced the rural West as the locus of the most rapid growth, and European immigrants as well as native-born Americans were flocking to the new jobs and opportunities the cities offered.

As the twentieth century dawned, the census takers could see political power shifting again—this time to the rapidly urbanizing and industrializing states in the Northeast and Midwest with their growing polyglot populations. From the

Civil War until World War I, Congress solved the decennial problem of reallocating political power among the states by increasing the size of the House of Representatives. In 1860 the House comprised 243 members; by 1910 there were 435. Areas with slow-growing or declining populations lost relative, but not absolute, political power in the House.

In the late nineteenth and early twentieth century, Congress expanded the administrative capacity of the census office. In 1880 the census superintendent received the authority to map the country, appoint local census supervisors, and test the enumerators for basic competency at their jobs. In 1890 the Census Office pioneered the machine tabulation (see *Pre-computer tabulation systems*) of census results. In 1902 the office became a permanent government bureau, and it joined the new Department of Commerce and Labor in 1903.

After the 1920 census, another apportionment crisis arose. The statisticians announced that a majority of Americans lived in urban areas, a development that threatened to undermine rural states' domination of national politics and rural towns' domination of state politics. The strikes and violence that erupted at the end of World War I were generally centered in the big cities, the home of immigrants and industrial workers, and such behavior deeply disturbed small-town and rural Americans. As the nation turned in revulsion from all things foreign, particularly European, Congress moved to restrict immigration and to delay reapportionment.

Congress had vowed in 1910 not to increase the size of the House beyond 435 members. When the census results showed that the great gainers from congressional reapportionment would be the large urban states—primarily in the Northeast and Midwest—Congress balked at passing an apportionment bill. Leaders from predominantly rural states refused to surrender political power to urban states. They argued that geography was the true basis for representation; that the urban states did not deserve representation for their noncitizen, foreign-born populations; and that urban political machines were corrupting traditional republican institutions. They also argued that because the census was taken in the immediate aftermath of World War I and in January—a month when farm workers were often absent from their land—the bureau had incorrectly allocated rural residents to cities where they were temporarily employed. For the remainder of the 1920s no bill passed, and for the only time in the history of the republic, Congress was not reapportioned.

In 1929 Congress finally passed a prospective bill, which would reapportion Congress in 1932 using the results of the 1930 census. But as part of the difficult compromise that made the bill possible, Congress removed the existing requirement that congressional districts be substantially equal in size. In short, Congress redistributed political power among the states but quietly permitted malapportioned districts within states in order to preserve rural and small-town dominance of Congress. By the early 1930s, it was not uncommon for congressional districts in large urban areas to encompass seven or eight times more people than those in rural areas. A similar pattern of apportionment held true at the local and state government level.

Malapportionment would remain the norm until the 1960s. In the meantime, the census was redirected to address new issues. The Census Bureau pioneered the collection of new information to cope with the problems of depression and war in the 1930s and 1940s. It used the first nondefense computer in the 1950s. With the growth of population-based federal aid and grant programs, census numbers came to be employed to administer a wide variety of laws and funding allocations at all levels of the federal system. The U.S. Bureau of the Census introduced probability sampling methods in 1940, and by 1950 it had separated the main census schedule into a "short form" questionnaire for all households and a "long form" sample to collect detailed characteristics of 16 to 25 percent of households. It also developed sample surveys to collect information between decennial counts, quality control procedures, methods to measure the accuracy of the basic census count and the quality of responses to individual questions, and mail enumeration procedures.

By the 1960s it was clear that the compromises of the 1920s had built major distortions into the apportionment and districting systems of the nation. Substantial numbers of Americans in urban and suburban areas were underrepresented in their state legislatures and in Congress. Older cities were losing population and no longer seemed to threaten the future of the republic. Nevertheless, legislatures dominated by rural members were unwilling to reapportion or redistrict. Thus, a series of carefully crafted test cases made their way through the court system.

In 1962 the Supreme Court ruled in *Baker v. Carr* that individuals could challenge the constitutionality of a malapportioned state legislature in court. The case led to a series of decisions that declared that state legislatures, local legislative bodies, and congressional districts had to be apportioned according to the rule that came to be called "one-person, one-vote." Citing the equal protection clause of the Fourteenth Amendment and the language of Article I, section 2 of the Constitution, the Court ruled that states must draw legislative districts such that they encompass an equal number of people as counted in the decennial census. Other methods of drawing legislative districts, which might use political or geographic boundaries, were invalid if those districts were not equal in population. As Chief Justice Earl Warren noted in his impassioned ruling in *Reynolds v. Sims* (1964), which restored population as the apportionment measure:

> Legislators represent people, not trees or acres. Legisla-
> tors are elected by voters, not farms or cities or eco-
> nomic interests. As long as ours is a representative form
> of government, and our legislatures are those instru-
> ments of government elected directly by and directly
> representative of the people, the right to elect legislators
> in a free and unimpaired fashion is a bedrock of our
> political system.

Thus, he concluded, "the right of suffrage can be denied by a debasement or dilution of the weight of a citizen's vote just as effectively as by wholly prohibiting the free exercise of the franchise." Since legislatures should be apportioned on the basis of one-person, one-vote, such "dilution" was unconstitutional. By the late 1960s, congressional and legislative districts around the country had been redrawn to meet the new guidelines, and underrepresented areas—mainly urban and suburban areas—had a dramatically increased level of legislative representation.

The Supreme Court requirement for legislative districts to be equal in population drew new attention to the quality of census data. Statisticians and demographers knew that the census counted some groups in the population more accurately than others, and demographers had developed a substantial technical literature on underenumeration and census accuracy. Minorities, the poor, and urban dwellers were counted less accurately than those people living in suburbs and middle-class areas of the country. Once local officials began to understand the implications of the one-person, one-vote decisions, they and Congress began to look much more closely at the quality of local-area census data. Officials in local areas that were undercounted or miscounted sought to improve the data, and census officials began to see interest in better data not only from demographers but also from ordinary citizens unschooled in the niceties of advanced statistical methods.

For most of the 1970s and 1980s, the census was embroiled in a complex set of controversies about improving the count. Congress, statisticians, local officials, and minority representatives demanded that the bureau count the population better in the first place and that it make plans to adjust the census in light of the inevitable undercounts. The bureau began to develop methods to improve the count and to experiment with adjustment methods to correct for undercounts. The budget for the census grew dramatically. New advisory committees worked on the planning efforts. The bureau successfully defended itself against fifty-four lawsuits after the 1980 census that accused the bureau of using improper and inadequate methods.

In the late 1980s, the U.S. Bureau of the Census developed what it hoped would be a statistically defensible method of adjusting the decennial census for the undercount, but it faced political resistance in the George H. W. Bush administration. Advocates for the new methods sued, and the courts mandated that the new methods be implemented in 1990. In 1991, the commerce secretary decided not to adjust the 1990 census results. In the 1990s the administration of Bill Clinton took the opposite tack, proposing a census design that included adjustment of the 2000 census, including the apportionment counts. Republican members of Congress sued to stop the Clinton plan. In *Department of Commerce v. United States House* (1999), the Supreme Court ruled that the current census statute prevented the use of sampling methods for reapportioning congressional seats after the 2000 census. The Census Bureau changed the design for the 2000 count so that the remaining census results, including the redistricting data, could be adjusted if the results indicated that adjusted data were more accurate. In 2001 the Census Bureau decided against adjustment, and the George W. Bush administration did not revive further efforts to adjust census results for undercount or to plan for such an eventuality in the 2010 census.

Nevertheless, the controversies over census accuracy indirectly led to other major innovations in census taking. Data users had begun to ask if it would be possible to collect the detailed characteristic data in the census more frequently. Furthermore, the mail response rate had dropped in the 1990 census and was lower for the long-form questionnaires than for the short-form questionnaires. As a result, the Census Bureau began a program to measure long-form characteristics separately from the short-form items that were required to fulfill the constitutional requirements of the census. This program, which began testing in the mid-1990s, would eventually be known as the American Community Survey. Further, increasing public resistance to the census and the ineffectiveness of previous pro bono advertising campaigns led to the adoption of major paid advertising efforts to promote public awareness for the 2000 and 2010 censuses. For 2010 this included using the new information-age tools of Facebook, Twitter, and YouTube. The U.S. Census Bureau's website became the locus of news, information, and promotion of the count, as well as the locus for finding census results. The American Community Survey replaced the long form in the 2010 census, and the 2010 count returned to the briefest set of questions since 1790 (see *American Community Survey: introduction*).

Innovation is likely to continue in the years ahead, still guided by the original purpose of the census. The census was and is a mechanism for distributing political power and economic resources among the various elements of the population. The founders created it because they needed a simple, automatic mechanism for apportioning legislative seats that was acceptable to all political factions. If we recognize this function, perhaps we can also set standards for resolving controversies and shaping technical improvements in the census.

Margo J. Anderson

ALPHABETICAL LIST OF ARTICLES

CONTRIBUTORS TO THE SECOND EDITION

Affiliations listed in italics. The articles are the personal work of the author(s); are copyrighted by CQ Press; and do not constitute official or authoritative documents by an author's agency, company, or educational institution.

ADAMS, MARGARET O'NEILL
National Archives and Records Administration (NARA)
National Archives and Records Administration
    (NARA)

ANDERSON, ALBERT F.
Public Data Queries Inc.
Dissemination of data: electronic products

ANDERSON, MARGO J.
University of Wisconsin–Milwaukee
Advertising the census
Census law
Censuses in other countries
Center of population
Decennial censuses: 1810 census
Decennial censuses: 1820 census
Decennial censuses: 1940 census
Disability
Dress rehearsal
Litigation and the census
Popular culture and the census
PUMS (Public Use Microdata Samples)
State and local censuses
Three-fifths compromise

AUSTIN, ERIK W.
ICPSR, University of Michigan
Archival access to the census

BAXTER, PAM M.
Cornell University
Dissemination of data: secondary products

BECKER, PATRICIA C.
APB Associates
Decennial censuses: 1970 census
Decennial censuses: 1980 census
Enumeration: field procedures
Housing
Tabulation geography

BENNETT, CLAUDETTE
U.S. Census Bureau
African-origin population
Race: questions and classifications

BISHOP, DEIRDRE DALPIAZ
U.S. Census Bureau
Geography: distribution of population

BOGGESS, SCOTT
U.S. Census Bureau
American Community Survey: data products

BOWIE, CHET
NORC at the University of Chicago
American Community Survey: questionnaire content

BRYANT, BARBARA EVERITT
University of Michigan (retired)
Decennial censuses: 1990 census

CHRISTOPHER, ED J.
*U.S. Department of Transportation, Federal Highway
    Administration*
Uses of the census and ACS: transportation

CITRO, CONSTANCE F.
National Academy of Sciences/National Research Council
Advisory committees
American Community Survey: using multi-year estimates
Content
Content determination
Coverage improvement procedures
Editing, imputation, and weighting
Enumeration: group quarters
Income and poverty measures
Long form
Related data sources
Sampling for content
Sampling in the census
Uses of the census and ACS: federal agencies

COHEN, MICHAEL L.
National Academy of Sciences/National Research Council
Coverage evaluation

COHEN, PATRICIA CLINE
University of California, Santa Barbara
Decennial censuses: 1830 census
Decennial censuses: 1840 census

COHN, D'VERA
Pew Research Center
Media attention to the census

CORK, DANIEL L.
National Academy of Sciences/National Research Council
Census testing
Internet data collection
Residence rules

CZAJKA, JOHN L.
Mathematica Policy Research
Federal administrative records

DEVINE, TIMOTHY J.
U.S. Census Bureau
Staffing

DIENSTFREY, STEPHEN J.
U.S. Department of Veterans Affairs (retired)
Veterans' status

EDMONSTON, BARRY
University of Victoria
Composition of the population
Internal migration

ELHAMI, SHOREH
Delaware County (Ohio) Auditor's GIS Office
Geographic information systems (GIS)

ERICKSEN, EUGENE P.
Temple University
Errors in the census

FIENBERG, STEPHEN E.
Carnegie Mellon University
Capture-recapture methods

FORSTALL, RICHARD L.
U.S. Census Bureau (retired)
Metropolitan areas
Urban areas

GAGE, LINDA
California Department of Finance
Uses of the census and ACS: state and local governments

GAINES, LEONARD M.
New York State Department of Economic Development
Dissemination of data: printed publications
Economic census
Uses of the census and ACS: state and local governments

GAQUIN, DEIRDRE A.
Consultant
Data dissemination and use
Summary files
Women in the decennial census

GATES, GERALD W.
U.S. Census Bureau (retired)
Confidentiality

GONA, DEBORAH A.
Gona & Associates
Grassroots groups
Not-for-profit organizations

GRANDA, PETER A.
ICPSR, University of Michigan
Archival access to census data

GRIFFIN, DEBORAH H.
U.S. Census Bureau
American Community Survey: methodology

GROVES, ROBERT M.
U.S. Census Bureau
Decennial censuses: 2010 census

HABERMANN, HERMANN
formerly U.S. Census Bureau and United Nations Statistics Division
Decennial censuses: 2020 census
International statistical system and its governance

HACKER, J. DAVID
Binghamton University
Civil War and the census
Decennial censuses: 1850 census
Decennial censuses: 1860 census
Decennial censuses: 1870 census

HARDCASTLE, JEFF
University of Nevada, Reno
Enumerating: rural areas
Rural areas

HARRIS-KOJETIN, BRIAN
Office of Management and Budget
Federal household surveys

HODGES, KEN
Nielsen
Private sector

HOGAN, HOWARD
U.S. Census Bureau
Accuracy and Coverage Evaluation

JACOBSEN, LINDA A.
Population Reference Bureau
American Community Survey: data products

KALTON, GRAHAM
Westat
American Community Survey: using multi-year
   estimates

KOMINSKI, ROBERT A.
U.S. Census Bureau
American Community Survey: implementation from
   2005
Education: changing questions and classifications
Languages spoken

LAMACCHIA, ROBERT A.
U.S. Census Bureau (retired)
Address list development
Geographic information systems (GIS)

LAVIN, MICHAEL R.
State University of New York at Buffalo
Depository libraries

LEE, SHARON M.
University of Victoria
Asian Americans
Native Hawaiian and Other Pacific Islander (NHOPI)
   population

LEVIN, MICHAEL J.
Harvard Center for Population and Development Studies
U.S. insular areas

LOBO, ARUN PETER
New York City Department of City Planning
Foreign-born population of the United States

LOVE, SUSAN P.
Consultant
American Community Survey: methodology

MAGNUSON, DIANA L.
Bethel University
Decennial censuses: 1880 census
Decennial censuses: 1890 census
Decennial censuses: 1900 census
Decennial censuses: 1910 census
Decennial censuses: 1920 census
Decennial censuses: 1930 census
Pre-computer tabulation systems

MAURY, WILLIAM M.
U.S. Census Bureau
Genealogy

MCCULLY, CATHY
U.S. Census Bureau
State and local governments: legislatures

MCDERMOTT, MONICA
University of Illinois, Urbana-Champaign
White or European-origin population
White population of the United States

MCMILLEN, DAVID
National Archives and Records Administration
Americans overseas
Apportionment and districting
Congress and the census

MESSER, CHRIS
*U.S. Department of Agriculture, National Agricultural Statistics
   Service*
Agricultural censuses

MULRY, MARY H.
U.S. Census Bureau
Post-enumeration survey

MURAKAMI, ELAINE
*U.S Department of Transportation, Federal Highway
   Administration*
Uses of the census and ACS: transportation

MURDOCK, STEVE H.
Rice University
Decennial censuses: 2010 census

NAYMARK, JOAN GENTILI
Target Corporation
Private sector

NEIDERT, LISA
University of Michigan
Dissemination of data: electronic products

PASSEL, JEFFREY S.
Pew Hispanic Center
Hispanic population
Hispanic/Latino ethnicity and identifiers
Immigration

PEMBERTON, DAVID M.
U.S. Census Bureau
Decennial censuses: 1950 census
Decennial censuses: 1960 census

POWERS, MARY G.
Fordham University
Occupation and education

PREWITT, KENNETH
Columbia University
Decennial censuses: 2000 census

RALEY, R. KELLY
University of Texas at Austin
Family and household composition of the population

ROBINSON, J. GREGORY
U.S. Census Bureau
Demographic analysis

ROTHWELL, CHARLES J.
National Center for Health Statistics
Vital registration and vital statistics

ROWE, JUDITH S.
Princeton University (retired)
Data products: evolution

RUGGLES, STEVEN
University of Minnesota
IPUMS (Integrated Public Use Microdata Series)

SALVO, JOSEPH J.
New York City Department of City Planning
Age questions in the census
American Community Survey: implementation from 2005
American Community Survey: introduction
Census tracts
Data capture
Decennial censuses: 2020 census
Local involvement in census taking
Uses of the census and ACS: state and local governments

SCARDAMALIA, ROBERT
RLS Demographics, Inc.
Enumerating rural areas
State data centers

SCHECHTER, SUSAN
NORC at the University of Chicago
American Community Survey: questionnaire content

SELTZER, WILLIAM
Fordham University
Human rights and population censuses
International coordination in population censuses

SNIPP, C. MATTHEW
Stanford University
American Indians and Alaska Natives

SPERLING, JONATHAN
U.S. Department of Housing and Urban Development
Census of Puerto Rico

STOREY, TIM
National Conference of State Legislatures
State and local governments: legislatures

THOMPSON, JOHN H.
NORC at the University of Chicago
Organization and administration of the census

VELKOFF, VICTORIA A.
U.S. Census Bureau
Population estimates and projections

WAITE, PRESTON JAY
U.S. Census Bureau (retired)
American Community Survey: development to 2004

WALLMAN, KATHERINE K.
Office of Management and Budget
Federal statistical system oversight and policy: intersection
    of OMB and the decennial census

WEINBERG, DANIEL H.
U.S. Census Bureau
Organization and administration of the census

WELLS, ROBERT V.
Union College
Colonial censuses
Decennial censuses: 1790 census
Decennial censuses: 1800 census

WEST, KIRSTEN K.
U.S. Census Bureau
Demographic analysis

ZEISSET, PAUL T.
U.S. Census Bureau (retired)
Economic census

CONTRIBUTORS TO THE FIRST EDITION

ALEXANDER, CHARLES (DECEASED)
American Community Survey

ALLEN, RICH
Agricultural censuses

BAILAR, BARBARA A.
Census testing

CASPER, LYNNE M.
Family and household composition of the population

CHAPA, JORGE
Hispanic population
Hispanic/Latino ethnicity and identifiers

DOYLE, PAT (DECEASED)
Federal household surveys

DUNTON, NANCY E.
PUMS (Public Use Microdata Samples)

FRYER, JANICE S.
Dissemination of data: printed publications

GOLDFIELD, EDWIN D. (DECEASED)
1950 census
1960 census

GRAY, ANN S.
Dissemination of data: secondary products

HARSHBARGER, DOROTHY S.
Vital registration and vital statistics

HEELEN, J. PATRICK
Census law

HIRSCHFELD, DONALD
Address list development

JENKINS, ROBERT M.
1940 census

KELLER, JAY K.
Staffing

KRALY, ELLEN PERCY
Foreign-born population of the United States

LAROCHE, BENOIT
Censuses in other countries

LONG, LARRY
Geography: distribution of the population

LOWENTHAL, TERRI ANN
Congress and the census
Media attention to the census

MCCLURE, PAUL
Genealogy

O'CONNELL, MARTIN
Family and household composition of the population

REEDER, FRANKLIN S.
Statistical policy and oversight

RICHE, MARTHA FARNSWORTH
2000 census

SIEGEL, PAUL
Small Area Income and Poverty Estimates (SAIPE)

SMITH, DANIEL SCOTT (DECEASED)
1810 census
1820 census

SPAR, EDWARD J.
Private sector

STIERS, GRETCHEN A.
Age questions in the census
Women in the decennial census

STUART, JOHN M.
Staffing

VOSS, PAUL R.
Rural areas

WRIGHT, TOMMY
Sampling for follow-up of nonresponding households

ENCYCLOPEDIA OF THE
U.S. CENSUS

Introduction to the American Community Survey

The decennial census long-form sample, which was the source of social and economic data for geographic areas and population groups in the United States from 1960 to 2000, has been replaced by the continuous American Community Survey (ACS). Like the long form, the ACS provides data on the social, economic, and housing characteristics of the population from a sample of the nation's households and group quarters. In several respects, the ACS represents a major advance over the census long-form sample by incorporating innovations that are meant to better address the information needs of the nation. These include the provision of data products for all geographic areas more than once a decade; the delivery of those products on a more timely basis—in the year after the data are collected; and the use of professional interviewers to help offset a decline in response and in the quality of data for many socioeconomic items on the long form.

Since 2005, the ACS questionnaire has been sent to a monthly sample of about 240,000 addresses in every county of the nation. (See the attached timeline of major events in ACS history.) The sample is combined or "rolled-up" for 12 months to produce annual estimates of characteristics for places of 65,000 or more population. Thus, for large places in the nation, a socioeconomic portrait is now available on an annual basis. For places of 20,000 to 65,000 persons, 36 months of sample is the minimum required to provide estimates. These "three-year period estimates" tell us the average number of high school graduates or people who drive to work, for example, over that period. For the smallest places, those with fewer than 20,000 people, 60 months of sample is needed to produce "five-year period estimates," which are averages for characteristics over a five-year period.

Like all innovations in their infancy, the ACS is a work in progress. The use of estimates for multi-year periods represents a new way of thinking about the way in which we paint portraits of the nation's communities. Making comparisons across different geographic areas and measuring changes over time

using these period estimates pose new challenges for all kinds of applications. Federal, state, and local officials, as well as members of the larger data user community, are now working on ways to incorporate these new data into policy formulation, needs assessments, and program planning and implementation. The challenge is how best to use these data, while dealing with issues regarding sample size, the addition of new variables to the survey, and changes in geographic boundaries over time.

The six entries in this new volume are designed to be a "what you need to know" about the ACS. There are two overarching entries, "ACS: Development to 2004" and "ACS: Implementation from 2005," which are meant to document aspects of ACS history and evolution that can serve as a framework for understanding the conceptual underpinnings of the survey. The entries on Questionnaire Content, Methodology, and Multi-Year Estimates are meant to provide a solid grounding in the basic "nuts and bolts" of the ACS. These entries include information on how the content development process works, the actual contents of the survey, some key aspects of the concepts and methods used to collect and compile the data, and the correct way to use multi-year estimates to compare different geographic areas. Finally, the Data Products entry provides information on the types of tabulations, profiles, and other specialized subject matter available from the ACS. This entry also provides information on where to find ACS data and the different pathways that are available to access the ACS.

Following the six entries is a combined bibliography, which is intended to provide the reader with a basis for further exploration on each topic. Together, the entries and the bibliography provide the reader with an essential primer on the ACS. Because the ACS program is in its infancy, data users need to pay careful attention to the ACS Web site, particularly the portion that documents errors in data products and any corrections (go to www.census.gov, then to American Community Survey, then to Data & Documentation, then to the Documentation page, then to User Notes and Errata, which are left-hand buttons on the Documentation page).

See also *Long form*

. . . . JOSEPH J. SALVO

Major Events in American Community Survey History

EVENT	YEAR
Use of a "rolling sample census" proposed by Leslie Kish before the House Subcommittee on Census and Population	1981
Decade Census Program (DCP) proposed by Roger Herriott and others at the Census Bureau for a rolling sample across states over a decade	1989
Response issues surrounding the 1990 census result in the creation of a Continuous Measurement (CM) program at the Census Bureau, with Charles Alexander as the chief architect	1992
Proposals call for initial sample of 500,000 households per month to create estimates for small areas, but budget requirements fix the initial sample at 250,000	1993
Staff appointed to test new continuous measurement approach, now renamed the American Community Survey (ACS). ACS testing begins in four counties	1995
Decision to retain the long-form sample in Census 2000; comparisons planned with the ACS	1996
ACS testing expands to 36 counties	1999
Census 2000 Supplementary Survey (C2SS) tests the operational feasibility of the ACS in more than one-third of U.S. counties	2000
First meeting of the Federal Interagency Committee for the ACS	2000
First national release of one-year estimates for geographic areas with 250,000 or more persons	2001
ACS-long form comparison studies completed	2004
ACS full national data collection for housing units begins (no group quarters included)	2005
First release of ACS one-year estimates of the population in housing units for all geographic areas with 65,000 or more persons	2006
ACS full national data collection begins for total population (housing units and group quarters)	2006
First ACS Content Test	2006
First release of ACS one-year estimates of total population (housing units and group quarters) for all geographic areas with 65,000 or more persons	2007
National Research Council Panel on the Functionality and Usability of the ACS (commissioned in 2004) publishes report "Using the American Community Survey: Benefits and Challenges"	2007
First release of three-year period estimates (2005-2007) of total population* for all geographic areas with 20,000 or more persons	2008
First major change to ACS content, including a revamped questionnaire format	2008
First in a series of Compass Handbooks published by the Census Bureau, providing guidance on use of ACS data	2008
Second ACS Content Test	2010
First release of five-year period estimates of total population* (2005-2009) for all geographic areas down to the census tract and block group level	2010
Planned sample size increase and new allocation of sample between large and small areas	2011

* Group quarters population for 2005 was estimated in order to derive total population for 2005-2007 and 2005-2009 periods.

American Community Survey: Development to 2004

The American Community Survey (ACS) uses a continuous measurement methodology that employs a monthly sample of the U.S. population, an innovation that traces its roots back to the 1980s. The ACS is designed to provide the same kinds of information previously provided by the decennial census long-form sample used for censuses from 1960 through 2000.

Why the ACS Was Developed

For decades, the long-form sample from the decennial census served as the only source of detailed social and demographic statistics for small areas and population groups in the United States. The long-form sample, however, had two major shortcomings.

First, since the information was collected as part of the census count, it was an added burden to the selected respondents and complicated the data collection effort by the Census Bureau. By 1990, the mail response rate for long-form recipients had dropped significantly below the rate for short-form recipients, increasing the costs of nonresponse follow-up (NRFU) and degrading the quality of the long-form data. In addition, because the census count is the Census Bureau's top priority, the editing, processing, and tabulation of long-form data had to take a back seat to the full count enumeration, delaying the release of long-form data for two or three years after the actual enumeration.

Second, perhaps the biggest drawback of the census long-form sample was that the data were collected only once every ten years. The sample provided a snapshot of one point in time for the decade and quickly became out-of-date in many communities throughout the nation. Couple this with the delay in release of the long-form data, and it became increasingly apparent that an alternative to the census long form was needed.

ACS Development—Initial Concepts

As far back as 1941, Philip Hauser, then at the Census Bureau (and its deputy director in 1947), proposed an "annual sample census" as a way to obtain continuously updated information for the population. In 1976, Congress passed a law requiring a mid-decade census beginning in 1985, but funding was never appropriated, and it failed to become a reality.

The concept of a rolling sample census, which became the ACS, was first proposed by Leslie Kish in a 1981 paper prepared for the Subcommittee on Census and Population of the U.S. House of Representatives Committee on Post Office and Civil Service. Kish proposed that an independent sample of one-tenth of the population be surveyed every year, cumulating the estimates over two or more years for detailed characteristics and small geographic areas.

In the late 1980s, as part of the early Census 2000 planning work, three options were identified to simplify the basic census and provide subnational demographic and housing data in a timelier manner throughout the decade: (1) a mid-decade census; (2) a rolling sample of states taken over a ten-year period; and (3) a large scale monthly sample survey. In 1989, a plan, called the Decade Census Program (DCP), envisioned a basic short-form-only census with the detailed social, economic, and housing data collected by a sample rolling across states during the decade with the goal of obtaining at least two measurements of data in each state, every decade. This proposal noted that most uses of small-area data involved comparisons within states; therefore, the absence of detailed data for every state in the same year was not considered to be a critical issue.

In the early 1990s, in response to not only renewed congressional interest in more up-to-date small-area data, but also to congressional distaste for the more burdensome long form and decreased mail response rates, the Census Bureau developed a proposal for a continuous measurement alternative to the long-form sample for the next census in 2000. Beginning in 1992, Charles Alexander, a statistician at the Census Bureau, led an effort to examine design alternatives that would eliminate the census long form. This work would soon develop into a proposal for a Continuous Measurement Survey (CMS), which included three major components:

1. a continuously updated Master Address File (MAF) to support survey sample selection;
2. a continuous intercensal survey using monthly samples to produce multi-year moving averages for small geographic areas such as census tracts and single-year estimates for larger areas; and
3. an estimates program that would produce control totals for the continuous survey.

These three components offered several major advantages for the Census Bureau. First, the decennial census enumeration itself would be simplified. Second, having a sample every month would put more emphasis on developing methods to regularly update the MAF as a frame for sample selection, which would, in turn, benefit the decennial census. Third, a continuous survey would allow for a permanent and much better-trained staff to collect data for complicated topics such as disability. The advantages for users would be more frequent and timely information for small geographic areas and population groups.

It was clear from the beginning that the new CMS, which now became known as the American Community Survey (ACS), would require an extensive development period, resulting in some trade-offs involving timeliness, reliability, and costs. One trade-off presented itself very early. Designers of the sample found that five-year estimates from the survey with comparable reliability to the census long-form sample would require a monthly sample of approximately 500,000 addresses, which would be costly. Ultimately, budget realities resulted in a reduced monthly sample of about 250,000 addresses. This reduction would have little effect on the reliability of single-year estimates for larger population areas, but reliability would suffer for the five-year estimates for smaller populations, Some early thought was given to expanding the monthly sample from about 250,000 to 400,000 in selected years as part of a cycle, but in the end no such sample expansion was introduced.

Assuming that about one-half of the sample each month would respond by mail, to control costs the designers proposed that both telephone and personal visit follow-ups be done using subsampling. In 1993, however, it was recommended that phone interviews be conducted for all eligible cases and that only personal visit follow-up cases would be subsampled. The ACS would also need to parallel the census long-form sample design parameters, particularly the oversampling of small governmental units.

ACS Development—1995–2004

In 1994, the Census Bureau established a staff to test the new approach. Throughout 1996 a questionnaire similar to the long form was fielded in four counties. The decision was made in the mid-1990s to retain the long-form sample in the Census 2000 and implement the ACS on a gradual basis so that its operational feasibility could be determined and the results compared with the 2000 results. The test sites were expanded to 36 counties in 31 sites for the years 1999–2004. In addition, a nationwide Census 2000 Supplementary Survey (C2SS) was successfully fielded during the 12 months of 2000 in more than one-third of U.S. counties; together, the C2SS and the sites obtained information during 2000 for about 587,000 housing units.

Monthly data collected in the test sites were used to produce three-year period estimates from the ACS centered on 2000 to be compared to the Census 2000 results for counties and census tracts. The C2SS permitted comparisons at the national level. The Census Bureau conducted ACS and Census 2000 comparability research in 2002–2004 and issued six comparison reports in 2004. Although the 2004 Evaluation Report Series noted differences, these evaluations provided support for the proposed change from the census long-form sample to the ACS model.

Around the same time, the Census Bureau contracted with researchers who possessed local knowledge of the ACS test areas to closely examine ACS and census sample data for selected counties. A number of studies used data from administrative records and other corroborating evidence to explore differences detected in ACS and Census 2000 data, for example, regarding house heating fuel and the year housing structure was built. This work found that the ACS information more closely resembled the administrative records data. Much of this work concluded that meaningful differences between the ACS and Census 2000 estimates at the local level were largely explained in favor of the ACS and were attributable to the use of professional interviewers who were better able to obtain information from respondents. Research on the rural and seasonal characteristics of the areas covered in the analysis confirmed that the ACS estimates would differ from the Census 2000 figures based on the different definitions of residence (usual residence in the census versus actual residence

for two months in the ACS). Finally, this research concluded that most statistically significant differences between the ACS and Census 2000 estimates would have limited implications for program development or targeting efforts by local officials.

In addition to the test sites, nationwide surveys similar to the C2SS were fielded in 2001–2004 and provided information for states, counties, and cities of 250,000 or more population. The ACS was fully implemented for housing units beginning in January 2005. Because of budget constraints, residents of group quarters (college dormitories, nursing homes, prisons, and other group living situations) were not added until a year later, in January 2006. The ACS is now in continuous operation with questionnaires being mailed to about 240,000 households each month in every county of the 50 states, the District of Columbia, and every *municipio* of Puerto Rico, with samples of group quarters being visited by interviewers.

Throughout the ACS development process, the Census Bureau worked closely with data users, particularly federal agency personnel who use census data to administer programs and distribute funds, to address their concerns about the new approach of continuous measurement. This outreach program included colloquia in 1995 and 1997 with federal statistical experts to explore the issues of the new design; a Rural Data Users Conference in 1998 to discuss specific concerns for small areas and populations outside cities; support for detailed studies at the Department of Housing and Urban Development (HUD) and the Department of Transportation (DOT) on issues related to their data applications; and, through the U.S. Office of Management and Budget (OMB), the creation of an interagency committee on the ACS to share information about plans with federal agencies. In addition, the Census Bureau solicited advice from Census Advisory Committees, informal town-hall-style meetings with data users, and a National Research Council Panel on the functionality and usability of ACS estimates.

See also *Long form; Sampling for content; Sampling in the census*

. . . . PRESTON JAY WAITE

American Community Survey: Implementation from 2005

The year 2005 is significant in the history of the American Community Survey (ACS) because it marks the end of more than a decade of testing and the beginning of what is generally regarded as full nationwide implementation. The 2005 implementation expanded earlier test samples to include all counties in the 50 states and the District of Columbia, as well as all *municipios* in Puerto Rico, for a total initial sample of about 2.9 million housing units. The 2005 sample did have one important limitation regarding coverage of the population—budget constraints restricted the sample to persons in housing units only, thus excluding persons in group quarters

(GQs). Starting in 2006, the sample was expanded to include residents in most types of GQs, which include facilities such as nursing homes, correctional institutions, military barracks, group homes, and college dormitories.

Beginning with the 2005 ACS and continuing every year thereafter, one-year estimates of demographic, social, economic, and housing characteristics are available for geographic areas with a population of 65,000 or more. These areas include the nation, all states and the District of Columbia, all congressional districts, approximately 800 counties, and 500 metropolitan and micropolitan statistical areas, among others—about 7,000 geographic areas in total. Starting in 2008, multi-year data products (for the period 2005–2007) were available for all areas of 20,000 or more—roughly an additional 7,000 areas. In late 2010, the Census Bureau began the release of the first five-year multi-year estimates (for the period 2005–2009) for all geographic areas down to census tract and block group levels. Since about 90 percent of all local governments in the nation have fewer than 20,000 people, 2010 was the first time these areas received any ACS data, all in the form of five-year period estimates.

Since its inception, the Census Bureau and data users have argued that one of the strengths of the ACS is the ability to make changes to the survey over time that will keep it in tune with national priorities and better meet the needs of data users. Changes have already been made to improve the content and data quality of the ACS and provide new tools and resources for data users.

Content Changes

The year 2008 was an important demarcation point in the ACS program because this would be the first year of a five-year estimate (for 2008–2012) centered on 2010, the date of the decennial census enumeration. Thus, any content changes that would be reflected in ACS estimates centered on 2010 for the smallest geographic levels would first have to appear in the 2008 data collection year. In turn, proposed 2008 content changes would have to be solicited, developed, and tested well before 2008. Therefore, preparations for new ACS data products for 2008–2012 actually began in late 2004, as part of meetings among members of the ACS Federal Interagency Committee, and culminated in the analysis of results from a large national content test held in 2006.

More than thirty federal agencies participated in the review of the ACS questionnaire and planning for the ACS 2006 Content Test. The goal was to improve questions and response categories and to evaluate alternatives for questions that showed some indication of a problem, for example, high missing data rates, estimates that differed systematically from other sources of the same information, or historically low reliability of reporting. The 2006 test also compared the ACS grid response format, in which a question such as age was asked of each household member, followed by another question, compared to the sequential questionnaire format planned for the 2010 census, in which all of the questions were asked of one household member before proceeding to the next person.

As a result of the input from federal agencies, subsequent Census Bureau cognitive testing, and the 2006 Content Test, the 2008 ACS data collection cycle saw the addition of new questions on marital history and health insurance coverage. Major conceptual changes also were made to the questions on disability, resulting in a break from earlier years of the ACS. In addition to new questions and questions with major modifications, about 30 minor modifications were implemented in 2008. Another change, designed to meet data needs of the National Science Foundation, was the addition of a question on field of study of bachelor's degree, but it could not be fully evaluated for inclusion in 2008. This new item was added in the 2009 data collection year.

The multi-year data product cycles of the ACS pose a unique problem for content and product changes. The new data collected in 2008 were available in the production year of 2009—but only for single-year data products for geographic areas of population 65,000 or greater. Since five years of ACS data are required for small geographic units with fewer than 20,000 residents, a new or modified question does not reach its full implementation until five full years of data are collected.

Given the logistical hurdles posed by content modifications, the Census Bureau decided to implement major changes only once every five years. Thus, the next major content redesign is focused on the year 2013. The ACS Federal Interagency Committee held meetings to determine needed changes that required testing. Topics considered for the ACS Content Test conducted in fall 2010 included Internet access and birthplace of parents. If all goes well, these questions will be included in the 2013 ACS, and users will see the first data products from these changes in late 2014.

Changes in Methodology/Data Collection

The major methodological change in the ACS since 2005 was the expansion of the survey to its "full implementation" level. Up until 2005, the survey was conducted as a large demonstration test. While data and associated products were processed and released to the public, these activities and products were part of the demonstration phase of the project.

This change to full implementation not only meant a sizable expansion of the initial sample, from 800,000 addresses to about 2.9 million, but also sample coverage of all 3,141 counties in the United States, as well as the 78 *municipios* in Puerto Rico. The workload for all ACS operations increased by more than 300 percent. Monthly mailouts from the National Processing Center (NPC) in Jeffersonville, Indiana, went from approximately 67,000 to 240,000 addresses per month. Telephone nonresponse follow-up (NRFU) workloads, conducted from three telephone call centers, expanded from 25,000 calls per month to approximately 85,000. More than 3,500 field representatives (FRs) across the country conducted follow-up visits at 40,000 addresses a month, up from 1,200 FRs conducting follow-ups at 11,000 addresses each month in 2004. In addition, full implementation saw the annual sample for Puerto Rico rise to approximately 36,000 addresses.

While virtually all continuing surveys of the Census Bureau limit their sample to the civilian non-institutional household population, in 2006, the ACS program was expanded to include sampling for residents in GQs. Concerns about privacy and the operational feasibility of repeated interviewing for an ongoing survey led to the decision to exclude some types of GQs, such as domestic violence shelters, soup kitchens, persons in targeted non-sheltered outdoor locations, and crews of commercial maritime vessels. Starting in 2006, the ACS sampled 2.5 percent of the population living in GQs for a total of approximately 20,000 GQ facilities and 195,000 people in GQs in the United States and Puerto Rico each year.

By 2008, the National Processing Center had switched data entry of the ACS mail form from a "key from paper" (KFP) approach to a "key from image" (KFI) method. Previously, clerks had keyed the data from mailed-back forms by reading the actual paper form and keying the information into a computer file. With the key from image method, the entire form was optically scanned and captured, which involved creating an image of the questionnaire, interpreting the check box entries with optical mark recognition (OMR) technology, and keying write-in responses from the images using a computerized system. The advantages of KFI include the potential for reduced costs and increased data capture accuracy.

While the initial yearly ACS sample is in the range of 2.9 million housing units, the actual sample upon which estimates are based is much smaller. One major reason for this attrition has to do with the fact that nonresponse follow-up is conducted on a *sample* of addresses that fail to respond by mail or telephone. Moreover, over the course of its implementation, the ACS has witnessed a general decline in mail and telephone response, further increasing the number of cases that require personal interviews and are therefore subject to subsampling. At present, the final sample that is used for the creation of estimates is in the range of about two million addresses per year or ten million cases over five years. This compares with approximately 16 million addresses in the 2000 long-form sample, which is one major reason why ACS estimates are less precise than those from the Census 2000 long-form sample.

In response, the Census Bureau has made several modifications to the survey sampling rate to improve statistical reliability of estimates for small geographic units as well as to optimize the sample overall. These modifications included increasing the sample for nonresponse follow-up in census tracts with low mail-back and telephone response. More recently, the overall size of the initial ACS sample was increased to 3.4 million addresses and a plan is being implemented to better distribute the sample by increasing the number of cases in small census tracts, while decreasing it in large tracts. In addition, the Census Bureau is reviewing the cost and efficiency of its sampling plan for persons in GQs. Finally, research has begun on the increased use of model-based estimation in an effort to improve the quality of small area data.

Changes in Data Products

As the ACS program moved into full implementation mode, the product set correspondingly began to evolve. Initially envisioned as a set of fairly basic two- and three-way tables (similar to those in the decennial census Summary Files 1 and 3), demands from both outside users and Census Bureau analysts led to an expansion of the detailed tables over a period of several years. In 2008, the first major increase in ACS data products was implemented. The number of Base Tables (also known as detailed tables) expanded to approximately 879. Ranking Tables increased to cover 64 additional population and housing characteristics; each includes a table, graphic representation, and chart of statistical significance. Thematic maps also became widely available for the first time. Subject Tables were also introduced in 2008. They are similar to the Census 2000 Quick Tables but contain much more detail than Quick Tables. Subject Tables display percent distributions rather than the estimates, except that the universe for each distribution is displayed as a numeric estimate (for example, a universe might be people aged 16 and older). Subject Tables allow for other measures such as medians and means where appropriate, and include the imputation rates for relevant measures. The Census Bureau issued Subject Tables in 42 subject areas, including education, employment, poverty, income, language, and housing.

Standard reports using ACS data also started to develop over time. Initially, a companion report to the annual poverty report based on Current Population Survey (CPS) data was issued. Since then, a series of reports have been issued on such topics as educational attainment, school enrollment, and fertility, using both the new ACS data and the historical data from the CPS. In 2009, the Census Bureau released a set of 16 "Briefs," short topical reports on specific data items, with the release of the one-year data products.

Quality measures have always been an important part of the ACS releases. The Census Bureau has updated the Quality Measures section of the ACS Web site to include national and state level quality measures for the 2007 and 2008 one-year estimates, joining the existing quality measures for the 2000 through 2006 ACS. The quality measures include sample sizes, coverage rates, response rates, and item allocation rates.

In an effort to better educate data users, the Census Bureau developed a series of 12 handbooks aimed at showing the appropriate use of ACS data. These *ACS Compass Products* include user-specific handbooks, fully scripted PowerPoint presentations, and an e-learning tutorial. Each handbook is designed to instruct and provide guidance to a particular audience. A web-based tutorial was released in 2010 and provides user-friendly training on the ACS, including "how to" demonstrations of accessing ACS data products in American Fact-Finder, the Census Bureau main portal to ACS data.

While standard data and information products constitute a large part of the continuing program of the ACS, the program also creates the potential for large numbers of specialized products. Historically, since only the decennial census could provide small-scale geographic information, "special tabs" were once-a-decade activities. With the ACS in place, these special products are likely to become more commonplace. Already, unique products looking at post-September 11, 2001, conditions in Lower Manhattan, as well as the states along the Gulf of Mexico after Hurricanes Katrina and Rita, have been provided to help planners and developers assess the impact of these major events.

On a more routine basis, various federal agencies, including the Equal Employment Opportunity Commission, the Department of Housing and Urban Development, the Justice Department, the Department of Education, and the Department of Transportation, have developed or are working to implement recurring special tabulations to support laws or legislative requirements of those agencies for particular data on small geographic areas. In fiscal year (FY) 2010 alone, 15 major special tabulation projects were under way. These products help to fulfill ACS's programmatic goal to provide timely data for decision-making and program applications. As the ACS data systems become more mature, it is likely that the demands for special products will continue to increase.

See also *Data products: evolution; Long form*

. . . . .   ROBERT A. KOMINSKI AND JOSEPH J. SALVO

American Community Survey: Methodology

The American Community Survey (ACS) methodology includes the set of methods and procedures that are used to select the survey's sample, collect and process survey interviews, and produce survey-based estimates. The Census Bureau conducts the ACS as part of the decennial census program under the authorization contained in Title 13 of the United States Code. As with the decennial count, Title 13 requires households to participate and for the Census Bureau to keep all information confidential. The ACS surveys the country's housing units and group quarters and the populations residing in them. In contrast to housing units, group quarters include such places as college residence halls, nursing homes, correctional facilities, and military barracks. The methods used to select and interview these two universes differ and are described separately below. The sample selection and data collection methods for the Puerto Rico Community Survey (PRCS) are similar to those used in the ACS.

All surveys require a frame from which a sample can be selected with known probability. The frame for the ACS is the Master Address File (MAF). The MAF is the Census Bureau's official inventory of known living quarters in the United States and Puerto Rico and is maintained throughout the decade by a series of automated, clerical, and field operations designed to reflect the changing housing inventory. The ACS samples of addresses are selected from the MAF to represent both the housing unit and group quarters populations. When the resulting interviews are combined, the survey data provide estimates of the characteristics of the total residential population.

Sample Selection and Data Collection for Housing Units

The ACS employs a two-phase sample design for housing units. In the first phase of sampling, an annual sample of about 2.9 million housing unit addresses is selected. To ensure the production of reliable estimates for the smallest geographic areas, the initial sampling rates are based on the estimated number of occupied housing units in each census block. The first-phase sampling rates for 2008 ranged from a low of 1.5 percent to a high of 10 percent of the addresses in each block. The sample is then divided into 12 panels of about 240,000 addresses each. Each month a new panel of sample addresses is introduced, and three sequential modes of data collection are used to collect the survey data for the panel over a three-month time period. Table 1 summarizes this mixed mode design. The mail mode is first. Each month the Census Bureau mails questionnaires to the new panel of housing unit addresses. The bureau accepts mail responses over the panel's full three-month data collection period. If the bureau does not receive a completed questionnaire from a household, they follow up with non-responding addresses initially by telephone, and then by selecting a subsample of the remaining non-responding addresses to visit in person. This overlapping panel design results in efficient continuous data collection within each mode throughout the entire year.

About 95 percent of the housing unit sample addresses are complete enough for mailing. The ACS uses four mailings to obtain as many mail responses as possible. An advance letter is sent a few days prior to the delivery of the ACS questionnaire, followed by a reminder postcard. A second questionnaire is sent to all nonresponding addresses about three weeks after the initial questionnaire. An instruction booklet accompanies the ACS questionnaire and toll-free telephone assistance is provided to help respondents complete the form. The ACS questionnaire is mailed in English, with Spanish questionnaires available upon request. Once the Census Bureau receives a questionnaire from the household in the mail, census staff scan the form and conduct an automated review to determine if the answers are sufficiently complete. If the form lacks sufficient

Table 1. American Community Survey Data Collection Schedule

SAMPLE PANEL	CALENDAR MONTH			
	JAN. 2010	FEB. 2010	MARCH 2010	APRIL 2010
Jan. 2010	Mail	Mail Phone	Mail Personal Visit	
Feb. 2010		Mail	Mail Phone	Mail Personal Visit
March 2010			Mail	Mail Phone

information, the bureau contacts the household by telephone to collect the missing data.

About five weeks after the initial mailout of questionnaires, the bureau identifies nonresponding addresses for follow-up by telephone. The bureau obtains telephone numbers from commercial vendors, and the nonresponding cases with an available telephone number are sent to the Census Bureau's telephone call centers. Interviewers at the call centers contact these cases and conduct computer assisted telephone interviews. The call centers recruit bilingual staff to conduct interviews in languages other than English. Telephone follow-up for each month's panel lasts about four weeks.

For 2008 and 2009, after the mail and telephone contacts, the Census Bureau received responses from about 51 percent of the initial sample. To reach the remaining households, the bureau initiates a second phase of sampling. The nonresponding addresses are subsampled to create a list of addresses that will have a personal visit from a census interviewer. Cases that could not be mailed to or contacted by telephone because the addresses were incomplete are also included in the universe that is subsampled. To account for the expected differences among geographic areas in levels of response by mail and telephone, there are four second-phase sampling rates, which range from a high of two-in-three to a low of one-in-three.

The Census Bureau's regional offices manage the personal visit follow-up. The interviewers use computer assisted methods. As with the call centers, the regional offices recruit staff with specialized language skills. Interpreters are also hired to assist with data collection. Personal visit follow-ups for each sample panel last about four weeks.

The combination of these three modes of data collection is very successful in obtaining completed interviews from the housing unit sample. The survey response rate, which is weighted to reflect the probabilities of selection of both the initial sample and the personal visit subsample, is about 97 percent, which means that interviews are not obtained for only about 3 percent of the *eligible* housing unit sample. This does not mean that 97 percent of the first phase sample is interviewed. Due to nonresponse, ineligible sample addresses, and

the second phase subsampling, only about 67 percent of the addresses selected in the *first phase* sample result in a completed interview.

Sample Selection and Data Collection for Group Quarters

Group quarters (GQs) and the people staying in them are sampled each year from the MAF. The smallest GQs are sampled in a similar manner to housing unit addresses, and all residents of the facilities selected for the sample are eligible to be interviewed. For large GQ facilities, sets of ten people are identified, and the final number to be interviewed is determined by the total number of residents in the facility. The annual GQ sample of about 20,000 facilities is divided into 12 monthly panels and results in a sample of approximately 195,000 persons for the year.

Data collection in GQs takes place in two phases. First, interviews are conducted with the contact person or administrator for each selected facility, and arrangements are made to conduct the interviews with residents. Second, a sample of residents to be interviewed is identified, which varies depending on the size of the facility. The collection of information from GQs is a very labor intensive process, involving field representatives at each stage, from the initial visit to verify the status of the facility to the actual interviews, which can involve multiple layers of approvals and different types of data collection. At some facilities, administrators may accept and distribute forms that are delivered and then picked-up by field representatives because of difficulties conducting personal interviews, for example, health issues among patients in nursing homes or other skilled nursing facilities. In other types of facilities, such as federal correctional institutions, approvals to conduct interviews need to be received ahead of time from the Federal Bureau of Prisons and interviews may be restricted to only certain months of the year. In addition, some interviews may take place over the telephone. The interview for GQs consists largely of the same questions asked of the general population, minus the housing information. Data collection for each monthly panel of GQs lasts about six weeks and does

---

WHO IS INTERVIEWED IN THE ACS?

Interview and residence rules define the scope of data collection by identifying the types of places included in a survey's sampling frame and the people eligible for inclusion. The ACS collects information about the population living in both housing units and group quarters, and its residence rules identify who should be interviewed at a sample address. Like the decennial census, the ACS interviews the population without regard to legal status or citizenship and excludes people only if the residence rules define their residence as somewhere other than the sample address.

The ACS uses a rule based on current residence. The people interviewed in an ACS sample housing unit are those who are living or staying in the unit when it is contacted, unless they are staying for only a short time, defined to be two months or less. In general, these short-term occupants are not eligible to be interviewed. Everyone residing in a group quarters when the facility is sampled and visited by an ACS interviewer is considered a resident and is eligible to be interviewed. In contrast, the decennial census determines a principal, or usual, place of residence on April 1, Census Day, defined as the place where a person lives most of the time.

not include a formal follow-up operation of non-responding residents.

These methods result in a high proportion of completed interviews from the GQ sample. The survey response rate, which is weighted to reflect the probabilities of selection, is about 98 percent, which means that interviews are not completed for about two percent of the eligible sampled group quarters population. However, given the difficulties associated with interviewing persons in institutions and other non-institutional arrangements, levels of missing data for questionnaire items are generally much higher for residents of GQs than for households.

Data Processing

Once the interviews are completed, the collected ACS data go through several steps before they are ready to be released as survey-based estimates. Some processes occur every month, but most happen only once a year. Electronic records of interviews conducted by telephone and in person arrive daily at the Census Bureau from the telephone call centers and regional offices, while paper questionnaires arrive daily by mail at the Census Bureau's National Processing Center. The information entered on the mailed-back forms is captured and converted to electronic computer records compatible with the telephone and personal visit records. The forms are scanned, creating a digital image of each, and the marked check box responses are read and interpreted from the image using optical mark recognition software especially designed to read entries on the ACS questionnaires. Many ACS responses on mail returns take the form of alphabetic write-ins, which are keyed from their digital images.

The data collected from mail, telephone, and personal visit interviews are accumulated each month, and certain responses are sent to coding operations. These operations convert race, Hispanic origin, ancestry, language, industry, occupation, place of birth, migration, and place of work responses into numeric codes, which are then added to their data records in preparation for the final processing that occurs at the end of the year. All data records undergo several checks to determine if they will be considered interviews and used to produce ACS estimates. The completeness of the records can range from all required information collected to all information missing. Records that do not include the required minimum amount of data are treated as noninterviews in the estimation process. Inconsistencies can also occur within interviews in which a response to one question contradicts a response to another. Content edits are applied to the ACS interview records that correct for both missing and inconsistent information.

Content edits are run once a year on the set of interviews conducted during the entire calendar year. The edits are designed by subject matter experts and specified by survey item. The purpose of the edits is two-fold: to apply rules that modify internally contradictory responses in a consistent way that helps maintain the quality of the data, and to deal with missing responses. Some edit rules are quite simple, as

when inconsistencies are identified and fixed: a person cannot be married if he/she is under the age of 15, and a person who reports their sex as male cannot respond to the fertility question as having given birth. In each case, flags identify these inconsistencies and rules are established to correct them. Other edits are very complicated and require comparisons of responses to several items. The consistency edit for housing value, for example, involves a joint examination of value, property taxes, and insurance. When the combination of variables is improbable, several variables may be modified to give a plausible combination with values as close as possible to the original. Edits are used to provide a value when a response is missing, which is done in two different ways: by assignment and by allocation. A value is considered an assignment when a response provided for a specific person or housing unit is used to generate the answer to a missing item for that same person or unit, as when a person's first name is used to assign a value for sex when it is missing. Certain values are more accurate when they are provided from another housing unit or person with similar characteristics. When a response is provided from the data record of another person or unit, the value is considered an allocation. For example, if a person fails to provide a response for the occupation question, that person's reported characteristics of age, sex, education, hours, and weeks worked are used as a basis for allocating an occupation from another person with similar characteristics. The Census Bureau monitors the levels of item allocation. Allocation rates are a key measure of data quality and are released each year concurrent with the survey-based estimates.

The final step in preparing the estimates to be published is called "disclosure avoidance." Disclosure avoidance measures are applied to the final data records to protect the confidentiality of survey respondents. The procedure used is called "swapping," in which a small percentage of household records are moved from one geographic area to another. The selection of households to be swapped targets the records with the highest risk of disclosure. All released data are created from the swapped data files.

Estimation

The ACS estimation process is based on pooling interview data collected over one year, three years, and five years, and results in three unique sets of ACS estimates. Each year the ACS actually collects data from about 1.9 million housing units and about 145,000 people living in group quarters facilities. This sample size is sufficient to support one-year estimates for the largest geographic areas—areas with populations of 65,000 or more. Three years of data collection are needed to produce estimates for areas with populations of 20,000 or more. Estimates for the full set of geographies, including areas as small as census tracts and block groups, require five years of data, or 60 months of interviews. Multi-year estimates are released every year based on new aggregations that exclude the data collected in the earliest year and include the data collected in the latest year. Table 2 illustrates

Table 2. Summary of American Community Survey Estimates and Release Schedule

DATA PRODUCT	POPULATION THRESHOLD	YEAR OF DATA RELEASE							
		2006	2007	2008	2009	2010	2011	2012	2013
		YEAR(S) OF DATA COLLECTION							
One-Year Estimates	65,000+	2005	2006	2007	2008	2009	2010	2011	2012
Three-Year Estimates	20,000+			2005–2007	2006–2008	2007–2009	2008–2010	2009–2011	2010–2012
Five-Year Estimates	All areas*					2005–2009	2006–2010	2007–2011	2008–2012

*Five-year estimates will be available for areas as small as census tracts and block groups.

SOURCE: U.S. Census Bureau.

the release schedule and the sets of interview data included in each year's release.

All housing unit and group quarters interviews completed from January 1 through December 31 of a specific year are used to produce the one-year estimates. The collected data are weighted to account for the ACS sample design and for survey coverage and nonresponse. The basic estimation approach is a raking ratio estimation procedure that results in the assignment of two sets of weights: a weight for each sample person record (both persons in housing units and in GQs) and a weight for each sample housing unit record. Ratio estimation is a method that uses auxiliary information to increase the precision of the estimates as well as correct for differential coverage of geographic areas and population groups. The ACS takes advantage of the availability of independent estimates of total housing units and the population by sex, age, race, and Hispanic origin that are produced by the Census Bureau's Population Estimates Program. This methodology results in ACS estimates that are consistent with these independent estimates for specified areas of geography.

The production of multi-year estimates follows a similar process. All interviews conducted from January 1 through December 31 of the three-year or five-year time period are pooled. New weights and noninterview adjustments are applied so that each year of data contributes proportionately to the multi-year estimates. Since these estimates cover a three- or five-year time period, the final adjustment is to a simple average of the independent housing and population estimates for the three- or five year time period.

ACS estimates are based on samples and are therefore subject to sampling error. Estimates of the sampling error associated with all ACS estimates are calculated and appear alongside published ACS estimates as margins of error.

See also *Long form; Sampling for content; Sampling in the census*

DEBORAH H. GRIFFIN
. . . . SUSAN P. LOVE

American Community Survey: Questionnaire Content

The determination of the particular questions on the American Community Survey (ACS), what is called "questionnaire content," is driven by mandates from Congress and the needs of federal agencies. In the process, the ACS also provides state and local government agencies, universities, private businesses, and other data users with essential information for geographic areas and population groups. There are four broad categories of questions covering the demographic, social, economic, and housing characteristics of the American population.

The U.S. Census Bureau coordinates the ACS content development and determination process for the ACS with the U.S. Office of Management and Budget (OMB) through an interagency committee comprised of more than 30 federal agencies. All requests for content changes are managed by the Census Bureau's ACS Content Council, which provides guidelines and oversight for pretesting, field testing, and implementing new content and changes to existing ACS content.

History of Content Development

The U.S Constitution mandates a decennial census, but it does not spell out a process for determining content. Early in the history of the census, members of Congress, statisticians, and other scholars urged that at the same time the population was enumerated, other important information should be collected. Thus, decennial censuses have always included both a "count" of persons and questions about persons in households and group quarters (GQs). Topics that were included and the kinds of questions asked have varied from decade to decade and often reflected policy-relevant issues of the time.

For Census 2000, the federal government classified all long-form content into three broad classes: (1) mandatory—a federal law required the use of decennial census data for a particular federal program; (2) required—a federal law or implementing regulation required the use of specific data, and the decennial census was the historical or only source, or the data were needed for case law requirements imposed by the U.S. federal court system; and (3) programmatic—the data were necessary for Census Bureau operational needs, and there was no explicit requirement for the use of the data under the mandatory or required categories. In general, questions that were classified as mandatory and required were approved for inclusion on the form; only a few programmatic questions were approved (for example, administrative questions such as telephone number were needed for operational purposes).

Shift from the Long Form to the American Community Survey

Each decennial census long form served as the foundation or starting point for the next decade's version. Thus, the initial content of the ACS at full implementation was based on the Census 2000 long form and, in general, was very similar. (New questions on the ACS included receipt of food stamps and whether any children were born in the last 12 months, asked of women between the ages of 15 to 50.) Even though the collection moved from a once-a-decade census to an annual survey, constraining the ACS content was deemed just as critical as it was for previous decennial census long-form questionnaires, due to the mandatory reporting requirement and the relatively high respondent burden.

To manage and provide oversight for the ACS content, the Census Bureau worked closely with OMB in July 2000 to establish a Federal Interagency Committee for the ACS, comprised of representatives from federal departments and agencies that use decennial census data. Working from the justification for the Census 2000 long form, federal agency representatives were asked to examine each question and provide the Census Bureau with the legal basis for requiring the data, the lowest geographic level required for the variables essential for cross-tabulation, and the frequency with which the data were needed.

This process continued throughout the decade and will continue in the future, in large part because the Census Bureau must justify ACS content as part of a regular cycle of evaluation by OMB. The Paperwork Reduction Act of 1995 (Public Law 104-13) requires that proposed information collections, such as surveys, be submitted to OMB for review and approval every three years.

Policy and Process Governing American Community Survey Content

The ACS is designed to produce detailed demographic, social, economic, and housing data every year. Because it accumulates data over time to obtain sufficient levels of reliability for dissemination for small geographic areas, the Census Bureau must minimize content changes. If a question changes significantly or has not been asked for long enough to accumulate three or five years' worth of data, then the data will not be available for dissemination for small areas.

In recent decades, statutory language requiring specific data was the primary justification for questions on the decennial census long form. In 2006, OMB, in consultation with Congress and the Census Bureau, adopted a more flexible approach to content determination for the ACS that focused more on OMB's role as the approving authority and less on using legislation to justify new or revised content. OMB's responsibility under the Paperwork Reduction Act requires that the practical utility of the data be demonstrated and that respondent burden be minimized, especially for the mandatory collection of information. In making ACS content determinations, OMB considers whether the data are needed frequently and at low levels of geography. They also consider whether there are other sources of the same data available that could meet a requestor's need. OMB approves new content on the basis of an agency's justification and program requirements. Legislation that specifies adding content to the ACS may also serve as justification.

The Census Bureau's ACS content policy is used as a basic guideline for all new question proposals from federal agencies and the Congress. The bureau does not solicit proposals for new or revised questions from the private sector, from state or local governments, or from the public at large. However, the process for obtaining OMB approval to continue ACS data collection requires that the Census Bureau notify the public of its proposed collection and provide the public with an opportunity to comment on content, burden, methodology, or other features of the survey. Thus, the Census Bureau often receives suggestions and input from internal and external groups, and the Federal Interagency Committee for the ACS obtains broad input from all federal agencies. Stemming from that input, the Census Bureau then coordinates the creation of subject area groups that include representatives from the Interagency Committee and the Census Bureau; these groups provide expertise in designing sets of questions and response categories so that the questions tested for possible inclusion or revision will meet the needs of data users.

American Community Survey Content Changes—Past and Future

The ACS content change process provides guidance for Census Bureau pretesting, including a field test, for all new or modified questions prior to incorporating them into the ACS questionnaire. As with most large surveys conducted by the federal government, changes in ACS content are always field tested prior to implementation. The Census Bureau submits the proposed questions to OMB for approval prior to testing. OMB approves testing for a new or revised question. Once the Census Bureau completes testing, OMB reviews and approves all changes to the instrument, including newly designed questions or revisions to existing questions.

Table 1. Subjects on the American Community Survey: 2005–2011

Population Items	
Age (and date of birth)	Income from earnings
Sex	Income from self-employment (non-farm plus farm self-employment)
Race	Income from Social Security or Railroad Retirement
Hispanic origin	Income from Supplemental Security Income
Relationship to household head	Income from public assistance
Marital status	Income from interest, dividends, rent, etc.
Marriage in the past 12 months *	Income from pensions
Number of times married *	All other income
Year of last marriage *	*Housing items*
Births in the past 12 months (for women ages 15–50)	Tenure–owned or rented
School attendance/educational attainment	Type of property (mobile home, single-family home, apartment, boat, RV, van, etc.)
Public or private school (for people enrolled in the past three months)	
Field of bachelor's degree ***	Value
Place of birth	Monthly rent
Citizenship	Does the rent include any meals?
Year of immigration	Number of rooms
Language spoken at home	Condominium status
How well English is spoken	Year household head moved into unit
Ancestry	Year structure built
Veteran status/period of service	Bathing facilities
Veteran's service-connected disability rating *	Toilet facilities
Place of residence one year ago	Hot and/or cold running water
Health insurance coverage *	Sink with a faucet
Disability —hearing impairment **	Kitchen facilities (stove or range)
Disability—vision impairment **	Kitchen facilities (refrigerator)
Disability—concentrating, remembering, or making decisions **	Telephone service, including cell phones
Disability—walking or climbing stairs **	Number of acres
Disability —dressing or bathing **	Sales of agricultural products in past 12 months
Disability—going outside of the home **	Business or medical office on property
Whether and how long responsible for grandchildren in home	Fuel used most for heating
Employment status	Electricity costs
Hours worked in preceding week	Gas costs
Occupation	Water costs
Industry	Oil, coal, kerosene, and/or wood costs
Class of worker	Food stamp receipt in past 12 months
Place of work	Mortgage payment (and whether includes taxes and insurance)
Means of transportation to work	Homeowners insurance
Commuting time and when usually left for work	Real estate taxes
Carpooling	Whether have second mortgage
On layoff or temporarily absent (if not employed last week)	Payment for second mortgage(s)/home equity loans
Looking for work in past four weeks	For mobile homes, total annual cost for taxes, site rent, registration fees, and license fees
Year last worked	
Weeks worked in past 12 months	Condominium fee
Hours worked per week in past 12 months	Number of bedrooms
Occupation, industry, class of worker	Automobiles, vans, and trucks

*Subject first added to the ACS in January 2008.

**Series substantially revised in January 2008, resulting in a break in series.

***Subject first added to the ACS in January 2009.

Note: Based on the results of the 2006 ACS Content Test, there were a number of improvements to wording and format of population and housing topics. See the following link for a more complete description of these changes: http://www.census.gov/acs/www/methodology/2006_summary_results/

In 2004, planning began for a major 2006 field test so that content changes in the ACS could be field tested before the 2008 ACS questionnaire was finalized. The 2006 ACS Content Test was the first opportunity to test revisions to the Census 2000 long-form-sample questions that provided the basis for the initial ACS questionnaire. The test included new questions on the subjects of marital history, health insurance coverage, and veterans' service-connected disability ratings. It also included many proposed revisions to topics on both the housing and population sections of the questionnaire.

The test methodology was designed to be similar to ACS data collection in the production phase. To measure response error, a computer assisted telephone interview content reinterview also was conducted. Simple response variance and gross difference rates, along with other data quality measures, such as item nonresponse rates and measures of distributional changes, served as indicators of the quality of the test questions relative to current ACS questions. The results of the test led to the implementation of the three new questions as well as a substantial number of revisions. A second, much smaller test was conducted in 2007 to test adding a question on undergraduate field of degree. The test proved successful, and the question was added to the ACS in January 2009. Table 1 lists the subjects on the ACS, since full implementation in 2005.

In September 2010, a new content test was conducted by the Census Bureau. Two new questions—computer and Internet access and parental place of birth—and several revisions to existing questions were tested. If testing demonstrates that these questions are viable, their earliest implementation would be in January of 2013.

See also *Content; Content determination; Long form*
. . . . CHET BOWIE AND SUSAN SCHECHTER

American Community Survey: Using Multi-year Estimates

Multi-year estimates for three-year and five-year periods are a product of the American Community Survey (ACS). These estimates, which provide continually updated information, must be used with care to understand what they do and do not represent.

The series of monthly samples that constitute the ACS can be combined in a variety of ways to produce survey-based estimates for geographic areas and population groups. Every year the Census Bureau produces three sets of estimates, for one-year, three-year, and five-year periods; the three sets of estimates are cumulated over 12, 36, and 60 months, respectively. The first time all three sets of period estimates were released was late 2010; the one-year estimates covered 2009, the three-year estimates 2007–2009, and the five-year estimates 2005–2009.

The reason to produce multi-year period estimates from the ACS is to cumulate the ACS sample over time in order to be able to provide estimates for small geographic areas. Only geographic areas with 65,000 or more people receive one-year (in addition to three-year and five-year) period estimates—one-year estimates for smaller areas would be much too imprecise to publish. Geographic areas with 20,000 or more people receive three-year (and five-year) period estimates, while the smallest geographic areas—small governmental units, census tracts, and block groups—receive only five-year period estimates (see Table 1).

Construction of Multi-year Estimates

The starting point for producing multi-year period estimates is to pool the survey data over the three or five years involved into a single file, in the same way that one-year data are pooled for the 12 months of data collected within a calendar year. Then, new weights are calculated for the combined sample to make the sample cases reflect the average total population for the relevant three- or five-year period. This procedure makes it possible to use a larger sample, not only to adjust for nonresponse to the survey, but also to control the estimates to independently derived population and housing unit totals. A larger sample is advantageous because the adjustments can be made for finer categories, such as age, sex, race, and ethnicity categories for the population controls. However, users must keep in mind that the estimates represent an average for the entire period and not for any particular month or year.

Other adjustments made to the three-year and five-year period data files are as follows.

The latest available geographic boundaries are used for all of the months in the combined sample. For example, if a city annexed a town in 2008, then its three-year period estimates for 2005–2007 would include all of the data collected within the *original* city boundaries for those three years, but its three-year period estimates for 2006–2008, 2007–2009, and so on would include all of the data collected within the *enlarged* city boundaries for all three of the relevant years.

The latest vintage of population and housing unit estimates are used as controls, including any corrections to prior year estimates. These controls are the averages of the population and housing unit estimates for the three- or five-year period.

A model-assisted weighting step is added to the weighting process to improve the precision of subcounty estimates. This step uses a generalized regression (GREG) approach, based on an administrative file of person characteristics by age, sex, race, and Hispanic origin maintained by the Census Bureau that is matched to the Master Address File (MAF). Note that the administrative data are not used directly in ACS estimates; they are used only in the weighting process.

Income amounts are adjusted for inflation. This adjustment is made because respondents to the ACS are asked to report their income for the prior 12 months. First, to put income amounts that are reported for differing 12-month reference periods on a comparable calendar-year basis, the Census Bureau expresses

Table 1. Major Geographic Areas and Type of American Community Survey Estimates Received

TYPE OF GEOGRAPHIC AREA	TOTAL NUMBER OF AREAS	PERCENT OF TOTAL AREAS WITH:		
		ONE-, THREE-, AND FIVE-YEAR ESTIMATES	THREE- AND FIVE-YEAR ESTIMATES ONLY	FIVE-YEAR ESTIMATES ONLY
States and District of Columbia	51	100.0	0.0	0.0
Congressional districts	435	100.0	0.0	0.0
Public Use Microdata Areas (PUMA)*	2,071	99.9	0.1	0.0
Metropolitan statistical areas	363	99.4	0.6	0.0
Micropolitan statistical areas	576	24.3	71.2	4.5
Counties and county equivalents	3,141	25.0	32.8	42.2
Urban areas	3,607	10.4	12.9	76.7
School districts (elementary, secondary, and unified)	14,120	6.6	17.0	76.4
American Indian areas, Alaska Native areas, and Hawaiian homelands	607	2.5	3.5	94.1
Places (cities, towns, and census designated places)	25,081	2.0	6.2	91.8
Townships and villages (minor civil divisions)	21,171	0.9	3.8	95.3
ZIP Code tabulation areas	32,154	0.0	0.0	100.0
Census tracts	65,442	0.0	0.0	100.0
Census block groups	208,801	0.0	0.0	100.0

* When originally designed, each PUMA contained a population of about 100,000. Over time, some of these PUMAs have gained or lost population. Due to the population displacement in the greater New Orleans areas caused by Hurricane Katrina in 2005, Louisiana PUMAs 1801, 1802, and 1805 no longer meet the 65,000-population threshold for one-year estimates.

SOURCE: U.S. Census Bureau (2008: Table 3). This tabulation is restricted to geographic areas in the United States. It was based on the population sizes of geographic areas from the July 1, 2007, Census Bureau population estimates and geographic boundaries as of January 1, 2007. Because of the potential for changes in population size and geographic boundaries, the actual number of areas receiving one-year, three-year, and five-year estimates may differ from the numbers in this table.

them in constant dollar terms by using the national Consumer Price Index for All Urban Consumers-Research Series (CPI-U-RS) for the latest calendar year covered by an estimate. For three-year period estimates for, say, 2007–2009, the incomes for people sampled in 2007 and 2008 (which were already adjusted to calendar 2007 or 2008 on a one-year basis) were adjusted to calendar year 2009 by the ratio of the annual average CPI for 2009 divided by the annual average CPI for 2007 or 2008, as the case may be. This adjustment expresses all of the reported income amounts for a given period (one year, three years, or five years) in a comparable manner with regard to purchasing power as of the most recent calendar year in the period. Such an adjustment should not be confused with a current-year estimate, given that incomes may grow faster (or more slowly) than prices.

For poverty estimates, the Census Bureau's method for determining poverty status for families and their members does not require adjusting income amounts for inflation. The Census Bureau compares the income of a family (or unrelated individual) for a 12-month reporting period, *not* adjusted for inflation, to an average of 12-month nominal dollar poverty thresholds by family size and type for that same period. (The official poverty measure is constructed in a similar manner except that the income and thresholds refer to a calendar year.) For a five-year period estimate, then, the poverty rate is the average rate of everyone in the sample over the five years.

Some housing costs are adjusted for inflation. While the Census Bureau makes no inflation adjustments for the one-year period estimates of housing value, rent, utilities, property taxes, and other housing costs, it does make such adjustments for the three-year and five-year period estimates. It adjusts housing costs for inflation by using the ratio of the annual average CPI value for the latest year of the three-year or five-year period to the annual average CPI value for the year for which the amounts were reported. These three-year and five-year period estimates for rent, housing value, utilities, and other housing amounts expressed in dollars for the latest year of the period are not the same as estimates for the latest year.

Some estimates are suppressed (that is, not published). The Census Bureau deletes entire tables or collapses the cells in tables containing one-year and three-year period estimates that are highly imprecise. Such suppression is not applied to five-year period estimates so that information for small areas is available for aggregation into larger areas. However, some small-area estimates are suppressed when the Census Bureau's Disclosure Review Board (DRB) determines that their release could lead to disclosure of data for an individual. Also, fewer tables of five-year period estimates are made available for block groups than for larger areas because of very small sample sizes.

Working with Multi-year Estimates

For geographic areas where one-year and multi-year period estimates are available from the ACS, users need to determine which set to use, considering the trade-off between having the most recent data possible (which favors one-year period estimates) and having the most precise data possible (which favors multi-year period estimates). When working with the multi-year period estimates, users need to take care to understand what they do and do not represent. For example, a five-year period estimate that 10 percent of people in a county or city live in poor families could reflect any of the following: a constant 10 percent across the five years; a steady increase from, say, 7 percent to 13 percent; a corresponding steady decrease; a rise and decline in the percentage across the years; and so on. To obtain an indication of the likely pattern that underlies a five-year (or three-year) estimate, users need to apply local knowledge of the conditions in the area over the period. They can also examine the published one-year estimates for a larger area that contains the area of interest.

Users of multi-year population counts also need to recognize that the counts (for example, the number of persons in poverty) are average counts across the period. Some small areas may appreciably increase or decrease in population size over a three- or five-year period, making it difficult to interpret an average count for the period.

Some considerations for users of multi-year ACS estimates for common applications are outlined below.

Precision. Even when ACS data are combined over five years, the resulting estimates are less precise than the comparable Census 2000 long-form-sample estimates, and are often highly imprecise. In particular, ACS five-year estimates for areas with small populations, such as census tracts and block groups within cities and other larger areas and small governmental jurisdictions (such as cities, towns, school districts, and some rural counties), can be subject to very high levels of sampling error. Equally, estimates of the characteristics for small

population groups in large areas, such as schoolchildren or disabled persons, can be very imprecise. In such cases, where possible, users are advised to aggregate estimates for smaller areas or population groups to form estimates for larger areas or groups.

Interarea comparisons. It is important not to mix and match ACS period estimates in making comparisons across geographic areas. For example, in comparing the percentage of poor people or employed people in each county of a state, it would be inappropriate to use one-year period estimates for large counties, three-year period estimates for medium-sized counties, and five-year estimates for small counties because economic conditions may have changed during the time period. An appropriate alternative would be to use five-year period estimates for all counties. If more recent estimates are desired, then one-year or three-year period estimates could be compared for large counties and for Public Use Microdata Areas (PUMAs, which are usually combinations of counties) for the remainder of each state.

Comparisons across time. For small geographic areas for which only multi-year period estimates are produced, the study of change over time is complicated. Users will be tempted to compare the change from one year to the next for small geographic areas by comparing overlapping three-year or five-year period estimates—for example, by comparing the percent of poor people for a small city in 2005–2007 with the percent of poor people in 2006–2008, or by comparing a census tract in 2005–2009 with 2006–2010. However, estimates of change based on differences between overlapping three-year or five-year period estimates are generally not useful—the reason is that the overlapping pairs of estimates contain much data in common (see Table 2). For example, estimates for 2005–2009 and 2006–2010 contain the same data for 2006, 2007, and 2008, so the only data that could generate a change are for 2005 and 2010. Yet for a small area that only has five-year period estimates available, the sampling variability of the difference between the two single years (2005 and 2010) is very large, and almost inevitably much larger than the difference itself, so that no conclusions can be drawn about the statistical significance of any difference. Furthermore, even with nonoverlapping estimates, the estimates of differences will generally be fairly imprecise. Analyses of change will be most productive for small geographic areas for which multi-year estimates must be compared only when major changes have occurred, or for large geographic areas for which one-year estimates are precise enough to be published.

A final point regarding differences between multi-year period estimates is that just like the estimates themselves, they can reflect a variety of patterns in the underlying one-year estimates. For example, a two percent change between two nonoverlapping three-year period estimates of the percent of poor people would occur if the estimate for each of the first three years was, say, 10 percent and that for each of the second three years was 12 percent. Alternatively, the two percent change could reflect an estimate of 10 percent for the first five

Table 2. Overlapping Years in Successive ACS Five Year Estimates, 2005-2011

ESTIMATE PERIOD	ACS YEARS						
	2005	2006	2007	2008	2009	2010	2011
4 Years of Overlap							
2005-2009	X	X	X	X	X		
2006-2010		X	X	X	X	**X**	
2006-2010		**X**	X	X	X	X	
2007-2011			X	X	X	X	**X**
3 Years of Overlap							
2005-2009	X	**X**	X	X	X		
2007-2011			X	X	X	**X**	**X**

X - Overlapping Year **X** - Unique Year (Non-overlapping Year)

years and an estimate of 16 percent for the sixth year. Users need to be aware of the possible underlying patterns and find ways to distinguish between them based on other sources or on ACS data at other levels of aggregation.

Despite their limitations, the multi-year period estimates are generally an improvement over the once-a-decade census long-form-sample estimates. Since they are updated every year, they provide a more recent picture of the characteristics of an area than is possible from the long-form sample.

See also *Long form; Sampling for content*

CONSTANCE F. CITRO
. . . . AND GRAHAM KALTON

American Community Survey: Data Products

Data products from the American Community Survey (ACS) include tables and maps that contain estimates of population and housing characteristics and computer files that contain individual person and housing data protected to ensure the confidentiality of respondents. Rather than collect information as part of the ten-year census cycle, the U.S. Census Bureau now collects detailed socioeconomic and housing information every year using the ACS. Sample size limits, however, require that multiple years of data be combined to provide reliable estimates for geographic areas with fewer than 65,000 people. Thus, the ACS provides three different sets of data products: one-year estimates (for areas with 65,000 or more persons), three-year estimates (for areas with 20,000 or more persons), and five-year estimates (for all areas). ACS data products are produced for geographic areas within the United States and Puerto Rico and are available through the Census Bureau's Web site.

Defining the Data Products

ACS data products were initially designed to be comparable to Census 2000 long-form sample products. However, based on extensive input from data users, the ACS data products have been redesigned and expanded, and additional tables have been added to reflect new content in the ACS that was not included in the Census 2000 long form. There are some differences between the data products provided for the one-year, three-year, and five-year ACS data. Table 1 provides a comparison of the ACS data products with the Census 2000 long-form sample products. These data are available through American FactFinder (AFF) on the Census Bureau's Web site, accessible either directly or as downloadable files.

The ACS was fully implemented in 2005, and one-year ACS data products are available for each year thereafter. Three-year ACS data products started in 2008, with the release of the 2005–2007 period estimates and subsequent releases for 2006–2008 and 2007–2009. The first five-year ACS data products for 2005–2009 were released at the end of 2010. Annual releases of one-year, three-year, and five-year ACS data products are planned for each year in 2011 and thereafter.

ACS data products can be divided into two broad categories: **tabulated data products** and **microdata files**. The tabulated data products contain precalculated estimates of frequently requested totals, percentages, means, medians, and ratios.

Table 1. Comparison of Census 2000 and ACS Data Products

DATA PRODUCT	GEOGRAPHIC AREAS COVERED			
	2000 CENSUS	ACS 1-YEAR (65,000+)	ACS 3-YEAR (20,000+)	ACS 5-YEAR (no threshold)
Data Profiles / Quick Tables	Selected	All	All	Selected
Narrative Profiles	N/A	All	All	Selected
Selected Population Profiles	N/A	Areas with pop >= 500,000	Areas with pop >= 500,000	N/A
Comparison Profiles	N/A	All	N/A	N/A
Detailed Tables	All	All	All	All
Subject Tables / Quick Tables	Selected	All	All	Selected
Ranking Tables	N/A	States, DC, Puerto Rico	N/A	N/A
Geographic Comparison Tables	All down to Census Tract	State, County, Place, Congressional District, CSA, AIAN Area and ANRC, CBSA, Urban/Rural, Urbanized Area	State, County, Place, Congressional District, CSA, AIAN Area and ANRC, CBSA, Urban/Rural, Urbanized Area	State, County, Place, Congressional District, CSA, AIAN Area and ANRC, CBSA, Urban/Rural, Urbanized Area
Thematic Maps	All	State, County, CSA, MSA, Congressional District, PUMA	State, County, CSA, MSA, Congressional District, PUMA	State, County, CSA, MSA, Congressional District, PUMA
Summary Files	All	All	All	All
Public Use Microdata Sample Files	States, DC, Puerto Rico, PUMAs	States, DC, Puerto Rico, PUMAs	States, DC, Puerto Rico, PUMAs	States, DC, Puerto Rico, PUMAs

NOTE: CBSA: Core Based Statistical Area; CSA: Combined Statistical Area; AIAN: American Indian and Alaskan Native; ANRC: Alaska Native Regional Corporation; PUMA: Public Use Microdata Area.

The microdata files, known as Public Use Microdata Sample (PUMS) files, contain a sample of the individual person and housing data and can be used to produce estimates not already published in the tabulated data products.

One important difference between ACS data products and Census 2000 data products is the inclusion of 90-percent margins of error (MOE) for all estimates in ACS tabulated data products. The MOE is a measure of the precision or reliability of an estimate. The larger the margin of error for an estimate, the less reliable or precise is that estimate. These margins of error can also be used to calculate 90-percent confidence intervals, which indicate that data users can be 90-percent confident that the true population value will usually fall within the range defined by the confidence interval. The margins of error in ACS tabulated data products provide an important tool to help data users understand the reliability of ACS estimates and to draw appropriate conclusions from the data. Measures of reliability are not provided in ACS PUMS files but can be calculated using either a standard formula or the replicate weights that are included in the files.

Tabulated Data Products

The range of ACS tabulated data products is very similar to that for Census 2000. Tabulated data products range from simple profiles for novice users with limited information needs to very detailed tables for advanced users requiring very specific types of information. Note that some of the tabulated data products for one-year ACS data are not provided for three- and five-year ACS data.

Data Profiles

Data Profiles provide four separate fact sheets on the broad demographic, social, economic, and housing characteristics for different geographic areas. Data Profiles display derived measures such as means and medians, estimated totals, and percent distributions. These are similar to the Census 2000 Data Profiles DP-1, DP-2, DP-3, and DP-4 provided in the Census 2000 Quick Tables data product.

Narrative Profiles

Narrative Profiles provide clear, concise, textual descriptions and graphical displays of selected measures included in the data profiles. They are a new data product for the ACS, which was not available for Census 2000 data.

Selected Population Profiles

Selected Population Profiles (SPPs) provide a predefined set of selected characteristics from the four Data Profiles for a specific race, Hispanic origin, ancestry, or country of birth population group. Many of the race, Hispanic origin, and ancestry group choices are similar to those included in the Census 2000 Summary Files 2 and 4. SPPs are produced for states, congressional districts, and all other geographic areas with a total population of 500,000 or more. However, for an area to receive a one-year SPP, it must also have a population of at least 65,000 in the race, ethnic, ancestry, or country of birth group of interest, and to receive a three-year SPP, it must have a population of at least 20,000 for the group of interest. Selected Population Profiles were not included in the Census 2000 data products and are not currently published for five-year ACS data.

Comparison Profiles

Comparison Profiles compare Data Profile estimates and distributions across time and denote statistically significant changes between the previous year's and the current year's estimates. The Comparison Profiles are currently only available for one-year estimates beginning with the 2006 ACS. There are four types of Comparison Profiles—demographic, social, economic, and housing—and they display the same characteristics as those included in the corresponding Data Profiles product. Comparison Profiles were not included in the Census 2000 data products.

Detailed Tables

The Detailed Tables provide the most in-depth ACS data available on all topics and geographic areas and serve as the source data for many other data products. Many detailed tables also have a corresponding "collapsed" version that contains less detail. Geographies that do not have enough respondents to support publication of the full detailed table may only receive the collapsed table. There are more than 1,400 tables in the ACS Detailed Tables product, including tables iterated or repeated for nine race and Hispanic origin groups, as well as tables that show how much of the data are allocated (that is, provided by Census Bureau edit routines because the data are missing).

Subject Tables

Subject Tables display detailed ACS data on a particular topic, such as employment, education, or income, generally drawn from multiple detailed tables. There are currently over 60 ACS Subject Tables, which are similar to those in the Census 2000 Quick Tables product.

Ranking Tables

Ranking Tables provide state rankings of key ACS variables. Ranking Tables can be displayed in three ways—as charts, tables, and tabular displays that allow for the testing of statistical significance. The data in the Ranking Tables come directly from the detailed tables. Ranking Tables are only produced for the one-year ACS data and were not included in the Census 2000 data products. There are currently over 90 ACS Ranking Tables.

Geographic Comparison Tables

Geographic Comparison Tables (GCTs) contain the same ACS variables that are included in the Ranking Tables, but compare other types of geographic areas in addition to states. They are produced for one-year, three-year, and five-year ACS data. GCTs are produced for states and substate geographies, including counties, places, congressional districts, and metropolitan areas.

Thematic Maps

Thematic maps provide graphical displays of the same ACS estimates available in the Geographic Comparison Tables and Ranking Tables. Different shades of color are used to display variations in the data across geographic areas. Data users can also highlight areas with statistically different values from a selected state, county, metropolitan area, or congressional district of interest.

Summary Files

Data users may want to download summary files because this product provides a level of flexibility for the user that is not available from American FactFinder (AFF), the Census Bureau's primary Web site for the dissemination of ACS data products. This flexibility can prove to be very useful, for example, when performing more complex aggregation of geographic areas or table cells. The standard summary files published as part of the one-year and three-year data products contain all of the Detailed Tables published on AFF and are available as a series of comma-delimited text files on the Census Bureau's File Transfer Protocol (FTP) Web site. The full set of Detailed Tables for the five-year data as well as the Detailed Tables for block groups are only available in the five-year ACS summary file product on the FTP site. The five-year Detailed Tables published on AFF are limited largely to those tables that are comparable to the Census 2000 tables down to the census tract level.

In addition to the standard ACS summary files, the Census Bureau plans to release a five-year race and Hispanic origin summary file that provides Detailed Tables for many race and Hispanic origin groups. This file will be similar to summary file 4 from 2000. Plans also include a five-year American Indian and Alaska Native Summary File that provides Detailed Tables for many American Indian and Alaska Native groups, similar to the product provided for Census 2000 data. These two additional ACS Summary Files are scheduled for release in 2012 using the five-year ACS data for 2006–2010.

Microdata Files

Microdata are untabulated records that contain information collected about individual people and housing units. The ACS Public Use Microdata Sample (PUMS) files are extracts or samples from the confidential microdata that avoid disclosure of information about households or individuals and allow users to generate estimates that are not available in the tabulated data products.

The only geography other than nation and state shown on a PUMS file is the Public Use Microdata Area (PUMA). PUMAs are special non-overlapping areas that partition a state. Each PUMA contains a population of at least 100,000 persons.

State governments drew the current ACS PUMA boundaries prior to Census 2000.

PUMS files are available as ASCII text files with comma-separated values (CSV) and in two versions of SAS data sets (PC-SAS files and UNIX files), and are published as part of the one-year, three-year, and five-year data products. The multi-year PUMS files combine annual PUMS files to create larger samples in each PUMA, covering a longer period of time. Tools are available to assist data users with the creation of tabulations, such as the Integrated Public Use Microdata Series (IPUMS) and the Census Bureau's Federated Electronic Research, Review, Extraction, and Tabulation Tool (DataFerrett).

Geography

Similar to the decennial census, ACS data products are published not only for legal and administrative areas, but also for statistical areas. Legal and administrative areas include states, counties, incorporated places, and congressional districts. Statistical areas are defined by the Census Bureau in cooperation with state and local agencies and include regions, divisions, census designated places (CDPs), census tracts, and block groups. Since several years of ACS samples are combined to produce the multi-year data products, the geographic boundaries for multi-year estimates are always the boundary as of January 1 of the final year of the period. For example, the geographic boundaries for the 2005–2009 ACS products are as of January 1, 2009. The boundaries for the 2006–2010 ACS products are as of January 1, 2010, the same as those for the 2010 census data products.

Generation of Data Products

Disclosure Avoidance

The Census Bureau's Disclosure Review Board (DRB) reviews all ACS data products to ensure that the confidentiality of respondents has been preserved. The Census Bureau uses several statistical methods during tabulation and the creation of the PUMS files—swapping of household records, top-coding, age perturbation or modification, and table suppression—to ensure that individually identifiable data will not be released.

Data Release Rules

In addition to disclosure avoidance procedures, data release rules based on the statistical reliability of the ACS estimates are applied to the one- and three-year data products. If more than half of the estimates in a table are not statistically different from 0 (at a 90 percent confidence level), then the table fails and is not published. In order to provide for the aggregation of small geographic areas, this data release rule does not apply to the five-year data products (although some level of suppression may still occur because of disclosure avoidance rules).

Custom Data Products

In addition to data products regularly released to the public, other data products may be requested by government agencies, private organizations and businesses, or individuals. To accommodate such requests, the Census Bureau operates a custom tabulations program for the ACS on a fee basis. Custom tabulation requests are reviewed by the DRB to assure protection of confidentiality before release. Once they are created, customized data products are available to anyone, on request. Examples of customized products include special tabulations for Lower Manhattan in New York City to help deal with the aftermath of the September 11, 2001, attacks, and for the Gulf Coast, in the wake of Hurricanes Rita and Katrina.

See also *Data products: evolution; Public Use Microdata Samples (PUMS); Summary files.*

SCOTT BOGGESS
. . . . AND LINDA A. JACOBSEN

Frequently Asked Questions about the American Community Survey (ACS)

1. In 2000 there was a decennial census long form with many questions on the social and economic characteristics of the population. I have heard that it no longer exists. What happened to the long form and what source is available to me now for these data?

The long form has been replaced by the American Community Survey (ACS). Rather than collect and release social and economic data once a decade at census time, the Census Bureau now contacts about 240,000 addresses each month to collect these data in the ACS and releases the data each year. This continuous measurement provides for annual updates of these important social and economic characteristics.

2. Does the American Community Survey (ACS) replace the decennial census?

No, it does not. The decennial census is still the source of official counts of population for reapportioning seats in the U.S. House of Representatives, for drawing congressional and other political districts, and for gauging compliance with laws related to voting and civil rights. Moreover, the decennial census counts by age, sex, race, and Hispanic origin are used as a basis for producing population estimates throughout the decade. These population estimates are used in formulas that allocate federal funds to states and localities and to "control" ACS data so that they match the official population estimates for geographic areas.

3. What kinds of data will be released from the 2010 decennial census and how do they differ from the data released from the ACS?

The 2010 decennial census data will only include age, sex, race, Hispanic origin, housing tenure (owner-renter), relationship to the household head (for example, spouse, child, unmarried partner), and type of household (for example, married couple; female householder, no spouse). The ACS includes these demographic characteristics as well as additional social, economic, and housing characteristics that will not be released as part of the 2010 census.

4. If the same data appear in the 2010 decennial census and in the ACS, which should I use?

The decennial census is the most accurate source of data for counts of population and housing because it is based on a full enumeration. If the data you want are available from the 2010 decennial census, they should be used. However, as time goes on, the 2010 decennial census data will quickly become out-of-date in many places, and the ACS may become the better choice.

5. Can I compare ACS data with data from Census 2000 for my area?

Yes, but not for all items. There are differences in some questions and reference periods that make some comparisons inappropriate. For a guide on making ACS comparisons with data from Census 2000, go to "Comparing ACS Data" under the "Guidance for Data Users" part of the Census Bureau's ACS website at: http://www.census.gov/acs/www/.

6. What is a "multi-year period estimate" and how does it differ from numbers I got from the long form in 2000?

In 2000, a sample of housing units received a long form, which contained the same demographic and housing questions asked at every housing unit plus more than 50 questions on social, economic, and housing characteristics, such as language spoken, education, income last year, and number of rooms in a house. The ACS questionnaire is very similar to this long form, but the data are collected over a period of months and then "rolled-up" on an annual basis. For some places (with at least 65,000 population), 12 months of data are sufficient to create estimates. For smaller places, more months of sample are needed to produce estimates: 36 months (three years) of data for places of 20,000 to 65,000 and 60 months (five years) of data for places with fewer than 20,000 people.

Decennial census data were collected over a fairly short time period—about four months—and are usually interpreted as presenting the characteristics of population and housing around April 1. The ACS one-year estimates are based on data collected over a full 12 months, and they should be interpreted as describing the average characteristics for that year. Similarly, ACS three-year and five-year estimates should be interpreted as representing the average characteristics for the three- or five-year period.

7. Sometimes geographic areas change their boundaries. What boundaries are used in the ACS when the data are for multi-year periods?

For multi-year periods, the geographic boundaries are taken from the latest year of the period. So, if data are presented for 2005–2009 for a city or town, the place's boundaries as of 2009 are used for the estimate.

8. I am interested in the census tract and block group data. I know that the Census Bureau sometimes changes the boundaries of these areas. How does this affect the 2005–2009 estimates for census tracts and block groups from the ACS?

The 2005–2009 ACS five-year estimates use census tract and block group boundaries from 2000. Starting with the release of the 2010 census data in 2011 and for all decennial census and ACS products in the coming decade, census tracts and block groups will change to new 2010 boundaries. Therefore, the 2005–2009 ACS five-year estimates for census tracts and block groups will be the last estimates to make use of 2000 boundaries. Information on these changes is available from the Census Bureau at the Redistricting web page: http://www.census.gov/rdo/.

9. What does MOE stand for?

MOE stands for margin of error. Both Census 2000 long-form estimates and ACS estimates are derived from a sample, and the estimates can therefore vary, plus or minus the MOE. This is frequently referred to as "sampling error" or the variability in a number based on the fact that it is taken from a sample and not an entire population. The ACS sample is smaller than the Census 2000 sample, so margins of error tend to be larger than those from the 2000 census long-form sample.

10. How do I know if data are reliable?

There is no hard- and- fast rule regarding reliability, since it depends on how the data are being used. A general rule is to calculate the upper limit (number plus the MOE) and the lower limit (number minus the MOE) and ask whether the number is useful for the purpose at hand, given that range. For some purposes, a broad range is acceptable, for example, to obtain a general sense of the population with difficulties speaking English. In other cases, the range may be unacceptable and other data sources should be consulted, as when an exact count of persons of limited English proficiency is needed for estimating budget expenditures or space for an instructional program.

11. My town has 42,000 residents. I have numbers for a three-year period (2007–2009) and for a five-year period (2005–2009) available. Which should I use?

It depends on what the numbers are being used for. The three-year numbers are more current, but the sample is limited to three years; conversely, the five-year numbers have a larger sample but are not as current. If you are examining employment or other economic characteristic, the three-year estimates are likely better because they exclude the boom years prior to the recent recession. On the other hand, if you are looking to get a figure for something that may not be as time-sensitive, such as the percent of the adult population who completed high school, sample size would likely trump the need to be current, so the five-year numbers may better serve your purpose. A good rule- of- thumb is to start with the three-year estimates and assess the margins of error for your application; if you think you need estimates with smaller margins of error, move to the five-year data.

12. Are data for census tracts and block groups available on American FactFinder (AFF)?

All ACS data products can be accessed from the AFF. The full complement of ACS tabulations is available for census tracts as tables in the American FactFinder. This includes profiles as well as more detailed tables. Block group tables are more limited and are only available in summary file format for download in the Download Center of AFF.

13. I have heard that the Census Bureau suppresses tables in an effort to minimize the release of unreliable estimates. How does this affect the release of the five-year estimates for census tracts and block groups from the ACS?

The Census Bureau has decided not to subject any of the five-year estimates to suppression based on their reliability. This is being done to encourage data users to use census tracts and block groups as building blocks for aggregation to larger customized geographic areas. Aggregation translates into larger samples and more reliable estimates and often results in areas that better suit specific applications. Keep in mind, however, that the one-year and three-year ACS data are subject to reliability thresholds, which may result in parts of tables or whole tables being suppressed.

14. Can the numbers from the 2005–2009 ACS be seen as representing the midpoint of that period—2007?

A. No. The estimates represent an average for the entire period and should not be associated with any single-year time point.

15. What are the Public Use Microdata Samples (PUMS) and when should they be used?

PUMS files are samples of individual records of census or ACS responses for households and people, stripped of identifying information (for example, names and detailed geographic codes). Unlike the tables reported for geographic areas in AFF, which are fixed, PUMS records can be used to create custom tabulations to answer more detailed questions, with the only major limitation being sample size. To ensure confidentiality, records in the PUMS files cannot be identified for geographic areas of fewer than 100,000 persons. Thus, the PUMS cannot be used to create custom tables for smaller geographic areas.

16. What is the PUMA Summary Level and why is it important?

PUMAs are Public Use Microdata Areas. They are nonoverlapping geographic areas, composed of census tracts that partition a state, each containing at least 100,000 persons. State governments drew the PUMA boundaries at the time of Census 2000. Since full implementation of the ACS in 2005, PUMAs have appeared as a summary level for the creation of tabulations online through American FactFinder (AFF). Thus, ACS data have been made available for the one-year and three-year period estimates at the PUMA level through AFF. In December of 2010, the first five-year PUMA estimates were made available through AFF. One-year and three-year PUMA estimates are useful when data are needed for substate areas (or subcounty or subcity areas in counties and cities with enough people to have two or more PUMAs) that are more up to date than the five-year data for census tracts and block groups.

BIBLIOGRAPHY

Evolution of the ACS

Alexander, Charles H. "Still Rolling: Leslie Kish's 'Rolling Samples' and the American Community Survey." *Survey Methodology* 28 (2002): 35–41.
———. "Determination of Sample Size for the Intercensal Long Form Survey Prototype." Internal Census Bureau Report CM-8. Washington, D.C.: U.S. Bureau of the Census, 1993.
———. "Overview of Research on the "Continuous Measurement" Alternative for the U.S. Census Bureau." Internal Census Bureau Report CM-11. Washington, D.C.: U.S. Bureau of the Census, 1993.
———. "Three General Prototypes for a Continuous Measurement System." Internal Census Bureau Report CM-1. Washington, D.C.: U.S. Bureau of the Census, 1993.
———. "An Initial Review of Possible Continuous Measurement Designs." Internal Census Bureau Report CM-2. Washington, D.C.: U.S. Bureau of the Census, 1992.
Herriot, Roger, David Bateman, and William F. McCarthy. "The Decade Census Program—A New Approach for Meeting the Nation's Needs for Sub-National Data." *Proceedings of the American Statistical Association, Social Statistics Section,* 1989: 351–355.
Horvitz, Daniel G. "Statement to the Subcommittee on Census and Population, Committee on Post Office and Civil Service, U.S. House of Representatives, May 1." Research Triangle Park, N.C.: Research Triangle Institute, 1986.
Johnson, Bruce, and S. Rowland. "Directions for the Future of the U.S. Decennial Census in the 21st Century." *Proceedings of the American Statistical Association, Social Statistics Section,* 1989: 329–334.
Kish, Leslie. *Using Cumulated Rolling Samples to Integrate Census and Survey Operations of the Census Bureau.* Washington, D.C.: U.S. Government Printing Office, 1981.
U.S. Bureau of the Census. *Measuring America: The Decennial Censuses from 1790 to 2000.* Washington, D.C.: U.S. Department of Commerce, 2002.
U.S. Department of Transportation, Bureau of Transportation Statistics. "Implications of Continuous Measurement for the Uses of Census Data in Transportation Planning." Washington, D.C., 1996.

ACS Methods and Tests

Gage, Linda. "Comparison of Census 2000 and American Community Survey 1999–2001 Estimates—San Francisco and Tulare Counties, California." Report submitted to U.S. Census Bureau, 2004.
Hough, George C., and David A. Swanson. "The 1999–2001 American Community Survey and the 2000 Census—Data Quality and Data Comparisons—Multnomah County, Oregon." Report submitted to U.S. Census Bureau, 2004.
National Research Council. "Using the American Community Survey: Benefits and Challenges." Panel on the Functionality and Usability of Data from the American Community Survey, Constance F. Citro and Graham Kalton, Editors. Committee on National Statistics, Division of Behavioral and Social Sciences and Education, Washington D.C.: The National Academies Press, 2007: Part II, Technical Issues.

Salvo, Joseph J., Arun Peter Lobo, and Timothy Calabrese. "Small Area Quality: A Comparison of Estimates—2000 Census and the 1999–2001 ACS—Bronx, New York Test Site." Report submitted to U.S. Census Bureau, 2004.

Salvo, Joseph J., Arun Peter Lobo, and Susan P. Love "Evaluating Continuous Measurement: Data Quality in the Bronx Test Site of the American Community Survey." *Journal of Economic and Social Measurement*, Vol.28, No.4, 2003.

Tersine, Anthony G., Jr., and Mark E. Asiala. "Methodology for the Production of American Community Survey Multiyear Estimates." *Proceedings of the Survey Research Methods Section,* American Statistical Association, 2007: 3018–3023.

U.S. Census Bureau. "Using the Data: Quality Measures." *American Community Survey.* Accessed October 2010. http://www.census.gov/acs/www/methodology/sample_size_and_data_quality/.

———. "Design and Methodology: American Community Survey, (ACS-DM1/09)." Washington D.C.: U.S. Government Printing Office, April 2009.

———. "Comparing Economic Characteristics with Census 2000." American Community Survey Evaluation Report Series, Report #5, 2004.

———. "Comparing General Demographic and Housing Characteristics with Census 2000." American Community Survey Evaluation Report Series, Report #4, 2004.

———. "Comparing Quality Measures: Comparing the American Community Survey's Three-Year Averages and Census 2000's Long Form Sample Estimates." American Community Survey Evaluation Report Series, Report #7, 2004.

———. "Comparing Selected Physical and Financial Housing Characteristics with Census 2000." American Community Survey Evaluation Report Series, Report #10, 2004.

———. "Comparing Social Characteristics with Census 2000." American Community Survey Evaluation Report Series, Report #9, 2004.

———. "Comparison for the American Community Survey 3-Year Average and the Census 2000 Sample for a Sample of Counties and Tracts." American Community Survey Evaluation Report Series, Report #8, 2004.

———. "The 2001–2002 Operational Feasibility Report of the American Community Survey." American Community Survey Evaluation Report Series, Report #6, 2004.

ACS Use and Products

National Research Council. *Using the American Community Survey: Benefits and Challenges.* Panel on the Functionality and Usability of Data from the American Community Survey, Constance F. Citro and Graham Kalton, Editors. Committee on National Statistics, Division of Behavioral and Social Sciences and Education, Washington DC: The National Academies Press, 2007: Part I: Using the American Community Survey and Part III: Education, Outreach and Future Development. http://www.nap.edu/catalog.php?record_id=11901.

ORC Macro. *The American Community Survey: Challenges and Opportunities for HUD.* Report submitted to the U.S. Department of Housing and Urban Development, 2002.

U.S. Census Bureau. "Data Products from the American Community Survey." http://www.census.gov/acs/www/Downloads/

———. "Data Dissemination." In *Design and Methodology American Community Survey*, Chapter 14, http://www.census.gov/acs/www/Downloads/

———. "Preparation and Review of Data Products." In *Design and Methodology American Community Survey*, Chapter 13. http://www.census.gov/acs/www/Downloads/

———. "Guidance for Data Users." *American Community Survey.* http://www.census.gov/acs/www/guidance_for_data_users/guidance_main/.

———. "Comparing 2008 American Community Survey Data." *American Community Survey.* http://www.census.gov/acs/www/guidance_for_data_users/

———. *A Compass for Understanding and Using American Community Survey Data: What PUMS Data Users Need to Know.* Washington, D.C.: U.S. Government Printing Office, 2009. http://www.census.gov/acs/www/guidance_for_data_users/

———. *A Compass for Understanding and Using American Community Survey Data: What Puerto Rico Community Survey Data Users Need to Know.* Washington D.C.: U.S. Government Printing Office, 2009. http://www.census.gov/acs/www/guidance_for_data_users/

———. *A Compass for Understanding and Using American Community Survey Data: What General Data Users Need to Know.* Washington, D.C.: U.S. Government Printing Office, 2008. http://www.census.gov/acs/www/guidance_for_data_users/

Accuracy and Coverage Evaluation

The Accuracy and Coverage Evaluation (ACE) is the program the Census Bureau used to measure the net undercount in Census 2000 by using a post-enumeration survey (PES) and capture-recapture statistical methodology. The bureau planned to correct the initial Census 2000 population figures for all blocks and groups in the nation for net undercount if the ACE estimates for the adjustment proved to be of high quality; however, this did not occur.

The ACE estimated the proportion of people missed by the census—that is, the gross omissions rate. It also estimated the proportion of census records that were included in error—that is, the gross erroneous enumerations rate. These proportions, together with the number of whole-person census imputations, were combined to measure the net undercount. The undercount was estimated nationally and by geographic area and demographic group.

Although seemingly well designed and executed, the initial estimates from the ACE, which were produced in March 2001, were flawed. The initial ACE estimate was a net undercount of 3.3 million people. Further research based on the ACE data and related evaluations produced a revised estimate of a 1.3 million census net *overcount*.

Background

The Census Bureau has long recognized that it is not possible to enumerate all the people in the census. The census misses some people. These omissions constitute the gross undercount. The census also sometimes counts the same person twice, counts babies born after the official census reference date, and so forth. Indeed, some census records do not refer to real people at all but instead refer to people made up by the census taker or by the respondent. These erroneous inclusions constitute the gross overcount. Still other census records are for people for whom no information could be obtained and whose data are imputed from another record. The difference between misses and erroneous inclusions and imputations constitutes the net undercount.

Beginning in the 1960s, the Bureau of the Census had increasing evidence that the net undercount was relatively larger for African Americans and other minorities—in other words, that there was a differential net undercount. At about the time of the 1980 census, the differential undercount became a political issue and the subject of litigation.

During the 1980s the Bureau of the Census developed improved tools to measure the number of people missed by the census for relatively large areas and large groups. Equally important, the bureau developed methods to potentially incorporate the adjustments into the detailed census tabulations.

These techniques were first carried out in the 1990 PES, which measured the net undercount and prepared corrected population measures for all areas within the United States. However, the results of the 1990 PES were not available until the spring of 1991, well after the December 31, 1990, legal deadline for the bureau to provide state population counts to the president and the Congress for use in reapportioning seats in the U.S. House of Representatives. The corrected population numbers were also produced after the legal date of April 1, 1991, when the bureau was required to release to the states detailed block-level population counts to be used for drawing congressional, state, and local political boundaries.

Planning for Census 2000

In planning for Census 2000, the Bureau of the Census had hoped to produce corrected population counts in time to deliver to the president on December 31, 2000. The basic census enumeration and the sample-based post-enumeration survey procedures were designed to work together to produce the most accurate population measures possible in time for this legal deadline, as well as the later April 1 redistricting deadline. Because of this combined approach, the survey was called the Integrated Coverage Measurement, or ICM.

The bureau implemented the ICM approach in its final dress rehearsal for Census 2000, conducted in two sites in 1998: Sacramento, California, and Menominee County, Wisconsin. It succeeded in completing the process on schedule—that is, producing adjusted population totals for these two sites in the required nine months after census day.

In January 1999, however, the Supreme Court ruled that the law governing the census, Title 13 of the United States Code, prohibits the use of sampling techniques to determine the state population counts used to apportion Congress. Because the ICM plan relied on sampling to produce the apportionment counts, the bureau quickly developed a different approach to Census 2000. It added several programs to improve the census enumeration in order to produce the most accurate state population counts possible by December 31, 2000, but without the use of sampling techniques. In addition, it conducted a post-enumeration survey with the goal of producing population counts by block and demographic group, corrected for net undercount, for release to the states by the April 1, 2001, deadline. This survey and the associated correction process together constituted the ACE program.

Measuring the Undercount

The ACE was designed to measure the net undercount of the bulk of the population who lived in housing units. It excluded those living at college, in prison, in hospitals, in homeless shelters, in other group housing arrangements, or on the street—about 3 percent of the total population. The process began by taking a random sample of census blocks. A block is a small unit of land bounded by visible features, such as an ordinary city block bounded by four streets. It can also be a "country block" bounded by two dirt roads, a creek, and an irrigation ditch. If the blocks had only a few housing units each, they were grouped with neighboring blocks to form block clusters.

The sampling process selected enough block clusters to obtain approximately 300,000 housing units for interview. The sample was selected from all 50 states and the District of Columbia, as well as Puerto Rico. The sample was also selected to ensure that all demographic groups were properly represented, including historically undercounted groups such as African Americans, Hispanics, Asians, Native Hawaiians, and American Indians.

In the sampled blocks or block clusters, all the ordinary census activities took place: census address listing, questionnaire delivery, nonresponse follow-up, coverage improvement, and the like. It was important that these blocks were enumerated with the same procedures and the same accuracy as any other similar census block.

The ACE program began by preparing blank maps of the sampled blocks, which showed roads and physical features only and not any of the housing units already listed by the main census address-listing operations. The ACE program's field interviewers visited each of these blocks in the fall of 1999 and prepared an independent listing of all housing units in the blocks.

In July 2000, after the census enumeration was largely completed, ACE interviewers began visiting each housing unit in the sample blocks. The ACE interviews were conducted using portable computers, in what is known as computer-assisted personal interviewing (CAPI), with the information transmitted electronically to census headquarters in Suitland, Maryland. Most interviews were in person, although some early interviews were conducted by telephone. The interviewers determined who was living in the housing unit on April 1, census day. They also gathered basic demographic information such as age, race, and Hispanic origin. The people interviewed during this process constituted the population, or P-sample.

When both the census enumeration and the ACE interviewing were complete, the two lists of census day residents were compared, or "matched," using both computer matching software and computer-assisted clerical matching. People whom the ACE workers interviewed but the census did not list constituted the census gross omissions in those blocks. Sometimes, the ACE work was rechecked to make sure that these were true census omissions. After follow-up, the ACE cases—that is, the P-sample—were classified as either enumerated or missed by the census.

Since the net undercount is the difference between the number missed by the census and the number counted in error and wholly imputed, the ACE workers also had to check a sample of census enumerations to see if they were correctly included. This sample of enumerations, or E-sample, was drawn from the same sample of blocks as the P-sample.

The ACE program checked to see if the E-sample included duplicate, fictitious, or other erroneous enumerations. The sampled block and surrounding blocks were searched for duplicates. All E-sample (census) records that matched P-sample (ACE) records were assumed to be verified and correct. Census records that did not match ACE records could be erroneous enumerations or they could be people missed by the ACE workers. Interviewers returned to the field to see if the people were real and whether they considered this address to be their "usual" residence as of census day. This was done at the same time as the P-sample follow-up to check on census omissions. After the follow-up interviewing was completed, census enumerations in these blocks—that is, the E-sample—were classified as either correctly or erroneously enumerated.

At the end of this process, the ACE estimated, within the sample blocks, the proportion of people missed by the census and the proportion of census records that were erroneous. This information was combined with the known census results into corrected estimates of the total population using the capture-recapture or dual-systems estimation method.

The estimation was done separately for distinct groups of people known as poststrata, defined based on factors known to affect the undercount, such as age, sex, race, and Hispanic origin. The poststrata definitions also considered other variables, such as region of the country and size of the town in which the person lived. Because, historically, families that own their own home are easier to count than those who rent, this characteristic was also taken into account. A poststratum might be, for example, Hispanic females, 18 to 29 years old, living in rented housing units in rural areas in the West.

Because census results are tabulated for small areas and for detailed demographic categories, the ACE program distributed the net undercount to all blocks in the nation by detailed demographic group. To do this, the ACE increased the count of a block proportionally to the number of people in each poststratum in each block. For example, if the ACE-corrected population was 10 percent higher than the census for a poststratum, then the count of all people in this poststratum in all blocks was increased by 10 percent. If this resulted in a whole number of people plus a fraction, as it usually did, the ACE process rounded the population count to a whole number of people. The ACE program also conducted a similar process to correct the census counts for the number of housing units.

ACE Evaluations and Revised Estimates

The initial March 2001 ACE estimates failed to even approximately measure the coverage error in Census 2000. The chief reason seems to have been a failure to measure the number of erroneous enumerations, especially duplicates. The ACE did not search for duplicates outside of the nearby neighborhood. Instead, it tried to determine whether the sample address was the resident's correct census (April 1) address, with the assumption that the other address would be coded as erroneous. However, for a large number of people in the census and the ACE, depending on when, where, and with whom the interview was conducted, two or more residences were reported as their correct—that is, usual—residence.

After both the census and the ACE were completed, the bureau was able to conduct a computerized search and match nationally, rather than just searching for duplicates in the sample and nearby blocks. This national search was possible because, for the first time, practically all names in the census were data captured. The ACE could now determine, for example, how many of the people who were classified by the E-sample as "correctly enumerated" were also enumerated somewhere else, including at another household or in a group quarters, which might be miles away from the E-sample address.

In one study, of an estimated 1.3 million E-sample people linked to a duplicate census enumeration outside the search area, 14 percent were coded as erroneous enumerations by the ACE. Since the ACE E-sample was a random sample, one would expect that for any pair of duplicates it would pick up the erroneous enumeration roughly half the time. From the significantly different proportions coded as correctly enumerated by the ACE from what would be reasonable, it was clear that the ACE had a strong tendency to misclassify enumeration status. This misclassification was due to the tendency of respondents to confirm people as living at an address who should have been counted as living somewhere else. For example, large numbers of parents of college students living in dormitories reported their child as living at home, to both the census and the ACE, even though census instructions clearly said not to. Further, both parents in a "joint custody" situation may have consistently reported the child as living in each of two households. This misreporting occurred in spite of the numerous, detailed, and specific probing questions about usual residence asked by the ACE.

The extended search for census duplicates discussed above formed the principal evidence for ACE error. Other evidence was also gathered, including a reinterview study. Based on this evidence, the Bureau of the Census produced, in 2003, a revised set of undercount estimates, known as ACE Revision II. Extensive analyses were conducted to reduce errors in the data and to develop new

models to estimate probabilities of correct enumeration and probabilities of residency status on census day for those cases with a duplicate link.

Final ACE Results

The revised ACE estimates suggest that Census 2000 produced a small net overcount of the population. The estimates also suggest that Census 2000 reduced the differential net coverage between race groups seen in previous censuses. The estimates found:

- A net overcount of the total household population of about one-half of 1 percent.
- A net overcount of 1.13 percent for non-Hispanic whites, but a net undercount of 1.84 percent for non-Hispanic blacks. Both of these estimates were found to be significantly different from zero. Net coverage estimates for all other race/Hispanic origin domains were not statistically different from zero.
- A net overcount of 1.25 percent for owners and a net undercount of 1.14 percent for nonowners. This differential net undercount by ownership status was estimated for every race/Hispanic origin domain with the exception of American Indians on reservations and Native Hawaiians and Other Pacific Islanders.

These results are for net census coverage. The gross errors of Census 2000, as with all previous censuses, were larger than the net coverage errors.

See also *Coverage evaluation; Errors in the count; Post-enumeration survey.*

. . . .   HOWARD HOGAN

BIBLIOGRAPHY

Hogan, Howard. "The 1990 Post-Enumeration Survey: An Overview." *The American Statistician* 46 (1992): 261–269.

———. "The Post-Enumeration Survey: Operations and Results." *Journal of the American Statistical Association* 88, no. 423 (1993).

———. "The Accuracy and Coverage Evaluation: Theory and Design." *Survey Methodology* 29, no. 2 (2003): 129–138.

Marks, E. S. "The Role of Dual System Estimation in Census Evaluation," *Developments in Dual Sysytem Estimation in Population Size and Growth,* K. Krotki ed. Edmonton, Canada: University of Alberta Press, 1979.

U.S. Census Bureau. *Technical Assessment of ACE Revision II, March 12, 2003* (2003). www.census.gov/dmd/www/pdf/ACETechAssess.pdf.

Wolter, K. M. "Some Coverage Error Models for Census Data." *Journal of the American Statistical Association* 81 (1986): 338–346.

Wright, T., and H. Hogan. "Census 2000: Evolution of the Revised Plan." *Chance Magazine* 12 (2000): 11–19.

Address List Development

The Census Bureau's address list and associated geographic information must be accurate and current if the modern census is to be taken efficiently and economically, and if the resulting data reported by small geographic areas are to accurately portray those areas. In a modern automated environment, this implies an accurate, integrated database that enables the Census Bureau to quickly tabulate the data and provide maps showing the boundaries of the tabulation areas.

The Traditional Census

As recently as the 1960 census, the U.S. Bureau of the Census enumerated the nation's population by the traditional door-to-door method, generally referred to as "conventional enumeration." This involved assigning a specific geographic area to an enumerator, who was responsible for accounting for all housing units and completing a census questionnaire for each unit and its occupants, if any. The enumerator was given a manually prepared census map of the assigned area and questionnaires to complete in face-to-face interviews with the residents of the assigned area. The bureau first used such maps nationwide for the 1890 census. Until the 1960 census, maps provided to the enumerators were copies of maps obtained from state and local agencies, with the bureau adding the required geographic boundaries. For the 1960 census, the bureau made its own base maps, called the Metropolitan Map Series (MMS), for a small number of urban areas.

With a growing population to enumerate, a shrinking labor pool as a source for its temporary census-taking staff, and the availability of computers to record and keep track of a variety of complex information, such labor-intensive efforts were no longer appropriate as the primary way to take a modern-day census. Also, more and more homes were receiving their mail at city-style addresses—that is, they had a house number and street name that were recognized by the U.S. Postal Service (USPS)—which would make it easier to identify and geographically code their locations. The process of linking an address to a geographic location, such as a census tract and block, is called geocoding, and it can be performed by computer algorithms using an Address Coding Guide (ACG). An ACG was a computerized address geocoding system that consisted of address range records for each side of each street segment within an area, with each record associated with a census block.

The Mail Census

In the 1960 census, for selected geographic areas, the bureau utilized the USPS to drop off census questionnaires but used enumerators to pick up the completed forms and assign the geographic location. After the 1960 census, the bureau decided that it would be effective to take much of the decennial census by mail. To take a mail census, it is necessary to know the geographic location for every questionnaire that is returned by mail, as well as the addresses for the housing units that do not mail back the questionnaire. Taking the census based on an accurate mailing list would ensure a more accurate count by identifying those housing units that required follow-up because the bureau had not received a questionnaire. To accomplish this, the bureau would need an accurate mailing list for areas with city-style addresses, which could then be used to geocode those addresses to the proper geographic areas for tabulation. The USPS would deliver the pre-coded questionnaires. To take much of the census by mail, the

bureau needed a list of city-style residential mailing addresses to which it could send its questionnaires. This list had to be as accurate, complete, and current (as of census day) as possible to ensure that a questionnaire could be delivered to every housing unit with a specific city-style mailing address; the bureau refers to this type of enumeration as mailout/mailback. For areas where city-style addresses were not used for mail delivery, each address had to be related to the location of its living quarters. This allowed the bureau to assign every housing unit and group quarters to its census geography, deliver a questionnaire to or find it to enumerate its residents (if any), and follow up to resolve problems and provide quality control. Thus, in addition to the geocoding and delivery aspects of the census, the bureau's list of residential addresses would serve as a device to control the enumeration, ensure complete coverage of all living quarters, identify which housing units should receive sample questionnaires, and record which ones required follow-up field visits.

Early Coding Efforts

Transportation and urban planning agencies developed the first computerized geographic coding systems in the late 1950s. To use address files for a decennial census, however, required a more complex and extensive system. The bureau's first effort to use an address list for census purposes took place in 1962 to support a mailout/mailback test census of Fort Smith, Arkansas, and Skokie, Illinois. In 1963 the bureau again tested the use of an address list in a test census in Huntington, New York, and investigated the availability and usability of commercial mailing lists.

For the 1963 economic censuses, the bureau identified the address ranges for all streets in incorporated places with 25,000 or more residents. The last address on each side of each street where it crossed the place boundary identified whether an establishment with a city-style address was inside or outside the place. The list was based on an address file purchased from a commercial vendor. (For the 1967 economic censuses, the bureau expanded the file to cover places with a population of at least 2,500.) For a 1965 test census in Cleveland, the bureau used a commercial mailing list whose addresses were geocoded by matching them against a rudimentary ACG. In 1967, to take a census of New Haven, Connecticut, the bureau used a more refined ACG that linked individual addresses to census geography. The procedures were further refined for the dress rehearsal censuses in preparation for the 1970 census.

For that census the bureau, in cooperation with local and regional government agencies, primarily regional transportation planning agencies, created ACGs for the 145 largest metropolitan areas. The combination of three factors—the geographic extent of the coverage of each ACG, the geographic extent of the USPS's city-delivery routes, and the availability of an address source—enabled the bureau's Geography Division to manually identify a boundary within which the bureau could prepare a computerized list of geocoded, mailable addresses. This boundary was called the "blue line" (simply because it had been drawn in blue pencil); the area it covered was referred to as the Tape Address Register (TAR) area because the geocoded addresses were maintained on magnetic tape. TAR areas covered the urban cores that had ACGs, estimated to contain about half the nation's population. The ACGs enabled the bureau to automate the assignment of 31.4 million city-style mailing addresses to their census geography.

The streets and areas recorded in the ACGs were related to an expanded set of MMS map sheets. These maps also showed census tract and block numbers, to which each address range—and, therefore, every address within that range—was assigned, together with the boundaries of higher-level geographic entities. For the first time, every block covered by the ACG was assigned a block number; previously, blocks were numbered only in areas that had contracted with the bureau for data at the block level (beginning with the 1940 Census of Housing). Elsewhere, the Bureau of the Census continued to use maps from various state and local governments, primarily transportation agencies. The bureau deleted unnecessary information and added census-specific information, including boundary information from the Boundary and Annexation Survey (BAS), which collected the governmental unit boundaries as of January 1 of each year.

The mailing addresses that the bureau recorded for the TAR areas came from two sources. The first source was a purchased file of city-style residential mailing addresses in ZIP codes identified by the bureau. Because TAR areas used city-style addresses for the delivery of mail, each mailing address had to consist of a house number and street name, and unit designation. The bureau geocoded the individual addresses using the ACGs; the bureau tried to geocode as many of the addresses not geocoded using both office and field operations.

The second source of addresses came from the USPS. In mid-1969, the USPS letter carriers "cased" bureau-prepared, addressed cards in their delivery slots—hence, the term *casing check*—for an "advance post office check." The carriers corrected errors, noted nonexistent addresses, and filled out "add cards" for missing residential addresses. Field staff tried to locate the added addresses so they could assign the proper geocodes. Another casing check was done with the preaddressed questionnaires. This was done yet one more time when the questionnaires for the census were actually delivered—the "time-of-delivery check."

The address file for the 1970 census included all the geocoded addresses from the commercial mailing list plus the first postal check, resulting in a geocoded Address Control File (ACF) that the bureau could use for the census.

In addition to the TAR areas, the bureau sent enumerators to list addresses in adjacent suburban areas that had a preponderance of city-style mailing addresses but did not meet the TAR requirements. This operation was referred to as "prelist." As in previous censuses, field staff recorded the address and other basic information for each of the living quarters in a book, now called an address register. Enumerators also assigned a number to each residential structure in the register and showed its location on a census map by "map spotting"

the number. This helped field staff find the unit for subsequent operations. However, the bureau did not add these addresses to the address file at this time, so the addresses were clerically geocoded and the questionnaires were addressed manually for mail-out. These addresses were subjected to the late post office checks. The bureau estimated that the mailout/mailback census covered about 60 percent of the population of the United States.

In areas that did not use city-style addresses for mail delivery—that is, where most residents used a postal route address or picked up their mail at a local post office—each housing unit was visited and enumerated. When the enumerator obtained or completed a questionnaire at each housing unit, he or she recorded the block number, address, and, if it was not a city-style address, a location and physical description for the unit in an address register; the enumerator also map-spotted the location of the unit on a census map. The block number was the basis for geocoding the questionnaire for data tabulation. The bureau did not record either the addresses or the map spots in a database.

To support the geographic coding of the place-of-work question, which depended on the location of nonresidential addresses, the bureau converted the ACGs to Geographic Base File/Dual Independent Map Encoding (GBF/DIME) Files, an improved file format that would allow for the insertion of coordinates and allow computers to display maps.

Addresses for the 1980 Census

The 1980 census did not retain the addresses from the 1970 census. Instead, the bureau obtained a new set of addresses using essentially the same basic methodology it used for the 1970 census, but this time it purchased the addresses from three vendors. The bureau again defined the TAR area based on a blue line determined by 276 GBF/DIME-Files, USPS "city delivery," and the availability of the commercial address list. The bureau used the GBF/DIME-Files to geocode the addresses. However, rather than relying solely on the advance post office check to report missing and erroneous addresses and to identify miscoded ones, the bureau decided to perform its own field check in the TAR areas—an operation referred to as "precanvass." Based on the information in its database, the bureau printed the addresses for each census block in address registers that covered one or more blocks. Using a census map, field staff visited each block to verify, correct, and update the list of TAR addresses and the information shown on the census maps. The bureau then revised the ACF to reflect the additions and changes, but it did not have the resources to update the GBF/DIME-Files with the updated map and address range information. The updated paper maps, however, were used in subsequent operations.

The bureau also expanded the area covered by the prelist. It added these addresses to the ACF, thereby enabling it to use the residential addresses in prelist areas in the same way that it did in TAR areas. The enumerators also map-spotted residential structures outside of TAR areas; again, the map spots were not carried to a database. Both TAR and prelist addresses were subjected to a late casing check and a time-of-delivery check by the USPS, requiring the bureau to geocode added addresses at the last minute. The bureau estimated that the mailout/mailback census covered about 95 percent of the nation's population.

Addresses for the 1990 Census

Major changes in the address list preparation and use resulted from the Topologically Integrated Geographic Encoding and Referencing System (TIGER) and the implementation of nationwide block numbering. For the first time the Bureau of the Census would create all of its own maps, utilize specialized maps designed for specific field operations, and not depend on a "one map fits all" design for data collection and dissemination. All field maps were computer-generated; the Geography Division developed software that determined all text placement, scaling, sheet layout, and insetting, as well as printing the maps on electrostatic plotters located in the Regional Census Centers. Quality control of the maps was performed after the maps were plotted.

Once again, the bureau did not retain the addresses from the previous census. The address acquisition process was essentially the same as for the previous two censuses, except that this time two vendors provided the addresses for the TAR areas. For the purchased addresses that did not match the TIGER file, the bureau undertook a massive clerical geocoding operation. Many of the prelist addresses, as well as all the TAR addresses, were subjected to an advance post office check. The USPS conducted a late casing check of all mailing addresses covered by the mailout/mailback census a few weeks before census day; however, this time there was no time-of-delivery check.

To develop, maintain, update, and finally use the address list for the census, the bureau used the ACF to uniquely identify each of the living quarters for the 95 percent of the nation's population included in the mailout/mailback and update/leave (U/L) enumeration areas. In U/L areas, new for 1990, bureau field staff (rather than the USPS) delivered the census questionnaires to the specific units identified by the prelist operation, because the addresses recorded for a significant number of housing units did not uniquely identify the intended unit. Therefore, it was more effective to have field staff, with copies of the annotated prelist maps and the information recorded by the listers in hand, deliver the questionnaires. Furthermore, at the same time, the field staff could update and correct the maps and the list of living quarters, simultaneously dropping off a questionnaire at each housing unit and identifying problem addresses (such as "burned down," "not a housing unit"). After the census, the bureau keyed into the ACF the approximately 5.5 million addresses the bureau collected in the areas covered by conventional enumeration procedures (called list/enumerate) for the 1990 census, as well as additions and corrections recorded in U/L areas. It also added addresses obtained by a pre-census and post-census Local Review operation offered to local officials so they could point out problems with the counts for their jurisdictions. The Pre-census Local Review was conducted in all mailout/mailback enumeration areas. The objective was to provide local government officials the

opportunity to review preliminary housing unit and special place counts for areas in their jurisdictions. The Bureau of the Census delivered counts of housing units to local officials to review and to identify and document discrepancies. Bureau staff then reviewed and attempted to resolve these discrepancies in the office and through selective recanvass of blocks. Detailed feedback was not provided to local governments, nor was any actual address information exchanged. A total of 21,048 governmental units were eligible to participate in the 1990 Precensus Local Review, and 16.3 percent of those governments participated. Approximately 121,000 blocks were challenged, and bureau field representatives recanvassed 52 percent of those blocks. The 1990 Pre-census Local Review added 367,313 housing units to the national housing inventory.

With nationwide block numbering, it was necessary for the bureau to assign a block suffix to the 3-digit block numbers used for data collection operations to uniquely identify tabulation blocks reflecting the January 1, 1990, governmental unit boundaries. The computer used the address ranges in TIGER, which had the final tabulation boundaries and geography, to perform this assignment in the TAR area; elsewhere, a clerical operation assigned the correct tabulation block suffix.

Addresses for Census 2000

The Bureau of the Census repeatedly had been requested by local governments to allow them to review the actual address list used in the decennial census. In 1994 Congress considered a proposal to enable the bureau to share the address list with the USPS, other federal agencies, and local governments with limited restrictions but outside the full confidentiality restrictions of Title 13 affirmed by the U.S. Supreme Court in *Baldrige v. Shapiro,* 455 U.S. 345 (1982). After a contentious public hearing on the issue, Congress passed Public Law 103–430, the Address List Improvement Act of 1994. This law requires the Bureau of the Census to allow representatives of local governments, after signing an agreement to maintain the confidentiality afforded by Title 13, an opportunity to review the census address list in advance of the census, propose updates and corrections, receive feedback on the disposition of proposed updates, and to appeal decisions by the bureau on those proposals to an independent appeals office established by the Office of Management and Budget. This program became known as the Local Update of Census Addresses (LUCA).

LUCA allowed officials who had sworn to maintain the confidentiality of the addresses to review the completeness of the address list for their jurisdictions. At the same time, they could update the maps. In areas within the blue line, they were asked to identify missing addresses; outside, they were asked to identify blocks with incorrect housing unit counts. In both cases the bureau followed up with field checks, updated its database and the Master Address File (MAF) with its findings, and provided feedback to the LUCA participants. About 47 percent of eligible localities participated, of which 63 percent provided address updates. Localities could appeal the bureau decisions on unacceptable addresses to the LUCA Appeals Office, which subsequently directed the bureau to include

93 percent of the appealed addresses into subsequent Census 2000 operations. About 44 percent of the accepted appealed addresses subsequently were included in the census results. As part of the LUCA program designed for city-style addresses, about 5.3 million addresses were submitted, of which 58 percent actually made it to the final census count.

For Census 2000 the bureau took several steps to create the most complete list of addresses and residential locations possible. For the first time, the bureau retained a substantial number of the addresses it had recorded and geocoded for the previous census. It did this by carrying forward to the MAF all of the addresses recorded in the 1990 census's ACF. In addition P. L. 103–430 enabled the USPS to provide its Delivery Sequence File (DSF) to the bureau. The DSF is the list of all addresses (including unit identifiers) with carrier route and delivery sequence information for which the USPS delivers mail. It also includes information on the residential/nonresidential nature of each address and whether mail is currently being delivered to the address. Rather than accepting every monthly update to the DSF, the bureau chose to obtain the DSF on an as-needed basis. To facilitate the bureau's use of these files and obviate the need for a casing check in ZIP codes with city-style mailing addresses, the USPS undertook two special efforts to ensure that its local post offices reported address updates on a timely basis. The Geography Division also used additional USPS files, such as the Zip+4 file and other internal USPS files, to maintain the MAF and TIGER.

In addition to adding the DSF addresses to the MAF, the bureau matched the DSF against the street name and address range information in the TIGER database. Geographic staff in the bureau's twelve regional offices—and, after their establishment from December 1997 to April 1998, the census-related Regional Census Centers—investigated unmatched cases by obtaining and reviewing reference materials in the office and visiting areas to resolve residual unmatched address ranges. It also offered to have local governments resolve unmatched cases by providing them with TIGER-derived maps and lists of address ranges (the TIGER Improvement Program). To ensure the completeness and accuracy of the addresses and their geocoding within the blue line—the mailout/mailback areas—the bureau had field staff check the addresses in a pre-canvass-like operation named "block canvassing."

In all but the most sparsely settled areas of the nation, including Puerto Rico, the bureau listed and map-spotted addresses outside the blue line. All the addresses were keyed into the MAF, and the map spots and numbers also were inserted into the TIGER database. As a result, the bureau could print block-based maps that showed the location of each residential structure—extremely useful when the map spots were referenced in later operations. For Census 2000, the bureau used large-format ink-jet printers and ledger-size laser printers to provide maps for the various field operations.

In order to ensure that it had current address and street information on census day, the bureau initiated the New Construction program, which asked local and tribal governments whose jurisdictions were within the blue line to inform the

bureau of any new housing units built between the bureau's last update of their address information and April 1, 2000. New Construction added 371,812 addresses, of which 175,020 were confirmed as valid addresses. Outside the blue line, census enumerators canvassed every block, generally beginning in mid-March 2000, to ensure the completeness of the address list and maps as they delivered a questionnaire to or enumerated each housing unit. Again, all updates of addresses and maps, including map spots, were carried to TIGER and the MAF.

As a result of improvements to its mapping capabilities, the bureau could create a variety of maps, at an appropriate size and scale and reflecting updates from previous operations, for every field and local input operation. Furthermore, these maps could now be printed at the Regional Census Centers and the local census offices on an as-needed basis. The same mapping capabilities enabled the bureau to print maps needed to accompany the data and also to make available to data users the ability to print their own maps from the public extract of the TIGER database, called the TIGER/Line files, and from map images in the PDF file, both available on the bureau's Web site.

For Census 2000 every geographic entity for which the bureau tabulated data is represented by one or more census blocks. With every residential address in the MAF assigned to a census block in the TIGER database, the bureau can allocate each response from a housing unit, group quarters resident, and other special populations to an individual census block. As all higher-level geography is associated with each block, Census 2000 data can be tabulated to any geographic entity in TIGER.

Addresses for the 2010 Census

In preparation for the 2010 census, the U.S. Census Bureau generally followed the same steps in preparing the address list. The Geography Division, however, undertook a major redesign of its geographic processing systems, integrating for the first time the information in the separate MAF and TIGER databases into a single, relational database using commercial software. This created both a spatial and address linkage and allowed an improved, efficient processing environment. Another major improvement for the 2010 census was the 2010 LUCA program, which was redesigned based on the evaluations from the Census 2000 program. A third major improvement was the realignment of the features in TIGER to conform to GPS accuracy, which enabled the acquisition of coordinates for the residential structures identified during address canvassing. Based on these structure coordinates, the tabulation geographic codes can be associated with each questionnaire and used for tabulation without having to rely solely on the residential address linked to an address range in TIGER.

The pre-census activities to update and correct the address list were similar to 2000; however, the Census Bureau used separate geography for the pre-census operations from the data collection operations. Except for three counties in Maine, the 2010 address canvass covered all of 49 states, the District of Columbia, and Puerto Rico. The densely settled portions of

Alaska also were covered. The address canvassers used a hand-held computer (HHC) that contained both the map data and the address list. These HHCs were specially designed for this purpose and included global positioning system (GPS) and cellular technology. For each residential structure, the address canvasser marked on the electronic map the location of the residential structure and attempted to collect the GPS coordinates. The HHC software associated the collection block number collected by the manual map spotting and from the GPS receiver with the residential address, including unit identifier, being canvassed. The data collected were transmitted to the Census Bureau data center via a cellular telephone network or, in remote areas, over telephone landlines using the built-in modem. The blue line was determined using a GIS application, and the mailout/mailback area was expanded based on the extent of the USPS city delivery area as well as the knowledge of the extent of city-style addresses in the MAF.

The 2010 LUCA program incorporated several improvements to encourage eligible governments to participate and to improve the quality and coverage of the MAF. The improvements included an effort to have all governments participate at the same time; the review period lengthened to 120 days from 90 days; increased participation options offered to allow governments to participate in the manner best for them, including non-Title 13 options; the provision of LUCA-specific GIS software to enable governments to update the MAF and TIGER electronically; and the extension of participation to representatives of state governments on behalf of their localities.

During the decade the Census Bureau included addresses from the periodic DSF matches, and addresses obtained from American Community Survey and Special Census field operations. However, the Census Bureau was not able to geocode all of the new addresses and identify new streets and address ranges with the assistance of major clerical operations as in Census 2000. Therefore, a substantial number of addresses, included in the MAF but without collection block codes, were not provided to LUCA participants and the Census Bureau depended on them to identify these addresses and provide their block codes. The subsequent address canvassing operation verified the LUCA submissions and provided the basis for the LUCA feedback. Again, LUCA participants could appeal any rejected addresses to the LUCA Appeals office. About 29 percent of the eligible governments participated (substantially fewer than in Census 2000), but they represented about 92 percent of the address universe, resulting in the same coverage as Census 2000. Updates were received from 79 percent of the participating governments, resulting in about 8 million new addresses being sent to address canvassing for verification. An additional 30 million addresses were matched to the MAF and were also sent to address canvassing for validation. The LUCA Appeals Office accepted 91 percent of the appealed addresses, and they were included in the mail delivery for late adds and the NRFU Vacant Delete Check.

The Census Bureau again conducted a New Construction program that allowed all governments within the mailout/mailback area to provide a list of addresses for newly constructed housing units. The bureau also continued to update the MAF from additional matches to the USPS DSF up to census day. The address updates from the Update/Leave operation, which used paper maps again produced on ledger-size laser printers, also were included in the MAF. Large-format field and publication maps again were produced on ink-jet printers.

Addresses Post-2010

The MAF supports not only the Decennial Census but also Census Bureau surveys, including the American Community Survey. The MAF continues to be updated by periodic matching to the USPS DSF and with updates from bureau field operations, including the targeted Community Address Updating System. The Census Bureau recognizes that updates from these sources alone are not sufficient to have a MAF that could support the 2020 census without another address canvass in 2019. Based on a pilot program as part of the MAF/TIGER Accuracy Improvement Project, the bureau determined that it was not cost-effective to have a contractor update the MAF. However, the bureau is considering additional processes during the decade to determine areas of change and to work with local governments to obtain new residential addresses from them and other primary and secondary sources.

See also *Data capture; Enumeration: field procedures; Geographic Information Systems (GIS); Geography: distribution of the population; Tabulation geography.*

ROBERT A. LAMACCHIA
. . . . . (WITH CONTRIBUTIONS BY DONALD HIRSCHFELD)

BIBLIOGRAPHY

Groves, Robert M. "2010 Census: A Status Update of Key Decennial Operations." Statement before the Subcommittee on Federal Financial Management, Government Information, Federal Services and International Security Committee on Homeland Security and Governmental Affairs, United States Senate, February 23, 2010.

Owens, Karen L. "Evaluation of the Local Update of Census Addresses 99 (LUCA 99) Final Report." Washington, D.C.: U.S. Census Bureau, 2000; Evaluation F.6, 2002.

U.S. Bureau of the Census. *1963 Economic Censuses: Procedural History.* Washington, D.C.: U.S. Government Printing Office, 1968.

———. "Chapter 2. Address List Development," *Programs to Improve Coverage in the 1990 Census.* Washington, D.C.: U.S. Government Printing Office, 1993.

———. *1970 Census of Population and Housing: Procedural History.* PHC(R)-1. Washington, D.C.: U.S. Government Printing Office, 1976.

———. *1980 Census of Population and Housing: History.* PHC80-R-2. Washington, D.C.: U.S. Government Printing Office, 1986–1989.

———. *1990 Census of Population and Housing: History.* 1990 CPH-R-2. Washington, D.C.: U.S. Government Printing Office, 1993–1996.

U.S. Census Bureau. *History: 2000 Census of Population and Housing (Volume 2).* PHC-R-V2. Washington, D.C.: U.S. Government Printing Office, 2009.

———. *2010 Census of Population and Housing: History.* Washington, D.C.: U.S. Government Printing Office, forthcoming.

———. *Evaluation of the Local Update of Census Addresses 98 (LUCA 98) Final Report, Census 2000 Evaluation F.3.* Washington, D.C.: U.S. Government Printing Office, 2003.

Vitrano, Frank A., Robin A. Pennington, and James B. Treat. *Census 2000 Testing, Experimentation, and Evaluation Program Topic Report No. 8, TR-8, Address List Development in Census 2000.* Washington D.C.: U.S. Census Bureau, 2004.

Advertising the Census

The census outreach and promotional campaign is designed to raise public awareness of the count and to encourage prompt and voluntary participation. The Census Bureau organizes a partnership program with state and local government and voluntary organizations, the private sector, and schools. It develops media materials to promote the census and conducts a direct mail campaign consisting of an advance letter, questionnaire sent to all households, and replacement questionnaires to areas with low mail response rates; it also organizes media events and special programs to raise public awareness. Starting at the 2000 census, the Census Bureau added a new feature to these activities and employed a paid advertising campaign to promote census awareness and participation. The 2010 campaign was budgeted at $133 million and was designed to expose the average American to 42 messages for the census. More than half the advertising budget was targeted to hard-to-count populations.

From 1950 to 1990 the bureau worked with the Advertising Council to produce radio and television commercials and print material to advertise the census. The advertising campaign also generated billboards, buttons, coffee mugs, signs, posters, brochures, pencils, and other memorabilia. An official logo was designed, and slogans developed to "brand" the count. The 2010 slogan emphasized the brevity of the form, informing the householder that there were "ten questions" which would require only "ten minutes" to complete. The advertising campaign for the 1970 census was the first to target ads to hard-to-count populations and minorities, and with each decade such targeted advertising has increased. By the 1990s the World Wide Web had become an important advertising venue. In 2010 the Census Bureau launched massive social media advertising efforts, including using blogs, Facebook, YouTube, Flickr, and Twitter page initiatives.

The advertising campaign has become increasingly elaborate and important to the overall design of the census plan since 1970, when the mail census first required residents to recognize and fill out a census form voluntarily and promptly. Before the development of the mail census in 1970, the enumerators who went door-to-door bore the primary burden of explaining the process to householders as they recorded the information. Since 1970 the mail census method has presumed that Americans are already aware of the census and are prepared to fill out the form when it arrives in the mail and, furthermore, that they know how to fill it out and send it in. At the household level, there are few incentives to fill out the form promptly and completely. Respondents receive little immediate direct benefit when they fill out the form, and the penalty for not filling it out is rarely invoked.

Householders can lose the form in piles of junk mail, or they may hesitate to fill it out because they are suspicious of the government's request for the information. The ad campaign is designed to educate and encourage participation.

Response rates to the mail census declined from the 1970 level of 78 percent to 65 percent in 1990, and Congress provided funding for paid advertising beginning in 2000. The initiative succeeded and the final mail participation rates in the census in 2000 and 2010 rose to 74 percent. (The denominator for the response rate includes residences that are determined to be vacant in the door-to-door enumeration that follows the mail-back phase. The denominator for the participation rate excludes those households and is a better measure of overall final response.)

In 2010, census officials continually emphasized that funding spent on advertising saved money, calculating that for every percentage point increase in the 2010 census mail-back response rate, the Census Bureau would save $85 million in follow-up with nonresponding households. Put differently, they noted that the government budgeted 42 cents in a postage-paid envelope to get a questionnaire back in the mail, but taxpayers would pay an average of $57 to count a household that had to be counted in person.

In earlier censuses public service ads were donated by the advertising industry and were displayed and broadcast as time and space permitted. The 2000 census advertising campaign was designed to guarantee coverage and to make an explicit claim for civic participation in the census. Advertisements described the benefits to local communities of good census data, the mechanics of the count, and how to fill out the form.

Starting in 2000, from mid-March to mid-April, after the census forms had been mailed to all residential addresses, the Census Bureau used its Web site to publish daily reports of response rates for states and all local jurisdictions in the country. The bureau also set targets for local areas to increase their response rates from the previous census. It listed those targets on the bureau Web site in the hope that competition between areas would be "news" and encourage local leaders to promote response.

Though the new advertising campaigns have contributed to increased public awareness of the census, the increased visibility of the census can also lead to unforeseen consequences. In early spring 2000, radio talk shows introduced extensive discussion of the count with a different message from the one the Census Bureau was promulgating. The talk show coverage spilled over into the print and television national electronic media in March and April 2000. It questioned why, if the census was mandated in the Constitution to provide a simple count of the population for political apportionment and legislative redistricting, householders had to provide additional detailed answers to the questions on the long form. These additional questions were challenged as an invasion of privacy, and many callers claimed they would not answer them. In 2010, skeptics of census confidentiality claims and the cost of the count also used the same social media to criticize the Census Bureau tweets and blogs, though such activities do not seem to have impaired the operations of the census itself.

See also *Confidentiality; Grassroots groups; Long form; Media attention to the census.*

. . . .   MARGO J. ANDERSON

BIBLIOGRAPHY

Bryant, Barbara Everitt, and William Dunn. *Moving Power and Money: The Politics of Census Taking*. Ithaca, N.Y.: New Strategist Publications, 1995.

Hillygus, D. Sunshine, Norman H. Nie, Kenneth Prewitt, and Heili Pals. *The Hard Count: The Political and Social Challenges of Census Mobilization*. New York: Russell Sage Foundation, 2006.

U.S. Bureau of the Census. "The Census Promotion Program." In *1980 Census of Population and Housing: History, Part B*. PHC80-R-2B. Washington, D.C.: U.S. Government Printing Office, 1986.

———. "The Census Promotional Program." In *1990 Census of Population and Housing: History, Part B*. 1990 CPH-R-2B. Washington, D.C.: U.S. Government Printing Office, 1995.

———. "The Public Information Program." In *1970 Census of Population and Housing: Procedural History*. PHC(R)-1. Washington, D.C.: U.S. Government Printing Office, 1976.

U.S. Census Bureau. "The Partnership and Marketing Program." In *History: 2000 Census of Population and Housing*. Vol. 1, chap. 4. Washington, D.C.: U.S. Government Printing Office, 2009.

———. Social Media. www.census.gov/aboutus/social_media.html.

Advisory Committees

Advisory committees provide input to planning and evaluation of the decennial census and the American Community Survey (ACS) from groups of people not directly employed by the Census Bureau who are chosen for their particular expertise or perspective and who serve on a volunteer basis. Since 1973 all advisory committees appointed by the executive branch have operated under the 1972 Federal Advisory Committee Act (FACA), which provides for open deliberations and advance notice of meetings in the *Federal Register*.

Input for the 2010 census was provided by advisory groups that reported to the Census Bureau. Also, as in past censuses input was provided by committees or groups responsible to private organizations. Examples from post–World War II censuses include the continuing Committee on Population Statistics of the Population Association of America, first established in 1956; several committees appointed by the American Institute of Planners to review plans for information systems and data series for the 1960 and 1970 censuses; and the ad hoc Technical Panel on the Census Undercount, appointed by the American Statistical Association in 1982. The advisory structure for the decennial census and the ACS has also involved the convening of consensus study panels by the National Academy of Sciences.

Early Advisory Efforts

Outside experts were first used to advise on census planning in 1849 at the behest of Joseph Kennedy, secretary of the newly created Census Board—consisting of the secretary of state, the attorney general, and the postmaster general—which was charged to draft legislation for the 1850 census. Kennedy invited Lemuel Shattuck of the American Statistical Association and Archibald Russell of the American Geographical and Statistical Society to Washington to help draw up the schedules for the census (the forms for obtaining data items), hitherto a function undertaken entirely by Congress. They recommended that the census schedules be expanded and restructured to collect data for each individual instead of summaries for each household. Also, they recommended that different schedules be developed for different elements of the census, such as free persons, slaves, people who had died in the preceding year, agriculture, manufacturing, and other "social" statistics (for example, information on schools, libraries, crime, religion). After extensive debate, Congress adopted most of the recommendations.

In November 1918 the first continuing formal advisory committee was appointed for the census: the Census Advisory Committee of the American Statistical Association (ASA) and the American Economic Association (AEA). The members were nominated by the two organizations and their appointments confirmed by the government. The joint committee originally consisted of people who had worked on the census and on obtaining statistics needed for mobilization of the economy for World War I. It continued as a joint ASA-AEA committee until 1937, as an ASA committee through 1973, and as a component committee of the Census Advisory Committee of Professional Associations through 2009.

During the early years of the joint committee, its members contributed substantially to policymaking for the census: they developed the form and content of census schedules, set priorities for special census studies, analyzed census data, and testified before Congress. For example, during a period of intense controversy over restricting foreign immigration in the 1920s, the Census Advisory Committee helped commission a study by the American Council of Learned Societies to revise key census estimates of the national origins of the population. The committee also participated in a debate on whether to conduct a second census in 1931 to measure unemployment, for which the 1930 census statistics were believed to be inadequate. Such a census was not conducted, but in 1937 Congress authorized voluntary registration of the unemployed, obtained by having postal carriers deliver forms to all residential addresses for unemployed workers to fill out and mail back. Later in 1937, at the behest of professional statisticians, postal carriers enumerated a 2 percent sample of households to ask about unemployment. The sample survey produced a 40 percent higher estimate of unemployed workers than did the voluntary registration.

Also providing considerable oversight and review of census issues during the early 1930s was the Committee on Government Statistics and Information Services (COGSIS), established by ASA and the Social Science Research Council. Meeting from 1933 to 1935, COGSIS helped promote professionalization of the Census Bureau's staffing, the introduction of new sampling methods for censuses and surveys, and the development of research and experimentation capabilities within the Census Bureau. The first chair of COGSIS, Stuart Rice, then president of ASA, became assistant director of the Census Bureau to help spearhead these changes.

Professional Advisory Committees

Since 1940 the advisory committee structure for obtaining outside professional review of census plans and results has expanded from the original joint ASA-AEA Census Advisory Committee. In 1946 the Census Advisory Committee of the American Marketing Association was established to review publicity and outreach plans for the census and data products for the user community. In 1960 the Census Advisory Committee of the American Economic Association was established to reforge a formal link with economists, who had not been represented on the ASA Census Advisory Committee after 1937. The Census Advisory Committee on Population Statistics was established in 1965, subsequently renamed the Census Advisory Committee of the Population Association of America. Over time, steps were taken to integrate the work of these four advisory committees (AEA, AMA, ASA, and PAA); from 1973 through 2009 they met as a single Census Advisory Committee of Professional Associations with four subcommittees. In 2010 the Professional Associations Committee was replaced by the Census Scientific Advisory Committee, with members chosen for their individual expertise and not as representatives of a particular association.

Other census advisory committees for specific areas have included the Census Advisory Committee on Privacy and Confidentiality, which met from 1972 to 1975, and the Census Advisory Committee on State and Local Area Statistics, which operated from 1964 to 1976. (These committees were disbanded as part of a government-wide effort to reduce the number of public advisory committees.)

Another professional advisory committee of note was appointed by the secretary of commerce in 1989 pursuant to an agreement between the parties in a lawsuit challenging the Commerce Department's 1987 decision that a postenumeration survey would not be used to adjust the 1990 census counts for net population undercoverage. The Special Advisory Panel consisted of eight members, four appointed from a list of experts recommended by the plaintiffs—(New York City and other local governments and citizen groups)—and four from a list developed by the Commerce Department. The panel was to advise on adjustment-related issues. The four members appointed by the plaintiffs issued a report that supported statistical adjustment; the other four members issued a contrary report. Although the Bureau of the Census director recommended adjustment, the secretary of commerce ultimately decided not to adjust the 1990 census counts.

Minority Advisory Committees

The Census Bureau first established formal advisory committees to advise on ways to reach minority groups and improve coverage for them for the 1980 census. Beginning with informal discussions in 1971, by 1976 three census advisory committees had been chartered for the African American, Asian and Pacific Islander, and Hispanic communities. (The Asian and Pacific Islander Committee was subsequently renamed the Asian, Native Hawaiian, and Other Pacific Islander Committee.) The American Indian and Alaska Native communities decided not to have a formal advisory group; instead, the Census Bureau held a series of regional meetings with these groups to explain the census plans and request input for improving the count. The three minority advisory committees met from 1975 to 1981. They were reconstituted in 1985, and a fourth committee was added for the American Indian and Alaska Native populations at that time.

National Academy of Sciences Review Panels

In addition to standing advisory committees, committees and panels of experts convened by the National Academy of Sciences/National Research Council (NAS/NRC) have reviewed census methods and results and have made recommendations for future censuses. The NAS is an independent, nonprofit honorary membership organization that was chartered by Congress in 1863 to provide scientific advice to the government on request. The NRC, established by presidential executive order in 1916 to involve the broader scientific community in advisory studies, is the principal operating arm of the NAS. Experts appointed to NAS/NRC study committees serve as volunteers; government agencies requesting studies by the NAS/NRC pay for committee members' travel and for staff and administrative costs. Since 1997, NAS/NRC committees have operated under Amendment 15 to the Federal Advisory Committee Act, which provides for fully open meetings when committees are gathering information but permits closed meetings to deliberate on recommendations and to draft report text.

The first involvement of the NAS/NRC with census issues concerned the formula used to reapportion the U.S. House of Representatives on the basis of census counts for each state. The Speaker of the House asked the NAS/NRC in 1928 to advise on the relative merits of two different methods of apportionment to help in framing a reapportionment bill. (For the only time in U.S. history, the Congress did not reapportion the House of Representatives after the 1920 census.) The NAS committee recommended a method of "equal proportions" (known as Hill's method), but legislation passed in 1929 continued the method of "major fractions" (known as Webster's or Willcox's method) that was used for reapportionment after the 1910 census. The reapportionment method was changed to Hill's method following the 1940 census, largely because that method would result in one more seat for the Democratic majority. Reapportionment scholars have criticized the NAS arguments supporting Hill's method.

The NAS/NRC was not asked to consider census issues again until 1969, when it convened the Committee on Problems of Census Enumeration at the request of the Bureau of the Census, the U.S. Office of Economic Opportunity, and the Manpower Administration of the U.S. Labor Department. The committee was charged to provide advice on ways to improve coverage of the population in the census and household surveys. Research dating back to the 1940s had documented that the census did not count everyone and that it disproportionately missed minorities, men, and people in younger age groups. In the 1960s, interest in coverage problems grew owing to the increasing importance of census and household survey data for civil rights enforcement (including equal representation under the Voting Rights Act of 1965), allocation of federal funds to states and localities, the documentation of conditions in cities, and related uses.

The Committee on Problems of Census Enumeration focused on ways to understand, measure, and reduce undercoverage in the census and surveys. Its 1972 report, "America's Uncounted People," also recommended research on methods to adjust small-area census counts to account for coverage errors.

In 1977 the Bureau of the Census asked the Committee on National Statistics (CNSTAT), a standing NAS/NRC committee established in 1972, to convene the Panel on Decennial Census Plans, chaired by demographer Nathan Keyfitz of Harvard University. The panel was charged with examining census coverage improvement plans; review proposed procedures for handling contested census counts; investigate the feasibility and implications of adjusting census counts, and subsequent population estimates, for undercoverage; and review the evaluations planned for the 1980 census. This panel, in its 1978 report, "Counting the People in 1980: An Appraisal of Census Plans," was the first to recommend not only research about undercoverage but also adjustment of population totals for states and local areas for the purpose of allocating federal funds.

Leading up to the 1990 and 2000 censuses, the bureau requested a series of CNSTAT panels to address issues of coverage and possible adjustment for coverage errors and to consider methods that could potentially improve the accuracy and reduce the costs of census operations:

- Panel on Decennial Census Methodology: 1984–1985, extended through 1988; chaired by John Pratt, Harvard Business School, and, later, Benjamin King, Florida Atlantic University; report issued 1985, "The Bicentennial Census: New Directions for Methodology in 1990."
- Panel to Evaluate Alternative Census Methods: 1992–1994; chaired by Norman Bradburn, University of Chicago; report issued 1994, "Counting People in the Information Age."
- Panel on Census Requirements in the Year 2000 and Beyond: 1992–1994; chaired by Charles Schultze, Brookings Institution; mandated by Congress in the Decennial Census Improvement Act of 1991; report issued 1995, "Modernizing the U.S. Census."
- Panel on Alternative Census Methodologies: 1996–1999; chaired by Keith Rust, Westat; report issued 1999, "Measuring a Changing Nation—Modern Methods for the 2000 Census."

While these panels differed in aspects of their scope and focus, they generally concurred on the following points: the potential for using statistical methods (specifically, dual-system estimation based on matching responses from a coverage evaluation survey to the census) to adjust census counts in order to make the data more accurate for many purposes;

the high costs and errors introduced by trying to achieve more complete coverage through special field operations; the potential cost-effectiveness of using sampling in field operations; the difficulties of using administrative records for the census; and the need for more research and data collection to inform planning and testing of methods for future censuses (for example, tracking a sample of housing units through the census process).

To evaluate the 2000 census and look forward to 2020 and also to consider various aspects of the American Community Survey, the bureau asked CNSTAT to convene the following six panels:

- Panel to Review the 2000 Census: 1998–2004; chaired by Janet Norwood, former commissioner of the Bureau of Labor Statistics; report issued 2004, "The 2000 Census: Counting Under Adversity."
- Panel on Research on Future Census Methods: 1998–2004: chaired by Benjamin King, Florida Atlantic University; report issued 2004, "Reengineering the 2010 Census: Risks and Challenges."
- Panel on Residence Rules in the Decennial Census: 2004–2006; chaired by Paul Voss, University of Wisconsin-Madison; report issued 2006, "Once, Only Once, and in the Right Place: Residence Rules in the Decennial Census."
- Panel on the Functionality and Usability of Data from the American Community Survey: 2004–2007; chaired by Graham Kalton, Westat; report issued 2007, "Using the American Community Survey: Benefits and Challenges."
- Panel on Correlation Bias and Coverage Measurement in the 2010 Decennial Census: 2004–2008; chaired by Robert Bell, AT&T Research; report issued 2008, "Coverage Measurement in the 2010 Census."
- Panel on the Design of the 2010 Census Program of Evaluations and Experiments: 2008–2010; chaired by Lawrence Brown, University of Pennsylvania; report issued 2010, "Envisioning the 2020 Census."

The Panel to Review the 2000 Census supported the bureau's decision not to adjust the 2000 census results for net coverage error because of the problems that surfaced with the coverage evaluation program in 2000, called Accuracy and Coverage Evaluation (ACE). (ACE estimates of net undercount differed significantly from those produced by the method of demographic analysis, and it was determined that ACE failed to detect numerous duplicate enumerations in the census.) The panel recommended that future coverage evaluation address gross and net errors in order to help improve future census operations. The Panel on the Design of the 2010 Census Program of Evaluations and Experiments recommended that the Census Bureau strive to substantially reduce the costs per housing unit, adjusted for inflation, in the 2020 census. It supported focused research on the potential for cost savings, without compromising data quality, from continuous updating of the Master Address File, the use of the Internet for census response, the use of administrative records in census operations, paperless nonresponse follow-up, and rigorous cost-benefit analysis to identify ways to scale back or eliminate ineffective census operations. The Panel on the Functionality and Usability of Data from the American Community Survey noted the benefits of continually updated information but also the challenges from the ACS design of multiyear estimates for small geographic areas based on sample sizes that are smaller than the 2000 census long-form sample.

Currently, the CNSTAT Panel to Review the 2010 Census, chaired by Thomas Cook, member of the National Academy of Engineering, is examining 2010 operations and making recommendations for major improvements to 2020 operations. Another CNSTAT panel, the Panel on Statistical Methods for Measuring Group Quarters in the ACS, chaired by Paul Voss, University of Wisconsin-Madison, is studying the problems of the ACS continuous design for estimates of the total and group quarters population in small geographic areas.

Advisory Committees for 2000

An especially elaborate structure of advisory committees was established for the 2000 census because of concerns about rising census costs and the perceived high stakes for Congress over the issue of whether to use statistical techniques to adjust the census results for population undercount. The Bureau of the Census's own advisory structure, consisting of the Census Advisory Committee of Professional Associations, with members nominated by the AEA, AMA, ASA, and PAA, and the minority advisory committees, continued from the past. The bureau also asked the NAS Committee on National Statistics to convene the Panel to Review the 2000 Census (see above).

The U.S. Department of Commerce set up an advisory structure for 2000 as well. The department's inspector general carried out several studies of census plans. In addition, in late 1991 the secretary of commerce appointed the 2000 Census Advisory Committee, with representatives from a wide range of organizations representing private-sector users; minority groups; professional associations; state, local, and tribal governments; and others. (Just some of the organizations represented were the American Civil Liberties Union, American Legion, American Sociological Association, Association of Public Data Users, Business Roundtable, Council of Chief State School Officers, Mexican American Legal Defense and Education Fund, National Association of Counties, and National Governors Association.) The committee also included ex officio, nonvoting members, including representatives of the congressional committees that handled oversight and appropriations for the census. The secretary's committee met several times a year and reviewed and made recommendations on all aspects of census planning.

Finally, in addition to continuing its practice in past censuses of holding frequent oversight hearings and periodically asking the U.S. General Accounting Office to study census plans

and budget proposals for 2000, Congress also established the 2000 Census Monitoring Board. The provision for the Monitoring Board was part of legislation passed in fall 1997 that represented a compromise between Congress and the Clinton administration on census issues. (The legislation called for the Bureau of the Census to plan a census both with and without sampling for nonresponse follow-up and coverage adjustment and provided for expedited judicial review of the constitutionality of using sampling to produce census counts for congressional reapportionment.) The Monitoring Board consisted of eight members, four appointed by House and Senate Republican leaders and four by the president in consultation with House and Senate Democratic leaders. The congressional and presidential appointees each had their own budgets and staffs and issued periodic reports to Congress on the progress of the census through fall 2001.

Subsequent to the findings of errors in the 2000 coverage measurement program, the possibility of adjusting census counts was taken off the table by the bureau director. As a consequence, the advisory structure for the 2010 census reverted back to historical norms, including the Professional Associations Committee (reconstituted in 2010 as the Census Scientific Advisory Committee); the minority advisory committees; the 2010 Census Advisory Committee (including the ACS in its purview), which was constituted similarly to the 2000 Census Advisory Committee but reported to the Census Bureau director rather than the Commerce Department secretary; and several CNSTAT panels.

See also *Accuracy and Coverage Evaluation; Apportionment and districting; Congress and the census; Content determination; Coverage evaluation; Sampling in the census.*

. . . . CONSTANCE F. CITRO

BIBLIOGRAPHY

Anderson, Margo J. *The American Census: A Social History.* New Haven: Yale University Press, 1988.

Anderson, Margo J., and Stephen E. Fienberg. *Who Counts? The Politics of Census-Taking in Contemporary America.* New York: Russell Sage Foundation, 1999.

Goldfield, Edwin D. *Review of Studies of the Decennial Census of Population and Housing: 1969–1992.* Paper prepared for the Panel on Census Requirements in the Year 2000 and Beyond, Committee on National Statistics, National Research Council, Washington, D.C., 1992.

U. S. Bureau of the Census. *1970 Census of Population and Housing Procedural History.* Washington, D.C.: U.S. Department of Commerce, 1976.

———. *1990 Census of Population and Housing History.* Part B, chap. 2, "Planning the Census." Washington, D.C.: U.S. Department of Commerce, 1995.

African-Origin Population

Blacks or African Americans (the terms are used interchangeably here) have been in America since the founding of the colonies. The first Africans (about 20) came to Virginia in 1619 as indentured servants; however, emigrant Africans arriving as indentured servants quickly gave way to Africans arriving as slaves. While the importation of slaves was banned by 1808, slavery continued on through the Civil War, finally ending with the enactment of the Thirteenth Amendment to the Constitution on December 18, 1865.

Slaves were brought to the American colonies primarily to work in the fields of southern farmers. In 1649 there were 300 black slaves in the Virginia colony; by 1671 there were 2,000. In 1700 the slave population of the American colonies was estimated at 28,000, with 23,000 slaves residing in the South. In 1750 there were 236,000 black slaves in the American colonies, and 87 percent of those lived in the South. At this time blacks composed about 20 percent of the population of the colonies, though they accounted for fully 40 percent of the population of Virginia.

The slave labor system in America stood in stark conflict with the ideals of freedom and equality proclaimed by the colonists and provoked great controversy. The presence of a large number of racially distinct people held in bondage created economic, social, and military problems, and many white Americans wanted to rid the country of both the "peculiar institution" of slavery and the slaves themselves. Slavery in the United States forced ideological debates about whether slaves should be returned to Africa or integrated into American life as free persons. The uncertainty over what to do with slaves and free blacks is reflected in the Constitution. For example, Article I, Section 2 apportioned representation and taxation using a formula that counted a slave as three-fifths of a free person. It also required the decennial census to collect population information distinguishing the slave and the free population.

In 1790, when the first census of the United States was conducted, there were 757,000 blacks in the United States, representing about 19 percent of the total population. At no other time in the history of the United States has the black population approached this percentage. In 1790, 60,000 blacks (9 percent) were "free persons of color." The terms used in the decennial censuses to categorize the African American population have changed at almost each census. The 2010 census and its questions on race continued this pattern of change.

1790 to 1860

The censuses from 1790 to 1840 were household censuses: only the names of household heads appeared on the schedule. Data on race or color were collected based on the observation of enumerators, who were assistants to United States Marshals. In 1790 the enumerators asked six questions, including the name of the head of the family and the number of persons in each household of the following descriptions: free white males of 16 years and upward, free white males under 16 years, free white females, all other free persons (by sex and color), and slaves.

In 1850 the Census Office began to use a schedule that separately identified each person. Officials created two separate forms, one for free persons and one for slaves. The enumerators listed each free individual by name and under the heading of "Color" identified him or her as "White," "Black,"

or "Mulatto." Slaves were listed by number and categorized as black or mulatto. From 1790 to 1860 the black population grew from 757,000 to 4.4 million. In 1860, blacks represented 14 percent of the total population. One in ten African Americans was free in 1860. In 1790 four states (Maryland, North Carolina, South Carolina, and Virginia) contained 87 percent of the slave population; by 1860 this proportion had declined to 33 percent.

1870 to 1920

After the Civil War the decennial census continued to collect data on the African American population. A column headed "Color" was used consistently. Beginning with the 1850 census, enumerators were provided specific instructions on how to fill in the "Color" column, and attempts were made to break down the black population into full-blooded blacks and mulattoes. Enumerators in 1870, for example, were cautioned to "be particularly careful in reporting the class mulatto," including "all persons having any perceptible trace of African blood."

"Race" was added to the column in the 1890 census, and additional instructions were provided to the enumerators to categorize "black." The 1890 census was the first to categorize the African American population by blood quantum. Instructions were given to enumerators specifying the appropriate classification of "black" (those who had three-fourths or more black blood), "mulatto" (those who had three-eighths to five-eighths black blood), "quadroon" (those who had one-fourth black blood), and "octoroon" (those who had one-eighth or any trace of black blood).

The 1900 census was the first in which the category "Negro or of Negro descent" appeared. Enumerators indicated the race of the respondent as black if he or she was a "Negro" or was of "Negro descent." The category "Mulatto" was dropped in 1900 but reintroduced in 1910 and used again in 1920. In the 1910 and 1920 censuses, the heading "Color or Race" continued to be used on the schedules to capture data on race.

The African American population grew from 4.9 million in 1870 to 10.5 million in 1920. Blacks composed about 13 percent of the total U.S. population in 1870; by 1920 this proportion had declined to about 10 percent. The country continued to be composed primarily of individuals of African or European descent, or both. Native Americans and people of other races composed less than 5 percent of the total population in the United States.

1930 to 1960

The African American population of the United States became more diverse by residence and origin in the twentieth century. In the early years of the century, blacks began to leave the South for other regions. Blacks from Jamaica, Barbados, and Trinidad began to move to America in small numbers, though restrictive immigration laws in the 1920s halted this trend.

The categories used by the Bureau of the Census to collect information on the race of the population from 1930 to 1960 continued to be listed in the column "Color or Race";

however, changes were made in the categorization of the population. In 1930 the mulatto category was eliminated and the "one-drop rule," or hypodescent rule, was used to categorize the black population by race. Enumerators were instructed to record "a person of mixed White and Negro blood as a Negro, no matter how small the percentage of Negro blood." Respondents who were part American Indian and part African American were recorded as Negro unless the American Indian blood predominated and the person was accepted as such in the American Indian community.

In the 1940 and 1950 censuses "Negro" was used on the census form to refer to the black population. It was also used in the 1960 census, though the question format was changed. Prior to 1960, self-enumeration had been used on a very limited scale; with the 1960 census, it became a major aspect of the decennial census. As a result of the use of self-identification, the format of the question on race changed. The question on race asked, "Is this person White, Negro, American Indian, Japanese, Chinese, Filipino, Hawaiian, Part Hawaiian, Aleut, Eskimo, (etc.)?"

The definition of "Negro" in the 1960 census was similar to that used in the 1930 census. Individuals of mixed African and European descent were considered Negro, and those of mixed African and American Indian descent also were considered Negro unless they were recognized as American Indian by that community. People of mixed racial parentage were classified according to the race of the "nonwhite" parent, and mixtures of nonwhite races were classified according to the race of the father.

The African American population grew from 11.9 million in 1930 to 18.9 million in 1960. According to the 1960 census, blacks represented about 10.5 percent of the total U.S. population, up from 9.7 percent in 1930. The majority of the growth in the black population was attributable to natural increase (births minus deaths).

1970 to 1990

For the 1970 census, about 60 percent of U.S. households (mostly urban) received a questionnaire in the mail, which they were to complete and return. In the remaining areas the data were collected by enumerators. When a respondent failed to return a questionnaire, data on race were obtained by an enumerator who showed the respondent a flashcard from which to choose the appropriate race. During personal visits and telephone interviews, enumerators asked respondents, "What is ———'s race?" In such cases, the respondent's race was assumed for all other related members of the household unless the enumerator learned otherwise. Data collected by self-identification were thought to be of higher quality than those obtained through enumerator observation.

The 1970 census question on race contained language that had been used in the past, and the racial categories were only slightly modified. The wording of the category "Negro" was changed to "Negro or Black" after a review of responses to the "Color or Race" item in several 1970 census pretests and after consultation with a number of national and regional organizations and individuals concerned with race relations in the United States. The term *Afro-American* also was considered but was found less widely used than *Black*.

The 1980 census employed self-enumeration to collect racial data. Unlike the previous census, the heading "Color or Race" was not used. The definition of the race groups was expanded to comply with the standards of the Office of Management and Budget (OMB) for federal data on racial and ethnic populations. In 1977 the OMB issued standards that all federal agencies were to use to collect, tabulate, and present data on race. These standards identified four race groups: White, Black, American Indian or Alaskan Native, and Asian or Pacific Islander. The directive also stated that additional race groups could be used to collect data if the additional groups could be collapsed back into the four minimum race groups. For census purposes, the category "Black" included respondents who indicated their race as black or Negro, as well as respondents who did not classify themselves in one of the specified race categories on the questionnaire but wrote in entries such as "Black Jamaican," "Black Puerto Rican," "Black West Indian," "Black Haitian," or Black Nigerian."

The 1990 census question on race, much like the 1980 question, included a number of sociocultural (or national origin) groups. It also included the heading "Race," and the instructions were improved to make the intent of the question clearer. The response category for blacks changed from "Negro or Black" to "Black or Negro" to reflect the increased use of the term *black* and the diminished use of the term *Negro*.

The African American population grew from 22 million in 1970 to almost 30 million in 1990. (The estimated undercount of the black population in the 1990 census was 4.4 percent.) Blacks composed about 12 percent of the total population, up from 11 percent in 1970. Changes in immigration laws allowed more immigrants to come from the African continent. Immigration also increased from the Caribbean and the West Indies. However, the growth of the black population was still due mainly to natural increase.

Between 1970 and 1980, migration patterns of blacks changed. During the 1940s, 1950s, and 1960s, millions of blacks left the South. After 1970, however, the trend reversed as more blacks stayed in the South and others returned to the South. By 1990 a majority of all blacks still lived in the southern region of the United States.

Census 2000

After the 1990 census, the OMB conducted a review of the statistical standards used to collect and tabulate federal data on race and ethnicity in response to criticism that the standards no longer accurately reflected the racial and ethnic diversity of the country. Children of interracial unions and their parents criticized standards that forced them to identify with only one race category. Others suggested that changes be made to the particular race categories identified in the standards. Some groups even questioned the need of the federal government to collect and tabulate data on race, stating that doing so promoted racism.

A number of significant innovations in the question on race appeared in Census 2000, including changes in the formatting and terminology of the question. Most notably, respondents were able to report themselves in one or more categories of race. These changes were the result of an extensive research and consultation process that began with an international conference convened by the Bureau of the Census and Statistics Canada in 1992, congressional hearings held in 1992 and 1993, and the OMB review of the statistical standards used by all federal agencies to collect, tabulate, and present data on race and ethnicity that began in 1993.

The question on race for Census 2000, much like the question on race in previous censuses, was asked of all respondents. It included fifteen response categories: White; "Black, African Am., or Negro"; American Indian or Alaska Native; Asian Indian; Chinese; Filipino; Japanese; Korean; Vietnamese; Other Asian; Native Hawaiian; Guamanian or Chamorro; Samoan; Other Pacific Islander; and Some other race. Respondents who marked the "American Indian or Alaska Native" category were asked to provide the name of their enrolled or principal tribe. People who reported "Other Asian," "Other Pacific Islander," or "Some other race" were also asked to write in their race.

Changes were made to the black response category on the race question as a result of consultation with community and national organizations. During the latter part of the 1980s, some members of the African American community suggested that the response category be changed to reflect the increased use of the term *African American*. Others suggested that *African American* be used alongside *Black,* and that *Negro* be dropped altogether. These suggestions came too late to be effectively tested and implemented in the 1990 census; however, after extensive research "Black, African Am., or Negro" became the response category for blacks in Census 2000.

The U.S. government has collected data on the black population since it began its census-taking activities in 1790. Over time the terminology for the response categories has changed considerably, from "free person" or "slave" to "Black," "Mulatto," "Quadroon," or "Octoroon" to "Negro" to "Black or Negro" to "Black, African Am., or Negro." The African American population grew from fewer than 1 million in 1790 to nearly 34.7 million in 2000. Unlike many other groups in this country, immigration has not been a major factor in the growth of the black population. Historically, about 85 percent to 90 percent of the growth in the black population of the United States has been due to natural increase. The censuses of years past have permitted the black population to identify with only one race group, albeit with some attempts to differentiate between full-blooded and mixed-blood descent. The Census 2000 option that allowed respondents to mark one or more racial group more clearly permitted blacks, as well as other racial groups, to identify their mixed racial heritage, which was based on the instruction "Mark [X] one or more races" to the question on race. Census 2000 showed 281.4 million people; of this total, 36.4 million, or 12.9 percent, reported as "Black" or "African American." ("Black, African Am., or Negro" was

the actual response category on the form.) This number included 34.7 million people, or 12.3 percent, who reported only "Black" or "African American." In addition, 1.8 million people, or 0.6 percent, reported "Black" or "African American" as well as one or more other races. Within the group reporting "Black" or "African American" and one or more other races, the most common combinations were "Black" *and* "White" (45 percent), followed by "Black" *and* "Some other race" (24 percent), "Black" *and* "American Indian" *and* "Alaska Native" (10 percent), and "Black" *and* "White" *and* "American Indian" *and* "Alaska Native" (6 percent). These four combination categories accounted for 85 percent of all blacks who reported two or more races.

The 2010 Census

The final 2010 race and Hispanic origin questions were the culmination of an extensive content testing and evaluation process that began early in the decade. A series of national tests were conducted to determine the exact wording of these questions. The goals of these tests were to (1) examine alternative versions of the Census 2000 race and Hispanic origin questions and their respective response categories, (2) assess the effect of dropping the "Some other race" response category to the question on race, (3) measure the effectiveness of revising the instructions to the race and Hispanic origin questions and expand the Note to Respondents to answer both questions, and (4) obtain information about respondents' reaction to added examples for selected response categories to these questions.

The above treatments were tested using both a two-question format (the Hispanic origin question, followed by the race question) and a three-question format (a shortened Hispanic origin question, followed by a shortened race question, followed by a modified ancestry question). Figure 1 provides examples of some of the questions used during the testing process. Because past research showed that small changes to one of these questions might affect the other, it was imperative to test the proposed changes as a package in the 2010 research and testing program.

With respect to the African American population, two major changes were tested—adding examples (such as Haitian, Negro, Nigerian) to the "Black, African Am., or Negro" response category and dropping the "Negro" term. Examples were included in the shortened question on race to test whether respondents understood the response categories. Although the term *Negro* appeared in the response category in Census 2000, more than 50,000 respondents wrote it in as well. Also, past qualitative research suggested that including the term provided a clue to some immigrants on how to respond to the question given the separate Asian and Pacific Islander subgroups listed in the question. Results of these changes were evaluated in the larger context of the question on race. Because there was no clear evidence to suggest that the above changes improved reporting of blacks to the question on race, it was decided to leave the "Black" response category as it appeared in Census 2000.

Figure 1. Examples of Alternative Race and Hispanic Origin Questions Tested Prior to the 2010 Census

Two Question Format (2004 Census Test)

Expanded Census 2000 "Spanish/Hispanic/Latino" language; added examples for Hispanic, Asian, and Other Pacific Islander; excluded "Some Other Race" category

Is this person of Spanish, Hispanic or Latino origin?
Mark ☒ "No" if not of Spanish, Hispanic or Latino origin.
☐ No, not of Spanish, Hispanic or Latino origin   ☐ Yes, Puerto Rican
☐ Yes, Mexican, Mexican Am., or Chicano   ☐ Yes, Cuban
☐ Yes, another Spanish, Hispanic or Latino origin — *Print origin, for example, Argentinian, Colombian, Dominican, Nicaraguan, Salvadoran, Spaniard, and so on.*
[Write-In Space]

What is this person's race? *Mark ☒ one or more races to indicate what this person considers himself/herself to be.*
☐ White
☐ Black, African Am., or Negro
☐ American Indian or Alaska Native — *Print name of enrolled or principal tribe.*
[Write-In Space]
☐ Asian Indian   ☐ Japanese   ☐ Native Hawaiian
☐ Chinese   ☐ Korean   ☐ Guamanian or Chamorro
☐ Filipino   ☐ Vietnamese   ☐ Samoan
☐ Other Asian — *Print race, for example, Hmong, Laotian, Thai, Pakistani, Cambodian and so on.*   ☐ Other Pacific Islander — *Print race, for example, Fijian, Tongan and so on.*
[Write-In Space]

Three Question Format (2005 Census Test)

Shortened Hispanic origin question; added "Hispanic origins are not races" instruction to race question; included narrative introduction to ancestry question

Is Person 1 of Hispanic, Latino, or Spanish origin?
☐ Yes ☐ No

What is Person 1's race? *Mark ☒ one or more races.*
For this census, Hispanic origins are not races.
☐ White or Caucasian
☐ Black, African Am., or Negro
☐ American Indian or Alaska Native
☐ Asian
☐ Native Hawaiian or Other Pacific Islander
☐ Some other race

People in the United States are from many countries, tribes, and cultural groups. What is Person 1's ancestry or tribe? *For example, Italian, African American, Dominican, Aleut, Jamaican, Chinese, Pakistani, Salvadoran, Rosebud Sioux, Nigerian, Samoan, Russian, etc.*
[Write-In Space]
☐ Don't know

Three Question Format (2005 Census Test)

Provided examples for Hispanic origin and all race categories; added ancestry write-in question without narrative explanation

Is Person 1 of Hispanic, Latino, or Spanish origin? *For example, Mexican, Puerto Rican, Colombian, etc.*
☐ Yes ☐ No

What is Person 1's race? *Mark ☒ one or more races.*
☐ White or Caucasian *(French, Scottish, etc.)*
☐ Black, African Am., or Negro *(Ethiopian, West Indian, etc.)*
☐ American Indian or Alaska Native *(Navajo, Athabascan, etc.)*
☐ Asian *(Asian Indian, Korean, etc.)*
☐ Native Hawaiian or Other Pacific Islander *(Fijian, Tongan, etc.)*
☐ Some other race

What is Person 1's ancestry or tribe? *For example, Italian, African American, Dominican, Aleut, Jamaican, Chinese, Pakistani, Salvadoran, Rosebud Sioux, Nigerian, Samoan, Russian, etc.*
[Write-In Space]
☐ Don't know

The 2010 census reported a total population of 308.7 million persons, of which 42 million, or 13.6 percent, were "Black" or "African American." Some 38.9 million (12.6 percent) reported only "Black" or "African American," while almost 3.1 million (1 percent) reported "Black" or "African American" and one or more other races. Among those reporting more than one race, the most common combinations were "Black" and "White" (59 percent), "Black" and "Some other race" (10 percent) and "Black" and "American Indian and Alaska Native" (9 percent). For the first time, in 2010, those reporting "Black" and "White" constituted the majority of all African Americans reporting more than one race.

The majority of the black population lived in the South. According to the 2010 census about 56 percent of the black-alone population resided in the South region, 18 percent lived in the Midwest, 17 percent lived in the Northeast, and 9 percent lived in the West.

The 10 states with the largest black populations in 2010 were New York, Florida, Texas, Georgia, California, North Carolina, Illinois, Maryland, Virginia, and Louisiana. Combined, these states represented 59 percent of the total black population. Six of these 10 states had black populations greater than 2 million: New York (3.1 million); Florida, Texas, and Georgia (about 3 million each); California (2.3 million); and North Carolina (just over 2 million). In the South, 11 states (Florida, Texas, Georgia, North Carolina, Maryland, Virginia, Louisiana, South Carolina, Alabama, Mississippi, and Tennessee) had black populations over 1 million and, when combined, they represented 52 percent of the nation's black-alone population.

See also *Race: questions and classifications.*

. . . . CLAUDETTE BENNETT

BIBLIOGRAPHY

Grieco, Elizabeth M., and Rachel C. Cassidy. "Overview of Race and Hispanic Origin: 2000." 2000 Census Brief C2KBR/01–1. Washington D.C.: U.S. Census Bureau, March 2001.

Humes, Karen R., Nicholas A. Jones, and Roberto R. Ramirez. "Overview of Race and Hispanic Origin: 2010." 2010 Census Brief C2010BR-02. Washington, D.C.: U.S. Census Bureau, March 2011. http://2010.census.gov/2010census/data/.

Joint Center for Political and Economic Studies. Annual Report. Washington, D.C.: Joint Center for Political and Economic Studies, 1992.

Lavraska, Paul, et al. "The Use and Perception of Ethno-Racial Labels: 'African American' and/or 'Black.'" Paper presented at the Bureau of the Census Annual Research Conference and CASIC Technologies Interchange, Arlington, Va., March 20–23, 1994.

Martin, Elizabeth M., Dave Sheppard, Michael Bentley, and Claudette Bennett. "Results of the 2003 National Census Test of Race and Hispanic Questions." Research Report Series (*Survey Methodology #2007–34*), Washington D.C.: U.S. Census Bureau, 2007.

McKinnon, Jesse. "The Black Population: 2000." Census Brief C2KBR/01–5. Washington D.C.: U.S. Census Bureau, August 2001.

Ploski, Harry A., and James Williams. *The Negro Almanac: A Reference Work on the African American.* 5th ed. Detroit: Gale Research, 1989.

U.S. Bureau of the Census. *Historical Statistics of the United States, Colonial Times to 1970.* Bicentennial ed., Part 2. Washington, D.C.: Government Printing Office, 1975.

———. *Negro Population 1790–1915.* Washington, D.C.: Government Printing Office, 1918.

———. *The Social and Economic Status of the Black Population in the United States, 1790–1978.* P23, No. 80. Washington, D.C.: Government Printing Office, 1980.

U.S. Census Bureau. *2010 Census of Population and Housing.* American Factfinder, Table P1, Race. Washington, D.C.: U.S. Government Printing Office, 2011. http://factfinder2.census.gov/main.html.

Age Questions in the Census

Since its beginnings in 1790, the decennial census has gathered information on age and as such has served for more than 200 years as a basic source of information on the age structure and changing distribution of ages in the U.S. population. The first census recorded the numbers of free white males under age 16 years and those age 16 years and over. Congress limited age categories to white men because it was interested in assessing the number who were able to work and were eligible for military service. The 1800 and 1810 censuses expanded the age information collected for white men and also white women: these two censuses counted the number of free white women and men under age 10 years; those age 10 to under 16 years; those age 16 to under 26 years, including heads of families; those age 26 years to under 45 years, including heads of families; and those 45 years and over, including heads of families. Between 1820 and 1840, these age categories were expanded to 13 different age groups, which signified an increased awareness that the U.S. population was aging. The 1820, 1830, and 1840 censuses also counted the number of free "colored" persons and slaves for a number of age categories. Starting in 1850, the census recorded the characteristics, including age, of individuals living in each household. Date of birth was not permanently added to the census schedule until 1960 (although it was included in the 1900 census).

In Census 2010, each respondent was asked, "What is this person's age and what is this person's date of birth?" with a request to report a baby as age 0 when the child was less than 1 year old. The respondent is instructed to specify his or her age in years on April 1, 2010, as well as the month, day, and year of birth. This question was asked in two parts to ensure that ages were reported accurately. Demographers have long been aware that people have a tendency to round their ages to a number ending in five or zero in response to a single question on age, a phenomenon known as "age heaping." Thus the question on date of birth provides a second piece of information to use in evaluating the answer to the question on age and for getting more accurate age data.

Data can be analyzed by any designated age categories; for example, data on income can be analyzed to examine the degree to which income levels vary by age. Data users also combine the answers to census questions to create age cohorts or average patterns by age. Current census information on age composition is useful because it can be aggregated to form cohorts of interest, to describe the patterns of living for a wide variety of groups—for example, children, teenagers, young adults, the middle aged, the elderly, the young old, the oldest old, to name just a few. Alternatively, characteristics of the population can be described by a single point estimate based on age—for example, a mean age at marriage or the median age of the population.

Many federal agencies, including the Departments of Commerce, Education, Labor, and Justice, use decennial census information on age to implement programs. Numerous federal statutes require the Census Bureau to collect information on age in order to implement and evaluate social programs for working-age adults, women of childbearing age, and the older population. Under the Voting Rights Act of 1965, the data on population of voting age are required for legislative redistricting. Community planners at both the state and local levels use census data, broken down by age, to evaluate future needs for child care, education, employment, and services for the elderly. At all levels of government, this information is used for equal opportunity purposes specified by the Age Discrimination and Employment Act of 1967 and the Older Americans Act of 1965.

Over the course of U.S. history, the age composition of the population has changed dramatically. In 1800 the median age of the population was around 16 years; now it is around 37 years. Life expectancy at birth has increased from about 40 years of age in 1800 to almost 78 years today. Moreover, substantial increases in those 65 years of age and over are projected for the nation over the next two decades.

See also *American Community Survey: questionnaire content; Composition of the population; Demographic analysis; Uses of the census and ACS: federal agencies.*

GRETCHEN A. STIERS
.... REVISED BY JOSEPH J. SALVO

BIBLIOGRAPHY

U.S. Bureau of the Census. *General Population Characteristics: Part I, United States Summary.* Washington, D.C.: Government Printing Office, 1983.
———. *Twenty Censuses: Population and Housing Questions, 1790–1980.* Washington, D.C.: Government Printing Office, 1978.
U.S. Census Bureau. *Subjects Planned for the 2010 Census and the American Community Survey: Federal Legislative and Program Uses.* Washington, D.C.: Government Printing Office, 2007.
Wright, Carroll D., and William C. Hunt. *The History and Growth of the United States Census.* Washington, D.C.: Government Printing Office, 1900.

Agricultural Censuses

Censuses of agricultural production have been conducted in the United States at least every ten years since 1840. Detailed information is collected on land use, total production of crops and livestock, value of sales, and farming practices of broadly defined American agricultural operations. Data on farm operation types and each operator's age, race, ethnicity, and sex also are collected. These periodic censuses are the only attempts to collect information from all farms in the United States and provide comprehensive data for all states and counties—data not available from any other source.

Each census of agriculture covers all 50 states, Puerto Rico, Guam, the U.S. Virgin Islands, and the Commonwealth of the Northern Mariana Islands. American Samoa is included in every other census of agriculture. Farm definition, report form content, timing, and survey procedures are adapted to local needs in conducting the censuses for these outlying areas. Specialty follow-on censuses or surveys have been conducted since 1890 to collect additional information about certain practices or specific economic factors using the regular census to identify a sampling frame.

The first specialty collection was the 1889 Census of Horticulture. The 2009 Census of Horticultural Specialties, conducted after the 2007 Census of Agriculture, is the eighth. Special irrigation surveys were conducted every decade starting in 1910 and have been a feature of each agricultural census since 1984. After the 1987 and 1997 censuses, the Agricultural Economics and Land Ownership Survey was conducted, which included questions addressed to farm landlords as well as the selected farmers. The Census of Aquaculture was conducted for the first time following the 1997 Census of Agriculture and in 2005 following the 2002 Census of Agriculture. Two new specialty programs, the 2008 Organic Production Survey and the 2009 On-Farm Renewable Energy Survey, used the 2007 Census of Agriculture as a sampling frame.

Definition of Farms

The first agricultural census, in 1840, did not include any definition of a farm, but every collection since, except for that in 1900, has used some definition. Since 1978, the farm definition has been any place that sells, or normally would have sold, at least $1,000 of agricultural commodities in the census year.

Department of Commerce funding concerns led to the announcement of a plan to change the farm definition from $1,000 in sales to $10,000 for the 1997 Census of Agriculture. That would have reduced the number of "farms" in the United States by 50 percent and removed as many as 80 percent in some states such as West Virginia. Funding authority was changed to the National Agricultural Statistics Service (NASS) of the United States Department of Agriculture (USDA) for fiscal year 1997, and full legislative authority was shifted to the USDA in the Census of Agriculture Act of 1997. NASS conducted the 1997 Census of Agriculture but used the Bureau of the Census services and systems for form printing, sending and receiving mail, data entry, basic editing, analysis, summary, and publication. NASS continues to use bureau services for forms printing, addressing, sending and receiving mail, and data entry.

The Questionnaire

The first agricultural census included 37 questions asked in face-to-face interviews with all people who indicated any agricultural activity on the population census. The number of questions increased substantially in 1880 (108 questions) and 1890 (255 questions). The 1840 questionnaire collected crop production data but no information on the area from which each crop was harvested, which greatly limited comparison with surveys conducted between censuses. This weakness

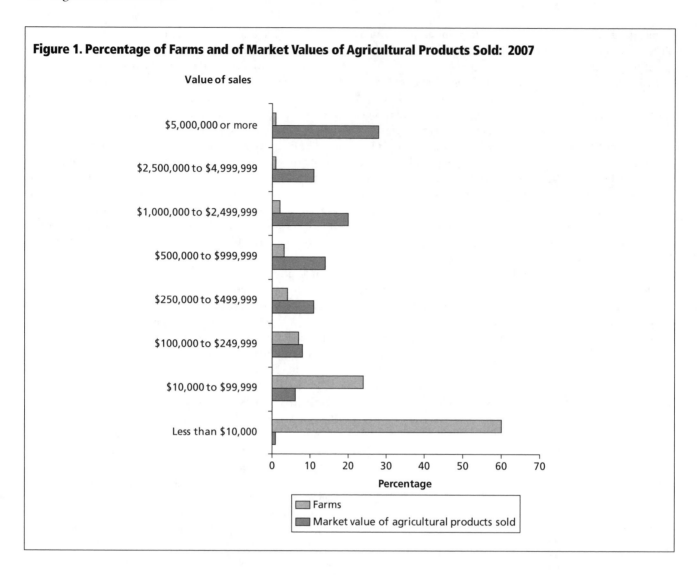

Figure 1. Percentage of Farms and of Market Values of Agricultural Products Sold: 2007

Value of sales

Percentage

Farms

Market value of agricultural products sold

continued until 1880, although questions were added in 1850 and 1860 to determine if production levels in those years correctly represented a typical production year.

Because of the broad interest in agriculture and the relatively rapid changes in crop acreage, livestock production patterns, and price levels, interest was often expressed in collection of agricultural data more often than every ten years. In 1896, Col. Carroll D. Wright, the commissioner of labor, called for an annual survey of agriculture and manufacturing. In 1909, Congress mandated that the Department of Commerce conduct a mid-decade agricultural census, but the 1925 census was the first mid-decade census. They have been conducted at approximately five-year intervals ever since.

The Census of Agriculture has been independent of the Census of Population since 1950. The population census had a question on its long form asking whether each residence is located on a farm. This information is now captured on the American Community Survey conducted by the Census Bureau, and it provides an estimate of the population with "actual sales of agricultural products."

Since agriculture in the United States varies so greatly, the agricultural census questionnaire must include many different categories. The basic questionnaire contains about 1,100 answer cells, but the median number of positive answer cells in the 2007 Census of Agriculture, by state, ranged from 82 to 97.

Data Collection

Census data were collected by face-to-face interviews until 1950. In that year, questionnaires, written in a personal interviewer style, were mailed out ahead of time. Farmers were asked to fill out the questionnaires and hold them for enumerators. This approach was used for most data collection through 1964. In 1969 farmers were asked to mail back the questionnaires for the first time. To ensure returns, the Bureau of the Census sent follow-up mailings. In 2007 a Web-based version of the questionnaire was offered for the first time.

In the 1970s a decision was made to coordinate agricultural census reference dates with other economic censuses. The shift was accomplished by conducting two four-year censuses in 1978 and 1982. Reference dates since have been for years ending in 2 and 7.

Figure 2. Farms by Market Value of Agricultural Products Sold: 1969 to 2007

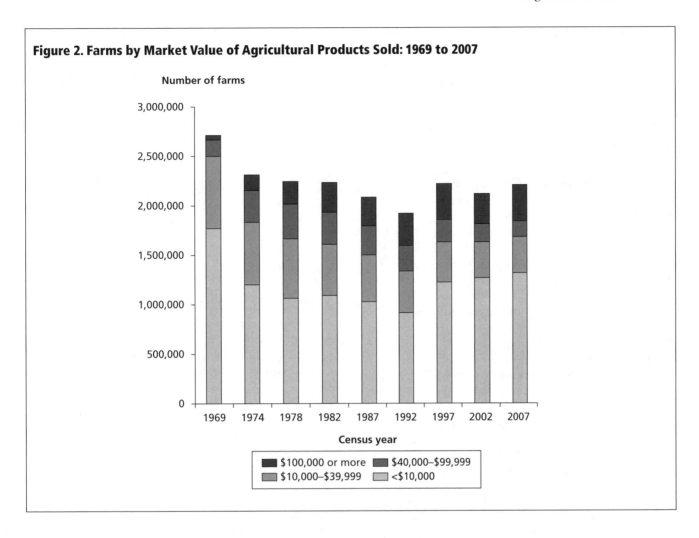

Number of farms

Census year

Legend:
- $100,000 or more
- $40,000–$99,999
- $10,000–$39,999
- <$10,000

Many list sources are used to create as complete a census mail list as possible; however, many small farming operations do not appear on any lists. Coverage evaluation studies have been conducted since 1945 using an independent area frame. Since 1987 the studies have used the NASS area frame that covers all land in the United States. Random sections of land are chosen, and the operators of that land are interviewed. Although these studies have shown that coverage of all farm operations has ranged from 84 percent to 93 percent, the coverage of total value of agricultural production has always exceeded 95 percent.

Follow-up telephone calls to farms that have not returned their form have been made since the 1969 census. Priority is given to large operations and counties with response rates less than 75 percent to maintain a response rate that provides quality statistics. Multiple attempts are made to contact nonrespondents as telephone follow-up continues up to a prescribed cut-off date.

Statistical Methodology

Census farm counts and totals have been adjusted for nonresponse since 1969. Nonresponse studies were conducted to estimate the number of nonrespondents who qualified as farms. Adjustments were made by increasing the weights of responding farms using nonresponse categories defined using economic size within county. In 2007 the adjustment methodology was changed to use data-mining techniques, in order to identify categories with statistically significant response rates on a set of administratively determined defining variables (mainly demographic and census list frame characteristics).

From 1945 to 1992 the results of the coverage evaluation studies were released in a separate publication well after the census results. In 1987 an appendix to the state and U.S. publications included estimates of farms not on the mailing list and their characteristics, including estimates of census undercoverage at the state level. The full results of the coverage evaluation were included in the appendices to the 1997 state and U.S. publications. Beginning in 2002, NASS began to "fully adjust" census farm counts and totals at the county level for coverage using multivariate calibration techniques. A set of defining variables was established for which incompleteness was measured from the area frame. These variables include farm counts for economic size, type of farm, and selective demographic characteristics plus land in farms. The sum of the list responses, adjusted for nonresponse, plus the estimate for list incompleteness, define target values for the variables. A calibration algorithm adjusted the weights of the responding farms to satisfy all targets. The 2002 fully adjusted farm counts and totals were published along with the comparable 1997 totals to help bridge this new methodology across censuses. Publication of fully adjusted farm counts and totals for the current census reference year and the previous census reference year continue for 2007 using the described methodology.

Availability and Uses of Census Data

Census of Agriculture publications are free on the Internet at www.agcensus.usda.gov/ as well as at federal depository libraries, NASS Field Offices, and many land-grant colleges and universities. Printed publications and CD-ROMs can be purchased. Reports for each of the 50 states include county and state data, whereas the *United States Summary* report includes data for each state with national totals.

Uses of Census of Agriculture data are quite varied. State and local government bodies have always used published data for a wide range of analyses. In recent years many government units have been interested in the data for farmland preservation and taxation issues. Census of Agriculture data are also used for research by sociologists, economists, and business analysts. All elected officials are interested in the makeup and economic attributes of their constituents. Special congressional district tabulations and products such as the *Agricultural Atlas of the United States, ZIP Code Tabulation of Selected Items,* and *State and County Profiles* are in high demand. Beginning in 2007 these items were made available only online. Additional publications created since 2007 include *American Indian Reservations, Watersheds, Race, Ethnicity, and Gender Profiles* and results from the follow-on surveys such as *Farm and Ranch Irrigation* and *Organic Production.*

Results from each agricultural census serve as part of a complete review of all NASS survey and administrative data for the years since the previous census. Thus the census totals are used not only as a benchmark but also as another indication that must be interpreted in light of any changes in census definitions, response rates, and data collection procedures. NASS uses agricultural census information for improving the sampling and conduct of surveys between censuses. In addition, NASS can maximize the value of the entire agricultural census and survey program by streamlining procedures, questionnaires, and data products. This helps reduce the survey burden on farmers and ranchers and provides unified service and products to all customers of agricultural statistics.

See also *Rural areas.*

. . . . CHRIS MESSER

BIBLIOGRAPHY

Allen, Rich, Vickie J. Huggins, and Ruth Ann Killion. "The Evolution of Agricultural Data Collection in the United States." In *Business Survey Methods,* ed. Brenda G. Cox, David A. Binder, B. Nanjamma Chinnappa, Anders Christianson, Michael J. Colledge, and Phillip S. Kott, 609–631. New York: Wiley, 1995.

Clark, Cynthia Z. F., and Elizabeth A. Vacca. "Ensuring Quality in U.S. Agricultural List Frames." *Proceedings of the International Conference on Establishment Surveys,* 352–361. Alexandria, Va.: American Statistical Association, 1993.

National Agricultural Statistics Service. *2007 Census of Agriculture.* Vol. 1, part 51. Washington, D.C.: U.S. Department of Agriculture, 2009.

Taylor, Henry C., and Anne D. Taylor. *The Story of Agricultural Economics in the United States, 1840–1932.* Ames, Iowa: Iowa State College Press, 1952.

U.S. Bureau of the Census. *1992 Census of Agriculture: History.* Vol. 2, part 4. Washington, D.C.: U.S. Department of Commerce, 1996.

Wright, Carroll D., and W. C. Hunt. *History and Growth of the U.S. Census: 1790–1890.* Washington, D.C.: U.S. Government Printing Office, 1900.

American Indians and Alaska Natives

As the first inhabitants of what is now the United States, American Indians and Alaska Natives are a legally, politically, and culturally unique part of the nation. No other group is explicitly recognized in the Constitution. An entire volume of the Code of Federal Regulations (CFR 25) is devoted to American Indian law; two congressional committees—one each for the House and the Senate—oversee relations with American Indians; and an agency within the executive branch is solely responsible for American Indians (the Bureau of Indian Affairs within the Department of the Interior).

In light of the special relationship that exists between American Indians and the federal government, it may be surprising that American Indians were not included in the early censuses of this country. For decades the United States government regarded American Indians as belonging to nations apart, and to some extent it continues to do so today. As a result, the decennial census did not enumerate American Indians until 1860 and paid virtually no attention to American Indian population characteristics until 1890.

The census clearly illustrates the peculiar status that American Indians have occupied throughout this country's history. The first census that counted American Indians (1860) distinguished "Indians taxed" from "Indians, not taxed." "Indians taxed" were individuals who had settled in or near Anglo-American communities, had adopted Anglo-American livelihoods and lifestyles, and were more or less assimilated in Anglo-American society. They resembled Anglo-Americans enough to be considered "citizens," and they could be taxed. "Indians, not taxed" were Indians who lived among their kinsmen in tribal communities, had not adopted Euro-American customs, and, because they were not "citizens" of the United States, were not called on to pay taxes. This distinction was eventually discarded in the late nineteenth century, when many American Indians were made citizens, and then, in 1924, the Indian Citizenship Act made all American Indians eligible for taxation.

Data Sources

Modern anthropology had an important influence on the types of information the Census Bureau first collected about American Indians. Anthropologists of this era were convinced, as were many others, that American Indians were destined for extinction. Guided by this belief, anthropologists in the late nineteenth century set out to observe, document, and collect every conceivable detail connected with the lifestyles and cultures of American Indians. This effort has come to be known as "salvage ethnography."

The Census Office issued its first major report devoted to American Indians in 1894, as part of the 11th decennial census in 1890. The report, titled *Report on Indians Taxed and Not Taxed in the United States, Except Alaska* (volume 17), was a remarkable document for at least two reasons. First, it was the first significant effort ever made to enumerate and collect data about the American Indian population. Second, this document was an exercise in salvage ethnography. In addition to the usual statistical data, this report also included maps, drawings, photographs, and detailed narrative accounts of tribal culture. No similar publication has ever been produced by the bureau.

In each decade since 1890, "American Indians" have been a feature in the decennial census. This does not mean, however, that data for American Indians improved significantly throughout the twentieth century. In fact, a great deal of information was available about American Indians at the end of the nineteenth century, somewhat less at the beginning of the twentieth, century, and relatively little for the mid-century decades.

Nonetheless, the decennial census has been and continues to be the preeminent source of data about the American Indian population. No other source contains as much information for the American Indian population in its entirety—urban and reservation—for so many different characteristics. This information can be found in two forms: special reports devoted to the American Indian population and in tabulations for the general population.

In the early part of the twentieth century, the Bureau of the Census published two special reports devoted to American Indians, one in 1915 and another in 1937, based on the 1910 and 1930 decennial censuses, respectively. These reports also contained a small amount of information about Alaska Natives. In 1940, 1950, and 1960, American Indians were enumerated in the census but virtually disappeared from most bureau publications. Data about American Indians did not appear in the main publications for states and other localities. In most instances, they were subsumed within the "Other Races" category of the bureau's racial classification. Data for American Indians (and other ethnic minorities) were published in special reports on the "non-white population" published in 1943, 1953, and 1963.

Likewise, American Indians were missing from most of the reports produced from the 1970 census. However, the bureau produced a special report devoted exclusively to American Indians and, to a lesser extent, Alaska Natives. The publications from the 1980 census were the first to regularly include American Indians and Alaska Natives in tabulations of racial characteristics. The bureau also produced, in 1983, a special subject report for American Indians and Alaska Natives, resembling the 1970 special report but containing much more detail. In addition to the regular census, a special supplementary questionnaire was distributed to reservation households. The results of this survey were published in yet another special report. The bureau did not sponsor a special reservation survey in the 1990 census. It did publish two special reports, however, one tabulated for reservations and another tabulated for tribes, in addition to including American Indians in all tabulations of racial characteristics.

After the 2000 census, a special file for the American Indian and Alaska Native populations was produced and made available on the bureau's American FactFinder. This file was the basis of a published report. At this time, there are plans to produce two reports and electronic data files for the American Indian and Alaska Native populations in connection with the 2010 census. One will contain population and housing characteristics iterated for many American Indian and Alaska Native tribes. These data are scheduled to be released late in 2012. Another file is slated to be released in 2013, similar to the data in the special file produced for American Indians and Alaska Natives after the 2000 census.

Population Characteristics

The content of information published about American Indians varied substantially across the twentieth century. In the early decades of the century, the Bureau of the Census paid considerable attention to the topic of "stock." Stock referred to tribal, linguistic, and blood quantum characteristics of the population. Blood quantum was of special concern to the bureau because of the government's long-standing interest in the so-called civilization and assimilation of American Indians. Blood quantum was a convenient measure of the Indian's progress toward being fully assimilated into the population at large. In particular, full-blood American Indians were sometimes considered to be backward and uncivilized, whereas persons with less than one-fourth blood quantum were considered to be fully civilized individuals, lacking any residual traces of American Indian cultural traits.

As the century passed, ideas about cultural inheritance receded in popularity. By mid-century, eugenics and its association with scientific racism were in disrepute and the bureau discontinued its publication of these data. Nonetheless, enumerators for the 1950 census were instructed to include as American Indians anyone who was one-quarter or more blood quantum. These instructions did not specify how blood quantum was to be ascertained.

The 1950 census was the last enumeration in which census workers ascribed racial ancestry to respondents. In the 1960 census, respondents themselves were asked to identify their racial background. For American Indians, this was perhaps the most significant innovation of the twentieth century. The importance of this change in procedure was reflected in growing numbers of persons reporting their race as American Indian.

From 1900 to 1950 the rate of growth in the American Indian population was slow and relatively stable. In 1900, American Indians numbered approximately 237,000. By mid-century, the population had grown 50 percent, reaching a total of 357,000. Compared with coming decades, this growth rate was very low. One reason is that although the American Indian population had a relatively high birth rate, they also had a high death rate. In 1940 the life expectancy at birth for American Indians was 51 years for males and 52 years for females. Another reason is that census coverage of American Indians was poor in many areas of the country, especially in urban areas. An evaluation of the 1940 census concluded that in areas in which there were concentrations of American Indians, such as reservations, the count of American Indians was reasonably acceptable. In other areas, it was most likely poor, with many persons of mixed–American Indian ancestry misclassified by census enumerators.

The introduction of racial self-identification eliminated enumerator errors and significantly improved the coverage of the American Indian population. Between 1950 and 1960, the American Indian and Alaska Native population grew from 377,000 to nearly 552,000, an increase of 51 percent in a single decade. This growth continued in the next decades with the Native American population expanding to 827,000 in 1970 (50 percent increase), 1.4 million in 1980 (71 percent increase), and 2.0 million in 1990 (43 percent increase).

Besides changes in census procedures, there are many possible reasons for these spectacular growth rates. One is that life expectancies increased dramatically for American Indians after World War II. The other is that the stigma attached to identifying with any race other than white diminished in the years after 1960, especially for persons with American Indian or Alaska Native heritage. Growing ethnic pride and awareness prompted many mixed-race persons who could have identified otherwise to choose instead to affiliate themselves with their American Indian ancestry. It is virtually impossible to ascertain the numbers of persons who changed their racial affiliation between the decennial censuses, but such individuals accounted for a substantial portion of the population growth for American Indians after 1960.

In the 2000 census, more than one race could be reported and data were tabulated for "American Indians alone," "American Indians and Alaska Natives alone," "American Indians in combination with another race," and "American Indians and Alaska Natives in combination with another race." The latter two groups represented individuals for whom two or more races were reported, one of which was American Indian or Alaska Native. The 2000 census enumerated 2,447,989 persons who were identified only as American Indians or Alaska Natives. An additional 1,867,876 persons were identified as American Indians or Alaska Natives in combination with another race, for a total of 4,315,865 persons with a reported American Indian or Alaska Native race. The 2010 census reported 2,932,248 American Indians and Alaska Natives (alone), and another 2,288,331 American Indians and Alaska Natives in combination with another race. Thus, the population with a reported American Indian or Alaska Native race has grown 21 percent since 2000.

See also *Native Hawaiian and Other Pacific Islander (NHOPI) population; Race: questions and classifications.*

. . . . C. MATTHEW SNIPP

BIBLIOGRAPHY

Ogunwole, Stella U. *We the People: American Indians and Alaska Natives in the United States.* 2000 Census Special Reports CENSR-28. Washington, D.C.: U.S. Department of Commerce, U.S. Census Bureau, 2006.

Sandefur, Gary D., Ronald R. Rindfuss, and Barney Cohen, eds. *Changing Numbers and Changing Needs: American Indian Demography and Public Health.* Washington, D.C.: The National Academies Press, 1996.

Shoemaker, Nancy. *American Indian Population Recovery in the Twentieth Century.* Albuquerque: University of New Mexico Press, 1999.

Snipp, C. Matthew. *American Indians: The First of This Land.* New York: Russell Sage, 1989.

Americans Overseas

Each census must arrive at a count of the total population, and it must also place each person at a specific location. For apportionment, that location needs only to be within a specific state. For drawing legislative districts, much more detailed information is required. The census thus must provide a precise and accurate count of each and every block in the nation. Consequently, "who gets counted where" is critically important and, in census terms, is defined as rules about residency.

The basic residency rule is that people should be counted at their "usual place of residence." Those away from home on census day are counted at their usual home. Similarly, those visiting the United States from other countries are not counted. However, those from other countries living in the United States on census day, regardless of citizenship, are counted.

People with two residences are counted at the residence where they stay "most of the time." Interpreting that seemingly straightforward rule can become difficult, however. For example, some small children spend equal time with their divorced parents who have joint custody. Members of Congress, meanwhile, are counted in their home district or state, even though they live and work in Washington, D.C., during the week. Residency rules are not so simple after all, and counting Americans overseas, who often have no U.S. residence, strains the system.

Since 1790 the census has been conducted by counting the persons living in each house. In 1790 determining who lived where was relatively straightforward compared with today but nonetheless was a complicated undertaking. As the population increased and society became more complex, determining who lives where became more difficult, and rules determining who gets counted where have become more important. A 1987 conference sponsored by the Council of Professional Associations on Federal Statistics produced a 375-page volume discussing census residency rules. Among the issues covered were where to count college students, students away at school below the college level, children in shared custody, and Americans overseas. In 1990 the Bureau of the Census produced a document specifying more than 30 rules for where individuals should be counted.

The inclusion in the census count of Americans overseas has become more controversial as the uses of census data have become more politically charged. Procedures for counting Americans overseas have evolved from relatively simple ones for counting "men at sea" in the mid-nineteenth century to the elaborate system of administrative procedures used in 1990 and 2000. In the early nineteenth century the census counted merchant seamen and military serving at sea or abroad. For most of the nineteenth century, when Americans overseas were counted, they were enumerated at their stateside home. The twentieth-century count of Americans overseas grew progressively more complicated and began to include private citizens as well as the military and merchant seamen. Controversy surrounded the plans for including Americans living overseas in the 2000 census.

Instructions for the inclusion of Americans overseas in the censuses from 1860 to 1990 are summarized in Table 1. While the tabulations from the 1830 and 1840 censuses show totals for Americans overseas, the first record of instructions for counting Americans overseas accompanies the 1860 census. Four conceptual categories are used to group Americans

Table 1. Instructions for Inclusion of Americans Overseas in Census, 1860–2010

CENSUS	MERCHANT SEAMEN	LAND-BASED ARMED FORCES	MILITARY AT SEA AND FEDERAL CIVILIAN EMPLOYEES	PRIVATE CITIZENS
1860	Enumerated at stateside home	Enumerated at stateside home	Not included overseas or stateside	No instructions provided
1870	Enumerated at stateside home	Enumerated at stateside home	Not included overseas or stateside	No instructions provided
1880	Enumerated at stateside home	Enumerated at stateside home	Not included overseas or stateside	No instructions provided
1890	No instructions provided	No instructions provided	No instructions provided	No instructions provided
1900	No instructions provided	Enumerated at stateside home	Enumerated at stateside home	No instructions provided
1910	Enumerated at stateside home	Included in overseas population	Included in overseas population	Enumerated at stateside home
1920	Enumerated at stateside home	Included in overseas population	Included in overseas population	Enumerated at stateside home
1930	Officers reported at home; crew reported at home port	Included in overseas population	Included in overseas population	Enumerated at stateside home
1940	Officers reported at home; crew reported at home port	Included in overseas population	No instructions provided	Enumerated at stateside home
1950	Included in overseas population if vessel at sea or in a foreign port	Included in overseas population	Included in overseas population	No instructions provided
1960	Included in overseas population if vessel at sea or in a foreign port	Included in overseas population	Included in overseas population	Included in overseas population
1970	Included in overseas population if vessel at sea with a foreign port as its destination or in a foreign port	Included in overseas population	Included in overseas population	Included in overseas population
1980	Not included in overseas population	Included in overseas population	Included in overseas population	Not enumerated
1990	Included in overseas population if in a foreign port or sailing from one foreign port to another	Included in overseas population	Included in overseas population	Not enumerated
2000	Not enumerated if in a foreign port, sailing from one foreign port to another foreign port, sailing from a U.S. port to a foreign port, or sailing from a foreign port to a U.S. port	Included in overseas population	Included in overseas population	Not enumerated
2010	Not enumerated if in a foreign port, sailing from one foreign port to another foreign port, sailing from a U.S. port to a foreign port, or sailing from a foreign port to a U.S. port	Included in overseas population	Included in overseas population	Not enumerated

overseas: (1) merchant seamen, (2) military at sea and land-based armed forces, (3) civilians working for the government, and (4) private citizens.

Counting Procedures

How Americans overseas are counted has varied considerably. For 1860 through 1880, census-takers were instructed to include merchant seamen and overseas military as residents of their stateside home. In 1890 no instruction was provided for counting Americans overseas. In 1910 military and federal civilian employees were counted in the overseas population, but merchant seamen and private citizens overseas during the census were included at their stateside home. As the twentieth century progressed, the rules for the inclusion of Americans overseas were modified from census to census. From 1990 to 2010 the count of Americans overseas included federal military and civilian employees and their dependents. Merchant seamen were included in the overseas population in 1990 if they were in a foreign port or sailing from one foreign port to another. Merchant seamen outside the United States were not enumerated in 2000 and 2010.

When Americans overseas have been included in the census, they have been counted as a separate population and reported separately (see Table 2). A major exception was made in both 1970 and 1990–2010, when federal military and civilian employees were included in the population of the states used for apportionment. In these cases, the Census Bureau yielded to pressure from Congress to change its procedures to forestall the passage of undesirable legislation. In 1970 the bureau sought to avoid being embroiled in the debate over the Vietnam War. In 1990 the bureau did not want to link the counting of Americans overseas with excluding undocumented aliens from the census.

Since 1995, groups representing Americans living overseas have lobbied the Census Bureau, without success, to count not just federal military and civilian employees overseas but all Americans overseas. The exceptions of counting federal military and civilian employees overseas, while well intentioned, have made it difficult for the Census Bureau to argue convincingly against the inclusion of all Americans overseas in the census. Proponents of counting private citizens overseas ask, "How can counting employees for the Department of Energy, and not Americans working for Exxon Mobil, be justified?" "Why include the 15 Americans working for the Overseas Battlefield Memorial Commission and not the thousands of Americans working overseas for the Red Cross?"

From 1990 to 2010 the Census Bureau used administrative records from the federal government to count Americans overseas. The bureau claims that no record system of comparable quality exists that could be used to account for private citizens overseas. The basis for differentiating between federal military and civilian employees and private citizens overseas is the ease of counting. For those Americans overseas who want to be included in the census, ease of counting does not justify being left out. The bureau, however, argues that it can use administrative records for enumerating federal military and civilian employees, and thus some have measure of completeness of the count. Those wishing to be counted point to the known weakness of the federal administrative records.

2010 Census

Pressure on the Census Bureau to count Americans overseas in Census 2010 began even before the 2000 census ended. In House Report 106–1005, the Appropriations Committee called on the secretary of commerce to produce a report on

Table 2. Americans Overseas, 1900–2010 Censuses

CENSUS	U.S. POPULATION ABROAD	TOTAL U.S. RESIDENT POPULATION	PERCENTAGE ABROAD
1900	91,219	75,994,595	0.12%
1910	55,608	91,972,266	0.06%
1920	117,238	105,710,620	0.11%
1930	89,453	122,775,046	0.07%
1940	118,933	131,669,275	0.09%
1950	481,545	150,697,361	0.32%
1960	1,374,421	179,323,798	0.77%
1970	1,737,836	203,302,031	0.85%
1980	995,546	226,542,199	0.44%
1990	925,845	248,718,301	0.37%
2000	576,367	281,421,906	0.20%
2010	1,042,523	308,745,538	0.33%

the "methodological, logistical, and other issues associated with the inclusion in future decennial censuses of American citizens and their dependents living abroad, for apportionment, redistricting, and other purposes for which decennial census results are used." Before that report could be issued, however, the apportionment process intervened.

As is always the case, the difference between the 435th seat and the 436th seat in the apportionment results was razor thin in 2000. North Carolina received the 435th seat, and Utah, which had expected its delegation to grow from three to four representatives, was allocated three. Utah sued, arguing that by including military and civilian government employees overseas, and not including Mormon missionaries serving overseas, the census gave unfair advantage to North Carolina over Utah. In March 2001, a three-judge panel from the U.S. Court of Appeals for the 10th Circuit ruled unanimously against Utah.

The Bureau of the Census issued the congressionally requested report at the end of September 2001. That report laid out the challenges of counting Americans overseas. The standard for comparison was the count of people in the United States, not the quality of the count of other Americans overseas. For example, the report questioned the feasibility of using administrative records because "none of these sources by themselves would give a complete, reliable estimate of the size of the Americans overseas universe."

The report to the Appropriations Committee was followed by a number of efforts to consider the feasibility of counting civilian Americans overseas, including a conference of experts, held in November 2001, and a field test in 2004. The field test produced results that were sufficiently problematic that the U.S. Government Accountability Office (GAO) recommended that Congress consider eliminating the funds for further research. The GAO went on to indicate that trying to count Americans overseas would only exacerbate what was already going to be a difficult census in 2010 (GAO-04–898). The test, conducted in France, Kuwait, and Mexico, cost about $1,450 per response compared with about $56 per household in the 2000 census—a cost that many thought was too high.

As Census 2010 drew near, Utah's congressional Republicans renewed their pressure. Representatives Jason Chaffetz and Rob Bishop introduced legislation that would require the Census Bureau to count Utah's missionaries, but the bill died at the end of the 110th Congress without action. In any case, population growth in Utah led to the state receiving a fourth congressional district in 2010.

See also *Apportionment and districting; Residence rules.*

. . . .   DAVID MCMILLEN

BIBLIOGRAPHY

Cork, Daniel L., and Paul R. Voss, eds. *Once, Only Once, and in the Right Place: Residence Rules in the Decennial Census.* Panel on Residence Rules in the Decennial Census, Committee on National Statistics, Division of Behavioral and Social Sciences and Education, National Research Council of the National Academies. Washington, D.C.: The National Academies Press, 2006. http://www.nap.edu/catalog.php?record_id=11727.

Council of Professional Associations on Federal Statistics. *Decennial Census Residence Rules. Proceedings of the December 15–16, 1986 Conference, Washington, D.C.* Washington, D.C.: U.S. Census Bureau, 1987.

Apportionment and Districting

Apportionment is the allocation to states of the seats in the House of Representatives, and *districting* is the drawing of geographic boundaries of the seats once each state's allocation has been defined.

The dynamics of apportionment played out between 1790 and 1940. Since 1940 there has been little controversy over apportionment. Districting, in contrast, has been increasingly controversial since 1940. The issue of drawing districts for state houses has been as important as that of congressional districting in developing the current standards used by the courts, including whether the Constitution permits states to adopt the federal model with one house based on population and one based on political boundaries. In general, the courts have insisted that both houses be based on population, although, in some cases they have allowed political boundaries to be a part, but not the sole determinant, of the districting process.

The distinction between apportionment and districting is central to the recent controversies surrounding the census, particularly in 2000. The 1999 Supreme Court decision in *Clinton v. Glavin* stated that Section 195 of Title 13 of the U.S. Code prohibited the use of sampling for apportionment purposes. Justice Sandra Day O'Connor went on to point out that the 1976 amendment to Section 195 changed that section from one that allowed the use of sampling for purposes other than apportionment to one that *required* the use of sampling for all other purposes, though to date, sample data have not been used for redistricting.

Apportionment from 1790 to 1910

Apportioning the seats in the House of Representatives according to the population of each state as measured by the census every ten years is part of what makes American democracy unique. The issue was central enough to making the new government work that the census was created in the first Article of the Constitution. But not long after the census of 1790, Congress realized that although the Constitution directed Congress to apportion the seats among the states, it did not say how to do it. Thus was born the first census controversy, as opposing sides lined up behind separate formulas for apportioning seats—one proposed by Alexander Hamilton, a Federalist from New York, and one supported by Thomas Jefferson, a Republican from Virginia. Indeed, President George Washington used the first presidential veto on the apportionment bill passed by Congress. His veto forced Congress to change the formula used for apportionment. These battles between North and South, between political parties, between geographic areas with large populations and those with small populations, and between urban and rural areas are central to nearly all controversy over apportionment and districting from 1790 to the present.

The conflict between the methods of Hamilton and Jefferson is the beginning of the politics of numbers in the United States, as well as illustrative of the extent that politicians will go to get their way when even one seat is at stake. Hamilton and his supporters proposed a House of 120 seats, up from the 65 apportioned in the Constitution, arrived at by dividing the total population of 3,615,920 by 30,000, the minimum number of persons per representative set in the Constitution. They then apportioned those 120 seats among the states by dividing the state population by 30,132, a number chosen so that the state quotas (population divided by 30,132) summed to 120. Of course, this left each state with a whole number of representatives and a fraction, or remainder (see Table 1). Each state was then apportioned the whole number from the quota, which apportioned 111 of the 120 seats. To distribute the remaining 9 seats, Hamilton gave 1 seat to each of the nine states with the largest fraction. Thus, Connecticut, Delaware, Massachusetts, New Hampshire, New Jersey, North Carolina, South Carolina, Vermont, and Virginia each got 1 extra seat. The other six states got none, despite the size of the fraction or remainder.

Jefferson argued that awarding the "extra" seats to some of the states based on the fractions remaining, in effect, resulted in two apportionment ratios—one for those states with the extra seats and one for all others. He argued that fairness called for each state to be apportioned with the same ratio and thus proposed a divisor of 28,500 (see Table 1). In effect, the Jefferson method simply dropped all fractions, awarding only the whole number of seats. The divisor was selected to sum to the predetermined size of the House, in this case 120 seats. After listening to the arguments in support of the congressional apportionment from Hamilton and arguments against that bill from Jefferson, President Washington vetoed the bill and sent Congress back to work. The attempt to override the veto failed, and Congress sent the president a bill apportioning 105 seats (as originally proposed by the Senate), using the Jefferson method. The Jefferson method remained the method used through the apportionment following the 1830 census.

By 1830 the bias in the Jefferson method was well known. Jefferson's method systematically gave preference to large states over small ones. Between 1790 and 1830, Delaware routinely had remainders over one-half but received two seats in only one of the five apportionments. New York, in contrast, was awarded a seat more than its whole number in each apportionment. As the debate began over the 1830 apportionment, many alternative methods for apportioning the seats in the House of Representatives were proposed, as were many different sizes for the House. It was Daniel Webster who became the champion of change. He proposed what is today considered the method

Table 1. Apportionment Formulas Proposed by Hamilton and Jefferson in 1790

STATE	HAMILTON		JEFFERSON	
	QUOTA	APPORTIONMENT	QUOTA	APPORTIONMENT
Connecticut	7.860	8	8.310	8
Delaware	1.843	2	1.949	1
Georgia	2.351	2	2.485	2
Kentucky	2.280	2	2.411	2
Maryland	9.243	9	9.772	9
Massachusetts	15.774	16	16.678	16
New Hampshire	4.707	5	4.976	4
New Jersey	5.959	6	6.301	6
New York	11.004	11	11.635	11
North Carolina	11.732	12	12.404	12
Pennsylvania	14.366	14	15.189	15
Rhode Island	2.271	2	2.402	2
South Carolina	6.844	7	7.236	7
Vermont	2.839	3	3.001	3
Virginia	20.926	21	22.125	22
Total	**120.000**	**120**	**126.874**	**120**

SOURCE: Michel L. Balinski, and H. Peyton Young. *Fair Representation: Meeting the Ideal of One Man One Vote.* 2nd ed. (Washington, D.C.: Brookings Institution Press, 2001) p.19.

with the fewest problems, although it is not the method in use today. Webster did not prevail in the 1830 debate; however, by 1842 (when the apportionment using the 1840 census actually became law), dissatisfaction with the Jefferson method, and with the ever-expanding House, resulted in the passing of a Senate bill that apportioned 223 seats using Webster's method (see Table 2). The 1840 apportionment is the only time in history that Congress has reduced the size of the House.

Prior to the 1850 census Rep. Samuel Finley Vinton, a Whig from Ohio, proposed a bill that would make the apportionment formula permanent law rather than the subject of partisan debate once the results were known. He proposed the Vinton method, a restatement of the method put forward by Hamilton, in which the size of the House was fixed and a divisor chosen. Seats were then allocated for the whole number for each state's quota. Any remaining seats were allocated to the largest remainders until all seats were apportioned. Between 1850 and 1900, the Vinton, or Hamilton, method was the law of the land, although it was never followed.

In 1850 the Vinton bill called for a House of 233 seats, but 234 seats were apportioned, with the extra seat given to California because of the rapid growth brought on by the gold rush. It was also the case that at 234, the methods of both Hamilton and Webster gave the same results. In 1860 the Hamilton/Vinton method was used to apportion 233 seats, and then 8 additional seats were distributed to northern states. In 1870 a House size of 283 was chosen, because at that point the Webster and Hamilton methods agreed. A few months later an additional 9 seats were distributed without the benefit of formula. The distribution of those additional seats proved to be the margin of presidential victory for Rutherford B. Hayes over Samuel J. Tilden in the Electoral College, even though Tilden had received more popular votes. Had the House been apportioned according to Hamilton's formula,

Table 2. U.S. House Size, Population, and Methods of Apportionment, 1790–2010

CENSUS	HOUSE SIZE	POPULATION (IN THOUSANDS)	AVERAGE POPULATION PER DISTRICT	METHOD OF APPORTIONMENT[a]	STATUTES AT LARGE CIT.
1790	105	3,929	37,419	Jefferson	1 Stat. 253
1800	141	5,308	37,645	Jefferson	2 Stat. 128
1810	181	7,240	40,000	Jefferson	2 Stat. 669
1820	213	9,638	45,249	Jefferson	3 Stat. 213
1830	240	12,866	53,608	Jefferson	4 Stat. 516
1840	223	17,069	76,543	Webster	5 Stat. 491
1850	234	23,192	99,111	Webster/Vinton	9 Stat. 428 and 10 Stat. 25
1860	241	31,443	130,469	Webster/Vinton	12 Stat. 353 and 12 Stat. 572
1870	292	39,818	136,363	Webster/Vinton	17 Stat. 28 and 17 Stat. 192
1880	325	50,156	154,326	Webster/Vinton	22 Stat. 5
1890	356	62,948	176,820	Webster/Vinton	25 Stat. 735
1900	386	75,995	196,878	Webster/Vinton	31 Stat. 733
1910	433	91,972	212,406	Webster	37 Stat. 13
1920	435	105,711	243,014	—	—
1930	435	122,775	282,241	Webster/Hill	46 Stat. 21
1940	435	131,669	302,687	Hill	54 Stat. 162 and 55 Stat. 761
1950	435	151,326	346,430	Hill	
1960	435	179,323	412,237	Hill	
1970	435	203,302	467,361	Hill	
1980	435	226,542	520,786	Hill	
1990	435	248,718	571,766	Hill	
2000	435	281,424	646,952	Hill	
2010	435	308,746	710,767	Hill	

[a]For brief explanations of apportionment methods, see Appendix, Methods of Congressional Apportionment.

as the law required, Tilden would have carried the Electoral College.

The 1870 apportionment was also the first observation of what became known a decade later as the Alabama Paradox, in which an increase in the size of the House results in a decrease in the number of seats allotted to a state. Rep. Ulysses Mercur (R-PA), in examining the apportionment of House sizes from 241 to 300, noted that in a House of 270 members Rhode Island received two seats, whereas in a House of 280 members it received only one—an increase in the size of the House should not result in one state losing a seat. He cited this paradox as yet another reason for favoring the Webster method, but at the time, his argument was ignored.

The Alabama Paradox was so named by the head of the census as materials were prepared for the 1880 apportionment. He noted that in using the Hamilton method, Alabama dropped from 8 seats to 7 between House sizes of 299 and 300 members. He proposed a variant of the Jefferson method as an alternative, but the large-state bias in his method was quickly noted and the proposal rejected. In the meantime, however, Congress had been alerted to one of the major flaws of the Hamilton method. In the end, a compromise was reached at a House size of 325—the point at which Hamilton and Webster agreed on the distribution of seats. A similar compromise was reached in 1890. A House of 356 seats was created because the two methods agreed on the distribution of those seats among the states, and at that size no state lost a seat.

Politics and the Alabama Paradox were the final undoing of the Hamilton method in 1900. Rep. Albert Jarvis Hopkins (R-IL), chairman of the Select Committee on the Twelfth Census, submitted a bill for apportioning a House of 357 seats. In every House size between 350 and 400 Colorado got 3 seats, except for a House of 357, at which point it got 2 seats. Colorado was a populist state, and Hopkins was an antipopulist. Congress passed an apportionment bill distributing 386 seats using Webster's formula. At 386 seats, no state lost a seat in the new apportionment. Michael L. Balinski and H. Peyton Young have identified two other paradoxes in apportionment formulas: the population paradox, in which a faster-growing state loses a seat to a slower-growing state, and the new state paradox, in which a seat shifts between two states when a new state is admitted.

Apportionment in the Twentieth Century

The 1910 apportionment was carried out using Webster's method. In 1911 Congress passed an apportionment bill that distributed 433 seats among the states and provided for 1 additional seat each for Arizona and New Mexico should they be admitted to the Union. (They were admitted in 1912.) A House of 433 members was chosen because that was the size at which no state would lose a seat.

Between 1910 and 1930 two sets of activities played out to remove apportionment from the controversy that characterized the nineteenth century. Following the 1920 census, which showed that for the first time in the country's history more people lived in cities than in rural areas, Congress was unable to agree on an apportionment formula. Congress complained bitterly about the quality of the census, arguing that the results could not possibly be correct. At the same time, there was heated debate within the academic community over the "best" method for apportionment. Those two sets of events led to the system that is in place today.

A reapportionment of the 435 seats in Congress by the Webster method in 1920 would have resulted in ten rural states losing 11 seats. California would have gained 3 of those seats, and Michigan and Ohio would have gained 2 each. This shift of power from rural to urban centers was strongly opposed by the rural interests in both the House and the Senate. It is difficult to exaggerate the rancor of this debate. Members criticized the Bureau of the Census for taking the census in January, when there was no work on farms. They blamed the 1920 recession and World War I, and they claimed that the farms were undercounted. Members opined on the superiority of rural inhabitants and the evils of the city. The cities were, after all, full of immigrants, they said. In the end, these interests conspired to prevent the reapportionment of the House—the only time in the 210-year history of apportionment that such has happened.

At the same time that politicians were arguing the merits of rural versus urban settings, rival factions of scholars were warring over apportionment methodology. One group, led by Walter Willcox, a professor at Cornell University, argued that Webster's method, or the method of "major fractions," as he called it, was the best approach. Willcox served as president of the American Statistical Association, the American Economic Association, and the American Sociological Association. These three groups represented the vast majority of professionals with expertise to bring to bear on apportionment methods. The opposing group, led by Edward Huntington, a professor at Harvard University, pushed the "method of equal proportions" first proposed by a classmate of his, Joseph Hill, then assistant director of the Bureau of the Census.

Willcox argued that Webster's method should be adopted because it met the fundamental constitutional objective of treating small and large states the same, and it had been the actual method used since at least 1860. Hill's method, Willcox argued, was biased in favor of small states. Huntington made the opposite claim. He argued that Hill's method was unbiased and that Webster's method favored large states. Confused by conflicting testimony, Congress turned to the National Academy of Sciences (NAS) for advice. In 1929 the NAS reported its support for Hill's method of equal proportions. The fundamental difference between the two methods is in what is used to measure the inequality between states. Huntington argued that the appropriate measure was the proportional difference in per capita representation, whereas Willcox advocated the use of the absolute difference in per capita representation. Balinski and Young argue that both Huntington and the NAS were wrong in characterizing Hill's method as neutral, or sitting in the middle of the five possible methods of apportionment. They point out, as did Willcox, that there are an infinite number of apportionment formulas and that Hill's and Webster's methods are both in the class they call divisor methods, as are the methods of Jefferson and others. They argue that of the possible divisor methods, Webster's method is "the only one that is perfectly unbiased."

In 1929 Congress was still apportioned on the basis of the 1910 census, despite a 34 percent increase in the population. Still, the controversy over reapportionment, and the sectional split between rural and urban representatives, remained. That year, the Senate passed a permanent reauthorization bill, but rather than specify a given method, the bill simply directed that the apportionment be done by the method used in the preceding census. Rural forces in the House seized on Huntington's criticisms of Webster's method as biased and unscientific in hopes of thwarting any apportionment bill. In the end, however, they managed only to modify the Senate bill to require that the president transmit to Congress the population of the states, the apportionment of representatives using the method used in the preceding apportionment, and the apportionment using both Webster's and Hill's methods. If Congress failed to act, then the apportionment based on the previous method would become law.

As it turned out, the apportionment of 435 seats based on the 1930 census resulted in no difference between Webster's and Hill's methods. The 1940 census was a different story. Using that census, the two methods differed only in the apportionment for Michigan and Arkansas. Hill's method gave Michigan 17 seats and Arkansas 7, whereas Webster's method gave Michigan 18 seats and Arkansas 6. Not surprisingly, an Arkansas representative introduced a bill calling for apportionment using Hill's method. That bill was supported by all Democrats except those from Michigan and opposed by all Republicans. By the end of 1941 Congress passed, and the president signed, legislation apportioning the House using Hill's method. Once again, politics won out over science and the majority party in Congress voted for the method that would give it one more seat. The method of equal proportions has been used ever since, and the House size has remained set at 435 members.

It was a large concession for Congress to pass a permanent apportionment bill in 1929, but that act is as important for what was left out as for what was included. Prior to 1929 Congress had included in apportionment bills the requirement that congressional districts be of roughly equal size, contiguous, and compact. That language was omitted from the 1929 bill, and the result was the redistricting mischief that prevailed for the next 30 years. The 1931 apportionment corrected the huge disparity in congressional district size that had grown from population growth and shifts between 1910 and 1930. By the time the Supreme Court ruled in *Baker v. Carr* (1962), however, that disparity had returned.

Drawing Congressional Districts

By and large, Congress has left the process of creating congressional districts within states to the state legislatures. In 1842, however, Congress passed legislation requiring states with more than one representative to divide the state into districts with one representative for each district, commonly known as single-member districts. During the second half of the nineteenth century the requirements of compactness and equal size were added. All these requirements died in 1929 when Congress passed the permanent apportionment act without such language. The requirement for single-member districts was reintroduced in 1967. Thus the history of redistricting can be separated into three distinct phases: 1790 to 1930, a period of modest federal guidance; 1930 to 1964, a laissez-faire period; and 1964 to the present, the period of the courts.

Between 1930 and 1964 neither Congress nor the courts would address the issue of equity of representative districts for either state governments or the U.S. House of Representatives. As a consequence, the size and shape of districts were at the whim of those creating them—in most states, the state legislature. The result was congressional districts of widely varying size. In many states the rural/urban divide that immobilized the U.S. House of Representatives during the 1920s dominated the state legislature throughout this period.

The first challenge to the disparity in size of congressional districts came in 1946. Kenneth Colgrove argued that he was denied equal protection of the law (under the Fourteenth Amendment) because as a resident of the 7th congressional district in Chicago he was among 900,000 people represented by a single member of Congress, whereas the 5th congressional district contained only about 100,000 people. Justice Felix Frankfurter wrote the opinion dismissing the case. Justice Frankfurter wrote, in *Colgrove v. Green* (328 U.S. 549 [1946]), that the question of district size was outside the jurisdiction of the Court because it was an issue of "peculiarly political nature." In 1962 the Supreme Court reversed the Frankfurter decision and ruled that state legislative districts of unequal size violated the equal protection clause of the Fourteenth Amendment. In 1964 the Supreme Court ruled that U.S. congressional districts should be of equal size and began the era of one-person, one-vote. At that time, Michigan had the smallest congressional district with a population of 177,431, and Texas had the largest with a population of 951,527 (a difference of 774,096). Texas also had the largest disparity between congressional districts, with a difference of 735,156 between the largest and the smallest district. The Supreme Court decision in *Baker v. Carr* (369 U.S. 186) in 1962 addressed the size of districts for state legislatures, whereas the decision in *Wesberry v. Sanders* (376 U.S. 1) in 1964 addressed the size of districts for the U.S. House of Representatives. A second difference between these cases is that *Baker v. Carr* relied on the Fourteenth Amendment, whereas *Wesberry v. Sanders* cited Article I, Section 2, of the Constitution, which states that representatives should be "apportioned among the several States . . . according to their respective Numbers." The Court thus held that in a House election, one person's vote should be worth as much as another's.

These decisions set in place the restructuring of legislative districts throughout the country. Congressional districts, which had a difference of more than 700,000 people between the largest and smallest in the 88th Congress (1963–1964), had a difference of fewer than 50,000 people by the 93d Congress

(1973–1974). By the 103d Congress (1993–1994) the difference had dwindled to about 5,000.

Although these lawsuits established the Court's jurisdiction over the size and shape of legislative districts and established the principle of one-person, one-vote, much was left unspecified, and Court decisions have refined the concept since.

One Person, One Vote: The Pressure for Accuracy

The census is required by the Constitution for apportioning the seats in the House of Representatives among the states, but there is no requirement either in the Constitution or federal law that census numbers be used to draw congressional or state district boundaries. Some states, as late as 1980, used voter registration data to define congressional districts, whereas other states, such as Massachusetts, conducted their own census to be used for districting. Still other states took census data from the U.S. census and modified it for districting purposes.

Nonetheless, the requirement that congressional districts be of equal size has put increased pressure on the census. Issues of census geography and census accuracy became intertwined in the political battles over drawing districts to give one side or the other a competitive advantage. As state legislatures struggled to create districts that would pass muster with the courts, they simultaneously struggled to maintain existing power structures and the integrity of existing political boundaries. That led to a need for more and more detail from the census.

The boundaries of states are relatively simple to deal with. No congressional district crosses state lines, and census geography always allows separate totals for each state. Below the state level, however, political boundaries and census geography often conflict. As a result of these demands, during the 94th Congress (1975–1976) a law was passed (Public Law 94–171) requiring the Bureau of the Census to provide to the states the age, sex, and race data for each census block within the state to be used in the redistricting process. These data files, or computer tapes as they were then, became commonly known as the P.L. 94–171 tapes, or the redistricting files. Drawing on this mandate, the bureau began a program to work with the states to ensure that the geographic boundaries used for census data were similar to those used by the state.

Defining a census block within a city is usually a simple task; however, even city blocks do not always conform to other boundaries. In some cases the boundary of a political jurisdiction runs down the middle of a street, splitting the block between two jurisdictions. As houses become more and more spread out, defining the boundaries of a block becomes increasingly difficult, and in most rural areas the concept of a block just does not exist. For the 1970 census, a large proportion of the country was not defined in terms of blocks but only in terms of larger geographical units—census tracts, places, census-designated places, minor civil divisions, cities, counties, and states. Since 1970 the Census Bureau has defined "blocks" for more and more of the United States. By 2000 the bureau had defined blocks for the entire country. By doing so, the bureau made the block the basic building block from which all other units can be constructed.

The process of building congressional districts varies from state to state, but as computers have become more powerful, more and more states have relied on them to draw and examine the effect of district boundaries. In 1970 the computing power needed to manipulate the geographic and census data necessary to draw congressional district boundaries was available to only a few. Many states still relied on paper maps, colored pencils, and books of tables. Today Geographic Information System (GIS) technology is widely available and has enabled the development of a healthy redistricting consulting business serving the political parties nationally.

Legal Developments since 1962

In addition to the Supreme Court decisions of 1962 (*Baker v. Carr*) and 1964 (*Wesberry v. Sanders*), the Voting Rights Act was passed by Congress in 1965 to protect the voting rights of minorities. Sections 2 and 5 of the Voting Rights Act are of particular importance to this discussion. Section 2 creates the right for individuals to challenge a districting plan and was amended in 1982 to allow individuals to prevail if they could prove that the effect of the districting was discriminatory, regardless of the intent. Section 5 requires 16 states (Alabama, Alaska, Arizona, California, Florida, Georgia, Louisiana, Michigan, Mississippi, New Hampshire, New York, North Carolina, South Carolina, South Dakota, Texas, and Virginia) to have their redistricting plans reviewed by the Department of Justice before they become effective. In addition, Section 5 requires "no retrogression" after redistricting: no minority could be worse off after redistricting than he or she had been before. Even if the minority could not prove to the court that retrogression had occurred, he or she could prevail if the minority could prove to the courts that the redistricting plan had a discriminatory purpose. The review by the Department of Justice proved to have as great an effect on redistricting as the provision of the act itself.

Since the Supreme Court laid out the principle of one person, one vote in 1964, the federal courts have spent a considerable amount of intellectual energy translating the principle into practice. The Supreme Court resisted entering the political fray of redistricting for the first 20 years and has moved very cautiously since. As a result, the Court often has been vague in explaining what would and would not constitute acceptable districting, and at times it has stepped back and changed direction.

Three issues have emerged as central to understanding what the Supreme Court will and will not accept in defining legislative districts: numerical equality among districts within a state; the use of "other" information, such as existing political boundaries; and majority-minority districts, or congressional districts in which the majority of voting-age residents are minorities, such as African American or Hispanic.

Supreme Court decisions in the late 1960s, the 1970s, and the 1980s pushed states toward greater and greater equality among congressional districts. In *Kirkpatrick v. Preisler* (394 U.S.

526 [1969]), the Court held that a Missouri reapportionment with a difference of approximately 35,000 between the smallest and largest was too great to provide equal representation. The same court, in *Wells v. Rockefeller* (394 U.S. 542 [1969]), threw out a New York redistricting plan that had a difference of approximately 53,000 persons from the smallest to the largest congressional district. Following the 1970 census, the Court invalidated a Texas redistricting plan in which the difference was only approximately 19,000 persons, or 4.1 percent (*White v. Weiser,* 412 U.S. 783 [1973]). Finally, in 1983, in *Karcher v. Daggett* (462 U.S. 725 [1983]), the Supreme Court invalidated a New Jersey plan in which the difference was less than 5,000 persons, and a difference of less than one-quarter of 1 percent from the ideal.

This series of Supreme Court decisions pushed state redistricting committees to greater and greater numerical equality among districts. The implication for state redistricting committees was that they had to use smaller and smaller geographic units to achieve this equality and simultaneously to achieve their political goals. For the Bureau of the Census these court cases meant increased political tension focused on census numbers and increased attention to errors in the census.

As the 1990 census approached, the Department of Justice pushed the 16 Section 5 states to create, wherever possible, majority-minority districts. The basis for this push was the Supreme Court's 1986 decision in *Thornburg v. Gingles* (478 U.S. 30 [1986]), in which the Court set out three standards necessary to prove that retrogression had occurred: the minority group must be able to demonstrate that it is sufficiently large and geographically compact to constitute a majority in a single-member district; the minority group must be able to demonstrate that it is politically cohesive; and the minority group must be able to show that the white majority votes sufficiently as a bloc to enable it to defeat the minority's preferred candidate.

The push for majority-minority districts, coupled with the Court's focus on numerical equality, produced in many states districts so oddly shaped that Elbridge Gerry's salamander from 1812 looked prosaic. The Supreme Court was still developing just what it would accept, and oddly shaped districts swelled their suspicion. In *Shaw v. Reno* (113 S.Ct. 2816 [1993]), the Court said, "We believe that reapportionment is one area in which appearances do matter. A reapportionment plan that includes in one district individuals who belong to the same race, but who are otherwise widely separated by geographical and political boundaries, and who may have little in common with one another but the color of their skin, bears an uncomfortable resemblance to political apartheid." (For an illustration of the majority-minority districts reviewed by the Court in *Shaw,* which examined North Carolina's 1st and 12th districts, see Figure 1.)

Politics and the Census

The controversy over numerical equality of districts and the appropriate building blocks for drawing districts led to questions about the accuracy and quality of the underlying census data. The Census Bureau routinely reports estimates of net undercount by race, ethnicity, age, and sex, and by the 1970s politicians recognized that the undercounts in the census could affect the districting process. In the 1980s, the bureau responded by proposing an adjustment methodology to correct for undercounts that used a second sample survey matched to the census to produce adjusted counts by blocks. The commerce secretary decided against the use of the adjusted counts after the 1990 census. Lawsuits by the City of New York and other jurisdictions supporting the adjusted data were unsuccessful. The Clinton administration developed the plan further to adjust the census in 2000, but again the methods were challenged, both technically and by Republican politicians concerned that the correction process could be manipulated for partisan advantage. The Republican Congress and the Democratic administration agreed on an expedited court review, and in January 1999 the Supreme Court ruled on the issues.

The distinction between apportionment and districting was central to these controversies. The 1999 Supreme Court decision in *Clinton v. Glavin* stated that Section 195 of Title 13 of the U.S. Code prohibited the use of sampling for apportionment purposes. Justice Sandra Day O'Connor went on to point out that the 1976 amendment to Section 195 changed that section from one allowing the use of sampling for purposes other than apportionment to one that *required* the use of sampling for all other purposes. Those two points allowed both sides to claim victory. Supporters of the use of adjusted census data using sampling pointed to the 1976 amendment and claimed that Section 195 required the use of sampling to produce the data used to draw congressional districts. At the time, opponents of sampling continued to argue that drawing congressional districts was simply an extension of the apportionment process, and the use of sampling is prohibited. By the time the adjusted data were to be released in spring 2001, the new Republican administration once again recommended against the use of adjusted data for Census 2000, citing both technical problems with the adjustment methodology and insufficient time to resolve the issues.

With the redistricting battles as a background, it is easier to understand why one of the principal attacks on sampling by Republicans has been the issue of accuracy at the block level. The demand for accuracy at the block level is made knowing that it is impossible for the Census Bureau to meet the test of producing more accurate data for all blocks through statistical adjustment. Yet both parties continue to advocate for block-level data, since it is much easier to draw congressional districts that both meet the test of numerical equality and maintain political advantage for one party or the other using census blocks as the basic unit of geography.

Census 2010

Several issues shaped the landscape for apportionment and districting leading up to the 2010 census. First, a Republican executive branch from January 2001 to January 2009 controlled the planning for the 2010 census, and Republicans from January 2001 to January 2007 controlled the legislative

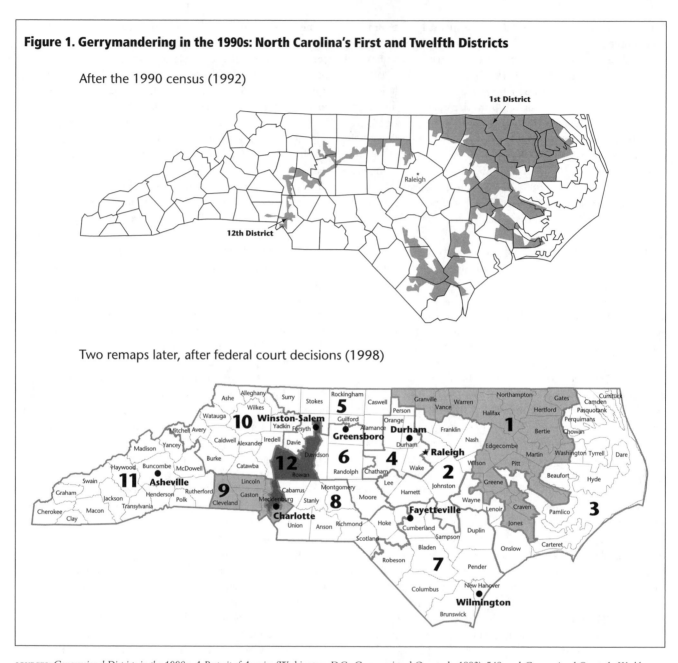

Figure 1. Gerrymandering in the 1990s: North Carolina's First and Twelfth Districts

After the 1990 census (1992)

Two remaps later, after federal court decisions (1998)

SOURCES: *Congressional Districts in the 1990s: A Portrait of America* (Washington, D.C.: Congressional Quarterly, 1993), 548; and *Congressional Quarterly Weekly Report,* April 5, 1997, 810.

NOTE: North Carolina's First and Twelfth Districts were drawn to give the state its first black representatives in 93 years. Elected in 1992, the two representatives were reelected in 1994 and 1996.

oversight of that planning. The unitary control of the legislative and executive branch minimized both the oversight of census planning and the battle over census methods. Thus, unlike the 2000 census, which was planned during a Democratic administration, the 2010 census was not designed to permit adjustment of the April counts for redistricting or other small-area data use. Second, Texas, under the leadership of the majority leader of the U.S. House, Tom DeLay, conducted a second redistricting in 2003 that shifted control of the state legislature into the Republican column and gave

Republicans a majority of the state's congressional delegation. Finally, two apportionment lawsuits by Utah challenged the Census Bureau's apportionment counts and required the courts to once again clarify issues of counting for apportionment disputes among states.

Planning the Census

The Census Bureau announced its plans for the 2010 census even as processing for the 2000 census was at its zenith. The plans rested on three changes. First, the census long form would be abolished, replaced by the American Community Survey (ACS). Second, a major investment would be made in the census geographic system, tracing new coordinates for every street in the United States. Third, the Census Bureau would develop handheld computers about the size of a circa 2000 cell phone that would be the primary data collection device for all households who did not return the census form by mail. The bureau implemented the ACS and the improvements in mapping, but the handheld computers were not implemented and in spring 2008, the bureau announced the return to the paper methods of 2000.

Preliminary indications are that the 2010 operational tasks were carried out successfully; however, no information on the census accuracy relative to districting will be available at the time the districting file is published in spring 2011. The first indication of the accuracy of the census came with the announcement of the apportionment counts in December 2010 and a comparison of those numbers with the population estimates provided by Demographic Analysis. That comparison is limited to state-level comparisons.

Unlike both 1990 and 2000, the evaluation component of the 2010 census will not produce results until well after both the apportionment and redistricting counts are released. The plans for evaluation of the 2010 census call for results to be issued in 2013. The robustness of the 2010 evaluation will be limited by the relatively small sample size for the post-enumeration survey.

The Texas ReRedistricting
Perhaps the most entertaining redistricting event following the 2000 census was the second districting of the Texas congressional districts in 2003. Following the 2000 census, the Texas legislature and governor could not agree on a redistricting. Consequently, a three-judge panel appointed by the federal court drew districts based on those existing in the previous decade. Republicans, believing that the 1991 redistricting allowed Democrats to unfairly control a majority of the house seats in the state, chafed at this plan. Rep. Tom DeLay, then majority leader in the House of Representatives, set out to undo the plan, first by electing a majority of Republicans to the Texas House and then by getting the state legislature to redraw the districts.

Representative DeLay succeeded in both ventures. In 2002 a majority of Republicans were elected to Texas House seats, giving Republicans control of the state House, Senate, and governorship. That majority then set about redrawing the congressional districts, which had been put in place just two years before. This "reredistricting" drew howls of complaint from Texas Democrats. Eventually, the "DeLay" plan was adopted. In 2004, the Texas delegation had 21 Republicans and 11 Democrats, replacing a delegation of 17 Democrats and 15 Republicans.

Politicians and pundits alike tend to exaggerate the power of redistricting to control the makeup of the House of Representatives. In 1991, Republicans in almost every state decried the Democrats' use of redistricting to keep them forever in the minority. In 1994, Republicans took control of the House

of Representatives. Similarly, commentators predicted that the extreme political gerrymandering in place following the 2000 census would disadvantage Democrats. In 2006, Democrats regained control of the House.

Utah Lawsuits
On the judicial landscape, Utah, which missed a fourth seat in the House by fewer than 1,000 inhabitants, sued twice. As is almost always the case, in 2000 the number of persons that separated the state getting the 435th seat and the state that held the 436th position was very small. Fewer than 1,000 inhabitants separated North Carolina (435) and Utah (436).

Utah first challenged the failure to include Mormon missionaries serving overseas during the census while including military, which, they argued gave North Carolina an advantage. North Carolina got the 435th seat. When that failed, Utah challenged the use of imputation in the census.

Utah's second suit fared better in reaching the Supreme Court for arguments; however, it too failed (*Utah v. Evans*, 536 U.S. 452 [2002]). In its second suit, Utah challenged the use of imputation in the census, arguing that imputation was a form of sampling, which was prohibited by the Court in its 1999 decision. In rebuffing Utah's claim, Justice Stephen Breyer, writing for the majority, ruled that imputation did "not represent an overall approach to the counting problem that will rely on data collected from only a subset of the total population, since it is a method of *processing* data (giving a value to missing data), not its collection." He further argued that imputation "does not rely upon the same statistical methodology generally used for sample selection." Finally he concluded that imputation "has as its immediate objective determining the characteristics of missing individual [cases], not extrapolating characteristics from the sample to the entire . . . population."

Apportionment and Districting after the 2010 Census
In December 2010 the Census Bureau announced the results of the April count. Eight states gained 12 seats in Congress; 12 states lost seats. Redistricting will proceed in 2011 for the 2012 election cycle. Despite efforts to make congressional districts the same size within states, there remains significant state-to-state variation. Congressional districts in 2010 will range from 527,624 (RI) to 994,416 (MT). For the seven single-member states (AK, DE, MT, ND, SD, VT, WY), Wyoming has the smallest population (568,300) and Montana the largest. The remaining 43 states are evenly distributed about the mean of 710,767, with 20 states having districts smaller than the average and 23 with districts larger than the average. The smallest districts (RI) are 25 percent smaller than the average district, while the largest districts in multidistrict states are 11 percent larger than the average. Montana's single district is 40 percent larger than the average district size. Thirty of the 43 multidistrict states have districts that are within 5 percent of the average (17 states above the mean and 13 states below the mean).

Several questions about the 2010 redistricting process remain. Will there be a challenge to the accuracy of the 2010 census? The decennial growth rate in the first decade of the 21st century declined 26.5 percent from the previous decade; however, it is too soon to tell if that is an early indicator of the accuracy of the count. How will the events in Texas and Utah following the 2000 census affect 2010 redistricting? How will voting rights enforcement be altered by the design of the 2010 census? In previous censuses, the Justice Department relied on long-form data for enforcement of the provisions of the Voting Rights Act. Those data are now collected in the American Community Survey, and the available data for Justice Department use have characteristics quite different from long-form data. Legislators, the political parties, demographers, and census officials will likely have a spirited debate about the quality, accuracy, and relevance of ACS data to the decennial redistricting process.

See also *Congress and the census; Tabulation geography.*

. . . . .DAVID McMILLEN

BIBLIOGRAPHY
Balinski, Michel L., and H. Peyton Young. *Fair Representation: Meeting the Ideal of One Man, One Vote.* 2nd ed. Washington, D.C.: Brookings Institution Press, 2001
Hanson, Royce. *The Political Thicket: Reapportionment and Constitutional Democracy.* Englewood Cliffs, N.J.: Prentice-Hall, 1962.
Toobin, Jeffrey. "Drawing the Line—Will Tom Delay's Redistricting in Texas Cost Him His Seat?" *New Yorker* (March 6, 2006): 32–37. www .newyorker.com/archive/2006/03/06/060306fa_fact.
U.S. Census Bureau. *Strength in Numbers: Your Guide to Census 2010 Redistricting Data from the U.S. Census Bureau.* www.census.gov/rdo.

Archival Access to Census Data

There are several major sources of information from recent and past censuses. Two of these are recognized archives whose mission is to preserve and provide access to such information. Using one of more of these sources, individuals may examine data from all of the nation's censuses, from the first in 1790 to the most recent.

Types of Census Information

Information from the decennial censuses is available in three forms: printed, microform, and electronic. Here we will concentrate on the third form in which census data are available, the electronic format. Although the Census Bureau began using electronic data-processing equipment for its tabulations as early as 1890, it was not until the 1960s that census information became publicly available in electronic form. Beginning with the 1970 census, electronic data products were routinely prepared and distributed by the Census Bureau for each decennial census. Those products took two forms: information on individuals (names were withheld to prevent identification) and summary or aggregate information. These are commonly known as Public Use Microdata Samples (PUMS)

and Summary Tape Files (STFs), respectively. For the censuses before 1970, electronic census information was created from the printed and microform products of earlier censuses, not by the Census Bureau but by several academic organizations, often working in conjunction with the bureau. For those years the same two formats of information, individual-level and summary, were created.

The chief advantage of census information in electronic form is the ability to manage, search, and manipulate these massive data resources with the aid of computers. Additionally, users can access or obtain electronic census information remotely, without having to travel physically to a site where the information is located or stored (such as a library or other repository). Finally, a dispersed network of organizations provides convenient access to electronic census information, offering choices for those who wish to use data in this form.

Major Sources of Census Information

The first major source of electronic census information is the U.S. Census Bureau, which maintains a large number of data files, chiefly from the most recent decennial censuses. Copies of these files can be acquired from the bureau. In addition, the bureau's World Wide Web site (www.census.gov) facilitates search and display of discrete items of census information for all areas of the country. The Census Bureau's network of State Data Centers, located in each state, affords yet other means of access to (mostly current) census information in electronic form.

The Census Bureau is required by law to deposit its official electronic products (as well as other material) with the U.S. National Archives and Records Administration (NARA). NARA is the official federal government repository for census data, with a mission to preserve these data as official records of the U.S. government. This organization is therefore a second source of electronic census information. NARA's holdings of electronic material are chiefly concentrated in the period since 1960. Its Web site (www.archives.gov) provides information on how to obtain copies of electronic census data files.

A third source of electronic census data is less well known to nonspecialists. That is the Inter-university Consortium for Political and Social Research (ICPSR), a worldwide academic membership organization based at the University of Michigan. This repository preserves and provides access to both contemporary and historical information from the first census in 1790 to the present. Aggregated (summary file) historical data in the ICPSR's holdings were key-entered by ICPSR staff or academic teams under the direction of economist Michael Haines (Colgate University) using printed reports from the 1790–1960 censuses. Data files were prepared containing more than 12,000 indicators, recorded for every state and for each of the 3,400 counties or county-equivalents that have ever existed across the nation's history. Included in these data files are social, demographic, and economic characteristics of the population, as well as economic activities (agriculture, manufacturing, retail and wholesale trade), religious institution and membership, and country of origin of immigrants. Individual-level (PUMS) data also are available from this source, as are summary data from the censuses of 1970 to the present. The ICPSR holdings of historical and contemporary census data are accessible online (www.icpsr.umich.edu) for downloading by personal computers (PCs); copies of specific files also can be provided, on request, on removable media. In addition, the ICPSR Web site provides links to related sites that offer other forms of access to census data.

Access to Census Data Files

Two means of access to census data files afford considerable flexibility for those wishing to use these data. The first requires some conversance with manipulating statistical data files with the help of computer software. Census information in electronic form is most commonly stored in "data files" that record characteristics of persons and households (for PUMS files) or tabulations of census-gathered characteristics that are summarized and recorded for geographic areas (summary files). These data files are largely numeric and require the use of computer software to interpret and display the information contained in them. These files can be ordered or downloaded from the sources listed above (as well as from other organizations) and then manipulated on PCs. Accompanying each data file will be two ancillary sets of information: *technical documentation* (text describing the data file and its contents that permits a user to understand the data storage format and all of the items of information contained in the file) and a *database dictionary* or *format statements* (electronic instructions that tell computer software how to read the data file). The ancillary information is typically delivered in electronic format as well.

A second means of access to census data files is more user-friendly. This form of access is through the growing number of online information utilities that now serve a variety of users. These utilities provide menu-driven options to extract census data without the need to download full data files and all of their documentation. Instead of creating their own datasets to work within statistical analysis software packages, users can visit a Web site that will do much of the work for them. These new utilities have proved extremely popular in recent years and have made census data in general more accessible to larger segments of the population. The Census Bureau maintains one of these online utilities (called American FactFinder), which allows users to obtain information from many sources, including the 1990, 2000, and 2010 decennial censuses. From viewing one-page summary sheets of basic population characteristics to examining the generation of sophisticated thematic and reference maps, one can utilize this tool without having to manipulate any original data files. Researchers may access a wider range of historical information through the Historical Census Data Browser, maintained by the Geospatial and Statistical Data Center at the University of Virginia (http://mapserver.lib.virginia.edu/). This site allows users to search census data from 1790 through 1960 and examine such topics as ethnicity, race, education, agriculture, the economy, and even information about the slave population. Finally, the National

Historical Geographic Information System (NHGIS), housed at the Minnesota Population Center (www.nhgis.org/) provides aggregate census data and GIS-compatible boundary files for the United States between 1790 and 2000. One of the exciting features of this site is that it includes state, county, and census tract boundary files that reflect the geographical characteristics of the United States at each period in which data were collected. Users can both generate maps from the site directly or download the appropriate boundary files to use with a Geographical Information System (GIS) software package.

Issues in Using Archival Census Data

Census data covering more than 200 years of the nation's history provide an unmatched resource for research and discovery of a wealth of topics. The electronic data files in particular permit examinations of changes over time in the size, distribution, and characteristics of the U.S. population. Several caveats, however, should guide the use of these collections of information. First is the number and size of available census data files. Many thousands of discrete files have been prepared from the U.S. decennial censuses. A considerable number of these files are massive, containing millions of data records or thousands of observations at a single point in time. Consultation with experts, or technical experience in using such files, is often necessary to avoid time-consuming and frustrating searches for needed information and its extraction from such large files.

Three methodological issues complicate the use of census data, particularly the comparison of data over time. The first is the changing definitions of terms used in different censuses for measuring concepts and describing population characteristics. Care needs to be paid to the varying definitions of attributes or categories of information over the years, including such basic concepts as "race," "occupation," and "ethnicity." (Integrated Public Use Microdata Series [IPUMS], described elsewhere in this volume, provides some assistance with this problem.) Those who examine summary data recorded for various geographic areas will confront a second issue, changing territorial or geographic boundaries. The nation's counties (and even states) have frequently changed their boundaries, and smaller geographic units have been even more volatile. A third methodological issue is census "underenumeration," or the failure to count and then record information for all persons residing in the country at the time of a census. Progressively better census-taking methods have reduced the undercounting, although undercount rates remain high for some groups. Yet for all censuses, researchers interpreting reported figures must contemplate the effect of persons missed or left out of the tabulations.

See also *IPUMS (Integrated Public Use Microdata Series); National Archives and Records Administration; PUMS (Public Use Microdata Samples).*

. . . .   ERIK W. AUSTIN AND PETER A. GRANDA

BIBLIOGRAPHY

Anderson, Margo. *The American Census: A Social History*. New Haven, Conn.: Yale University Press, 1988.

Clubb, Jerome, Erik W. Austin, and Michael W. Traugott. "Demographic and Compositional Change." In *Analyzing Electoral History: A Guide to the Study of American Voter Behavior*, ed. Jerome M. Clubb, William H. Flanigan, and Nancy Zingale, 105–136. Beverly Hills, Calif.: Sage Publications, 1981.

Sharpless, John B., and Ray M. Shortridge. "Biased Under-enumeration in Census Manuscripts: Methodological Implications." *Journal of Urban History* 1 (August 1975): 409–439.

U.S. Bureau of the Census. *Twenty Censuses: Population and Housing Questions, 1790–1980*. Washington, D.C.: U.S. Government Printing Office, 1979.

Asian Americans

"Asian Americans" are people who report as Asian in response to the race question on the census and other surveys that follow federal standards for collecting and presenting data on race and Hispanic origin. Data on race have been collected since the first census, in 1790. Chinese immigrants arrived on the West Coast at the time of the California gold rush and were identified in the 1850 and 1860 censuses by country of origin. In 1870 the census added Chinese to the race categories. Japanese became a category in 1890 and Filipino and Korean by 1920.

Federal standards for collecting racial statistics have changed over time. In recent years, Statistical Directive 15, issued by the Office of Management and Budget (OMB) in 1976, led to a combined Asian/Pacific Islander racial category in the 1980 and 1990 censuses. Current practices follow revised guidelines issued by the OMB in 1997. Beginning with the 2000 census, the combined Asian/Pacific Islander racial category was separated into two—"Asian" and "Native Hawaiian and Other Pacific Islander"—and people were able to report more than one race. Because of these changes, data from the 2000 census and subsequent sources such as the American Community Survey (ACS) are not directly comparable with data from earlier censuses.

To reflect current practices, data reported here from the 2000 census and the ACS on Asian Americans include all persons who report Asian race alone or in combination with one or more other races (that is, "White," "Black/African American," "American Indian or Alaska Native," or "Native Hawaiian and Other Pacific Islander"). People who report as Asian on the census race question encompass diverse religions, languages, and ethnic backgrounds, such as Asian Indian, Chinese, Filipino, Japanese, Korean, and so forth.

Population Size and Growth

In 2010 there were 17.3 million Asian Americans, representing 5.6 percent of the U.S. population (see Table 1). While a relatively small percentage of the total U.S. population, the Asian American population has increased at a faster rate than the total population in recent decades. For example, between 1980 and 1990, while the total population grew by about 10 percent, the Asian American population almost doubled. Since 2000 the Asian American population has grown by 45 percent.

Of the 17.3 million people reporting Asian race alone or in combination with one or more other races in 2010, 85 percent reported Asian race alone, and the remainder reported Asian race in combination with one or more other races. Racial intermarriage is the main reason for more than one race reporting: 2000 census data show that about 16 percent of married Asians have a non-Asian partner. The children of intermarried Asians are increasingly more likely to report more than one race.

Projections by the U.S. Census Bureau suggest that the Asian American population will continue to grow at a faster pace than the total population. While the total U.S. population is projected to increase by almost 157 million people between 2000 to 2050 (or a 56 percent change), the Asian American population is projected to increase by 28.5 million, or a 235 percent change (see Table 2). According to these projections, Asian Americans would be just over 9 percent of the projected total population of 439 million in 2050.

The factors behind population growth are natural increase (births minus deaths) and net international migration (immigrants arriving minus emigrants departing). Immigration has been the main driver of the rapid growth of the Asian American population since 1980. According to U.S. Census Bureau estimates of components of population change between 2000

Table 1. Growth of Total U.S. and Asian American Populations, 1980–2007 (numbers in thousands)

	1980		1990		% INCREASE	2000[a]		2010		% INCREASE
	NO.	%	NO.	%	1980–1990	NO.	%	NO.	%	2000–2010
Total U.S.	226,625	100.0	248,712	100.0	9.8	281,422	100.0	308,341	100.0	9.7
Asian	3,457	1.5	6,876	2.8	98.9	11,899	4.2	17,321	5.6	45.0

[a] Beginning with the 2000 census, people could report more thes one race. The numbers for 2000 and 2010 include people who reported Asian race alone or in combination with one or more other races. Racial data from the 2000 and 2010 censuses and the ACS are not directly comparable with earlier censuses.

SOURCES: 1980 and 1990: S. M. Lee, "Asian Americans: Diverse and Growing," *Population Bulletin* 53, no. 2 (Washington, D.C.: Population Reference Bureau, 1998); 2000: T. J. Reeves and C. E. Bennett, "We the People: Asians in the United States," Census 2000 Special Reports (Washington, D.C.: U.S. Census Bureau, 2000); 2010: U.S. Census Bureau, "Overview of Race and Hispanic Origin: 2010," March 2011.

Table 2. Projected Change in Population Size of Total U.S. and Asian American Populations, 2000–2050 (numbers in thousands)

	2000–2050		2000–2025		2025–2050	
	No.	%	No.	%	No.	%
Total U.S.	156,852	56.0	75,294	27.0	81,558	23.0
Asian[a]	28,484	235.0	12,283	101.0	16,201	66.0

SOURCE: Table 7, "Projected Change in Population Size by Race and Hispanic Origin for the United States: 2000 to 2050" (NP2008-T7). Washington, D.C.: Population Division, U.S. Census Bureau, 2008.

[a] Includes Asian race alone or in combination with one or more other races.

and 2008, net international migration accounted for 54 percent of growth of the Asian American population, compared with 36 percent of total U.S. population growth. The role of immigration becomes evident when we examine the nativity and citizenship of Asian Americans in a following section.

Changing Ethnic Composition

The substantial growth of the Asian American population since 1980 has been accompanied by significant changes in the ethnic composition of the population, as shown in Table 3.

As recently as 1980, Chinese, Filipinos, and Japanese were the largest ethnic groups in the Asian American population. By the 1990 census, however, two new groups—Korean and Asian Indian—had become as large as the Japanese community, each

representing 0.3 percent of the U.S. population. Chinese and Filipinos were still the two largest groups in 1990, at 0.7 and 0.6 percent of the total, respectively.

In 2000 and 2007, the largest Asian group was the Chinese, at about 1.0–1.1 percent of the U.S. population. Filipinos and Asian Indians were the next largest groups, each at 0.9 percent of the total. Japanese, Koreans, and Vietnamese each made up about 0.4–0.5 percent of the total, and people of "other Asian" backgrounds made up another 0.6 percent of the total U.S. population. The main changes were the relative declines of the Japanese American population, while other groups such as Asian Indians, Koreans, and Vietnamese increased absolutely and as a proportion of the Asian American population.

Table 3. Changing Composition of the Asian American Population, 1980–2007 (numbers in thousands)

	1980		1990		2000[a]		2007[a]	
	NO.	% OF U.S. POPULATION	NO.	% OF U.S. POPULATION	NO.	% OF U.S. POPULATION	NO.	% OF U.S. POPULATION
Detailed group								
Total Asian	3,457	1.5	6,876	2.8	11,859	4.2	14,863	4.3
Asian Indian	387	0.2	787	0.3	2,065	0.7	2,635	0.9
Chinese	812	0.4	1,649	0.7	2,858	1.0	3,420	1.1
Filipino	782	0.3	1,420	0.6	2,385	0.9	2,850	0.9
Japanese	716	0.3	866	0.3	1,152	0.4	1,093	0.4
Korean	357	0.2	797	0.3	1,227	0.4	1,492	0.5
Vietnamese	245	0.1	593	0.2	1,212	0.4	1,562	0.5
Other Asian	166	0.0	765	0.3	1,306	0.4	1,946	0.6

SOURCES: 1980 and 1990: S. M. Lee, "Asian Americans: Diverse and Growing," *Population Bulletin* 53, no. 2 (Washington, D.C.: Population Reference Bureau, 1998); 2000: T. J. Reeves and C. E. Bennett, "We the People: Asians in the United States," Census 2000 Special Reports, (Washington, D.C.: U.S. Census Bureau, 2004); 2007. Author's analysis of 2006–2007–2008 American Community Surveys (ACS) Public Use Microdata Samples.

[a] Numbers for 2000 and 2007 include people who reported Asian race alone or in combination with one or more other races. Rows do not sum to the total because people who reported more than one Asian category—for example, Chinese and Vietnamese—are tabulated once in each category but only once in the total. The number for each detailed group includes people who reported that group alone or in combination with one or more other Asian group or race.

Table 4. Geographical Distribution of Total U.S. and Asian American Populations, 2007 (in percentages)

	TOTAL	ASIAN AMERICAN
Northeast	18.3	20.0
New England	4.8	3.7
Middle Atlantic	13.6	16.3
Midwest	22.0	11.9
East North Central	15.4	8.8
West North Central	6.6	3.2
South	36.6	20.9
South Atlantic	19.2	12.2
East South Central	5.9	1.5
West South Central	11.5	7.2
West	23.1	47.2
Mountain	7.1	4.5
Pacific	16.0	42.7

SOURCE: Author's analysis of 2006–2007–2008 ACS PUMS.

Immigration has played a key role in the growth of the Asian American population and in altering its ethnic composition. During the 1980s and into the early 2000s, immigration from Asia accounted for 30 to 40 percent of all legal immigration to the United States. China, the Philippines, Vietnam, India, and Korea were the leading countries of origin for Asian immigrants during these years, while immigration from Japan was negligible. For example, between 1989 and 2003 an annual average of about 52,000 people arrived from the Philippines, about 43,000 each from China and India, and 37,000 from Vietnam, compared with just 6,000 from Japan. Future generations of Asian Americans will include more people reporting Korean, Asian Indian, and Vietnamese origins and fewer reporting Japanese origin.

Geographical Distribution

Compared with the total U.S. population, the Asian American population is distinctive in its concentration in the West (see Table 4). Almost half of the Asian American population resides in the Western region, compared with 23 percent of the total U.S. population. Within the Western region, almost all of the Asian American population (43 of 47 percent) resides in the Pacific states of Alaska, California, Hawaii, Oregon, and Washington. Two regions where there are lower percentages of Asian Americans compared with the total population are the Midwest and the South.

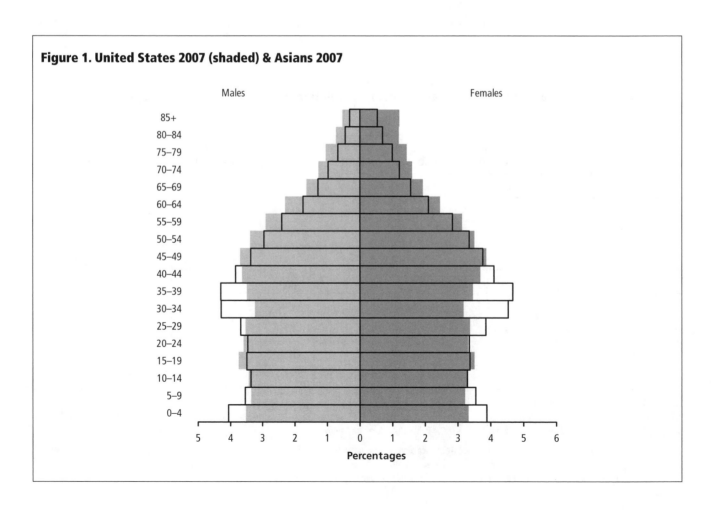

Figure 1. United States 2007 (shaded) & Asians 2007

The five states with the highest percentages of Asian Americans are California (33 percent), New York (10 percent), Texas (6 percent), Hawaii (5 percent), and New Jersey (5 percent).

Age and Sex

Age and sex are basic variables in describing any population. Using median age as an indicator, the Asian American population is younger (median age = 33) than the total U.S. population (median age = 36). While the Asian American median age is lower than that of the total population, there are differences within the Asian American population. The median age of Japanese Americans is 39, three years older than the national median age. Chinese Americans have the same median age as the national median, at 36, while other Asian groups have lower median ages; for example, the median age for Asian Indians is 32, and it is just 27 for "other Asians."

An examination of the age-sex pyramid using data from the 2006–2007–2008 ACS (see Figure 1) shows higher percentages of Asian Americans at the younger ages of 0–4 and 5–9 and prime adult working ages of 25–29, 30–34, 35–39, and 40–44. In contrast, there are noticeably higher percentages at the older ages for the total U.S. population.

The Asian American sex ratio (number of males for every 100 females) is 94, which is lower than the national sex ratio of 97. The lower Asian American sex ratio is likely related to many factors, including a higher percentage of females among Asian immigrants and a longer life expectancy among Asian American females.

Place of Birth or Nativity and Citizenship

Given the important role of immigration in the growth and changing ethnic origins of the Asian American population, it is not surprising that higher percentages of the Asian American population are foreign born and are not U.S. citizens (see Table 5). While close to 88 percent of the total U.S. population are native-born citizens, less than 40 percent of the Asian American population are native-born citizens. More than one-third are naturalized citizens, and 27 percent are not U.S. citizens.

Japanese Americans have the highest percentage of native-born citizens, at 68 percent, while Asian Indians have the lowest, at 29 percent. The percentage of naturalized citizens is high for all Asian groups, ranging from close to 30 percent for the "other Asian" group to 47 percent among Vietnamese. Japanese are the exception, with just 10 percent naturalized citizens; this is probably related to the temporary assignment of Japanese employees to U.S.-based corporate offices—for example, in the auto industry. For Asian Indians 39 percent are not U.S. citizens, and 31 percent of Koreans are not U.S. citizens, probably because of the recency of immigration and residence requirements to qualify for naturalization.

Home Language and English-Language Proficiency

Since the majority of Asian Americans are foreign born, it is not surprising that while over 80 percent of the U.S. population speak English as their home language, less than 30 percent of Asian Americans report English as their home language

Table 5. Nativity and Citizenship, Total U.S. and Asian American Populations, 2007 (in percentages)

	NATIVE-BORN CITIZEN	FOREIGN-BORN, NATURALIZED CITIZEN	FOREIGN-BORN, NOT CITIZEN
Total U.S.	87.5	5.3	7.2
Total Asian	39.4	34.0	26.5
Asian Indian	28.7	32.9	38.5
Chinese	35.7	38.1	26.2
Filipino	43.6	35.6	20.8
Japanese	68.1	10.1	21.8
Korean	32.7	36.0	31.2
Vietnamese	35.0	46.9	18.2
Other Asian	48.3	27.4	24.3

SOURCE: Author's analysis of 2006–2007–2008 ACS PUMS.

(see Table 6). Japanese Americans have the highest percentage speaking English as their home language (61 percent), and Vietnamese have the lowest percentage (16 percent).

Among people who do not speak only English, over 56 percent of the total population and 54 percent of Asian Americans report speaking English very well. Higher-than-average levels of Asian Indians and Filipinos report speaking English very well, while below-average levels (about 40 to

Table 6. Home Language and English-Language Proficiency, Total U.S. and Asian American Populations, 2007 (in percentages)

	ENGLISH ONLY HOME LANGUAGE	SPEAKS ENGLISH VERY WELL[a]
Total U.S.	80.4	56.2
Total Asian	29.3	53.5
Asian Indian	22.5	71.4
Chinese	22.3	44.3
Filipino	40.9	67.4
Japanese	61.4	48.4
Korean	26.1	41.1
Vietnamese	15.6	39.5
Other Asian	29.8	53.6

SOURCE: Author's analysis of 2006–2007–2008 ACS PUMS.

[a] Asked of people who do not speak only English.

Table 7. Educational Attainment, Total U.S. and Asian American Populations, 25 Years and Older, 2007 (in percentages)

	LESS THAN HIGH SCHOOL	HIGH SCHOOL GRADUATE	SOME COLLEGE	BACHELOR'S DEGREE OR MORE
Total U.S.	15.5	29.7	27.4	27.4
Total Asian	14.2	17.3	19.9	48.6
Asian Indian	9.8	11.2	10.9	68.1
Chinese	18.4	15.8	14.8	51.0
Filipino	8.0	16.6	29.0	46.5
Japanese	6.3	20.9	27.4	45.4
Korean	9.3	19.8	19.7	51.2
Vietnamese	27.1	23.4	22.4	27.1
Other Asian	21.0	21.6	22.8	34.6

SOURCE: Author's analysis of 2006–2007–2008 ACS PUMS.

44 percent) of Chinese, Korean, and Vietnamese report speaking English very well.

Educational Attainment

Educational attainment of the Asian American population is remarkably high, compared with the total U.S. population (see Table 7). Almost 50 percent of Asian Americans have a bachelor's degree or higher level of education, compared with 27 percent of the national population. However, the percentage with less than a high school education is similar, around 14 to 15 percent.

There are large differences across Asian groups. Asian Indians have the highest percentage of those obtaining a bachelor's degree or higher level of education (68 percent), followed by Chinese and Koreans (51 percent). The Vietnamese have the lowest percentage of those with a bachelor's degree or higher level of education (27 percent, which is the same as the total

U.S. percentage) and also have the highest percentage of those having less-than-high-school education (27 percent, which is higher than the 16 percent for the total U.S. population).

Future Prospects

Continued immigration and a younger age structure will contribute to faster growth of the Asian American population compared to the total U.S. population. As the Asian American population continues to grow, so will its diversity along many dimensions. Unless U.S. immigration policies are substantially changed, immigration will remain the primary factor for continued growth of the Asian American population. Natural increase will become more important, however, in future years as the number of Asian Americans increases, reaches reproductive ages, and have children.

See also *Grassroots groups; Native Hawaiian and Other Pacific Islander population; Race: questions and classifications.*

. . . . SHARON M. LEE

BIBLIOGRAPHY

Grieco, Elizabeth M., and Rachel E. Cassidy. "Overview of Race and Hispanic Origin." Census 2000 Brief. Washington, D.C.: U.S. Census Bureau, 2001.

Lee, Sharon M. "Asian Americans: Diverse and Growing." *Population Bulletin* 53, no. 2 (1998).

———. "Racial Classifications in the U.S. Census: 1890–1990." *Ethnic and Racial Studies* 16, no. 1 (1993): 75–94.

Lee, Sharon M., and Barry Edmonston. "New Marriages, New Families: U.S. Racial and Hispanic Intermarriage." *Population Bulletin* 60, no. 2 (2005).

Mezey, Naomi. "Erasure and Recognition: The Census, Race and the National Imagination." *Northwestern University Law Review* 97 (2003): 1701–1768.

Reeves, Terrance J., and Claudette E. Bennett. "We the People: Asians in the United States." Census 2000 Special Reports. Washington, D.C.: U.S. Census Bureau, 2004.

U.S. Census Bureau. "Projections of the Population and Components of Change for the United States: 2010 to 2050" (Tables 1, 6, 7). Washington, D.C.: Population Division, U.S. Census Bureau, 2008.

———. "Cumulative Estimates of the Components of Resident Population Change by Race and Hispanic Origin for the United States: April 1, 2000, to July 1, 2008" (NC-EST2008-05). Washington, D.C.: Population Division, U.S. Census Bureau, 2009.

U.S. Department of Homeland Security. Yearbook of Immigration Statistics: 2003 (Table 3). Washington, D.C.: U.S. Government Printing Office, 2004.

Black Americans

See *African-origin population*

Capture-Recapture Methods

The U.S. decennial census process produces what is commonly referred to as a "complete count." The U.S. Census Bureau has traditionally dealt with counting problems by building many follow-up and checking procedures into the census process to catch errors and make sure that households are counted. Nonetheless, considerable evidence, accumulated over decades, documents the existence of a systematic undercount in the decennial census, one that differentially affects different population groups. A substantial technical literature exists tracing the undercount and statistical methods to measure it. For the 1980 census, for example, as Robert E. Fay reported, the bureau determined that there were at least 6 million erroneous enumerations in the census, of which as many as 1 million were fabrications and as many as 2.5 million people were erroneously included twice at the same location. Given the bureau's report of a net undercount of 1.4 percent, or 3.2 million people, in 1980, an estimated 9.2 million people were omitted from that year's census count. By adding omissions to erroneous enumerations, we get a total of 15.2 million gross errors in counting individuals, which corresponds to almost 7 percent of the official 1980 census total. For 1990 the estimates of gross error ran even higher than in 1980, with about a 10 percent gross error being cited by Eugene P. Ericksen and Teresa K. DeFonso as well as many others. For 2000 the net undercount was substantially lower and estimates of the gross error rate were similarly down, but new problems arose, especially those associated with the large number of imputations and duplicate enumerations, as documented in the 2004 report from the Committee on National Statistics of the National Research Council, *The 2000 Census: Counting Under Adversity*.

The controversies surrounding the differential undercount of blacks and other minorities have made the flaws in the counting systems painfully clear and have led to proposals for fundamentally new ways to count, derived from different statistical traditions. This new methodology involves a form of systematic double counting, not just checking to make sure that the count is accurate, and it uses sampling. The traditional methods rely for their validity on careful bureaucratic procedures, the administrative chain of command, legal sanctions for nonresponse, and public cooperation of respondents. The new methods rely on the principles of statistical theory and probability for validity.

Dual-systems estimation was the method of choice adopted by the methodologists at the Census Bureau for the 1990 decennial census. Its basic premise is the use of two sources of information to arrive at a better estimate of the population than could be obtained from one source alone. The procedure is an old one, widely accepted among statisticians, and has been used for a host of practical population estimation problems. It is most familiar in the context of estimating the size of wildlife populations, in which it is known as the capture-recapture technique. A hypothetical example of fish counting adapted from Margo Anderson and Stephen E. Fienberg shows how the technique can be applied to a counting problem associated with public policy.

Fish in a Lake

State X has only two types of fish in its lakes, red fish and blue fish (with apologies to a favorite author, Dr. Seuss), and we would like to know how many of each there are and how they are distributed across the lakes in the state. We begin by going to one lake where we attempt to catch and count each fish in the lake on two successive occasions. To keep track of which fish were counted the first time, we mark each fish caught before releasing it. As the fish are caught the second time, we can then determine, for each fish, whether it was counted in the first attempt. We can use the information from these two counts to derive a more accurate estimate of the size of the fish population than the ones we made from either of the two counts alone.

It turns out that the first time we went out, the weather was sunny, and the fish were somewhat difficult to catch. As a result, we counted only 150 fish. The second day was cloudy, and the fish were easier to catch; as a result we were able to catch 200 fish. Further, of the 200 fish counted the second time, 125 bore marks indicating that they had been among the 150 fish counted the first time. There are thus three distinct classes of fish that have been counted: fish caught both the first time and the second time (which in this example number 125), fish caught the first time but not the second (25 in this example, or the total number of fish caught the first time minus the number of marked fish recaught the second time), and fish caught the second time but not caught the first time (75 here, equaling the total number caught the second time minus the number of marked fish caught the second time). The total number of fish in the three classes is 225. Note that we have observed all 225 fish directly and that this number exceeds the number of fish observed in either of the two counts separately. A convenient way to display the data is in the form of a 2 × 2 table with rows corresponding to presence and absence in the first attempt and columns corresponding to presence and absence in the second attempt (see Table 1).

The task at hand is to estimate those not caught either time. This can be done as long as the two fish counts are independent random samples. A random sample by its nature permits us to estimate the incidence of any observable characteristic in the larger population from which the sample is drawn. In this case, the characteristic of interest is that of having been captured in the first count. The examination of our random sample—the second count—showed that 125 out of 200 fish, or five-eighths of the sample, had been captured in the first count. Generalizing from the sample, we can conclude that the total number of fish counted the first time, 150, is five-eighths of the total population—that is,

$$150 = \frac{5}{8} \times \hat{N}$$

Table 1. Example: Two Counts of Fish in a Lake

		DAY 2: CLOUDY		
		IN	OUT	TOTAL
Day 1: Sunny	In	125	25	150
	Out	75	?	??
	Total	200	?	??

where $\hat{N}$ is the estimate of true population size N. To arrive at our estimate, a little high school algebra suffices:

$$\hat{N} = \frac{8}{5} \times 150 = 240$$

Of this estimated 240 total population, 225 have been observed in one or the other or both of the two counts. Thus, we infer that there are 15 fish in the population that were not counted either time.

We now observe that 30 red fish were counted the first day and 40 the second day; conversely, 120 blue fish were counted the first day and 160 counted the second day. We are interested in what would happen if we made separate calculations for red fish and blue fish. To do this, we work with a table divided into two parts, one for red fish and one for blue fish (see Table 2). By looking at the two parts of the table we see that

- red fish appear to be less numerous than blue fish (there are only 50 red fish observed but there are 175 blue fish).
- more fish, both red and blue, are caught on the cloudy second day than on the sunny first day (40 red fish on day 2 versus 30 on day 1; 160 blue fish on day 2 versus 120 on day 1).
- on the sunny first day, the catchability rate for the red fish is less than for the blue fish (20/40 = 50 percent for red versus 105/160 = 65.6 percent for blue).
- on the cloudy second day, the catchability rate for the red fish is also less than for the blue fish (20/30 = 66.7 percent for red versus 105/120 = 87.5 percent for blue).
- the catchability rates for the cloudy day exceed those for the sunny day for both red and blue fish.

If we now apply the same logic to the red and blue fish separately, we get

$$\hat{N}_r = \frac{40}{20} \times 30 = 60$$

and

$$\hat{N}_b = \frac{160}{105} \times 120 = 182.85$$

Since our estimate for blue fish involves a fraction and we only count whole fish, we use $\hat{N}_b = 182$. We now have as our estimate of the total number of fish in the lake $\hat{N} = \hat{N}_r + \hat{N}_b = 242$. By taking into account the types of fish and the different patterns of "catching" fish, we learn that our original estimate of the total number of fish, 240, should be raised to 242.

What will happen for a different lake where the proportions of red and blue fish are different? The same approach works no matter what the composition of the lake, but if catchability

Table 2. Example: Comparing Two Counts of Red Fish and Blue Fish

		RED FISH					BLUE FISH		
		DAY 2: CLOUDY					DAY 2: CLOUDY		
		In	Out	Total			In	Out	Total
Day 1: Sunny	In	20	10	30	Day 1: Sunny	In	105	15	120
	Out	20	?	?		Out	55	?	?
	Total	40	?	??		Total	160	?	??

rates for red and blue fish vary according to the location of the lake (for example, in the northern as opposed to the southern part of the state), then we will need to gather separate data.

Finally, we ask whether we really need to count all the fish in all the lakes twice to get an estimate of the total numbers of red and blue fish. One possibility is to carry out one count for all the lakes on the same day but then on the second day use only a sample of the lakes for the north and a sample for the south. We can then apply the catchability rates from the second day's sample to the remaining lakes separately for the two parts of the state and separately for red and blue fish in each of the lakes.

Dual Systems and the Census Counting Problem

This method for counting fish can also be used to measure the size of a human population—in our case the first attempt to measure the population size is the census, and the second is a special sample. For example, suppose we are trying to estimate the number of people living on a block in the Bedford-Stuyvesant neighborhood of Brooklyn. This neighborhood in New York City was estimated to have one of the highest net undercounts in the nation in 1990; the congressional district that includes Bedford-Stuyvesant had a net undercount that ranked in the top ten nationwide.

The first count of the population could be a list of the names and addresses of people counted in the census. Assume that 300 people were counted by the census on this particular block. For the second count of the population, let us imagine a specially commissioned, independent count carried out with even greater care than the census and yielding 400 people. In the hypothetical Bedford-Stuyvesant block, this second count will surely include many of the same 300 people counted by the census (although the second count does not need to be bigger than the first for the method to work). We determine how many people were counted both times by comparing the list of names and addresses in the first count with the list of names and addresses in the second count and matching those that are the same. Suppose that through matching these two lists, we find that 250 people out of 400 counted in the second count on this block were also included in the census count. The three observed categories of the population, and their sizes, are thus the 250 counted both times, the 50 counted the

first time but not the second, and the 150 counted the second time but not the first. Thus, we have observed a total of 450 people. If the second count is a random sample of the population of the block as a whole, then the fraction of members of the second count included in the census (250 out of 400, or 5/8) is an estimate of the fraction of the total population of the block counted in the census. Finally, we can estimate that the total population is the number of people counted in the census, or 300, divided by 5/8. This yields an estimate of the total population of 480 people. Thus, the estimated census undercount in this hypothetical block is 180 people out of 480, or three-eighths of the population.

The numbers here are hypothetical, and they are the same as in the example of fish in the lake, except that all the counts are doubled. And just as there were red and blue fish in the lake, there are people from different population groups in our block in Bedford-Stuyvesant—for example, blacks and non-blacks—so we will need separate estimates for the numbers of each group in this block. The breakdown this time might be quite different, as in Table 3.

The vast majority of people in the block are black, and the estimates for the total numbers of blacks and nonblacks in the block are

$$\hat{N}_{\text{black}} = \frac{360}{214} \times 262 = 440.74$$

and

$$\hat{N}_{\text{nonblack}} = \frac{40}{36} \times 38 = 42.2$$

Again, counting only the whole numbers of people, we get a total of 440 + 42 = 482. The result is slightly higher than our earlier estimate of 480 from the two groups combined because the catchabilities are so different and the numbers so disproportionate. There is a very serious differential undercount in this hypothetical block, however, with $100 \times [1 - (262/440)]$ = 40.5 percent of the blacks being missed compared with only $100 \times [1 - (38/42)]$ = 9.5 percent of the nonblacks being missed.

Because the undercount rate varies among different kinds of blocks, we must estimate separate undercount rates for blacks and nonblacks for each of a sample of blocks. We

Table 3. Count and Recount of Hypothetical Census Block

		BLACK					NONBLACK		
		RECOUNT					RECOUNT		
		IN	OUT	TOTAL			IN	OUT	TOTAL
Census	In	214	48	262	Census	In	36	2	38
	Out	146	?	?		Out	4	?	?
	Total	360	?	??		Total	40	?	??

would not, for example, expect our dual-systems estimate of the undercount rates of a block in Bedford-Stuyvesant to tell us much about the undercount rates in an expensive suburb. Accordingly, in selecting the sample, one starts with a list of all the blocks or equivalent-size rural units in the United States, then groups the blocks into categories, or *strata,* according to their demographic characteristics. Such characteristics might include racial composition, proportion of homeowners to renters, and average household size. Rates of undercount are determined for each stratum by measuring the undercount of a sample of blocks within the stratum by dual-systems estimation. The undercount rate of these blocks is then applied to the other blocks throughout the country in that stratum. The actual correction of the census counts consists of adjusting the raw census count for each stratum to compensate for the estimated undercount in that stratum.

The Census Bureau itself was an early user of this type of methodology. In particular it matched the results from a sample to the census records for coverage evaluation in connection with the 1950 decennial census, although official reports did not provide a full implementation of the dual-systems estimation. In 1980 the bureau implemented a version of the dual-systems method using data from the Current Population Survey for the second count and not a specially designed post-enumeration survey. In 1990 the Census Bureau took an independent count of the populations of each of a large number of blocks nationwide and then matched those counted to the records of the census for those blocks. This second count was known as a "post-enumeration survey," or PES. In the 2000 census, the Census Bureau again used essentially the same methodology and the second survey was called the Accuracy and Coverage Evaluation survey (ACE). C. Chandra Sekar and W. Edwards Deming, Karol J. Krotki, and Stephen E. Fienberg provide additional background and references to the original uses of the methodology and to technical details and discussions.

Dual-Systems Model Assumptions and Their Empirical Base

The dual-systems estimation method is based on a set of assumptions linked to a very explicit statistical model. Following are the three assumptions most widely discussed:

- *Perfect matching.* The individuals in the first list can be matched with those in the second list, without error.
- *Independence of lists.* The probability of an individual being included in the census does not depend on whether the individual was included in the second list.
- *Homogeneity.* The probabilities of inclusion do not vary from individual to individual.

Perhaps the greatest problem with the dual-systems approach as it was used in conjunction with the 1980 census was the rate of matching errors (the failure of the "perfect matching" assumption). There are two kinds of matching errors: false matches and false nonmatches. False matches produce an underestimate of the population size. By contrast, if individuals in the sample cannot be matched with their records in the census, then the population size is overestimated.

The matching problem as it emerged in the context of the coverage evaluation program for the 1980 census was discussed at length in the analyses reported by Robert E. Fay and his colleagues and was the focus of a major research program in the 1980s, which included the development of new computer-based matching algorithms by Matthew Jaro. Approximately 75 percent of the 1990 PES records were matched using these algorithms, and clerical matching then took care of most of the remaining records. Special features of the redesigned PES reduced other difficulties associated with the matching process. Yet there was still a residual group of nonmatches, some of which were real matches. Thus, the bureau statisticians set about finding a suitable statistical approach to allocating the residual group to the match and nonmatch categories. (See Nathaniel Schenker for a description of the details of their approach.)

The failure of the "independence of lists" assumption is known as correlation bias. In the presence of positive correlation bias (being missed in the census is positively correlated with being missed in the second list), the traditional capture-recapture population estimate tends to underestimate the actual population size, but, as Howard Hogan suggested, the approach yields an improvement over the unadjusted value. The only direct statistical method available to measure the extent of correlation bias involves a generalization of the dual-systems approach to multiple lists and the estimation techniques developed for multiple-capture problems developed in the works by Stephen E. Fienberg and by Yvonne M. M. Bishop, Stephen E. Fienberg, and Paul W. Holland cited in the bibliography. This alternative is more complex and has been used only in the 1988 test census in analyses by Alan M. Zaslavsky and Glenn S. Wolfgang and not as part of the full-scale census process. As part of the coverage evaluation process for the 1990 census, William R. Bell of the Census Bureau produced several indirect estimates of correlation bias, all of which reaffirmed what had widely been assumed, that correlation bias appears to be positive.

Heterogeneity, or difference, of capture probabilities for both the census and the sample is clearly an issue in any real population setting. The issue is not so much whether the "homogeneity" assumption is violated but the extent to which it is and the implications for the results of dual-systems estimation. What is quite clear is that the correlation between census and sample catchabilities and the effects of heterogeneity are confounded in the simple dual-systems estimation model, since in a 2×2 contingency table with a missing cell, there are no degrees of freedom left over to separate the two. Only since the 1990 census have statisticians begun to address the precise nature of the effects of heterogeneity. Joseph B. Kadane, Michael M. Meyer, and John W. Tukey presented an interesting and detailed model for heterogeneity and describe its implications.

Statisticians now understand that the problem of heterogeneity can be handled in at least two very different ways. One might model the effects of heterogeneity, or one can attempt to reduce them directly by stratification or grouping the data into small, relatively homogeneous groups. The latter strategy, stratification, was built into the design for the 1990 PES, and it reduced but did not eliminate the concern at the Census Bureau about heterogeneity. The tricky thing here is that there is a trade-off between making the strata smaller and thus more homogeneous, on the one hand, and making sure that the counts in the 2 × 2 table used for dual-systems estimation are large enough to make the assumptions of the estimation statistically valid, on the other hand.

As part of the follow-up to the PES, the Census Bureau examined several indirect measures of the effect of residual heterogeneity. One can use a statistical-modeling approach that actually attempts to account for individual-level heterogeneity, but it requires matching three or more sources rather than just the two in the dual-systems approach. John N. Darroch and his colleagues, Stephen E. Fienberg and his colleagues, and Daniel Manrique-Valier and Fienberg described alternative approaches to the estimation of heterogeneity based on multiple lists, which may be of value in future censuses. Multiple-systems estimation has now been used extensively for estimating casualties in the human rights context as Patrick Ball and Jana Asher and Kristian Lum and colleagues have documented.

Modifying Dual-Systems Methods for the U.S. Decennial Census

Two major modifications to the basic dual-systems approach are required for it to be useful for census adjustment purposes. The traditional dual-systems method deals only with the problem of omissions and does not touch the problem of erroneous enumerations. In the 1970s and 1980s, the Census Bureau developed extensions to the basic methodology to correct for erroneous enumerations. The bureau counts erroneous enumerations by doing a check of those included in the census for the sample blocks and subtracts them out of the counts for dual-systems estimation.

If we break the block-level data down by racial and ethnic groups, which is a major goal of the dual-systems approach, the counts in the 2 × 2 table become very small. Thus, we need to aggregate data across selected blocks according to some type of stratification scheme. To estimate the missing people for the nation as a whole, we employ a complex stratified sample of blocks, so we need to "weight" the counts from different blocks according to the sample design when we combine them.

Because we take only a sample of such blocks, and it is only for them that we can produce adjustment factors based on dual-systems estimation, we need to be able to generalize from the sample, appropriately aggregated, to all the other blocks in the nation. This is a simple task in principle but quite tricky in practice. The method of choice has turned out to be a version of traditional regression estimation from sampling

theory. In the traditional theory, one applies regression-based adjustments only to the units of the sample or their aggregates. For the 1990 census adjustment calculations, these same adjustments were applied to blocks not in the sample as well. This has been labeled by some as the "synthetic adjustment assumption." It not only provides a solution to the generalization problem but also helps address the issue of how much to aggregate the sample data to form the strata for estimation purposes.

To some extent we have simplified the description of some of the basic ideas of the dual-systems estimation technique, and we do not wish to disguise the difficulties that some statisticians have claimed are inherent in the methodology. Lawrence D. Brown and his colleagues described many of the concerns with and criticisms of the methodology as implemented in 1990. Nonetheless, the vast majority of assessments of the 1990 implementation of the method conclude that the results were superior for most purposes to the raw census counts. Mary H. Mulry and Bruce D. Spencer carried out the original analyses, demonstrating the superiority of the adjusted data. Anderson and her colleagues provided a response to the critique of Brown and his colleagues. And a report from the National Research Council (NRC) edited by Michael L. Cohen, Andrew A. White, and Keith F. Rust took stock of the 1990 adaptation of the methodology.

Following the 2000 census, Constance F. Citro, Daniel L. Cork, and Janet L. Norwood evaluated the outcome of the proposed use of dual-systems estimation for adjustment. David A. Freedman and Kenneth W. Wachter continued their critique of the dual-systems methodology for undercount adjustment, and Wachter proposed scaling down the follow-up survey and perhaps replacing it with data from the American Community Survey. Lawrence Brown and Zhanyun Zhao proposed alternative estimators of the undercount that focus on the role of imputations and the homogeneity assumptions. For 2010, the Census Bureau proceeded with a similar approach but planned to use the results only for coverage evaluation, not for adjustment.

Though the U.S. Census Bureau has rejected the use of capture-recapture or dual-systems methodology for adjustment, other countries have adopted either this methodology or variations on it for adjustment in a census context. Examples include Australia, Brazil, Israel, and the United Kingdom. Similar uses in a somewhat more limited context in Macedonia, South Africa, Suriname, and Uganda have been documented by the United Nations Statistical Division.

See also *Coverage evaluation; Post-enumeration survey.*

. . . . STEPHEN E. FIENBERG

BIBLIOGRAPHY

Abbott, Owen. "2011 UK Census Coverage Assessment and Adjustment Strategy," *Population Trends* 127 (2007): 7–14. www.statistics.gov.uk/downloads/theme_population/PopulationTrends127.pdf.

Anderson, Margo J., Beth Osborne Daponte, Stephen E. Fienberg, Joseph B. Kadane, Bruce D. Spencer, and Duane L. Steffey. "Sampling-Based

Adjustment of the 2000 Census–A Balanced Perspective." *Jurimetrics* 40 (2000): 341–356.

Anderson, Margo J., and Stephen E. Fienberg. *Who Counts? The Politics of Census-Taking in Contemporary America.* Rev. ed. New York: Russell Sage Foundation, 2001.

Ball, Patrick, and Jana Asher, "Statistics and Slobodan: Using Data Analysis and Statistics in the War Crimes Trial of Former President Milosevic." *Chance* 15, no. 4 (2002): 17–24.

Bell, William R. "Using Information from Demographic Analysis in Post-Enumeration Survey Estimation." *Journal of the American Statistical Association* 88 (1993): 1106–1118.

Bishop, Yvonne M. M., Stephen E. Fienberg, and Paul W. Holland. *Discrete Multivariate Analysis: Theory and Practice.* New York: Springer Science+Business Media, 2007. First published 1975 by MIT Press.

Brown, James, and Nicola Tromans, "Methodological Options for Applying Dual System Estimation in the 2011 Census." Technical Paper 22. Office of National Statistics, UK, 2007. www.s3ri.soton.ac.uk/isi2007/papers/Paper22.pdf.

Brown, Lawrence D., Morris L. Eaton, David A. Freedman, Stephen P. Klein, Richard A. Olshen, Kenneth W. Wachter, Martin T. Wells, and Donald Ylvisaker. "Statistical Controversies in Census 2000." *Jurimetrics* 39 (1999): 347–375.

Brown, Lawrence, and Zhanyun Zhao. "Alternative Formulas for Synthetic Dual System Estimation in the 2000 Census." In *Probability and Statistics: Essays in Honor of David A. Freedman,* IMS Collections, Vol. 2, 90–113, ed. Deborah Nolan and Terry Speed. Beachwood, Ohio: Institute of Mathematical Statistics, 2008.

Chandra Sekar, C., and W. Edwards Deming. "On a Method of Estimating Birth and Death Rates and the Extent of Registration." *Journal of the American Statistical Association* 44 (1949): 101–115.

Citro, Constance F., Daniel L. Cork , and Janet L. Norwood, eds. *The 2000 Census: Counting Under Adversity.* Washington, D.C.: Panel to Review the 2000 Census, Committee on National Statistics, National Research Council. Washington, D.C.: The National Academies Press, 2004. http://www.nap.edu/catalog.php?record_id=10907.

Cohen, Michael L., Andrew A. White, and Keith F. Rust. *Measuring a Changing Nation: Modern Methods for the 2000 Census.* Washington, D.C.: The National Academies Press, 1999. http://www.nap.edu/catalog.php?record_id=6500.

Cowen, Charles D., and Donald Malec. "Capture-Recapture Models When Both Sources Have Clustered Observations." *Journal of the American Statistical Association* 81 (1986): 347–353.

Darroch, John N., Stephen E. Fienberg, Gary F. V. Glonek, and Brian W. Junker. "A Three-Sample Multiple-Recapture Approach to Census Population Estimation With Heterogeneous Catchability." *Journal of the American Statistical Association* 88 (1993): 1137–1148.

Ericksen, Eugene P., and Teresa K. DeFonso. "Beyond the Net Undercount: How to Measure Census Error." *Chance* 6 (1993): 38–43.

Fay, Robert E. "Evaluation of Census Coverage from the 1980 Post Enumeration Program (PES): Census Population and Geocoding Errors as Measured by the E-Sample." In *1980 Preliminary Evaluation Results Memorandum,* no. 119. Washington, D.C.: U.S. Bureau of the Census, 1988.

Fay, Robert E., Jeffrey S. Passel, J. Gregory Robinson, and Charles D. Cowan. *The Coverage of the Population in the 1980 Census.* Washington, D.C.: U.S. Bureau of the Census, 1988.

Fienberg, Stephen E. "The Multiple-Recapture Census for Closed Populations and the 2k Incomplete Contingency Table." *Biometrika* 59 (1972): 591–603.

———. "Bibliography on Capture-Recapture Modeling with Application to Census Undercount Adjustment." *Survey Methodology* 18 (1992): 143–154.

Fienberg, Stephen E., Matthew S. Johnson, and Brian W. Junker. "Classical Multilevel and Bayesian Approaches to Population Size Estimation Using Multiple Lists." *Journal of the Royal Statistical Society A* 162, part 3 (1999): 383–405.

Freedman, David A., and Kenneth W. Wachter. (2003). "On the Likelihood of" Improving the Accuracy of the Census Through Statistical Adjustment. In *Science and Statistics. A Festschrift for Terry Speed,* IMS

Lecture Notes, Vol. 40, ed. Darlene R. Goldstein, 197–230. Beachwood, Ohio: Institute of Mathematical Statistics, 2003.

Gersh, Mark, and Ken Strasma. *1990 Census Undercount by Congressional District.* Washington, D.C.: National Committee for an Effective Congress, 1999.

Hogan, Howard. "The 1990 Post-Enumeration Survey: Operations and Results." *Journal of the American Statistical Association* 88 (1993): 1047–1060.

Hogan, Howard, and Kirk M. Wolter. "Measuring Accuracy in a Post-Enumeration Survey." *Survey Methodology* 14 (1988): 99–116.

Jaro, Matthew. "Advances in Record-Linkage Methodology as Applied to Matching the 1985 Test Census of Tampa, Florida." *Journal of the American Statistical Association* 84 (1989): 414–420.

Kadane, Joseph B., Michael M. Meyer, and John W. Tukey. "Yule's Association Paradox and Stratum Heterogeneity in Capture-Recapture Studies." *Journal of the American Statistical Association* 94 (1999): 855–859.

Kamen, Charles S. *The 2008 Israel Integrated Census of Population and Housing: Basic Conception and Procedure.* Jerusalem, Israel: Central Bureau of Statistics, 2005.

Krotki, Karol J., ed. *Developments in Dual System Estimation of Population Size and Growth.* Edmonton, Canada: University of Alberta Press, 1978.

Lum, Kristian, Megan Price, Tamy Guberek, and Patrick Ball. "Measuring Elusive Populations with Bayesian Model Averaging for Multiple Systems Estimation: A Case Study on Lethal Violations in Casanare, 1998–2007." *Statistics, Politics, and Policy* 1, no. 1 (2010): article 2. doi: 10.2202/2151–7509.1005.

Manrique-Vallier, Daniel, and Stephen E. Fienberg. "Population Size Estimation Using Individual Level Mixture Models." *Biometrical Journal* 50 (2008): 1–13.

Mulry, Mary H., and Bruce D. Spencer. "Accuracy of the 1990 Census and Undercount Adjustments." *Journal of the American Statistical Association* 88 (1993): 1080–1092.

Nascimento Silva, Pedro Luis do. "Reporting and Compensating for Non-Sampling Errors for Surveys in Brazil: Current Practice and Future Challenges." Chap. XI in *Household Sample Surveys in Developing and Transition Countries.* Department of Economic and Social Affairs, Statistics Division, Studies in Methods Series F No. 96. New York: United Nations, 2005. http://unstats.un.org/unsd/hhsurveys/pdf/Chapter_11.pdf.

Schenker, Nathaniel. "Handling Missing Data in Coverage Estimation with Application to the 1986 Test of Adjustment Related Operations." *Survey Methodology* 14 (1988): 87–98.

Seuss, Dr. [Theodore Geisel] *One Fish Two Fish Red Fish Blue Fish.* New York: Random House, 1960.

United Nations Statistics Division. *Post Enumeration Surveys Operational Guidelines: Technical Report.* New York: Department of Economic and Social Affairs, Statistics Division, United Nations, 2010. http://unstats.un.org/unsd/demographic/standmeth/handbooks/Manual_PESen.pdf.

Wachter, Kenneth "The Future of Census Coverage Surveys." In *Probability and Statistics: Essays in Honor of David A. Freedman,* IMS Collections, Vol. 2, 234–245, ed. Deborah Nolan and Terry Speed. Beachwood, Ohio: Institute of Mathematical Statistics, 2008.

Wolter, Kirt M. "Some Coverage Error Models for Census Data." *Journal of the American Statistical Association* 81 (1986): 338–346.

Zaslavsky, Alan M., and Glenn S. Wolfgang. "Triple-System Modeling of Census, Post-Enumeration Survey, and Administrative-List Data." In *1990 Proceedings of the Section on Survey Research.* Alexandria, Va.: American Statistical Association, 1990, 279–288.

Census Law

Census law, or the law pertaining to the decennial census of population, is grounded in the U.S. Constitution. The constitutional mandate to take a census every ten years is implemented by various acts of Congress that direct the manner of its conduct and the information to be collected.

The Constitution

The decennial census is the foundation on which our democratic system of government is built. The founding fathers realized that critical to the success of their efforts to create a new form of government was the development of processes for allocating political power among the states and for raising sufficient funds to support the federal government. Solutions to both representation and funding were reached through compromise.

The allocation of political power among the states was a particularly sensitive issue. The smaller states were concerned they would be dominated by the larger, faster-growing states. This led to the Great Compromise: The legislature would have two houses. In the House of Representatives, representation would be based on the size of a state's population, thereby protecting the interests of the larger states. In the Senate, each state would have two representatives, regardless of population size, thereby protecting the rights of the smaller states.

Given the differences among the states in population size, landmass, and natural and economic resources, a procedure was needed to determine each state's financial contribution to the federal government. The Framers of the Constitution quickly discovered that ability to contribute, or wealth, was an elusive concept. They were able to agree on neither the elements constituting wealth nor the manner of evaluating those elements. Eventually they decided to use population size as a proxy for wealth. This did not resolve the problem, however, because the southern states insisted that slaves be included for purposes of representation. Again, a compromise was reached by agreeing to include three-fifths of the slave population. Thereafter, direct taxes (taxes on land and buildings primarily) were imposed in proportion to each state's population.

Having agreed on population as the basis for a state's political representation and its financial support of the federal government, the next challenge for the Framers was to agree on a means for determining the size of a state's population. After extensive debate, the Framers decided that a census of population should be taken every ten years (Article 1, section 2, clause 3).

By basing both representation and funding on the size of a state's population, the Framers created a disincentive for states to inflate their census counts. Although a state would want its population count to be high for purposes of apportionment, the opposite would be true for determining the amount of its contribution through direct taxation by the federal government.

With the abolition of slavery and the adoption of the Fourteenth Amendment, the language requiring that each slave would be counted as only 3/5ths of a person was deleted. The adoption of the Sixteenth Amendment, providing for a personal income tax as a means of funding the federal government, resulted in two significant changes for the census. First, the size of a state's population would not affect the amount of its contribution through direct taxation by the federal government, thereby removing the disincentive against attempts to inflate a state's population count. Second, all residents, including Indians who formerly were not taxed, were to be counted.

Early Acts of Congress: Census Laws of 1790 to 1870

Since the first census, in 1790, Congress has passed laws directing how and by whom the census shall be taken. The first census law, the Act of March 1, 1790 (1 Stat. 101), set the tone and the parameters for censuses to follow. It established the residence rules (a person is to be counted where he or she usually resides), collected information beyond that needed to apportion the House, and made participation in the census mandatory.

Under the 1790 census law the information collected was limited in scope, asking for only the name of the head of the household, the numbers of free white males 16 and up and those under 16, and the numbers of white females, all other free persons, and slaves. Indians not taxed were excluded. At the outset the census was used to collect information beyond that necessary to apportion the House. It was conducted by U.S. marshals and their assistants, under the direction of the secretary of state, Thomas Jefferson.

Persons were to be counted where they usually resided, those without a "settled place of residence" were to be counted where they resided on census day, and those "occasionally absent at the time of the enumeration" were to be counted as residing in their place of usual residence. This procedure for designating residence, essential to meeting the constitutional purpose of apportioning the House, has been carried forward to the present day, with minor revisions to reflect changes in living patterns.

Participation in the census was required. The law directed that every person over age 16 years, whether or not the head of a family, must provide the information to the best of his or her knowledge, "on pain of forfeiting twenty dollars." Participation in the census continues to be mandatory to this day.

Subsequent early census laws expanded the scope of inquiries on a gradual basis and made moderate adjustments to the procedures for conducting the census. The 1800 census law, the Act of February 28, 1800 (2 Stat. 11), called for a breakdown of free white males and free white females into five age groups. The statute also specified that the census was to include the "territory of the United States northwest of the river Ohio, and of the Mississippi territory." Of particular interest to those concerned with privacy and confidentiality was the requirement that the marshals' assistants post a copy of census information, by name of family, "at two of the most public places within [the district], there to remain for the inspection of all concerned."

The 1810 census law, the Act of March 26, 1810 (2 Stat. 564), continued along the same lines as the 1800 census with the additional requirement that a personal visit be made to each dwelling. This requirement continued until the 1970 census.

The 1820 census law, the Act of March 14, 1820 (3 Stat. 548), extended the age breakdown to slaves and "free coloured persons" and required the designation of "persons in agriculture, commerce, and manufactures" and enumeration of "foreigners not naturalized."

The 1830 census law, the Act of March 23, 1830 (4 Stat. 383), called for a more extensive age breakdown and for data on persons who were "deaf and dumb" and those who were blind.

The 1840 census law, the Act of March 3, 1839 (5 Stat. 331), in addition to requiring information about those who were "deaf and dumb" and those who were blind, required information on those who were "insane and idiots," distinguishing those who were public charges. It also required information on those who were receiving pensions for Revolutionary or military service. Further, information was to be collected "in relation to mines, agriculture, commerce, manufactures, and schools, as will exhibit a full view of the pursuits of industry, education and resources of the country."

The 1850, 1860, and 1870 censuses were all taken under the same law, the Act of May 23, 1850 (9 Stat. 428). This law moved the responsibility for conducting the census from the secretary of state to the secretary of the interior. The draft questionnaires were appended to the census law, but the secretary of the interior gained discretion to change and edit the forms. The 1860 and 1870 schedules included changes, most dramatically the elimination of the "slave schedule" in 1870 after the Civil War. Although participation continued to be mandatory and a personal visit to each dwelling was required, posting of the census information was not required. Instead the marshals' assistants were required to provide the original census returns to the clerk of the county court and two copies were to be sent to the marshal.

The Era of Information Expansion: Census Laws of 1880 to 1920

A new law was passed for the 1880 census, the Act of March 3, 1879 (20 Stat. 473), which increased exponentially the number and kinds of questions asked, most notably in areas focusing on the nation's economy. The 1850 census had included 15 subjects of inquiry and 138 questions seeking specific details. This scope held, with minor changes, for the 1860 and 1870 censuses. In contrast, the 1880 census included 23 subjects of inquiry and 13,010 questions seeking specific details under the various subjects. Most of these questions were inquiries about particular industries and were contained on separate census forms (for example, there were 5,779 inquiries about the insurance industry alone). Even so, more than 250 questions were inquiries about individuals or the institutions dealing with them.

Not only was the scope of the census expanded to encyclopedic proportions, but also the structure for conducting the census was changed radically. A census office was established in the Department of the Interior, to be headed by the superintendent of the census, who would be appointed by the president with the advice and consent of the Senate. The secretary of the interior was to appoint supervisors of the census within each state and territory. The supervisors were to employ enumerators "without reference to their political or party affiliations."

The 1880 census also introduced the first steps in ensuring the confidentiality of the respondents' information. The enumerator was required to take an oath that he would "not disclose any information . . . obtained by me to any person or persons, except to my superior officers." The law also provided a penalty for improper disclosure, making it a misdemeanor with a fine up to $500. These protections were limited, however, as reflected in the requirements of a subsequent modification, the Act of April 20, 1880 (25 Stat. 760), directing the enumerators to file a list of names (with age, sex, and color of all persons enumerated by him) with the county and to correct the enumeration "on such reliable information as he may obtain, all omissions and mistakes in such enumeration, and to that end he may swear and examine witnesses."

A personal visit to each dwelling was required, but for the first time authority was given to collect what has come to be known as last-resort information. If no one could be found at home, the enumerator could obtain the required information from neighbors.

The same scope and process pertained, for the most part, to the 1890 census law, the Act of March 1, 1889 (25 Stat. 760). A total of 13,161 separate inquiries were made, more than 400 of which sought information about individuals or the institutions dealing with them. Again, many of these inquiries were on separate census forms. The issue of privacy was again affected by a provision expressly authorizing the superintendent of the census to furnish incorporated municipalities, cities, towns, villages, and the like with a copy of the names (with age, sex, birthplace, and color or race) of all persons within these jurisdictions.

The 1900 census law, the Act of March 3, 1899 (30 Stat. 1014), called for a census office in the Department of the Interior but explicitly stated that it should not be considered as providing for a permanent census bureau. The director of the census was given "discretion as to the construction, and form and number of inquiries necessary to secure the information." Confidentiality was again qualified by further expanding the availability of the data. The law authorized release to the governors of the states and territories, as well as to municipal governments, of the names (with age, sex, color or race, and birthplace) of all persons within these jurisdictions.

The Act of March 6, 1902 (32 Stat. 51) established a permanent Census Office, which continued to be located temporarily in the Department of the Interior. The bureau moved to the Department of Commerce and Labor in 1903, and it remained in the Department of Commerce when Commerce and Labor were separated into two separate departments by the Act of March 4, 1913 (37 Stat. 736).

The Era of Methodological Innovation: Census Laws of 1930 to the Present

The 1930 census law, the Act of June 18, 1929 (46 Stat. 21), formed the basis for what was codified on August 31, 1954, as Title 13 of the U.S. Code, the Census Act (68 Stat. 1012). Although it ushered in what might be considered the modern era, the 1930 census law continued many of the provisions contained in earlier authorizing legislation. A personal visit to each dwelling was required, and the enumerators still had the authority to seek last-resort information. Participation was mandatory. Any enumerator who disclosed census information without authority from the director was subject to fines and imprisonment.

A major innovation came with the provision for confidentiality. Under previous statutes, only economic data were protected by a provision directing that the data be used solely for statistical purposes, prohibiting publication that would permit identification of data provided by a particular respondent, and permitting only sworn employees of the Census Office to examine the individual reports. This protection was now extended to all information collected under the census law. Complete protection was not afforded, however, because the provision authorizing release to governors of states and territories and courts of record, as well as to individuals for "genealogical and other proper purposes," remained in effect. This apparent gap was corrected in a 1976 amendment (P.L. 94–521) that eliminated the authority to provide data to governors and courts of record and permitted release to individuals only if the requested data were their own or were requested by their authorized agent or in connection with their estate. Census confidentiality was upheld by the Supreme Court in *Baldrige v. Shapiro,* 455 U.S. 345 (1982).

As survey research methodology has developed in the past half century, Congress has periodically authorized changes in the law to facilitate innovation. In 1964 Congress eliminated the requirement that the enumerators personally visit each dwelling (P.L. 88–530). This law permitted the first mailout/mailback census in 1970. Essential to the mailout/mailback procedure was development of a complete and correct address list. The Census Bureau works closely with the U.S. Postal Service to ensure that every reasonable effort is made to include all addresses in the country. For Census 2000 another improvement was added authorizing the Census Bureau to furnish state and local governments with a copy of the census address list and the opportunity to revise it (P.L. 103–430) through the Local Update of Census Addresses (LUCA) program. The state and local government officials participating in this program are prohibited from using the information for any other purpose and are sworn to uphold census confidentiality. In 2002 Congress passed the Confidential Information Protection and Statistical Efficiency Act (CIPSEA) (P.L. 107–347) to permit data sharing among the Census Bureau, the Bureau of Economic Analysis, and the Bureau of Labor Statistics while protecting data confidentiality. To date, that law has had its primary impact on the development of economic statistics.

Arguably, the most important innovation of the modern era is the authorization to use sampling in collecting census data. In sampling, only a portion of the total universe of respondents (for the census, the universe is all persons residing in the country) is queried. Information obtained from this portion (a systematic random sample) is used to make an estimate for the total universe. In 1957, Congress gave discretionary authority to the secretary of commerce to use sampling, if deemed appropriate, "except for the determination of population for apportionment purposes" (P.L. 85–207). This provision, codified as Sect. 195 of Title 13, U.S. Code, was amended by Congress in 1976 (P.L. 94–521) to require the secretary to use sampling, if deemed feasible, with the caveat remaining that it could not be used for apportionment of the House. The Supreme Court held in *Department of Commerce v. House of Representatives,* 119 S.Ct. 765 (1999), that Sect. 195 precluded the use of sampling for apportionment of the House. Regardless of the limitation imposed by Sect. 195, sampling has permitted the Census Bureau to greatly reduce the burden placed on respondents in completing the census. In Census 2000 the vast majority of households (approximately five in six) received the short form, which asked for only very basic information. Most of the demographic data collected in the census was asked on a sample basis using the long form. In the 2000s the Census Bureau replaced the long form portion of the decennial count with a continuous measurement sample survey, the American Community Survey. The 2010 census was a "short form"-only census.

See also *Confidentiality; Litigation and the census; Three-fifths compromise.*

J . PATRICK HEELEN
. . . . .REVISED BY MARGO J. ANDERSON

BIBLIOGRAPHY
Bowen, Catherine Drinker. *Miracle at Philadelphia.* Boston: Little, Brown, 1966.
Farrand, Max, ed. *The Records of the Federal Convention of 1787.* New Haven, Conn.: Yale University Press, 1966.
Killian, Johnny H., ed., and Leland E. Beck, assoc. ed. *The Constitution of the United States of America. Analysis and Interpretation.* Washington, D.C.: U.S. Government Printing Office, 1987.
Rossiter, Clinton, ed. *The Federalist Papers.* New York: New American Library, 1961.
Wright, Carroll D. *The History and Growth of the United States Census.* Prepared for the Senate Committee on the Census. Washington, D.C.: Government Printing Office, 1900.

Census of Puerto Rico

The 2010 census marked the 100th anniversary of decennial census taking in Puerto Rico by the Census Bureau. Although a special census was conducted by the U.S. War Department in November 1899—one year after the island's acquisition from Spain following the Spanish-American War—it was not until the 1910 census that Puerto Rico was fully represented as a census area of the United States for the decennial censuses. Many counts and censuses of the island were taken in the previous 400 years under the auspices of the Spanish crown, but they were not taken with the same decennial regularity. The 2010 census reported a population of 3.7 million, a 2.2 percent decrease from 2000 and the first recorded decline in the island's population since the bureau began enumerating Puerto Rico a century ago.

Since the 1910 census, and particularly during the past half century, Puerto Rico has become increasingly integrated into the bureau's statistical and geographic operations and products. Recent decennial census programs and related operations in Puerto Rico, including the new Puerto Rico Community Survey, generally have followed the same set of procedures as in the 50 states and the District of Columbia. Without regard to a person's legal immigration status or citizenship, the bureau counts all people whose usual place of residence is in Puerto Rico.

Similar to the District of Columbia and the noncontiguous territories of the United States, and in accordance with Title 13 of the U.S. Code, Puerto Rico is treated *de facto* as a state equivalent for statistical purposes. Unlike with the District of Columbia, however, Puerto Rico's population is not officially recognized by Congress as part of the total U.S. resident population. Different from other nonstate island areas, such as Guam and the U.S. Virgin Islands, but similar to the 50 states and the District of Columbia, the bureau conducts all aspects of the census in Puerto Rico. The 1958 Memorandum of Understanding (MOU), and its ongoing amendments, between the bureau and the government of the Commonwealth of Puerto Rico ensure close coordination and collaboration in the planning, conduct, and promotion of the Puerto Rico censuses.

The primary differences between census operations, activities, and products in Puerto Rico and the states have resulted from many factors, such as its unique political status, social and economic planning needs, Spanish language and culture, geographic issues, and addressing system. Although the most apparent differences are language, culture, and political status, the primary technical obstacles to greater consistency with stateside programs and products during the past few censuses have been Puerto Rico's unique addressing system and its special data content needs. Clarification and simplification of its geographic entities for the 1990 census, adoption of the stateside questionnaire for the first time in Census 2000, and establishment of the Puerto Rico Community Survey have made the addressing situation *the* primary technical challenge to full integration with stateside programs and processes.

Puerto Rico Community Survey

One of the major changes in census taking for 2010 was the replacement of the census long-form sample with the American Community Survey (ACS), which, for Puerto Rico, is called the Puerto Rico Community Survey (PRCS). In essence, the PRCS provides communities with reliable demographic, housing, social, and economic data on an annual basis versus the traditional ten-year snapshots from the decennial census. Detailed information on the PRCS and its impact on the data user community are well documented in other articles within this encyclopedia. Effective utilization of this new source of intercensal data for Puerto Rico will require an understanding of the PRCS in general, sampling and statistical issues particularly for smaller geographic areas, and the hierarchy of legal/statistical entities in Puerto Rico.

Data Content

Puerto Rico's unique status historically has caused the bureau to treat data content somewhat differently from its treatment in the states. Although census questionnaires used for previous decennial censuses generally have followed the stateside version (both the short and long forms), the bureau made some modifications to accommodate socioeconomic, cultural, language, and climatic differences according to provisions of the 1958 MOU between the commonwealth and the bureau. For Census 2000, the governor's office requested that the Census Bureau use the stateside questionnaire in Puerto Rico (albeit primarily printed and conducted in Spanish and with minor differences in terminology), and the same protocols continued for the 2010 census, including the new ACS questionnaire. Standardizing the questionnaire facilitates data processing and ensures greater consistency with stateside data delivery schedules and data products.

The adoption of the stateside decennial and ACS questionnaires is one of the more significant differences between earlier and more recent censuses that will affect data users and policymakers. All changes made for the stateside census questionnaire for the 2010 census also applied to Puerto Rico. Major differences in data comparability resulted from different questionnaires used by Puerto Rico for the 1990 and previous censuses. One of the most interesting changes resulting from the alignment of the questionnaires for the past two censuses concerns the use of Hispanic origin and race questions. The race question had not been asked since the 1950 census, when it was based on enumerator assignment rather than self-identification.

Enumeration Methodology

For the past several censuses, data-collection and data-processing methodologies in Puerto Rico generally have been much more labor intensive than their counterparts in the states. Although Puerto Rico contains metropolitan areas and urbanized areas with greater population densities than most similar areas stateside, the bureau continues to enumerate the island's population using canvassing methodologies that apply to only very sparsely settled areas in the states, where mail delivery typically does not use house numbers and street names.

The primary reason for the use of data collection methodologies associated with sparsely settled areas in the United States is the existence of a street-naming and addressing system in Puerto Rico that is not compatible with Census Bureau address-matching requirements and current capabilities. For example, the U.S. Postal Service's addressing standards for Puerto Rico require an additional address line not used stateside to distinguish addresses with the same house number and street name in the same ZIP code. Other characteristics of the street-naming and addressing system in Puerto Rico that require special handling and additional computer-programming resources include variant street-naming and addressing conventions. As a result of these and other situations, data collection has been more costly and, owing to the nature of highly labor-intensive operations, potentially more error prone than the mailout/mailback methodologies used in the states.

The 1990 and previous censuses used a list/enumerate methodology, where all housing units received an unaddressed short-form census questionnaire from the U.S. Postal Service (USPS). The 1990 census address list for Puerto Rico, called the Address Control File, was created at the time of enumeration. Census enumerators visited all housing units, listed their addresses in registers and marked their approximate location, and added missing streets and street names to Bureau of the Census maps. This served to geographically code each address to its census block, the basic unit for all decennial census data tabulations. They completed questionnaires for vacant housing units and interviewed respondents if the questionnaires were not complete. For one of every six housing units, enumerators were responsible for completing a long-form questionnaire.

Census 2000 and the 2010 census used an Update/Leave methodology, whereby an addressed questionnaire is left at a housing unit by a census enumerator. The questionnaire was filled out by any adult household member and mailed to the local office of the Census Bureau. Nonresponding housing units, including those that were vacant, were visited and enumerated by census enumerators. Self-response, enabled by the new Update/Leave data collection methodology, has been shown by census studies stateside to yield higher-quality data than those obtained through enumerator interviews.

Using an Update/Leave operation for the 2010 census required the bureau to develop an address list prior to questionnaire delivery. An island-wide address-listing operation was conducted in 2009 to add and delete addresses from Census 2000 operations to generate the 2010 census address list, called the Master Address File (MAF). Coverage, currency, and data quality of the MAF are critical for all census operations and used to design the sampling frame for all census demographic surveys and the PRCS. Following the address-listing operation, the MAF was used to control questionnaire delivery and return, and the Census Bureau's Topologically Integrated Geographic Encoding and Referencing (TIGER) database was used to generate maps with housing unit locations for follow-up operations. Linkage between the locations for all housing units in the MAF and TIGER for Puerto Rico enabled internal census staff to more easily check and review potential address-listing problems.

A major advance for the 2010 census in Puerto Rico, similar to stateside operations, was the adoption of advanced location-based technology to collect the latitude/longitude coordinates of all housing unit locations. Field listers used handheld units that were global positioning system (GPS) enabled to view census maps and annotate the address and "front door" location of every housing unit. Owing to several issues, not all housing unit locations could be captured with GPS by the handheld devices, so some map spot locations were manually entered. This advance enabled improved data quality and follow-up operations. Similar to the policy in the states, this address information is not publicly available, because of Title 13 restrictions.

Address canvassing in Puerto Rico had slightly different procedures than those of the 50 states and the District of Columbia. In the states the lister was encouraged to find the address of the living quarters by observation, with speaking to a member of the household as a last resort. In Puerto Rico the lister was encouraged to find the address by speaking to someone in the household, with observation being a last resort.

Unlike areas in the United States that have mail delivery to city-style addresses, the MAF for Puerto Rico was created with less input from postal or local sources After the 2000 census, the Census Bureau entered into a contract with a private firm, the only nongovernmental entity with access to Title 13 data, to help fix address-listing processing errors from 2000 decennial operations in Puerto Rico and ensure the MAF could support more automated address processing for the PRCS and the 2010 census operations. Census field listers played a major role in updating and correcting the MAF during the Update/Leave operation. Unlike in the states, the bureau did not use the USPS's Delivery Sequence File of city-style addresses, because of quality and coverage limitations and the inability of the bureau's address-matching software to deal with Puerto Rico's unique addressing conventions. As such, the creation and quality of the MAF were dependent on accurate listings and map updates by field staff. Although not specifically covered by Public Law 103–430, under the Census Address List Improvement Act (1994), which enables address list sharing between the bureau and local governments, all *municipio* (county equivalent) governments were invited to check the census address list and related maps to ensure coverage and quality; 35 of the 78 *municipios* chose to participate in this process. The delivery of census questionnaires by census enumerators provided an additional opportunity to enhance the MAF and the TIGER databases.

It is well known that for a variety of reasons, large, labor-intensive clerical operations, in themselves, can lead to higher error rates than more automated operations. In Puerto Rico this problem is compounded by language difficulties. Although supervisory and field staff in Puerto Rico are required to be Spanish speaking, the information acquired in both map update and address-listing operations is transcribed and entered into computers in large, labor-intensive operations by staff that may know little, if any, Spanish or may not be cognizant of the unique aspects of census geography or postal addressing in Puerto Rico.

Geography

The bureau reports data by legal/administrative and statistical geographic entities. Legal/administrative entities include the commonwealth (state equivalent), *municipio,* barrio/barrio-pueblo (minor civil division equivalent), and subbarrio (no statistical equivalent stateside). Statistical areas are, for the most part, similar and conform to the same technical criteria as their stateside counterparts. *Zonas urbanas* and *comunidades* are census-designated places that are unique to Puerto Rico, which does not have legally incorporated places.

Puerto Rico's current legal/administrative geography is the result of historical factors and legal actions taken by the commonwealth legislature, whereas statistical geography is the result, in most cases, of interaction between the Census Bureau and the Puerto Rico Planning Board. Prior to both the 1980 and 1990 censuses, there was some confusion in understanding Puerto Rico's legal and statistical entities. This situation, which led to actual errors in the 1970 data tabulations for barrios, derived from several factors, such as alternative use of terms to define similar entities, use of same names to identify different entities, errors in original delineation or description of boundaries, and translations between English and Spanish. Understanding the unique legal/administrative and statistical entities in Puerto Rico remains a critical issue for census operations and data users.

Perhaps no other situation better dramatizes Puerto Rico's situation between two worlds and between past and present than the barrio geography. Barrios maintain a political and cultural function, but they have no planning or economic function. The growing availability and use of data by ZIP code, census tract, block group, and block, and the unfamiliarity of urban Puerto Ricans with the sub-*municipio* barrio nomenclature, have led to several statistical and data collection concerns. In a growing number of cases the original barrio boundaries no longer separate communities. Barrio boundaries often do not follow visible features, and the same name may exist for barrios in adjacent *municipios*. Unlike *municipios,* they are often not identified by signs or even known by residents of the barrio. This situation is especially acute where there has been new suburban growth at the barrio boundary, where residents are recent arrivals, or where residents live in *urbanizaciones* (named housing developments).

Data Products

Prior to 2000 most data products offered to the 50 states and the District of Columbia also were available for Puerto Rico, including redistricting data files (although Puerto Rico is not covered by Public Law 94–171). However, data for Puerto Rico generally were not included in the nationwide products or summaries and, because of the addressing situation discussed earlier, some stateside data products (for example, the 1990 Summary Tape File 3B, which contains ZIP code–level data) were not available for Puerto Rico. In 2000, however, Puerto Rico was treated as a state equivalent and included in all data products for which data were available, both electronic and hard copy; and the same is true for 2010. Moreover, Puerto Rico is fully integrated into most of the bureau's geographic data products. The only notable difference in products is related to the address limitations in the bureau's geographic files for Puerto Rico. As such, the Census Tract/Street Index and similar address-related products have not been available for Puerto Rico, and the TIGER/Line files do not have the same level and quality of attribute coding as stateside files with city-style addressing.

It is important that data users thoroughly acquaint themselves with the unique aspects of the geography of Puerto Rico before making use of the data. Of special concern is an understanding of the hierarchy of geographic designations, including *municipio, ciudad* (in census products prior to 1990), *zona urbana,* urbanized area, and metropolitan area. For example, data for San Juan can be referenced under all these headings, with each referring to a different geographic area.

Looking toward the Future

Data from the 2010 census of Puerto Rico, including the PRCS, appear in all stateside census products and online through the census Web site. Online access for data from Puerto Rico includes user-requested Spanish interfaces. This represents a change from 1990 and earlier censuses, when separate machine-readable and printed products were created for Puerto Rico and the outlying areas.

In an effort to achieve a more robust integration of Puerto Rico with stateside decennial census programs, operations, and products, problems arising from Puerto Rico's unique addressing conventions will be tackled and resolved through ongoing public and private partnerships begun during the 1990s. The enhancement and standardization of addressing by the USPS and *municipio* officials will be accompanied by the development of a continually updated and enhanced MAF through cooperative efforts between the postal service, the bureau, the Puerto Rico Planning Board, the *municipio* governments, the island's emergency-911 program, and other public and private partners. Greater usage of signs on roads for legal boundaries by the commonwealth and *municipio* governments also will enhance the bureau's data collection efforts and resultant data quality as well as meet many local planning needs.

These developments, and a corresponding enhancement of the bureau's Master Address File and address-matching capability to handle Puerto Rico's unique addressing conventions, will make it easier to conduct the PRCS and other Census Bureau programs. The PRCS provides demographic and economic data products annually for geographic areas as small as the census block group. Enhancing the MAF and the TIGER database also will enable Puerto Rico to participate fully in all future plans, procedures, and technology-based solutions implemented in the states.

The census of Puerto Rico serves many uses. It is essential for the redistricting of Puerto Rico's legislature and the distribution of billions of dollars in federal grants for social and economic programs. The census is the primary source of long-term reliable data for the government, business, and academic community. The 2010 census of Puerto Rico also offers the nation a statistical portrait of the commonwealth at the end of 110 years as a U.S. territory, after 100 years of census taking by the Census Bureau, and at the birth of a new millennium. Regardless of whether Puerto Rico becomes the 51st or 52nd state, acquires independence, retains its current status, or chooses another unique relationship with the United States, the results of the 2010 census and the ongoing PRCS will help to evaluate and forge new strategies to better meet the needs of the people of Puerto Rico.

See also *American Community Survey: methodology; American Community Survey: data products.*

. . . . JONATHAN SPERLING

BIBLIOGRAPHY

Sperling, Jonathan. "Census Geography in Puerto Rico: A Technical Addendum to the 1990 Census." *Caribbean Studies* 23 (Fall 1990): 111–130.

U.S. Bureau of the Census. "Puerto Rico, Virgin Islands, and the Pacific Island Territories." In *1990 Census of Population and Housing History.* Washington, D.C.: U.S. Government Printing Office, 1996.

U.S. Census Bureau. *A Compass for Understanding and Using American Community Survey Data: What Puerto Rico Community Survey Data Users Need to Know.* Washington, D.C.: U.S. Government Printing Office, 2009.

Census Testing

The 1910 census—eight years after the formation of the permanent Bureau of the Census—included what might be considered the first major experiment or test conducted in tandem with a decennial count, through the distribution of informational "advance schedules" by enumerators in cities with populations over 100,000. Not yet intended as a means for self-response to the census, the 1910 advance schedules were an attempt to see whether the distribution heightened awareness of the census and eased the eventual interview. The 1910 activity was followed in 1940 and, particularly, 1950 by fuller programs of testing and experimentation; since then, some program of testing has been part of the regular process of planning the decennial count.

Forms of Census Testing

As they have evolved over recent decades, census-testing activities have taken three basic forms:

- Every census since 1950 has included a suite of tests, experiments, and evaluations conducted during the census itself. Content tests have ranged from basic tests of alternative questionnaire wording or layout to (in the 2000 census) the fielding of the Census 2000 Supplementary Survey (C2SS) to assess the feasibility of conducting the census and what became the American Community Survey (ACS) at the same time.
- The Census Bureau has routinely held large-scale census tests—essentially, "test censuses" or operational trials—prior to the decennial census, usually including one or more dress rehearsals. These tests have varied as to whether they include actual fieldwork (for example, non-response follow-up) in a small number of sites or whether they use a national mail sample. In the testing cycle prior to 2010, the Census Bureau alternated between mail-only operational trials and test censuses including fieldwork in each of the years 2003 through 2006.
- Finally, the Census Bureau occasionally fields other tests during the decade that may focus on new techniques or

methodology but that are not conducted at the full-census scale. Occasionally, these have been tests directly mandated by Congress, such as a 2004 test on the feasibility of counting Americans residing overseas. In the earlier census testing cycles, the bureau was more prone to use other surveys or testing opportunities for such experimental work, including supplements to the Current Population Survey or bundling experimental procedures into off-year special censuses commissioned by localities. However, after a September 1976 pretest conducted as part of a special census in Camden, New Jersey, culminated in legal challenges and investigation, the bureau has largely refrained from testing methods in special censuses.

Profiles of Census Testing

Mailout/Mailback Methodology

Arguably, the most visible and tangible "success" arising directly from programs of census testing was the implementation of a census relying primarily on the mail. The fundamental shift from an enumerator-based, canvassing-type census to a primarily mailout/mailback census was a massive one in census methodology; it was also one with an extensive history of careful, preliminary testing. The earliest steps toward the eventual mail methodology date back to 1890, when a supplemental questionnaire on residential finance was mailed to households with a request for mail return; similar finance-based surveys were conducted by the Bureau of the Census in 1920 and 1950. Information on special populations in the census (including the blind and deaf) was collected through mail questionnaires in 1910, 1920, and 1930.

During the 1950 census, ten district offices in Ohio and Michigan were selected to participate in an experiment focusing primarily on the effect of enumerators on census response. In six of the districts, experiments included use of a household questionnaire rather than a person-level census "schedule" and use of self-enumeration (questionnaire completion by respondents) rather than enumerator interview. The results of this experiment—suggesting, in part, that the traditional, all-interview-based census was no more accurate than a 25 percent sample—gave strong impetus to continued investigation of a mail-based census, lessening the enumerator effect.

Additional pretesting continued during the buildup to the 1960 census, including a mailout-only test in Hartford City, Indiana, in November 1957 and fuller tests of both mailout and mailback data quality in Memphis, Tennessee, and Lynchburg, Virginia, in early 1958. Ultimately, the 1960 census settled on a strategy of mailing short-form questionnaires to residential households but asking respondents to hold on to them for the eventual enumerator visit. As tested in the 1960 census dress rehearsal (in two North Carolina counties in spring 1959), households that were given the long-form questionnaire by enumerators were asked to return them by mail to their local census office. The formal testing and experimentation program conducted during the 1960 census included a postal coverage improvement study to try to identify households missed from the initial mailing. It also included a three-phase Response Variance Study, which revisited the question of enumerator effects; that work suggested that the mailed questionnaires reduced the variability in the responses to levels about one-quarter of those observed in 1950 when enumerators collected the information.

The Bureau of the Census prepared for the 1970 census anticipating wider use of the mail, and it became authorized to conduct the first primarily mailout/mailback census when a requirement that enumerators personally visit every home was stricken from census law in 1964. In readying for 1970, the bureau conducted a series of escalating tests of the mailout/mailback, field-based nonresponse follow-up methodology between 1962 and 1967. The tests varied the type of areas covered (including small cities in Fort Smith, Arkansas, and Huntington, New York, in 1962 and 1963; big cities and dense housing structures in Cleveland and Detroit in 1965 and 1967; focused ethnic and linguistic communities in St. Louis Park, Minnesota, and Yonkers, New York, in 1966) and methodologies used to determine mailing address lists (for example, comparing complete address canvassing, knocking on every door, to knocking only when necessary or in instances of confusion, in the Wilmington, Delaware, area throughout 1966). The bureau also used a tiered set of dress rehearsals as a final check on competing designs: a last try at traditional nonmail techniques in two Wisconsin counties and two mail-based control strategies in Dane County, Wisconsin, and Trenton, New Jersey, varying in the degree to which questionnaire processing and nonresponse follow-up planning were performed by enumerators in local offices or by clerks in more centralized locations.

Based on the preliminary testing, the bureau set out to cover some 60 percent of the household population by mailout/mailback methods in the 1970 census. Research studies in the formal testing and evaluation program included a National Edit Sample to compare data content in mailout/mailback and conventional enumeration areas; another response variance study to examine enumerator effects; and experimental work in ten district offices (in more rural areas) to study the effects of expanding mailout/mailback beyond the 1970 levels. Based on the various tests, the fraction of the population covered by mailout/mailback has grown in subsequent censuses.

Enumeration Strategies for Nonmail Areas

In recent decennial censuses, block-by-block designation of the nation into as many as nine types of enumeration areas (TEAs) has been used to define the initial approach that will be made with respondents in those areas. By far, the mailout/mailback TEAs are the most populous, concentrating on urban areas. But the other TEAs—in which enumerators still deliver questionnaires and may conduct interviews—continue to span the majority of the land area of the United States; these other TEAs have typically evolved from decades of testing.

Update/leave enumeration, in which enumerators may check and update address list entries during their visits but simply leave questionnaire packets for the respondents to complete and return by mail, was first tested in a significant way in one of the formal experiments of the 1980 census. Five local offices (Dayton, Ohio; northeast central Chicago; Yakima, Washington; Greenville, North Carolina; and Abilene, Texas) were designated to use update/leave, and were paired for comparative analysis with offices in nearby areas. The method received continued testing in 1986, particularly in a group of eight counties in central Mississippi, and it was retained for use in the 1990 censuses (and those that have followed). The 1988 dress rehearsal for the 1990 census—in particular, the part of the dress rehearsal conducted in the greater St. Louis area—expanded the toolkit, when pretest work suggested higher-than-expected levels of undeliverable addresses. For such areas, where mail delivery or the quality of the underlying address list was suspect, the bureau chose to test a variant approach dubbed *urban update/leave* as an alternative to mailout/mailback. The approach having worked favorably in the dress rehearsal, it was retained for use in the 1990 census and has endured as one of the TEAs.

Refining Residence Rules

An early "success" of rigorous census testing arose in planning for the 1950 census. Census practice since the 1880 census had favored counting college students at their parental homes, but the changing dynamics of the college population in the post-war years raised the question of the adequacy of this rule. Through two supplements to the Current Population Survey (in 1946 and 1948) and questions in at least one special census (Wilmington, North Carolina, in 1946), the Bureau of the Census concluded that college students enrolled at schools away from home were frequently omitted from their parents' household rosters. Accordingly, for the 1950 census the bureau reversed its residence rule for college students to count those students at their school location, a change that has continued to hold in every subsequent census.

Changing Census Technology

Another recurring theme in census testing has been preparation for and assessment of changes in the basic technology of conducting and tabulating the census. Although the 1950 census was tabulated in part by electronic computer, the 1960 census was the first in which the computer was an integral part of the process, and a series of tests led to the development of the Census Bureau's film optical sensing device for input to computers (FOSDIC) platform. Rather than keypunch all data, the bureau designed questionnaires for which most of the information could be recorded by filling in a circle; microfilmed versions of those questionnaires could be translated onto magnetic computer tape by FOSDIC equipment, developed by the National Bureau of Standards for the Census Bureau. Following their use in the 1960 census, FOSDIC techniques were tested for speed improvements; a test focused on the use of a motorized Plexiglas cover that held down the folds on the questionnaire and allowed the camera operator to have both hands free to move documents. Through this switch, the Census Bureau was able to double operator throughput. In testing for the 1970 census, the bureau also had to confront the challenge of designing census questionnaires that were both capable of FOSDIC processing and easy for census respondents to understand and complete on their own, and testing of alternate computer-readable questionnaires played into many of the preparatory tests.

During the 1980s the bureau continued to test automation of many of the data collection operations. A major innovation tested was optical mark recognition (OMR) as a data capture technique, which would convert responses on the questionnaire directly to digital data. Although the test results were favorable, OMR was not used in 1990; however, bar codes on questionnaires were scanned. Testing of OMR continued, and it was used in 2000, joined by optical character recognition (OCR), or automated parsing of alphanumeric characters by computers. OCR permitted—for the first-time and revolutionary (for census research purposes)—automated data capture of census respondents' full names.

As the bureau testing programs moved toward increased use of the mail in the 1960–1980 cycles, the bureau also necessarily began to test alternative strategies for developing address lists and for geocoding—associating addresses with specific geographic locations. Work on address coding in an April 1967 census test in the New Haven, Connecticut, area in turn led to development of the Dual Independent Map Encoding (DIME) approach for spatial databases, essentially starting the process of viewing geocoding as an exercise in topology, piecing together points, lines, and polygons with associated metadata. The DIME approach ultimately led to the development of Geographic Base Files (called GBF/DIME files) for the 1980 census, covering urban centers in most metropolitan areas. Further testing—and then pairing with electronic versions of U.S. Geological Survey topographical maps—contributed to the mid-1980s development of the nationally comprehensive Topologically Integrated Geographic Encoding and Referencing (TIGER) system. The bureau's development of TIGER is deservedly a highlight in the agency's history of technological innovation and spawned the modern geographic information systems industry.

Testing for 2010 and Beyond

To prepare for the 2010 census, the Census Bureau adopted the strategy of concentrating principally on a small number of large-scale tests, alternating in different years between mail-only "National Census Tests" sent to nationally representative samples and limited-site "Census Tests" that did include field enumerator work.

- National Census Tests: The 2003 mail-only test included a sample of about 250,000 households, with mixes of experimental treatments covering two main topics. First, the test varied response mode and contract strategies, trying different means to permit respondents to reply either by the Internet or by an automated telephone-based interactive voice response (IVR) system rather than the mail. Second, the test tried different wordings of the race and Hispanic origin questions; in particular, coming out of the first-time experience with multiple-race reporting in the 2000 census, the bureau

was concerned about the effects of the explicit inclusion of "some other race" as a category in the question on race. On that front, the test received attention from Congress: the Census Bureau's appropriations for fiscal year 2005 included a provision forbidding "the collection of census data on race identification that does not include 'some other race' as a category" (P.L. 110–161). Bound by that provision, the 2005 National Census Test considered other refinements of the race and Hispanic origin questions but focused its attention (in a sample of about 420,000 households) on alternative questionnaire layouts, including a bilingual English-Spanish questionnaire and several different layouts of the "Question 1" (household count) instructions and format.

- Census Tests: The 2004 Census Test was fielded in parts of Queens, New York, and in a four-county region in Georgia, while the 2006 Census Test was fielded in the Austin, Texas, area and the Cheyenne River Indian Reservation in South Dakota. Involving fieldwork, the tests are notable as the Census Bureau's first large-scale deployment of handheld computer devices, assembled by the bureau from commercial off-the-shelf components (in 2002, the bureau had done very limited pilot testing on reading TIGER maps on handheld devices in southeast Virginia). The 2004 test used the handhelds primarily for nonresponse follow-up interviewing; the 2006 test added map reading and updating capabilities. The tests contributed to the Census Bureau's final decision to use handhelds in 2010 and to award its Field Data Collection Automation (FDCA) contract.

- Dress Rehearsal: A final, large-scale census test was the 2008 dress rehearsal in San Joaquin County, California, and a nine-county region around Fayetteville, North Carolina. The pre-census address canvassing for the dress rehearsal, in spring 2007, was the first operational trial of the custom handheld computers developed under the FDCA program, and consequently it became the first exposure to problems with the handhelds' development that precipitated the 2010 census "replan" in the first half of 2008.

In addition to those scheduled tests, the Census Bureau conducted two other major tests prior to the 2010 census. At the urging of Congress, the bureau conducted an Overseas Enumeration Test in France, Kuwait, and Mexico, in July 2004. Although rough estimates suggested that on the order of 1.15 million American citizens might reside in the selected countries, the test generated very low response (5,390 questionnaires), suggesting that relying on advertisements in English-language media and asking Americans living overseas to contact an embassy or consular office to obtain the questionnaire "would not yield sufficient response". In early 2006 the Census Bureau mounted an ad hoc Short Form Mail Experiment covering about 24,000 households, testing revised wording about which household member should be listed as "Person 1" on the census form, an end-of-the-form reminder to try to make sure that the person completing the census form included himself or herself on the form, and slightly different mailing schedules and implied deadlines for response.

The 2010 Census Program of Evaluations and Experiments (CPEX), conducted during the census itself, included five formal experiments: an alternative questionnaire experiment with 19 experimental panels, 15 of which varied the wording, structure, or example set of the race and Hispanic origin questions; a nonresponse follow-up contact strategy test in which field enumerators were given questionnaires with space for only four or five contacts rather than the normal six; a deadline messaging and compressed schedule experiment in which advance letters, reminder postcards, and the census questionnaire mailing package itself included varied wording or suggested a deadline for response; a privacy notification experiment varying the advisory on the cover letter accompanying the questionnaire; and a "heavy-up" publicity experiment that steered additional media and promotional resources to selected markets.

Looking ahead to the 2020 census, the Census Bureau has expressed interest in avoiding the rigid schedule of large-scale tests that dominated the 2010 testing cycle, instead seeking out more continuous, small-scale testing throughout the decade.

See also *Address list development; American Community Survey: development to 2004; Data capture.*

. . . . DANIEL L. CORK

BIBLIOGRAPHY
Anderson, Margo J. *The American Census: A Social History.* New Haven, Conn.:Yale University Press, 1988.
National Research Council. Panel on Research on Future Census Methods. *Reengineering the 2010 Census: Risks and Challenges.* Daniel L. Cork, Michael L. Cohen, and Benjamin F. King, eds. Committee on National Statistics, Division of Behavioral and Social Sciences and Education. Washington, D.C.: The National Academies Press, 2004. Available at http://www.nap.edu/catalog.php?record_id=10959.
————. *Envisioning the 2020 Census.* Panel on the Design of the 2010 Census Program of Evaluations and Experiments. Lawrence D. Brown, Michael L. Cohen, Daniel L. Cork, and Constance F. Citro, eds. Committee on National Statistics, Division of Behavioral and Social Sciences and Education. Washington, D.C.: The National Academies Press, 2010. Available at http://www.nap.edu/catalog.php?record_id=12826.
U.S. Bureau of the Census. *1960 Censuses of Population and Housing: Procedural History.* Washington, D.C.: General Printing Office, 1966.

Census Tracts

Census tracts are small geographic units delineated for the presentation and analysis of decennial census data. They are a form of statistical geography, as opposed to geography created exclusively for legal, political, or administrative purposes. Census tracts are intended to permit meaningful analyses of small areas over time and, as such, have relatively permanent boundaries.

Origins

The census tract concept was conceived by Walter Laidlaw in the first decade of the twentieth century. At that time many of the nation's cities were developing into major metropolitan areas, the result of huge immigrant flows. Social, religious, and government organizations were attempting to understand these changes and meet the needs of the burgeoning population. Laidlaw, an ordained Presbyterian minister, observed that little scientific knowledge existed about the neighborhoods of New York. Largely unaware of the changes occurring, the churches of the city were unable to take advantage of new opportunities. As director of the Population Research Bureau of the New York Federation of Churches, Laidlaw was sensitive to the dilemma faced by those attempting to gauge neighborhood change. In an article first published by the Federation of Churches and later summarized in the preface of the 1910 census tract report for New York, Laidlaw argued for a permanent geography not susceptible to the political manipulation of wards and assembly districts. He advocated a scientific map system, one capable of fitting addresses to new statistical areas that were small and similar in physical size with permanent boundaries that provided for comparisons from one census to another. For populated areas, tracts were set at approximately 40 acres, while for areas with little or no population, no acreage was specified and natural boundaries were used. For the Lower East Side of Manhattan, this translated into tracts that averaged about eight city blocks.

Laidlaw's efforts brought him to Washington, D.C., in 1907, where he persuaded the Bureau of the Census to include a code for census tracts on the punched cards that would be created for the 1910 census. Eight cities would have census tract codes for 1910, but local organizations would have to supply funds and labor for the actual compilation and presentation of data. Laidlaw worked closely with the bureau to compile data for New York City census tracts and presented these data as part of the 1910 census results. The New York State Census of 1915 and, retroactively, the New York State Census of 1905 were compiled using 1910 census tracts. In addition, the 1910 census tracts were adopted by the New York City Department of Health as "sanitary districts," in an effort to monitor public health.

With the support of the Tenement House Department of New York City and the New York City Department of Health, Laidlaw worked on refinements to his tract concept over the next decade. The result was designation of 3,427 census tracts that would be the foundation for the 1920 census, a big jump from the 705 census tracts drawn for 1910. In October 1919 the New York City Census Committee was formed to take over the work of the Population Research Bureau of the Federation of Churches. It consisted of a broad group of business, government, religious, and social welfare organizations, of which Laidlaw was the executive director. The group raised more than $65,000 for the compilation, tabulation, and publication of tract data for 1920. This volume grouped data for more than 3,400 census tracts into more than 1,600 neighborhoods because many census tracts at the time were still unpopulated.

The work of the New York City Census Committee was a prototype for things to come, so much so that the Cities Census Committee was formed in 1924. The two elements for what would later become the census tract program were falling into place: an interested local party and formal cooperation by the Bureau of the Census; however, the federal government still assumed no direct financial responsibility for the undertaking. Getting the bureau to acknowledge that these data were essential to the national interest and should be made a part of the decennial census collection and publication program was the task at hand. It is at this juncture, in the 1920s, that Howard Whipple Green's work complemented Laidlaw's earlier efforts.

Green, a statistician, recognized the need for data from small areas when he attempted to study the movement of the black population in Cleveland in 1924. After examining data for wards from the 1910 and 1920 censuses, he quickly realized that boundary changes made such work impossible to carry out. Green had also heard the laments of the Cleveland Health Council about problems posed by the absence of base data from which to calculate mortality and morbidity rates over time for neighborhoods. After visiting with Laidlaw, Green was convinced that census tracts were the key to the future of small-area data analysis. Unable to obtain enough funds from the Health Council, Green garnered the interest of the *Cleveland Plain Dealer,* based on the business potential of census tracts in describing the market to potential advertisers. With Green's help, Cleveland went on to obtain tabulations from the 1910 and 1920 censuses. The Cleveland Health Council efforts also enhanced the state of the art by providing data for areas outside of the city and by publishing a census tract street index. Word of the efforts in Cleveland spread, and other cities became interested in pursuing small-area data analysis. By 1930, 18 cities had requested that decennial census data be coded at the census tract level.

Then, in 1931, the American Statistical Association (ASA) established the Committee on Census Enumeration Areas, with Howard Whipple Green as chair. Its assignment, unofficially sanctioned by the Bureau of the Census, was to promote census tract coding in all cities with more than 250,000 residents. The census tract movement now had organized support that would be reinforced in myriad meetings of the ASA and in other forums in which the ASA was a participant. This support was critical to the future of the program because the Great Depression strangled efforts by local organizations to come up with the dollars to support compilation of tract data. As a result of the movement promulgated by the ASA committee in general and Green in particular, it became clear that census tracts were here to stay and that the activity had become sufficiently broad in the range of its participants to warrant creation and administration of a formal program by the bureau. In 1940 the bureau, for the first time, coded and published census tract bulletins for 64 cities. The formal program that was created was based on a unique foundation of unprecedented federal-local cooperation. The task of delineating tracts and monitoring their boundaries from decade to decade was to be the work of local census tract committees, functioning in concert with Bureau of the Census geographers. Manuals, developed through federal-local cooperative efforts at several points in the 1930s, outlined the purpose of the program and suggested how local communities could participate.

As the program grew, it increasingly required national coordination. This was achieved in 1955, when the bureau took responsibility for appointing local liaisons for the tract program. The idea was for a local committee to subdivide a jurisdiction into small areas as homogeneous as possible in population and housing. These subdivisions were submitted to the bureau, which then coded, tabulated, and published the data, along with a census tract map. Local committees also encouraged organizations to code their administrative records by census tract, originally through the use of locally prepared address coding guides and, more recently, through geographic information systems that permit electronic geocoding.

Criteria and Use

When first established, census tracts were designed to be relatively homogeneous with respect to population characteristics, economic status, and living conditions and be in a certain population size range, most recently set at between 2,500 and 8,000 inhabitants. Visible permanent features are used to delineate boundaries of census tracts—that is, features that can be readily identified in the field and are not subject to change as a result of political or administrative considerations. Census tracts are almost always numbered consecutively within county boundaries.

Laidlaw's initial idea was to make census tracts of approximately equal area. Over time, however, this criterion proved to be impractical as more and more of the nation became covered with tracts. In 1990, census tracts covered 80 percent of the nation's population but just 25 percent of its land area. Counties that did not have census tracts were covered with block-numbering areas (BNAs); the concept started in 1940 because the Bureau of the Census needed a way to group blocks in cities that did not have census tracts. In 1990 the bureau created BNAs for all counties that did not have census tracts and published the same data for BNAs as for tracts. In 2000, for the first time, all counties in the nation were subdivided by census tract.

Covering the geography of the nation with census tracts means that the areal size of tracts varies widely, depending on the density of settlement. Although tracts are designed to be homogeneous from the standpoint of social, economic, and housing conditions when first delineated, there is little guarantee that this will continue over time, especially in areas with high population turnover. In spite of the fact that tracts are based on permanent features, physical changes in road and housing infrastructure, changes in street patterns (for example, street closings), or the absence of physical boundaries in large housing developments (for example, those consisting of cul-de-sacs and no continuous through streets) can all result in tracts with unusually large or small populations. Moreover, special conditions, such as the presence of ships in port, observations made during the actual enumeration that bring to light problems with tract boundaries (for example, errors in the bureau's tract boundary configuration), and requests by local jurisdictions to correct the location of misplaced census tract boundaries have all resulted in the creation of tracts with little or no population.

Census tract boundaries do actually change in some cases; however, when tracts are added together or subdivided, the original boundaries are usually maintained. Tracts can be split because of large growth in population or housing or be combined, as when areas experience large population declines or housing losses that are not likely to be reversed. The guiding principle, however, is to maintain tract boundaries because tracts exist to chronicle population and housing change, holding geography constant. Thus boundaries are altered in ways that permit them to be reconfigured for comparisons over time: a tract that was recently split into two parts can be reassembled into a single geographic unit for comparison with an earlier census; or a single census tract in the latest census, formed by combining two tracts from an earlier census, can then be compared with that combined area. Land use can change dramatically over time, as when formerly agricultural, industrial, or commercial areas are developed for residential use, causing the tract configuration to change. Areas may undergo rapid housing development, requiring a whole new template of census tracts to be created where a single census tract (or no census tract) may have existed earlier.

The mix of conditions that presents itself to local census tract liaisons is almost limitless. Thus the decisions on tract delineation from census to census, although subject to criteria that attempt to achieve some level of standardization, need to be carefully evaluated with respect to the range of conditions present in a jurisdiction. The speed of population growth, level of housing development, changes in socioeconomic composition, and shifts in land use are just a few of the key conditions that need to be measured when evaluating how to configure and reconfigure census tracts.

The 2010 Participant Statistical Areas Program (PSAP) permitted designated participants to review and suggest modifications to the boundaries for block groups, census tracts, census county divisions, and census designated places for reporting data from the 2010 census. Minimum and maximum thresholds were established for population and/or housing units, as in previous periods; however, with the implementation of the American Community Survey (ACS) in 2005, these thresholds were more strictly enforced because of efforts by the Census Bureau to obtain a sufficient sample for all geographic areas.

See also *Geographic Information Systems (GIS); Local involvement in census taking; Tabulation geography.*

. . . . JOSEPH J. SALVO

BIBLIOGRAPHY

Association of Public Data Users. *A Guide to State and Local Census Geography, 1990 CPH-I-18.* Washington, D.C.: U.S. Bureau of the Census, 1993.

Bowser, Benjamin P., Evelyn S. Mann, and Martin Oling, eds. *Census Data with Maps for Small Areas of New York City 1910–1960,* Cornell University Libraries. Woodbridge, Conn.: Research Publications (now Primary Source Media), 1981.

Green, Howard Whipple. "A Period of Great Growth and Development, 1926–1946." Paper presented at the annual meeting of the American Statistical Association, Special Session on the Golden Anniversary of Census Tracts, Detroit, 1956.

Kaplan, Charles P., and Thomas L. Van Valey. *Census 80: Continuing the Factfinder Tradition.* Washington, D.C.: U.S. Bureau of the Census, 1980.

Laidlaw, Walter, ed. *Statistical Sources for Demographic Studies of Greater New York, 1910.* 2 vols. New York: New York Federation of Churches, 1913.

New York City 1920 Census Committee. *Statistical Sources for Demographic Studies of Greater New York, 1920.* New York: City Census Committee, 1923.

Swift, Arthur L., Jr. "Doctor Laidlaw's Vision: The Early Years." Paper presented at the annual meeting of the American Statistical Association, Special Session on the Golden Anniversary of Census Tracts, Detroit, 1956.

U.S. Bureau of the Census. *Geographic Areas Reference Manual.* Washington, D.C.: U.S. Government Printing Office, 1994.

U.S. Census Bureau. Participant Statistical Areas Program (PSAP) Participant Information. Washington, D.C.: U.S. Government Printing Office, June 2008.

Censuses in Other Countries

Census taking has been used in all types of societies as a tool to understand better their physical and cultural dimensions. In the same way that representation of daily activities went from petroglyphs to live television coverage, census methodology has evolved over time from rounding up people from a village to mailout/mailback technology, albeit at different paces from country to country.

In most countries census taking is done by enumerators going from door to door asking the householder basic questions on the demographic and socioeconomic characteristics of the members of the household. In some countries this operation is done in one day, whereas in others it is spread out over weeks. The enumerator records the information, which is then captured using various methods. For the 2000 round of censuses, the information gathered by the enumerators was transferred in many cases from imaged documents to computers by optical character recognition. Several countries also opt to compile population counts manually and produce them very quickly after census day. These counts are generally preliminary in nature and as such are subject to review once the questionnaires are processed. This door-to-door methodology is the only one applicable in countries where the rate of literacy is low, postal communication is not reliable, or communication with the householders is otherwise difficult. Most South American, African, and Asian countries used this methodology with slight variations in the conduct of their census.

In most Western countries, where postal communication is effective and the literacy rate relatively high, census questionnaires are either delivered to the household by an enumerator or sent by mail, the latter method requiring the existence of an accurate address register. Householders are asked to complete the questionnaire and return it to the enumerator (either by mail or by handing it back to the enumerator who comes back to pick it up). Missing questionnaires are followed up until an acceptable rate of response is achieved. Data are generally transferred to computers by imaging the questionnaires and by using a combination of optical character recognition, optical mark recognition, and keying techniques from the images.

In some European countries, mostly in northern Europe, population and demographic information is obtained from population registers created and maintained to administer the country. In some countries, such as Finland and Denmark, the information held in registers suffices, whereas in other countries, such as Norway, the register information needs to be completed by and combined with traditional basic census information.

The United Nations Statistics Division compiles information on censuses taken around the world and facilitates the international exchange and sharing of knowledge and information on census taking. For the 2010 census round encompassing the years 2005 to 2014, the division estimates that 225 countries will conduct population counts using traditional census methods, sample surveys, administrative records, or population registers. By 2014 almost 99 percent of the world's population of about 6.9 to 7 billion people will be included in a count. The most common years to take a count are 2010 and 2011. In addition to the United States, Mexico, China, Indonesia, the Russian Federation, and Brazil are among the countries taking censuses in 2010. Most European countries, and the nations of the British Commonwealth, take censuses in 2011.

Censuses are used for apportionment of legislative bodies and for economic and social planning. The questions asked in various nations and the methods of conducting the counts reflect the policy issues of the particular country. Religious identification is asked, for example, on the Indian census. A proposed racial or ethnic classification has been controversial in France, and concerns about the intrusiveness of questions have arisen during the current census round in Canada. Many developed nations have begun to plan for replacement of the traditional house-to-house enumeration with a population count based on administrative records. The United Kingdom has indicated that its 2011 count will be the last traditional census. How and whether such changes in census taking are implemented globally will be the subject of technical and political debate in the 2010s.

See also *International coordination in population censuses; International statistical system and its governance.*

BENOIT LAROCHE
. . . . REVISED BY MARGO J. ANDERSON

BIBLIOGRAPHY
Alonso, William, and Paul Starr. *The Politics of Numbers*. New York: Russell Sage Foundation, 1987.
United Nations Statistics Division, 2010 World Population and Housing Census Programme. http://unstats.un.org/unsd/demographic/sources/census/2010_PHC/default.htm.
U.S. Census Bureau, International Statistical Agencies. www.census.gov/aboutus/stat_int.html.

Center of Population

Census officials invented the concept of the center of population in the 1870s to illustrate trends in the distribution and migration of the American population over time. Considered the center of population gravity, the center of population is the point on which the United States would balance if it were a plane without weight and its population were distributed on the plane as if each individual had the same weight. Each individual would exert on the central point a force proportional to the individual's distance from it. Calculating the point is complex and involves first allocating the population to square degrees of latitude and longitude and then determining where the United States would "balance."

The center of population provided one of the first visual illustrations of population change in the census. Officials originally used the calculation in statistical maps published with tabular results of the census to illustrate the westward migration of the population. From the first census in 1790 to the ninth in 1870, the point moved from Maryland to southern Ohio. Officials saw its steady westward trajectory as natural. They continued the maps in later census publications and extended the concept to calculate centers of population for population subgroups, such as the white, foreign-born, and African American populations.

In the twentieth century, as the nation industrialized in the Northeast and Midwest, the point's decennial migration slowed considerably. The center of population had moved to eastern Indiana by 1890 and remained in Indiana through 1940. Since then, rapid population growth in the South and Southwest has given the point a southwestern trajectory. In early 2000 the center of population rested in Phelps County, Missouri. The 2010 center of population is near Plato, Missouri.

Americans have attributed symbolic meaning to the place where the center of population is located and have celebrated the site with commemorative markers. After the 1990 census, for example, a marker was erected in Steelville, Missouri, the Crawford County seat, 9.7 miles northwest of the true center of population, and in 2000 a similar marker was placed at Edgar Springs, Missouri.

Concepts related to the center of population include the median center of population and the geographic center of area of the United States. The median center is found at the intersection of two median lines: one a north-south line (a meridian of longitude) chosen so that half the population lives east of it and half west, and the other an east-west line (a parallel of latitude) selected so that half the population lives north of it and half south. The median center of population for the 2000 census resided in Indiana, where it was for most of the twentieth century. The geographic center of area represents the point at which the surface of the United States would balance if it were a plane of uniform weight per unit of area. In early 2000 that point fell in Butte County, South Dakota, as it has since the 1960 census, after Alaska and Hawaii became states. The geographic center of the coterminous United States (48 states and the District of Columbia) is in Smith County, Kansas.

See also *Geography: distribution of population.*

. . . . MARGO J. ANDERSON

BIBLIOGRAPHY

National Atlas of the United States. "2000 U.S. Population Centered in Missouri." www.nationalatlas.gov/articles/history/a_popcenter.html.

U.S. Census Bureau, Geography Division. Centers of Population Computation for 1950, 1960, 1970, 1980, 1990, and 2000. Issued April 2001. www.census.gov/geo/www/cenpop/calculate2k.pdf.

Citizenship

See *Congress and the census; Foreign-born population of the United States; Immigration.*

The Civil War and the Census

The American Civil War and the growing sectional strife in the decades preceding it had an important influence on the census. Congressional debate over the 1850 census was concurrent with the acrimonious debate over the Compromise of 1850. Southern senators, keenly aware of the growing controversy over slavery and fearing detailed analyses of the South's "peculiar institution," were able to restrict the information the census collected on the nation's slave inhabitants. The final census bill approved by the Senate eliminated several questions from the proposed slave schedule that were deemed to be too sensitive, including each slave's name, birthplace, "degree of removal from pure blood," the number of children each woman had borne, and whether the children were still living.

The war and its political ramifications also had a significant impact on several postwar censuses. The 1870 census included two questions on "Constitutional Relations" mandated by Section 2 of the Fourteenth Amendment, which was intended to reduce congressional apportionment in states restricting newly freed blacks' right to vote. In 1890 veteran groups and the growing federal commitment to support Union veterans and their widows with pensions convinced Congress to ask "Whether [the respondent was] a soldier, sailor, or marine during the civil war (U.S. or Confederate), or widow of such person" in the population schedule. An additional special schedule of inquiry was conducted to record the names, military units, and length of service of men who served in the Union forces and had survived to the 1890 census. The 1910 census asked whether the individual was a survivor of the Union or Confederate forces.

The 1860 Census Office played an important role in the conduct of the war. Following the bombardment of Fort Sumter in April 1861, census supt. Joseph C. G. Kennedy prepared a report for President Abraham Lincoln on the number of men age 18 to 45 in the free states, the slave states, the "border" states, and the territories. The report showed the North had an overwhelming advantage in manpower—69 percent of men of military age resided in the free states, compared with just 9 percent in the slave states. The Census Office loaned clerks to the War Department for statistical work, conducted analyses of the Confederacy's ability to manufacture explosives, and prepared statistical maps for generals in the field showing local demographic and economic information. Gen.

William Tecumseh Sherman relied on census maps with livestock and crop production information from the 1860 census during his march through Georgia in 1864. The data allowed the army to abandon traditional supply lines and live off the land, and thus move faster than traditional armies. "No military expedition was ever based on sounder or surer data," he contended. In a thank-you letter to Superintendent Kennedy after the war, Sherman contended that the campaign "demonstrated the value of these statistical tables and facts, for there is a reasonable probability that, without them, I would not have undertaken what was done and what seemed a puzzle to the wisest and most experienced soldiers of the world." The 1860 census was also used to assess direct taxes to finance the war, prepare reports on the potential cost of paid emancipation, and help policymakers plan for the "reconstruction" of the post-war South.

However, on the most fundamental problem facing the post-war United States—the future of the freed slaves—the Census Office was of little help. In his introduction to the 1860 census, Kennedy, reflecting the racism of nineteenth-century white society, contended that competition with whites would lead to the "gradual extinction" of the black population.

The American Civil War was the most costly conflict in the nation's history. An estimated 620,000 military deaths occurred during the Civil War—roughly equal to the combined number of deaths suffered in all American wars though the Korean War. The human cost was borne most heavily by the South, which lost 18 percent of its white male population age 13 to 43 in 1860 to the North's 6 percent. The South also suffered a large but uncounted number of civilian deaths from famine, disease, and guerrilla warfare. Mortality was especially high among the refugees who fled the advancing Union Army and the tens of thousands of blacks who escaped from slavery to enlist in the Union forces or to live in "contraband" camps behind army lines.

Post-war censuses also reveal a dramatic reduction in wartime fertility. Military mobilization, the death of hundreds of thousands of young men, and the economic disruptions of the war resulted in a deficit of approximately 500,000 to 700,000 white births between 1862 and 1866 (8–11 percent of the expected total). The war also had a dramatic impact on the black population. For the first time, the nation's nearly 4 million slaves were able to form and maintain families without fear of disruption by owners and to live where they wanted. Although most blacks remained in their local area, many newly freed blacks chose to move to urban areas, swelling the population of many southern cities.

See also *Decennial censuses: 1850 census; Decennial censuses: 1860 census; Decennial censuses: 1870 census; Decennial censuses: 1890 census.*

. . . .   J. DAVID HACKER

BIBLIOGRAPHY

Anderson, Margo J. *The American Census: A Social History.* New Haven, Conn.: Yale University Press, 1988.

Hacker, J. David. "The Human Cost of War: White Population in the United States, 1850–1880." PhD diss., University of Minnesota, 1999.

Magnuson, Diana Lynn. "The Making of a Modern Census: The United States Census of Population, 1790–1940." PhD thesis, University of Minnesota, 1995.

Vinovskis, Maris A. "Have Social Historians Lost the Civil War? Some Preliminary Demographic Speculations." *Journal of American History* 76 (1989): 34–58.

Colonial Censuses

Residents of England's colonies in America acquired much experience with census taking before the first federal census of 1790. In all, 124 censuses were produced between 1623 and 1775, covering 21 colonies from Newfoundland in the north to Barbados in the Caribbean. Of these censuses, 46 were for 9 colonies that became part of the original 13 states. Virginia was the first colony in which a census was taken (1623), though enumerating the people there would not last long into the eighteenth century. In contrast, New York first had its population counted in 1698 but then had 9 more censuses by 1771. That colony was one of 5 to count its population in the 1770s. Other European countries also had censuses taken in their American colonies, as counts exist for territories originally under French and Spanish control that were eventually incorporated into the United States. Here, however, the focus will be on the English experience.

The censuses were intended to be enumerations of all the people living in a colony, setting them apart from estimates of population derived from militia rolls and tax lists, as well as pure guesses. Although colonial authorities in London often indicated an interest only in military and economic aspects of populations such as size and racial composition, the censuses vary significantly in the scope and detail reported to England. Some provided little more than the total counted; others, such as the one taken in New Jersey in 1772 under the direction of Benjamin Franklin's son William, offered sophisticated compilations of data that went well beyond what the imperial authorities desired. Many included greater detail about the composition of populations than the 1790 census.

How the Censuses Were Taken

With the exception of a few local counts, every census taken in an American colony was the result of a request for information from England. In the seventeenth century, these requests frequently reflected a basic ignorance about what the colonies were like and how strong they were. Because the colonies were intended to profit the mother country, it was essential to learn who and what was there to be exploited. At the same time, the colonial censuses emerged at a time when men involved in public affairs were beginning to appreciate the value of accurate data collected in numerical form. Thus censuses were often only one of many kinds of information requested.

Over the course of the seventeenth century, census taking became a more common part of colonial administration. The first censuses in Virginia (1623–1624, 1624–1625) were taken in response to concerns in England about the viability of that colony. The results were not promising, since the population was only just over 1,200, despite the migration of several thousand people since 1618. But as the survival of Virginia became more certain, the requests for counting the people subsided. In 1654 Thomas Povey, a prominent London merchant with interests in trade in the Caribbean, proposed a council of trade and plantations with responsibilities to collect data, including information on population. After 1670 the newly formed Council for Foreign Plantations elicited 10 censuses in the next 14 years. But the most impressive results for colonial censuses came with the creation of the Board of Trade in 1696, as 88.7 percent of all colonial counts occurred after the board assumed supervision of colonial affairs. In all, 20 censuses were taken between 1623 and 1700; another 52 date from between 1701 and 1750, and the years between 1751 and 1775 saw an additional 52 censuses. As administrative control became better established, collection of information moved from a focus on one colony at a time to more general "queries" to all royal governors.

Most queries focused on the size and growth of the population and its racial composition. The latter was a major concern regarding the economic and military viability of the Caribbean colonies. Governors were responsible for collecting the evidence and sending it back to England in a usable form. Over time, governors and their local legislative assemblies added categories into which the population was to be divided. The most common were to distinguish race (or between free and enslaved), sex, and age, with 16 and 60 (the years of militia duty) the ages most often used to define different parts of the population. Broad age categories frequently were applied not only to white males, as in the 1790 census, but also to women and slaves. Censuses within a colony often were similar to those taken earlier in that colony. Although the final report sent to London was frequently only a table or two of results broken down by the major civil divisions in the colony, the process of taking a census could produce extraordinarily detailed findings. Some fragments of original manuscripts exist (most often in American archives), in which every member of a family or household is listed by name and age, allowing remarkably complex analysis of family structures and other relationships.

Most governors tried to respond promptly to requests from London, facing reminders of their duties if they were too slow in producing results. The governors had to rely on the cooperation of their colonists, from citizens responding to questions to local officials recording and forwarding data to legislatures agreeing to pay for the process. This was not always easily obtained. William Franklin's 1772 census for New Jersey covered only the western half of the colony because the tax assessors in the east refused to do the job without pay. Occasionally the Old Testament story of a plague following King David's efforts to take a census was used to explain citizens' resistance. Suspicions over the possible use of censuses by tax collectors may have encouraged some to provide false information. Gov. Archibald Hamilton of the Leeward Islands had to delay a census because of the presence of pirates who were too powerful for him to confront. Several times Pennsylvania governors used past apathy to excuse present dereliction of duty.

Once the data were collected, the governor had to send them to London in an appropriate form. Several years after the Board of Trade chided one Virginia governor that "'Many' and 'Few' are too indeterminate expressions," it was forced to inform his successor that the lists he sent noting the names of every child and slave were "too particular and voluminous." But even when governors produced the right amount of detail, the uncertainty of trans-Atlantic voyages could lead to the loss of a census. Lord Cornbury (Edward Hyde), governor of New York and New Jersey (1702–1708), was reprimanded for failure to send censuses to England, even though surviving fragments in American archives indicate he took at least some of them.

Using the Censuses

Throughout the seventeenth century, imperial officials made use of the censuses to determine what they had on the other side of the Atlantic and to ensure that their possessions were economically and militarily secure. Although early reports must have produced anxiety about the survival of some of the colonies, most settlements in America were thriving by 1700. Following the creation of the Board of Trade in 1696, English policymakers used the censuses as part of their effort to gain greater control over the colonies by emphasizing their economic potential. The most sophisticated analysis of census materials occurred in 1721, when a long report stressed the remarkably rapid growth of populations in America and, in conjunction with the belief that such growth meant economic benefit, offered suggestions on ways to sustain or even increase it. The report also took note of any groups of a population that might pose a potential threat in a given region. The same themes were repeated during the remainder of the colonial period, though often in a perfunctory fashion. In 1763, as England considered revisions in its colonial policies, two officials offered quite different solutions to the concern that rapid growth might eventually undermine the colonies' loyalty to the mother country.

By the middle of the eighteenth century, a number of Americans remarked with favor on the rapid growth that was everywhere evident. Benjamin Franklin; Ezra Stiles, president of Yale College; and Edward Wigglesworth, Harvard College professor of divinity, all pointed with pride to such growth. They saw this as evidence that life was better in America than in England, even predicting that the colonies' population would exceed England's by 1825. If not encouraging revolution, such views certainly made it conceivable.

The growth of the population in American colonies still attracts attention today, for it documents one of the most impressive population "explosions" in history, with numbers doubling approximately every 25 years from 1700 to 1860. At the same time, the censuses demonstrate the remarkable complexity of England's empire in America, with highly diverse populations in colonies from Canada to the Caribbean. The most obvious variation was the racial composition, as the proportion of people of African origin in each colony ranged from almost none to well over 90 percent. But the censuses

have allowed historians to examine the age and sex composition in some detail and, in a significant number of instances, structures of the family and household.

See also *Congress and the census; Decennial censuses: 1790 census.*

. . . . ROBERT V. WELLS

BIBLIOGRAPHY

Demos, John P. *A Little Commonwealth: Family Life in Plymouth Colony.* New York: Oxford University Press, 1970.

Dunn, Richard S. *Sugar and Slaves: The Rise of the Planter Class in the English West Indies, 1624–1713.* Chapel Hill: University of North Carolina Press, 1972.

Greene, Evarts B., and Virginia D. Harrington. *American Population before the Federal Census of 1790.* New York: Columbia University Press, 1932.

Sutherland, Stella H. *Population Distribution in Colonial America.* New York: Columbia University Press, 1936.

Voorhies, Jacqueline K., comp. *Some Late Eighteenth Century Louisianians: Census Records, 1758–1796.* Lafayette: University of Southwestern Louisiana Press, 1973.

Wells, Robert V. *The Population of the British Colonies in America before 1776: A Survey of Census Data.* Princeton, N.J.: Princeton University Press, 1975.

Composition of the Population

Population composition refers to the distribution within a population of one or more individually defined traits that influence population comparisons or demographic phenomena. The individual traits or variables to which population composition refers are usually those believed to have major significance for the uses of population data. Thus, while there are a large number of variables of potential interest for study in demography, there are a limited number that are relevant for use in compositional studies.

To a large degree, compositional elements relevant for study are those characteristics of individuals that are enumerable by conventional census-taking techniques. In earlier U.S. censuses, enumerable meant that nonprofessional census personnel could collect the information. In recent U.S. censuses, enumerable means that adults in households are able to provide information on a mail questionnaire or personal or phone interview.

The individual characteristics to which composition generally refers include sex, age, marital status, place of birth, education, occupation, labor force status, industry, relation to head of household, and other such features. This overview article offers general discussion of age, sex, nativity, and race and ethnicity.

Age and Gender

Age and sex are pivotal characteristics in analyses of composition. The distributions of other characteristics are usually contingent in one way or another on age and sex distributions. This results not only from the fundamental social and economic importance of sex and age but also from their independent variability. As inherent biological properties of individuals, sex and age do not determine marital status, education, or other demographic characteristics. But other demographic processes are often linked to the life cycle and, hence, develop a pattern that is often revealed by the age and sex profiles.

Figure 1. Median Age of the U.S. Population, 1820–2050

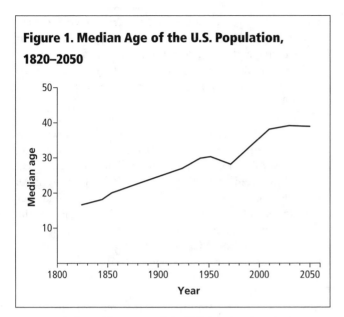

SOURCES: U.S. decennial censuses and the 2008 American Community Survey; 2050 population projection from the U.S. Census Bureau, 2008.

A basic procedure in analyzing age structure is to learn what proportion of the population is at each stage of the life cycle, how these proportions have been changing, how they differ from place to place, and what factors are responsible for the age composition and its changes.

The median age of the population gives a quick and approximate measure of the age of a population. The median age indicates the age that divides the population into two equal parts: 50 percent of the population is above the median age, and 50 percent is below it.

As shown in Figure 1, the median age of the U.S. population was only 16.7 years in 1820 and rose to 38.0 years in 2008. Thus, during a period of almost 19 decades the median age increased by 21.3 years, or about one year per decade. The rise in the age was most rapid between 1900 and 1950, caused

principally by fertility declines. Between 1950 and 1970 this trend of the previous 150 years duration was interrupted; the median age in 1960 and 1970 was lower than it had been in 1950. This unique reversal is attributed to the reversal in the long-term downward trend in fertility that took place starting in 1944 to 1946.

Despite the fact that the median age is a useful measure for indicating generally the age level of a population, it cannot give detailed information about age structure or the distribution of the population among various stages of the life cycle. A more informative picture is to study the proportions of the population for a general set of age groups, such as childhood (age 0 to 8), youth (age 9 to 17), adulthood (age 18 to 64), and the elderly (age 65 and older).

Using these age categories, Table 1 displays U.S. population following the changes in its percentage composition for the U.S. population. More than a century ago, in 1880, the U.S. population was much younger, with a larger proportion of the population in the childhood and youth ages, fewer in the adult years, and dramatically fewer in the elderly years. In 2008, about six out of ten residents are adults, about one out of four are children or youth, and about one out of eight are elderly.

If present low birth rates continue, the median age will increase and the absolute and relative population who are 65 years of age and older will expand. Current population projections indicate that the median age of the U.S. population will increase from 36 years in 2008 to 40 years in 2050.

The U.S. population in 2050 will likely have, in relative, not absolute terms, slightly fewer persons in the childhood and youth years and fewer persons in the adult years. The decreases will be counterbalanced by unprecedented growth of persons in the elderly years, increasing to about one in five persons in the population.

Sex

For the first time in history, the United States had a preponderance of women in 1950. Until 1950 males had outnumbered women. The extent of the imbalance was only slight.

Table 1. Percentage Distribution of the U.S. Population by Major Life Cycle Age Groups, 1880–2050

Major Stages of the Life Cycle	1880	1940	2008	2050
Childhood (0–8 years)	24	14	12	12
Youth (9–17 years)	19	16	12	12
Adulthood (18–64 years)	53	63	63	56
Elderly (65 years and older)	3	7	13	20
Total	100%	100%	100%	100%

SOURCES: U.S. decennial censuses and the 2008 American Community Survey; 2050 population projection from the U.S. Census Bureau, 2008.

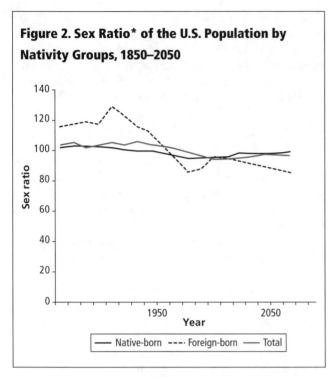

Figure 2. Sex Ratio* of the U.S. Population by Nativity Groups, 1850–2050

NOTE: * Males per 100 females

SOURCE: Historical reconstruction of the U.S. population described in Passel and Edmonston, 1994; U.S. 2000 census and 2008 American Community Survey; 2050 population projection from Edmonston and Passel, 1994.

Instead of being divided 50–50, males were 49.4 percent of the total population in 2008.

It is conventional to describe a population's sex composition in terms of the sex ratio, or the number of males per 100 females. From 1850 to 1910 the sex ratio of the total population of the United States fluctuated between 102 and 106. From 1910 to 1970 it declined steadily and dropped to 95 in 1970.

Both the native and foreign-born populations have had a distinctive sex ratio history. The native-born population had a sex ratio near 100 between 1870 and 1950 and was always below the general sex ratio for the nation (see Figure 2). In 1950 its sex ratio was exactly the same as that of the national average.

The sex ratio for the foreign-born population showed a preponderance of males until 1960. During the years of heavy immigration to the United States at the turn of the twentieth century, immigrants were predominantly male. Consequently, the sex ratio for the foreign-born population during that time was extraordinarily high. In 1850 for example, the foreign-born population had a sex ratio of 124. In 1910 it was 129. In the period from 1920 to 1960, as the volume of immigration was curtailed, the number of female immigrants came to equal and surpass that of males. By 1960 the sex ratio for the foreign-born had declined to 94.

Women will continue to outnumber men in future years, but the relative surplus of women will remain relatively unchanged. The principal cause of the tendency of women to outnumber men is the greater longevity of women. If present demographic trends continue and if the gap in life expectancy narrows between women and men, the sex ratio of the overall population will remain at about 96 between 2000 and 2050.

The sex ratio for the overall population represents a balancing between the sex ratios for the foreign- and native-born components of the population. Because U.S. immigration includes a surplus of women, the foreign-born population will become more predominantly female as immigration continues and as the foreign-born population ages (a greater number of older women than men will survive). The sex ratio of the native-born population is expected to shift slightly upward, from 96 in 2000 to 98 in 2050, as the gap in life expectancy between males and females narrows.

Nativity

Nativity has a social significance that reaches into many spheres of study. The foreign-born have a distinctive age structure and tend to be selected from several major countries of origin. Furthermore, the foreign-born often evidence differences in English-language abilities, fertility, settlement patterns, and other social and economic characteristics.

Immigrants have arrived in the United States throughout its entire national history, with a great deal of variation from the peaks of the 1900s and of the 1980s and 1990s to the valleys of the 1930s. Immigration increased steadily in the decades after World War II, since the United States enjoyed a high degree of political freedom and economic prosperity, compared with Europe and many other countries. The 1965 changes in U.S. immigration law prompted even further increases as the United States began to receive large numbers of new immigrants from Asia and Latin America.

Figure 3 shows the size of the foreign-born population in the United States, from 1850 to 2050. Immigrants affect the composition of the population in several ways. They change the racial/ethnic makeup of the population *if* they differ from the resident population. Immigrants *always* affect the generational composition, since they increase the size of the first generation (that is, the foreign-born population). The foreign-born population derives principally from past levels of immigration but is also affected by the effects of emigration and mortality.

The size of the foreign-born population in the United States reflects the changing course of immigration over time. Approximately 2.2 million foreign-born persons resided in the United States in 1850, constituting 9.7 percent of the total population. With the continuing heavy volume of immigration in the late nineteenth century, the foreign-born population grew steadily, reaching a peak of 14.4 million in 1930. At the same time, the foreign-born population increased as a proportion of the U.S. population, reaching the peak proportion of 14.8 percent in 1890.

Figure 3. Foreign-Born Population of the United States and the Percentage of Foreign-Born Population in the Total Population, 1850–2050

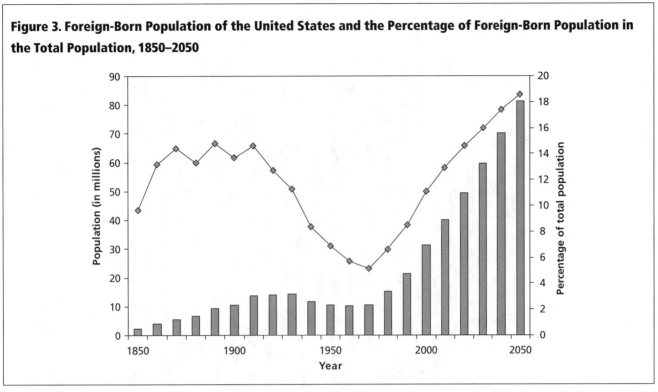

NOTES: The bars represent the "Foreign-Born" population, with the scale shown on the left; the line represents the percentage of the population, with the scale shown on the right.
SOURCES: Historical reconstruction of the U.S. population described in Passel and Edmonston, 1994; U.S. 2000 census and the 2008 American Community Survey; 2050 population projection from Passel and Cohn, 2008.

With the diminution of immigration from about 1918 to 1946, the foreign-born population decreased in both numbers and proportions as mortality reduced the aging wave of immigrants. By 1970 the foreign-born population had decreased to 10.5 million, accounting for only 5.1 percent of the total population.

The large increase in immigration that began in the 1960s produced a rapid turnaround in the 40-year decrease of the foreign-born population. By 2008 the number of foreign-born persons residing in the United States reached the highest levels in the history of the country, almost 38 million. Relative to the rest of the population, however, the foreign-born population is slightly less than the highest levels attained from 1860 to 1920: Just over 12 percent of the population was foreign-born in 2008 versus 13 to 15 percent at the end of the nineteenth century.

Population projections suggest that the foreign-born population of the United States will increase from 37.0 million in 2008 to 54.4 million in 2025, and 81.3 million in 2050, assuming current trends in fertility, mortality, and international migration rates. Under similar assumptions for the growth of the native-born population, these projections forecast an increase of the foreign-born population, as a percentage of the total population, from 12.5 percent in 2008, to 15.3 percent in 2025, and 18.6 percent in 2050.

Race and Ethnicity

Race and ethnic characteristics of the U.S. population have long had special importance. Although "race" is not now regarded as a meaningful biological concept, this fact should not overlook the social and economic correlates of self-reported racial and ethnic identity in U.S. society. Population statistics provide much of the basis for factual study of the conditions under which racial and ethnic groups live and the ways in which their relative positions are changing. For much demographic analysis of the U.S. population, ethnic and racial origins are basic variables that are included as statistical controls before studying the effect of other variables.

Throughout most of its history, the United States has often been considered an essentially biracial society, composed of the white majority and a black minority, along with a marginalized American Indian population. In 1790 the United States' population was recorded as 81 percent white and 19 percent black (the U.S. census did not distinguish other racial groups until 1850). This situation is now changing. The United States is becoming a more diverse society. Figure 4 presents information on the percentage composition of the U.S. population, by race and Hispanic origin from 1850 to 2050.

We focus on 1900, the first year for which adequate data on the five "racial" groups have been developed (shown in Figure 4). At the turn of the twentieth century, the U.S.

Figure 4. Racial Composition of the U.S. Population, 1850–2050

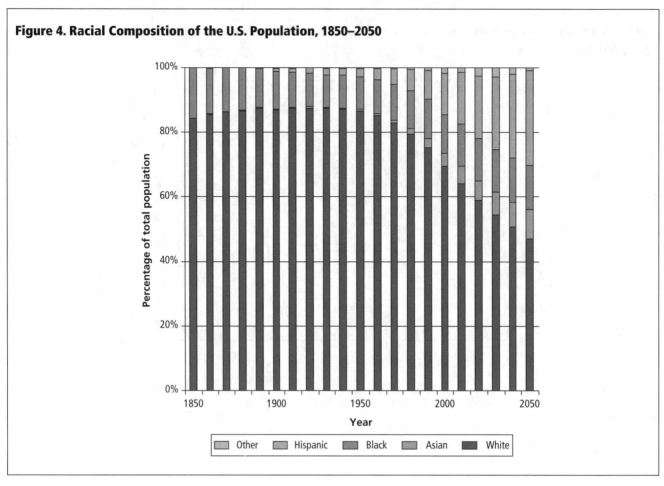

SOURCE: Historical reconstruction of the U.S. population described in Passel and Edmonston, 1994; U.S. decennial censuses and the 2008 American Community Survey; 2050 population projection from Passel and Cohn, 2008.

population was 87 percent white, 12 percent black, and about 1 percent other racial groups. The 1900 census counted about 240,000 American Indians, 240,000 Asians (primarily Chinese, Japanese, and Hawaiians), and 660,000 Hispanics (predominantly Mexican-origin population).

All racial groups increased numerically from 1900 to 1960, although the relative shifts were small. By 1960 the white population's share had dropped only slightly, from 87 to 85 percent. The proportion of blacks in the population had decreased slightly, from 12 to 11 percent. The other three racial/ethnic groups had increased their combined proportion from about 1 to 4 percent.

Since 1960, shifts in origins of immigrants have led to substantial absolute and relative increases in the Asian and Hispanic populations. Over the past 50 years, the combined proportion of Asians, Hawaiians, Pacific Islanders, and Hispanics increased from 4 percent in 1960 to more than 20 percent in 2008. These groups, which accounted for just over 1 million people in 1900, had grown to a total of more than 61 million by 2008.

As a result of rapid growth of the Asian and Hispanic groups, the composition within the minority population is also changing. The minority population of the United States was predominantly black during the nineteenth century, with a small number of persons of other races, along with the diverse American Indian population. While the black population has increased at a modest pace, the Asian and Hispanic groups have grown at much more rapid rates during the past three decades. Consequently, the proportion of minority population that is black has been dropping steadily, decreasing from 70 percent in 1960 to 38 percent in 2008. Although the black population is expected to increase during the next 40 years, it should remain fairly steady at 13 to 14 percent of the total population.

With a continuation of current levels of immigration, the racial/ethnic composition of the United States will continue to change and the minority population will increase. Two groups are likely to experience substantial growth during the next 40 years: Asians and Hispanics. The Asian population will grow at annual rates exceeding 1 percent for the next 50 years, increasing from 13 million in 2008 to 39 million in 2050, or 9 percent of the total population.

The Hispanic population—assumed to have the largest share of immigration, in part because of having the major share of illegal immigration—will grow substantially over the next 50 years. The Hispanic population will increase at annual rates exceeding 2 percent, growing from 45 million in 2008, or 15 percent of the projected total population, for the next four decades, at which time Hispanics would number 128 million, or 29 percent of the projected population, in 2050. The Hispanic population passed the black projected population to become the largest minority group in the nation in 2001.

Population projections of the racial and ethnic composition need to be viewed with caution, however. An increasing proportion of children are born to parents of different racial or ethnic origins. Some of these children choose to identify themselves with two or more racial backgrounds, while others prefer to identify themselves with only a single racial background. Racial self-identities are sometimes blurry and often dynamic. The way that grandchildren of current Americans identify themselves in 2050 may be different from what is currently commonplace.

See also *Internal migration; Immigration; Race: questions and classifications; Women in the decennial census.*

. . . . BARRY EDMONSTON

BIBLIOGRAPHY

Edmonston, Barry, and Jeffrey S. Passel. "The Future Immigrant Population of the United States." In *Immigration and Ethnicity: The Integration of America's Newest Arrivals,* ed. Barry Edmonston and Jeffrey S. Passel. Washington, D.C.: Urban Institute Press, 1994.

Passel, Jeffrey S., and Barry Edmonston. "Immigration and Race: Recent Trends in Immigration to the United States." In *Immigration and Ethnicity: The Integration of America's Newest Arrivals,* ed. Barry Edmonston and Jeffrey S. Passel. Washington, D.C.: Urban Institute Press, 1994.

Passel, Jeffrey S., and D'Vera Cohn. *U.S. Population Projections: 2005–2050.* Washington, D.C.: Pew Research Center, Pew Hispanic Center, 2008.

U.S. Census Bureau. *U.S. Population Projections by Age, Sex, Race, and Hispanic Origin : July 1, 2000–2050.* Washington, D.C.: U.S. Census Bureau, 2008.

Confidentiality

The Census Bureau's long-standing commitment to confidentiality in its laws, its policies, and its practices shows how strongly it believes that its core business depends on protecting confidentiality and privacy. Confidentiality is a component of employee training; it is emphasized in all communications with respondents; it is integrated into data processing and transmission operations; and it is the first consideration in decisions about which data to release to the public.

Throughout the twentieth century confidentiality has been tested by the courts, by congressional actions, and by actions of other government agencies. In each case the Census Bureau has prevailed to maintain or strengthen its statutory protections.

In its practices the Census Bureau strives to improve its procedures and the products it disseminates while ensuring that confidentiality is not compromised. This often involves trade-offs between efficiency and data use on the one hand and confidentiality on the other.

Legal Protections

Legal confidentiality protections for census data are contained in Title 13 of the United States Code. Section 9 states that information provided by respondents to Census Bureau surveys and censuses may be used for statistical purposes only, that published information may not identify a particular establishment or individual, and that no one other than sworn officers or employees may see individual reports. Section 214 provides for severe penalties, including large fines and up to five years in prison, for Census Bureau employees who breach confidentiality. One of the strongest confidentiality protections for any government agency, the current census law dates back to 1929, when it was amended to address concerns about the weaker protections afforded data on individuals compared with data on businesses.

Before the 1929 amendment, the confidentiality protections of the census law were less stringent. For example, in 1917 the bureau director released transcripts of the 1910 census to the Department of Justice, to local draft boards, and to individuals in cases in which the individuals had been arrested for draft evasion. The census law at that time permitted such use of census records.

Arguably, the most significant test of confidentiality of census records involved the government response to the Japanese attack on Pearl Harbor. Section 1402 of the Second War Powers Act of 1942 authorized government access to data produced by the Commerce Department (including the Bureau of the Census) "for use in connection with conduct of the war." Until 2000 there was some question as to whether the bureau had contributed data to the war effort. Based on their research between 2000 and 2007, Margo Anderson and William Seltzer reported that the bureau had provided tabulations to the War Department to assist in the internment of Japanese Americans and also complied with a request by the Treasury secretary for names and locations of people of Japanese ancestry residing in the Washington, D.C., area. Although legal under the Second War Powers Act, which expired in 1947, the release of confidential information for a nonstatistical use violated the trust established with census respondents.

In 1947, a request by the attorney general to obtain census information on certain individuals suspected of being communist sympathizers resulted in the bureau's refusal to comply. In 1950 representatives of the Secret Service approached a bureau official seeking census records for a neighborhood in the northwest section of the District of Columbia, which was being considered for a temporary residence for President Harry S. Truman during a renovation of the White House. The official provided only tabulations that characterized the neighborhood, not the specific people residing there. During the summer of 1980, the Federal Bureau of Investigation (FBI), with a court order, showed up at the Colorado Springs Census District Office seeking access to all census records. This was in response to a former enumerator's allegation that questionnaires and payroll forms had been falsified. Following a tense standoff between Bureau of the Census and FBI personnel, the bureau director called the FBI director and offered to assist the investigation in a way that ensured confidentiality of the census forms.

The courts have also played a role in defining and reshaping the census law. In 1961 the Supreme Court ruled (in *St. Regis Paper Co. v. United States*) that copies of census forms retained by a respondent were not protected in the same way as the original forms submitted to the Bureau of the Census. This was in spite of the fact that the bureau had asked its business respondents to retain completed file copies for future reference. As a result of this ruling, Congress strengthened the census law to bring copies of completed forms under the same legal protections as the originals. In 1982 the Supreme Court ruled (*Baldrige v. Shapiro*) that census addresses collected and used by the bureau were exempt from disclosure, by way of either civil discovery or the Freedom of Information Act. This ruling responded directly to suits filed by Essex County, New Jersey, and Denver, Colorado, to obtain the bureau's address lists to compare with their own lists in support of their lawsuit alleging an undercount.

A legal exception to confidentiality of census records is the law that covers the National Archives. Historically, the archivist has made available to genealogists and researchers many records on individuals after 50 years (later reduced to 30 years). Census records were precluded from release because of the strict interpretation of the confidentiality law. Beginning in 1952 the director of the Bureau of the Census and the archivist agreed that census records collected under a pledge of confidentiality could be made publicly available after 72 years. This was later codified in the archives law (Title 44 of the United States Code). There is some disagreement about the significance of this time period. Most believe that it was the average life span of a person in 1952. Others argue that it is only significant as the time between the census of 1870 and its public release in 1942.

Another exception to census confidentiality is Public Law 103-430, the Census Address List Improvement Act of 1994. Under this law the Census Bureau is permitted to share its address register with state and local officials for the purpose of updating the census address list. Local officials who are designated as census liaisons are entitled to see only those addresses pertinent to their local jurisdictions. They are subject to the same confidentiality provisions and penalties as are regular census employees.

In a case demonstrating the potentially harmful consequences of legislation that ignored existing statutes, the USA PATRIOT Act of 2001 gave the government new powers to obtain personal information to combat terrorism. The Patriot Act specifically included certain information maintained by the National Center for Education Statistics and raised questions about whether other statistical agencies could continue to withhold personal information under preexisting legislation. To assuage concerns from respondents to the 2010 census, the chairs of the Congressional Asian Pacific American, Black, and Hispanic Caucuses sought and received a ruling from the Department of Justice that the Congress did not intend to override the protections of Title 13 and that census confidentiality protections were not diminished by the Patriot Act.

Providing Access to Data

Protecting confidentiality is critical but must be accomplished within the basic mission of the Census Bureau—to provide data to inform the nation. This involves a trade-off between providing access to research data and ensuring confidentiality. Generally, the more detailed the data, the greater the risk of disclosure. Traditionally, the Census Bureau has provided census data in tabulations at the block level for only the few items on the short form and at the block group and tract levels for a sample of households using the long form and, beginning in 2005, the American Community Survey. Beginning with the 1960 census, the bureau began providing Public Use Microdata Sample files representing a proportion of the population so that users could generate their own tables and estimate statistical models.

The technique for protecting confidentiality in census tabulations before 1990 involved cell suppression. Table cells with too few cases were made blank to protect the identity of the individuals with those characteristics. Data users did not like this approach because it left gaps in the data and severely limited their analysis. Beginning in 1990, for short-form data, the Bureau of the Census began using data swapping in tables of frequency data (the number or percentage of the population with certain characteristics). A sample of households is selected and matched on a set of selected key variables with households in neighboring geographic areas (census blocks or tracts) that have similar characteristics. The swapped households are similar (number of adults, number of children, and racial and Hispanic composition) to those they are replacing. Usually, the swap occurs within the tract, and therefore has no effect on tabulations at the tract level and above. With swapping a user cannot be certain that the individual cell represents a particular person.

Microdata files from the census long-form sample and the American Community Survey for public use consist of small (less than 5 percent) samples of the population. This sampling adds considerable confidentiality protection. To protect confidentiality further, the Census Bureau removes individual identifiers (such as name and address), modifies distinguishing characteristics (such as high levels of income), and restricts geographic identifiers (such as name of city) to ensure that only population areas of at least 100,000 persons are identified. These disclosure limitation techniques are designed to protect against attempts to identify specific individuals on a file either directly or through links to other data sources.

The Internet

The Census Bureau has developed innovative ways to collect and disseminate data interactively over the Internet. Doing so is not without risk, however. Security is threatened by intruders who attempt to intercept data transmissions or break through security systems, or firewalls, to get to unprotected data. For Census 2000, respondents could file their census short forms over the Internet. Authentication was assured by requiring each household to enter its 23-digit control number from the mailed census form before entering the information through a firewall to a template on the Census Bureau's World Wide Web site. The data were encrypted and sent directly to Census Bureau computers, where they were immediately brought behind a second firewall to ensure that hackers, should they get through the main firewall, could not get to the completed forms. Because of performance and security concerns, the bureau did not highlight Internet reporting and very few people chose this option. For Census 2010, the Census Bureau decided not to provide an Internet option because of a judgment that it would not increase overall response and would not provide cost savings necessary to justify its expense and because of the public's growing concerns over information privacy and the challenges in protecting the information provided. However, the Census Bureau is testing the use of the Internet for response to the American Community Survey and is planning to test the use of the Internet for the 2020 census.

The American FactFinder (AFF) is the Census Bureau's online data retrieval system designed to allow users to extract tables from the confidential files. The AFF was developed to provide safe and easy access to data from the 2000 census, American Community Survey, and other Census Bureau programs. The AFF makes extensive use of firewalls to protect source data. Output consists of printed reports and press releases, summary tables, and custom tables. All data provided through the AFF undergo a disclosure review and may be swapped to protect confidentiality. Data provided in the AFF are similar to the summary data products provided on paper and the computer tapes produced from the 1990 census. The Advanced Query System (AQS) of the AFF that was developed for the 2000 census provides the most innovative—and perhaps risky—advance over 1990 census data products. The AQS allows users to submit requests electronically for user-defined tables. The request passes through a firewall, where it is processed on the previously swapped, recoded, and top-coded microdata. Software analyzes the resulting table to make sure there are no disclosures resulting from this request solely or in combination with any previous request. However, access to the AQS for 2000 was limited to State Data Centers and Census Information Centers. For 2010 the Census Bureau is replacing the AQS with the Microdata Analysis System, which, in addition to table generation, will allow users to perform various statistical analyses.

The Census Bureau's reputation for protecting privacy is well known; nevertheless, the external environment and the concerns raised by new technologies have led the bureau to examine its data-handling policies and procedures and its ability to communicate its commitment to keeping personal information confidential. To better understand public attitudes and foster awareness, the Census Bureau began a research program in the early 1990s focused on measuring the public's attitudes toward confidentiality. This research has shown that the public does value confidentiality but that it is cynical about the government's promises. In response to this public relations problem, the Census Bureau has set about to focus attention on its excellent record for protecting confidentiality, reinforce its own "culture of confidentiality" internally, and undertake an outreach and education program designed to change public opinion. To strengthen its controls over data access and use, the bureau formalized its Data Stewardship Program in 2002 by adopting a set of privacy principles and associated polices that are administered by an executive-level committee.

See also *American Community Survey: data products; American Community Survey: methodology; Archival access to the census; Dissemination of data: electronic products; Litigation and the census; Summary files.*

. . . . GERALD W. GATES

BIBLIOGRAPHY

Bohme, Frederick G., and David Pemberton. "Privacy and Confidentiality in the U.S. Censuses—A History." Census Bureau paper presented at the annual meeting of the American Statistical Association, Atlanta, Ga., August 18–21, 1991.

Gates, Gerald, and Deborah Bolton. "Privacy Research Involving Expanded Statistical Use of Administrative Records." In *Proceedings of the Government Statistics Section*. Alexandria, Va.: American Statistical Association, 1998.

Griffin, Richard, Alfredo Navarro, and L. Flores-Baez. "Disclosure Avoidance for the 1990 Census." In *Proceedings of the Section on Survey Research Methods*, 516–521. Alexandria, Va.: American Statistical Association, 1989.

Seltzer, William, and Margo Anderson. "After Pearl Harbor: The Proper Role of Population Data Systems in Time of War." Paper presented at the annual meeting of the Population Association of America. Los Angeles, Calif., March 23–25, 2000.

———. "Census Confidentiality under the Second War Powers Act (1942–1947)." Paper presented at the annual meeting of the Population Association of America, New York City, March 29–31, 2007.

U.S. Department of Justice. Letter from Ronald Weich to Naydia Velazquez, Chair of Congressional Hispanic Caucus. Dated March 3, 2010.

Zayatz, Laura, Jason Lucero, Paul Massell, and Asoka Ramanayake. "Disclosure Avoidance for Census 2010 and American Community Survey Five-year Tabular Data Products." Washington, D.C.: Statistical Research Division, U.S. Census Bureau, 2009.

Congress and the Census

The Constitution of the United States (Article 1, section 2) requires that a census be conducted every ten years, gives Congress the authority to determine how the census will be conducted, and defines the political purpose of the census—apportionment of seats in the House of Representatives among the states. From the beginning Congress has played an important role in how the census is shaped.

In 1790, Congress passed legislation defining how the first census would be conducted. United States marshals were charged with collecting information from each household starting in August 1790. They had nine months to complete the task. Copies of the census schedules were posted in public places to assure their accuracy. Congress directed that the marshals collect the name of the head of each household, the number of free white males 16 years and over [as per 108b] and under 16, the number of free white females, the number of other free persons, and the number of slaves. President George Washington reported the population of each state to the Congress in October 1791 so that Congress could apportion representation among the states. Congress quickly learned that just having a population count did not assure a fair distribution of power. After much debate, and the first presidential veto, an apportionment was agreed on in April 1792. Alexander Hamilton's method of apportionment was replaced by Thomas Jefferson's method, shifting one seat from Delaware to Virginia. Two principles emerged from the first census. First, the census would collect both the number and characteristics of the population, however rudimentary. Second, the census numbers were to be collected for the purpose of apportionment.

Throughout the nineteenth century, Congress expanded the number of individual characteristics collected as well as the geographic detail in the census. Congress also debated apportionment methods, discovered that the census could contain errors that resonated with ongoing political controversies, and authorized ever larger administrative structures and expenditures for the decennial count. By 1903 the Bureau of the Census was established as a permanent agency in the Department of Commerce and Labor (later, the Department of Commerce), where it remains. Today the agency director reports to the undersecretary for economic affairs in the Economics and Statistics Administration. Through the nineteenth century Congress continued to exercise close legislative and fiscal oversight of the census. As late as the 1920s, Congress was still preparing a new law authorizing the count each decade.

Census data showing the increased number of immigrants during the early twentieth century, control of Congress by rural states and districts, and growing anti-immigration sentiments among the public led Congress to the maelstrom that was the 1920 census and reapportionment. The 1920 census showed a shift of power from the rural Midwest to the urban centers of the country. Reapportionment would have shifted 11 seats from 10 rural states to 8 states with major urbanized areas. To mitigate the effects of this shift, the size of the House would have to be increased to 483, and just the decade before CONGRESS had agreed to freeze the house size at 435. Throughout the 1920s, Congress refused to face this changing demographic reality, and for the only time in the history of the country, Congress failed to reapportion the House of Representatives. The election in 1928 was based on congressional districts and apportionment created from the 1910 census.

In April 1929, President Herbert Hoover called Congress into a special session. High on the agenda were an apportionment bill and legislation authorizing the 1930 census. During the decade, Congress had debated which formula to use for apportionment even though many members of congress preferred to wait until the numbers were in before choosing a formula, including? the exclusion of aliens from the apportionment, invoking Section 2 of the 14th Amendment, which would have penalized Southern states that failed to enfranchise freed slaves. All attempts at compromise had failed. In June 1929, Congress passed a bill that authorized the 1930 census and provided for reapportionment following that census, although the bill called on the Bureau of the Census to report apportionment based on both formulas under consideration. But the bill also set the seeds for the next apportionment crisis by eliminating the requirements that congressional districts be compact, contiguous, and of approximately equal size.

Despite the establishment of a permanent census agency and a provision for apportionment, Congress continued to pass laws to implement the census, codifying the rules governing the modern-day census in 1954. The language of Title 13 of the United States Code, which sets the statutory requirements for the decennial census, is broad and relatively brief. Congress vested responsibility for the census in the secretary of commerce, who in turn, by administrative order, delegated authority to the director of the Bureau of the Census to plan, prepare for, and implement the once-a-decade population count. By granting broad authority to the commerce secretary (and, by implication, the director of the bureau), Congress relieved itself of the burden of constructing an increasingly complex census process every ten years, a process that now requires ongoing research and development, planning, and preparation. Most technical and operational decisions are left to the executive branch, allowing members of Congress to focus their attention on policy-oriented questions of cost-efficiency, content, and, not surprisingly, the coverage of certain population groups for the purpose of determining the House's composition through the apportionment process. However, given its constitutionally prescribed roles as both manager and chief beneficiary of the census, Congress continues to direct specific census operations through changes in the law, even at times against the advice of experts at the Census Bureau and external scientific organizations. And when the Census Bureau believes that technical considerations outweigh political ones, battles fought at the highest levels of policymaking can ensue.

The primary consequences of the census are political in nature. Consequently, disputes in Congress over census methods or coverage of the population are usually fought along partisan or geographic lines. The landmark equal representation decisions handed down by the U.S. Supreme Court starting in the 1960s placed added burdens on the census, as state legislatures were required to draw congressional and other political district boundaries in a way that equalized the population of districts within each state. Suddenly, detailed data on the population of very small areas, including characteristics such as race and voting age, became essential for the decennial post-census exercise of redistricting. Already a process laced with partisan maneuvering, redistricting was elevated to an art form in the decades following the 1970 census as rapid advances in technology allowed politicians to determine which neighborhoods—even which specific blocks—should be assigned to particular districts to benefit prospective candidates from one political party or the other.

Party allegiance started to emerge publicly and clearly in the years leading up to the 1990 census, when, with backing from experts convened by the National Academy of Sciences, the Bureau of the Census announced that it planned to conduct a post-enumeration survey to measure the expected undercount and possibly adjust the initial results to improve the accuracy of the count. The Commerce Department, under the administration of Republican president Ronald Reagan, quickly moved to quash the idea, setting off protests from many Democratic lawmakers, who at the time controlled the leadership positions as the majority party in Congress. At the time, and throughout the 1990 census itself, both Republicans and Democrats in Congress refrained from accusing the other side of opposing or supporting a statistical adjustment to correct the disproportionate undercount of racial minorities and the poor, based on partisan interests. But a growing belief among party loyalists on both sides of the political aisle that their political opponents viewed the debate over adjustment strictly in partisan, not scientific, terms was simmering not far beneath the surface. When the controversy over the use of statistical methods to correct the census undercount resurfaced in 1996, with the bureau's unveiling of its plan for Census 2000, the political tables were turned; Democrat Bill Clinton was in the White House and Republicans were in control of both houses of Congress.

Geographic interests on some issues affecting census methods and operations have also played a significant role in several census controversies over the past 40 years. Lawmakers from states with absolute or relative declines in their populations and states with significant minority populations have often viewed disputes over census methods in terms of the political and fiscal consequences for their home territory. As the secretary of commerce considered whether to statistically adjust the 1990 census numbers, for example, members of Congress from states that were in danger of losing a congressional seat tried to gauge how such a change would affect the apportionment outcome, before deciding whether to support or oppose the new method. A recurring controversy over whether to exclude undocumented residents from the census state totals used for apportionment was fought largely along geographic lines, with many Democrats and Republicans from states with large immigrant populations (such as California, New Mexico, and Texas) opposing such an exclusion

and with lawmakers from states with relatively low numbers of immigrants (such as Indiana and Pennsylvania) supporting the change.

In addition to partisan and geographic concerns, interest group pressure has become an increasingly significant factor in determining how Congress views the Census Bureau's plans for each decennial census. Constituent and interest group involvement in the census decision-making process increased as more fiscal resources, enforcement of civil rights, and the promise of political representation became inextricably tied to the census results through the proliferation of formula-based government programs, Supreme Court decisions, and sweeping federal laws (such as the Voting Rights Act of 1965) designed to carry out the new rights that emerged from the Court's findings.

The series of hallmark desegregation, voting rights, and affirmative action cases in the 1950s, 1960s, and 1970s empowered more segments of the population and galvanized their advocates toward involvement in the legislative process as a way to ensure a fair share of resources for their communities. These advocates knew the importance of the census in determining the allocation of funds and guaranteeing equal representation. They used their growing political clout to urge legislative action that would ensure adequate funding for the census, new methods to address the chronic undercount, and the availability of demographic and economic data to track the progress of their communities.

Finally, with the start of the so-called information age in the 1980s, businesses realized the need for detailed data to guide investment decisions and to track the need for goods and services among different population subgroups. Already savvy players in the legislative process, business representatives also used their influence with both Congress and executive branch agencies to ensure the availability of useful data from the census.

Authorization and Oversight

Congress controls the conduct of the census through two basic legislative processes: authorizations and appropriations. The authorizing process involves enactment of laws that define what an agency must or can do, what it may not do, and how it should carry out its responsibilities. An authorization often sets a maximum funding level for a government activity, but the law governing the work of the Census Bureau includes no such restriction. This "open-ended authorization" has elevated the importance of the appropriations process in shaping the design and content of the decennial census. Congress has sanctioned or opposed census plans and methods in recent years by allocating or withholding funds in the annual bill that appropriates money for the Census Bureau, and by specifying how those funds can be spent.

Closely related to the authorizing process and usually carried out by the same committee is the oversight function of Congress. While not necessarily seeking to amend existing law or enact new ones, the authorizing committees and subcommittees often hold hearings to review the progress of federal activities, evaluate the success of programs, probe concerns about the misuse of funds or activities that may not be in accordance with the law, and assess the need for new programs or changes in the authorizing statutes governing federal activities.

Despite the enormous political consequences and high profile of the decennial census, Congress has not always afforded the census the level of attention an activity of such massive scope and cost usually receives. At times over the past several decades, the work of the Census Bureau appears to have been an afterthought in the organization of authorizing committees in both the House and Senate. In the House the Committee on Post Office and Civil Service—established in 1946—had responsibility for overseeing activities of the bureau until 1995, when a new Republican majority eliminated the entire panel and all its subcommittees. Since the 1970 census, jurisdiction over the bureau's work shifted from one subcommittee to another as the committee reorganized from time to time. The census often competed for the attention of subcommittee members with other unrelated issues within the Post Office and Civil Service committee's broader jurisdiction, including federal government workforce issues, postal employee concerns, and federal holidays. In the 1970s the Subcommittee on Manpower and Human Resources was responsible for overseeing the census and authorizing its activities, as necessary. In the 1980s and early 1990s, the new Subcommittee on Census and Population signaled a desire to pay closer attention, on an ongoing basis, to census planning and preparation, as well as other statistical activities of the Bureau of the Census and federal government. In 1993, two years before the demise of the Committee on Post Office and Civil Service, the subpanels were reorganized once again, resulting in the new Subcommittee on Census, Statistics, and Postal Personnel.

The new Republican majority assumed control of all committee and subcommittee chairmanships in the 104th Congress (1995–1997), representing a sweeping change in how the House and Senate would be run. In the House most of the standing committees were renamed and several were eliminated altogether. With the old Committee on Post Office and Civil Service gone, responsibility for census authorization and oversight shifted to the renamed and reorganized Committee on Government Reform and Oversight (renamed the Committee on Government Reform in the 106th Congress).

Democrats had controlled the House for 40 years as the majority party, and nearly all House Republicans had served only as minority party members in that chamber. Throughout the legislative branch–where in the Senate, Republicans also assumed majority status—Republican leaders had their hands full rearranging offices, hiring staff, and setting their policy agenda; hence, even though the Bureau of the Census was preparing for its final tests in 1995 before settling on a plan for the 2000 census, members of Congress had many other issues on their minds. Census planning was not a priority, and responsibility for overseeing the census process was tucked away,

almost as an afterthought, in the Subcommittee on National Security, International Affairs, and Criminal Justice.

In early 1998, realizing that oversight of the upcoming census required more fiscal and personnel resources, House Republicans created the Subcommittee on the Census under the Government Reform and Oversight Committee. The jurisdiction for the new panel was limited to the work of the Bureau of the Census, allowing it to devote its resources to overseeing census preparations and considering legislative proposals to modify or add census operations.

In the last several decades the Senate took only sporadic interest in significant policy debates affecting the design, coverage, and content of the census. It followed an unwritten but traditional rule of deferring to the House in matters affecting reapportionment and redistricting, and, therefore, the composition of the House itself.

From the 1970s to the present, the Senate assigned authorizing responsibility for the census in much the same haphazard fashion as the House. Jurisdiction over the census rests with the Committee on Governmental Affairs. At times the committee has elected to retain that responsibility, while at other times it has vested one of its subcommittees with jurisdiction over the census. As in the House the census has sometimes been assigned to a subcommittee with jurisdiction over a wide range of unrelated government activities, making it difficult for members of the panel or their staff to devote significant time to the census. For example, in the 1970s the Subcommittee on Energy, Nuclear Proliferation, and Federal Services was responsible for overseeing the census. In the late 1980s, after a committee reorganization, the census was assigned to the new Subcommittee on Government Information and Regulation (renamed the Subcommittee on Government Regulation and Information in the early 1990s), signaling a recognition that the census is part of a broader federal statistical system providing lawmakers with information to support policy decisions. However, in 1995, when Republicans took control of leadership posts and committee chairs as the new majority party, the Committee on Governmental Affairs decided not to assign the census to a subcommittee, giving members of the full panel a leading role in overseeing plans for the 2000 census.

Appropriations

Congress also has used the appropriations process to direct changes in the design and content of the decennial census that it could not accomplish through changes in the Census Bureau's authorizing statute. The practice became more prevalent in the mid- to late-1990s, as the Republican-controlled Congress clashed with the Democratic administration over major aspects of the proposed 2000 census plan, making it more difficult to amend the law in the face of presidential veto threats.

Every year Congress must pass and the president must sign spending bills that provide money to run all federal government activities in the next fiscal year. The government's activities are divided into 13 broad budget accounts; the Committee on Appropriations of each chamber must steer the 13 spending bills through the legislative process.

Funding for the Census Bureau is included in an appropriations bill covering the Departments of Commerce, State, and Justice, the federal Judiciary, and several independent agencies including the Legal Services Corporation and the Small Business Administration. (The Census Bureau is an agency of the Commerce Department.) Congress divides up the total amount of money available for spending on discretionary federal programs (for example, programs that are not entitlements, such as Social Security) among the 13 budget accounts, in an annual budget resolution. Within each large budget category, diverse programs also must compete with one another for funds during the annual appropriations process.

The decennial census has not been immune from the competition for fiscal resources, despite its constitutional grounding. In the years between censuses, appropriators have been less generous in allocating funds for census research and planning, often preferring to spend available funds on other priority programs in the same budget account, such as the Justice Department's law enforcement initiatives and the Commerce Department's trade promotion activities. Congressional interest in the census heightens as serious preparations get under way for each count, usually two years before the census year. Even then, the Census Bureau is not guaranteed its full appropriation request. Preparations for the census require sharp increases in funding over a relatively short period (the years ending in "9," "0," and "1"), a cycle not well suited to a budget process that generally contemplates only modest annual increases, no increases at all, or decreases in funding for existing programs.

Nevertheless, the "must-pass" nature of the annual funding bills makes them a logical vehicle for directing changes in census policy. If the administration disagrees strongly with the amount of appropriated funds or a restriction on census methods, the president must veto the entire funding bill, potentially delaying funds for equally important but unrelated federal programs.

Congress uses the annual Commerce appropriations bill to influence census plans by "earmarking" a portion of the funds for a specific activity, such as advertising, or by prohibiting the expenditure of funds on an activity. It also provides more detailed guidance to the Census Bureau in committee reports. Although legally nonbinding, the "report language" explains the intent of the bill and often includes more detail than the bill itself as to how the overall funding for each program should be spent. Appropriators also express their views on the general direction of census plans in the committee reports, noting their concern about the number of questions on the census long form or Census Bureau staffing levels, for example. Occasionally, the reports direct the Census Bureau to take certain steps, such as including American citizens living overseas in the census; however, the Census Bureau is legally required to comply only with bill language that is signed into law.

Independent Agencies and Organizations

Congress often turns to independent, nonpartisan agencies of the legislative branch, or other independent government organizations, to help it oversee and monitor the census process. Several of these organizations have helped legislators identify strengths and weaknesses in the census process. They also have recommended new methods for research or testing, evaluated the results of census tests, assessed the fiscal and political consequences of various census methods, and analyzed cost estimates of census operations.

The U.S. Government Accountability Office (GAO) (formerly, the U.S. General Accounting Office) is the investigative and audit agency of the legislative branch. Primarily at the request of the census authorizing committees, the GAO has evaluated census plans and procedures, analyzed management practices, and monitored census operations in real time, for the past several decades. Its findings and recommendations are conveyed in testimony at congressional hearings or in written reports.

Congress also relies on the Congressional Research Service (CRS), an arm of the Library of Congress, for legal analyses of statutes governing the census, research into the uses of census data, and historical narratives of census methods and legislative activity affecting the count. The CRS also monitors the effect of population change on congressional apportionment.

The National Academy of Sciences is a congressionally chartered, private, nonprofit corporation that advises the federal government on issues requiring technical and scientific expertise. At the request of Congress or federal agencies, the academy's National Research Council convenes panels of experts to study scientific aspects of policies and programs. Since the 1970s the council's Committee on National Statistics has studied census methods and content requirements, and it has issued several exhaustive reports that include recommendations for new census methods and future research. In the early 1990s two separate panels concluded that the Bureau of the Census could not reduce the persistent, differential undercount of racial minorities without employing sampling and statistical methods to supplement traditional counting operations. Congressional opponents of sampling, however, essentially discounted the panels' findings, a clear demonstration of Congress's ultimate authority to decide how the census should be conducted.

Determining Census Content

Another key decision that must be made for each census is the type and amount of information to be collected. For much of census history, Congress established the precise topics to be covered and the questions to be asked in the law enacted before each decennial count. As the nation grew and became more complex, Congress increasingly relied on the census for a wide range of demographic, social, housing, and economic information to help it evaluate conditions, assess need, and address both national and local problems.

As with much of the census planning process in recent history, Congress delegated more authority over content determination to the Commerce Department, but it retained clear lines of oversight through reporting mechanisms in the law. The Census Act of 1954 (Public Law 83-740) grants the secretary of commerce broad authority to conduct the census "in such form and content as he may determine." It also requires the secretary to report to Congress, no later than three years before census day, the subject matters that will be included in the next census. No later than two years before each census, the secretary must report the questions that will be included on the census forms. These reporting requirements have given Congress specific opportunities to review the proposed topics to be covered, as well as the questions that will appear on the census forms, before the questionnaires are finalized and printed in the year prior to the census.

While the law provides for notification to Congress of proposed census content, it does not explicitly require Congress to approve the topics or questions proposed by the Census Bureau. The absence of a formal approval process has given the Census Bureau some flexibility in deciding what data to collect and how to collect them. At times Congress has been forced to pass legislation to add topics or modify questions when either the Census Bureau or the U.S. Office of Management and Budget (OMB), which is currently responsible for approving all federal data-collection activities under the Paperwork Reduction Act of 1980 (Public Law 96-511), objected to the changes on technical or policy grounds.

For example, prior to the 1990 census, the OMB decided that some of the questions initially proposed by the Bureau of the Census on home heating fuel and other housing characteristics should be eliminated to reduce the burden of response on the public, much to the dismay of the utility and housing industries. In addition, in the standard question on race, the Census Bureau decided to ask Asian and Pacific Islander Americans to write in their specific country of origin, instead of providing a list of countries that respondents could simply check off, as it had in the 1980 census. Supporters for the existing questions objected. Congress passed legislation to ensure the collection of particular information on home heating and plumbing and to require a check-off format for Asian Americans. President Ronald Reagan refused to sign the legislation, but in the end Congress prevailed. When the 101st Congress convened in January 1989, the Bureau of the Census informed the relevant authorizing committees that it had decided to modify the race question, as set forth in the failed legislation, and to retain the questions on home heating equipment and plumbing facilities.

The controversy over the 1990 census forms illustrated the precarious balance of power between Congress and the bureau under the broad delegation of authority to the executive branch in the Census Act of 1954. This balance can affect all aspects of census planning, preparation, and implementation.

More often in recent decades, Congress has guided the content of the census forms without resorting to legislative battle with the Census Bureau. It has successfully expressed its interest in collecting certain information informally through consultations with the bureau. For example, several legislators persuaded the bureau to tabulate the number of Taiwanese Americans in the 1990 census, after overcoming State Department objections that designating Taiwanese as having an independent national origin might undermine the United States' official position of not recognizing the independence of Taiwan from the People's Republic of China.

Congress also has guided the content determination process by including directives in the committee reports that accompany the Census Bureau's annual spending bill. Following the 1990 census, influential members of the House appropriations committee were convinced that the number of questions asked in the census (particularly on the long form) contributed to declining response rates. For several years the committee's legislative reports included strong language directing the Census Bureau to reduce the amount of data collected in the census. That clear evidence of congressional intent, while not having the force of law, convinced the bureau to scale back the length of both the short and long forms for the 2000 count.

But since delegating substantial authority over census design and content to the bureau in the Census Act of 1954, Congress has influenced census content primarily through authorizing statutes for federal grant-in-aid programs, the number of which exploded in the post–World War II period. A significant number of these programs used population and other socioeconomic data to distribute funds to the states and cities; the census, or other government surveys that rely on the census to produce reliable estimates, was often the only source for the data.

Programmatic Uses of Census Data

Concerns about reapportionment and redistricting have been a primary but not exclusive factor driving congressional activity on census issues. The desire for a wide range of demographic, social, and economic information about the nation's population increased substantially in the latter half of the twentieth century. Lawmakers sought information for increasingly smaller units of geography both to evaluate the need for federal resources or intervention at the state and local level and to distribute funds according to program formulas once they identified those needs.

According to the GAO, $185 billion in federal aid was distributed in 1998 to states or substate areas based in whole or in part on census data. Most population-based federal assistance is allocated according to formula grants. Large formula grant programs include Foster Care, Highway Planning and Construction, Employment and Training for Dislocated Workers, and Child Care and Development Block Grants; Medicaid reimbursements to states also rely on census population figures. Eligibility for some aid programs, such as Community Development Block Grants, is based on population size. Federal aid also is available through program grants, which fund specific projects such as research or planning. Examples of program grants that are distributed based on census data include Rural Development Grants and Head Start. Some direct lending and guaranteed lending programs, such as loans for rural electrification and water and waste disposal, depend at least in part on census data to establish eligibility.

While population is the most common factor in federal aid formulas, other characteristic data collected in the census are used to distribute funds or establish eligibility for grants. The number of people with incomes below the poverty level is a factor in some programs that target disadvantaged families or children, while census data on commuting patterns are used to allocate transportation funds. Other factors used to allocate funds or determine eligibility for funds are unemployment, per capita income, age, and counts of specific population subgroups, such as migrant children.

Typically, the authorizing statutes for federal grants-in-aid programs specify the source of the data to be used in determining the distribution of funds. Some programs require the use of decennial census data, while others require only the most recent data available. In the latter case, updated population estimates produced annually by the Census Bureau often are used. Formulas that rely on certain data but do not specify the source often are viewed as de facto requirements to collect the information in the census when no other reliable or cost-effective source exists.

The Twenty-First Century Census

The partisan battle over Census 2000 began in 1996, lasted well into the next decade, and thus also affected the planning for Census 2010. Some Republicans in Congress saw the administration's "one-number census" in 2000 as a cleverly designed plan to "fix" the census to give Democrats an advantage for redistricting. The Clinton administration portrayed its 2000 census plan as one built on scientific principles that incorporated sampling for nonresponse to reduce costs and a post-enumeration survey to correct for persons missed and for persons counted twice. Republicans argued that sampling for any purpose was both illegal and unconstitutional. Their position was that sampling in the census is not permitted by Title 13 of the U.S. Code Section 195, which says, "Except for the determination of population for purposes of apportionment of Representatives in Congress among the several states shall, if he considers it feasible, authorize the use of the statistical method known as 'sampling' in carrying out the provisions of this title." Further, they argued, the Constitution calls for an "actual enumeration" and the use of sampling is not that. The administration argued that the attorney general said the law permitted sampling and that nothing in the Constitution addressed the issue. In hearings and consultations in 1996, neither the congressional critics nor the administration budged from their positions.

In 1997, the appropriations process became the battleground for the dispute. Republicans attempted to attach anti-sampling language to a mid-year emergency appropriations bill aimed primarily at helping flood victims in the Midwest and Northwest and supporting extended military operations in Bosnia. President Clinton vetoed the measure, and the Republican leaders relented and removed the anti-sampling language from the emergency bill. Later in 1997 the issue arose again as Republicans included an anti-sampling provision in the fiscal year 1998 Commerce Department spending bill. Intense negotiations at the highest levels of Congress and the White House resulted in a compromise agreement that essentially required the Bureau of the Census to prepare both for its original census plan and for a census without any sampling methods. It also authorized Congress to challenge the proposed sampling methods in court and created an eight-member Census Monitoring Board to oversee the census. Included as part of the fiscal year 1998 Commerce appropriations bill, the November 1997 agreement represented the most extensive use of the appropriations process to direct census plans since enactment of the modern census statute in 1954.

In January 1999 the Supreme Court issued its ruling in *Department of Commerce v. U.S. House of Representatives,* the lawsuit authorized in the 1998 appropriations process. Sampling violates the provision in Title 13 of the U.S. Code, the Court ruled. The Bureau of the Census was forced to redesign the 2000 census to conduct nonresponse follow-up at all addresses for which a census form was not returned by mail. This change added $1.7 billion to the cost of the census. The plans for conducting a survey following the census to provide estimates to correct the census could still be implemented, but those results could not be used for the apportionment counts to be delivered at the end of December 2000. The partisan battle over the 2000 census continued through the conduct of the census in 2000. Republicans in Congress and on the Census Monitoring Board criticized the census planning and execution and the content of the census long form at every opportunity.

The 2000 presidential election changed the political landscape for the census. After the release of the apportionment counts, a Republican administration, supported by a Republican Congress, controlled the release of 2000 census data. Simultaneously, the Bureau of the Census began to question the results coming in from the Accuracy and Coverage Evaluation (ACE) survey. Two months later the bureau announced that there were sufficient questions about the quality of the ACE survey data that a major effort was needed to study the methodology and the results it produced. The survey would not be used to correct the census counts for errors of omission or erroneous inclusion. Redistricting numbers were released in March 2001, and the remaining data products flowed on a regular schedule. The Republican Congress praised the census and moved on to other issues.

The Bureau of the Census immediately began planning the 2010 census. In 2001, the bureau announced that the 2010 census would be conducted on handheld computers about the size of a small paperback book and about as thick as a package of cigarettes. The census questionnaire on these machines would be the shortest since the early nineteenth century. Only the basic questions needed for apportionment and districting would be asked. Everything else would be diverted to a new survey, the American Community Survey. This new census would cost over $11 billion, almost twice the $6.5 billion cost of the 2000 census and four times the cost of the 1990 census.

These dramatic innovations did not draw much attention from Congress. From January 2001 to January 2009, a Republican executive branch controlled the planning for the 2010 census, and from January 2001 to January 2007, Republicans controlled the legislative oversight of that planning. Thus the partisan suspicion that motivated congressional attention and characterized census planning in the 1990s evaporated. Ironically perhaps, the lack of close congressional scrutiny during the mid-decade planning phase for the 2010 census may have increased the cost of the 2010 count considerably. Throughout the decade both the GAO and the Department of Commerce inspector general repeatedly warned that the handheld computer project was a high risk. Between January 2004 and July 2006, the GAO and the Department of Commerce inspector general issued nine reports warning of technical and managerial problems with the handheld initiative. At the time the reports received little attention.

The scrutiny of the project by Congress changed dramatically when the Democrats took control of the House and Senate in the 2006 elections, and the flaws in the project became obvious. In the spring of 2008, the secretary of commerce announced that the Census Bureau would abandon the handheld computers and revert to pencil and paper for the field data collection, a change that would add about $3 billion to the cost of the census. The handhelds were used for address canvassing, but the 2010 census was conducted much like the 2000 census.

Census supporters routinely express frustration that the Congress does not pay sufficient attention to the census during the middle of the decade. Since 1990, planning for the next census has begun before the current census closes its books. The census, supporters argue, is a 12-year cycle. Planning and design are done early in the decade. Most critical decisions are completed by year 6 in the decade to allow for testing in year 7, finalized design in year 8, and production in years 9 and 10. Census data are released in years 11 and 12. Congress does not begin examining the census until most of the design decisions have been made, and then members want to tinker with the design. This can be as minor as adding a question to the census questionnaire to the full-scale battle leading up to the 2000 census. To be responsible, supporters argue, Congress should focus its oversight energies during the planning and design phase in years 1 through 6 and leave the Census Bureau alone to implement that design.

Given the history of Congress and the census, and the purposes for which the census is conducted, it is likely that there will always be political pressures on the conduct of the census. The stakes for Congress are too high for it to be otherwise.

See also *Apportionment and districting; Census law; Content; Content determination.*

. . . . DAVID MCMILLEN

BIBLIOGRAPHY
Anderson, Margo J. *The American Census: A Social History.* New Haven, Conn.: Yale University Press, 1988.
U.S. General Accounting Office. *Decennial Census: Overview of Historical Census Issues.* GAO/GGD-98-103. Washington, D.C.: U.S. Government Printing Office, May 1998.
————. *Formula Grants: Effects of Adjusted Population Counts on Federal Funding to the States.* GAO/HEHS-99-69. Washington, D.C.: U.S. Government Printing Office, February 1999.
U.S. House of Representatives. Title 13—Census. http://uscode.house.gov/download/title_13.shtml

Constitution

See *Census law; Introduction; Three-fifths compromise.*

Content

To fulfill the purposes of congressional apportionment specified by the U.S. Constitution, the decennial census of population need count only the number of persons (before 1870, the number of free and slave persons) in each state. From the beginning, however, members of Congress and others inside and outside the federal government recognized the value of having the census collect additional content to inform program administration, policy development, and general public understanding.

The first census in 1790 had very limited content. U.S. marshals in each judicial district obtained for each household a count of the number of free white males 16 years of age or older, free white males under 16 years, free white females, all other free persons, and slaves. The 22nd census in 2000 had much more extensive content. All households were asked on the short form about the age, race, Hispanic origin, sex, and household relationship of each household member, and whether the housing unit was owned or rented. In addition, about one-sixth of households were asked on the long form to answer another three dozen questions for each person (two-thirds of the questions pertained to people age 15 or older) and another two dozen questions for the housing unit. The 2010 census was a short-form-only census because the additional questions asked of the long-form sample in censuses from 1960 through 2000 were now ascertained on a continuous basis in the American Community Survey, which began full implementation in 2005.

In the decades between 1790 and 2000, the content of the census expanded and changed in response to changing needs for information about particular groups (for example, immigrants, farmers, veterans, people with disabilities) and for information relevant to particular issues (for example, education, transportation). Some topics have appeared in almost every census, and most censuses have covered a wide range of topics.

Statistical sampling, in which questions are asked of samples of households instead of all households, was used in censuses beginning in 1940 on a small scale and greatly expanded in censuses from 1950 through 2000 to reduce the costs and public burden of providing all of the information that was needed from the census. For the 1990 and 2000 censuses, concerted efforts were made not to increase and, if possible, to scale back the number of questions, so that these censuses had somewhat fewer questions than were asked in 1980. In 2010, only ten questions were asked for each household—the total number of people living in the house or apartment, whether anyone who stayed there on April 1, 2010, was left out of the total count, a telephone number for the household, whether the housing unit was owned or rented, and, for each household member, the age and date of birth, sex, household relationship, race, ethnicity, and whether the person sometimes lived at another residence (for example, college housing). Additional questions previously asked on the census long form are now included in the American Community Survey.

Listed below (in italics) are the short-form population items in the 2010 census and the long-form population items in the 2000 census, with a summary of their appearance in earlier censuses. Question wording and detail vary, often substantially, across censuses. (See *American Community Survey: questionnaire content* for the questions included in that survey beginning in 2005; see *Long form,* Table 1, for an item-by-item comparison of population and housing census content in 1960 to 2000.)

2010 Census Short-Form Population Items

Age, race, and sex
Asked in every census from 1790 to 2010 (race question in 2000 and 2010 permits respondent to mark one or more races; date of birth asked in addition to or in place of age in 1900 and 1960 to 2010).

Hispanic origin
Asked in 1930 (in the race question) and in 1970 to 2010.

Relationship to head of household
Asked in 1880 to 2010.

Whether sometimes lives or stays somewhere else
Asked in 2010 (to assist in identifying duplicate enumerations).

2000 Census Long-Form Population Items

Ancestry
Asked in 1980 to 2000.

Citizenship and year of immigration
Citizenship asked in 1820, 1830, 1870, 1890 to 2000; year of immigration asked in 1900 to 1930, 1970 to 2000; year of naturalization asked in 1920; eligibility to vote asked in 1870.

Disability (several questions)
Items related to physical or mental disabilities asked in 1830 to 1890, 1900 (supplemental schedules), 1910, 1920 to 1930 (supplemental schedules), 1970 to 2000.

Education (school attendance, including whether public or private, and highest grade completed)
School attendance asked in 1850 to 2000; public or private school asked in 1960 to 2000; educational attainment asked in 1940 to 2000; literacy asked in 1840 to 1930; vocational training asked in 1970.

Employment status last week
Asked in 1930 to 2000; duration of unemployment asked in 1880 to 1910, 1930 (supplemental schedule), 1940, 1950, 1980.

Hours usually worked per week last year
Asked in 1980 to 2000; hours worked last week asked in 1940 to 1990.

Income (total and by source, such as wages, Social Security)
Asked in 1940 to 2000; categories expanded over time.

Language (whether speak a language other than English at home; how well does respondent speak English)
Language asked in 1890 to 1940, 1960 to 2000; how well does respondent speak English asked in 1980 to 2000; language of parents asked in 1910, 1920.

Marital status
Asked in 1880 to 2000; other marriage-related questions asked in 1850 to 1910, 1930 to 1980; number of children living asked in 1890 to 1910; number of children ever born asked in 1890 to 1910, 1940 to 1990.

Occupation and industry of current employment, class of worker
Occupation asked in 1850 to 2000; industry asked in 1820, 1840, 1910 to 2000; class of worker asked in 1910 to 2000; occupation, industry, and class of worker five years ago asked in 1970; activity five years ago asked in 1970, 1980.

Place of birth
Asked in 1850 to 2000; place of birth of parents asked in 1870 to 1970.

Place of work and *transportation to work* (several questions)
Asked in 1960 to 2000.

Responsibility for grandchildren
New question in 2000.

Prior residence (five years ago) and *farm residence* (housing item)
Prior residence asked in 1940 to 2000; farm residence asked in 1890 to 2000; year moved into present residence asked in 1960, 1970, 1980 to 2000 (housing item); whether previously a farm resident asked in 1940, 1950.

Veteran status (including period of service) and *years of military service*
Veteran status asked in *1840, 1890, 1910, 1930* to *2000*; period of service asked in *1930, 1950* to *2000*; years of military

service asked in *1990, 2000*; questions on dependents of veterans asked in *1890, 1940*.

Weeks worked last year
Asked in 1940 to 2000.

Year last worked
Asked in 1960 to 2000.

The 2000 census long form included one new question (responsibility for grandchildren) and significant changes to previous questions (for example, disability), but it did not include some questions that were asked in earlier censuses—for example, occupation five years ago and vocational training (asked in 1970), value of real estate (asked in 1850 to 1870), and value of personal property (asked in 1860 and 1870). Further, censuses from 1850 through 1930 included not only general population questions but also one or more supplemental schedules (forms for interviewers to record answers). In 1850 to 1890, questions were asked on a supplemental schedule about people who died in the previous year. In 1880 to 1930, detailed questions were posed on one or more supplemental schedules for such groups as people with disabilities or people who were residents of institutions. (Recent censuses include residents of institutions, who are categorized by type of institution, but no special questions were formulated for them.) In 1880 to 1910, there were supplemental schedules for Native Americans. The 1930 census included a supplemental schedule on unemployment.

The population census has often been conducted in conjunction with other censuses. In 1810 the population census was augmented by a census of manufactures. In later decades censuses of agriculture, mining, governments, business, and transportation were conducted at the same time as the population census, but these censuses are now conducted in years that do not conflict with the census of population.

Since 1940 the population census has included a census of housing as an integral component—see list of short-form and long-form housing items in the 1960 to 2000 censuses in *Long form,* Table 1, and in the American Community Survey, beginning in 2005, in *American Community Survey: questionnaire content.* In censuses from 1950 through 2000, a survey of residential financing was conducted in conjunction with the population and housing census; and in 1960 and 1970 a survey of components of change in the housing stock (for example, new additions, demolitions) was conducted in conjunction with the population and housing census.

See also *American Community Survey: questionnaire content; Content determination; Housing; Long form; Related data sources; Sampling for content.*

. . . . CONSTANCE F. CITRO

BIBLIOGRAPHY

U.S. Census Bureau. "Population and Housing Inquiries in U.S. Decennial Censuses, 1790–1970." Working paper no. 39. Washington, D.C.: U.S. Department of Commerce, 1973.

———. *Residential Finance Survey: 2001.* Census 2000 Special Report No. 27. Washington, D.C.: U.S. Department of Commerce, 2005.

National Research Council. Committee on National Statistics, *Modernizing the U.S. Census,* Panel on Census Requirements in the Year 2000 and Beyond. Barry Edmonston and Charles Schultze, eds. Washington, D.C.: The National Academies Press, 1995 (see particularly Chapter 6). Available at http://www.nap.edu/catalog.php?record_id=4805.

———. *The 2000 Census—Counting under Adversity,* Committee on National Statistics. Panel to Review the 2000 Census. Constance Citro and Janet Norwood, eds. Washington, D.C.: The National Academies Press, 2004 (see particularly Chapter 7). Available at http://www.nap.edu/catalog.php?record_id=10907.

Content Determination

The process of determining the content of the decennial population census (the questions asked) involves many players. Members of the U.S. Congress were largely responsible for setting the content of the first few censuses, under the constitutional mandate that a census be conducted every ten years "in such Manner as they shall by Law direct," and Congress continues to play a role in content determination today. However, other agencies and groups increasingly assumed important roles in content determination. In recent censuses extensive testing also contributed to decisions about including items in the census and about the best ways to ask questions so as to obtain valid responses. The resulting information collected in censuses up through 2000 reflected the balance of forces about which questions appeared most needed to support public policy, provide time series for analysis, and serve the general public understanding.

With the advent of the American Community Survey (ACS), which replaces the decennial census long-form sample with continuous measurement of the population, the process of content determination is taking two somewhat distinct paths. The 2010 census included a short set of questions designed to obtain an accurate count of every American and to obtain such basic information as age, sex, race, ethnicity, and household relationship. The ACS, which was first tested in 1996 and became fully operational in 2005, includes content that is very similar to that obtained on the "long form" used in censuses from 1960 through 2000, but that content has evolved and continues to evolve to meet changing societal needs.

History

For the first census in 1790, members of Congress debated the merits of including additional questions beyond the minimal constitutional requirement to ascertain the number of free and slave persons (excluding Native Americans not taxed). James Madison argued for asking not only for basic demographic information, such as age and sex, but also for such information as occupation to help understand the economic makeup of the country. The final law stipulated more limited content; specifically, for each household, the numbers of free white males by age (16 and over and under age 16), free white females, all other free persons, and slaves.

Groups such as the American Philosophical Society lobbied Congress to expand the number of questions for the

1800 census; however, the only new items comprised a finer breakdown of the white male and female populations by age, Congress having decided that additional questions were either unnecessary or unconstitutional. The 1820 census marked the first time that Congress agreed to a census inquiry about the economic composition of the population. The question asked the number of household members principally engaged in agriculture, manufacturing, or commerce.

President John Quincy Adams, who had directed the 1820 census when he was secretary of state, made several suggestions for the 1830 census that were adopted, including the addition of further detail on age. Congress also added questions on the numbers of people who were deaf, blind, or "dumb."

For the 1850 census, a Census Board, consisting of the secretaries of state and interior and the postmaster general, was set up to draft legislation for the census. The board enlisted the aid of expert advisers, who recommended that the census schedules (forms) be expanded and restructured to collect data for each individual instead of collecting summaries for each household. They also recommended that different schedules be developed for free persons, slaves, people who had died in the preceding year, agriculture, manufacturing, and other "social" statistics (for example, information on schools, libraries, crime, religion). After extensive debate, Congress adopted most of the board's recommended changes, which significantly added to the census content. (An exception was that southern senators blocked the inclusion of many of the proposed new questions for slaves.)

The 1850 census legislation governed the content of the 1860 census. For the 1870 census a House select committee, headed by James Garfield, with advice from outside experts, recommended adding new questions on marital status, immigration, and other topics, but most of its recommendations were not adopted.

The 1880 census saw increased lobbying on the part of academics, businesses, and other groups, as well as members of Congress, to add, modify, or drop specific questions from the census. By the 1920 census, such requests had proliferated. A new player—the joint Census Advisory Committee of the American Statistical Association and American Economic Association—was formed in 1918. This committee helped the Bureau of the Census (established as a permanent agency in 1902) sort through and prioritize the myriad requests for new questions on the census.

The Census Act of 1929 authorized the director of the census to select the census items, subject to approval by the secretary of commerce. The bureau then faced directly the tension between keeping the census content relatively simple and consistent over time and the interest of many groups and individuals in adding "their items" to the census. Beginning with the 1930 census the bureau used public conferences to solicit input and involve interested parties in the development of census content.

The advent of modern statistical sampling methods made it possible to accommodate more questions in the census, without incurring the costs and public burden of asking everyone to respond. For the first time, in the 1940 census six new questions were asked of only 5 percent of the population instead of everyone. Subsequent censuses greatly expanded the use of sampling for content. Beginning in 1960, separate "short" and "long" forms were used for mail delivery to households. The short form contained the items asked of all households; one or more long forms included the short-form items plus sample items asked of only some households.

Census Content Determination Today

Congress remains an important player in the determination of census content for the modern census. By provisions of the Census Act of 1954, the Census Bureau is required to submit to Congress a list of topics to be included in the census three years before census day (April 1) and a list of specific questions two years before census day. Following the 1990 census Congress expressed strong interest in simplifying the short form and even eliminating the long form, on grounds that the length and complexity of the forms contributed to undercoverage of the population. The Census Bureau conducted extensive testing on "user-friendly" short and long forms and also developed plans for a new American Community Survey. The advent of the ACS made it possible to drop the long form beginning in the 2010 census.

Congress also occasionally intervened on specific questions. For example, in the 1990 census race question, the bureau wanted Asian and Pacific Islander Americans to write in their specific country of origin instead of checking a box from a list of countries. Pressure from Congress and the Asian American community, which stemmed from concern about the likely poor quality of write-in entries, led the bureau to adopt a check-off list for 1990 similar to that used in 1980. In 2005, Congress explicitly mandated that the census and the ACS must retain a "some other race" category.

Beginning with the 1960 census, a federal interagency council, organized by the U.S. Office of Management and Budget (OMB), played a major role in determining census content. Because of the growth in federal programs that use census data to allocate funds to states and localities and other federally mandated uses of census data (for example, for civil rights enforcement), primacy was given in recent censuses to questions that were needed for federal program purposes. The interagency councils and their subcommittees provided forums for agencies to debate and establish priorities. One such interagency group pressed successfully in the 1970 census to have a question on Hispanic origin added at a very late date to one of the long forms used in that census (the 5 percent form). Input on census content also continued to be obtained from a broad range of groups and individuals through such mechanisms as formal advisory committees, public meetings, conferences, and other contacts.

The OMB has a formal role in the determination of census content because of the requirement in the 1942 Federal Reports Act that it clear all federal agency questionnaires intended for more than nine people. In 1987 the OMB did not approve the 1990 census dress rehearsal questionnaire, citing public burden, and ordered a reduction in the planned sample size for the long form, the deletion of several questions, and the placement of some housing items on the long form instead of the short form. Opposition from Congress and the census data user community to these changes resulted in a compromise whereby only a few questions were deleted or moved from the short to the long form. Also, the overall long-form sample size was maintained, although a smaller sampling fraction was used in more densely settled areas.

In the mid 1990s the OMB led a process to revise *Statistical Policy Directive No. 15—Race and Ethnic Standards for Federal Statistics and Administrative Reporting*, first issued in 1977. After extensive testing and public input, the OMB issued revised *Standards for Maintaining, Collecting, and Presenting Federal Data on Race and Ethnicity* in 1997. The updated directive maintained a two-question format for race and Hispanic origin, included separate categories for Asians and for Native Hawaiian and other Pacific Islanders, and allowed respondents to select more than one racial category. These changes were implemented in Census 2000, which made other changes in the format and specific wording of the race and ethnicity questions on the basis of extensive testing.

For the 2000 census, the decision was made to limit the census content almost entirely to items that were mandated in federal legislation for such purposes as fund allocation or required for federal purposes in that the census was the only source of needed data. Further, to be included on the short form, the item had to be needed at the smallest level of census geography, the census block. Federal agencies played a key role in determining which census items were mandated, required, or only loosely tied to federal programs. The Bureau of the Census also surveyed nonfederal groups about their uses of census items and commissioned case studies of data applications from the Association of Public Data Users. Input from these efforts helped support the retention of some items in the 2000 census that were not specifically mandated or required for federal programs. Overall, the result was a significant reduction in the length of the short form as well as some changes in the long form. (See *Long form*, Table 1, for the short-form and long-form population and housing items in the 1960 to 2000 censuses.)

The Census Bureau carried out extensive research and experimentation on the appearance and content of the forms for recent censuses. A mail survey of a large sample of housing units conducted several years before the census, the National Content Test, was used to test alternative question wording and the feasibility of including proposed new or modified questions. Other tests of question wording and questionnaire format were carried out through small-scale surveys, cognitive research in which small groups of respondents were walked through the questionnaire or in other ways probed to see how they interpreted questions, and experiments with alternative questionnaires during the census itself. These kinds of tests and research are important to increase the likelihood that respondents will interpret the questions as they are intended and provide valid answers.

ACS Content Determination

The ACS was planned to include the content of the census long form, but from the beginning there have been changes to the content. For example, the first 1996 test questionnaire included new questions on receipt and value of food stamps in the previous 12 months and whether women age 15–50 had given birth to any children in the past 12 months.

In 2000 the OMB and the bureau established the ACS Federal Interagency Committee with more than 30 members; its first task was to verify the justification for each question planned for the 2003 ACS. However, there was no specified process by which further content changes would be made in the ACS. Agencies that wanted to add a question were informed that legislation would be required. The National Science Foundation's Science Resources Statistics (SRS) Division sought congressional approval to add a question on field of bachelor's degree, in order to facilitate an NSF-sponsored survey on scientists and engineers that had traditionally used the long-form question on occupation to develop the sample. Relevant congressional committees indicated that the OMB should specify and oversee a process for questionnaire changes to the ACS. Consequently, the OMB in 2006 issued a memorandum specifying a more flexible process for modifying the ACS content. Under this process, ACS content can be modified only once a year; to add or modify questions, the changes must be reviewed by relevant agencies and then pretested, including a field test, and, finally, approved by the OMB. A 2006 ACS Content Test provided the basis in 2008 for rewording several questions, including those on disability, and adding questions on service-connected disability, marital history, and health insurance coverage. A 2007 ACS Content Test provided the basis for adding field of bachelor's degree beginning in 2009. No further content changes are to be made until 2013.

See also *Advisory committees; American Community Survey: questionnaire content; Congress and the census; Long form; Sampling for content; Federal statistical system oversight and policy: intersection of OMB and the decennial census.*

. . . . CONSTANCE F. CITRO

BIBLIOGRAPHY

Anderson, Margo J. *The American Census: A Social History.* New Haven, Conn.: Yale University Press, 1988.

Magnuson, Diana L. "Who and What Determined the Content of the U.S. Population Schedule over Time." *Historical Methods* 28 (winter 1995): 11–26.

National Research Council. *Using the American Community Survey: Benefits and Challenges.* Panel on the Functionality and Usability of Data from the American Community Survey, Constance F. Citro and Graham Kalton, eds. Committee on National Statistics. Washington, D.C.: The National Academies Press, 2007. Available at: www.nap.edu/catalog .php?record_id=11901.

———. *Using the American Community Survey for the National Science Foundation's Science and Engineering Workforce Statistics Programs.* Panel on Assessing the Benefits of the American Community Survey for the NSF Division of Science Resources Statistics, Committee on National

Statistics. Washington, D.C.: The National Academies Press (2008). Available at: www.nap.edu/catalog.php?record_id=12244.

U.S. Bureau of the Census. "Planning the Census." In *1990 Census of Population and Housing History,* part B, chap. 2. Washington, D.C.: U.S. Department of Commerce, 1995.

U.S. Census Bureau. *Design and Methodology of the American Community Survey* (Chapter 5). Washington, D.C.: U.S. Department of Commerce, 2009.

———. *Questions Planned for the 2010 Census and American Community Survey.* Washington, D.C.: U.S. Department of Commerce, 2008.

Coverage Evaluation

As was suspected by George Washington with respect to the first census in 1790 and is clear to anyone who has considered the matter since then, the decennial census does not obtain a complete count. Although most people are included only once and at the proper address, many people (and households) are missed, and others are included more than once or are otherwise included erroneously (for example, those born after census day). In other words, the decennial census experiences *undercounts* and *overcounts.* There are also those who are included but at the wrong address, which does not affect the count for the nation as a whole but, depending on the level of geography used by the application and the distance between the two addresses, may produce an undercount and an overcount in two different areas.

The difference between undercounts and overcounts for the nation or a given demographic group or region—almost always expressed as a percentage—is the *net undercount.* When the net undercount is uneven across groups or regions, the census is subject to a *differential (net) undercount,* typically expressed (for a group or region) in relation to the national level of net undercount. This is an important statistic, since many of the key uses of census counts are to determine population shares. If a demographic group or an area experiences the same percentage net undercount as the nation as a whole, then there is no effect on the shares for that group or area, but if a group or area experiences a large differential net undercount, then its share will be smaller than it should be in comparison with other groups or areas.

The measurement of undercounts and overcounts is a vital component of an overall assessment of census quality, not only to inform data users but also to learn about ways to improve the quality of the census. To support both of these purposes, the U.S. Census Bureau has used *coverage evaluation* programs to measure the degree of census net undercount since at least as far back as the 1950 census. These programs make use of previous censuses, surveys, and administrative records to measure differential net undercount at various levels of geographic and demographic aggregation as well as to understand the mechanisms of census omission, double counting, and other errors. The important uses for which census counts are produced, and the existence of these coverage evaluation programs, have periodically raised the possibility of using the information from these programs to "adjust" the census for net undercount—that is, to use the information from these programs to improve the accuracy of the census counts.

The Major Types of Coverage Evaluation Programs

Demographic Analysis

Demographic analysis (DA) makes use of the following "accounting" equation to estimate net undercount for the current census for a particular demographic group:

Current census count (DA estimate) =
    Previous census count (adjusted for net undercount as measured by DA)
+ Intercensal births
+ Intercensal immigration
− Intercensal deaths
− Intercensal emigration

In recent censuses, since birth records have been considered to be relatively complete only since 1935, the above equation has been used only for people born after 1935. For the population age sixty-five and over, Medicare records have been used to measure net undercount. For those in between, various extrapolation methods involving use of information from multiple censuses and sex ratios (ratios of the number of males to the number of females for a specified demographic group) have been used. For the 2010 census, it was possible to estimate coverage of the population age sixty-five to seventy-five not only by using Medicare records but also by using the accounting equation.

Demographic analysis was the preferred method for assessing census completeness starting with the 1950 census and continuing at least through the 1970 census. It is still valuable in providing independent check totals at the national level for some demographic groups in comparison with estimates from other methods.

Post-Enumeration Survey and Dual-Systems Estimation

The method now primarily relied on by the Census Bureau for coverage evaluation of the census is the use of a post-enumeration survey (PES) coupled with dual-systems estimation (DSE). The original idea was to take a random sample of areas and conduct a second "census" in those areas with better enumerators. Then the ratio of the census count to the survey count would measure census completeness. This approach was found to be unsatisfactory because the survey count did not achieve uniformly superior coverage to the census, perhaps because the survey did not enjoy the same imprimatur as the census in the public eye. Therefore, this "do it again, better" idea was replaced by "do it again, independently," a method suggested first in 1949.

This method, improved and expanded by the Census Bureau for decennial census application, involves two sample surveys. The first, the so-called *P-sample,* is a sample of blocks (or block clusters) for which an address list is created through a separate listing process. After most census operations are completed (therefore the term *post-enumeration*), enumerators obtain an interview at each P-sample address. These post-enumeration survey interviews are matched to the census enumerations for the PES blocks, with four types of individuals comprising the entire population: those in the census and in the PES, those in the census and not in the PES, those in the PES and not in the census, and those in neither the census nor the PES. These four types of individuals are represented in a 2 × 2 contingency table.

In Table 1, N denotes the total population count. All cells but the n_{22} cell (sometimes referred to as the "fourth" cell) can be directly estimated. The estimation of N—equivalent to estimation of the n_{22} cell—is based on three separate assumptions. First, it is assumed that each individual has the same probability p_c of being included in the census and that each individual has the same probability p_p—possibly different from p_c—of being included in the post-enumeration survey. This is the so-called *homogeneity assumption*. Second, given the separate operations of the census and the PES, it is assumed that inclusion in the census is independent of inclusion in the PES. Third, it is assumed that the matching is accurate.

If these assumptions are at least approximately true, then one can estimate N as follows. Since the probability of being included in the census overall is n_{1+} / N, and the probability of being included in the census for those included in the PES is n_{11} / n_{+1}, then except for sample variation, these probabilities should be equal. Equating these probabilities and re-expressing the resulting equation gives the following estimate for the total population count: $N = (n_{1+} n_{+1}) / n_{11}$.

Although the assumption of independence is generally considered to be sound, the Census Bureau has long recognized that the enumeration probabilities are not constant (homogeneous). Therefore, post-enumeration strata are used to group individuals in an effort to have more homogeneous inclusion probabilities within these strata. The data for the 1990 and 2000 censuses were based on age, race, sex, ethnicity, census region, and whether an individual owned or rented his or her residence.

Major complications are that erroneous enumerations, duplicates, and people counted in the wrong location inflate the census count and that census imputations (responses for nonresponding households that are filled in using information for neighboring households of similar type) cannot be matched. To account for these, a second sample survey

operation, the *E-sample,* takes place in parallel with the P-sample. The E-sample is a sample of census enumerations for the PES blocks. These enumerations are rechecked for validity and for whether they are represented in other responses (duplicates). Letting E_{cen} denote the number of valid census enumerations as measured for the PES blocks, letting II denote the number of census imputations, and letting EE denote the number of erroneous and duplicate enumerations in the PES blocks, we get the final dual-systems estimation formula as used by the Census Bureau (within post-enumeration strata):

$$DSE = \left[\frac{(n_{1+} - II)(n_{+1})}{n_{11}} \right] \left[1 - \frac{EE}{E_{cen}} \right]$$

The final estimated net undercount percentage for a post-enumeration stratum is 1 minus the ratio of the census count to the DSE count—for example, $1 - (98/100)$ gives a net undercount of 2 percent (a net overcount correspondingly is represented as a negative; for example, $1 - (100/98)$ gives a minus 2 percent). The estimate of the net undercount percentage for a geographic area is then a weighted linear combination of the net undercount percentages for the pertinent poststrata, weighted by the percentage that each post-enumeration stratum represents in the given area.

Because DSE provides particularly poor estimates of "fourth cells" for male minority group members due to *correlation bias* (that is, the propensity to be missed in both the census and the PES at higher rates than independence would provide for), there have been efforts to combine demographic analysis and DSE approaches for coverage measurement of these groups. The final DSE estimates from the 2000 census used sex ratios to adjust the DSE estimates for black and Hispanic males in certain age groups.

Reverse Record Check

The Canadian census, taken every five years, makes use of the following procedure to evaluate census net undercount. A sample is put together, composed of the following four subsamples: (1) a sample of enumerations from the previous census, (2) a sample of intercensal immigrants, (3) a sample of intercensal births, and (4) a sample of omissions from the previous census. Sample (4) can never be a true sample; it is identified from a small matching operation based on information from the reverse record check of the previous census. The sample is then traced to present-day addresses, and it is determined whether each individual was a resident of Canada as of census day and therefore should have been counted in the census. This alternative count is compared with the census count to measure net undercount. A small-scale matching then is only used to create the fourth sample component, which is needed to evaluate the subsequent census. With each subsequent application of a reverse record check, the fourth sample will become closer to a true sample, because the undercounted population not represented initially is gradually reduced by death and emigration.

Table 1. Individuals in and out of Census Count and Post-Enumeration Survey

	PES		
	In	Out	Total Census Count
Census In	n_{11}	n_{12}	n_{1+}
Out	n_{21}	n_{22}	
Total PES count	n_{+1}		N

Megalist, Super Census, Systematic Observation

Three additional ideas for coverage evaluation, some of which have been tested but none ever implemented on a national scale, are megalist (including composite list and multilist), super census, and systematic observation. In the process called *composite list,* many administrative record lists are merged, and duplicates are weeded out. Then, after the people are traced to current addresses if necessary, the merged list is matched to the census. The results of the matching operation are input into dual-systems estimation. A related approach, referred to as *multilist,* is not to merge the lists but to match them individually to the census and each other and then use what is known as triple or higher systems estimation (based on a higher dimensional contingency table), which is a generalization of dual-systems estimation.

The *super census* process makes use of repeated enumeration attempts, and possibly administrative records, to obtain what is considered to be a complete count of a sample of areas, comparable in size to a sample for a post-enumeration survey. These counts are then weighted up to provide estimates of the total population count. There is no matching to the census, only a comparison of counts for areas as in a reverse record check.

In *systematic observation,* some census employees are each given several months to obtain a complete list (including only basic demographic information and addresses) of the residents of a small area, possibly comprising one or two census blocks. Once obtained, this list is matched to the census enumerations in those areas. Even if the number of areas was relatively small, this procedure would provide information, much of it anecdotal, on the causes of census undercounts and overcounts. One would then use ratio estimation for estimation strata (similar to post-enumeration strata) to develop estimates of census net undercount for larger areas and demographic groups.

A Quick History of Coverage Evaluation in the U.S. Census

Coverage evaluation was first made possible during the mid-twentieth century as a result of the development of sample survey methodology and the improvement in the accuracy and completeness of vital statistics records. In 1950 the Census Bureau used a post-enumeration survey, made up of a list sample and an area sample, based on the "do it again, better" idea. The area sample was used to measure omissions of whole households, and the list sample was used to measure omissions within households and other errors. Enumerations from both the list and the area samples were matched to census records. Also, the 1950 census was evaluated for net undercount using demographic analysis.

In 1960 the Census Bureau again used a post-enumeration survey, and it had a design similar to that used in 1950. In addition, record checks (comparisons with aggregate counts based on administrative records) of the numbers of college students and the elderly were carried out. A small study of a reverse record check was also conducted in 1960. However, difficulty in tracing the sample to current addresses as a result of the ten-year gap between censuses made it clear that this method was not promising for evaluating the U.S. decennial census.

Given the discrepancy between demographic analysis estimates of net undercount, considered to be reliable for 1960, and those from the PES based on the "do it again, better" method, coverage evaluation for the 1970 census relied primarily on demographic analysis. In addition, a match study between the Current Population Survey (CPS) and the census and some record checks provided additional information for targeted groups—namely, the elderly and males age twenty to twenty-nine living in the District of Columbia.

In 1980 the Census Bureau first used a post-enumeration survey with the "do it again, independently" methodology. The PES used the April and August samples from the CPS. The entire process—that is, both the sample and the estimation—was referred to as the Post-Enumeration Program, or PEP. It was hoped that this program would provide details on census net undercount for relatively small geographic areas and demographic groups. The 1980 census also was the first to use an E-sample. Unfortunately, data collection problems with PEP meant that a match status between the CPS and the census could not be determined for about 8 percent of the individuals. In addition, difficulties in using the August CPS sample-based estimates arose because of people changing residences. As a result, different treatments for nonresponse caused relatively wide variations in estimates of net undercount. Demographic analysis was again used in 1980. However, the relatively large amount of undocumented immigration (very roughly measured) was thought to reduce the utility of these estimates, especially for nonblack populations.

In 1990 the Census Bureau again focused its efforts on coverage evaluation through use of a PES with dual-systems estimation in addition to demographic analysis. (One of the tests leading up to the 1990 census, the Forward Trace Study, had again shown the difficulty in tracing addresses over a ten-year time frame, making it clear that a reverse record check would be difficult to implement.) In 1990 the post-enumeration survey, instead of being based on the CPS, used a stand-alone sample survey of 165,000 housing units. Through use of a stand-alone survey, some of the operational problems that occurred in 1980, especially with respect to nonresponse and unresolved matching but also with respect to questionnaire design and timing, were reduced. After a substantial computer-programming error was eliminated and some additional fine-tuning was done in 1992, the report by the Census Bureau's Committee on Adjustment of Postcensal Estimates defended the reliability of the PES estimates for areas of 100,000 and higher but did not fully support their use for smaller areas. Demographic analysis was again used, mainly as a control total to help corroborate the PES results.

Leading up to the 2000 census, the initial plans were to produce a "one-number" census, in which the DSE estimates would be regarded as the official census estimates, assuming that no serious deficiencies were discovered in those estimates and that they would be available in time to satisfy the legislative requirements for apportionment and redistricting. At that point, the coverage evaluation program was known as integrated coverage measurement, or ICM. The sample size of the post-enumeration survey was to be 700,000 households to support direct state estimates of net undercount. Then in 1999 the Supreme Court ruled that the "Census Act" (Title 13 of the United States Code) precluded use of sampling to produce census counts for apportionment. The Court left open the possibility, however, of using adjusted counts for redistricting and other purposes. As a result of this decision, the plan to use sampling for nonresponse follow-up in the census had to be dropped in favor of the traditional 100 percent follow-up; correspondingly, there was no justification for such a large post-enumeration survey, which was reduced in size to 300,000 households. This new coverage evaluation program was referred to as Accuracy and Coverage Evaluation, or ACE. Various problems with the ACE estimates of net undercount, including a large number of duplicate census enumerations not identified as such by ACE, resulted in the use of unadjusted census counts for all census data products. The ACE problems with duplicates were first suggested through comparisons with demographic analysis and subsequently confirmed by a first-time nationwide matching operation of the census to itself. Demographic analysis was also of only limited use due to uncertainty regarding the large number of undocumented immigrants who had entered the United States in the preceding decade.

For the 2010 census, the coverage evaluation program, referred to as Census Coverage Measurement (CCM), again focussed on data collected through a post-enumeration survey. The CCM post-enumeration survey sample size was about 165,000 households. In addition, demographic analysis, relatively unchanged from previous decades except that ranges of estimates were being produced for the first time, was providing independent estimates for some demographic groups at the national level.

Two important changes were made between ACE and CCM. First, the DSE formula can be rewritten as

$$DSE = \left(n_{1+} - II\right)\left[\frac{n_{+1}}{n_{11}}\right]\left[1 - \frac{EE}{E_{cen}}\right]$$

and used to reinterpret the DSE as the product of a slight modification of the census counts multiplied by two ratios: the reciprocal of the percentage of PES cases that match to the census and the percentage of census cases that are correct enumerations. So rather than base the estimation on a 2×2 contingency table, dual-systems estimation simplifies to the estimation of two logistic regressions of similar form

$$\log\left[\frac{p_i}{1 - p_i}\right] = \beta_0 + \sum_{j=1}^{p} \beta_j X_{ij}$$

where X_{ij} are predictors at the person level, and β_j are parameters that indicate what impact different predictors

have on the log odds either for (1) matching to the census or (2) being a correct census enumeration. Key advantages of the use of logistic regression are that the predictors can be continuous and only the predictors that are important can be retained, unlike the situation in 2000 where many small interactions were effectively retained through use of the enumeration poststrata. These models can be applied at the individual level, and therefore enumeration poststrata are no longer needed, since the estimated count for a geographic region can be defined as the sum over the nonimputed census cases of terms in which the estimated probability of a correct enumeration is divided by the estimated probability of a census match.

The second major change from ACE to CCM is that the focus of CCM is no longer on providing adjusted counts for redistricting and fund allocation. Instead, the major focus is on census improvement. Therefore, the goal has moved from just estimating net undercount to estimating the individual components of census errors, such as omissions, duplications, counts in the wrong location, and erroneous enumerations. The goal is further to link estimates of the probability of these errors to their possible causes, which may include personal and neighborhood characteristics as well as census operations. It turns out that census net undercount estimates are still needed to estimate census omissions, so it will still be necessary to estimate net undercount even absent an independent interest in that summary statistic.

The CCM net undercount estimates will not be available until sometime in 2012. Unless this date is changed, using adjusted census counts—should there be interest in doing so—will be restricted for the 2010 census to funding allocation programs and other intercensal uses, and the data will not be available for redistricting.

Weaknesses (and Strengths) of PES and Other Methods of Coverage Evaluation

Demographic Analysis

Demographic analysis relies not only on records of births and deaths that are of a high degree of accuracy but also on information on documented immigration, emigration, and undocumented immigration; the latter two are measured indirectly and with considerable error. Therefore, for groups that are likely to emigrate and immigrate (especially illegally), the resulting estimates can have appreciable error. Further, given the lack of historical use of ethnicity on birth and immigration records (although recently there have been efforts to change this), demographic analysis cannot provide useful estimates of net undercount for the Hispanic population over age twenty. Possibly the most important limitation for demographic analysis is that given the lack of reliable information on interstate migration, it is not currently possible to provide useful estimates of net undercount for subnational areas. Finally, only estimates of net undercount are available. There are no estimates of gross omissions or gross overcounts, which limits the information on how to reduce over- and undercounts in the next census.

Given the relative infrequency of immigration and emigration for blacks, demographic analysis is still widely believed to provide, at the national level, the best measurement of census net undercount for blacks. Also, the total population count from demographic analysis is still of interest in assessing overall census completeness.

Reverse Record Check

The greatest worry when using a reverse record check in the United States is the difficulty in tracing addresses from the previous census to the current time period. This alone makes application of a reverse record check difficult to justify. In addition, the incompleteness of information on immigration, especially undocumented immigration, and the failure of the sample of census omissions to be a random sample from that population are two additional concerns. Also worthy of mention is that there is no separate measurement of census gross undercount or gross overcount, which limits the information on how to improve coverage for the subsequent census (although an analog to the E-sample has been added to recent reverse record checks in Canada to address this).

Still, assuming the tracing problem could be addressed, the relatively small amount of matching needed and the relative lack of statistical modeling give this method interesting advantages. Clearly, the tracing problem is less pronounced for the Canadian quinquennial census.

Composite List, Super Census, and Systematic Observation

The composite list method relies on several difficult assumptions, including that the various lists contain identifiers which facilitate matching and that few data are missing for the variables used for matching. In addition, it assumes that the addresses on the lists are the addresses of residence and that the matching is accurate. Also, the merged list must not have much differential undercoverage. Finally, the composite list method makes use of dual-systems estimation, so the assumptions discussed above also need to obtain to a reasonable extent if this technique is to be applied safely. The multilist approach has similar problems.

The serious weakness of the super census method is that a very large number of areas must be sampled so that the variance of the resulting estimate of net undercount is low enough to be useful. This weakness could cause super census to be extremely expensive. In addition, depending on the methods used, this procedure could suffer from the same problem of failing to exceed census coverage that is typical of the "do it again, better" approach.

The systematic observation method is obviously greatly dependent on finding a large number of individuals who are capable of gaining the trust of a small group of people in a relatively short amount of time. Also, it is possible that the same problem of failing to exceed census coverage could weaken this methodology in a large-scale application. Finally,

the estimates from systematic observation have a large variance because of the necessarily small size of the program.

Post-Enumeration Survey and Dual-Systems Estimation

A post-enumeration survey making use of dual-systems estimation has several weaknesses. Of primary concern is whether the error rate for confirmed matches and nonmatches of the matching operation can be kept very low. Also, although the unresolved match rate was reduced from the 1980 to the 1990 and 2000 censuses, given the relatively low amount of undercoverage, the treatment of unresolved matches has to be of extremely high quality to provide reliable estimates of undercoverage. A second weakness, related to the first, is that it is very difficult to estimate undercoverage for people who move in or out of the PES blocks between the census and the PES interview. In dealing with this issue, the Census Bureau has made use of different methods of defining the universe that is being counted; the two pure strategies are to count either (1) those present in the PES blocks on census day (PES-A) or (2) those present during the time of the PES interview (PES-B).

Besides errors in matching and the problem with people who move, the largest source of bias in dual-systems estimation is likely due to *correlation bias*. Recall that one of the assumptions underlying dual-systems estimation is that the probabilities of inclusion in the census and PES (within post-enumeration strata) are constant. Correlation bias is the correlation, generally expected to be positive, between the probabilities of individuals being included in the census and the PES. (The failure of the independence assumption is also sometimes said to cause correlation bias. The effect of this failure is the same as that from correlation bias, so it is difficult to distinguish between them in practice.) Except for unusual situations, correlation bias will result from heterogeneity in both sets of probabilities of inclusion. It can be shown that positive correlation bias will cause the adjusted census counts themselves to be underestimates of the true counts. This weakness has been addressed mainly by using either more or different post-enumeration strata. However, the benefits of doing so are limited because the size of the PES limits the number of post-enumeration strata that can be specified and because the information that is available on the census short form for defining post-enumeration strata is limited in the first place.

To address the problem of correlation bias, it is worth mentioning three alternative methods that avoid making either the independence assumption or the homogeneity assumption. One approach is to add a third measurement system, usually using administrative records, referred to as *triple systems estimation*. This is similar to the multilist approach, in which one of the lists is enumerations from the post-enumeration survey. A second approach is called *census plus,* which uses field reconciliation of discrepancies between the census count and the PES count to achieve a "true" count at the household level. This method was tested during the mid-1990s and was found to present some difficulties in implementation. Finally, as discussed above, the use of logistic regression, with sufficiently effective predictors, by modeling at the individual level could reduce the extent of correlation bias.

Other difficulties with dual-systems estimation can only be touched on here. First, since the census counts have no sampling variability but the PES counts do, it is not uncommon (when considering the 2×2 contingency table) in the smaller post-enumeration strata for n_{1+} to be smaller than n_{11}, which makes it difficult to interpret the n_{12} cell. This problem is eliminated through the use of logistic regression. A second weakness, if the DSE estimates were to be used for adjustment, concerns the methods used to "carry down" the estimates to low levels of geography. The method used from the 1980 to the 2000 censuses is referred to as *synthetic* estimation. Again, the use of logistic regression would eliminate this problem (ignoring the general concerns of the validity of these models). Were the DSE estimates to be used for redistricting, a significant additional weakness that became evident in the 2000 ACE is that the amount of fieldwork and matching makes it difficult, if not impossible, to complete the estimation and perform a careful review before the deadline for delivery to the states of block-level counts.

Although such statements can be considered controversial, it seems widely acknowledged, at least for areas of more than 100,000 people and for large demographic groups, that a PES is informative about census undercount and overcount and that there is currently no other approach for the U.S. Census that can provide this information. However, for people who, for one or another reason, are counted neither in the census or the PES, dual-systems estimation is problematic, and the only reasonable alternatives for estimating their number are likely to rely on the use of administrative records.

Key Findings for Recent Censuses
Trends in Census Undercoverage

In the 1950 census, the PES measured a net national undercount of 1.4 percent, whereas demographic analysis measured a net national undercount of 4.1 percent. The differential undercount of blacks compared with nonblacks was measured by demographic analysis to be 3.7 percent.

In the 1960 census, the PES measured a net national undercount of 1.9 percent, the reverse record check measured a net national undercount of between 2.5 and 3.1 percent, and demographic analysis measured a net national undercount of 3.1 percent. The differential undercount between blacks and nonblacks was measured by demographic analysis to be 3.9 percent.

In the 1970 census, there was no PES. Demographic analysis measured a net national undercount of 2.7 percent. The differential undercount between blacks and nonblacks was measured by demographic analysis to be 4.3 percent.

In the 1980 census, the PES, making use of dual-systems estimation for the first time, measured a net national undercount of between 0.8 and 1.4 percent, depending on the assumptions used. Demographic analysis measured a net

national undercount of 1.2 percent. The differential undercount between blacks and nonblacks was measured by demographic analysis to be 3.7 percent.

In the 1990 census, the PES measured the differential undercount as 1.6 percent. Demographic analysis measured the differential undercount to be 1.7 percent. The differential undercount between blacks and nonblacks was measured by demographic analysis to be 4.4 percent.

In the 2000 census, the ACE (Revision II) measured the net national undercount as −0.5 percent—in other words, a national census net overcount. Demographic analysis measured a net national undercount of 0.1 percent. The differential undercount between blacks and nonblacks was measured by demographic analysis to be 2.5 percent.

Five sets of demographic analysis estimates for the 2010 census have been released. The midpoint of the range, 308,475,000 people, differs by less than 0.1 percent from the 2010 census count of 308,745,000 people.

Who Is Missed?

Based on the results of dual-systems estimation and other sources, Eugene P. Ericksen and his colleagues identified several likely causes of census omissions, including illiteracy or households in which English is not the primary language, general unfamiliarity with surveys, housing units without a clear individual address, and households in high-crime areas. Leslie A. Brownrigg and Manuel de la Puente listed the following characteristics as contributing to census omissions: mobility, language problems, concealment, irregular relationship to head of household, and resistance to government interaction. One of the best predictors of census net undercount in 1990 and 2000 for larger geographic areas was low census mail return rate. The demographic groups that experience the greatest percentage net undercount are black males (and probably Hispanic males), with net undercount rates for the 2000 census for black males of 5.2 percent, compared with 0.5 percent for nonblack females (from demographic analysis).

One important question is whether census omissions are primarily due to missed housing units or to missed individuals within otherwise enumerated housing units. Howard Hogan identified four categories: (1) one or more people missed in a housing unit in which other people were enumerated in the census, (2) everyone missed in a housing unit listed in the census address list, (3) a missed housing unit in a building that was included in the census address list, and (4) a missed housing unit that was not listed in the census address list. If one considers people missed in otherwise enumerated structures to be the first two categories, about two-thirds of the 1990 census misses were for people living in listed housing units.

Census overcounts are also a substantial problem. Hogan reported that in the 1990 census, based on the E-sample, 14 million erroneous enumerations were due to duplications, fictitious enumerations, geocoding errors, people enumerated at the wrong address, census enumerations without names, and other causes. (This compares to 18 million estimated omissions.) Of these 14 million, approximately 4 million were duplicate enumerations.

See also *Accuracy and Coverage Evaluation; Capture-recapture methods; Demographic analysis; Errors in the census; Post-enumeration survey.*

. . . .   MICHAEL L. COHEN

BIBLIOGRAPHY

Alho, Juha M., Mary H. Mulry, Kent Wurdeman, and Jay Kim. "Estimating Heterogeneity in the Probabilities of Enumeration for Dual-System Estimation." *Journal of the American Statistical Association* 88 (1993): 1130–1136.

Anderson, Margo J., and Stephen E. Fienberg. *Who Counts: The Politics of Census-Taking in Contemporary America.* New York: Russell Sage Foundation, 1999.

Brownrigg, Leslie A., and Manuel de la Puente. *Alternative Enumeration Methods and Results: Resolution and Resolved Populations by Site.* Washington, D.C.: U.S. Bureau of the Census, 1993. Available at http://www.census.gov/srd/papers/pdf/lab92-01.pdf.

Coale, Ansley. "The Population of the United States in 1950 Classified by Age, Sex, and Color—A Revision of Census Figures." *Journal of the American Statistical Association* 50 (1955): 16–54.

Committee on Adjustment of Postcensal Estimates. *Assessment of Accuracy of Adjusted versus Unadjusted 1990 Census Base for Use in Intercensal Estimates.* Report to the Bureau of the Census. Washington, D.C.: U.S. Bureau of the Census, 1992.

Ericksen, Eugene P., Leobardo F. Estrada, John W. Tukey, and Kirk M. Wolter. *Report on the 1990 Decennial Census and the Post-Enumeration Survey.* Report submitted by members of the Special Advisory Panel to the Secretary of the U.S. Department of Commerce. Washington, D.C.: U.S. Bureau of the Census, 1991.

Fein, David. "The Social Sources of Census Omission: Racial and Ethnic Differences in Omission Rates in Recent U.S. Censuses." PhD diss., Princeton University, 1989.

Hogan, Howard. "The 1990 PES: Operations and Results." *Journal of the American Statistical Association* 88 (1993): 1047–1060.

Kostanich, Donna. *A.C.E. Revision II: Design and Methodology,* DSSD A.C.E. Revision II Memorandum Series, # PP-30. Washington, D.C.: U.S. Bureau of the Census, 2003.

National Research Council. *The Bicentennial Census: New Directions for Methodology in 1990.* Panel on Decennial Census Methodology. Committee on National Statistics, Commission on Behavioral and Social Sciences and Education. Edited by Constance F. Citro and Michael L. Cohen. Washington, D.C.: The National Academies Press, 1985.

———. *The 2000 Census: Counting Under Adversity.* Panel to Review the 2000 Census, Committee on National Statistics, Division of Behavioral and Social Sciences and Education. Edited by Constance F. Citro, Daniel L. Cork, and Janet L. Norwood. Washington, D.C.: The National Academies Press, 2004. Available at http://www.nap.edu/catalog.php?record_id=10907.

———. *Coverage Measurement in the 2010 Census.* Panel on Correlation Bias and Coverage Measurement in the 2010 Decennial Census, Committee on National Statistics, Division on Behavioral and Social Sciences and Education. Edited by Robert M. Bell and Michael L. Cohen. Washington, D.C.: The National Academies Press, 2009. Available at http://www.nap.edu/catalog.php?record_id=12524.

Robinson, J. Gregory, Bashir Ahmed, Prithwis das Gupta, and Karen A. Woodrow. "Estimation of Population Coverage in the 1990 United States Census Based on Demographic Analysis." *Journal of the American Statistical Association* 88 (1993): 1061–1071.

U.S. Census Bureau, 2010 Demographic Analysis Research Team. *The Development and Sensitivity Analysis of the 2010 Demographic Analysis Estimates.* Washington, D.C.: U.S. Census Bureau, 2010. Available at http://www.census.gov/newsroom/releases/pdf/20101206_da_revpaper.pdf.

U.S. Census Bureau. "2010 Demographic Analysis Estimates" [news conference, including tables and figures]. December 6, 2010. http://www.census.gov/newsroom/releases/archives/news_conferences/120610_demoanalysis.html.

Coverage Improvement Procedures

Recent censuses have included special programs to improve the coverage of the population. These programs are in addition to efforts to obtain a more complete count through advertising and quality control of census field operations.

The U.S. Census Bureau first adopted special coverage improvement procedures for the 1970 census on the basis of three assumptions: (1) the need for greater accuracy in the population count than had been achieved in the past because of use of the data for legislative redistricting under "one-person, one-vote" court requirements and for federal fund allocations; (2) the perception that it was becoming increasingly difficult to obtain a complete count in the absence of additional coverage efforts; and (3) the belief that new methods would be required to achieve improvements in coverage. By contrast, the 1950 and 1960 censuses were planned on the assumption that undercoverage was largely because enumerators failed to follow instructions. Consequently, simplifying procedures and increasing training and quality control were stressed. However, evaluation of the 1960 census results indicated that much undercoverage stemmed from reasons that would not likely be addressed by such approaches as better enumerator training. These reasons included some people being fearful of being counted and some people not being strongly attached to a particular household.

1970 Census

Programs to encourage public cooperation with the census, particularly among hard-to-count groups, were important components of the Census Bureau's strategy to obtain complete coverage in 1970. These programs included public information efforts and community education programs, assistance centers set up in twenty cities that the public could call or visit to get help with filling out census forms, and instruction sheets and questionnaires in Spanish and Chinese in some locations. Special efforts to improve enumerator performance in the twenty largest cities were also adopted.

The Census Bureau also implemented specific coverage improvement programs designed to add housing units and persons to the count. Several programs were carried out prior to census day (April 1) to correct the address list used for mailing questionnaires. A post-census check of the address list in selected areas was also carried out. Other coverage improvement programs in 1970 included a recheck of housing units originally classified as vacant to determine whether they were occupied; a cross-check of respondents' answers to a question on the number of living quarters at their address against the census address list; a check of persons who reported a change of address to the U.S. Postal Service during the census enumeration period; a "Missed Persons" campaign that placed cards in community centers, carry-out restaurants, barbershops, and similar locations to try to obtain minimal information from people with no fixed address; and a "Were You Counted?" campaign to encourage people not originally counted to come forward.

Many of the coverage improvement programs in the 1970 census were carried out selectively in areas in which they presumably would be most effective. Two programs, the National Vacancy Check and the Post-Enumeration Post Office Check of the address list in selected areas of sixteen southern states, were carried out for samples of addresses, and the results were used to add people and housing units to the census count. The 1970 census is the only census in which statistical sampling procedures were used to add people to the count.

The special coverage improvement programs in 1970 added about 3 percent to the cost of the census and about 6 percent to the total population count. The most effective programs in adding people were the address checks carried out prior to census day. The National Vacancy Check also added (imputed) a significant number of people to the count.

1980 Census

The 1980 census coverage improvement strategy exhibited three differences from that of 1970. First, substantially more resources were put into coverage improvement in 1980 than in 1970. Programs aimed at increasing public cooperation—particularly among hard-to-count groups—such as special publicity efforts, assistance centers, and foreign-language questionnaires, were greatly expanded, as were the number and extent of programs designed specifically to add housing units and persons to the count. (The cost of specific coverage improvement programs in 1980 was about six times the cost of such programs in 1970 in constant dollars.)

Second, the Census Bureau made a deliberate decision to conduct most specific coverage improvement programs on a nationwide basis and to avoid the use of sampling and imputation. However, some programs were implemented selectively in areas specifically designated for the purpose. Third, new programs were adopted to tackle the problem of undercoverage of people in otherwise enumerated households.

Several coverage improvement programs in 1980, similar to those in 1970, were designed to improve the address list prior to census day. The address list was also rechecked in some areas after census day. A vacant/delete check was carried out on a 100 percent basis to recheck the status of housing units that were originally thought to be vacant or not a residential address. In a new local review program, the Census Bureau provided the opportunity for local officials to assess preliminary housing unit and population counts.

Programs that were carried out during the census enumeration period to improve the count of persons included a casual count operation, in which Census Bureau staff visited places in central cities frequented by transients who might otherwise be missed; rechecks of responses to questions on the number of units in the building and the roster of people in the household; a "Were You Counted?" program similar to that of 1970; and a Nonhousehold Sources Program. The last program—an innovation in 1980—involved matching several administrative lists to census records for selected areas in urban district offices. Census field staff followed up on people on the lists who were not found in the census to determine if they should be added to the count. The lists used were driver's license records, immigration records, and (in New York City only) public assistance records.

Overall, the specific coverage improvement programs that were implemented in 1980 added about 8 percent to the total population count—a somewhat higher percentage than in 1970. Most of the added people resulted from the improvements to the address list that were achieved by the pre–census day address checks. The vacant/delete check also added a significant number of people to the count and reduced the differential undercount of minorities, although it appears to have overcounted some people as well. The other post–census day coverage improvement programs added very few people to the count.

1990 Census

Coverage improvement programs in the 1990 census were similar to those in the 1980 count, although some 1980 programs were dropped and new programs were added. Specific coverage improvement programs in 1990 included address list checks prior to census day and, for the first time, a pre-census local review, in which local governments in mailout/mailback areas reviewed census maps and counts of addresses by block to look for discrepancies with their own information.

Other specific coverage improvement programs in 1990 were

- enumeration of shelters and street locations where the homeless might be found;
- 100 percent recheck of housing units originally classified as vacant or nonresidential (the vacant/delete check);
- parolee/probationer check, in which parole and probation officers were given census questionnaires to distribute to people under their jurisdiction, the responses were cross-checked against the census records, and people were added to the count if no match was found (administrative lists of parolees and probationers were also checked against census records);
- "Were You Counted?" campaign;
- recanvass of blocks containing about 15 percent of housing units that were thought to have new construction or other structures that might have been missed; and
- post-census local review program (more extensive than in 1980) in which local governments were sent preliminary housing unit counts by block to assess. The Census Bureau recanvassed blocks with significant differences between the census count and local information.

As in 1970 and 1980, most of the people added to the count from specific coverage improvement programs in 1990 were the result of the pre–census day address check programs. The vacant/delete check also added two million people, but evidence indicates that some of them had already been counted. The parolee/probationer check had a very high rate of erroneous additions to the count.

2000 Census

As originally planned, the 2000 census would have scaled back the use of specific coverage improvement programs while expanding such programs as foreign-language questionnaires, walk-in and telephone assistance, and targeted outreach and publicity to hard-to-count population groups and areas. Cutbacks would have involved programs for improving the address list as well as specific programs for improving the count after census day.

The original plan for the census Master Address File (MAF) was to update the 1990 census list with information from the U.S. Postal Service and to recheck the list in selected areas. Also, legislation was enacted to allow the Census Bureau to share the address list with local governments and obtain their input through a Local Update of Census Addresses (LUCA) program. Late in the decade, it became clear that more checks were needed to obtain a high-quality address list, so a complete canvass of the MAF was carried out by Census Bureau staff. In addition, addresses provided by localities through the LUCA program were added to the MAF and rechecked by Census Bureau staff.

Originally, the use of specific coverage improvement programs during the census enumeration period was to be limited on the assumption that an Integrated Coverage Measurement (ICM) program would result in corrected population counts by December 31, 2000. (The ICM corrections for census undercounts and overcounts would result from matching the responses of a coverage evaluation survey to the census responses.) However, the U.S. Supreme Court ruled that survey sampling procedures could not be used for the population counts for reapportionment of congressional seats. Hence, the Census Bureau planned to deliver unadjusted population counts by December 31, 2000, with adjusted counts to come later. (The adjustments would be based on matching an Accuracy and Coverage Evaluation [ACE] survey—smaller than the originally planned ICM survey—with census records.)

Consequently, the Census Bureau expanded the planned recheck of units initially designated as vacant or nonresidential. Originally, this recheck was to be conducted of a 30 percent sample of vacant units; instead, the recheck was carried out on a 100 percent basis. Other coverage improvement programs included telephone follow-up of certain types of households (for example, those that provided information for fewer than the total number of people reported to be living in the household), procedures to enumerate homeless and transient populations, and a "Be Counted" program in which questionnaires were made available at local sites. A computer-based unduplication operation was implemented in summer 2010 when it became apparent from checks in selected localities that there was substantial duplication of addresses; this special operation ultimately deleted 1.4 million housing units and 3.6 million people from the count.

2010 Census

The 2010 census used many of the same coverage improvement procedures as in previous censuses. A complete canvass of the MAF was carried out in 2009; handheld computers were used to verify the information. An extensive LUCA program was also carried out as in the 2000 census.

Other coverage improvement programs were similar to those in 2000. They included a 100 percent recheck of units classified as "vacant or delete"? by enumerators in nonresponse follow-up, telephone follow-up of certain types of households (for example, those that provided information for fewer than the total number of people reported to be living in the household or containing members who sometimes lived at another address), procedures to enumerate homeless and transient populations, and a "Be Counted" program in which questionnaires were made available at local sites. In addition, the communications and outreach program provided advertising, translated questionnaires, and other materials in many more languages than in previous censuses.

The costs and benefits of census coverage improvement programs have not been carefully assessed in recent censuses. The utility of many such programs has been questioned by panels of the National Academy of Sciences.

See also *Accuracy and Coverage Evaluation; Advisory committees; Editing, imputation, and weighting; Enumeration: field procedures; Sampling in the census.*

. . . . CONSTANCE F. CITRO

BIBLIOGRAPHY

Ericksen, Eugene P., Leobardo F. Estrada, John W. Tukey, and Kirk M. Wolter. *Report on the 1990 Decennial Census and the Post-Enumeration Survey.* Report submitted by members of the Special Advisory Panel to the Secretary of the U.S. Department of Commerce. Washington, D.C.: U.S. Bureau of the Census, 1991.

National Research Council. *The Bicentennial Census: New Directions for Methodology in 1990.* Panel on Decennial Census Methodology, Committee on National Statistics, Commission on Behavioral and Social Sciences and Education. Edited by Constance F. Citro and Michael L. Cohen. Washington, D.C.: The National Academies Press, 1985.

———. *The 2000 Census: Counting Under Adversity.* Panel to Review the 2000 Census, Committee on National Statistics, Division of Behavioral and Social Sciences and Education. Edited by Constance F. Citro, Daniel L. Cork, and Janet L. Norwood. Washington, D.C.: The National Academies Press, 2004. Available at http://www.nap.edu/catalog.php?record_id=10907.

———. *Envisioning the 2020 Census.* Panel on the Design of the 2010 Census Program of Evaluations and Experiments, Committee on National Statistics. Edited by Lawrence D. Brown, Michael L. Cohen, Daniel L. Cork, and Constance F. Citro. Washington, D.C.: The National Academies Press. Available at http://www.nap.edu/catalog.php?record_id=12865.

U.S. Bureau of the Census. *Census 2000 Operational Plan Using Traditional Census-Taking Methods.* Washington, D.C.: U.S. Government Printing Office, 1999.

Data Capture

Data capture is the transferring of data from census questionnaires into a format that is suitable for processing. It is that part of a census operation that lies in between the collection of data and the preparation of tabulations.

Prior to 1850

From the first census in 1790 until 1830, federal marshals charged with taking the census did not make use of standard census schedules, or forms, nor were there any uniform tallying instructions. The marshals and their assistants were required to submit aggregate counts, not the actual census forms, to officials in Washington, D.C. Not until 1830 were uniform schedules distributed to marshals and returned and checked by clerks in Washington.

The population census schedules used prior to 1850 recorded information for an entire household on a single line, with individual columns providing specific information on characteristics—for example, the number of persons 16 to 26 years of age in the household. All data were reported for the entire household, including aggregated information for the individuals contained within. Thus clerks added together the data on the census schedules themselves, making the tallying process much like the construction of tabulations. The results of these tallies would then be further aggregated into summaries for various geographic areas.

1850 to 1890

Starting with the 1850 census, information was presented on the census schedule, line-by-line for each person in the household. Rather than adding together preaggregated data for households, the task now changed to counting individual responses. Tallies were constructed in order to create the classifications that would later lead to finished tabulations; clerks tallied the number of occurrences of a characteristic (for example, males, persons 10 to 15 years old, farmers), sometimes by passing through the forms several times. Thus there was little distinction between creating tallies and creating tabulations. What clerks tallied were essentially table cells that were then checked for inconsistencies and printed as a final product. As the content of the census grew increasingly complex, tally systems became unwieldy and prone to duplication, as when tallies needed to be repeated many times in order to achieve consistency between tabulations.

A first rather modest advance came just after the 1870 census, when Charles W. Seaton created a device to make manual tallying faster. Seaton was chief clerk of the 1870 and 1880 censuses and became census superintendent between 1881 and 1885. The device consisted of a series of rollers on a wood frame, through which a lengthy tally sheet would pass. The objective of the "Seaton Device" was to make portions of the tally sheet that were physically distant appear close together for several different items on the schedule. This enabled the clerk to make physical tally marks at six or more spots on the tally sheet simultaneously, without physically moving around the tally sheet to find different items. Despite increases in productivity, this device still required manual tallying.

It wasn't until the 1880s that the first ideas regarding automated alternatives to manual tallying started to be seriously considered. The nation's population was growing dramatically in the nineteenth century, and the number of items on the census schedules followed suit. More data were compiled for an increasingly large population. Charles Pidgin and William Hunt devised a plan to transcribe data for the 1885 census of Massachusetts in a way that presented all information for each person on a single card. These cards (or "chips," as they were sometimes called) could then be color-coded or flagged with other markers that permitted them to be sifted and sorted in a host of ways. Although the time needed to create these "cards" was more substantial than that embodied in the traditional tally system, the payoff in flexibility for later compilation and tabulation more than offset the initial investment. And, indeed, the rich level of detail found in the 1885 census of Massachusetts provides ample testimony that this idea had a future.

Consolidation of information for an individual on a single card meant that key sorts, such as those by age and sex, needed to be done only once and could be retained for later use. The traditional tallying system required that some sorts, even basic ones by age and sex, be done over and over again. Most important of all, however, this new mode of processing separated tallying from tabulation for the first time.

1890 to 1930

The removal of data from census schedules using an independent data capture process was first used in the 1890 census. Data for individuals from census schedules were coded onto cards that would later be mechanically processed to produce tabulations. The idea was to create perforations in cards, with each spot representing a questionnaire response. "Punched cards," as they came to be known, were then passed over a series of electronic contacts that would "count" or, in effect, "read" the responses; data could then be compiled in a variety of ways to produce aggregates that formed the cells of tabulations. This idea was the brainchild of Herman Hollerith, who later founded International Business Machines (IBM). Hollerith received guidance on the ultimate applications of his new ideas from John Shaw Billings, a colleague who had a special interest in vital statistics data.

The schedules for the 1890 census were different from those used in earlier decades. A separate tally sheet was now provided for each family or household with questions running down the table stub and separate columns for each individual. "Punching clerks" recorded responses by creating perforations with a hand punch. In time, however, various punching machines were developed to make this task quicker and easier. The "gang punch" device made multiple perforations at the same time, as when a card needed to receive codes for a predetermined enumeration district or other geographic area. Innovations with each successive census permitted higher levels of output within the punching operation. Keypunch machines, on which operators hit keys to record responses as holes in cards, came into use. As keypunching became more efficient, operations involving different sets of cards became more common, as with the creation of "family cards" in the 1900 and 1910 censuses or "occupation cards" in 1920.

Although the tabulation of data had advanced significantly as a result of Hollerith's innovation, it is important to recognize that the job of data capture was more labor intensive than ever. More census questionnaire items needed to be coded onto cards for an increasingly larger population.

1940 to 1990

Science brought innovations into the 1940 census in many areas, such as the incorporation of sampling. So, too, with data capture methods. A new machine, "the reproducer," permitted mass transfer of information punched on one set of cards to another. A new IBM machine not only could accumulate information from consecutive cards but also could now add across different fields on the same card, creating important totals and subtotals that earlier required separate punching operations. Special cards were created for many new items, such as labor force and migration, which were obtained on a sample basis.

The most significant period for innovation in data capture occurred in the 1950s, with the advent of machines that permitted more direct entry and compilation of data from the questionnaires. Card-to-tape machines were developed as part of the emerging technology associated with the electronic computer; the large-scale effort associated with punched cards, however, was still present in 1950, but that would soon change. In 1951 the census of Canada used what was referred to as "mark-sense" schedules; cards were punched by mechanical means from questionnaires on which enumerators had made marks. This system was considered for the 1950 U.S. Census,

but time constraints made its full adoption impractical. During the 1950s, however, the U.S. Bureau of the Census, in conjunction with the National Bureau of Standards, developed FOSDIC, the film optical sensing device for input to computers. FOSDIC was capable of "reading" information from a negative microfilm copy of census questionnaires and transferring responses to magnetic tape for processing. The data on the tape were then put into a computer for compilation and tabulation. Questionnaires made use of "index marks," solid black squares printed on the questionnaire, followed by a series of circles containing responses. After finding the black mark, a light beam scanned the circles and determined which ones were filled in.

Since FOSDIC used microfilmed questionnaires, this meant that the actual questionnaires, once shot, could be stored away from the main processing operation. Microfilm was more compact and efficient, resulting in faster and more accurate data capture. By some estimates data capture increased sixtyfold with the advent of FOSDIC. The development of this new capture mode may have overcome the huge burden of manual punching, but it put more pressure on field staff. Enumerators now had to make sure that responses were recorded in a way that FOSDIC could accept. In addition, a professional programming staff of specially trained people had to be maintained for processing, including groups of clerks who needed to manually edit input from "write-in" responses. Still, in the 1950s, advances in data capture had outpaced those of the previous 70 years.

The advent of computers meant that programs could be developed to compile, edit, and tabulate data. By 1970 innovations in FOSDIC efficiency and advances in computing permitted the bureau to handle an increasing number of questionnaires. Mailout/mailback was now the primary method of data collection, and the level of demographic and geographic detail available from the data was unprecedented. The Bureau of the Census's facility in Jeffersonville, Indiana, received questionnaires from some 399 district offices between May and September 1970—425 truckloads, with a gross weight of 6.1 million pounds. Questionnaires were checked in, sorted, and microfilmed. The microfilm was then developed on site by a private contractor and shipped to bureau headquarters in Suitland, Maryland, for FOSDIC processing. All told, about 77,000 rolls of microfilm were scanned in short-form questionnaire processing, with some 30 percent of the rolls requiring reprocessing, mostly because of poor markings made by respondents and bureau coders. "Diaries," control counts of population and housing and key operational items (for example, codes for rejected questionnaires), were created as processing evaluation tools. These diaries were especially handy for the evaluation of clerical coding operations that translated questionnaire write-in responses into marked circles for FOSDIC input.

In 1980 more accurate FOSDIC processing was developed. At the same time, the bureau started to use more efficient strategies for getting questionnaires to the processing centers. It was not until 1990, however, that the bureau fully implemented concurrent processing—the conversion of questionnaire data on an individual form-flow basis, with editing and correction being done in the field. Rather than wait for all questionnaires to be received before engaging in large-scale data capture efforts, 1990 saw capture take place on a flow basis, as questionnaires were received. Prior to this time, automated processing at the bureau's Processing Centers (seven in 1990) usually did not occur until manual-collection offices had completed their work and were ready to close and ship questionnaires. The Processing Centers were then responsible for turning the questionnaire responses into machine-readable data using FOSDIC technology. This included the labor-intensive job of keying write-in entries; although word-recognition technology now permitted computers to code many responses, several hundred clerks were still needed to assign codes to responses that could not be directly coded via computer (500 clerks alone at the Jeffersonville Processing Center). A clerical staff of almost 1,100 was needed to code industry and occupation in the Kansas City Processing Office in 1990.

More powerful computer hardware and innovative software replaced earlier diaries with elaborate coverage, content, and consistency editing. Questionnaires with missing or multiple answers were more readily identified, and later on programs were developed to check for gross inconsistencies among items, permitting bureau staffers to quickly gauge the quality of responses and initiate corrective measures.

2000 and Beyond

The 2000 census brought with it several important changes in data capture. Although the bureau had used private contractors for some aspects of its earlier capture efforts, private sector involvement in 2000 data capture was unprecedented. The days of homegrown innovations at the bureau had given way to more cost-efficient, commercially developed technologies. Three of the four data capture centers for Census 2000 were supported by private sector contractors, with the sole government site being the bureau's National Processing Center in Jeffersonville. These centers made use of advanced optical scanning technologies, including optical character recognition (OCR). A suite of software extracted information from forms that contained a combination of machine printing, hand printing, optical marks, and bar codes. Images of each questionnaire were created, and modern "diaries" were established, with pertinent management systems information that permitted an evaluation of operations and initial assessments of response quality.

The data capture system for 2000 (DCS-2000) captured information from more than 120 million census questionnaires. The DCS-2000 scanned questionnaires and created digital images that served as input to further data processing. In effect, the system directly scanned forms and converted them into ASCII (American Standard Code for Information Interchange) text. As in times past, images that could not be recognized by the OCR technology needed to be examined by census workers and manually entered into the system.

The bureau's approach to data capture in 2000 represented the logical next step in a history that has attempted to take advantage of innovations as a way of making data collection and capture more cost effective. Continuing in this tradition, plans for the 2010 census began with a series of proposals to further automate the data collection process, in an effort to streamline operations and make the more labor-intensive parts of the census paperless. The goal was to automate and integrate major field operations for 2010 (the system was called Field Data Collection Automation, or FDCA), with the key feature being more than one-half million handheld computers for collecting responses from households that did not return their questionnaires by mail.

While the data capture centers would still process the paper forms that were mailed back, the bureau planned on reducing costs by directly capturing information collected during personal interviews through the regular transmission of digital files from the field, thereby eliminating the need for paper maps and address lists for the two largest field data-collection operations—address canvassing and the nonresponse follow-up. (The Census Bureau also considered using the Internet for data-collection purposes, but this option was ultimately rejected because of security issues.) While handheld devices were successfully used in the address canvass, their deployment for nonresponse follow-up never materialized. Problems involving poor communication between the bureau and private sector vendors over the specifications for these devices and their performance requirements proved too overwhelming. In April 2008 a decision was made to drop the use of handheld devices in the actual enumeration, meaning that the 2010 census would be a primarily paper-based enumeration, which (unlike 2000) included a targeted second mailing of questionnaires.

Three capture centers in Phoenix, Ariz.; Baltimore, Md.; and Jeffersonville, Ind., received some 175 million paper census forms, which were put through optical scanners that converted them into electronic images. The images then went through an automated quality check to make sure that they were of sufficient quality to proceed (those that were not were subject to manual inspection and correction, one of many such points in the capture process). Once certified, the electronic images were then converted into readable data using OCR and intelligent character recognition (ICR), processes that "read" the scanned images. Both OCR and ICR assign scores to each field based on the probability that they were successfully recognized and on other considerations related to consistency and completeness. Images that have fields with problems are then sent for manual review, where clerks "key from image" as a means of fixing problems, which may be as simple as a stray mark on the form. Quality assurance is incorporated into these operations by taking samples of images that have been keyed-in and repeating the procedure with different clerks. Once the images have been read and the data captured, a "check-out" process occurs, where receipt of data from the images and the key-from-image processes have been confirmed. Once confirmed, the forms are shredded and then recycled.

See also *Pre-computer tabulation systems.*

. . . . JOSEPH J. SALVO

BIBLIOGRAPHY

Truesdell, Leon E. *The Development of Punch Card Tabulation in the Bureau of the Census: 1890–1940.* Washington, D.C.: U.S. Bureau of the Census, 1965.

U.S. Census Bureau. *Field Data Collection Automation (FDCA): Program Scope, Processes, and Automation Considerations.* Washington, D.C.: U.S. Government Printing Office, 2005.

———. *1990 Census of Population and Housing: History, Part C.* CPH(R)-2C. Washington, D.C.: U.S. Government Printing Office, 1995.

———. *United States Censuses of Population and Housing, 1970: Procedural History.* PHC(R)-1. Washington, D.C.: U.S. Government Printing Office, 1976.

———. *United States Censuses of Population and Housing, 1960: Processing the Data.* Washington, D.C.: U.S. Government Printing Office, 1962.

U.S. Department of Commerce, Office of the Inspector General. *Census 2010: Revised Field Data Collection Automation Contract Incorporated OIG Recommendations, but Concerns Remain Over Fee Awarded during Negotiations.* Final Report CAR 18702. Washington, D.C.: U.S. Government Printing Office, 2009.

U.S. General Accounting Office. *2000 Census: New Data Capture System Progress and Risks.* GAO/AIMD-00-61. Washington, D.C.: U.S. Government Printing Office, 2000.

Data Dissemination and Use

Data dissemination refers to the processes and products used to distribute the results of the census. In the early years of our nation, this consisted simply of a formal handing over of the official counts from the president or the secretary of state, who were responsible for conducting the census, to the Congress. The numbers were then used for reapportionment, the constitutional purpose of the census. The single printed report from the 1790 census consisted of 56 pages. With each census, the process became more complex and the dissemination broader. By the middle of the nineteenth century, the content of the census questionnaire had grown to include information beyond the basic population, age, sex, and race counts, and reports were printed in large quantities and distributed to federal officials, state governors members of congress, and colleges and universities. By the end of the twentieth century, census data had become a vast resource, integral to many societal institutions, including Congress, government agencies, universities, and commercial organizations.

Two changes have had major impacts on data dissemination in the twenty-first century. First, Internet access to vast amounts of data, with print-on-demand capability, has replaced most printed documents and electronic products. Second, the decennial census long form has been replaced by the American Community Survey (ACS), resulting in annual data for detailed characteristics, greatly reducing the amount of information from the decennial census.

Data Products and Tools

In the twenty-first century the Internet has become the principal dissemination medium for census data, though DVDs are also widely used, and the language of data dissemination has largely shifted from "data products" to "data access tools." Printed reports were the only data products from 1790 through 1950, starting with the simple 56-page report

from the 1790 census, later including elaborate hand-drawn colored maps and graphics, and by 1990 growing to about 450,000 pages in multiple volumes with detailed characteristics for geographic areas, ranging from the nation to the city block. Computerized data were introduced with the 1960 census, but it was not until the 1990 census that reductions in the number of printed reports occurred as more data were distributed through electronic means. The printed products from the 2000 and 2010 censuses are primarily Census Briefs—short printed overviews of particular population characteristics—and Special Reports that provide detailed analysis of specific topics. The multiple volumes of data tables for all geographic areas are now produced as PDF computer files and can be printed on demand.

The technological developments of the mid-twentieth century resulted in many new forms of data dissemination. Tabulating machines, precursors of today's computers, were invented in the late nineteenth century for the purpose of processing census data. By 1960 computers had become integral to the census process, and the bureau began to distribute data on computer tape. At about the same time, some data were distributed on microfiche. In more recent decades the development of TIGER/Line files with geographic and cartographic information has spurred the growth of geographic information systems (GIS) and mapping software. TIGER (Topologically Integrated Geographic Encoding and Referencing) files contain neither maps nor data but a digital database of geographic features that can be used in mapping and GIS software.

Computerized data products developed for the 1960 through 1990 censuses consisted primarily of Summary Files (SFs) and Public Use Microdata Samples (PUMS) on magnetic tape for use with mainframe computers. SFs are computerized summaries of the data. They include predefined frequency counts or tabulations for all geographic entities recognized or defined by the Census Bureau. They are used most often to analyze characteristics of specific geographic areas. PUMS contain basic coded information about a sample of individuals and households. PUMS users can employ statistical software to develop tabulations not available in the SFs. PUMS are used most often to analyze detailed characteristics of people and households for the nation, states, and other large geographic areas. Because PUMS contain information about individuals, the geographic identification was, until 1980, restricted to areas with 250,000 or more people to protect the confidentiality of the respondents. That limit was then dropped to areas of 100,000 or more in population. In addition to these standard data products, the Census Bureau produces special tabulations, paid for by the requester, for user-defined geographic areas or subject-matter tables. All special tabulations are subject to the Census Bureau's usual standards, ensuring that confidential information is not revealed.

With the 1990 census, electronic data products were expanded to include CD-ROMs and online access. SFs and PUMS were released on CD-ROM (compact disc, read-only memory) shortly after the tape versions. The CD-ROMs were much smaller and less expensive than the tapes. At a time when use of personal computers was exploding in offices and homes, these CD-ROMs quickly supplanted the tape files as the medium of choice. Online access to selected data via the Census Bureau's Cendata system provided an early step in the direction of the large-scale Internet dissemination of the 2000 census. By 1999 the Census Bureau's World Wide Web site had evolved into a comprehensive source of key data products. With different formats for different products, the Web site provides access to or information about all of the Census Bureau's data products.

American FactFinder (AFF), the Census Bureau's online database, was introduced in 1998 and provided basic access to the 2000 and 1990 census data. AFF has since expanded and evolved to the point where it now provides much more comprehensive access to data from the decennial censuses, the American Community Survey (ACS), and many other data sources. Just as the Internet has revolutionized access to information of all kinds, AFF has revolutionized the Census Bureau's definition of data products. A new user can quickly find fact sheets and maps, while an experienced user can interact with AFF's interface to develop complex customized data products at no cost. In addition to its table-making capabilities, AFF can be used to download large files—Summary Files and Public Use Microdata Files—and to find relevant documents and definitions. Since the ACS has replaced the long form, AFF must add large new databases each year. Because the data user community has expanded well beyond the data professionals who worked with the earlier electronic products, the Census Bureau has developed very detailed guidelines for interpreting the data, including margins of error for all numbers derived from the ACS sample.

Microform products (microfilm and microfiche) are miniaturized photographs of the printed reports that must be read through a special viewer. Used primarily in dissemination of the 1980 and 1990 censuses, microform products benefited libraries and other users because they required much less space than printed reports and also included additional data from the SFs that were not in any printed report. Microfilm was also used internally as the Census Bureau's storage medium for the original census schedules and questionnaires, but scanned digital images were used for the 2010 census. Carefully guarded for 72 years after each census, these images are then made available to the public through the National Archives. During the 72 years when the original census data are not public, the Census Bureau offers the Age Search Service, for a fee, whereby individuals can obtain transcripts of selected data from these records. Information is released only to the named person, his or her heirs, or legal representatives. These transcripts, which may contain information on a person's age, sex, race, state or country of birth, and relationship to the householder, can be used as evidence to qualify for Social Security or other retirement benefits, for passport applications, to prove relationship in settling estates, for genealogical research, and other uses when a birth certificate is not available.

Data Uses and Users

Beyond the constitutional purpose of reapportioning Congress, census data are used for a variety of public and private purposes. Many federal, state, and local laws require that funds be distributed based on the census counts. Billions of federal and state dollars each year are transferred to local governments based on census data. Census data are also used for planning community, private, and public facilities and services, such as schools, shopping centers, health facilities, and residential developments. Many federal and state government agencies have units that analyze census data and publish special reports. The Census Bureau itself publishes a large variety of analytical reports. Local government agencies often distribute area profiles and maps and maintain Web sites that often include links to the Census Bureau's Web site. Larger cities frequently use census data to conduct detailed analyses of many aspects of their populations. Universities and private research organizations produce studies that use census data and related resources, particularly in the fields of demography, sociology, economics, and urban planning. In recent decades increasing numbers of commercial organizations use census data for assessing the markets for their products. A large industry of demographic data companies repackages census data, maintains Web sites, and sells products such as area profiles for marketing, topical maps, specialized data books, and electronic files.

Data products can be obtained directly from the Census Bureau or through other organizations. Libraries are perhaps the most common source of census data. The Federal Depository Library Program originated in the early nineteenth century and now consists of more than 1,200 libraries. These libraries maintain copies of selected census data products and offer access to federal electronic databases. In addition, the Census Bureau has established formal networks of data users to ensure widespread availability. The State Data Center program establishes a lead agency and affiliates in each state to maintain and distribute census data within the state. Often the State Data Centers are also depository libraries. National Census Information Centers are nonprofit organizations that focus on minority concerns. They facilitate data access for their constituencies. Business and Industry Data Centers, usually within chambers of commerce or small-business development centers, are established to promote development by providing access to economic data.

Members of many associations share an interest in the quality of the census data that are critical to their organizations. The American Statistical Association has monitored census data and other federal statistical programs for more than 150 years. The Association of Public Data Users was founded in 1975 specifically to foster interaction among users of then newly available electronic data products. Since 1980, the

Council of Professional Associations on Federal Statistics has provided a forum for these and many other associations to learn about and exchange information on federal statistics and current developments in census data.

See also *Archival access to the census; Depository libraries; Dissemination of data: electronic products; Dissemination of data: printed publications; Pre-computer tabulation systems; PUMS (Public Use Microdata Samples); State Data Centers; Summary Files.*

. . . .   DEIRDRE A. GAQUIN

BIBLIOGRAPHY
Anderson, Margo J. *The American Census: A Social History.* New Haven, Conn.: Yale University Press, 1988.
Kaplan, Charles P., and Thomas L. Van Valey. *Census '80: Continuing the Factfinder Tradition.* Washington, D.C.: U.S. Government Printing Office, 1980.
U.S. Bureau of the Census. "Census Product Catalog." Last revised September 22, 2009. www.census.gov/mp/www/cat/.
———. "Data Access Tools." Last revised August 2, 2010. www.census.gov/main/www/access.html.
———. "History." Last revised July 29, 2010. www.census.gov/history.
———. *1990 Census of Population and Housing: Guide, Part A. Text.* Washington, D.C.: U.S. Government Printing Office, 1992.

Data Products: Evolution

Throughout the history of the United States, the decennial census has reflected the changing social, political, and economic interests of the country. The published reports have reflected the needs of government, academic, and public data users, and the format has reflected the technology available at the time. Today little of the data is available in printed form; most is available on the Internet. The annual updates from the American Community Survey (ACS) are now combined with the data from the decennial census. Data for individual geographic areas are easily available using the American Fact-Finder. More complex requests are less easily fulfilled.

The Early Censuses

The decennial census that directed the reapportionment of Congress, the redistricting of state and local territories, and the collection of taxes was mandated in Article I of the Constitution. The data collection forms were not standard, and only a limited number of questions were asked in the early censuses. Neither privacy nor confidentiality was of concern. The law required no formal reports or publication of data. It demanded only the posting of the census schedules in "two of the most public places within each jurisdiction, there to remain for the inspection of all concerned…" and "that the aggregate amount of each description of persons" for every district be transmitted to the president. Nonetheless, even the 1790 census resulted in a single 56-page report based on six inquiries.

In 1907–1908, the Bureau of the Census published 12 volumes titled *Heads of Families at the First Census of the United States Taken in the Year 1790.* These volumes also contain the names of heads of families from all states included in the census except Delaware, Georgia, Kentucky, New Jersey, and Tennessee, the schedules for which were burned in 1812.

The 1800 census was similar in scope and method to the 1790 count except that the marshals made their reports to the secretary of state rather than to the president; also, data were collected for additional age groups. Until the creation of standardized forms in 1830, marshals included items on occupation or ethnic origin at will and summarized the data as they thought appropriate. As a result, published tables were not consistent across specific states or counties.

Statisticians and members of Congress recognized that the 1810 census was a potential source of information on the economic state of the nation. Earlier voluntary efforts to collect such data had been largely unsuccessful. Although the 1810 census of manufactures was hardly error-free, a two-volume report, one on demographics and one on industry, was published in 1811. Questions on citizenship were added in 1820, and a similar pair of volumes was published. In 1830 the manufacturing census was abandoned and efforts were concentrated on the collection of population data.

Once there were three data points to compare (1790, 1800, and 1810), unofficial but highly useful publications compared the condition of the country over time. This type of comparison became an ongoing part of the official census publications. It would be many years before a permanent Bureau of the Census would be established, but this type of analytic work eventually became an ongoing part of its responsibility

Although standardized forms were initiated in 1830, errors and inconsistencies in the data were still apparent. Corrected editions of both volumes from 1830 were issued, but the publication of corrected editions was not the general rule.

The Temporary Census Office

In 1850 a centralized Census Office was authorized for decennial data collection. It was established before each census was conducted and, until the end of the century, was disbanded once the results had been tabulated and published.

The number of census publications increased with the 1850 census. Both a huge volume containing limited data for states, counties, and towns and a far briefer abstract of detailed national data appeared in 1853. A separate compendium, containing retrospective census data, was published in 1854. Mortality data were covered in a publication of 1855, and a digest of the statistics of manufacture based on the seventh census appeared in 1858. A similar group of publications followed the 1860 census with the addition of a separate volume on agriculture.

The remainder of the publications from the eighth census appeared between 1864 and 1866. The 1870 census publications were organized similarly. The still widely used *Statistical Abstract of the United States* (*Statistical Abstract*) was first published in 1878. Only in 1880 were separate volumes produced for special subjects with separate parts for individual states. The result was more than 22 volumes, each with numerous sections. Fifteen volumes and more than 200 bulletins and reports were produced in 1890. More data were being collected and more tables published.

There was a growing emphasis on social statistics. Censuses just prior to the Civil War requested more information about slaves. As the century progressed, more data became available on people with physical and mental disabilities, on people in jails, and on occupations, marital status, and ethnic origin. Detailed questions on incarceration reached their peak numbers in 1880 and 1890. Throughout this period, efforts were made to standardize the data-collection geography and hence the reporting geography.

Before the 1880 census, authorizing legislation provided that the Census Office be placed within the Department of the Interior and that a superintendent be appointed for each census. Francis Walker was appointed superintendent for the 1880 census, and he was eager to make this tenth census a landmark effort. Accordingly, he produced more than 300 bulletins containing preliminary figures early in the decade; individual volumes for the population, manufactures, agriculture, and vital statistics of the nation; and additional volumes addressing industrial and economic growth. These latter volumes, written by experts, combined statistics with explanatory text. These publications represented monumental efforts—all of the tabulations were performed manually by clerks. With a growing population and a growing demand for detailed reports, it was 1888 before the final results of the 1880 census were published.

Efforts to automate the tabulation process were encouraged. Herman Hollerith, the developer of the punched card, easily won a competition among three alternate methods. Using Hollerith's equipment only for the population section, the Census Office in 1890 was able to complete most of its work in less than half the time it had taken in 1880.

With the Hollerith Electric Tabulating Machine, it was possible to perform more complex tabulations than in the past. In addition to an increased number of preliminary and special bulletins, detailed volumes contained both statistics and analyses on such subjects as population; "the insane, feeble-minded, deaf, dumb and blind"; "crime, pauperism and benevolence"; vital and social statistics; agriculture; manufacturing; mineral industries; churches; Indians; insurance; real estate mortgages; "farms and homes"; transportation; and "wealth, debt and taxation."

A Permanent Census Office

The new Bureau of the Census was moved to the Department of Commerce and Labor in 1903, where it undertook a number of nontraditional projects. Among these were the compilation of immigration data; special censuses of Cuba, the Philippines, and Oklahoma (likely in preparation for Oklahoma's admission to the Union as the 46th state in 1907); the completion of an official register of the United States; special reports on marriage and divorce; and several interpretive volumes on population growth. Business and economics became a main focus of the bureau, and surveys in this area became more frequent.

The 1910 census was the first completed under the auspices of a permanent Bureau of the Census. The data collected were similar to those of previous censuses, and the final publications were similar as well. However, the data that were ready first were made available initially as press releases and

then as official bulletins. By 1914 the bureau had published 11 volumes, plus numerous specialized population and economic bulletins and state supplements. For the first time census data were provided for small subdivisions of cities or neighborhoods. In order to do this, census tracts were delineated in eight large cities, including New York, which had initially requested small-area data.

Items from earlier censuses are available in library catalogs under "U.S. Census Office," but those since 1910 (the 13th census) and those after are organized under "U.S. Bureau of the Census." In 1938 the Bureau of the Census assumed responsibility for the publication of the *Statistical Abstract*, originally published in 1878 and still the most widely used statistical publication.

The Modern Census

The 1940 census reflected dramatic changes in all areas of census operations. Reflecting the interests of the Depression years, the bureau expanded the number of questions on employment and unemployment, internal migration, and income. A census of housing was taken at the same time. The combined effort has been known ever since as the Census of Population and Housing. The additional housing questions provided more data on the quality of the nation's housing and on the need for a public housing program.

Advanced statistical techniques, such as sampling, were introduced as standard procedures. As a result preliminary returns were published more than eight months before the complete tabulations, and it was possible to publish more detailed tables and to review tabulations with greater efficiency. The wartime pressures on the Census Bureau resulted in an even greater number of publications than had been produced in the 1930s, and for the first time, tables for small-area socioeconomic data were produced for the 60 cities tracted at the time.

There was already some standardization of the publication program, with the use of such report titles as "Number of Inhabitants" and "Detailed Characteristics of the Population." There were also census tract reports, special subject reports, and procedural reports. Maps were published, and volumes included appendices with definitions of census terms. The 1940 census resulted in an unprecedented number of printed reports.

Sampling was extended to the housing census in 1950. Subsequently, sampling design varied from census to census, with the common goal of producing accurate estimates of population and housing characteristics for areas as small as census tracts. The number of questions asked of the entire population was reduced to that necessary to identify the population and to avoid duplication. The resultant publications included a variety of working and technical reports in addition to the standard tabular reports and the procedural history.

Standard metropolitan statistical areas (SMSAs) were defined for the 1950 census and census county divisions for the 1960 census; census tracts were included for areas within SMSAs. This meant that until 1990, when the entire nation was covered by tracts or block-numbering area (BNA) equivalents, there were more small-area data for the urbanized parts of the country than for the rural ones.

The use of census data for the allocation of government funds continued, and the reapportionment issue reemerged in the courts. As a result, census reports grew more detailed. The major innovation in 1950 was the initiation of a survey of residential financing. Similar surveys were conducted for the rest of the century. Surveys of components of housing change were included with the 1960 and 1970 censuses.

The Bureau as a Service Agency

Before 1960 the bureau was first and foremost a production agency; its product was a set of printed volumes that summarized the results of each census. Relatively little attention was paid to issues of data access or use. In addition to the published volumes, special tabulations were available on a limited basis only. In response to a growing interest in census data by external users, a service unit was created at the bureau to deal directly with user needs and to distribute standard data products.

The 1960 census saw the beginning of the transition to machine-readable products. Special extracts were created to meet the needs of both governmental and nongovernmental users. Since there was no program for the distribution of standard off-the-shelf tape products, data requests were costly and time-consuming. Among the special products requested by other government agencies were the Journey to Work and the Equal Employment Opportunity (EEO) files.

The first public use samples (actual census form responses without personal identifiers), the 1/10,000 and the 1/1,000 samples, met the needs of those who wished to create their own tabulations or perform other types of data analysis. These were initially released on punched cards to a selected group of academic data users. Because these data lacked household identifiers, it was essential that the cards be kept in chronological order. Subsequently these data were released on magnetic tape. The bureau also released standard tapes with limited tabular data for census tracts.

The data on these tapes were not subject to the kind of checking and validating that is now a routine part of the bureau's operation; however, they met the needs of many users. Documentation was limited and data were difficult to use, since no packaged software was yet available for statistical analysis. Because no plans were made to archive these data, most of the census tract data are no longer available in machine-readable form.

Based on input from both internal and external advisory groups, in 1970 the bureau designed a series of data products to supplement the standard printed volumes. To introduce these products, they initiated a serial newsletter, "Small-Area Data Notes," and issued a two-volume *Census User's Guide* to document the aggregate data products known as the "counts."

Because the costs of printing and paper had already skyrocketed, the computer tapes contained substantially more data than the printed reports. They were usually issued well before their printed equivalents. However, printed reports were more widely available and were easier and cheaper to use. As a result the 1970 and 1980 censuses resulted in more printed reports than ever before. Major users of census data found the tapes to be more efficient. The public-use sample data allowed users to create their own extracts and tabulations for larger geographic areas.

The first, second, and third counts were based on 100 percent data: enumeration districts, census tracts, and blocks, respectively. The fourth, fifth, and sixth counts were based on sample data. The fourth count was the most heavily used because it included all of the socioeconomic and detailed housing items for almost all levels of geography. The fifth count provided limited sample data for three-digit and five-digit ZIP codes and for enumeration districts. The sixth count contained detailed tables for large geographic areas such as states, metropolitan areas, and large cities. Anticipating a decline in the use of printed materials, the bureau, then under the direction of Vincent Barabba, cut the size of its print order for the 1970 census; however, the publicity associated with the tape products only increased the use of printed as well as of machine-readable census data. Data were also available on microfiche.

Prior to the 1970 census, the bureau established the Data Access and Use Laboratory. Outside the bureau, Jack Beresford established the nonprofit Data Use and Access Laboratories (DUALabs) to make the tape data more accessible and more usable. Funded by the Ford Foundation, in cooperation with the Center for Research Libraries, DUALabs produced compressed versions of the 1970 count data; its MOD software was used at major research libraries and for internal use at several large corporations and municipal planning departments. Its compression algorithm reduced the tape required by 90 percent, and COBOL software made access to the data easy for experienced computer users. Use of data in this format declined with the demise of large IBM mainframes. Count data, which have been preserved, are available from the National Archives.

In addition to the count data, the bureau released a complex group of six 1/100 public use samples: State; SMSA and County Group; and Neighborhood Characteristics, each for the 15 percent and the 5 percent samples. A 1/1,000 and a 1/10,000 file were made available for each of these samples. All of these data were distributed on either 800 bpi or later on 1600 bpi magnetic tapes, and while each of the 1/100 samples required 33 reels of tape, each of the 1/1,000 required only three reels of tape and each of the 1/10,000 only one. The major problem with these data was their hierarchical format (household, family, and individual), but extracts were readily analyzed using the statistical packages that were by then widely available. A new sample of the 1960 census made these data more comparable with the 1970 state sample. Later, thanks to the efforts of Halliman Winsborough of the University of Wisconsin, public use samples from the 1940 and 1950 censuses were produced in machine-readable form from microfilm records.

Several geographic products were also made available for use with the count and public use sample data. These included files for identifying SMSAs, counties, places, census tracts, and enumeration districts; a collection of printed maps for use in locating county groups, census tracts, and enumeration districts; and the geographic area code index, which provided quick access to codes for counties, places, and townships.

During the 1970s an increasing awareness of the value of census data emerged for the comparative study of areas of all sizes and of rare populations. In 1980, efforts were made to eliminate several standard printed reports. Although the block statistics program was expanded substantially, the reports from it were made available only on tape and on microfiche. Efforts to eliminate tract reports met with great objections from documents librarians and planners and, as a result, were published as they had been in the past. The "detailed characteristics" reports were not included in the original 1980 publication program but were subsequently published; these reports were finally eliminated in 1990. The number of printed special and subject reports was decreased in 1980 but made available on tapes and CDs as Subject Summary Tapes (SSTs) in 1990. The counts were renamed Summary Tape Files (STFs), and the public use samples became Public Use Microdata Samples, or PUMS. The age of microcomputers was only beginning and computer-readable data were still being released on magnetic tape. In response to strong user demands, the format of the STFs was changed so that each record began with a geographic segment. Medians were computed, and the data suppression codes were replaced with a different method of disclosure avoidance.

As a result of a change in the sampling design, PUMS was less complicated in 1980. They used three samples instead of six and the County Group sample was released for 5 percent of the population. However, it was still not possible to identify places with populations of less than 100,000.

Census 2000 Products: New Media for Data Delivery

The initial plan for the 1990 census was to produce products that closely resembled those from the 1980 census; however, by the time the bureau started to prepare the 1990 products, it was obvious that most depository libraries and many individual users had access to microcomputers. As a result, CD-ROMS containing the Public Law 94-171 data for reapportionment and redistricting, selected STFs, and SST files, PUMS, and geographic products were available for less money and were the media used for depository library distribution. Microfiche was eliminated, and economic census data and a limited amount of 1980 decennial census data were also made available on CDs. Four printed volumes remained: *General Population Characteristics; Summary Social, Economic and Housing Characteristics; General Housing Characteristics;* and *Detailed Housing Characteristics. Tract Reports* and *Detailed Social and Economic Characteristics* were eliminated. In 2000 there were only three printed reports: *Summary Population and Housing Characteristics; Summary Social, Economic and Housing*

Characteristics; and *Population and Housing Unit Counts.* All of these reports were available for both the United States and for each of the individual states. Although STFs continued to be available on various media, other means of data access became more common.

As browsers such as Mosaic, Netscape, and Explorer, and subsequently Firefox, Safari, and others, provided data users with Internet access, the bureau experimented with various forms of online access. Among the initial ones were Ferret, a system for creating data extracts, and the data extraction system developed at the University of Minnesota for use with Microdata, including the 1990 PUMS. Selected 1990 summary data for STF1 and STF3 could be displayed for multiple geographic areas using Lookup.

The American FactFinder is the newest database engine and the one in current use. Although originally designed for use with the economic censuses, it was further developed for the 1990 census and subsequently for the 2000 census. It is now used to obtain data for individual communities using both the 2010 census and the American Community Survey data. It is also possible to use the Internet to obtain EEO data and State and County Quick Facts, which are updated on a regular basis.

As the bureau prepared to tabulate data for 2000, it also developed methods for making selected historical census data available online by searching on "historical" and on selected census years. Although the PUMS data are now widely available on the census Web site (census.gov) and elsewhere, notably at the Web site of the Integrated Public Use Microdata Series (IPUMS; http://usa.ipums.org/usa/), it is not possible to access pre-1990 summary tables online easily. However, summary files from earlier censuses (1970–1990) are available from the National Archives, from the Inter-University Consortium of Political and Social Research (ICPSR), and from other academic data libraries. Printed reports going back to 1790 can be obtained at federal depository libraries or the U. S. Government Printing Office, or they can be printed through "print on demand" by the Census Bureau.

Bit by bit printed reports are being eliminated: the block data reports in 1980, the tract and detailed characteristics reports in 1990, and the social and economic characteristics reports in 2010. The only printed reports currently planned from the 2010 census data are summary housing and population characteristics, population and housing counts, and selected special reports and census briefs. However, since the American Community Surveys have replaced the census "long form," there are several ACS reports, easily printed from the ACS home page, that contain the type of data previously provided in the social and economic characteristics reports. In addition, a great deal of ACS data is available for selective downloading. Comprehensive lists of data products for both the census and the ACS are available on the Internet.

Over the decades the community of census data users has grown enormously. As the usefulness of these data has become more obvious, their accessibility has also increased. Just as it was impossible to predict 30 years ago what census dissemination would be like today, so too it is impossible to know exactly what the combination of data requirements and technological innovation will produce in the future. The very idea of what constitutes a useful "data product" will certainly change as the environment in which these products are made available grows more virtual and more interactive.

See also *Dissemination of data: electronic products; Dissemination of data: printed publications; Dissemination of data: secondary products; Summary files.*

. . . . JUDITH S. ROWE

BIBLIOGRAPHY

Anderson, Margo J., and Stephen E. Fienberg. *Who Counts? The Politics of Census-taking in Contemporary America*. New York: Russell Sage Foundation, 1999.

Cassedy, James H. *Demography in Early America: Beginnings of the Statistical Mind, 1600–1800*. Cambridge, Mass.: Harvard University Press, 1969.

Dodd, Donald B. *Historical Statistics of the States of the United States: Two Centuries of the Census, 1790–1990*. Westport, Conn.: Greenwood Press, 1993.

Eckler, A. Ross. *The Bureau of the Census*. New York: Praeger, 1972.

Greene, Evarts Boutell, and Virginia D. Harrington. *American Population before the Federal Census of 1790*. Baltimore: Genealogical Pub. Co., 1993.

Schmeckebier, Laurence Frederick. *The Statistical Work of the National Government*. Baltimore: Johns Hopkins University Press, 1925.

Truesdell, Leon E. *The Development of Punch Card Tabulation in the Bureau of the Census, 1890–1940: With Outlines of Actual Tabulation Programs*. Washington, D.C.: U.S. Government Printing Office, 1965.

U.S. Bureau of the Census. *Historical Statistics of the United States, 1789–1945*. Washington, D.C.: U.S. Department of Commerce, 1949.

———. *1970 Census Users' Guide*. Part I. Washington, D.C.: U.S. Department of Commerce, 1970.

———. *1970 Census Users' Guide*. Part II. Washington, D.C.: U.S. Department of Commerce, 1970.

———. "Population and Housing Inquiries in U.S. Decennial Censuses 1790–1970." Working Paper 39. Washington, D.C.: U.S. Department of Commerce, 1973.

———. "Public Use Samples of Basic Records from the 1970 Census: Description and Technical Documentation." Washington, D.C.: U.S. Department of Commerce, 1972.

U.S. Congress. Office of Technology Assessment. *Federal Information Dissemination in an Electronic Age: Informing the Nation*. Washington, D.C.: U.S. Government Printing Office, 1988.

Wright, C. D., and W. C. Hunt. "The History and Growth of the United States Census." Prepared for the Senate Committee on the Census. Washington, D.C.: U.S. Government Printing Office, 1900.

Decennial Censuses: 1790 Census

The population of the United States, as reported in the 1790 census, was 3,929,625, which was used to apportion 105 seats in the House of Representatives among the 15 states. Although census taking was familiar to many Americans from the colonial period, the 1790 census was the first time that the population of all the states was counted at the same time.

The census resulted from the ratification of the Constitution in 1788. As part of a compromise over representation, the Constitution required that an "actual enumeration" be taken within three years of the first meeting of Congress and within every ten years thereafter, for purposes of allocating seats in the House of Representatives, direct taxes, and votes in the Electoral College. The relative proportions among the states were to be based on the size of the free population (white and black) and, "excluding Indians not taxed, three-fifths of all other persons" (meaning slaves).

The Constitution had assigned 65 seats in the House to the 13 original states on the basis of population estimates. Because of concerns that the size of the House was too small to represent the country adequately, Congress moved promptly to take the census. On May 18, 1789, the House of Representatives began work on a bill to take the census; the final version was signed into law by President George Washington on March 1, 1790. It stipulated that the count should begin August 1, 1790, and should be completed within nine months. Although the Constitution required only that the population be divided into free, slave, and Indians not taxed, James Madison, then in the House, argued that greater detail would aid in passing useful legislation. At minimum, he wanted to know the total of adult, white males—that part of the population most involved in the political life of the country. As a result the census separated the free population into white males age 16 and above and below the age of 16, white females, and all other free persons. Slaves were counted with no distinctions by age or sex; Indians were excluded from the count by the law. Madison also urged that occupations be recorded because he believed political interests often reflected economic divisions. Others disagreed, arguing that the people would be suspicious of too many questions about their economic status, that many individuals worked in a variety of occupations, and so would be hard to classify, and that collecting the extra data was unnecessary, useful only for "idle people to make a book." Local counts were made by household, with the head listed by name and the rest of the family counted under the appropriate headings. Although the final law required more information than the minimum specified in the Constitution, the first census contained less detail than many colonial censuses.

The census was taken under the supervision of local federal marshals, who were empowered to hire assistants, as needed. Most assistants were paid at the rate of $1 per 150 people counted. In towns of more than 5,000, the rate was reduced to $1 per 300, while in thinly settled areas the rate increased to $1 per 50. The assistants were not provided with printed forms. Total cost of the census was $44,377. Failure to provide information to the census-takers could lead to a $20 fine. To ensure accuracy, all assistants were required to post their tabulations in public places for inspection and correction. When the marshals were satisfied with the results, they forwarded them to Secretary of State Thomas Jefferson, who passed them on to President Washington. Washington presented a table of the population to Congress on October 27, 1791, though reports from South Carolina had not yet been received. Vermont and the Southwest Territory, neither part of the original area to be counted, both managed to get their totals to the government before South Carolina. A 56-page

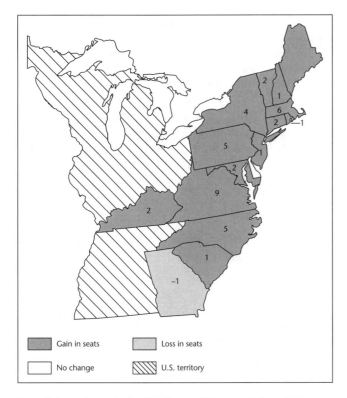

Gain in seats   Loss in seats

No change   U.S. territory

State Gains or Losses in the U.S. House of Representatives, 1790

book containing considerable detail was published in 1791. Partial results had appeared in the press before then. Preservation of some of the original manuscripts provides specific information about town and county populations as well as the size of families, which was useful to scholars who later returned to the local sources.

As the results arrived at the capital, Jefferson and others remarked that the total was probably too low, estimating the true number might approach 4.1 million—representing about a 5 percent undercount. Jefferson and Washington were among many who thought a larger number projected the strength of the country and a promising future among the nations of the world. They had almost no interest in other details, such as 17.8 percent of the total population being slave, 50.9 percent of all whites being male, or 49.0 percent of white males being under the age of 16. These proportions were familiar from the colonial period and so, presumably, did not merit comment.

See also *Colonial censuses; Congress and the census; Decennial censuses: 1800 census.*

. . . . ROBERT V. WELLS

BIBLIOGRAPHY

Anderson, Margo J. *The American Census: A Social History.* New Haven, Conn.: Yale University Press, 1988.

Cohen, Patricia Cline. *A Calculating People: The Spread of Numeracy in Early America.* Chicago: University of Chicago Press, 1982.

Greven, Philip J., Jr. "The Average Size of Families and Households in the Province of Massachusetts in 1764 and in the United States in 1790: An Overview." In *Household and Family in Past Time,* ed. Peter Laslett and Richard Wall, 547–560. Cambridge: Cambridge University Press, 1972.

U.S. Bureau of the Census. *A Century of Population Growth: From the First Census of the United States to the Twelfth, 1790–1900.* Washington, D.C.: U.S. Government Printing Office, 1909.

Decennial Censuses: 1800 Census

The 1800 census counted 5,308,483 people in the United States. That total was used to apportion 141 seats in the House of Representatives to the 16 states. (Ohio received one seat in 1803, upon its admission to the union.)

The 1800 census was similar to that of 1790 in many ways. The law implementing the taking of the census in 1800 again relied on federal marshals and their assistants as enumerators. After the marshals had collected the data, checked for errors, and arrived at totals, they sent the final versions for each state to the secretary of state, who in turn presented them to the president for submission to Congress. The official version was published in a 74-page volume, though newspapers provided summaries to their readers. An estimated 900 enumerators were involved in taking the census, about 250 more than in 1790; the total cost was $66,000, an increase of $22,000 from the first census. But because of the increase in population, the estimated cost per capita rose only from 1.1 to 1.2 cents.

As Congress prepared for the census, both the American Philosophical Society and the Connecticut Academy of Arts and Sciences urged expanding the number of questions to provide a more complex and useful picture of the American people. In addition to reviving James Madison's appeal for information on occupations, rejected in 1790, they suggested greater detail on age as well as recording nativity (place of birth) and marital status. Although Congress did agree to collect more information on age, it decided that additional questions were either unnecessary or unconstitutional. The white population, both male and female, was divided into the following categories by age: under 10, 10 to under 16, 16 to under 26, 26 to under 45, and 45 and up. The reasons for these particular divisions are unclear, as colonial censuses used 10 and 16 to set off children, but never both, and 60 was the most common maximum age used before 1775. Perhaps young men between 16 and 26 were the prime choices for military service, but that does not explain the other divisions. Heads of families were included in the appropriate category by age and sex, in addition to being listed in the census schedule. Once again, no details were required for either other free persons or slaves.

The 1800 census was taken amid one of the most controversial presidential elections in American history. As a result the political correspondence of the period is more concerned with the election and the subsequent decision in the House to select Thomas Jefferson as president

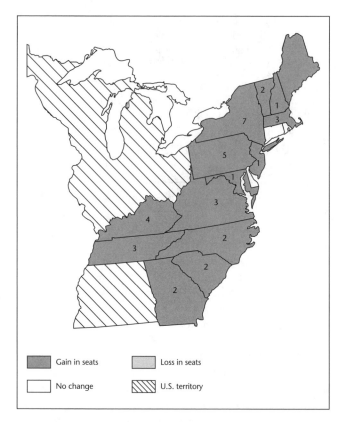

Gain in seats   Loss in seats

No change   U.S. territory

State Gains or Losses in the U.S. House of Representatives, 1800

over his running mate, Aaron Burr, than with the census. Three secretaries of state oversaw the 1800 count. Federalist Timothy Pickering served as secretary of state through mid-1800 and was the target of the Republicans in 1799, as Congress debated whether census legislation allowed the secretary too much freedom in establishing regulations for taking the census. President John Adams replaced Pickering with John Marshall, who served until President Jefferson and Secretary of State James Madison took office in the spring of 1801. After Madison replaced Marshall, he had to prod new marshals in several states to complete the work of their predecessors and to reassure them that the Treasury Department would pay them. In May 1801, Tench Coxe, a Jefferson supporter and writer on statistical matters, unsuccessfully urged Madison to have the president request that the public voluntarily report desired data on occupation and nativity. Madison also received requests for copies of the census from Treasury secretary Albert Gallatin and the American ambassador to London, Rufus King.

Jefferson made reference to the census in his first State of the Union message in 1801, noting with pride that the population had doubled in just over 22 years. In the midst of diplomatic problems caused by the Anglo-French conflict that would ultimately give rise to the War of 1812, Jefferson observed that Americans did not take pleasure from their rapid growth because of "the injuries it may enable us to do to others," but because of what it meant for the settlement of "the extensive country still remaining vacant . . . [and] the multiplications of men susceptible of happiness, educated in the love of order, habituated to self-government, and valuing its blessings above all price."

In addition to rapid growth, Jefferson and others could have noted such national characteristics as 101 men for every 100 women, 49.5 percent under the age of 16, 12.2 percent age 45 or older, 17.0 percent held in slavery, and 2.1 percent free blacks. Variations from one state to another were readily apparent, though largely ignored, regarding not only size and racial composition but also age and sex. By and large, the New England states were whiter, older, and more female than other parts of the country.

See also *Decennial censuses: 1790 census; Decennial censuses: 1810 census; Decennial censuses: 1820 census.*

. . . . ROBERT V. WELLS

BIBLIOGRAPHY
Anderson, Margo J. *The American Census: A Social History.* New Haven, Conn.: Yale University Press, 1988.
Cassedy, James H. *Demography in Early America: Beginnings of the Statistical Mind, 1600–1800.* Cambridge, Mass.: Harvard University Press, 1969.
Cohen, Patricia Cline. *A Calculating People: The Spread of Numeracy in Early America.* Chicago: University of Chicago Press, 1982.

Decennial Censuses: 1810 Census

The population of the United States according to the 1810 census was 7,239,881. By the end of the 1810s, 186 seats in the House of Representatives had been allocated among the 23 states.

Under the direction of the secretary of state, the federal government instructed the marshals and their assistants to collect information about the population as of Monday, August 6, 1810. The five months originally set for the enumeration were extended until June 3, 1811, for assistants to make their returns and until July 1, 1811, for the marshals to complete the work. Two publications were issued after the census: a 180-page folio volume devoted to population and a 233-page quarto volume on manufacturing, prepared and summarized by political economist and former high federal official Tench Coxe of Philadelphia. The total cost of the census, including printing, was $178,444.67, or two cents per person enumerated.

In the 1810 census only the names of heads of families were recorded. For the first time, the law required that an inquiry be made at every dwelling house or to the head of every household. The categories of information collected were identical to that of the preceding census. Free white males and females were separately tallied into the five age groups of under 10 years of age, 10 to 15, 16 to 25, 26 to 44, and 45 and older. The numbers of slaves and other free persons—primarily free blacks and taxed American Indians—were recorded with no distinction made as to sex or age.

Since 1800 the population had grown by 36 percent. The United States remained a rural society in 1810. The share of

A cartoon-map of a Massachusetts legislative district (*Boston Gazette*, March 26, 1812) approved by Governor Elbridge Gerry. Drawing district lines for political advantage has become known as "gerrymandering".

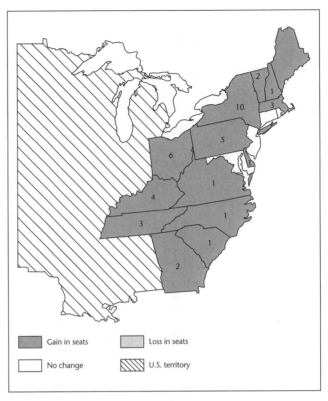

State Gains or Losses in the U.S. House of Representatives, 1810

the urban population, places with 2,500 or more people, crept forward from 6.1 to 7.2 percent of the total population. There were 46 such towns and cities in 1810 compared with 33 in 1800. Because of Thomas Jefferson's purchase of the Louisiana Territory from France in 1803, which nearly doubled the area of North America under the control of the United States, population density declined from 6.1 to 4.3 enumerated persons per square mile between 1800 and 1810. All segments of the population increased rapidly. The size of the enslaved population expanded by 33 percent during the first decade of the nineteenth century, and one-sixth of Americans were held in slavery in 1810. The percentage of free blacks in the total population of color increased from 10.8 to 13.5 between 1800 and 1810. During the decade Congress approved the first law limiting immigration to the United States. The forced importation of blacks in the slave trade, which the Constitution had allowed to continue legally for 20 years, was finally ended in 1808.

In his introduction to the volume on industrial statistics, Coxe pointed to numerous imperfections and omissions but eschewed any attempt to estimate the correct figures. Information was collected on more than 200 products and production facilities, such as mills and tanneries, and was tabulated for states and smaller civil divisions. The tables effectively conveyed an impression of the diversity and widespread nature of industrial production in the country. Overall, however, Coxe admitted and later commentators concurred that the effort was unsuccessful in documenting the aggregate of industrial activity in the United States.

The constitutionally pertinent population, based on counting slaves as three-fifths of free persons, of the average congressional district increased slightly from 33,000 to 35,000, but no state lost a representative. Gaining ten seats, New York replaced Virginia as the state with the most members of Congress, a rank it would hold for 160 years until California emerged after 1970 as the most populous state. Pennsylvania and Ohio both gained five seats, and Kentucky added four. The share of House seats held by the South declined for the first time, from 46 to 44 percent, but the regions still had equal numbers of senators. Politicians and commentators began to take note of what was to become a trend toward northern population dominance. A major aspect of the Missouri Compromise of 1820 was the paired admission of Missouri as a slave state and Maine, previously a noncontiguous district of Massachusetts, as a free state.

The results of the 1810 and other early censuses of the United States were most important in shaping a vision of growth and progress in the country and in providing the demographic framework for the conflict between the North and South.

See also *Census law; Decennial censuses: 1800 census; Decennial censuses: 1820 census; Dissemination of data: printed publications.*

DANIEL SCOTT SMITH
. . . . REVISED BY MARGO J. ANDERSON

BIBLIOGRAPHY

Anderson, Margo J. *The American Census: A Social History.* New Haven, Conn.: Yale University Press, 1988.

Coxe, Tench. *A Statement of the Arts and Manufactures of the United States of America, for the Year 1810.* New York: Norman Ross Publishing, 1990, ©1814.

Inter-University Consortium for Political and Social Research (ICPSR). *Historical, Demographic, Economic, and Social Data: The United States, 1790–1970.* Part No. 3. Ann Arbor, Mich.: ICPSR, 1984. County-level computer file available to persons at ICPSR-affiliated institutions. www.icpsr.umich.edu.

U.S. Secretary of State. *Aggregate Amount of Persons within the United States in the Year 1810.* New York: Norman Ross Publishing, 1990, ©1811.

Wright, Carroll D. *The History and Growth of the United States Census.* Washington, D.C.: U.S. Government Printing Office, 1900.

Decennial Censuses: 1820 Census

The population of the United States was 9,638,453 at the time of the 1820 census. A total of 213 seats in the House of Representatives were apportioned among the 24 states.

Under the supervision of Secretary of State John Quincy Adams, the federal government instructed the marshals and assistants to record the facts about the population located in their customary residences as of Monday, August 7, 1820. The enumerators were given six months to complete their interviews, whether done at each dwelling or with a household head elsewhere. Because of delays, Congress in March 1821 had to extend the deadline until September 1 of that year. The total cost of the census, including printing, was $208,525.99 or just over two cents per person enumerated. Published were a 160-page folio volume of population data and a 100-page volume of information on manufacturing. Neither the process of counting nor the publication of the results generated controversy or even much commentary.

Although the House of Representatives grew by 27 seats, the constitutionally pertinent population of the average congressional district, based on counting slaves as three-fifths of free persons, grew as well—from 35,000 after the 1810 census to 40,000 after the 1820 census. Four states—Connecticut, Delaware, Vermont, and Virginia—lost one representative from their delegations. Consequent to rapid growth in the Middle Atlantic region, the delegations from New York and Pennsylvania, the two largest, grew from 50 to 60, and Ohio in the West expanded its number of representatives from 6 to 14. The trend toward more rapid population growth in the North than in the slave states continued. State legislatures were not required to use the results from the census in laying out the boundaries of congressional districts. On average, nevertheless, districts varied only 11 percent from the state average in those states having two or more districts.

As was the case until the 1850 census, only the names of heads of families were recorded. The instructions asked the enumerators to delineate the white population into five age groups for females (under 10, 10 to 15, 15 to 25, 26 to 44, and 45 and older) and six for males (16- and 17-year-olds separately recorded). Aliens who had not been naturalized were

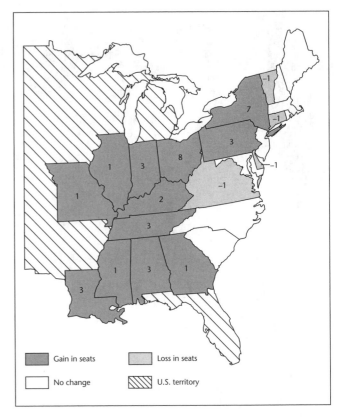

State Gains or Losses in the U.S. House of Representatives, 1820

included both in the age categories and in a separate tally. They numbered more than 53,000 nationally. For the first time Congress required age and sex cohort breakdowns for the slave and free colored population. They mandated four categories instead of the five or six used for the white population. The age categories also had different breakpoints (under 14, 15 to 25, 26 to 44, and 45 and older). The resulting published tables permitted age and sex comparisons between the slave and free colored population but made comparisons with the white population difficult. Finally, some 4,631 American Indians who paid taxes were separately recorded.

Since 1810 the population had grown by 33 percent and the size of the House of Representatives by 14 percent. The United States remained an overwhelmingly rural, agricultural society. The population in towns and cities expanded at virtually the same rate as that in the countryside. Only 7.2 percent resided in the 61 places that had 2,500 or more in population. Because of a high birth rate, the population remained youthful. The median age of the entire population was only 16.6 years, an increase of 0.6 years since 1810. The enslaved population expanded by 29 percent over the course of the 1810s. Some 16 percent of enumerated Americans were slaves at the time of the fourth census, while 13 percent of African Americans were legally free.

Congress had rejected the respective requests of James Madison and Thomas Jefferson that a question about occupation be included in the first and second census. The 1820 census for the first time tallied the principal activities of persons, including those of slaves, into 3 broad and exclusive categories. In his instructions, Adams recognized that many in the relatively unspecialized American economy were engaged in more than one sector. Some 83 percent were in agriculture; 14 percent in manufacturing, including such hand labor as was carried out in households; and 3 percent in commerce. In a separate folio volume of 100 pages, 14 categories of information on each separately enumerated manufacturing establishment were detailed. Among these inquiries were the numbers of men, women, and children employed, the amount of capital invested, and the total wages paid. These returns were, however, incomplete, and economic historians have found them of limited use.

The 1820 census represented another increment in the gradual expansion of the decennial count's scope and documented the continuing rapid growth of the American population during the first half of the nineteenth century.

See also *Decennial censuses: 1810 census; Decennial censuses: 1830 census*

DANIEL SCOTT SMITH
. . . . REVISED BY MARGO J. ANDERSON

BIBLIOGRAPHY

Anderson, Margo J. *The American Census: A Social History.* New Haven, Conn.: Yale University Press, 1988.

Parsons, Stanley D., William W. Beach, and Dan Hermann. *United States Congressional Districts 1788–1841.* Westport, Conn.: Greenwood Press, 1978.

U.S. Secretary of State. *Census for 1820.* Washington, D.C.: Gales and Seaton, 1821.

———. *Digest of Accounts of Manufacturing Establishments in the United States, and of Their Manufactures.* Washington, D.C.: Gales and Seaton, 1823.

Wright, Carroll D. *The History and Growth of the United States Census.* Washington, D.C.: U.S. Government Printing Office, 1900.

Decennial Censuses: 1830 Census

According to the 1830 census, the population of the United States was 12,866,020 (including 5,318 persons on ships and thus not in any state or territory). A total of 240 seats in the House of Representatives were apportioned among the 24 states.

An enumeration bill establishing the census of 1830 was passed on March 23, 1830. As in previous censuses, this one called for the enumeration of households under the household head's name, with all residents classified by sex, age categories, race, and civil condition (free or slave). The broad three-part occupational categorization inaugurated in the 1820 census was dropped. On the suggestion of John Quincy Adams, who had directed the 1820 census when he was secretary of state, the 1830 census further refined age classifications. Adams, as president, argued for ten-year intervals up to 100 and over in his fourth annual message to Congress in December 1828, on the grounds that this would allow for highly interesting "comparative tables of longevity." Congress enacted this suggestion, but for white males and females only. Thirteen age columns for whites replaced the five from 1820, bounded by the ages 5, 10, 15, 20, 30, 40, 50, 60, 70, 80, 90,

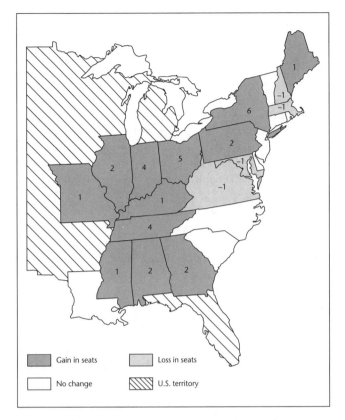

State Gains or Losses in the U.S. House of Representatives, 1830

and 100. Slightly altered age categories were also established for blacks, both slave and free, dividing them into six groups instead of the four used in 1820 and including a column for those over 100. The broad boundaries (10, 24, 36, 55, and 100) did not easily allow longevity by race to be compared. The undifferentiated grouping of all blacks between 55 and 100 particularly hampered potential study of life expectation for blacks.

Congress added one new inquiry to the 1830 census. Assistant marshals were asked to gather data on the numbers of deaf, dumb, and blind, sorted by race, and, except for the blind, by three age categories (under 14, 14 to 24, 25 and up). As in 1820, a column identified foreigners not naturalized. Congress also moved the date of the census ahead two months, to June 1 instead of August 1 as in 1820, on President Adams's suggestion that this would permit a longer stretch of good weather for the house-to-house enumeration. Congress allowed six months for the process to be completed. An amended act passed on February 3, 1831, extended the terminal date for aggregating returns until August 1, 1831. The amendment also directed the secretary of state "to note all the clerical errors in the returns" and publish the corrections along with the aggregate returns of the marshals.

President Andrew Jackson's secretary of state, Martin Van Buren, directed the census. For the first time, the State Department provided a printed schedule for the enumerators. The uniform schedule measured 18 1/2 by 16 inches, with columns printed on both the front and back. As before, marshals and assistant marshals in the field were to conduct the census, and they were directed by Congress to obtain information "by actual inquiry at every dwelling house." A penalty of $20 was charged to anyone over 16 who refused to answer census questions. The assistant marshals prepared two copies of the returns and posted them in public places for inspection and verification. One copy was then deposited with the local district court and the other sent to the State Department, along with the marshal's aggregation of the district's returns.

In 1830 the U.S. population was 8.8 percent urban, 18 percent African American, and 15.6 percent slave.

In 1832, Washington, D.C., printer Duff Green published the population returns. Three thousand books were produced, with copies distributed to colleges and historical societies. The aggregation by county and state was followed by a long "errata" section containing the corrections made by temporary clerks hired by the State Department to double-check the calculations of the marshals.

See also *Decennial censuses: 1820 census; Decennial censuses: 1840 census.*

. . . . PATRICIA CLINE COHEN

BIBLIOGRAPHY

Bohme, Frederick G. *200 Years of U.S. Census Taking: Population and Housing Questions, 1790–1990.* Washington, D.C.: U.S. Government Printing Office, 1989.

Wright, Carroll D. *The History and Growth of the United States Census,* Prepared for the Senate Committee on the Census. Washington, D.C.: U.S. Government Printing Office, 1900.

Decennial Censuses: 1840 Census

The 1840 census tallied the U.S. population at 17,069,453, leading to an apportionment of 223 seats in the House of Representatives among the 26 states. The American population was 10.8 percent urban, 16.8 percent African American, and 14.6 percent slave.

An enumeration bill establishing the census of 1840 was passed in the closing days of the Twenty-fifth Congress, in February 1839. With strong bipartisan support, lawmakers duplicated the language of the 1830 census act, providing for the enumeration of households under the household head's name, with all residents classified by sex, age categories, race, and civil condition (free or slave). For whites, the age categories were bounded by the ages 5, 10, 15, 20, 30, 40, 50, 60, 70, 80, 90, and 100; for blacks, both slave and free, the category boundaries remained as they had been in 1830, at ages 10, 24, 36, 55, and 100. (A proposal by Rep. William Slade, a Vermont Whig, to count the black population by age categories comparable to those of whites failed even to come to a vote.) The enumeration bill continued the practice, started in 1830, of gathering information on the numbers of "deaf, dumb, and blind", sorted by race.

Congress added three new inquiries to the 1840 census. One stipulated a count of the numbers of "insane and idiots,"

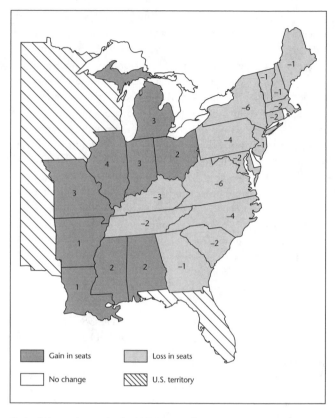

State Gains or Losses in the U.S. House of Representatives, 1840

Gain in seats   Loss in seats

No change   U.S. territory

distinguished by race and mode of support (at public or private charge). A second called for a list, by name and age, of all pensioners still drawing government support for Revolutionary War service, information vital for forecasting future pension payments and for checking the accuracy of the pension rolls. A third amendment, at once ambitious, unprecedented, and unspecified, directed that "statistical tables" should be returned, containing "all such information in relation to mines, agriculture, commerce, manufacturers, and schools, as will exhibit a full view of the pursuits, industry, education, and resources of the country."

Previous federal censuses had been directly supervised by the secretary of state, but this time Secretary John Forsyth hired William A. Weaver to superintend the entire job, from preparing the schedule to publishing the results. For the population schedule Weaver devised an oversize, two-sided form with 74 columns, including the question on pensioners and the notation of deaf, dumb, blind, insane, and idiot persons. Weaver designated seven occupational categories (mining, agriculture, commerce, manufacturing, learned professions, ocean navigators, and navigators on internal waters), and he added seven columns for tallying schools and scholars (in colleges, academies, common schools). A final column recorded persons over the age of 20 who could not read or write. These inquiries went to satisfy the desire for fuller economic and educational statistics. To answer thoroughly the congressional call for a "full view" of the country's resources, Weaver prepared a second schedule consisting of 214 inquiries about production and investment in economic enterprises including mining, agriculture, horticulture, commerce, fisheries, forestry, and manufacturing. The resulting compilation yielded figures for the number of swine, retail stores, bushels of potatoes, and employees in cotton manufacturing, among another 200 economic statistics, for every census district in the country.

The census began on June 1, 1840; returns came in slowly, and aggregation in Washington, D.C., proceeded even more slowly. In February 1841 the Senate requested a progress report, a call repeated by the House in summer 1841. In October the state tallies of population were made public, both in an official government publication and in privately published statistical almanacs. In 1842 the economic statistics were printed by two printing firms, Blair & Rives and Thomas Allen.

Two controversies quickly engulfed the 1840 census. One, relatively minor, concerned the two rival firms that had printed the volume of economic statistics. One firm had held exclusive government printing contracts for a decade under Democratic rule, but the 1841 inauguration of a Whig presidential administration led a new secretary of state, (Daniel Webster), to promise the lucrative job to a Whig printer. Congressional hearings to sort out the contract dispute generated a significant byproduct: exceptional documentation about methods used to process the census at the Department of State.

A second controversy of national proportions arose over the detection of peculiar patterns of rates of insanity and idiocy by race. Close inspection of the published data by insanity expert Dr. Edward Jarvis of Massachusetts revealed an apparent precipitous rise in black insanity neatly correlated with geography. The ratio of insane blacks to all blacks in Maine was 1 in 14; in Louisiana, the ratio was 1 in 5,650. Ratios for each state, arrayed from far north to far south, exhibited an amazingly uniform gradient. Overall, the North's ratio was 1 in 162.4, while the South's was 1 in 1,558. The corresponding ratio for whites showed almost no North/South difference. Charges of fraud, data tampering, and incompetence greeted this finding in publications in the North, but some Southern essayists defended the data, linking it to other data on poverty and crime to support their view that freedom was very harmful to blacks.

That the data were clearly in error could be easily shown in 1842: Insane blacks were tallied in northern towns where no black population existed. Yet William Weaver defended the integrity of his procedures; the data tallies had been made by assistant marshals working independently across the country, ruling out conspiracy. Southern politicians such as John C. Calhoun, the new secretary of state in 1842, found it too useful a piece of ammunition in slavery debates to repudiate. The errors likely resulted from the complex layout of the manuscript population schedule, with its three-tiered headings obscuring the racial sort in the insanity and idiocy columns. But the data were never officially disavowed or corrected.

See also *Decennial censuses: 1830 census; Decennial censuses: 1850 census; Disability.*

. . . . PATRICIA CLINE COHEN

BIBLIOGRAPHY

Cohen, Patricia Cline. *A Calculating People: The Spread of Numeracy in Early America.* New York: Routledge, 1999.

Deutsch, Albert. "The First U.S. Census of the Insane (1840) and Its Use as Pro-Slavery Propaganda." *Bulletin of the History of Medicine* 15 (1944): 469–482.

Grob, Gerald. *Edward Jarvis and the Medical World of Nineteenth-Century America.* Knoxville: University of Tennessee Press, 1978.

Decennial Censuses: 1850 Census

The population of the United States in 1850 census was 23,191,876. A total of 234 House seats were apportioned among 31 states. In the ten years since the preceding census, the American population increased 35.9 percent, equivalent to an average annual growth rate of 3.1 percent and a doubling of the population every 22.6 years. The rapid population growth of the 1840s abetted and was stimulated by one of the most dramatic periods of territorial expansion in the nation's history. Florida, Texas, Iowa, and Wisconsin were admitted to the Union, and new territories were established in California, Minnesota, New Mexico, Oregon, and Utah (California was admitted as a state on September 9, 1850, bringing the total number of states to 31). The new territories in the West increased the area of the United States to 2,991,655 square miles, an increase of 67 percent from 1840. Although the addition of new territories caused the nation's overall population density to fall from 9.8 inhabitants per square mile in 1840 to 7.9 in 1850, states east of the Mississippi River experienced increased population densities and rapid urbanization. The total population living in urban places—defined as incorporated places of 2,500 or more inhabitants—increased from 10.8 to 15.3 percent.

Demographics

Of the 23.2 million inhabitants of the United States in 1850, 19.6 million (84.3 percent) were classified by census enumerators as "White" and 3.6 million (15.7 percent) as "Black" or "Mulatto." Approximately 88.5 percent of the white population in 1850 was native born. Among the foreign-born population, immigrants from Ireland predominated (43 percent of all foreign-born whites), followed by Germany (26 percent), England (12 percent), Scotland (3 percent), France (2 percent), and Wales (1 percent). The vast majority of the black and mulatto population lived in servitude: 3.2 million (89.0 percent) were enumerated as slaves and just 0.4 million (11.0 percent) were enumerated as "free coloreds." Despite the high percentage of the black population held in bondage and the virtual absence of immigration, the black population increased by 26.6 percent in the 1840s, an average annual rate of 2.4 percent.

Improvements in Census Taking

The 1850 census marked a major turning point in American census taking. It was the first census to use the individual as the basic unit of enumeration and the first census to be tabulated and analyzed exclusively in Washington, D.C. Previous censuses, in contrast, had been conducted on the household

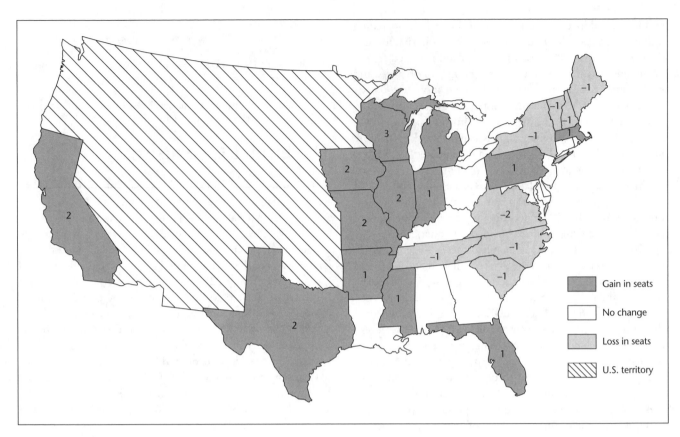

State Gains or Losses in the U.S. House of Representatives, 1850

level and relied on field enumerators to make initial tabulations. The 1850 census was also the first census to have a Census Board overseeing pre-enumeration issues, the first to include a question on place of birth, and the first to ask detailed information on age and occupation. As a result the 1850 census serves as a baseline from which to evaluate the immense social and economic transformations of the late nineteenth and the early twentieth century, including the impact of immigration, internal migration, industrialization, and urbanization on the American population.

The creation of the Census Board in 1849 and the appointment of Joseph C. G. Kennedy as its secretary profoundly shaped the 1850 census. Kennedy and members of the Census Board solicited outside advice on what should be asked on the census, how it should be conducted, and how the results should be reported. Many of the nation's statisticians were convinced that the cumbersome 80-column form used in the 1840 census resulted in a significant number of errors, and they suggested the need for radical change. Late in 1849, Lemuel Shattuck of the American Statistical Association and Archibald Russell of the American Geographical and Statistical Society were invited to Washington to help Kennedy design the 1850 schedules. The result, modeled after Shattuck's 1845 census of Boston, was a dramatic expansion in the scope and design of the census. Each individual in the population—free and slave—was to be given his or her own line on

the new forms. The number of questions grew; to be recorded was every individual's name, age, sex, color, occupation (if male and over 15 years of age), value of real estate owned, state or country of birth, whether married within previous year, whether attended school in previous year, literacy (if over 20 years of age), and whether "deaf, dumb, blind, insane, idiotic, pauper, or convict." The slave schedule initially was conceived as including most of the questions on the schedule for free inhabitants. It also was to include a question on the number of children each woman had borne, whether the children were still living, and the name of the owner. Unfortunately, southern senators, fearing detailed analyses of slavery, were able to delete many of the proposed questions from the schedule when the census bill came up for debate. The final slave schedule approved by the Senate identified each slave by number only. In addition, it included questions on the age, sex, and color of each slave; whether the slave was deaf, dumb, blind, insane, idiotic, or a fugitive from the state; the name of the owner; and the number of slaves manumitted (freed).

The 1850 census was conducted in the field by 45 marshals and 3,231 assistant marshals. Marshals were responsible for subdividing their districts into "known civil divisions" and ensuring that assistant marshals accurately completed the schedules. Assistant marshals were responsible for the enumeration, traveling door to door to complete the six different census schedules (free population, slave inhabitants, mortality, agriculture, manufacturing, and social statistics). Under the new census act, the raw completed schedules were returned to Washington for tallying. It soon became apparent that condensing the new schedules for publication was a formidable task. Kennedy eventually increased the size of the Census Office staff from 70 to over 170 to process the returns. Even so, publication of the results was delayed and Congress was soon accusing Kennedy of "incompetence" and "extravagance." In retrospect, difficulties in processing the 1850 census are understandable in light of the dramatic changes in census content and procedure and the rudimentary processing capabilities of the mid-nineteenth century. Kennedy, however, lost his job after Franklin Pierce won the presidency in 1852. He was replaced by James D. B. DeBow, a southern Democrat, statistician, and renowned editor. DeBow oversaw the publication of a 1,000-page volume on population statistics in 1853, a condensed edition called the *Compendium* in 1854, and a volume on the statistics of mortality in 1855, after which the Census Office was officially disbanded. Joseph C. G. Kennedy was appointed three years later to publish the results of the manufacturing census.

See also *Decennial censuses: 1840 census; Decennial censuses: 1860 census; Decennial censuses: 1870 census.*

. . . .   J. DAVID HACKER

BIBLIOGRAPHY

Anderson, Margo J. *The American Census: A Social History.* New Haven, Conn.: Yale University Press, 1988.

Carter, Susan, et al. *Historical Statistics of the United States.* Millennial ed. New York: Cambridge University Press, 2006.

Census Office. *Abstract of the Statistics of Manufactures, According to the Returns of the Seventh Census.* Washington, D.C., 1858.

———. *Mortality Statistics of the Seventh Census of the United States.* Washington, D.C.: A. O. P. Nicholson, 1855.

———. *The Seventh Census of the United States: 1850. Embracing a Statistical View of Each of the States and Territories, Arranged by Counties, Towns, Etc.* Washington, D.C.: Robert Armstrong, 1853.

———. *Statistical View of the United States, Being a Compendium of the Seventh Census.* Washington, D.C.: A. O. P. Nicholson, 1854.

Magnuson, Diana Lynn. "The Making of a Modern Census: The United States Census of Population, 1790–1940." PhD thesis, University of Minnesota, 1995.

Wright, Carroll, and William C. Hunt. *History and Growth of the United States Census.* Washington, D.C.: Government Printing Office, 1900.

Decennial Censuses: 1860 Census

According to the 1860 census, the population of the United States was 31,443,321. A total of 241 seats in the House of Representatives were apportioned among 34 states. The census revealed that the American population continued to grow rapidly. Between 1850 and 1860 the population increased 35.6 percent, equivalent to an average annual growth rate of 3.0 percent. Minnesota and Oregon were admitted as new states, and territories were established in Colorado, the Dakotas, Kansas, Nebraska, Nevada, and Washington (Kansas was admitted to the Union on January 29, 1861, bringing the total number of states to 34). The area of the United States increased to 3,021,295 square miles, resulting in a population density of 10.6 inhabitants per square mile. Although most Americans continued to reside in rural areas, an increasing percentage chose to live in incorporated towns and cities. The total population living in urban places increased from 15.3 percent in 1850 to 19.8 percent in 1860.

Demographics

Of the 31.4 million inhabitants of the United States in 1860, 26.9 million (85.6 percent) were classified by census enumerators as "White," 4.4 million (14.1 percent) as "Black" or "Mulatto," 35,000 (0.1 percent) as "Chinese," and 44,000 (0.1 percent) as "Indians"—indicating only those Native Americans living off reservations and no longer maintaining tribal affiliations. Heavy immigration in the previous decade, especially from Ireland, Great Britain, and northwestern Europe, increased the percentage of the white population that was foreign-born from 11.5 percent in 1850 to 15.2 percent in 1860. The vast majority of the black and mulatto population lived in servitude: 3.95 million (89.0 percent) were enumerated as slaves and just 0.49 million (11.0 percent) were enumerated as "free coloreds." The total black population increased by 22.1 percent in the 1850s, an average annual rate of 2.0 percent, down from the 2.4 percent average annual increase in the previous decade.

The Census and Slavery

The 1860 census was taken in the year preceding the outbreak of the U.S. Civil War. In part the war was the result of demographic forces evident in the census. Rapid population growth, western migration, and the territorial expansion of the United States in the early nineteenth century routinely raised the divisive issue of whether to allow slavery in newly acquired territories. Less rapid growth in the South helped undermine the precarious balance of power achieved in the antebellum period. Between 1790 and 1860 the South's share of seats in the House of Representatives fell from 46 percent to 35 percent. The relative decline of the southern population allowed Abraham Lincoln in win the presidential election in 1860 even though he was not on the ballot in the South. The census data also reveal that the North and South were becoming more demographically distinct. Although the northern and southern white populations were similar in ethnic composition in 1830, seven out of every eight immigrants in the intervening period settled in the free states. As a result, the South's white population in 1860 was ethnically more homogeneous than the North's. The North also underwent more rapid urbanization and industrialization: 26 percent of northerners lived in urban areas, and 40 percent had non-farm occupations. In the South only 10 percent lived in urban areas, and 84 percent worked in agriculture. Most importantly, the North and South differed in their racial composition. Ninety-five percent of the nation's black population in 1860 lived in the South, comprising 34 percent of the population. In contrast, blacks composed only 1 percent of the population of the free states. The 1860 census data also reveal the immense political problem of slavery and its abolition. The

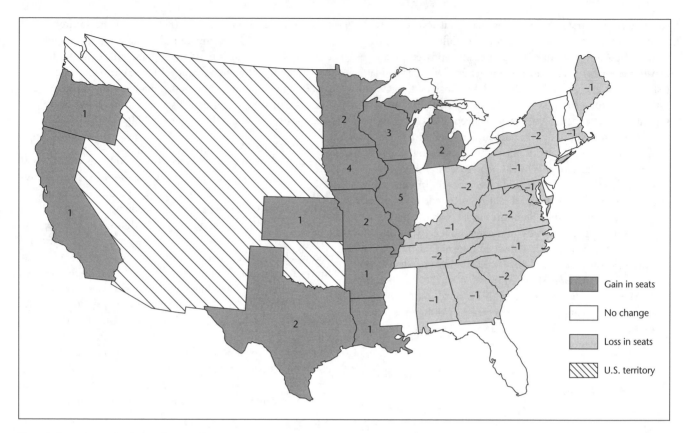

State Gains or Losses in the U.S. House of Representatives, 1860

nearly 4 million slaves in the United States were "worth" approximately $1.2 billion, nearly 20 times the size of the federal budget.

The late 1850s were replete with acrimonious attacks on and defenses of slavery. Although little information on the South's "peculiar institution" could be obtained from the 1850 census, abolitionists and proslavery pundits alike used census data to bolster their arguments. Both sides misused the small amount of data that was available. Despite the heightened interest in the use of census data for social and economic analysis, no significant changes were made in the administration, content, or processing of the 1860 census. Congress did not pass any new legislation, and the 1860 census was taken under the 1850 Census Act. Joseph C. G. Kennedy was again appointed as census superintendent, and though he made a few modest changes to the schedules and instructions to assistant marshals to remedy misunderstandings in the 1850 census, there appears to have been little or no debate on the changes in Congress. The inquiry "profession, occupation, or trade" of males over 15 years of age was extended to females over 15 years of age, and a new question on personal wealth—"value of personal estate"—was added to the existing question "value of real estate."

The 1860 census was conducted in the field by 4,417 assistant marshals. From his experience processing the 1850 census returns, Kennedy was prepared for the large task of condensing the 1860 returns for publication. When the completed schedules

began to arrive in the fall of 1860, he quickly increased the size of the clerical staff. At its maximum, the size of the office force reached 184, a small increase from 1850. In addition to cross-tabulating the returns and publishing the results, the Census Office assisted in the northern war effort. Kennedy prepared a report for President Lincoln on the number of men age 18 to 45 in the free, slave, and "border" states to compare the potential military strength of the Union and Confederacy. The 1860 census was also used to assess direct taxes to finance the war. Finally, the 1860 census was used to reallocate the House of Representatives after the abolition of the slavery and the end of the Three-fifths Compromise.

The cost of the 1860 census was $3.47 million, or eight cents per capita. Kennedy oversaw the publication of three census volumes: a preliminary report published in 1862, the official population report in 1864, and a volume on agriculture also published in 1864. Additional volumes on manufactures and the statistics of mortality and property were published under the direction of the secretary of the interior in 1865 and 1866, respectively. The combined published reports totaled 1,969 pages, up from 1,423 pages in 1850.

See also *Civil War and the census; Decennial censuses: 1850 census; Decennial censuses: 1870 census.*

. . . .   J. DAVID HACKER

BIBLIOGRAPHY

Anderson, Margo J. *The American Census: A Social History*. New Haven, Conn.: Yale University Press, 1988.

Carter, Susan, et al. *Historical Statistics of the United States*. Millennial ed. New York: Cambridge University Press, 2006.

Census Office. *Agriculture of the United States in 1860; Compiled from the Original Returns of the Eighth Census*. Washington, D.C.: U.S. Government Printing Office, 1864.

———. *Manufactures of the United States in 1860; Compiled from the Original Returns of the Eighth Census*. Washington, D.C.: U.S. Government Printing Office, 1865.

———. *Population of the United States in 1860; Compiled from the Original Returns of the Eighth Census*. Washington, D.C.: Government Printing Office, 1864.

———. *Preliminary Report on the Eighth Census*. Washington, D.C.: Government Printing Office, 1862.

———. *Statistics of the United States, (Including Mortality, Property, &c.,) in 1860; Compiled from the Original Returns and Being the Final Exhibit of the Eighth Census*. Washington, D.C.: A. O. P. Nicholson, 1866.

McPherson, James M. "Antebellum Southern Exceptionalism: A New Look at an Old Question." *Civil War History* 29 (1983): 230–244.

Magnuson, Diana Lynn. "The Making of a Modern Census: The United States Census of Population, 1790–1940." PhD thesis, University of Minnesota, 1995.

Wright, Carroll, and William C. Hunt. *History and Growth of the United States Census*. Washington, D.C.: Government Printing Office, 1900.

Decennial Censuses: 1870 Census

The 1870 census put the U.S. population at 38,558,371. The total was revised later to 39,818,449 to adjust for a suspected undercount in 13 southern states. A total of 292 seats in the House of Representatives were apportioned among 37 states. Between 1860 and 1870 the population increased 22.6 percent (26.6 percent after adjustment for the suspected southern undercount), at that time the lowest decennial growth rate in the nation's history. Kansas, Nebraska, Nevada, and West Virginia were admitted as new states, and new territories were established in Arizona, Idaho, Montana, and Wyoming. The area of the United States remained at 3,021,295 square miles, resulting in a population density of 13.0 inhabitants per square mile. The total population living in urban places increased from 19.8 percent in 1860 to 25.7 percent in 1870.

Of the 38.6 million inhabitants of the United States originally enumerated in 1870, 33.6 million (87.1 percent) were classified by census enumerators as "White," 4.9 million (12.7 percent) as "Black" or "Mulatto," 63,000 (0.1 percent) as "Chinese," and 26,000 (0.1 percent) as "Indians Taxed"—meaning only those Indians living off reservations and no longer maintaining tribal affiliations. Continued immigration increased the percentage of the white population that was foreign-born from 15.2 percent in 1860 to 16.4 percent in 1870. Only the 1890 census recorded a higher percentage of foreign-born whites (16.6 percent). The 1870 census was the first census to record complete information for the newly freed black population. The total black population increased by 9.9 percent in the 1860s, down dramatically from the 22.1 percent increase in the previous decade.

Changes to the Constitution and the Census

The 1870 census was also the first census to apportion Congress after the passage of the Thirteenth Amendment, which abolished slavery and ended the Three-fifths Compromise. Confederate defeat in the Civil War and the abolition of slavery resulted in the South receiving a bonus of about 15 seats in the House of Representatives. The expected southern windfall explains in part northern Republican support for black suffrage and the Fourteenth Amendment, Section 2 of which reduced each state's apportionment by the percentage of males age 21 and older who were denied the right to vote on grounds other than rebellion or other crime.

Although Section 2 of the Fourteenth Amendment was never implemented, a House Select Committee was formed to investigate using the census to administer its political penalties. The committee, headed by James A. Garfield of Ohio, went further—calling on statistical experts for advice and proposing a major revision of the legislation governing the census. Garfield and the committee hoped that the elimination of Schedule No. 2 (Slave Inhabitants) would free up space to add new questions and refine existing ones. In addition to the new questions mandated by the Fourteenth Amendment regarding the abridgment of citizenship rights, the committee proposed adding a question on the relationship of each person to the head of the family, a question on each person's marital status, and a number of other questions regarding language spoken, religion professed, and whether parents were of foreign birth. Garfield also proposed changing the compensation system for enumerators, shortening the time allowed for the enumeration from months to days, and shifting the responsibility for the field enumeration from the U.S. marshals to field supervisors appointed for each congressional district. Passage of the Fifteenth Amendment, which nullified state laws restricting black suffrage, eliminated the ostensible reason for the census reforms, and the proposed legislation failed. In the end a few additions were made to the population schedule. The category "Chinese" was added to the question on "Color" through administrative action; literacy was divided into two questions intended to distinguish reading and writing capabilities; and new questions were added on month of birth (for individuals born within the year), month of marriage (for individuals married within the year), whether father was of foreign birth, whether mother was of foreign birth, whether a male citizen of the United States 21 years of age and upward, and whether a male citizen of the United States 21 years of age and upward whose right to vote was denied or abridged on grounds other than rebellion or other crime. The new schedules no longer inquired as to whether the individual was a pauper or convict. The census was administered under the 1850 law.

New Leadership

The 1870 census was taken under the supervision of Francis Amasa Walker, a 29-year-old relative newcomer to Washington, D.C., and a distinguished veteran of the Civil War. Walker's prior experience with the census was limited to a few months helping

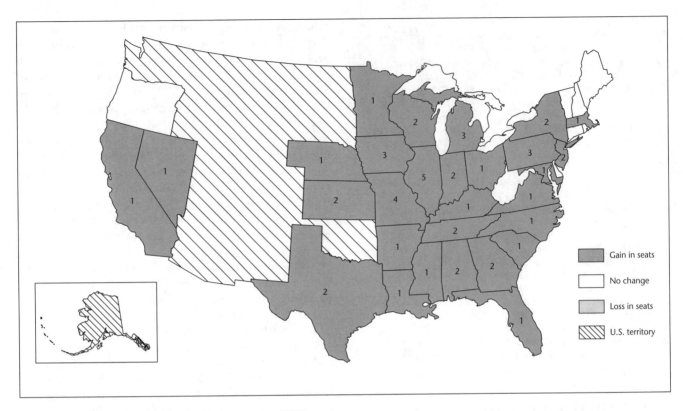

State Gains or Losses in the U.S. House of Representatives, 1870

to draft a new census bill as a member of Garfield's staff. Despite his relative inexperience, Walker was the first superintendent to bring a modern, statistical approach to the census. He complained about his lack of control over the 62 marshals and 6,530 assistant marshals, but he was able to eliminate the practice of "farming out" subdivisions and "taking the census" at election and courts days, practices believed to have been prevalent in the South in previous censuses. Walker believed that marshals were poorly trained for their duties as enumerators and that assistant marshals were often appointed for reasons of patronage with no regard to their qualifications. In Washington, where he was able to assert control, Walker almost tripled the size of the office staff to 450 in an effort to publish more detailed tabulations and shorten the time to publication. Although Walker exceeded his budget and had to return to Congress for more funds, the main volume on the statistics of population was published in 1872, one to two years earlier than in previous censuses. Three more volumes were published in 1872, and a statistical atlas was published in 1874. The combined published reports totaled 3,421 pages, up from 1,969 pages in 1860.

The 1870 count seemed to confirm Walker's rather dim view of the census field staff. Complaints of excessive undercounts in New York and Philadelphia resulted in the unusual step of the president ordering a recount. City boosters in Philadelphia believed that as much as a third of its population had not been enumerated. The recount, taken in the winter, when the population was more likely to be indoors, and with rigorous efforts on the part of city officials to ensure full enumeration, resulted in an increase of only 2.5 percent. New York's recount found only 2 percent more people. Ten years later, when the 1880 census was conducted, a more serious deficiency was discovered in the 1870 census's enumeration of the South. The population of most southern states had grown so dramatically that several observers charged the census with fraud in the form of overcounting. An investigation conducted by census geographer Henry Gannett, however, concluded that the 1870 count was too low, a result of the unsettled conditions in the Reconstruction South and the appointment of poorly trained enumerators, some of whom were said to be poorly educated blacks or "carpetbaggers" unfamiliar with the local terrain. The 1890 Census Office later estimated the 1870 undercount in the South at 1.26 million, or 10.1 percent of the southern population. Although no modern investigation has been conducted to verify the undercount estimates—which ignored the potential demographic impact of the Civil War and assumed linear population growth between 1860 and 1880—the 1890 Census Office's adjusted total for the 1870 population (39.8 million) is preferred by most historians and is typically cited in official census publications.

See also *Civil War and the census; Decennial censuses: 1850 census; Decennial censuses: 1860 census; Decennial censuses: 1880 census.*

. . . . J. DAVID HACKER

BIBLIOGRAPHY

Anderson, Margo J. *The American Census: A Social History*. New Haven, Conn.: Yale University Press, 1988.

Carter, Susan, et al. *Historical Statistics of the United States*. Millennial ed. New York: Cambridge University Press, 2006.

Census Office. *A Compendium of the Ninth Census*. Washington, D.C.: Government Printing Office, 1872.

————. *Ninth Census, Volume I: The Statistics of the Population of the United States*. Washington, D.C.: Government Printing Office, 1872.

————. *Ninth Census, Volume II: The Vital Statistics of the United States*. Washington, D.C.: Government Printing Office, 1872.

————. *Ninth Census, Volume III: The Statistics of the Wealth and Industry of the United States*. Washington, D.C.: Government Printing Office, 1872.

————. *Statistical Atlas of the United States Based on the Results of the Ninth Census*. New York: J. Bien, 1874.

Hacker, J. David. "The Human Cost of War: Population and Family Structure in the Era of the American Civil War." PhD thesis, University of Minnesota, 1999.

Magnuson, Diana Lynn. "The Making of a Modern Census: The United States Census of Population, 1790–1940." PhD thesis, University of Minnesota, 1995.

Wright, Carroll, and William C. Hunt. *History and Growth of the United States Census*. Washington, D.C.: Government Printing Office, 1900.

Decennial Censuses: 1880 Census

The population of the United States in 1880 was 50,155,783. A total of 332 House seats were apportioned among the 38 states. The area of the country was 3,021,295 square miles. For the census, 150 supervisors and 31,382 enumerators conducted fieldwork. The tenth census was administered by the Department of the Interior from Washington, D.C. Francis Amasa Walker served as superintendent of census from 1879 to 1881, with Charles W. Seaton serving from 1881 to 1885. The total cost of the census was $5,790,000.

The content of the census, dictated by the Census Act of March 3, 1879, required enumerators to return responses to 26 questions. The schedule contained eight questions on home and personal qualities, four on marital status, two on occupation, six on health, three on education, and three on nativity. Of particular significance were the questions regarding the relationship of each person to the head of the household and the civil condition of each person (single, married, widowed, or divorced). Walker and others concerned with the census of population had lobbied for these queries since before 1870.

The Census Act of 1879 and the April 20, 1880, amendment ushered in a new era of administering the census and marked a high point in census innovation and experimentation. First, the 1879 legislation eliminated the marshals, who fulfilled decennial canvassing duties, and replaced them with a much larger field force appointed exclusively and temporarily for the task of enumerating the population.

The new law divided the country into specially drawn supervisors' districts, instead of judicial districts, as administrative units for overseeing census taking. Responsibility for dividing the country into 150 census districts, each with its own resident supervisor, lay with the census superintendent, contingent on the approval of the secretary of the interior. Supervisors' districts did not cross state or territorial lines. Supervisors were nominated by the president, in consultation with the superintendent, and were confirmed by the Senate. The secretary of the interior designated the number of supervisors to be appointed for each state and territory, but each state was to have at least one. Under the new census law, supervisors were required to be residents of the state or territory of their appointment.

In addition to supervisors' districts, the 1879 census law required the use of smaller and more clearly defined enumeration districts (in 1870 enumeration districts were limited to 20,000 people; in 1880 they were cut to 4,000). The task of defining enumeration districts fell on census supervisors who followed specific rules defined by the Census Office. One of the most important tasks of the census supervisors was the selection of enumerators. The census law and Superintendent Walker set general guidelines for supervisors to follow in choosing canvassers. Simply, supervisors were required to solicit and encourage qualified applicants and to make appointments based on each applicant's merit.

Second, the 1879 law bolstered the administrative position of the superintendent of the census within the Department of the Interior. Prior to 1879 the position of superintendent of the census had only the sanction of appropriation acts. According to the new census law, the superintendent was to be appointed by the president, with the advice and consent of the Senate, and the post terminated when the census returns were compiled and published. Almost immediately after his appointment, Walker began the task of assembling his clerical staff in Washington. One of Walker's first appointments was Charles W. Seaton as chief clerk. The 1880 census machinery, which reached a peak of 1,495 employees, was more than triple the size of the 1870 clerical staff.

Additional changes in census law included shortening the enumeration period to the first two weeks in June, significantly increasing the penalty for noncompliance with the census from $30 to $100, and issuing preliminary results of the census. Beginning with the 1880 census, the Census Office experimented with issuing periodic bulletins containing preliminary results of the population count. The experiment was so successful that the Census Office continued its use in successive censuses and expanded it to include other principal results.

Superintendent Walker exerted considerable influence over the development and implementation of procedures governing training and overseeing his field staff. Many of Walker's procedural innovations in 1880 would be used and refined in succeeding censuses. A decade before, Walker had experienced great frustration over his inability to adequately train and supervise his vast field staff for enumerating the census. Walker rectified this situation for the 1880 census. Supervisors and enumerators received instructions regarding responsibilities, pay rates, commissions and oaths, and details outlining completing a census schedule prior to the enumeration period. All enumerators were required to report each day, via a standard form on postal cards, to the central office in Washington and their district supervisor. These daily reports indicated the number of hours and minutes engaged in the service as well as

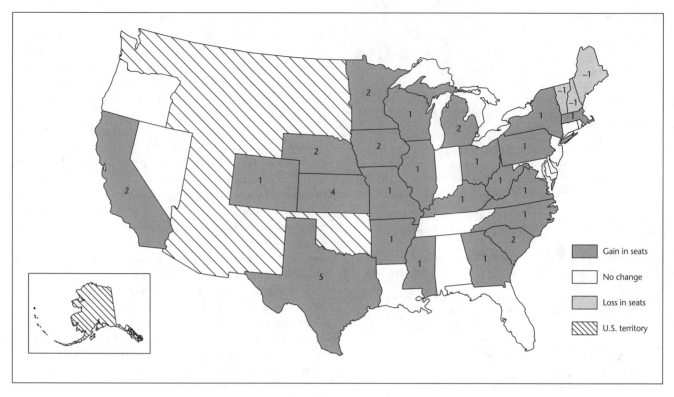

State Gains or Losses in the U.S. House of Representatives, 1880

Legend:
Gain in seats
No change
Loss in seats
U.S. territory

the number of persons, farms, manufacturing establishments, and deaths enumerated that day. Given the widespread efforts to check the quality of the first few days' fieldwork, Walker likely dictated this step to the supervisors.

The Census Office produced a record number of publications at the close of the 1880 census: 22 quarto volumes, a compendium in two parts, and a monograph. The total number of pages in published reports was 21,458.

See also *Decennial censuses: 1870 census; Decennial censuses: 1890 census.*

· · · · · · · · · · · · · · ·   DIANA L. MAGNUSON

BIBLIOGRAPHY

Anderson, Margo J. *The American Census: A Social History.* New Haven, Conn.: Yale University Press, 1988.

Holt, W. Stull. *The Bureau of the Census: Its History, Activities, and Organization.* Washington, D.C.: Brookings Institution, 1929.

Magnuson, Diana L. "The Making of a Modern Census: The United States Census of Population, 1790–1940." PhD diss., University of Minnesota, 1995.

Wright, Carroll D., and William C. Hunt. *The History and Growth of the United States Census.* Washington, D.C.: U.S. Government Printing Office, 1900.

Decennial Censuses: 1890 Census

According to the 1890 census, the population of the United States was 62,947,714. Included in the enumeration were the territories of Idaho, Oklahoma, and Wyoming. A total of 357 seats in the House of Representatives were apportioned among the 42 states. The area of the country was 3,021,295 square miles. For the census 175 supervisors and 46,804 enumerators conducted fieldwork. The 11th census was administrated by the Department of the Interior from Washington, D.C., and was overseen by Robert P. Porter, who served as superintendent of census from 1889 to 1893, and Carroll D. Wright, who served from 1893 to 1897. The total cost of the census was $11,547,000.

The content of the Census of Population, as stipulated by the Census Act of March 1, 1889, required enumerators to return responses to 30 household questions. The schedule contained 5 questions regarding personal description; 2 each regarding marital status, occupation, and health; 3 regarding education; 6 regarding nativity; 5 regarding home and farm ownership; and 1 question each regarding veteran status, ability to speak English, female fertility, whether a prisoner, convict, homeless child, or pauper, and the supplemental schedule. Five groups of inquiries made their first appearance on the 1890 population schedule: fertility, citizenship, ability to speak English, and ownership of homes and farms. The fertility and citizenship queries had been lobbied for in past census debates. The "mother of how many children" and "number of these children living" questions were used in the Massachusetts and Rhode Island state censuses in 1885 with relative success. The inclusion of the queries regarding citizenship, "number of years in the United States," "whether naturalized," and "whether naturalization papers have been taken out" had been urged on Congress in past decades. National concern with the enormous number of immigrants entering

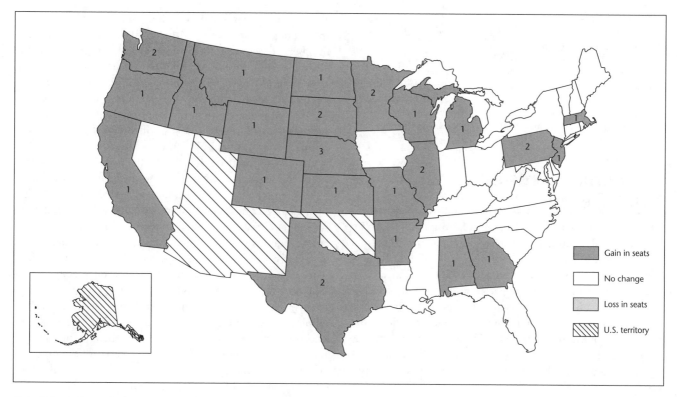

State Gains or Losses in the U.S. House of Representatives, 1890

the United States from southern and eastern Europe during this period likely contributed to the inclusion of these questions, as well as the question on ability to speak English. The scope of the 1890 enumeration was greater than that of any previous census.

Administratively speaking, the structure of the census machinery began what would be a trend of institutional expansion. The Census Act of 1889 provided that the secretary of the interior could appoint a chief clerk, a disbursing clerk, two stenographers, ten chiefs of division, 90 clerks of classes one through four (clerks were classified according to job description and pay scale), and as many clerks, copyists, and computers as deemed necessary. In addition, the secretary of the interior was authorized to appoint watchmen, messengers, and charwomen. The maximum number of census office employees for the 1890 census was 3,143.

The adoption of the family schedule in 1890 permitted experimentation with its use as a prior schedule. The schedules were distributed to all known households prior to the official date of enumeration, and on enumeration day an enumerator retrieved the completed schedule and answered any questions. Despite initial praise for this innovation, the use of separate forms for each household was cumbersome and the 1900 census of population schedule returned to the familiar format.

The 1890 census was taken under the model of training and oversight instituted by Francis A. Walker for the tenth census. The only discernable differences in the training and oversight of field staff in 1890 from the 1880 enumeration were the creation of a "supervisors correspondence" position within the Census Office (held by a single special agent) and an increase in the detail of supervisor and enumerator instructions.

For the first time in census history, the work of tabulating census results was carried out by automatic tabulating machinery. Herman Hollerith invented the "Hollerith system," which utilized a single punched card for each person enumerated. Details from the population schedule were transferred to cards via a punched hole. The cards were then run through an electric tabulating machine that counted the date entered on them. The Hollerith system afforded the Census Office not only greater accuracy and speed in compiling the results but also the opportunity to manipulate various combinations of population statistics heretofore impossible. Thus the published results of the 1890 census of population are much more detailed than those of previous censuses.

The Census Office produced a record number of publications at the close of the 1890 census of population: 24 volumes, a compendium in three parts, an abstract, and a statistical atlas. The total number of pages in published reports was 26,408.

Most of the raw schedules from the 1890 census were destroyed in a fire in 1921. The 1890 forms are the only ones that have not been substantially preserved for later uses by genealogists and historical analysis.

See also *Decennial censuses: 1880 census; Decennial censuses: 1900 census; IPUMS (Integrated Public Use Microdata Series); National Archives and Records Administration (NARA); Precomputer tabulation systems.*

. . . .   DIANA L. MAGNUSON

BIBLIOGRAPHY

Anderson, Margo J. *The American Census: A Social History.* New Haven, Conn.: Yale University Press, 1988.

Holt, W. Stull. *The Bureau of the Census: Its History, Activities, and Organization.* Washington, D.C.: Brookings Institution, 1929.

Magnuson, Diana L. "The Making of a Modern Census: The United States Census of Population, 1790–1940." PhD diss., University of Minnesota, 1995.

Wright, Carroll D., and William C. Hunt. *The History and Growth of the United States Census.* Washington, D.C.: U.S. Government Printing Office, 1900.

Decennial Censuses: 1900 Census

The 1900 census put the U.S. population at 75,994,575. Included in the enumeration were the territories of Hawaii and Oklahoma. A total of 391 seats in the House of Representatives were apportioned among the 45 states. The area of the country was 3,021,295 square miles. For the census 300 supervisors and 52,871 enumerators conducted the fieldwork. The 12th census was administered by the Department of the Interior from Washington, D.C. William R. Merriam was director of the census from 1899 to 1903, with Simon N. D. North serving from 1903 to 1909. The total cost of the census was $11,854,000.

The content of the Census of Population, provided for by the Census Act of March 3, 1899, required enumerators to return responses to 28 questions. The schedule contained 12 questions regarding home and personal characteristics; 3 each regarding nativity, citizenship, and ownership of home; 2 regarding occupation; 4 regarding education; and

1 regarding the number on the farm schedule. Three of these queries were new to the 1900 census: date of birth, number of years married, and year of immigration to the United States. Questions about the health status of Americans were moved from the population schedule to a separate schedule. In addition, the economic censuses, which became more elaborate in the late nineteenth century, were shifted to a different year so as not to compete in terms of resources with the population census.

The administrative machinery of the 1900 census remained relatively constant with that of the preceding two censuses. Several legislated changes should be noted, however. First, the title of the head of the Census Office was changed, from superintendent to director of census. Second, a new position, assistant director of the census, was created with the stipulation that it be filled by "an experienced practical statistician." The assistant director was to serve only during the three-year decennial census period (beginning the year before the census). Third, power to appoint and remove Census Office employees was shifted from the secretary of the interior to the director of the census, significantly strengthening the administrative position of the director of the census. All the director's appointees, with the exception of enumerators, special agents, and the lowest paid laborers, were required to pass noncompetitive examinations to assume their posts. The maximum size of the 1900 census office force was 3,447.

The 1900 census was taken under the model of training and oversight instituted by Francis A. Walker for the 1880 census with two notable innovations, the enumerator examination and the street book. Prior to 1900, supervisors made

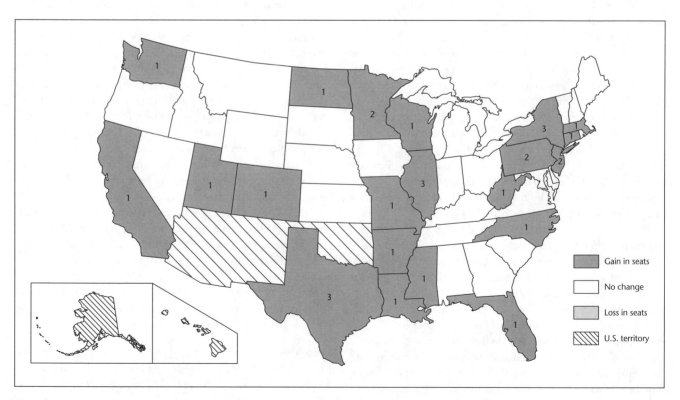

State Gains or Losses in the U.S. House of Representatives, 1900

enumerator appointments based on their own judgment of the character and competency of each applicant. For the 1900 census, enumerator applicants were required to submit to a written, nonproctored examination. The street book remained part of the enumerator's portfolio for succeeding censuses. The Census Office used the street book to aid in the enumeration of larger municipalities and to counter any complaints against the accuracy of the returns. The street book facilitated organization and completeness of the canvass on the part of the enumerator; canvassers used it to account for every house, building, or place of abode in their enumeration district. Supervisors in turn used the street book to verify the completeness of each enumerator's canvass. Just as in 1890, the 1900 decennial census of population saw an increase in the volume of instructions for facilitating training and oversight of supervisors and enumerators.

Electrical tabulating machines, first introduced at the 1890 census, were again employed in the compilation of the 1900 results. The practicality the machines demonstrated a decade earlier convinced census officials to employ their use on a large scale in 1900, and the innovations of the automatic feeder and sorting machine increased their effectiveness.

In 1902 Congress enacted the Permanent Census Act, which made the census bureau a permanent agency within the Department of the Interior. One year later the Census Office became part of the newly created Department of Commerce and Labor. It was generally appreciated that the enormity of the task assigned to the Census Office warranted an intercensal period, to both complete the previous census and prepare for the next. The Census Office produced ten volumes and an abstract of the 1900 census. The total number of pages in published reports was 10,925.

See also *Decennial censuses: 1890 census; Decennial censuses: 1910 census; Pre-computer tabulation systems.*

. . . .   DIANA L. MAGNUSON

BIBLIOGRAPHY

Anderson, Margo J. *The American Census: A Social History.* New Haven, Conn: Yale University Press, 1988.

Holt, W. Stull. *The Bureau of the Census: Its History, Activities, and Organization.* Washington, D.C.: Brookings Institution, 1929.

Magnuson, Diana L. "The Making of a Modern Census: The United States Census of Population, 1790–1940." PhD diss., University of Minnesota, 1995.

Decennial Censuses: 1910 Census

The population of the United States in 1910 was 91,972,266. Included in the enumeration were the territories of Hawaii and Puerto Rico. A total of 435 House seats were apportioned among the 46 states. The area of the country was 3,021,295 square miles. For the first time in 80 years, the date of enumeration was changed from June 1 to April 15. For the census 335 supervisors and 70,286 enumerators conducted fieldwork. The 13th census was administered by the Department of Commerce and Labor from Washington, D.C. Edward Dana Durand was director of the census from 1909 to 1913, with William J. Harris serving from 1913 to 1914 and Samuel L. Rogers from 1915 to 1921. The total cost of the census was $15,968,000.

The Census Act of July 2, 1909, required enumerators to return responses to 32 questions. The schedule contained 11 questions on home and personal characteristics; 3 on nativity; 2 on citizenship; 1 on language; 5 on occupation; 3 on education; 4 on home ownership; 2 on health; and 1 on service in the Civil War. An amendment to the 1909 census act, passed on March 24, 1910, added a question on mother tongue for the foreign-born population. The enumerator recorded the mother tongue of the respondent and the respondent's mother and father, thus bringing the total number of questions on the 1910 schedule to 34.

The establishment of a permanent Bureau of the Census—first within the Department of the Interior in 1902 and then as part of the Department of Commerce and Labor in 1903—affected the 1910 census of population in several important ways. First, having a permanent bureau facilitated an unusually early start on the 1910 decennial census planning. Second, after 1903 the secretary of commerce and labor appointed a special advisory commission on the recommendation of the director of the census. Responsibilities of the special advisory commission included evaluating the conditions surrounding census work and preparing a report to educate Congress before it enacted legislation for the 1910 census. Third, a permanent Bureau of the Census afforded the bureau intercensal periods to become more sophisticated in its administrative structure, interpret the results of the enumeration, and prepare for the next census.

The structure of the 1910 census closely resembled that of its immediate predecessor. A few refinements dictated by the new census law are noteworthy. First, the director was empowered to appoint by recommendation a geographer, a chief statistician, an appointment clerk, a private secretary, two stenographers, and eight expert chiefs of division, all without examination by the secretary of commerce and labor. Only the assistant director was appointed by the president with the advice and consent of the Senate. Breaking from the tradition of previous censuses, the remaining positions of 200 clerks of classes one through four—clerks, copyists, skilled and unskilled laborers—and charwomen were appointed by the director of the census in the order of their rating on eligibility lists and in accordance with civil service rules. This change in the method of appointing lower-level office employees was considered a vast improvement over the old practices that were largely based on patronage. The maximum size of the bureau force was 3,738.

Creation of the permanent Office of the Census did not significantly alter enumeration procedures. Refinements in the selection process and in training and oversight of field staff, however, continued to be the trend. Supervisors were required to apply for the positions and were theoretically chosen based on their qualifications. Once appointed to their positions, supervisors received copious written instructions and were required to attend training conventions held in major cities

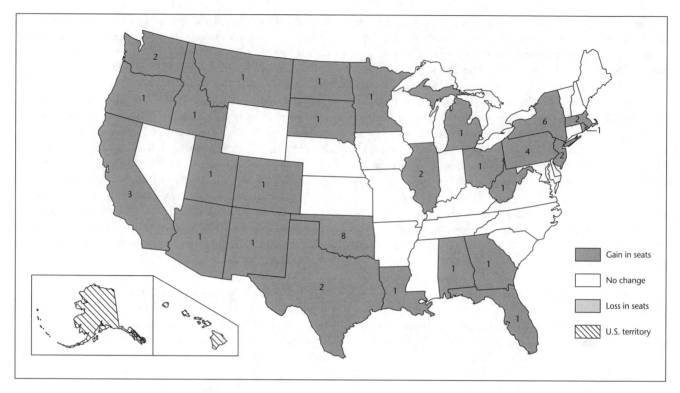

State Gains or Losses in the U.S. House of Representatives, 1910

across the United States. At these conventions the director or assistant director of the census, accompanied by the chief statistician for population or the chief statistician for agriculture, gave oral instructions to the supervisors and answered their questions. Beginning in 1910, persons seeking enumerator posts were required to submit an application to their respective supervisors and take a competitive proctored exam. Enumerators received a carefully revised instruction manual, oral instructions from their supervisors, and continuous supervision and instruction over the course of the enumeration period. A new member of the field staff, the inspector, became an extension of the supervisor. Inspectors were hired to help supervisors maintain constant contact with enumerators and to provide information and oversight.

The establishment of the permanent bureau also permitted census officials in Washington to begin systematic analysis of the accuracy of the results of the enumeration. Officials noted various anomalies and, in the case of the count of Tacoma, Washington, recounted the city and prosecuted local officials for "census fraud." Tacoma's official population was reduced by 33,296 to 82,972 because of the discovery of "padding" of answers by the local census takers. In previous decades, census officials had suspected such padding but in a temporary agency lacked the capacity to correct the suspected errors.

The Bureau of the Census published 11 volumes as well as additional studies and bulletins, including *Abstract of the Census; Statistical Atlas of the United States; The Blind Population in the United States, 1910; Deaf-Mutes in the United States; and*

Indian Population in the United States and Alaska, 1910. The total number of pages in published reports was 11,456.

See also *Decennial censuses: 1900 census; Decennial censuses: 1920 census.*

. . . .   DIANA L. MAGNUSON

BIBLIOGRAPHY

Anderson, Margo J. *The American Census: A Social History.* New Haven, Conn.: Yale University Press, 1988.

Holt, W. Stull. *The Bureau of the Census: Its History, Activities, and Organization.* Washington, D.C.: Brookings Institution, 1929.

Magnuson, Diana L. "The Making of a Modern Census: The United States Census of Population, 1790–1940." PhD diss., University of Minnesota, 1995.

Decennial Censuses: 1920 Census

The 1920 census put the U.S. population at 105,710,620. Included in the enumeration were the territories of Guam, Hawaii, the Panama Canal Zone, Puerto Rico, and Samoa. House seats were not reapportioned following the 1920 census. The area of the country was 3,021,295 square miles. For only the second time in 90 years, the enumeration date of the census was changed; the canvass was moved up from April 15 to January 1. A total of 372 supervisors and 87,234 enumerators conducted fieldwork for the census. Women were employed as supervisors for the first time; three received original appointments, and two were appointed to fill vacancies. The census was administered by the Department of Commerce from

Nonapportionment of the 1920s

The 1920s was the only decade in American history in which the House and Electoral College were not reapportioned according to population changes. The reasons for this are numerous and complex. The size of the House increased at every apportionment since the beginning of Congress, except in 1840. There were physical limitations of the House chamber to hold even the 435 seats allotted in 1910. However, the apportionment debate centered not only on practical gains and losses of congressional seats and power but also on serious social and political feelings and demographic questions that cut to the heart of a changing America.

The apportionment debate began as usual after the report of the 1920 census data. The basic controversy centered on two propositions: (1) expand the House once more to accommodate all states and ensure no losses of seats; or (2) fix the House size at 435 and reapportion accordingly. The debate began in 1921 and lasted virtually the entire decade. Many of the arguments used were as old as the Republic with respect to the size of the House and political representation.

Those arguing for an increased size of the House put forth the following rationale:

1. The recent enfranchisement of women meant an increase in the size of the average constituency and the need for more representatives.
2. More representatives would better serve democracy, since they could be located closer to their constituents.
3. More representatives would keep power from being concentrated in the hands of a few.
4. The mathematical formula was generally unfair.
5. The census figures were inaccurate, especially in rural areas.
6. The nation was disrupted by World War I and an accurate count was not made.[1]

Those arguing for keeping the size of the House at 435 and for passing an apportionment bill immediately put forth the following rationale:

1. More representatives would lessen the efficiency of the House operation.
2. More representatives would decrease the amount of debate time for all.
3. More representatives would incur additional cost.
4. There should be fair redistribution of representatives and districts.
5. The American people and media supported reapportionment.
6. The Constitution mandated action on reapportionment every ten years.

One argument to increase the size of the House or to delay apportionment was new to the debate or at least was brought up in a consistent and vitriolic way as never before in American history. This argument concerned the growth of the city and its influence on American politics and culture. In the floor debate the urban-rural conflict was brought out, usually by fearful rural representatives, as one significant theme. City values were corrupting fundamental native "American" religious and moral life. City bosses were corrupting American political life. Cites were filled with immigrants wishing to repeal prohibition. Cities were filled with immigrants wishing to repeal the new restrictive immigration laws. The hostility toward the city brought out the fear of changing economic, cultural, social, demographic, and technological realities of twentieth-century America.

An analysis of roll call voting on the various apportionment bills suggests that the representatives from states likely to lose seats wanted an increased House size or no apportionment at all. These states were usually rural agricultural states (see maps showing state gains or losses in 1910 and 1930). Representatives from states likely to increase in seats favored fixing the size of the House and passing an apportionment bill. These states usually had urban industrial areas and other growing areas. The states that had no change in seats were critical. Rural "no change" states seemed to vote against reapportionment, especially from the Democratic rural South. Urban "no changers" tended to support reapportionment, many from the Republican Northeast.[2]

In spite of the constitutional and legal questions involved, Congress did not pass an apportionment bill after the census. The 1922 elections were held with the same numbers given to each state in 1910. Throughout the 1920s apportionment was debated on and off, with the same forces in the House and Senate aligning and blocking passage of a bill. As the time for a new census came near, sentiment arose to once again make apportionment automatic with the census as in 1850 and 1860. With President Herbert Hoover's support, a bill was passed in 1929 to incorporate apportionment in the census with automatic calculations based on a House fixed at 435 seats. This system of automatic reapportionment has been in effect since that time.

1. Charles W. Eagles, *Democracy Delayed: Congressional Reapportionment and the Urban-Rural Conflict in the 1920s* (Athens, Ga.: University of Georgia Press, 1990), 33–62; Lawrence F. Schmeckebier, *Congressional Apportionment* (Washington, D.C.: Brookings Institution, 1941), 120–124.
2. Eagles, *Democracy,* 85–115.

Source: Kenneth C. Martis and Gregory A. Elmes, *The Historical Atlas of State Power in Congress, 1790–1990* (Washington, D.C.: Congressional Quarterly, 1993), 163–165.

Washington, D.C. Samuel L. Rogers (1915–1921) and William Mott Steuart (1921–1933) served as directors of the census. The total cost of the census was $25,117,000.

The Census Act of March 3, 1919, required enumerators to return responses to 29 questions. The schedule contained 10 questions on home and personal characteristics; 2 on home ownership; 3 each on citizenship and education; 7 on nativity and mother tongue; and 4 on occupation.

Administratively the 1920 census machinery closely followed that of the 1910 census. Two changes affecting the organization of the Bureau of the Census are noteworthy. First, the 1919 law authorized the director of the census to appoint as many temporary clerks in classes one through nine as necessary, provided that they had passed an examination guided by Civil Service Commission rules. Second, the 372 supervisors provided for under the new census law were to be appointed by the secretary of commerce on the recommendation of the director. Since the Census Act of 1879 supervisors were appointed by the president with the advice and consent of the Senate. The maximum size of the census office force in Washington was 6,301.

The administration of the 1920 census, the 14th decennial census, continued the process of refining the training and oversight of census field staff. The bureau carefully revised all schedules, forms, and instructions for field staff. In an effort to facilitate greater accuracy of the enumeration, the trend toward greater contact between the director of the census and his supervisors continued. The innovation of supervisors conferences directed by census administrators, begun in 1910, was continued. Greater personal contact was also built into the training and oversight of enumerators by their respective supervisors. Supervisors in large cities were authorized to employ one or two inspectors to provide daily support in overseeing enumerators.

Probably the most significant result of the 1920 tabulation was the bureau report that a majority of Americans, for the first time in U.S. history, lived in "urban" places (defined as having populations of 2,500 or more). The statistic raised controversy among the American public. Three concerns emerged, as "old stock" American statistical analysts contemplated this momentous demographic change. First, a decline in the rural population and a gain in the urban population were perceived as a harbinger of the end of political liberty. Jeffersonian republican political theory had relied on the virtue of independent yeoman farmers and artisans to sustain political liberty and institutions, and these population groups were a declining proportion of the national population. Second, the constitutionally mandated reapportionment mechanism automatically shifted political power from those areas of the country with declining populations to those with growing populations. Until the last quarter of the nineteenth century, this power had shifted westward. After the 1920 census, states with large urban populations (located primarily in the Northeast) clearly would be the apportionment winners. Third, urban growth was being fueled by immigration, not natural reproduction of native-born Americans. Nativists feared the impact of urban immigrant working-class political power on the national scene.

Within this milieu a debate over the method of apportionment postponed the passage of the 15th census bill, providing for the 1930 census, until June 1929 (see box, "Nonapportionment of the 1920s"). The language of the bill directed that a present Congress could not bind a future Congress, but apportionment would not be delayed.

The Bureau of the Census published a number of volumes by the end of the 1920 census period: 11 major volumes, *Abstract of the Fourteenth Census, Statistical Atlas of the United States, Children in Gainful Occupations, Deaf-Mute Population of the United States, Blind Population of the United States,* as well as bulletins, technical reports, and a monograph series of special analyses. See www.census.gov/prod/www/abs/decennial/1920.html for details. The total number of pages in published reports was 14,550.

See also *Decennial censuses: 1910 census; Decennial censuses: 1930 census.*

. . . . DIANA L. MAGNUSON

BIBLIOGRAPHY

Anderson, Margo J. *The American Census: A Social History.* New Haven, Conn: Yale University Press, 1988.

Holt, W. Stull. *The Bureau of the Census: Its History, Activities, and Organization.* Washington, D.C.: Brookings Institution, 1929.

Magnuson, Diana L. "The Making of a Modern Census: The United States Census of Population, 1790–1940." PhD diss., University of Minnesota, 1995.

Decennial Censuses: 1930 Census

The population of the United States in 1930 was 122,775,046. Included in this enumeration were the territories of Guam, Hawaii, the Panama Canal Zone, Puerto Rico, Samoa, and the Virgin Islands. A total of 435 seats in the House of Representatives were apportioned among the 48 states. The area of the country was 3,021,295 square miles. The enumeration date was moved to April 1, 1930, from the January 1 date of the 1920 census. For the census 575 supervisors and 87,756 enumerators conducted fieldwork. The census was administrated by the Department of Commerce from Washington, D.C., and under the supervision of census director William Mott Steuart (1921–1933). The total cost of the census was $40,156,000.

The content of the Census of Population, provided for by the Census Act of June 18, 1929, required enumerators to return responses to 32 questions. The schedule contained 15 questions regarding home and personal qualities; 2 each regarding education, veteran status, and employment; 3 each regarding nativity, citizenship, and occupation and industry; and 1 each regarding mother tongue and the number on the farm schedule. While the majority of the queries were "standard" and represented merely an amplification of past questions and categories, 2 questions—on homemaker status and radio set ownership—reflected Congress's growing interest in the changing status of women and the new "consumer economy" in the first quarter of the twentieth century. As the census was being tabulated, the economic crisis that came to be called the Great Depression began to grip the nation and Congress, and the public called for data on unemployment from the 1930 count. In January 1931 the Bureau of the Census did an additional special census of unemployment and published the results with the decennial publications.

The 1930 census was administered much like its immediate predecessor; however, the 1929 census law did make a few significant changes. First, two assistant directors, appointed by the secretary of commerce on the recommendation of the director of the census, were provided for in the new legislation. Since 1899, census legislation had required the appointment of a single assistant director by the president, with the advice and consent of the Senate. For the 15th decennial census, one assistant director acted as the executive assistant to the

State Gains or Losses in the U.S. House of Representatives, 1930

director and performed the duties previously assigned to the chief clerk; the other assistant director served as the technical and statistical adviser to the director and was required to possess experience in statistical work. Second, the 1929 census legislation empowered the director of the census to hire as many temporary employees as deemed necessary for the work during the decennial census period. In addition, the director fixed the rates of compensation for all temporary clerical employees. Third, civil service rules were applied to the appointment process of special agents; supervisors, supervisors' clerks, enumerators, and interpreters were exempt from civil service examination.

An alteration in the 1929 census law regarding the apportionment process had important ramifications for the 1930 and future censuses. A protracted and contentious debate over the issue held up passage of the census bill until June 1929. The final compromise bill required an automatic apportionment if, as in the 1920s, Congress took no action. The bill

stipulated that a present Congress could not bind a future Congress. However, apportionment could not be delayed.

In an effort to increase the accuracy of the canvass, as well as expedite training and oversight of enumerators' work, the bureau increased the total number of supervisors from 372 to 575. As in previous twentieth-century censuses, supervisors received advance instructions for carrying out the details of the enumeration. These instructions were again in the form of pamphlets, supplemental written instructions in the form of letters, and oral instructions given at conferences. The bureau facilitated constant communication between the bureau in Washington and the supervisors. Enumerators received a revised pamphlet of instructions as well as oral instructions from their respective supervisors and field assistants. In 1930, inspectors were called field assistants but served the same purpose of instructing and advising enumerators.

The Bureau of the Census published a total of 32 volumes by the end of the 1930 decennial census period, including 6 volumes on the population, 2 on unemployment, and an abstract. The total number of pages in published reports was 35,700.

See also *Decennial censuses: 1920 census; Decennial censuses: 1940 census.*

. . . .   DIANA L. MAGNUSON

BIBLIOGRAPHY
Anderson, Margo J. *The American Census: A Social History.* New Haven, Conn.: Yale University Press, 1988.
Holt, W. Stull. *The Bureau of the Census: Its History, Activities, and Organization.* Washington, D.C.: Brookings Institution, 1929.
Magnuson, Diana L. "The Making of a Modern Census: The United States Census of Population, 1790–1940." PhD diss., University of Minnesota, 1995.

Decennial Censuses: 1940 Census

The population of the continental United States in 1940 was 131,669,275. A total of 435 seats in the House of Representatives were apportioned among the 48 states, using the method of equal proportions.

Developments in the 1930s

The Bureau of the Census faced drastic staff reductions after completion of the 1930 census, but the election of Franklin D. Roosevelt in 1932 brought new government programs and expanded demand for statistical information. The Roosevelt administration worked closely with professional organizations to create a plan for improved collection of statistical data.

The Committee on Government Statistics and Information Services (COGSIS) was created in 1933 under the sponsorship of the American Statistical Association (ASA) and the Social Science Research Council (SSRC), with funding from the Rockefeller Foundation. COGSIS operated from June 1934 to December 1935, providing statistical advisory services to the secretaries of agriculture, commerce, interior, and labor, and offering an opportunity for reorganization and coordination of federal statistical services.

COGSIS influenced the bureau in two ways. First, the committee responded to a request from William Lane Austin, director of the census, to survey the bureau's work in the field of population. COGSIS solicited confidential comments from users of population data, reviewed the population schedule and tabulation procedures, and made various recommendations. Second, vital bureau personnel came from COGSIS. Stuart A. Rice, president of ASA and chair of COGSIS in the summer of 1933, served as assistant director of the bureau from 1933 to 1935. He was instrumental in the hiring of Calvert L. Dedrick, a former researcher at the SSRC and staff member of COGSIS who was named assistant chief statistician in 1937. Dedrick played a central role in Morris H. Hansen's beginning work in the area of sampling.

Congress approved a national unemployment census in 1937, on the basis of a voluntary registration of unemployed and partially employed persons. A temporary agency was established under the direction of John D. Biggers to carry out the unemployment census. Biggers requested that Director Austin provide the personnel for the operation. He assigned Dedrick and several other bureau staff to the project.

Along with many other statisticians, Dedrick had opposed voluntary registration for conducting the census, arguing that it would bias the results. He convinced Biggers that a "check census" was necessary, and a 2 percent sample representing the 80 percent of the population served by postal delivery routes was designed. The household enumeration of this sample was the first nationwide use of probability and area sampling to canvass a population from which no lists were available. Results from the probability sample were used to estimate error rates in the voluntary figures. The bureau was also involved in editing and tabulating the results, offering valuable experience for the 1940 census.

Preparations for the 1940 Census

In the Census Act of 1929, the director of the bureau gained responsibility for developing specific census questions, subject to approval by the secretary of commerce. In early 1939 Austin requested the chief statisticians of the various bureau divisions to develop a schedule for the 1940 census. A tentative schedule was presented for public discussion at conferences in March and April. These also covered the use of sampling techniques for inclusion of questions not appearing on the main population schedule. In addition, a technical advisory committee held meetings on the proposed schedule in late spring 1939. On the basis of these efforts, preliminary schedules, instructions, and other forms were tested in a special census in Indiana in August 1939.

Reflecting the economic problems of the era, the 1940 census brought added emphasis to questions of the national labor force. The first complete classification of work status for all persons 14 years of age and over in a specific week (March 24–30, 1940) was introduced to replace the concept of "gainful worker" used in 1930. Number of weeks worked in 1939 was added to further measure unemployment. A new, 11-category scheme of occupational classification developed by Alba M. Edwards was introduced, and a new industrial classification based on the Standard Industrial Classification was used.

Two questions on income in 1939 were recommended for inclusion on the 1940 population schedule: (1) the amount of wages or salary received and (2) whether more than $50 was from sources other than wages or salary. These questions generated some public criticism and adverse publicity. Sen. Charles W. Tobey of New Hampshire called on the secretary of commerce to delete the questions but this was refused. Tobey then introduced a Senate resolution requiring deletion of the questions; however, Senate leadership did not allow the resolution to get out of committee. In response to the controversy, the bureau developed a confidential reporting form for income questions, but only 200,000 were used. The 1940 census also introduced new questions on children born to ever-married women, highest grade of school completed, and place of residence five years earlier. These were among the recommendations made by COGSIS.

State Gains or Losses in the U.S. House of Representatives, 1940

A major innovation of the 1940 census was incorporation of sampling as an integral component of enumeration. Sampling procedures were used to gather supplementary information from 1 out of every 20 persons. Two lines on the 40-line population schedules were designated for the asking of supplementary questions appearing at the bottom of the form. Five different styles of schedule were used to reduce possible effects of line bias.

Austin and Leon Truesdell, chief of the Population Division, opposed use of sampling, while Assistant Director Vergil D. Reed and Dedrick favored the procedure. With his chief economic adviser in favor of sampling, Commerce Secretary Harry Hopkins decided to allow its use. Philip M. Hauser, assistant chief statistician in the Population Division, and Dedrick planned the implementation of sampling in consultations with Hansen and sampling expert Fredrick F. Stephan, then secretary-treasurer of the ASA. The bureau also used the services of W. Edwards Deming of the Department of Agriculture.

By approval of Congress on August 11, 1939, the 16th decennial census included a housing census, the first nationwide inventory of housing. The housing census was conducted in conjunction with the population census and gathered information on the number, characteristics, and geographical distribution of dwelling structures and units in the continental United States, Alaska, Hawaii, Puerto Rico, and the Virgin Islands.

Enumeration, Processing, and Reporting

Enumeration of the population began on April 2, 1940, and was designed for completion within two weeks in any incorporated place of at least 2,500 persons in 1930 and within 30 days in all other places. Inhabitants were enumerated at their usual place of residence. On April 8, 1940, field staff went to all hotels, tourist facilities, and one-night lodging houses and left forms for self-enumeration of guests. These were collected the following day. A staff of approximately 120,000 enumerators, 529 district supervisors, and 104 area managers was responsible for conducting the enumeration.

After district supervisors issued preliminary population counts for every county and each city of 10,000 persons or more, completed enumeration forms were shipped by registered mail to the bureau. Hand counts of the population and housing schedules were then compared with field counts.

Coding and verification of the population and housing schedules were performed in phases, with a separate step for treatment of the occupation, industry, and class of worker data. As part of coding in 1940, the bureau developed and implemented a method for allocating unknown ages. Under the direction of Deming, sampling was also incorporated into the verification of coding and card punching. Based on error records, sample verification was used for coders and punchers who achieved certain accuracy standards.

Tabulation procedures involved a number of counts made from a variety of punched cards: individual, supplementary (sample) individual, fertility (ever-married women), sample family, dwelling, household, and mortgage. Results from counts were published as series of state and U.S. summary preliminary bulletins, which were later bound together as volumes.

Entry into World War II had an impact on the operation of the bureau and work on preparation of final reports. The Second War Powers Act of March 1942 authorized the secretary of commerce to make information on census schedules available to war agencies. The bureau became chiefly involved in preparing statistics for defense and war agencies. Advance releases were provided on foreign-born Germans and Italians in the United States and on Japanese in the United States and Hawaii. Special releases were also prepared on a number of labor force–related issues. A planned program of special reports and publication of a statistical atlas had to be abandoned. Designs for widespread distribution of 1940 census publications were curtailed. Instead, about 1,600 libraries throughout the nation were designated as depository centers for Bureau of the Census publications.

In 2012 the National Archives will open the manuscript schedules from the 1940 census to the public for genealogical and research use.

See also *Confidentiality; Decennial censuses: 1930 census; Decennial censuses: 1950 census; National Archives and Records Administration (NARA); Sampling for content.*

ROBERT M. JENKINS
. . . . REVISED BY MARGO J. ANDERSON

BIBLIOGRAPHY

Deming, W. Edwards, and Leon Geoffrey. "On Sample Inspection in the Processing of Census Returns." *Journal of the American Statistical Association* 36 (September 1941): 351–360.

Eckler, A. Ross. "Employment and Income Statistics." *Journal of the American Statistical Association* 36 (September 1941): 381–386.

———. *The Bureau of the Census.* New York: Praeger Publishers, 1972.

Jenkins, Robert M. *Procedural History of the 1940 Census of Housing and Population.* Madison: University of Wisconsin Press, 1985.

Decennial Censuses: 1950 Census

The 1950 census revealed that the population of the United States, comprising the 48 states and the District of Columbia, was 150,697,361. This census also covered the territories of Alaska, American Samoa, Guam, Hawaii, the Panama Canal Zone, the Trust Territory of the Pacific Islands (enumerated by the U.S. Navy), and the U.S. Virgin Islands, as well as the Commonwealth of Puerto Rico. Following the census, 435 seats in the House of Representatives were reapportioned among the 48 states.

General Background

For many decades most of the censuses, including the censuses of agriculture, manufactures, mineral industries, business, and, since 1940, housing, were taken in the same year and were considered to compose the decennial census. By 1950 the manufactures, mineral industries, and business censuses had been moved to other years and were no longer part of the decennial census. The Census of Agriculture remained part of the 1950 decennial census but was shifted to a different cycle in 1954. This article focuses on the censuses of population and housing.

The 1950 census was taken as the nation was recovering from the dislocations of World War II, while continuing some trends that were launched or accelerated by the war—for example, the increase in labor force participation of women. The latter part of the 1940–1950 decade was marked by an upsurge in population growth, fed by increasing birth rates and immigration. The 1950 census aimed to measure the effects of these and other social and economic developments.

The 1950 census was taken in accordance with the constitutional requirement (Article I, Section 2) that a census be conducted within every ten-year period. The manner in which the Census of Population was taken was prescribed by the Act of June 18, 1929. Congress authorized the periodic taking of a decennial housing census in the Act of July 15, 1949. (The legislation authorizing the first housing census in 1940 did not provide for subsequent censuses.)

Planning the Census

While Congress appropriated $200,000 for census planning in July 1947, preparations had begun the previous year. Bureau employees reviewed the uses of data from previous censuses, consulted with data users, considered requests for new information, prepared budget estimates, and, in a series of experiments with supplements to the Current Population Survey and other surveys and special censuses, tested question wording, schedule design, enumerator instructions, and revisions of such concepts as dwelling unit and usual residence. Test censuses were conducted in two counties in Missouri in April and May 1948; in several counties in Kentucky and Illinois and in Minneapolis, Minnesota, in October 1948; and in South Carolina, rural areas throughout the country, and Atlanta, Georgia, in May 1949. The Bureau of the Budget (now the Office of Management and Budget) coordinated federal government input on proposed census plans and procedures.

State Gains or Losses in the U.S. House of Representatives, 1950

One trend that influenced the planning for the 1950 census was the growing suburbanization of the population. A new designation of "urbanized area" was adopted, to apply to cities of 50,000 or more together with their closely built-up adjacent territory. These fringes were classified as urban. In a related development, recognizing that large unincorporated places were becoming increasingly important in the population distribution, the Bureau of the Census decided to identify those not within the boundaries of urbanized areas and to compile separate statistics for them. The newly developed concepts and measurements affected the definitions of urban and rural, converting some areas from rural to urban. The urban population for 1950 under the old definition was 59 percent of the total population; under the new definition it was 64 percent.

During the 1940s the Bureau of the Census cooperated with the Bureau of the Budget and other federal agencies in establishing a set of standard metropolitan areas to replace the variety of definitions of big-city areas that had been used in

various government programs. The new definitions were to be used for all statistical purposes by all agencies. Unlike the bureau's metropolitan districts and urbanized areas, which required detailed census geography, the standard metropolitan areas were made up of whole counties (towns in New England) so that any data available by counties could be compiled for standard metropolitan areas. These new areas were used in the publications of the 1950 census.

The 1950 census was the first to use a more refined set of definitions of household, family, and individual, each subdivided into various types. The new definitions were adopted by the bureau in 1947 and used since then in censuses and surveys.

The instructions to enumerators continued to allow anyone to be designated as head of the household for relationship classification purposes—that is, to determine the status of other household members in terms of "relationship to head." However, if a woman was listed as head and her husband was present, he was reclassified as the head when the completed schedule was reviewed in the census office. At the time, the number of such cases was small.

The Questionnaire

The basic schedule for the 1950 census, form P1, was a white, 10-by-22-inch sheet printed in green ink on both sides. The front included space for population information for 30 persons, with a separate line for each person. The reverse side, the housing schedule, contained spaces for information for 12 dwelling units that housed the persons enumerated on the population side of the form.

Population questions asked of all respondents were age, sex, race, relationship to head of the household, marital status, birthplace, citizenship, farm residence, and, for those over 14 years of age, occupation, industry, class of worker, employment status, and the number of hours worked the previous week.

The rising costs of data collection, additional demands for information, and improved techniques led to the increased use of sampling in 1950. The sample size was increased, and more questions were put on a sample basis. Questions at the bottom of the population schedule were asked for the one person in five whose name fell on a sample line that was indicated in black. There were five printings to vary the sample lines. The person whose name fell on the last sample line was also asked additional questions.

Among the inquiries on the population schedule shifted from 100 percent coverage in 1940 to the sample in 1950 were school attendance and educational attainment, place of residence the previous year, duration of unemployment, and the number of weeks worked the previous year. New questions on the duration of marriage and the number of years widowed, divorced, or separated were added to the sample. The questions on income were also moved to the sample in 1950, but respondents were asked to provide more detail on specific amounts of income received in several different categories. It thus became possible to tabulate total income for individuals instead of just wage or salary income and to tabulate family income. The income data related to the calendar year 1949.

As in 1940, a separate form was available for use by a respondent who did not wish to divulge the income information to the local enumerator. This confidential income report form was handled somewhat differently than the 1940 version. It was a self-mailing piece that the householder was asked to complete and send to the census office.

The housing census of 1940 had posed all questions on a 100 percent basis. In 1950, 18 items were asked on a 100 percent basis, but many others were moved to the sample. These included inquiries on electric lighting, heating equipment, fuels used for cooking and heating, refrigeration, and ownership of radios. New questions on the presence of television sets and a kitchen sink were added to the sample. A sample survey, the Survey of Residential Financing, was conducted as a supplement to the housing census.

The housing sample was somewhat different from the 20 percent population sample. A 20 percent sample was obtained for certain items, but instead of asking one household in every five to answer all the sample items, the sample questions were divided into five groups. Each household responded to one of the five groups of questions.

Data Collection

To take the decennial census, the Bureau of the Census added six area offices and 391 district offices to the eight area offices and 67 district offices the agency used for current surveys. Eighteen more district offices were opened in the territories and possessions.

Each area office covered three or four states (or parts of states) and was responsible for between 13 and 41 district offices. Area office managers and their assistants were career civil servants. The rest of the decennial field staff consisted of temporary personnel. Area managers and their assistants selected district office supervisory staff from lists provided by the local member of Congress or by state and local organizations.

The boundaries of most district offices coincided with those of congressional districts and contained an average population of 350,000. District offices had to be open and staffed by March 1, 1950, and were expected to complete their work by June 30.

Crew leaders and enumerators had to pass a written test, be U.S. citizens, have a high school education or its equivalent, and be able to perform the duties assigned. Veterans received a special preference. Most of the 133,000 enumerators employed as of March 31, 1950, in the continental United States were homemakers. Enumerators were paid at a fixed rate of $1 per hour or at a piece rate designed to yield about $1 per hour.

Each enumerator collected census information from the inhabitants of an area called an enumeration district. For the 1950 census, about 230,000 enumeration districts were defined for the United States and its territories. Enumeration districts were delineated in a manner that permitted enumerators to complete their work in the time allotted and allowed the data from enumeration districts to be aggregated into all the legal, political, and administrative areas for which census statistics were to be published.

The bureau established special enumeration procedures and questionnaires (individual and military census reports, which contained only the population questions) to include people who were traveling during the census, had no fixed residence, or were members of the armed forces or merchant marine.

Repeating a special feature of the 1940 census, enumerators were required to fill out an "infant card" for every infant born in the first quarter of 1950. It was used in a post-census evaluation of the completeness of the count of infants, who were considered especially liable to be overlooked in the enumeration of "persons," and also for the evaluation of the completeness of birth registration. In addition to their use for evaluation, the infant cards served as a coverage improvement device because they reminded the enumerator to ask about infants and provided an extra-pay incentive for enumerating them.

For most previous censuses the instructions to enumerators told them to enumerate college students at their parental homes, even if they lived most of the year in or near the college. Beginning in 1950 such college students were to be counted as residing in the college area. This change, in the interest of getting a more complete and geographically accurate count, also had the effect of being beneficial to college towns by increasing their population counts.

As the enumeration was completed, district office supervisors announced the population of each city of 10,000 or more and of each county. Supervisors emphasized that these preliminary counts would not be final until those enumerated away from home could be added. By law, the bureau had to provide final figures to the president by December 1, 1950, eight months after the start of the census.

Data Products

The 1950 Census of Population and Housing resulted in the publication of nearly 73,000 pages of printed reports. The first population reports to appear were the preliminary counts released by district offices for the cities and counties within each district. Appearing as early as June 1950, the preliminary data were superseded, beginning in the fall of 1950, by the advance reports, which were the first to provide final population totals. The first advance reports gave population figures for the continental United States by regions, divisions, and states. The state population totals were those reported to the president on November 2, 1950, together with the number of representatives to which each state was entitled in the Eighty-third and subsequent Congresses. Later advance reports provided final population figures for various legal, political, and administrative areas.

Detailed information from the population census was published in four series: *Number of Inhabitants, Characteristics of the Population, Census Tract Statistics,* and *Special Reports.* The *Number of Inhabitants* volumes presented population figures for each state, for its constituent counties, for minor civil divisions within each county, and for all towns.

Characteristics of the Population gave general characteristics of the population (for example, age, sex, race, nativity, citizenship, educational attainment, marital status, country of birth, income, and so on) for counties, places of 2,500 or more inhabitants, urbanized and metropolitan areas, and other geographic units. Detailed characteristics were presented for large areas of each state, such as cities and standard metropolitan areas of 100,000 or more inhabitants.

Census Tract Statistics reports were published separately for each area and included a variety of population and housing data for each census tract. *Special Reports* presented data that were too detailed to report in the regular volumes. They generally referred to the country as a whole or to large regions and covered such topics as employment and personal characteristics, occupational and industrial characteristics, family characteristics, the institutional population, and nativity and parentage.

The publications of the Census of Housing also included preliminary and advance reports. District offices released preliminary housing unit counts beginning in July 1950. Final figures for housing characteristics first appeared in the advance reports, beginning in August 1951.

The bureau published detailed data from the housing census in five series. The *General Characteristics* volumes provided data on occupancy and tenure of housing units, type of structure, race and number of occupants, condition and plumbing facilities, number of rooms and persons per room, rent, and value of owner-occupied units. *Nonfarm Housing Characteristics* contained cross-tabulations of housing characteristics by monthly rent, value, sex and age of household head, type of household, and family income. For occupied housing units in 119 farming areas, *Farm Housing Characteristics* presented cross-tabulations of housing characteristics with such variables as year built, heating equipment, plumbing facilities, number of occupants, and sex and age of household head. The statistics in *Residential Financing* described the financial characteristics of mortgages and the characteristics of property owners. The fifth series reported *Block Statistics* for 209 cities with populations of 50,000 or more.

The Bureau of the Census increased the number of cities for which it tabulated and published statistics for city blocks, from 191 in 1940 to 209 in 1950. Begun on an experimental basis a decade earlier, block statistics became a regular part of the decennial publication program with the 1950 census.

For the first time since the 1920 census, the bureau published monographs. The publishing program was sponsored by the Bureau of the Census and the Social Science Research Council, and it produced 13 books, written by specialists on such subjects as the changing population, immigration, families, children, labor force, income, and housing.

Evaluating the Census

The 1950 census included the first post-enumeration survey (PES). It consisted of two samples, one of areas to measure completeness of coverage of housing units and the other of households to measure completeness of coverage of persons within enumerated units and to evaluate the quality of the content of the census returns. The PES estimated the gross census undercount to be 3.4 million persons and the net undercount to be 2.1 million, or 1.4 percent of the enumerated total. This first evaluation attempt, based on a small sample and estimation techniques that would be improved for later censuses, was deemed to be an inadequate appraisal. Demographic analytical studies indicated that a more valid estimate of the net undercount in the 1950 census might have been 5 million to 5.5 million. Some years after the census, the bureau made public an estimate of the national net undercount based on a more thorough study. The estimate was 4.1 percent, compared with a retroactive estimate of 5.4 percent for 1940.

Another evaluation matched the 1950 census returns with corresponding returns from the April 1950 Current Population Survey (CPS), a monthly large sample survey conducted by the bureau, that asked many of the same questions as the population census. Among the findings of the matching study were that response variability and response bias were greater for the census than for the CPS and that labor force participation estimates were significantly higher in the CPS. The CPS enumerators were considerably more experienced than the temporary workers hired for the census fieldwork. The CPS-census match was repeated in succeeding censuses.

Selected Findings from the 1950 Census

The population of the United States according to the 1950 census increased by 14.5 percent over the 1940 figure. This was twice as great a percentage increase as that for the 1930–1940 decade, when the economic depression held down population growth. During the depression some demographers had predicted that the U.S. population would level off at about 150 million. Had they been correct, the 1950 total would have become the ceiling; however, they were wrong.

The resident population totals as of April 1 in the census of 1950 (as well as 1940 and 1960) included the armed forces within the country but excluded the armed forces and others outside it. This exclusion was not consistent among all the decennial censuses.

The increase in population growth in the decade of the 1940s was fed by a resurgence in birth rates in the latter part of the decade, as well as a resurgence in net immigration. Of the increase in population of about 19 million, 90 percent was attributed to natural increase and 10 percent to net immigration. Despite some rebound in immigration, the percentage of the U.S. population that was foreign-born continued its long-term decline, to 6.9 percent in 1950.

The influence of depression, war, and post-war recovery was reflected in changes in the age distribution of the population. Measured from about the beginning of the depression in 1930 to the time of the 1950 census, the population age 5 to 19 declined, despite the increase in the total population. The number under age 5 increased by 42 percent, reflecting the early years of the post-war baby boom. The long-term increase in the older population continued, with substantial increases in the age group 45 to 64 and especially the age group 65 and over.

The average size of households continued its long-term decline, from 5.7 persons in 1790 to 3.4 persons in 1950.

The 1950 census showed a continuing trend toward population concentration in metropolitan areas, reaching a level of 57 percent metropolitan. The most rapid increase was in the coastal areas. The percentage of increase in metropolitan-residing population was more than twice as great for blacks as for whites. The fastest-growing states in order according to the size of percentage of growth in the decade ending in 1950 were California, Arizona, Florida, and Nevada. The fastest-growing region, by far, was the West, at a rate three to four times as great as the other regions.

In general, housing improved during the decade of the 1940s. More homes were equipped with basic plumbing facilities and household conveniences. A booming economy, favorable tax laws, a rejuvenated home building industry, and easier financing encouraged a great increase in home ownership. For the first time more than half of the occupied homes were owner-occupied. The proportion of units with electric lighting increased from 79 percent in 1940 to 94 percent in 1950. Fewer units were crowded. Yet 1950 still saw a nation in which more than one-third of the housing lacked complete plumbing.

See also Data capture; Decennial censuses: 1940 census; Decennial censuses: 1960 census.

EDWIN D. GOLDFIELD
AND DAVID M. PEMBERTON

BIBLIOGRAPHY

Goldfield, Edwin D. "Innovations in the Decennial Census of Population and Housing: 1940–1990." Commissioned paper prepared for the Year 2000 Census Panel Studies. Washington, D.C.: National Research Council, Committee on National Statistics, August 1992.

"The Minnesota Historical Census Projects." *Historical Methods* 28 (Winter 1995).

Taeuber, Conrad, and Irene B. Taeuber. *The Changing Population of the United States.* New York: John Wiley and Sons, 1958.

Taeuber, Irene B., and Conrad Taeuber. *People of the United States in the 20th Century.* Washington, D.C.: U.S. Government Printing Office, 1971.

U.S. Bureau of the Census. *The 1950 Censuses—How They Were Taken.* Procedural studies of the 1950 censuses, no. 2. Washington, D.C.: U.S. Government Printing Office, 1955.

———. *Population and Housing Inquiries in the U.S. Decennial Censuses, 1790–1970.* Working paper 39. Washington, D.C.: U.S. Government Printing Office, 1973.

———. *200 Years of U.S. Census Taking: Population and Housing Questions, 1790–1990.* Washington, D.C.: U.S. Government Printing Office, 1989.

Decennial Censuses: 1960 Census

According to the 1960 census, the population of the United States, including the contiguous 48 states, the District of Columbia, and the newly admitted states of Alaska and Hawaii, was 179,323,175. This census also covered the Commonwealth of Puerto Rico and the territories of American Samoa, Guam, the Panama Canal Zone, the U.S. Virgin Islands, and a number of smaller islands. The high commissioner of the Trust Territory of the Pacific Islands conducted a census in 1958; the Bureau of the Census tabulated its results and released the data together with the rest of the information from the 1960 census. Following the census, all 435 seats in the U.S. House of Representatives were reapportioned among the 50 states.

General Background

The demographic situation of the nation at the time of the 1960 census was marked by a continuation of the recovery in the population growth rate following the end of World War II, but with the beginning of a slackening in the rate of growth. The unemployment rate was relatively low, and the employment rate for women was climbing upward, already higher than the temporary peak during World War II.

The growth of the United States (defined as the contiguous 48 states and the District of Columbia) was augmented by the admission to statehood of Alaska and Hawaii in 1959. In this article, numbers for 1960 are for the United States including Alaska and Hawaii; comparisons of 1960 with 1950 or earlier dates are for the coterminous United States, excluding Alaska and Hawaii.

The 1960 census was taken in accordance with the constitutional requirement (Article I, section 2) that a census be conducted within every ten-year period. The statute that authorizes the bureau to take the population and housing census is Title 13 of the United States Code. Legislated in 1954, Title 13 consolidated a number of laws authorizing various bureau activities into a single statute.

Planning the Census

While congressional appropriations earmarked for the 1960 decennial census began in fiscal year 1958, the bureau had begun planning for the census as early as 1955. Bureau staff consulted with the agency's advisory committees and representatives of business, professional, and civic organizations; evaluated requests for new information; and tested elements of census taking, such as question wording, questionnaire design and content, and enumeration and sampling procedures in a series of supplements to ongoing surveys and special censuses. The Bureau of the Budget (now the Office of Management and Budget) coordinated federal governmental input on proposed census plans and procedures.

Experimentation with self-enumeration in the decennial census, to replace the conventional door-to-door canvass and interviewing by enumerators, continued during the 1950s and resulted in considerable use of mail and self-enumeration in the 1960 census. However, a heavy reliance still remained on door-to-door canvassing and enumerator follow-up, especially in rural areas.

In the research that led to the introduction of mail and self-enumeration, measures of enumerator variability when enumerators were used were contrasted with the variability found when self-enumeration was used. High rates of enumerator error, often consistent through the enumerator's work area, characterized all but the simplest questions. This suggested that the census could be more accurate if self-enumeration could be used as much as was feasible. Nonsampling errors, such as those made by enumerators, were typically greater than sampling errors. Thus more accurate statistics could be obtained on a sampling basis than on a 100 percent basis for many questions if the nonsampling errors made by enumerators could be sufficiently reduced by using self-enumeration.

In the 1960 census, the definition of "head of household" continued to display a gender bias. The head of a household was the person reported as such, except that in the case of a married couple, the husband was always considered the head.

With the substantial changes for the 1950 census in geographical concepts and measurements and in residential rules (for example, where to count college students), the preparation for the 1960 census in these matters consisted mainly of updating, refinement, and expansion of coverage. A considerable increase was evident in the number of census tracts, to more cities and to the outlying portions of metropolitan areas.

There were 23,365 tracts delineated for 1960, almost twice as many as for 1950.

The Questionnaire

For 1960 the 100 percent and sample questions were placed on two separate questionnaires (the "short form" and the "long form"). The main reason was to allow for more rapid processing and publication of the 100 percent statistics.

Previous censuses had used a line schedule as the main data-collection form. For example, the 1950 form was a large sheet with 30 lines for persons on one side and space for housing information for 12 units on the reverse. The 1960 census used a separate questionnaire for each household and its housing unit. The use of mail and self-enumeration necessitated a separate form for each household.

The changes in questionnaire content were more numerous in 1960 than in 1950. New population questions included commuting (place of work and means of transportation to work), length of residence, whether school enrolled in was public or private, for whom worked (for example, company name—to be coded by industry classification in the data-processing procedure), date of first marriage, and more specific household relationship information. The question on age in previous censuses was replaced by a question on month and year of birth to reduce the biases, such as a tendency to round, in age reporting. With self-enumeration for most of the population, the question on race became largely one of self-identification rather than observation by the enumerator. Only the questions on relationship, sex, race, month and year of birth, and marital status were asked of all persons. All other population items were collected on a 25 percent basis (every fourth household). The housing unit or group quarters was the sampling unit; everyone living in that unit became a member of the sample.

New housing questions were access to housing unit, presence of cooking equipment, water heating fuel, clothes washing machine, clothes dryer, air conditioning, home food freezer, number of bathrooms, source of water, sewage disposal, telephone, automobiles, number of bedrooms, basement, elevator, mobility of trailers, and duration of vacancy for vacant units. Added to the Survey of Residential Financing, which had been introduced in 1950, was the Survey of Components of Change, which measured the quantitative and qualitative impact of basic changes that occurred in the housing inventory during the decade 1950–1960. The two inquiries constituted a large-scale sample survey conducted in the fall of 1959 and early 1960 as a part of the housing census. In the basic housing census, 14 questions were asked for all housing units and 30 questions were asked on a sample basis, either 25 percent, 20 percent, or 5 percent. The 20 percent and 5 percent samples were subdivisions of the 25 percent sample (every fourth housing unit—the same sample as for the population inquiry).

Data Collection

During the late 1950s, the Bureau of the Census maintained 17 permanent regional offices to support data collection for special censuses and current surveys. To collect the information

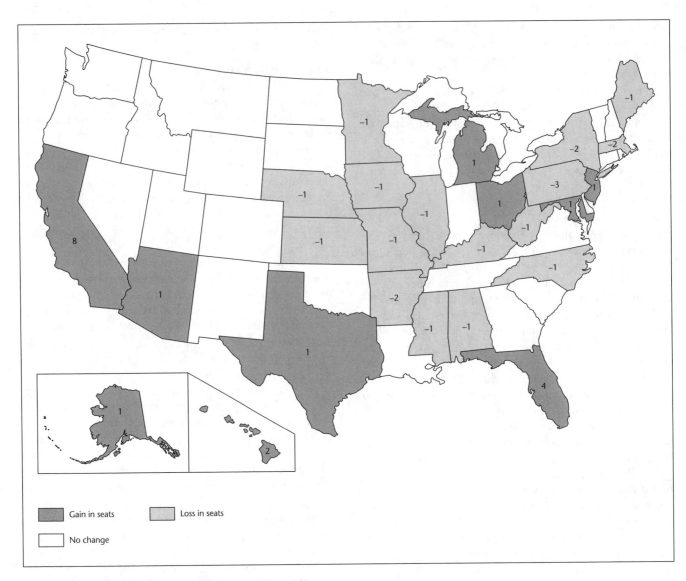

State Gains or Losses in the U.S. House of Representatives, 1960

for the 1960 decennial census, the bureau set up 399 temporary district offices throughout the 50 states and the District of Columbia. (Six additional district offices were established in Puerto Rico and one each in American Samoa, Guam, the Panama Canal Zone, and the U.S. Virgin Islands.) District office managers reported to one of the 17 regional offices. The main factor in determining the number of district offices in each region was population density.

The area for which each district office was responsible was divided into crew leader districts, and the latter were subdivided into enumeration districts. Each crew leader supervised an average of 15 or 16 enumerators. The population of enumeration districts ranged from 100,000 to 200,000 people. Peak employment for enumerators came to 156,966 on April 7, 1960; the largest number of crew leaders employed on a given day was 10,271, also on April 7.

In the 1960 census the bureau used a two-stage procedure in areas composing 82 percent of the population. Advance forms containing the 100 percent questions were delivered by mail. Enumerators visited all households and transcribed the 100 percent items to a FOSDIC (film optical sensing device for input to computers) machine-readable form. If the advance form had not been completed, the enumerator obtained the information and filled out the FOSDIC form. About 60 percent of the advance forms had been filled out before the enumerator's visit. At every fourth household the enumerator left a sample long form to be completed by the household and mailed back to the census district office. The mail response rate for the sample questions was 77 percent. Follow-up enumerators visited households that had not mailed back the forms. In the 18 percent remainder of the country, mainly rural, where the two-stage procedure was not used, a single-stage procedure was employed. Advance forms were mailed out and then were followed by enumerators' visits to all households to fill out the short forms and the sample long forms.

In 1960 a major formal program of quality control was instituted for the fieldwork. It provided supervisors with definite procedures for detecting and, when necessary, rejecting unacceptable work.

For tabulation and publication, some of the population statistics were based on a subsample of one-fifth of the collected 25 percent sample questionnaires. Sampling yielded economies in cost and tabulation time. Sampling rates depended on the size of the geographic areas or population and housing categories being tabulated and on the degree of reliability needed.

The use of household questionnaires and households as the sampling units made possible the collection and compilation of better and more extensive household and family statistics.

Data Products

The 1960 decennial census produced approximately 138,000 pages of census reports. Most were released between 1961 and 1963, but specialized volumes continued to come out until well into the decade.

The first reports to be published were the preliminary counts of states, counties, and incorporated places of 1,000 or more inhabitants. Appearing between May and September of 1961, these preliminary reports were superseded beginning in August by the advance reports, which contained final population counts for each state and a number of geographic units within each state. Later advance reports provided final figures for personal characteristics such as age, sex, race, and marital status and for some economic and social characteristics, by state and other geographic areas.

Detailed information from the population census was published in four series of volumes. The first series, with the overall title of *Characteristics of the Population,* was divided into four subseries. The first subseries, *Number of Inhabitants,* contained final population counts from the 100 percent questionnaires for states, counties, standard metropolitan statistical areas, urbanized areas, incorporated places, minor civil divisions, and unincorporated places with at least 1,000 inhabitants.

The second subseries, *General Population Characteristics,* provided final 100 percent data for age, sex, marital status, race, and relationship to household head for states, counties, standard metropolitan statistical areas, urbanized areas, places with 1,000 or more inhabitants, and minor civil divisions.

The third subseries, *General Social and Economic Characteristics,* presented data taken from the sample questionnaire on such variables as nativity, mother tongue, school enrollment and years of school completed, family composition, veteran status, employment status, occupational and industry group, and income. These data were given for states, counties, standard metropolitan statistical areas, urbanized areas, and urban places. The fourth subseries, *Detailed Characteristics,* provided cross-tabulations for 100 percent and sample data for many of the topics treated in *General Social and Economic Characteristics* for larger geographic areas such as states, large counties, and cities.

The second series of reports from the population census, *Subject Reports,* consisted of detailed cross-tabulations for the United States and its regions for such variables as race, fertility, marital status, families, education, employment, occupation, industry, and income. The third series, *Selected Area Reports,* presented selected characteristics for specialized geographic areas and for Americans overseas. *Supplementary Reports* presented population data for a variety of geographic areas, miscellaneous types of data, and selected tables from earlier publications.

The 1960 Census of Housing produced a series of preliminary and advance reports, followed by several series of final reports. The preliminary reports contained preliminary housing-unit counts on a state-by-state basis for many urban places. Advance reports presented final data on housing units by tenure, race of occupants, number of rooms, rent, and other variables for standard metropolitan statistical areas and some places.

Final reports from the Census of Housing were published in seven series. The first, *States and Small Areas,* presented occupancy and structural characteristics, equipment and facilities, and financial characteristics of housing units or their occupants for states, counties, standard metropolitan statistical areas, and other geographic areas. The *Metropolitan Housing* series of reports provided cross-tabulations of housing and household characteristics for the United States and most standard metropolitan statistical areas. The *City Blocks* series contained a limited amount of housing data for each block in cities with 50,000 or more inhabitants and for 172 other urban places.

The fourth series, *Components of Inventory Change,* was released in two parts and described changes in the nation's housing stock. *Residential Finance* also had two parts and presented information on home finance and characteristics of some types of owner-occupied housing and on rental and vacant properties. *Housing of Senior Citizens* contained cross-tabulations of household and housing characteristics for housing units having one or more household member age 60 years or older. *Special Reports for Local Housing Authorities* focused on the social and economic characteristics of respondents living in substandard housing and on the characteristics of the housing.

A joint population and housing series, *Census Tract Reports,* was part of a new series that combined data from both censuses. A new methodological series described some census operations, evaluated census procedures, and presented results from experiments.

An innovation for the 1960 census was the production of public-use samples from the census returns. These were samples of the basic records for individual persons, households, and housing units, with the identifying information, such as name, address, and detailed geography, removed to preserve confidentiality. The bureau made these data available to the public on computer tapes, so that researchers could make their own special tabulations. The first samples were released on tape, and also on punch cards, in 1963. The series has been extended forward and backward, to succeeding and preceding censuses.

A related innovation for the 1960 census was the production of summary tapes for public use, containing more subject and geographic detail than the printed reports. They fall under the same confidentiality rules as the printed report data. They were made available on a small scale for the 1960 census and greatly expanded for succeeding censuses.

Following the example of the 1950 census, a program was established for a series of monographs to follow the 1960 census, again with the cooperation of the Social Science Research Council. It produced five books, a considerably smaller number than the 1950 program. The 1960 monograph series was published by the U.S. Government Printing Office.

Evaluating the Census

The 1960 census operation featured many evaluations and research projects looking toward improvements for future censuses as well as evaluations of the quality of the 1960 census. From the many studies proposed, 22 were selected for implementation. This emphasis on researching, experimenting, and analyzing enabled the bureau to learn, and share with the public, more technical knowledge about the workings of censuses than had occurred in earlier censuses and to get an early start on planning for the 1970 census.

Litigation

The issue of privacy was raised in the case of the *United States v. William Rickenbacker* in 1961–1963. The defendant argued that his refusal to respond in the 1960 census, and his advocacy of a boycott of the census, was justified because the census, for which answers are required under penalty of law, was an unreasonable invasion of privacy. The U.S. District Court reached a decision in favor of the government and found Rickenbacker guilty of violating the census law. He received a suspended sentence of 60 days' imprisonment and a fine of $100 and was placed on probation for one day. The Court of Appeals upheld the action, stating, "The authority to gather reliable statistical data reasonably relating to governmental purposes and functions is a necessity if modern government is to legislate intelligently and effectively." This was the final judgment in the case because the Supreme Court declined to review it.

Selected Findings from the 1960 Census

The population of the United States (including the new states of Alaska and Hawaii) according to the 1960 census increased by 18.5 percent over the 1950 figure of 151,325,798, with states-to-be Alaska and Hawaii added in. This was the greatest percentage increase since the 1900–1910 decade and is higher than any increase for decades subsequent to 1960, at least to date. In absolute terms, the increase of nearly 28 million people is the greatest for any decade in the history of the United States. Credit for the record goes mainly to the post–World War II baby boom, plus the resumption of immigration. In the 1950–1960 decade, as in the preceding decade, natural increase accounted for 90 percent of the total increase and net immigration for 10 percent.

The percentage of the population that was foreign-born continued its decline, to 5.4 percent in 1960. State-to-state migration continued to increase. In 1960, 16.9 percent of the

U.S.-native population of California had been born in other states, a far higher proportion than that of any other state of the coterminous United States.

Population growth continued to be concentrated in urban, especially metropolitan, areas. The percentage urban increased from 64.0 percent in 1950 to 69.9 percent in 1960. In that period the percentage urban for the black population increased from 62.4 percent in 1950 to 73.2 percent in 1960. After a long history of the black population being concentrated in the rural South, blacks had become more urban than whites.

Although women's rate of participation in the labor force continued to increase, it still was far below that for men. In 1960 the proportion of men 14 years of age and over in the labor force was 77.4 percent; for women it was 34.5 percent.

The fastest-growing states in order according to the size of percentage of growth in the decade ending in 1960 were Florida, Nevada, Alaska, and Arizona. The West continued to far outstrip the other regions in rate of population growth.

The housing census showed that the rate of residential construction in the 1950–1960 decade continued almost unabated from the previous decade. Home ownership gained impressively; the proportion of homeowners was higher than at any other date for which data on tenure were collected. Quality of housing improved. The percentage of housing units lacking plumbing decreased significantly in the decade from slightly over 35 percent to about 17 percent. The percentage of "crowded" (based on persons per room) housing units continued to decrease. Television sets became a staple of the American home, with 87 percent of the occupied units having at least one set, an increase from 12 percent in 1950.

See also *Data capture.*

EDWIN D. GOLDFIELD
. . . . AND DAVID M. PEMBERTON

BIBLIOGRAPHY

Goldfield, Edwin D. "Innovations in the Decennial Census of Population and Housing: 1940–1990." Commissioned paper prepared for the Year 2000 Census Panel Studies. Washington, D.C.: National Research Council, Committee on National Statistics, August 1992.

"The Minnesota Historical Census Projects." *Historical Methods* 28 (Winter 1995).

Taeuber, Irene B., and Conrad Taeuber. *People of the United States in the 20th Century*. Washington, D.C.: U.S. Government Printing Office, 1971.

U.S. Bureau of the Census. *1960 Censuses of Population and Housing: Procedural History*. Washington, D.C.: U.S. Government Printing Office, 1966.

———. *Population and Housing Inquiries in the U.S. Decennial Censuses, 1790–1970*. Working paper 39. Washington, D.C.: U.S. Government Printing Office, 1973.

———. *200 Years of U.S. Census Taking: Population and Housing Questions, 1790–1990*. Washington, D.C.: U.S. Government Printing Office, 1989.

Decennial Censuses: 1970 Census

Shortly before the 1970 census, the population of the United States passed the 200 million mark. The 1970 count of 203,302,031 represented an increase of more than 13 percent, or almost 24 million people since 1960. This level of growth could not match the 18.5 percent increase recorded between 1950 and 1960, and it was indicative of what would become a pattern of slower growth in the nation's population in the last few decades of the twentieth century.

Changes in Population Growth

Two factors lay behind the decline in the growth rate. First, the baby boom was over. Demographers define this period of high birth rates as 1946 to 1964, with its peak in 1957. By 1970 the nation was well into a "baby bust." This meant that far fewer children were being born than in previous decades. At the same time, the oldest baby boomers were growing up and moving out of their parental homes. Unlike their parents, however, many were deferring marriage and childbirth to later ages.

Second, the immigration rate, while slightly higher than in the immediately previous decades, was still low (1.7 immigrants per 1,000 U.S. population). In later decades, the immigration rate would rise sharply. Immigrants, and their children born in the United States, contribute significantly to overall population growth.

The large number of children born in the baby-boom years lowered the population's median age to 28 years—that is, half the people in the United States were younger and half were older. This was the lowest median age figure since 1930 (in 2000, the median age was almost 36 years). The strength of the young population, particularly of children under age 18, meant that the nation's resources were concentrating on education, including building schools. The 2000 picture was significantly different.

Census Innovations

The 1970 census was most remarkable for two innovations: the mailout/mailback census and the routine dissemination of data in electronic form. The mailout/mailback method was used for the first time in a population and housing census. Covering major urban areas and some adjacent counties, preaddressed census questionnaires were delivered to about 60 percent of the nation's housing units on March 28, 1970. Householders were asked to fill in the questionnaires and mail them back to the local census office on census day (April 1).

The mailing list for the preaddressed questionnaires was assembled from commercial sources, augmented by checks both by postal carriers and by census field staff. The addresses were then processed through the Address Coding Guide (ACG), which coded them to census tract, block, and other geographic identifiers. The ACG was the forerunner of the Topologically Integrated Geographic Encoding and Referencing (TIGER) system.

Because commercial lists were available only in major urban areas, the remainder of the country was enumerated through the conventional methods used in earlier censuses, where the address list was constructed and geographically coded by enumerators as they conducted the census on a door-to-door basis.

As in 1960, the census questions were divided between a "short form" and a "long form." The short-form population items, asked in every household, were name, relationship to head of household, color or race, age, month and year of birth, and marital status. Short-form housing items were living quarters at address (subsequently referred to as "units in structure"), telephone, direct entrance, complete kitchen facilities, number of rooms, a set of plumbing questions (piped hot water, toilet, bathtub or shower), basement, tenure (own or rent), housing value, and rent. The plumbing items, which became the subject of great controversy before the 1980 and 1990 censuses, were critical to measuring housing quality. In 1970 many Americans still lived in housing that lacked these basic amenities.

The long form went to 20 percent of the households (the other 80 percent received only the short form). The long form was split into two questionnaires. The majority of items were included on both, but a special subset of questions was asked only in 15 percent of the households, while another subset went to only 5 percent.

The 1970 census continued use of a 1960s innovation: the FOSDIC (film optical sensing device for input to computers) system for capturing the data from the paper questionnaire for processing. FOSDIC was much more efficient than the older method, keypunching IBM cards for every questionnaire and reading the punched cards into the computer; however, the FOSDIC questionnaire required respondents to fill in circles for most of the responses. The questions were laid out in two columns on oversized pages in a booklet. They could be intimidating for those with lower education or literacy levels as well as for older persons with sight problems. These considerations were much more critical in a mailout/mailback census than they were in a census where paid enumerators filled out the questionnaires.

The second major innovation of 1970, Summary Tape Files (STFs), represented the first routine delivery of data in electronic format. The STFs were used on mainframe computer systems, which were the standard of the time. The STFs contained far more data than could be or would be included in printed reports. Users could use the computer to aggregate data across different geographic areas (such as groups of census tracts), create new statistics from the existing tables, and calculate percentages and other statistical presentations of the data for publication. The data could be arranged in a variety of ways to suit the needs of the user. The concept of "data intermediaries" was born, as some demographers and planners became experts at working with the data on STFs and delivering the information to end users.

Using the STFs required programming. Most users, even intermediaries, were not in a position to create their own software. The most important person to facilitate addressing this problem was John C. "Jack" Beresford, an innovative and far-thinking young Bureau of the Census employee who advanced the concept of data delivery in this electronic format. After observing that the bureau had no plans to create software to accompany the data files, he formed a company known as DUALabs (Data Use and Access Laboratories) to ensure that methods for using summary tapes would be created. Initially supported by a group of public-and private sector clients who planned to use the STFs, DUALabs later received a grant from

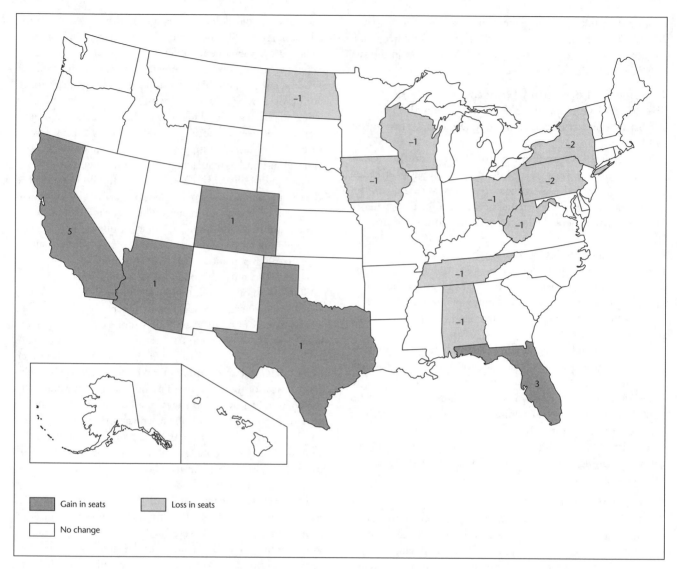

State Gains or Losses in the U.S. House of Representatives, 1970

the Ford Foundation to spread these techniques to the nation's colleges and universities. The MOD series, as the software was named, became the prototype method for handling summary data. In addition, the documentation prepared by DUALabs became the standard for describing the structure and content of the 1970 Summary Files.

The 1970 Summary Files should be viewed as experimental. Many of the lessons learned were incorporated into the 1980 STFs and continued into the twenty-first century. They were controversial because many bureau staff members feared release of the data in this form would lead to breaches of confidentiality. These fears proved to be unfounded. Summary Files made the transition from the mainframe to the personal computer. They remain the prime method for comprehensive data dissemination from the decennial census as well as the American Community Survey. The "detailed tables" provided on the Census Bureau's American FactFinder are, as a group, equivalent to Summary Files.

Public Use Microdata Samples (PUMS) files had been produced for the 1960 census, but they were small samples with limited geographic identification. In 1970 six 1 percent samples were released on computer tape—three that were drawn from the census records for households that returned the 15 percent long form and three that were drawn from the census records for households that received the 5 percent long form. Three different geographic identification schemes were used. For the first time, users could prepare their own tabulations for such areas as states and Standard Metropolitan Statistical Areas and counties or groups of counties. However, no area was identified in the files unless it had a population of at least 250,000.

See also *Data products: evolution; Dissemination of data: electronic products; Summary Files.*

. . . . PATRICIA C. BECKER

BIBLIOGRAPHY
U.S. Bureau of the Census. *Data Collection Forms and Procedures,* 1970 Census Report PHC(R)-2. Washington, D.C.: U.S. Government Printing Office, 1971.
———. *Statistical Abstract of the United States, 1998.* Washington, D.C.: U.S. Government Printing Office, 1998.

Decennial Censuses: 1980 Census

The population of the United States in 1980 was 226,545,805. This represented an increase of some 23 million people, or more than 11 percent, over 1970. The demographic picture of the nation was dominated by the emergence of the baby-boomer generation as adults, forming their own households and participating in the labor force. Female labor force participation, especially among women with young children, increased dramatically in the 1970s. At the same time, women were having fewer children, with more than 1 million fewer births in 1975 than in 1957, the peak year of the baby boom.

Average household size had dropped significantly, as a result of three major factors: (1) the low birth rate, (2) an increase in single-person households caused by deferred marriage and a growing divorce rate, and (3) a growing elderly population. Almost 24 percent of households contained only one person, compared with 17 percent in 1970.

Other notable changes in the nation's socioeconomic and demographic patterns during the 1970s included a significant increase in the proportion of children living with only one parent, a marked decrease in the number of school-age children, and a great decline in population growth in the nation's Northeast and Midwest regions (the "Rust Belt"). By 1980 the nation had a new demographic pattern, different from 1970 and earlier, which was to persist for at least the next 20 years.

Expansion of Existing Methods
The 1980 census continued and expanded on the innovative methods introduced in 1970 and established several new procedures. Mailout/mailback census methods were extended to areas containing more than 95 percent of the nation's housing units. A new procedure, called Local Review, enabled local officials to examine census housing unit counts. The Summary Tape Files (STFs) and the Public Use Microdata Samples (PUMS) continued as the major form of data delivery in electronic format. The issue of census undercount, and possible adjustment, moved from the academic domain into the political arena. A new file, the Public Law 94-171 Redistricting File, was mandated by law to provide data at the census block level for the entire nation. For this reason census block numbering became universal.

The census questionnaire continued to be divided into a "short form" and a "long form," but the split long-form sample used in 1960 and 1970 was eliminated. Cost considerations led to a smaller sample size; only one in six households received the long form, instead of the 20 percent in the 1970 sample and 25 percent in 1960. Special provisions were made for small communities (under 2,500 persons), where a 50 percent sampling fraction was used to improve the quality of income and poverty data utilized in revenue sharing and other government programs.

In 1978 a bill was introduced in Congress that would have separated the long-form questions from the census, instead calling for a separate survey of a sample of households later in the year. Both the Bureau of the Census and the professional community opposed this idea. It would have generated extra costs for poorer quality data, because census promotional activity and the sense of a legal mandate to respond would be absent at the time of the later survey. The bill did not survive a committee vote.

After the 1980 census was completed, President Ronald Reagan in 1981 mandated an across-the-board budget cut of 12 percent. As a consequence, the bureau was forced to delay coding of long-form information and to cut by half coding of the journey to work and migration questionnaire items. The result was poorer data for use in transportation planning in defining metropolitan areas and in analyzing migration patterns within smaller metropolitan areas.

New Requirements and Enhanced Products
The 1980 census was the first that was required to produce data by race and Hispanic origin to conform with Directive 15, issued by the Office of Management and Budget (OMB) in 1977. The data requirements for the PL 94-171 file included a count of the total population and the population 18 and older by each of five race groups (White, Negro or Black, Asian and Pacific Islander, American Indian, and Other) in total and for persons who also reported a Hispanic origin. These items were required to meet the data needs of the Voting Rights Act. Thus, for the first time, Hispanic origin and race categories other than Negro or Black received prominent attention on the questionnaire and in the early tabulations.

Another reason for heightened concern over the population distribution by race was the growing understanding that the population missed by the census, the undercount, was disproportionately composed of minority group members. Many interest groups argued that the census should be adjusted to compensate for the undercount. In the opinion of professionals at the bureau, however, the methods to achieve fair and equitable adjustment were not yet available, and so bureau director Vincent Barabba announced shortly before census day that no census adjustment would be made in 1980. This announcement spurred numerous lawsuits, which occupied bureau staff in court well into the 1980s. In the end, however, there was no 1980 census adjustment.

The 1980 census products program included most of the reports that had traditionally been published as books, as well as four major Summary Tape Files, three Public Use Microdata Samples (PUMS) files, and a large number of special products designed for specific governmental needs. One of the PUMS files provided a very large 5 percent sample of the population; also the population size cutoff for identifying areas in the PUMS files was lowered from 250,000 in 1970 to 100,000 in 1980. Learning from the lessons of the 1970 tape products,

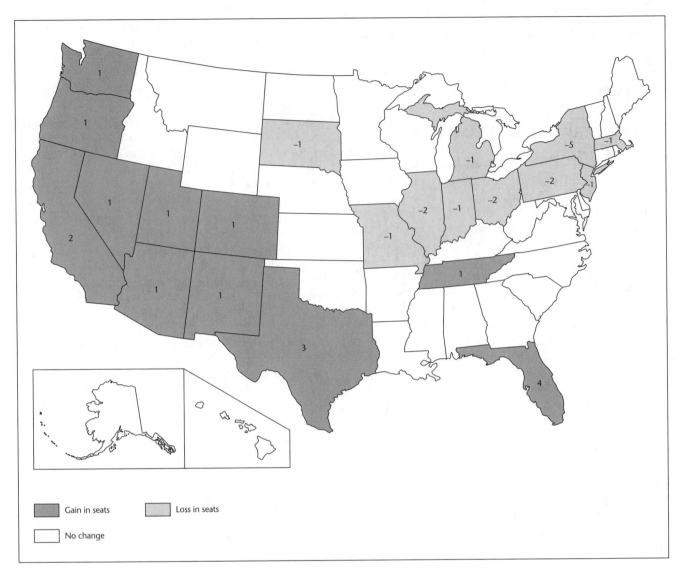

State Gains or Losses in the U.S. House of Representatives, 1980

bureau staff worked hard, and with significant success, to standardize the files and improve their documentation.

The special products included the Equal Employment Opportunity file created for the U.S. Office of Civil Rights to assist in setting goals for affirmative action plans and validating discrimination claims. Another important file was the Census Transportation Planning Package (CTPP), designed for the Department of Transportation and distributed to metropolitan and state planning agencies. The STF3 ZIP Code file was produced as a special product funded by a consortium of private sector data vendors; under the agreement, the files were released to the public after 18 months. The School District Database provided tabulations for use by the education community.

Microfiche was used extensively to provide information that was not formally printed. This included a data set for every residential block in the nation. Microfiche was also the vehicle used to make the tables available from two of the

summary files, STF1 and STF3, readable and printable. These were widely distributed to libraries and to agencies affiliated with the State Data Center (SDC) program.

The SDCs were created under joint statistical agreements between the Bureau of the Census and the states. Each state was permitted to name a number of affiliates, based on their population size. Both the core agencies and the affiliates received complimentary copies of all census publications on tape and in print. In exchange, they were expected to provide census data service to local users and to document the level of service in annual reports. The SDC participants around the country elected a Coordinating Council, whose members traveled periodically, at bureau expense, to meet at bureau headquarters in Washington, D.C.

In tandem with the SDC program, the bureau decided to create its own software package, CENSPAC, for use in processing the STFs. The decision generated substantial controversy and, in the end, did not work out well. The software's full potential was never realized, and after some time the bureau decided to discontinue further work on it. STF users created their own software, used packages such as SPSS or SAS to access the data, or used an upgraded version of the MOD series software created by DUALabs (Data Use and Access Laboratories) for the 1970 census.

See also *Data products: evolution; Dissemination of data: electronic products; State Data Centers; Summary Files.*

. . . . PATRICIA C. BECKER

BIBLIOGRAPHY

Anderson, Margo J. *The American Census: A Social History.* New Haven, Conn.: Yale University Press, 1988.

Choldin, Harvey. *Looking for the Last Percent.* New Brunswick, N.J.: Rutgers University Press, 1994.

U.S. Bureau of the Census. *Changes in American Family Life.* Report P-23, No. 163. Washington, D.C.: U.S. Government Printing Office, August 1989.

———. *The Coverage of Housing in the 1980 Census.* Census Report PHC80-E1. Washington, D.C.: U.S. Government Printing Office, 1984.

———. *History, Part A.* Census report PHC80(R)-2A. Washington, D.C.: U.S. Government Printing Office, 1986.

———. *Statistical Abstract of the United States, 1998.* Washington, D.C.: U.S. Government Printing Office, 1998.

Decennial Censuses: 1990 Census

The 1990 census counted 249,632,692 people, of whom 248,709,873 were resident in the United States and 922,819 were overseas military, and federal employees, as well as [to emphasize these are diplomats & other fed. emps. overseas] their dependents. The count showed a growth of 9.8 percent over the decade since the 1980 census, 3 percent of this as the result of immigration. The census apportioned 435 seats in the House of Representatives among 50 states.

Population growth was very unevenly distributed, as it had been during the prior decade. Three states—Iowa, Wyoming, and West Virginia, plus the District of Columbia—actually lost population, while four had gains of over 30 percent. These were Nevada, Arizona, Alaska, and Florida. By region, the West grew by 22.3 percent, the South by 13.4 percent, the Northeast by 3.4 percent, and the Midwest by only 1.4 percent.

The Census Bureau conducts many ongoing demographic surveys and produces population estimates over the course of the decade. The results of the census, therefore, produced few surprises. There were, however, two major ones: Both the Hispanic and Asian populations had increased far more than had been estimated. Hispanics (who can be of any race according to federal government definitions) zoomed from 6.4 to 9.0 percent, a growth of 53 percent in the decade, and Asians from 1.5 percent to 2.9 percent, a growth of 108 percent.

The 1990 census was a technological triumph and a public relations disaster. It was a mix of technological breakthroughs and innovations that have changed census taking since, coupled with reuse of the basic mailout/mailback procedures that had been employed in the 1970 and 1980 censuses. Those procedures included the mailing of questionnaires

to all households with street addresses plus multiple, in-person, follow-up calls on households that did not return their questionnaires. There were special procedures for counting those with rural, nonstreet addresses, those living in shelters or on the street, transients, prisoners/parolees, and other special groups. Some of those procedures proved no longer adequate given the changes in society: more racial and ethnic diversity, new immigrants, less sense of the need for "civic" participation, and more varied household structures than in prior decades. Whereas in 1970, 78 percent of households returned the mailed questionnaires and 75 percent in 1980, in 1990 only 63 percent returned them by the deadline for follow-up calls (although another 2 percent came in later). The Bureau of the Census had anticipated a drop to 70 percent, but the remainder of the shortfall meant over 6 million additional households had to be contacted in person.

The Technological Triumphs

The 1990 census had four big wins: (1) creation of a computerized mapping system for all 7 million blocks in the nation that became the base for geographic information systems (GIS), (2) creation of a computerized Master Address File (MAF) that censuses since have updated and used, (3) advancement and improvement of statistical methodology for measuring undercount, and (4) delivery of the data in a form that anyone with a personal computer could use. The latter represented democratization of the data. The census also had some smaller wins in bar coding of questionnaires and distributed data processing. There were no data processing glitches in taking the 1990 census, with over 100 million questionnaires processed in a few months' time.

Creation of the mapping system called TIGER (Topologically Integrated Geographic Encoding and Reference system) was a rare example of federal agency cooperation under a tight deadline. The bureau and the U.S. Geological Survey (USGS) produced a geographic information system (GIS) with every point along every street, highway, stream, river, railroad, and local boundary in the country computer digitized by latitude and longitude. Whereas for prior censuses, enumerators set off with local maps of varying quality, now there was a national system that could print maps on demand. Since neither the bureau nor the USGS can patent or copyright work produced at taxpayer expense, TIGER became a public asset. It spawned a multibillion-dollar GIS industry as the mapping system underlying every computer product that produces maps of the United States, including those used by 911 emergency services.

The 1990 MAF was the first census address list ever computerized. While people move, most buildings do not. The MAF became a permanent tool for Census Bureau use for censuses and surveys, updated regularly with U.S. Postal Service lists and construction and demolition data.

The 1970 and 1980 censuses were available to data users on tapes. These data tapes required large mainframe computer systems, systems available only to those in large corporate, academic, or government environments. The decade of the 1980s saw the proliferation of personal computers. The 1990 census was made available on CD-ROMs, usable by any group or individual with a PC and CD-ROM reader. Thus census data

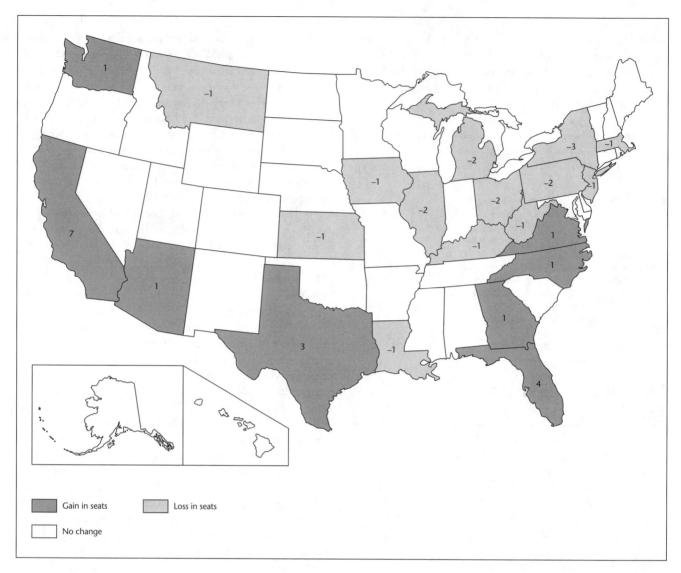

State Gains or Losses in the U.S. House of Representatives, 1990

became accessible to the taxpayers who paid for these data. Although delivery of 1990 data on CD-ROMs in 1991 was a technological breakthrough, by 1995 census data moved to the Internet at www.census.gov. This was a move that could not have been envisioned at the time the census was taken.

Litigation and Controversy Create Public Relations Disaster

Hanging like a black cloud over the 1990 census was litigation demanding that census counts be adjusted for undercount. This pushed the bureau into making great strides in research-ing any undercount. The first lawsuit was filed in 1988, two years before census taking began, by the City of New York, State of New York, Chicago, California, Los Angeles, Dade County, Florida, and a number of organizations and individu-als who joined in as plaintiffs (eventually numbering about 50). The lawsuit created a negative media environment for both census taking and the final results of the census. Reporters,

cartoonists, and comedians alike took up a litany that the bureau could not count accurately. In all, 21 suits were filed contesting the 1990 census, most of them over the under-count. The last was settled in 1996.

The bureau used two kinds of research to estimate the size of undercount in the census, Demographic Analysis (DA) and the Post-Enumeration Survey (PES), coupled with an estima-tion technique called dual-systems estimation (using com-parisons of survey results to census counts of sampled areas). DA uses non-census data such as births, deaths, immigration, and migration records. DA is usable for national estimates, and estimates for blacks and nonblacks, but cannot provide data on geographic changes and other demographic character-istics. The DA estimate of the undercount was 1.8 percent, slightly larger than the DA estimate of 1.2 percent for the previous (1980) census. Between 1940, when DA was first used, and 1980, the difference in undercount between blacks and nonblacks was steadily reduced. It was a setback that both the undercount and the racial difference in it increased for 1990 despite substantially more effort to count hard-to-enumerate groups.

The PES produced estimates of the population by 1,392 nonoverlapping groups defined by age, race, ethnicity, home owner/renter, geographic areas, and types of areas. It determined which of these groups had been undercounted, and by how much, and which had been overcounted (counted twice), as well as those not counted. The initial estimate, made by June 1991 as required by the lawsuit, was a net undercount of 2.1 percent. This was refined after further research and finalized in August 1992 as a net undercount of 1.6 percent made up of an undercount of approximately 8 million persons and an overcount of approximately 4 million. The undercount was differential by demographic groups (see Table 1). The 1990 PES, coupled with dual-systems estimation, produced the most thorough analysis ever of the size and location characteristics of undercounted and overcounted segments of the population.

The decision of whether or not to adjust the census count—as called for by the New York et al. plaintiffs—was the biggest controversy of the 1990 census. The suit required that the decision be made by July 15, 1991, seven and one-half months after the counts for the nation and the states were delivered to President George H. W. Bush. Until the adjustment decision was made, every count delivered was marked as subject to correction.

The Bureau of the Census formed a committee of nine of its senior statisticians and demographers, who, along with academic consultants, conducted many tests and analyses of the data. The census director, Dr. Barbara Everitt Bryant, was an ex officio member of the study team. There was also an advisory panel of eight—four appointed by the plaintiffs and four by the Department of Commerce—who reviewed the data. The director and this panel were to advise the secretary of commerce, who had ultimate authority to decide whether to statistically adjust the count as enumerated.

By a 7–2 vote, the bureau study group voted that adjustment would improve the accuracy of the 1990 census. The census director agreed with her research team and so advised the secretary. The court-mandated panel split 4–4, and the undersecretary for economic affairs advised against adjustment. With advisors divided and unconvinced by the research, Secretary of Commerce Robert M. Mosbacher chose not to adjust.

Mosbacher's decision was appealed, but in 1993 Judge Joseph McLaughlin of the U.S. District Court for the Eastern District of New York ruled that Mosbacher's decision was not "arbitrary and capricious." In a footnote he said that if he had been ruling de novo—that is, not on the basis of "arbitrary and capricious,"—he might have favored adjustment. McLaughlin's decision was vacated at the next court level, the U.S. Court of Appeals, but then upheld by the Supreme Court.

Whatever the merits of improving accuracy by statistical adjustment, or cutting census costs by sampling and estimating the population that does not return mailed questionnaires, both have since proved not to be feasible politically. After looking at plans for the 2000 census, Republicans in the

Table 1. Undercount in the 1990 Census (according to the Post-Enumeration Survey and Dual-Systems Estimation)

Population segment	% Net undercount
TOTAL	1.58
Residents of	
Owner-occupied housing	0.07
Renter-occupied housing	4.31
Race:	
Whites (non-blacks)	1.18
Males	1.52
Females	0.85
Blacks	4.43
Males	4.90
Females	4.01
Asian/Pacific Islanders	2.33
Males	3.44
Females	1.25
American Indians	4.52
Males	5.18
Females	3.86
Ethnicity:	
Hispanic (of any race)	4.96
Males	5.51
Females	4.39
Age:	
0–17	3.28
18–29	2.99
30–49	1.36
55+ (overcounted)	−0.92

SOURCE: Barbara Everitt Bryant, *Moving Power and Money: The Politics of Census Taking* (Ithaca, N.Y.: New Strategist Publications, 1995), 151, 164.

House of Representatives wrote language into the bill for the Commerce Department to expedite a challenge to statistical adjustment methods and require that only direct enumeration could be used for apportioning the House of Representatives. Litigation followed in 1998, and the House position was upheld by the Supreme Court in January 1999. The decision prevented use of adjustment for apportionment but left the door open for using adjusted data for redistricting.

The Cost of the Census

Cost for the ten-year cycle, 1984–1993, for planning, testing, census rehearsals, taking of the census, data processing, tabulating and distributing results, and evaluation was $2.6 billion, a sum that sent some congressional appropriators into orbit because the cost was more than that for which population growth plus inflation could account. Most of the additional money was spent trying to reduce the undercount. Looked at another way, the cost of the 1990 census was only $10.40 per person, or about $1 per year for data that would be used for a decade.

The 1990 Census Legacy

Many things worked well in the 1990 census. It counted a net of over 98 percent of the population. The evaluations of under- (and over-) counts were the most thorough ever. The legacies of the 1990 census were permanent assets in the TIGER mapping system and the Master Address File. Anyone with access to the Internet had the data the 1990 census produced at his or her fingertips. Because of the growth in personal computers and the introduction of the Internet, 1990 data were more widely used than those for any prior census.

Evaluation showed some changes that needed to be made for the future and have been used for 2000 and 2010. The questionnaire needed to be graphically redesigned to make it user friendly, not just data processing friendly. The bureau went one census too long in depending on public service announcements to alert the public to the timing and importance of the census. Massive commercial advertising campaigns, recommended from evaluation of the 1990 census, improved questionnaire return rates in the subsequent censuses. Based on recommendations coming out of 1990, the law that kept the Master Address File totally confidential was changed to allow sharing of local census address lists with local governments for pre-census checking purposes to improve accuracy. The same change in law allowed sharing lists between the Census Bureau and the U.S. Postal Service for use in updating the Master Address File.

See also: *Address list development; Coverage evaluation; Decennial censuses: 1980 census; Decennial censuses: 2000 census; Litigation and the census.*

. . . .   BARBARA EVERITT BRYANT

BIBLIOGRAPHY

Anderson, Margo J., and Stephen E. Fienberg. *Who Counts? Census Taking in Contemporary America.* New York: Russell Sage Foundation, 1999.

Bryant, Barbara Everitt, and William Dunn. *Moving Power and Money: The Politics of Census Taking.* Ithaca, N.Y.: New Strategist Publications, Inc., 1995.

Choldin, Harvey. *Looking for the Last Percent.* New Brunswick, N.J.: Rutgers University Press, 1994.

Hogan, Howard. "The 1990 Post-Enumeration Survey: Operation and Results. *Journal of the American Statistical Association* 88 (September 1993): 1047–1060.

National Academy of Sciences, Committee on National Statistics. There have been three panels evaluating the 1990 census and making recommendations for the 2000 census. All have published both interim and final reports available from The National Academies Press, Washington, D.C. http://nap.edu/

TIGER: The Coast-to-Coast Digital Map Data Base. Washington, D.C.: U.S. Department of Commerce, Bureau of the Census, November 1989.

Decennial Censuses: 2000 Census

The 2000 census counted 281,421,906 persons resident in the United States on April 1, 2000, a 13.2 percent increase since 1990. To accomplish the task, the Bureau of the Census faced a host of familiar issues. These included the operational challenges presented by counting a mobile, diverse, and sometimes indifferent population; the political significance of the numbers that would be used to apportion power for a decade, and annually allocate approximately $250 billion in federal funds until the next census; and an unusually partisan and intense political argument about an old problem: the difficulty of counting everyone. Census science was politically debated, even attacked as unconstitutional. The Supreme Court had to weigh in twice in two years.

Despite the controversy, the census did its job—producing good numbers relevant to the multiple tasks for which those numbers are used, starting with the most basic constitutional obligation: reapportionment of Congress. Reapportionment saw ten states lose congressional seats, with two of these, New York and Pennsylvania, losing two each. Arizona, Florida, Georgia, and Texas increased their congressional delegation by two, and four other states each gained one seat. The census results reduced the political power of the industrial states of the North and increased it in the South and West.

Preparing for Census 2000

In preparing for the census 2000 the bureau took into account that easy-to-count households—for example married couples living together—were less numerous than in prior censuses, and hard-to-count households—single persons or those with unrelated people living together—proportionally more numerous. Immigration rates had increased in the previous 20 years; by 2000 the foreign-born represented 10 percent of America's population. Not all of these 28 million or so recent immigrants spoke English, not all of them were in the country legally, and not all understood or cared about the census. Response rates in all mail surveys had fallen sharply in the last two decades; there were growing privacy concerns. Civic engagement was in steady decline, as was trust in government.

This census atmosphere prompted a number of operational innovations. Households received three mailings: an advance notice, the form itself, and a postcard thanking those who had responded and reminding others to do so. Multiple ways were provided for response—by mail, phone, or the Internet; going to a walk-in assistance centers; or using the "Be Counted" forms placed in convenient community locations. Questionnaires were printed in five commonly used languages, in addition to English. Telephone assistance centers were similarly multilingual, as was the door-to-door enumerator staff in the follow-up phase to the mail-back operation.

Also new was a major paid advertising campaign. With a budget of $165 million, a highly concentrated advertising campaign increased awareness and encouraged high rates of cooperation. Paid advertisements were designed by a leading

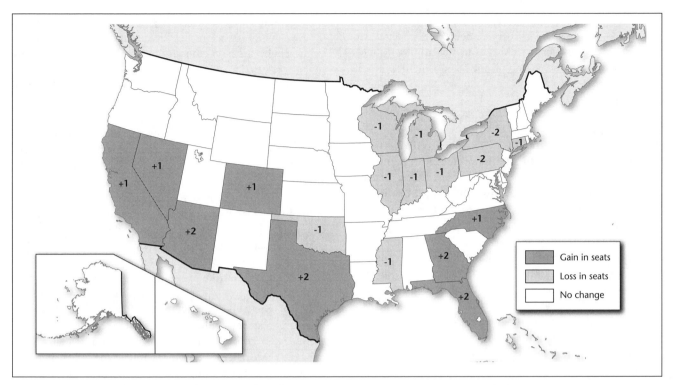

State Gains or Losses in the U.S. House of Representatives, 2000

Madison Avenue firm, working closely with specialty firms experienced in reaching minorities and recent immigrant groups. Approximately 50 languages were used across every major outlet available—TV, radio, newspapers, magazines, billboards, placement of posters in dozens of high visibility spots, and even an ad during the Super Bowl in January 2000.

The bureau also established an unprecedented number of partnerships with state and local governments, community groups, and businesses, totaling 140,000 in all. It had nearly 600 staff working full time on the partnership effort and a budget of $143 million for the program. Promotional dollars were also contributed by hundreds of local and state governments, private businesses, and other groups.

Public Cooperation with the 2000 Census

As the census got under way, a "1990 plus 5%" campaign was launched to challenge every city, county, and state to improve its 1990 census response rate by 5 percent. The key element in the campaign was to report every day on the census website the response rate for 39,000 jurisdictions in the country. These rates were widely cited in the press, with *USA Today* daily reporting the national totals as well as the response rate for each of the 50 states.

All this effort paid off well above expectations. The high response rate also improved the mail-back participation rate. The denominator for the response rate includes residences that are determined to be vacant in the door-to-door enumeration that follows the mail-back phase. The denominator for the participation rate excludes those households and is a better measure of overall final response. The census was

budgeted on the assumption of a mail-back participation rate of approximately 71 percent; the final result was 74 percent. This effectively halted a three-decade-long decline in census form return rates. During the phase of maximum publicity, the percentage of the population aware of the census exceeded 90 percent.

The Persistent Differential Undercount Challenge

Improved public cooperation with the census in the mail-back phase, and even in the door-to-door follow-up phase, can occur without making serious headway on the persistent problem of census coverage—that is, counting everyone in the country once, and only once, and in the right place. Censuses everywhere in the world are plagued by missing some households and counting others twice. A higher rate of the former than the latter produces a net undercount. Across the second half of the twentieth century, the U.S. census had steadily reduced this net undercount, a triumph of improved census-taking methodology.

Harder, however, was erasing the differential undercount problem—that is, missing some regions or some groups at higher rates than others. Because the benefits distributed on the basis of census counts—congressional seats and federal funds—are proportionate to population shares, a differential undercount necessarily produces unfair outcomes. Regions or groups included in the census proportionate to their true share of the total population are treated fairly; those counted at rates less than their true share are penalized—treated unfairly.

The differential undercount in America's census had been presented for a half-century in terms of its racial dimension, proportionately lower counts of minorities than of the white population. Consequently, it became deeply intertwined with the politics of racial justice. This was particularly pronounced as the 2000 census was being planned, and it figured heavily in partisan battles over census methodology and "sampling" in the decennial census.

Sampling in the Census Design

As usual, in 2000 all traditional methods available to the bureau would be used. In addition, the bureau considered two ways in which sampling might be used. The first was known as sampling for nonresponse follow-up—that is, sampling the population that failed to return a form in the mail. The plan involved maintaining a constantly updated record of the percentage of households reached in every census tract. Until at least 90 percent of the households had been counted, this effort would continue. When the 90 percent threshold was reached, the bureau would sample the remaining unenumerated households and concentrate its funds and expertise on reaching every household sampled. The results from the sample would then produce estimates of the size and characteristics of the nonsampled households. This, it was believed, would lower costs and increase accuracy.

Sampling was, secondly, planned for assessing the size and demographic composition of the minority groups differentially undercounted. The basic design involved a large post-enumeration survey, which would be used to adjust basic census numbers, at the block level, to ensure that any undercounted group was represented in the final census numbers proportionate to its actual share of the total population. This census design was announced in early 1996 and was directly challenged largely along partisan lines. Opposition focused on adjusting the differential undercount.

Partisan Politics and Supreme Court Ruling

The Democratic Party supported the use of sampling to improve the undercount. While recognizing that an increase in urban and minority populations would likely increase their number of electoral districts, Democrats emphasized how the differential undercount violated the constitutional mandate to count everyone, and they stressed that the census should include any statistical methods designed to improve its accuracy. The Republican Party was resolutely opposed to sampling, claiming that it was unconstitutional, that it lent itself to political manipulation, and that it was vulnerable to technical difficulties that might introduce more error than it removed.

In 1999 the dispute reached the Supreme Court, which ruled (5–4) that language in the census statute prohibited the Census Bureau from using sampling to produce state-by-state apportionment counts. It did not rule that sampling itself was unconstitutional, nor did the decision prohibit sampling and adjustment for purposes other than apportionment, such as drawing congressional district lines following apportionment. Consequently, it did not end the partisan battle; it shifted it to whether the adjusted data would be used in the redistricting process.

The Census under Scrutiny

Census operations came under intense scrutiny, fueled in large part by the suspicion among the Republican majority in Congress that the Clinton administration could manipulate the adjustment process and thereby increase the number of Democrats elected to Congress.

Beyond the bureau's own collection of eight different advisory committees, a number of congressional committees were given jurisdiction over one or another aspect of the census. As part of a compromise struck between the Congress and the White House during the legal and budgetary battles in 1998, the first ever Census Monitoring Board was also appointed. This board was evenly divided between Republicans and Democrats, had its own $3 million budget and professional staff, and held the tasks of monitoring the census, holding hearings, and periodically issuing reports on the census.

In addition, various agencies and government departments, including the General Accounting Office, the Office of Management and Budget, and the Commerce Department (the parent agency of the Bureau of the Census), all involved themselves in oversight and monitoring of census affairs. More than 10,000 local governments examined the bureau's address list and supplied corrections, while governments and community organizations across the country were quick to report to local media any problems detected in how well the census was going.

The Census Results

The census in 2000 was well funded. A Republican-led Congress, partly to deflect charges that it opposed sampling because it did not want a fair count of the nation's minorities, provided funding for the advertising and outreach campaign noted above. It also provided funding directed to reach the hard-to-count population. The outcome surprised many. Based on the comparison of the census and the post-enumeration survey, the net undercount was less than 1 percent. The differential undercount rates also dropped, though the key white-black difference was at 3 percent (a white overcount of 1.13 and a black undercount of 1.84).

There was some skepticism about these estimates, as the bureau did report technical problems in the post-enumeration survey and the adjustment methodology. The bureau therefore concluded that at least within the time available, it could not improve the census by sampling and statistically adjusting the results. This was an unexpected ending to a decade-long political controversy. Discussion of the use of sampling in the decennial environment has to date not resumed, though the American Community Survey is, of course, a sample, and that survey in turn uses sampling for nonresponse follow-up.

Privacy, Confidentiality, and Census Taking

Suspicion regarding the nature and confidentiality of the census was inflamed during Census 2000, when talk show hosts, local leaders, members of Congress, and even a presidential candidate suggested that the long form was intrusive and contained questions the government had no right to ask.

This flared up into a mini-crisis in the middle of taking the census, leading to outright refusal and high rates of skipping particular questions, such as income or amount of rent paid.

The Multiple-Race Option in Census 2000

The politics of social justice find in the census a powerful ally, since it provides the denominator against which to assess who is being given equal opportunity and who is not. Here the dramatic change in the 2000 census was the addition of the multiple-race option. Americans were no longer forced into a limited number of racial groups. Although only 6.8 million people used the multiple-race option in the 2000, a more fluid and contested racial classification emerged that will undoubtedly work its way into our increasingly diverse and multicultural society in profound ways.

The Census and Democracy in the Twenty-first Century

Fashioning democratic principles to govern a multicultural society in the twenty-first century will necessarily require a robust and impartial census. Census 2000 reflected the difficulties in achieving this goal. The long partisan fight over sampling and statistical adjustment threatened to undermine public trust in the Census Bureau as a politically neutral and high-quality statistical agency. The long-standing integrity of the census and the bureau held, but barely.

See also *American Community Survey: development to 2004; American Community Survey: introduction; Coverage evaluation; Decennial censuses: 1990 census; Decennial censuses: 2010 census; Litigation and the census; Race: questions and classifications.*

. . . . KENNETH PREWITT

BIBLIOGRAPHY

Citro, Constance F., Daniel L. Cork, and Janet L. Norwood, eds. Panel to Review the 2000 Census, National Research Council, *The 2000 Census: Counting under Adversity.* Washington, D.C.: The National Academies Press, 2004. Available at http://www.nap.edu/catalog.php?record_id=10907.

Thomas A. Louis, Thomas B. Jabine, and Marisa A. Gerstein, eds. Panel on Formula Allocations, National Research Council. *Statistical Issues in Allocating Funds by Formula.* Washington, D.C.: The National Academies Press, 2003.

Jones, Nicholas A., and Amy Symens Smith. "The Two or More Races Population: 2000. Census 2000 Brief (C2KBR/01-6)." Washington, D.C.: U.S. Census Bureau, November 2001.

Prewitt, Kenneth. *Politics and Science in Census Taking.* New York: Russell Sage Foundation; Washington, D.C.: Population Reference Bureau. 2003.

———. "The U.S. Decennial Census: Politics and Political Science." *The Annual Review of Political Science* 13 (May 2010): 246. http://polisci.annualreviews.org.

———. "What Is Political Interference in Federal Statistics?" In "The Federal Statistical System: Its Vulnerabilities Matter More Than You Think," ed. Kenneth Prewitt. *Annals of the American Academy of Political and Social Science* 631 (September 2010): 225–238.

Decennial Censuses: 2010 Census

The 2010 census was the 23rd census of the population of the United States. This census was the largest census effort in history and among the most methodologically and technologically sophisticated. It counted 308,745,538 people, an increase of 9.7 percent over the total counted in 2000 (the smallest percentage increase since 1940). Based on the census results, eight states gained one or more seats in the U.S. House of Representatives (Arizona, Florida, Georgia, Nevada, South Carolina, Texas, Utah, Washington), and ten states lost seats (Illinois, Iowa, Louisiana, Massachusetts, Michigan, Missouri, New Jersey, New York, Ohio, Pennsylvania). Prior to its completion, the 2010 census was also contentious (as many censuses have been) and the most expensive in the history of U.S. census taking.

Given the extensive and costly nature of the census process and the multitude of uses of census data, it is clearly essential to evaluate the 2010 census. At the time of this writing, results from demographic analysis indicate that the national census count was about the same as the median estimate derived from vital registrations of births, deaths, and estimated net legal and illegal immigration. However, such crucial elements as the post-enumeration sample survey for population groups and subnational geographic areas have yet to be completed for the 2010 census, so that an in-depth evaluation of the success of the census must await examination in future documents.

The 2010 Census Process

The 2010 census process unfolded largely as planned, despite the fact that the nonresponse follow-up (NRFU) procedures had to be markedly changed from what was originally intended earlier in the decade. The main processes for the 2010 census began with the Local Update of Census Addresses (LUCA) program, conducted between August 2007 and April 2008. Local jurisdictions submitted 38 million addresses, with 79 percent of these matching addresses already on the Census Bureau's Master Address File (MAF) and 21 percent, or roughly 8 million addresses, added as new records to the MAF, which was continuously updated during the decade from the U.S. Postal Service Delivery Sequence File.

During 2008 the bureau also opened 12 regional census offices in its 12 regional census areas and began the selection and opening of 150 early local census offices (LCOs), including an office in Puerto Rico, to support the address canvassing and group quarters validation operations. Address canvassing (AC) began in March of 2009 and was completed in July 2009, with group quarters validation beginning in September 2009 and extending through October. During August through December 2009, an additional 344 local census offices, including 8 LCOs in Puerto Rico, were opened to complete the infrastructure development needed for the census.

During AC, more than 140,000 field workers checked 144.8 million addresses using handheld computers that allowed them to capture global positioning system (GPS) coordinates for the units. Overall, the AC process took actions on 155.4 million entries, with about 63 percent verified as is; 13 percent identified as delete, duplicates, or nonresidential; 7 percent added to the MAF as new records; and 16 percent resulting in some change to an existing address. The end result was a MAF of approximately 134.4 million addresses to be used for enumeration. A comparison of the 2008 housing unit estimates extrapolated to 2009 with the corrected MAF found that the MAF included 2.8 million (2.1 percent) more units than the independent estimates. This compares with the 6 million (roughly 5 percent) more units on the 2000 MAF, compared with extrapolated independent estimates.

The main enumeration processes began in early 2010 and proceeded largely as planned. All enumeration activities (including mailout/mailback, Remote Alaska, update/enumerate, group quarters enumeration, shipboard vessel enumeration, nonresponse follow-up, and vacant/delete check) were completed by early September of 2010.

The largest of these activities, nonresponse follow-up (NRFU), is the process of sending an enumerator to addresses from which no response has yet been obtained. As this process began, there were 48.6 million housing units in the NRFU workload. About 2 million late mail returns were later eliminated, but, nevertheless, follow-up operations employed more than 600,000 persons at one time. Over the course of all operations, a total of 1.4 million positions were filled (some people filled more than one position).

The final population count was delivered to the president on December 21, 2010; delivery to the states of redistricting data began in February and was completed by April 1, 2011. Remaining tests and evaluations, including the Census Coverage Measurement to determine the net and gross level of undercount, will be completed by the end of 2012.

Despite challenges in the use of technology and in the development of some control systems, the operational phase of the 2010 census appears to have been successful. Given the long-term decline in responses to mail surveys, the 2010 census obtained a good mail response rate. As of mid-September 2010 the response rate was 64.6 percent, compared with 67.2 percent in 2000. However, because the denominator of the response rate includes all mailed forms and does not subtract those returned as undeliverable (which are largely vacant units, of which there were many more in 2010 than in 2000), the Census Bureau developed a new measure it called the participation rate, in which the denominator is adjusted for undeliverable forms. The 2010 mail participation rate was now estimated at 74 percent, compared with 74 percent for the short form in 2000. When both short and long forms of the 2000 census are included, the participation is lower than that of the short-form-only 2010 census. Whichever rate one utilizes, it is evident that the Census Bureau appears to have done a good job in convincing Americans to respond by mail, using both direct and targeted mailings, with 28 states meeting or exceeding Census 2000 rates and 11 states within one point of their 2000 rates.

2010 Census Innovations

The 2010 census was innovative in many respects. It introduced timely and recurring data collection efforts, used computer technology not previously available, and added steps to the data collection process that reflected methods long used in other survey data collection efforts but were new to the large-scale data collection involved in the census.

The American Community Survey. After several decades of combining a short form to obtain the items used for reapportionment and redistricting with a long form to collect a much more extensive set of data on socioeconomic and other variables from a sample of residents, the Census Bureau, with support from its user community, chose to implement the American Community Survey (ACS). One reason for the change was that Census Bureau professionals and user groups became convinced that if the long-form sample were not replaced, it threatened the timely completion and accuracy of the basic census products. The continuous, large-scale ACS became operational in 2005. (See articles in this volume on the history, content, methodology, and other aspects of the ACS.)

New and Improved Pre-census and Census Programs and Processes. Several pre-census procedures differed significantly in 2010 from predecessor censuses. For example, group quarters' locations were verified in the 2010 census, and the Master Address File was maintained throughout the intercensal period to improve its coverage and accuracy. The LUCA program, in which local jurisdictions are given the opportunity (under appropriate provisions to protect confidentiality) to review the MAF, was expanded to include a more comprehensive review of group quarters locations, and the materials to be used in reviews were improved. The Census Partnership Program, which hires local persons to promote the census and encourage participation through a variety of activities with local area residents and officials, was enhanced and expanded in 2010. Building on initial plans to hire approximately 700 partnership specialists across the county, American Recovery and Reinvestment Funds made it possible to increase that number to 2,700 partnership specialists.

The 2000 census was the first to use paid advertising to encourage response. The 2010 census represented a substantial increase in that effort, with over $350 million in general and targeted advertising being spent to advertise in a wide variety of venues, including additional funds for targeted advertising and the Census in Schools program.

Questionnaire Design and Administration. Dropping the long form from the 2010 census eliminated a major source of resistance to the census and allowed for the introduction of several innovations in the design and administration of the census questionnaire. The short-form questionnaire included two new questions that had not been included in previous censuses. One of these asked the person completing the form if there was anyone who was staying at the residence who was not listed (question 2), and the other (question 10) asked whether there was anyone living at the residence who was listed but who usually lived elsewhere. "Yes" answers to these questions triggered telephone follow-up to try to reduce the omission of household members on the form (to reduce undercount) and to avoid the listing of persons who were not members of the household (to reduce overcount).

The questionnaire was also printed in more languages than ever before, with the availability of the form in different languages noted on the material included with the mailing of the form. In addition, for the first time more than 12 million residences in census tracts with high concentrations of Spanish-speaking residents received bilingual (Spanish/English) questionnaires, and questionnaire assistance was provided in a more than 60 languages.

An innovation long overdue was the inclusion of a second mailing of a questionnaire to a targeted set of residences, including all 15 million addresses in MO/MB areas for which low response was expected and 25 million nonresponding addresses in areas for which medium response was expected. The use of a second questionnaire mailing has been found to improve response rates in many surveys used in a variety of other contexts but had not been seen as feasible owing to the large number of questionnaires involved and the operational complexity of implementing two mailings. With the elimination of the long form, and improvements in the printing industry, capacity was made available for this innovation. It worked effectively in the 2010 census and, along with reminder postcards and substantial advertising, resulted in a response rate equal to that in previous censuses.

Census Technology. The 2010 census was often heralded as the census that would become fully automated. Long known for its development of computer technology (having employed the first civilian computer in history, mark-sensing technology, and mapping systems such as the Topologically Integrated Geographic Encoding and Referencing [TIGER] system), the Census Bureau engaged in an ambitious process to use handheld computers for address canvassing (AC) and nonresponse follow-up (NRFU). Because the census is a census of housing units from which data on households and their members are obtained, ensuring a good census requires a complete, and nonduplicative, list of occupied housing units. AC, which involves verification of the existence and occupancy of units at each address, is critical. Similarly, the NRFU process, which involves attempts to obtain answers to the census questionnaire from households who did not return mailed questionnaires, is of vital importance.

Preplanning for the 2010 census had incorporated the use of handheld computers for both AC and NRFU. The utility of using such technology was evident. Responses could be electronically and nearly instantaneously transferred to central data processing, exact locations for housing units could be obtained using GPS technology, and whether considering data on the number and location of housing units (from AC) or on basic characteristics of the population (from NRFU), the saving in labor and in paper processing and handling could be extensive.

Difficulties in the comprehensive use of the handhelds became evident in early 2008, when the director, deputy director, and a special adviser to the director found that the pretests of the handhelds showed unacceptable levels of performance that could threaten the entire census. Over a period of a month, a task force created by the director and chaired by a former acting director and deputy director revealed that

it was unlikely the two major tasks of address canvassing and nonresponse follow-up could be completed successfully with the use of the handhelds. The final set of recommendations of the task force (reviewed and endorsed by a task force of experts impaneled by the secretary of commerce and several sets of outside experts) was that the handheld technology should be used in AC but that NRFU should return to a paper-based operation. Although this required an extensive and expedited development of numerous census processes and systems, including a paper-based operations control system (PBOCS) and a substantial increase in budget, it was a late-course correction that was essential if the census was not to be delayed.

Although not as extensive as had been hoped, technology use and development occurred in all census operations with improvements in address canvassing, questionnaire processing, census mapping, and other processes.

Challenges of the 2010 Census: Lessons Learned and Questions Remaining

As the distribution of 2010 census data has proceeded, it is possible to identify some of what has been learned from the 2010 census processes that should be considered in planning for the 2020 census and beyond. Given that most evaluations of the census have not been completed, there are clearly additional lessons yet to be learned that cannot be delineated here.

The Challenge of Multiple Sources. The 2010 census is the first census in modern times in which the collection of a complete head count, which is used not only for reapportionment and redistricting but also for updated population estimates throughout the decade, was separate from the collection of small-area characteristics for fund allocation, program planning, and many other purposes in the American Community Survey. How the differences in residence rules, reference periods, sample size (comparing the ACS with the old long-form sample), and other dimensions of the two data sets may affect their intended uses is not yet fully understood. A concerted research program to examine these differences methodologically and statistically should be a critical priority in the coming years.

The Challenges of Security and Accessibility. Twice during the 2010 planning process, consideration was given to allowing response through the use of the Internet, which was used on a very small scale in the 2000 census. Given the widespread use of the Internet for financial and other transactions, it appeared illogical not to allow response to the census through the Internet. However, the risk to public cooperation with the census from an inadvertent release of confidential data during the census process was obvious, and the potential for a breach, if Internet access were to be allowed, was deemed to be relatively high by experts from the most sophisticated security firms in the nation. The next census must allow such access, and potential problems related to it must be a major area of research between 2010 and 2020.

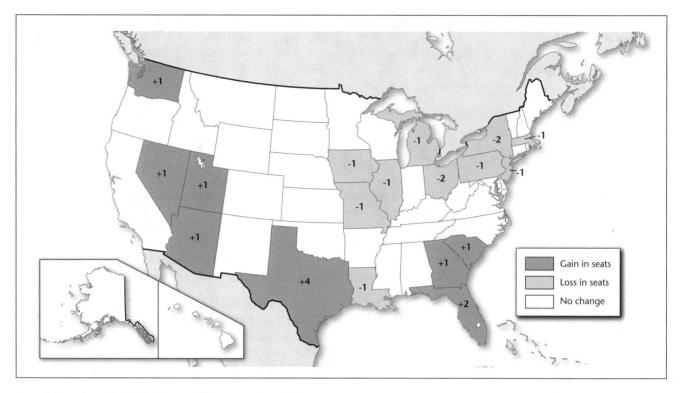

State Gains or Losses in the U.S. House of Representatives, 2010

The Challenge of Resources. The costs per household for completing the census continue to increase. In 1970 the cost per housing unit in 2009 dollars was $17; it was $33 by 1980, $43 by 1990, and $70 by 2000. The actual cost of the 2010 census was about $95 per housing unit, and it could be 30–60 percent higher by 2020 (assuming continuation of the trends since 1980). Although there is no doubt that the data are essential for the operation of our participatory democracy, attempts to reduce costs are essential. This is a consideration that will weigh on the decisions of future leaders of the census and of future administrations and Congress.

The Need for Expanded Research. The Census Bureau has recently raised the prominence and increased the professional leadership of its research directorate. This is a major step forward, but more remains to be done. The bureau once played a leading role not only in statistics but also in demography, survey research, geographic analysis, and other areas. This preeminence paid dividends in the ability of the bureau to recruit the best and most able in all these areas. Recruitment has remained strong, but the bureau will do well to further increase its research effort. The U.S. Census Bureau methods and procedures have been the gold standard of international census activities, and keeping that position will require continued investment in the science of census taking.

Conclusion

The 2010 census has been successfully completed, thereby continuing a tradition that is now more than 230 years long. Each decade the people of the United States through a temporary or permanent census office have completed what no other nation has been able to do for such a long period of time, and that is to create an ongoing set of data that serve as the basis for their representative government. For each census there have been challenges met and challenges passed on to future censuses. The same is true of the 23rd census of the United States. Nevertheless, through the support of the American people and the expertise of census professionals, the count of Americans in every part of the nation has been produced to guide the government for yet another decade of U.S. history.

See also *Address list development; Advertising the census; Apportionment and districting; Census testing; Content determination; Coverage evaluation; Demographic analysis; Enumeration: field procedures; Enumeration: group quarters; Internet data collection; Post-enumeration survey.*

. . . .   STEVE H. MURDOCK AND ROBERT M. GROVES

BIBLIOGRAPHY

Anderson, Margo. *The American Census: A Social History.* New Haven, Conn.: Yale University Press, 1988.

Anderson, Margo, and Stephen Fienberg. *Who Counts? The Politics of Census-Taking in Contemporary America.* New York: Russell Sage, 1999; revised and updated 2001.

Eckler, A. Ross. *The Bureau of the Census.* New York: Praeger, 1972.

Groves, Robert H. "2010 Census: A Status Update of Key Decennial Operations." Testimony before the Senate Subcommittee on Federal Financial Management, Government Information, Federal Services and International Security, Committee on Homeland Security and Governmental Affairs, October 7, 2009.

Hillygus, Sunshine, Norman H. Nie, Kenneth Prewitt, and Heili Pals. *The Hard Count: The Political and Social Challenges of Census Mobilization.* New York: Russell Sage Foundation, 2006.

Jackson, Arnold. "2010 Census Progress Report." Paper presented at the meeting of the Texas Economic and Demographic Association, Houston, Tex., September 16, 2010.

Murdock, Steve H. "Critical Budget Issues Affecting the 2010 Census." Testimony before the House Subcommittee on Information Policy, Census and National Archives of the Committee on Oversight and Government Reform, July 30, 2008.

———. "2010 Census Status Update." Testimony before the House Committee on Oversight and Government Reform, June 11, 2008.

———. "Census in Peril: Getting the 2010 Decennial Back on Track." Testimony before the U.S. Senate Committee of Homeland Security and Governmental Affairs, March 8, 2008.

National Research Council *Reengineering the 2010 Census: Risks and Challenges.* Committee on National Statistics, Panel on Research on Future Census Methods. Edited by Daniel L. Cork, Michael L. Cohen, and Benjamin F. King. Washington, D.C.: The National Academies Press, 2004.

———. Committee on National Statistics, *Once, Only Once and in the Right Place.* Panel on Residence Rules in the Decennial Census. Edited by Daniel L. Cork and Paul Voss. Washington, D.C.: The National Academies Press, 2006.

———. Committee on National Statistics, Panel on the Functionality and Usability of Data from the American Community Survey. *Using the American Community Survey: Benefits and Challenges.* Edited by Constance F. Citro and Graham Kalton. Washington, D.C.: The National Academies Press, 2007.

———. Committee on National Statistics, Panel on the Design of the 2010 Census Program of Evaluations and Experiments. *Envisioning the 2020 Census.* Edited by Lawrence D. Brown, Daniel L. Cork, Michael L. Cohen, and Constance F. Citro. Washington, D.C.: The National Academies Press, 2010.

U.S. Census Bureau. *American Community Survey: Design and Methodology.* Washington, D.C.: U.S. Department of Commerce, 2006.

———. "Demographic Analysis Tables and Figures." Released at the 2010 Demographic Analysis Conference, Washington, D.C., December 6, 2010.

Decennial Censuses: 2020 Census

Although the constitutionally mandated objective of the decennial census seems straightforward—to enumerate the population for reapportionment of the seats in the House of Representatives—the form and conduct of the census enumeration have been subject to controversy and to the demographic, social, economic, and political trends within American society. In the early 21st century, apprehension regarding government intrusion, logistical hurdles related to increasing race and ethnic diversity, persistent issues regarding undocumented immigrants, and more complex household and living arrangements all combined to make the 2010 census among the most challenging ever. These considerations, combined with observable declines in the response rate on all surveys, will bring serious enumeration challenges in the 2020 census.

The cost of the 2010 census was about 40 percent higher than for 2000, with a total expenditure in the range of $12.9 billion. If current methods were carried forward to 2020, estimates are that the cost of the decennial census would rise to some $25 billion, which is widely regarded as untenable. Even if the dollars were appropriated, the Census Bureau and outside experts alike have expressed doubt that the quality of the census could be improved using current methods. Further, there is general agreement that the current census process is not nearly as cost efficient as it needs to be. As a result, a consensus emerged after the 2010 census that the entire process needed to be fundamentally revamped.

In response, the Census Bureau adopted a more empirical approach aimed at making a series of decisions in a number of major methodological and operational areas, using a process that employs dozens of small research projects. The idea was to evaluate operational choices, early on in the decade, which could then be developed into an integrated package on which an evaluation of efficiencies and costs could be based. This approach permits a plan for 2020 to be built based on the balance between the need for both high-quality data and reduced cost while managing what are the inherent risks of a large, complex operation. This research-oriented approach was strongly advocated by the National Research Council's Panel on the Design of the 2010 Census Program of Evaluations and Experiments. It represents a sea change from the past, when disparate and more ad hoc evaluations of individual procedures resulted in risky and incremental changes, the costs and benefits of which were not clearly known.

Current thinking is that changes are needed in several key areas of census procedures and operations, with an overall vision of a census that makes better use of technological innovations and alternative sources of data, permitting movement away from the current labor-intensive, paper-driven enterprise. For the 2020 census, in broadest terms, this means:

1. Creating a process to update the address list which is less costly and produces higher quality results.
2. Establishing more efficient mix of response modes
3. Engineering the system of field data collection in a more cost-efficient way

The Address List

The Census Bureau's objective in the decennial census is to count all residents of the United States and to attach each person to a place—an address or facility. Residents need to be tied to a place because the determination of political representation requires it. This makes the construction of a list of addresses the cornerstone of the decennial census.

The Master Address File (MAF) is a list of housing units, each record consisting of an exact address—number, street, and apartment. Each response in the decennial census needs to be tied to a specific geographic reference point to conduct congressional reapportionment among the states and for drawing political districts based on population within states (redistricting). Therefore, while being counted is essential, it is equally critical that those who are counted are reliably put in a valid geographic location.

The current system of MAF updates is limited to accessing data from the U.S. Postal Service, along with a program called the Community Address Updating System (CAUS) for rural areas. While useful, the Census Bureau has found that the Postal Service updates are not sufficient to convey all of the information required on new housing or housing that has changed. As a consequence, the Census Bureau in the past has had to conduct a complete canvass of all addresses in the nation prior to the enumeration.

The once-a-decade canvass is one reason for the high price tag of decennial operations. At present, the Census Bureau is evaluating the efficiency of its address-updating operations, including the Address Canvass, Postal Service updates, Local Update of Census Addresses (LUCA) program, New Construction Program, Vacant/Delete Check, and a variety of other operations to see which are effective and cost efficient. One of the most engaging options is based on the need for a continuously updated MAF. After the 1990 census, a decision was made to create a separate survey for the content that had been collected on the census long form, which was part of the decennial census. As a result the American Community Survey (ACS) was created. The survey goes to about 3 million households annually, which are selected from the MAF. This means that the representativeness of the survey is contingent on an updated MAF. Continuous updating would require a cooperative agreement with local governments to satisfy Title 13 disclosure requirements, where local records (for example, property tax information, certificates of occupancy) are provided to the Census Bureau on a regular basis. This sharing of information on a continuous basis may be far more cost effective in updating the MAF. The goal would be to preclude the need for a one-shot canvass of the nation in the year prior to the census enumeration and to provide the Census Bureau with local sources of information to better update the MAF.

Modes of Response and New Avenues for Nonresponse Follow-up

In addition to the fact that achieving compliance with a request to mail back a census form has grown more difficult with time, there is the very real question as to whether the current mailout/mailback strategy needs to be augmented with other modes of contact with the nation's residents. Witness the declining importance of the U.S. Postal Service as a vehicle for personal communication and business, in a society where daily living has become increasingly electronic and paperless. In response, the Census Bureau is examining research on ways to engage respondents via electronic means, such as contacting households to inform them how and when to respond to the census, by sending e-mail or voice mail for example. Social networking sites on the Internet may provide avenues for response, provided that the disclosure and address list hurdles could be overcome (for example, matching electronic addresses from e-mail and cell phones to physical addresses). Secure sites, where respondents could enter information, have been used successfully in other countries, and the application of this approach in the United States is being investigated. One goal could be to match response options to the everyday infrastructure that people use to conduct their lives by making electronic modes of response that are commonly used to pay bills or check the status of a credit card account available for answering the census.

At the same time, the Census Bureau has been investigating the means by which nonresponse follow-up can be more efficiently conducted. While studies on the effectiveness of the current nonresponse follow-up methods will be done for 2010, there is already consensus that the current practice of conducting in-person follow-up by multiple visits to a home using paper questionnaires is not very cost efficient. The evidence is not clear that the seemingly endless cycle of follow-up (up to six times in most places) produces quality data, especially when "last resort" measures are implemented through the use of proxy responses from neighbors. Instead, the Census Bureau is evaluating the use of administrative records that can be employed to shorten the follow-up process and preclude the use of "last resort" measures, through the use of databases that may yield higher-quality data at the same or less cost. It is likely that recordkeeping systems will continue to evolve to a point where substantial segments of the population can be "counted" by virtue of their inclusion in selected databases, such as those for Medicare recipients or persons residing in selected facilities. The Census Bureau continues to conduct research on record-matching technologies to identify those situations where enough content and record standardization exist to implement a "count" through the use of administrative recordkeeping systems. In addition, there is research being conducted on the efficacy of using other surveys, such as the ACS, to "fill-in-the-holes" for households as an alternative to multiple in-person visits in nonresponse follow-up.

It is also clear that the concept of "place of residence" is far too vague and amorphous for what is needed to produce high-quality data and the rules that have been developed to define a person's "residence" have become more and more tenuous and problematic with time. This is a function of different living arrangements and residential preferences, making it more and more difficult to definitively put people in a single place. Increasingly, children are involved in more complex residential living situations, frequently spending time in multiple locations with each parent or with grandparents. There is often confusion over the residences of students and multiple residences in the general population, especially with displacement as a result of human-created or natural disasters and economic dislocation. With multiple residences many census respondents become easily confused about where they are supposed to be enumerated. This has become an intractable problem that is likely to grow more complicated in the years ahead.

The National Research Council's Panel on Residence Rules in the Decennial Census has found that current census residence rules are too complex and difficult to communicate, from the standpoint of both enumerator training and those who respond. This was attributed to lack of a clear conceptual base and concise focus on what constitutes residence. As a result, research is being conducted on a "questions, not instructions" approach that emphasizes the gathering of information, for example on where children or spouses lived throughout the year. This would shift the burden of deciding what constitutes "usual residence" from respondents to the Census Bureau. The census form would collect sufficient information from respondents to allow the bureau to determine residence during processing and editing. Therefore, instead of "instructing" respondents and enumerators to determine residence a priori, residence can be determined "after the fact," using information ascertained on the questionnaire itself.

Technology and Field Data Collection

The decennial census is a huge engineering and logistical operation involving hundreds of processes that are deeply interconnected. The 2010 census was conducted through almost 500 local census offices that supervised the work of several hundred thousand field enumerators. While a standardized approach to training and operations is an important goal, the Census Bureau recognizes that tailored local approaches are frequently the key to success. The dilemma, then, is to engineer enough centralized control to standardize operations while permitting some degree of local autonomy to take care of "nonstandard" situations. Determining the optimal point on this continuum depends on the outcome of several cost-efficiency studies, based on the 2010 census, which involve the technologies available to track and support field infrastructure. A hybrid approach with some level of decentralized decision making and enough centralized control to encourage standardization is the likely goal; however, the Census Bureau must have technology that permits it to institute such a plan and to permit real-time evaluation for quality control.

Already apparent is that for those households enumerated in person the transfer of data to and from paper forms has required substantial resources that may be better spent elsewhere. The use of handheld computer devices would permit nonresponse follow-up to be paperless, making the path from enumeration in the field to data capture less labor intensive. Information from questionnaires would be sent directly from the handheld devices to data capture centers for preliminary evaluation, with any anomalies reported back for immediate remediation (for example, missing questionnaire responses). The technologies are already in place to conduct the enumeration in this fashion. Better ability to manage contracts and develop sound business practices with the private sector should enable the Census Bureau to maximize the potential benefits of this technology for use in 2020.

See also *Address list development; Data capture; Enumeration: field procedures; Geographic Information Systems (GIS); Internet data collection.*

. . . .   JOSEPH J. SALVO AND
HERMANN HABERMANN

BIBLIOGRAPHY

National Research Council, Committee on National Statistics, Division of Behavioral and Social Sciences and Education, Panel to Review the 2010 Census. *Change and the 2020 Census: Not Whether But How.* Edited by Thomas M. Cook, Janet L. Norwood, and Daniel L. Cork. Washington, D.C.: The National Academies Press, 2011.

National Research Council, Committee on National Statistics, Division of Behavioral and Social Sciences and Education, Panel on the Design of the 2010 Census Program of Evaluations and Experiments. *Envisioning the 2020 Census.* Edited by Lawrence D. Brown, Michael L. Cohen, Daniel L. Cork, and Constance F. Citro. Washington, D.C.: The National Academies Press, 2010.

National Research Council, Committee on National Statistics, Division of Behavioral and Social Sciences and Education, Panel on Residence Rules in the Decennial Census. *Once, Only Once, and in the Right Place: Residence Rules in the Decennial Census.* Edited by Daniel L. Cork and Paul R. Voss. Washington, D.C.: The National Academies Press. 2006.

Obenski, Sally M., and D. H. Weinberg. "Early 2020 Census Planning." Paper presented to the Census Advisory Committees, Washington D.C., 2010.

Demographic Analysis

In the United States, methods of demographic analysis have historically been used for measuring coverage trends between censuses and differences in coverage by age, sex, and race at the national level. Demographic analysis (DA) estimates support the notion of a long-term reduction in the census net undercount rate over the last sixty years, yet demographic analysis also indicates a persistent and disproportionate undercount of certain demographic groups (such as black men).

Demographic analysis represents a macro-level approach to evaluating censuses, where analytic estimates of differences from the census are derived by comparing aggregate sets of data, or counts. In general, DA population estimates are developed for the census date by analysis of various types of demographic data essentially independent of the census, such as administrative statistics on births, deaths, and immigration; estimates of emigration and immigration not measured by the administrative statistics; and Medicare data. The difference between the DA estimated population and the census count is then assumed to represent an estimate of the net census undercount (or overcount).

Description of the Demographic Analysis Method

The particular analytic procedure used to develop the DA estimates for the various demographic subgroups depends primarily on the nature and availability of the required data. Two techniques were used to produce the estimates for 2010, one for the population under age 65 and another for the population 65 and over.

Age Group Components

Ages under 65. DA estimates for the population below age 65 are based on the compilation of historical estimates of the components of population change: births (B), deaths (D), immigration (I), and emigration (E). Presuming that the components are measured accurately, the population estimates (P_{0-64}) are derived by the basic demographic accounting equation applied to each birth cohort:

$$P_{0-64} = B - D + I - E$$

The actual calculations are carried out for single-year birth cohorts. For example, the estimate of the population age 40 on April 1, 2010, is based on births from April 1969 to March 1970 (adjusted for underregistration), reduced by deaths to the cohort in each year between 1970 and 2010, and increased in increments by estimated immigration and emigration of the cohort over the 40-year period.

The historical data on births come from the vital registration system. These data have been available for all states since about 1933. The extent of under-registration has been empirically quantified, and correction factors are used. Births represent by far the largest component in the equation above. The component of deaths is based on administrative records. These records are relatively complete. Data on immigration up to 2000 come primarily from the Department of Homeland Security's Office of Immigration Statistics (formerly known as the Immigration and Naturalization Service), as well as the analysis of census data on the foreign-born. Estimates of immigration since 2000 are based on data on the foreign-born from the American Community Survey. The number of emigrants is estimated using analytical methods. Estimates of emigrants and undocumented immigrants are the two components subject to the greatest uncertainty.

Age 65 and Over. Administrative data on aggregate Medicare enrollments are used to estimate the population age 65 and over (P_{65+}):

$$P_{65+} = M + m$$

where M is the aggregate Medicare enrollment and m is the estimate of under-enrollment. Although Medicare enrollment data are generally presumed to be quite accurate, adjustments are made to the basic data to account for groups who are omitted and to remove persons erroneously included (deceased). For 2010, two sets of estimates were developed for the population age 65–74, one based on the component method used for people under age 65 and the other based on Medicare enrollment. It will be possible to compare the two methods for more and more of the population age 65 and older in subsequent censuses.

Development of Historical Estimates for Multiple Censuses

The foundation of the demographic method is the logical consistency and relation of the underlying data. With the use of components of change (births, deaths, and net immigration), the estimated population for a birth cohort can be carried forward through time for comparison with each census as the cohort ages (for example, the cohort of people who were age 0–4 in 1950, 10–14 in 1960, 20–24 in 1970, 30–34 in 1980, 40–44 in 1990, 50–54 in 2000, and 60–64 in 2010).

The multiple series of DA estimates for cohorts across censuses are linked through the components of population change. This linkage of the estimates provides a consistent basis to judge changes in patterns of the differences over time and to assess the plausibility of the demographic estimates themselves.

Limitations of the Demographic Estimates

The aggregate administrative data and estimates in the equations above are corrected for various types of errors. Many assumptions go into the estimation process, some of which can be validated and some of which are based on quite limited information.

Births are by far the largest component of population change involved in the DA system; thus even relatively small errors in the estimates of births and the assumptions used to correct for under-registration can have significant effects. The adjustments for birth under-registration are based on three tests of registration completeness (1940, 1950, and 1964–1968). The estimated level of completeness was 92.5 in 1940 (81.9 percent for black births), 97.9 in 1950 (93.7 for black births), and 99.2 by 1964–1968. Factors for other years are derived by interpolation and extrapolation. In particular, the estimated number of black births depends on the quality of the correction factors. An investigation and subsequent revision of the 1940 birth registration results led to a downward adjustment to the time series of black births in the years 1935–1950 and lowered the estimated net undercount for those black cohorts. Also, algorithms need to be developed to assign the race of the child (the birth certificate gives only the race of the parent). Inconsistencies in the race classification of the birth with the reported race of the child in the census is another source of error in the DA estimates.

With the exception of a correction for infant deaths occurring in years prior to 1960, death statistics are used without any adjustments for misreporting of age, sex, or race, or for under-registration. Immigration and emigration, while smaller overall components than births and deaths, are subject to more relative error because of the greater uncertainty of some specific estimated elements.

The overall accuracy of the demographic estimates depends on the quality of the demographic data and the corrections. The internal consistency of the demographic estimates permits trends and changes in enumeration patterns over time to be estimated more precisely than the exact level of net undercount or overcount in any given census.

Historical Trends, 1960–2000

Table 1 presents estimates of percent net undercount as measured by DA for the decennial censuses from 1960 to 2000. The net undercount in the census of 2000 was estimated to be 0.1 percent, barely different from the census count and well below the estimated 3.1 percent undercount in 1960. The estimated undercount has declined for blacks (from 6.6 percent in 1960 to 2.8 percent in 2000) and nonblacks (2.7 percent net undercount to a 0.3 percent net overcount). Net undercount estimates are not yet available for population groups from the census of 2010, but the midpoint of the range of DA estimates released in early December 2010 differs by less than 0.1 percent from the total population count released later in that month.

Despite the overall declines in the implied net undercount, the rate for blacks has remained persistently higher than the rate for nonblacks in each census between 1940 and 2000. In fact, the excess of the estimated net undercount rate for blacks has hovered in the range of 3.1 to 4.4 percentage points over these censuses (see last row of Table 1).

Table 1. Demographic Analysis Estimates of Percentage Net Undercount, by Race: 1960–2000

RACE	1960	1970	1980	1990	2000
Percent					
Total	3.1	2.7	1.2	1.6	0.1
Black	6.6	6.5	4.5	5.5	2.8
Nonblack	2.7	2.2	0.8	1.1	−0.3
Percentage Point Difference					
Black − Nonblack	3.9	4.3	3.7	4.4	3.1

NOTE: A minus sign denotes a net overcount.

SOURCES: 1960–1980 for Total, Black, and Nonblack from J. Gregory Robinson, Table 6 in U.S. Census Bureau, "Accuracy and Coverage Evaluation: Demographic Analysis Results," in *DSSD Census 2000 Procedures and Operations Memorandum Series B-4*, March 1, 2001.

1990–2000 for Total, Black, and Nonblack from J. Gregory Robinson, Table 6 in U.S. Census Bureau, "ESCAP II. Accuracy and Coverage Evaluation: Demographic Analysis Results," in *Executive Steering Committee For A.C.E. Policy II, Report No. 1*, October 13, 2001.

Table 2 gives a perspective on how the relatively high estimated net undercounts for black men and black children contribute disproportionately to the well-known differential undercount for all blacks. The pattern of relatively high undercounts of adult black men age 20 to 64 in 2000 repeated the pattern from 1960 to 1990. Indeed, crude historical demographic estimates of percentage net undercount that extend back to 1880 demonstrate the persistent nature of the net undercount for this group. Note, however, that the estimated

Table 2. Demographic Analysis Estimates of Percentage Net Undercount for Blacks: 1960–2000

RACE, SEX, AND AGE	1960	1970	1980	1990	2000
Percent					
Total	6.6	6.5	4.5	5.5	2.8
Black Men 20–64	13.4	13.1	11.3	11.3	8.4
Black (0–9)	5.4	8.1	7.0	7.2	3.4
Other Black	4.4	2.9	0.4	1.9	−0.4

NOTE: A minus sign denotes a net overcount.

SOURCES: 1990–2000 for Black Men 20–64, from Table 7 in J. Gregory Robinson, Arjun Adlakha, and Kirsten K. West, "Coverage of Population in Census 2000: Results from Demographic Analysis," paper presented at the Annual Meeting of the Population Association of America, Atlanta, Georgia, May 8–11, 2002.

1960–1980 for Black Men 20–64, Black (0–9), and Other Black from Howard R. Hogan and J. Gregory Robinson, Table 2, in *What the Census Bureau's Coverage Evaluation Programs Tell Us about Differential Undercount* (Richmond, Va.: Bureau of the Census Research Conference on Undercounted Ethnic Populations, 1993).

1990–2000 for Black (0–9) and Other Black from unpublished tabulations.

net undercount was reduced substantially from 1990 to 2000 for all groups of blacks.

History of Demographic Analysis

Demographic analysis has a long history in the Census Bureau. The first demographic-based analysis of the census counts focused on the 1940 census and specific demographic subgroups. One study by the Bureau of the Census in 1944 indicated significant differences in the coverage of black and nonblack children. Another study, by Daniel O. Price, examined the completeness of the 1940 census for young men age 21 through 35 using figures from the first compulsory draft registration, which started on October 16, 1940. Price created comparable census figures by using demographic analysis to age the census count on April 1 to October 16, 1940. Black men were estimated to be undercounted by 13 percent, compared to 3.1 percent for all men in that age group.

In the 1950s, Ansley Coale used the demographic accounting equation (combining birth, death, and migration statistics) to create an estimate of the true population against which the 1950 census could be evaluated. Coale used different analytic procedures for different age groups and assumed age misstatements and errors of omission to form similar patterns from one census to the next. He was the first to identify age-sex patterns of coverage as well as race differences.

In 1966, Jacob S. Siegel and Melvin Zelnik evaluated the completeness of the 1960 census using the DA method. Again, different analytical procedures were applied to different age-sex groups. The age, sex, and race patterns of estimated undercount for 1960 were found to be similar to those in the 1950 census. Up to age 50, DA indicated that the enumeration was less complete for men than for women. Up to age 60 or 65, the enumeration of nonwhites was less complete than the enumeration of whites.

By the 1970 census, the DA results had become a standard for measuring trends and differentials in coverage. Other developments occurred around this time. Data from the Medicare system became available for improving the DA estimates of the population age 65 and over. Finally, by using state-of-birth data, subnational estimates were developed for the first time.

The DA methodology continued to be developed, new data sources were incorporated, and estimated components of change were improved for the coverage evaluations of the 1980 and the 1990 censuses. In 1980, an explicit estimate of the number of undocumented residents was included as a demographic component for the first time. In 1990, explicit measures of uncertainty in the DA estimates were developed.

Research on methodological improvements and refinements to the DA estimates continued with the 2000 Census. Considerably more attention was paid to estimating the component of net international migration. The DA program was expanded to produce estimates on a timely basis (during the census process) and to extend the scope of demographic indicators below the national level. The program also included the use of demographic benchmarks, such as housing-unit

Table 3. Range of Demographic Analysis Estimates of the U.S. Resident Population, 2010

LOW	LOW MIDDLE	MIDDLE	HIGH MIDDLE	HIGH
305,684,000	307,415,000	308,475,000	310,038,000	312,713,000

NOTE: The Census 2010 U.S. resident count, released December 21, 2010, is 308,745,538.

SOURCE: Table 3 in U.S. Census Bureau, "Demographic Analysis Tables and Figures," released at 2010 Demographic Analysis Conference, Washington, D.C., December 6, 2010.

estimates, as a tool to provide assessments early in the census process.

The 2010 DA estimates for the total population and age, sex, and black/nonblack groups were released on December 6, 2010, just a few weeks prior to the release of the census counts for the 50 states for reapportionment. The 2010 DA effort included a sensitivity analysis of the impact of altering various assumptions used in the DA estimates. While the sensitivity analysis does not provide a measure of the accuracy of the DA estimate based on an explicit probability model, it should allow for a meaningful assessment of the plausible range of the DA estimates. Given the uncertainty of the DA estimates, the differences from the 2010 Census counts will not be treated as direct measures of net coverage. Rather, the pattern of the DA and the 2010 Census differences by age, sex, and race will be assessed for evidence of relative weaknesses in census coverage for particular demographic groups. The range of 2010 DA estimates is shown in Table 3.

See also *Coverage evaluation; Federal administrative records*

. . . . J. GREGORY ROBINSON AND KIRSTEN K. WEST

BIBLIOGRAPHY

Bureau of the Census. "Standardized Fertility Rates and Reproduction Rates." *Population. Differential Fertility, 1940 and 1910. Sixteenth Census of the United States: 1940.* Washington, D.C.: U.S. Department of Commerce, U.S. Bureau of the Census, 1944.

Coale, Ansley J. "The Population of the United States in 1950 Classified by Age, Sex and Color—A Revision of Census Figures." *Journal of the American Statistical Association* 50, no. 269 (1955): 16–54.

Fay, Robert E., Jeffrey S. Passel, and J. Gregory Robinson. "The Coverage of Population in the 1980 Census." In *Evaluation and Research Reports.* PHC80-E4. Washington, D.C.: U.S. Government Printing Office, 1988.

Himes, Christine L., and Clifford C. Clogg. "An Overview of Demographic Analysis as a Method for Evaluating Census Coverage in the United States." *Population Index* 58, no. 4 (1992): 587–607.

Hogan, Howard R., and J. Gregory Robinson. *What the Census Bureau's Coverage Evaluation Programs Tell Us about Differential Undercount.* Richmond, Va.: Bureau of the Census Research Conference on Undercounted Ethnic Populations, 1993.

Passel, Jeffrey S. "Age-Period-Cohort Analysis of Census Undercount Rates for Race-Sex Groups, 1940–1980: Implications for the Method of Demographic Analysis." In *Proceedings of the Social Statistics Section of the American Statistical Association*, 326–331. Washington, D.C.: American Statistical Association, 1991.

———. *Demographic Analysis: A Report on Its Utility for Adjusting the 1990 Census.* Washington, D.C.: The Urban Institute, 1990.

Price, Daniel O. "A Check on Underenumeration in the 1940 Census." *American Sociological Review* 12 (1947): 44–49.

Robinson, J. Gregory. "Accuracy and Coverage Evaluation: Demographic Analysis Results." In *DSSD Census 2000 Procedures and Operations Memorandum Series B-4*. Washington, D.C.: U.S. Bureau of the Census, 2001.

———. "ESCAP II. Accuracy and Coverage Evaluation: Demographic Analysis Results." In *Executive Steering Committee For A.C.E. Policy II, Report No. 1*. Washington, D.C.: U.S. Bureau of the Census, 2001.

Robinson, J. Gregory, Arjun Adlakha, and Kirsten K. West. "Coverage of Population in Census 2000: Results from Demographic Analysis." Paper presented at the Annual Meeting of the Population Association of America, Atlanta, Ga., May 8–11, 2002.

Robinson, J. Gregory, Bashir Ahmed, and Edward W. Fernandez. "Demographic Analysis as an Expanded Program for Early Coverage Evaluation of the 2000 Census." In *Proceedings of the Annual Research Conference*, 166–200. Arlington, Va.: U.S. Bureau of the Census, 1993.

Robinson, J. Gregory, Bashir Ahmed, Prithwis Das Gupta, and Karen A. Woodrow. "Estimation of Population Coverage in the 1990 United States Census Based on Demographic Analysis." *Journal of the American Statistical Association* 88 (1993): 1061–1071.

Robinson, J. Gregory, and Howard Hogan. "Differential Coverage in the United States Census of Population: An Historical Review." *Proceedings of Statistics Canada Symposium 90* (1990): 67–78.

Jacob S. Siegel. "Estimates of Coverage of Population by Sex, Race, and Age: Demographic Analysis." In *Census of Population and Housing: 1970 Evaluation and Research Program*. PHC(E)-4. Washington, D.C.: U.S. Government Printing Office, 1974.

Siegel, Jacob S., and Melvin Zelnik. "An Evaluation of Coverage in the 1960 Census of Population by Techniques of Demographic Analysis and by Composite Methods." In *Proceedings of the Social Statistics Section of the American Statistical Association*, 71–85. Washington, D.C.: American Statistical Association, 1996.

U.S. Census Bureau. "Demographic Analysis Tables and Figures." Released at Demographic Analysis Conference, Washington, D.C., December 6, 2010.

U.S. Census Bureau, Demographic Analysis Research Team. "The Development and Sensitivity Analysis of the 2010 Demographic Analysis Estimates." 2010. www.census.gov/newsroom/releases/pdf/20101206_da_revpaper.pdf.

Depository Libraries

One way to locate and use current or historical census data is to visit a depository library. The Federal Depository Library Program (FDLP) is a cooperative venture between the United States Government Printing Office (GPO) and America's library community. Authorized by Title 44, Chapter 19 of the U.S. Code, the purpose of the FDLP is to make government information readily accessible to the general public at no direct cost to the user. Under the provisions of the program, the GPO provides participating libraries with publications and databases at no charge; in turn, the libraries agree to provide access to materials and to help the public use them. Approximately 1,250 depository libraries currently operate in the United States and its territories.

History of the FDLP

As far back as 1813, Congress recognized the fundamental importance of distributing government information to as wide an audience as possible. At that time a law was passed that required the federal government to distribute one copy of every congressional publication to each college and university in the nation, as well as to the official historical society of each state. The newly formed American Antiquarian Society, which began actively collecting such publications in 1814, is widely regarded as the country's first depository library. A truly national network for distributing government publications began to take shape in the 1850s, when a series of resolutions and laws established the necessary components, including the transfer of pertinent responsibility from the Department of the Interior to the newly established Government Printing Office in 1861. Landmark legislation in 1895 further centralized printing and distribution activities, increased the scope and number of depository libraries, established an ongoing publications catalog, and reduced duplication and waste in the system. The FDLP as it exists today took shape through the passage of the Depository Libraries Act of 1962. Changes in the 1970s further expanded the types of libraries eligible for depository status and incorporated microfiche as a significant means of distributing publications. Beginning in the 1990s, Congress, the Government Printing Office, and the library community have worked toward establishing a coherent policy of handling electronic information, including the passage of major legislation in 1993 and 2002.

Depository Basics

A library can obtain depository status in one of two ways. By law certain types of libraries are eligible to become a depository on request; these include the official state library for each state, federal and state appellate court libraries, federal agency libraries, and accredited law school libraries. The second method is to be nominated by the institution's congressional delegation. Each congressional district is entitled to two depository libraries created in this way, and the state is entitled to two additional depositories nominated by its senators. In practice, not all congressional districts have two such depositories—some have three, others have only one. This situation results from a combination of local needs and the history of congressional redistricting in the area.

The law specifies two types of depository libraries: regional and selective. Regional depositories are required to receive all depository materials published by the GPO and to keep them in perpetuity. Each state is entitled to two regional depositories, but because of the cost of maintaining regional status, most states have only one. At present, there are 49 regional depositories in the United States, including 7 that share joint responsibility for 2 or more smaller states or territories.

Selective depositories, as the name suggests, may choose which categories of publications they wish to receive, in keeping with the local libraries' collecting policies and needs. Selective depositories may also discard older publications deemed no longer useful, although the library must follow GPO guidelines for doing so. All selective depositories are encouraged to accept a small "core collection" of important designated publications, such as the *Budget of the U.S. Government*. At present, decennial census publications for the library's home state are included on the core list, as are the Census Bureau's *County and City Data Book* and *Statistical Abstract*.

FDLP law specifies that the GPO must provide depository libraries with designated documents free of charge. In turn, depositories agree to process and shelve the materials in a manner and timeliness similar to other library materials; to provide the requisite computers, microform readers, and other equipment necessary to use the materials; and to provide the general public with assistance in locating and using the publications.

Technically, depository materials are owned by the government, not the individual libraries. The law requires depository libraries to provide all members of the public access to those materials, even if an individual is not otherwise entitled to use that library. For example, regular access to a university library might be restricted to students, faculty, and alumni of the school, but anyone who wishes to do so has the right to use that library's depository publications.

Individual libraries may determine local circulation policies for their depository collections. Some libraries allow depository materials to be borrowed; others limit access to in-library use only. The GPO also allows depositories to organize their collections according to local policies. Some libraries intershelve depository publications with all other books, magazines, and library materials. Many libraries keep their depository collections separate, typically in a "government documents" department. GPO inspectors visit every depository library at least once every seven years to ensure that the institution is following FDLP policies and guidelines.

It is important to remember that depository libraries, even regional ones, are not comprehensive repositories for every government document. Many government publications are "non-depository" titles. The law requires the GPO to assign depository status only to publications of "public interest or educational value." Researchers can use the Internet to determine the depository status of GPO publications by consulting the *Catalog of U.S. Government Publications* at http://catalog.gpo.gov/. This resource contains entries for all GPO publications issued from 1976 to the present. (The online version has replaced its print predecessor, the *Monthly Catalog of U.S. Government Publications*, which ceased publication in December 2004.) Over time, the GPO hopes to enhance the online *Catalog* with listings for all government materials published prior to 1976.

For smaller print runs, individual agencies can arrange their own printing, bypassing the GPO completely, and many of these items never find their way to libraries. A second limitation is that some materials designated as depository publications fall through the cracks somehow and never get distributed to libraries. It should be noted that the Census Bureau has a strong tradition of cooperating with the GPO, and nearly all of the bureau's important publications are distributed through the depository program.

Benefits of Using Depository Libraries

Depository libraries offer several major benefits to people looking for census data: depositories are conveniently located across the United States, access to them is free and open to everyone, and depository librarians are familiar with census publications, terminology, and concepts, and they are happy to share that knowledge with anyone, from casual user to serious researcher. In addition, a typical depository library will receive related statistical data from a host of other federal agencies, such as the Bureau of Economic Analysis or the Bureau of Labor Statistics. Most depository libraries also purchase commercially produced databases, printed indexes, and other resources to enhance the usefulness of their census materials.

Larger depository collections offer several advantages beyond what might be found through the Census Bureau's regional offices or its State Data Centers. First, major depositories collect census information for the entire country, whereas other organizations might limit coverage to their home state. Second, many libraries have maintained depository status for a century or more, creating a rich collection of retrospective census materials unavailable elsewhere.

An obvious question that comes to mind is why we need depository libraries if everything from the government is now on the Internet. The short, but perhaps obvious, answer is "Everything is not on the Internet." Although the government's official policy, promulgated in the U.S. Office of Management and Budget's circular A-130 (February 1996), encourages government agencies to distribute public information electronically, a large number of publications have not yet made the transition from a paper environment; this is especially true of many retrospective historical collections. However, the Census Bureau stands at the forefront of Internet publishing, including its American FactFinder database system. The bureau has scanned many retrospective decennial census publications from 1790 forward (found at www.census.gov/prod/www/abs/decennial/ and other locations), but some are not yet available in electronic form.

A second answer is that the continued existence of depository libraries provides a safeguard against the increasing pressures on federal agencies to charge fees for electronic data. Furthermore, depository librarians are expert at organizing information in all its forms, and some of the best Web-based guides and directories of government information have been created by depository libraries. Finally, although the GPO and other agencies post government publications online, this does not guarantee that people will be able to locate them. Depository librarians are skilled at navigating the complexities of the government publication system. They can assist individuals in locating needed information, recommend related resources, and help users understand what is found.

Locating the Nearest Depository Library

The majority of depository libraries are housed in colleges, universities, or community colleges. Others can be found at large public libraries or in specialized organizations, such as federal agency libraries, official state libraries, court libraries, or historical societies.

Census users can locate their nearest depository by consulting the GPO's *Federal Depository Library Directory* on the Internet (http://catalog.gpo.gov/fdlpdir/FDLPdir.jsp). This Web-based interactive directory is searchable by state, city, ZIP code, telephone area code, or congressional district. Users can also search by library, institution, or librarian name. Search results can be limited by library type (regional or selective), library size, or the year the library was first designated as a depository. Directory listings include each depository library's address, telephone and fax numbers, names of key staff members, and links to the library's Web site.

Depository Libraries Today and Tomorrow

The biggest challenge facing the Federal Depository Library Program is electronic publishing. From the 1990s forward, traditional printed products represent a small percentage of the information for which the GPO is responsible. Most documents are now disseminated electronically via the Internet. Because of this increased availability, and because of the costs of maintaining depository status, a number of libraries have opted out of the FDLP in recent years, while others have downsized their depository selections.

A continually growing collection of current and historical electronic publications can be found at the GPO's Federal Digital System (FDsys) digital repository system (www.gpo.gov/fdsys/), formerly known as GPO Access. FDsys includes a fairly sophisticated search interface; users can limit search results by date and by publication categories, such as congressional hearings or GAO reports. In addition to FDsys, most federal organizations maintain their own extensive Internet resources. Federal statistical reporting agencies, such as the Bureau of Labor Statistics, the National Center for Health Statistics, and of course the Census Bureau, maintain especially robust Web sites.

Many publications formerly available as tangible paper products now exist only in electronic form. In one sense this extensive use of the Internet makes government publications more accessible than ever before. Still, the decentralized, ever-changing nature of the Web, together with its enormous size, can make it difficult for users to locate needed information from the government. Recognizing these concerns, Congress passed the Government Printing Office Electronic Information Access Act of 1993. The law recognizes the GPO's responsibility for cataloging and publishing the government's electronic publications, a task that the GPO is addressing via the *Catalog of U.S. Government Publications*, FDsys, and other means. A more sweeping law, the E-Government Act of 2002, addresses electronic distribution of government information by all federal agencies.

A related concern is that many government publications fall outside the scope of the FDLP system. Depository librarians estimate that approximately 50 percent of current publications are bypassed in this way. In addition, some government-produced electronic publications are not free to the general public but are sold on a per-document basis or as an ongoing electronic subscription. Examples include government-funded scientific and technical reports distributed via the National Technical Information Service and the Census Bureau's own USA Trade Online database. Whether because of legislative mandate or agency budget constraints, such fee-based products are likely to proliferate in the coming years. This is a potential concern for census users because most of the bureau's electronic information is currently free but that may not always be the case.

What does the future hold for depository libraries? This is a topic of debate within the library community, but most believe that libraries will continue to play an important role in government information for a variety of reasons. The GPO's ambitious plans to digitize all retrospective government publications are moving more slowly than originally envisioned. To assist with this massive project, depository libraries have entered into a variety of partnerships with the GPO to help digitize and catalog retrospective documents. More importantly, experienced depository librarians possess the skills and specialized training needed to help users locate the information they need. The Government Printing Office and the library community will continue working with Congress and with agencies such as the Census Bureau to ensure that important electronic products will be available to visitors of depository libraries at no cost and that historical archives of electronic publications will be preserved and made accessible for future generations.

See also *Data dissemination and use; Data products: evolution; Dissemination of data: printed publications; National Archives and Records Administration (NARA).*

. . . . MICHAEL R. LAVIN

BIBLIOGRAPHY

Bernholz, Charles D. "Federal Government Documents: Dead or Alive." *Government Information Quarterly* 25 (January 2008): 57–60.

Morehead, Joe. *Introduction to United States Government Information Sources.* 6th ed. Englewood, Colo.: Libraries Unlimited, 1999.

Pettinato, Tammy R. "Legal Information, the Informed Citizen, and the FDLP: The Role of Academic Law Librarians in Promoting Democracy." *Law Library Journal* 99 (Fall 2007): 695–716.

Ragains, Patrick. "Fixing the Federal Depository Library Program." *American Libraries* 41 (May 2010): 36–38.

Schonfeld, Roger C., and Ross Housewright. *Documents for a Digital Democracy: A Model for the Federal Depository Library Program in the 21st Century.* New York: Ithaka S+R, 2009. www.ithaka.org/ithaka-s-r/research/documents-for-a-digital-democracy.

Shuler, John, Paul T. Jaeger, and John Carlo Bertot. "Implications of Harmonizing the Future of the Federal Depository Library Program within e-Government Principles and Policies." *Government Information Quarterly* 27 (January 2010): 9–16.

U.S. Federal Depository Library Program. *FDLP Desktop.* www.fdlp.gov.

U.S. Government Printing Office. *Regional Depository Libraries in the 21st Century: A Preliminary Assessment (Final Report to the Joint Committee on Printing).* Washington, D.C.: U.S. Government Printing Office, December 2008. http://purl.access.gpo.gov/GPO/LPS108524.

Washington University Federal Depository Library. *History of Government Documents.* St. Louis, Mo.: University Libraries, Washington University, 2006. http://library.wustl.edu/units/westcampus/govdocs/onlinedisplay/doc-history.html.

Disability

Since 1830, the census has asked a variety of questions on the disability status of the population, and it currently collects disability data on the American Community Survey. The questions were not uniform over the years, nor were questions asked consistently from 1830 forward. Reporting of the results of questions on disability also varies widely from census to census. Data users thus need to take particular care in examining the format of particular questions and understanding their intent, since concepts of disability, as well as the legislative responsibilities of the federal government with regard to disabled Americans, have changed over the years. Current federal policy is defined by the Americans with Disabilities Act (1990). The act defines *disability* as a "physical or mental impairment that substantially limits one or more of the major life activities."

Disability Questions

The questions on disability on the American Community Survey were last revised in 2008. Two questions ask for yes or no responses as to whether the respondent is "deaf" or has "serious difficulty hearing" or is "blind" or has "serious difficulty seeing even when wearing glasses." Three questions ask respondents age 5 years or older, if "because of a physical, mental, or emotional condition," they "have serious difficulty concentrating, remembering, or making decisions"; "have serious difficulty walking or climbing stairs"; or "have difficulty dressing or bathing." Respondents 15 years or older are asked whether "because of a physical, mental, or emotional condition," they "have difficulty doing errands alone such as visiting a doctor's office or shopping." Veterans are also asked for their "VA service-connected disability rating."

The 2000 census long form contained two areas of questions on an individual's disability status. The first asked for yes or no answers to whether the person has "any of the following long-lasting conditions: Blindness, deafness, or a severe vision or hearing impairment" and whether the individual had "a condition that substantially limits one or more basic physical activities such as walking, climbing stairs, reaching, lifting, or carrying." The second asked if a "physical, mental, or emotional condition lasting 6 months or more" caused the individual to have "any difficulty" in "learning, remembering, or concentrating" or in "dressing, bathing, or getting around inside the home." For persons 16 years of age or more, the questions asked if the person had difficulty "going outside the home alone to shop or visit a doctor's office" or "working at a job or business."

The questions identify the number of persons of working age who could be limited from working by a "long-lasting condition." They also identify the number of individuals who could need help or care in managing daily activities because of a "long-lasting condition."

Prior census questions addressed similar concerns, albeit at different levels of detail. The 1830 census, which collected data by household only, asked for the number of individuals in the household who were "deaf and dumb" in three age cohorts: under 14, from 14 to 24, and 25 and up. The information was gathered for whites and separately for slaves and the free colored. The 1830 census also asked for the numbers of blind whites and blind free coloreds and slaves but did not ask for age breakdowns. The 1840 census added questions on the number of "insane and idiots," by race, and whether they were "at public charge" or "at private charge"—that is, cared for privately or in public institutions. In the parlance of the day, an "insane" person was mentally ill and an "idiot" was "feeble-minded" or mentally retarded. By 1880 disability questions on the main population questionnaire had increased to six, and the enumerator was asked to record for each individual counted whether the person was, "on the day of the enumerator's visit, sick or temporarily disabled, so as to be unable to attend to ordinary business or duties"; "blind"; "deaf and dumb"; "idiotic"; "insane"; or "maimed, crippled, bedridden, or otherwise disabled." From 1880 to 1930 the decennial census also used "supplemental schedules" on the disabled, which collected a wide variety of additional data. Questions on disability were not asked on the main population census form for the census of 1900 and for the counts from 1920 to 1960; they were resumed in 1970 on the long form.

Question Debates

The questions used to gauge disability have been the subject of much debate in modern census taking. After the 1970 census a post-census disability survey tested the reliability of data collected in the 1970 count. The survey re-asked a sample of census respondents about their disability status as of census day 1970. A sizable number of respondents who earlier reported disabilities no longer did so in the survey, leading many to question the reliability of responses. Some researchers proposed dropping the questions for 1980. Organizations serving the disabled community pointed out that the decennial census was the only source of small-area data on disability and put pressure on the bureau to retain the items. They were continued in 1980.

During the 1980s, content specialists sought to create a question that went beyond the 1970 item, which focused exclusively on disabilities related to work. An item was needed that could encompass the entire population, not just those who were in the working ages. As a result an item was added that asked about health conditions lasting six or more months that made it difficult or impossible to use public transportation. Post-censal studies showed, however, that the responses to the new public transportation disability item were difficult to interpret. Planners, for example, viewed the data from this item as too general, especially in light of the wide differences among communities in the types of public transportation that were referred to in the question. Ultimately, the Health and Disability Interagency Working Group recommended that the public transportation disability item be dropped from the 1990 census, and the transportation planners concurred. In addition to the questions on work disability, two items were added in 1990: health conditions lasting six months or more that affected mobility and self-care. These items were regarded as more useful as a measure of disability for the overall population, including those who have low levels of labor force participation, such as the elderly.

Rates of Disability

About 10 percent of the noninstitutionalized American population of working age (ages 16 to 64) reported a difficulty in 2009. Disability rates rise with age; roughly half of Americans over age 65 report a disability. Data on the number and characteristics of disabled Americans are also collected in periodic surveys such as the Survey of Income and Program Participation (SIPP) and the Current Population Survey, as well as through administrative records of agencies charged with caring for the disabled. SIPP provides the most detailed federal survey data. For persons 15 years old or over, the SIPP disability questions cover limitations in functional activities (seeing, hearing, speaking, lifting and carrying, using stairs, and walking), in activities of daily living, or ADLs (getting around inside the home, getting in or out of a bed or chair, bathing, dressing, eating, and toileting), and in instrumental activities of daily living, or IADLs (going outside the home, keeping track of money or bills, preparing meals, doing light housework, and using the telephone). SIPP also obtains information on the use of wheelchairs and crutches, canes, and walkers; the presence of certain conditions related to mental functioning; the presence of a work disability; and the disability status of children. According to SIPP, from 2002, 51 million noninstitutionalized Americans (about 18 percent of the population) have a disability; 34 percent of those with disabilities were age 65 or older.

In the past a much smaller proportion of the population reported the particular mental and physical categories of disability asked on the census. Between 1850 and 1880 the total deaf, dumb, blind, insane, and idiotic population ranged from 0.2 to 0.5 percent of the total population. The 1880 census counted 0.68 percent of the population, about 341,000 people, as "maimed, crippled, bedridden, or otherwise disabled."

See also *Composition of the population; IPUMS (Integrated Public Use Microdata Series); Uses of the census and ACS: federal agencies; Veterans' status.*

. . . .   MARGO J. ANDERSON

BIBLIOGRAPHY

Integrated Public Use Microdata Samples. http://usa.ipums.org/usa/.

U.S. Bureau of the Census. *Americans with Disabilities: 2002.* Household Economic Studies. Current Population Reports. P70-107. May 2006. www.census.gov/prod/2006pubs/p70-107.pdf.

———. *Population and Housing Inquiries in U.S. Decennial Censuses, 1790–1970.* Working paper no. 39. Washington, D.C.: U.S. Government Printing Office, 1973.

U.S. Census Bureau. *Disability among the Working Age Population: 2008 and 2009.* American Community Survey Brief. ACSSB/09-12. September 2010. www.census.gov/prod/2010pubs/acsbr09-12.pdf.

Dissemination of Data: Electronic Products

The advances in computation, communication, and information technology over the past 50 years have had a dramatic impact on the dissemination and use of census data. These changes will be discussed on a decade-by-decade basis to present a snapshot of the use of census products over time. What were the impediments to usage? How did the Census Bureau leverage technology to improve access to data? Did the Census Bureau meet the needs of all users?

A revisionist view of electronic products is also presented. Major infrastructure projects, especially out of the Minnesota Population Center (MPC), have revitalized the early electronic products from the 1960s and on. In fact, the MPC has created electronic products from the earliest census forward—that is, 1790–2000. The National Historical Geographic Information System (NHGIS; www.nhgis.org) provides an interface to all of the tabular products from the Census Bureau. Likewise, the Integrated Public Use Microdata Series (IPUMS; www.ipums.org) provides access to a harmonized version of the census microdata samples from 1850 on. Both of these projects and many other interfaces not referenced have markedly increased the reuse of these older products. It is safe to say that the 1960 data have been used more in recent years than when the files were first released.

Census data are protected under Title 13. This does not mean that the public cannot access data from the Census Bureau. The history of the dissemination of electronic products illustrates the increasing access to census data over the past 50 years. However, during this era the likelihood of respondent disclosure has also increased. The future of the dissemination of electronic products depends on the Census Bureau remaining ahead of disclosure threats. Access to data is important to our participatory democracy, and yet it is never guaranteed.

Finally, while data products can come in many forms—punch cards, magnetic tapes, CD-ROMs, or downloads from a Web browser—appropriate use of these electronic products requires knowledge of census concepts, including geography and an adequate level of statistical literacy. Most barriers to access have disappeared, but the knowledge requirement remains. This is the new barrier for electronic products.

Until the 1960 census, printed reports issued by the Bureau of the Census were the primary source of information from the decennial censuses. These reports presented tabulations and summary statistics for a variety of geographic and census-defined areas as well as selected subpopulations. The printed reports were often sufficient for persons seeking specific demographic information about a geographic or political area. However, printed reports have two major shortcomings: (1) they may not have precisely the information a user desires; and (2) the printed reports cannot be easily used for analyses and comparisons across large numbers of areas or characteristics. Electronic products provided a solution to the shortcomings of printed reports. But it was a solution with a caveat—users needed dollars, time, and expertise to extract information from the machine-readable files.

Census data have proven to be relevant to a broad range of concerns of interest to researchers, planners, and the commercial community. While the primary constitutional purpose of the decennial census is to provide population counts required for the allocation of seats in the House of Representatives to the states, the uses of the data now extend far beyond that initial purpose. Much of the content of the census questionnaire is linked to the requirements of federal agencies for planning, monitoring, and evaluating programs. For example, items on income and other economic data are used by a number of federal agencies.

Technology, Dissemination, and Users

The Census Bureau has a strong history of innovation in information processing. The 1890 census was tabulated using punched cards and counting hardware designed by Herman Hollerith, a bureau employee. The technology later became the foundation for International Business Machines (IBM) Corporation. Stored program digital computing technology was first described in the late 1930s. Morris Hansen and others at the bureau realized the substantial reductions in tabulating time that could be gained by using electronic pulses rather than mechanical holes to sense data. In 1948 the bureau contracted with the Eckert-Mauchly Computer Corporation (EMCC) to design a machine for statistical purposes. When the UNIVAC (UNIVersal Automatic Calculator) computer was delivered by Remington-Rand, EMCC's successor, to the Bureau of the Census in March 1951, it was too late to help with much of the 1950 census processing.

However, having a computer on hand for the planning and processing of the 1960 census put the bureau in the lead on data processing when compared with other federal agencies and even large corporations. Other improvements in technology, such as magnetic tape as a storage medium and film optical sensing device for input to computers (FOSDIC) processing as a means to transfer data to machine readable form, also contributed to the move to electronic processing and dissemination of data.

Mainframe computing technology evolved through the 1970s and 1980s with the capability to handle increasingly larger data sets at increasingly faster speeds. Software for managing and analyzing data also was developed during this period. Then, in the 1990s, came desktop computers with processing and data storage capabilities that exceeded those of earlier mainframes, client-server networks, parallel processors, read-only compact disks (CD-ROM), the Internet, browsers, and the World Wide Web (WWW). The consequences of these recent developments filtered into the dissemination of 1990 census data in the last years of the decade and became more fully apparent with the release of the 2000 census data.

The 1960s

In 1960 the Bureau of the Census released to the public for the first time data that could be directly manipulated by the user to produce reports and analyses. The tabular data for 1960 were distributed in electronic formats similar to those used in subsequent censuses. Documentation and support were minimal. Data Use and Access Laboratories (DUALabs), created as a private organization by Jack Beresford, former chief of the bureau's Data Access and Use Laboratory (DAUL), distributed and supported the summary tape data from the 1970 census.

Releasing microdata meant that users would be allowed to produce their own tabulations and statistics. This raised the issue of respondent disclosure or confidentiality. Initially, the data were released with the understanding that they would not be redistributed, but by the end of the decade the bureau was willing to enlarge the sampling fraction for the microdata files tenfold and treat the files as publicly accessible.

The microdata files were released in 1960 as one-in-one-thousand (1/1,000) and one-in-ten-thousand (1/10,000) samples. The card files comprised 180,000 and 18,000 cards, respectively. Only the 1/1,000 was released on tape—13 reels in UNIVAC format and 7 reels in IBM format. Standards for storing data on magnetic tape were not yet defined. Use of the tapes typically required custom programming to handle the physical and logical layout of the data on the tapes. No software was available for managing or analyzing data.

As a note, in the early 1970s the Bureau of the Census rereleased the 1960 microdata. The intent was to provide a 1/100 sample for 1960 structured similarly to the 1970 public use sample that was forthcoming. DUALabs documented, disseminated, and supported this 1960 Public Use Sample (PUS), as it was referred to in the DUALabs documentation. The 1960 PUS was structured hierarchically (person-level records nested within housing-level records) with larger numbers of items and more detailed geography than were included in the original 1960 releases from the bureau. Although copies of the original 1960 microdata files from the bureau still exist, most users of 1960 microdata use the 1/100 PUS released by DUALabs in 1973 or the IPUMS version of the data from the Minnesota Population Center.

While most users of census data at this time had some familiarity with census data and data concepts, they now needed to understand data structures and data management and have access to programming assistance. They also needed access to computing equipment capable of handling the media. An overall consequence was that significant planning was required to extract information from the machine-readable files. Generating a simple extract from the seven tape reels of the 1960 1/1,000 file, for example, could require several days of programming time and thousands of dollars of computing costs.

Storage requirements were an important consideration when distributing data on media such as cards and magnetic tape. To reduce the number of cards or tapes required, steps were usually taken to limit the number of characters, bytes, or columns. In 1960 these included restricting the number of items made available, coding two or more items into one character position, and using overpunches (+ or -), multiple punches, and non-numeric codes to allow larger numbers of responses to be coded into one character position. Each of these presented difficulties to the users of the files. At some user sites the original files were expanded to eliminate the non-numeric data. Attempts were made at using data compression techniques to reduce the storage requirements, but the operating systems available in the 1960s typically required that data be uncompressed and stored back on magnetic media prior to use, negating the major virtue of compression.

The 1960 data introduced users to sample weights. Housing data were gathered from 25 percent, 20 percent, or 5 percent samples of the housing units. Users performing their own analyses on the microdata needed to weight properly any given housing item to produce correct population estimates.

The 1970s

The response of users to the release of the 1960 data in machine-readable formats and the evolving computer technology encouraged the bureau to increase the number of summary and microdata files to be made available from the 1970 census. A series of summary tapes covering the First, Second, and Third Counts (100 percent items) and the Fourth through Sixth counts (sample or long-form items) were created. Each count was subdivided into subfiles with varying degrees of geographic detail. Population and housing tabulations were released in separate files for some counts. The tapes were generally released by state. In total, more than 2,000 summary tapes were available from the 1970 census. The sheer quantity of data available presented problems to users. DUALabs released compressed versions of the census files. This reduced the count of tapes by a factor of ten but still left users with multiple-reel data sets to handle and the additional need of uncompressing the data before they could be accessed and analyzed.

Users faced other problems. Tabulations in the Summary Tape Files (STFs) were typically defined for specified populations with as many as five-way tabulations presented. Extracting specific numbers desired from specific tabulations was challenging. With the release of so much data with such fine geographic detail, maintaining user confidentiality became a concern in 1970. The policy adopted for the 1970 STFs was to suppress either complete tables or portions of them if counts were sufficiently small to risk a breach of confidentiality. As with the 1960 products, people do not use the original media anymore—they get tabular data from the NHGIS or similar providers.

Magnetic tape technology improved rapidly in the late 1960s and early 1970s. Tape was commonly available in 7-track at 556 and 800 bytes per inch (bpi) densities and 9-track at 800 bpi. Standards for the logical structure of data on tape were beginning to emerge, but users had no guarantee that a tape they acquired could be read by the computer system to which they had access.

Public Use Microdata Samples (PUMS) files also were released in 1970. Six 1/100 files were created. The 1970 long form was distributed in two versions, 1 to 5 percent and the other to 15 percent samples of housing units. Three levels of geographic detail were also created: state, county group, and neighborhood characteristics. Thus 5 percent and 15 percent PUMS files were made available for each geographic level.

The 1970 PUMS differed in structure from the original 1960 microdata file in that the housing and person data were ordered hierarchically. This structuring of the data posed a significant challenge to users. Statistical packages were becoming available, but data management capabilities were limited and, in general, they could not directly handle hierarchical file structures.

The 1980s

The changes in computing technology in the 1970s, while significant, had primarily quantitative rather than qualitative effects on the ability of users to work with census data. This tended to be true in the 1980s as well. More tabulations were released in the STF series, and larger samples were available from the PUMS. A new data product, Special Tabulations, was introduced in the 1980s. These were user-requested tabulations that were not available in the published data. They were created on a cost-reimbursable basis once the Disclosure Review Board determined that there were no confidentiality issues with the request. The product became a public use file after six months of exclusive use by the requestor.

The 1/1,000 sample from 1960 that was increased to six 1/100 samples from the 1970 census became 1/100 and 5/100 PUMS in 1980, with a total of more than 15 million person and housing records included in the 1980 5 percent (5/100) PUMS. Higher tape densities (6250 bpi) allowed significantly larger quantities of data, approximately 160 MB, to be stored per reel. Fewer reels of tape were required for the distribution of the STFs, and the 5 and 22 reels required for the 1 percent and 5 percent PUMS, respectively, were more manageable than the dozens of reels required for the 1970 PUMS.

Tape standards were well defined. Multiple-reel data sets could be handled more easily and reliably than previously. However, users continued to rely on work files in the form of extracts from the full data sets and rarely created their own extracts. Mainframes were too costly for the inefficient, error-prone routines that a typical user might write.

By the end of the 1980s and into the 1990s, computing environments underwent significant changes as the consequences of the revolution in microprocessor and network technologies became apparent.

The 1990s

The changes in computing, networking, and information technology during the 1990s had both quantitative and qualitative ramifications for users. Computing power and data storage capacities increased dramatically to the point that a data set such as the 5 percent PUMS with 18 million housing and person records could be stored on the disk of a desktop personal computer (PC) and processed at speeds greater than those of the mainframes of a few years earlier. Users could work directly from the full data set with less need for creating and maintaining extracts and work files. Two gigabytes (GB) of RAM and tens of GB of hard disk storage could be installed on an affordable PC running at 550 MHz and higher speeds.

Users who had succeeded in handling the 1980 files generally found it easier to work with the 1990 data. The Bureau of the Census used record-swapping techniques rather than suppression to protect confidentiality in the STFs. The development of read-only compact disk (CD-ROM) technology provided a medium for the low-cost distribution of massive amounts of data. A single CD-ROM could store 640 MB of data, approximately the capacity of four high-density open reel tapes. Digital versatile disks (DVD) extended those capacities tenfold by the end of the decade.

STF1, STF3, and the Public Law 94-171 files as well as the 1 percent and 5 percent PUMS became available on CD-ROM. The bureau developed software to facilitate extracting data from the disks, including GO, Extract, and QuickTab, which allowed users to work more easily with STFs and microdata.

The Internet and the World Wide Web (WWW) were the most dramatic developments of the 1990s. They made massive amounts of information and data readily accessible to millions of people. At the beginning of the decade, the Internet allowed computers worldwide to establish computer-to-computer links. File transfer protocol (FTP) provided a mechanism for moving large amounts of data from one computer to another, significantly reducing the need to transfer data by tape or other media. The evolution of standard communication protocols made possible the development of Mosaic, the first of the network browsers, which the National Center for Supercomputer Applications (NCSA) at the University of Illinois demonstrated in 1993. Netscape, Internet Explorer, and similar commercial products soon followed.

Other developments took advantage of the technological revolution. Because the Census Bureau is always looking ahead to the next census, plans for a new way to disseminate data were well under way in the early 1990s. Those plans came into fruition by the close of the decade, owing in large part to the evolution of the WWW and Web browsers.

Early in the decade, William P. Butz and J. Michael Fortier of the bureau proposed the development of a system that could store the full national census online within a computing environment that had the capability to analyze data and generate reports on demand. The concept simmered for a few years until 1996, when the bureau proposed the development of the Data Access and Dissemination System (DADS).

This system, which has evolved into the American Fact-Finder (AFF), was intended to provide easy access to much of the 1990 census data that were published or distributed as STF files. The technical capabilities existed to allow custom tabulations and analyses to be generated in real time from either the sample data or complete data files. The feasibility of doing so was demonstrated by several projects around the country that allowed users to work interactively with PUMS, Current Population Survey (CPS), and similar microdata files. Called "Advanced Query", the custom reporting capabilities never advanced beyond the prototype stage.

Initial funding constraints for the development of this system were overcome when the Department of Commerce adopted the Concept of Operations (CONOPS) model for supporting developmental activities rather than purchasing off-the-shelf capabilities. The Bureau of the Census was designated as one of the pilot sites in 1996, with DADS one of three projects proposed by the bureau.

Perhaps the most significant consequence of the technology of the 1990s was what has been termed the democratization of census data. Access to and use of census data were no longer restricted to those who possessed the expertise and resources to acquire, manage, and analyze data from STF and PUMS files. The Web and the resources accessible via the Web opened access to the information in census data to any person familiar with browsers.

The 2000s

The first decade of the new millennium witnessed the maturation of the technological innovations that had their seeds in the previous decade. DADS evolved into the American FactFinder, which became more than just a way to disseminate data; it also dramatically reduced the emphasis or promotion of published census volumes and subject reports. These were available from the Census 2000 portal as PDF files for perusal online or to print, although the census volumes ran to hundreds of pages. The subject reports were snapshots in comparison with the more extensive subject-based reports from earlier censuses, which often ran to hundreds of pages.

American FactFinder allowed users to pull off selected tables for a geography (state) or multiple geographies (all counties in the nation, for example) and download the data as a spreadsheet. The tables ranged from exactly the tables one had found previously in the summary table products (Detailed Tables) to tables that more closely resembled the printed products (Population Profiles and Quick Tables). The output ranged from a nicely formatted Excel table suitable for printing to a database table with the geographies as rows and the items as columns.

While American FactFinder could be said to democratize data by providing access to summary file data to users with nothing more than a Web browser, the likelihood of the novice user coming away from the bureau site with what they needed was low. First, the user would have to know that long-form data were behind the SF3 and SF4 choices. Second, while the bureau provided search capabilities for tables, novice users would not necessarily succeed if they used terms such as "living together" or "gay marriages." Even American Fact-Finder required that users have a basic knowledge of the types of information the census collected as well as some understanding of census geography—for example, the distinction between a census place and a metropolitan area. The bureau realized this so the main bureau page also provided a Quick Facts area, where visitors could type in a geographic location to get a summary of statistics about that locality. Depending on the location selected—for example, state or populous county versus a small-population location—the user was pointed to a profile from American FactFinder.

The bureau also met the needs of high-volume users with a "Download Center" available via American FactFinder. This interface allowed users to download data for all geographies in a summary type—for example, census tracts—instead of the AFF limit of 7,000 areas. However, the Download Center offered only 12 major summary levels among more than 60 summary types.

The other major users of census data were those who wanted access to microdata. A popular way to access microdata was by way of the IPUMS from the Minnesota Population Center. This interface, developed in the mid-1990s, allowed users to select the items they wanted via a Web interface. The user would then download the data and accompanying setup files for statistical software, such as SPSS, SAS, or Stata and do their analysis on the items and cases of interest.

A small unit within the Census Bureau had also developed an extraction interface (DataFerrett). This interface had the same capabilities as the IPUMS interface but required users to download the client to their desktop. Both interfaces provided access to more than just census data, although primarily federally based data. DataFerrett provided access to data in its original raw form, whereas the IPUMS data were harmonized, making it easier to examine variables over time.

The Census Bureau responded to the concerns of archivists and high-volume users with a release of bulk raw data not tied to an interface such as American FactFinder. As in the past, the bureau made these available via magnetic tapes, CD-ROM/DVDs, and FTP. The format of the summary files changed from earlier releases. Instead of a fixed format file with thousands of columns of data, the release was issued as multiple files, primarily comma delimited ASCII data. The microdata were released in hierarchical comma delimited files.

The Census Bureau expanded its Research Data Center (RDC) program, giving researchers working within secure computing environments access to the full decennial long form, the short form, and the ACS, among other data sets. The initial impetus for the RDCs was to provide access to data from the economic census, but by the early 2000s, the bureau had begun making data from the decennial census available through the RDCs. Eleven RDCs were supported in 2010. The limitations on access to the RDCs were developed to fully protect the confidentiality of respondents while allowing researchers to use results from the full files for a variety of research purposes, the most common of which was the use of the data for statistical modeling. The restrictions limited access to a relatively small number of researchers who typically worked in academic research environments.

The 2010 census was a short-form only census, so the data products were far fewer. These included the Public Law 94-171 used for redistricting purposes, Summary Files 1 and 2 (SF1 and SF2), and a short-form PUMS file. These products were available via FTP and through American FactFinder. The more popular information released in 2010 were data gathered as part of the American Community Survey (ACS).

The ACS was designed to serve as a replacement for the decennial long form. It differed markedly from the decennial censuses in that it was based on continuous measurement with monthly surveys and thus provided a steady flow of data into the Census Bureau. As a consequence more current housing and population data were available over the course of the decade than had been available from the decennial censuses. Users did not have to wait ten years to receive new census reports. However, the ACS presented users with some concerns not posed by the decennial files. Because the survey was continuous, the data did not represent a single point in time. Results from the ACS were aggregated over time with single-year, three-year, and five-year results reported from the AFF and released in the microdata files. The size of a geographic area determined whether data were available in a one-year, three-year, or five-year aggregation. All states met the 65,000-population threshold for annual releases, but only 800 or so counties out of more than 3,000 met this threshold.

As with decennial data, most of the interface to these data was via the American FactFinder. There were a few notable changes to the interface. First, because there was no long-form/short-form distinction, the confusing SF1, SF2, and so forth, nomenclature disappeared. Instead, the user was confronted with a choice of a year (2008) or a range (2006–2008). Second, the results also came with both population counts and margins of error. Third, the types of reports expanded to include such choices as ranking tables, geographic comparison tables, and selected population profiles. The Data Profiles even included a "narrative" that put text alongside tables to help novice users with the interpretation of tables.

The 2010 release of the five-year ACS file was unlike other ACS products. These were not subject to the reliability thresholds in evidence with the one-year and three-year products, which prevented tables from being displayed because the number of sample cases was too small. The Census Bureau realized that many users of small census geographies such as census tracts will combine them to create a neighborhood profile, which will usually meet the Census Bureau's recommendations for data quality.

The ACS Web site (www.census.gov/acs/www) gave much more support via tutorials and guides than was ever provided to users of the decennial census. The *ACS Compass Handbooks* are an example of the latter. These explained how to use ACS data depending on whether one was a journalist, a teacher, or a researcher. The tutorials provide very explicit instructions, including screenshots, on how to obtain ACS data on the AFF.

2010 and Beyond

The revolution in information technology over the past 50 years has had a significant impact on who uses census data and how the data are used. For the first 30 years of that period, the primary effect was to allow those using machine-readable files to accomplish more. More data were available, the data could be managed and analyzed more rapidly, and more complex and sophisticated analyses could be performed. Over the past 20 years, many of the obstacles to accessing and using decennial census and ACS data have been removed or diminished to the point that novice users can accomplish tasks that once required access to costly mainframe computing resources and extensive technical knowledge and skills.

Most of this recent change has come with the advent of the Internet. Information can now be located from the desktop. Data can be drawn from CD-ROMs, from the Census Bureau's home page or from other public, private, and commercial sites that make census data available.

Certain needs and directions for the future are apparent. Large numbers of persons will have access to information from the census. Intelligent and meaningful use of this information still requires users to have a sound understanding of census geography and statistical concepts. A massive educational, training, and support program will be necessary if that understanding is to be developed in the public at large. The Census Bureau is aware of this challenge. The Compass series of handbooks and the tutorials available from the ACS Web site are a good start; however, the existence of the guides and tutorials may not be obvious to users who come to the data via the American FactFinder.

In addition, even with the guidance the Census Bureau has provided, users will at times become confused. All of the numbers generated from the AFF are official statistics, but two different users can end up with different results when looking up the same fact. Is the difference due to a single-year estimate (2007) versus a multiyear estimate (2006–2008), or did one number come from the decennial census (2010) and the other from the ACS 2010 file? Is it a poverty measure based on the ACS, the Current Population Survey, or some hybrid alternative?

Confidentiality will continue to be another area of concern for the Census Bureau. All of the tables released on the AFF have met data disclosure requirements, but users may think they have identified someone in a table. With microdata files, it is easy to generate tables with cells containing single individuals. The Census Bureau has multiple links to statements describing its statistical procedures aimed at introducing uncertainty (aka "noise") into the data, but do users understand these explanations or even see them? What does a data disclosure mean when multiyear estimates are being examined? The future challenge will be to help the public understand what the Census Bureau does to protect individual privacy in the data it provides. Expect the Census Bureau to continue to explore other options for respondent disclosure.

Another concern for the Census Bureau is the growing reluctance of the public to participate in surveys. While the ACS is mandatory, as is the decennial census, a vocal minority questions the constitutional basis of these data collection efforts. It is quite clear that many who complain about these invasions of privacy are users of census products. The Census Bureau has a public relations dilemma when people who use census information are complaining about its collection. To counter these concerns and to address the ever-escalating costs of the decennial census, the Census Bureau is exploring the use of administrative records. These will never replace the census, which is a constitutional requirement, but they can and will improve future census operations.

The coming decade will see a continuing increase in the use of census data and products. The Internet and the Web have made almost unlimited quantities of data and information, good and bad, readily available to the public. Much effort is needed to make it easier for users to find what is needed and to make sense of it when found.

See also *American Community Survey: data products; Data products: evolution; Dissemination of data: printed publications; Summary Files.*

. . . . ALBERT F. ANDERSON AND LISA NEIDERT

BIBLIOGRAPHY
Anderson, Margo J. *The American Census: A Social History.* New Haven, Conn.: Yale University Press, 1988.
Hawala, Sam, Laura Zayatz, and Sandra Rowland. "American FactFinder: Disclosure Limitation for the Advanced Query System." *Journal of Official Statistics* 20 (March 2004): 115–124.
Minnesota Population Center. *National Historical Geographic Information System: Pre-release Version 0.1.* Minneapolis: University of Minnesota, 2004.
Procedural History: 1960 Census of Population and Housing. www2.census .gov/prod2/decennial/documents/1960/proceduralHistory/1960proce duralhistory.zip
Procedural History: 1970 Census of Population and Housing. www2.census. gov/prod2/decennial/documents/1970/proceduralHistory/1970proced uralhistory.zip
Procedural History: 1980 Census of Population and Housing. www2.census .gov/prod2/decennial/documents/1980/proceduralHistory/1980proce duralhistory.zip
Procedural History: 1990 Census of Population and Housing. www2.census. gov/prod2/decennial/documents/1990/history/Chapter1-14.zip
Procedural History: 2000 Census of Population and Housing. www.census .gov/history/pdf/Census2000v1.pdf and www.census.gov/history/pdf/ Census2000v2.pdf
Ruggles, Steven, J. Trent Alexander, Katie Genadek, Ronald Goeken, Matthew B. Schroeder, and Matthew Sobek. *Integrated Public Use Microdata Series: Version 5.0.* Machine-readable database. Minneapolis: University of Minnesota, 2010.
Title 13, U.S. Code. Protection of Confidential Information. www.census .gov/geo/www/luca2010/luca_title13.html
Zayatz, Laura. "Disclosure Avoidance Practices and Research at the U.S. Census Bureau: An Update." *Journal of Official Statistics* 23 (June 2007): 253–265.

Dissemination of Data: Printed Publications

Beginning with the first census in 1790 and continuing until the present, the results of census enumerations have been published in printed products. Early on, James Madison, Thomas Jefferson, and others recognized that information about the labor force, manufacturing, and agriculture would be useful not only to their contemporaries but also to future generations. The form and content of subsequent printed publications have reflected their farsightedness as each succeeding census has included more statistics on economic and social issues. Following the establishment of a permanent Bureau of the Census in 1902, printed reports were issued with greater frequency and on far more diverse topics than was envisioned in the nineteenth century. Advances in technology and the more complex needs of a larger and expanding population have combined to increase the bureau's statistics-gathering activities and capabilities, resulting in a burgeoning quantity of printed reports during the twentieth century. Paradoxically, at the beginning of the twenty-first century the role of printed reports is being eclipsed by CD-ROMs and the Internet.

The Earliest Census Reports

The first printed census publication, the report of the first census, taken in 1790 by the federal marshals, consisted of a 56-page octavo pamphlet. Statistics in the report included the number of persons in the judicial districts, the number of free white males age 16 and over, the number of free white males under 16, free white females, all other free individuals, and slaves. It was delivered to President George Washington in 1791, and one copy was forwarded to each of the clerks of the district courts. Printing was contracted out to a private firm, as were all the census printed products until the eighth census (1860), when the Government Printing Office was assigned the responsibility for printing census publications.

Nineteenth-Century Census Reports

Beginning with the census of 1800, the marshals reported the results of the census to the secretary of state, instead of the president; the secretary of state then forwarded the reports to Congress and the president. The second census printed report was published as a 70-page folio volume in 1801. The population reports of the third census, in 1810, were still relatively brief, consisting of a 180-page volume, published in 1811. The 1810 census contained the first statistics on manufactures. Although the threat of war at the time prompted the report, it led Congress to want to know more about the industrial capacity of the American manufacturing sector. Published in 1813, the relatively brief report (233 pages) included the kind, quantity, and value of goods manufactured; the number of establishments; and the number of machines used under certain circumstances. The data were not consistent from area to area, but this report represented a first attempt at gathering industrial statistics. The collection of these data was supervised by the secretary of the Treasury.

The fourth census (1820) also included industrial statistics but was hampered, like the third census, by the incompleteness of the returns from the various districts. For the first time legislation authorizing the census of 1820 included a provision that one copy of the report be provided to each of the colleges and universities in the United States as well as to members of Congress, officers of the government, and judges of the United States courts. The inclusion of colleges and universities in the dissemination scheme ensured that the data would reach beyond government officials and set a precedent that would continue through the establishment of the Federal Depository Library Program. The cost of printing these reports was $11,014; postage to disseminate them came to $1,229.

The printed results of the fifth census (1830) were presented in a large folio of 163 pages. It was so poorly printed that

Congress mandated its reprinting under the direct supervision of the secretary of state. The defective printing and the reprinted edition were then bound together for dissemination along with population figures from the censuses of 1790, 1800, 1810, and 1820 by counties as well as statistics by districts. This time the cost of printing rose to $18,473 and postage to $7,098.

The four-volume census of 1840 was the last census to be limited in scope to information about population only. Although the earlier attempts at collecting and publishing statistics about manufacturing had not been totally successful, lawmakers and scholars recognized the importance of broadening the scope of the data collected and disseminated in the reports.

With each succeeding decennial census taken between 1850 and 1900, the size and number of printed reports increased, reflecting the expanding subject coverage of the census, the growth of the population, the expansion of the economic sector, and the more widespread interest in statistical data on the part of public officials, scholars, and others. The format of printed reports was inconsistent from census to census, primarily because activities ceased at the completion of each census owing to the lack of permanent staff. Thus there was little or no advanced planning for the next census, record-keeping was haphazard, and the data included many errors, especially in the sixth census (1840). However, the results of the eighth census, taken in 1860, were published in a four-volume format in which the first volume was devoted to population, the second to statistics on agriculture, the third to statistics on manufacturers, and one on miscellaneous statistics. This publication pattern would continue into the twentieth century.

Throughout the nineteenth century, the content of the reports increased with each census. The first information on manufactures was included in the census of 1810; information about agriculture, mining, and fisheries first appeared in the census of 1840; and information on social issues such as taxation, churches, pauperism, and crime was included in the census of 1850. With each succeeding decennial census, the scope of the data that were collected and disseminated in the printed reports expanded. Maps first appeared in the ninth census, in 1870. The number of reports dramatically increased with the censuses of 1880 and 1890. This is exemplified by the fact that the number of volumes in the 1880 census ballooned to 22, more than in all eight censuses that preceded it.

Almost from the beginning, complaints had been made that the publication of the reports was delayed beyond all reasonable expectations. These delays culminated with the tenth census in 1880, when the earliest reports were not published until 1883 and the last report was published in 1888. Some of these problems had been addressed in legislation of 1879 and 1880, which established a Census Office in the Department of the Interior, provided for a superintendent of the census to be appointed by the president, and transferred responsibility for taking the census from the marshals to 150 supervisors. Not addressed was the problem of the lack of a permanent staff; the terms of the supervisors ended with the completion of each census. New technological developments in the form

of punched cards and electric tabulating machines began to address the problem of tardy reporting of the results with the 1890 census. These machines were primitive by today's standards, but they were improved and used to tabulate and compile census data until the introduction of the computer in the mid-twentieth century. Statistics that were tabulated and compiled first could be published as they were ready, in the form of press releases and preliminary reports. This was especially important for high-demand products such as total population counts of cities, counties, states, and the nation as a whole.

Printed Census Reports in the First Half of the Twentieth Century

As the new century dawned, Congress finally passed legislation in 1902 establishing the Bureau of the Census as a permanent unit within the Department of the Interior. (With reorganizations in 1903 and 1913, the bureau moved to the Department of Commerce and Labor.) The most important aspect of this legislation, which would have a far-reaching effect on the printed reports, was that the Census Bureau was now an ongoing organization with a permanent staff. This change enabled the staff to engage in long-term planning and to respond much more quickly to new demands and needs for data products. A permanent bureau also allowed for more flexibility in the intervals at which data could be collected and published. For example, data on agriculture had been included in the decennial census as far back as the census of 1840, and printed reports dealing with agricultural information were included in each of the decennial censuses through 1920. Following the census of 1910, it was recognized that the data would be more useful if it were collected and published more frequently than every ten years, so plans were made for a quinquennial Census of Agriculture beginning in 1915. The outbreak of World War I, however, postponed the beginning of the five-year census until 1925.

By the turn of the twentieth century, statisticians, political leaders, and scholars also recognized that statistical data from other sectors of the economy should be collected and disseminated in printed reports that were independent of the decennial Census of Population. The first economic census, the Census of Business, was conducted in 1929. The results of this census included printed reports with data on retail and wholesale trade, service industries, and construction. Data on these subjects were also collected and disseminated in censuses for 1933, 1935, and 1939. After an interruption for World War II, the Census of Business was taken in 1948, 1954, 1958, 1963, 1967, and every five years since.

With the publication of the 1940 census, the presentation of the data collected in the decennial census was reorganized for the first time since the census of 1850. The statistics collected on population were presented in the Census of Population, which was structured into four volumes: *Number of Inhabitants; Characteristics of the Population; The Labor Force;* and *Characteristics by Age, Marital Status, Relationship, Education, and Citizenship.* Housing data were separated from population data and published in a separate Census of Housing report. Statistics on economic activity were published in printed reports on agriculture, manufactures, mineral industries, business (including one volume on retail trade, one on wholesale trade, and one on service establishments). These would later evolve into six of the separate quinquennial economic censuses. The 1940 census was also notable because it was the first census to include printed reports containing demographic and socioeconomic statistics for census tracts in the 60 cities that had been subdivided into tracts.

A key concept that was greatly expanded on during the twentieth century is that of census geography. Early censuses mainly included reports of data by political units: states, counties, townships, cities, and so forth. But collecting data just within political boundaries is not always precise enough to provide an accurate and useful count, especially in rural areas close to cities. Therefore, the bureau developed geographic units that are defined independently of political boundaries. Printed reports now contained tables of statistics for metropolitan statistical areas, census tracts, urbanized areas, and other geographical subdivisions created by the bureau in cooperation with local leaders. Another outcome of this concern with geography is that the Census Bureau has compiled thousands of maps of detailed urban and rural areas.

In order to achieve consistency between and within census reports, it became necessary to provide standardized definitions of terms, concepts, and geographic units. Almost every census printed report now contains an appendix in which detailed explanations, information about historical comparability, and definitions are provided for *housing unit, census tracts, ancestry,* and many other important terms.

The use of sample data enabled the bureau to publish reports on a wider variety of subjects than had been possible or practical before. In the 1940 census, for the first time several questions were asked of a sample of people instead of everyone. Building on this experience with sampling, the 1950 census included collection and dissemination of sample data from 20 percent of the population and 3.3 percent of the population. There are four numbered volumes in the 1950 census, as there were for the 1940 census, but with different titles and organization. Volume 1, *Number of Inhabitants,* consists of 54 reports, including a United States summary, and reports for each state, the District of Columbia, and the territories and possessions. Volume 2, *Characteristics of the Population,* provides additional data for the same geographical areas as volume 1. Volume 3, *Census Tracts,* contains the reports for the 64 areas that had been divided into tracts. Volume 4, *Special Reports,* contains 19 reports on economic and family characteristics, national origin and race, mobility of the population, and other subjects.

The 1960 census included more data, presented in more reports, than any census that preceded it. Volume 1, *Characteristics of the Population,* consists of 59 parts, including a United States summary and 55 reports for states and outlying areas. Volume 2, *Subject Reports,* is made up of 33 reports on social and economic characteristics by nativity, parentage, and country of origin. Volume 3, the *Selected Area Reports,* consists of 5 reports of statistical data for places, including state

economic areas, size of place, Americans overseas, standard metropolitan statistical areas, and type of place. A fourth and unnumbered volume contains the census tract reports for 180 standard metropolitan statistical areas. Data on housing are contained in the reports of a companion but separate Census of Housing.

The publication of printed reports of the Census of Population and Housing reached its zenith with the censuses of 1970 and 1980. Following the four-volume pattern established during the previous 30 years, each had the volumes *Characteristics of the Population, Subject Reports, Census Tract Reports,* and *Supplementary Reports* in addition to numerous other reports in print as well as microfiche format. By 1990 budget constraints within the federal government resulted in a drastic reduction in the number of printed reports. They included four volumes: *General Population Characteristics,* which includes complete count data on race, Hispanic origin, age, marital status, and so forth, for states, counties, places, and county subdivisions; *Summary Social, Economic, and Housing Characteristics,* which contains data derived entirely from sample counts ranging from 12 to 50 percent for states, counties, places, and county subdivisions; *General Housing Characteristics,* which contains complete count data on such topics as unit value or rent, number of rooms, tenure, vacancy for states, counties, places, and county subdivisions; and *Detailed Housing Characteristics,* which contains more extensive data than *General Housing Characteristics* based on sample data.

Technology and the Modern Census

Arguably the most important technological development in the history of the census occurred with the incorporation of the computer into the collection, tabulation, and production of census reports. The 1950 Census of Population and Housing and the 1954 economic censuses marked the first use of the computer to process data. During the 1950s, the bureau's attention remained on the production of the census reports in a timely manner, and the use of the computer was seen as a way to accomplish this goal. Not only could computers be used to tabulate the data, but also they were used to produce the printed reports. The 1960 Census of Population and Housing was the first decennial census in which the computer took the place of the old punched card system for tabulating the data.

Besides increasing the speed at which the data could be tabulated and published in the printed reports, the use of the computer also made it possible for reports to be generated on topics of a much higher degree of specificity. As the Census Bureau became more user oriented, technology enabled it to provide special reports on demand to particular user groups.

Up to and including the 1960 census, most census reports were published as printed reports either as ink on paper or, later in the twentieth century, on microfiche. During the transition era starting in 1970, census publications began to be issued in a variety of formats, including print, microfiche, CD-ROM, computer tape, and floppy disk, and on the Internet. Publication in electronic formats has been shrinking the central role formerly occupied by printed reports. There are several reasons for this. Publications in print format are static: pages can be copied, but the data cannot be manipulated. Data published electronically on CD-ROM or magnetic tape, or on the Internet, can be manipulated to fit the specific needs of the user by means of specialized programs. Data products that are published on the Internet can be used conveniently in one's office, home, or other location without taking up the storage space necessary for printed reports. Similarly, electronic data products on the Internet are often cheaper for the individual to use. All these factors are compelling reasons for the dramatic reduction in printed reports for data collected in the 1990 and later censuses of population, the economic censuses, and other report series. Reflective of this, the results of the 2000 census included three volumes for each state and the following national volumes in print format: *Census 2000: Summary Population and Housing Characteristics; Census 2000: Summary Social, Economic, and Housing Characteristics;* and *Census 2000: Population and Housing Unit Counts.* Most of the other data gathered in the 2000 census was distributed in electronic format.

The 2010 census collected only basic demographic and housing data. Fewer data tabulations and a reliance on the Internet as the main vehicle for dissemination have resulted in few printed reports from the census. The major printed report from the 2010 census is the *Population and Housing Unit Counts Report Series,* which contains selected data on population and housing unit counts, population density, and area measurements for geographic areas down to the place level for each of the states, the District of Columbia, Puerto Rico and a U.S. summary. Another printed report from the 2010 census is the *Characteristics of American Indians and Alaska Natives by Tribe,* with data for the nation and states. The remaining printed reports are the *2010 Census Briefs* and *2010 Census Special Reports,* both of which contain analyses of specific topics and data for the nation, states, and largest places.

Additionally, the *Summary Population and Housing Characteristics Report Series* contains tables on each of the variables included in the 2010 census along with population density and area measurement for each state, the District of Columbia, Puerto Rico, and a national summary. Instead of being printed as a hardcopy report, this report series is available as PDF files for download and printing by the user.

Some important statistical publications were originally published by other government agencies and later transferred to the Census Bureau. Perhaps the most widely used census report, the *Statistical Abstract of the United States,* was first published in 1878 by the Department of the Treasury. The early editions of this report reflected data gathered primarily by that agency. Between 1903 and 1937 various statistics-gathering agencies expanded the scope of its coverage; in 1938, the bureau began issuing the publication. It is a compendium census report in which data from many different agencies on a wide variety of topics are assembled in one recurring source. It and other compendia like it are particularly useful to students

and others who want an easy-to-use source of comparative statistical information. Less frequently published companions to the *Statistical Abstract of the United States* are the *City and County Data Book* and the *State and Metropolitan Area Data Book.*

Resources on Printed Products

For more comprehensive information on the printed reports in all the censuses through 1980, the user should consult Suzanne Schulze's three-volume work, *Population Information in Nineteenth Century Census Volumes; Population Information in Twentieth Century Census Volumes, 1900–1940;* and *Population Information in Twentieth Century Census Volumes, 1950–1980.* The most complete listing of census publications from the 1st through the 16th censuses remains *Catalog of United States Census Publications, 1790–1945,* by Henry J. Dubester. It has been reprinted several times; the most recent edition, *Dubester's U.S. Census Bibliography with SuDocs Class Numbers and Indexes,* by Kevin L. Cook, also includes supplemental entries, a title index, a series index, and a Superintendent of Documents Classification Number index. Between 1945 and 1984 the Bureau of the Census published the *Bureau of the Census Catalog,* in which were listed all the publications, in all formats, issued by the bureau. This publication was followed by the *Census Catalog and Guide,* which was published annually until 1998 and, like its predecessor, lists all the publications of the bureau. Starting in 1999, the catalog was available only online through the Census Bureau's Web site.

See also *Data dissemination and use; Data products: evolution; Dissemination of data: electronic products; Dissemination of data: secondary products.*

JANICE S. FRYER
. . . . REVISED BY LEONARD M. GAINES

BIBLIOGRAPHY

Cook, Kevin L. *Dubester's U.S. Census Bibliography with SuDocs Class Numbers and Indexes.* Englewood, Colo.: Libraries Unlimited, 1996.

Dubester, Henry J. *Catalog of United States Census Publications, 1790–1945.* Washington, D.C.: U.S. Government Printing Office, 1950.

Farrington, Polly-Alida. *Subject Index to the 1980 Census of Population and Housing.* Clifton Park, N.Y.: Specialized Information Products, 1985.

Kaplan, Charles P., and Thomas L. Van Valey. *Census '80: Continuing the FactFinder Tradition.* Washington, D.C.: U.S. Government Printing Office, 1980.

Lavin, Michael R. *Understanding the Census: A Guide for Marketers, Planners, Grant Writers and Other Data Users.* Kenmore, N.Y: Epoch; Phoenix, Ariz.: Oryx Press (distributor, library ed.), 1996.

Lavin, Michael R., Jane Weintrop, and Cynthia Cornelius. *Subject Index to the 1990 Census of Population and Housing.* Kenmore, N.Y.: Epoch Books, 1997.

Schulze, Suzanne. *Population Information in Nineteenth Century Census Volumes.* Phoenix, Ariz.: Oryx Press, 1983.

———. *Population Information in Twentieth Century Census Volumes, 1900–1940.* Phoenix, Ariz.: Oryx Press, 1985.

———. *Population Information in Twentieth Century Census Volumes, 1950–1980.* Phoenix, Ariz.: Oryx Press, 1985.

U.S. Bureau of the Census. *Bureau of the Census Catalog of Publications, 1790–1972.* Washington, D.C.: U.S. Government Printing Office, 1974.

————. *Bureau of the Census Catalog, 1973–1984.* Washington, D.C.: U.S. Government Printing Office, 1973–1984.

————. *Census Catalog and Guide, 1985–.* Washington, D.C.: U.S. Government Printing Office, 1985–.

Wright, Carroll D. *History and Growth of the United States Census.* Prepared for the Senate Committee on the Census. Washington, D.C.: U.S. Government Printing Office, 1900.

Dissemination of Data: Secondary Products

Secondary products of the decennial censuses are produced for special purposes outside the scope of the primary decennial census report series and summary files, to the extent that there *are* primary products, since that concept is not recognized nor used by the Census Bureau. The reports and products that are declared and funded prior to the census can be regarded as planned or primary products. In general, primary products supply basic counts and summary data for all aspects of the census and include what are termed *statistical summary data files* and *subject reports*. Because the content of the census varies over time in response to social needs and political pressures, primary and secondary products cannot be differentiated on the basis of content or subject matter. Furthermore, what may be a special topic in one census year can be part of the primary reports in the next. The difference between secondary products and primary products is determined by how the products are defined by the Census Bureau. Secondary products can be defined as being products that are not part of the primary series and are created to meet special needs of nongovernmental bodies, the internal requirements of the Census Bureau, or the needs of other government agencies. Creation and production of these tabulations are often requested by and funded by other agencies to support mandated programs or for research within the agencies.

Today, metropolitan, state, and federal governments use secondary data products to meet the requirements of many federal programs and to supply data needed for federal grants. In some cases state and local funding may require census data found in these products, and some products are necessary to the private sector in meeting statutory requirements. The best known of these are the Equal Employment Opportunity data, but financial institutions also use census products to meet the reporting requirements of the Home Mortgage Disclosure Act of 1975. Statistical data are needed in formula-based grant programs, and population statistics influence a vast amount of targeted dollar outlays. Income and housing data are also important in the distribution of federal funds. Secondary products also facilitate academic research and provide additional materials to both for-profit businesses and not-for-profit organizations.

History

The ability to create secondary products was realized in 1850, when the census began to collect individual-level data. This made post-census tabulations possible, although difficulties in performing tabulations meant that few special reports were created in the nineteenth century. The first large-scale special uses of the census began during the Civil War, when the Census Office supplied special tabulations and reports directly to the War Department. From that time through the 1950s secondary reports were frequently prepared in response to pressing social and economic issues. Beginning with the 1900 census, secondary products became commonplace. Among the many reports from the 1900 census were *Child Labor in the United States* and a compendium titled *Supplementary Analysis and Derivative Tables, Twelfth Census of the United States,* which dealt mainly with African Americans and included "The Negro Farmer," by W. E. B. Du Bois. Following the 1910 census came reports such as *Deaf-Mutes in the United States* as well as a similar report dealing with the blind. Many special reports of this time were prepared by Joseph A. Hill, chief statistician in the Division of Revision and Results, Bureau of the Census. For example, his "Occupations of the First and Second Generations of Immigrants in the United States: Fecundity of Immigrant Women" was published in 1911 as a report of the Immigration Commission. Immigration would also be an important issue surrounding the census of 1920, as would the growth of cities and child labor. Included here are the reports *Immigrants and Their Children; Children in Gainful Occupations at the Fourteenth Census of the United States; Farm Population of the United States;* and *An Analysis of the 1920 Farm Population Figures, Especially in Comparison with Urban Data.* These are all examples of census products that reflect the concerns of the day. Following the 1930 census was a series of reports dealing with the unemployed based on a special unemployment schedule that was used in that enumeration, a reflection of the economic crises of that era. Other reports published early in the twentieth century were *Women in Gainful Occupations, 1870–1920* (1929), *The Negro Population, 1790–1915* (1918), *Paupers in Almshouses, 1910,* and *Prisoners and Juvenile Delinquents in the United States, 1910* (1918).

In the 1940s, secondary products focused on housing, the labor force, and internal migration. Reports from the 1940 census included *The Labor Force (Sample Statistics) Employment and Family Characteristics of Women, Housing Special Reports Series H-46,* and *Internal Migration: Color and Sex of Migrants.* Also from 1940 was a special report dealing with education: *Educational Attainment by Economic Characteristics and Marital Status.* In 1950 there was continued interest in housing issues, as demonstrated by the publication of *Special Tabulation for Local Housing Authorities, Series HC-6.* The 1960 census products included the first special transportation planning product, *Transportation Planning Data for Urbanized Areas,* based on the 1960 census, as well as reports dealing with poverty and aging. The Housing and Home Finance Agency published *Senior Citizens and How They Live: An Analysis of 1960 Census Data.* Following the 1960 census, primary publications dealing with racial minorities were produced. Thus what had been a special or secondary topic became a primary one.

Since 1970 many of these supplemental or special reports have been issued both in print and as data files. In 1980 many of the data products were included as part of the Summary Tape Files (STFs) only, but the print reports were issued under separate titles. In 1990 there was a large increase in the number of secondary products and programs or series under which these products can be found. With the release of public-use versions of the microdata files and geographical cross-referencing facilities, it is possible to create tabulations for many special populations on many topics or to create the standard tables for nonstandard geographic areas. Still, secondary data products remain a valued source for business, governments, and research.

It is difficult to identify, let alone locate, complete listings of historical special subject reports. The annual *Census Catalog and Guide* (covering 1980–1998) provides a fairly comprehensive list of secondary report and data products. For products from the 1970 census, *Directory of Data Files* was first issued in 1979 with loose-leaf updates running through 1984. Those based on the 1990 and 2000 censuses and American Community Surveys are largely available on the bureau's Web site. Older special reports are out-of-print but still available in many libraries. Increasingly, they are being scanned and made more widely available through such services as Internet Archive, Google Books, and the Census Bureau's own Web site.

Current Subject Areas

From 1970 through 2000 the subject areas covered by secondary products have remained reasonably consistent, with a few exceptions. These subject areas include aging, educational attainment, commuting or journey to work, fertility, minorities and ethnic groups, native language, poverty, disabilities, employment status, occupation and industry, and work experience. A number of special reports deal with housing and its costs, as well as characteristics of residents: housing of the elderly, persons served by emergency and transitional shelters, rental housing, mobile homes, condominium housing, and racial and ethnic neighborhood segregation. The Subject Summary Tape Files, or SSTFs, series provided a wide range of population and housing items such as age, citizenship, educational attainment, employment status, and detailed housing characteristics. Reports based on the 2000 census recognized the increasing complexity of household relationships and family composition by producing reports on the characteristics of married-couple and unmarried-partner households, and the presence of children in households.

Other subject-based secondary products covering topics such as migration, marriage and living arrangements, foreign-born citizens living abroad, and income and earnings are used by various Census Bureau divisions and programs. The population estimates and projections programs use many census items. Among them are details about the demographics of the population at the time of the census and data on household structure, family relationships, childbearing and women of childbearing age, migration, and persons in group quarters. Since 1970 the bureau has produced modified counts of age/race and sex data, or "MARS" files, which incorporated adjustments to compensate for errors in the census tabulations, especially for the very young, very old, and persons of nonspecified races. In some cases these files also included adjustments made to counties or other areas that may have

challenged Census Bureau numbers and were able to have their population counts revised.

Other Products

The 1990 Special Tabulation Project (STP) provided small-area data dealing with veterans, aging, and housing. These tabulations were funded by the Veterans Administration, the Administration on Aging, and the Department of Housing and Urban Development. There were more than 100 other special tabulations, some providing unique detail and cross-tabulations. Most of these were announced in Census Bureau publications of the time but were never available and have become difficult to locate as time passes. For example, STP 89, *Characteristics of Displaced Homemakers and Single Parents,* was released on diskette in 1993 and was available from the Decennial Programs Coordination Branch. That branch no longer exists. Computer printouts were available from the Population Division and the Housing and Household Economic Statistics Division (HHES). The HHES repackaged a set of listings for sale as a group. This set, *The Historical Poverty Tables,* contains comparisons of poverty characteristics from the 1970, 1980, and 1990 censuses.

Mandated programs dealing with equal employment have led to the creation of special products to meet the needs of employers. The Equal Employment Opportunity (EEO) file (1980 and 1990) provides detailed occupation, race, sex, and Hispanic origin counts for states, counties, metropolitan areas, and large cities. There is a separate table for educational attainment, age, and sex. In 1990 two supplemental EEO files were funded by external sources, and the data from that work are made available to the public. Owing to fiscal exigencies, a consortium of four federal agencies (Equal Employment Opportunity Commission, Department of Justice, Office of Federal Contract Compliance Programs, and Office of Personnel Management) funded the Census 2000 special EEO tabulation.

Secondary data products dealing with transportation, journey to work, place of work, and vehicle availability have been produced since the questions were first asked in 1960. These files and reports find many uses at the national, state, and local level. They are used to define labor markets and to meet mandated programs, many dealing with the Clean Air Act. From 1970 to 2000 the Department of Transportation distributed special census tabulations designed to aid transportation planners in their Census Transportation Planning products (known as the Census Transportation Planning Package, formerly the Urban Transportation Planning Packages for the years 1970 and 1980). The Office of Rural Health Policy at the Department of Health and Human Services sponsored the creation of STP64, *Census Tract of Work by Census Tract of Residence,* the results of which were used to define Rural-Urban Commuting Areas. Related to this is Census 2000 STP86, *County of Residence by County of Work,* commissioned by the Bureau of Economic Analysis, detailing county-to-county worker flows.

Data on education, sponsored by the National Center for Education Statistics (NCES), have been made available by the Census Bureau and the private sector. Since 1940 the bureau has prepared special data products dealing with educational attainment. Similar data are found in the Current Population Survey supplemental questions on that topic and the Current Population Report Series. In 1970, the NCES funded tabulations by school district for 1st Count and 5th Count data files but contracted with Applied Urbanetics to compile some tables from the 1970 4th Count at the school district level. The bureau produced a block group to school district geographic equivalency for districts with at least 300 students. For each block group or enumeration district, Office of Education school district codes were given. In 1980 the Bureau of the Census was the contracting agent for school district–level summaries and a geographic reference file, but in 1990 the NCES turned to the private sector to deliver census data tabulations at the school district level.

More recently, a Voting Rights Determination File based on the 2000 census supported requirements of the Voting Rights Act Amendments of 1992 to identify political subdivisions subject to its language assistance requirements. Special tabulations by nongovernment units include a 2000 census file on citizenship status, race, and Hispanic origin sponsored by Election Data Services. The Guttmacher Institute supported a series of 1990 census special tabulations (STP20) on race, Hispanic origin, marital status, and poverty status.

See also *American Community Survey: data products; Data products: evolution; Dissemination of data: electronic products; Dissemination of data: printed publications; Summary Files.*

. . . . PAM M. BAXTER

BIBLIOGRAPHY

U.S. Bureau of the Census. *Bureau of the Census Catalog of Publications, 1790–1972.* Washington, D.C.: U.S. Department of Commerce, Social and Economic Statistics Administration, Bureau of the Census, 1974. www.census.gov/prod/www/abs/catalogs.html.

———. *Census Catalog and Guide.* Washington, D.C.: U.S. Department of Commerce, Bureau of the Census. [Preceded by *Bureau of the Census Catalog.* Annual 1964–1984.] Annual. Available in print for 1980–1998. www.census.gov/prod/www/abs/catalogs.html.

———. *Directory of Data Files.* Washington, D.C.: U.S. Department of Commerce, Bureau of the Census, 1979. With updates through 1984.

Dress Rehearsal

The dress rehearsal is the last major test of census procedures before the decennial census and is therefore the culmination of all the planned innovations for that census. The Census Bureau chooses several sites around the country and mounts a full-scale census in each of these local areas. The 2008 dress rehearsal for the 2010 census took place at two sites, San Joaquin County, California, and the city of Fayetteville, North Carolina, and the surrounding nine-county region in North Carolina.

Throughout the decade the bureau conducts small-scale tests of changes in census procedures planned for future censuses. It also conducts such tests during the enumeration itself. These include tests of instructions, question wording, question order, employment and training procedures, and other census elements. Once a census plan is designed, all these elements are tested again in the dress rehearsal. The bureau evaluates the operational plan in the dress rehearsal to anticipate and identify problems with the enumeration and to make final changes to the plan before the full April enumeration. The dress rehearsal takes place about two years before the enumeration to allow for a full evaluation.

The bureau began to include tests of census procedures, including the dress rehearsals, before the 1940 census. In August 1939 it took a special census of St. Joseph and Marshall Counties, Indiana, which it used to finalize plans for the April 1940 count. In later years the dress rehearsal became the culmination of a decade or more of smaller procedural tests.

See also *Census testing.*

. . . . MARGO J. ANDERSON

Economic Census

The economic census is an enumeration of business establishments in the United States. It provides a detailed portrait of the nation's economy once every five years, for years ending in "2" and "7."

Data from the economic census serve as the foundation for the nation's system of statistics about the functioning of the American economy. While many monthly, quarterly, and annual surveys provide the numbers most closely watched by private and government economists for the latest in economic trends, the once-every-five-years economic census provides the statistical controls and sampling frames that make many of those surveys possible. Further, the census yields rich data products of its own, providing far greater precision and geographic detail than are possible from the more frequent surveys and making possible many applications ranging from economic research to business-to-business marketing. It also collects information found nowhere else, such as electricity usage by different manufacturing industries and selling floor area of grocery stores.

Data Collection

Most of the data in the economic census are collected by mail. Forms in the 2007 Economic Census were mailed to 4.7 million businesses at the end of 2007, and companies were asked to report their activity during all of that calendar year. Over 500 variations of the census form were sent, each customized to particular industries or groups of industries, so that companies could respond in terms meaningful to their own kind of business.

Some very small businesses are not sent census forms to complete. In the 2007 Economic Census, instead of sending out 3 million forms to very small employers and 21 million forms to businesses without paid employees (nonemployers), the Census Bureau adapted information to the extent possible from the administrative records of other federal agencies.

The economic census is mandated by law under Title 13 of the United States Code (sections 131, 191, and 224). The law requires firms to respond and specifies penalties for firms that fail to report. The law also requires the Census Bureau to maintain confidentiality. Individual responses may be seen only by those sworn to protect the data. No data are published that could reveal the identity or activity of any business.

The economic census traces its beginnings to the 1810 decennial census, when questions on manufacturing were included with those for population. Coverage of economic activities was expanded in subsequent censuses to include mining and some commercial activities. The 1905 Census of Manufactures was the first time a census was taken separately from the regular decennial population census. Censuses covering retail and wholesale trade and construction industries were added in 1930, as were some service trades in 1933. The 1954 Economic Census was the first time the various censuses were integrated: providing comparable census data across economic sectors, using consistent time periods, concepts, definitions, classifications, and reporting units. Censuses were taken for 1958 and 1963 and, starting in 1967, have continued at five-year intervals.

Basic Concepts

The core data from the economic census are summarized in terms of business establishments— for example, the number and aggregate employment of establishments in a certain kind of business located in a certain area. An establishment, as defined for census and survey purposes, is a business or industrial unit at a single geographic location that produces or distributes goods or performs services, such as a single store or factory.

Classifying economic activity establishment by establishment is only one of three alternatives. Some census results are classified by company or firm (an entity owning or controlling any number of establishments, including those of subsidiary firms). But because different establishments within the same company can be located in different areas or be engaged in different kinds of business, the establishment basis of reporting yields more precise information than data reported in terms of companies.

Users frequently want data in terms of particular products produced or sold, a third way to classify economic activity. Census forms ask for dollar volume of sales for key products appropriate to each industry, but these data are limited to avoid placing an unreasonable record-keeping burden on businesses. Further, many of the statistics collected in the economic census, such as employment or capital expenditures, are associated with particular establishments but cannot generally be reported separately for individual product lines. Thus, only selected tables present statistics by product line. Most of the basic census statistics reflect the classification of establishments, not companies or products.

Classifying Industries and Products

Economic census data are classified by industry according to the North American Industry Classification System (NAICS), a scheme developed together with Canada and Mexico. NAICS replaced the Standard Industrial Classification (SIC) system developed in the 1930s. NAICS classifies North America's economic activities at two-, three-, four-, and five-digit levels of detail, and the U.S. version of NAICS further defines industries to a sixth digit (see Table 1).

NAICS categorizes each establishment by the principal activity in which it is engaged. Some establishments engage in more than one kind of activity and thus may not fit neatly into a single industry category. Nonetheless, each establishment is classified into only one NAICS category on the basis of its primary activity. Its secondary activities are still counted, for example, toward total sales, but they do not affect the classification. For instance, the total sales of furniture retailers (NAICS 44211) in a given area should not be interpreted as the total sales of furniture. Stores in that industry may sell other items in addition to furniture, and other kinds of businesses, such as department stores (NAICS 45211), also sell furniture. This is an inevitable limitation of the establishment basis of classification.

Despite their limitations, standardized industry classification systems have major advantages. Their widespread use, inside and outside the government, promotes uniformity and comparability in the presentation of statistics collected by various federal and state agencies, trade associations, and private research organizations.

The Census Bureau also classifies products, and, in the case of manufacturing and mining, products are classified in a manner consistent with the industry structure. Since 1997 the first six digits of the ten-digit product code are the same as the NAICS code for the industry with which the product is most frequently associated. Broad product or service lines also are provided for retail and wholesale trade and other service industries, although their numbering is independent of the industry code. Product lines for service industries are based on the new North American Product Classification System (NAPCS).

Coverage of the Census

Economic censuses have never covered all of the economy. After a significant expansion in 1992, the economic census, together with the censuses of agriculture and governments conducted separately, covers roughly 98 percent of economic activity.

The 2007 Economic Census covered 1,064 of the 1,175 industries in NAICS. Specific exclusions are noted in Table 2.

The economic census does not generally include government-owned establishments, even when their primary activity would be classified in industries covered by the economic census. Because of these exclusions, economic census data for industries in many sectors might appear to be incomplete, for

Table 1. NAICS Hierarchic Structure

NAICS LEVEL	NAICS CODE	DESCRIPTION
Sector	31-33	Manufacturing
Subsector	312	Beverage and Tobacco Product Manufacturing
Industry group	3121	Beverage Manufacturing
Industry	31211	Soft Drink and Ice Manufacturing
U.S. industry	312112	Bottled Water Manufacturing

NOTE: NAICS = North American Industry Classification System.

Table 2. NAICS Sectors and Their Coverage in the 2007 Economic Census

NAICS CODE	ECONOMIC SECTOR[a]
11	Agriculture, Forestry, Fishing, and Hunting (Separate Census of Agriculture, conducted by the Department of Agriculture, covers farming but excludes agricultural services, forestry, and fisheries)
21	Mining
22	Utilities
23	Construction
31–33	Manufacturing
42	Wholesale Trade
44–45	Retail Trade
48–49	Transportation and Warehousing (census excludes U.S. Postal Service and rail transportation)
51	Information
52	Finance and Insurance (census excludes funds and trusts)
53	Real Estate and Rental and Leasing
54	Professional, Scientific, and Technical Services
55	Management of Companies and Enterprises
56	Administrative and Support, Waste Management, and Remediation Services
61	Educational Services (census excludes elementary and secondary schools, colleges, and professional schools)
62	Health Care and Social Assistance
71	Arts, Entertainment, and Recreation
72	Accommodation and Food Services
81	Other Services (Except Public Administration) (census excludes labor, political, and religious organizations, and private households)
92	Public Administration (Separate Census of Governments does not present data according to NAICS)

NOTE: NAICS = North American Industry Classification System.

[a] The economic census covers all industries except where noted. For a complete list of industries, see www.census.gov/naics.

example, with the exclusion of public utilities, government-operated bus and subway systems, or public libraries.

Another limitation to the coverage of the economic census is that most of the statistics apply only to establishments with payroll; that is, they omit small, single-establishment companies with no paid employees—what are sometimes called "mom and pop" businesses. This limitation is a practical one because the census is conducted by mail and the best records for developing the mailing list of businesses come from the federal payroll tax (Social Security) system. To gauge the number and sales of nonemployer businesses—those not covered by payroll tax records—the Census Bureau obtains data from the Internal Revenue Service derived from business income tax returns. Most economic census reports summarize statistics about only those establishments with paid employees.

On the one hand, statistics on manufactures are not much affected by the exclusion of establishments without employees. On the other hand, in retailing, services, and construction, establishments without paid employees—for instance, door-to-door salespeople, consultants, independent contractors—are relatively common. In 2007, nonemployer establishments

accounted for about 2.2 percent of retail sales nationwide, 16.6 percent of other services (except public administration) receipts, and 8.4 percent of construction receipts. Certain small industries, such as barbershops, are dominated by nonemployers, and in a number of others—such as real estate agents and brokers, tax return preparers, child day care providers, taxi services, beauty shops—nonemployers account for more than 20 percent of all receipts.

Geographic Areas

The most detailed economic census data are provided for the United States as a whole. Key statistics, albeit progressively fewer, are available for states, metropolitan and micropolitan areas (MAs), counties, and places. Only limited data are provided for ZIP codes. Places (including incorporated cities, towns or townships in selected states, and census designated places) were published for 2007 if they had either 5,000 residents or 5,000 workers, although the criteria for included places have changed over time. No economic census data are published for census tracts or other small areas. The level of geographic detail varies by sector, as shown in Table 3.

Table 3. Geographic Areas in the 1997 Economic Census

SECTOR	STATES	METROPOLITAN AND MICROPOLITAN AREAS	COUNTIES	PLACES 5000+	ZIP CODES
Mining	X				
Utilities	X	X			
Construction	X				
Manufacturing	X	X	X	X	X
Wholesale Trade	X	X	X	X	
Retail Trade	X	X	X	X	X
Transportation and Warehousing	X	X			
Information	X	X	X	X	
Finance and Insurance	X	X	X	X	
Real Estate and Rental and Leasing	X	X	X	X	
Professional, Scientific, and Technical Services	X	X	X	X	X
Management of Companies and Enterprises	X				
Administrative and Support, Waste Management, and Remediation Services	X	X	X	X	X
Educational Services	X	X	X	X	X
Health Care and Social Assistance	X	X	X	X	X
Arts, Entertainment, and Recreation	X	X	X	X	X
Accommodation and Food Services	X	X	X	X	X
Other Services (Except Public Administration)	X	X	X	X	X

Within a given area, the more economic activity there is, the more detail is available. Thus, a county with many factories is likely to have more industry detail in a manufacturing census report than a county with fewer manufacturers. All of the data are scrutinized closely to avoid possible disclosure of information about particular firms. This can be frustrating for a user who finds that a desired number has been replaced with a "(D)" for "disclosure" and therefore must rely on data at a higher level of aggregation.

Economic Census Products

Economic census results are published primarily through the interactive American FactFinder system accessible at www.census.gov. Data from the 2007 Economic Census were published across a two-and-one-half-year period beginning early in 2009 and continuing through mid-2011.

Types of Reports

Table 4 illustrates data published in the *Economy-Wide Key Statistics* (EWKS) file. It features the four "key statistics"—establishments, sales or receipts, payroll, and employment—common to most economic census tables. Economic census data are distributed by industry, geography, and, in some cases, other variables. Table headnotes, column headings, and row labels are linked to explanatory material—methodology, reliability, and definitions of terms.

Detailed Reports. Most economic census reports are issued sector by sector.

- Industry Series provide national totals on individual industries and their products. The data are preliminary and are superseded by later reports.
- Geographic Area Series provide detail as illustrated in Table 4. They include data for the nation, states, and substate areas listed in Table 3, except ZIP codes.
- Subject Series and Summary Series provide national and, in some cases, state data on special topics including Product Lines, Concentration Ratios, and Establishment and Firm Size.
- ZIP Code Statistics (selected sectors, see Table 3) include counts of establishments by sales size by industry.

Other Reports. Several reports are published with economy-wide scope. The Advance Report is the first report published from each census, with only broad NAICS categories shown at the national level; its data are preliminary and are superseded by later reports. Nonemployer Statistics, compiled largely from tax return data, is the only source for information about more than 20 million small businesses not included in other census reports. Island Areas reports include data corresponding to the Geographic Area Series for Puerto Rico, the Virgin Islands,

Table 4. Sample Data in Economy-Wide Key Statistics

GEOGRAPHIC AREA NAME	2007 NAICS CODE	MEANING OF 2007 NAICS CODE	NUMBER OF EMPLOYER ESTABLISHMENTS	EMPLOYER SALES, SHIPMENTS, RECEIPTS, REVENUE, OR BUSINESS DONE ($1,000)	ANNUAL PAYROLL ($1,000)	NUMBER OF PAID EMPLOYEES FOR PAY PERIOD INCLUDING MARCH 12
California	44-45	Retail trade	114,438	455,032,270	44,328,924	1,683,023
California	441	Motor vehicle and parts dealers	11,323	105,835,001	9,019,038	212,872
California	4411	Automobile dealers	3,888	90,791,581	6,878,747	143,863
California	44111	New car dealers	2,318	85,479,903	6,554,240	134,251
California	44112	Used car dealers	1,570	5,311,678	324,507	9,612
California	4412	Other motor vehicle dealers	1,520	6,867,436	753,953	19,141
California	44121	Recreational vehicle dealers	325	2,663,752	274,053	6,315
California	44122	Motorcycle, boat, and other motor vehicle dealers	1,195	4,203,684	479,900	12,826
California	441221	Motorcycle, ATV, and personal watercraft dealers	626	2,534,465	306,706	8,129
California	441222	Boat dealers	390	1,223,683	127,164	3,505
California	441229	All other motor vehicle dealers	179	445,536	46,030	1,192

American Samoa, Guam, and the Commonwealth of the Northern Mariana Islands.

The Economy-Wide Key Statistics file consolidates the industry and geographic data published in most of the foregoing series and grows with successive releases across a two-year period.

Franchise Establishment Statistics documents the number and impact of establishments operating under the trade name of a franchisor.

Business Expenses shows various types of operating expenses, including supplemental labor costs, energy costs, taxes, and a variety of purchased services including advertising, legal and accounting services, and repairs. Data are available only for retailers, merchant wholesalers, and services firms.

Bridge and Comparative Statistics reports are discussed below in the section on Assembling Time Series.

Survey of Business Owners. The Survey of Business Owners, conducted in conjunction with the economic census, measures the extent of business ownership by gender, veteran status, Hispanic origin and race—whites, blacks, Asians, Native Hawaiians and Other Pacific Islanders, and American Indians and Alaska Natives. Data on the major categories are published for the same areas shown in Table 3 except ZIP codes. Also in the series are Characteristics of Business Owners tables, including age, education, hours worked, and whether born in the United States, and Characteristics of Businesses tables, identifying home-based and family-owned businesses, financing, franchising, and other variables.

Access to Microdata: Special Tabulations and Studies

One of the most popular forms of data release for users of demographic data from the Census Bureau is the public-use microdata file. Samples from the bureau's various household surveys, including the Census of Population and Housing, are made available to data users after detailed geographic information has been removed and other modifications are made to reduce the potential that any respondent could be identified. Public-use microdata files allow users to retabulate the data in a variety of ways to examine different relationships that may not be highlighted in published tables.

Unfortunately, the typical business establishment is far more identifiable than the typical household. Government agencies that regulate or tax businesses, as well as trade associations, publishers of business information, and other private entities frequently maintain large amounts of information about many specific businesses. Some of this information is made publicly available (for example, in classified telephone directories or in reports to shareholders). Thus any file of microdata about unidentified business establishments from a census would have some potential for being matched to information from other sources to indirectly identify, and thus disclose, confidential information about at least some specific businesses. In the absence of methods to keep such records anonymous, there can be no public-use microdata files about firms or establishments from the economic census.

The Census Bureau has developed the Longitudinal Research Database (LRD) of business establishments, with data assembled to cover both census and intervening years to the extent available. These and other microdata files are not available for public use, but the Census Bureau has a special staff (the Center for Economic Studies) to work with economic microdata. Appropriately funded outside researchers can be sworn in as Census Bureau staff to work with the data at Census Bureau Research Data Centers in various locations around the nation, but data publication requires the same kind of scrutiny to avoid disclosure of confidential information that applies to all other Census Bureau products.

Assembling Time Series Data
One of the preeminent virtues of the economic census program is that comparable data have been collected at fixed intervals and with consistent definitions across decades. Nonetheless, the reports from any one census typically include little historical data. Left to the user is the assembly of time series—such as the growth of retailing in a particular area or trends in a particular manufacturing industry.

Acquiring Reports from Previous Censuses
The American FactFinder system makes available data only for the most recent censuses: 2007 and 2002. Those data published as PDF documents for 2002, 1997, and 1992 are available on the census Web site. Collections of older printed reports are maintained at certain major libraries, and individual reports may be borrowed through interlibrary loan. The Census Bureau Library has a complete collection of printed economic census reports and is able to provide scans of selected pages. At least one depository library in each state also has a complete collection of the printed economic census reports.

Many of these data were also published on disc. CD-ROM or *DVD-ROM* coverage of the 2002 and 1997 Economic Census is complete, and CD-ROMs for 1992 and 1987 exclude only "miscellaneous subjects" reports. The files issued on disc, as well as selected files back to 1977, are now available for download at www.census.gov/econ/census12/historical-data.html.

Industry Comparability: 1997 Conversion to NAICS from SIC
The implementation of NAICS in 1997 caused major disruptions in the availability of comparable information across time periods. The SIC system was updated three times (in 1967, 1972, and 1987), and each time a significant number of new industries was introduced into the existing framework. What was different for 1997 was that the whole framework changed.

While data for nearly half of the SICs in use in 1992 could be derived from 1997 NAICS industries, a substantial number of industries cannot be much more than approximated under NAICS. That makes the 1997 Economic Census particularly important because census questionnaires identified industry components finely enough that data could be categorized under either NAICS or SIC; and as a result certain key data could be published according to the old system as well as the new. The report *Comparative Statistics, 1997 and 1992* (www.census.gov/epcd/ec97sic/E97SUS.HTM) presented the number of establishments, sales, employment, and payroll for each SIC for the nation and each state, for both 1997 and 1992. Thus, basic SIC-by-state time series can be carried backward from 1997 to 1987 and farther to the extent that particular industries were not affected by SIC changes in 1987, 1972, and 1967.

With some limitations due to revisions in 2002 and 2007, the NAICS time series can go forward from 1997, but it cannot generally go backward to earlier years because many NAICS categories require information that was not collected in 1992 and earlier censuses. For instance, NAICS 45321, Office Supplies and Stationery Stores, differs from SIC 5943, Stationery Stores, primarily by the addition of certain office supply stores that were previously classified in wholesale trade. Census questionnaires prior to 1997 did not separately differentiate office supply stores from other kinds of office supply wholesalers, so NAICS 45321 cannot be estimated for prior periods.

The Census Bureau estimated some national-level NAICS time series back to 1992. That project, intended to support time series for monthly surveys, was limited to broad industry categories within manufacturing, retail trade, and wholesale trade.

Users have access to correspondence tables between the old and new systems at the NAICS Web page (at www.census .gov/naics; select "Concordances"). These tables show for each NAICS industry the SIC categories or parts thereof that are included in the larger (NAICS) category and for each SIC industry the NAICS industries or parts thereof to which their establishments were likely to be reclassified. The 1997 Economic Census report *Bridge between 1997 NAICS and 1987 SIC* (www.census.gov/epcd/ec97brdg/) takes that correspondence a significant step further by showing the number of establishments, sales, employment, and payroll at the national level for each of those intersections between the old and new systems. For example, that *Bridge* report shows that the number and sales of those office supply stores that were transferred into retail trade from wholesale trade increased sales of the new retail Office Supply and Stationery Stores category by nearly tenfold over the SIC industry of the same name.

The *Bridge* tables are so powerful that one might be tempted to "update" historical figures from SIC to NAICS by applying proportions derivable from the tables. The user should employ such "synthetic estimation" with caution, however, since nationwide proportions may not reflect relationships in particular geographic areas or in prior time periods. Also many new industries reflected in NAICS—for example, satellite telecommunications—did not exist to a significant extent in prior periods.

At broader levels of classification, the changes between SIC and NAICS were further confounded by the rearrangement of the hierarchy. The Service Industries division of the SIC

was subdivided into five new sectors and parts of four others. Less noticeable, but perhaps more troublesome, were shifts affecting sectors—such as manufacturing, wholesale trade, and retail trade—that retained their status as sector titles in NAICS but were affected by changes in scope. Retail trade was smaller under NAICS than under SIC just because eating and drinking places, which accounted for roughly 10 percent of SIC-based retail sales and a third of SIC-based retail employment, were transferred to the new Accommodation and Food Services sector. Retail losses were offset partially by transfers between retail and wholesale trade, such as the office supply stores mentioned above. Manufacturing also shrank somewhat under NAICS because significant components were reclassified elsewhere.

Industry Revisions within NAICS: 2002, 2007, and 2012

Industry revisions are a regular feature of NAICS, out of the conviction that the old SIC system was allowed to get out of touch with the changing economy. Thus, users can expect some changes every five years, typically very minor in scope relative to the massive change that was undertaken in 1997.

For 2002, industries were redefined within construction and wholesale trade, and there was some rearrangement of industries within the information sector. Several new industries were defined within information and retail trade without disrupting the availability of data comparable to that published for 1997. These modifications did not affect the comparability of sector totals.

Changes between 2002 NAICS and 2007 NAICS were relatively minor but do affect four sector totals. NAICS 2007 introduced two new industries: biotech research and development and executive search services. At the same time several industries in the information sector were consolidated: paging into wireless telecommunication; cable program distribution and most ISPs into wired telecommunication; Web search portals into Internet publishing and broadcasting. Real estate investment trusts (REITs) were dispersed and mostly moved from the finance and insurance sector to real estate.

The 2012 Economic Census will see the introduction of new NAICS categories for solar, wind, geothermal, and biomass electric power generation, but the most significant change will be the substantial consolidation of industries within the manufacturing sector, reducing 473 industries to 366.

For each period of changes there are three resources:

- Correspondence tables on the NAICS Web site, generally available before the reference year
- *Bridge between [year] NAICS and [prior year] NAICS*, showing essentially the same changes as the correspondence tables, but with statistics that allow the significance of each change to be evaluated, generally available three to four years after the reference year. (For 1997 NAICS to 1987 SIC, see www.census.gov/epcd/ec97brdg/. For 2002 NAICS to 1997 NAICS, see www.census.gov/ econ/census02/data/bridge/. Bridge tables for 2007 are available from the Census Bureau's American FactFinder.)

- *Comparative Statistics, [year] and [prior year]*, a presentation of the latest economic census data reclassified according to the previous system for direct comparison with data from the previous census. (For Comparative Statistics 1997 and 1992, see www.census.gov/epcd/ec97sic/E97SUS.HTM. For 2002 and 1997, see www.census.gov/econ/census02/data/comparative/USCS.HTM. Comparative tables for 2007 are available from the Census Bureau's American FactFinder.)

Scope of Economic Census Programs

Prior to 1992 the economic census program covered significantly less of the American economy. In 1987 and earlier years, the census did not include finance, insurance, and real estate; and it included only selected transportation industries within the transportation, communication, and utilities sector. The addition of those components boosted census coverage from roughly 76 percent of the gross domestic product in 1987 to about 98 percent in 1992. The coverage of service industries expanded in 1967, 1977, and 1987.

In 2002 the economic census expanded to include four relatively small industries previously out of scope: landscape architecture, landscaping services, veterinary services, and pet care.

In 2007 the economic census expanded to include all scheduled passenger air transportation. Even with these additions, total coverage still rounds to 98 percent.

Geographic Comparability

Most students of economic trends confine themselves to looking at the nation, states, and counties. County boundary changes are few and far between, while many metropolitan areas, places, and ZIP codes change boundaries over time. Metropolitan areas are redefined after each population census, and new criteria are generally introduced at that point. Most metropolitan areas tabulated for 2007 are defined the same as they were for 2002, while most multicounty metro areas changed boundaries between the 1997 and 2002 censuses.

The boundaries of cities, and other places may have been modified owing to annexations or other changes during the intervening period. In 2007 the scope of places published changed, including census designated places for the first time but excluding small incorporated places with 2,500 to 4,999 inhabitants that had been included in earlier censuses.

Sources for More Information

The Census Bureau Web site at www.census.gov provides a wide variety of informational material about the economic census and related data. The NAICS Web site has already been referenced. The economic census page, also linked from the Census Bureau home page, includes a "User Guide" tab, under which is comprehensive information about the data, including key concepts, geography, methodology, and tips for finding data. Slide shows and videos provide alternative ways of learning about the data.

Both the economic census and NAICS sites are part of the broader business and industry section at www.census.gov/econ. That site links to many related data sets, including monthly and annual data that complement the economic census, albeit generally with less detail. Key among the data-finding resources is an industry search that directs the user to all of the various data sets available for a particular industry.

See also *Data products: evolution; Income and poverty measures; Occupation and education; Private sector; Related data sources.*

. . . . . . PAUL T. ZEISSET AND LEONARD M. GAINES

BIBLIOGRAPHY

Ambler, Carole A., and James E. Kristoff. "Introducing the North American Industry Classification System." *Government Information Quarterly* 15 (1998).

Boettcher, Jennifer C., and Leonard M. Gaines. *Industry Research Using the Economic Census: How to Find It, How to Use It.* Westport, Conn.: Greenwood Press, 2004.

Zeisset, Paul T., and Mark E. Wallace. *How NAICS Will Affect Data Users.* Lanham, Md.: Bernan Press, 1997. Also available at www.census.gov/epcd/www/naicsusr.html.

Editing, Imputation, and Weighting

Two related steps in processing census and American Community Survey (ACS) questionnaires are editing and imputation. The purpose of editing is to reconcile an inconsistent or anomalous answer or to assign a value for a missing item from other information provided by a person or household; the purpose of imputation is to supply a value for a missing item by using information obtained from another person or household. A third processing step for the census long-form sample and the ACS is weighting the data for responding households and persons to equal the total population. Throughout the history of the census, the volume of data has spurred technological innovation to automate as much of the processing as possible. Computerization has taken over much of the editing that was formerly carried out by clerical review, although some clerical editing is still performed. Computerization has also made it possible to develop sophisticated imputation and weighting techniques.

Terms and Techniques

Editing in the census has traditionally referred to review and modification of a response or filling in a missing response for a person or household from other information for the same person and household or by following the logic of the questionnaire. ("Editing" as used in the ACS—see "American Community Survey: methodology"—includes not only consistency edits and assignments but also imputation.) For example, if a minor under age 18 is listed as the first (reference) person for a household in the census or the ACS, either the person's age may be increased or another older person may be designated as the reference person and the minor given an appropriate household relationship code, depending on the information provided for everyone in the household. Consistency and logical edits are also applied to items included only in the ACS (or in the census long-form sample through 2000). For example, if the marital status of the person listed as the spouse of the first person in the household is reported as "divorced," the entry will be changed to "now married," or if an entry is provided for a person under age 16 for an item that pertains to people 16 years of age and older (for example, occupation), the entry will be changed to an appropriate "not applicable" code. For missing entries in the census or the ACS, edits are used whenever possible to *assign* values on the basis of other information provided by the same person or household. For example, a person's given name may be used to provide a value for "sex" if that item was left blank.

Imputation in the census or ACS refers to providing a response for a missing item by using not only other information for the person or household but also information from another similar person or household. Imputation is sometimes distinguished in the census as "allocation" versus "substitution": *allocation* is the imputation of values (answers) for missing data items when some of the person's characteristics are known; *substitution* is the imputation of values for all items when the only information known is that a person or housing unit is present. Allocations are the only type of imputation in the ACS, which does not include households in the final sample for which nothing is known about the occupants.

Two imputation techniques that have been used in computerized processing of census data are the "cold deck" method and the "hot deck" method. Cold decks were originally sets of punched cards that contained numeric values representing known distributions of the answers to questions from earlier censuses or surveys. The term *deck* continued to be used even after the distributions were provided to computers in other forms. The distribution of values in a cold deck does not change. Each value is used in sequence to allocate missing data, and the sequence is repeated as often as necessary. For example, if other data show that 40 percent of married men have served in the military, then a cold deck might contain the following random sequence of ten values to impute veteran status for married men in the census: 1, 2, 1, 1, 2, 2, 2, 2, 1, 2 (four 1's representing yes, served in the military, and six 2's representing no, did not serve). If 21 married men did not respond to the item, then the cold deck values would be assigned in order. The first man would receive a value of 1, the second man a value of 2, and so on. The 10th man in this example would receive a value of 2, and the 11th man would be assigned a 1, which is the first value in the sequence. Consequently, to assign values for military service for all 21 married men, the first value in the sequence would be used three times (for the 1st, 11th, and 21st man), and the other nine values would be used twice.

Hot decks, which are used in both the ACS and the census, are distributions of values that are constantly altered as questionnaires are processed and data for the latest person or housing unit are substituted for the values already in the hot deck matrix. Imputation (allocation) of a missing entry is made from the latest value stored in the matrix that fits other known characteristics of the person or housing unit. For example, a person reported as a 20-year-old male relative for whom

marital status was not reported would be allocated the same marital status as the latest such person processed. When no information is available about the persons in a housing unit counted in the census, people in a previously processed housing unit are selected as a substitute and all their basic characteristics are duplicated. When it is not even known whether a housing unit is occupied or vacant in the census, an imputation is first performed to assign occupancy status.

Compared with cold decks, hot decks have the advantage of using data from the current census or survey that is being processed rather than a previous census or survey; also, hot decks preserve more of the variability that characterizes the population. Further, hot decks, by using information for similar, recently processed people or housing units, take advantage of commonalities of characteristics among small geographic areas. Today, cold decks are not used in census processing except to determine the starting values for the distributions for hot decks.

Weighting in the long-form sample and the ACS (and in sample surveys, generally) refers to the development of values for each person and household that when applied to the raw data will yield estimates for the total population or total households. In the simplest case, such as a simple random sample of 1 in 10 of 600 college students in a professor's class, all of whom respond, each of the 60 sampled persons will have the same weight of 10, and tabulations of the data, such as the estimated number of men and women in the class, will be 10 times the raw count in the sample. In the census long-form sample and the ACS, the weighting process is more complicated: the value of the weight for an individual person or household takes into account the use of different sampling rates, the failure of some households to respond at all, and an adjustment so that the weighted totals from the sample equal control totals from the complete census count for the long-form sample and from census-based population estimates for the ACS.

Editing, imputation, and weighting are designed to make census and ACS data more complete and accurate; however, the procedures used may introduce error. Rates of allocation and substitution are published for each census, and the ACS Web site provides allocation rates for each item each year for the nation and states, but there have been no systematic studies of error from editing or imputation. Similarly, estimates of sampling error are provided for the long-form sample and the ACS, but error introduced by imputation or by errors in control totals is not accounted for.

Analysis of allocation rates for the 1990 and 2000 censuses found that they were lower for questionnaires returned by households in the mail than for questionnaires obtained by enumerator follow-up and that they were lower for short-form items, such as age and sex, than for long-form items, such as income and place of work. The ACS has achieved higher item response rates than the census long-form sample and therefore lower imputation rates; in the ACS, imputation rates for many items are lower for questionnaires obtained by enumerators than for mailed-back questionnaires. One reason is that the ACS interviewers are much more highly trained than are temporary census enumerators; they also use computer-assisted interviewing.

History of Editing and Imputation

For the censuses of 1790–1820, U.S. marshals and their assistants tallied (added up) the responses to census questions from households in their districts without further review of their work in Washington, D.C. For the 1830 and 1840 censuses, temporary clerks were hired in Washington to examine the marshals' returns and note errors. Clerks took over the job of tallying the returns and organizing the data for publication beginning with the 1850 census. Electromechanical punched card tabulating machines were used as early as the census of 1890 to automate the process of tallying people in various response categories; however, armies of clerks still had the job of recording the census responses on punched cards for input to the tabulating equipment.

Over the decades, more and more editing was performed by clerks in the process of encoding census responses for punching onto cards. For example, elaborate rules were developed for coding occupation, which provided for editing (modifying) some responses on the basis of other information about the person. In some censuses, occupation entries believed to be inappropriate for the gender or race of the respondent, and therefore believed to be erroneously reported, could be changed during editing to other categories believed to be appropriate and more likely correct (for example, "tailor" for a woman respondent might be changed to "seamstress").

For the first 150 years of census taking, there was no imputation for missing data. (In place of imputation, census publications carried counts of "not reported" for specific items.) The first use of imputation occurred in the 1940 census, when a method was devised to impute age for persons for whom age was not reported on the schedule. (W. Edwards Deming, who subsequently became a world-renowned industrial adviser on quality control, originated the method.) The procedure—similar to a cold deck—involved randomly selecting a value for age from an appropriate deck of cards, selected according to what other information was known about the person for whom age was missing.

For the 1950 census new multicolumn punched card sorting machines were used to automate the editing and coding of employment status, which depended on often inconsistent or incomplete responses to multiple questions. A "decision table" was devised that specified an employment status code (for example, "employed," "unemployed," "not in the labor force") for each of the possible combinations of answers and missing values to the relevant questions. This table was wired into the multicolumn sorters. Clerks punched the actual responses onto cards, and the employment status code was produced automatically by running the cards through the sorters.

The advent of high-speed computing technology significantly expanded the opportunities for sophisticated editing and imputation of census data. The UNIVAC I computer, developed under contract to the Census Bureau, was delivered in time for some of the last tabulation work on the 1950 census. Improved UNIVAC models were used to perform the majority of the data processing for the 1960 census, and the sophistication of computerized data processing has increased for each subsequent census.

The 1960 census used computers for data editing and to impute values for missing responses from cold and hot decks. The 1970 census used editing and imputation techniques similar to those employed in the 1960 census but made much fuller use of hot decks. The 1980 census saw the development of even more sophisticated hot deck imputation procedures that imputed one or more related data items on the basis of a large number of known characteristics instead of the one or two characteristics that were used in the past. Data users benefited from tabulations and Public Use Microdata Samples that contained imputed values instead of missing data codes; without imputation, cross-tabulations of more than one item would be restricted to the number of cases that had responses to all items in the tabulation and could be biased as a result.

Even after the introduction of computers for census data processing, there has still been a clerical editing stage. In the 1990 census, clerks reviewed the paper questionnaires and made changes in specified instances (for example, if a write-in response was provided instead of a filled-in answer box, the clerk would fill in the appropriate box whenever possible). For missing or inconsistent data, clerks telephoned households to obtain more complete information. Finally, when a questionnaire "failed edit" and the household could not be reached by telephone, the questionnaire was included in the workload for enumerators to follow up in person. (A questionnaire could "fail edit" if it contained incomplete or inconsistent information about the number of people residing at the household or if too many content items were blank.) Only after these steps were completed were the data recorded and put through further editing and imputation by computer.

In the 2000 census, a clerical "coverage edit follow-up" (CEFU) operation was carried out after the data had been scanned into the computer to ascertain that selected households were completely counted with regard to the number of persons. For households for which the computer detected coverage problems (for example, the household reported five persons but only provided information for two of them), clerks telephoned the households to obtain more information. Content edits, for missing or incomplete responses to specific items, were handled solely by computer. A similar process was followed in the 2010 census, which expanded the criteria for identifying possible coverage problems. The ACS has a callback procedure for mailed-back questionnaires that fail content as well as coverage edits.

History of Weighting

The use of sampling for certain questionnaire items, which began on a small scale in the 1940 census, necessitated the use of weighting to enable the sample responses to represent the total population. The 2000 census was the last to include a long-form sample in which about 17 percent of households were asked additional questions; weights for the 2000 long-form sample were developed to produce estimates for specified population groups and geographic areas that agreed with the census population counts as a whole. A goal of the weighting was to minimize the variation in weights, which in turn would minimize the variation in sampling error across population groups and geographic areas. Adjusting the weights to match complete-count controls would also minimize the variation. Weights were constructed separately for people in households, group quarters residents, service-based enumerations (for example, people enumerated in shelters), and vacant housing units. To the extent possible, weights for each group were constructed separately by sampling rate (which varied from 1 in 2 in the smallest governmental units to 1 in 8 for large census tracts) and such characteristics as household size and type, age, sex, race, and ethnicity. Weights were controlled to the complete census counts for these groups within small geographic areas defined to be block groups or census tracts with at least 400 long-form-sample person records.

Weighting in the ACS is a complex, multistage operation that is carried out separately for household members and group quarters residents. The weighting for households for one-year period estimates includes more than ten steps, of which the most important adjust for the inverse of the sampling rate, for unit nonresponse, to account for the subsampling of households visited by enumerators to obtain their information, and to achieve agreement with housing unit and population controls from the Census Bureau's population estimates program for July 1 of the reference year. The controls for total housing units and population by age, sex, race, and ethnicity are implemented for counties or group of counties; in addition, beginning in 2009, total population controls are implemented for places with at least 5,000 people. The need to use controls from population estimates introduces a source of error that did not affect the long-form-sample estimates. Moreover, the need to use controls for relatively large geographic areas (because of the smaller ACS sample size) means that ACS total population estimates for small cities, towns, counties, census tracts, and block groups may differ when, for example, comparing 2010 ACS estimates with 2010 census counts.

ACS three-year and five-year period weights use weight factors that are similar to the one-year factors up to the point of applying controls, when averages of the three-year or five-year population estimates are used as controls. A model-assisted procedure is also used to reduce the variation in sampling error for ACS subcounty multiyear estimates. ACS weights for group quarters residents are developed by using state-level controls by type of group quarters.

See also *American Community Survey: methodology; Data capture; Data dissemination and use; Long form; Pre-computer tabulation systems; Sampling for content.*

. . . . CONSTANCE F. CITRO

BIBLIOGRAPHY

Goldfield, Edwin D. "Innovations in the Decennial Census of Population and Housing: 1940–1990." Paper delivered to the Panel on Census Requirements in the Year 2000 and Beyond, Committee on National Statistics, National Research Council, Washington, D.C., October 1992.

National Research Council. Using the American Community Survey: Benefits and Challenges. Panel on the Functionality and Usability of Data from the American Community Survey. Constance F. Citro and Graham Kalton, eds. Committee on National Statistics, Division of Behavioral and Social Sciences and Education. Washington, D.C.: The National Academies Press, 2007. Available at http://www.nap.edu/catalog.php?record_id=11901.

———. The 2000 Census: Counting Under Adversity. Panel to Review the 2000 Census. Constance F. Citro, Daniel L. Cork, and Janet L. Norwood, eds. Committee on National Statistics, Division of Behavioral and Social Sciences and Education. Washington, D.C.: The National Academies Press, 2004. Available at http://www.nap.edu/catalog.php?record_id=10907.

U.S. Census Bureau. *American Community Survey Design and Methodology.* Washington, D.C.: U.S. Department of Commerce, 2009. See especially Chapters 10–12.

Education: Changing Questions and Classifications

Without interruption, one or more questions about education have been asked in every decennial census since 1840. Despite some changes in the questions over time, there is a remarkable degree of consistency in their basic format. Most of the changes that have taken place reflect responses to shifts occurring in U.S. society at large, and corresponding data needs.

School Enrollment and Literacy, 1840–1930

The first questions about education appear in the 1840 census. Enumerators were asked to record the number of persons attending "universities and colleges," "academies and grammar schools," and "primary and common schools." Included in this enumeration was the "number of students at public charge." The focus of these questions was not persons in households but, rather, the number of persons in *schools*. Immediately following these questions was another item intended to identify "Persons over the age of 20 who could not read and write."

In 1850 a major change was made to the counting procedure, one that would remain in place in roughly the same form for the next nine censuses. In this census a question about school enrollment was asked for the persons in each household. The yes or no question, "Attended school within the last year," was accompanied by instructions that it was to be asked of all persons and should not include Sunday schools.

From 1850 to 1930, these two concepts—school enrollment and literacy—constituted the scope of measurement regarding education in the decennial census. The choice of these questions reflects a nation undergoing major changes in public education and literacy efforts, as well as national concern about a growing immigrant population. In some years ability to read and write was determined by separate questions (1870–1920), in other years by a single item (1840–1860, 1930). For the 1890 and 1900 censuses, those attending school in the previous "census year" (year prior to June 1) were asked to report the number of months in school. For 1910, 1920, and 1930, census schedules asked whether respondents attended school at any time since September 1 of the previous year. In several of these censuses, a question about the ability to speak English immediately followed the reading and writing questions.

Enrollment and Attainment: 1940–1980

The next major change in census education questions occurred in the 1940 census. An entirely new aspect of education—attainment, or completed education—was queried for the first time. (Since there was only one questionnaire at this time, the question was a "100% item"—asked of all persons.) The question concerning the "highest grade of school attended" allowed for responses ranging from "none" to the "5th or higher year" of college. Other changes were incorporated as well. In 1940 the reference date for school enrollment was shortened from anytime in the previous school year to March 1, just one month prior to census enumeration day; in 1950 the date was changed to February 1 and has remained there since then. Finally, the focus of all schooling was designated as "regular school," defined as schooling that would lead to a high school or college degree.

In 1950 the new attainment question was modified so that the current grade of attainment response could also be used to infer the current level of enrollment. At this point the school enrollment and educational attainment questions became to some degree "linked," since estimating enrollment level clearly required one to use some of the information from the attainment item.

Over the next several censuses these combined enrollment and attainment questions were modified to continue to capture and reflect emerging social changes. In 1960 the school enrollment categories were expanded to include a separate category for "private or parochial" schools. In 1970 "parochial" was a separate category; in 1980 it became "private, church-related"; and in 1990 (and 2000) the independent category for church-related schooling had disappeared altogether, subsumed in the category "private school, private college."

Another source of change since the major revision in 1940 relates to the categories of educational attainment. In 1970 the category "nursery school" was added to the questionnaire, reflecting the increased use of nursery schools for young children. In 1980 the upper bound was expanded, including categories for single years of college up through the eighth year.

The 1970 census included an attempt to measure "vocational schooling," which by the Bureau of the Census definition was presumed to be outside the designation of "regular schooling." This two-part question assessed whether the person had "ever completed a vocational training program" and the "main field" of vocational training. Evaluation of the responses to this question after the census was completed revealed very high rates of inconsistency in response to the questions, and the item was dropped from future censuses.

Changes since 1990

In the past few decades, a number of important changes have been made in measuring education. In the 1990 census the focus of educational attainment was switched from "years of schooling completed" to "highest degree or level." Research conducted after the 1980 census had concluded that the "years of school" concept was too vague at the college level, with many people reporting not a completed level of schooling but, rather, the amount of time—number of calendar years—spent in school. The research showed that individuals could much more reliably report a completed earned degree than they could the usual or required amount of time it took to get the degree. The 1990 census thus switched to a redesigned attainment question, with grades below the high school completion level and degree categories (for example, bachelor's, master's, doctorate) above the high school completion level.

Since the enrollment and attainment questions from 1940 to 1980 were designed to be somewhat interdependent, the creation of the new attainment question based on degrees impacted the school enrollment data as well. Enrollment data for individual elementary and secondary grades were no longer possible with the new question, resulting in an actual loss of enrollment information from previous censuses.

With the transition of the long-form census data content to the American Community Survey (ACS), the opportunity arose to make further refinements in education data. Early cycles of the ACS development phase (1996–1998) saw the testing of revised enrollment reference periods, as well as modified attainment and enrollment categories. In an attempt to provide comparability with 2000 census data items, some of these test changes were ultimately abandoned (for example, a "vocational/technical/business" enrollment and attainment category, and the ability to write-in specific grade of enrollment). As such, from 2000 through 2007, the ACS education items mirrored those used in the 2000 (and 1990) censuses.

As a result of the 2006 National Content Test, two changes in education items were made. First, the write-in of specific grades 1–11 was restored, thus providing the ability to provide single grade-specific enrollment and attainment data. Second, attainment categories were more clearly "clustered" and high school graduates were broken into two categories: those with a "regular high school diploma" and those with a "GED or alternative credential."

In 2009, a completely new question, collecting data on the field of bachelor's degree, was added to the ACS questionnaire to meet the need for estimates of the nation's science and engineering human resources, as well as providing information for a variety of science and engineering surveys conducted by the National Science Foundation. This item collects write-in responses, which are then coded into 189 unique field entries for tabulation purposes. Data for this item first appeared for the 2009 ACS data products, which were released in the fall of 2010.

Research continues on other education-related issues, including the growing variety of non-baccalaureate certifications and educational programs. The 170-year history of education questions in the census clearly illustrates their critical role as an instrument of social measurement and change. As the social definition of education continues to evolve, it is likely that so too will the measurement recording tool.

See also *Content determination; Long form.*

. . . . ROBERT A. KOMINSKI

BIBLIOGRAPHY

Crissey, Sarah, Kurt Bauman, and Alan Peterson. "Evaluation Report Covering Educational Attainment." 2006 ACS Content Test Report 2b. Washington, D.C.: U.S. Census Bureau, 2007.

Kominski, Robert. *Evaluation of the 1980 Decennial Census Education Questions.* 1980 Census Preliminary Evaluation Results Memorandum No. 104. Washington, D.C.: U.S. Bureau of the Census, 1985.

Kominski, Robert, and Paul Siegel. *Measuring Educational Attainment in the 1990 Census.* Paper presented at the annual meeting of the American Sociological Association, Washington, D.C., 1987.

U.S. Bureau of the Census. *200 Years of U.S. Census Taking: Population and Housing Questions, 1790–1990.* Washington, D.C.: Government Printing Office, 1989.

Woltman, Henry. *Accuracy of Responses for Vocational Training.* 1970 Census Preliminary Evaluation Results Memorandum No. 42. Washington, D.C.: U.S. Census Bureau, 1974.

Electronic Products

See *Data dissemination: electronic products.*

Enumerating Rural Areas

Since 1790, when the census was conducted by U.S. marshals and their assistants, rural areas served to illustrate the many challenges for taking the census. To be sure, census procedures have evolved, but the difficulties of carrying out the census enumeration in rural America remain. The central issues for enumerating the rural population revolve around key operational, logistical, and resource issues that determine the accuracy of counting lower density, geographically dispersed populations. The rural population of the nation was more than 59 million in 2000, accounting for about 20 percent of the nation's population. At the same time, rural America accounted for more than 95 percent of the nation's land area. Traversing an area of this size in an effort to enumerate one-fifth of the nation's population is nothing less than a herculean task.

Table 1 shows differences in the geographic size, population, and population density of rural and urban areas by census region (the Census Bureau uses population density in defining urban populations, and any area not defined as urban is considered rural). Differences in size, travel distance, and dispersion of residents all must be factored into census operations.

Against this backdrop, there are three functional operations that the Census Bureau must perform nationwide to conduct a complete and accurate census: address listing, review, and canvassing; the actual enumeration; and the promotional program to highlight the importance of the census and timely response.

Address Listing, Review, and Canvassing

Development of a nationwide Master Address File (MAF) is the foundation of the enumeration process in the United States. If the Census Bureau can identify the address and physical location of every dwelling unit in the country, the goal of a complete and accurate census count can be attained. However, there are a variety of issues related to address identification and physical location that impact both urban and rural addressing. Urban areas are densely settled, and individual structures may contain multiple units and hidden units that are not individually addressed. At the same time, urban areas are most often covered by city-style addresses (number, street name, apartment number), which make identification, delivery of mail, and enumeration easier.

Addressing in rural areas takes on many different forms. While city-style addressing has expanded throughout the nation owing to county level implementation of Emergency-911 systems, many areas are still covered by rural addressing: post office boxes, rural route box numbers, cluster boxes for mobile home parks, or even narrative descriptions of physical characteristics.

Table 1. Urban and Rural Population and Density by Census Region for 2000

REGION	TOTAL	URBAN	RURAL	PERCENTAGE RURAL POPULATION	TOTAL SQUARE MILES	TOTAL URBAN SQUARE MILES	TOTAL RURAL SQUARE MILES	URBAN POPULATION DENSITY*	RURAL POPULATION DENSITY*
Northeast	53,594,378	45,221,152	8,373,226	16%	181,324	17,186	164,139	2,631	51
Midwest	64,392,776	48,098,662	16,294,114	25%	821,733	20,770	800,963	2,316	20
South	100,236,820	73,004,919	27,231,901	27%	919,885	37,839	882,046	1,929	31
West	63,197,932	56,033,576	7,164,356	11%	1,871,141	17,527	1,853,614	3,197	4
West, excluding Alaska	62,571,000	55,622,319	6,948,681	11%	1,207,874	17,261	1,190,613	3,222	6
Alaska	626,932	411,257	215,675	34%	663,267	266	663,002	1,548	0.3

* Persons per square mile.

SOURCE: U.S. Census Bureau, Census 2000, Summary File 1, Tables P2, Urban and Rural and GCT-PH1 Population, Housing Units, Area, and Density.

Moreover, in urban areas, the identification of hidden housing units can be a challenge in rural areas. What the U.S. Postal Service needs to deliver mail is not always what the Census Bureau needs to physically locate and enumerate a dwelling unit. This is especially true in rural areas where the post office does not perform house-to-house delivery.

Address listing in the development of the MAF begins years before the census enumeration through a variety of sources. Most important is the U.S. Postal Service Delivery Sequence File (DSF), but even it has deficiencies that are especially critical in rural areas. The DSF is reasonably good for updating city-style addressing, but less so in rural areas. Not all jurisdictions require permitting, nor do they assign city-style addressing. As a result, the Census Bureau must use alternative field operations to capture these addresses throughout the decade. These operations are conducted by the Census Bureau's regional offices, and in the past decade the completeness of these operations suffered from a lack of funding, thereby affecting the initial quality of the MAF for rural areas.

In addition to a complete listing of addresses, the Census Bureau needs an accurate geographic base, or map, that defines the actual physical location of units. The geographic system for ensuring consistency between addresses and geographic location is called the Topologically Integrated Geographic Encoding Reference (TIGER) file. An important goal for the 2010 census was to improve the accuracy of the TIGER file (the TIGER Enhancement Program) so that the exact coordinates of a dwelling unit could be referenced to its accurate map location. For rural areas the improvement of TIGER was critical because these were the exact areas where the quality of the geographic base map was least accurate. Earlier versions of TIGER may not have accurately matched the location of local road networks and their naming systems. Given these limits, local governments in most rural areas would need to rely on the Census Bureau's field canvassers, who would list addresses and update the maps in the year prior to the census enumeration.

In 1994 Congress passed the Census Address List Improvement Act, which allowed the Census Bureau to share the MAF (which is confidential under Title 13 of the U.S. Code) with local governments for the review and updating of addresses and geography through the Local Update of Census Addresses (LUCA) program. This is a voluntary program with participation offered to every unit of local government. To participate, the local government must ensure protection of the address data, conduct the address review in a manner consistent with the Census Bureau's guidelines and requirements, and do so at its own expense. While the benefits of participation can be significant in terms of creating a complete and accurate address list and improving the geographic base map, local governments often do not have the extra staff, data, or fiscal resources to participate. This is particularly true of small rural areas, where staff may work only part-time and there is a lack of awareness of the importance of the census in general and the address review program in particular. Another important issue is the availability of local data upon which to review the bureau's

addresses. Tax parcel records are often the only source of data and may or may not capture the existence of multiple units, legal or illegal, and likely do not identify separate addresses for multiple dwelling units required by the bureau.

The Census Bureau conducted the 2010 Census LUCA program in a way that reflected the fundamental distinction between city-style and non-city-style addresses. City-style addresses have a house number and street name that are recognized by the U.S. Postal Service (USPS)—which usually makes it easy to identify and geographically code the physical location of the unit address. Non-city-style addresses are prevalent in areas where mail is delivered to rural routes with box numbers or to post office box numbers. While this typology does not equate with rural and urban per se, it does distinguish addresses that need to be treated differently in the enumeration.

There were several options available for local governments to review addresses in LUCA depending on the resources available and the types of addresses that existed in a jurisdiction. Many rural local governments with non-city-style addresses participated in LUCA by reviewing block *counts* of housing units provided by the Census Bureau rather than individual addresses. In these cases, the local governments did not have to worry about the confidentiality of individual addresses, but they were also then unable to know whether their count of addresses reflected the same units as those in the Census Bureau's count. In addition, particular problems arose in rural areas if the bureau showed only the old non-city-style addresses for a block that might have recently converted to city-style addressing. Local governments were instructed to provide those new city-style addresses, but it was often difficult to match the old and new addresses. And, again, it was not possible to know if the local government records identified the same unit addresses as the Census Bureau. The timing of LUCA (August 2007 to April 2008) was another important issue because the complete results of the TIGER Enhancement Program were not always available for evaluation. In this case, the local government's base map may be more accurate than the Census Bureau's, making the comparison of addresses difficult and causing local governments to expend their resources to update map features that may have been already captured by the Census Bureau.

Address canvassing is the final step in the creation of a complete and accurate MAF, and it took place between March and July 2009. In this operation Census Bureau field office staff, operating out of the more than 150 Early Local Census Offices, visited every street and every housing unit address in the nation, verifying its address and location. This operation was conducted between March and July 2010.

Enumeration of Rural Areas

Rural territory and even small rural communities often get their mail through their local post office box. These areas do not have house-to-house mail delivery and are perfect examples of how the missions of the U.S. Postal Service and the Census Bureau differ. The USPS has to get mail delivered and, in fact, is specifically instructed to return as undeliverable any questionnaire addressed to a post office box. On the other hand, the Census Bureau has to deliver a questionnaire, by mail or by field delivery, to each unit at that unit's physical location. Physical location is not important to the USPS but is critical to the Census Bureau, where the unit must be placed accurately in order to tabulate data to the block level and meet legal requirements for congressional reapportionment and state redistricting. This presents a significant problem for the enumeration of rural areas. During list development and address canvassing, the Census Bureau needs to identify these unit addresses (post office box and rural route addresses) and reconcile the postal address, or any non-city-style address for that matter, with the physical location of the unit.

The 2010 census enumeration was conducted through four main methods: mailout/mailback, update/leave (U/L), update/enumerate (U/E), and remote Alaska enumeration. Every community and block in the entire country was assigned to one of these four types of enumeration areas (TEAs). These names reflect the method used by the Census Bureau to deliver the questionnaire to each housing unit, and the assignment of TEAs was determined by the Census Bureau's regional offices in cooperation with headquarters staff.

While some rural territory has city-style addressing and is enumerated through the mailout/mailback method, U/L and U/E are the most common methods of enumerating rural and remote areas where it is difficult to compile an accurate address list. The U/L operation is used in areas where homes do not have city-style addresses but rather have rural route delivery and post office boxes that are not tied to a specific location. There census workers visit each housing unit to update the address list, add in missing addresses, and leave the questionnaire for residents to complete and mail back. This operation is intended to solve the post office box delivery problem, because the Census Bureau will get a questionnaire

to the housing unit regardless of whether the USPS conducts house-to-house delivery. This method also allows for the Census Bureau to verify the physical location of the unit for processing in TIGER. In 2010 this process was used in several counties along the Gulf Coast still recovering from Hurricane Katrina.

The U/E procedure is used in remote, sparsely populated, and hard-to-visit areas. In this operation the Census Bureau combines the address listing/updating and the actual enumeration of the population. In the most rural areas, this often involves searching for housing units, as there is no preexisting address list. This operation was also conducted in many resort areas where there were believed to be high concentrations of seasonally vacant units, some American Indian reservations, and *colonias* on the U.S.-Mexico border.

Table 2 shows an example of how the TEAs were distributed across communities by size, using places in Nevada to illustrate. A place might have more than one TEA within its area, and this designation and delivery method might conflict with local USPS operations. For example, Storey County, Nevada, was initially designated for mailout/mailback operations, but all mail delivery there is by post office box. These types of situations are not uncommon and adversely impact rural enumeration by forcing the Census Bureau into more labor- and cost-intensive operations while confusing local residents and officials.

Given the remote nature of some rural locations, physical conditions such as inclement weather, the quality of roads, and sometimes-unsafe conditions combine with already difficult census operations to adversely impact the completeness and accuracy of the census. These conditions often lead to delays in the enumeration, which makes the nonresponse follow-up operations more critical and expensive. In rural areas with high concentrations of seasonal population, delays in enumeration

Table 2. Type of Enumeration Area by Size of Place for Nevada: 2009

SIZE OF PLACE	NUMBER OF PLACES	TOTAL POPULATION	RURAL	TYPE OF ENUMERATION AREA*			
				MAILOUT/ MAILBACK	UPDATE/LEAVE: RURAL	LIST/ ENUMERATE	MILITARY
250,000 to 499,999	1	478,434	312	1	1	0	0
100,000 to 249,999	6	930,929	6,251	6	2	1	3
50,000 to 99,999	2	118,803	3,746	2	1	2	0
25,000 to 49,999	1	26,958	0	1	0	0	0
10,000 to 24,999	8	130,317	24,633	8	4	2	0
5,000 to 9,999	11	86,130	13,223	9	7	3	1
less than 4,999	42	79,241	35,280	17	27	11	4
Totals	71	1,850,812	83,445	44	42	19	8

SOURCE: U.S. Census Bureau, Census 2000, Summary File 1, Table P2

*Sum of enumeration types may not equal total number of places because multiple methods can be used in the same place.

and follow-up can result in different application of residency rules and counting population in a location other than their "usual place of residence." For example, a questionnaire could be delivered (by mail or census delivery) in late March but the residents, who spend more than six months at that location, may not return the form before leaving for their summer residence. In follow-up this unit will be found vacant. At the same time, the destination unit used for summer residence could also be found vacant in follow-up operations if the residents do not arrive before the unit is captured. Owing to the higher proportion of seasonal units in rural areas, these inconsistencies in enumeration methods and operations adversely affect the census counts.

Census Promotion for Rural Areas

The average American is not aware of the importance of the decennial census and his or her need to participate, because it is a once-a-decade national event. Issues of privacy, distrust of government, and the perceived intrusiveness of the questions need to be overcome if the Census Bureau is to maximize civic participation. For the 2010 census, the Census Bureau used two avenues to educate the public and thereby improve responsiveness to the census: an extensive media campaign and local partnerships to facilitate cooperation and response.

In mid-March 2010 the bureau launched a $133 million media campaign designed to accomplish four goals: boost the mail response rate, improve accuracy, reduce the differential undercount, and improve the public's cooperation with enumerators. This national campaign targeted specific population clusters and media outlets. Rural America was identified as part of the "All Around Average I" cluster whose defining characteristics included 35.3 percent of all occupied housing units, the second-highest mail response rate and a low hard-to-count score in 2000; a large percentage of rural population; and skewing toward homeowners and older residents. Message testing indicated that agriculture and rural life issues were "hot-button" topics to use in media campaigns, and television was identified as the primary vehicle for message delivery because of the prevalent viewing habits focused on variety shows, soap operas, movies, and sitcoms. However, the fact that the cluster including rural America already had a high response rate in the 2000 census and scored low on indicators identifying hard-to-count characteristics meant that rural areas would not receive the same attention as their urban counterparts. This media campaign was an important part of delivering the Census Bureau message, but its primary focus was not on the issues related to rural enumeration.

A second component of the bureau's promotional program was to develop partnerships with local governments, civic groups, and special interest groups and to directly engage community leaders in support of the census effort through the establishment of complete count committees. However, the effectiveness of these partnerships was more limited in rural areas because of limited census bureau and community resources.

Each of the bureau's regional offices staffed a partnership program designed to help local officials establish Complete Count Committees and mobilize local resources to educate residents. Targeting of these efforts was based on the Census Bureau's Planning Database, which correlated tract-level characteristics with indicators related to response rates and difficulty of enumeration. This effort was quantified in a hard-to-count score, which guided the allocation of partnership staff and funding. Low-response and hard-to-count areas are predominantly low-income and minority communities; therefore, most of the effort focused on urban issues. Fortunately, with the passage of the American Recovery and Reinvestment Act of 2009, there were additional partnership specialists and assistants hired across the country, which helped to expand the program to more rural areas.

Through the Partnership Program, the Census Bureau encouraged the creation of Complete Count Committees, but the ability for a local government to create an effective Complete Count Committee or to promote the census was dependent on a number of factors. These included support by elected officials, staff support and resources, interested community organizations, and local media. Rural communities may not have local papers, radio stations, or television stations to air targeted messages, and that made promotional activities within some communities more difficult. While community partnership specialists helped to raise awareness and had a positive impact on the enumeration efforts, this program still suffered from a lack of resources and awareness of its importance. Local officials, particularly those in small rural communities, simply have too many competing demands for staff and fiscal resources; therefore, few actually participated in the promotional effort.

Summary

Rural America represents only about 20 percent of the nation's population, but the important issues driving a complete and accurate census are no less important proportionately in rural versus urban areas. Risks for underenumeration, geographic misallocation, and finding "hidden" dwelling units are just as high and require continued research and effort on the part of the Census Bureau to address rural issues.

In 1790 the U.S marshal assistants faced challenges that included uncertain maps, unimproved roads and trails, and at times hostile respondents in conducting the first census as they ventured into rural areas. The technology may have changed, but many of the same issues still remain.

See also *Address list development; American Community Survey: methodology; Enumeration: field procedures; Rural areas.*

. . . . JEFF HARDCASTLE AND ROBERT SCARDAMALIA

BIBLIOGRAPHY
Cork, Daniel L., and Paul R. Voss, eds. *Once, Only Once, and in the Right Place: Residence Rules in the Decennial Census.* Washington, D.C.: The National Academies Press, 2006.
Leithauser, Gail. "2010 Census Field Operations." SDC National Annual Training Conference, Suitland, Md., October 14–16, 2009." www.census.gov/sdc/leithauser.ppt.
National Center for Frontier Communities. www.frontierus.org/2000census.htm

Scott, Ann Herbert. *Census U.S.A. Fact Finding for the American People, 1790–1970*. New York: Seabury Press, 1968.

U.S. Census Bureau, "Chapter 6. Survey Rules, Concepts and Definitions." In *Design and Methodology American Community Survey*, April 2009. www.census.gov/acs/www/Downloads/survey_methodology/acs_design_methodology_ch06.pdf.

———. "LUCA Promotional Workshop." www.census.gov/geo/www/luca2010/luca_promo_work.pdf.

———. "2010 Census Integrated Communications Campaign Plan," August 2008. http://2010.census.gov/partners/pdf/2010_ICC_Plan_Final_Edited.pdf.

———. "2010 Census Local Census Offices with Type of Enumeration Areas." www.census.gov/geo/www/maps/tea2010/teamap.html.

Enumeration: Field Procedures

The process of collecting data in the field is at the heart of the decennial census. Almost all of the population is enumerated at the location where each person lives. Field procedures are created and designed to accomplish this task.

1960 Census

The 1960 census was a transitional census in terms of the procedures used for the enumeration. It was the last census conducted with what has since become known as the "conventional" method, one that had been in place for more than 150 years. The most important feature of this method was the absence of a list of addresses, or housing units, prior to the census. Instead, enumerators created an address list at the same time that they enumerated the population. The 1960 census also was the first census to use the post office to assist in the enumeration and to use separate short and long forms for individual households. A major innovation in 1960 was the use of the film optical sensing device for input to computers (FOSDIC). FOSDIC allowed the data collected for each person and household to be read directly into a computer, avoiding the time-consuming intermediate step of keypunching the information onto IBM cards.

The 1960 procedures called for census crew leaders (enumerators who were in charge of several lower-level enumerators) to travel over the enumeration districts to which they had been assigned. An enumeration district was composed of blocks or otherwise-defined geographical territories that were considered an appropriate assignment area for a single enumerator. The crew leaders verified the accuracy of their enumerators' maps, marked their routes, prelisted the first 25 housing units for the purpose of checking later on the enumerators' work, and identified "special places," such as hotels and hospitals, which required a different type of enumeration procedure.

During the last ten days in March 1960, the post office delivered two documents to each occupied housing unit in the country. These were not identified by address but simply dropped at each unit's mailbox. One document, the Advance Census Report, was a brief questionnaire containing the short-form, or "100-percent," questions. The other document was a statement requesting that householders fill out the questionnaire and retain it for the enumerator's visit.

Beginning on April 1 in most parts of the country, enumerators visited each housing unit. If the questionnaire had been filled in, the enumerator transferred the information contained on it to the "FOSDIC Schedule," which was designed to be used with the computerized tabulation equipment of the Bureau of the Census. If the questionnaire had not been filled in, the enumerator obtained the information directly from the respondent; in addition, he or she collected information on housing through direct observation.

Enumerators also carried listing books in which they recorded the address or description of each place visited, the name of the head of the household, and the total number of persons enumerated. Where necessary, they recorded the fact that a unit was vacant or indicated that a specific location required another visit.

Twenty-five percent of households were selected for inclusion in the long-form, or "25-percent," sample. In the enumerators' listing books, households were listed on a repeating series of lines labeled A, B, C, and D. All households that appeared on the lines labeled "A" were included in the long-form sample. In 82 percent of the country, the long-form sample data were collected in a two-stage enumeration process. Geographically, most of the two-stage areas were in the Northeast and Midwest, the upper South, eastern Texas, and along the West Coast. The remaining 18 percent, located in low-density areas primarily in the Deep South and Rocky Mountain areas of the country, were covered in one stage in which both short- and long-form data were collected in the same visit. In the two-stage households that had been selected into the sample, the enumerator left a questionnaire with the sample questions. Respondents were asked to fill it in and mail it back to the local district office.

A variety of procedures were used in special situations. Individuals in group quarters were enumerated on a special form; 25 percent of these respondents were asked to fill in the sample questionnaire for the enumerator to pick up. Other procedures covered transients in hotels and motels and in missions, flophouses, and similar places with very low rent. Military and maritime personnel were enumerated through their military installations. Data on Americans abroad were collected through the Departments of Defense and State. Finally, "Were You Counted?" forms were made widely available. The 1960 census was the first to count students living away at college as part of the college community's population rather than assigning them back to their parental addresses. Younger children in boarding schools were counted at their parental homes.

Close-out procedures were employed after three visits to a housing unit failed to yield an interview. In single-stage households, information was obtained from neighbors, hired help, or an apartment house manager. Similar procedures were used when interviews could not be completed in two-stage households. In either case, questionnaires and preaddressed postage-free envelopes were left at the unit so that respondents could provide the information by mail.

The 1960 census was conducted through 399 district offices spread among 17 permanent regional field offices. The total number of job positions exceeded 170,000.

The 1970 Census

The 1970 census brought a major procedural innovation: introduction of the mailout/mailback method of census enumeration. This new procedure was used in major metropolitan areas, which, while accounting for only a small proportion of U.S. geography, covered 60 percent of the nation's 70 million housing units. The remainder of the country was enumerated using procedures similar to those used in 1960, except that the long-form sample data questions were administered at the same time as the short-form data items.

The address list of 42 million mailout/mailback housing units was compiled in advance of the census. It began with commercial mailing lists and was updated by postal carriers on their individual routes. All computer processing was done using computer tapes on a bureau mainframe. An Address Coding Guide (ACG) was developed independently and used to assign census geographic information (census tract and block, city, county, and congressional district) to each address. Individual serial numbers and codes for district office and enumeration district were added. Twenty percent of households were randomly assigned to receive long-form questionnaires. Finally, address labels and address registers (ARs) were generated. The census forms were mailed on March 28, 1970.

In mailout/mailback areas where commercial lists were not available or where there was no city-style delivery system, census workers conducted a special listing operation prior to the census to create the address list. The subsequent compilation and addressing work was accomplished manually in the district offices.

Two additional post office checks were performed on the address lists; after each, missing address information was forwarded to the district offices for AR updates and manual questionnaire addressing. In 21 inner-city areas, district office personnel conducted a precanvass operation to double-check the master AR once more.

The sampling fraction for long-form data was reduced from 1 in 4 for the 1960 census to 1 in 5 for the 1970 census. In addition, this "20-percent" sample was split further into two groups. Three out of four of the 20 percent sample households (or 15 percent of all households) received one questionnaire, while one in four (or 5 percent) received a somewhat different questionnaire. Thus, the census delivered four data sets: a 100 percent sample, a 20 percent sample, a 15 percent sample, and a 5 percent sample.

After sufficient time had passed for most mailed questionnaires to be logged in at the district offices or at the bureau's central processing office in Jeffersonville, Indiana, the first follow-up stage began with enumerators visiting addresses from which no mail response had been recorded. A second follow-up stage commenced when the first was completed, with close-out procedures used after that.

Data collection procedures in special situations were, generally, a continuation of the 1960 census methods. Special coverage procedures, however, were new in 1970. The bureau had released coverage information after the 1960 census, and the concept of "undercount" was just emerging as a public issue. Special public information materials were prepared for minority and selected ethnic groups. Intensive efforts were made to work with representatives of community organizations, social agencies, and civil rights groups who interacted with hard-to-count populations. Another first was the creation of a staff of outreach workers, recruited from and targeted to inner-city communities. Questionnaires and some instructional materials were translated into Spanish and Chinese to assist in enumerating non-English-speaking residents. Local communities formed Complete Count Committees, which assisted in outreach and promotion and in distribution of the "Were You Counted?" forms designed to enumerate people who were otherwise missed.

Post-census evaluation indicated that these methods did improve coverage. The housing-unit missed rates declined from 3.1 percent in 1960 to 2.2 percent in 1970. Most of this improvement was due to better coverage of occupied units. The research also showed that coverage was significantly better among the commercial mailing list units (0.9 percent missed) than among those units listed by census workers in prelist or conventional census operations (2.6 percent missed).

The 1970 census was conducted through 393 district offices managed through 12 permanent regional offices. The total staffing level was about 185,000.

The 1980 Census

Census officials deemed the 1970 mailout/mailback method successful. It was extended to more than 95 percent of the country's housing in 1980, with conventional methods used only in the northern sections of New England and the Midwest, and in most sections of the Rocky Mountain states. As in 1970, addresses were compiled through two different means. In urban areas with city-style postal delivery, commercial lists comprised the TAR (Tape Address Register), which was then checked by the post office and geocoded using the Geographic Base File/Dual Independent Map Encoding (GBF/DIME), a file that had been created during the intervening decade as a replacement for the 1970 census's ACG. An additional post office check and a precanvass operation provided further updates.

The sampling fraction for 1980 long forms was again reduced, this time to an overall 1 in 6. However, small governmental units (estimated to have a population count of under 2,500) were sampled at 1 in 2 in order to improve the quality of income and poverty data used in revenue-sharing formulas.

A 1980 innovation was implementation of the Local Review program, which provided local officials an opportunity to check the housing counts at the enumeration district level. Problems in geocoding precluded the pre-census stage of the program from being carried out. In the post-census phase local communities received a printout showing population, housing unit, and group quarters counts in each enumeration district (rather than census block, as originally planned) within their boundaries.

Each local community had ten working days to submit responses to the local district office, suggesting areas that appeared to be undercovered and providing detailed "hard evidence" in the form of address information to support its claims. The program's logistics were difficult, as the post-census responses often arrived just as the local district office was in close-out mode. Census evaluations noted that the program provided questionable benefits, though many local community evaluations indicated otherwise. About 32 percent of the eligible governments participated, with half of those reporting potential problems requiring investigation

The remaining mailout/mailback area was prelisted, as it had been in 1970. These addresses were keyed into the computer in 1979. In both TAR and prelist enumeration districts, address registers and mailing labels were generated by computer. Methods in the conventional census areas followed the pattern established in earlier censuses.

Follow-up procedures were generally the same as in 1970. The task was more difficult, however, because in a much larger proportion of households no one was at home during the day. This necessitated a greater number of calls in the evening and on weekends. The local review materials were created at the end of the first follow-up stage.

Special places and other types of nonhousing-unit living situations were enumerated as in previous census operations. Some special attention was paid to achieve earlier enumeration in places where there was significant population turnover in April, such as in college dormitories. Military personnel were generally counted in the community where they were stationed or based, except for two Navy fleets, whose personnel were included in the overseas population.

Coverage improvement activities were again expanded over the previous census. A total of 14 different programs were executed, 11 of which took place during the data collection time frame. (A description of each activity, along with an evaluation of its effectiveness, may be found in Census Report PHC80-E3, listed in the bibliography.) Programs such as the Spanish-language questionnaire, the establishment of assistance centers, the "Were You Counted?" campaign, and the vacant/delete check, in which enumerators revisited each housing unit categorized as vacant or nonresidential to double-check its status, were judged successful and carried forward to the 1990 census.

Regional Census Centers were established in each of the 12 regional office cities for the express purpose of carrying out decennial census activities. These centers coordinated and supervised a total of 409 district offices. An estimated 460,000 people were employed during some stage of the field operation, with 270,000 working during the peak follow-up weeks in April and May.

1990 Census

The overall 1990 field enumeration design was much the same as that used in 1980. Of the five field enumerations discussed in this article, the 1990 enumeration saw the least amount of change in method from the preceding census.

The master address list used for the mailout/mailback operation (now called the Address Control File, or ACF) included about 86.2 million housing units comprising over 85 percent of the national total. Of these, 55 million came from the TAR obtained from commercial mailing lists. This address list was improved through the advance post office check (APOC) and a precanvass operation.

The remaining mailout/mailback addresses were obtained through a prelist operation. Originally planned to include 32 million housing units, it was reduced to 27.8 million. The remaining addresses were designated for the update/leave operation, in which census enumerators checked the address list and delivered the questionnaires at census time. Respondents were asked to mail back these questionnaires. This list, too, was improved through APOC activities. The number of addresses added through APOC and fieldwork totaled nearly 1.2 million.

Finally, about 5.7 million housing units were covered through the list/enumerate procedure, similar to the pre-1970 conventional census method. Postal carriers delivered unaddressed short form questionnaires called ACRs (Advance Census Reports). Enumerators collected them and asked additional questions in those households selected randomly to receive the long form.

As in 1980, the long-form questions were asked, overall, in 1 in 6 households. Oversampling (at a rate of 1 in 2) was used in very small communities, while very large census tracts were reduced to 1 in 8. Follow-up procedures were similar to previous censuses, as were methods for enumerating special places.

The Local Review program was again implemented to provide an opportunity for local input into the quality of the address list. The geographic coding systems worked properly, so that participating local governments were able to evaluate the housing counts at the block level both before and after the census. About 30 percent of local governments participated. Upon evaluation the program was deemed a success both in terms of improvement to the address lists (units added and deleted and geographic corrections) and in terms of the opportunity it offered to local government officials.

The 1990 census was conducted in 13 regional census centers supervising 463 district offices. More than 550,000 temporary workers were hired to conduct the field enumeration work.

Census 2000

Over the three-census period since the inception of the mailout/mailback method in 1970, there was a continuing decline in the final mail return rate, which represents the proportion of occupied households that return the form. The first use of mailout/mailback techniques in the 1970 census produced a final mail return rate from occupied households of 87 percent; that is, about seven out of eight households returned the form by mail and did not require a follow-up visit in the field. The comparable figures were 81 percent in 1980 and 74 percent in 1990.

The initial mail response rate for all units on the address list, including those found to be vacant or nonresidential and those that could not receive their mail at a city-style address (number, street, apartment number), was even lower. For example, the rate calculated on this basis was 78 percent in 1970, 75 percent in 1980, and 65 percent in 1990. Reversing this decline, or at least holding level at the 1990 rate, was a major concern in Census 2000 planning. As a result, there was considerable sentiment to reengineer census methods. Significant bureau, federal agency, and advisory resources were devoted to these efforts in the early 1990s. The result was significant change in the census design. Much of this change was facilitated by an extraordinary growth in technology that permitted entirely new ways of conducting census activities.

The first major change involved the replacement of the FOSDIC system, first implemented in 1960. The system's technical requirements forced creation of census forms that were not considered user-friendly. After much experimentation, the Bureau of the Census developed a form that could be read into a computer via optical scanning. This made it possible to read letter characters and numbers rather than just filled-in circles, greatly improving form design options.

A second change involved the passage in 1994 of the Census Address List Improvement Act. This legislation drastically altered the method by which the Master Address File (MAF) was created. The law permitted address sharing in two different ways. First, it authorized the U.S. Postal Service to share its Delivery Sequence File (DSF) with the bureau. Improvements in technology had also meant a more efficient delivery system at the Postal Service, which now maintained its own master file complete with nine-digit ZIP coding to facilitate efficient mail delivery. The law made it possible for the bureau to create its initial MAF from a combination of the 1990 ACR and the DSF.

The 1994 law also permitted the bureau, with confidentiality restrictions, to share its MAF with local governments. This program, designated Local Update of Census Addresses, or LUCA, was much more extensive than the Local Review program it replaced. Local governments, if they chose to participate, could actually check each MAF entry by address against local files. The program was slow in getting out to the governments, however, and was plagued by missed deadlines and extremely tight schedules.

Another technological change affecting Census 2000 was connected to the development of the 911 emergency services system during the 1985–1995 period. These systems, heavy users of geographic information systems (GIS) techniques, require city-style addresses. Consequently, thousands of communities had converted from rural route/box number postal delivery to house numbers and street names. Initial MAF planning assumed that these systems would become nearly universal in time for Census 2000 use; however, many rural households opted to keep their post office boxes for mail delivery even though they were identified with house numbers for 911 purposes.

These problems notwithstanding, the 2000 MAF was the most complete address list ever to be used in a mailout/mailback census. The Census Bureau plans to maintain the file on a permanent basis and to use it as a sampling frame for the American Community Survey and perhaps other current survey programs.

Field enumeration procedures for 2000 were similar to those used in 1990. The number of list/enumerate housing units was reduced to fewer than 1 million. Update/leave techniques were employed in areas where city-style addressing was not consistently in place; concerns over the completeness of this list led the bureau to conduct a complete review and update at the time of census form delivery in March 2000. The older prelist activity, where address lists were built by census enumerators for use in mailout/mailback, was generally eliminated.

The response rate decline led to another major change: a paid advertising campaign. In 1990 and earlier, the bureau had relied on public service announcements that were not well targeted. Beginning in late 1999, a $167 million professionally created campaign got under way. Its initial goal was to acquaint Americans with the upcoming census and with the reasons why they should participate. A later phase, beginning in April, was designed to promote cooperation in the nonresponse follow-up stage. Another aspect of the campaign focused on privacy and confidentiality issues. In addition to the paid campaign, the bureau also worked hard to promote Census 2000 coverage in the media.

The response rate in 2000 was equal to that of 1990 but not a significant improvement. There remained a major difference between short-form recipients and those who had been asked to respond to the long form. After a period of research and analysis, the bureau declared that there had been no undercount, although most professionals considered this simply to be a result of balancing undercount with overcount and that the undercount problem was not solved, since the characteristics of the undercounted population differ greatly from those who are subject to being counted twice.

Census 2010

All of these considerations led to a major census reengineering project, resting on three corners: a short-form enumeration, implementation of the American Community Survey (ACS) to obtain "long-form" data, and improvements in the Master Address File (MAF) and Topologically Integrated Geographic Encoding and Referencing (TIGER) accuracy. The decision to drop the long form in favor of the ACS was made early in the decade, although the ACS was not fully implemented nationwide until 2005.

Early 2010 plans also called for much of the data collected in the field to be managed via handheld computers. Enumerators would record changes in the maps (for example, new streets), add new housing and make corrections in the MAF during the block canvass phase, and record census responses during the census follow-up stage. In 2008 it became apparent that software development for the handheld computers would be inadequate to use them for nonresponse follow-up. Thus in 2010 the "old-fashioned" paper and pencil method was used for this work. However, other improvements were implemented, including selected mailing of replacement questionnaires and use of bilingual questionnaires in neighborhoods with at least 20 percent Spanish-speaking households.

Going into the 2010 census, there were many concerns about the potential response rate, given significantly increased fears of loss of privacy and confidentiality among the American public and the power of the Internet to spread false information. The advertising campaign worked to counteract these problems. In the end the mail participation rate to this short-form-only 2010 census was 74 percent, equal to the rate for all households in 2000, some of which received a long form. Moreover, because participation rates were at the high end of expectations, the 2010 census came in under budget.

See also *Address list development; Coverage improvement procedures; Enumeration: group quarters; Housing.*

. . . .   PATRICIA C. BECKER

BIBLIOGRAPHY

Abramson, Florence H. "Census 2000 Testing, Experimentation, and Evaluation Program Summary Results." Washington, D.C.: U.S. Census Bureau, 2004. http://www.census.gov/pred/www/

The National Research Council. Modernizing the U.S. Census. Panel on Census Requirements in the Year 2000 and Beyond. Barry Edmonston and Charles Schultze, eds. Committee on National Statistics Commission on Behavioral and Social Sciences and Education. Washington, D.C.: The National Academies Press, 1995. Available at http://www.nap.edu/catalog.php?record_id=4805.

———. *Once, Only Once and in the Right Place.* Panel on Residence Rules in the Decennial Census. Daniel L. Cork and Paul Voss, eds. Committee on National Statistics, Division of Behavioral and Social Sciences and Education. Washington, D.C.: The National Academies Press, 2006. Available at http://www.nap.edu/catalog.php?record_id=12244.

U.S. Bureau of the Census. *Census 2000 Operational Plan Using Traditional Census-Taking Methods.* Washington, D.C.: U.S. Government Printing Office, January 1999.

———. *Procedural Report on the 1960 Censuses of Population and Housing,* Working Paper No. 16. Washington, D.C.: U.S. Government Printing Office, 1963.

U.S. Bureau of the Census, Census of Population and Housing: 1970. *Data Collection Forms and Procedures* (PHC(R)-2). Washington, D.C.: U.S. Government Printing Office, 1971.

———. *The Coverage of Housing in the 1970 Census* (PHC(R)-5. Washington, D.C.: U.S. Government Printing Office, 1973.

U.S. Bureau of the Census, Census of Population and Housing (1980). *History, Part A* (PHC80-R-2A). Washington, D.C.: U.S. Government Printing Office, September 1986.

———. *Programs to Improve Coverage in the 1980 Census* (PHC80-E3). Washington, D.C.: U.S. Government Printing Office, January 1987.

U.S. Bureau of the Census, 1990 Census of Population and Housing. *History* (2990 CPH-R 2A-D) Parts A-D. Washington, D.C.: U.S. Government Printing Office, October 1993 (Part A), October 1995 (Parts B and C), March 1996 (Part D).

———. *Programs to Improve Coverage in the 1990 Census* (1990 CPH-E-3). Washington, D.C.: U.S. Government Printing Office, November 1993.

U.S. Government Accountability Office. *2010 CENSUS: Census Bureau's Decision to Continue with Handheld Computers for Address Canvassing Makes Planning and Testing Critical.* GAO 08-936. Washington, D.C.: U.S. Government Printing Office, July 2008.

Enumeration: Group Quarters

The decennial census enumerates people who live in housing units, such as single-family homes, town homes, apartments, condominiums, and mobile homes, each of which is a separate living quarters. In addition, and unlike household surveys, the census enumerates people living in other kinds of situations. In the 2010 census the "group quarters population" included people living in nonmilitary group quarters (for example, nursing homes, prisons, college dormitories), people living on military installations and ships, people in transitory locations at the time of the census (for example, staying at recreational vehicle campgrounds, traveling with fairs and carnivals), and people living in job-specific housing such as migrant and seasonal farmworker camps. In recent censuses, a service-based enumeration portion of group quarters enumeration has included some segments of the population experiencing homelessness or living in some types of shelters.

In 2000 the group quarters population amounted to 7.8 million people, or 2.8 percent of the population enumerated in that census. By type, 1.4 percent of the population lived in such institutions as nursing homes, long-term-care facilities for people with physical or mental disabilities, and prisons; 0.7 percent were college students in dormitories; and 0.6 percent lived in military barracks, rooming houses, and other types of group quarters, including 0.06 percent enumerated at shelters for the homeless. The 2010 census counted 8 million people in group quarters, or 2.6 percent of the population. In contrast to most household surveys, college students living away from home and in campus housing were to be counted at the college location in the census, not at the location of their parents' residence.

The American Community Survey (ACS), the successor to the census long-form sample, includes almost all of the group quarters population and follows the census residence rules for college students in dorms and other people living in group quarters. The ACS excludes people living in circus quarters, in recreational vehicles in a campground, and in domestic violence shelters; it also excludes merchant marine crews and people who might be found at soup kitchens, mobile food van sites, or specific street locations where the homeless are known to congregate.

Group Quarters (Nonmilitary)

Nonmilitary group quarters include college dormitories, nursing homes, long-term-stay hospitals, convents, monasteries, orphanages, boarding and rooming houses, jails, prisons, institutions for people with mental and physical disabilities, and others. Prior to the 2010 census, special places, such as a university campus, were distinguished from group quarters, such as a particular dormitory on campus. In 2010 the special places versus group quarters distinction was dropped.

To enumerate people in group quarters, the Census Bureau first builds a list of them. For the 2010 census the bureau included housing units and group quarters in its Master Address File, updating operations from the outset instead of building a separate group quarters inventory as in 2000. A group quarters validation operation conducted in fall 2010 involved visits to addresses identified as "other living quarters" during the address canvassing operation in spring 2009 to determine whether each such address was a group quarters (and the type of group quarters), a housing unit, or nonresidential.

A group quarters advance visit was carried out in February and March 2010 to inform the group quarters contact person of the upcoming enumeration, address privacy and confidentiality concerns, and identify any security issues. The actual group quarters enumeration took place in April–May 2010; interviewers visited group quarters, developed a control list of all residents, and distributed questionnaires called individual census reports (ICRs) for completion. The enumerators later returned to pick up the ICRs and, when needed, provide assistance in completing them. In some instances in which residents could not enumerate themselves (for example, some nursing home residents), administrative records were used to complete the enumeration. At a small number of facilities, such as jails and prisons, the facility staff conducted the enumeration. They were sworn in as special census employees for this purpose to protect the confidentiality of the census information.

The ICRs included a question on whether the respondent usually lived at the group quarters and, if not, to provide an alternative residence. However, not all types of group quarters were considered eligible for this "usual home elsewhere" provision; for example, the alternative address could be used to count a person found at a residential and noncorrectional treatment facility, a religious group quarters location, or a shelter for victims of natural disasters, but residents of correctional facilities or college or university campus housing were only eligible to be counted at the group quarters.

A similar group quarters (or special places) operation had been carried out in previous recent censuses. The procedures in 2010 were designed to improve on the 2000 procedures, which were not well controlled, resulting in errors of omission and duplication. In addition, nonresponse rates were high for many items on the 2000 long-form ICR; nonresponse rates to these items are much reduced in the ACS group quarters data collection, although they are still higher than the rates for household members. In the nineteenth and the early twentieth century, censuses included supplemental schedules, or forms, that ascertained detailed information about residents of certain kinds of institutions, such as prisons, institutions for people with disabilities, and almshouses.

Military and Maritime Enumeration

For the 2010 census, the Census Bureau worked with the U.S. Department of Defense and U.S. Coast Guard to identify both housing units and group quarters on military installations and ships assigned to a homeport in the United States. Service members living in on-base housing, such as barracks, received military census reports styled after the ICRs completed by other group quarters residents; contacts with base personnel and distribution of the questionnaires were brokered through designated liaisons. Families of service members and personnel living in housing near but outside the boundaries of military bases were to be counted by usual census methods (for example, mailout/mailback questionnaires), as were people living in actual housing units within military installations. The bureau also worked with the U.S. Maritime Administration to identify maritime vessels in operation at the time of the census and arrange to mail questionnaires to those ships; the personnel living on board (and naval personnel) completed another slight variant of the basic ICR, the shipboard census report.

In addition, the Department of Defense and other federal agencies were asked to provide counts of their employees assigned overseas and their dependents by home state from personnel records of the agencies. Such counts, which included people on board military ships assigned to a foreign homeport, were included in the 2010 census population totals for states for reapportionment of the U.S. House of Representatives.

Transitory Locations and Migrant Workers

Enumeration at transitory locations for the 2010 census (called transient night or T-Night in previous censuses) involved census field staff interviewing people at such sites as commercial and public campgrounds, recreational vehicle campgrounds or parks, fairs and carnivals, campgrounds at racetracks, and marinas. Each person enumerated during this operation was given the opportunity to report a usual residence at some other location. To enumerate migrant workers in the 2010 census, the Census Bureau worked with local officials and community-based organizations to identify camps and other locations at which migrant and seasonal farmworkers were expected to be found at census time.

Transient night has been included in previous recent censuses. Prior to the 1990 census, hotels and motels were among the locations visited, but such places were largely dropped beginning in 1990 because tests showed that visiting them added very few uncounted persons. Censuses prior to 1990 also included missions and flophouses in T-night operations.

The Homeless

The 2010 and 2000 censuses used an operation called service-based enumeration (SBE) to count people with no usual residence who might otherwise be missed. For 2010, efforts were focused successively over the last three days of March 2010 on shelters, soup kitchens, and specifically identified nonsheltered outdoor locations. There was no attempt through SBE to provide a total count of the homeless or of users of the service facilities visited.

For the 2010 census, the Census Bureau worked with local governments and community-based organizations during 2009 to identify lists of service locations open at census time. Census staff then made an advance visit to SBE locations two to six weeks prior to enumeration to update information about the location and explain the process. Using simplified enumeration procedures and questionnaires, bureau staff conducted a one-time enumeration at shelters on the evening of March 29, 2010. They did the same during the day, March 30, at soup kitchens and at stops made by mobile food vans with regular schedules. Enumerators also visited outdoor locations where people live and eat, as identified by local officials and community groups, in the early morning of March 31.

In addition to the SBE operations, people with no usual residence could pick up and complete "Be Counted" questionnaires, either from boxes of the questionnaires placed at various public locations or at questionnaire assistance centers (staffed, for the first time in the 2010 census, by paid part-time workers). These sites were typically located in places such as public libraries, shopping centers, and health care clinics.

The 1990 census was the first to include special procedures to try to count homeless people: the operation used in 1990 was called Shelter and Street Night (S-Night). Local governments were asked to identify locations at which homeless people stayed, such as shelters, bus and train stations, abandoned buildings, hotels and motels used to house homeless people, other very inexpensive hotels and motels, and street locations at which homeless people congregated. "Phase 1" enumeration was conducted in the evening hours of March 20 at shelters and low-cost hotels and motels. "Phase 2" enumeration was conducted between 2 A.M. and 4 A.M., March 21, at pre-identified street locations, abandoned buildings, and places of commerce. In selected cities, enumerators stayed outside selected abandoned buildings until 8 A.M. to enumerate people as they left the buildings.

The S-Night operation attracted considerable media attention and was controversial because the results were viewed as an undercount of the homeless. In some large cities, media hindered the operation by converging on large shelters and places of commerce, such as New York's Grand Central Station. Some coverage problems were identified, which were apparently largely due to incomplete location lists provided by local governments. Some additional locations were identified and enumerated on March 21 and 22, 1990. In all, 34,000 sites were canvassed. The total count of people enumerated at shelters was 178,000; those enumerated at street locations totaled 49,000.

See also *American Community Survey: methodology; Americans overseas; Content; Enumeration: field procedures; Residence rules.*

. . . . CONSTANCE F. CITRO

BIBLIOGRAPHY

National Research Council. The 2000 Census: Counting Under Adversity. Panel to Review the 2000 Census. Constance F. Citro, Daniel L. Cork, and Janet L. Norwood, eds. Committee on National Statistics, Division of Behavioral and Social Sciences and Education. Washington, D.C.: The National Academies Press, 2004. Available at http://www.nap.edu/catalog.php?record_id=10907.

———. Once, Only Once and in the Right Place. Panel on Residence Rules in the Decennial Census. Daniel L. Cork and Paul Voss, eds. Committee on National Statistics, Division of Behavioral and Social Sciences and Education. Washington, D.C.: The National Academies Press, 2006. Available at http://www.nap.edu/catalog.php?record_id=12244.

U.S. Census Bureau. *Census 2010 Operational Plan*. Washington, D.C.: U.S. Department of Commerce, 2010.

———. "Field Enumeration." Chap. 6 in *1990 Census of Population and Housing: History*. Washington, D.C.: U.S. Department of Commerce, 1993.

———. *Population and Housing Inquiries in U.S. Decennial Censuses, 1790–1970*. Working Paper No. 39. Washington, D.C.: U.S. Department of Commerce, 1973.

Errors in the Census

Just as no book is free of typographical errors and no highway free of cracks, every census has errors. Although the large majority of American households return census forms that are complete and correct, errors can and do occur. For example, some people do not receive census forms because their addresses were inadvertently left off the Census Bureau's mailing list. Elsewhere, the person filling out the form omits some people while counting others. Still others get counted twice. The problems of "hard-to-find" addresses, ambiguous rules for defining "usual residence," and a mobile population combine to make a perfect census count an impossible ideal.

In general, two types of errors occur within the census. *Omissions* refer to people who should have been counted but were not. *Erroneous enumerations* refer to those who were counted but should not have been included. The *net undercount* is the difference between omissions and erroneous enumerations. In past censuses the net undercount has usually been positive, but in Census 2000 it was negative because there were more erroneous enumerations than omissions. Should the numbers of omissions and erroneous enumerations be the same, the net undercount for the nation would equal zero, but there could still be serious problems in many local areas. Omissions and erroneous enumerations tend to occur in different types of places. Omissions are especially likely to occur among low-income racial minorities living in urban areas. Rates of erroneous enumeration, although high among low-income racial minorities, are also high in vacation home areas and among other families maintaining a second residence, perhaps for a commuter marriage.

In 2000 the net overcount was estimated to be 0.5 percent, or 1.3 million people. There were an estimated 5.8 million duplicates and additional numbers of omissions and other erroneous enumerations. The Census Bureau's undercount estimate for blacks was 1.84 percent, and for Hispanics it was either 0.71 or 3.17 percent, depending on the "correlation bias" assumption (correlation bias refers to the tendency of groups to be consistently missed in the census and the adjusted counts as well). In contrast, for the predominantly white "All Others" category, there was an overcount of 1.09 percent. This creates a racially differential net undercount.

How Omissions Occur

There are two general types of omission: whole household and partial household. A whole household omission occurs when the entire housing unit is left off the mailing list used by the Census Bureau. Some housing units are missed because no one finds the building. Others are missed because they are located in structures that appear to contain only one residence but actually contain several. For example, a three-story house, originally built for one family, is converted into apartments. From the outside the census-taker sees only one door and one mailbox and does not search for, or find, the extra housing units to update the mailing list.

Housing units for the poor can be hard to find. Old apartment buildings, sometimes located in high-crime areas, may not have separate mailboxes or identifiable numbers for the individual apartments. Many poor people, often undocumented immigrants, live in such places as garages and tents located in the backyards of friends or relatives. Their addresses are not listed, and they are not counted. Of course, homeless people, attached to no specific housing unit, cannot be included in the Census Bureau's mailing list. There are other procedures, admittedly imperfect, to try to count the homeless.

Partial household omissions occur when the census form arrives at a household but not everyone is counted. Some people are omitted because they are temporary residents. For example, a recently arrived immigrant from Mexico stays with a relative while looking for a job. Others are omitted because they spend time at more than one address. For example, a child with a single parent may live with a grandparent during the week while the parent works. The grandparent, thinking that the "usual" residence is at the parent's house, does not count the child. The parent, thinking that "usual" means "most of the time," does not count the child either. In general, more distant relatives and unrelated borders are less likely to be counted than members of the nuclear family living at a particular address.

How Erroneous Enumerations Occur

Ambiguities about the term *usual residence* cause some people to be omitted, but others are counted twice or at the wrong location. As they are for rates of omission, rates of erroneous enumeration are higher for persons not in the nuclear family of the household head.

When the Census Bureau prepares its mailing list, it has no way of knowing which addresses are second homes for a particular family. It mails the census forms to every address on the mailing list and waits for the returns. Census forms are frequently returned from "second homes" in spite of the "usual residence" instruction. Thus "second count" erroneous enumerations can take place in a vacation home or in an apartment used by one spouse in a commuter marriage. They also occur for retirees who spend the winter in Florida and the summer in the North. Similarly, a family moving around the April 1 census day may dutifully return its form at the original address. When the family arrives at the new address and finds a second census form, it might send that one in, too.

Erroneous enumerations also take place in rural areas where houses do not have street addresses. Census-takers must rely on descriptions of houses, and they sometimes confuse houses that have and have not already been counted, causing double counting.

Mailbacks, Omissions, Erroneous Enumerations, and the Net Undercount

The mailback rate is a good indicator of census-taking difficulty. Areas with low mailback rates require more of the energy and financial resources of the Census Bureau, and the census process takes longer there. By comparing areas with high and low mailback rates in the 1990 census, we get a good picture of how the incidences of omissions and erroneous enumerations combine to produce a differential net undercount across areas.

As shown in Figure 1, the mailback rates for most geographic areas varied from 55 to 85 percent. Rates of omission were strongly, and negatively, correlated with the mailback

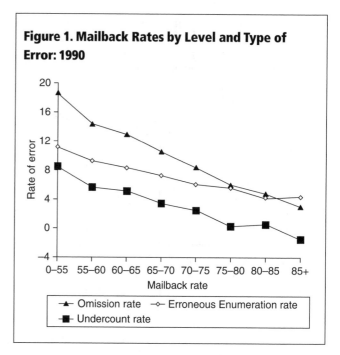

Figure 1. Mailback Rates by Level and Type of Error: 1990

SOURCE: U.S. Bureau of the Census

rate. Where the mailback rate was lower, fewer people were eventually found. The differences in omission rate were substantial, ranging from 3 to 18 percent.

Rates of erroneous enumeration were also negatively correlated with the mailback rate, again reflecting the greater difficulty of census taking when the mailback rate was low. The differences in the erroneous enumeration rate were not as extreme as for the omission rate. They ranged from 4 to 10 percent.

Combining omissions and erroneous enumerations, the net undercount was largest in low mailback areas and declined as the mailback rate increased. Indeed, those areas with the highest mailback rates showed a slight overcount.

The Bureau's Experience in Census 2000

Census 2000 marked the first time that erroneous enumerations outnumbered omissions and the census count was too large. This continues a trend, since the gap between omissions and erroneous enumerations has been narrowing over the past several censuses. There are four good hypotheses about why there are so many erroneous enumerations.

The first hypothesis concerns the Master Address File. Whole household omissions are a major source of census error, and the Census Bureau has worked hard to find and list more housing. Their efforts included the Local Update of Census Addresses (LUCA) program, which added 2 million addresses to the count in Census 2000. The 2000 LUCA program was successful in areas such as New York City, which had the resources to create alternative lists of addresses from sources not available to the bureau. The success of this program led to New York City having a population above 8 million for the first time in its history. Unfortunately, other cities without the resources of New York City were unable to duplicate its success. Overall there were millions of housing unit omissions and duplications; they nearly offset each other, and the overall housing unit undercount in 2000 was 0.3 percent. The frequency of these errors is increased by the lack of clear addresses on buildings and ambiguities in distinguishing different housing units in the same building. In Census 2000 a substantial number of person duplications occurred in buildings that were duplicated within the same or a nearby block as the original unit.

However, as there was a slight net undercount of housing units nationwide, the Census 2000 overcount cannot be attributed to duplications on the Master Address File.

The second hypothesis concerns the use of "coverage improvement" programs such as the vacant/delete check, in which housing units originally counted as unoccupied are checked to make sure the original designation is correct. In past censuses, rates of erroneous enumeration were very high for such programs, and they did not reduce omissions very much. As a consequence the bureau decided in Census 2000 to end data collection at an earlier date than in the immediately previous censuses and to impute missing cases by computer. There were 5.77 million imputations in the 2000 census, compared with 1.97 million in the 1990 census. Use of imputation no doubt reduced the number of erroneous enumerations that had been associated with coverage improvement and other "late stage" data collection efforts in the 1990 census. This is not a likely reason why the bureau obtained an overcount in Census 2000.

The third hypothesis focuses on problems with non-response follow-up (NRFU). The NRFU included those addresses where householders had not returned their census forms and counting conditions were sometimes difficult. The NRFU counted 44 percent of blacks and 39 percent of Hispanics but only 26 percent of whites in 2000. In many cases householders did not provide the necessary data to census-takers. The bureau collected NRFU data from householders in 80 percent of cases, and the remaining 20 percent, 4.5 million households, were counted by proxy. The proxy-counted data were often incomplete, because only 40 percent of the proxy respondents given long forms on Census 2000 provided enough information to be counted as "data defined"—that is, one member of the household had at least two sample data items reported. This is in addition to the 5.77 million imputed records that were created by a computer.

Because the proxy and imputed cases include so little personal information, the bureau could not accurately match them against survey data to estimate their omission and erroneous enumeration rates. It is reasonable to believe that at least some of the proxy respondents and imputed persons duplicated others who had already been counted by either a householder or census-taker. Duplicated addresses make this possibility even more likely. This hypothesis can be neither

ruled out nor substantiated. It probably accounts for at least some of the overcount.

The fourth hypothesis concerns the possible increase in "second residences" such as vacation homes, "commuter apartments," and shared child custody arrangements. The numbers of such homes have increased substantially in recent years, and they logically explain some of the overcount in 2000.

How the Census Bureau Treated Duplicates in Census 2000

The Census Bureau had not anticipated the increased numbers of duplicates in Census 2000. When it became aware of the excess counting it created a computer matching procedure to match and eliminate duplicated households. It originally identified 6.01 million person records in such households and took them out of the count. It later replaced 2.37 million of these, so a total of 3.64 million duplications were eliminated from the census.

As part of its evaluation program, the bureau estimated that the 2000 census included an even larger number of duplications than it had originally thought—as many as 8.7 million duplications before the deletions described above occurred. The bureau also learned that it had more success removing duplicate cases where the original and its duplicate were close together than when they were farther apart. When the duplicates were located in the same or nearby blocks, the bureau identified and eliminated 50 percent of them. It also eliminated 11 percent of duplicates located elsewhere in the same county but only 3 percent of duplicates located outside the same county. In sum, the bureau did a better job of removing nearby duplicates than other, farther away duplicates. This led to overcounting in areas where the farther away duplicates were located.

Error and the 2010 Census

The story of Census 2000 is that whites were overcounted while blacks and Hispanics were undercounted, and there was once again a racially differential undercount. To improve counting in 2010 and later censuses, the bureau attempted to better identify housing units, to actually contact and count a larger share of the NRFU population, and to figure out how to identify and delete duplicate counts, especially when the duplications are not in the same or nearby blocks. The Census Coverage Measurement (CCM) methodology for estimating census errors in the 2010 census will render a judgment on the effectiveness of these methods. The 2010 CCM program will provide estimates of net coverage error, as well as the components of that error (omissions and erroneous enumerations) for housing units and persons in housing units. This will yield estimates of net coverage error for selected geographic areas and demographic groups, as well as for key census operations. Given the importance of the duplication issue in the 2000 census, the Census Bureau is making a special effort to evaluate these errors in 2010. The methodology is very similar to that used for 1980, 1990, and 2000, with some additional features involving changes in post-stratification methods and adjustments for correlation bias for selected subgroups. Results of the CCM are expected in 2012.

See also *Accuracy and coverage evaluation; Post-enumeration survey; Coverage evaluation; Demographic analysis.*

. . . . EUGENE P. ERICKSEN

BIBLIOGRAPHY

Ericksen, Eugene P. "Census Goals: Management Choices and Prospects for Accuracy." *Public Performance and Management Review* 33 (2009): 156–172.

Moul, Darlene. "Nonresponse Follow-up for Census 2000," Census 2000 Evaluation H.5. Washington, D.C.: U.S. Census Bureau, 2002.

Mule, Thomas. "ACE Revision II Results: Further Study of Person Duplication." U.S. Census Bureau revised ACE Estimates Memorandum Series PP-51. Washington, D.C.: U.S. Census Bureau, 2002.

Mulry, Mary H., and Tamara S. Adams. "Overview of Evaluations of the 2010 Census Coverage Measurement Program." Paper Presented at the Joint Statistical Meetings in Washington, D.C., August 2009.

National Research Council. *The 2000 Census: Counting Under Adversity.* Panel to Review the 2000 Census. Constance F. Citro, Daniel L. Cork, and Janet L. Norwood, eds. Committee on National Statistics. Washington, D.C.: The National Academies Press, 2004. Available at http://www.nap.edu/catalog.php?record_id=10907.

U.S. Census Bureau. "The Design and Coverage Measurement Program for the 2010 Census." DSSD 2010 Census Coverage Measurement Memorandum Series #2010-B-07. December 2008. www.census.gov/coverage_measurement/post-enumeration_surveys.

Family and Household Composition of the Population

Basic demographic information collected about household members—including the number of members; their relationship to each other; and each person's sex, age, and marital status—is used to describe the composition of families and households. "Composition" describes the structure of families and households—the set of statuses and associated roles that are important for the functioning of society. American families and households have diverse and complex structures. For example, households can contain married couples, unmarried couples, single mothers, children, grandparents, other relatives (such as brothers, sisters, or in-laws), roommates, or simply one person living alone. Family and household composition is the result of demographic processes or family-related events such as marriage, divorce, and childbearing. Changes in the timing, number, or sequences of these events transform family and household composition. Examining the composition of households allows us to monitor how families and households are changing.

The household-based census is primarily designed to obtain social, demographic, and economic information about all the people living at a residence. Consequently, it can be used only to examine the family relationships of people living together at a given point in time. For example, census data can tell us how many families contain grandchildren living with their grandparents, but it cannot tell us the total number of grandparents in the United States because most grandparents do not live with their grandchildren.

Some Useful Definitions

U.S. households and families exhibit a wide variety of living arrangements: to discuss them, some definitions of key concepts are needed. A *household* can contain one or more people—everyone living in a housing unit makes up a household. In most cases, the person who owns or rents the residence is known as the *householder*. For the purposes of examining family and household composition using census data, the U.S. Census Bureau has defined two types of households: family and nonfamily. A *family household* has at least two members related by blood, marriage, or adoption, one of whom is the householder. *Families* consist of all related people in a family

household. A *nonfamily household* can be either a person living alone or a householder living only with nonrelatives.

Families can be maintained by married couples or by a man or woman with no spouse at home and may or may not contain children. In contrast, nonfamily households can only be maintained by a man or woman with no relatives at home. In censuses conducted through 1990, *children* included sons and daughters by birth, stepchildren, and adopted children of the householder regardless of the child's age or marital status. *Own children* differ from *children* in that they are never married and are under the age of 18. Note that according to these definitions, nonfamily households cannot contain children or own children of the householder; all individuals under 18 years in nonfamily households are simply unrelated individuals.

When we want to know about the different types of families and households and how they have changed, we look at the composition of households and families. When we want to know about the relationships and characteristics of people in households, we examine the living arrangements of the individual. For example, if we wanted to know about children and families, we could ask, "How many families have children?" But we could also ask, "How many children live in families?" In the first case, we are interested in family composition; in the second, we are interested in living arrangements.

Trends in Family and Household Size and Composition

According to the 2000 census, there were 105.5 million households in the United States, up from 63.6 million in 1970. Traditionally, families have accounted for a large majority of all households. In 1940, only one out of ten households was a nonfamily household. Figure 1 shows that the proportion of nonfamily households increased steadily until 1970, increased steeply between 1970 and 1990, then remained steady in the 1990s. Part of the increase in nonfamily households up to 1990 was due to the growth in one-person households—people living alone. The proportion of households containing one person increased from 18 percent in 1970 to 25 percent in 1990 but did not increase between 1990 and 2000. The growth in one-person households, combined with declines in the proportion of households that contain five or more people, led to a reduction in household size. Between 1940 and 2000, the average number of people per household declined from 3.7 to 2.6.

Changes in marriage and divorce were important contributors to the increase in nonfamily households and to declines in the size of American families and households between 1970 and 1990. The postponement of marriage after 1960 led to a substantial increase in the percentage of young, never-married adults. Between 1970 and 1990, the percentage of women age 30 to 34 who had never married increased from 7 percent to 18 percent. For men this figure increased from 11 to 26 percent. The delay of marriage meant that young adults in 1990 were less likely than in the past to be living with their spouses and more likely to be living alone, with a cohabiting partner, or with roommates. Meanwhile, the proportion of divorced people more than doubled from 3 percent to 7 percent for men and from 4 percent to 10 percent for women from 1970 to 1990. Increases in divorce also reduced the size of households and families; divorce generally separates one household into two smaller households.

Figure 1 indicates that the growth in nonfamily households and decline in household size observed since 1940 stopped in 1990. Yet marriage continued to decline so that in 2000, 22 percent of women and 30 percent of men ages 30–34 had never married. The percentage of men and women divorced also increased, but only slightly, up to 9 percent for men and 11 percent for women. Continued delays in marriage should have led to a modest increase in the percentage of nonfamily households, but shifts in the age composition of the population counterbalanced this trend. Those ages 35–64 are substantially less likely than older or younger adults to live alone. As mentioned above, delays in marriage contribute to a high proportion of young adults living alone. Among households maintained by someone under 25, 51 percent do not include a family member. Additionally, significant improvements in the health and economic well-being of the elderly have increased life expectancy and the quality of life for both men and women. This, combined with the fact that women continued to outlive men by a significant number of years, contributes to a greater proportion of one-person nonfamily households among the elderly. Among households maintained by someone over age 75, 55 percent are nonfamily households. In contrast, only one in four households maintained by someone ages 35–64 does not include family members. During the 1990s the percentage of the population ages 35–64, the group most likely to live in family households, increased from 34 percent to over 38 percent.

Trends in fertility could also potentially influence trends in household size, but recently fertility rates have been relatively stable. In 2000, 48 percent of families included own children, the same as in 1990. Yet the context of fertility has changed substantially over time, and almost 40 percent of births 2010 are to unmarried women. Consequently, a decreasing proportion of children live with married parents. In 1970, 88 percent of families with children had married parents; this decreased to 76 percent in 1990 and to 72 percent in 2000. Trends in young children's household contexts have changed in parallel. In 1990, 82 percent of children under age three lived in a family with married parents; in 2000 this had declined to 77 percent. Continued growth in nonmarital fertility since 2000 has likely contributed to further growth in the proportion of children living with an unmarried parent. Whereas divorce once was the primary factor contributing to changes in children's family and household contexts, today delays in marriage and growing nonmarital fertility are increasingly important. High proportions of births to unmarried women, combined with low levels of marriage following a nonmarital birth, imply that children will spend fewer years living with their own mother and father and will likely experience a greater number of family and household transitions before they reach adulthood.

Same-Sex Households

In 1990 the census questionnaire added "unmarried partner" to the list of types of relationships a household member might have to the householder. This made it possible to identify

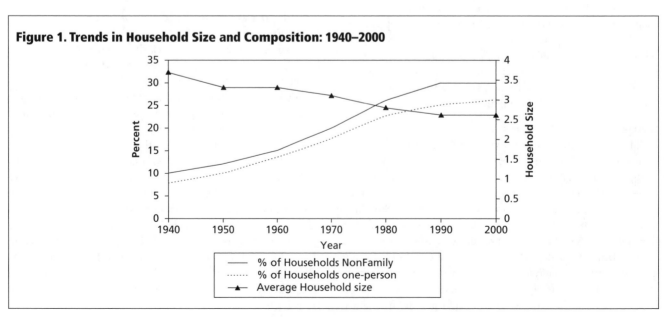

Figure 1. Trends in Household Size and Composition: 1940–2000

— % of Households NonFamily
...... % of Households one-person
—▲— Average Household size

source: Decennial Censuses of Population, 1940-2000.

unmarried couples (also known as cohabiting couples) using census data. When combined with information on the sex of each household member, these data allow us to distinguish households maintained by heterosexual cohabiting couples from those maintained by gay and lesbian cohabiting couples. Additionally, some gay and lesbian couples identify themselves as married and their relationship to each other as husband or wife. These data raise many important methodological and political issues.

Until recently, the Census Bureau recoded married same-sex households as same-sex cohabiting households for its official data releases and reports because the federal government did not recognize same-sex marriage. In 2009, well after the Census Bureau had established editing procedures for the 2010 census, the Commerce Department determined that the Bureau no longer needed to follow this rule. Thus, for the 2010 census the bureau released two types of data. In the first set, it followed the original plan to continue to edit records so that same-sex individuals who reported that they were married were recoded as cohabiting. In the second set, classifications used the originally coded relationship.

Limitations of Census Data for Studying Family Composition

Census data provide a snapshot of the population at one point in time. They are excellent for describing changes in the structure of households and families because they are comparable across time and are large enough to allow analysis of extremely small groups in very small areas. However, because the 2010 census did not collect marital status and the census has never collected cohabitation status, these data miss married and cohabiting individuals who are not householders and thus are not a good source of information on the number of married or cohabiting couples, regardless of whether they are same-sex or opposite-sex. Additionally, census data are not adequate for describing the processes or events that change these structures. Standard measures of process include marriage, remarriage, divorce, fertility, and mortality rates; these measures are not currently available in the census. Administrative data collected by the National Center for Health Statistics are used to construct these vital statistics rates.

The American Community Survey (ACS) is another new source of information on family events. Starting in 2008, the ACS began collecting individual-level data on the year of most recent marriage, on divorce, and on childbearing. These data have the advantage of combining events as well as population bases, which will be valuable for calculating rates. The ACS can be pooled across multiple years for the calculation of rates for smaller population subgroups or geographic areas. As it accumulates more years of data, the ACS will come to represent an important resource for describing changes in family processes, yet even the ACS has limitations. Often family demographers are interested in information about relationships such as cohabitation and in exploring the linkages between social and economic factors and family processes. For these types of analyses, the census, the ACS, and administrative data are limited. The National Survey of Family Growth, the Survey of Income and Program Participation, Fragile Families, and the National Longitudinal Surveys, are more appropriate data sources for investigating these complex issues.

See also *Federal household surveys.*

. . . .   R. KELLY RALEY

BIBLIOGRAPHY
Carlson, Marcia, Sara McLanahan, and Paula England. "Union Formation in Fragile Families." *Demography* 41 (2004): 237–261.
Martin, Joyce A., Brady E. Hamilton, Paul D. Sutton, Stephanie J. Ventura, Fay Menacker, Sharon Kimeyer, and T. J. Mathews. *Births: Final Data for 2006.* National Vital Statistics Reports 57, no 7. Hyattsville, MD: National Center for Health Statistics, 2009.
Sweet, James A., and Larry L. Bumpass. *American Families and Households.* New York: Russell Sage Foundation, 1987.
Raley, R. Kelly, and Elizabeth Wildsmith. "Cohabitation and Children's Family Instability." *Journal of Marriage and the Family* 66 (2004): 210–219.

Federal Administrative Records

Records collected and maintained by federal agencies for the purpose of administering programs that affect broad segments of the population include some of the same kinds of information captured in the decennial census. The Census Bureau considered a number of potential uses of administrative records for the 2000 and 2010 censuses, and while none was adopted, research to evaluate prospective applications to future censuses continued. This article discusses the strengths and limitations of federal administrative records as an alternative or supplement to the information collected on a census form, reviews the Census Bureau's initial plans for administrative record use in the 2000 census, describes actual administrative record use in 2000 and 2010, and lays out several issues that must be addressed if administrative records are to play a role in the conduct of future censuses.

Major Federal Administrative Records

Each year the Internal Revenue Service (IRS) receives more than 140 million tax returns and more than a billion "information documents." Filers of tax returns and their dependents represent an estimated 92 percent of the entire U.S. population. Information documents—which include the statements that employers, financial institutions, and government agencies file to document wages, investment income, retirement income, and other benefits—cover an additional several percent of the population. With respect to items requested on the 2010 census form, both tax returns and information documents provide a current address, while tax returns also provide relationship to the filer. Both sets of documents also include Social Security numbers for nearly all persons represented, making it easy to link the tax information to demographic data maintained by the Social Security Administration (SSA). With these additional data, tax returns would approximate the content of the 2010 census form.

The SSA Numerical Identification System (Numident) file contains data collected from applications for Social Security numbers and replacement cards as well as applications to change the name associated with a previously issued number. Data recorded on the Numident besides the Social Security number include the date of birth, sex, race, Hispanic origin, country of birth, and all names associated with that number. The number of persons covered by the Numident file received a boost following the Tax Reform Act of 1986, which mandated the reporting of Social Security numbers for all dependents age five and older—a requirement that was soon expanded to age one and older. Most children now receive Social Security numbers through an application process that is coordinated with the registering of births.

The SSA Master Beneficiary Record contains benefit payment data for the 51 million people who receive Old-Age, Survivors, or Disability Insurance (OASDI) benefits. These data include current mailing addresses and benefit amounts. Because these data are used to issue payments, they are updated continuously as changes are reported.

The SSA Master Earnings File contains histories of annual earnings from jobs covered by Social Security—including self-employment. This file, which is updated from employers' annual reports of covered earnings, includes data for more than 180 million persons. The employer submissions provide the SSA with a source of current address for persons who are not yet beneficiaries.

The Health Insurance Master Record, maintained by the Centers for Medicare & Medicaid Services (CMS), is the primary administrative database for the Medicare program, which provides health insurance coverage to nearly all persons 65 and older and to younger persons with qualifying disabilities. The file covers 38 million aged beneficiaries and 8 million non-aged disabled beneficiaries and contains name, mailing address, sex, a limited race classification, age, and disability (if under 65).

The Delivery Sequence File (DSF) is a database of names and mailing addresses maintained by the U.S. Postal Service (USPS) to assist in the management of mail delivery. An authoritative source of accurate address information for mail delivery, the DSF is a valuable resource for both the USPS and its customers. While the DSF contains no demographic information on the persons associated with individual addresses, it provides a key input to the census Master Address File (MAF). Updated continuously with address changes and delivery applications submitted by USPS clients, the DSF has played a growing role in census enumeration.

Some federal agencies compile administrative records that are collected by the states and transmitted to Washington, D.C., to fulfill a legal obligation or as part of a federal-state cooperative effort. For example, the Medicaid program provides health insurance coverage to more than 60 million Americans annually through individual state programs, which receive federal reimbursements. As part of their reporting requirements, all states must now submit quarterly files of individual case record data directly to CMS. Another example is the vital statistics system. Following federal guidelines,

each state compiles records of births and deaths and submits these data to the National Center for Health Statistics, which constructs and publishes national statistics on the number and characteristics of births and deaths. The Supplemental Nutrition Assistance Program (SNAP, formerly the Food Stamp Program), administered nationally by the Food and Nutrition Service of the U.S. Department of Agriculture, serves more than 18 million low-income households throughout the nation. SNAP records are often cited as a potentially important resource for census use because they provide extensive data on households that often fall below the tax-filing threshold, but the states and localities that operate the program do not ordinarily share their administrative records with the federal government.

Limitations of Administrative Records

Despite the broad population coverage and census-relevant content of federal administrative records, these data have important limitations—particularly in the areas of data quality and timeliness. The addresses reported on tax returns are not always residential or consistent with the census concept of usual place of residence. An estimated 10 to 20 percent represent post office boxes, business addresses, or addresses of tax preparers. An unknown fraction of the remainder represents locations other than the census residence. In addition, children who are away at college may be reported on tax returns as living at home (that is, claimed as dependents), whereas the census would count them at their college addresses.

The tax-filing unit does not correspond, exactly, to a census household. Although most households contain a single filing unit, households with multiple filing units or with both filers and nonfilers who are not claimed as dependents are not uncommon. By sorting tax returns on the address field, filing units can be aggregated into households—subject to the completeness of the address information. Apartment unit numbers missing from some of the returns filed from multi-unit residences, for example, would result in separate households being combined erroneously. Furthermore, when filing units are aggregated in this manner, it may not be evident which unit contains the householder or how the members of one unit are related to a householder in another unit. Filing units may also include persons who reside in different households—as in the college student example cited above or when married couples live apart but file joint returns. In addition, filing-unit composition is based on the preceding calendar year (the tax year) rather than the filing date. Marital status is defined as of December 31, whereas dependents can satisfy the residency test in the first half of the tax year. Furthermore, dependents who died at any time during the previous year are still counted in the filing unit, and filers themselves may have died during the year, leaving a filing obligation for their surviving spouses or estates.

Perhaps the most important limitation of federal administrative records involves the race and Hispanic origin data on the Numident. The infrequency with which these data are collected—just once in a lifetime for most individuals—precludes a consistent and current measure of racial and ethnic identity across the population. The Office of Management and Budget

(OMB) revises its racial classification periodically, and the Census Bureau follows the OMB directives, but the Numident data generally reflect the classification used by the SSA at the time each individual applied for a Social Security number. Prior to 1980 the racial classification included only three categories: "black," "white," and "other." Hispanic origin was not identified. In 1980 the SSA adopted the five-category classification mandated by OMB at the time, replacing the "other" category with "Hispanic origin" (intended to take precedence over "black" or "white"), "Asian or Pacific Islander," and "North American Indian or Alaskan Native." The current application for a Social Security number, reflecting the latest OMB directive, includes separate questions on race and Hispanic origin and allows the applicant to select multiple races from seven options.

The most serious limitation of Numident race data arises from the program initiated in 1990 to allow parents to obtain Social Security numbers for their newborn infants in conjunction with registering their births. Although the race of both biological parents (but not the newborn) is collected for the birth certificate, these data are requested in a confidential portion of the birth registration questionnaire that is not shared with the SSA. By the year 2010, well over a quarter of the records in the Numident lacked a race classification, and by 2020 this fraction is likely to exceed one-third.

The lag in data availability due to agency processing schedules is another important limitation of administrative records. Each year the IRS provides the Census Bureau with a file containing data extracted from all tax returns processed through late September. The file is received too late to be used in a census conducted in that year. Barring a change in what the IRS provides to the Census Bureau, and when, the Census Bureau would have to substitute the previous year's file in any census application. With about 12 percent of the population moving in a given year, a comparable fraction of the tax return addresses could be expected to be out-of-date and, therefore, inappropriate for use in a census. Furthermore, the relationship data would be at least 15 months rather than 3 months out-of-date, close to 2 percent of the filers and dependents would be deceased, and all of the children born in the 15 months before an April 1 census day would be missing.

Yet another limitation of administrative records, at least potentially, is that their contents are controlled by the agencies that maintain the files and, therefore, are subject to change without regard to their census use. Just as tax reform added children's Social Security numbers to the tax return, another tax law change could remove them—or, as happened in Canada, eliminate the reporting of dependents altogether.

With the addition of state records from federal programs that focus on the low-income population, it is possible that the coverage of administrative records could approach or even surpass that of a traditional census. Nevertheless, certain segments of the population may be systematically undercounted. Recent immigrants, who are precluded from participation in some of the major state and federal programs, are the most prominent example. Homeless persons are another. If administrative records were intended to replace the census enumeration, the attainment of complete or at least unbiased coverage would be very important. With a more limited role, complete and unbiased coverage would be less critical.

Census 2000

In its April 1996 "Plan for Census 2000," the Census Bureau announced that administrative records would contribute to the 2000 census in several ways. These applications included updating the MAF; assisting with the enumeration of special population groups (such as American Indians, Alaska Natives, people in group quarters, and people in remote areas); providing an alternative to in-person follow-up for about 5 percent of the households that do not return their census forms; augmenting the household rosters used in the coverage evaluation interviews; and filling in missing items on the long form. Ultimately, however, all of these applications were eliminated from the census plan, and, except for address listings from the U.S. Postal Service, military records on Armed Forces members stationed overseas, and administrative records for some group quarters, such as some prisons and nursing homes, administrative records were not used in Census 2000.

To support potential uses of administrative records in 2010, the Census Bureau focused its intercensal research on records from a small number of primarily federal sources. Building on efforts that were initiated prior to the 2000 census, the Census Bureau constructed a database of administrative records named StARS (Statistical Administrative Records System) and evaluated its coverage properties. The inputs to StARS were drawn from six sources: IRS tax returns and information documents, Department of Housing and Urban Development files, and Medicare, Selective Service, and Indian Health Service records. In creating the first version of StARS, the Census Bureau unduplicated 900 million administrative records, reducing them to 290 million unique individuals. The 1999 and 2000 versions of StARS were compared with records from the 2000 census. The results documented known or suspected weaknesses of administrative records—for example, underrepresentation of the young, mislocation of young adults and the institutionalized, and overestimation of the elderly. In subsequent years the Census Bureau continued to update and refine StARS as part of a growing program of administrative records research, which has included expanded efforts to link administrative records and survey data in order to improve understanding of measurement error in both sources.

Census 2010 and Beyond

Despite this ongoing research, administrative records played no greater role in the 2010 census than in its predecessor. A forthcoming evaluation of the latest administrative records database against the 2010 census data will document the advances made in coverage and content since 2000 and provide critical information on the viability of administrative records for population enumeration, as the Census Bureau plans for the 2020 census.

Several issues must be addressed if administrative records are to play an important role in the 2020 census. First, there must be an unambiguous determination that an enumeration from administrative records qualifies as an actual enumeration under the U.S. Constitution. Second, additional legal questions are raised by the use of administrative records for purposes other than those for which they were collected; census applications may require legislation giving official recognition to statistical uses of such data and ensuring that the Census Bureau has continued access to key records and specific content. Third, in light of growing threats to the privacy and confidentiality of commercial and government records, the public attitude toward prospective census uses must be taken into consideration. Fourth, the processing cycles for key administrative records may have to be altered to meet the census schedule whenever the substitution of earlier data would seriously reduce data quality. Fifth, a mechanism for obtaining a contemporary measure of racial and ethnic identification across the population must be identified.

See also *Address list development; Coverage improvement procedures; Enumeration: group quarters.*

. . . . JOHN L. CZAJKA

BIBLIOGRAPHY

Centers for Medicare & Medicaid Services. *Data Compendium.* 2009 ed. http://www.cms.gov/datacompendium/.

Food and Nutrition Service. "Program Information Report: U.S. Summary, FY 2009 to FY 2010" [Excel spreadsheet]. Alexandria, Va.: U.S. Department of Agriculture, May 2010. http://www.fns.usda.gov/fns/key_data/may-2010.xls.

Internal Revenue Service. *Statistics of Income, Individual Income Tax Returns, 2008.* Washington, D.C.: Internal Revenue Service, 2010.

The National Research Council. Counting People in the Information Age. Panel to Evaluate Alternative Census Methods. Duane L. Steffey and Norman M. Bradburn, eds. Committee on National Statistics, Commission on Behavioral and Social Sciences and Education. Washington, D.C.: The National Academies Press, 1994. Available at http://www.nap.edu/catalog.php?record_id=4796.

———. Envisioning the 2020 Census. Panel on the Design of the 2010 Census Program of Evaluations and Experiments. Lawrence D. Brown, Michael L. Cohen, Daniel L. Cork, and Constance F. Citro, eds. Committee on National Statistics, Division of Behavioral and Social Sciences and Education. Washington, D.C.: The National Academies Press, 2010. Available at http://www.nap.edu/catalog.php?record_id=12865.

———. Modernizing the U.S. Census. Panel on Census Requirements in the Year 2000 and Beyond. Barry Edmonston and Charles Schultze, eds. Committee on National Statistics, Commission on Behavioral and Social Sciences and Education. Washington, D.C.: The National Academies Press, 1995. Available at http://www.nap.edu/catalog.php?record_id=4805.

———. Preparing for the 2000 Census: Interim Report II. Panel on Alternative Census Methodologies. Andrew A. White and Keith F. Rust, eds. Committee on National Statistics, Commission on Behavioral and Social Sciences and Education. Washington, D.C.: The National Academies Press, 1997. Available at http://www.nap.edu/catalog.php?record_id=5886.

Sailer, Peter, and Michael Weber. *The IRS Population Count: An Update.* Proceedings of the Section on Survey Research Methods. Alexandria, Va.: American Statistical Association, 1998.

Social Security Administration. "Medicare Enrollment: National Trends; 1966–2008." In *Social Security Bulletin: Annual Statistical Supplement, 2009.* Baltimore, Md.: Social Security Administration, 2010. http://www.cms.gov/MedicareEnRpts/Downloads/HISMI08.pdf.

Federal Household Surveys

Historically, the decennial census provided sufficient information on the population of the United States not only to satisfy the requirements of enumeration and apportionment but also to support program planning at all levels of government and demographic and economic research in the private sector and academia. However, this information was updated only every ten years and thus was insufficient to answer all of the questions posed by Congress, policymakers, and researchers about the population, its characteristics, behaviors, and well-being. To acquire more timely information and to answer more in-depth questions, the Census Bureau and other federal agencies since the 1940s have relied principally on sample surveys that collect much more detailed information than is possible in a census but on considerably fewer households and people. Survey respondents are sampled in a manner that permits the results to be generalized to the full population with a known degree of sampling variability.

Beginning in 2010, the census is limited to collecting only basic demographic information for every household. The more detailed information that was previously collected in the full census (prior to 1940) or in a large sample of the population (on the "long form") is now being collected in the continuous American Community Survey (ACS), which is covered extensively in other articles in this volume.

In addition to the ACS, the federal government sponsors a number of household surveys that provide regularly updated information on the changing social, economic, and other characteristics of the U.S. population. Many of these surveys are conducted by the Census Bureau; others are conducted by the sponsoring agency or by private survey research firms. Survey information is used to allocate federal funds, evaluate programs, and inform policymakers. Some federal household surveys are narrowly focused on a specific topic or special subpopulation—for example, veterans—while others are broad, multipurpose surveys.

The decennial census, the ACS, and other federal household surveys complement each other, with each serving different purposes. The census, in addition to providing benchmark population counts every ten years, often provides the primary lists of households that will be sampled in a survey; the ACS provides a broad range of continually updated information for subnational geographic areas; and other household surveys provide detailed information in particular topic areas but with less geographic and demographic detail.

What Is a Survey, and How Is It Different from a Census?

Robert Groves and his coauthors define a sample survey as a "systematic method for gathering information from a sample of entities for the purposes of constructing quantitative descriptions of the . . . population of which the entities are members." A survey can be taken of virtually any population, provided that a list of objects or units in that population (that is, the "universe") and a way to find them are available. For example, households, businesses, or farms can be surveyed. Federal surveys of the U.S. population tend to sample households or other organizations that provide services to that population, such as schools or hospitals, and then ask specific questions about individuals within the household or organization. For practical reasons, the universe may be more narrowly prescribed either to focus on the portion of the population that is of greatest interest or to enable the survey to be conducted in a more efficient manner. For example, the universe for many federal household surveys is the civilian noninstitutionalized population in the United States instead of the total resident population; however, some federal surveys include additional subpopulations in their universes. For example, a survey of the elderly may include people living in nursing homes.

Ideally, the subset of the in-universe population selected for a sample resembles the full in-universe population for the characteristics of interest to the survey so that conclusions drawn from a survey can be applied to the entire population. Asking questions of a subset of the population instead of the full population allows the collector to ask more questions, given a fixed budget, than could be asked of every unit.

The ACS and the Current Population Survey (CPS) represent examples of federal household surveys. The ACS is exceptional because of its large sample size (in 2010, the ACS obtained information from 1.9 million households) and the availability of information for small geographic areas. The other household surveys discussed in this article are more modest in size and may also be more ambitious in the amount of information collected. For example, the CPS is a key federal household survey that provides the monthly unemployment rate as well as providing the vehicle for supplemental surveys, such as the Annual Social and Economic (ASEC) Supplement. The ASEC provides annual estimates of the poverty rate and of people not covered by health insurance. The CPS has a monthly sample of approximately 60,000 households.

Why Use a Survey Instead of a Census?

The official census is limited in its content and timing, and thus it cannot be used to address many important political, economic, and social issues beyond enumeration and apportionment. Some issues require more in-depth sets of questions than those included in the decennial census to measure all facets of the problem. Consider, for example, an assessment of the impact of a change in taxes across the population at different income levels. Such a study of tax issues requires detailed information on income and population characteristics along with all the information included on federal income tax forms used to calculate tax liabilities before and after a proposed or actual change in the law. In addition, some population characteristics, such as the unemployment rate, can change rapidly and thus need more frequent measurement than could be collected from the whole population in a timely and regular manner. (In the case of the unemployment rate, the CPS is conducted monthly.)

Data collection efforts have fixed budgets and often do not have sufficient funds to collect much information on all people. Furthermore, the Paperwork Reduction Act directs the government to minimize the burden of data collection on the population as a whole, which can be done by questioning the minimum number of people needed to accurately address an issue. Trade-offs exist among the accuracy of the results, the cost, the sample size, and the design. However, modern sampling and estimation techniques are employed to yield precise estimates needed to address many important issues, even with small to modest sample sizes. For example, the Consumer Expenditure Survey relies on a sample of fewer than 30,000 addresses to describe the spending patterns of over 310 million people in the United States.

Survey results produced by the Census Bureau, as well as other government agencies and private firms, are used in many ways by researchers, the media, nonprofit organizations, marketing firms, and all levels of government. Researchers often use survey data to assess the impact of policy changes implemented in the past, such as the major changes to social welfare programs that were introduced in 1996. The media, the federal government, and other institutions routinely use survey data to describe the population and its characteristics, such as the number of people and families living below the poverty level or the number of people who are disabled or who are college graduates. Researchers rely on analyses of underlying trends in the population covered by federal surveys to predict future patterns or to make decisions about future operations. Users of the data also simulate answers to "What if?" questions, such as "What would happen to the Social Security trust fund if the age requirement for receiving Social Security retirement benefits was increased?"

To support this statistical research, federal agencies release survey results to the public. Under the 2002 Confidential Information Protection and Statistical Efficiency Act (CIPSEA) and other legislation, such as Title 13 of the United States Code, which applies to the Census Bureau, federal agencies are required to strictly protect the confidentiality of individuals responding to the questions asked in surveys. Therefore, the data released can be in aggregate form (tables) or in the form of anonymous microdata (a file having one record per sample member where identifying information is suppressed). The Census Bureau provides access to publicly available data from the federal household surveys included in Table 1 through the Internet and through direct purchase arrangements.

How Does the Decennial Census Relate to Federal Household Surveys?

Federal surveys of the U.S. population often yield estimates about people and their characteristics, such as the number of people with health insurance coverage or the unemployment rate among different population groups. However, the underlying sampling method does not directly sample the population. Instead, the survey samples housing units, school districts, or other institutions providing services to the population. For many of the federal surveys in Table 1, the sample is based on addresses (such as 123 Main Street) obtained from the decennial census, and questions are asked of some or all of the people who reside at each of the chosen addresses.

The samples in Table 1, drawn from addresses in the decennial census, typically use the most recent decennial census supplemented with information on new housing construction subsequent to the census. The master list of addresses from which the sample is drawn is referred to as the frame. To minimize the cost of data collection while maximizing the precision of the survey estimates, the selection of addresses from the frame is not based on a simple random sample. Instead, the sample selection process involves several stages of selection at successively lower levels of geography (referred to as multistage sampling). First, the frame is often stratified by state or region or Metropolitan Statistical Area status to ensure adequate representation of these geographic areas or adequate sample sizes for these areas. Second, for household surveys conducted in person by interviewers, the addresses selected are typically clustered in smaller areas or segments based on geography to reduce travel between cases.

The decennial census also plays a key role in preparing estimates from survey results, a role described more fully in the last section of this entry.

How Long Has the Federal Government Been Conducting Surveys?

Federally sponsored surveys of the U.S. population date back to the nineteenth century. Early measures of trends in the cost of living were derived from annual surveys of income and expenditures conducted by the U.S. Department of Labor between 1888 and 1891. Periodic surveys of income and expenditures continued through the twentieth century and evolved into the Consumer Expenditure Survey, which was formalized in the early 1970s and was made continuous beginning in 1980. Until the formal survey was introduced, the expenditure surveys did not rely on the decennial census as the frame. The early expenditure surveys also did not rely on the same multistage probability sampling techniques currently in use.

The sampling methods now in use routinely by the federal government date back to the 1930s. The Financial Survey of Urban Housing began in 1934 using a sample of housing units drawn by randomly selecting blocks from large and small cities and then interviewing people in all units in the selected blocks. The Study of Consumer Purchases, conducted in 1935–1936, relied on a multistage design (then called double sampling). At the same time, the federal government conducted the National Health Survey using a sample of housing units selected from 83 cities and 23 rural counties.

In 1943 the Census Bureau conducted the Monthly Report on the Labor Force using the more sophisticated form of multistage sampling currently in use for the surveys in Table 1. This report was developed as a continuation of a series of surveys designed to study unemployment in the United States. It was renamed in 1947, in conjunction with the transfer of the project to the Census Bureau and the redesign of the sample, as the Current Population Survey, and its scope expanded beyond labor force issues.

What Do Federal Household Surveys Measure?

Most surveys have a specific focus (such as employment, health, crime victimization, etc.) guiding the content determination and the selection of the sample. Despite the wide variety of topics of federal household surveys, many of them also collect basic demographic and economic characteristics of people, such as age, race, sex, marital status, familial relationships, educational attainment, income, and labor force activity. The level of detail varies depending on the objectives. For example, surveys often will contain some measure of income of the household or of the people in the unit. This topic could be addressed using a single question (for example, "What is the total income you received from all sources last year?") or using a series of highly detailed questions of each person on specific sources of income, amounts, and distribution within the year (as is true for the Survey of Income and Program Participation [SIPP]). The objective of the more detailed questions is to increase the accuracy of the estimate of total income or to provide details needed for analysis or both.

Most surveys query people on topics that the respondents know firsthand. Occasionally, and with permission from the respondent, data collectors supplement this personal information with information obtained directly from establishments that serve the respondents, such as health care providers. The surveys in Table 1 generally rely on self-reported information asked directly of respondents or information provided by another knowledgeable person serving as the sample member's proxy.

The sample selection process generally restricts units to residential addresses that are occupied and whose occupants are in the civilian population. Thus, the resulting sample estimates apply to the civilian noninstitutionalized population of the United States. There are exceptions, however. For example, the New York City Housing Vacancy Survey covers unoccupied units and covers the targeted geographic area of New York City.

How Are the Data Collected?

The questions posed to respondents in federal surveys are contained within a questionnaire or instrument. The questions could be administered like the decennial census, where the questionnaire is mailed to the respondent who fills out the answers and mails it back. By their nature, these mail surveys are "self-administered"; that is, there is no interviewer to read the questions, and the questions are printed on paper. The National Survey of College Graduates is an example of a mail survey, although it also uses telephone interviews to follow up with sample members who do not respond initially.

Other surveys can be administered by an interviewer who reads each question and records the results. The interviewer can come in person to the respondent's home or contact the respondent by telephone. Telephone interviewers may be centrally located at one or a few phone centers or dispersed throughout the community. The SIPP is conducted

Section 1 — History of Technology

1790 Ledger with Paul Revere

The first decennial census followed soon after the ratification of the United States Constitution; an accurate population count was essential to the new nation's representative government. In its first century, 1790 to 1890, the census was a manual enterprise, unaided by machinery. Apart from the use of printing presses to disseminate statistical summaries, the entire operation was documented in longhand. Pictured here is an enlargement of the page below from the 1790 census ledger, preserved at the National Archives. Fourth from the top is the name of Paul Revere.

See *Congress and the census, Decennial censuses: 1790 census.*

Source: AP/Wide World

The Return for SOUTH CAROLINA having been made since the foregoing Schedule was originally printed, the whole Enumeration is here given complete, except for the N. Weftern Territory, of which no Return has yet been publifhed.

1790 Census National Summary

After all enumerators had reported their results to their U.S. marshal, and all U.S. marshals had reported back to Washington, the results were summed and printed for dissemination to Congress, the administration, and the public. To the right is a printed summary of results for the 1790 census.

See *Congress and the census, Decennial censuses: 1790 census.*

Source: National Archives

DISTICTS	Free white Males of 16 years and upwards, including heads of families.	Free white Males under fixteen years.	Free white Females, including heads of families.	All other free perfons.	Slaves.	Total.
Vermont	22435	22328	40505	255	16	85539
N. Hampfhire	36086	34851	70160	630	158	141885
Maine	24384	24748	46870	538	NONE	96540
Maffachufetts	95453	87289	190582	5463	NONE	378787
Rhode Ifland	16019	15799	32652	3407	948	68825
Connecticut	60523	54403	117448	2808	2764	237946
New York	83700	78122	152320	4654	21324	340120
New Jerfey	45251	41416	83287	2762	11423	184139
Pennfylvania	110788	106948	206363	6537	3737	434373
Delaware	11783	12143	22384	3899	8887	59094
Maryland	55915	51339	101395	8043	103036	319728
Virginia	110936	116135	215046	12866	292627	747610
Kentucky	15154	17057	28922	114	12430	73677
N. Carolina	69988	77506	140710	4975	100572	393751
S. Carolina	35576	37722	66880	1801	107094	249073
Georgia	13103	14044	25739	398	29264	82548
	807094	791850	1541263	59150	694280	3893635

Total number of Inhabitants of the United States exclufive of S. Weftern and N. Territory.	Free white Males of 21 years and upwards.	Free Males under 21 years of age.	Free white Females.	All other Perfons.	Slaves.	Total.
S.W. territory N. Ditto	6271	10277	15365	361	3417	35691

Herman Hollerith, Inventor of Punch Card

The modern U.S. census is largely the product of two contemporaneous processes: rapid population growth, fueled in part by immigration; and rapid technological advance. To the left is an image of Herman Hollerith (1860–1929), American statistician and inventor of punch cards and the electrical tabulating machines to read them. His machines were used for the censuses of 1890 and 1900. The company that he founded would become International Business Machines (IBM).

See *Data capture; Decennial censuses: 1900; Pre computer tabulation systems.*

Source: National Archives

Herman Hollerith Counting Machine

The first machinery used for tabulating census was invented in 1872 by invented by Charles W. Seaton, the chief clerk of the Census Office, and used in 1880. However, the process began to change even more dramatically around 1890, when the predecessors of modern computers began to appear. Shown here is the first complete tabulating system of Herman Hollerith, with the "counting" mechanism to the left, the "contact" mechanism in the center, and the "sorting box" to the right.

See *Data capture; Data products: evolution; Decennial censuses: 1900.*

Autosorting Machine from 1910s

With the U.S. population continuing to grow, the first decades of the 20th century witnessed increasing innovation in each step of processing completed Census forms. A photo dated between 1909 and 1920 shows a larger machine that automatically sorts the survey cards.

See *Data capture; Decennial censuses: 1900; Pre computer tabulation systems.*

Source: Library of Congress, Prints & Photographs Division, [LC-USZ62-101226]

Drawing Census Tracts

The division of metropolitan areas into "census tracts" was first proposed by Walter Laidlaw, director of the Population Research Bureau of the New York Federation of Churches. By 1930, the date of this photo, eighteen cities had requested that decennial census data be coded at the census tract level.

See *Census tracts; Decennial censuses: 1930*

Source: National Archives

1940 Punchcards
Source: National Archives

Closeup of Punchcard
As late as the 1940 census, punchcards were still in use.

See *Decennial censuses: 1940 census; National Archives and Records Administration (NARA)*

Source: National Archives

UNIVAC in Operation

After World War II, tabulating machines gave way to true computers. The Census Bureau was the first civilian government agency to acquire a computer, taking receipt of a Universal Automatic Computer (UNIVAC) on March 31, 1951. The new technology was used to tabulate part of the 1950 census and all of the 1952 Economic Census.

See *Editing and imputation*

Source: National Archives

UNIVAC Technician Joyce Cade
In this photo, dated October 19, 1955, computer technician Joyce Cade pauses while replacing a vacuum tube on a UNIVAC computer during the compilation of results from the 1954 Census of Business. The first UNIVAC computers had a clock speed of about 2.25 MHz and five thousand vacuum tubes.

See *Editing and imputation*

Source: Corbis/Bettman

Processing Center
Data processing today utilizes the latest technology. Much of the survey information collected by the Census Bureau is processed at the Bureau's National Processing Center in Jeffersonville, Indiana, pictured here.

See Data capture; State data centers

Source: U.S. Census Bureau

Albert Einstein and a Census Taker
Questions about education in some form have been included in every census since 1840. In 2009, a completely new question, asking for the field of one's bachelor's degree, was introduced in the American Community Survey. In this April 13, 1950 photo, taken in Princeton, New Jersey, Professor Albert Einstein answers questions for census taker Erna L. Cromwell. His answer to the question of attained education was likely "5th or higher year" of college.

See *Education: Changing questions and classifications*

Source: Robert K. Cromwell (Corbis/Bettman)

Enumerating Special Populations
In addition to enumerating "households," the census enumerates two major types of "group quarters"—institutional and non-institutional. The institutionalized population basically includes people in correctional institutions, nursing homes, and other institutions where they are under the care of trained staff who have responsibility for their safekeeping and supervision. Non-institutional group quarters include college dormitories, military quarters, homeless shelters—and religious convents. This photo was taken during the 2006 Census test.

See *Dress rehearsal; Enumeration: group quarters*

Source: U.S. Census Bureau

Data Collection with Laptop
Enumerators have been greatly assisted in data collection by the advent of mobile computing technology. Laptops can be used to compile and correct information gathered from in-person visits.

See *Internet data collection*

Source: U.S. Census Bureau

Data Collection with Mobile Computing Device
In the 2010 Census, the bureau moved away from updating addresses by paper and pencil and towards using handheld computers equipped with GPS (Global Positioning System) software. The spread of GPS and Geographic Information Systems (GIS) softwares have required a significant effort to integrate with the Census Bureau's Topologically Integrated Geographic Encoding and Referencing (TIGER) database, which was first developed in the 1980s.

See *Address list development; Geographic information systems (GIS)*

Source: U.S. Census Bureau

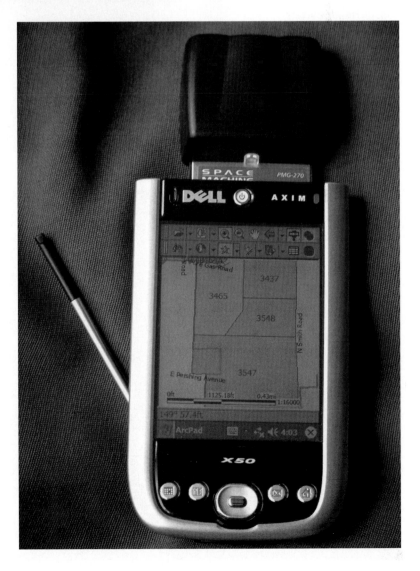

Section 3: Central Operations

Robert Groves, Census Director

Nominated by President Barack Obama and confirmed by the Senate, Robert Groves began his tenure as director of the U.S. Census Bureau on July 15, 2009. Groves had been a professor at the University of Michigan and director of its Survey Research Center, as well as research professor at the Joint Program in Survey Methodology at the University of Maryland. He was the Census Bureau's Associate Director for Statistical Design, Methodology and Standards from 1990 to 1992. Groves' mentor, Leslie Kish, first proposed the rolling sample survey that became the American Community Survey.

See *American Community Survey: Development to 2004; Decennial censuses: 2010 Census*

Source: U.S. Census Bureau

Census Headquarters

The Census Bureau's new headquarters building in Suitland, MD officially opened on August 7, 2006. The agency had previously been housed in the same building—Federal Office Building 3 (FOB-3)—since 1942.

See *Organization and administration of the census*

Source: U.S. Census Bureau

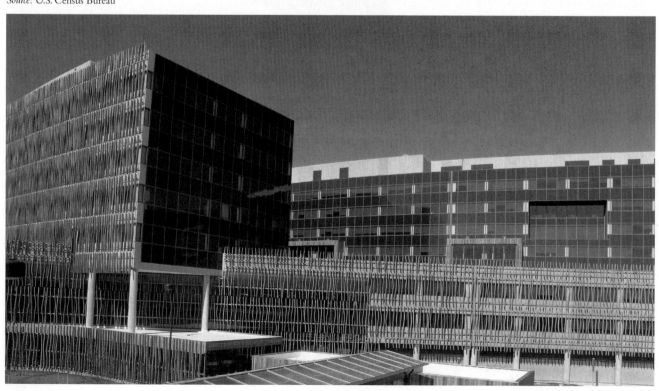

Vital Statistics Department

Vital statistics—records of birth, death, marriage, and divorce—were first published for the entire United States with the 1850 census. This picture is of the vital statistics division of the U.S. Census Bureau, dated between 1910 and 1930. The Bureau worked to standardize birth and death registry in the first half of the twentieth century, before handing the compilation of vital statistics to the National Office of Vital Statistics in 1946 (since 1960, the National Center for Health Statistics or NCHS).

See *Demographic analysis; Vital registration and vital statistics*

Source: Library of Congress, Prints & Photographs Division, [LC–USZ62-134542]

Tabulating Census Data

In an undated photo, workers in warehouse-like conditions tabulate data.

See *Data capture*

Source: National Archives

Mary C. Oursler, Official Custodian of Census Records, U.S. Census Bureau

Unverified caption from Harris & Ewing collection: U.S. census expert finds out ages of persons whose births have not been registered. Washington, D.C., Nov. 27. Statistical data might be dry for most persons but Miss Mary C. Oursler, Official Custodian of Census Records, U.S. Census Bureau, finds it the spice of her job. She is an expert at discovering the ages of persons whose births have not been registered, dig up data in heirship cases as well as for criminal cases in importance. Miss Oursler has been on her present job for the last twenty years. 11/27/37.

See *Archival access to census data; Vital registration and vital statistics*

Source: Library of Congress, Prints & Photographs Division, photograph by Harris & Ewing, [LC-DIG-hec-23699]

Unemployment Questionnaire

One of the first uses of sampling by the U.S. Bureau of the Census was an unemployment questionnaire sent to 2% of the U.S. population in 1937. From 1940 to 2000, the Bureau used sampling in the decennial census, differentiating between short and long forms. Beginning in 2005, the American Community Survey (ACS) replaced the long-form as a census mechanism. The original, unverified caption from Harris & Ewing dates this photo from October 7, 1937, and claims that "3,000,000 of the questionnaires are being printed daily at Uncle Sam's big printing plant."

See *National Archives and Records Administration (NARA); Sampling for content*

Source: Library of Congress, Prints & Photographs Division, photograph by Harris & Ewing, [LC-DIG-hec-23452]

Section 4: Advertising and Promoting the Census

The Census and the Military

This poster encourages participation in a "military census" in June of 1917, probably conducted by the state of New York, two months after the United States entered World War I. While the U.S Census is not used for military purposes, it has recorded military veteran's status: intermittently from 1840 to 1950 (the data was not always published due to low response rates), and continually since 1960. The veteran's status question moved to long form in 2000 and to the American Community Survey thereafter.

See *Veteran's status*

Source: Library of Congress, Prints & Photographs Division, WWI Posters, [LC-USZC4-8370]

The Census Assures Confidentiality of Responses

Congress, through the statutes that govern the collection and use of census data, guarantees the confidentiality of Census records. One of the few major exceptions occurred during World War II, when the Bureau of the Census prepared small area tabulations of the West Coast Japanese American population to assist in their evacuation and internment. Since then, the Bureau has defended confidentiality on a number of occasions. Among the latest: for the 2010 Census, the chairs of the Congressional Asian-Pacific American, Black, and Hispanic Caucuses sought and received a ruling from the Department of Justice that census confidentiality protections were not diminished by the 2001 Patriot Act.

See *Confidentiality*

Source: U.S. Bureau of the Census, The 1950 Censuses: How They Were Taken (Washington, D.C.: U.S. Government Printing Office, 1955), iv.

"It's OK Boys. You can tell him everything... He's the Census Man!"

Farming and the Census

Censuses of agricultural production have been conducted in the United States at least every ten years since 1840. The full census of agriculture is now conducted every five years by the Department of Agriculture. The population census had a question on its long form asking whether each residence is located on a farm. This information is now captured on the American Community Survey.

See *Agricultural censuses*

Source: National Archives

"Children Count Too" Campaign

Promotions for the 2010 census went well beyond posters, and included a number of public appearances by U.S. Census Bureau Director Robert Groves. On March 9, 2010 he met with Nickelodeon's Dora the Explorer and families at Mary's Center in Washington, D.C., to announce the launch of "Children Count Too," a public awareness campaign to remind parents to include their young children on the 2010 Census form. Overall, the 2010 campaign was budgeted at $133 million and was designed to expose the average American to 42 messages for the census.

See *Advertising the census; Popular culture and the census*

Source: U.S. Census Bureau

census2010@tacl.org   (626) 551-0227

IT'S IN **OUR HANDS**

Minority Groups Promote the Census

In addition to the advertising campaign conducted by the Census Bureau, many independent groups and organizations promote the enumeration. For the Taiwanese American Cultural League (TACL), such advertising is vital because their community is not among the official listing of ethnic groups used by the census. In this poster, TACL picks up the 2010 theme, "It's in your hands," and encourage Taiwanese Americans to write-in their identification under "Other Asian."

See *Advertising the census; Asian American population; Grassroots groups; Non-profit organizations*

Source: Taiwanese American Cultural League

so remember:

☑ Other Asian – *Print Race*
TAIWANESE

for more information please visit:
www.census2010.tacl.org

be recognized. be counted. april 1st.

Census Ads Woo Immigrants

The census is responsible for documenting the ethnic and racial composition of the population. Hispanic men in Madera, California, wait to be chosen for basketball teams beside a census poster that says answers given on census forms are confidential, on March 18, 2000. The Census Bureau has gone to great lengths in recent enumerations to convince migrant workers, indigenous people, and undocumented immigrants to fill out census forms. Distrustful of the government and fearful of the Immigration and Naturalization Service, migrant workers and undocumented immigrants are chronically undercounted in the census.

See *Hispanic population; Immigration*

Source: AP/Wide World

U.S. Population Estimator

The Census Bureau produces population estimates annually disaggregated by age, sex, race, and Hispanic origin for the nation, states, and counties. The Federal-State Cooperative for Population Estimates (the FSCPE) was created in the late 1960s to help coordinate this work between the bureau and the states. As this photo shows, the bureau also has a "population clock" at the Suitland, MD headquarters that reached the 300 million mark on Tuesday, Oct. 17, 2006.

See *Center of population; Population estimates and projections*

Source: AP/Wide World

by interviewers either in person or by telephone. When conducting the SIPP interview by phone, interviewers are dispersed throughout the community, most likely calling from their homes instead of calling from a central location.

The questions administered in surveys can be recorded on paper, as noted for mail surveys, or automated on a computer. The latter method is referred to as computer assisted interviewing (CAI). CAI surveys have become the norm for large, ongoing federal household surveys. CAI permits the use of the complex skip patterns that are often necessary to obtain the kind of detailed information requested in federal household surveys, while asking only questions that are relevant to the respondents. In addition, CAI instruments permit the customization of questions to the members and characteristics of the households and the use of consistency and edit checks to improve the quality of information that is collected.

CAI surveys can be interviewer administered, conducted either in person using a laptop computer or by telephone using a shared computer, such as those at central telephone centers. CAI surveys can also be self-administered, using instruments disseminated to respondents by telephone, by the Internet, or on a computer disk. The federal surveys discussed in Table 1 currently do not have a component administered through the Internet, although that option is under consideration by the Census Bureau.

Respondents to federal surveys are typically people age 15 years and older residing at selected addresses who meet the selection criteria unique to each survey. Depending on the objectives of the survey, the respondents may include just one person from the household reporting for the entire unit, all people meeting the age cutoff, or a sample of people from the household. Occasionally, and only when it is important to improve the accuracy of the responses, questions are directed to children under age 15. For example, the National Crime Victimization Survey (NCVS) administers questions to crime victims age 12 and older. The National Health Interview Survey allows any person age 18 or older to provide demographic characteristics for all household members and to provide characteristics of the family. One adult is then selected at random from each NHIS household to be administered a sample adult section of the instrument, and proxies for that respondent are not allowed. Finally, one sample child is selected at random from the NHIS household for information collected in the sample child section of the instrument, but in this case adults are allowed to provide the information on the selected child.

How Often Are Surveys Repeated?

Just as surveys can vary in their content and focus, they can vary in the number of repetitions and the interim time between repetitions. Surveys can occur one time and provide a single picture of a cross section of the population (cross-sectional), or they can be repeated over time, yielding a series of estimates that can be used to analyze trends (time series).

There are two types of repeated surveys: surveys that follow and reinterview the same unit over time (longitudinal) and surveys that rely on newly selected samples of the full population each time they are administered (repeated cross-sectional). A number of federal surveys, such as the CPS, reflect a hybrid approach. In the CPS, addresses selected for interview are visited for 4 months in a row, retired for 8 months, and then revisited for 4 more months, potentially being surveyed a total of 8 times over a 16-month period. Although this sounds like a longitudinal survey, it is not because it does not follow people when they move. The SIPP, meanwhile, is a purely longitudinal study. It selects a sample of people for its first round of interviewing and then attempts to follow those people over time (as long as they remain alive and within the universe of the survey). In addition to being a longitudinal survey, the SIPP is refreshed every few years when the Census Bureau selects a new sample of people to follow.

How Does the Quality of Survey Data Compare to Census Data?

Statistical theory says that basing a study on a sample instead of a full population will provide results with known precision or error due to sampling. The error associated with the use of a sample instead of a census is referred to as sampling error, and the level of sampling error varies depending on how the sample is selected and the sample size.

Formulas determining variation of the sample estimates from the population estimates quantify the amount of sampling error in a given survey. For example, for each of its surveys, the Census Bureau publishes a Source and Accuracy Statement that documents the level of sampling error and its impact on survey-based estimates. Typically, estimates are provided with a variety of statistics that indicate the degree of uncertainty of the estimates, such as confidence intervals or standard errors, and are suppressed from publication if deemed unreliable based on these measures.

The quality of the data collection process is crucial to the reliability of the estimates ultimately produced from a survey. Aside from sampling error, all censuses and surveys have some amount of nonsampling error. Nonsampling error refers to the deviation of the results from the truth for reasons other than the use of a sample to collect the data. The sources of census and survey errors include coverage errors, nonresponse errors, measurement errors, and processing errors.

Coverage errors can result when the frame from which the sample is selected is not complete. Nonresponse errors may occur when there is nonresponse to the survey or census. Measurement errors may occur when respondents do not understand the question being asked or do not correctly recall the information. Measurement errors can also arise from interviewers, such as the interviewer incorrectly recording the respondent's answer or not asking the question as worded. Errors can arise in the flow of the instrument—that is, in determining the appropriate question to pose during the interview—and data processing errors can inadvertently change the answers after data collection.

Some of these forms of nonsampling error introduce bias into the survey estimates. Bias is a measure of the persistent

Table 1. Federal Surveys of U.S. Households Using Decennial Census Results and Conducted by the Census Bureau

CHARACTERISTIC	AMERICAN HOUSING SURVEY (AHS)		CONSUMER EXPENDITURE SURVEY (CE)	
	NATIONAL SURVEY	METROPOLITAN SURVEY	QUARTERLY INTERVIEW SURVEY	DIARY SURVEY
Purpose	Inform housing policy and housing program design and evaluation		Update Consumer Price Index, support poverty measurement, analyze consumer expenditures	
Frame	Decennial census + new construction		Decennial census + new construction	
Current Size	62,000 addresses (2009)	2,400 addresses (one metropolitan area, 2009)	60,000 addresses over four quarters	12,600 addresses over the year
Frequency	Biennially (odd years)	Biennially (odd years, beginning in 2007, previously even years)	Quarterly (continuous monthly interviewing); each address is in the survey for five quarters with first quarter used as *bounding* interview	Two weekly diaries (two-week reference period is designated throughout the year so all weeks are covered)
Interviewing Mode	Personal visit and telephone; automated instrument		Personal visit; automated instrument	Combination of personal visit and self-administered paper diary
Respondent	One adult resident age 16 and over (occupied unit) or owner or proxy (unoccupied unit)		One adult in the consumer unit age 16 and over (consumer units defined by household member relationships and sharing of expenses)	
Sponsor	U.S. Department of Housing and Urban Development		U.S. Bureau of Labor Statistics	
History	National survey began as Annual Housing Survey in 1973 based on 1970 census; metropolitan survey began in 1974 with 60 areas interviewed on a rotating basis (20 areas each year); biennial surveys began in 1982 (national survey) and 1996 (metropolitan survey); frame updated to 1980 census in 1985; sample size fluctuated with available funds; automation introduced in 1997; mobile home frame updated and assisted-living unit frame introduced from 2000 census		Began in 1979 based on 1970 census; frame updated to 1980 census in 1985, to 1990 census in 1995–1996, and to 2000 census in 2004–2005; automation (quarterly survey) introduced in 2003; major redesign currently under way (Bureau of Labor Statistics Gemini project; see http://www.bls.gov/cex/geminiproject.htm)	
Weighting Controls	Housing unit controls derived from the decennial census and changes in the housing stock within a decade		Population controls derived from the decennial census adjusted for births, deaths, immigration, and emigration within a decade	

CHARACTERISTIC	CURRENT POPULATION SURVEY (CPS)		
	BASIC LABOR FORCE SURVEY	ANNUAL SOCIAL AND ECONOMIC SUPPLEMENT (ASEC)	OTHER SUPPLEMENTS
Purpose	Provide monthly estimates of employment, unemployment, and labor force characteristics; disability questions added beginning in June 2008	Provide annual estimates of income, poverty, work experience, and health insurance coverage	Periodic estimates of other topics, such as child support, civic engagement, fertility, food security, housing vacancy (quarterly estimates), Internet use, school enrollment, tobacco use, veterans' characteristics, volunteering, voting
Frame	Decennial census + new construction		
Current Size	72,000 addresses per month; about 112,000 adults per month	Hispanic oversample plus expanded sample (about 100,000 addresses and 210,000 adults); began in 2000 to support state-level estimates of children's health insurance coverage	Usually one month of sample
Frequency	Monthly (week of the 19th); addresses are in sample for 4 months, out for 8 months, and in again for 4 months	Annually in February, March, April	Annually (with exceptions) in various months
Interviewing Mode	Personal visit and telephone; automated instrument		
Respondent	One adult age 15 year and over responds for the unit and for each person in the unit (with some exceptions)		
Sponsor	Bureau of Labor Statistics and Census Bureau		Various agencies

(Continued)

Table 1. (*Continued*)

History	Monthly survey began in 1942 based on 1940 decennial census; underlying frame updated every ten years with most recent samples based on 2000 census; early samples drawn from an area frame with address sampling introduced with the 1960 census frame; sample size fluctuated over the years with maximum of 85,000 households per month (basic) in 1980; began with national sample design and switched to state-based sample in 1984
Weighting Controls	Population controls derived from the decennial census adjusted for births, deaths, relocation, immigration, and emigration within a decade

	NATIONAL CRIME VICTIMIZATION SURVEY (NCVS)		
CHARACTERISTIC	**BASIC**	**POLICE PUBLIC CONTACT SURVEY (PPCS)**	**SCHOOL CRIME SUPPLEMENT (SCS)**
Purpose	Provide estimates of crime victimization	Provide estimates of interaction with police and police use of excessive force	Provide information on school-related victimization
Frame	Decennial census + new construction		
Current Size	51,000 addresses, about 100,000 people aged 12+ per year	56,000 addresses, about 96,000 people aged 16+	10,000 households, 11,000 students
Frequency	Semiannually (with interviewing spread evenly over six-month period); addresses are in sample for 7 interviews	Triennially; last survey in 2005	Biennially (with some exceptions)
Interviewing Mode	Personal interviews; automated instrument introduced in July 2006 (automated telephone instrument used in previous years)		
Respondent	Each person age 12 and over in interviewed unit	Designated sample member	Students age 12 to 18 enrolled in primary or secondary schools
Sponsor	Bureau of Justice Statistics		National Center for Education Statistics
History	Basic survey began in 1972 based on 1970 decennial census; sample frame updated every ten years with most recent frame based on 2000 census; sample size fluctuated in response to available funds; PPCS supplement began in 1996; SCS began in 1999 with predecessor surveys in 1989 and 1995; major redesign of basic NCVS is under way		
Weighting Controls	Population controls derived from the decennial census adjusted for births, deaths, immigration, and emigration within a decade		

CHARACTERISTIC	**NATIONAL HEALTH INTERVIEW SURVEY (NHIS)**	**NATIONAL SURVEY OF COLLEGE GRADUATES (NSCG)**
Purpose	Provide estimates of the amount and distribution of illness and utilization of health care services; includes core and supplemental questions	Provide estimates of the numbers and characteristics of U.S. scientists and engineers
Frame	Sample areas selected based on 2000 population	For the 2010 NSCG, samples from the 2009 American Community Survey, 2008 NSCG, and 2008 National Survey of Recent College Graduates
Current Size	36,000 households (oversamples of Asians, blacks, Hispanics, and people age 65 and over in minority households)	100,000 adults (65,000 from the ACS)
Frequency	Annually (with interviewing spread evenly over the year)	Biennially (longitudinal survey that will follow subsample of the 2010 NSCG with periodic refreshment of the sample from the ACS)
Interviewing Mode	Personal interviews; automated instrument	Combination of mail, Internet, and computer-assisted telephone interviews
Respondent	One adult age 18 and over responds for family and household questions; selected other adults respond to additional questions on designated adults and children	Designated sample members (noninstitutionalized adults under age 76 with bachelor's or higher degree living in the United States or its territories during the survey reference week); oversampling of ACS respondents with science and engineering bachelor's degrees
Sponsor	National Center for Health Statistics	National Center for Science and Engineering Statistics
History	Began in 1957 based on 1950 decennial census; frame updated in 1972, 1985, 1995, and 2006; automation introduced in 1996; various topical modules included over the years on topics of import for health services research (for example, Cancer Control Module, Child Health Mental Supplement, and Child Health Mental Services were among the topical modules in 2010)	Predecessor to the NS was the National Survey of Natural and Social Scientists and Engineers conducted in the 1970s and 1980s based on the 1970 and 1980 census long-form samples; the 1993 NSCG and the 2003 NSCG were the baseline surveys for the 1990s and 2000s—both were drawn from the census long-form sample, and subsamples were followed up over the decade

(Continued)

Table 1. (*Continued*)

Weighting Controls	Population controls derived from the decennial census adjusted for births, deaths, immigration, and emigration within a decade	Weighted to the source of the sample case (ACS or 2008 surveys)
CHARACTERISTIC	**NATIONAL SURVEY OF FISHING, HUNTING, AND WILDLIFE-ASSOCIATED RECREATION (FHWAR)**	**NEW YORK CITY HOUSING VACANCY SURVEY (NYCHVS)**
Purpose	Provide estimates of fishing, hunting, and wildlife-related activities to aid in managing fish and wildlife resources	Estimate the vacancy rate for New York City's rental stock and the characteristics of housing and residents in the city
Frame	2010 decennial census	Decennial census, new construction lists, and other local information on the formation of rental units
Current Size	60,000 households for 2011 screener interview	18,000 units
Frequency	Household screener with three follow-up interviews, once every four months, of household members who participated or expected to participate in these activities to get reports of their actual participation; entire survey repeated approximately every five years	Triennially (with some exceptions)
Interviewing Mode	Personal and telephone interviews; automated instrument	Personal interview; paper instrument
Respondent	Adult household member for the screener, designated sample adult for follow-up	Adult resident (occupied units); owner, manager, or proxy (vacant units)
Sponsor	Fish and Wildlife Service of the U.S. Department of the Interior	New York City Department of Housing Preservation and Development
History	Began in 1955 and repeated at approximately five-year intervals; prior to 1996, the follow-up survey was administered once with recall period of five to sixteen months; wildlife-watching survey introduced in 1980	Began in 1962 based on 1960 decennial census; repeated approximately every three years; updated frame every decade with new decennial census results
Weighting Controls	Population controls derived from the decennial census adjusted for births, deaths, immigration, and emigration within a decade	Housing unit controls derived from the decennial census, adjusted for changes in the rental housing stock within a decade
	SURVEY OF INCOME AND PROGRAM PARTICIPATION (SIPP)	
CHARACTERISTIC	**1984–2008 PANELS**	**SURVEY OF PROGRAM DYNAMICS (SPD)**
Purpose	Describe patterns of income and benefit receipt and amounts in the United States and other special topics	Estimate the impact of the welfare reform legislation of 1996
Frame	2000 decennial census + new construction	1992 and 1993 SIPP samples
Current Size	42,000 interviewed households in Wave 1 of 2008 panel	18,000 households
Frequency	Every four months for four years; includes core questions (income, program participation, and work experience by month) and topical modules (personal history, childcare, wealth, program eligibility, child support, use and cost of health care, disability, school enrollment, taxes, annual income)	Once per year for six years; similar topics as SIPP with a focus on welfare dependency
Interviewing Mode	Personal and telephone interviews; automated instrument	
Respondent	Household members age 15 and older, who are followed over the life of the panel or survey	
Sponsor	U.S. Census Bureau	
History	Predecessor surveys took place in 1978; 1979 based on 1970 decennial census frame; first SIPP panel introduced in 1984 based on 1980 census frame, followed sample adults for up to 2.5 years; subsequent panels of varying sizes and lengths introduced in 1985–1993 based on 1980 census frame; 1996 panel based on 1990 census frame followed sample adults for 4 years; 2001 panel followed sample adults for 3 years; 2004 panel followed sample adults for 4 years based on 2000 census frame; major redesign under way (see http://www.census.gov/sipp/dews.html).	Sample members from 1992 and 1993 panels of SIPP followed and interviewed once per year between 1997 and 2002; thereafter SPD funding was used to increase the size of the 2004 and 2008 SIPP panels
Weighting Controls	Population controls derived from the decennial census adjusted for births, deaths, relocation, immigration, and emigration within a decade	

SOURCE: U.S. Bureau of the Census, Demographic Surveys Division, *Survey Abstracts* (Washington, D.C., March 2010).

deviation of the estimate from the true value and can be measured by the comparison of the survey estimates with reliable independent estimates. A form of bias that is typical in surveys is underreporting of income relative to an independently derived benchmark. For example, John Czajka reports that the 2005 Current Population Survey ASEC estimate of the amount of Social Security income received by the U.S. civilian noninstitutionalized population was about 90 percent of an independently derived benchmark.

The Census Bureau and other data collection organizations employ a large number of quality assurance techniques to minimize errors in survey results and to ensure that high-quality data are produced. Typically, sample surveys devote more resources to minimizing nonsampling errors than would be practicable if the collection were a census, yielding higher-quality information.

How Are Estimates Derived from a Survey?

Regardless of the focus, federal surveys employ complex sampling algorithms; that is, the selection is not as simple as every tenth person in a row. Sample members are clustered in a way that minimizes the cost of data collection while maximizing the precision of the estimates. Thus, certain special techniques of estimation (primarily weighting) are required to use these data. Federal survey data typically contain weights for people, weights for the units sampled (that is, addresses), and weights for one or more groupings of people within the units sampled. Population estimates are derived by totaling these weights over the sample members. Following is some important information on weights.

- In a simple random sample, if the sampling process selects one out of every five units from the full universe, then each selected sample unit represents five members of the universe (the selected unit and four others). Hence, the unit can be said to have a weight of five (which is the inverse of the rate of selection), and whenever that sample member is counted in an analysis, it is counted five times. In the case of complex sample designs, the weight still represents the inverse of the rate of selection. However, the rate of selection—and hence the weight—varies across sample members.

- Weights are used to compensate for noninterviewed units. If all people eligible for an interview at a selected address either cannot or will not be interviewed, the result is a unit noninterview. If left uncorrected, the weighted estimates likely will be biased. To minimize the impact of unit noninterviews on estimates derived from surveys, the weights of interviewed units are adjusted to compensate for the missing noninterviewed units.

- Counting people in interviewed units based on the unit weight, even adjusted for nonresponse, does not always result in unbiased estimates of people because of undercoverage and the luck of the draw. Therefore, it is common for federal surveys to have person weights that are derived from unit weights but adjusted so that, when totaled over all people in the universe, they equal

the numbers in the estimates from the Census Bureau's Population Estimates Program. These estimates are derived from the decennial census updated to account for births, deaths, immigration, and emigration since the last census.

Aside from creating weights to support estimation, the Census Bureau and other survey organizations employ other processes to minimize nonsampling error in survey estimates. Typically, all new questions to be added to a survey are pretested unless already proven successful in another survey. Pretesting research is designed to address the issue of whether respondents interpret questions as intended and can provide appropriate answers. Additional techniques to test the validity of the questionnaire wording include cognitive techniques, focus groups, and expert review.

Some forms of nonsampling error can be minimized after the data are collected, such as the error associated with missing responses because of refusal, lack of knowledge, or an instrument flow problem. Just as the assignment of weights includes a correction for noninterview and errors in the original frame, the assignment of data to questions with missing responses reduces the impact of missing data on the resulting estimates. This assignment of answers to questions with missing responses is referred to as imputation. The success of imputation in reducing nonsampling error is a function of the approach used to impute the missing data, the amount of missing data to be imputed, and the extent to which and the way in which people with missing data differ from people with reported data.

In addition to imputing information not originally reported, the Census Bureau and other data collection agencies edit information if good reason exists to suspect it was reported or recorded in error. For example, if a respondent reported not being enrolled in school and then reported attending college, the answers are inconsistent, and one is likely to be incorrect. Data collectors often rely on experts in subject areas (such as an expert in education in this case) to make an assessment of which answer is more likely to be correct and then edit the data accordingly.

Summary

Many federally sponsored surveys of the U.S. population rely on the decennial census either directly or indirectly. The surveys in Table 1 are those that rely directly on the decennial census for selecting the sample and controlling the estimates produced from the surveys. Although Table 1 focuses on surveys administered by the Census Bureau, numerous other federally sponsored surveys are conducted by private firms. These firms often rely at least indirectly on published estimates from the decennial census to control their estimates and establish their sample frames.

See also *American Community Survey: methodology; American Community Survey: questionnaire content; Data products: evolution; Editing, imputation, and weighting; Long form.*

. . . . BRIAN HARRIS-KOJETIN

BIBLIOGRAPHY

Bohme, Frederick G. "The Census Bureau's Current Programs: A History." Unpublished draft manuscript. U.S. Bureau of the Census, 1979–1981.

Czajka, John C. "SIPP Data Quality." Appendix A in *Reengineering the Survey of Income and Program Participation*. Edited by Constance F. Citro and John Karl Scholz, Panel on the Census Bureau's Reengineered Survey of Income and Program Participation, Committee on National Statistics, National Research Council. Washington, D.C.: The National Academies Press, 2009. Available at http://www.nap.edu/catalog.php?record_id=12715.

Duncan, Joseph W., and William C. Shelton. *Revolution in United States Government Statistics: 1926–1976*. Washington, D.C.: U.S. Department of Commerce, Office of Federal Statistical Policy and Standards, 1978.

Groves, Robert M., Floyd J. Fowler Jr., Mick P. Couper, James M. Lepkowski, Eleanor Singer, and Roger Tourangeau. *Survey Methodology*. 2nd ed. Hoboken, N.J.: John Wiley and Sons, 2009.

U.S. Bureau of the Census, Demographic Surveys Division. *Survey Abstracts*. Washington, D.C.: U.S. Bureau of the Census, 2010. Available at http://www.census.gov/aboutus/surveyabstracts.pdf.

Federal Statistical System Oversight and Policy: Intersection of OMB and the Decennial Census

The United States has what is frequently referred to as a "decentralized" statistical system. This decentralized system includes a total of nearly 100 agencies spread across virtually every department (and independent agency) of government. A substantial portion of the U.S. official statistics output is produced by 13 agencies that have statistical work as their principal mission. These agencies include the Census Bureau; the Bureau of Economic Analysis; and the Bureau of Labor Statistics; along with the National Centers for Education Statistics, Health Statistics, and Science and Engineering Statistics; the National Agricultural Statistics Service; the Economic Research Service; the Bureaus of Justice and Transportation Statistics; the Energy Information Administration; the Internal Revenue Service's Statistics of Income Division; and the Social Security Administration's Office of Research, Evaluation, and Statistics. The heads of some of these agencies are appointed by the president with Senate confirmation, while others are career civil servants. Some of the appointed agency heads have fixed terms, while others do not. These agencies operate on the basis of separate statutes that authorize, or in some cases require, the secretaries of departments to collect and publish statistical data on particular subjects. Exclusive of funding for the decennial census, approximately 40 percent of resources dedicated to statistical work in the United States (or about $2.5 billion annually) are expended by the principal statistical agencies. The remaining work is carried out by more than 80 agencies that conduct statistical activities in conjunction with another program mission, such as providing services (for example, medical care benefits for the elderly and the poor) or enforcing regulations (for example, with respect to the environment, transportation, or occupational safety).

With its decentralized system, the United States has had for more than 70 years a chief statistician located in the Executive Office of the President who has a number of key policy and coordination responsibilities. The chief statistician is authorized by law and executive orders to carry out budget reviews, information collection approvals (including for the census and the American Community Survey), standard setting, and other statistical policy and coordination activities. The statutory authorities of the chief statistician currently derive from the Paperwork Reduction Act of 1995, the Budget and Accounting Procedures Act of 1950, and executive orders, as described below.

Statutory Authorities for the U.S. Chief Statistician

Sec. 3504(e) of the Paperwork Reduction Act of 1995 (44 U.S.C. 3504) assigns to the director of the Office of Management and Budget (OMB) nine "statistical policy and coordination" functions. These are to

"(1) coordinate the activities of the Federal statistical system to ensure—

"(A) the efficiency and effectiveness of the system; and

"(B) the integrity, objectivity, impartiality, utility, and confidentiality of information collected for statistical purposes;

"(2) ensure that budget proposals of agencies are consistent with system-wide priorities for maintaining and improving the quality of Federal statistics and prepare an annual report on statistical program funding;

"(3) develop and oversee the implementation of Government-wide policies, principles, standards, and guidelines concerning—

"(A) statistical collection procedures and methods;

"(B) statistical data classification;

"(C) statistical information presentation and dissemination;

"(D) timely release of statistical data; and

"(E) such statistical data sources as may be required for the administration of Federal programs;

"(4) evaluate statistical program performance and agency compliance with Government-wide policies, principles, standards and guidelines;

"(5) promote the sharing of information collected for statistical purposes consistent with privacy rights and confidentiality pledges;

"(6) coordinate the participation of the United States in international statistical activities, including the development of comparable statistics;

"(7) appoint a chief statistician who is a trained and experienced professional statistician to carry out the functions described under this subsection;

"(8) establish an Interagency Council on Statistical Policy to advise and assist the Director in carrying out the functions under this subsection that shall—

"(A) be headed by the chief statistician; and

"(B) consist of—

"(i) the heads of the major statistical programs; and

"(ii) representatives of other statistical agencies under rotating membership; and

"(9) provide opportunities for training in statistical policy functions to employees of the Federal Government under which—

"(A) each trainee shall be selected at the discretion of the Director based on agency requests and shall serve under the chief statistician for at least 6 months and not more than 1 year; and

"(B) all costs of the training shall be paid by the agency requesting training."

Section 103 of the Budget and Accounting Procedures Act of 1950 (31 U.S.C. 1104[d]) directs the president to develop programs and prescribe regulations to improve the compilation, analysis, publication, and dissemination of statistical information by executive agencies. Executive Order No. 10253, as amended, delegates these functions to the director of OMB, to be redelegated to the administrator of the Office of Information and Regulatory Affairs. This agency houses the Statistical and Science Policy Office, which is headed by the chief statistician.

Executive Order No. 10033 of February 6, 1949, as amended, assigns the director of OMB responsibility for determining, with the concurrence of the secretary of state, what statistical information shall be provided in response to official requests received by the U.S. government from any international organization of which the United States is a member, and what agency is to provide the information.

These authorities initially were established administratively in the late 1930s and were subsequently mandated in legislation dating essentially from the 1940s. In addition, government-wide protections for the confidentiality of data collected for statistical purposes were set forth in the Confidential Information Protection and Statistical Efficiency Act of 2002.

In light of this highly decentralized system, the United States has essentially had a "culture of collaboration" among the statistical agencies for many decades. The primary role of the Office of Information and Regulatory Affairs' Statistical and Science Policy Office is to provide oversight, coordination, and guidance for federal statistical activities. Staff members identify priorities for improving federal statistical programs, establish government-wide statistical policies and standards, and evaluate statistical programs for compliance with OMB guidance. In carrying out these responsibilities, the chief statistician has certain tools to enhance coordination, collaboration, and comparability. In particular, locating the statistical policy coordination function in OMB means that the chief statistician is directly involved in the budget development, legislative review, and information collection review processes.

Development of Budgets for Statistical Programs

One of the most important responsibilities of the Office of Management and Budget is its central role in the federal budget process. The director of OMB is responsible for preparing the president's budget that is transmitted to the Congress each year. The process of creating the president's budget involves not only examining agency budget proposals to ensure their economy and efficiency but also ensuring consistency with the policies and priorities of the current presidential administration. During OMB's review, questions are raised about the cost, utility, and feasibility of agency proposals. Using their knowledge of statistical agency programs and priorities, the statistical and science policy staff members formulate long-range plans to improve the performance of federal statistical programs so that robust measures are available for use by public and private decision makers. They also play a critical role in ensuring that budget proposals of the agencies are consistent and mutually supportive where appropriate.

In general, OMB tends to consider resources for statistical activities to be within the context of the responsibilities of individual departments—there is no overall "statistics budget" that is allocated to the statistics-producing agencies. However, the Statistical and Science Policy Office has the opportunity to recommend funding levels for each area of statistical activity and to advocate for resources that will address high-priority improvements for particular agency statistical programs or for related programs within and across agencies. Examples include the American Community Survey and the decennial census or the Bureau of Economic Analysis National Income and Products Accounts, which obtain input data from various agencies across the system.

Establishment and Enforcement of Standards

Statistical and science policy staff members ensure the quality, integrity, and accessibility of federal government statistical methodologies, activities, and products through the issuance of government-wide policies, guidelines, standards, and classifications that are developed in collaboration with the federal statistical agencies. These standards are of various types:

- **Core** standards and guidelines for statistical surveys focus on ensuring high-quality surveys and encourage agency best practices.
- **Guidelines** on protection of confidential statistical information include recommendations for a common pledge of confidentiality and promulgate best practices.
- **Classification** standards, such as industry and occupational classifications, standards for classification of data on race and ethnicity, and standards for the designation of geographic areas including Metropolitan and Micropolitan Statistical Areas, provide a "common language" for collecting and presenting data across the agencies of the decentralized statistical system.
- **Data-release** standards govern the release of official statistics. These include standards for the release of principal economic indicators (such as gross domestic product, trade data, construction statistics, and employment and unemployment statistics) that establish strict rules to separate data release by a statistical agency from policy interpretation of the information. They also include complementary standards for the release of other official statistics such as those on poverty, education, health, and crime.
- **Data access and pricing** standards provide, generally, that information produced by the federal government must be available to all on an equitable and timely basis.

User charges may be assessed to recover the cost of dissemination but *not* to cover costs associated with the original collection or processing of the data.

Approval of All National Data Collections

A key tool for monitoring and enforcing the government-wide use of the standards and classifications is the information collection review process. Under the Paperwork Reduction Act (PRA), all information that an agency proposes to collect from ten or more members of the public, whether from individuals, households, establishments, educational and nonprofit institutions, organizations, or other levels of government, must be approved by OMB. This review is not limited to surveys or to "statistical" agency data collections; rather, it extends to *all* collections of data, whether they originate for statistical, administrative, or regulatory uses. All agencies must submit all proposed information collections to OMB (about 8,000 are currently active). Furthermore, collections are approved for a maximum of three years and must be approved again if the sponsoring agency plans to continue them.

The intent of the PRA was, among other things, to minimize the "paperwork" burden that results from the collection of information by or for the federal government and to ensure the greatest possible public benefit from information created, collected, maintained, used, shared, and disseminated by or for the federal government. The law gave OMB broad authority to carry out this mandate, which applies regardless of medium—oral interview, paper form, or electronic submittal—and whether or not the collection is voluntary or mandatory. In effect, this means that virtually every survey and census proposed by a federal agency must be submitted to OMB for review and approval. Central to this process is the requirement for consultation with members of the public and with other affected agencies. Public comment is solicited to evaluate whether the proposed collection of information is necessary for the proper performance of the functions of the agency, including determining whether the information will have practical utility; assessing the accuracy of the agency's estimate of the burden of the proposed collection of information; enhancing the quality, utility, and clarity of the information to be collected; and minimizing the burden of the collection of information on respondents.

While most of the burdens of responding to government data collection requests—and indeed most of the government's data collection requests—are not statistical in nature, statistical data collections are an important component of the government's data collection activities and are subject to the requirements of the PRA. Surveys and other data collections are reviewed to ensure that they conform to proper statistical methodology, standards, and practices; to ensure that statistical methods are appropriate to intended uses; to monitor agencies' use of classification standards; to coordinate collections carried out by various agencies; to prevent duplicative requests; and to reduce respondent burden.

The PRA also provides OMB with the authority to designate a central collection agency to obtain information needed by two or more agencies and to direct an agency to make the information it collects available to another agency.

OMB and the Census

OMB's interaction with the decennial census program is characterized by involvement in each of the roles described above—reviewing and recommending the budget resources that will be allocated for the decennial census and the American Community Survey (ACS); ensuring that classification standards are appropriately embraced in the census and ACS forms and that other standards for quality, confidentiality, and data release are honored; and reviewing and approving the forms before they are implemented by the Census Bureau. In addition, the Congress in the 1990s assigned to OMB a unique role with respect to the decennial census address lists. As part of the Local Update of Census Addresses (LUCA) program, the Congress called upon the OMB director, working through the chief statistician, to develop and implement a process whereby local jurisdictions could appeal the address lists compiled by the Census Bureau. For both the 2000 and 2010 decennial censuses, OMB designed and oversaw implementation of the Census Address List Appeals Office, a temporary activity associated with the conduct of each of these censuses.

With respect to the administration's recommendations to the Congress for the budget for the decennial census program, the statistical and science policy staff work closely with the Census Bureau to determine the soundness of the estimates of the resources that will be needed. They also work with colleagues in the budget offices at OMB to ensure that the Census Bureau request is given appropriate attention during formulation of the president's budget. For the decennial census and the ACS, these ongoing programs require both year-to-year discussions as well as longer-term multi-year assessments of the life-cycle costs for the activities envisioned.

With respect to implementation of government-wide statistical standards and to the review and approval of the forms ultimately used for the decennial census and the ACS, the involvement of OMB is ongoing and includes many dimensions. For example, it is often the case that census tests serve as the venue in which new terminology or categories are considered for occupations or for race and ethnicity. Another activity generally led by OMB, in collaboration with the Census Bureau, is the determination of content that ultimately will be incorporated into the decennial census and the ACS. For several decades it has been policy that the content for the decennial census (and more recently for the ACS, in its role as the replacement for the decennial census long form) would be limited to questions that were required by law or regulations. Given the limited "real estate" available on these forms and the role they play in serving needs across the government, such criteria for limiting the content were—and are today—essential. Through collaboration with an interagency committee, most recently cochaired by OMB and the Census Bureau, these criteria have guided the determination of the decennial census and the ACS content. Ultimately, OMB is responsible for ensuring that the approved information collection forms meet quality standards, will provide data that have practical utility, respect privacy and confidentiality concerns, and minimize burden on the responding public.

See also *Content determination.*

. . . . KATHERINE K. WALLMAN

BIBLIOGRAPHY

The National Research Council, Committee on National Statistics. "Appendix A: Organization of the Federal Statistical System," and "Appendix B, Legislation and Regulations That Govern Federal Statistics." In *Principles and Practices for a Federal Statistical Agency, 4th ed.*, ed. Constance F. Citro, Margaret E. Martin, and Miron L. Straf. Washington, D.C.: The National Academies Press, 2009. Available at http://www.nap.edu/catalog.php?record_id=12564.

U.S. Office of Management and Budget. "Chapter 19: Strengthening Federal Statistics." In *Budget of the U.S. Government: Fiscal Year 2012*, 341–344. Washington, D.C.: U.S. Government Printing Office, 2011. Available at http://www.whitehouse.gov/sites/default/files/omb/budget/fy2012/assets/topics.pdf.

U.S. Office of Management and Budget, Statistical and Science Policy Office, Office of Information and Regulatory Affairs. *Statistical Programs of the U.S. Government: Fiscal Year 2011.* Washington, D.C.: U.S. Government Printing Office, 2010. Available at http://www.whitehouse.gov/sites/default/files/omb/assets/information_and_regulatory_affairs/11statprog.pdf.

Foreign-Born Population of the United States

The foreign-born are U.S. residents who were born outside the United States and its outlying territories and whose parents were also foreign-born. They include people in a variety of immigration categories who fulfill the residency rules of the census, including permanent resident aliens, naturalized citizens, and some temporary migrants such as foreign students and exchange visitors. They also include persons illegally residing in the United States. Excluded from the foreign-born are persons born abroad of American parents.

A question on birthplace has been asked in each census since 1850, as well as in the American Community Survey (ACS), and has been used to distinguish U.S. natives from people of foreign birth.

Trends in Birthplace and Parentage

In 1850 the foreign-born numbered 2.2 million, accounting for just under 10 percent of the total population (see Table 1). The share of the foreign-born increased during subsequent decades, reaching a high of nearly 15 percent in 1890. The huge immigrant flows from southern and eastern Europe that started in the 1880s and continued into the 1920s dramatically swelled the foreign-born population. By 1930 the foreign-born population had peaked at 14.2 million, but due to the even greater increase in the native-born population, the foreign-born share had fallen to under 12 percent. The restrictive immigration laws of the 1920s and the economic hardships of the Great Depression caused immigration to slow to a trickle until

Table 1. U.S. Foreign-born Population: 1850–2008

YEAR	TOTAL POPULATION	FOREIGN-BORN	FOREIGN-BORN (%)
1850	23,191,876	2,244,602	9.7
1860	31,443,321	4,138,697	13.2
1870	38,558,371	5,567,229	14.4
1880	50,155,783	6,679,943	13.3
1890	62,622,250	9,249,547	14.8
1900	75,994,575	10,341,276	13.6
1910	91,972,266	13,515,886	14.7
1920	105,710,620	13,920,692	13.2
1930	122,775,046	14,204,149	11.6
1940	131,669,275	11,594,896	8.8
1950	150,216,110	10,347,395	6.9
1960	179,325,671	9,738,091	5.4
1970	203,210,158	9,619,302	4.7
1980	226,545,805	14,079,906	6.2
1990	248,709,873	19,767,316	7.9
2000	281,421,906	31,107,889	11.1
2008	304,059,728	37,960,935	12.5

SOURCES: Campbell Gibson and Kay Jung, *Historical Census Statistics on the Foreign-Born Population of the United States: 1850 to 2000.* Working Paper 81 (Washington, D.C., U.S. Bureau of the Census, 2006). 2008 American Community Survey.

about 1935. In fact, between 1930 and 1934 more people departed than entered the country. The total foreign-born population declined for the next four decades, falling to 9.6 million in 1970, or under 5 percent of the population. The Immigration Act of 1965, which opened up immigration from non-European countries, resulted in a dramatic resurgence in immigration. As a result, the foreign-born population climbed to 14.1 million in 1980 and more than doubled to 31.1 million in 2000. By 2008 it numbered nearly 38 million, an all-time high, comprising nearly 13 percent of the U.S. population.

A larger category, the foreign-stock, combines first- and second-generation immigrants—that is, the foreign-born and their U.S.-born children. Data on the total foreign-stock population are only available for the 1890–1930 and 1960–1970 censuses. Between 1890 and 1930 the foreign-stock population nearly doubled from 20.8 million to 40.3 million, accounting for approximately one-third of the U.S. population at both the start and end of the period (see Table 2). The decline in immigration after 1930 resulted in a corresponding drop in the foreign-stock population, which fell to 33.6 million by 1970, or just under 17 percent of the total population.

As noted, the foreign-stock population is composed of the foreign-born and their U.S.-born children, who could have both parents or just one parent who was foreign-born. During the early decades of the twentieth century, the foreign-born comprised between 35 and 42 percent of the foreign-stock population, and between 40 and 44 percent of

Table 2. Foreign-stock Population: 1890–1930 and 1960–1970

| | | | | DISTRIBUTION OF FOREIGN-STOCK (%) | | | | |
| | | | | | | NATIVE-BORN | | |
YEAR	TOTAL POPULATION	FOREIGN-STOCK	FOREIGN-STOCK (%)	FOREIGN-STOCK	FOREIGN-BORN	BOTH PARENTS FOREIGN-BORN	ONLY FATHER FOREIGN-BORN	ONLY MOTHER FOREIGN-BORN
1890	62,622,250	20,781,945	33.2	100.0	44.5	39.0	11.4	5.0
1900	75,994,575	26,038,397	34.3	100.0	39.7	40.9	12.9	6.4
1910	91,972,266	32,480,839	35.3	100.0	41.6	39.9	12.2	6.4
1920	105,710,620	36,715,938	34.7	100.0	37.9	42.9	12.4	6.7
1930	122,775,046	40,286,278	32.8	100.0	35.3	43.5	13.9	7.4
1960	179,325,675	34,050,442	19.0	100.0	28.6	41.4	18.9	11.0
1970	203,210,158	33,575,232	16.5	100.0	28.6	NA	NA	NA

NOTE: NA = Not available

SOURCE: Campbell Gibson and Kay Jung. *Historical Census Statistics on the Foreign-Born Population of the United States: 1850 to 2000.* Working Paper 81 (Washington, D.C., U.S. Bureau of the Census, 2006).

the foreign-stock population consisted of native-born individuals both of whose parents were born abroad. The balance included the native-born with only one foreign-born parent, and the immigrant parent was much more likely to be the father than the mother.

As immigration declined after 1930, the proportion of foreign-born people in the foreign-stock also fell. By 1970 it had dipped to just 29 percent, with the second generation comprising the remainder.

Geographic Origin

The continent of birth of the foreign-born population is available for the 1850–1930 and 1960–2000 censuses and the 2008 American Community Survey (see Table 3). In the 1800s, a period of generally open-door immigration to the United States, Europe accounted for the overwhelming share of the foreign-born. In 1850, for example, 92 percent of the foreign-born population was from Europe, while only 7 percent came from North America (essentially Canada). For the next five decades Europe and Canada contributed over 97 percent of the foreign-born population. The dominance of these two areas was assured when the United States banned the entry of Chinese and Japanese labor in 1882 and 1907, respectively, and virtually barred all Asian immigration in 1917. At the end of World War II these restrictions were slightly eased, but national-origin immigration quotas continued to favor Europe in general and countries in northern and western Europe in particular.

The Immigration Act of 1965 was a watershed in that the quota system was eliminated, creating opportunities for immigration from all countries. As a result, the proportion of Latin Americans and Asians in the immigration stream to the United States soared, while the share of Europeans declined. By 2008 Latin Americans and Asians composed 53 percent and 27 percent, respectively, of the total U.S. foreign-born population,

whereas Europeans made up just 13 percent. Thus, the dominance of European birthplace, evident among the foreign-born in the mid-nineteenth century, had waned by the start of the twenty-first.

The changing continents of origin were also reflected in the country of birth of the foreign-born (see Table 4). In 1850 the most frequently reported country of birth among the 2.2 million foreign-born was Ireland, with 962,000 people. This was followed by Germany (584,000), Great Britain (379,000), and Canada (148,000). Eight of the top ten source countries were European. By 1930 the major source countries of the foreign-born reflected the growing presence of immigrants from southern and eastern Europe. Italy was the top source country with 1.8 million people, followed by Germany, Canada, Poland, and Great Britain. By 2008 no European country was among the top ten source countries, and the ascendance of Latin America and Asia was evident in the rankings. Mexico, with 11.4 million people, was by far the most frequently reported country of birth, followed by China, the Philippines, India, and Vietnam.

Demographic Characteristics

Table 5 shows the age and gender characteristics of the foreign-born population since 1870. Immigrants disproportionately enter the United States in their prime working ages and tend to be younger than the general population. But their median age climbs as their length of stay in the country increases. The median age of the overall foreign-born population is thus influenced by both the level of immigration to the United States and the aging of earlier immigrant cohorts. The median age of the foreign-born population stood at 35 in 1870 and rose to 44 in 1930. With the precipitous drop in immigration in the 1930s and 1940s, the foreign-born population aged because it was not being replenished by younger immigrants. By 1960, with people age 65 and over comprising nearly one-third of the total foreign-born population,

Table 3. Continent of Birth of the Foreign-born Population: 1850–1930 and 1960–2008

YEAR	TOTAL FOREIGN-BORN*	DISTRIBUTION OF CONTINENT OF BIRTH (%)					
		EUROPE	ASIA	AFRICA	OCEANIA	LATIN AMERICA	NORTH AMERICA
1850	2,202,625	92.2	0.1	0.0	0.0	0.9	6.7
1860	4,134,809	92.1	0.9	0.0	0.1	0.9	6.0
1870	5,563,637	88.8	1.2	0.0	0.1	1.0	8.9
1880	6,675,875	86.2	1.6	0.0	0.1	1.3	10.7
1890	9,243,535	86.9	1.2	0.0	0.1	1.2	10.6
1900	10,330,534	86.0	1.2	0.0	0.1	1.3	11.4
1910	13,506,272	87.4	1.4	0.0	0.1	2.1	9.0
1920	13,911,767	85.7	1.7	0.1	0.1	4.2	8.2
1930	14,197,553	83.0	1.9	0.1	0.1	5.6	9.2
1960	9,678,201	75.0	5.1	0.4	0.4	9.4	9.8
1970	9,303,570	61.7	8.9	0.9	0.4	19.4	8.7
1980	13,192,563	39.0	19.3	1.5	0.6	33.1	6.5
1990	18,959,158	22.9	26.3	1.9	0.5	44.3	4.0
2000	31,107,573	15.8	26.4	2.8	0.5	51.7	2.7
2008	37,960,773	13.1	27.3	3.8	0.6	53.1	2.2

NOTE: * With a stated continent of birth

SOURCES: Campbell Gibson and Kay Jung. *Historical Census Statistics on the Foreign-Born Population of the United States: 1850 to 2000.* Working Paper 81 (Washington, D.C., U.S. Bureau of the Census, 2006). 2008 American Community Survey.

Table 4. Top 10 Source Countries of the Foreign-born: 1850, 1930, and 2008

	1850			1930			2008	
1	Ireland	961,719	1	Italy	1,790,429	1	Mexico	11,412,668
2	Germany	583,774	2	Germany	1,608,814	2	China*	1,913,443
3	Great Britain	379,093	3	Canada	1,310,369	3	Philippines	1,684,802
4	Canada	147,711	4	Poland	1,268,583	4	India	1,622,522
5	France	54,069	5	Great Britain	1,224,091	5	Vietnam	1,138,039
6	Switzerland	13,358	6	Soviet Union	1,153,628	6	El Salvador	1,094,993
7	Mexico	13,317	7	Ireland	744,810	7	South Korea	1,030,691
8	Norway	12,678	8	Mexico	641,462	8	Cuba	974,657
9	The Netherlands	9,848	9	Sweden	595,250	9	Canada	818,920
10	Italy	3,679	10	Czechoslovakia	491,638	10	Dominican Republic	771,910

NOTES: * Includes the mainland, Taiwan, and Hong Kong. Data are based on political boundaries existing at the specified time points.

SOURCES: Campbell Gibson and Kay Jung. *Historical Census Statistics on the Foreign-Born Population of the United States: 1850 to 2000.* Working Paper 81 (Washington, D.C., U.S. Bureau of the Census, 2006). 2008 American Community Survey.

Table 5. Age Distribution and Sex Ratios of the Foreign-born Population: 1870–2008

YEAR	TOTAL	AGE DISTRIBUTION (%)				MEDIAN (YEARS)	SEX RATIO*
		UNDER 15	15 TO 44	45 TO 64	65 + AGE		
1870	5,567,229	8.4	65.8	21.8	4.0	34.6	117.4
1880	6,679,943	6.5	58.6	28.8	6.1	38.3	119.1
1890	9,249,547	8.0	57.0	27.5	7.5	37.1	121.2
1900	10,341,276	5.0	58.0	27.8	9.2	38.5	119.5
1910	13,515,886	5.7	59.9	25.5	8.9	37.2	131.1
1920	13,920,692	4.0	56.4	29.9	9.7	40.0	122.9
1930	14,204,149	2.5	50.2	35.3	12.0	43.9	116.6
1940	11,594,896	0.7	33.4	47.8	18.0	51.0	111.8
1950	10,347,395	1.9	23.1	48.6	26.3	55.9	103.3
1960	9,738,091	5.2	24.7	37.5	32.6	57.2	95.6
1970	9,619,302	6.3	34.7	27.0	32.0	52.0	84.4
1980	14,079,906	8.8	48.4	21.6	21.2	39.9	87.8
1990	19,767,316	7.5	56.8	22.0	13.6	37.3	95.8
2000	31,107,889	7.4	58.2	23.7	10.7	37.6	99.0
2008	37,960,935	5.3	53.5	29.0	12.3	40.8	100.4

NOTE: * Males per 100 females

SOURCE: Campbell Gibson and Kay Jung. *Historical Census Statistics on the Foreign-Born Population of the United States: 1850 to 2000.* Working Paper 81 (Washington, D.C., U.S. Bureau of the Census, 2006). 2008 American Community Survey.

the median age reached a high of 57. After passage of the Immigration Act of 1965, immigration once again increased, and the median age of the foreign-born declined. By 1990 the share of people age 65 and over declined to 14 percent of the total foreign-born, and the median age had dropped to 37. Despite continued immigration, the median age had increased to nearly 41 by 2008, partly a reflection of the aging of earlier immigrant cohorts.

Historically, males have accounted for a disproportionate share of immigrants entering the United States, and this disparity has skewed the sex ratio (number of males per 100 females) of the overall foreign-born population. In the 1880 foreign-born population, for example, males outnumbered females, with a sex ratio of 119 males per 100 females. This sex ratio became even more skewed as southern and eastern European immigrants entered the country. Their sex ratios were among the most lopsided of any period, and by 1910 the sex ratio for the foreign-born population had increased to 131. As immigration dipped in the 1930s and early 1940s, women outnumbered men in the immigration flow for the first time. For a few years after World War II, war brides entering the country made the immigrant stream even more disproportionately female. By 1950 the

sex ratio of the total foreign-born population had dropped to 103, and by 1970 it had reached a low of 84. Nearly one-third of the foreign-born in 1970 were elderly, and due to higher male mortality they were disproportionately female, thus skewing the overall sex ratio of the foreign-born. The Immigration Act of 1965, which made family reunification the main path of entry to the United States, witnessed the continued, though reduced, dominance of the immigrant stream by women. In 1980 the sex ratio of the foreign-born population stood at 88. It increased to 96 in 1990, and by 2008 there were an equal number of males and females among the foreign-born.

Region and State of Residence

Table 6 provides information on the foreign-born population's regional patterns of residence, as documented in censuses between 1850 and 2000 and in the 2008 American Community Survey. For the four major U.S. regions—the Northeast, Midwest, South, and West—population counts for the total and foreign-born populations are shown, as is the percentage of each region that is foreign-born.

Historically, the South has had the smallest proportion of foreign-born. It was just 3 percent in 1850 and declined for

Table 6. Number and Percentage of Foreign-born for U.S. Regions: 1850–2008

YEAR	NORTHEAST			MIDWEST			SOUTH			WEST		
	TOTAL POPULATION	FOREIGN-BORN	FOREIGN-BORN (%)	TOTAL POPULATION	FOREIGN-BORN	FOREIGN-BORN (%)	TOTAL POPULATION	FOREIGN-BORN	FOREIGN-BORN (%)	TOTAL POPULATION	FOREIGN-BORN	FOREIGN-BORN (%)
1850	8,626,851	1,325,543	15.4	5,403,595	650,375	12.0	8,982,612	241,665	2.7	178,818	27,019	15.1
1860	10,594,268	2,023,905	19.1	9,096,716	1,543,358	17.0	11,133,361	392,432	3.5	618,976	179,002	28.9
1870	12,298,730	2,520,606	20.5	12,981,111	2,333,285	18.0	12,288,020	399,975	3.3	990,510	313,363	31.6
1880	14,507,407	2,814,520	19.4	17,364,111	2,916,829	16.8	16,516,568	448,532	2.7	1,767,697	500,062	28.3
1890	17,401,545	3,888,177	22.3	22,362,279	4,060,114	18.2	19,830,813	530,346	2.7	3,027,613	770,910	25.5
1900	21,046,695	4,762,796	22.6	26,333,004	4,158,474	15.8	24,523,527	573,685	2.3	4,091,349	846,321	20.7
1910	25,868,573	6,676,283	25.8	29,888,542	4,690,461	15.7	29,389,330	740,011	2.5	6,825,821	1,409,131	20.6
1920	29,662,053	6,846,363	23.1	34,019,792	4,607,794	13.5	33,125,803	868,354	2.6	8,902,972	1,598,181	18.0
1930	34,427,091	7,201,674	20.9	38,594,100	4,359,876	11.3	37,857,633	818,614	2.2	11,896,222	1,823,985	15.3
1940	35,976,777	6,102,546	17.0	40,143,332	3,358,966	8.4	41,665,901	639,788	1.5	13,883,265	1,493,596	10.8
1950	39,341,610	5,287,165	13.4	44,281,175	2,707,390	6.1	47,085,880	767,320	1.6	19,507,445	1,585,520	8.1
1960	44,681,702	4,574,743	10.2	51,623,773	2,276,959	4.4	54,963,470	962,920	1.8	28,056,726	1,923,521	6.9
1970	49,044,015	4,119,681	8.4	56,564,917	1,873,561	3.3	62,792,882	1,316,205	2.1	34,808,344	2,309,855	6.6
1980	49,135,283	4,505,923	9.2	58,865,670	2,114,190	3.6	75,372,362	2,894,757	3.8	43,172,490	4,565,036	10.6
1990	50,809,229	5,231,024	10.3	59,668,632	2,131,293	3.6	85,445,930	4,582,293	5.4	52,786,082	7,822,706	14.8
2000	53,594,378	7,229,068	13.5	64,392,776	3,509,937	5.5	100,236,820	8,608,441	8.6	63,197,932	11,760,443	18.6
2008	54,924,779	8,264,367	15.0	66,561,452	4,255,979	6.4	111,718,549	11,674,124	10.4	70,854,948	13,766,465	19.4

SOURCES: Campbell Gibson and Kay Jung. Historical Census Statistics on the Foreign-Born Population of the United States: 1850 to 2000. Working Paper 81 (Washington, D.C., U.S. Bureau of the Census, 2006). 2008 American Community Survey.

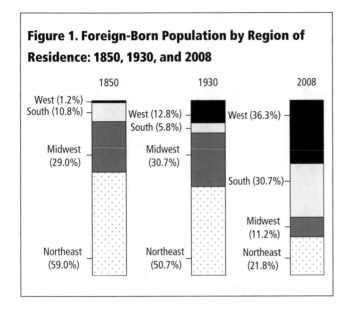

Figure 1. Foreign-Born Population by Region of Residence: 1850, 1930, and 2008

SOURCE: Campbell Gibson and Kay Jung. *Historical Census Statistics on the Foreign-Born Population of the United States: 1850 to 2000*, Working Paper 81 (Washington, D.C., U.S. Bureau of the Census, 2006). 2008 American Community Survey.

most of the early decades of the twentieth century, reaching a low of under 2 percent in 1940. In contrast, a large proportion of the population of the Northeast and West has been foreign-born. For example, in 1850 15 percent of the population of each of these regions was foreign-born. The absolute sizes of these foreign-born populations, of course, were quite different. In 1850, 1.3 million people of foreign birth lived in the Northeast, compared to just 27,000 in the western states. The proportion of foreign-born increased dramatically in both regions in the following decades. In the Northeast the huge flows from southern and eastern Europe boosted the foreign-born share to a high of 26 percent in 1910. In the West, high levels of immigration,

primarily recruited foreign workers, caused a dramatic increase in the proportion of foreign-born, which rose to 32 percent in 1870. Restricted Asian immigration precipitated a decline in the share of the foreign-born population in the following decades. The Midwest historically has also had a high foreign-born component. Its proportion of foreign-born increased during the last decades of the nineteenth century—reaching a high of 18 percent in 1890—but has largely fallen in subsequent decades.

The drop-off in immigration in the 1930s and 1940s brought large decreases in the proportion of foreign-born. By 1970 the percentages of foreign-born in the Northeast (8 percent), Midwest (3 percent), and West (7 percent) had reached all-time lows. As immigration bounced back after the Immigration Act of 1965, the proportion of foreign-born began to rise again. In 2008 the West had the highest percentage of foreign-born (19 percent), followed by the Northeast (15 percent), South (10 percent), and Midwest (6 percent).

Since 1850 there have also been shifts in the geographic distribution of the foreign-born population, reflecting changes in both the settlement patterns of immigrants and the population at large. In 1850, 59 percent of the foreign-born population lived in the Northeast, 29 percent in the Midwest, 11 percent in the South, and just 1 percent in the West (see Figure 1). By 1930 the share of the foreign-born population living in the Northeast had declined to 51 percent, with both the Midwest and the West increasing their share of the population to 31 percent and 13 percent, respectively. Changes in immigrant sources brought about by the Immigration Act of 1965—specifically, the increasing flows from Asia and Mexico—have resulted in a dramatic redistribution of the foreign-born population. Asians settle disproportionately in the western states, and Mexicans primarily immigrate to the West and South. By 2008 the West accounted for the largest share of the foreign-born (36 percent), and the rising share of the South (31 percent) exceeded that of the Northeast, which had fallen to 22 percent. Just 11 percent lived in the Midwest.

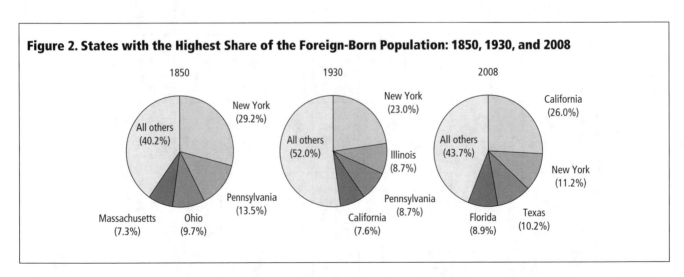

Figure 2. States with the Highest Share of the Foreign-Born Population: 1850, 1930, and 2008

SOURCE: Campbell Gibson and Kay Jung. *Historical Census Statistics on the Foreign-Born Population of the United States: 1850 to 2000*, Working Paper 81 (Washington, D.C., U.S. Bureau of the Census, 2006). 2008 American Community Survey.

Table 7. U.S. Foreign-born Population by Citizenship Status: 1920–1950 and 1970–2008

YEAR	TOTAL FOREIGN-BORN*	NATURALIZED	NATURALIZED (%)
1920	13,119,216	6,489,883	49.5
1930	13,704,296	7,919,536	57.8
1940	10,759,917	7,280,265	67.7
1950	9,615,610	7,562,970	78.7
1970	9,739,723	6,198,173	63.6
1980	14,079,906	7,110,475	50.5
1990	19,767,316	7,996,998	40.5
2000	31,107,889	12,542,626	40.3
2008	37,960,935	16,329,909	43.0

NOTE: *With citizenship status reported. Data for 1950–2000 are sample data.

SOURCES: Campbell Gibson and Kay Jung. *Historical Census Statistics on the Foreign-Born Population of the United States: 1850 to 2000.* Working Paper 81 (Washington, D.C., U.S. Bureau of the Census, 2006). 2008 American Community Survey.

These shifts in the regional distribution of the foreign-born population are further illustrated by data on the states with the largest share of that population in 1850, 1930, and 2008 (see Figure 2). In 1850 most of the foreign-born population lived in the northeastern and midwestern states of New York (29 percent), Pennsylvania (14 percent), Ohio (10 percent), and Massachusetts (7 percent). By 1930 the four top states included New York, with 23 percent of the foreign-born population, as well as Illinois and Pennsylvania (each with 9 percent), and, for the first time, California (8 percent) was ranked among the largest destinations of the foreign-born, a position it has not relinquished. Indeed, in 2008, 26 percent of the foreign-born population lived in California, while New York's share had dropped to 11 percent. Texas (10 percent) and Florida (9 percent) rounded out the top four, a reflection of the growing immigrant presence in the South.

Citizenship Status

The foreign-born acquire U.S. citizenship through the process of naturalization. In recent decades a person wishing to become naturalized had to be at least 18 years of age, have been lawfully admitted for permanent residence in the United States, and have continuously resided in the United States for at least five years (three years if naturalizing as a spouse of a U.S. citizen). The rate of naturalization tends to increase with more time spent in the United States, with the longest resident foreign-born having the highest rate of naturalization.

In 1920, the first census year for which data are available, one-half of the foreign-born were naturalized U.S. citizens, but by 1950 nearly four in five foreign-born residents were naturalized (see Table 7). Since immigration had slowed in the prior two decades, most of the foreign-born had arrived decades earlier, affording them ample time to naturalize. As the pace of immigration increased in subsequent decades, the overall percentage of the foreign-born population that was naturalized declined, reaching a low of 40 percent in 2000. Though large flows to the United States have continued in the first decade of the twenty-first century, the percent naturalized has increased, reaching 43 percent in 2008. This trend suggests that the inclination to naturalize has increased.

See also *Immigration.*

. . . . ARUN PETER LOBO
with CONTRIBUTIONS by ELLEN PERCY KRALY

BIBLIOGRAPHY

Gibson, Campbell, and Kay Jung. *Historical Census Statistics on the Foreign-Born Population of the United States: 1850 to 2000.* Working Paper No. 81. Washington, D.C.: U.S. Census Bureau, 2006. Available at http://www.census.gov/population/www/documentation/twps0081/twps0081.pdf.

Lobo, Arun Peter. "Unintended Consequences: Liberalized U.S. Immigration Law and the African Brain Drain." In *The New African Diaspora in North America: Trends, Community Building, and Adaptation,* ed. Kwadwo Konadu-Agyemang, Baffour K. Takyi, and John Arthur, 189–208. Lanham, Md.: Lexington Books, 2006.

Lobo, Arun Peter, and Joseph J. Salvo. "Changing U.S. Immigration Law and the Occupational Selectivity of Asian Immigrants." *International Migration Review* 32, no. 3 (1998): 737–760.

Salvo, Joseph J., and Arun Peter Lobo. "The Federal Statistical System: The Local Government Perspective." *Annals of the American Academy of Political and Social Science* 631, no. 1 (2010): 75–88. doi:10.1177/0002716210374414.

U.S. Census Bureau. *A Compass for Understanding and Using American Community Survey Data: What State and Local Governments Need to Know.* Washington, D.C.: U.S. Government Printing Office, 2009.

Warren, Robert, and Ellen Percy Kraly. *The Elusive Exodus: Emigration from the United States.* Population Trends in Public Policy No. 8. Washington, D.C.: Population Reference Bureau, 1985.

Genealogy

Genealogy surely was very low in the Founding Fathers' order of priority when they included a mandated census in the Constitution. In fact, the census's connection with genealogy remained largely muted until the late nineteenth century when the nation had proved its durability by surviving a civil war, defeating an internal enemy, expanding its boundaries from sea to sea, and becoming an emerging player on the international scene. Only then did Americans of European extraction begin to show widespread interest in researching their nation's history and tracing their roots back to the nation's earliest settlers.

Although the New England Historic Genealogical Association was more than a generation older, it was the Daughters of the American Revolution (DAR), founded in 1890, who truly spurred the national interest in genealogy. DAR required women aspiring to become members to trace their lineage from ancestors "who aided in achieving American independence." Early censuses offered a starting place for the necessary genealogical research.

Record Availability

Even though the 1840 census produced a listing by state of Revolutionary War pensioners—including widows—that helped some potential DAR members, for the most part genealogists seeking information on their ancestors were and remain hard-pressed to find much specific information in the censuses before 1850. Until then, instructions to enumerators directed them to enumerate by household and to ask the full name only of the "head of household" (usually the oldest male living there). All other residents were listed by general age bracket, sex, and color. Relation to the head of household was not requested.

Despite the lack of personal data requested in the early censuses, genealogical research today benefits significantly from the survival of the original census questionnaires, also known as schedules. These schedules provide handwritten entries penned by census-takers documenting respondents' answers to questions, and in many instances they include revealing marginalia added by the enumerator. Most of the original census schedules from 1790 through 1840 are available in original form at the National Archives. The 1850 through 1880 schedules have been returned to the states, and the originals from 1900

through 1940 were destroyed after being microfilmed. Several state records as well as records from specific censuses have been lost over time for a variety of reasons (including some being burned by British soldiers during the sacking of Washington, D.C., in 1814). Not infrequently the earliest census records for territories and states are missing in whole or in part. But the most damaging loss by far was caused by a fire in 1921 that destroyed almost all of the 1890 schedules. One possible benefit of the 1921 fire was that it served as a major prod to establish a national archives that could provide secure storage to documents critical to the history of the country. The National Archives building opened in 1935, and in less than a decade it had begun accessioning census schedules and had established itself as a key resource for genealogists using census records.

National Archives

The National Archives began to accession Census Bureau records in 1942 and opened these records to researchers that year. The initial group of records brought into the archives included the population schedules through the 1870 decennial census. The 1880 schedules were opened to the public in the 1950s. Responding to post-war concern about confidentiality—exemplified by the passage of the Federal Property and Administrative Services Act, which placed a 50-year limit on the release of federal records—the chief executives of the Archives and the Census Bureau debated time limits for the release of confidential census information. Following an exchange of letters in October 1952, they agreed to a 72-year time limit for disclosing private census information. The so-called "72-year rule" was codified in 1978, more than 25 years after the original agreement.

As the repository for census schedules and records, the Archives are responsible for preparing them for research use. Entire sets of census microfilms are available to researchers at the National Archives in Washington, D.C.; at National Archives branches; and at major genealogical research libraries. State libraries typically have census microfilms for their own and adjoining states, as do many large public libraries. In addition, microfilms can be accessed via interlibrary loan or may be purchased, either directly from the Archives or from commercial vendors.

Schedules and Indices

Census schedules are arranged by year, state, or territory, and then by local jurisdiction, first by county or city and then by smaller civil division. Sometimes the divisions were devised by the Census Bureau and its predecessor agencies. Within the schedules themselves, the information is arranged by household, usually in the order visited by the census-taker. In some early instances, households are listed alphabetically.

This arrangement of census schedules encouraged the creation of indices that would assist researchers in quickly pinpointing households by county, city, and manuscript page. Print indexes have been published commercially for all states through 1850 and for many states in subsequent years. These books are usually available in any library or archive that owns census microfilms.

A different type of index, the Soundex, covers the census schedules for 1880, 1900, 1910, 1920, and 1930. The Soundex system was developed in the years right after the end of World War I. The original coding for the system was adapted for census use by the Works Projects Administration in the 1930s and renamed American Soundex. The system was based on the sounds in names and was intended to help federal agencies locate households by the sound instead of the spelling of surnames. Soundex uses an alphanumeric code based on four key letters in each surname. Like the schedules themselves, the Soundex was handwritten and is most accessible to researchers via microfilm.

Genealogical Data in the Census

Prior to the 1850 census, the only names listed by enumerators were those of the predominantly white male heads of households. Hence, adult free African Americans and women were named in the schedule only if they headed households. Other free persons were listed only by the number of each sex in each age group; these age categories became narrower by 1830 and 1840. Slaves were also tallied, by number and sex, on the main schedule.

Beginning with the 1850 census, the instructions to the enumerators directed them to include the names, ages, and states or countries of birth of all whites and free blacks in each household. Also beginning in 1850, census schedules requested the identities of persons who attended school within the previous year, adults who could not read or write, and the profession and value of real estate holdings for each individual (often left blank for all but heads of households). Heading 13 on the 1850 schedule inquired whether any of the respondents noted was deaf and dumb, blind, insane, idiotic, a pauper, or a convict.

In both 1850 and 1860, slaves were enumerated on a separate schedule, where they are listed only by sex and age under their owner's name. A heading in the slave schedule also inquired whether a numbered slave was deaf and dumb, blind, insane, idiotic, a pauper, or a convict. The 1870 census, the first after the end of the Civil War and the passage of the Thirteenth Amendment to the Constitution, called for the listing of names of all persons from all racial groups in each household—the categories then being "white," "black," "mulatto," "Chinese," and "Indian."

Beginning in 1850, censuses requested respondents to include vital records for individuals and more details about family relationships. As a result, indicators are found of births within the year prior to the census day (1870–1880), marriages within the year (1850–1880), number of years married (1900–1910), number of children born to each woman and number still living (1900–1910), foreign-born parents (1870), mother tongue for foreign-born parents (1910), and parents' birthplaces (1880–1920). In 1900 only, the census includes the month and year of birth for each person. Deaths within the year were recorded in separate "mortality" schedules from 1850 to 1880 and for 1885. (The 1885 census was a result of what many in Congress hoped would become the first of many regular semi-decennial censuses. It did not, but for the few jurisdictions that did participate, the 1885 census produced valuable genealogical information.) Before 1880, the census did not formally specify the relationship of people enumerated to the head of household.

The Census and Other Sources of Genealogical Data

The census is of greatest genealogical value when used in conjunction with other records, such as tax lists, wills, deeds, marriage registers, family Bibles, and other years of the census itself. Even the pre-1850 schedules can help one track family movements and gather clues—though few specifics—regarding ages and number of children. Furthermore, it was not uncommon for enumerators to include useful information in the margins of the schedules. For example, even though they were instructed to list slaves only by number and sex, some enumerators included the names of slaves in marginalia written on the schedule. Moreover, examining schedules instead of relying on indexes lets one identify a household's neighbors, some of whom may be part of an extended family.

Reliance upon census schedules does have its problems, however. Probably the most serious of these is that census records have many potential sources of error. Until 1960, census schedules were filled out by enumerators who wrote down respondents' answers. Census-takers might mishear or misspell information, or they might overlook or double-count individuals and neighborhoods. Occasionally a census-taker recorded more or less information than was required. Also, because household information was typically gathered from only one person, guesswork might replace knowledge about ages and birthplaces. Lies might even creep into responses. As a result, census records should not be taken as fully accurate and should be corroborated by other records.

Additionally, errors in the schedules can be compounded by transcriptions, including indexes. A compiler may misread handwriting, make typographical errors, or overlook some of the data. Researchers should refer to the actual schedules whenever possible. Anything but the original handwriting is a step removed from the respondent.

While the national decennial censuses are the genealogical mother lode so far as censuses are concerned, they are far from being the only censuses. Numerous jurisdictions, including most states and many cities, have requested U.S. government census enumerators to conduct censuses for them throughout our history. Additionally, some colonies conducted their own censuses prior to the Revolution. Many of these enumerations were taken in mid-decade years and offer genealogical insights not present in the decennial censuses.

In cases where census schedules do not survive or are somehow insufficient, alternative records of comparable value may exist. Immigration records, including ship manifests, can provide basic demographic information about new arrivals. Beginning in 1900 and continuing until 1930, census schedules asked whether respondents were naturalized citizens. The answers to these questions appear on the relevant schedules. The naturalization records themselves are available either in state archives or the National Archives, depending on the year of naturalization, and are excellent sources of genealogical information. Beginning in the early twentieth century, states began to collect and retain so-called "vital statistics"—births, deaths, marriages, and the like—which can include key genealogical data. These are usually available from state vital records offices. Military records also frequently include important genealogical information. Military records through 1912 are available at the National Archives. Records from World War I to the present are at the National Personnel Records Center in St. Louis, Missouri.

Tax lists have been published as substitutes for lost censuses by several states, most notably Virginia/West Virginia in 1790 and Kentucky in 1790 and 1800. The lists generally include all taxpayers, not just the heads of household who appear in censuses. Where they survive, lists cover each year, allowing one to pinpoint the date a person died or left the community. In some states, they also predate the 1790 census. Tax lists are typically found in state archives and, like the census, are accessible via microfilm. Some have been published or indexed.

New Technology and the Use of Census Schedules

Twenty-first-century genealogists are blessed with many advantages their forbears lacked. Information about obtaining paper-based guides to genealogical research, complete with instructions to novices about getting started, is available on the Internet. The Census Bureau Web site (www.census.gov/history/www/reference/genealogy/) includes a link to all decennial censuses, publications, and information about censuses open to the general public. An updated edition of *Measuring America: The Decennial Censuses from 1790 to 2000* (to be published in 2012) will include the questionnaires and all instructions to the enumerators from the censuses for 1790 to 2010. This update to the 2002 edition will benefit genealogists by explaining the reasoning behind the inclusion of many questions.

Those testing the genealogical waters for the first time would be well advised to reference one or more of the many different electronic guides on the Internet before starting research. Simply entering something like "genealogical records available online" in a search engine will open the door to many indices and how-to books that explain how to find genealogical information from census records and how different censuses altered the nature of the information included

in the questions. Indices such as the National Archives and Records Administration (NARA) genealogy pages for census records include information on all the decennial enumerations, including questions asked and special features. The Census Bureau has undertaken the USGenWeb Census Project, which intends to transcribe all federal census schedules and make the data available to the public for free.

A number of commercial vendors provide extraction forms—essentially clean copies of the schedules used in the various censuses—which enable genealogists to place information taken from a schedule in a space on the extraction form that is appropriately and clearly labeled. In addition to some free services, commercial vendors offer a number of useful products that can be purchased online. In addition to making available an ever-expanding breadth of genealogical information online, computer interfaces ease searches and general navigation through the numerous pages associated with genealogical research.

See also *National Archives and Records Administration (NARA); State and local censuses.*

. . . . WILLIAM M. MAURY

BIBLIOGRAPHY
Heritage Quest Online. www.heritagequestonline.com.
National Archives and Records Administration. Guide to Census Records. www.archives.gov/.
Szucs, Loretto Denis, and Mathew Wright. *Finding Answers in U.S. Census Records.* Orem, Utah: Ancestry, 2002.
U.S. Census Bureau. History. www.census.gov/history/.
U.S. Census Bureau. *Measuring America: The Decennial Censuses from 1790 to 2000.* POL/02-MA(RV). Washington, D.C.: U.S. Government Printing Office, 2002. Available at http://www.census.gov/prod/2002pubs/pol02marv.pdf.

Geographic Information Systems (GIS)

Geographic information systems (GIS) can be defined in many ways. A commonly accepted definition for GIS is a computer-based technology for capturing, storing, analyzing, maintaining, and displaying data that are linked to locations. GIS merges cartography, statistical analysis, and database technology. When implemented appropriately, it increases efficiency and improves decision-making capabilities. GIS is used in numerous applications, including natural resources and environmental analysis, urban planning, infrastructure assessment and development, criminology and public safety, economic development, and population/geo-demographic studies.

A Brief History of GIS

The history of using computers for mapping and spatial analysis goes back to the late 1950s and early 1960s. This period saw parallel development of these uses of computers inside and outside the United States in various sectors such as academia, government, and the military. Due to the concurrency of these developments, the exact origins of GIS has been the subject of some debate.

The first known automated mapping application was produced in 1957 by Swedish meteorologists and British biologists. However, many consider the birth of the operation of the first true GIS to have occurred in 1962 in Ottawa, Ontario, Canada, under Dr. Roger Tomlinson. The system was called Canada Geographic Information System (CGIS) and was established to compile and analyze Canada's national land inventory.

Another almost parallel activity started in 1964 at the Harvard Laboratory for Computer Graphics and Spatial Analysis. This lab was established under the direction of Howard Fisher, who along with other Harvard researchers developed the first raster GIS (where information is stored in cells or pixels) called the SYnagraphic Mapping System (SYMAP). The development of SYMAP was started at Northwestern Technology Institute and completed in the Harvard lab.

Later on and during the 1970s, other teams at the Harvard lab developed ODYSSEY, a vector-based software (where information is stored in point, line, and polygon features) that owes more of its topological content to the U.S. Census Bureau's Geographic Base File/Dual Independent Map Encoding (GBF/DIME) Files. Scott Morehouse, the developer of ODYSSEY, would later join Jack Dangermond's Environmental Systems Research Institute (ESRI) to develop ARC/INFO, which is one of the most widely used GIS systems today. It is important to mention that many of today's veteran GIS leaders and pioneers have either worked at or been otherwise associated with the Harvard lab.

Another GIS pioneer was the U.S. Census Bureau. Researchers at the bureau's New Haven Census Use Study developed the GBF/DIME Files in 1967. The GBF/DIME project was an enormous undertaking that eventually revolutionized GIS.

Throughout the 1960s and 1970s, the use of GIS was limited to a relatively small group of scientists and researchers, mostly due to the high cost of computer hardware and software. These developments took place mostly in the natural resources and transportation communities, where natural resource developments centered on raster-based solutions and the transportation community used vector-based solutions. One of the early raster software programs was called Geographic Resources Analysis Support System (GRASS) and was developed by the Army Corps of Engineers' Construction Engineering Research Laboratory (CERL) in the late 1970s.

During the 1980s the development of the personal computer, the decline in the cost of hardware and software, and the increase in computer-processing power resulted in a sharp increase in the acquisition, development, and application of GIS in many disciplines. It also encouraged more extensive use of spatial analysis and the development of more tools. Furthermore, for the first time the development of the nationwide Topologically Integrated Geographic Encoding and Referencing (TIGER) files by the Census Bureau enabled GIS software vendors to supply a national spatial database at no cost.

The rapid growth of GIS continued into the 1990s and 2000s, and a large number of local governmental and private entities in the United States and around the world use GIS technology today for numerous applications.

Early GIS–Related Activities: ACG and GBF/DIME at the Census Bureau

Prior to the 1960 census, the U.S. Census Bureau required that its enumerators visit each household in the United States and ask the residents to fill out a questionnaire. When visiting each household, enumerators worked with paper maps that identified their designated areas and the geography necessary for tabulation. The enumerators manually assigned the basic geographic codes to each questionnaire to allow for subsequent tabulation. The maps were obtained from various sources, including transportation and regional planning agencies. The Census Bureau then added to the maps the geographic area boundaries and codes that were required to collect and tabulate the data.

Metropolitan Map Series (MMS) map sheets (paper maps) were first developed for a small number of Metropolitan Areas (MAs) for the 1960 census and were extended to additional areas for the 1970 census to support the first mailout/mailback census. The first consistent set of maps developed by the Census Bureau, these showed all of the streets and other features and governmental unit boundaries required to conduct, tabulate, and present data from the census. The Address Coding Guides (ACGs) were developed through a cooperative program with local agencies, primarily transportation-planning agencies, which also used ACGs to code their origin-destination surveys.

While the Geography Division staff at the bureau were busy developing ACGs, another part of the bureau was developing ways to demonstrate the utility of census data. In 1965 the Census Advisory Committee on Small-Area Data was established. The advisory committee established the Census Use Study (CUS) in New Haven, Connecticut, which started its operation in 1966. In 1967, the CUS team started experimenting with computer mapping and started Geographic Base File (GBF) research. They also were using SYMAP and other early computer-mapping applications to demonstrate the utility of census data for health planning, education, and other applications.

The CUS determined that the ACGs did not permit a more comprehensive system of editing techniques using the capabilities of the computer, and they did not contain features that would permit greater use of the file. For example, important data that appear on the bureau's MMS maps, such as railroad tracks, drainage features, and coordinate information that allows for computer mapping, were not on the file.

The team came up with a unique approach in which each street was registered as a series of line segments and each intersection as a node point (numbered), and therefore an entire region could be viewed as a series of interrelated nodes, lines, and enclosed areas. Other features, such as streams or jurisdictional boundaries, could also be defined in terms of segments and nodes. By having street segments encoded in terms of the areas to the left and right of them as well as the nodes that they connected (to node, from node), the topology was encoded with redundancy that allowed automated checking for consistency. Importantly, each record also identified a segment of a feature on a map by its node points (intersections or terminations of selected map features), address ranges, and associated geographic codes. These files were digitized by determining x,y-coordinate values for each node point. This approach was called Dual Independent Map Encoding (DIME), and the geographic file, together with the maintenance and user programs, was referred to as the GBF/DIME System.

In summary, GBF/DIME Files were an improvement over ACGs in two ways. First, they applied the topological principles of points, lines, and areas having a mathematical relationship that linked them together, whereas the ACGs were simply a collection of records with no linkage other than identification of the census tract and block number that were associated with the address range along one side of a street segment. Second, the lines in the GBF/DIME Files represented all map features—railroads, streams, invisible boundaries, and the like—rather than just streets and roads.

The Census Bureau used ACGs to code the questionnaires for the 1970 census but converted most of the ACGs to GBF/DIME Files to allow the coding of the 1970 place-of-work responses, which depended upon nonresidential address ranges. Again, local agencies assisted the Census Bureau with the conversion of files through the Address Coding Guide Improvement Program (ACGIP). The Census Bureau subsequently inserted coordinates into the file to support civil defense emergency route evacuation and shelter planning.

The Census Bureau continued GBF/DIME development during the 1970s to support the 1980 census. The Correction, Update, Extension (CUE) program again worked with local planning agencies, using matching funds from the Census Bureau by way of Joint Statistical Agreements. For the first time, the Census Bureau instituted quality evaluation of the source materials used by local agencies, which included an assessment of the census block–level geocoding accuracy of the completed files. The acceptance level was set at 95 percent or better block-level coding accuracy. That means a local entity's data sets were only accepted if 95 percent of addresses were correctly coded/located at the census block level; otherwise, the data sets were rejected. For the few areas where local agencies were unwilling to participate, the Census Bureau established a coding operation in its Pittsburg, Kansas, facility. For the 1980 census, the files covered the urbanized cores of 276 Metropolitan Statistical Areas.

Where the MMS maps used to create the GBF/DIME Files did not exist, the bureau continued to utilize maps obtained primarily from state and local transportation agencies. They used traditional mapmaking techniques, employing overlays and making composite negatives. The maps were produced using diazo machines, which are ammonia-based machines that reproduce on paper, Mylar, and vellum. However, the preparation of the maps for the 1980 census was delayed, resulting in rushed production and introducing errors that were discovered after the 1980 census. Data-tabulation

geography did not match the geography on the maps, producing errors such as block numbers appearing in the data that did not appear on the maps and vice versa.

Once the coordinates were inserted into the GBF/DIME Files, the data necessary to create maps were present, but the maps themselves were crude. This was because all segments were a series of straight lines; curved features could not be accurately represented. Nonetheless, these files were primarily used by planning agencies to code local files to census geographic areas, thus permitting local data to be used with census data both for creating maps and for geocoding and further analysis.

The TIGER Database: 1980s and 1990s

For both the 1970 and 1980 censuses, the ACGs and the GBF/DIME Files could not be used to produce maps. The census maps and the lists of geographic entities ("geographic reference files") were developed separately. The result was that information in different files could be out of sync. Thus, a map might display information differently from the data, or a geographic code in one file might not match the code for the same area in another file. Furthermore, as in previous censuses, census maps were drawn by hand or obtained from local sources. If an operation required maps that covered smaller or larger areas, they were copied as reductions or enlargements of the basic maps. Many maps had to be reused in the field for several operations because they contained the annotations and updates from previous operations. Also, the area assigned to each enumerator generally was used for all census operations, even though this might mean that some assignments in late operations would be less than optimal, as when assignment areas were too small. Finally, the geographic coverage of both the ACGs and the GBF/DIME Files constituted less than 2 percent of the nation's land area.

In 1981 the U.S. Bureau of the Census undertook a review of the 1980 census geographic operations. From this review, the bureau determined that it needed a single, integrated geographic support system that could not only geocode the address list but also produce the paper maps and the master reference files that controlled census tabulations. Such a database, it believed, would ensure that the geographic products were consistent. The initial proposal envisioned a 20-year development for a spatial database of the United States. Even though no computerized map of the United States existed, the bureau decided that it would need to be developed for the 1990 census. Although professional geographic experts informed the bureau that the software and data did not exist and that, in their opinion, the map could not be developed in time for the 1990 census, the bureau went ahead with its plan to develop the first nationwide digital map, including roads, railroads, hydrography, and census-required geographic areas.

This computer file also needed to have the capability to link every housing unit and group quarters to its correct geographic entities; to provide the maps and geographic controls needed for the bureau's collection, tabulation, and dissemination of census data; and to be updated quickly and easily to reflect new information needed for various operations. The result was the TIGER database (at that time referred to as the TIGER file). Basically, this is a computer-readable, seamless map of the United States and its territories that the bureau can use to catalog and identify the relationships between attributes of the geographic entities for which it collects, tabulates, and disseminates data. It can also geocode addresses so they are assigned to these entities, and it can produce a variety of maps that display that exact same census geography or specially selected items.

The bureau derived part of the TIGER file from the 1980 GBF/DIME Files. However, as noted above, these usually included only large urban centers, which covered only a small portion of the United States. In order to include map features and their attributes for the rest of the area covered by the bureau's periodic censuses and surveys, the bureau initiated a cooperative arrangement with the U.S. Geological Survey (USGS). Key to success of TIGER was the use of USGS 1:100,000 scale maps, which were designed to be converted to digital format. USGS scanned the planimetric layers and tagged all but the roads. The Census Bureau tagged the roads with the detailed USGS codes, which the USGS distributed as Digital Line Graph (DLG) files. The Census Bureau simplified the USGS codes for TIGER, as it did not need the more detailed codes for census operations. For Alaska, Hawaii, Puerto Rico, and the Island Areas, the bureau developed this information in a separate operation. In addition to recording basic map features in their correct locations, the TIGER file included the names of named features, contained city-style address ranges for those street segments whose living quarters received their mail at those addresses, and identified and delineated the boundaries of every geographic entity for which the bureau collected and tabulated data.

It is important to note that TIGER provided the first seamless nationwide street centerline coverage of the United States, Puerto Rico, and Island Areas. The public products from the TIGER database were called TIGER/Line files because they represented all of the lines in the database. The six-record-type TIGER/Line format was based on discussions with potential data users who had requested that TIGER "look like GBF/DIME." In February 1989, the bureau released a prototype TIGER/Line file for a single county. The demand for the entire nation was immediate, so the bureau released the entire nation on magnetic tape at a cost of $175 per reel. The initial purchasers made some suggestions on format and content, and the bureau responded in subsequent versions by adding additional record types to incorporate the point and polygon information not initially included. Because government data are not copyrighted, GIS software vendors and others were able to build upon the TIGER data and often distributed it free with their GIS software. TIGER/Line files do not include demographic data or any mapping software, and selected versions are available free of charge on the Internet.

The first major users of the TIGER/Line files were the state legislatures and other organizations involved in redistricting efforts in each state. The Census Bureau's Redistricting Data Program worked closely with the National Conference of State Legislatures to teach legislative staff how to utilize the TIGER/Line files in their GIS systems, which were tailored for redistricting. A very small number of states had used early GIS software for the 1980 redistricting cycle with data sets they had constructed. Almost all of the other states in 1980 relied on the acetate overlay and grease pencil to develop the new legislative and congressional district plans. With TIGER/Line files available for the 1990 redistricting cycle and the availability of block-level population counts nationwide, GIS technology drove redistricting efforts.

The first release of the TIGER/Line Shapefiles (2007 version) was in March of 2008, and the bureau plans to release a new edition of these files approximately once per year. The TIGER/Line Shapefiles are also available free of charge on the Internet. The TIGER database is part of the larger TIGER System, which also includes the applications, specifications, procedures, computer programs, and related source materials required to build, use, and maintain the database. Figure 1 is an example of a 2010 block map generated from the TIGER/Line data set.

TIGER Modernization: 2000 to Present

The development of a nationwide digital data set such as the TIGER database was an enormous undertaking and success for the bureau. The TIGER files were a unique resource and contained a wealth of geographic data attributes unavailable in earlier data sets of similar nature. Also, the bureau had to develop mapping software, mainly because no commercial software that allowed for totally automated mapping was available. Automated computer mapping produces a specific map type for a county without any human intervention, including scaling, insetting, sheeting, and text placement.

As with all sources of GIS data, TIGER data were not suitable for use at scales larger than that from which the source data were compiled. In the case of TIGER data, 1:100,000 is a regional scale not recommended for use on the larger scale used for smaller geographic areas. Furthermore, the accuracy of TIGER line work was found to be inconsistent, especially in Metropolitan Areas (MAs) where GBF/DIME Files along with USGS maps were used to compile the TIGER files.

It is important to note that the bureau's mission to count and profile the nation's people and institutions did not require very high levels of positional accuracy in its geographic products. Its files and maps were designed to show only the relative positions of various features, and that objective was met very successfully.

However, this inherent misalignment became problematic as local governments obtained GIS systems and started assembling more accurate data sets. Overlaying TIGER on top of the local data revealed its shortcomings further (see Figure 2). More importantly, it reduced the ability of local governments to provide adequate and effective feedback to the bureau. Further, TIGER's misalignment prevented the bureau from

Figure 1. Block Map Generated from TIGER/Line Data: 2010

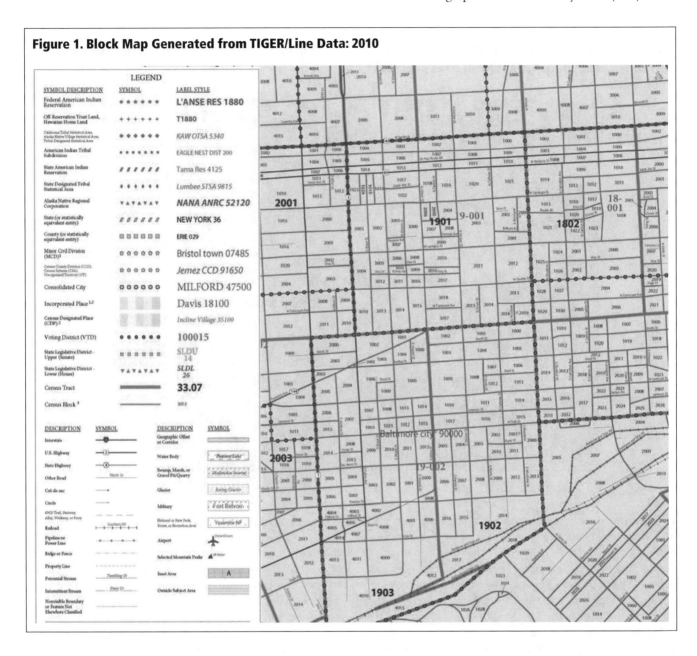

using global positioning system (GPS) devices for logging the accurate location of each address as well as assigning accurate census geography to an address (census tract, block group, or block). Finally, since TIGER was developed using in-house software, it was difficult to find enough programmers to perform all the tasks, and some of its operations were limited.

In order to rectify the above shortcomings, the bureau came up with three objectives for improving TIGER in the post-2000 period. These were to (1) accurately locate every street and other map feature in the TIGER data base; (2) implement a modern processing environment for the Master Address File (MAF)/TIGER System using commercial off-the-shelf (COTS) products; and (3) expand and encourage geographic partnership programs with state, local, and tribal governments to update the MAF/TIGER databases.

To meet the first objective, the bureau awarded a contract for the MAF/TIGER Accuracy Improvement Project. This project was successfully completed in 2008 using a combination of local GIS files, direct collection of street centerlines using GPS receivers, and extraction of street centerlines from imagery. For the first time, the bureau included in its TIGER/Line Shape files metadata associated with each feature so that the data user could determine the source of the coordinates. In some cases, preexisting features in TIGER were not realigned because the feature was not in the higher-quality source file or could not otherwise be acquired. The street centerline accuracy requirement was 7.6 meters, based on the assumption that the GPS receivers used by the 2010 census field staff would have 3-meter accuracy. Unlike the 95 percent geocoding accuracy of the GBF/DIME Files, successful capture of

Figure 2. Overlay of TIGER/Line Data on Local GIS Data for Portion of Delaware County Ohio (TIGER lines in dashed white; local government lines in black.)

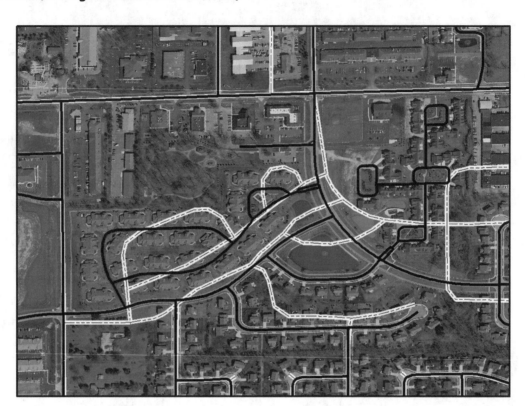

a residential structure would result in 99 percent accuracy for the geographic codes assigned to the questionnaires associated with that structure.

It is important to note that except for areas where local digital files were used, realigned TIGER did not improve the coding capability but actually decreased its capability because of the realignment work. The MAF associated with TIGER did not lose any previously assigned codes, however.

The second objective was to modernize the computing environment for the MAF and TIGER. This objective also was successfully completed and resulted in the merger of the information from the separate MAF and TIGER databases into a single relational database using COTS database software. The bureau was able to produce the digital files and totally automate paper map generation for the 2010 census using the new MAF/TIGER system. However, the bureau again had to develop its own unique application software, including totally automated mapping software.

The third objective resulted in providing a PC-based GIS tool for participants in the Local Update of Census Addresses (LUCA) program, the statistical areas (census tracts, CCDs, and so forth) program, and the annual Boundary and Annexation Survey (BAS). The participants received a program-specific GIS application, the MAF/TIGER Partnership Software, for the development and submission of their proposal. The Census

Bureau contracted with a major GIS vendor to customize its COTS product for each participant program. In addition to the PC-based software, the contract also included the development of a Web-based application for the annual BAS. Along with the software, participants received program-specific TIGER shape files, computer-based training, program documentation, and access to a help desk at the Census Bureau.

Use of Mobile and Handheld Devices for the 2010 Census

Automated Listing and Mapping Instrument (ALMI) is a post–Census 2000 system of files and software used by the bureau to enable regional-office field staff to update the address information in the MAF and the street, address location, and related information in the TIGER database for an area. The field staff uses laptop computers to view address and map information derived from the TIGER database and the MAF and to record updates and corrections to those files. It is important to note that although the ALMI software does have GPS capability, the bureau chose not to purchase the supporting hardware. ALMI was used in the 2010 census for a small number of blocks where the handheld computers (HHC) could not be used (primarily blocks with a very large number of housing units). ALMI was and continues to be used to support the American Community Survey (ACS) to update the MAF and street features through the mostly rural Community Address Updating System (CAUS).

For the 2010 Census, HHCs were designed to Census Bureau specifications and equipped with GPS. Initially, the bureau intended to use them for all of its canvassing operations, nonresponse follow-up (NRFU), and Census Coverage Measurement (CCM). However, due to problems experienced during the 2007 address-canvassing dress rehearsal operation and problems between the consultant and the Census Bureau in the identification of requirements, a decision was made not to use HHCs for NRFU and CCM, effectively terminating NRFU and CCM HHC software development. Some of the problems reported by canvassers included issues related to transmission, the device freezing up, problems with map spotting (collecting mapping coordinates), and difficulties working on blocks with a very large number of housing units. The HHCs successfully completed the 2010 address canvassing operation, ending up with an address list of approximately 134 million addresses, where the vast majority of them had a structure coordinate.

Mapping Applications for the 2010 Census

In 2010 the bureau launched a Web application called *Take 10 Map*, which reported census mail participation rates—the percent of forms mailed back by households that received them—on a daily basis by geographic area (http://2010.census.gov/2010census/take10map/). The interactive mapping site used an easy-to-use interface and allowed for data download on a daily basis. Later on, immediately after the states' total population figures became available, the bureau launched another mapping application that showed the total population figures at the state level, comparisons between censuses starting with the 1910 census, and the number of seats gained or lost at the state level (http://2010.census.gov/2010census/data/index.php).

American FactFinder (AFF) is another Web-based interactive searchable database that allows the user to compile census data into tables, maps, and downloadable files that can be viewed or printed. A large selection of premade tables and maps satisfies many information requests. The AFF permits creation of thematic maps at varying levels of census geography (tract, block group, block) and other jurisdictional levels (county, city, township, etc.). The ability to map a vast number of census attributes in an easy-to-use environment is a very useful component of AFF.

It is anticipated that similar mapping applications will be launched to display a variety of decennial census and ACS information in the coming decade. Local governmental entities as well as many nongovernmental organizations will make use of the latest GIS Web applications to make their regions' census information available to their constituents.

See also *Address list development; Geography: distribution of population; Tabulation geography.*

. . . . . SHOREH ELHAMI AND ROBERT A. LAMACCHIA

BIBLIOGRAPHY

Burrough, P. A. *Principles of Geographic Information Systems for Land Resources Assessment.* Oxford, U.K.: Clarendon Press, 1986.

Chrisman, N. R. *Exploring Geographic Information Systems.* New York: John Wiley & Sons, 1997.

Cooke, D. F. "Topology and TIGER: The Census Bureau's Contribution." In *The History of Geographic Information Systems: Perspectives from the Pioneers.* Edited by T. W. Foresman. Upper Saddle River, N.J.: Prentice Hall PTR, 1998.

DeMers, M. N. *Fundamentals of Geographic Information Systems.* New York: John Wiley & Sons, 1997.

Environmental Systems Research Institute. *What is ArcGIS?* Redlands, Calif.: Environmental Systems Research Institute, 2001.

Longley, P. A., M. F. Goodchild, D. J. Maguire, and D. W. Rhind. *Geographic Information Systems and Science.* 2nd ed. New York: John Wiley & Sons, 2001.

Mark, D. M., Chrisman, N., Frank, A. U., McHaffie, P. H., Pickles, J. *The GIS History Project.* www.ncgia.buffalo.edu/gishist/bar_harbor.html.

U.S. Bureau of the Census. *1963 Economic Censuses: Procedural History.* Washington, D.C.: U.S. Government Printing Office, 1968.

———. *1970 Census of Population and Housing: Procedural History.* PHC(R)-1. Washington, D.C.: U.S. Government Printing Office, 1976.

———. *1980 Census of Population and Housing: History.* PHC80-R-2. Washington, D.C.: U.S. Government Printing Office, 1986–1989.

———. *1990 Census of Population and Housing: History.* 1990 CPH-R-2. Washington, D.C.: U.S. Government Printing Office, 1993–1996.

U.S. Census Bureau, *History: 2000 Census of Population and Housing* (Volume 2). PHC-R-V2. Washington, D.C.: U.S. Government Printing Office, 2009.

———. *2010 Census of Population and Housing: History.* Washington, D.C.: U.S. Government Printing Office, forthcoming.

Geography: Distribution of Population

Analyzing the spatial distribution of a population entails identifying *where* people live so as to gain insight into *how* they live. When the first census was conducted in 1790, the U.S. population was 3.9 million people. The majority of the population was concentrated along the Atlantic coast, and about 5 percent of the population lived in urban areas. At the start of the twenty-first century, the population had grown to over 281 million people. The distribution of the population had spread across the United States to the Pacific coast, and over 80 percent lived in Urbanized Areas (UAs). With each census, the mean center of population has moved further west and further south, from Chestertown, Maryland, in 1790 to Phelps County, Missouri, in 2000. The 2010 census enumerated 309 million people in the United States, and the center of population continued to move southwestward into Texas County, Missouri, near the Village of Plato.

1890–1929

Low-density counties and small towns grew rapidly early in the twentieth century. Big cities, especially in the Northeast and Midwest, were also growing as their expanding factories attracted the "new immigrants" whose southern- and eastern-European origins distinguished them from earlier immigrants from northern and western Europe. Improved transportation and communication enabled some cities to become service centers for expanding "hinterlands."

Immigration to the Northeast and Midwest in the late nineteenth and early twentieth centuries supplied needed labor and may have slowed movement of African Americans from the South, a region then dependent on low-wage labor to harvest crops. After World War II, agricultural mechanization and other changes in the South resulted in many African Americans moving to other regions just as demand for factory labor was falling in the North.

In 1920, the census showed the United States to be more urban than rural. Moreover, some large cities presented a stark image of unforeseen density and heterogeneity. Partly for these reasons, Congress was reluctant to use the 1920 census for its central purpose, the reapportionment of the House of Representatives. This was the only decade in which reapportionment did not occur as a result of the decennial census.

1930–1990

Early in the twentieth century, some cities began to spill over their boundaries as new technology, in the form of streetcars and automobiles, encouraged the growth of suburbs. The Great Depression of the 1930s slowed suburbanization in much of the country and changed how the public viewed the migrants whose movements had redistributed the U.S. population in previous decades. Past views of migrants as heroic pioneers or individuals taking advantage of new opportunities gave way to images of people forced off the land by conditions in the Dust Bowl and seeking to fill too few job openings in California and the West. In the end most of the migrants stayed in the West, with many finding defense-related jobs during World War II.

Immediately after World War II, policies designed to foster economic growth seemed necessary to keep the country from slipping back into depression. Investing in roads encouraged automobile production and new housing construction on open land just beyond city boundaries. Such public investment appealed to veterans who needed housing for the baby boom they were creating. Programs that seemed to favor suburban growth also facilitated the exodus of whites from cities just as growing numbers of African Americans were arriving from the rural South. The causes and consequences of suburbanization and segregation of the races continue to be key issues in population geography today.

This new settlement pattern—cities surrounded by suburban rings—prompted efforts to identify Metropolitan Areas (MAs) in a standard way throughout the country. When MA standards were implemented after the 1950 census, it became evident that the United States had reached a milestone: a majority of the population lived in MAs of 50,000 or more people.

However, in the 1950s and 1960s many core cities started to lose population rapidly, and by the 1970s many had lost one-half of their peak population, which they had typically reached around World War II. The 1970 census showed that suburbanites outnumbered residents of central cities. At that point, the metaphor for many MAs was a doughnut—a core that was losing population and a suburban fringe that was growing rapidly. In many MAs the hole in the doughnut grew larger as older, inner suburbs started to lose population.

By the close of the twentieth century, overall population redistribution was seen to be an increasingly dynamic process that was subject to new, external forces. These included the effects of trade agreements, globalization of production processes, and technological changes that altered workplace-residence relationships. The most consistent redistributive trend since World War II has been the growth of population on the fringes of MAs, creating "edge cities" where urban development sprawls into rural landscapes and MAs fuse together.

2000 and Beyond

Census 2000, the nation's twenty-second census, documented a population jump of nearly 33 million people, the largest ever population increase from one census to the next. The highest rates of growth occurred in the West and South, and at the start of the twenty-first century the majority of the U.S. population was living in those regions. Migration from the Northeast and Midwest to the Sun Belt states was fueled in part by better employment prospects, affordable housing, and a warmer climate. In addition, immigration from Latin America and Asia contributed to growth in states such as California and Texas.

California remained the nation's most populous state in 2000 with nearly 34 million people, but for the first time in the state's history it sent more migrants to other states than it received. As a consequence, its growth during the decade lagged behind that of most other western states. New York City maintained its position as the largest city in the United States, reaching the 8 million mark for the first time, while Los Angeles housed nearly 4 million in the nation's second-largest city.

The 2010 census documented yet another major milestone: the U.S. population had surpassed the 300 million mark for the first time. The population continued its shift to the West and South, with the largest state—California—now possessing in excess of 37 million residents, followed by Texas (25.1 million), New York (19.4 million), and Florida (18.8 million). Despite a dramatic slowing of growth in many areas of the nation in the latter part of the decade because of a deep economic recession, the 2000–2010 period saw continued strong growth in the South (14.3 percent) and West (13.8 percent) and more modest growth in the Northeast (3.2 percent) and Midwest (3.9 percent). The fastest-growing states in the nation were Nevada (35 percent), Arizona (25 percent), Utah (24 percent), and Idaho and Texas (21 percent each). It remains to be seen whether the severe economic downturn and the collapse of the housing market in many places will curb the migration patterns that have continued to redistribute the population to the southern and western states.

See also *Center of population; Tabulation geography*

. . . .   DEIRDRE DALPIAZ BISHOP

BIBLIOGRAPHY

Frey, William H. "The New Geography of Population Shifts." In *State of the Union: America in the 1990s (Volume 2: Social Trends)*, ed. Reynolds Farley, 271–336. New York: Russell Sage Foundation, 1995.

Hobbs, Frank, and Nicole Stoops, U.S. Census Bureau. *Demographic Trends in the 20th Century*. Census 2000 Special Reports, Series CENSR-4. Washington, D.C.: U.S. Government Printing Office, 2002. Available at http://www.census.gov/prod/2002pubs/censr-4.pdf.

Nucci, Alfred, and Larry Long. "Spatial and Demographic Dynamics of Metropolitan and Nonmetropolitan Territory in the United States." *International Journal of Population Geography* 1, no. 2 (1995): 165–181. doi:10.1002/ijpg6060010205.

Perry, Marc J., and Paul J. Mackun. "Population Change and Distribution: 1990 to 2000." Census 2000 Brief C2KBR/01-2. Washington, D.C.: U.S. Department of Commerce, 2001. Available at www.census.gov/prod/2001pubs/c2kbr01-2.pdf.

Plane, David, and Peter Rogerson. *The Geographical Analysis of Population: With Applications to Planning and Business*. New York: John Wiley & Sons, 1994.

U.S. Census Bureau. 2010 Census Data. http://2010.census.gov/2010census/data/.

Grassroots Groups

Grassroots groups have played increasingly significant roles in shaping the content, operations, and outreach efforts associated with decennial censuses. They have raised awareness of group-specific interests, needs, and opportunities and have actively promoted and mobilized locally for the count. By their very nature, increased numbers, and varying stakes in the outcomes, they also have stepped up the intensity of demands, issues, and debates associated with the census.

For all of the national planning and processing that goes into the decennial census, its success still hangs on the prospect that local people will be found, will respond, and will become part of the official count and data bank. The ease and effectiveness with which this has happened in recent censuses—given the increasingly varied and hard-to-reach populations in the United States and, in some cases, wariness about the motives and purposes for conducting the count—have depended upon many factors.

Especially since the 1970 census, and with growing frequency and urgency heading into both the 2000 and 2010 counts, the message from many advocacy groups to the Census Bureau has been that effective planning, creating working relationships with community organizations, and engaging local groups in the enumeration process are critical to a successful count. Ignore or underuse local groups who are familiar with the people, languages, and neighborhoods, and the potential for inaccuracy, mistrust, and undercounts increases. The message from these groups to their constituencies has been that their political representation, share of population-dependent government dollars, and civil rights hang in the balance. If their members are not counted, for whatever reason, the potential loss is substantial.

Thousands of these groups exist across the country. They are defined not only by geographic and political boundaries but also by shared issues, interests, loyalties, and characteristics.

These shared characteristics include but are not limited to race, ethnicity, age, gender, socioeconomic status, sexual orientation, disability, and veteran status. All such groups, along with the rapidity with which they can form, inform, and mobilize like-minded members, have come to factor one way or another into the conduct and applications of and messages associated with the decennial census.

The groups themselves vary in size and in the level and nature of their organizational structure and influence. Over time, the term *grassroots* has evolved to encompass not only citizen-based organizations and small political and governmental units but also larger "conglomerates," high-profile institutions with a broader, often national, reach that implement and thrive through local affiliates and chapters. For these larger organizations, their ability to speak with authority on the national platform (in the case of the census, in congressional hearings and on national advisory committees) comes in part because of the significant needs they can identify, the numbers they can muster, and the rapidity with which they can activate their members.

Since the middle of the last decade, the establishment and rising use of social media, blogging, video sharing, and other networking utilities on the Internet (such as Facebook, YouTube, and Twitter) have offered an electronic platform for stepped-up interactions and message delivery within these organizations. In addition, this technology has facilitated the creation of virtual groups that can mobilize around issues and, sometimes, around misinformation about those issues.

Whatever their structure or origins, the growing savvy and tenacity of grassroots groups and their national advocates have made them formidable supporters and vocal opponents of proposals and policies regarding the content, operations, and applications of recent censuses. Moreover, these groups have brought a new dynamic into decennial census planning and outreach. However, the same qualities that give grassroots organizations an edge in advising on and tending to local details of census preparations, promotion, and operations also promote narrower perspectives, making national-level compromise among their competing interests challenging. Moreover, their effective, face-to-face (or cell phone to smart phone to computer), quick-response manner of moving through tasks runs against the grain of the bureaucratic framework that gives order to the massive census operations.

Evolving Relationships between Grassroots Groups and the Census Bureau

The New Deal, post–World War II, and Great Society programs relied on decennial data for allocations and implementation and thus helped to fuel interest in and demands on the census. The train of events arising from revenue sharing (the distribution of federal revenues to states), the dramatic demographic changes of the 1980s, the census undercounts, and the rekindling of "decentralization" as the way to attend to the "people's business" fired up community-based organizations, minority organizations, and national and regional coalitions of these groups. Organizational representatives were provided several occasions to vocalize group concerns and enumerate the missed opportunities and missteps in the counts.

Testimony presented in congressional hearings repeated many of the same themes: the traditional approach to counting the population was not in sync with the growth and transformation of society; the census was not employing methods that would reach the people who were the hardest to enumerate; effective systems were not in place to work with the smaller units of government that could serve as resources; and ethnic and other civic organizations were not effectively utilized to ensure that enumerators spoke the languages of the residents in the neighborhoods.

In response to critiques regarding the extent of its reach into localities, the Census Bureau cited the enormous number of census-awareness programs involving community-based organizations and advocacy groups that supported the census and encouraged member and client participation. More than 50,000 organizations participated in the census effort in 1990 alone. But grassroots groups and national confederations of these organizations pointed out that effective outreach called for a deeper understanding of the social and political infrastructures within communities, what it takes to connect with specific populations, and how to fashion productive relationships. Cities that had appealed to a variety of community organizations and other grassroots groupings, for example, had more successful census count campaigns, according to municipal leagues. Groups cited, in particular, the role of neighborhood associations, which are increasing in number and are expected to be even more influential in future censuses.

Minority community organizations, too, argued that many racial and ethnic advocacy groups were uniquely situated to promote their constituents' participation because of their community base and the perception that they would focus on important group issues. With this credibility, the groups would be able to convince their communities that the census was a legitimate government effort to gather data and that confidentiality would be maintained. At the same time, the grassroots organizations could provide direct assistance on census operations, including helping to answer constituent questions, distributing materials in appropriate languages, and recommending techniques intended to elicit strong response rates.

Other groups and networks cited the benefits of solidifying long-term relationships and trust between the Census Bureau and communities. They argued that census outreach to the grassroots level should be ongoing and not comprised of isolated, independent campaign activities taking place in the years just prior to the count. To have the grassroots fully engaged in the count, they noted, interactions between the bureau and the communities should be continuous and deal with many aspects of census outreach and operations—from the policies and courtesies associated with retaining census workers and enumerators locally to the development of census questionnaires that reflect a sensitivity to and understanding of the varied populations and their circumstances.

Over the years, many national advocacy groups with grassroots cores or otherwise strong links to community-based organizations moved out in front on the issues of census outreach and operations and of promoting grassroots opportunities for improving awareness and, ultimately, the count itself. After the 1990 census experience, the NAACP (National Association for the Advancement of Colored People), which through its network of state and local affiliates had informally engaged in joint efforts with the bureau since the 1970s, coupled an offer of assistance with its recommendation that the bureau's National Services Program mount an extensive campaign to identify and engage a range of national- and community-based public and private organizations. These organizations provide direct assistance not only to ethnic and racial minorities but also to the homeless, the disabled, documented and undocumented aliens, public assistance recipients, and other demographic groups.

The Mexican American Legal Defense and Educational Fund (MALDEF), which also had partnered with the bureau and conducted census awareness campaigns since the 1970 census, announced its plans to expand those efforts going into the 2000 census. It sought to reach about three million parents through schools and churches and three million young adults through community organizations, youth centers, sporting events, and concerts.

Ultimately, the 2000 Census Partnership Program reflected the sense that a solid foundation for implementation of the census had to be built at the grassroots level, with partners who knew their local conditions and circumstances and had the local connections to encourage participation in the census. By census day 2000, 140,000 partners had signed on, the vast majority of them community-based groups such as churches, neighborhood associations, and service clubs. Building on lessons learned through internal evaluations and a U.S. General Accounting Office (GAO) review of the 2000 partnership operations, the bureau implemented the 2010 program with a more defined partner-selection process and a catalogue of "partner toolkits" and resource materials for targeting key groups. A month before census day, the bureau announced that 200,000 partners had joined in the effort. The hope is that these engaged partners would also support, promote, and inform about the mechanics and benefits of the American Community Survey (ACS), which has replaced the decennial census long form.

Moreover, active, inclusive representation of grassroots-dependent organizations on the census advisory committees—notably, the 2010 Census Advisory Committee and the Race and Ethnic Advisory Committees—continued to focus attention on the most effective methods for reaching the hardest-to-enumerate populations and forging solid working relationships with the bureau. Groups as varied as the American-Arab Anti-Discrimination Committee, Association of MultiEthnic Americans, National Association of Towns and Townships, National Association of Counties, National

Congress of American Indians, and National Urban League, among many others, provided input.

Grassroots Groups Using the Decennial Data

Although the spotlight has been on the roles they have played in planning, in education and awareness programs, and in the enumeration process, grassroots groups and many of their national advocates have been highly visible in the debates over census content and the uses of decennial data to further their causes. In just one example of congressional testimony on the questions that were to be included in the 2000 census, a representative of a coalition of ethnic organizations argued that it was imperative for the groups, run mostly by volunteers, to be able to know who or where their communities are, how to mobilize them, and in this instance, how to help them in the process of becoming citizens or increasingly involved in civic life. The ancestry data generated in the census were invaluable to their efforts.

Following the 1990 count, the Census Bureau initiated a program to get the decennial data and data from other programs back into underserved communities that might not otherwise have had access to census data. The Census Information Center Program, an effort that involves national-level, community-based organizations in partnership with the bureau, makes census information and data available to the participating organization for analysis, policy planning, and further dissemination through a network of regional and local affiliates. The member network includes American Indian and Alaska Native, Asian American, Hispanic, Native Hawaiian and other Pacific Islanders, emerging populations, children, and rural-based organizations.

See also *Advertising the census; Local involvement in census taking; Not-for-profit organizations; State and local governments: legislatures.*

. . . .   DEBORAH A. GONA

BIBLIOGRAPHY

Ehrenhalt, Alan. *Democracy in the Mirror: Politics, Reform, and Reality in Grassroots America.* Washington, D.C.: Congressional Quarterly Press, 1998.

U.S. Congress, House Committee on Government Operations and Committee on Post Office and Civil Service. *Problems with the 1980 Census Count: Joint Hearing before the Commerce, Consumer, and Monetary Affairs Subcommittee of the Committee on Government Operations and the Census and Population Subcommittee of the Committee on Post Office and Civil Service, House of Representatives, Ninety-sixth Congress, Second Session, July 31, 1980.* Washington, D.C.: U.S. Government Printing Office, 1980.

U.S. Congress, House Committee on Government Reform and Oversight. *Oversight of the 2000 Census: Revisiting the 1990 Census; Hearing before the Subcommittee on the Census of the Committee on Government Reform and Oversight, House of Representatives, One Hundred Fifth Congress, Second Session, May 5, 1998.* Serial 105-159. Washington, D.C.: U.S. Government Printing Office, 1998.

U.S. Congress, House Committee on Post Office and Civil Service. *The Role of Community and Advocacy Organizations during the 1990 Census and in Planning for the 2000 Census: Hearings before the Subcommittee on Census and Population of the Committee on Post Office and Civil Service, House of Representatives, One Hundred Second Congress, First Session, October 29 and 30, 1991.* Serial 102-32. Washington, D.C.: U.S. Government Printing Office, 1992.

U.S. General Accounting Office. *2000 Census: Review of Partnership Program Highlights Best Practices for Future Operations; Report to Congressional Requesters.* GAO-01-579. Washington, D.C.: General Accounting Office, 2001. Available at www.gpo.gov/fdsys/pkg/GAOREPORTS-GAO-01-579/pdf/GAOREPORTS-GAO-01-579.pdf.

U.S. Government Accountability Office. *2010 Census: Key Efforts to Include Hard-to-Count Populations Went Generally as Planned; Improvements Could Make the Efforts More Effective for Next Census; Report to Congressional Requesters.* GAO-11-45. Washington, D.C.: U.S. Government Accountability Office, 2010. Available at www.gao.gov/new.items/d1145.pdf.

Hispanic Population

The Hispanic population of the United States reached 49.5 million in 2010, representing 16 percent of the U.S. population according to estimates from the U.S. Census Bureau. The Hispanic population's rapid growth since 2000—40 percent—exceeded that of all other major race/ethnic groups. In 2001 the Hispanic population became the nation's largest minority group, surpassing the African American population. In 2010 Hispanics accounted for about 45 percent of the minority population (that is, the population that is not "white, nonhispanic").

The large-scale immigration that began in the 1970s has been a major factor in the rapid growth of the Hispanic population, which has increased more than fivefold from less than 10 million in 1970. In each decade from the 1970s through the 1990s, there were more Hispanic immigrants than Hispanic births so that by 2000, about 42 percent of all Hispanics were foreign-born and immigrants constituted a majority (56 percent) of working-age Hispanic adults. This dynamic changed in the first decade of the 2000s as Hispanic births outnumbered Hispanic immigrants for the first time since the 1960s. As a result, the foreign-born percentage began to decline from the 2000 peak to 38 percent in 2010.

The Hispanic population is projected to grow significantly faster than the rest of the population; by 2050, Hispanics are expected to comprise 30 percent of the U.S. population. Although immigration is projected to remain a significant source of Hispanic population growth in the first several decades of the twenty-first century, births will be the largest source of population growth and an increasing one. Hispanic births now account for almost one-quarter of all births; by 2050, their share is projected to approach 40 percent. The increasing numbers of births eventually will lead to increasing numbers of U.S.-born Hispanic adults. Foreign-born Hispanics will continue to be an important component of the population, but their share is expected to drop to 33 percent among all Hispanics in 2050 and 40 percent among working-age Hispanics.

Hispanic Subgroups

The Hispanic population is defined through "self-identification" that focuses on distinct national origin subgroups: Mexican, Puerto Rican, Cuban, Central and South American countries, and other Hispanics. The Mexican-origin population is by far the largest, accounting for almost two-thirds of all Hispanics according to the 2009 American Community Survey (ACS). The Puerto Rican–origin population of the United States (excluding the population living in Puerto Rico) represents slightly over 9 percent of the total, persons with origins in Central America account for a little more than 8 percent, and those from South America are about 6 percent of the total. Cubans and Dominicans each represent about a 3 percent share of all Hispanics. The remaining 5 percent of the Hispanic population includes Spaniards; "Spanish Americans"; persons giving generic responses such as "Latino," "Spanish," "Hispano," or "Hispanic"; and persons with other national-origin backgrounds.

Through the 2000 census, the largest three Hispanic national-origin groups had been Mexican, Puerto Rican, and Cuban. By 2009 sustained immigration from Central America and lowered immigration from Cuba resulted in Salvadorans passing Cubans and Dominicans to become the third largest Hispanic group. Hispanic groups differ substantially in terms of nativity, age, and other characteristics. About five out of eight Cubans and Central or South Americans are immigrants. Among the Mexican-origin population, about three out of eight are immigrants. Only about one in six other Hispanics are immigrants. Less than 1 percent of the Puerto Rican–origin population is foreign-born because persons born in Puerto Rico are U.S. citizens at birth.

The wording and placement of the question used to identify the Hispanic population can affect the reporting of the number of Hispanics and their distribution across national origin groups. With the increasing share of U.S.-born Hispanics, it is possible that a "pan-Hispanic" identity will emerge to subsume the individual national origin groups. However, current research shows that young adult Latinos—the group at the vanguard of generational changes—have a strong preference for identifying first with their national origins as opposed to other possible identities.

Age Distribution

Hispanics are a relatively young population. More than one-third are under age eighteen, compared with about 23 percent of nonhispanics. Within the Hispanic population, however, there are substantial differences in age composition, principally attributable to fertility differences. About 36 percent are under 18 in the Hispanic subgroups with the highest fertility—Mexicans and Puerto Ricans. Among Cubans, only about 20 percent are under 18, whereas the Central and South American group is intermediate at 28 percent. The large youth population for Hispanics leads to a lower median age than other race/ethnic groups; Hispanics, at 28 years (in 2009), have a significantly lower median age than do nonhispanic race groups—41 for whites, 32 for blacks and American Indians, and 37 for Asians.

The younger the age group, the higher the percentage of that group is Hispanic. Among newborns, 26 percent are Hispanic. The school-age population (6 to 17 years) is 22 percent Hispanic. Among young adults (25 to 44 years), about 19 percent are Hispanic. For seniors (ages 65 and over), only about 7 percent are Hispanic. The dynamics of aging and population progression mean that the Hispanic share within each age group will increase in the future as the more highly Hispanic young cohorts age into older groups.

Immigration

Immigration has played an important role in the emergence of the Hispanic population as the nation's largest minority group. Since 1965 more than 40 million immigrants have arrived in the United States, and about half have been Hispanic. The foreign-born population (that is, the immigrant population of the country) increased from slightly less than 10 million in 1970 to about 40 million in 2010. Hispanics made up less than 20 percent of the immigrant population in 1970 and almost half in 2010. These figures include both legal immigrants and unauthorized immigrants.

Unauthorized immigrants in 2010 accounted for 11.2 million of the country's 40.2 million foreign-born residents, or 28 percent of all immigrants. Hispanics represented over three-quarters of the unauthorized immigrant population in 2010, with 58 percent having come from Mexico alone. Among legal foreign-born residents, Hispanics account for 38 percent of the total; again Mexico, with 21 percent of legal immigrants, is by far the largest single source.

The Hispanic share of unauthorized and legal immigrants changed little in the last decade. Rather the growth in Hispanic immigrants has tracked growth in total immigrants very closely. The number of unauthorized immigrants in the United States increased steadily from 3.5 million in 1990 to more than 12 million in 2007. Annual growth averaged about 500,000 per year with some variations but no declines. The trends changed markedly after 2007 when the United States entered the Great Recession. The unauthorized immigrant population dropped by 1 million to 11.1 million in 2009 and remained constant there. The number of unauthorized Mexicans also peaked in 2007 at about 7 million and declined to 6.5 million in 2010. This trend reversal marked the first recorded significant decline in the unauthorized immigrant population without an accompanying legalization program.

There is an ongoing debate about the relative roles of increased enforcement of immigration laws versus the state of the U.S. economy in the post-2007 decrease in the unauthorized immigrant population. During most of the last two decades, enforcement increased markedly with a much larger Border Patrol (both in agents and budgets), more high-tech fencing separating Mexico and the United States, and more interior enforcement at U.S. worksites. Even in the face of this growing enforcement, the unauthorized population increased steadily. Population growth and estimated inflows increased sharply in periods of economic expansion and low unemployment in the United States (for example, the late 1990s and mid-2000s). Conversely, inflows diminished when U.S. unemployment rates were high and the economy was in recession (for example, 2002–2003 or 2007-2009). The very strong correlation of unauthorized immigration with U.S. employment conditions supports the notion that the unauthorized immigrants are coming to work in the United States at wages that are high by home-country standards even though low by U.S. standards. Conditions in Mexico can play a role as well. In particular, it seems that high interest rates in Mexico can encourage unauthorized immigration to the United States as an alternative means of financing purchases and investments.

Nativity, Citizenship, and Generations

Immigration has naturally played an important role in producing the generational structure of the Hispanic population. The multidecadal history of sustained immigration has led to a buildup of the foreign-born population, but as immigrants have had children in the United States, the second generation (that is, U.S.-born children of immigrants) has begun to grow rapidly. The generations have very different age structures and differentially impact the nature of the Hispanic population and its characteristics.

In 2010 about 38 percent of Hispanics were foreign-born; this figure peaked in 2000 at 42 percent and has decreased since then because of the rapid growth of the second generation. The U.S.-born children of immigrants constitute 29 percent of Hispanics (up from 27 percent in 2000), and the third-and-higher generations represent 32 percent. There are more legal Hispanic immigrants (21 percent of all Hispanics) than unauthorized immigrant Hispanics (17 percent of the total).

Only a minority of Hispanic immigrants have become U.S. citizens through naturalization—about two in every nine foreign-born Hispanics are naturalized U.S. citizens. However, this share does not offer a complete picture of naturalization behavior because so many Hispanic immigrants are unauthorized and are thus not eligible to become U.S. citizens. Among legal Hispanic immigrants, slightly over 40 percent have naturalized. This share is lower than the naturalization rate among nonhispanics (60 percent).

Hispanic generations (foreign-born, U.S.-born children of immigrants, and U.S.-born children of U.S. natives) have very different age structures, educational characteristics, and other characteristics. Because of these differences, a static view of Hispanic characteristics can be misleading about future prospects for the population. Immigrants tend to enter the United States as young adults, so only a very small percentage of immigrants are children. The median age of immigrant Hispanics is almost 39 years compared with the overall Hispanic median age of 27 years; unauthorized immigrants are younger than immigrants in general with a median age of 33 years. Second-generation Hispanics have a median age of only 13 years. This group will be aging into adulthood over the next several decades and will provide much of the Hispanic growth in the future. The third-and-higher generations have a median age of 22 years.

Language

A significant share of the Hispanic population aged five and over (76 percent) speaks a language other than English at home; 40 percent of Hispanics are "bilingual"—speaking English "very well" and speaking Spanish at home—while 37 percent do not speak English "very well." The latter group is referred to as the "limited English proficient" (LEP) population or "English language learners" (ELL). There are major differences in the ability to speak English by age and by nativity. Among Hispanic children ages 5 to 17 years, about 1 in 6 is ELL, about one-third speak only English, and half speak both English and Spanish. Generally, older children tend to speak English better. Among U.S.-born children ages 12 to 17, only 8 percent are not fluent in English; among older immigrant children, about one-third are ELL.

Among Hispanic adults, English is almost universal. About 42 percent speak only English, 49 percent are bilingual, and only 9 percent do not speak English very well. Immigrant Hispanics are considerably less likely to speak English, although English-language ability improves the longer the immigrant has lived in the United States. Fully 87 percent of Hispanic immigrants living in the United States for five years or less are ELL, but for immigrants resident in the country for at least 21 years, the ELL share drops to 62 percent. This difference is reflected in the percentage who are bilingual as well. For those Hispanic immigrants in the country for less than six years, about 10 percent speak Spanish and English very well; after 21 years in the country, one-third are bilingual.

Educational Attainment

Hispanic adults have significantly less education than other race/ethnic groups. Relatively low educational attainment affects other aspects of life and is reflected in the occupational distribution of the population and in low income. Over the last decade, a trend toward improved levels of educational attainment is apparent. These improvements are the result of two reinforcing trends: (1) younger age groups maturing into adulthood have more education than older groups, and (2) the U.S.-born generations, which are increasing as a share of Hispanic adults, are much better educated than the immigrant groups.

Over one-third (36 percent) of Hispanic adults ages 25–64 have not graduated from high school according to data from the March 2010 Current Population Survey (CPS). Although this represents an improvement from 42 percent in 2000, it is much higher than for other groups—6 percent of white nonhispanics, 12 percent of African Americans, and 8 percent of Asians. At the higher end of the educational spectrum, about one in seven Hispanic adults (14 percent) in this group have a college degree compared with 36 percent of whites, 21 percent of blacks, and 54 percent of Asians. The improvements from better-educated younger cohorts are very apparent. In 2010, among elderly Hispanics aged 71 years or more, 57 percent did not graduate from high school. For the 25- to 34-year-old group that share was 33 percent, which is still very high but a substantial improvement over their elders.

U.S.-born Hispanics are much better educated than their immigrant counterparts. In 2010, 17 percent of native-born Hispanics ages 25–64 had not graduated from high school compared to 42 percent of legal Hispanic immigrants and 58 percent of unauthorized immigrants in this age group. While the share with a college degree is higher among native Hispanics (19 percent) than legal immigrants (15 percent) or unauthorized immigrants (6 percent), it is still well below the levels for other race/ethnic groups.

Younger Hispanics show continued improvement in educational attainment over the older groups as well as a strong trend toward higher attainment over time. In the decade between 2000 and 2010, the high school dropout rate among young adult Hispanics (ages 18–24 years) fell by almost half from 35 percent to 20 percent. While this dropout rate is still much higher than that of the next highest group (African Americans at 12 percent), the gap has shrunk considerably in just ten years. This trend toward improvement is also apparent in the share of young high school graduates who go on to college. Here the improved Hispanic rate (from 53 percent in 2000 to 62 percent in 2010) has achieved parity with that of African Americans.

Employment and Earnings

The labor force participation rate for Hispanic men (calculated for the population ages 16 and over) is significantly higher than for nonhispanic men (76 percent versus 69 percent in 2010); for women, Hispanics have slightly lower labor force participation than for nonhispanics (55 percent versus 58 percent). The difference for women is attributable to the much higher tendency among Hispanics to have children and to stay at home with them. About 18 percent of adult Hispanic women are not in the labor force but have young children in the household, compared with only 8 percent of nonhispanic women. Even with overall higher labor force participation rates, Hispanics in March 2010 had a much higher unemployment rate (13.0 percent) than nonhispanics (9.8 percent). The rate for Hispanics is lower than for nonhispanic blacks (16.7 percent).

Even though Hispanic men have higher labor force participation rates than other groups, the median personal income for Hispanics is considerably lower than for nonhispanics. Hispanic men earn only about 63 percent of the personal income of nonhispanic men ($22,000 versus $35,000 in 2009). The gap for Hispanic women is somewhat less, but their personal income is 26 percent lower than for nonhispanic women ($15,800 compared to $21,400). Median earnings for Hispanic men and women are lower than for any of the other major race/ethnic groups. Within the Hispanic population, Mexican-origin men and women have lower median incomes than do any of the other Hispanic subgroups.

Poverty Level

The low incomes for Hispanics translate into a high share living in poverty—25 percent of all Hispanics lived in families with 2009 incomes below the poverty line. This is two-and-a-half times the share of white nonhispanics living in poverty and roughly the same as African Americans (26 percent) and American Indian/Alaska Natives (27 percent). For children (under age 18), the shares are much higher—33 percent of Hispanics versus 12 percent of white children and 35 percent of African Americans. Among Hispanic groups, the Mexican-origin population has the highest share living below poverty at 28 percent; Cubans have the lowest share at 17 percent. Puerto Ricans (22 percent) and Central and South Americans (21 percent) fall in between.

Families and Households

Hispanics are considerably more likely than nonhispanics to live in households headed by couples with their children under 18 (36 percent of Hispanic households versus 22 percent of nonhispanic households). Over half of Hispanic households (54 percent) include children under 18 versus under one-third of nonhispanic households (31 percent). This difference is a reflection of the much younger age structure in the Hispanic population coupled with their greater tendency to marry and somewhat higher than average fertility. Mexican-origin households are the most likely to include children under 18 (59 percent), whereas Cuban households are similar to nonhispanic households in that 32 percent include children.

Among families with children, single-parent, female-headed families are slightly more common among Hispanics (29 percent of all families with children) than among nonhispanic families with children (24 percent). Female-headed families are most common among Puerto Ricans (45 percent of families with children) and nonhispanic African American families (53 percent). Mexican-origin families have the lowest share of such families (26 percent) among the Hispanic subgroups.

Geographic Distribution

The rapidly increasing Hispanic population exhibits two seemingly contradictory aspects of geographic distribution across the country: a high degree of concentration in a few areas yet increasing dispersion. Historically, Hispanics have been concentrated in nine states in four parts of the country:

1. The five southwestern states of Arizona, California, Colorado, New Mexico, and Texas—principally Hispanics of Mexican background, who constituted 60 percent of all Hispanics nationwide in 1980;
2. Illinois, mainly in the Chicago area—largely of Mexican origin and 4 percent of the U.S. Hispanic population in 1980;
3. Florida, historically in the Miami area—concentration of Hispanics of Cuban origin, who constituted 6 percent of the U.S. Hispanic population in 1980;
4. New York and New Jersey in the New York City area—mainly Puerto Ricans and Dominicans, who represented 15 percent of the U.S. Hispanic population in 1980.

Through the 1990 census, these nine states had 85–90 percent of the Hispanic population, depending on the year and the specific measure. This pattern began to change in the early 1990s as many Hispanics, especially immigrants already in the country, moved out of California to other states in response to a serious recession in California. These initial migrants set in motion further migration to new settlement areas in the intermountain West, Plains states, the upper Midwest, and southeastern states, many of which had never seen significant numbers of Hispanics or immigrants. By the late 1990s, new immigrant streams developed into these areas; this was facilitated by the strong U.S. economy and new migration networks pioneered by the initial settlers.

The new immigrant settlement patterns changed the distribution of the Hispanic population significantly during the 2000s. The number of Hispanics in the nine states with traditionally high Hispanic populations grew by 31 percent from 2000–2009, but these 37.5 million Hispanics represented 78 percent of the U.S. total. In the remaining states, the Hispanic population increased by 63 percent. By 2009 Georgia, Massachusetts, Nevada, North Carolina, Pennsylvania, Virginia, and Washington state each had more than 500,000 Hispanics; as a group, these states had seven times as many Hispanics as in 1980. Although the traditional states still have large shares of the Hispanic population (for example, California has more than one-quarter of the total U.S. Hispanic population), new settlements emerged in these states, too, as Hispanics dispersed from the Mexican border in Texas and into central and northern Florida, for example. The 2010 census has shown even more rapid growth in the new settlement areas as well as the emergence of more areas.

Hispanics are more likely to live in cities and Metropolitan Areas (MAs) than nonhispanics. In 2009, 93 percent of Hispanics lived in MAs, roughly the same percentage as in 2000. The share of nonhispanics living in MAs was considerably lower at 82 percent. Hispanics represent about 18 percent of the population in MAs compared with the overall national share of 16 percent and the 7 percent share in nonmetro areas. Half of all Hispanics nationwide live in the 11 MAs with 900,000 or more Hispanics: Chicago-Naperville-Joliet; Dallas–Fort Worth–Arlington; Houston–Sugar Land–Baytown; Los Angeles–Long Beach–Santa Ana; Miami–Fort Lauderdale–Pompano Beach; New York–Northern New Jersey–Long Island; Phoenix-Mesa-Scottsdale; Riverside–San Bernardino–Ontario; San Antonio; SanDiego–Carlsbad–SanMarcos; SanFrancisco–Oakland–Fremont. They represent one-third of the population in these areas, or twice the national share.

See also *Hispanic/Latino ethnicity and identifiers; Immigration; Race: questions and classifications*

JEFFREY S. PASSEL

BIBLIOGRAPHY

Anderson, Margo J., and Stephen E. Fienberg. *Who Counts? The Politics of Census-Taking in Contemporary America.* New York: Russell Sage Foundation, 1999.

Bean, Frank D., and Marta Tienda. *The Hispanic Population of the United States.* New York: Russell Sage Foundation, 1987.

Kandel, William, and John Cromartie. *New Patterns of Hispanic Settlement in Rural America.* Rural Development Research Report No. 99. Washington, D.C.: U.S. Department of Agriculture, Economic Research Service, 2004. Available at www.ers.usda.gov/publications/rdrr99.

Massey, Douglas S., ed. *New Faces in New Places: The Changing Geography of American Immigration.* New York: Russell Sage Foundation, 2008.

Passel, Jeffrey S., and D'Vera Cohn. *A Portrait of Unauthorized Immigrants in the United States.* Washington, D.C.: Pew Hispanic Center, 2009. Available at http://pewhispanic.org/files/reports/107.pdf.

———. *Unauthorized Immigrant Population: National and State Trends, 2010.* Washington, D.C.: Pew Hispanic Center, 2011. Available at http://pewhispanic.org/files/reports/133.pdf.

———. *U.S. Population Projections: 2005–2050.* Washington, D.C.: Pew Hispanic Center, 2008. Available at http://pewhispanic.org/files/reports/85.pdf.

Pew Hispanic Center. *Between Two Worlds: How Young Latinos Come of Age in America.* Washington, D.C.: Pew Research Center, 2009. Available at http://pewhispanic.org/files/reports/117.pdf.

Singer, Audrey. *The New Geography of United States Immigration.* Brookings Immigration Series No. 3. Washington, D.C.: Brookings Institution, 2009. Available at www.brookings.edu/~/media/Files/rc/papers/2009/07_immigration_geography_singer/.pdf.

Tienda, Marta, and Faith Mitchell, eds. *Hispanics and the Future of America.* Washington, D.C.: The National Academies Press, 2006.

Tienda, Marta, and Faith Mitchell, eds. *Multiple Origins, Uncertain Destinies: Hispanics and the American Future.* Washington, D.C.: The National Academies Press, 2006.

U.S. Census Bureau Population Estimates: County Characteristics; *Vintage* 2009. www.census.gov/popest/counties/asrh/.

———. Population Estimates: Resident Population; National Population Estimates for the 2000s. www.census.gov/popest/national/asrh/2009-nat-res.html.

———. U.S. Population Projections: 2008 National Population Projections. www.census.gov/population/www/projections/2008projections.html.

Hispanic/Latino Ethnicity and Identifiers

Despite the long history of Hispanic residents in the United States, the federal statistical system did not make a systematic effort to count all U.S. residents with some Hispanic heritage until the late twentieth century. The conceptualization of Hispanic ethnicity as operationalized in censuses through question wording and various other identifiers has changed many times over the past century and a half. These changes reflect shifts in the composition of the Hispanic population and some of the challenges in trying to count and describe this fast-growing population.

Since the 1980 census, the Hispanic population has been counted through self-identification with a direct question on Hispanic/Spanish/Latino origin or descent. Prior to the emergence of this concept, various combinations of immigrants' place of birth, parental birthplace, Spanish language usage, racial identification, and individual surnames were used to construct estimates of a population group similar to today's notion of the "Hispanic" population. In the late nineteenth and early twentieth century, almost the entire population that would be considered Hispanic by today's definition consisted of persons of Mexican origin concentrated in a few southwestern states (notably Texas, New Mexico, Colorado, Arizona, and California). Early measures focused specifically on this group. The emergence of a significant movement of persons from Puerto Rico to the continental United States in the 1950s and subsequent increased immigration from other parts of Latin America in the 1950s and 1960s rendered the initial measures inadequate. A variety of combined approaches were used in censuses from 1940 through 1970 until the self-identification method took hold.

The various methods reflect not only the changing nature of the Hispanic population but also a growing awareness on the part of the Census Bureau, data users, and the nation at large. Some of the early problems with self-identification resulted from a lack of awareness on the part of people in many parts of the country of the concept of hispanicity or a general unfamiliarity with the terminology being used. By 2010 California alone had more Hispanics than did the entire country in 1970. Fully 20 states had fewer than 10,000 Hispanics in 1970; in contrast, only Vermont in 2009 is estimated to have such a small number. In only 3 states do Hispanics represent less than 2 percent of the population in 2009 versus 28 states in 1980. This entry traces the development of historical measures of the Hispanic population and contrasts these early identifiers with the contemporary measure based on self-identification.

1850–1940: Immigrants, Race, and National Origin

Race has played a central role in U.S. census data since the inception of the census in 1790. Generally the question on race was concerned with differentiating white persons of largely European stock from blacks of African stock, either slave or free. With the beginnings of new immigration in the 1840s, the census added a question on nativity to count immigrants (and has done so in every census since). From 1880 through 1970, questions on parental birthplace were added to track the children of immigrants. The focus on immigration and its impact on the country also led to a question on "mother tongue" (that is, the language that respondents spoke at home as children) in censuses of 1910–1940 and 1960–1970. Generally these questions were tabulated only for immigrants and their children (that is, the first and second generations). As the nation's territory expanded across the continent in the 1870s and later, the race data were expanded to include American Indians and not just persons with African background.

These concepts tied to race and immigration status were not especially appropriate for counting Hispanics in the early years of the country. When Texas became a state in 1845, the first significant population of Hispanics was added to the country. Within a few years, more Hispanics became U.S. citizens with the acquisition of more land in the Southwest as a result of the Mexican War and California joining the Union in 1850. Many, perhaps most, of the initial Hispanic residents of the country did not immigrate in a traditional sense because they and their ancestors had been living in the same places for centuries. Not only did immigration concepts not fit this new population, the country's focus on race did not fit well either since these Hispanics were not descendants of African slaves but rather from European colonizers and the indigenous populations of Mexico and other parts of Central and South America. Nonetheless, the original Hispanic residents, their descendants, and the relatively small number of immigrants from Mexico were generally segregated from the European-origin population and were much poorer.

By 1930 there was a desire to differentiate the white, European-origin population from this Hispanic population. The result was the addition of the category "Mexican" to the race question. This approach did not work very well. Most of the Hispanics were U.S. citizens by birth, and many had parents and earlier ancestors who were born in the United States. Thus they were not "Mexican" because they had no ties to the nation of Mexico. Moreover, Mexicans were generally viewed as a subordinate group, and many, if not most, of the Hispanics considered themselves to be white.

The term preferred by many Hispanics at the time was "Latin," as in the League of Latin American Citizens (LULAC), an organization founded in Texas in 1929. This name was also thought to emphasize the U.S. citizenship of many Hispanics. The "Mexican race" conceptualization proved highly inadequate. Many people identified as being of Mexican birth or parentage failed to be counted by enumerators as Mexican. Moreover, the census data were often wildly inconsistent with data collected in 1929 and 1930 on births and deaths among the "Mexican race" population. Because of these and other data problems and litigation, the use of "Mexican" as a race category was dropped after the single usage in 1930.

1950–1970: Objective Identifiers and Classification

The 1950 census marked the next attempt to develop a classification scheme to count Hispanics. Migration from Puerto Rico started to be significant after World War II, adding a large group of Hispanics without roots in Mexico or the southwestern United States. Even though persons born in Puerto Rico had been considered U.S. citizens by birth since 1917, the country of birth and parentage tabulations were expanded to include Puerto Rico in addition to foreign countries.

Another objective identifier was added in 1950. Census respondents in five southwestern states (Texas, New Mexico, Colorado, Arizona, and California) that were originally part of Mexico were coded as "Spanish surname" if their names appeared on a list of purportedly Spanish surnames. This identifier has a number of well-known shortcomings. For one thing, it typically works much better for men than women. In the case of Spanish-surnamed women marrying men without Spanish surnames, the women are typically lost

to the Spanish-surname population. Moreover, their descendants would generally not have Spanish surnames.

Also, many surnames common in Mexico and Spain are common among people whose ancestors were from countries such as Portugal and Italy, where other Latin-based Romance languages are spoken. The lists used in the censuses of 1950–1970 were generally drawn from Mexican sources or other Latin American countries. Little regard was taken of names that were common (or even much more common) among persons with nonhispanic ancestry. The geographic restriction of the Spanish surname identifier to the Southwest improved its performance as an identifier of Hispanics, since there were few residents in this part of the country with roots in these nonhispanic countries.

Despite problems, a Spanish surname list was used through 1980. Improvements in the list, especially before the 1980 census, enhanced its performance as a Hispanic identifier. The Spanish surname identifier continues to be used in some non-census applications today, and further research with census data and surnames captured with optical-sensing tools has offered improvements in data quality. Surnames provide an objective measure that can be applied consistently across disparate data systems, such as birth and death records or voter or juror lists. The use of such a consistent identifier thus avoids some of the problems that plagued the Mexican race comparisons of 1930 census data with vital record systems. Moreover, the surname identifier can be applied retrospectively to data systems that did not collect other information to identify Hispanics.

The 1970 census marked the high point in the use of so-called objective measures to identify Hispanics from other data items. Six different Hispanic identifiers were constructed from data collected on two different long forms. These identifiers were designated as "Hispanic countries of foreign birth or parentage," "Spanish language," "Spanish mother tongue," "Spanish surname," "Spanish heritage," and, for the first time, "self-identification." By 1970 the Hispanic population had increased in number and diversity. Puerto Rican migration had continued to increase after World War II. There had been a large increase in the Cuban population following the exodus after the 1959 revolution. Migration from Mexico had begun to increase following the Great Depression, and the U.S.-born segment of the population was increasing.

The Spanish-language items were used in innovative ways. Use of Spanish and Spanish mother tongue was coded for all respondents, not just those of foreign birth or parentage. All persons in a household where the head or spouse had Spanish as a mother tongue were counted as having a Spanish-language background.

A new identifier was constructed for the "Spanish heritage" population. In the five southwestern states, the "Spanish heritage" population included the "Spanish language" population plus persons with Spanish surnames. In New York, New Jersey, and Pennsylvania, persons born in Puerto Rico or with Puerto Rican parentage were included in the

"Spanish heritage" population. Finally, in the rest of the states, the identifier was equated with the new, expanded concept of "Spanish language."

1970 and Beyond: Standardizing Subjective Self-Identification as Spanish/Hispanic Origin

In the 1970 census, respondents in the 5 percent sample were asked the question "Is this person's origin or descent [blank]?" The possible responses were "Mexican," "Puerto Rican," "Cuban," Central or South American," "Other Spanish," and "No, none of these." (Note that the question did not explicitly ask respondents if they were of Spanish or Hispanic origin.) Analysis of responses to this item showed both the strengths and weaknesses of the identifier. Unlike other identifiers, especially those based on language, the origin question distinguished among Mexicans, Puerto Ricans, Cubans, and the other groups. It also identified persons who did not speak Spanish and respondents who were neither foreign-born nor of foreign parentage. However, the item had a high nonresponse rate (mainly by persons not of Hispanic origin). Moreover, many nonhispanic residents of central and southern U.S. states identified themselves as being of "Central or South American" origin. These respondents were apparently not familiar with the concept being asked about because (a) the question did not specify Hispanic or Spanish origin explicitly, and/or (b) there were very few Hispanics living in their states. Comparison of the 1970 counts with data from pre- and post-census surveys suggested that perhaps as many as 1 million of the 9.1 million persons identified with this question were not of Hispanic origin. Notwithstanding this high degree of overstatement, the Spanish-origin population was the smallest of the six populations measured with Spanish identifiers and much smaller than the probable size of the Hispanic population in 1970 as indicated by subsequent historical analyses.

Despite some of these disadvantages, the self-identification concept had broad appeal because it separated Hispanic identity from immediate reliance on language, birthplace, and parentage. Tests in other survey environments showed that the quality of data collected could be improved substantially. The growing importance of the Hispanic population and the advantages of this identifier coincided with political and legal considerations. In 1976 Congress passed the Roybal Resolution (P.L. 93-311), which required the use of a self-identified Hispanic question on federal censuses and surveys. The use of this identifier was further promulgated by Office of Management and Budget *Statistical Policy Directive No. 15*, which was first released in 1977. Directive 15 defined the concepts used for self-identification of race and Hispanic origin. Although the directive suggests the use of two separate questions, it permits a combined race and Spanish-origin question. However, data collected from a combined question are significantly different than data collected using separate race and Hispanic questions. Separate race and Hispanic-origin questions have

become the standard in federal surveys and censuses and most other applications. Many analyses combine the data from two questions into a single Hispanic origin/race variable, but the data almost always come from separate questions.

Since the 1970s, self-identification has become the accepted standard for determining Hispanic origin. Some version of the question has been part of the short form in the 1980 and later censuses and part of the American Community Survey (ACS), which achieved full operational status in 2005. A number of changes in the question itself and in the response category have improved the quality of data collected.

Beginning with the 1980 census, the wording of the question was changed to make it explicitly about Hispanic origin—"Is this person of Spanish/Hispanic origin or descent?" In 2000 the term *Latino* was added to the question to reflect the growing popularity of the term. Over time, the terms *Hispanic* and *Latino* gained broader acceptance and were more widely used than the term *Spanish*. In the 2008 ACS, the Hispanic-origin question referred to "Hispanic, Latino, or Spanish origin." This question was on the 2010 census questionnaire and is planned for use in future applications of the ACS.

To help reduce nonresponse by persons not of Hispanic origin, the "No, not of [Hispanic] origin" response was placed before the specific Hispanic responses because most of the population is not of Hispanic origin. The "Mexican" response category was expanded after the 1970 census to make it more inclusive by encompassing "Mexican-American" and "Chicano." The "Mexican-American" label has undergone several changes. In 1980, it was formulated as "Mexican-Amer." This formulation apparently attracted some nonhispanic respondents to identify as "American" in parts of the country with few Hispanics. Subsequent census and ACS questionnaires have shortened the label to "Mexican Am." To minimize this problem after the response problems in the 1970 census, all variants used in 1980 and later censuses and the ACS have eliminated the response category of "Central or South American."

One other modification has been added to help identify persons of "Other Hispanic" origin and to make up for the elimination of the "Central or South American" category. Since 1990 the "Other Hispanic" category has included an option for the respondent to write in a specific response. These responses are then coded to provide information on national origins beyond Mexican, Puerto Rican, and Cuban, as well as provide the opportunity for respondents to identify with broader, more generic categories such as "Hispanic" or "Latino."

One final change designed to improve data from both the race and Hispanic-origin questions has been to place the Hispanic-origin question immediately *before* the race question. This placement, begun in the 2000 census, encourages persons not of Hispanic origin to respond to both questions. With the original ordering, many did not respond to the Hispanic-origin question because they felt they had already answered in response to the race question. A specific instruction to answer both questions was added to the 2000 questionnaire. This ordering is also designed to encourage persons of Hispanic origin to pick a specific race rather than provide a "Hispanic" response to the race question. Beginning in the 2008 ACS, an explicit instruction was added to tell respondents that Hispanic-origin responses are not considered to designate race. These changes apparently had an impact on responses to the 2008 ACS, with a much smaller share of persons of Hispanic origin providing "Hispanic" responses to the race question. However, this pattern appears to have been short-lived, as data from the 2009 ACS and early results from the 2010 census show a reversion to response patterns from earlier versions of the question.

The Hispanic population has grown very rapidly in the last four decades and is projected to continue growing well into the future. The Hispanic population as of 2010 shows a high propensity for marriages to nonhispanics. With increasing intermarriage, more descendants will have mixed heritage with Hispanic origins from one parent and nonhispanic origins from the other. Subsequent generations have more potential for dilution of Hispanic heritage. Ultimately, the future size of the Hispanic population will depend heavily on the retention of Hispanic identity by persons with mixed backgrounds. Simulations suggest that growth could be much faster than the measured demographic changes if persons with mixed backgrounds choose to self-identify as Hispanic. On the other hand, intermarriage could lead to slower growth if persons with mixed backgrounds choose not to identify as Hispanic. Moreover, the characteristics of the future population could be affected by patterns of self-identification. Similar considerations will also apply to another major census question that is increasingly recognized as subjective—race.

. . . .   JEFFREY S. PASSEL

See also *American Community Survey: questionnaire content; Content determination; Race: questions and classifications.*

BIBLIOGRAPHY

Anderson, Margo J., and Stephen E. Fienberg. *Who Counts? The Politics of Census-Taking in Contemporary America.* New York: Russell Sage Foundation, 1999.

Bean, Frank D., and Marta Tienda. *The Hispanic Population of the United States.* New York: Russell Sage Foundation, 1987.

del Pinal, Jorge. "Treatment and Counting of Latinos in the Census." In *The Latino Encyclopedia,* ed. Richard Chabrán and Rafael Chabrán. New York: Marshall Cavendish, 1996.

del Pinal, Jorge, and Audrey Singer. "Generations of Diversity: Latinos in the United States." *Population Bulletin* 52, no. 3 (1997): 1–48.

Gibson, Campbell, and Kay Jung. "Historical Census Statistics on Population Totals by Race, 1790 to 1990, and by Hispanic Origin, 1970 to 1990, for the United States, Regions, Divisions, and States." Working Paper Series No. 56, September 2002. Available at www.census.gov/population/www/documentation/twps0056/twps0056.html.

Hayes-Bautista, David E., and Jorge Chapa. "Latino Terminology: Conceptual Basis for Standardized Terminology." *American Journal of Public Health* 77, no. 1 (1987): 61–68. Available at www.ncbi.nlm.nih.gov/pmc/articles/PMC1646816/pdf/amjph00252-0063.pdf.

Hernandez, Jose, Leo Estrada, and David Alivirez. "Census Data and the Problem of Conceptually Defining the Mexican American Population." *Social Science Quarterly* 53, no. 4 (1973): 671–687.

Passel, Jeffrey S. "Census History: Counting Hispanics." Social & Demographic Trends project of the Pew Hispanic Center. March 3, 2010. http://pewresearch.org/pubs/1513/census-counting-hispanics-history-of-difficulties/.

Passel, Jeffrey S., Wendy Wang, and Paul Taylor. "Marrying Out: One-in-Seven New U.S. Marriages Is Interracial or Interethnic." Social & Demographic Trends Project of the Pew Research Center. June 4, 2010. http://pewsocialtrends.org/2010/06/04/marrying-out/.

Siegel, Jacob S., and Jeffrey S. Passel. *Coverage of the Hispanic Population in the 1970 Census: A Methodological Analysis.* Current Population Reports, Series P-23, Special Studies No. 82. Washington, D.C.: U.S. Department of Commerce, Bureau of the Census, 1979.

Teller, Charles H., Jose Hernandez, Leo Estrada, and David Alvirez, eds. *Cuantos Somos: A Demographic Study of the Mexican-American Population.* Mexican American Monographs, No. 2. Austin: Center for Mexican American Studies, University of Texas at Austin, 1977.

U.S. Census Bureau. American Community Survey: Questionnaire Archive. www.census.gov/acs/www/methodology/questionnaire_archive/.

U.S. Census Bureau. *Measuring America: The Decennial Censuses From 1790 to 2000.* POL/02-MA(RV). Washington, D.C.: U.S. Government Printing Office, 2002. Available at www.census.gov/prod/www/abs/ma.html.

Word, David L., and R. Colby Perkins Jr. *Building a Spanish Surname List for the 1990's—A New Approach to an Old Problem.* Technical Working Paper No. 13. March 1996. www.census.gov/population/documentation/twpno13.pdf.

Homelessness

See *Enumeration: group quarters*

Housing

Housing is complementary to population in the decennial censuses of population and housing and the American Community Survey (ACS). It is both the framework for collecting information about people and a subject of interest in its own right.

While a few items regarding housing were collected on censuses going back to 1890, the first official Census of Housing was conducted in 1940. During the Great Depression of the 1930s, new construction had virtually come to a halt, existing structures were deteriorating, and many families were living doubled-up. The poor conditions and need for corrective action were voiced by President Franklin D. Roosevelt when, in his second inaugural address in 1937, he said, "I see one-third of a nation ill-housed."

The requirements to assess the condition of housing stock and to judge the effect of New Deal legislation led Congress to authorize the Census of Housing. The law stated, in part:

> Be it enacted by the Senate and House of Representatives of the United States of America in Congress assembled; that to provide information concerning the number, characteristics (including utilities and equipment), and geographical distribution of dwelling structures and dwelling units in the United States, the Director of the Census shall take a census of housing in each State . . . at the same time, and as part of the population inquiry of the sixteenth decennial census.

A committee composed principally of federal government agency representatives developed a set of questions. This first Census of Housing laid a comprehensive foundation for the content of future censuses, and many of the same inquiries continued into the 2000 census. The 1940 questionnaire items may be classified into three broad groups. First, facilities and equipment items included toilet facilities, bathtub or shower, electric light, refrigeration, radio, heating equipment, and cooking fuel. Second, physical characteristics included size and type of structure, exterior material, need of major repairs, year built, rooms, and water supply. Third, financial characteristics items included value, rent, utility cost, mortgage status, present debt, mortgage payments, taxes included, interest rate, and type of mortgage holder.

Over time, some questions were dropped for lack of use or because the information could not be collected accurately, while others were added as the data needs of the nation changed. The content of the Census of Housing reflects changing technology and housing standards. For example, as electric lighting became nearly universal, including questions about it was no longer important. The item on television sets was added in 1950 but then dropped in 1980 when TV, too, had become nearly universal. Condominium, cooperative, and congregate housing categories were identified and tabulated as these alternative housing forms became more common and important to the understanding of the total housing stock.

A major procedural change, beginning in 1970, had a significant impact on the collection of housing data. Questionnaires delivered by mail and designed for self-enumeration could not capture information on housing condition. Other housing concepts had to be translated to question language and levels of detail that could be handled by the public. Applying the definition of a housing unit to individual structures became more dependent on how addresses were recorded on mailing lists and less subject to determination by an enumerator. In general, the impact of this change from field enumeration to mailout/mailback questionnaires was more serious for housing data items than for population items.

The mailout/mailback censuses of 1980 and 1990 included housing items on both the short (full-count) and the long (sample-count) forms. Respondents were asked whether they owned or rented their units (tenure), the monthly rent of rental units, the market value of the property in owner units, the type of structure, and other items. Questions on plumbing facilities were moved from the 1980 short form to the 1990 long form.

Another major change took place in 2000. Because of congressional pressure to shorten the questionnaire, housing content on the short form was reduced to one item: tenure (rent/own). This item remained because it is required for calculation of the census undercount. All other housing items were moved to the long-form questionnaire.

The Housing Unit Definition

The concept of *housing unit* has an official definition that has changed over the past several decades. Whatever official definition is in place for a particular census, however, its implementation in address-list development makes a significant difference in the data that are later tabulated and published.

The Census Concept: 1960 to 2000

The housing unit concept, defining the units within which the population is enumerated, is crucial to the conduct of the census as well as to using the data the census produces. The definition establishes the control unit for census sample surveys as well as the standard to be applied in local surveys and other research. At its heart, the definition establishes the criteria for what constitutes living together and living separately among people living under one roof, for what is housing and what is something else (now called *group quarters*), and for what is part of the housing stock and what is not.

The definition of a housing unit has changed in small but significant ways over time. In 1960 it was this:

> A housing unit is a group of rooms or a single room occupied as separate living quarters by a family. However, a housing unit might also be occupied by a group of unrelated persons living together or by a person living alone. Vacant living quarters intended for occupancy as separate living quarters are also housing units. A housing unit is separate when *its occupants did not live and eat with any other household and when there was either . . . direct access from the outside or through a common hall, or a kitchen or cooking equipment for the exclusive use of the occupants* [emphasis added].

There were two exceptions. If a unit was occupied by five or more persons who were unrelated to the head of the household or to each other, the unit was a "group quarters." Unusual structures such as trailers, boats, and railroad cars were not classified as living quarters unless they were occupied.

The 1960 census was conducted by trained enumerators who could observe the arrangement of housing units in structures. However, to ensure more accurate application of the definition of *housing unit* to individual units than in 1950 and earlier, a number of questions designed to provide proper classification were included on the questionnaire. Thus, question H3 determined whether the unit was a "regular structure" or a "trailer"; H4 identified whether there was direct access from the outside or through a common hall, or only through another unit; H5 recorded the presence of a kitchen or cooking equipment for the exclusive use of the occupants.

The definition of a housing unit changed only slightly between 1960 and 1970. Units were required to have either direct access (defined as above) or "complete kitchen facilities" (now defined as a sink with piped water, a range or cook stove, and a refrigerator) for the exclusive use of the occupants. Units that had only cooking equipment such as a hot plate and that lacked direct access were not separate housing units.

Two small but significant changes were made in the definition of a housing unit for the 1980 census. First, the population criterion for distinguishing between housing units and group quarters was raised from five (in addition to the householder or the person in charge) to nine. This had the effect of defining slightly more housing units and meant that small group homes and communes (with between six and ten people) would be enumerated as housing units. Second, cooking equipment was removed from the definition. This meant that to qualify as a separate housing unit, the living quarters had to have direct access from the outside or through a common hall.

The housing unit definition established in 1980 continued in force for 1990. The 1980 question on number of units at an address was dropped; instead, the item on units in a structure was moved to the 100 percent or short form. The item on direct access was also dropped. Thus, no questions on the 1990 census form check directly for features that identify the criteria for the housing unit definition.

Three changes were made to the definition for the 2000 census. First, the concept of "eating separately" was effectively eliminated; no items on the questionnaire asked about eating arrangements. Second, the "number of nonrelatives" criterion for conversion of housing units to group quarters was eliminated, which meant that larger buildings used as group homes, fraternity houses, and the like could be enumerated as housing units. Third, vacant rooms in permanent resident hotels were no longer counted as housing units.

Restated, the 2000 definition was this:

A housing unit is a house, an apartment, a mobile home or trailer, a group of rooms, or a single room occupied as a separate living quarters, or if vacant, intended for occupancy as separate living quarters. Separate living quarters are those in which the occupants live separately from any other individuals in the building and which have direct access from outside the building or through a common hall. For vacant units, the criteria of separateness and direct access are applied to the intended occupants whenever possible.

The Census Concept: Beyond 2000

This 2000 definition continued in use, unchanged, through implementation of the American Community Survey (ACS) and the 2010 census. However, as a practical matter it has become increasingly more difficult to apply the definition in multi-unit structures, at the same address, without clear apartment number designations. The goal in the decennial census is to enumerate the population, and it matters little whether a group of people is enumerated in one or multiple housing units at the same address.

Address List Development

Address list development is an integral part of the census because the population is enumerated at addresses, representing housing units, on the address list. Before the widespread use of mailout/mailback procedures beginning in 1970, enumerators created the address list in the process of conducting the census. From 1970 to 1990, most of the mailout/mailback address list (called the Master Address Register, or MAR) was constructed initially from commercial lists purchased from mailing companies. Several procedures served to update this list, including a block canvass conducted by census enumerators and an address check by postal carriers.

A completely new procedure was created for the 2000 census. In geographic areas with city-style addresses (house numbers, street names, and apartment numbers), the Master Address File (MAF) was created through a combination of the 1990 census MAR and the U.S. Postal Service's Delivery Sequence File (DSF). During the decade of the 2000s, the Census Bureau attempted to maintain the MAF with periodic updates from the DSF, combined with some field-based updates using the Community Address Updating System (CAUS) in more rural areas. The MAF is the sampling frame for the ACS. However, prior to both the 2000 and 2010 censuses, a comprehensive enumerator-conducted block canvass checked the MAF for accuracy.

In geographic areas where residents receive their mail through post office boxes or rural route delivery, a different procedure is required. Enumerators compile lists of most housing in these areas prior to the census. This permits census questionnaires to be delivered by address or by location/description at the time of the census, a process known as Update/Leave (U/L). Respondents then complete and mail back the questionnaires in the same fashion as do respondents in city-style areas.

In remote, difficult-to-reach areas, a procedure called list/enumerate requires that enumerators visit each housing unit, create the list, and complete the enumeration. This procedure, which was used for the entire census in 1960, applied to less than 1 percent of the nation's housing in 2000 and 2010.

Group Quarters

Group quarters are defined as places where people live that are not housing units. The Census Bureau identifies two major types: *institutional* and *noninstitutional*.

All people not living in housing units are classified by the Census Bureau as people living in group quarters. We recognize two general categories of such people: (1) "institutionalized population" and (2) "noninstitutionalized population." The institutionalized population basically includes people in correctional institutions, nursing homes, and other institutions. They are generally under the care of trained staff who have responsibility for their safekeeping and supervision. The noninstitutionalized population includes people who live in group quarters other than institutions, such as college dormitories (including college quarters off campus) and military quarters (including barracks and dormitories on base, transitional quarters on base, and military ships). Homeless and domestic abuse shelters are also group quarters, as are long-term-care hospitals.

Census staff visit these places in advance to identify their characteristics and return to them at census time to distribute questionnaire packets. In some cases, the enumeration is made from the facility's administrative records. Persons who have no place of residence (that is, the homeless) are enumerated at street locations or at service facilities such as soup kitchens and medical clinics.

Issues in Housing Unit Definition

The housing unit definition is inherent in all tabulations of housing data in the census and the ACS. Housing units are either occupied or vacant. People live either in households (occupied housing units) or in group quarters (a tabulation category that includes the homeless). Tabulations have not changed much over time; changes in applications of the definition are the most important consideration.

Most occupied and vacant units are either single-family houses (attached, detached, or manufactured housing in mobile home parks), apartment buildings being occupied as intended when they were built, or small multi-unit structures with separate addresses for each unit. These units are easy to define and record properly in a listing. However, some units are located in problematic structures. There are buildings that look like single-family houses but have been subdivided, sometimes with apartments in the attic or basement. These pose problems because extra units may not have apartment numbers that can be used for questionnaire delivery and nonresponse follow-up (NRFU). Sometimes, non-residential buildings such as warehouses have been converted to residential use, and apartments may be hidden from view. Hotels being used as housing for permanent residents present another problem; this is the category of housing often called single room occupancy (SRO). When comparing the census count of the housing stock with a locally developed inventory, it is important to note problems in structures of the types described above.

Another problem concerns the application of the housing unit definition to determine whether or not a structure and its vacant unit(s) is in or out of the housing stock. The traditional definition (found only in instructions to enumerators) says that a housing unit exists if it is "protected from the elements." In new housing construction, this means that there are a roof and windows to keep the rain out. In the case of deteriorating housing on its way out of the inventory, application of this criterion is less clear. In any event, the determination is made by an enumerator and, in census activities, may be subject to high variability. This and the other problems outlined previously are especially difficult to deal with because they tend to be concentrated in large cities with older housing stock and are disproportionately occupied by households with low income. Failure to identify and enumerate these units properly is one component of the census undercount.

The definition of a housing unit and the resulting census count of housing units may be used in many different activities. Three important ones are (1) creating a sampling frame in an area-sampling design for local surveys, (2) implementing the building permit method used for intercensal population estimates, and (3) preparing for and conducting the Local Update of Census Addresses (LUCA) program prior to the decennial census. The problems described above must be understood and their impact must be incorporated into the design for these activities.

Housing Data Items

Some housing data items that are tabulated and published in census products come directly from the questions themselves, while others are new variables calculated from the response to two or more questions.

Tenure

Tenure is the formal name for the question that asks householders if their home is owned with a mortgage, owned free and clear, rented for cash rent, or occupied without payment of cash rent. It measures the concept called *home ownership*, an important benchmark of prosperity in American society. The item remained on the short form for 2000 and 2010, permitting tabulation at the census block level. It is highly accurate and not subject to change from one census to another.

Condominiums and Cooperatives

Condominiums and cooperatives, as types of home ownership, are variations from the usual "own free and clear" or "own with a mortgage" situations. Most homes are "fee simple," which means that the title to the property includes a defined parcel of land and all of its improvements (house, garage, barn, and so on). In a *condominium*, each owner owns his or her own living space (from the walls in) and a share of the common space defined in the condominium agreement. However, home values for condominiums can be considered in the same category as home values for "fee simple" properties.

Cooperatives are buildings or parcels of buildings that are entirely jointly owned. Each member, when purchasing living quarters, is buying a share of the cooperative. Co-ops, as they are called, often require two payments. One goes to the cooperative association so that it can pay its mortgage and other bills. The other is for the lender from whom the co-op buyer borrowed the money required to purchase a share of the cooperative association. This payment reflects both the growing equity held by the cooperative and the appreciated market value of the property. Census items about value and rent costs do not work well for co-op occupant shareholders.

Type of Structure/Units in Structure

Structure type refers to the kind of building in which a housing unit is located. The census cannot describe every variety of building but instead concentrates on the major categories into which most housing may be classified. Most structure type categories in the census are defined by the number of units in the building. The questions that define type of structure have been on either the short form or the long form in different censuses. They are now only on the ACS.

Value and Contract Rent

The value of owner-occupied single-family homes and contract rent for renter-occupied units are the only socioeconomic indicators available for housing. Collected as complete count items through 1990, they were tabulated at the census block level and for communities of every size.

Combined with other housing cost items and household income, they provide important information on housing affordability. As with several other housing items, value and contract rent were on the long form in the 2000 census and remain in the ACS, with the universe for tabulations now expanded to all owner-occupied housing units.

Value is the respondent's estimate of what the owner-occupied unit would bring if sold on the open market (that is, the current market value). The value of vacant for-sale homes is estimated by census enumerators. The statement of value is not tested or confirmed in any way by independent estimates such as a survey of homes sold or the value established by the tax assessor.

Contract rent information is based on a fact that is well known to the respondent. Thus, it is reasonably reliable. The major problem is variability in the items included in rent, some of which are taken into account when considering gross rent. In small areas (such as census tracts or small communities) where the rental housing stock is a mixture of single-family houses and apartment units (some furnished and some not), a mean or median figure is not particularly useful. In these instances, cross-tabulations by structure type and calculations of gross rent provide a more accurate statement of housing cost.

With the growth in senior citizen population, a wider variety of housing options is being created to meet their needs. Congregate housing, collected and reported in 1990 for the first time, is one variation. Subsidized housing with group services is another; no census data are available to distinguish such units from ordinary apartments. The American Housing Survey provides greater detail on these alternative forms of housing tenure and more opportunity for analysis.

Contract rent is the amount of money a tenant, or renter, has agreed to pay the landlord each month. For vacant units, it is the asking rent. The rent may or may not include such items as water, heat and other utilities, or furniture.

Value and contract rent are relatively straightforward variables that have changed little in concept over time. The most important change is related to inflation; the range of estimated value and of contract rents has grown substantially over the 40-year period in question. The value item is subject to significant error because the accuracy of the respondent's estimate of a home's value varies based on many factors. Comparison with more objective statements of value, such as the tax assessor's valuation or a list of comparable sale prices, may yield large differences. Nonetheless, the value variable is useful because it provides a comparative measure across small geographic areas.

Analysis of median value at the census tract level, at least in one city (Detroit), has shown a consistent pattern when compared with assessors' figures. The rent item, which is much more accurate on its face, is combined with household income to determine the proportion of households that are paying a large share of their income for housing. This variable is used in determining federal housing funding for such activities as rent subsidies.

Year Built

This question asks: "About when was this building first built?" Choices range from the year prior to and including the census, two 5-year time periods in the preceding decade, and then entire decades (for example, 1960 to 1969, 1950 to 1959) back to the oldest building category: "1939 or earlier." This oldest building category has remained unchanged for several censuses and continues into the ACS.

The accuracy of year-built responses varies widely. First, homeowners are much more likely to know the answer than are renters. Second, accuracy declines with the age of the house; that is, a response of "1999 or 2000" is much more likely to be correct than a response of "1940 to 1949." Thus, data users should not interpret these responses as absolute. Local property tax or building department records are much more likely to provide accurate data on the age of housing in the community. However, as with the value item, comparisons between different geographic areas will likely be reasonable.

Length of Residence

The length of time since a household moved into its current quarters is measured through a question that asks: "When did **Person 1** move into this house, apartment, or mobile home?" As with year built, several time-period choices are offered. The 2000 census offered several time-period choices, ending with "1969 or earlier." The ACS question is open-ended, asking the respondent to write the year into a four-box figure.

This item works well in one-person households and in others where all the members of the household moved in at the same time (other than children born later). Historically, it posed problems for the respondent, and became less accurate, when the two householders in a household moved in at different times. For example, if a single woman lived in a house with her children and, upon marriage, her husband moved in, his length of residence in the house is different from hers. From an analytic perspective, the response should reflect her move-in date, but often the husband's move-in date will have been reported. The ACS item eliminates any confusion by limiting the response to "Person 1," but the analytic problems remain. The aggregate distribution of this item provides useful information about small areas such as census tracts. It is of less interest at state and higher levels.

Rooms and Bedrooms

A question on rooms has been in the census since 1940, while a separate item on bedrooms has been asked since 1960. In the number of rooms item, respondents are instructed not to count bathrooms, porches, halls, foyers, balconies, or half rooms. The result is a reasonable report of number of rooms, yielding data tabulations that closely match local records. The bedrooms item clearly tells respondents to count the number that they would list if the house or apartment were on the market for sale and rent. Again, this yields reasonable data. The items continue, unchanged, into the ACS.

Housing Facilities

The plumbing facilities questions were historically among the most controversial items on the census questionnaire, leading to accusations that "the census is in our bathroom" and the like. From 1940 to 1970, the items were broken up—separate questions were asked about toilets, bathing facilities, and hot and cold piped water. In 1980 the questions were combined into a single short-form question on "complete plumbing facilities," instructing respondents to mark "yes" if all three items were included. Largely because of the controversial nature of the item, it was moved to the long form in 1990 and continued there in 2000. The ACS asks, specifically, "Does this house, apartment, or mobile home have . . ." with subitems for hot and cold running water, a flush toilet, and a bathtub or shower.

Complete kitchen facilities, defined as a sink with piped water, a range or stove, and a refrigerator, were part of the housing unit definition through 1970. When the concept was removed from the definition in 1980, the question was moved to the long form, where it has remained ever since. In the ACS, inquiries about a sink with a faucet, a stove or range, and a refrigerator are each included in the overall facilities question described above.

The item on telephone service has been on the census since 1960, usually on the long form. In the ACS the respondent is simply asked to enter a telephone number on the front page of the form. The respondent is not asked whether the number is for a cell phone or a landline at the residence.

All of these inquiries about facilities are measures of housing quality—of the degree to which the standard of having all of them is met in various parts of the country and in rural as compared to urban areas.

Heating Fuel

This long-form item, which provides critical information for determining the need for infrastructure to support access to heating fuel, has been asked in each census since 1940. Understandably, the responses vary widely both by section of the country and by the degree of urbanization. It is of less interest in cities and suburbs in the Northeast and Midwest, where almost all homes are heated by natural gas. It is very important in rural areas, which may not have access to a utility system, and in areas of the South where these utilities are unevenly available. The item continued unchanged into the ACS.

Number of Automobiles

This is a question about the household, not the housing unit, but has been included in the housing section of the questionnaire since 1960. It is of critical use in transportation planning, as well as in planning social services for households that neither have cars nor good access to public transportation. The 2000 form of the question was "How many automobiles, vans, or trucks are kept at home for use by members of your household?" This means that vehicles that are not owned by the household, such as company cars, are still included in the total if a household member drives them home each night. The ACS item is similar.

Housing Costs

Most of these items were first asked in 1940. On the 2000 long form, they included the annual cost of electricity, gas, water and sewer, and other heating fuels. Since 1980, homeowners have also been asked about their mortgage payments and whether those payments include taxes or insurance, a second mortgage or home equity loan and its monthly payments, and the cost of real estate taxes and insurance. Since 1990, condominium owners also have been asked to disclose their monthly fees, which also serve to identify condominium status. Similar questions are aimed at mobile home owners. The product of all these items is the total housing cost sustained by the household—that is, what it costs per month or per year to live in the home. The information is critical for analysis and support of federal and other housing programs.

These items continue into the ACS, but the form of the questions is somewhat changed because the ACS is a year-round survey. Thus, the "last month" cost of electricity and gas is collected. The ACS also includes questions on real estate taxes and the annual payment for fire, hazard, and flood insurance. Another set of questions asks for the monthly mortgage payment on the property, whether or not there is a second mortgage or home equity loan, and the monthly payment on the second mortgage or home equity loan if there is one. Mobile home owners are asked for the total annual costs of personal property taxes, site rent, registration fees, and license fees for the mobile home and its site.

See also *Content determination; Family and household composition of the population; Local involvement in census taking; Long form.*

· · · · · · · · · · · · · · · · · PATRICIA C. BECKER

BIBLIOGRAPHY

U.S. Bureau of the Census. *1980 Census of Population and Housing: Users Guide, Parts 1–3.* PHC80-R1. Suitland, Md.: U.S. Department of Commerce, 1982–1983.

———. *1990 Census of Population and Housing: Content Determination Reports; Housing: Financial Characteristics.* CDR-13. Washington, D.C.: U.S. Department of Commerce, 1990.

———. *1990 Census of Population and Housing: Content Determination Reports; Housing: Occupancy and Structural Characteristics.* CDR-11. Washington, D.C.: U.S. Department of Commerce, 1990.

———. *1990 Census of Population and Housing: Content Determination Reports; Housing: Plumbing, Equipment, and Fuels.* CDR-12. Washington, D.C.: U.S. Department of Commerce, January 1989.

———. *Census of Population and Housing 1970: Evaluation and Research Program 5; The Coverage of Housing in the 1970 Census.* PHC-E-5. Washington, D.C.: U.S. Government Printing Office, 1973.

———. Census Questionnaire Content, 1990. www.census.gov/apsd/www/cqc.html.

———. *Procedural Report on the 1960 Censuses of Population and Housing.* Working Paper No. 16. Washington, D.C.: U.S. Department of Commerce, 1963.

U.S. Census Bureau. American Community Survey: Questionnaire Archive. www.census.gov/acs/www/methodology/questionnaire_archive/

———. "Revised Housing Unit Definition for Census 2000." Decision Memorandum No. 8. Washington, D.C.: U.S. Department of Commerce, 1997.

———. *United States Census 2000.* Form D-2. www.census.gov/dmd/www/pdf/d02p.pdf.

Human Rights and Population Censuses

In the United States, as in many other countries around the world, population censuses have been an important tool for both advancing and repressing human rights. Given this dual role, it is not surprising that human rights advocates are sometimes divided or confused in their general assessment of population censuses. This article first reviews the important role that population censuses can play in advancing human rights, both at the individual and societal level. It then reviews how population censuses have been used to limit human rights and target vulnerable population groups for serious human rights abuses. In its final section, the article identifies some of the complex interactions among factors that make a population census most useful in the cause of advancing human rights and those factors that may contribute to possible harm.

The Population Census as a Tool for Advancing Human Rights

The Universal Declaration of Human Rights identifies over two dozen basic human rights. These rights are political, social, and economic in nature. Among them are the right to life, liberty and security of person; to recognition everywhere as a person before the law; to freedom of movement and residence within the borders of each state; to leave any country, including one's own, and to return; to a nationality; to marry and to found a family; to own property; to freedom of thought, conscience, and religion; to freedom of opinion and expression; to freedom of peaceful assembly and association; to take part in the government of one's own country, directly or through freely chosen representatives; to social security; to work; to free choice of employment; to just and favorable conditions of work and to protection against unemployment; to a standard of living adequate for health and well-being; to security in the event of unemployment, sickness, disability, widowhood, old age, or other lack of livelihood in circumstances beyond one's control; to education; and to free participation in the cultural life of the community.

Population censuses can play an important role in helping to secure and safeguard many of these basic human rights, both at an individual and a societal level. At the individual level, censuses have been useful in establishing place of birth, age, and relationships among family members. These facts can, in turn, be critical in establishing citizenship and the qualifications to vote, entitlement to social security and other retirement benefits, entitlement to free or subsidized education, settling estates, and securing passports (thus ensuring the right to travel for persons lacking birth certificates). For example, in the United States, the U.S. Census Bureau provides an "age search" service to the public that involves searching the confidential records pertaining to the persons making the request, their minor children, or their deceased parents, from the federal population censuses of 1910–2001. Such a search of census records was critically important for millions of Americans who needed documentation in the late 1930s and the 1940s

to work in defense plants or for other reasons because so many births went unregistered at that time. For a fee of $65, the Census Bureau will still carry out such a search and issue an official transcript of the results that is recognized for many legal and administrative purposes in the United States. For further information, see www.census.gov/genealogy/www/data/agesearch/index.html.

Census records in other countries with poorly functioning birth registration systems have helped persons establish their citizenship and related rights. In addition, in circumstances where many basic government records and services were destroyed due to war or civil disturbances, census records have helped the reconstruction of civil society by providing authoritative documentation on the status of many members of the population. For example, after the civil conflicts in the former Yugoslavia ended, population census records helped to establish the voter lists that were used in the critically important postconflict elections. These records also were used to develop the estimates of mortality that were used as evidence in the trials of the perpetrators of genocide and other serious human rights crimes.

Equally important, census results, either in the form of simple tabulations or as input to complex statistical analysis, have been used in support of political and legal advocacy to advance many of these same human rights. The cornerstone of such advocacy often rests on the right of "equal protection of the law" provided for in both the Universal Declaration of Human Rights and in the U.S. Constitution. Census-based tabulations and statistical analysis can often provide firm evidence, even at state or county levels, of both equality and inequality in such areas as education, employment, and housing. They can also contribute to the documentation of progress, or the lack thereof, in achieving many basic human rights. Finally, census results play a decisive role in apportioning political power in the United States at the national, state, and local levels each decade.

The Population Census as a Threat to Human Rights

Unfortunately, as important as population censuses have been in helping to secure many human rights, they have also been used to deprive persons of many basic human rights, again both individually and as members of targeted vulnerable population subgroups. Extreme cases include the use of data and data systems to target vulnerable population subgroups for major human rights crimes, including genocide and crimes against humanity. Over the years there have been many examples of such misuse in countries around the world, including in the United States. To better understand this phenomenon, it is helpful to distinguish three sources of such misuse: (a) macrodata, (b) mesodata, (c) and microdata.

Macrodata

Macrodata are tabular outputs and statistical analyses used to discredit or stigmatize victim populations. Examples include the use of outputs from nineteenth-century U.S. population censuses to demonstrate that free African Americans and persons of mixed race had far higher levels of "imbecility" than did African American slaves and the use of analogous data sets in Germany and South Africa to show Jewish "criminality" and black "immorality." Examples aimed at discrediting still other groups are too numerous to mention. Of course, some may be difficult to distinguish from legitimate social analysis and commentary. In the United States, such uses of data and analysis, however faulty, are generally protected under the First Amendment, as is most hate speech. Under the laws of a number of other countries, including Canada and several democratic countries in Western Europe, people can be prosecuted for producing or disseminating hate speech, including hate speech containing statistical analysis. In general, macrodata cannot be used directly to target individuals for human rights crimes.

Mesodata

Mesodata are statistical results presented at such a fine level of geographic disaggregation that the results may be used in conducting field operations at the local level. Mesodata can and have been used to target members of vulnerable population groups for human rights crimes. The borderline between macrodata and mesodata is not always clear-cut. In part it depends on the size of the geographic units in question, in part on the distribution of the target population among these units, and in part on the intended operational uses of the data. For example, census aggregates showing the number of persons belonging to a target population in an individual small village may be operationally useful, while similar data for a large city would need to be broken down further by tract, ward, or even block to be operationally useful. One example of the use of mesodata to assist in aiming operations at vulnerable populations is the use of dot maps showing Jewish population densities derived from the 1930 Dutch Census in planning Nazi-inspired anti-Jewish street violence in Amsterdam during the early stages of German occupation in World War II. Another example is the use of special enumeration district-level tabulations of the Japanese American population from the 1940 U.S. Population Census in the detailed operational planning of the roundup of that population in the western United States in 1942.

Microdata

Microdata are the information contained in the individual unit records for each member of the population covered. Initially at least, such unit records usually contain or are linked to identifying information such as name and address. National population censuses or population registration systems are a frequent source of microdata used in large-scale human rights crimes. Some examples include the identification of Jews and Romany for deportation to death camps during World War II, the identification of persons classified as "African" or "Colored" for the purposes of implementing apartheid in South Africa, the development of lists of the Tutsi population in Kigali to assist in the 1994 Rwandan genocide, and the forced migration of persons considered to have "bad class" origins in China during the Cultural Revolution.

For further information on the examples cited here as well as information about other instances of the use of data and statistical systems to assist in efforts aimed at the deprivation of human rights, see Seltzer and Anderson (2008), Table 13.1. That source provides a comprehensive listing of known instances of such misuse involving mesodata and microdata.

Balancing Benefits and Dangers

Given the important role that population censuses can play in advancing human rights and the potentially serious threats to human rights that these same censuses can also pose, how does one carry out a useful census that is safe in terms of human rights? The answer to this question is a complex one involving legal, administrative, operational, technical, political, and social dimensions.

A few examples illustrate how some of these factors interact.

To the extent that data, particularly on variables used to target vulnerable populations (for example, race, ethnicity, citizenship, or religion) are gathered by sampling rather than in a full count, the potential risk for the worst kinds of misuse is substantially reduced. On the other hand, small-area tabulations based on a complete count census using these very same variables are often needed to plan and evaluate private- and public-sector programs designed to address political, social, or economic inequalities and to assess the progress of disadvantaged populations in attaining equality.

In general, population subgroups who perceive themselves as particularly vulnerable do not want to be explicitly identified in the census, while those who perceive themselves as particularly disadvantaged do want to be explicitly identified. Those groups who perceive themselves as both vulnerable and disadvantaged often express considerable disagreement as to the best policy.

It is generally recognized that a strong statistical confidentiality law, backed up by effective policies and procedures and maintained by a staff committed to the ethical principle of protecting respondents from harm arising from cooperating with a census, is the best protection against misuse.

Further discussion of these issues may be found in some of the entries cited in the bibliography below and in the items posted to https://pantherfile.uwm.edu/margo/www/govstat/integrity.htm.

See also *Apportionment and districting; Census law; Civil War and the census; Confidentiality; Sampling for content; Tabulation geography; Uses of the census: federal agencies; Uses of the census: state and local governments; Vital registration and vital statistics.*

. . . . WILLIAM SELTZER

BIBLIOGRAPHY

El-Badry, Samia, and David A. Swanson. "Providing Census Tabulations to Government Security Agencies in the United States: The Case of Arab Americans." *Government Information Quarterly* 24, no. 2 (2007): 470–487. www.doi:10.1016/j.giq.2007.02.001.

Leadership Conference on Civil and Human Rights Education Fund. *Counting in the Wake of a Catastrophe: Challenges and Recommendations for the 2010 Census in the Gulf Coast Region* (2009). Available at www.civilrights.org/publications/gulf-coast-census/.

Seltzer, William. "Population Statistics, the Holocaust, and the Nuremberg Trials." *Population and Development Review* 24, no. 3 (1998): 511–552. Available at https://pantherfile.uwm.edu/margo/www/govstat/seltzer .pdf.

Seltzer, William, and Margo Anderson. "Using Population Data Systems to Target Vulnerable Population Subgroups and Individuals: Issues and Incidents." In *Statistical Methods for Human Rights*, ed. Jana Asher, David Banks, and Fritz J. Scheuren, 273–328. New York: Springer, 2008.

United Nations. *Universal Declaration of Human Rights*: *UN General Assembly Resolution 217 A (III), adopted December 10, 1948*. Available at www .ohchr.org/EN/UDHR/Pages/Language.aspx?LangID=eng.

U.S. Census Bureau. *Subjects Planned for the 2010 Census and American Community Survey: Federal Legislative and Program Uses; United States Census 2010* (2010). Available at www.census.gov/acs/www/ Downloads/operations_admin/Final_2010_Census_and_American_ Community_Survey_Subjects_Notebook.pdf.

Immigration

The role of immigration in the formation and development of the United States can hardly be overstated. From colonial times to the present, the population of the country has been shaped and reshaped, both in size and racial/ethnic composition, by expanding and contracting waves of immigrants. The latest wave of immigration, dating roughly from 1965, has dramatically reshaped the country. Over half of the nation's population growth since 1965 is attributable to post-1965 immigrants and their U.S.-born descendants. As a result of the largely Asian and Latin American origins of the immigrants, the racial/ethnic composition of the country has changed; the share of the country's population made up by the white nonhispanic majority decreased from about 84 percent in 1965 to approximately 65 percent in 2010.

The nation's continuing interest in immigration is reflected directly in the decennial census. Despite the ebbs and flows of immigration, a question on country of birth has appeared in every census from 1850 through 2000. This is the longest continuous run for any question other than the basic demographic questions on age, sex, and race. With the replacement of the long-form census sample by the American Community Survey (ACS) for the 2010 census, the questions on country of birth and citizenship were moved to the ACS. Information needed to assess the impact of immigration has been provided by other, related census and ACS questions.

Information on U.S. citizenship, which is perhaps the major difference between natives and immigrants, is now collected by legal mandate, but the topic was not always covered in previous censuses. A citizenship question appeared very early, in 1820 and 1830, but was omitted in 1850, 1860, and 1880 even though a question on country of birth was asked. (A related question on year of naturalization appeared in 1920 and reappeared in the 2008 ACS.) The ability to speak a language other than English was a question topic (in various forms) from 1890 to 2000, with the exception of 1950.

The pace of immigration is one of the key factors affecting not only the size of the foreign-born population but also its impact on the United States. More recent immigrants tend to be less well integrated, meaning they are less likely to be U.S. citizens or to speak English and are more likely to have lower incomes, for example. Data on year of immigration allow

measurement and assessment of such factors. A question on year of immigration appeared in the censuses of 1890 to 1930 and 1970 to 2000. For Census 2000 and the ACS after 2005, the wording of this question was altered to permit collection of better (that is, more accurate) data.

Immigration Policy

The broad outlines of contending forces in U.S. immigration policy have been apparent from early times. On the one hand, Americans wish to admit those who will benefit the United States economically and socially while excluding those likely to become public burdens, but on the other hand, Americans wish to provide sanctuary for political and economic refugees. Notwithstanding these common themes, the bases for admission and, especially, exclusion have been defined differently throughout the country's history. Until the 1870s, the United States had virtually open immigration. The first broad controls were qualitative in nature, excluding criminals and prostitutes (1876), the physically and mentally ill (1891, 1907), and those likely to become paupers (1907). A distinctive feature of the increasingly exclusionary bent of American immigration law over the period from 1882 to 1924 was its racially based character; the Chinese Exclusion Act of 1882 barred Chinese people, the Gentlemen's Agreement in 1907 expanded these exclusions to Japanese people, and in 1917, all Asians and illiterates were barred.

In 1921 and 1924, the first *quantitative* restrictions on immigration were imposed, ultimately leading to a ceiling of 150,000 per year on European immigration. The ethnically based nature of the restrictions was reinforced as admission was structured to maintain the putative "national origins" character of the United States in 1790. This provision had the effect of severely limiting immigration from southern and eastern Europe, which became the point of origin of most immigrants after 1890 but had produced relatively few immigrants before then.

The restrictions on immigration officially lasted until the passage of the Immigration Act of 1965, which marked the beginning of a new, more inclusionary era in immigration policy. Nevertheless, legislative changes in the 1940s and 1950s began to chip away at the draconian character of the national origins provisions and to allow immigration outside the official quota system. In particular, the Displaced Persons Acts of the late 1940s led to the admission of over 400,000 immigrants from Europe in the late 1940s and 1950s. The McCarran-Walter Act of 1952, while officially retaining the national origins quota system, also removed the racial bars to naturalization and created new programs for admission of family members of current residents and individuals with economic skills needed in the United States.

The Immigration Act of 1965 repealed the discriminatory national origins quota system altogether and replaced it with a uniform limit of 20,000 immigrants per country for all countries outside the Western Hemisphere. The law continued a preference system based on family unification and job skills and, for the first time, imposed a limit on Western Hemisphere (and especially Mexican) immigration. Further amendments in 1976 brought the Western Hemisphere under the 20,000-per-country limit with somewhat larger, special quotas for the neighboring countries of Mexico and Canada. The new laws set the stage for massive shifts in the origins of legal immigrants and for large-scale illegal immigration.

The period from 1980 to 1990 saw a complete restructuring of U.S. immigration policy beginning with the Refugee Act of 1980. This act set up a permanent and systematic procedure for admitting refugees and asylees. It committed the country to receiving a substantial number of refugees while bringing the legal definition of *refugees* in line with international standards, instead of more narrow ideological standards. The Refugee Act of 1980 reinforced the shift in national origins away from Europe.

The Immigration Reform and Control Act of 1986 (IRCA) focused on illegal immigration. IRCA contained the first penalties for employers who knowingly hired illegal immigrants. At the same time, it created two large programs to grant legal status to certain illegal immigrants who had worked or lived in the United States for significant periods of time. Ultimately, about 2.7 million formerly illegal immigrants, mostly Mexican, became legal through IRCA's amnesty programs, further reinforcing the shifting origins of immigration.

The Immigration Act of 1990 was the culmination of a decade of reform. This act represented a major liberalization of legal immigration policy, increasing total admissions by 40 percent (including a tripling of employment-based immigration, emphasizing skills).

Notwithstanding the reforms of the 1980s, immigration remained a focus of congressional attention in the 1990s. Three laws passed in 1996 had significant implications for immigration and immigrant policy: the Antiterrorism and Effective Death Penalty Act, the Personal Responsibility and Work Opportunity Reconciliation Act (PRWORA), and the Illegal Immigration Reform and Immigrant Responsibility Act. Despite widespread calls for reductions in the level of legal immigration, Congress did not alter admission levels with these new laws but instead placed restrictions on immigrants' rights. Requirements for sponsoring immigrants were tightened and made enforceable, and penalties affecting subsequent legal admission could now be enforced against illegal immigrants. However, the most noteworthy provisions of the laws affected immigrants' rights and responsibilities. For the first time, eligibility for a broad range of social programs, which had been open to most legal residents of the country, was limited to U.S. citizens. Furthermore, the federal government, while barring some immigrants from all programs, ceded to the states the right to determine eligibility standards affecting other immigrants.

There has been little change in official immigration policy since the mid-1990s, notwithstanding a broadly recognized need to overhaul the country's immigration system in the face of the reemergence of large-scale unauthorized immigration in the post-IRCA era (at least from 1990 to 2007) and long backlogs for legal admission. No consensus emerged on the nature of needed reforms, and an attempt to legislate comprehensive immigration reform, in the form of the McCain-Kennedy bill, failed to pass the Senate in 2007. Increased enforcement of existing immigration laws and passage of various measures by states and localities were the de facto responses to the lack of policy reform at the federal level. The number of Border Patrol agents increased from about 2,500 in the early 1990s to about 20,000 in 2009. More elaborate fencing backed up with various types of sensors and other technology was installed along almost one-third of the 2,000-mile U.S.-Mexico border. Local jurisdictions in many parts of the country passed laws designed to restrict or bar unauthorized immigrants from living and working in their communities; examples include Prince William County, Virginia; Hazleton, Pennsylvania; New Carrolton, Texas; and Lexington, Nebraska. In 2010 Arizona passed a controversial law that greatly increased local law enforcement's involvement in immigration enforcement; many other state legislatures took up similar legislation afterward. Even in the face of very widespread reaction to unauthorized immigration, the national commitment to legal immigration remained unchanged as an average of 1.1 million legal immigrants per year were admitted for permanent residence in the decade before 2010.

The passage of the USA PATRIOT Act (Patriot Act) in 2001 had a significant impact on U.S. immigration activities and on the data available. The Patriot Act disbanded the agency formerly tasked with enforcement of the country's immigration laws, the U.S. Immigration and Naturalization Service (INS), which had been housed in the U.S. Department of Justice. Most of the functions of the INS were transferred to the new U.S. Department of Homeland Security (DHS). U.S. Customs and Border Protection (CBP) and U.S. Immigration and Customs Enforcement (ICE) took over enforcement functions that had been performed by the Customs Service, the Border Patrol, and various other enforcement agencies. The U.S. Citizenship and Immigration Services (USCIS) took over naturalization services and other administrative functions. From a statistical perspective, the Patriot Act changed a number of elements of the former INS, and it strengthened statistical reporting on immigration. The Office of Immigration Statistics (OIS) develops, analyzes, and disseminates statistical information needed to inform policy and assess the effects of immigration in the United States. OIS began to issue a broader range of estimates and data, including a regular series of annual estimates of the number of unauthorized immigrants in the United States. This was the first official regularly issued estimate of this population.

Immigration Numbers and Patterns

The impact of immigration can be assessed with two complementary demographic concepts: *stocks* and *flows*. Immigration flows are the numbers of immigrants coming into and going out of a country. As a result of the flows (and mortality), the number of immigrants living in a country changes; this foreign-born population represents the stock of immigrants in the country. Immigrant stocks are measured with census or survey data. Immigration flows are generally measured with data and estimates on admissions, arrivals, and exits but may also be assessed with survey measures of dates of arrival and as differences in immigrant stocks over time.

Immigration flows increased steadily from the 1820s until the Civil War, with mass immigration beginning in the late 1840s as 1.7 million immigrants arrived during the decade, fleeing political turmoil and famines in northern Europe and Ireland (see Table 1). Through World War I, immigration continued, with steady increases being interrupted by changes in economic and political conditions on both sides of the Atlantic. Thus, immigration decreased during the Civil War (to 2.3 million for the 1860s, down from 2.6 million for the 1850s) and increased only slightly during Reconstruction (to 2.8 million in the 1870s). Immigration surged to 5.2 million during the 1880s but fell to 3.7 million in the 1890s, with further increases being interrupted by several economic panics in the United States. With economic prosperity in the 1900s, immigration again increased, this time to 9.0 million for the decade; during the 1905–1914 period, immigration averaged more than 1 million per year, a level not to be seen again until the 1990s. However, for the entire decade of the 1910s, immigration decreased to 6.0 million because of the effects of World War I in Europe. Europe was totally absorbed with the war, and all the "mechanisms" of immigration—transportation and immigration agreements between nations—disrupted. Moreover, anti-immigrant sentiment was already building with the creation of the Dillingham Commission in 1907 and the literacy test implemented in the following decade.

Two major sources of immigrants were evident during the long period of mass immigration from the 1840s through the 1910s. Through the 1880s, by far the largest numbers of immigrants came from Germany, Ireland, and the United Kingdom (including Northern Ireland). During this era, smaller but significant numbers also came from Scandinavia and other countries of northern and western Europe. A shift in origins began during the 1880s and occurred on a large scale by the 1890s. From 1890 to 1920, the principal sources of immigration were countries in southern and eastern Europe, including but not limited to Italy, Russia (which sent mainly Jewish immigrants), Poland, and Austria-Hungary. Concerns about U.S. ability to integrate immigrants from these new source regions led to ethnically based restrictions embodied in the legislation of 1921 and 1924. These laws, which included the first numerical

Table 1. Immigration to the United States, 1821–1830 to 2001–2010 (in millions)

IMMIGRATION DECADE	LEGAL IMMIGRATION				
	ALL TOTAL	CANADA	EUROPE AND OTHER	OTHER[a]	ALL
1821–1830	0.1	0.1	0.1	0.0	—
1831–1840	0.6	0.6	0.5	0.1	—
1841–1850	1.7	1.7	1.6	0.1	—
1851–1860	2.6	2.6	2.5	0.1	—
1861–1870	2.3	2.3	2.2	0.1	—
1871–1880	2.8	2.9	2.7	0.2	—
1881–1890	5.2	5.2	5.1	0.1	—
1891-1900	3.7	3.7	3.6	0.1	—
1901–1910	9.0	8.8	8.2	0.6	0.2
1911–1920	6.0	5.8	5.1	0.7	0.3
1921–1930	4.1	4.1	3.4	0.7	—
1931–1940	0.5	0.6	0.5	0.1	—
1941–1950	1.0	1.0	0.8	0.2	—
1951–1960	2.5	2.5	1.7	0.8	—
1961–1970	3.8	3.3	1.5	1.8	0.5
1971–1980	7.0	4.5	1.0	3.5	2.5
1981–1990	10.0	6.0	0.9	5.1	4.0
1991–2000	14.5	8.0	1.4	6.6	6.5
2001–2010	15.0	9.0	1.2	7.8	6.0

SOURCE: Department of Homeland Security, *2009 Yearbook of Immigration Statistics* (Washington, D.C.: Office of Immigration Statistics, 2010); author's estimates. Legalized immigrants included as unauthorized at entry.

— = Not applicable.

a Mainly immigrants unauthorized at entry (may have later acquired legal status), estimated by author.

limits on immigration and national origin quotas that favored northern and western Europe, placed severe limits on immigration from other parts of Europe and the rest of the world. As a result, immigration flows began to drop in the late 1920s so that only 4.1 million immigrants arrived in the 1920s, with the majority coming by 1924.

By the 1930s the Great Depression had reduced economic opportunities in the United States and resources available to potential migrants abroad. As a result, immigration levels plummeted. For the entire decade of the 1930s, only about half a million persons moved to the United States—less than in any decade since the 1820s and less than six months' worth of immigration in most of the 2001–2010 decade. Furthermore,

more people emigrated from the country than immigrated during the 1930s, yielding the only decade in the nation's history with net out-migration. The very low levels of immigration continued during World War II, with only about 1 million immigrants coming during the 1940s.

After the war and the passage of the Displaced Persons Acts, more normal patterns of immigration resumed. The national origins system and the numerical limits of the Immigration Act of 1924 were retained in the McCarran-Walter Act of 1952. The national origins quotas favored northern and western European immigration, and continued to severely limit immigration from Asia. Legal immigration during the 1950s averaged about 250,000 per year, with roughly two-thirds of the immigrants coming from Europe and Canada (see Table 2).

The Immigration Act of 1965 changed the nature of immigration to the United States, ushering in the current era of high immigration. The repeal of the national origins quota system and the dropping of the ban on Asian immigration opened the United States to more of the world. As a result, immigration levels increased even though the numerical ceilings were kept in place. Under the previous immigration regime, not all slots were filled because the demand to enter from northern and western Europe was not great. However, a sizable demand was evident in the newly opened areas, and the proportion of immigrants from Asia and Latin America increased significantly after 1965.

By the 1960s, average annual immigration had increased to more than 300,000 per year; in the 1970s, it reached 450,000 per year. By the 1970s, immigration from Europe had dropped numerically to roughly half the level of the 1950s and accounted for only about one-fifth of total legal immigration. Asia now accounted for 35 percent of legal immigrants and Latin America, including Mexico, for 40 percent.

What is striking about the changes engendered by the Immigration Act of 1965 is that they were generally unanticipated. The rationale for the elimination of national origin quotas and the opening of Asian migration was largely the civil rights notion of nondiscrimination rather than immigration-specific justifications. Few politicians or commentators envisioned the subsequent shift of origins from Europe to Asia. Moreover, the increases in immigration levels were generally not anticipated either.

These trends continued after the 1970s, but other policy changes contributed to further increases in immigration and to more changes in the origins of immigration flows to the United States. The Refugee Act of 1980 placed refugees outside the preference system, leading to a slight increase as annual legal immigration reached 600,000 per year in the 1980s. The admission of large numbers of Southeast Asian refugees beginning in the late 1970s and early 1980s reinforced the trends set in motion in 1965. Many Asians came as refugees, but others came directly under the preference system, and some relatives of Southeast Asian refugees filled preference slots. During the

Table 2. Origins of Legal Immigrants, 1951–1960 to 2001–2010

DECADE	TOTAL	EUROPE AND CANADA	ASIA	MEXICO	OTHER LATIN AMERICA	ALL OTHER
Number of Immigrants (in thousands)						
1951–1960	2,520	1,760	150	300	260	40
1961–1970	3,320	1,560	430	450	830	50
1971–1980	4,490	970	1,590	640	1,170	120
1981–1990a	5,980	890	2,680	680	1,530	200
1991–2000a	7,700	1,430	2,850	1,140	1,860	410
2001–2010	10,560	1,570	3,590	1,700	2,450	1,240
Percentage of Immigrants						
1951–1960	100	70	6	12	10	2
1961–1970	100	47	13	14	25	2
1971–1980	100	22	35	14	26	3
1981–1990a	100	15	45	11	26	3
1991–2000a	100	19	37	15	24	5
2001–2010	100	15	34	16	23	12

SOURCE: U.S. Department of Homeland Security, *2009 Yearbook of Immigration Statistics* (Washington, D.C.: Office of Immigration Statistics, 2010); author's estimates for 2010.

a Excludes Immigration Reform and Control Act of 1986 legalizations.

1980s, about 45 percent of legal entrants, or almost 2.7 million immigrants, were from Asia. This figure is larger than total legal immigration during the 1950s.

The Immigration Act of 1990 expanded legal immigration by roughly 40 percent, from about 500,000 per year to 700,000. Much of the increase was allocated to employment-based immigration, which roughly tripled, with an emphasis on highly skilled immigrants. The impact of these changes and past immigration flows is very apparent; although more immigrants were admitted directly, the larger foreign-born population in the United States was able to sponsor more immediate family members (especially spouses) under various unification provisions. In the 1990s, annual legal immigration averaged almost 800,000 per year and increased further to more than 1 million per year in the 2000s, or more than double the flows of the 1970s and four times the level of the 1950s.

Unauthorized Immigration

Another source of concern over immigration and some confusion surrounding the meaning of the data is unauthorized immigration (also known as illegal or undocumented immigration)—that is, the entry and settlement in the United States of persons not authorized by the legal admissions system. Although some records from the first half of the twentieth century refer to concerns with illegal immigration, these mainly involve the movement of farm labor from Mexico to the United States. Special authorizations of "temporary" migrants such as the Bracero Program, which the United States and Mexico authorized in 1942, created new streams of immigrants. This program was initially intended to recruit agricultural labor during wartime and was later extended to immigrants from other Western Hemisphere nations. Almost 5 million workers came under the auspices of the program until it was discontinued in 1964. The end of the Bracero Program, in conjunction with the limits on Western Hemisphere immigration in the Immigration Act of 1965, meant that the continuing migration patterns between Western Hemisphere nations (particularly Mexico) and the United States created a migration flow outside of the legal provisions of American immigration law.

Contemporary concern about this phenomenon dates from the mid- to late 1970s, when serious political discussion of the size of the unauthorized alien population began. The number of unauthorized immigrants living in the United States appears to have been severely overstated, however. One of the earliest recorded conjectures was by INS commissioner Raymond Farrell, who testified in 1972 that 1 million illegal aliens were in the country. Although this figure was apparently just a guess, unsupported by empirical work, subsequent research suggests he may have been reasonably close to the actual number at the time. However, this estimate was not accepted at all. By 1976 the next INS commissioner placed the number at 4 million to 12 million, again without empirical support. While the actual unauthorized population did not approach the upper part of this range for another 30 years, the numbers were large and growing.

Undocumented immigration streams had two principal roots. The first, motivating a large majority of these early unauthorized immigrants, was the long-standing demand for labor, especially in agriculture, in the southwestern United States. Mexicans, mostly men, gladly met this demand. The second stream of undocumented immigrants is related to increasing international flows of migrants and travelers. As more people moved to the United States, more of their friends and relatives came to visit. More tourists came to the United States, too. Some people who entered the United States with a temporary status simply decided to stay in the country. Most unauthorized immigrants are so-called clandestine entrants who sneak into the country, usually across the Mexican border. However, visa abusers, or persons who enter legally with a document permitting them to be in the United States for a specific period of time but who then fail to leave, probably account for at least 40 percent of unauthorized immigrants. By the mid-1980s, immediately before the passage of IRCA, the unauthorized population reached a peak of roughly 4 million to 5 million (see Table 3). In the late 1980s, IRCA's legalization programs granted legal status to about 2.7 million formerly unauthorized immigrants. As a result, the size of the unauthorized population decreased substantially, dropping to about 3.5 million in 1990.

Table 3. Unauthorized Immigrants Living in the United States, 1980–2010

DATE	UNAUTHORIZED POPULATION (IN MILLIONS)	PERCENT FROM MEXICO
2010	11.2	58
2009	11.1	60
2008	11.6	59
2007	12.0	58
2006	11.3	57
2005	11.1	57
2004	10.4	58
2003	9.7	56
2002	9.4	55
2001	9.3	51
2000	8.4	55
1990	3.5	58
1986	4.5	65
1980	3.0	55

SOURCE: Estimates based on Current Population Surveys 1986, 2001–2010 and decennial censuses 1980–2000 using residual techniques. See Passel and Cohn (2011) and earlier sources.

IRCA also introduced measures intended to control illegal immigration. Specifically, it increased enforcement along the U.S.-Mexico border and made the knowing employment of unauthorized immigrants illegal for the first time. IRCA was notably unsuccessful in controlling growth in the illegal population, however. After a short hiatus, the undocumented population began to increase again at a rate roughly the same or even higher than in the pre-IRCA period: 200,000–300,000 per year in the early 1990s. By the late 1990s, the very strong U.S. economy created so many jobs that the flow of unauthorized immigrants to the United States increased substantially. Census 2000 revealed a significantly larger than expected foreign-born population resulting from previously unmeasured immigration. Estimates based on the 2000 census showed that the unauthorized population had increased to more than 8 million.

After the rapid growth leading up to 2000, the unauthorized population continued to increase by an average of 500,000 per year through 2007. At that time the number of unauthorized immigrants living in the country reached 12 million. This proved to be a peak value as the number of new unauthorized immigrants coming into the United States fell dramatically, apparently in response to the Great Recession of 2007–2009. The number leaving the country may have increased as well, but the evidence here is less clear. The result was the first sustained decrease in the unauthorized population (other than through a legalization program), with the numbers dropping to just over 11 million in 2009 followed by a leveling off in 2010.

Mexicans have represented more than half of the unauthorized immigrant population since it has been measured. Other parts of Latin America, most notably El Salvador, Guatemala, and Honduras, account for about one-quarter of the unauthorized population, but no other single country accounts for as much as 5 percent of the immigrants. Almost every country that sends significant numbers of legal immigrants to the United States sends some unauthorized immigrants as well.

The unauthorized population largely consists of young, working families. Unauthorized immigrants are much younger than other immigrants or natives; in 2010 the median age of adult unauthorized immigrants (that is, those ages 18 and over) was 36.2 years as compared to 46.1 years for legal immigrants and 46.5 years for U.S. natives. Even though a large majority of unauthorized adults are men (55–60 percent during the 2000s), unauthorized-immigrant households are much more likely to be family households with children. In 2010, 46 percent of unauthorized-immigrant households were headed by a couple with children as compared to 34 percent of legal immigrant households and only 21 percent of native-born households. About half of the native/unauthorized difference can be attributed to the relative youth of the unauthorized population and the remainder to higher fertility rates among the immigrants. With the increasing numbers of unauthorized immigrant households, the total number of children has grown considerably, and an increasing share are U.S. citizens by virtue of being born in the United States. In 2000 slightly less than 60 percent of the 3.6 million children of unauthorized immigrants were U.S.-born; by 2010 the total number of children had grown to 5.5 million, and more than 80 percent were U.S-born.

Legal Status of the Immigrant Population

The legal status of the immigrant population in U.S. censuses and surveys continues to be a source of confusion and controversy. While the census and ACS classify immigrants as "naturalized citizens" or "aliens," they make no further distinctions with regard to legal status. Yet myriad categories are of interest to analysts and policymakers. The main immigrant populations of interest to most observers, in roughly decreasing order of size, are the following:

- Naturalized citizens who were formerly legal permanent residents (about 14.6 million in 2010);
- Legal permanent resident aliens, or LPRs (12.4 million);
- Unauthorized immigrants (11.2 million);
- Legal temporary aliens or nonimmigrant residents (1 million to 1.5 million);
- Refugees, asylees, and parolees (at most several hundred thousand who will generally transition to LPR status within a few years of admission).

These groups have substantially different characteristics, are affected by different laws and policies, and are changing at different rates.

Legal aliens, or aliens admitted for permanent residence as defined here, are those persons who are not U.S. citizens and are regular family-based and employment-based immigrants. They also include aliens who acquired legal status under IRCA. For most of the first decade of the twenty-first century, more than 1 million new LPRs were admitted to the country each year. Notwithstanding this substantial addition of new LPRs each year, the total number present in the United States hardly changed during the decade, fluctuating between 11.9 and 12.4 million. Each year, several hundred thousand LPRs emigrate from the country, and more than 100,000 die.

The change in the LPR population is also due to naturalization, as LPRs who change their status do so by becoming U.S. citizens. Beginning in the mid-1990s, the number of LPRs naturalizing increased substantially. Before 1990 about 100,000 to 200,000 persons became naturalized U.S. citizens each year. By 1995 that number had increased to almost 500,000. Since then, an average of 700,000 LPRs have become U.S. citizens through naturalization each year. Consequently, the naturalized citizen population living in the country has been growing significantly, increasing from 10.7 million in 2000 to 14.9 million in 2010. This population is the only group within the foreign-born population that has been growing consistently throughout the last decade; the unauthorized alien population increased through 2007 but has decreased since then, while the number of LPRs remained essentially unchanged as did the legal temporary population.

Nonimmigrants are aliens admitted to the United States for specific, temporary periods and for specific purposes. There are solid data on annual admissions of nonimmigrants, but population estimates of this group are somewhat problematic because no agency keeps track of how many nonimmigrants depart or change to other immigration statuses. More than 90 percent of nonimmigrant admissions are temporary visitors for business or pleasure (that is, tourists), with more than 75 percent of the total being tourists. These temporary visitors are not entitled to take up residence in the United States; if they do so, they fall into the unauthorized immigrant category. The largest group of nonimmigrants entitled to live in the country is foreign students and visiting faculty; temporary workers constitute another large group. Smaller groups of nonimmigrants include diplomatic personnel, treaty traders, au pairs, and the like. Because these nonimmigrants are considered residents of the United States, albeit temporary, they are included in decennial census counts. Current estimates suggest that about 1.5 million nonimmigrants are living in the United States at any given time, but only half to three-quarters of them appear in the census and survey data.

The Mexican-born population in the United States, including both legal and unauthorized residents, has become significant for both the United States and Mexico because of its sheer size. This group reached approximately 12.5 million by 2007 and has remained at roughly that level, representing about 30 percent of all immigrants in the United States. The 6.5 million unauthorized Mexicans account for about 58 percent of all unauthorized residents and 53 percent of the Mexicans in the United States. Mexicans are also the largest group of legal immigrants, representing about 21 percent of that group. More striking, however, is the fact that Mexican immigrants in the United States represent more than 10 percent of Mexico's population.

Unauthorized immigrants have been a problematic feature of decennial enumerations since 1980. In each of the last four censuses, legislation has been proposed and lawsuits have been filed to exclude unauthorized aliens from the census counts used to apportion congressional representation (for example, *F.A.I.R. et al. v. Klutznick et al.* for the 1980 census and *Ridge et al. v. Verity et al.* for 1990). In the lawsuits and legislative justification, proponents of excluding the unauthorized aliens have argued that the presence of these aliens on the census rolls has increased representation in states with higher concentrations of unauthorized aliens and diluted the representation of citizens in states with fewer of them. They have further argued that this dilution violates the constitutional provisions for representation and the "one man, one vote" Supreme Court decisions of the 1960s. The opponents of exclusion have countered with several arguments. One argument addressed the impracticality of identifying and excluding unauthorized aliens and the necessity of using estimates rather than counts to do so. A more direct and substantive argument was that the Constitution's apportionment prescription was not restricted to citizens or potential voters but included the entire population (originally the entire free population plus three-fifths of the slave population

but later changed to encompass the entire population). Thus, unauthorized aliens, as part of the population of a state, should affect the number of representatives assigned to that state.

None of the proposed legislation to exclude unauthorized immigrants from the apportionment population has passed, and the lawsuits have been decided on narrow, technical grounds. Specifically, the plaintiffs have been ruled not to have "standing" to bring the suits because the damages alleged were both prospective and not specific. Several courts, including the U.S. Supreme Court, have addressed the substance of the cases through dicta by stating that the intent of the Constitution was to provide representation to "persons" rather than to "citizens" or to the potential voting population.

. . . . JEFFREY S. PASSEL

See also *Composition of the population; Foreign-born population of the United States; Internal migration.*

BIBLIOGRAPHY

Bean, Frank D., Barry Edmonston, and Jeffrey S. Passel. *Undocumented Migration to the United States: IRCA and the Experience of the 1980s.* Washington, D.C.: Urban Institute Press, 1990.

Daniels, Roger. *Guarding the Golden Door: American Immigration Policy and Immigrants since 1882.* New York: Hill and Wang, 2004.

Fix, Michael, and Jeffrey S. Passel. *Immigration and Immigrants: Setting the Record Straight.* Washington, D.C.: Urban Institute Press, 1994. Available at www.urban.org/publications/305184.html.

Gibson, Campbell, and Kay Jung. *Historical Census Statistics on the Foreign-Born Population of the United States: 1850 to 2000.* Working Paper No. 81. Washington, D.C.: Population Division, U.S. Census Bureau, 2006. Available at www.census.gov/population/www/documentation/twps0081/twps0081.html.

Hoefer, Michael, Nancy Rytina, and Bryan C. Baker. "Estimates of the Unauthorized Immigrant Population Residing in the United States: January 2010." Department of Homeland Security Office of Immigration Statistics, *Population Estimates*, February 2011. www.dhs.gov/xlibrary/assets/statistics/publications/ois_ill_pe_2010.pdf.

Lee, Margaret Mikyung, and Erika K. Lunder. *Constitutionality of Excluding Aliens from the Census for Apportionment and Redistricting Purposes.* CRS Report for Congress R41048. Washington, D.C.: Congressional Research Service, Library of Congress, 2010. Available at http://assets.opencrs.com/rpts/R41048_20100120.pdf .

Passel, Jeffrey S. *Unauthorized Migrants in the United States: Estimates, Methods, and Characteristics.* Organisation for Economic Co-operation and Development (OECD) Social, Employment and Migration Working Papers No. 57. Paris, France: OECD, 2007. Available at www.oecd.org/dataoecd/41/25/39264671.pdf.

Passel, Jeffrey S., and Rebecca L. Clark. *Immigrants in New York: Their Legal Status, Incomes, and Taxes.* Washington, D.C.: Urban Institute Press, 1998. Available at www.urban.org/url.cfm?ID=407432.

Passel, Jeffrey S., and D'Vera Cohn. *Unauthorized Immigrant Population: National and State Trends, 2010.* Washington, D.C.: Pew Hispanic Center, 2011. Available at http://pewhispanic.org/files/reports/133.pdf. Also see related reports in bibliography.

U.S. Census Bureau. *Measuring America: The Decennial Censuses from 1790 to 2000.* POL/02-MA(RV). Washington, D.C.: U.S. Government Printing Office, 2002. Available at www.census.gov/prod/2002pubs/pol02marv.pdf.

U.S. Department of Homeland Security. Yearbook of Immigration Statistics. www.dhs.gov/files/statistics/publications/yearbook.shtm.

U.S. Immigration and Naturalization Service, Office of Policy and Planning. *Estimates of the Unauthorized Immigrant Population Residing in the United States: 1990 to 2000.* www.dhs.gov/xlibrary/assets/statistics/publications/Ill_Report_1211.pdf.

Income and Poverty Measures

Questions on annual income were first asked of everyone in the 1940 census; in every subsequent census through 2000, income questions were asked of a sample of the population with increasing detail requested. The American Community Survey (ACS), the replacement for the census long-form sample survey (which was not part of the 2010 census), collects data on income similar to the data collected in the 2000 census. The censuses from 1970 to 2000 and the ACS since its inception have also provided estimates of the numbers of people in families with incomes below the official poverty thresholds. The concept underlying the census and ACS income questions is that of regular, before-tax money income.

Income in the 1940 Census

The decennial population census obtained measures of socioeconomic status for 150 years; for example, the 1850 census asked about occupation and value of real estate owned. However, no questions about income were asked in the census until 1940 when, to help understand the effects of the Great Depression, two questions about income were added to the population schedule used by enumerators. The two questions, asked of all people age 14 and older, asked for (1) the amount of wage and salary income earned in 1939, and (2) whether or not the person had more than $50 of other income in that year.

The U.S. Bureau of the Census anticipated public objection to the questions and acted as follows to minimize burden and maximize response: (1) the questionnaire asked for a specific dollar amount only for wage and salary income, which many workers knew was already reported to the government for Social Security purposes; (2) the questionnaire did not require people with more than $5,000 of wages and salaries to specify the exact amount they earned; (3) people who did not want to let the enumerator (who might be a neighbor) know their income could ask for a confidential income form to fill out and mail back; and (4) the income questions were the last ones asked.

The inclusion of income questions in the census generated some adverse publicity and congressional hearings; however, public cooperation was excellent. The nonresponse rate to the wage-and-salary income item was only 2 percent, and only 0.5 percent of the 40 million people who reported such income used the confidential form.

Income Questions from 1950 to 2000 and in the ACS

The 1950 census used sampling to reduce the burden of the census considerably. The income questions were obtained for a 20 percent sample of people age 14 and older who were asked for amounts of wages and salaries, net self-employment income, and income from other sources in 1949. Enumerators asked the sample questions of every fifth person by using "line schedules" that included a line for each household member. If the head of a family fell into the sample, that person was also asked about the income of other family members from wages and salaries, self-employment, and other sources.

In the 1960 census, the format changed from line schedules to household questionnaires, including both short and long forms. Table 1 shows the income questions asked on the long form for the 1960–2000 censuses, the population asked to provide income information, and the sample size.

The ACS, which became fully operational in 2005, collects income for the previous 12 months from people age 15 and older in the sample of about 2 million households each year, using the same categories as did the 2000 census long form. Because the income-reporting period varies depending on the month when the household (or group quarters resident) receives the questionnaire, the data collected in a calendar year, say 2010, may represent income received in the previous calendar year (for example, all of 2009 for households responding in January 2010) or income received partly in the previous calendar year and partly in the current year (for example, December 2009 through November 2010 for households responding in December 2010). To make the income amounts comparable in real dollars, the Census Bureau adjusts them using the average of the Consumer Price Index for Urban Consumers-Research Series (CPI-U-RS) for the calendar year.

Poverty Measures

The U.S. Bureau of the Budget (now the U.S. Office of Management and Budget) adopted a measure of poverty for official use in 1969. The measure had first been developed for 1963 by Mollie Orshansky of the U.S. Social Security Administration. Poverty statistics were first tabulated from census data in 1970; annual poverty statistics are published each fall from the Current Population Survey (CPS) Annual Social and Economic (ASEC) Supplement and the ACS. The Census Bureau recommends that the CPS ASEC and the ACS poverty statistics be used for national and subnational analyses, respectively.

Official poverty rates are based on comparing before-tax money income for a family or unrelated individual to the appropriate poverty threshold to determine if the family or individual falls below the threshold. Oversimplifying for ease of description, the thresholds were developed using the cost of a minimum adequate diet times three to allow for other needed consumption. The thresholds vary based on the total number of persons and children in the family and (for one-person and two-person families) based on whether the head of the family is over or under age 65. (Originally there were also separate thresholds for farm versus nonfarm families and single-parent families headed by women versus other types of families.) The thresholds assume that children and the elderly require less income than working-age adults. Also, while the thresholds assume that larger families need more income than smaller families, they recognize economies of scale. For example, larger families can make more efficient use of food purchases, with less waste; conversely, smaller families need such basic living spaces as kitchens just as much as do larger families.

Table 1. Income Questions on the 1960–2000 Census Long-Form Questionnaires

CENSUS AND INCOME REPORTING PERIOD	1960 (1959 INCOME)	1970 (1969 INCOME)	1980 (1979 INCOME)	1990 (1989 INCOME)	2000 (1999 INCOME)
Population asked to respond and sample size	People age 14 and older; 25 percent sample	People age 14 and older; 20 percent sample	People age 15 and older; average 19 percent sample	People age 15 and older; average 17 percent sample	People age 15 and older; average 17 percent sample
Income questions	Wages and salaries	Wages and salaries	Wages and salaries	Wages and salaries	Wages and salaries
	Net self-employment income (nonfarm + farm)	Net self-employment income (nonfarm)	Net self-employment income (nonfarm)	Net self-employment income (nonfarm)	Net self-employment income (nonfarm + farm)
	NA	Net self-employment income (farm)	Net self-employment income (farm)	Net self-employment income (farm)	NA
	NA	Social Security or railroad retirement	Social Security or railroad retirement	Social Security or railroad retirement	Social Security or railroad retirement
	NA	Public assistance or welfare income	Supplemental Security Income, Aid to Families with Dependent Children, or other welfare	Supplemental Security Income, Aid to Families with Dependent Children, or other welfare	Any public assistance from the state or local welfare office
	NA	NA	NA	NA	Supplemental Security Income
	NA	NA	Interest, dividends, royalties, and net rent	Interest, dividends, royalties, net rent, and estate and trust income	Interest, dividends, royalties, net rent, and estate and trust income
	NA	NA	NA	Pension income	Pension income
	All other income	All other income	All other income	All other income	All other income
	NA	NA	Total income	Total income	Total income

NOTES: "NA" means income source included in "all other income"; wording of public assistance category changed in 2000 to reflect the 1996 "welfare reform" legislation that replaced Aid to Families with Dependent Children (AFDC) with a block grant program to the states, Temporary Assistance to Needy Families (TANF).

SOURCE: Compiled by author from review of census questionnaires.

Each year the thresholds are adjusted for inflation based on the change in the Consumer Price Index for All Urban Consumers (CPI-U). A variant of the official thresholds is published each year by the Assistant Secretary for Planning and Evaluation, U.S. Department of Health and Human Services, for use in establishing income eligibility for the Supplemental Nutrition Assistance Program (SNAP) and other public assistance programs.

The poverty measure was extensively critiqued in a 1995 report prepared by a panel of the National Academy of Sciences/National Research Council (NAS/NRC). The report recommended that the official measure be replaced with a new measure with the following features:

- Thresholds updated for changes since the 1960s in the real standard of living for basic necessities and adjusted for geographic differences in the cost of housing;
- Thresholds reflecting a limited budget for basic necessities, including food, clothing, shelter, and utilities plus

a little more, developed from expenditures reported by two-adult/two-child families in the Consumer Expenditure Survey of the U.S. Bureau of Labor Statistics (BLS) and adjusted for other families by use of an equivalence scale;

- Income measured as after-tax disposable income available for consumption of basic necessities, defined as regular cash income after taxes plus benefits from SNAP (formerly food stamps), school meals, housing subsidies, and other noncash assistance programs and minus medical out-of-pocket expenses, child support payments, dependent-care expenses of working parents, and transportation and other work-related expenses.

Since the 1995 report, the Census Bureau, with assistance from BLS, has developed a large number of experimental poverty measures that are based on the report's recommendations. The experimental measures vary aspects of the thresholds and the income concept (for example, including dependent-care costs in the thresholds instead of as a deduction from income) to show various factors' effects on the poverty level.

Recently, states and cities have begun to use the ACS with other data sources to implement the NAS/NRC recommendations. New York City pioneered the development of a new poverty measure that enables city officials to determine the effects of such initiatives as local tax credits that are not reflected in the official measure. In March 2010 an Obama administration Interagency Technical Working Group on Developing a Supplemental Poverty Measure outlined a Supplemental Poverty Measure (SPM), which would be published annually by the Census Bureau in cooperation with BLS. The SPM would largely reflect the recommendations of the NAS/NRC 1995 report; it would not replace the official poverty measure but would supplement it. Funding has not yet been appropriated for this initiative, although the SPM will be made available as an experimental poverty measure in fall 2011.

Concept and Quality Issues

The basic income concept in the 1940–2000 censuses, the ACS, and also the official poverty measure from the CPS ASEC—namely regular, before-tax money income—has been stable across time. The concept excludes lump-sum money income, such as capital gains or inheritance. It also excludes any income amounts that could be attributed to the value of assets; for example, many economists argue that homeowners' incomes should include imputed amounts for the flow of services they receive from ownership.

More important for comparative analysis across time and population groups, the census income concept excludes in-kind benefits, which have grown substantially over the past few decades. For example, the SNAP, Medicare, and Medicaid programs did not exist in 1960 and were barely in place by 1970 but are now providing billions of dollars of benefits to substantial portions of the population. Privately provided fringe benefits, such as group health and life insurance, also have become much more common. There are difficult questions around how to value in-kind benefits, particularly for medical care, but there is no doubt that the money-only income concept underestimates available economic resources for families and individuals, particularly in censuses since 1970.

The census income concept is also a pretax concept. It therefore ignores changes in tax burdens that have occurred over the years and that affect population groups differently. For example, the recent expansion of the Earned Income Tax Credit, which helps low-income working families, is not captured in income and poverty statistics from past censuses, the ACS, or the CPS ASEC.

Several sources of error affect the quality of responses to the census and ACS income questions. These sources include sampling error, which varies from census to census according to the sampling rates used (in the 1980–2000 censuses, rates varied by size of place, as they do for the ACS); nonresponse to the income questions, which has increased over time; errors in the procedures the Census Bureau uses to impute missing responses (currently, 30 percent of income is imputed in the

CPS ASEC and 20 percent in the ACS); and respondent errors, such as underreporting and overreporting.

In making decennial census income data available to users, the Census Bureau top-codes dollar amounts; that is, it reports dollar amounts up to a limit and then provides a broad top category. For example, in the 1980 census Public Use Microdata Samples (PUMS) files, income amounts were generally shown in dollars up to a top category of "$75,000 or more." In the 1990 and 2000 census PUMS files, the top category varied by type of income and state of residence, as it also does in the ACS. The purpose of top-coding is to protect the confidentiality of individual responses.

See also *American Community Survey: questionnaire content; American Community Survey: using multi-year estimates; Confidentiality; Editing, imputation, and weighting; Federal household surveys; Long form; Sampling for content.*

. . . . CONSTANCE F. CITRO

BIBLIOGRAPHY

Citro, Constance F. *The Concept of Income in the U.S. Decennial Censuses: 1960–90.* Arlington, Va.: Association of Public Data Users, 1996.
Czajka, John L., and Gabrielle Denmead. *Income Data for Policy Analysis: A Comparative Assessment of Eight Surveys; Final Report.* Prepared for the Office of the Assistant Secretary for Planning and Evaluation, U.S. Department of Health and Human Services. Washington, D.C.: Mathematica Policy Research, 2008. Available at http://aspe.hhs.gov/sp/reports/2008/incomedata/report.html.
National Research Council. *Experimental Poverty Measures: Summary of a Workshop.* Planning Group for the Workshop to Assess the Current Status of Actions Taken in Response to Measuring Poverty: A New Approach. John Iceland, ed. Committee on National Statistics, Washington, D.C., The National Academies Press, 2005. Available at http://www.nap.edu/catalog.php?record_id=11166.
———. *Measuring Poverty: A New Approach.* Panel on Poverty and Family Assistance: Concepts, Information Needs, and Measurement Methods. Constance F. Citro and Robert T. Michael, eds. Committee on National Statistics, Washington, D.C.: The National Academies Press, 1995. Available at http://www.nap.edu/catalogue.php?record_id=4759.
NYC Center for Economic Opportunity. *The CEO Poverty Measure: 2005–2008.* Working Paper. New York: NYC Center for Economic Opportunity, 2010. Available at www.nyc.gov/html/ceo/downloads/pdf/ceo_poverty_measure_v5.pdf.
Short, Kathleen S. "Who Is Poor? A New Look with the Supplemental Poverty Measure." SEHSD Working Paper No. 2010-15, prepared for the 2011 Conference of the Allied Social Science Associations, Society of Government Economists. Washington, D.C.: U.S. Census Bureau, 2011. Available at www.census.gov/hhes/povmeas/methodology/supplemental/research.html.
Short, Kathleen S., Thesia Garner, David Johnson, and Patricia Doyle. *Experimental Poverty Measures: 1990 to 1997.* Current Population Reports, Consumer Income, No. P60-205. Washington, D.C.: U.S. Government Printing Office, 1999. Available at www.census.gov/prod/99pubs/p60-205.pdf.
U.S. Census Bureau. "Observations from the Interagency Technical Working Group on Developing a Supplemental Poverty Measure." March 2010. www.census.gov/hhes/www/poverty/SPM_TWGObservations.pdf.
———. Supplemental Poverty Measure Federal Register Notice. www.census.gov/hhes/www/poverty/methods/spm_fedregister.html.

Internal Migration

Americans are very mobile. During a single year, more than 45 million or about 14 percent of the nation's population move from one residence to another—about 12 percent move within their state of residence, and 2 percent move from one state to another. Relatively few Americans spend their entire lives in their communities of birth, and many move from one state to another more than once. Internal migration is not the movement of only a few residents or an aimless wandering but a common occurrence with definite patterns related to economic and social changes.

Internal migration is an inherent feature of population changes associated with employment mobility. Within the United States, some communities have expanding employment opportunities, while other communities have stable or declining economic opportunities. As a result, some younger persons are born and raised in communities that offer little promise of satisfactory employment as adults. Internal migration both provides a mechanism for improving one's personal employment prospects and maintains a better connection between available workers and job opportunities. Migration is a vital demographic process for a dynamic economy.

The process of internal migration has important consequences for the communities of departure and arrival. Along with the effects of migration on employment, migrants themselves influence the housing markets, schools, public services, and retail establishments in both communities. In communities where the numbers of births and deaths are relatively similar, internal migration is often the most important demographic factor in changing local population size and characteristics of the community.

Measurement of Internal Migration

Demographers usually consider two types of internal migration. One type is local movement; this involves people, called *movers*, who change residence within the community. The second type is migration; this involves people, called *migrants*, who change community of residence. Movers migrate locally and usually do not disrupt their regular daily social and economic ties. Migrants change their community of residence and generally interrupt their social and economic ties with their original community. Census data define movers as people who change their place of dwelling and migrants as people who change their county of residence.

Types of Migrants

Although migrants often move for economic reasons, not all mobility is related to employment. Families often move within a community because of the desire to change their housing, to be closer to work, to send their children to a preferred school, to be closer to suitable transportation, and for other reasons. People often move between communities, on the other hand, for economic reasons because job opportunities are an important motivation. A large number of young adults move to seek job training and attend college. Retirees select places to settle based on available suitable housing, climate, and desirable amenities.

Lifetime Migration

A common, basic measure of mobility is to compare current residence to the place of residence at birth. Figure 1 presents the percentages of persons born in the United States who lived in a state other than their state of birth from 1850 to 2008. In the middle of the 1800s, about one-fourth of U.S. residents lived in a different state than their state of birth. From 1850 to 1900, there were steady declines in the proportion of residents

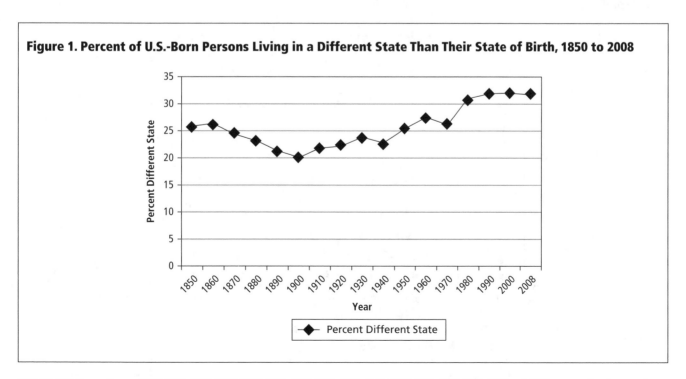

Figure 1. Percent of U.S.-Born Persons Living in a Different State Than Their State of Birth, 1850 to 2008

SOURCES: U.S. Census Bureau, 1850, 1860, 1870, 1880, 1900, 1910, 1920, 1930, 1940, 1950, 1960, 1970, 1980, 1990, 2000, and 2008 census microdata samples (data tabulated by author); 1890 data are estimated by interpolation from 1870, 1880, 1900, and 1910 data.

who had moved to a different state from their state of birth, in spite of the popular perception that many Americans were moving, especially westward, during this period. In 1900 an overwhelming number of Americans, about 80 percent, lived in their state of birth.

Migration between states increased in the first decades of the twentieth century, except for the 1930s, when many remained in their birth state during the Great Depression. Interstate migration increased greatly during World War II, when millions of Americans moved because of military service. By 1950 the proportion of Americans living in a state other than their state of birth had increased to more than one-fourth. During the 1950s and afterward, the pace of interstate migration increased. By 1980 the percentage of Americans living in a state other than their state of birth had increased to almost 31 percent, and it remained at about 32 percent in 1990, 2000, and 2008.

Variations in Mobility Status

Since 1940 the census has asked a question on where the respondent lived five years earlier. The responses permit demographers to classify the population into five mobility groups. *Nonmovers* are those living in the same residence as five years previously. *Nonmigrant movers* are those living in a different residence in the same county. *Intrastate migrants* are those living in a different county in the same state. *Interstate migrants* are those living in a different state. *External migrants* are those who have immigrated from outside the United States. Figure 2 displays the mobility status of residents in the United States from 1940 to 2008, based on mobility during the five-year period prior to the decennial census or the 2008 American Community Survey. (The ACS asks about migration in the previous year, so these data were used to estimate a five-year migration rate for Figure 2 in order to allow comparison to decennial census data.)

There have been changes in the mobility status of U.S. residents during the last seven decades. The percentage of all movers increased from 38 percent in 1940 to about 44 percent in 1950, remained between 50 and 55 percent during the 1950–1990 period, and decreased to 40 percent in 2000 and 39 percent in 2008. By 2008 the percentage of nonmovers had reached the highest level of the past 50 years, with almost 6 in 10 persons remaining in the same dwelling over a 5-year period.

The percentage of nonmigrant movers has declined during the past 70 years, from 24 percent in 1940 to 22 percent in 2008. The percentage of intrastate migrants increased from 6 percent in 1940 to almost 10 percent in 1980 before decreasing to less than 9 percent in 2008. Overall, about 1 in 12 American residents move within their state during an average five-year period. Interstate migration rates increased from 6 percent in 1940 to 9 percent in 1960 and peaked at 10 percent in 1980. They then decreased to less than 9 percent in 2000 and 2008.

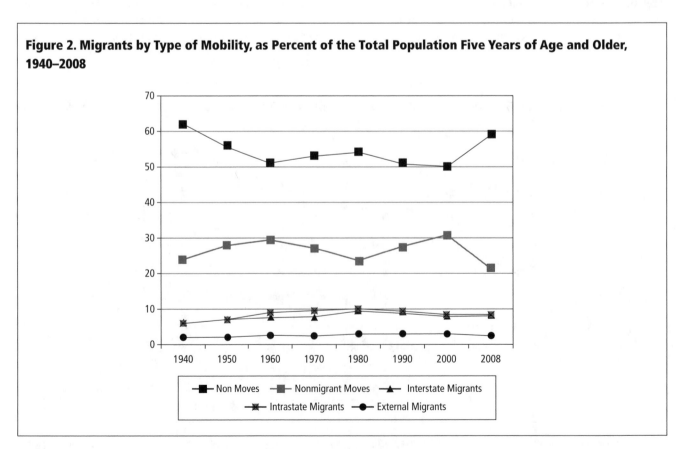

Figure 2. Migrants by Type of Mobility, as Percent of the Total Population Five Years of Age and Older, 1940–2008

SOURCES: U.S. Census Bureau, 1940, 1950, 1960, 1970, 1980, 1990, 2000, and 2008 census microdata samples (data tabulated by author).

External migrants constitute the smallest percentage of American residents. About 2 to 3 percent of U.S. residents have moved from outside the United States during an average five-year period.

Interstate Migration

Over an average five-year period, more than 7 million American residents move from one state to another. Interstate migration involves movement both into and out of states. Net interstate migration is the difference between in-migrants and out-migrants. During the 2007–2008 period, three states (Texas, North Carolina, and Arizona) experienced the largest net interstate in-migration. The largest net interstate out-migration was witnessed by New York, California, and Michigan.

Patterns of interstate migration for the 2007–2008 period have been similar to those of previous periods for some states. There has been net in-migration to North Carolina, Arizona, and Georgia in recent years. There has been net out-migration from New York, California, Illinois, and New Jersey since 1995. The level of net migration for Florida and Nevada, however, has shifted. Both states experienced changes from large net in-migration to modest net out-migration in the past decade.

The number of in-, out-, and net interstate migrants is typically largest for the most populous states. Calculating migration rates per 1,000 residents produces statistics that take population size into account. During 2007–2008, the highest rates of net in-migration were experienced by Montana, Utah, and North Carolina. High rates of net out-migration occurred in Alaska, the District of Columbia, and Wyoming.

During 2007–2008 the single largest interstate flow was 77,000 migrants from California to Texas. This was a result of greater employment opportunities in Texas relative to California. The second-largest migration stream was 57,000 migrants who moved from New York to Florida. The third-, fourth-, and fifth-largest streams were 52,000 from New York to New Jersey, 49,000 from California to Arizona, and 49,000 from Florida to Georgia, respectively.

Age and Sex Selectivity of Migration

Some groups are more likely to move than others. The study of groups that are more likely to move is referred to as the selectivity of migration.

During recent years, men and women appear to have been equally mobile. Overall, 15 percent of men and women were movers during the one-year periods of 1999–2000 and 2007–2008. More than 12 percent of men and women moved within their states of residence, and almost 3 percent were interstate migrants.

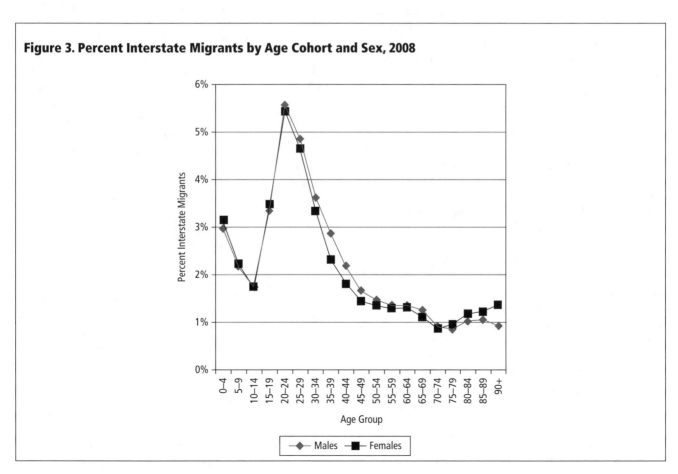

Figure 3. Percent Interstate Migrants by Age Cohort and Sex, 2008

Persons in their late teens, twenties, and early thirties are more mobile than the general population. Persons who are 55 years of age and older are less mobile than the general population. As shown in Figure 3, younger men and women have higher interstate migration rates than the overall average. In the one-year period prior to the 2008 ACS, more than 5 percent of younger adults moved from one state to another. By way of contrast, about 1 percent of the population 65 years of age and older changed their state of residence during 2007–2008.

The mobility of children and youth age 17 years and younger reflects the movement, both local and migratory, of their parents. The higher mobility rates of younger adults (those above 17 years) reflects completing secondary education, going to college, seeking work, enlisting in military service, or moving based on personal preferences. Mobility among younger adults is also affected by choices about marriages or partnerships, which typically involve the change of residence for one or both persons.

Education Selectivity

The most mobile segment of the population appears to be that with above-average educational attainment. The rates of local mobility, as indicated for nonmigrant movers, are highest for persons with some college or university, are slightly lower for those at the upper end of educational attainment, and are lowest for those at the lower end. For migration and especially for interstate migration, the highest rates are for those with a university degree or more; rates are much lower for those with less than a high school education. One-year (2007–2008) rates of interstate migration exceed 3 percent for persons with university degrees; this is twice the rate for persons with less than a high school degree.

Occupation Selectivity

Mobility patterns vary greatly for occupational groups. One of the most mobile segments of the population includes managers and professionals. The least mobile occupational groups are technicians, supervisors, and skilled clerical workers. If more specific occupational groups are analyzed for levels of 2007–2008 interstate migration, three occupations are found to be much more mobile than the overall average: police and others in protective services, natural and applied scientists, and chefs and cooks. Each of these occupations moves from one state to another at levels almost twice the overall average. Three specific occupations are relatively less mobile, with interstate migration rates that are about one-half the overall average: laborers in manufacturing, processing, and utilities; contractors and supervisors in trades and transportation; and workers in primary industries (such as mining, agriculture, and fishing). This pattern probably results from the available job opportunities for particular occupations and from particular companies requiring their employees to migrate.

Household Income Selectivity

Demographic research has not devoted much attention to the relationship between mobility and income. Interstate migration patterns during 2007–2008 suggest that lower-income persons are more likely to be mobile than higher-income persons. The inverse relationship between household income and mobility is evident for both local mobility and migration. Much of this variation is probably due to the younger age of mobile persons (household income is lower among younger adults), but the difference is probably not due solely to the different age compositions of various household income groups. A mobile person may have moved after losing his or her job and thus report a lower income for the year prior to the census. Both the change of household income and the mobility may result from employment opportunities. If moving requires a person to be out of work, even temporarily, this can act to reduce household income for mobile persons. Because available census data do not collect information about income at the beginning of the migration interval—2007 in the case of the 2008 ACS—the conclusions one can draw from observed relationship between income and mobility are limited.

Nativity Selectivity

Immigration and internal migration overlap in two areas. Immigrants often settle in areas with growing economic opportunities, which are the same areas that attract internal migrants. Also, after settling in the United States, immigrants also move within the country. If we compare the U.S.-born to the foreign-born people who resided in the United States in 2007, we look primarily at the population who may have moved internally during the 2007–2008 period. In this case, the comparison reveals that the foreign-born population had lower percentages of movers (11.9 percent compared to 12.7 percent for the native-born) and lower rates of interstate migration (2.1 percent compared to 2.5 percent). These mobility patterns for the foreign-born have two implications. Once foreign-born persons have decided to emigrate to the United States, they still need to decide upon where they will settle in the United States. Their selection of a settlement destination is influenced by social and economic factors, as well as by the locations of immigrant reception centers and other programs that may make one place more desirable than others. It is also clear that immigrants continue to move around the United States even as they adjust to life in a new country, although they do not move as frequently as other residents.

Conclusion

Internal migration is one of the fundamental processes of population change. It is a critical mechanism that changes communities, altering population size and characteristics for both the community of origin and the community of destination.

Internal migration is unquestionably one of the most impressive features of the American population. Mobility at the local and state level is such a routine occurrence that it is easy to overlook the ways in which it changes communities across the nation. The movement of a person from one community to another changes the population at both the origin and the destination. Not only does the movement of people subtract and add residents for the communities of origin and destination, respectively, but the communities are changed by the characteristics of the internal migrants. Migration is a process of cultural change and social integration. The person who migrates from one community to another provides a link between the two communities, at least temporarily. If the new arrival is "different" from members of the new community of settlement, he or she may be the first of many arrivals who will become a new social group, either assimilating into the new community over time or changing the community itself.

With lower rates of natural increase in recent years, internal migration has become a more important component of population change at the state, metropolitan, and local level. Unlike fertility and mortality, however, the determinants of internal migration change quickly, producing sudden positive or negative migration flows. As a result, the internal migration patterns evident in the 2000–2008 period are intricately related to the social and economic structure of this period. The ACS will continue to provide information on internal migration in future years.

See also *Immigration; Composition of the population.*

. . . . BARRY EDMONSTON

BIBLIOGRAPHY

Gregory, James N. *The Southern Diaspora: How the Great Migrations of Black and White Southerners Transformed America.* Chapel Hill: University of North Carolina Press, 2005.

Perry, Marc J. *Domestic Net Migration in the United States: 2000 to 2004; Population Estimates and Projections.* Current Population Reports No. P25-1135. Washington, D.C.: U.S. Government Printing Office, 2006. Available at www.census.gov/prod/2006pubs/p25-1135.pdf.

International Coordination in Population Censuses

If Ambrose Bierce had ever been asked to define international coordination in census taking, his definition might have read something like the following: (1) an idealized arrangement, often advocated but never achieved, under which all countries would adopt the same census content, timing, and outputs, almost invariably those of the country of the proposer; (2) a misnomer for international cooperation in census taking.

The primary obstacle to true international coordination in census taking is that population censuses are basically national undertakings carried out for largely national purposes. Accordingly, while the notion of a unitary global census operation with a single set of questions, field and processing procedures, and outputs has been repeatedly proposed in one form or another over the decades, and has been repeatedly ignored, more modest but important efforts are now well established. These efforts, better characterized today as international cooperation than international coordination, include the organized exchange of census data and census experience among national census authorities in different countries; the development, adoption, and dissemination of international recommendations for concepts, definitions, and classifications for use in population censuses; and different forms of technical assistance and training

designed to help developing or other countries facing special challenges in carrying out their censuses.

The modern history of international cooperation on population censuses began in the middle of the nineteenth century, initially in the context of a series of quasi-diplomatic international statistical congresses. When that system of congresses broke down around 1870, the work on collaboration was continued under the auspices of the newly established International Statistical Institute (ISI). Census-related work in this period covered such subjects as agreement on the meaning of the de jure and de facto concepts of census enumeration and the initial development of a standard occupational classification.

As the new millennium was about to dawn, notions of a single world census caught the imaginations of statisticians in several countries. For example, in 1899, John Howard Dynes wrote a paper assessing the feasibility of conceiving the 1900 U.S. census as part of a "census of the world." Not surprisingly, because of the many obstacles to comparability identified by Dynes himself, nothing came of this effort.

After World War I, the ISI continued to promote the exchange of information and the development of new international standard statistical definitions and classifications. However, in the 1920s and thereafter, the primary locus of work on developing and promoting standard international definitions and classifications for statistical use, including those relating to population censuses, shifted to international organizations such as the League of Nations, followed by the United Nations (UN) and the International Labour Organization.

Other vehicles for promoting coordination in work on censuses, particularly in the 1930s and 1940s, were the administrative systems of countries with large colonial empires. By its very nature, a colonial regime might be seen as providing an ideal setting for comparatively rigorous coordination of statistical work. Nevertheless, while considerable uniformity was achieved in the timing of census enumerations (for example, throughout the British Empire, censuses were generally taken in years ending in one), census methods and content varied widely depending on local conditions and needs.

Since the end of World War II, international coordination and international cooperation in the population census field have operated through four primary means: (1) UN resolutions and recommendations pertaining to population and housing censuses; (2) multilateral and bilateral exchanges and syntheses of information on census content, methods, and problems among national census authorities; (3) financial and technical assistance and related training provided to developing countries and other countries needing special assistance; and (4) overall, more knowledgeable and better-trained census users. Each of these means is reviewed, in turn, in the balance of this article.

United Nations Recommendations and Related Documentation

On July 22, 2005, the United Nations Economic and Social Council, on the recommendation of its Statistical Commission (a body consisting of representatives, usually the chief governmental statisticians, from 24 member states of the UN that reports directly to the Economic and Social Council), inaugurated the 2005–2014 census decade. It did so by adopting a formal resolution aimed at "ensuring that Member States conduct a population and housing census at least once during the period from 2005 to 2014" and urging

> Member States to carry out a population and housing census and to disseminate census results as an essential source of information for small-area, national, regional and international planning and development and to provide census results to national stakeholders as well as the United Nations and other appropriate intergovernmental organizations to assist in studies on population, environment, and socio-economic development issues and programmes.

This resolution—E/2005/13 (2010 World Population and Housing Census Programme)—provided the framework for the global UN population and housing census recommendations adopted in 2008 by the Statistical Commission. The recommendations, published as *Principles and Recommendations for Population and Housing Censuses, Revision 2*, provided basic definitions of census terminology and concepts, as well as guidance on methodology, census content, and outputs, including tabulations.

Roughly comparable resolutions and global census recommendations have been initiated by the Statistical Commission every ten years since the 1950 census decade that ran from 1945 to 1954. (Prior to the 1980 census decade, separate recommendations were issued for population censuses and housing censuses.) Although these global UN recommendations potentially could provide considerable scope for international coordination in census timing, content, and methods, increased awareness that national data needs and conditions of enumeration vary markedly among countries has reduced the emphasis on achieving a unitary model for population censuses. For example, in the first several census decades, an effort was made to encourage at least approximate simultaneity in the timing of enumeration. Thus, the resolution adopted in connection with the 1970 census decade recommended that countries carry out their censuses "preferably around the year 1970." Beginning with the census decade of the 1980s, the emphasis shifted to the importance of fixed periodicity of census enumerations within each country, and the reference to a desired year of enumeration was dropped. The approach with respect to census content has been more episodic. In the 1950s to 1970s considerable emphasis was placed on recommending a specific list of topics for inclusion. For the next several census decades, there was a more pragmatic approach to the choice of content. In the 2010 census decade, however, the UN recommendations again urged more uniformity in content.

Multilateral and Bilateral Exchanges of Information

An important and growing aspect of international cooperation in census taking is the exchange of relevant information and experience among groups of countries facing the common challenge of conducting a timely, reliable, and cost-effective population census to satisfy diverse user needs. At the global level, this work has led to the production of handbooks and other technical studies by the UN Statistics Division and the statistical services of the specialized agencies. Since 1945 the exchange of census information and experience has been of particular importance at the regional level under the auspices first of the Conference of European Statisticians, the Economic Commission for Europe, and the Organization of American States. Subsequently, the statistical services of other UN regional commissions and the European Union, as well as of a wide variety of subregional groups of countries, also provided important focal points for the collection, distillation, and dissemination of census experience.

Financial and Technical Assistance and Related Training

Other potential means for promoting, at least indirectly, international coordination in census taking are the various programs of technical assistance provided to countries that have planned and carried out population censuses since 1945. Many of the components of this assistance (particularly training, advisory services, and the provision of data processing equipment and services) have had a tendency to encourage the replication of the census methods and content of those providing the assistance. However, in terms of achieving a high degree of overall international coordination, the impact of such assistance has been diminished by the fact that most multilateral technical cooperation programs have valued a certain degree of diversity as a matter of principle. On the other hand, these programs are a prime example of effective international cooperation in the population census field.

More Knowledgeable and Better Trained Census Users

A factor that can be expected to have a growing impact on census outputs and content, and eventually census methods, is the growing body of reasonably knowledgeable census users in all parts of the world. Such users, while recognizing that a unitary census model of census operations may be irrelevant to their needs, have a growing interest in similar data, including internationally comparable data, which are aggregated or analyzed in similar ways and often for similar purposes. Thus, in the long run, these users may well be the most powerful advocates for improved international coordination of the concepts, classifications, and definitions used in population censuses.

See also *Censuses in other countries; Census of Puerto Rico; Content determination; International statistical system and its governance; IPUMS (Integrated Public Use Microdata Series).*

. . . . WILLIAM SELTZER

BIBLIOGRAPHY

Bierce, Ambrose. *The Devil's Dictionary*. Oxford, UK: Oxford University Press, 1999. First published 1911 by Doubleday.

Dynes, John Howard. "Development of the Plan for a Census of the World." *Publications of the American Statistical Association* 6, no. 48 (1899): 357–371.

Seltzer, William. "Statistical Standards and National, Regional and Global Requirements and Capabilities." In *American Statistical Association: 1996 Proceedings of the Section on Government Statistics*. Washington, D.C.: American Statistical Association, 1996.

United Nations, Department of Economic and Social Affairs, Statistics Division. *Principles and Recommendations for Population and Housing Censuses, Revision 2*. Statistical Papers Series M, No. 67/Rev. 2. New York: United Nations, 2008. Available at http://unstats.un.org/unsd/demographic/sources/census/docs/P&R_Rev2.pdf.

United Nations Statistical Commission. *Report on the Thirty-sixth Session (1–4 March 2005)*. Economic and Social Council, Official Records 2005, Supplement No. 4. New York: United Nations, 2005. Available at http://unstats.un.org/unsd/statcom/doc05/Report-English.pdf.

Westergaard, Harald. *Contributions to the History of Statistics*. London, UK: P. S. King and Son, 1932.

International Statistical System and Its Governance

Statistics was among the early fields in which international cooperation took an organized form. Adolphe Quetelet (1797–1874), a famous Belgian statistician, understood that the statistics of countries needed to be compared and that a key task of statisticians should be to make the data internationally comparable by introducing standard definitions and data collection techniques. The first International Statistical Congress (ISC) was in Brussels in 1853. At that meeting the ISC started to examine the establishment of an international classification of diseases, thus beginning the process of international standard classifications. The idea behind the ISC was to arrive at binding statistical procedures on the basis of majority decisions. This approach was not successful, and the ISC was discontinued. However, the underlying forces that argued for international comparability still existed, and in 1885 the International Statistical Institute (ISI) was established as an organization. It did not have an official status with countries as did the ISC, but it had the goal of giving useful advice to statisticians around the world and to governments. However, not until the United Nations (UN) was established after World War II did the international statistical system now in place begin to evolve. The remainder of this article discusses the membership and structure of this international system, its governance, and the benefits of such a system.

Membership and Structure

National Statistical Offices

Every country collects statistical information, often called official statistics, about itself. The nature and extent of the information that is collected, the confidentiality provisions, and the extent to which the information is disseminated vary from country to country. Typically, an agency of the government is charged with collecting official statistics, and to a greater or lesser degree these collections are supported by tax revenues.

Countries collect statistical data for three reasons. The first is to provide information to government decision makers to assist in the operation of the government. This information can help legislators craft new laws or can help government

employees perform the executive functions of the government. The second is to provide information on the state of the nation to the general public, including the business community as well as private citizens. Finally, statistical information is collected and disseminated by the government as a public good. This information, usually economic, needs to be provided by an agency that is viewed as trustworthy, and its value to one user does not diminish its value to another user.

As might be expected from the diversity of nations, there is a concomitant diversity of national statistical offices. Some statistical offices have fewer than 50 people on staff, while others employ thousands. The degree of centralization is also quite variable. Although no country has completely centralized its national data collection activities, the degree of centralization ranges widely. On one end of the scale, a chief statistician is directly responsible for the collection and production of the full range of official statistics in such areas as population, education, health, the economy, and the environment. At the other end are more- or less-coordinated decentralized systems in which individual agencies, including the central bank, are responsible for individual data sectors. Moreover, in many countries, different layers of government collect data that they may or may not report to the national statistical office. Data collection efforts by the business community and nongovernmental organizations are also ubiquitous. In most cases, these are considered to be outside the national statistical system, although these relationships are in flux. In some systems, those in charge of official statistics may be political appointees serving at the pleasure of the government, while in other systems, those responsible are senior civil servants, who usually enjoy long tenures.

International Statistical Agencies

Only since the end of World War II have the statistical offices of most international agencies become major players in the global system. These include agencies such as the Organisation for Economic Co-operation and Development (OECD), the International Monetary Fund (IMF), the World Bank, and the United Nations (UN). These agencies perform to a greater or lesser degree the following functions:

- They obtain data from around the world and publish them; such data are usually, but not always, produced by national statistical offices;
- They work with national statistical offices to develop international statistical standards, which are subscribed to on a voluntary basis;
- They provide technical advisory services to developing countries.

The statistics divisions of these organizations share a common discipline and a strong commitment to public service. Unlike the national statistical offices, they do not, however, have an official set of principles. The strongest bond among them comes from a shared commitment to develop and implement voluntary international standards, and one should not underestimate the degree to which these organizations can cooperate in the pursuit of common objectives. The joint publication of the Revised System of National Accounts—adopted by the UN Statistical Commission, the Statistical Office of the European Union (Eurostat), IMF, OECD, and the World Bank—is significant testimony to the common bonds linking statistical organizations across the world.

On the other hand, each international agency has an executive board of countries, which varies in membership. Even if the same country has a seat on more than one board, entirely different parts of the country's government usually represent it on the different boards. For example, the representative of the U.S. Department of the Treasury serves on the IMF executive board, while the U.S. Department of State is charged with responsibility for the UN. At times, the statistical divisions of international agencies are given inconsistent direction, weakening the ties among them.

Unlike the ISC, the current structure of the global statistical system is characterized by its voluntary nature. It is useful to think of this system as a network in which the nodes or members of the system include national statistical offices and the statistical offices of international agencies. These include the Regional Economic and Social Commissions of the UN, such specialized agencies of the UN system as the International Labour Organization (ILO) and the World Health Organization (WHO), statistical arms of central banks and agencies such as the African Development Bank and the Asian Development Bank, and Eurostat. Increasingly the statistical components of regional economic organizations, such as the South African Development Community, and of nongovernmental organizations are also members. In addition, professional organizations such as the ISI play an important role in the global statistical system. This diverse and inclusive membership is intentional, as befits a system in which both membership and compliance are generally voluntary and actions depend on consensus. Such consensus can only work if the global statistical system includes all the relevant actors. One significant exception to the voluntary principle is the supranational organization Eurostat. It has standards-setting and certain regulatory and compliance authority over its members. As the European Union evolves, the relationships between Eurostat and its members and between Eurostat and the other members of the global statistical community are also evolving. In addition, some international agencies require the reporting of statistical information, and encourage member countries to comply with international standards.

Governance

Because of its global role, the UN occupies a central place in the international statistical system. The UN Statistical Commission is the world's forum in which to identify global problems, to decide on priorities for standards development, and to adopt standards on a consensus basis. The Statistical Commission is one of the oldest technical bodies in the UN; it was created in 1946 in recognition of the importance of developing comparable statistical standards for use around the world. The attendees at the annual meeting of

the Statistical Commission are usually the chief technical representatives for statistics in their respective countries. The Statistical Commission also serves as a board of directors for the global system. Although it is comprised of only 24 official members, who are elected on a rotating basis, all member countries are invited to attend the annual meeting of the Commission, and more than 100 countries and international statistical agencies usually attend. Votes are not taken; actions are taken on a consensus basis. As with most bodies, those members who take the time to understand the problems of their colleagues, who work with them on solutions, who have a reputation for being thoughtful and cooperative, and who deliver quality work are usually the most influential. Therefore, a country's size is not the most important factor in determining its influence on the Commission. Often, countries with relatively small populations have great influence in developing international standards.

Benefits

Despite differences in cultures, forms of government, languages, and legal traditions among the members, powerful forces prevent the international statistical system from flying apart. The first is that statistics is an academic discipline, and most of those involved in the global system have a grounding in a common curriculum of mathematics, statistics, demography, and/or economics. Statisticians have developed their own common language, which often transcends political systems and levels of development and unites people from different countries and cultures.

Perhaps even more important, however, is the common ethos that exists among members. In the final analysis, the defining test of the existence of a global network is a shared belief in a set of common attitudes and characteristics. Given the diversity of political, social, and cultural values among the member states of the UN, it is remarkable that a set of principles exists which codifies a shared ethos defining and binding together official statisticians regardless of where they are. Such a set of principles was adopted by the UN Statistical Commission on April 14, 1994. In developing and affirming these principles, the national statistical offices recognized that the public will trust official statistics only if the statistical agencies themselves adhere to a set of fundamental principles which respects the rights of citizens. The Commission affirmed that the quality of official statistics depends largely on the cooperation of citizens, enterprises, and other respondents in providing appropriate and reliable data needed for statistical compilations and on cooperation between users and producers of statistics to meet users' needs. The ten principles to which the member states agreed are as follows:

1. Official statistics provide an indispensable element in the information system of a democratic society, serving the Government, the economy and the public with data about the economic, demographic, social and environmental situation. To this end, official statistics that meet the test of practical utility are to be

compiled and made available on an impartial basis by official statistical agencies to honor citizens' entitlement to public information.

2. To retain trust in official statistics, the statistical agencies need to decide according to strictly professional considerations, including scientific principles and professional ethics, on the methods and procedures for the collection, processing, storage and presentation of statistical data.

3. To facilitate a correct interpretation of the data, the statistical agencies are to present information according to scientific standards on the sources, methods and procedures of the statistics.

4. The statistical agencies are entitled to comment on erroneous interpretation and misuse of statistics.

5. Data for statistical purposes may be drawn from all types of sources, be they statistical surveys or administrative records. Statistical agencies are to choose the source with regard to quality, timeliness, costs and the burden on respondents.

6. Individual data collected by statistical agencies for statistical compilation, whether they refer to natural or legal persons, are to be strictly confidential and used exclusively for statistical purposes.

7. The laws, regulations and measures under which the statistical systems operate are to be made public.

8. Coordination among statistical agencies within countries is essential to achieve consistency and efficiency in the statistical system.

9. The use by statistical agencies in each country of international concepts, classifications and methods promotes the consistency and efficiency of statistical systems at all official levels.

10. Bilateral and multilateral cooperation in statistics contributes to the improvement of systems of official statistics in all countries.

The existence of a set of fundamental principles benefits all members. Each country can use such principles as necessary to argue, for example, for the confidentiality of statistical data and for the professional independence of the national statistical office. The global statistical system serves to reinforce the effectiveness of all the members. The shared language of mathematics and dependence on the related academic disciplines enables all the members to learn from one another.

In addition to these benefits, there are other pragmatic reasons for the existence of a global statistical system. Wallman and Evinger (2008) have described the following motivations for countries to adopt international statistical standards:

- Countries may find it more efficient to use existing international standards than to develop their own national standards for official statistics.

- In some countries, implementation of internationally accepted statistical standards may be an instrument with which to shield statistical activities from political interference and thus to maintain the integrity and strengthen the credibility of the statistical process.

- Adoption of international standards can facilitate comparisons of information for smaller geopolitical units, such as provinces or states.

- Member countries of some international organizations, such as the IMF, are required to report a range of data and are encouraged to comply with international frameworks and classifications.

- International standards provide a framework for comparing and assessing a country's situation vis-à-vis other countries; international standards have fostered such intercountry comparisons by facilitating the organization of international databases.

Although these shared principles foster strong bonds among national statistical offices, there are still differences in how these offices operate. For example, in the implementation of the System of National Accounts, at one end of the spectrum are those countries whose resources and sophisticated techniques permit the compilation of extended accounts (including, for example, institutional sector accounts describing complex financial transactions). At the other end are those countries that have to focus on such basic macroeconomic aggregates as the calculation of gross national income, national disposable income, national savings, and net lending and borrowing. These differences exist not only in national accounts but also in many other areas, including the application of survey methodology. One of the major challenges faced by the global system is the task of bringing the capacities of national statistical offices closer to one another and ensuring that the benefits of the global statistical system are shared equally.

See also *Confidentiality; Federal statistical system oversight and policy: intersection of OMB and the decennial census.*

. . . .   HERMANN HABERMANN

BIBLIOGRAPHY

Kenessey, Zoltan. "International Statistical Organization." In *The Future of Statistics: An International Perspective*, ed. Zoltan Kenessey, 113–116. Voorburg, Netherlands: International Statistical Institute, 1994.

United Nations Economic Commission for Europe. ECE–World Bank Seminar on the Application of the Fundamental Principles of Official Statistics. Almaty, Kazakhstan, April 28–29, 2003.

United Nations Economic and Social Council. *Implementation of the Fundamental Principles of Official Statistics: Report of the Secretary-General.* E/CN.3/2004/21. New York: United Nations, 2003. Available at http://unstats.un.org/unsd/statcom/doc04/2004-21e.pdf.

United Nations Statistical Commission and Economic Commission for Europe. Resolution on fundamental principles of official statistics in the Economic Commission for Europe (draft). *Report of the Thirty-Ninth Plenary Session,* June 17–21, 1991.

United Nations Statistics Division. *Fundamental Principles of Official Statistics.* Adopted in the Special Session of April 11–15, 1994. http://unstats.un.org/unsd/methods/statorg/FP-English.htm.

Wallman, Katherine K., and Suzann K. Evinger. "International Standards for Compilation of Statistics: The Gap between Standards Adoption and Standards Implementation. *Statistical Journal of the IAOS* 25, nos. 1–2 (2008): 3–10.

Internet Data Collection

The 2000 census in the United States was among the first in the world to include an option to respond via the Internet. Other early adopters in the 2000 round of censuses worldwide included Singapore (2000), Spain (2001), and Switzerland (2001). In subsequent years, other population censuses adopted online response—notably Canada's 2006 census, which yielded an Internet response rate of close to 20 percent—while others began planning to implement Internet response in the 2010 round of censuses. However, in 2006, although Internet use was growing, the U.S. Census Bureau ruled out online response as an option for the census in 2010. The Census Bureau fielded a major test of online response in the American Community Survey (ACS) in 2011 (an earlier test of online response in the ACS was conducted in 2000–2001), and it has suggested that online response will be an option in 2020.

The 2000 Census Online Response Option

The Internet response option in the 2000 census came together very swiftly, without the benefit of prior large-scale testing. Online response was considered for the 1998 dress rehearsal but ultimately abandoned "due to security concerns"; however, the option was revived in late 1998 by a U.S. Department of Commerce directive (Whitworth 2002, 1). Due to insufficient time, online response was only offered for the English-language version of the 2000 census short-form questionnaire. Programming of the form was kept as simple as possible for compatibility with different Web browsers. Consequently, the online form was essentially presented as a single screen page rather than walking respondents through separate questions on different Web pages. Hence, real-time editing and confirmation steps were not used, nor were skip patterns used to move respondents through the questionnaire.

In part because of the late development of the option and in part to keep the Internet workload under control, the Internet response option was not publicized. To access the electronic questionnaire, respondents needed to have in hand the paper questionnaire that they had received in the mail. Following a link from the main census Web page, they were asked to enter the 22-digit census ID printed on the paper form's label (thus ensuring a linkage to a specific mailing address). If the 22-digit ID was confirmed as valid, then the questionnaire appeared onscreen.

During the period of availability—March 3 to April 18, 2000—89,123 submissions of census ID numbers were made on the Web site. Of these, 74,197 were valid census IDs, and 66,163 led to questionnaire data being retained for processing. That 16.7 percent of the overall Internet responses were failures (invalid IDs)—close to the roughly one-in-six coverage of the census long-form sample—suggests that many of these failures might have been attempts to complete the long form online. After final processing, 63,053 households representing 169,257 persons were included in the census through the Internet form.

The Census Bureau's formal evaluation of the Internet response option deemed it "an operational success." Moreover, the evaluator pushed for further research, arguing that this "research focus not necessarily on how to implement the form itself, but how to promulgate the Internet form as an option and convince the public that there is sufficient data security" (Whitworth 2002, 17).

Experimentation and Testing

Internet response was also included as part of the Response Mode and Incentive Experiment (RMIE) conducted concurrently with the 2000 census. The RMIE compared samples of households replying via paper, an interactive voice response (IVR) system (a fully automated telephone interview), or the Internet. The "incentive" portion tested whether the offer of a 30-minute telephone calling card boosted the response rates for the different modes. Summarizing the experiment, Caspar and Shaw (2003) noted low usage of the Internet option with or without the incentive but nonetheless argued in favor of further work on an online response option. Even under "conservative assumptions," they suggested that the Census Bureau "might save between one and six million dollars in postage costs alone if between three percent and 15 percent of the sample uses the web rather than the mail survey," making Internet response "cost-effective even if a relatively small proportion of respondents [use] it" (25).

Internet response was also included in the mailout-only National Census Tests in 2003 and 2005, with no field follow-up component. The 2003 test included 16 panels, 7 of which tested revisions of the census questions on race and Hispanic origin and 8 of which included different packages of response modes and contact strategies (for example, sending a replacement questionnaire or a telephone reminder call, soliciting responses by telephone, or soliciting responses via the Internet). The Census Bureau concluded that offering the option of responding by telephone or the Internet along with the mailout of a paper questionnaire neither increased nor decreased the response rate. However, attempts to "force" respondents to use either of the electronic response modes by not including a paper questionnaire resulted in lower response rates. In terms of data quality, item nonresponse rates were significantly lower for the Internet responses than for paper returns for almost all items. The 2005 test was similar in structure and included interface improvements to both the telephone and Internet response options. The 2005 test performed comparably to the options used in 2003 and did not yield major gains in new response relative to paper questionnaires.

Decision for 2010

Very early signals on direction for the 2010 census suggested a strong role for the Internet. An initial planning framework for the 2010 census listed "expanded use of Internet and telephone systems . . . to make it easier for people to complete their questionnaire" (Angueira 2003, 3) among the key improvements for the next census. The strategy document continued: "Our expectation is that we can increase the response rate even further by developing and implementing the optimal mix of contacts and response options. . . . We can significantly increase the number of forms that move directly into data capture without needing to be scanned in a data capture center" (Angueira 2003, 5–6). Indeed, the initial scope of work for the Census Bureau's Decennial Response Integrated System (DRIS) for 2010—awarded to Lockheed Martin in October 2005—included requirements to facilitate questionnaire assistance by Internet or telephone and to permit census response (to both the 2008 dress rehearsal and the 2010 census form) by all three modes of telephone, Internet, and paper.

However, the results of the 2003 and 2005 tests, which did not show a response advantage for the Internet—combined with concern over the inherent risks and lack of guaranteed major cost savings—led the Census Bureau to reverse course. The bureau's decision not to pursue online enumeration was formalized in a July 2006 decision memorandum. Earlier, on June 6, census director Louis Kincannon testified to a U.S. Senate subcommittee that "our research, as well as our own experience and knowledge of the experiences of other countries," led the bureau to conclude that "we do not believe Internet data collection would significantly improve the overall response rate or reduce field data collection" (5). Kincannon added that the bureau had concluded from its consultations with "the statistical offices of Australia, Canada, and New Zealand"—all of which had included Internet response in their most recent censuses—that "it was not possible [for those countries] to accurately anticipate the response rate" (5) and accordingly reduce the overall cost of paper data-capture operations. Ultimately, the bureau judged Internet response to be too risky: "At this point in the decade, efforts to develop an Internet response option would divert attention and resources from tested and planned improvements such as the second mailing" (6).

In 2007 a Census Bureau-commissioned report from the MITRE Corporation summarized the major risks seen by the bureau. Most fundamental was the notion that something could go awry with the Internet option, such as a widely publicized hacking of the census site or establishment of a "phishing" site purporting to be the census. This could cause voluntary response to the census to decline, strain nonresponse follow-up (NRFU) capabilities, and raise the overall cost of the census. MITRE also noted that the bureau's DRIS contractor had found that it could not provide an Internet response facility in time for testing in the 2008 dress rehearsal, meaning it would have to go into the main 2010 census without a large-scale test.

The Census Bureau reiterated its opposition to online enumeration in 2010 in its responses to a U.S. Department of Commerce, Office of Inspector General assessment of the bureau's plans for group quarters enumeration. Noting that only 719 college student census report forms were returned in the part of the 2006 Census Test in Travis County, Texas—an area where about 7,000 college students should be found—the inspector general recommended online enumeration as a means of appealing to the Internet-savvy college generation. However, the Census Bureau's reaction to the draft recommendation suggested that it had no plans to change direction.

Toward the 2020 Census

In October 2009, Census Bureau Director Robert Groves announced the addition of some new research programs to the planned 2010 Census Program of Experiments and Evaluations. Among these was a small-scale Internet measurement reinterview survey, asking the basic census questions via a Web-based instrument to discern the differences between answers obtained via the Internet and those obtained via a paper questionnaire. Subsequent public statements from the Census Bureau on the shape of the 2020 census have implied that consideration of online response is inevitable over the next decade, though whether and to what extent the Internet will be pushed as a response option remains unclear.

Other nations that, like the United States, still conduct a traditional census (as opposed to reliance on a population register or other methods) have aggressively pursued online response. Notably, the Canadian 2011 census was designed to build on what Statistics Canada views as a successful implementation of online response in 2006. Most Canadian households (approximately 60 percent) did not receive a paper questionnaire as their first contact with the census. Instead, they received a letter with an access code and instructions for completing the census online (along with contact information to request a paper questionnaire, if desired). A reminder letter urged nonresponding households in that group to reply via the Internet, with a paper questionnaire only being mailed if there was no response to the reminder letter. Through its sequencing of "waves" of response, Statistics Canada boosted overall response via the Internet to well over 40 percent, according to preliminary estimates.

See also *Data capture; Enumeration: field procedures; Enumeration: group quarters.*

. . . .   DANIEL L. CORK

BIBLIOGRAPHY

Angueira, Teresa. "Re-engineering the Decennial Census: The Baseline Design for 2010." 2010 Census Planning Memoranda Series, Number 14, Version 1.5. Washington, D.C.: U.S. Census Bureau, 2003. Available at http://www.census.gov/procur/www/fdca/library/2010-planning/2010%20Census%20Business%20Architecture%20-%20Entire.pdf, pp. 94–102.

Caspar, R., and K. A. Shaw. *Synthesis of Results from the Response Mode and Incentive Experiment: Final Report.* Census 2000 Testing, Experimentation, and Evaluation Program. Washington, D.C.: U.S. Bureau of the Census, 2003. Available at http://websm.org/uploadi/editor/1139406277RMIE_Synthesis.pdf.

Griffin, D. H., D. P. Fischer, and M. T. Morgan, U.S. Bureau of the Census. "Testing an Internet Response Option for the American Community Survey." Paper presented at the annual conference of the American Association for Public Opinion Research, Montreal, Quebec, Canada, May 17–20, 2001. Available at www.census.gov/acs/www/Downloads/library/2001/2001_Griffin_01.pdf.

Kincannon, C. L. "The 2010 Decennial Census Program." Testimony before the Subcommittee on Federal Financial Management, Government Information and International Security Committee on Homeland

Security and Governmental Affairs, U.S. Senate, June 6, 2006. Available at http://hsgac.senate.gov/public/_files/060606Kincannon.pdf.

National Research Council. "Appendix B: Internet Response Options in Selected Population Censuses." In *Experimentation and Evaluation Plans for the 2010 Census: Interim Report*, Panel on the Design of the 2010 Census Program of Evaluations and Experiments, Lawrence D. Brown, Michael L. Cohen, and Daniel L. Cork, eds., 75–92. Committee on National Statistics, Washington, D.C.: The National Academies Press, 2008. Available at http://www.nap.edu/catalog.php?record_id=12080.

National Research Council. *Envisioning the 2020 Census.* Panel on the Design of the 2010 Census Program of Evaluations and Experiments, Lawrence D. Brown, Michael L. Cohen, Daniel L. Cork, and Constance F. Citro, eds. Committee on National Statistics, Washington, D.C.: The National Academies Press, 2010. Available at http://www.nap.edu/catalog.php?record_id=12865.

Whitworth, E. *Internet Data Collection: Final Report.* Census 2000 Evaluation A.2.b. Washington, D.C.: U.S. Government Printing Office, 2002. Available at http://www.census.gov/pred/www/rpts/A.2.b.pdf.

IPUMS (Integrated Public Use Microdata Series)

IPUMS is an acronym for Integrated Public Use Microdata Series, a coherent individual-level Web database consisting of 496 million individuals drawn from 280 national censuses and surveys of 61 countries in the period from 1800 to the present. It is accessed at www.ipums.org. By putting all samples in a common format, imposing consistent variable coding, and carefully documenting changes in variables over time, IPUMS allows comparative studies and analyses of historical change. IPUMS includes information about both individuals and households in a hierarchical structure so researchers can construct new variables based on information from multiple household members. Because it is microdata as opposed to summary aggregate data, IPUMS allows researchers to create tabulations tailored to particular research questions and to carry out individual-level multivariate analyses. Among key research areas are economic development, poverty and inequality, industrial and occupational structures, household and family composition, the household economy, female labor force participation, employment patterns, population growth, urbanization, internal migration, immigration, nuptiality, fertility, and education.

IPUMS provides comprehensive documentation, including detailed analyses of the comparability of every variable across all censuses. Data and documentation are distributed through an online data-access system at www.ipums.org, which provides powerful extraction and search capabilities to allow easy access to both metadata and microdata. The IPUMS project also supports an online data analysis system on its Web site. The project is funded by the National Science Foundation and the National Institutes of Health, so all data and documentation are available to researchers without cost.

Origins and Development

IPUMS began as an integrated series of U.S. census microdata, and the U.S. data remain the most intensively used component of the database. IPUMS currently describes the characteristics of 170 million Americans. It includes data from every surviving decennial census since 1850, combining high-precision historical census samples with microdata produced by the Census Bureau since 1960. The only census year missing from the series is 1890, whose data were destroyed by fire. For 1880, 1900, and 1970 onward, currently available samples include at least 6 percent of the population, and all census years cover at least 1 percent of the population. Projects currently underway are expanding the existing samples for 1850, 1930, and 1960.

In 2010 the scope of the U.S. census was sharply reduced. The Census Bureau eliminated the detailed long-form census questionnaire, and the census now includes a few basic inquiries on age, sex, race, and the relationship of each person to the householder. Information about such topics as income, education, housing, migration, and disability is instead provided by the American Community Survey (ACS). With virtually the same questions as the Census 2000 long-form questionnaire, the ACS provides data on about 2.9 million households and 20,000 group-quarters facilities each year. The ACS has released an annual Public Use Microdata File since 2000, and IPUMS has incorporated these samples. For most purposes, ACS samples are closely comparable to those from censuses, so the shift from census to surveys introduces only minor discontinuities into the data series. For researchers needing a longer series of annual data, IPUMS also provides a coherent version of the Current Population Survey (CPS), the widely used survey produced by the U.S. Bureau of Labor Statistics (BLS). CPS microdata are available for every year since 1962. They cover virtually all the subject areas in the decennial census and the ACS but provide much greater detail in certain areas, such as work status, but less detail on smaller geographic areas.

The U.S. component of IPUMS is designed to encourage analyses that incorporate multiple census years to study change over time. The census has always contained certain core questions that are generally comparable over the entire time span of the database. Other questions have come and gone. Table 1 describes many of the subject areas covered by the U.S. census since 1850 (these topics usually correspond to multiple variables in the database). In general, the IPUMS samples include all the census questions available in each year, but for the period from 1940 onward, some detail is suppressed in order to preserve respondent confidentiality. In particular, geographic detail is far superior in the pre-1940 samples. In fact, the samples for the period prior to 1940 include the names and addresses of the respondents. On the other hand, topics such as income, educational attainment, and migration have only been covered by the census for the last six decades of the twentieth century. All IPUMS samples also include a common set of constructed variables to allow easy data manipulation. Most important among these is a set of family interrelationship variables, which have proven broadly useful in the construction of consistent family composition and own-child fertility measures.

IPUMS across the Globe

Since 2000 IPUMS has added microdata from around the world. Large quantities of machine-readable microdata survive from census enumerations of the past five decades, but few files are available to researchers and most are at risk of becoming unreadable. The first goals of the IPUMS-International project are to preserve machine-readable census

Table 1. Availability of Select IPUMS-USA Subject Areas, 1850–2000*

	1850	1860	1870	1880	1900	1910	1920	1930	1940	1950	1960	1970	1980	1990	2000
Household Record															
State	X	X	X	X	X	X	X	X	X	X	X	X	X	X	X
County	X	X	X	X	X	X	X	X	.	.	.	.	.	.	.
County group/microdata area	.	.	.	.	.	.	.	.	.	.	P	X	X	X	X
State economic area	X	X	X	X	X	X	X	X	X	X	P	.	.	.	.
Metropolitan area	X	X	X	X	X	X	X	X	X	X	.	X	X	X	X
City	X	X	X	X	X	X	X	X	X	X	.	.	X	X	X
Size of place	X	X	X	X	X	X	X	X	X	X	.	.	X	X	X
Urban/rural status	X	X	X	X	X	X	X	.	.	.	X	X	X	X	X
Farm	X	X	X	X	X	X	X	X	X	X	X	X	X	X	X
Ownership of dwelling	.	.	.	.	X	X	X	X	.	.	X	X	X	X	X
Mortgage status	.	.	.	.	X	X	X	.	.	.	.	.	X	X	X
Value of house or property	.	.	.	.	.	.	.	X	X	X	X	X	X	X	X
Monthly rent	.	.	.	.	.	.	.	X	X	X	X	X	X	X	X
Total family income	.	.	.	.	.	.	.	.	X	X	X	X	X	X	X
Person Record															
Relationship to household head	.	.	.	X	X	X	X	X	X	X	X	X	X	X	X
Age	X	X	X	X	X	X	X	X	X	X	X	X	X	X	X
Sex	X	X	X	X	X	X	X	X	X	X	X	X	X	X	X
Race	X	X	X	X	X	X	X	X	X	X	X	X	X	X	X
Marital status	.	.	.	X	X	X	X	X	X	X	X	X	X	X	X
Age at first marriage	.	.	.	.	.	.	.	X	.	X	X	X	X	.	.
Duration of marriage	.	.	.	.	X	X	.	.	X	.	.	.	.	.	.
Times married	.	.	.	.	X	X	.	.	X	X	X	X	.	.	.
Children ever born	.	.	.	.	X	X	.	.	X	X	X	X	X	X	.
Birthplace	X	X	X	X	X	X	X	X	X	X	X	X	X	X	X
Parents' birthplaces	.	.	.	X	X	X	X	X	X	X	X	X	.	.	.
Ancestry	.	.	.	.	.	.	.	.	.	.	.	.	X	X	X
Years in the United States	.	.	.	.	X	X	X	X	X	.	.	X	X	.	X
Mother tongue	.	.	.	.	X	X	X	X	X	.	X	X	.	.	.
Language spoken	.	.	.	.	X	X	X	X	.	.	.	.	X	X	X
School attendance	X	X	X	X	X	X	X	X	X	X	X	X	X	X	X
Educational attainment	.	.	.	.	.	.	.	.	X	X	X	X	X	X	X
Literacy	X	X	X	X	X	X	X	X	.	.	.	.	.	.	.
Employment status	.	.	.	.	.	X	.	X	X	X	X	X	X	X	X
Occupation	X	X	X	X	X	X	X	X	X	X	X	X	X	X	X
Industry	.	.	.	.	.	X	X	X	X	X	X	X	X	X	X
Class of worker	.	.	.	.	.	X	X	X	X	X	X	X	X	X	X
Weeks worked last year	.	.	.	.	.	.	.	.	X	X	X	X	X	X	X
Weeks unemployed	.	.	.	X	X	X	.	.	X	X	.	.	.	.	.
Total personal income	.	.	.	.	.	.	.	.	.	X	X	X	X	X	X
Wage and salary income	.	.	.	.	.	.	.	.	X	X	X	X	X	X	X
Value of personal or real estate	X	X	X	.	.	.	.	.	.	.	.	.	.	.	.
Migration status	.	.	.	.	.	.	.	.	X	X	X	X	X	X	X
Veteran status	.	.	.	.	.	X	.	X	X	X	X	X	X	X	X
Surname similarity code	X	X	X	X	X	X	X	X	X	X	.	.	.	.	.
Name	X	X	X	X	X	X	X	X	.	.	.	.	.	.	.

NOTE: X = available in that census year; P = available in a future data release.

SOURCE: "Variable Availability" in Steven Ruggles, J. Trent Alexander, Katie Genadek, Ronald Goeken, Matthew B. Schroeder, and Matthew Sobek. *Integrated Public Use Microdata Series: Version 5.0* [Machine-readable database]. Minneapolis: University of Minnesota, 2010. http://usa.ipums.org/usa-action/variableAvailability. do?display=Household#h-tech.

Table 2. Availability of International Microdata Samples in IPUMS, September 2010

Argentina	1970·1980·1991·2001	Mali	1987·1998
Armenia	2001	Mexico	1960·1970·1990·1995·2000·2005
Austria	1971·1981·1991·2001	Mongolia	1989·2000
Belarus	1999	Nepal	2001
Bolivia	1976·1992·2001	Netherlands	1960·1971·2001
Brazil	1960·1970·1980·1991·2000	Norway	1865·1875·1900
Cambodia	1998	Pakistan	1973·1981·1998
Canada	1871·1881·1891·1971·1981·1991·2001	Palestine	1997
Chile	1960·1970·1982·1992·2002	Panama	1960·1970·1980·1990·2000
China	1982·1990	Peru	1993·2007
Colombia	1964·1973·1985·1993·2005	Philippines	1990·1995·2000
Costa Rica	1963·1973·1984·2000	Portugal	1981·1991·2001
Cuba	2002	Puerto Rico	1970·1980·1990·2000·2005
Ecuador	1962·1974·1982·1990·2001	Romania	1977·1992·2002
Egypt	1996	Rwanda	1991·2002
France	1962·1968·1975·1982·1990·1999	Saint Lucia	1980·1991
Ghana	2000	Senegal	1988·2002
Greece	1971·1981·1991·2001	Slovenia	2002
Guinea	1983·1996	South Africa	1996·2001·2007
Hungary	1970·1980·1990·2001	Spain	1981·1991·2001
India	1983·1987·1993·1999·2004	Sweden	1900
Iraq	1997	Switzerland	1970·1980·1990·2000
Israel	1972·1983·1995	Tanzania	1988·2002
Italy	2001	Thailand	1970·1980·1990·2000
Jordan	2004	Uganda	1991·2002
Kenya	1989·1999	United Kingdom	1851·1881·1991·2001
Kyrgyz Republic	1999	Venezuela	1971·1981·1990·2001
Malaysia	1970·1980·1991·2000	Vietnam	1989·1999

SOURCE: "IPUMS Sample Information" in Steven Ruggles, J. Trent Alexander, Katie Genadek, Ronald Goeken, Matthew B. Schroeder, and Matthew Sobek. *Integrated Public Use Microdata Series: Version 5.0* [Machine-readable database]. Minneapolis: University of Minnesota, 2010. https://international.ipums.org/international/samples.shtml.

microdata files wherever possible and to obtain permission to disseminate anonymous samples of the data to researchers. Then—just as in the original IPUMS project—the Minnesota Population Center (MPC) converts the data into a consistent format, supplies comprehensive documentation, and makes microdata and documentation available through a Web-based data dissemination system.

The national statistical agencies of over 90 countries have designated IPUMS to preserve, integrate, and disseminate their census microdata, and the project has acquired a massive collection of hundreds of national censuses and surveys spanning the past five decades. Through the North Atlantic Population Project, the project has also teamed with national archives and historical research centers of 13 countries to develop historical census microdata, often capitalizing on electronic census transcriptions originally digitized for genealogical analysis. As of 2010, IPUMS had released microdata on 326 million persons outside the United States drawn from 165 censuses and surveys of 59 countries. The MPC estimates that the size of the database will double over the next five years. Table 2 summarizes current and planned IPUMS-International data releases. The project began releasing data in 2003. Current information on the IPUMS-International release schedule is available at www.ipums.org.

See also *American Community Survey: data products; PUMS (Public Use Microdata Samples).*

. . . .   STEVEN RUGGLES

BIBLIOGRAPHY

Goeken, R., C. Nguyen, S. Ruggles, and W. L. Sargent. "The 1880 U. S. Population Database." *Historical Methods* 36, no. 1 (2003): 27–34. Available at http://users.pop.umn.edu/~ruggles/1880.pdf.

Minnesota Population Center, IPUMS USA. IPUMS Documentation: User's Guide. http://usa.ipums.org/usa/doc.shtml.

Languages Spoken

Questions about languages spoken and English-language ability have been a part of decennial census data collections for over 100 years. Over time, the questions asked have changed as data needs and interests have evolved. Beginning with the 1890 census, individuals were asked if they could speak English and, if not, the "language or dialect spoken." Associated with these early questions were items about English literacy—that is, the ability to read and write in English.

Language Questions: 1910–1970

Starting with the 1910 census, the focus changed to the concept of "mother tongue," the language spoken in one's home while growing up or before coming to the United States. For several censuses (1910–1940), questions about the use of non-English languages were asked only of the foreign-born, and the specific questions were slightly different in each implementation. In 1950 language data were not collected for the general population; American Indians were asked a series of six yes/no questions about English and other language ability. The 1960 census saw a return to the mother tongue concept (for foreign-born persons only), with a variant of this item also asked in 1970.

Redefining Language Data: 1980

After many decades of constantly shifting language items, the 1980 census marked the emergence of the language questions now in use. These items represented a marked change from the mother tongue concept. Instead of focusing on the language of the parents or the language spoken while growing up, this new three-part question attempted to address emerging policy concerns about the English-language ability of a nation with a growing immigrant population.

The questions first implemented in the 1980 census asked:

(1) Does this person speak a language other than English at home? [Yes/No]
(2) What is this language? [This is a write-in response.]
(3) How well does this person speak English? [Very Well, Well, Not Well, Not at All]

In effect, the question gets to three different aspects of language use: use of a non-English language in a daily (home) context; for those who reported speaking a non-English language at home, the actual language spoken; and a self-reported assessment about English-language ability.

Write-in responses to the second part of the question are assigned values by an automated coding routine (with expert resolution of entries that cannot be directly coded), which was first developed for the 1970 census and has been continually improved since then. Currently, there are about 120,000 entries in the autocoder, many of which deal with spelling variations. The Census Bureau codes these write-in entries into 382 distinct codes, about one-half of which are American Indian and Alaska Native languages.

The questions introduced in 1980 were a result of testing a variety of alternatives, some of which were examined in the 1976 National Content Test. Variants focused on language use in a mixture of locales, different types of self-assessment, and a range of functional tasks (for example, reading a newspaper or writing a postcard—both in English or the other reported language).

Uses of the Data

These new questions were put to almost immediate use in the early 1980s when the Census Bureau had to meet its legislative responsibility to provide coverage determinations for Section 203(c) of the Voting Rights Act (1965). This section of the law allows for the provision of bilingual ballots in areas with sufficient numbers of persons of a single "language minority." Up to this point in time, language minorities were chosen on the basis of the race question, as the law specified. In reauthorizing the law, the bureau was instructed to make use of the new questions if possible to better target areas with special language needs.

Coincidentally, around this time the Census Bureau was conducting the English Language Proficiency Survey (ELPS) for the U.S. Department of Education. This survey consisted of a series of age-graded literacy tests to determine English-language ability in daily tasks, such as reading signs, following instructions, and other routine activities. Included in the survey was the same three-part language question used in the 1980 census. Analysis of the data for adults on the relationship between failing the test and self-reported English-speaking ability showed that the failure rate for persons reporting to speak English "Very Well" was about the same as that of native English speakers, while the failure rates for persons in the other three categories ("Well," "Not Well," and "Not at All") were significantly higher. With these findings, the bureau suggested that language minority groups deemed to have difficulties speaking English be defined as those persons who reported that they spoke a language other than English at home and who reported an English-speaking ability of less than "very well." Despite a growing Hispanic population in the United States, using these new guidelines, the 1982 determinations for the Section 203(c) targeted 200 groups in 197 counties, as compared to 402 groups in 384 counties in the determinations of 1975.

Subsequent reauthorization of the Voting Rights Act supported continued use of the "English-ability" component of the question using the 1990 and 2000 census results. As often happens when there are limited sources of data on a topic, other organizations began to use the "less than very well" criterion as a means of identifying limited English proficient (LEP) populations for a wide variety of policy and program needs, particularly at small geographic levels. Reanalysis of the English-ability item using data from the 1986 National Content Test has reinforced the utility of this question as a useful indicator of English-language ability.

Language Data in the ACS

With the transition to the American Community Survey (ACS), the language question has been moved along with all other long-form data collection items to this ongoing national survey. Language questions are asked of all persons ages five and over. A recent Census Bureau report using data from the 2007 ACS showed that over 55 million persons reported speaking a language other than English at home, an increase of 140 percent from the 1980 census numbers. While Spanish is the dominant non-English language reported (34.5 of 55 million), 6 other languages were reported by more than a million people. These languages are Chinese (2.5 million), French (2 million), Tagalog (1.5 million), Vietnamese (1.2 million), German (1.1 million), and Korean (1.1 million). About 44 percent of these 55 million speakers of other languages also reported that they spoke English less than "very well." The data also demonstrated a highly variable spread of languages spoken across the country; for example, 71 percent of Armenian speakers are in the Los Angeles metropolitan area, and 25 percent of the Hmong speakers are in metropolitan Minneapolis.

Language data in the census data collections have gone from being indicators of national origin and background to more applied indicators of language diversity and English-language needs. As issues surrounding language continue to evolve and data needs change, it is quite possible that, once again, census questions may need to change as well.

See also *Long form.*

. . . . ROBERT A. KOMINSKI

BIBLIOGRAPHY

Congressional Record. Vol. 128, June 18, 1982, pp. H3840, S7104.

Kominski, Robert A. "Final Report: Documentation of Voting Rights Act Determinations." Unpublished internal memorandum to Paul Siegel, U.S. Bureau of the Census, Washington, D.C., February 4, 1985.

————. "How Good Is 'How Well'? An Examination of the Census English-Speaking Ability Question." Paper presented at the 1989 Annual Meeting of the American Statistical Association, Washington, D.C., August 6–11, 1989. Available at www.census.gov/population/socdemo/language/ASApaper1989.pdf.

Shin, Hyon B., and Robert A. Kominski. *Language Use in the United States: 2007.* American Community Survey Reports, no. ACS-12. Washington, D.C.: U.S. Government Printing Office, 2010. Available at www.census.gov/population/www/socdemo/language/ACS-12.pdf.

Litigation and the Census

Litigation related to census taking methods and procedures has generally fallen into five categories: (1) prosecutions of householders for refusing to respond to census questions; (2) prosecutions of enumerators or census employees for failing to do their jobs; (3) challenges to or defenses of the confidentiality of information on the individual census forms; (4) challenges to the Census Bureau to remedy the differential undercount of subgroups of the population; and (5) challenges to the sampling procedures proposed for taking the census. The suits, which span censuses conducted from 1790 (the year of the first count) to the present, illustrate the complexities and ambiguities in census taking. They also provide an evolving set of standards for determining the count's accuracy and precision and for assessing the relative responsibilities of the public and the government for conducting the census.

Taking the census has always required residents to cooperate with the census-taker and provide the requested information. Today, the federal government relies on households to respond voluntarily and to return the census forms they receive in the mail. But Congress determined at the outset of the republic that responding would be mandatory for all residents and that individuals who refused to comply would be subject to legal penalties. The Act of March 1, 1790 (first census law) contained such a penalty, permitting the assistant U.S. marshal to sue a household head in federal court for $20 if the individual refused to provide information. Several suits were filed in South Carolina under this provision. Such prosecutions have been extremely rare over the centuries. The penalty in 2010 for willfully refusing to fill out the census form was $100. The penalty for giving false information was $500, though Title 18 of the United States Code Sections 3571 and 3559 in effect amend Title 13 of the United States Code Section 221; they change the fine for anyone over age 18 who refuses or willfully neglects to complete the questionnaire or answer questions posed by census-takers from a fine of "not more than $100" to "not more than $5,000."

Similarly, census enumerators who violated their oaths and failed to do their jobs properly could also be legally prosecuted. In 1790 assistant U.S. marshals were fined $200 for not completing their work competently and on time. The current census statutory language (Title 13) levies a fine of up to $2,000 and imposes a sentence of five years in jail on enumerators who neglect their duties or submit false information. Among those who have been prosecuted and convicted under these provisions are the enumerators who in 1910 systematically padded the population of Tacoma, Washington, by over 35 percent.

Another major area of litigation affecting the census focuses on the confidentiality of the answers reported on census forms. In the nineteenth century, census forms were considered open records. They were either posted at county courthouses for correction or were provided, in whole or in part, to local governments for reference and preservation. Beginning in the late nineteenth century, as census officials became increasingly concerned about privacy, they sought to clarify and define census confidentiality. They did so by prosecuting enumerators or employees who revealed information on the forms. By 1929 they also had inserted in the statutory language statements specifying that census information be used "for statistical purposes" and barring publication of any data that might reveal information on "any particular establishment or individual." By the 1960s these provisions had been expanded to prevent courts from subpoenaing copies of individual census forms.

Lawsuits over Counting Procedures

A new type of challenge to the census emerged with the count of 1970, when the Census Bureau itself was sued. Local officials claimed that the bureau's procedures, particularly those affecting the mail census, would prevent some groups from being accurately counted. These suits did not fare well in federal court. District court judges decided that the bureau, in implementing its responsibilities under Title 13, had the authority to determine count procedures and methods. But the courts also ruled that the bureau had a new responsibility—that those procedures and methods be fair to all of society's constituencies. After 1970 such suits proliferated as the courts became involved in determining counting procedures that previously had been considered only in legislative or administrative venues.

Several suits, for example, have challenged the bureau's rules for determining who is included in the population counts. The bureau faced district court challenges in 1980 and 1990 from plaintiffs who wanted it to exclude undocumented aliens from the apportionment population counts (*FAIR v. Klutznick,* 486 F. Supp. 564 [1980]; *Ridge v. Verity,* 715 F. Supp. 1308 [1989]). In 1990 the state of Massachusetts, seeking a U.S. Supreme Court ruling, challenged the inclusion of overseas military personnel in the state counts for congressional apportionment (*Franklin v. Massachusetts,* 505 U.S. 788 [1992]). Similar suits were filed by the state of Utah after the 2000 census, challenging the Census Bureau's practices for counting the overseas population and its imputation procedures (*Utah v. Evans,* 536 U.S. 452 [2002]). The decisions in these cases upheld the authority of the bureau to determine counting procedures.

The most serious of the suits challenging census procedures have involved the census undercount. In the 1960s and 1970s, Census Bureau evaluation studies demonstrated that the census counted whites, persons in suburban areas, and the middle class more accurately than it did minorities, persons in urban areas, and the poor. In 1980 the bureau faced over 50 lawsuits filed by state and local governments seeking to correct the differential undercount. The plaintiffs sought to ensure that undercounted constituencies retained political representation and economic resources. The most serious of the challenges were brought in district court by the city of Detroit (*Young v. Klutznick,* 497 F. Supp. 1318 [1980]) and the city and state of New York (*Carey v. Klutznick,* 508 F. Supp. 420 [1980]). Both suits tried to stop the bureau from reporting the official census results on schedule, in December 1980, and to force it to adjust the counts in light of the known undercount. Although in both cases the courts initially sided with the plaintiffs, the decisions were later stayed, and the 1980 census results were released to the president on time.

The suits did not die with the release of the 1980 results. Most were withdrawn or dismissed after the census, but the New York litigants continued to press their case, claiming that census procedures had not been properly implemented and that even if they had been, the undercount should be corrected. They asked for a trial to determine if the bureau could adjust the 1980 census results to correct for errors in the count. If it could, they argued, the bureau should issue a second or revised set of data.

That trial took place in 1984. Three years later Judge John Sprizzo ruled in *Cuomo v. Baldrige* (674 F. Supp. 1089 [1987]) that the procedures used by the bureau were not "arbitrary and capricious" as defined in the Administrative Procedure Act (APA) of 1946. The judge accepted the testimony of high-level bureau officials and outside experts that the methods used to measure error in the 1980 census were not accurate enough to be used to adjust the count. The ruling upheld the authority of the bureau to determine the procedures for taking the census but implicitly left open the door to further litigation if plaintiffs could demonstrate that bureau procedures were arbitrary and capricious.

In the 1980s the bureau conducted a major research project to improve the adjustment methods so that they could be used to adjust the 1990 census if the differential undercount recurred. In 1987 the bureau announced its intention to implement the new adjustment procedures by adding a recently designed post-enumeration survey (PES) to the 1990 operational plan. The U.S. Department of Commerce, the bureau's parent agency, overruled this plan, and in 1988 New York City and a coalition of other local governments and interest groups sued the bureau and the Commerce Department, asking the court to reinstate the new adjustment procedures, including the PES. The plaintiffs and the Commerce Department in 1989 reached a stipulation agreement to continue with the plans for the survey and a possible adjustment of the 1990 census. The parties also created a special panel to monitor census procedures and make recommendations to the commerce secretary, who was to recommend by July 1991 whether the 1990 census results should be adjusted.

In July 1991 Commerce Secretary Robert A. Mosbacher declined to adjust the 1990 census. The secretary admitted that a differential net undercount of minorities and persons in some jurisdictions had existed in the 1990 census, but he also claimed that the proposed adjustment methods were not sufficiently accurate to improve the unadjusted counts. In response, the New York City plaintiffs returned to court, asserting that Mosbacher's decision had been arbitrary and capricious under the APA. After hearing arguments in May 1992, the district court in 1993 held that the decision of the commerce secretary had not been arbitrary and capricious. The judge also noted, however, that if he had been asked to decide the case de novo—that is, from the beginning—he would have ordered the census adjusted. The New York City plaintiffs appealed the decision to a circuit court, which in summer 1994 reversed the ruling. In 1995 the U.S. Department of Justice and the states of Pennsylvania, Wisconsin, and Oklahoma appealed the circuit court's ruling to the U.S. Supreme Court. The Court in March 1996 decided in favor of the commerce secretary (*Wisconsin v. City of New York,* 517 U.S. 1 [1996]).

Sampling Methods Challenged

By the second half of the 1990s, a substantial body of litigation had upheld the authority of the bureau and the Commerce Department to make decisions about census procedures. In 1997 Congress issued a new challenge to that authority. That year the Clinton administration and the Republican-controlled Congress disagreed on procedures for taking the 2000 census. Congress wrote language into the census appropriations bill allowing members of Congress and aggrieved individuals to sue the administration and the bureau and granting them expedited hearings if they felt that the proposed census plans would result in an inaccurate, invalid, or unconstitutional census. Early in 1998 Speaker of the House Newt Gingrich (R–GA) and the Southeastern Legal Foundation filed separate district-court suits under these provisions, charging that the plans for using statistical sampling in the nonresponse follow-up (NRFU) phase and the PES of the 2000 census violated the Constitution and the current provisions of Title 13.

In January 1999 the U.S. Supreme Court (*Department of Commerce v. U.S. House,* 525 U.S. 316 [1999]) ruled that Title 13 prevented the use of sampling to determine the population counts for apportionment. The Court thus struck down the use of statistical sampling in the NRFU phase of the count. The Court acknowledged that other provisions of Title 13 required the bureau to use sampling as the preferred counting method. The bureau interpreted the ruling to require the use of unadjusted counts for apportioning seats in the U.S. House of Representatives among the 50 states and to permit adjustment if the results of the Accuracy and Coverage Evaluation (ACE) survey component of the Census 2000 plan indicated that the census results would be improved by adjustment. In early 2001 the Census Bureau recommended against the use of adjusted data for the redistricting files. The sampling and adjustment controversy did not reemerge in the 2010 census. The operational plan for the census included a sample PES for census evaluation but not for adjustment of the reported results.

See also *Apportionment and districting; Capture-recapture methods; Census law; Confidentiality; Demographic analysis; Postenumeration survey.*

. . . .   MARGO J. ANDERSON

BIBLIOGRAPHY

Anderson, Margo J., and Stephen E. Fienberg. *Who Counts? The Politics of Census-Taking in Contemporary America.* New York: Russell Sage Foundation, 2001.

Brown, Lawrence D., Morris L. Eaton, David A. Freedman, Stephen P. Klein, Richard A. Olshen, Kenneth W. Wachter, Martin T. Wells, and Donald Ylvisaker. "Statistical Controversies in Census 2000." *Jurimetrics* 39 (Summer 1999): 347–375.

Choldin, Harvey M. *Looking for the Last Percent: The Controversy over Census Undercounts.* New Brunswick, N.J.: Rutgers University Press, 1994.

U.S. Census Bureau. "Legal Issues." In *History: 2000 Census of Population and Housing.* Vol. 2, chap. 11. Washington, D.C.: U.S. Government Printing Office, 2009. Available at www.census.gov/history/pdf/Census2000v2.pdf.

Local Involvement in Census Taking

The decennial census is a federal enterprise, the result of an extraordinary consensus among the framers of the Constitution that the distribution of political representation should be based on a census that employs uniform standards to enumerate the nation's population. Yet census taking involves an essential paradox: the federal government conducts the decennial census, but the census is inherently a local enterprise that is closely dependent on cooperation between federal and local entities.

The more than 100 years of experience in local census taking in the colonies provided those who met in the 1780s to form the laws of the new republic with a wealth of experience in the practices and outcomes of locally conducted censuses. The British had mandated colonial censuses, and 46 of them were conducted in 9 of the original 13 colonies. At no time during the colonial period was a census of *all* colonies attempted, however, and no uniformity existed in the questions asked or methods used in these censuses. By 1787 it became obvious to the Continental Congress that sharing obligations (for example, taxes) and rights (for example, political representation) based on population was the path of choice, but absent fair counts of population for all colonies, such a path would prove useless. Also obvious were the diverse interests that localities had in particular outcomes, as evidenced by the debate over the definition of a "person" for census purposes and the status of slaves. All recognized that a federal-level coordinating body was necessary to conduct a uniform census at regular intervals. This federal coordination, however, would not remove the inherent tension among localities, which over the next 200 years would vie for the influence and power connected to the census.

A big part of census history involves how local governments have tested their relationships with federal authorities since 1790. Although numerous issues have permeated the dialogue between the federal government and local organizations, most of these can be encompassed under two broad headings: census accuracy and the advent of small-area data.

Census Accuracy

Even the earliest attempts to enumerate the population of the colonies were fraught with response problems as a result of religious beliefs, fear of government reprisals, and sheer lack of physical access to the territory of the newly formed nation. In the nineteenth century, each census brought with it allegations of procedural problems and undercounts by state and local governments, especially as the census field operation expanded. Although questions regarding undercounts had occurred at earlier points, it was in 1870 that census superintendent Francis Amasa Walker had to contend with major allegations by many cities that the decennial census did not count everyone. These complaints sometimes resulted in a recheck of the census enumeration, which did sometimes result in higher counts, as was the case in New York City, Philadelphia, and Indianapolis in 1870.

In other instances, however, these allegations not only proved false but, upon closer scrutiny, revealed large-scale fraud sponsored by local organizations attempting to boost their counts. In Minneapolis and Saint Paul, for example, allegations that schedules were lost in the 1890 census resulted in a re-enumeration that revealed widespread fraud by census enumerators who had attempted to boost population counts. As a result, both cities saw substantial reductions in their official population counts. Civic involvement in census taking became more formalized in the twentieth century, with the advent of local-area census committees and increased awareness of the decennial census as a planning tool. Many of these committees were genuinely helpful in the census taking effort, but some were sponsors of fraudulent practices that systematically padded counts, all in the name of locally inspired "civic chauvinism." Writing in 1911, after the Census Bureau became a permanent entity within the U.S. Department of Commerce and Labor, the bureau's director Edward Dana Durand reported deliberate conspiracies to inflate the enumeration in some cities. One of the most notable examples, according to his report, was in Tacoma, Washington, where the original count of more than 116,000 in the 1910 census was reduced to about 84,000 after a second enumeration was conducted.

Despite attempts by some local groups to manipulate returns, undercounts in many localities were increasingly apparent. In Durand's 1911 account to the secretary of commerce and labor, he went on record about the issue of undercount by alluding to the problem of achieving absolute accuracy, given the vast physical area and enormous population of the nation. Indeed, he reported that a recheck of the 1910 enumeration in some cities did yield evidence of undercount. It was not until 1940, however, when modern statistical methods were first used in census taking, that the Census Bureau began formally to evaluate census accuracy by attempting to quantify the magnitude of the undercount and its effects, especially by race. By doing this, the bureau entered a period of increased

awareness, which led to several programs aimed at formally including local governments in the census process.

These programs included campaigns aimed at gaining local support for full participation in the census, especially after 1960, when the mailout/mailback method became the primary mode of response. Declines in mailback response with each passing decade prompted the bureau to form local committees, composed of influential government officials and community leaders, to plan and implement local publicity and outreach campaigns. According to the Census Bureau, about 9,800 of the 39,000 local governments responded to the call for Complete Count Committees in 1990, with some 5,600 actually participating in the program. In 1990 the Census Bureau also used 181 "partnership specialists" to directly engage local community organizations in support of the census. By 2000 the number of local partnership specialists employed in the field grew to 564. While this increase was substantial, the number of community organizations involved in the census effort grew even faster. In 2010 the Census Partnership Program initially employed 680 partnership specialists throughout the nation. The American Recovery and Reinvestment Act (ARRA) provided $1 billion to help the Census Bureau conduct a successful census in 2010. Some $120 million of this allocation was used to enhance the 2010 Census Partnership Program, mainly by increasing the number of partnership specialists working with local community organizations to 2,700.

Another effort aimed at involving local governments in making the census more accurate was local review. The local review program began in 1980, when local governments were permitted to review housing unit counts before they became final so that deficits in the enumeration could be identified. The idea was to incorporate local knowledge and data to make the address list used in the enumeration more accurate before the census itself was taken (pre-census local review) and to review the preliminary housing unit counts from the actual enumeration before they became final so that problems in the field could be identified and fixed (post-census local review). The local government was given a limited period (usually 30 to 60 days) to respond with challenges based on local data. Title 13 of the United States Code, which protects the confidentiality of census respondents, prohibited the disclosure of individual addresses on the list in both 1980 and 1990, so local governments were not able to sort out problems at the address level, nor was the Census Bureau required to provide detailed feedback on the final disposition of these challenges. According to the U.S. General Accounting Office (GAO), 32 percent of eligible governments participated in pre-census local review in 1990. The GAO concluded that the three-quarters of those eligible governments not participating lacked the required data and staff resources to do so. As a result, the local review program had, even by the most optimistic accounts, only spotty success.

Determined to provide local governments with better access to addresses used in the census, Congress passed the Address List Improvement Act in 1994, which permitted local governments to receive and review the actual address list used to mail questionnaires in advance of the 2000 census. Representatives of local governments signed an agreement not to disclose any information from the address list and to use it solely for the purpose of making the census more accurate. Despite this new incentive, the resource limitations of local governments once again acted to inhibit uniform and effective participation in the Local Update of Census Addresses (LUCA) program in 2000. About 9,900 local governments provided at least some address information, in the form of actual addresses or challenges to block counts, in the 2000 LUCA program. This represented about 25 percent of the 39,000 eligible local governments.

Unlike in 1980 and 1990, no comprehensive post-census review of counts was offered to local governments in 2000 because earlier post-census review programs were not cost-effective, according to the Census Bureau. Instead, a more limited program, called Count Question Resolution (CQR), offered local governments an opportunity after the census to correct errors in boundaries, geocoding, and other census processing that affected the accuracy of the enumeration. Any errors that were found and resulted in changes to census counts were issued in the form of corrected totals for population and/or housing, but summary data files and other data products released by the bureau were not altered to reflect these changes. The corrected figures, however, were used as the basis for subsequent population estimates.

Once again, the Census Bureau has provided localities with opportunities for input into the 2010 census, through the following programs: a LUCA program; the New Construction Program, which allowed localities to submit information on units constructed immediately prior to the census enumeration; and the Count Review Program, consisting of a final check of housing unit addresses (pre-census) and a check of group quarters facilities afterward (post-census). In addition, a post-census CQR program similar to the program in 2000 was offered in 2010. While there is considerable evidence that the 2010 LUCA program was implemented more effectively than the 2000 program, once again, the labor-intensive nature of participation and the resource constraints of local governments resulted in less than optimal levels of participation. Some 8,100 governments, or about 21 percent of all those eligible to participate in the 2010 LUCA program, submitted address information. While the large majority of addresses in the nation was represented in the LUCA program in both 2000 and 2010, fewer governments participated in LUCA in 2010. However, comparisons with 2000 are complicated by the fact that larger governmental entities, such as states, were permitted to submit addresses on behalf of their component localities in 2010 but not in 2000.

Another by-product of the heightened awareness of census accuracy was a series of lawsuits brought by localities in regard to the 1980 and 1990 censuses. Such litigation was now possible given the existence of statistical and demographic methods documenting the persistence of differential undercount by race and the creation of statistical algorithms to address the problem. Localities entered into extensive litigation in an attempt to force the Census Bureau to correct the undercount via statistical methods. By and large, localities were unsuccessful in their attempts to force a statistical adjustment of census numbers. The issue of statistical adjustment emerged prior to the 2000 census, with many localities concerned about undercounts. The issue of the use of sampling for statistical adjustment for reapportionment, in fact, was put before the U.S. Supreme Court. The Court ruled that such methods could not be used for reapportionment purposes.

A big debate ensued about adjustment of counts for redistricting and other purposes. After intense examination of the topic by Census Bureau statisticians, the U.S. Department of Commerce ruled that unadjusted counts of the population would be the only data issued from the 2000 census. The Census Bureau itself now determined that the scientific basis for an adjustment was too uncertain to proceed. This rendered the issue almost moot for localities as the bureau began preparations for 2010, since the absence of a consensus on appropriate methods for adjusting the census largely precluded any realistic possibility of a 2010 adjustment.

The Advent of Small-Area Data

As the twentieth century began, the nation's cities were entering a period of unprecedented growth, absorbing large numbers of migrants from the nation's rural areas and immigrants from southern and eastern Europe. This high level of growth posed a dilemma for many local governments, which were concerned about controlling the spread of communicable diseases, providing shelter for many new arrivals, and maintaining order. Whereas the federal government focused on broad changes to the nation, such as the disappearance of the frontier, and to changes at the state level for reapportionment purposes, local organizations became increasingly concerned about changes in their communities.

Local governments became more aware of their vested interests in the census counts and began to request data for small areas. In some cities, such as New York and Cleveland, the demand for small-area data translated into locally sponsored programs of data tabulation for new units of geography, which came to be known as census tracts. For more than 30 years, tabulations of small-area data from the decennial censuses were created as a direct result of the commitment to local data analysis on the part of local organizations. Groups such as the New York Federation of Churches and the New York City 1920 Census Committee designed the small-area tabulations that later became the foundation for the census tract program, as adopted by the Census Bureau in 1940. Until that time, the program was funded by local entities in New York, Cleveland, and other cities that found the information essential for addressing problems in their rapidly growing communities.

The creation of small-area data became synonymous with local involvement in census taking efforts. When the bureau formally instituted the census tract program in 1940, it established a link between federal and local organizations that remains firm to this day. By accepting the responsibility to prepare data for locally defined units, the federal government created a program that depended heavily on local input. Changes in census tract designations are done jointly with localities, usually with local governments or their designated representatives.

When the new era of federal funding began in the 1960s and 1970s, involvement in this program peaked because small-area data were now being used to allocate funds for a variety of purposes, including community-development initiatives. Today, the Census Bureau actively incorporates local-area geographic knowledge into census work. Local-area census tract committees are responsible for designating tract boundary changes before each census, based on a series of ground rules established by the Census Bureau in an attempt to achieve standardization and comparability over time. The most recent effort by the Census Bureau to solicit input on small-area geography for 2010 is called the Participant Statistical Areas Program (PSAP), in which local participants are permitted to redefine small geographic areas for data-reporting purposes, based on thresholds established by the Census Bureau.

See also *Census tracts; Coverage evaluation; Grassroots groups; Litigation and the census; State and local censuses; State and local governments: legislatures.*

. . . . JOSEPH J. SALVO

BIBLIOGRAPHY

Alterman, Hyman. *Counting People: The Census in History.* New York: Harcourt, Brace and World, 1969.

Barrows, Robert G. "The Ninth Federal Census of Indianapolis: A Case Study in Civic Chauvinism." *Indiana Magazine of History* 73, no. 1 (1977): 1–16.

Groves, Robert M. "2010 Census: Master Address File, Issues and Concerns." Testimony before the Subcommittee on Information Policy, Census, and National Archives, Committee on Oversight and Government Reform. United States House of Representatives, October 21, 2009. Available at www.census.gov/newsroom/releases/archives/directors_corner/.

National Research Council. *Assessment of the 2000 Census LUCA Program.* Working Group on LUCA. Washington, D.C.: Committee on National Statistics, 2001. Available at www7.nationalacademies.org/cnstat/LUCA%20Report.pdf.

Stevens, L. Nye. "Expanding the Role of Local Governments: An Important Element of Census Reform." Testimony before the Subcommittee on Census and Population, Committee on Post Office and Civil Service, U.S. House of Representatives, June 15, 1991. Available at http://archive.gao.gov/d38t12/144153.pdf.

Superintendent of the Census. *Report of the Superintendent of Census to the Secretary of the Interior for the Six Months Ending December 31, 1890.* Washington, D.C.: U.S. Government Printing Office, 1891.

U.S. Bureau of the Census. "Field Enumeration." In *History: 1980 Census of Population and Housing.* Part B, chap. 5. Washington, D.C.: U.S. Government Printing Office, 1986.

———. "Field Enumeration." In *History: 1990 Census of Population and Housing.* Part A, chap. 6. Washington, D.C.: U.S. Government Printing Office, 1993. Available at www2.census.gov/prod2/decennial/documents/1990/history/Chapter_06.pdf.

———. *Report of the Director to the Secretary of Commerce and Labor Concerning the Operations of the Bureau for the Year 1909–10.* Washington, D.C.: U.S. Government Printing Office, 1911.

U.S. Department of Commerce, U.S. Census Bureau. "2010 Census Partnership: American Recovery and Reinvestment Act Program Plan." Washington, D.C.: U.S. Census Bureau, 2010. Available at www.census.gov/recovery/docs/2010-Census-ARRA-Program-Plan-Partnerships.doc.

U.S. General Accounting Office. *2000 Census: Review of Partnership Program Highlights Best Practices for Future Operations.* GAO-01-579. Washington, D.C.: U.S. Government Printing Office, 2001. Available at www.gpo.gov/fdsys/pkg/GAOREPORTS-GAO-01-579/pdf/GAOREPORTS-GAO-01-579.pdf.

U.S. Government Accountability Office. *2010 Census: The Bureau's Plans for Reducing the Undercount Show Promise, but Key Uncertainties Remain.* GAO-08-1167T. Statement of Robert Goldenkoff, Director, Strategic Issues. Washington D.C.: U.S. Government Printing Office, 2008. Available at www.gao.gov/new.items/d081167t.pdf.

Long Form

The long form is a questionnaire that was sent to a sample of addresses in the 1960–2000 censuses. Long forms contained the "short-form" person and housing items that all households were asked to provide together with additional items that only the households in the long-form sample were asked to provide. Short-form items were generally limited to basic demographic and housing items; long-form items covered such topics as income, employment, veteran status, transportation to work, education, and others (see Table 1).

The long form provided a way to obtain more information from the census than was needed for the basic head count without burdening the entire population; it also reduced the costs of the census compared to the cost of a single long questionnaire for everyone.

The Long Form in Censuses Between 1960 and 2000

The 1960 census first introduced the concept of "short" and "long" forms or questionnaires. In the 1940 and 1950 censuses, some items were obtained from a sample of households, but separate forms were not employed. The use of mail delivery to help conduct the 1960 census necessitated the development of separate forms.

In 1960 the U.S. Postal Service dropped off questionnaires at all households containing the short-form or 100-percent items. Enumerators then visited these households to obtain the short-form answers. At every fourth household (25 percent of all households) in areas of the country that contained about 80 percent of the housing, the enumerator left a long-form questionnaire to be filled in and mailed back by the household to the local census offices (LCOs). Different forms were used in large cities (defined as 50,000 or more people) and other areas; each contained several questions unique to the form. In the remaining, more rural areas that contained about 20 percent of the housing, the enumerators asked the long-form questions on the spot. In these areas, enumerators asked 20 percent of households one set of housing questions and 5 percent of households another set. Some housing items and all population items were asked of both groups, producing a 25 percent sample for those items. In the more urban areas, households in the long-form sample filled out all items for the type of place—large city or other. Enumerators working in the LCOs transcribed the answers to computer-readable forms, transcribing the answers for 25 percent, 20 percent, or 5 percent of households, depending on the item.

Table 1. Questions on the Long-Form Decennial Census: 1960–2000

QUESTIONNAIRE ITEMS	1960	1970	1980	1990	2000
Population Items					
Age (and/or date of birth)	S	S	S	S	S
Sex	S	S	S	S	S
Race	S	S	S	S	S
Hispanic origin		L[b]	S	S	S
Relationship to household head	S	S	S	S	S
Marital status	S	S	S	S	L
Age at or date of first marriage	L	L[b]	L		
Married more than once	L	L[b]	L		
If remarried, was first marriage ended by death?		L[b]	L		
Number of children ever born to mother	L	L	L	L	
School attendance/educational attainment	L	L	L	L	L
Public or private school (for people currently enrolled)	L	L[a]	L	L	L
Vocational training		L[b]			
Place of birth (short-form item in New York State in 1960)	L	L	L	L	L
Place of birth of mother and father	L	L[a]			
Citizenship (short-form item in New York State in 1960 and not asked elsewhere in that year)		L[b]	L	L	L
Year of immigration		L[b]	L	L	L
Language spoken at home (before came to U.S. if born abroad, in 1960; as a child, in 1970)	L	L[a]	L	L	L
How well English spoken			L	L	L
Ancestry			L	L	L
Veteran status/period of service (for men in 1960 and 1970)	L	L[a]	L	L	L
Years of military service				L	L
Place of residence 5 years ago (state of residence 5 years ago only on 5-percent long form in 1970)	L	L[a, b]	L	L	L
Year moved to present residence (see housing item on year household head moved into unit)		L	L[a]		
Work disability		L[b]	L	L	L
Transportation disability			L		
Disabled for going outside the home alone				L	L
Disabled for taking care of personal needs				L	L
Other disabilities (involving eyes, ears, cognition, mobility)					L
Duration of disability		L[b]			
Whether and how long responsible for grandchildren in home					L
Employment status	L	L	L	L	L
Hours worked in preceding week	L	L	L	L	
Occupation	L	L	L	L	L
Industry	L	L	L	L	L
Class of worker	L	L	L	L	L
Place of work	L	L[a]	L	L	L
Means of transportation to work	L	L[a]	L	L	L
Commuting time (and when usually left for work in 1990, 2000)			L	L	L
Carpooling				L	L	L
Year last worked	L	L	L	L	L
Weeks worked in preceding year	L	L	L	L	L
Hours worked per week in preceding year			L	L	L
Weeks unemployed in preceding year			L		
Activity 5 years ago		L	L		
Occupation, industry, class of worker 5 years ago		L[b]			
Income from earnings	L	L	L	L	L
Income from nonfarm self-employment (nonfarm plus farm self-employment in 1960 and 2000)	L	L	L	L	L
Income from farm self-employment		L	L	L	
Income from Social Security		L	L	L	L
Income from Supplemental Security Income					L
Income from public assistance		L	L	L	L
Income from interest, dividends, rent			L	L	L
Income from pensions				L	L
All other income (also total income in 1980, 1990, 2000)	L	L	L	L	L
Housing items					
Tenure—owned or rented	S	S	S	S	S
Type of property (for example, whether includes a business; short-form item in large cities, long-form item otherwise in 1960; single-family homes only in 1980, 1990, 2000)	S[c]	S	S	S	L

(Continued)

Table 1. *(Continued)*

QUESTIONNAIRE ITEMS	1960	1970	1980	1990	2000
Value (short-form item in large cities, long-form item otherwise in 1960)	S	S	S	S	L
Contract rent (short-form item in large cities, long-form item otherwise in 1960)	S	S	S	S	L
Does the rent include any meals?				S	L
Number of rooms	S	S	S	S	L
Access to unit	Sc	S	S		
Condition (sound, deteriorating, dilapidated)	Sc				
Condominium status			S	L	L
Bathing facilities	S	S			
Toilet facilities	S	S			
Whether hot and/or cold piped water	S	S			
Complete plumbing facilities			S	L	L
Kitchen, cooking facilities; complete kitchen facilities	S	S	L	L	L
Telephone available	L	S	L	L	L
Basement	La	S			
Number of units at address		S	S		
Number of units in structure	La, c	L	L	S	L
Farm residence/sales of farm products (asked only outside large cities in 1960; for single-family homes only in 2000)	L	L	L	L	L
Number of stories (asked only in large cities in 1960; combined with question on elevator)	La	Lb	L		
Elevator (asked only in large cities in 1960; combined with question on number of stories)	La	Lb	L		
Second home		Lb			
Whether trailer home mobile or fixed	L				
Year household head moved into unit (replaced population item on year moved in)			L	L	L
Year structure built	L	L	L	L	L
Utilities (for renters only in 1960 and 1970)					
Electricity costs	L	L	L	L	L
Gas costs	L	L	L	L	L
Water costs	L	L	L	L	L
Oil, coal, etc., costs	L	L	L	L	L
Does the rent include land used for farming (asked only outside large cities in 1960)?	L				
Mortgage payment (and whether includes taxes and insurance)			L	L	L
Homeowners insurance			L	L	L
Real estate taxes (for owners only)			L	L	L
Whether have second mortgage			L	L	L
Payment for second mortgage(s)/home equity loans				L	L
Condominium or mobile home fee				L	L
Number of bathrooms	La	La	L		
Number of bedrooms	Lb	Lb	L	L	L
Heating equipment	L	L	L		
Cooking fuel		Lb	L		
Heating fuel	Lb	Lb	L	L	L
Water heating fuel		Lb	L		
Sewage disposal (asked only outside large cities in 1960)	La	La	L	L	
Source of water (asked only outside large cities in 1960)	La	La	L	L	
Air conditioning	Lb	La	L		
Automobiles (20-percent item in large cities, 5-percent item outside large cities in 1960; includes vans and trucks in 1990 and 2000)	La, b	La	L	L	L
Vans or trucks			L		
Clothes washer; clothes dryer	Lb	Lb			
Dishwasher		Lb			
Home food freezer	Lb	Lb			
Radio sets (battery-operated only in 1970)	Lb	Lb			
Television sets	Lb	Lb			
Whether television equipped for UHF		Lb			

NOTE: S indicates short form; L indicates long form.

aIndicates the 15-percent long form in 1970 and items that were transcribed on a 20 percent basis in 1960.

bIndicates the 5-percent long form in 1970 and items that were transcribed on a 5 percent basis in 1960.

cItem obtained by enumerator observation.

SOURCE: Extracted from Table A.2 in National Research Council (1995) and Appendix B in National Research Council (2004).

In 1970 households were sent either a short form (80 percent of households) or one of two versions of the long form. Each long form contained the 100-percent population and housing items and a common set of items asked of 20 percent of households. One version, however, also included a set of questions asked of 15 percent of households, and the other a set asked of 5 percent of households.

The use of more than one long form in the 1960 and 1970 censuses, with some questions in common and other questions unique to the form (what is termed *matrix sampling*), reduced the burden on individual households of filling out the questionnaire. However, multiple long forms complicated the data processing and made using census data products more difficult.

In 1980 only one long form was used, but different percentages of households received it, depending on the population size of their place of residence. In places with an estimated population of 2,500 or more, one in every six households received the long form; in smaller places, one in every two households received it. The overall sampling rate was approximately 19 percent. The primary reason for changing from a uniform 20 percent sampling rate to rates of 50 percent for small places (which account for about 5 percent of the population) and 16.7 percent for all other places was to provide reliable per capita income data for use in allocating federal funds to 39,000 state and local jurisdictions under the provisions of the 1972 State and Local Fiscal Assistance Act. (This act is often referred to as General Revenue Sharing, a program that distributed several billion dollars each year from 1973 through 1987.)

In 1990 about one in every six households (17 percent) received the long form. Three different sampling rates were used to provide somewhat more reliable estimates for small areas and to decrease respondent burden in more densely populated areas. The sampling rate was one in two housing units (50 percent) in governmental units such as counties and towns with an estimated 1988 population of less than 2,500. Outside these areas, the sampling rate was one in six housing units (17 percent) in census tracts and equivalent areas with a pre-census housing count of fewer than 2,000 housing units (fewer than about 5,200 people) and one in eight housing units (13 percent) in larger census tracts and equivalent areas.

In 2000 the overall sampling rate was once again about one in six housing units, but four sampling rates were used to reflect the goal of smoothing the rates and, therefore, the reliability of the estimates from the sample data (more so than in 1990). Specifically, in 2000 the sampling rate was one in two (50 percent) for governmental units with fewer than 800 housing units (fewer than about 2,100 people); one in four (25 percent) for governmental units with 800–1,200 housing units (about 2,100–3,100 people); one in eight (13 percent) for census tracts with 2,000 or more housing units (about 5,200 people or more); and one in six (17 percent) in all other areas. Governmental units that were oversampled in 2000 included school districts, in addition to counties, towns, and townships. School districts were oversampled because of the need for reliable estimates of poor school-age children for the purpose of allocating federal funds to school districts under Title I of the Elementary and Secondary Education Act.

Replacing the Long Form with the American Community Survey

The American Community Survey (ACS) is a large-scale, continuing monthly sample survey of U.S. households, conducted primarily by mail, which collects information similar to that previously provided by the census long-form sample. The ACS, after a long period of testing, was fully implemented beginning in 2005. From 2005 to mid-2011, the ACS sampled 240,000 housing units each month, for an annual sample size of about 2.9 million housing units spread across all counties in the nation. The 5-year sample size was about 15 million housing units, which is somewhat smaller than the 2000 census long-form sample size of about 18 million housing units. Beginning in June 2011, the sample was increased to 295,000 housing units each month or close to 18 million housing units over five years. However, because the ACS by design interviews about one-third of households that do not respond to the survey by mail or telephone, the effective sample size for analysis over a five-year period is expected to be about 11.5 million housing units. The ACS also includes a sample of people living in group quarters, such as correctional facilities, nursing homes, military barracks, college dormitories, and other group quarters.

Due to the advent of the ACS, there was no long-form sample in the 2010 census—that census asked only ten questions of every household. One reason for replacing the census long-form sample with the ACS the interest of data users in more up-to-date estimates for states and smaller geographic areas on such topics as poverty, education, and employment. Also, dropping the long-form sample encourages higher mailback response rates (recipients of the long form in 2000 mailed back their questionnaires at significantly lower rates than recipients of the short form) and simplifies census operations.

See also *American Community Survey: questionnaire content; Content determination; Sampling for content.*

. . . . CONSTANCE F. CITRO

BIBLIOGRAPHY

National Research Council., "Assessment of Basic and Long-Form Sample Data." In *The 2000 Census: Counting Under Adversity*, Panel to Review the 2000 Census, Constance F. Citro, Daniel L. Cork, and Janet L. Norwood, eds., 269–302. Committee on National Statistics, Washington, D.C.: The National Academies Press, 2004.

———. "Census Content." In *Modernizing the U.S. Census,* Panel on Census Requirements in the Year 2000 and Beyond, Barry Edmonston and Charles L. Schultze, eds., 113–139. Committee on National Statistics, Washington, D.C.: The National Academies Press, 1995.

———. "Planning the 2020 Census: Cost and Quality." In *Envisioning the 2020 Census*, Panel on the Design of the 2010 Census Program of Evaluations and Experiments, Lawrence D. Brown, Michael L. Cohen, Daniel L. Cork, and Constance F. Citro, eds., 21–58. Committee on National Statistics, Washington, D.C.: The National Academies Press, 2010.

Mailing the Census

See *Address list development; Data capture.*

Marriage

See *Family and household composition of the population*

Media Attention to the Census

The past decade has seen major changes in media attention to the census, due mainly to two causes. One is the transformation of the media landscape, which has altered the pace and nature of journalism. The second is the Census Bureau's rollout of the American Community Survey (ACS), which has provided new, widely used mid-decade data for states and localities.

Changes in the Media Environment

There has been notable shrinkage in recent years of audiences and advertising revenue for traditional media such as printed newspapers and network television news. Users and revenue have migrated to new media such as blogs, social networks, and Web sites. Increasingly people receive information from all such media sources on their cell phones or other mobile devices. These developments have had a major influence on the content and form of news that Americans consume.

The newspaper industry's circulation has declined for two decades, but losses accelerated in the last half of the 2000s as the national economy deteriorated. According to the Pew Research Center's Project for Excellence in Journalism (PEJ), during the years 2007–2009, the newspaper industry's advertising revenue declined 43 percent, full-time newsroom employment declined 27 percent, and paid circulation declined 17 percent. At many newspapers, the growth in Web site traffic offset the decline in print circulation, but advertising and other revenue did not grow enough to compensate for losses stemming from decreased sales of print editions.

Viewership of evening news shows on the three major commercial television networks, which has been in decline for decades, averaged 22.3 million people in 2009. This was down from 31.9 million people in 2000, according to Nielsen Media Research figures cited by PEJ. All three networks cut their news divisions. Cable television, meanwhile, has grown in viewership, profits, and spending.

These trends have had important implications for coverage of the Census Bureau and its data products. The decline in traditional media has weakened these outlets' depth and influence. Staff reductions have caused newsroom workloads to increase and have reduced the number of Washington, D.C.-based journalists who write about the federal government. The rise of cable television and online news sites has promoted a 24/7 news cycle that emphasizes speed and brevity. Combined, these trends have increased demand for shorter, more superficial stories. There are fewer opportunities for journalists to develop and use the expertise necessary to make sophisticated use of census data.

A larger, more diverse media universe favors two-way interaction and personal voice over institutional authority. New media include a wide variety of outlets such as Web sites that repackage or comment on stories from other sources, social media, such as Twitter, through which users exchange short messages about topics of mutual interest, and online sites that focus on one topic or one individual's opinions. These sites measure success not by paid circulation but by the number of users who click on their offerings.

The media environment has become more diverse in other ways as well. Growing numbers of print and broadcast outlets have pursued audiences among the nation's expanding immigrant population, although this sector has also faced economic troubles. In some cities, the top-rated television news show in 2009 was on a Spanish-language channel.

Among print, broadcast, and online media, visual presentation and user involvement have become more prominent. Colorful charts and video stories have become routine. Graphics increasingly have allowed users to explore numbers such as census data in greater depth. Web sites often give users the opportunity to comment on postings and exchange views with other users.

Coverage of the Census Bureau

Media coverage of the Census Bureau and its work generally has been driven by journalists' preference for stories about competition, controversy, and change. Recent alterations in the news industry have sharpened these tendencies.

Most original reporting is still done by traditional media, but their weakened position means they have less of a role in determining which news stories Americans see. According to an analysis by PEJ, bloggers "tend to gravitate toward events that affect personal rights and cultural norms—issues like same-sex marriage, the rationing of health care or privacy settings on Facebook, while traditional media news agendas are more event-driven and institutional" (Pew Research Center 2010a, "The Blogosphere"). New media are more likely to be ideologically based, while traditional media journalism strives for nonpartisan presentation.

One generality that continues to be true is that except for specialized publications, the media have not given sustained attention to the Census Bureau's preparations for the decennial census or to debates over its mid-decade budget. Mainstream journalists are often averse to writing stories about process rather than outcome. Additional barriers to coverage are that the Census Bureau's planning stages often involve decisions which are highly technical and of little immediate consequence to Americans.

The lack of attention by journalists parallels the usual lack of more than cursory oversight of the census by Congress until the bureau has put its plan in place. When members of Congress focus a critical eye on the Census Bureau, however, they usually draw media attention. For example, the agency's problems with handheld computers (HHCs) in the late 2000s became the focus of congressional scrutiny and were covered extensively.

As the next census count draws near, high interest in the decennial census by both political parties is guaranteed because of the census's role in providing data used to apportion congressional seats (and to allocate federal dollars). The confluence of politics and census taking is of great interest to journalists; new media, especially sites with a political point of view, have often pushed these stories aggressively. When Republicans expressed concerns that the Democrat-controlled White House could manipulate census taking to its advantage, the story won extensive coverage. One instance in which this occurred was in the context of the nomination of U.S. Sen. Judd Gregg (R-NH)—and then his withdrawal—as secretary of the Commerce Department, which includes the Census Bureau. Several months later, coverage of the nomination of Robert M. Groves as Census Bureau director included stories on Republican criticism of the bureau's partnership (later severed) with a community organization accused of voter-registration fraud.

Compared with the 2000 census, there was less media attention to congressional oversight of the enumeration itself in 2010. In part that was because in 2000, Congress was controlled by Republicans who held frequent hearings to examine—and criticize—the Census Bureau and, by extension, the Democrat-controlled White House. In 2010 the Democrats were in charge of Congress and the White House, so there was less friction on which to report.

During the early weeks of census taking in 2010, journalists focused on threats to high participation. They took note of a boycott called for by some conservatives and wrote about the possibility that unauthorized immigrants would be reluctant to fill out their forms, fearing the information could be used to deport them. Those stories faded when the Census Bureau provided statistics indicating that the 2010 rate of participation was on track to equal or surpass the 2000 rate. Another theme of coverage was potential problems with the temporary workforce hired by the Census Bureau. There was ongoing media interest in tracking assaults on census workers (whether due to anticensus hostility or other reasons), as well as potential criminals who might be hired.

News coverage of the taking of the census peaked during the week that included census day, April 1. According to statistics compiled by PEJ, the 2010 census ranked as the fourteenth most prominent news story for the week of March 29–April 4, 2010. The story filled 2 percent of the "newshole," which is the space and time devoted to print, online, and broadcast news coverage as tracked by the PEJ News Coverage Index. The top story that week was the U.S. economy, which filled 10 percent of the newshole. Research by the Census Bureau and other organizations indicated that most Americans were aware of the 2010 census, and news media exposure (along with advertising) played an important role in what they learned.

The Census Bureau had considerable success during the 2010 enumeration in generating stories that reported daily changes in local, state, and national participation rates. Media accounts often compared the participation rates with those in 2000. These stories played to the media's interest in reporting about competition; many stories in local media compared their community's response rate with the national participation rate.

The bureau's 2010 census strategy used new modes of delivery both to inform the news media and to reach out directly to Americans in ways that had not been possible in previous counts. The bureau posted video stories on its Web site, and the bureau's director blogged about the taking of the 2010 census. For the first time, the agency set up accounts on social media sites including Facebook, Twitter, and YouTube, to publicize its activities. Major news releases about the 2010 census were issued in Spanish as well as English.

The Census Bureau, like other government agencies, has sometimes wrestled with how to respond to the challenges of the new media environment. Agency staff scrambled to keep track of blogs in which temporary census employees wrote about their experiences. In some cases, agency staff warned the employees that such writings could violate the law against disclosing confidential data. Bureau officials debated among themselves how quickly and directly they should respond to criticisms in a new media world that placed a premium on speed. As the census taking season went on, they increasingly engaged in answering their critics.

Coverage of Census Data

Census Bureau data are widely used to support stories about demographic, social, and economic trends, both locally and nationally. The use of data from the Census Bureau has increased dramatically with the annual release of estimates from the ACS, which provides data for states and localities that previously had not been available between decennial censuses. Journalists also showed increasing interest through the decade in the bureau's annual population estimates for states and counties. This has increased the bureau's visibility and placed new demands on its staff.

Population growth, racial or ethnic change, and migration among states, regions, and localities are topics that are perennially popular with the media and that rely on census data. So are subjects such as family structure and educational attainment. Census data also increasingly are used to illustrate stories about issues in the political realm—immigration, for example. In urban areas, commuting data are used to illustrate traffic problems.

The national economic recession raised interest among journalists in using census data to monitor national and local conditions by looking at changes in measures of well-being. The annual Census Bureau news conference to release income, poverty, and health insurance coverage estimates has generated large amounts of coverage in recent years. The large 2010 census workforce became the focus of debate over its role in temporarily countering unemployment.

Much of this coverage is driven by the media's search for stories about change and competition. At the national level, journalists gave high attention to the announcement that the U.S. population had reached 300 million people in 2006. At the community level, journalists have written frequently about the ups and downs of local population change. Stories often compare one locality's gain or loss of population to gains or losses in other communities, and they make frequent use of ranking tables provided by the Census Bureau. Journalists generally have taken the view that growth is good, even though it may be accompanied by problems such as school crowding or traffic.

In writing about census data, contrary to their usual professed skepticism, journalists tend to accept the reliability of the numbers at face value, except for stories about local jurisdictions that challenge their census counts. The premium that the news media places on documenting change, combined with many journalists' lack of statistical expertise, also has led some journalists to overstate the amount of change. In some cases, stories have cited differences in the estimates for two geographical areas or two points in time, when those differences were not statistically significant.

One positive development is that a growing number of journalists have acquired experience in computer assisted data analysis and mapping that make use of census numbers. Professional associations and journalism schools have sponsored training classes for journalists (including freelance writers) in how to extract and use data from the 2010 census and ACS.

As a scientific and research agency, the Census Bureau has been slow in the past to communicate effectively to the media (and other users) about technical matters. But in recent years it has reached out more to all users, offering assistance on how to use its data properly. Census Bureau staff have issued item-specific guidance to journalists (and other users) about when it is appropriate to compare estimates. The bureau has published

a handbook for the media on using the ACS. Such efforts will be a continual challenge, however, because of frequent turnover in the ranks of journalists and the increasing pace of daily news gathering.

See also *American Community Survey: implementation from 2005; Advertising the census; Grassroots groups.*

. . . . D'VERA COHN

BIBLIOGRAPHY

Cohn, D'Vera. "News Coverage of the 2010 Census." *Pew Social & Demographic Trends*, April 8, 2010. http://pewsocialtrends.org/2010/04/08/news-coverage-of-the-2010-census/.

Davis, Richard. *A Symbiotic Relationship Between Journalists and Bloggers.* Discussion Paper Series, no. D-47. Joan Shorenstein Center on the Press, Politics and Public Policy, Harvard University. Cambridge, Mass., 2008. Available at www.hks.harvard.edu/presspol/publications/papers/discussion_papers/d47_davis.pdf.

Pew Research Center Project for Excellence in Journalism. *New Media, Old Media: How Blogs and Social Media Agendas Relate and Differ from the Traditional Press* (2010a). Available at www.journalism.org/analysis_report/new_media_old_media/.

———. *The State of the News Media 2010: An Annual Report on American Journalism* (2010b). Available at www.stateofthemedia.org/2010/.

U.S. Census Bureau. *A Compass for Understanding and Using American Community Survey Data: What the Media Need to Know.* Washington, D.C.: U.S. Government Printing Office, 2008. Available at www.census.gov/acs/www/Downloads/handbooks/ACSMediaHandbook.pdf.

Metropolitan Areas

The term *Metropolitan Area* (MA) generally means a large city, including its suburbs. As presented in census publications since 1950, MA refers to a set of geographic areas defined under various labels by the Office of Management and Budget (OMB) as a standard for federal statistical agencies in their presentation of data. The term has developed mostly independently of the related term *metropolis*, meaning a city of major importance in its country or region. Many officially defined MAs in the United States are not metropolises in that sense.

As recognized by the OMB, the general concept of a Metropolitan Statistical Area (MSA) is a functional one. OMB defines an MSA as a large population nucleus or core plus adjacent communities having a high degree of economic and social integration with that core. Integration is measured using census data on commuting to work. In general, entire counties form the MSA building blocks so that besides a city and its built-up suburbs, most MSA definitions include smaller satellite communities and considerable open country. Thus, *metropolitan* should not be confused with *urban*; an MSA generally includes at least one Urbanized Area (UA) but also rural population as defined by the census, while many small cities and towns are classified as urban but are not included in any MA.

Beginning with the MSAs defined after the 2000 census, OMB extended its metropolitan delineations to embrace smaller Micropolitan Statistical Areas. It termed the combined sets Core Based Statistical Areas (CBSAs), while retaining the general concept under which all these areas are recognized and delineated. The population outside any CBSA is termed *non-metropolitan*, and many census publications contain extensive data on the total metropolitan and nonmetropolitan population of the United States and the individual states. Within each CBSA, data generally are presented for the principal city or cities (known in earlier censuses as *central cities*) based on corporate boundaries and for the MSA remainder outside these cities. Although the latter category often is interpreted as representing the *suburbs*, the census itself has avoided that term, probably reflecting the lack of public consensus on what constitutes a suburb.

The delineations undergo extensive updating after each census. However, because detailed census commuting data do not become available until the second year after the enumeration, decennial census output since 1960 generally has presented delineations that do not yet reflect the changes in commuting patterns of the preceding decade. This lag also has been reflected in the redesign of many census surveys. For example, the CBSA delineations reflecting 2010 commuting data from the ACS are not scheduled to be released until 2013, which is after the five-year ACS data for 2008–2012 will have become available.

Only a few other countries defined MAs officially in 1950, but by 2010 many were doing so at least for their capital cities, sometimes with criteria and terminology borrowed from U.S. practice.

Recognizing and Delineating MAs

Although the MA term itself did not emerge until the early 1900s, the recognition of an urban area larger than the official city existed as early as 1790, when Philadelphia already had several large built-up suburbs. The 1905 Census of Manufactures presented data on 13 "industrial districts" defined in terms of subcounty Minor Civil Divisions (MCDs) such as townships, districts, and (in certain states) towns.

In the decennial census, MAs first were officially defined in 1910 as *Metropolitan Districts* (MDs). The definitions generally were in terms of MCDs and followed a functional approach, not limited to the continuously built-up area. In the absence of comprehensive data on commuting between core cities and suburbs, the MDs included outlying MCDs chiefly on the basis of a population density of at least 150 persons per square mile.

The MDs were updated and the list of qualifying areas expanded in the 1920–1940 censuses, but their definitions by subcounty units severely limited their usefulness for the compilation of nondecennial data, many types of which were not available below the county level. This, in parallel with continuing suburban expansion, prompted the U.S. Bureau of the Census and other federal agencies to develop various mutually inconsistent metropolitan definitions using whole counties. As a result, in 1949 the U.S. Bureau of the Budget (later renamed the Office of Management and Budget [OMB]) established specific criteria to define Standard Metropolitan Areas (SMAs) for presentation in 1950. The Bureau of the Budget was advised in this effort by an interagency committee, with most of the technical support provided by the Bureau of the Census.

Establishing the SMA criteria called for four fundamental decisions: (1) what geographic building blocks to use, (2) how large an area had to be to qualify as an SMA, (3) how to define the core, and (4) how to determine the inclusion of units beyond the core. Generally, the SMAs were defined in terms of counties and included every city of at least 50,000, with a city's county constituting the core. In the New England states, where use of counties would have forced some sizable unrelated cities into single SMAs, an SMA and its core were defined in terms of MCDs (towns and cities), which were locally well known and often used for statistical tabulations. Although the use of county building blocks would lead to some crudeness in the definitions, this was judged to be outweighed by the large amount of statistical data that could be made available by county and hence by SMA.

The participating agencies decided that if at least 15 percent of resident workers commuted on a daily basis, then additional counties should be added to the core county. They chose this cutoff after examining available data for specific areas. Since there were no national commuting data, agencies made decisions on the basis of local surveys of varying methods and coverage.

Besides meeting the commuting cutoff as a measure of integration, counties had to meet certain requirements of "metropolitan character," such as having less than one-third of their labor force engaged in agriculture and at least half their population in contiguous MCDs with at least 150 persons per square mile. Other criteria provided rules for identifying central cities and for titling the SMA. In all, 169 SMAs were defined for 1950, comprising 265 counties and 208 New England MCDs; there also were 3 SMAs defined in Puerto Rico.

Developments Up to 1980

Some changes were made in these criteria in the 1950s, 1960s, and 1970s. After 1960, census commuting data provided an improved basis for measuring integration. Requirements concerning the percentage of a county's workforce engaged in agriculture were dropped after that measure ceased to affect the definitions, and the criterion of metropolitan character required counties with high commuting rates also to meet minimum levels of population density, percent urban population, and/or recent growth. The size requirement for the qualifying city was broadened to allow first for twin-city pairs, and then for a city with many contiguous densely populated areas if the combination exceeded 50,000 in population. The result of these changes, in conjunction with national population increases and substantial migration to large and small cities, was a sizable increase in the number of official areas—to 214 in 1960 and 245 in 1970. The term *Standard Metropolitan Area* was changed to *Standard Metropolitan Statistical Area* (SMSA) in 1959.

As the MAs became better known, some local areas wanted to achieve independent metropolitan status, although they did not qualify for it under either the underlying concept or the official SMSA criteria. However, in 1959 the New York SMSA was reduced by splitting off its New Jersey portion as several separate SMSAs; the Chicago area underwent similar surgery. The pre-1959 extent of these two areas were recognized as Standard Consolidated Areas (SCAs), establishing a two-level metropolitan hierarchy (SMSAs within SCAs). Likewise, Orange County, California, was allowed to secede from the Los Angeles SMSA in 1963, though no Los Angeles SCA was established then. Finally, in 1972 the Nassau-Suffolk SMSA on Long Island was detached from the New York area, although it did not even contain a qualifying central city.

These conspicuous disparities between the MA concept and its official implementation were addressed during the pre-1980 review of the standards. The census-defined UA was adopted as the basis for the MA core, which would consist of all counties with at least half their population in the UA. But it became clear that once defined officially, MAs of the size of Nassau-Suffolk, New York; Newark, New Jersey; and Orange County, California; could not easily be abolished without local concurrence.

The result was the full recognition in the criteria of a two-level hierarchy of areas, with rules, based mainly on commuting ties, for defining subareas termed Primary Metropolitan Statistical Areas (PMSAs). Any area containing PMSAs was labeled a Consolidated Metropolitan Statistical Area (CMSA), and all other areas became MSAs. Besides standardizing the recognition of Nassau-Suffolk and the other seceding areas as PMSAs, these criteria permitted recognizing as PMSAs certain other areas whose separate qualification had been overtaken by heavy commuting to large neighboring areas. Recognition of any PMSA required support from local opinion, which the OMB obtained through congressional offices. The OMB also consulted with congressional offices on some area titles and other issues.

The 1980 criteria also tightened the rules for including outlying counties after comments were received that many counties which had been deemed metropolitan were really rural, even though they had a high percentage of workers commuting. This issue reflected a significant broadening of commuting during the 1960s and 1970s around many smaller cities as the interstate highway system was extended. There were 334 official MAs reported in the 1980 census, but the updating based on that census increased the total to 351 in June 1983, including 253 separate MSAs and 22 SCSAs comprising 76 PMSAs.

By the 1980s, the MAs had achieved a high degree of recognition, which served to multiply the interests eager to achieve particular MA configurations. While this sometimes had statistical aspects—for example as submetropolitan cities campaigned to be recognized as MAs—more often it resulted from some federal agency adopting the MA boundaries to determine eligibility under a nonstatistical program.

Developments from 1990 to 2010

The 1990 census reported a total of 355 official areas. The 1990 review made few changes in the criteria, but with the MA system in its fifth decade, many users saw room for improvement. Some felt that the standards should be less

complicated, even though they also recognized that metropolitan structure had become more complex.

The extensive decentralization of population and employment experienced by most MAs after 1950 had largely been accommodated by the criteria, since most new outlying job centers still were within the UA and hence within the core used to define the area. The expansion of the outlying zone of significant commuting, however, added more counties to MAs that were locally perceived as rural. Such outlying counties accounted for an increasing share of metropolitan territory, even though more than nine-tenths of the metropolitan population still was accounted for by the central counties, as had been the case ever since 1950. In addition, commuting increasingly linked formerly separate metropolitan centers such as Washington-Baltimore and others with large populations, thus demonstrating the importance of the criteria for determining whether such nearby city pairs should be recognized as single areas.

During the 1990s, the OMB and the Census Bureau undertook an extensive investigation of the MA standards and possible modifications thereto, commissioning proposals by some outside scholars and soliciting opinions at two conferences. There continued to be a consensus on the need for a functionally conceived set of official metropolitan definitions in terms of counties, although ideally there would also be one in terms of subcounty units. The UA was confirmed as the starting point for delineations, and commuting was accepted as the most useful available measure of integration, with varying views about what percentage level of commuting should be required. It was recognized that the New England subcounty definitions could be replaced by county definitions. There was also broad agreement that the "nonmetropolitan" category should have some standard official subdivisions, but little consensus on how these should be determined.

After due deliberation, OMB issued extensively revised standards in December 2000. They continued to recognize those MSAs that had UA cores with populations of at least 50,000, and they also recognized Micropolitan Statistical Areas based on UAs with populations of 10,000 to 49,999. They dubbed the two sets collectively as CBSAs. All CBSAs, including those in New England, were delineated in terms of counties, but an ancillary set of New England City and Town Areas (NECTAs) was also delineated.

Counties outside an area's central core qualified for inclusion in a CBSA if at least 25 percent of their resident workers commuted to the central core or if 25 percent of their jobs were held by commuters from the core. The earlier requirements of population density, recent growth, and so on, were eliminated. Two adjacent CBSAs qualified to merge if the central core of one qualified as outlying to another. Relaxation in the criteria for identifying principal cities resulted in longer titles for many CBSAs.

Originally, as in 1980, OMB intended to eliminate separately identified metropolitan units, such as the PMSAs within major MAs, but the final standards for 2000 allowed for recognition of Metropolitan Divisions. (NECTA Divisions in New

England) within MSAs of at least 2.5 million in population. However, the parent areas in such cases remained designated as MSAs rather than being given a distinctive label. Former PMSAs not qualified as Metropolitan Divisions no longer had separate recognition, and the term was dropped.

Adjacent CBSAs were combined if their employment interchange was at least 25 percent and could be combined if interchange exceeded 15 percent, provided local opinion was in favor of combination. The individual areas in such Combined Statistical Areas (CSAs) retained their identity as CBSAs; local opinion was considered in determining CSA titles. The 2000 standards also eliminated a rule that would retain as an MSA an area whose UA population had fallen below 50,000.

The 2000 census reported 349 MAs but after the 2003 updating of the definitions this increased to 361 MSAs. This embraced 232.6 million people or 82.6 percent of the 2000 U.S. total population, compared with 84.9 million and 56.1 percent in the SMAs in 1950. There were also the 573 new micropolitan areas, accounting for another 10.5 percent of the 2000 census total and leaving only 6.9 percent of the population outside CBSAs.

OMB issued revised standards in June 2010 for use after the 2010 census. As in 1990, changes in the standards were minimal in view of the extensive changes made for the preceding census. With the CBSAs update after the 2010 census, all cases of adjacent CBSAs with employment interchange rates between 15 and 25 percent will be combined as CSAs, without reference to local opinion. Updating between censuses will be limited essentially to the recognition of newly qualifying CBSAs, and the term *definition* used hitherto for the criteria for determining MA and CBSA boundaries has been replaced by *delineation*.

See also *Urban areas.*

. . . . RICHARD L. FORSTALL

BIBLIOGRAPHY

Dahmann, Donald C., and James D. Fitzsimmons, eds. *Metropolitan and Nonmetropolitan Areas: New Approaches to Geographical Definition.* Working Paper Series, no. 12. Washington, D.C.: U.S. Bureau of the Census, 1995.

Federal Committee on Standard Metropolitan Statistical Areas. "Documents Relating to the Metropolitan Statistical Area Classification for the 1980's." *Statistical Reporter* (August 1980): 335–384.

Forstall, Richard L., Richard P. Greene, and James B. Pick. "Which Are the Largest? Why Lists of Major Urban Areas Vary So Greatly." *Tijdschrift voor Economische en Sociale Geografie* 100, no. 3 (2009): 277–297. doi:10.1111/j.1467-9663.2009.00537.x.

Office of Management and Budget. "Standards for Defining Metropolitan and Micropolitan Statistical Areas." *Federal Register* 65, no. 249 (2000): 82228–82238. Available at www.whitehouse.gov/sites/default/files/omb/fedreg/metroareas122700.pdf.

Thompson, Warren S. *Population: The Growth of Metropolitan Districts in the United States, 1900–1940.* Washington, D.C.: U.S. Government Printing Office, 1948.

U.S. Bureau of the Census. *Industrial Districts: 1905; Manufactures and Population.* 1905 Census of Manufactures, Bulletin no. 101. Washington, D.C.: Government Printing Office, 1909.

Mortality

See *Vital registration and vital statistics.*

National Archives and Records Administration (NARA)

The National Archives of the United States, established in 1934, holds in trust a vast information resource: the unique and irreplaceable records of the U.S. government. Dating from the First Continental Congress and the earliest period of our federal history, the records come in many forms. They include textual records on paper, microfilm/microfiche, and electronic media. They also include nontextual records—such as architectural drawings, maps and other cartographic records, motion pictures, sound recordings, still pictures, videotape recordings—electronic data files, and publications. As of September 2010, a series-level description for 68 percent of the records in the National Archives can be accessed in the Archival Research Catalog (ARC) at www.archives.gov/research/arc.

NARA acquires, preserves, and makes available for research records of enduring value created or received by organizations of the executive, legislative, and judicial branches of the federal government. Researchers can review textual and nontextual archival holdings or copies of them at NARA's buildings in the Washington, D.C., area or at NARA's presidential libraries or regional records services facilities nationwide. Reproductions of NARA's holdings are available on a cost-recovery basis. A selection of scanned images from NARA's textual and nontextual holdings and a selection of "born digital" records are available online. More information for researchers is available at www.archives.gov/research/.

The Bureau of the Census and the National Archives

Among the reasons advanced for the establishment of a permanent census bureau, as well as for a national archives, was the prevention of the loss of valuable records. During the nineteenth century, a census office was established for each decennial census and was disbanded when its work was completed. Given this discontinuity, and in the absence of a national archives until well into the twentieth century, the preservation of records from the censuses was inconsistent. In fact, the fire in January 1921 at the U.S. Department of Commerce building, which destroyed most of the 1890 decennial census schedules, significantly influenced the movement to establish an archives.

By the time the Census Office became permanent in 1902, the organization of census-related documentation was made up of three main classes: (1) *records,* consisting of all documentation other than schedules and published reports, including unpublished tabulations; (2) *schedules*, the documents on which individual census data were recorded; and (3) *publications*. In 1942 the National Archives formally appraised records and schedules of the Bureau of the Census as having long-term value. This evaluation was in response to an offer by the bureau to transfer to archival custody records of various censuses from 1800 to 1930, the population schedules from 1790 to 1870, and some nonpopulation census schedules. The National Archives accepted these historical materials in March 1942, noting that the records documented the administrative and organizational history of the census agency and that the schedules had well-established value to historians, sociologists, economists, genealogists, and the general public. In the 1930s and 1940s, the Census Bureau microfilmed the original schedules from the censuses from 1840 to 1880, the few schedules that were extant from 1890, and then the 1900–1940 schedules. The 1942 appraisal only partially resolved the issues of the bureau's archives because it did not address the population schedules for 1880 and after or the duplication of the schedules on microfilm. Resolution of these issues came early in the next decade.

In 1951 the National Archives and Records Service concluded that the microfilm form was adequate as the archival record of the census schedules after 1870. Following this decision, the Census Bureau and the National Archives agreed that the bureau would transfer the positive microfilm copies of schedules for 1840–1880 and the paper schedules for 1880 to the Archives. They also agreed that the bureau would transfer the master negative set of microfilm of the schedules for 1840–1940 to the Federal Records Center. The microfilmed schedules would be preserved as the permanent records of the decennial census schedules, and the bureau would transfer its positive microfilm copies for the 1890–1940 schedules to the National Archives in the coming years, as it no longer needed them. Similar decisions have applied to the schedules of later decennial censuses. Finally, the bureau and the Archives agreed that the Federal Records Center would acquire the original paper schedules of the 1950 Census of Population and Housing and would microfilm them. The paper schedules would be destroyed after successful completion of the microfilming.

In 1952 the archivist of the United States, Wayne C. Grover, and the director of the Bureau of the Census, Roy V. Peel, agreed in an exchange of letters to procedures for eventual public release of the population schedules. In 1950 the Congress had passed the Federal Property and Administrative Services Act, imposing a 50-year limit on public release of federal records unless the archivist determined that records should be closed for a longer period. In his testimony when this law was under consideration, the archivist referred to population census schedules as an example of records that might be closed for more than 50 years, noting that eventually they would be made available to researchers.

Subsequently, the director of the bureau wrote to the archivist, proposing nondisclosure of information in the population census schedules for a period of 72 years following the enumeration of each decennial census. In his letter of October 10, 1952, the archivist agreed. Thus the "72-year rule" on the confidentiality of the population census schedules was mutually accepted by the National Archives and the Bureau of the Census. It balanced public release of federal records with the tradition of confidentiality of the census schedules for an extended period. The confidential nature of contemporary census information had evolved gradually during the latter part of the nineteenth century, and in the 1920s the bureau ruled that schedules from censuses prior to 1880 were publicly releasable. In fact, population schedules for the first nine censuses had been deposited in public places to ensure their accuracy.

The 1952 agreement facilitated the release of information from the 1880 census to researchers. The bureau transferred to the National Archives the paper census schedules for the 1880 census and the microfilmed schedules for the 1840–1940 censuses. Rather than retain the 1880 paper schedules, the National Archives donated them in 1956 to the Daughters of the American Revolution (DAR), which subsequently sent some of them to nonfederal depositories nationwide. As agreed, the paper schedules from the 1950 census were destroyed after microfilming. The bureau has transferred microfilmed schedules for the 1960 and 1970 censuses more recently, and transfers of the records for subsequent censuses will follow. In 1978, responding to controversy and objections from the bureau to the National Archives' 1972 opening of the 1900 census schedules to researchers, Congress codified the 72-year rule into law.

In the mid-1970s, the Bureau of the Census, working with staff from the National Archives Machine-Readable Records Division, inventoried and proposed the disposition of the data files (the machine-readable or electronic records) of its Demographic Fields programs. In response, the National Archives appraised these materials and agreed to permanent retention of the decennial Public Use Microdata Samples (PUMS) files and the final decennial Census Summary Tape Files (STFs), including both publicly released files and some tabulations

that would be subject to the 72-year rule. The appraisal archivist noted that these electronic files were the versions of the decennial census that the bureau and other federal agencies had used, just as they had earlier relied on published and unpublished tabulations that had been on paper. Also, the organization of the electronic files by geography enhanced their informational value.

Decennial Census Records and Schedules in the National Archives of the United States

NARA arranges its holdings according to the archival principle of *provenance,* the principle that provides that records be attributed to the agency that created or maintained them and be arranged as they were filed when in active use. At NARA, application of the principle of provenance takes the form of numbered record groups, each comprising the records of a major government entity. The records of the Bureau of the Census and its predecessors form Record Group 29 (R.G. 29) and span the history of the United States from 1790 to the present. The balance of this entry describes the R.G. 29 archives related to the Censuses of Population and Housing.

Textual Records

Administrative. The temporary Census Office for the second through the sixth decennial censuses (1800–1840) was in the U.S. Department of State. The temporary Census Office for the seventh through the twelfth decennial censuses (1850–1900) was in the U.S. Department of the Interior. Administrative records in the National Archives from the Census Office document the fourth through the twelfth censuses (1820–1900).

A permanent Census Office was established in the Department of the Interior in March 1902 and transferred to the newly established U.S. Department of Commerce and Labor in 1903. The name of the office was changed to the U.S. Bureau of the Census later in 1903. Administrative records in the National Archives from the Bureau of the Census include Records of the Office of the Director (1882–1983), the Census Advisory Committee of the American Statistical Association (1919–1963), and the Administrative Services Division. The latter includes records of the chief clerk (1912–1950) relating to census machine equipment, wartime activities, and procedures for taking the 1920–1940 censuses, as well as correspondence, memoranda, and reports from 1900 to 1980. The textual records also hold microfilm copies of 1792–1917 census publications in the Records of the Publications Division and the records of Bureau Directors William Mott Steuart (1922–1932) and William Lane Austin (1933–1941).

Records of the Geography Division include descriptions of enumeration districts (EDs; 1830–1950), as well as publications relating to census mapping activities and the origin and use of the census tract (1947–1952). Other series of administrative records include Records of the Office of the Assistant Director for Statistical Standards (1850–1975), Records of the Assistant Director for Demographic Fields (1870–1982), and Records of the Director of Public Information (1890–1980).

Decennial Population Schedules. NARA preserves 3,100 volumes of manuscript schedules of decennial population censuses (1790–1870); typescript copies of the 1810 and 1820 population schedules from the Ohio and Michigan Territories; 1,150 volumes of photostatic copies of the 1800–1830 population schedules; manuscript schedules of the slave population in 1850 and 1860; four volumes of schedules of a special census of American Indians in 1880; seven volumes of damaged schedules from the 1860 and 1880 censuses; fragments of manuscript population schedules of the eleventh census (1890); and territorial population schedules for Minnesota (1856–1857), Arizona (no date available), and Seminole County, Oklahoma (1907). There are no schedules for some states and territories for the first four censuses, and the returns of some enumerators for later censuses are also missing. NARA also holds 37,770 microfilm rolls with population schedules from 1790 to 1950; the microfilm rolls from more recent censuses are even more voluminous. The National Archives is offering online access to scanned digital images of the 1940 population schedules as of April 2, 2012. This is the first time that NARA is not releasing the decennial census schedules on microfilm.

Nontextual Records

Maps. NARA preserves census ED maps (1880–1970). They consist of approximately 110,000 printed, photocopied, and manuscript maps of cities, counties, lesser political units, and unincorporated areas. Only a small number are extant for 1880 and 1890, but availability increases with each decade. These maps show the boundaries and the numbers of enumeration districts that were established to administer and control census data collection. Wards, precincts, incorporated areas, urban unincorporated areas, townships, census supervisors' districts, and congressional districts may also appear on some maps. The content of ED maps varies greatly among states and over time. The base maps that were used to portray the EDs were obtained locally and include postal maps; general land office maps; soil survey maps; and maps produced by city, county, and state government offices as well as commercial map companies. NARA also has an incomplete set of published and manuscript maps and atlases produced by the Bureau of the Census to illustrate cartographically the findings of the decennial censuses (1860–1970). The earlier statistical atlases show population by race and nationality, vital statistics, wealth, employment, handicapped groups, agriculture, irrigation and drainage, congressional districts, slaves (1860), and types of forest trees. Later maps show the distribution or percentage of the general population, ethnic population, older Americans, income, poverty areas, owned and rented housing, migration, high school education, retail sales, mineral industries, and the value of farm products.

Motion Picture Films. NARA has 43 moving-image titles in R.G. 29. They include training films for enumerators for the sixteenth census (1940); *Know Your U.S.A.*, a film relating to the 1940 census; and a 1940 film about the punch card and tabulating operations of the Census Bureau. *Counting the*

Jobless explains the 1937 Census of Unemployment. NARA has a theatrical trailer on the 1950 population census; a film on the test of a mailed census (no date available); a National Educational Television series concerning the 1960 census, which illustrates the history and work of the Census Bureau; television public information films and spots for the 1960 and 1980 population censuses; and two other Bureau of the Census releases: *Age/Sex Distribution of the Population 1905 to 2025* and *We the People.*

Sound Recordings. R.G. 29 includes 22 sound recording titles. Among them are *Uncle Sam Calling—Story of the 1940 Census,* a three-part interview with Dr. Roy V. Peel (August 2, 1950), as well as the 1950s public service piece by the Golden Gate Quartet singing *There's A Man Going 'Round Taking Names.* Other audio records include public information sound recordings (1959–1960); excerpts from the 1980 Census Users Conference in Little Rock, Arkansas; and the 1990s public service announcement *The 1990 Census Is You*, which accompanies a slide presentation of the same title used to publicize and encourage participation in that year's census.

Still Picture Records. Series of still picture holdings in R.G. 29 include 302 photographic prints and lantern slides showing tabulating machines used by the Bureau of the Census from 1890 to 1950, recording activities relating to the enumeration of the Navajo (circa 1939), and documenting the programs and activities of the Bureau of the Census during the 1940 and 1980 population censuses. Also included in the holdings are the slide presentation *The 1990 Census Is You* and 20 filmstrips that were used to train enumerators for the 1950 and 1960 censuses. In addition, NARA preserves 29 posters encouraging the participation, particularly of ethnic minorities, in the 1980 census.

Data Files

Public Use Microdata Sample (PUMS) Files. The Bureau of the Census produced PUMS files from the long-form census schedules of the 1960–2000 censuses, and they are included among NARA's R.G. 29 electronic records holdings. Since the records in the PUMS files do not include any names of persons or households or any other personal identifiers, and because the geographic identifiers are at a level of aggregation that was designed to ensure complete confidentiality, the PUMS files are fully open. The bureau also transferred to NARA the PUMS files of the 1940 and 1950 censuses, which were created by a University of Wisconsin–Madison project. The National Science Foundation also transferred the public use sample from the 1900 census, which was created by an NSF-funded University of Washington project. Finally, in R.G. 453, Records of the Commission on Civil Rights, NARA preserves the 1970 census PUMS extract files for Puerto Rican and southwestern Spanish-surname persons and households that the Bureau of the Census provided for the Commission.

Census Summary Statistic Files. Summary statistic files contain basic tabulations of census statistics for various legal, administrative, and geographic areas. The bureau began distributing summary statistic files in electronic form with the 1970 census. It has transferred to NARA complete collections of the tabulations known as the first, fourth, and fifth counts of the 1970 census; Public Law 94-171 and STF1, STF2, STF3, and STF4 from the 1980 census; and complete sets of all publicly released STFs and Summary Files (SFs) from the 1990 and 2000 census programs. In R.G. 381, Records of the Community Services Administration, NARA preserves two separate series of statistical tabulations from the 1970 census. One has tabulations for Standard Metropolitan Statistical Area (SMSA) poverty neighborhoods in 107 large central cities; the other records a selection of socioeconomic data for states and counties, based upon Office of Economic Opportunity criteria. Similarly, in R.G. 419, Records of the National Institute of Education (NIE), NARA preserves a data file created for NIE's 1975–1978 Compensatory Education Study that consists of county-level poverty estimates based on 1970 census data. Another electronic version of summary statistics, some of which come from the 1940–1980 decennial censuses, is the County and City Data Book electronic files in R.G. 29. NARA also preserves a complementary series in R.G. 512, Records of the Health Resources and Services Administration, in their Bureau of Health Manpower Area Resources Files. NARA's holdings of these electronic records include data from the 1940s to the 1990s, which include some decennial census data. Finally, Donald Bogue, emeritus professor of sociology, University of Chicago, has donated to NARA summary statistic files compiled largely from Census Bureau paper publications with data for census tracts from the 1940–1970 censuses.

Cartographic. NARA's electronic records also include data files that the Bureau of the Census created specifically for geographic analysis. They include the Master Enumeration District List files (with coordinates) for the 1970 census, the Geographic Base File/Dual Independent Map Encoding (GBF/DIME) Files for the 1980 census, and the Topologically Integrated Geographic Encoding and Referencing (TIGER)/Line files from the 1990 and 2000 census programs. In addition, NARA has reference maps and the *Congressional District Atlas*, 108th and 109th Congresses of the United States, in PDF format from the 2000 census program.

Publications

In addition to the Bureau of the Census publications held as part of R.G. 29, NARA preserves a major collection of Bureau of the Census publications in R.G. 287, which is the Record Group known as Publications of the U.S. Government. The core collection of Bureau of the Census publications came to the National Archives in 1972 when the U.S. Government Printing Office transferred its library collection, sometimes known as the Public Documents Library. It includes multi-volume sets of books and magazines, monographs, guides, manuals, circulars, bulletins, indexes, reports, regulations, maps, charts, and posters. The R.G. 287 publications serve as the nation's "record" copy of government publications that are widely distributed, including to federal depository libraries, and it also includes selected publications unavailable in the depository library system.

See also *Archival access to the census; Confidentiality; Depository libraries; Genealogy; IPUMS (Integrated Public Use Microdata Series); PUMS (Public Use Microdata Samples).*

. . . . MARGARET O'NEILL ADAMS
. . . . WITH THEODORE J. HULL,
. . . . . CONSTANCE POTTER, AND RODNEY A. ROSS

BIBLIOGRAPHY

Publications about the national archives and records administration

McCoy, Donald R. *The National Archives: America's Ministry of Documents, 1934–1968.* Chapel Hill: University of North Carolina Press, 1978.
———. "The Struggle to Establish the National Archives in the United States." In *Guardian of Heritage: Essays on the History of the National Archives,* ed. Timothy Walch, 1–15. Washington, D.C.: National Archives and Records Administration, 1985.

Finding aids describing decennial census records in the national archives

National Archives and Records Administration. 1790–1890 Federal Population Censuses Catalog of NARA Microfilm. www.archives.gov/research/census/publications-microfilm-catalogs-census/1790-1890/index.html (accessed July 2011).
———. 1900 Federal Population Census Catalog of NARA Microfilm. www.archives.gov/research/census/publications-microfilm-catalogs-census/1900/index.html (revised 1996).
———. 1910 Federal Population Census. www.archives.gov/research/census/publications-microfilm-catalogs-census/1910/index.html (revised 1982).
———. 1920 Federal Population Census. www.archives.gov/research/census/publications-microfilm-catalogs-census/1920/index.html (revised 1992).
———. *1970 Census (Nineteenth Census) of Population and Housing: Electronic and Special Media Records Services Division Reference Report* (2005). Available at www.archives.gov/research/census/1970-statistics.html.
———. *1980 Census (Twentieth Census) of Population and Housing: Electronic and Special Media Records Services Division Reference Report* (2010). Available at www.archives.gov/research/census/1980-statistics.html.
———. *1990 Census (Twentifirst Census) of Population and Housing: Electronic and Special Media Records Services Division Reference Report* (2006). Available at www.archives.gov/research/census/1990-statistics.html.
———. Archival Research Catalog (ARC). www.archives.gov/research/arc/ (accessed July 16, 2011).
———. *Census Tract Data Files, 1940–1970 (Elizabeth Mullen Bogue Files): Electronic and Special Media Records Services Division Reference Report* (2007). Available at www.archives.gov/research/census/census-tract-data.html.
———. *Guide to Genealogical Research in the National Archives.* 3rd ed. Washington, D.C.: National Archives and Records Administration, 2001.
———. *Guide to Holdings of the Still Picture Branch of the National Archives and Records Administration* (1990). Compiled by Barbara Lewis Burger. Available at www.archives.gov/research/guides/still-pictures-guide.html.
———. How to Research the Microfilm. http://1930census.archives.gov/beginSearch.asp.
———. *Records of the Bureau of the Census, Record Group 29, 1790–1996, 29.1–29.7* (1996). Compiled by Robert B. Machette, Jan Shelton Danis, Anne B. Eales, et al. Available at www.archives.gov/research/guide-fed-records/groups/029.html.

———. *Records of the Bureau of the Census, Record Group 29.* Preliminary Inventory 161. Compiled by Katherine H. Davidson and Charlotte M. Ashby. Washington, D.C.: National Archives and Records Administration, 1997.

———. Resources for Genealogists. www.archives.gov/research/genealogy/.

National Archives and Records Service. *Preliminary Inventory of the Cartographic Records of the Bureau of the Census: Record Group 29.* Preliminary Inventories no. 103: National Archives Publication no. 58-6. Compiled by James Berton Rhoads and Charlotte M. Ashby. Washington, D.C.: National Archives and Records Service, 1958.

Articles related to decennial census records in the national archives

Adams, Margaret O., and Thomas E. Brown. "Myths and Realities About the 1960 Census." *Prologue* 32, no. 4 (2000). www.archives.gov/publications/prologue/2000/winter/1960-census.html.

Blake, Kellee. "First in the Path of the Firemen: The Fate of the 1890 Population Census." *Prologue* 28, no. 1 (1996). www.archives.gov/publications/prologue/1996/spring/1890-census-1.html.

Collins, James P. "Native Americans in the Census, 1860-1890." *Prologue* 38, no. 2 (2006). www.archives.gov/publications/prologue/2006/summer/indian-census.html.

Crawford, Rebecca. "The Forgotten Federal Census of 1885." *Prologue* 40, no. 3 (2008). www.archives.gov/publications/prologue/2008/fall/1885-census.html.

Green, Kellee. "The Fourteenth Numbering of the People: The 1920 Federal Census." *Prologue* 23, no. 2 (1991): 131–145.

Hendricks, David, and Amy Patterson. "Genealogy Notes: The 1930 Census in Perspective." *Prologue* 34, no. 2 (2002). www.archives.gov/publications/prologue/2002/summer/1930-census-perspective.html.

Pemberton, David M. "'Blisters on My Heels, Corns on My Toes': Taking the 1930 Census of Population." *Prologue* 34, no. 4 (2002). www.archives.gov/publications/prologue/2002/winter/1930-census.html.

Prechtel-Kluskens, Claire. "Genealogy Notes: 'Plans of Division': Describing the Enumeration Districts of the 1930 Census." *Prologue* 35, no. 3 (2003). www.archives.gov/publications/prologue/2003/fall/1930-eds.html.

Native Hawaiian and Other Pacific Islander (NHOPI) Population

Native Hawaiian and Other Pacific Islander (NHOPI) Americans include people who report as NHOPI in response to the race question on the census and other surveys that follow federal standards for collecting and presenting data on race and Hispanic origin. Data on race have been collected since the first census in 1790. Statistical Directive 15, issued by the Office of Management and Budget (OMB) in 1976, led to a combined "Asian/Pacific Islander" racial category in the 1980 and 1990 censuses. The OMB issued revised guidelines in 1997. Beginning with the 2000 census, the combined "Asian/Pacific Islander" racial category was separated into two—"Asian" and "Native Hawaiian and other Pacific Islanders"—and people were allowed to report more than one race. Because of these changes, data from the 2000 census and subsequent sources such as the American Community Survey (ACS) are not directly comparable with those of earlier censuses.

To reflect current practices, data reported here from the 2000 and 2010 censuses and the ACS on NHOPI Americans include all persons who report NHOPI race alone or in combination with one or more other official races—that is, white, black/African American, American Indian or Alaska Native, or Asian. NHOPI Americans encompass diverse peoples with different languages and cultures whose origins are in any of the Pacific Islands—for example, Hawaii, Guam, Samoa, Fiji, and Tonga.

Population Size and Growth

The NHOPI population is the smallest of the five official racial populations of the United States. Because of its small size, we use the three-year period estimates of 2006–2008 for the detailed analyses.

In 2010 there were 1,225,195 NHOPI Americans, representing 0.4 percent of the U.S. population (see Table 1). The NHOPI population increased at a faster rate than the total U.S. population between 2000 and 2010. While the total population grew by almost 10 percent, the NHOPI population grew by 42 percent.

In 2000 and 2010, 44 percent of people who reported NHOPI race reported NHOPI race alone, meaning that the majority of NHOPI people, or 56 percent, reported more than one race in the census.

U.S. Census Bureau projections indicate that the NHOPI American population will grow at a faster pace than the total U.S. population (see Table 2). While the total U.S. population is projected to increase by almost 157 million people between

Table 1. Growth of Total U.S. and Native Hawaiian and Other Pacific Islander (NHOPI) Populations, 1980 to 2010 (numbers in thousands)

	1980		1990		% INCREASE	2000ᵃ		2010ᵃ		% INCREASE
	NO.	%	NO.	%	1980–1990	NO.	%	NO.	%	2000–2010
Total U.S.	226,625	100.0	248,712	100.0	9.7	281,422	100.0	308,746	100.0	9.7
NHOPI	269	0.1	398	0.2	47.9	861	0.3	1,225	0.4	42.2

SOURCES: S. M. Lee, "Asian Americans: Diverse and Growing," *Population Bulletin* 53, no. 2 (Washington, D.C.: Population Reference Bureau, 1998); P. M. Harris and N. A. Jones, "We the People: Pacific Islanders in the United States," *Census 2000 Special Reports* (Washington, D.C.: U.S. Census Bureau, 2005); U.S. Census Bureau, "Overview of Race and Hispanic Origin: 2010," *2010 Census Briefs* (March 2011).

ᵃ The numbers for 2000 and 2010 include people who reported Native Hawaiian and Other Pacific Islander alone or in combination with one or more other races.

Table 2. Projected Change in Population Size of Total U.S. and Native Hawaiian and Other Pacific Islander (NHOPI) Populations, 2000 to 2050 (numbers in thousands)

	2000–2050		2000–2025		2025–2050	
	NO.	%	NO.	%	NO.	%
Total U.S.	156,852	56.0	75,294	27.0	81,558	23.0
NHOPI[a]	1,664	182.0	730	80.0	934	57.0

SOURCE: Table 7, Projected Change in Population Size by Race and Hispanic Origin for the United States: 2000 to 2050 (NP2008-T7) (Washington, D.C.: Population Division, U.S. Census Bureau, 2008).

[a] Includes Native Hawaiian and Other Pacific Islander race alone or in combination with one or more other races.

2000 and 2050 (a 56 percent increase), the NHOPI American population is projected to increase by 1.7 million (a 182 percent increase). According to these projections, the NHOPI population will be about 0.59 percent of the projected total population of 439 million in 2050.

The factors behind population growth are natural increase (births minus deaths) and net international migration (immigrants arriving minus emigrants departing). Natural increase is the main factor in NHOPI population growth. U.S. Census Bureau estimates of components of population change indicate that between 2000 and 2008, natural increase accounted for 77 percent of NHOPI population growth, compared to 62 percent of total U.S. population growth over the same period. This is related to the younger age structure of the NHOPI population, as discussed below.

Detailed Groups

Though the NHOPI population is just a small percentage of the total U.S. population, it is made up of several smaller subgroups, some of which are not large enough to register detailed information in the ACS.

The three largest NHOPI subgroups are Native Hawaiian, Samoan, and Guamanian (see Table 3). Native Hawaiians were 0.14 percent of the U.S. population in 2000 and 0.12 percent in 2007, and they remain the largest NHOPI group. Samoan and Guamanian are the next two largest groups, at about 0.02 percent of the total population in 2007.

Geographical Distribution

The NHOPI population is heavily concentrated in the West (see Table 4). About 78 percent of the NHOPI American population resides in the western region, compared with 23 percent of the total U.S. population. Over 67 percent resides in the Pacific states of Alaska, California, Hawaii, Oregon, and Washington. About 13 percent of NHOPI Americans reside in the South. Two regions where there are few NHOPI Americans are the Northeast (4 percent) and the Midwest (6 percent).

The highest percentages of NHOPI Americans live in five states: Hawaii (35 percent), California (25 percent), Washington (5 percent), and Texas and Utah (3 percent each).

Table 3. Native Hawaiian and Other Pacific Islander (NHOPI) Population, by Detailed Group, 2000 and 2007

	2000		2007	
	NO.	% OF U.S. POPULATION	NO.	% OF U.S. POPULATION
Detailed Group				
Total NHOPI[a]	860,965	0.31	850,086	0.30
Native Hawaiian	400,435	0.14	353,822	0.12
Samoan	128,183	0.05	88,701	0.02
Guamanian	91,380	0.03	95,156	0.02
Tongan[b]	36,982	0.01	NA	NA
Fijian[b]	14,159	0.01	NA	NA
Other Pacific Islander	215,890	0.07	493,427	0.16

SOURCES: Data for 2000 are from P. M. Harris and N. A. Jones, "We the People: Pacific Islanders in the United States," in *Census 2000 Special Reports* (Washington, D.C.: U.S. Census Bureau, 2005); data for 2007 are from author's analysis of 2006-2007-2008 ACS PUMS.

[a] The total is less than the sum of the rows because people who reported one or more NHOPI category or in combination with other races are tabulated once in each category (for example, Native Hawaiian and Samoan are tabulated once in each category but only once in the total). The number for each group includes people who reported the group alone or in combination with one or more other NHOPI group or with one or more other races.

[b] The ACS did not provide data on people who reported each of these two groups alone or in combination with other NHOPI groups or with one or more other races.

Age and Sex

Age and sex are basic variables used in describing populations. The NHOPI American population is considerably younger (median age = 26) than the national population (median age = 36). While the NHOPI American median age is 10 years lower than that of the total population, there are differences within the NHOPI American population. Native Hawaiians have the highest median age of all NHOPI groups, with a median age of 30. The median ages of other NHOPI groups are lower: 24 for Samoans, 27 for Guamanians, and a remarkable 19 for "other NHOPI" Americans.

An examination of the age-sex pyramid (see Figure 1) shows substantially higher percentages of NHOPI Americans at the younger ages. The differences are particularly large for children, youths, and young adults from ages 0 to 24. In contrast, there are substantially lower percentages at older ages, from ages 40 to 44 and older, than in the national population.

The NHOPI American sex ratio (the number of males for every 100 females) is 98, compared to a sex ratio of 97 for the total population. The slightly higher NHOPI American

Table 4. Geographical Distribution of Total U.S. and Native Hawaiian and Other Pacific Islander (NHOPI) Populations, 2007 (in percent)

	TOTAL	NHOPI
Northeast	18.3	3.8
New England	4.8	0.9
Middle Atlantic	13.6	2.9
Midwest	22.0	5.6
East North Central	15.4	3.2
West North Central	6.6	2.4
South	36.6	13.1
South Atlantic	19.2	6.7
East South Central	5.9	1.7
West South Central	11.5	4.6
West	23.1	77.5
Mountain	7.1	10.2
Pacific	16.0	67.3

SOURCE: Author's analysis of 2006, 2007, 2008 ACS PUMS.

Table 5. Nativity and Citizenship, Total U.S. and Native Hawaiian and Other Pacific Islander (NHOPI) Populations, 2007 (in percent)

	NATIVE-BORN CITIZEN	FOREIGN-BORN, NATURALIZED CITIZEN	FOREIGN-BORN, NOT CITIZEN
Total U.S.	87.5	5.3	7.2
Total NHOPI	85.9	5.7	8.4
Native Hawaiian	98.6	0.7	0.7
Samoan	85.1	7.3	7.7
Guamanian	86.4	5.7	7.8
Other Pacific Islander	77.4	9.5	13.1

SOURCE: Author's analysis of 2006, 2007, 2008 ACS PUMS.

sex ratio is related to the fact that the NHOPI category has a younger age structure; younger age groups contain more males than older age groups.

Place of Birth or Nativity and Citizenship

NHOPI Americans born in Hawaii, Guam, or American Samoa are considered native-born U.S. citizens, while most people born on other Pacific Islands (for example, Fiji, Tonga, or Western Samoa) are not considered native-born U.S. citizens unless one or both parents are U.S. citizens.

The percentage of NHOPI who are native-born U.S. citizens (86 percent) is quite similar to that of the total U.S. population (see Table 5). Just 8 percent of NHOPI are not U.S. citizens. Almost all Native Hawaiians are native-born U.S. citizens, as are over 85 percent of Samoans and Guamanians. About 13 percent of "other NHOPI" are not U.S. citizens.

Figure 1. Age-Sex Pyramid, United States and Native Hawaiian and Other Pacific Islander Populations, 2007

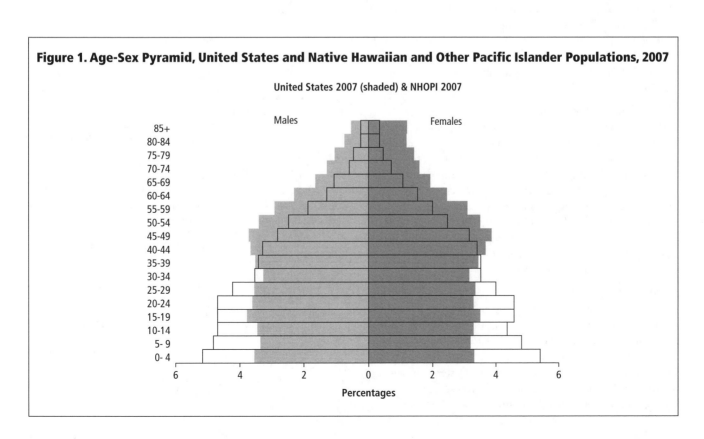

Table 6. Home Language and English Language Proficiency, Total U.S. and Native Hawaiian and Other Pacific Islander (NHOPI) Populations, 2007 (in percent)

	ENGLISH ONLY HOME LANGUAGE	SPEAKS ENGLISH VERY WELL[a]
Total U.S.	80.4	56.2
Total NHOPI	71.1	71.0
Native Hawaiian	89.0	84.1
Samoan	48.6	73.9
Guamanian	63.9	67.2
Other NHOPI	64.8	66.8

SOURCE: Author's analysis of 2006, 2007, 2008 ACS PUMS.

[a] Asked of people who do not speak only English.

Table 7. Educational Attainment, Total U.S. and Native Hawaiian and Other Pacific Islander (NHOPI) Populations, 25 Years and Older, 2007 (in percent)

	LESS THAN HIGH SCHOOL	HIGH SCHOOL GRADUATE	SOME COLLEGE	BACHELOR'S DEGREE OR MORE
Total U.S.	15.5	29.7	27.4	27.4
Total NHOPI	13.2	36.2	33.4	17.2
Native Hawaiian	10.6	37.2	34.3	17.8
Samoan	14.7	39.8	34.6	11.0
Guamanian	19.0	32.9	31.6	16.5
Other NHOPI	14.0	29.9	32.3	23.7

SOURCE: Author's analysis of 2006, 2007, 2008 ACS PUMS.

Home Language and English-Language Proficiency

About 71 percent of NHOPI report speaking English only, compared with 80 percent of the total population (see Table 6). There are differences across NHOPI groups. Almost 90 percent of Native Hawaiians report speaking English only, compared to less than half of Samoans. About two-thirds of Guamanians and "other NHOPI" speak only English.

Among NHOPI who do not speak only English, 71 percent report speaking English very well. Eighty-four percent of Native Hawaiians who do not speak only English speak English very well. Among Samoans, who have the lowest percentage speaking only English, 74 percent of those who do not speak only English speak English very well. Two-thirds of "other NHOPI" who do not speak only English report speaking English very well.

Educational Attainment

NHOPI Americans are less likely to have a bachelor's degree or other higher education: 17 percent versus 27 percent of the total U.S. population (see Table 7). Thirteen percent of NHOPI Americans have less than a high school education, 36 percent are high school graduates, and 33 percent have some college education. Higher percentages of Guamanians have less than a high school education compared to other NHOPI groups and the total U.S. population. The "other NHOPI" category has the highest percentage (24 percent) with a bachelor's degree or more education.

Future Prospects

The NHOPI population is unique in many ways. It is the smallest of the five official racial populations of the United States and is heavily concentrated in a few Pacific states in the western region of the country. It has a much younger age structure. Its size and age structure imply faster-than-average growth of the NHOPI population in future years through two related mechanisms. First, smaller populations tend to have higher intermarriage rates, and if children of intermarried NHOPI parents identify and report as NHOPI, they will add to the NHOPI population through racial-identity reporting. Second, younger populations grow faster through natural increase as more people will move into the reproductive years. U.S. Census Bureau projections indicate that the NHOPI population could increase to 0.59 percent of the U.S. population by 2050. Even so, the NHOPI population will remain the nation's smallest racial population.

See also *American Community Survey: questionnaire content; Race: questions and classifications.*

. . . . SHARON M. LEE

BIBLIOGRAPHY

Grieco, Elizabeth M., and Rachel C. Cassidy. *Overview of Race and Hispanic Origin: 2000.* C2KBR/01-1. Washington, D.C.: U.S. Census Bureau, 2001. Available at www.census.gov/prod/2001pubs/c2kbr01-1.pdf.

Harris, Philip M., and Nicholas A. Jones. *We the People: Pacific Islanders in the United States.* CENSR-26. Washington, D.C.: U.S. Census Bureau, 2005. Available at www.census.gov/prod/2005pubs/censr-26.pdf.

Lee, Sharon M. "Intermarriage Trends, Issues, and Implications." In *Multiethnicity and Multiethnic Families: Development, Identity, and Resilience,* ed. Hamilton McCubbin, Krystal Ontai, Lisa Kehl, Laurie McCubbin, Ida Strom, Heidi Hart, Barbara Debaryshe, Marika Ripke, and Jon Matsuoka, 15–42. Honolulu: Le'a Publications, 2010.

Lee, Sharon M., and Barry Edmonston. "New Marriages, New Families: U.S. Racial and Hispanic Intermarriage." *Population Bulletin* 60, no. 2 (2005). Available at www.prb.org/pdf05/60.2newmarriages.pdf.

U.S. Census Bureau. U.S. Population Projections: Summary Tables 1, 6, and 7. www.census.gov/population/www/projections/summarytables.html.

———. Population Estimates: Cumulative Estimates of the Components of Resident Population Change by Race and Hispanic Origin for the United States; April 1, 2000 to July 1, 2008 (NC-EST2008-05). www.census.gov/popest/national/asrh/NC-EST2008-compchg.html.

Not-for-Profit Organizations

Not-for-profit organizations, which occupy the realm between the profit-making private sector and the governmental public sector, collectively have been labeled the *independent sector*, the *third sector*, the *voluntary sector*, and even the *invisible sector*. Overall, though, and especially in recent years, not-for-profits hardly have been invisible when it comes to their opinions about the conduct and content of the decennial census, their use of census data, and their interest in promoting an accurate count.

The not-for-profit world of American organizational life is huge and complex. The sector includes an estimated 1.5 million agencies, organizations, institutions, and projects with vastly varied roles, purposes, and efficiencies, from multi-billion-dollar umbrella agencies raising funds to advance specific causes to storefront churches delivering services to neighborhoods. Today, the sector is estimated to employ 9 percent of the American workforce and to make up 5 percent of the gross domestic product.

The not-for-profit world includes social- and human-services agencies, churches, schools, colleges and universities, research institutes, hospitals, foundations, social-action and civil-rights movements, arts and cultural organizations, community development groups, associations and mutual benefit societies, and a host of others. Not-for-profits have had a major impact on the history of the United States, helping to shape social and cultural values, playing mediating roles between large bureaucratic institutions and individuals, and providing services to millions of citizens.

In its vast work, the not-for-profit sector consumes, analyzes, and applies the results of the decennial census and intercensal estimates and is now doing the same with the detail that the American Community Survey (ACS) provides. Some organizations within the sector even function as not-for-profit "extensions" of the for-profit world, playing important roles in the economic and political realms and distributing value-added, census-derived information that is pertinent to their members.

In the 1970s not-for-profits began laying their claim as stakeholders in the decennial census, coming to sit at the "census decision table" to ensure the preservation and inclusion of aspects of the census that were important to their constituencies. Over time, these groups have examined and commented forcefully on census operations and conduct to ensure that those they represent are not unduly disadvantaged by the results, and they have called attention to specific interests or changes in society demonstrated within the ranks of their members, constituencies, and clientele.

Stakeholders on the User and Recipient Ends of the Decennial Data Application Spectrum

Despite the broad range of organizational types and functions that comprise the sector, the *not-for-profit* label most often is associated with charities and the delivery of social and human services. Food, shelter, day care, residential care, health care, legal services, job training, and hundreds of other services are provided by thousands of organizations. Some, like the United Way, Salvation Army, and Big Brothers/Big Sisters, are part of national networks; others are based in a single jurisdiction and operate independently; many are multipurpose agencies operating direct-service, advocacy, and education programs.

These nonprofits use demographic, socioeconomic, and other data from the decennial census and intercensal estimate programs not only to target clientele, plan and implement appropriate programs and services, and measure performance in communities but also to identify and make the case for their worth to donor populations and foundations, meet preconditions for grant support, and ensure their share of governmental dollars that are allocated on the basis of census data. Data from smaller geographic areas often serve to draw comparisons within and between communities and act as benchmarks to validate local surveys of need conducted by community-based organizations.

Nonprofits' interest in the census, though, reaches beyond their own use of the data to the implications of how the decennial census is conducted and how the results affect them and those they represent. It was in the early stages of discussion on the form and content of the 1980 census, even before the 1970 census was completed, that a broad-based coalition of groups, including not-for-profits, demanded to be part of the formal planning process. That phenomenon continued and expanded through the planning for the 2000 and 2010 censuses.

Representatives of social- and human-service-oriented not-for-profits, advocacy groups, and racial and ethnic civil rights groups with a national reach have argued on a variety of census-related issues, not least among them the likelihood that persons of color and the rural and urban poor will be disproportionately represented among those left uncounted. These and other segments of the population, which are more heavily served by nonprofits, are missed more often than others in the count. This, in turn, compounds the consequences of undercount because it decreases the ability of these organizations and the communities they assist to sustain service requests in the face of lower funding based on lower official numbers.

Over the years, groups like the National Association for the Advancement of Colored People (NAACP), the Mexican American Legal Defense and Educational Fund (MALDEF), the National Council of La Raza, the National Urban League, the National American Indian Council, the National Indian Education Association, and the Coalition for an Accurate Count of Asian and Pacific Islanders, among many others, have been vocal on undercount issues and energetic in other census-related activities. But so have other not-for-profits and major public interest groups representing state and local governments and government officials, including the U.S. Conference of Mayors, the National League of Cities, the National Association of Counties, the National Conference of State Legislatures, and the National Black Caucus of State Legislators. Through policy conferences, resolution adoptions, and congressional testimony, not-for-profits such as these have often taken alternate sides on the use of statistical sampling to augment the traditional census count, requested population adjustments to known undercounts, and noted difficulties with pre-census and post-census review periods. Along with not-for-profits in other functional areas, they have encouraged stronger community-level partnerships with the Census Bureau in planning, promoting awareness of, and implementing the decennial census. Building on the 2000 experience, the 2010 Census Partnership Program attracted 200,000 partners to the effort, the vast majority of them community-based organizations.

Post-census evaluations likely will reveal that multiple factors contributed to an unprecedented mobilization among not-for-profit organizations to promote participation in the 2010 Census. However, grim economic conditions nationally, coupled with state and local governmental budget cuts, were a significant part of the dynamic, according to sector representatives. Not-for-profits worked to make sure their clientele—often comprised of historically hard-to-count populations—got the message that the census would be safe, would be necessary for their political representation, and would benefit them directly. In many instances, charitable foundations, individually or in concert with counterparts, provided the dollars for census outreach.

A few of the numerous examples of not-for-profit involvement leading to the 2010 Census are (1) Nonprofits Count!, a nationwide campaign to mobilize organizations to get involved with the census, with special emphasis on traditionally undercounted communities; (2) an expansion of the Ya Es Hora ("Now Is the Time") civic participation campaign launched by the National Association of Latino Elected and Appointed Officials (NALEO) Educational Fund, to include NALEO's national initiative to achieve a full Latino count in 2010; and (3) The Funders Census Initiative, an ad hoc working group committed to stimulating interest in the census among funders and their grantees.

See also *Advisory committees; Grassroots groups.*

. . . .   DEBORAH A. GONA

BIBLIOGRAPHY

Fessler, Pam. "Charities Spend Millions on Census Outreach." NPR.org, March 9, 2010. www.npr.org/templates/story/story.php?story Id=124496951.

O'Neill, Michael. *The Third America: The Emergence of the Nonprofit Sector in the United States.* San Francisco: Jossey-Bass, 1989.

Tobin, Gary A. *Social Planning and Human Service Delivery in the Voluntary Sector.* Westport, Conn.: Greenwood Press, 1985.

U.S. Congress, House Committee on Post Office and Civil Service, Subcommittee on Census and Population. *The Role of Community and Advocacy Organizations during the 1990 Census and in Planning for the 2000 Census. Hearings before the Subcommittee on Census and Population of the Committee on Post Office and Civil Service, One Hundred Second Congress, First Session, October 29 and 30, 1991.* Serial no. 102-32. Washington, D.C.: U.S. Government Printing Office, 1992.

Occupation and Education

Questions about occupation and education have been included in some form in every census for over 170 years. As long ago as the first census in 1790, debates about content of the census reflected a view that knowledge about the social and economic composition of the population was needed in order to plan for the development of a new society. Numerous proposals were made before occupation and literacy became part of the information collected in the 1820 and 1840 censuses, respectively. Since then, and especially since 1950, occupation and education have been important indicators of societal change and of differences in the social and economic status of various American populations.

Occupation

Three broad classes of occupation—"agriculture," "commerce," and "manufactures"—were the basis for the first official occupational count in 1820. Today we would view these as industrial classifications; that is, one's *occupation*, or what work one does, is separated from the *industry* in which one performs the work. Although enumerators were instructed to assign more specific occupations to each broad group, only the three broad categories can be identified in the 1820 census.

The increasing division of labor in American society can be observed in the growing number of occupational classifications in subsequent censuses. No occupational information was collected in 1830, but in 1840 seven occupational categories were included: "mining"; "agriculture"; "commerce"; "manufactures and traders"; "navigation of the ocean"; "navigation of canals, lakes, and rivers"; and "learned professions and engineers". Although these categories were more representative than the earlier three, they omitted servants, government officials, clerks, and others. Also, the census enumerated families rather than individuals in 1840 and listed the number of persons in each family who were in each broad occupational class.

A major change occurred in the 1850 census, when enumeration shifted from the family to the individual. Separate schedules were provided for free persons and for slaves. Information on occupation was acquired only for free males over age 15, but greater occupational detail was collected. In 1850, 323 specific occupations were classified under 10 headings.

In 1860, women as well as men over age 15 were asked their occupations, and the increasing complexity of the economy was reflected in the classification of 584 detailed occupations. Between 1870 and 1930, persons age 10 and over were included in the occupational inquiry, reflecting the prevalence of child labor in the United States. In 1940 and later, the age limit was 14 years and over, reflecting the effect of child labor laws that prohibited or limited the paid employment of children.

Other modifications reflected further changes in the American economy and labor force. Separate questions on occupation and industry were introduced in 1910, and the number of detailed categories shifted each decade. These changes in coverage and in the census categories of occupations occurred because of an expanded economy, a greater division of labor, the emergence of new jobs, the disappearance of others, and some major shifts in broad occupational areas. In 1790 the nation was predominantly agricultural. By the mid-twentieth century, it had become predominantly industrialized and commercial. In the twenty-first century, it has become increasingly a service economy with continuing changes in job categories. By looking at the proportion of people in each occupational group, one can observe these broad social and economic changes. For example, the change from a largely rural to a largely urban population is evident in the declining percentage of "gainful workers" in agriculture, from 86 percent in 1820, to less than 60 percent by 1860, to 37 percent by 1900, and to 18 percent in 1940, when the "gainful worker" concept was last used in a census. From 1940 on, when employment was described in terms of labor-force concepts (specifically "employed, unemployed, and not in the labor force"), the decline in agricultural workers continued until it reached only about 4 percent of the male civilian labor force by 1980. Other occupations were dropped from the classification as technological advances made them obsolete.

As workers moved from farm to nonfarm work, the composition of nonfarm work changed throughout the twentieth century. Work in the service trades grew, as did the proportion of operatives, craftspeople, and related workers; on the other hand, the number of laborers declined. The most significant rise in the twentieth century was observed in white-collar occupations, from about 18 percent of all workers in 1900 to over 40 percent by 1980.

Occupational trends were usually described in detail for men or for the total population until 1970, when the increasing involvement of women in the labor force required separate tabulations for men and women. The percentage of women who were in the labor force increased from 18 percent in 1890, to 52 percent in 1980, to about 60 percent in 2000. Trends in the occupational distribution of women differed from those of men. There was a notable drop in private household workers, such as housekeepers, from 1900 to 1980 and significant declines in the "operative" category as well. In contrast, trends among women were similar to those among men in the number of farm workers and other manual types of work as well as white-collar occupations. Some convergence was evident by 1980, although many more women were still in clerical and service work, whereas men were concentrated in managerial and craft occupations. This convergence continued through 1990 and 2000.

In response to these societal changes, the Census Bureau made changes in the occupational classifications each decade, including two major changes since 1950. The 1950 and 1960 classifications are similar. A major reclassification and expansion of detailed occupation/industry/class-of-worker categories occurred in the 1970 census, from 466 categories in 1960 to 589 in 1970. In 1980 another major change occurred when the Census Bureau changed to a classification system designed to be consistent with the Standard Occupational Classification (SOC) developed for use by all government agencies. The system was introduced in 1977 and revised several times. The 1980 and 1990 census classifications are almost identical, and relatively few changes were made for Census 2000, making historical comparisons relatively easy.

The Census 2000 occupational classification was based on the 1998 revision of the SOC, which contained 822 detailed occupations. These were aggregated to 509 in the 2000 census detailed occupation classification and were generally comparable to the 501 in the 1990 census. Historical comparisons of occupational distributions between 1990 and 2000 may be made as both were based on a one-in-six sample of households actually enumerated in the census. "Crosswalks," or bridges, between the two have been created. Historical comparisons with the 2010 census may be more problematic because major changes in the source of occupation data occurred at that time.

In 2010 every household was sent a ten-question short form similar in format to what had been done over the past several decades. The long form, which had been sent to a one-sixth sample of households since 1960 to obtain detailed social and economic data (including occupation and education), was dropped. It was replaced for 2010 by the American Community Survey (ACS) in the form of combined files of separate monthly sample surveys of about 240,000 addresses. This major change affected all census users who compare the social and economic characteristics of the American population over time. Census data have been used to measure and compare, for example, changes in the occupational distribution and educational levels of men and women and of minority and majority populations, and they have been used to decide practical matters such as locating a school. Instead of data products for a single point in time, users now have multi-year period estimates for one-year, three-year, or five-year intervals, which must be reconciled with the earlier single-point-in-time data from the long form.

The ACS data for a single year are combined from 12 monthly surveys. This continuous design of the ACS raises some issues that must be addressed by researchers who want to compare, for example, the occupational distributions of black men and white men in 2000 and 2010. First, how do the data for the one-, three-, and five-year periods in the ACS compare to the point-in-time data from the 2000 long-form sample? Multi-year averages may mask short-term changes in the characteristics of groups. Second, what are the extent and effects of the greater sampling errors in the ACS compared to long-form estimates? The ACS may not meet generally accepted error rates for small areas and/or small population groups, such as recent college graduates or smaller ethnic groups, because of the smaller size of the ACS samples (in the range of 2 percent of addresses annually compared to the approximately one-sixth long-form sample). Because of the larger sampling errors, users will need to develop strategies such as collapsing data categories or combining data for tracts or block groups. The Census Bureau has developed a large variety of ACS data products that meet or exceed the product detail provided earlier for the 2000 census long form. This includes several Public Use Microdata Sample (PUMS) products, which provide users with the capacity to construct custom tabulations for specific occupational categories.

Education

Information on literacy, meaning the ability to read and write in at least one language, was first collected in 1840 and was collected in each census through 1930. The distinction between literate and illiterate persons, while not significant in recent years, differentiated a significant proportion of the population in earlier decades. In 1840, 22 percent of the population was illiterate. The illiteracy rate declined over the years to 11 percent by 1900 and to just over 4 percent by 1930. More recent censuses focused on school enrollment and educational attainment.

School enrollment statistics have been included in each census since 1850, primarily for younger persons. The proportion of the "school-age population" enrolled in school increased dramatically during the twentieth century. Between 1940 and 1990, the proportion of persons ages 5–24 (defined as the school-age population) who were enrolled in school increased from 58 percent in 1940 to 70 percent in 1990. Recent trends have shown people enrolling earlier and staying longer. In 1990, 30 percent of three- and four-year-olds were enrolled in preschool, and 80 percent of five- and six-year-olds were enrolled in school; these figures compare to 49 percent and 91 percent, respectively, in 2000. At the other end of the age spectrum, about one-third of persons ages 20–24 and 12 percent of those ages 25–34 were enrolled in school in 1990, compared to almost 36 percent and 12 percent, respectively, in 2000.

The wording of the enrollment questions on the decennial censuses changed over time in response to this increased enrollment. "College" was added to the enrollment question in 1930. In 1940, the question of whether the person had been enrolled in the previous year was changed to whether the person had been enrolled since March 1 of the census year, and the question on the highest grade attended was expanded to include the highest grade of school completed. In the 1950 census, the reference date for school enrollment was changed to February 1, where it has remained ever since. In 1960 a question on whether enrollment was in public or private school was added, and in 1990 the question on level of attendance was changed to request the highest degree or highest level completed. In 2000 school enrollment information was collected for people ages 3 and over rather than 5 and over. As a result, historical comparisons published by the bureau for recent decades tend not to define a "school-age population" as ages 5–24 or 3–24 but to describe enrollment in terms of the percentage of the population age 3 and over, which was 27.3 percent in 1990 and 28.4 percent in 2000. Because of changes in the wording of the questions, enrollment figures at some specific levels above high school are not strictly comparable.

Educational attainment is a good measure of socioeconomic achievement for adults who have passed the usual school-completion age, which is generally defined as age 25 and over. The educational attainment of persons in this age group increased dramatically throughout the twentieth century, particularly during the last half of the century. Over 80 percent of the adult population had completed high school or more in 2000, compared to 75 percent in 1990 and only about 25 percent in 1940. In addition, almost one-fourth of the adult population had completed four or more years of college in 2000, compared to one-fifth in 1990 and compared to only 5 percent in 1940. Part of the increase in educational attainment is undoubtedly due not only to changing occupational requirements but also to changing laws requiring that larger proportions of young people remain in school, first until age 14 or 15 and then, in most states, until age 16. Thus, persons born after 1930 were required to be in school long enough to complete at least eight years of school, if not high school. The results are evident in any breakdown of educational attainment by age. For example, in 2000 among persons ages 25–29, 84 percent had completed high school or more, compared to only 61 percent of persons age 75 and over.

In 1990 a significant change occurred in the way the educational attainment question was asked. In the censuses of 1940–1980, educational attainment was measured in terms of years of school completed. In 1990 the question was asked in terms of completion of specific degrees, so that in 1990, one could say that 75 percent of the adult population had received a high school diploma, compared to 1940, when about 25 percent reported completion of four years of high school. This change was perceived as an improvement because some people complete four years of high school without receiving a degree. Also, the increased attainment levels required more detail on achievement at the upper end of the education measures.

For the first time, the 1990 census identified the number of adults who had received bachelor's, master's, doctoral, or professional degrees. By 2000 the question included 16 educational levels, from "no schooling" to "professional degree" or "doctorate degree." In 1990, 20 percent of the population had received a bachelor's degree or higher, and about 7 percent of adults age 25 and over reported that they had received master's, doctoral, or professional degrees. By 2000, these percentages had increased to 24.4 percent and 8.9 percent, respectively. In general, the data show that the United States experienced major improvements in the education of its population in the last half of the twentieth century, in terms of both the proportion going to and staying in school and the proportion receiving high school and college diplomas and degrees.

That improvement is not the same for all population groups. As noted, there are age-related differences in educational attainment, but there have also been, and continue to be, differences by gender, race, and ethnicity. As of 2000, the differences in educational attainment between men and women were relatively small. For example, about 26 percent of men and 23 percent of women had a bachelor's degree or more. In contrast, although the educational attainment of major race and ethnic groups in the population had improved since 1960, some significant differences remained. In 2000, the Asian groups had, for example, the largest proportion of college graduates of all groups: 44 percent compared to 24 percent of all persons age 25 and over. In contrast, only 10 percent of the Hispanic or Latino-origin population had bachelor's degrees or more.

Differences also exist in terms of educational achievements of the populations of different regions and states within the United States. A good measure of disadvantage is the proportion of school dropouts, or of persons age 25 years and over who are not enrolled in school and who are not high school graduates. With increasing educational attainment, all states had lower high school dropout levels in 2000 than in previous decades. Considerable variation in the dropout rate remained, however, ranging from 33 percent in Alabama to about 18 percent in New Hampshire. The states with the highest dropout rates were in the South and West, generally. High school completion is a basic measure of educational attainment and almost a necessity to obtain a job with any possibility for future advancement. Hence, there is still room for improvement in educational attainment.

The wording of questions on education in the ACS is similar to that on the 2000 census long form. And with the addition of "field of degree" information starting with the 2009 ACS, information on the educational attainment of the nation will be further enhanced. Still, historical comparisons of education involving the ACS must address some of the same issues noted above in the "Occupation" section, with respect to larger errors associated with smaller sample size and comparisons of single-point-in-time data from the decennial censuses to multi-year period estimates from the ACS. Regardless, data on occupation and education will continue to be collected through the ACS and, with creative analytic decisions, will continue to be valuable for research aimed at social and economic planning for the twenty-first century.

See also *Education: changing questions and classifications; Long form.*

. . . . MARY G. POWERS

BIBLIOGRAPHY

Bauman, Kurt J., and Nikki L. Graf. *Educational Attainment: 2000.* C2KBR-24. Washington, D.C.: U.S. Government Printing Office, 2003. Available at www.census.gov/prod/2003pubs/c2kbr-24.pdf.

Bradley, Dana, and Katherine Earle. "Developing and Explaining the Crosswalks between Census 1990 and 2000 Industry and Occupation Codes." Proceedings of the Annual Meeting of the American Statistical Association, Atlanta, Ga., August 5–9, 2001.

Day, Jennifer Cheeseman, with assistance from Amie Jamieson. *School Enrollment: 2000.* C2KBR-26. Washington, D.C.: U.S. Government Printing Office, 2003. Available at www.census.gov/prod/2003pubs/c2kbr-26.pdf.

Kominski, Robert, with assistance from Andrea Adams. *We the Americans: Our Education.* WE-11. Washington, D.C.: U.S. Government Printing Office, 1993. Available at www.census.gov/apsd/wepeople/we-11.pdf.

Nam, Charles B., and Monica Boyd. "Occupational Status in 2000: Over a Century of Census-Based Measurement." *Population Research and Policy Review* 23, no. 4 (2004): 327–358. doi:10.1023/B:POPU.0000040045.51228.34.

Nam, Charles B., and Mary G. Powers. *The Socioeconomic Approach to Status Measurement: With a Guide to Occupational and Socioeconomic Status Scores.* Houston, Texas: Cap and Gown Press, 1983.

National Research Council. *Using the American Community Survey: Benefits and Challenges.* Panel on the Functionality and Usability of Data from the American Community Survey. Constance F. Citro and Graham Kalton, eds. Committee on National Statistics, Division of Behavioral and Social Sciences and Education. Washington, D.C.: The National Academies Press, 2007. Available at http://www.nap.edu/catalogue.php?record_id=11901.

U.S. Census Bureau. *A Compass for Understanding and Using American Community Survey Data: What Researchers Need to Know.* Washington, D.C.: U.S. Government Printing Office, 2009. Available at http://www.census.gov/acs/www/guidance_for_data_users/handbooks/.

Organization and Administration of the Census

Each census of the United States requires the mobilization of an "army" of temporary workers to collect the information needed to fulfill the constitutional mandate for a census: Article I, section 2 says, "The actual Enumeration shall be made within three Years after the first Meeting of the Congress of the United States, and within every subsequent Term of ten Years, in such Manner as they shall by Law direct." The U.S. census, begun in 1790, is the longest continuously administered census in the world. During the peak week for employment in 2010, the Census Bureau employed 585,729 temporary field enumerators, 6,799 temporary office workers, and 6,382 temporary workers in its paper data capture centers (PDCCs), in addition to hundreds more permanent workers. These temporary employees helped to locate over 130 million housing units, count more than 305 million people, and process more than 1.5 billion pieces of paper. The Census Bureau accomplished this feat under intense political, social, and legal scrutiny, while trying to chronicle the ever-changing demographic face of America.

The 2010 census was a "reengineered" census. The Census Bureau attempted to make three radical changes in census taking between 2000 and 2010. It was fully successful in two of those changes but only partly successful in the third.

The first change was to eliminate the long form—questions asked only of a sample of the population—a feature of the census since 1940. This was accomplished in 2005 by launching the American Community Survey (ACS), a monthly survey of households and (in 2006) of people living in group quarters (roughly 3.5 million addresses per year as of June 2011) that collects Census 2000 long-form data (with a few topical additions). By accumulating data from the ACS from five consecutive years, estimates are provided for geographic areas as small as block groups, as well as for small population groups. Since this is an ongoing survey, long-form-equivalent information has become available every year starting in 2010, instead of just once per decade, for small geographic areas.

The second major change was to update the geographic framework of the census—both the Master Address File (MAF) and the Topologically Integrated Geographic Encoding and Referencing (TIGER) system spatial (map) database. The MAF was updated continuously through the 2000s, using the U.S. Postal Service Delivery Sequence File (DSF) for city-style addresses and using the Census Bureau's Community Address Updating System (CAUS) for rural addresses. The MAF was further updated for the 2010 census through a nationwide address canvassing operation in mid-2009. TIGER was updated by a contractor, which aligned all the street features in every U.S. county, and in Puerto Rico and all Island Areas, with global positioning system (GPS) coordinates. Then the address canvassing operation obtained GPS coordinates for all housing units.

The third change was to automate as many 2010 census operations as possible. While automated processing of the actual census forms has been around for quite a while—for example, the Census Bureau invented the film optical sensing device for input to computers (FOSDIC) for the 1960 Census—the intention was to use handheld computers (HHCs) for most data collection operations. Due to problems encountered with the HHC software in the 2007 dress rehearsal for the address canvassing operation, the Census Bureau removed HHC-based data collection for nonresponse follow-up (NRFU) from the contractor's portfolio and built its own operations-control system for paper-based data collection, the same methodology that has been used for NRFU for many decades. This change added perhaps $1.5 billion to the cost of the 2010 census, but in the opinion of the Census Bureau and its parent agency (the U.S. Department of Commerce), it reduced the risk of an unsuccessful census.

Management Structure

At the time of the 2010 census, the Census Bureau was organized into eight directorates, each under an associate director. Each associate director reported to the director through the deputy director. All of these directorates were involved in some way in the 2010 census. Although the roles played by each directorate were crucial to the census, three positions were particularly key:

- The director, a political appointee who is ultimately responsible to the president (through the secretary of commerce) and to Congress (Dr. Robert Groves became director in July 2009).
- The associate director for decennial census (ADDC), who oversaw all decisions for planning, budget, and operations.
- The associate director for field operations, who oversees data collection by the Field Division, which for the 2010 census encompassed 12 regional offices (ROs), 12 regional census centers (RCCs), a Puerto Rico area office, 494 local census offices (LCOs), and the aforementioned army of temporary enumerators.

The Office of the ADDC directed and provided planning and coordination of the 2010 census, aided principally by the assistant director for ACS and decennial census and the chief of the Decennial Management Division (DMD); the latter served as the program manager for the census. The decennial directorate managed and coordinated all funding for decennial-related operations. Under the ADDC were DMD, the Geography Division, the Decennial Statistical Studies Division (DSSD), and the Decennial Systems and Contracts Management Office (DSCMO); all but the last reported to the associate director through the assistant director. DSCMO was divided into the following two offices during the operational phase of the census: the Decennial Systems and Processing Office (DSPO) and the Decennial Automation and Contracts Management Office (DACMO).

The DMD provided overall direction for program planning and coordination of the decennial census; assigned functional responsibility to divisions; determined program priorities; and developed budget requirements, schedules, and a cost- and progress-reporting and control system. It monitored and documented program and budget status; served as the primary point of contact on the decennial census program with the Census Bureau's outside oversight groups, such as the U.S. Government Accountability Office (GAO), the U.S. Department of Commerce Office of the Inspector General, and congressional oversight committees; developed census methodology plans and organized test and research programs (with DSSD); and recommended policy for decennial program issues. DMD also ran the census risk-management process and chaired the Census Integration Group (CIG) and the Risk Review Board.

The Geography Division plans, coordinates, and administers all geographic and cartographic activities needed to facilitate the Census Bureau's statistical programs throughout the United States (including Puerto Rico). For the 2010 census, its work also included the four U.S. Island Areas. The DSSD develops and coordinates the application of statistical techniques in the design and conduct of decennial censuses.

The DSSD managed all quality-control operations for the 2010 census and is running the 2010 Census Coverage Measurement (CCM) program. It also is responsible for many of the evaluations and assessments of the 2010 census, including (in collaboration with others at the Census Bureau) reports on the experiments embedded within that census.

The DSPO managed all headquarters hardware for the 2010 census, including the hardware needed for the universe control and management (UC&M) system, the response processing system (RPS), and DMD's cost and progress system, excluding the hardware for the MAF/TIGER database (which is managed by the Geography Division). It was also responsible for the software to manage the 2010 census, including UC&M, RPS, and the paper-based operations control system (PBOCS).

The DACMO managed the development and implementation of major Census 2010 contracts, including development and implementation of a data capture system; acquisition of hardware, software, telecommunications, and integration services required to support the temporary offices; acquisition of other support such as printing of census forms; conduct of telephone questionnaire assistance (TQA) and telephone coverage follow-up; and development of the tabulation and dissemination systems.

The Office of the Associate Director for Field Operations plans and conducts data collection for other censuses and surveys as well as the decennial census. Within this directorate are the Field Division, the National Processing Center (NPC), the Technologies Management Office (TMO), and the ROs covering the United States and Puerto Rico. The Field Division plans, organizes, coordinates, and carries out the Census Bureau's data collection in the field. The 12 RCCs set up for 2010 operated a national network of 494 temporary offices from which employees collected the census data. Census operations in American Samoa, the Commonwealth of the Northern Mariana Islands, Guam, and the U.S. Virgin Islands were conducted by the Census Bureau out of its headquarters in partnership with the government of each Island Area. The Census Bureau supplied a liaison and funding and handled processing and tabulation, while the local governments handled data collection.

The NPC, located in Jeffersonville, Indiana, conducts statistical-processing operations for current and special surveys and censuses and provides related administration and logistics services for its programs. The NPC also ran one of the three PDCCs used to scan, key, and transmit 2010 census questionnaires. The TMO develops and implements computer assisted data collection and related support operations and oversees the development of automated questionnaires for computer assisted interviewing (CAI) and related systems and applications in support of critical data collection programs, such as operations control systems. The TMO was responsible for designing the software to manage and collect the personal interview portion of the 2010 CCM program.

The director and deputy director are responsible for the highest level of decision making that substantially affects budget, program success, or policy. They work under the direction and with the advice of the undersecretary of commerce for economic affairs, the secretary of commerce, and the Office of Management and Budget (OMB).

The 2010 Decennial Leadership Group (DLG) consisted of senior executive staff responsible for the operational level of decision making and oversight. The DLG was chaired by the associate director for decennial census, and during operations it included the assistant director for ACS and decennial census, the associate director for field operations, and the chiefs of DMD and the Field Division. It also included other associate directors as appropriate (depending on the topic).

The CIG was the primary governance group for the 2010 census. It was composed of division chiefs of all key involved divisions, as well as a substantial number of important contributing divisions and offices. The CIG performed high-level program integration across divisions and functional teams and resolved issues escalated from the teams. The CIG also operated as the 2010 Census Change Control Board and the 2010 Census Risk Review Board.

The operations and systems teams were chartered cross-divisional structures that were responsible for the planning and monitoring of the 2010 census operations and their supporting systems; a team might be responsible for more than one of the 44 high-level operations. Implementing the 2010 census involved several types of teams made up of both headquarters staff and contractors. Team leaders prepared any team status reports. These included quarterly briefings of the CIG during the development phase on accomplishments, upcoming activities, issues, risks, and testing, and weekly or daily briefings during ongoing operations. The team leader was responsible for resolving conflicts in schedules, resources, and other areas of responsibility, elevating issues for CIG resolution only when necessary. Leaders from all teams met on a biweekly basis to vet and resolve integration issues.

Operational responsibility rested with Census Bureau divisions, and they were all responsible for resource management within their budgets for the 2010 census as established by DMD. This included both resource balancing to ensure sufficient resources were applied to the highest-priority operations and activities as well as succession planning to remove the unacceptable risk of having single points of failure in the staffing plan. Division chiefs were to make every effort to resolve issues brought to them from the team leaders or assistant division chiefs before raising the issue to the CIG.

Recently, the Census Bureau made several organizational changes, which have implications for planning the 2020 census. A new associate director for 2020 census position has been created with responsibility for 2020 planning and the operation of the ACS, while the ADDC continues to oversee the completion of all 2010 census data products and evaluations. The twelve permanent ROs are to be reorganized into six offices over an eighteen-month period beginning in the summer of 2011.

Research

Prior to the 2010 census, research on census methodology was managed at Census Bureau headquarters under the

Table 1. Major Census Tests, 2002–2008

YEAR	CENSUS TEST
2002	Field test of prototype handheld computers
2003	Test of various self-response options, their effects on overall response rates and data quality, and the impact of various changes to the race and Hispanic origin questions
2004	Field test of new methodologies, including handheld computers
2004	Overseas Enumeration Test to examine the feasibility, quality, and cost of enumerating private American citizens living overseas
2005	Test of content-related issues
2006	Test of the systems and infrastructure needed to support the census design, including coverage measurement
2007	Bilingual (English-Spanish) forms test
2007–2008	Intended as "dress rehearsal" for all methods and systems for 2010; included all operations through mailout plus data capture, response processing, and dissemination of a prototype redistricting data file

SOURCE: U.S. Census Bureau, Decennial Statistical Studies Division.

ADDC and the associate director for research and methodology (ADRM). Research for 2020 planning is under the new associate director for the 2020 census and the ADRM. The major means for testing census methods and for obtaining operational information for the full deployment of the census has been the dress rehearsal, also managed by the ADDC for 2010. Significant tests of various aspects of census taking were conducted in advance of the 2010 dress rehearsal (see Table 1).

The dress rehearsal for the 2010 census was conducted on April 1, 2008, at two sites. One was Fayetteville, North Carolina, and its surrounding counties because this site had a mix of city-style, rural-route, and box-number address types, and its population had a large proportion of both African Americans and the military. The other was San Joaquin County (Stockton), California, because of its population diversity. Because of the difficulties the automation contractor had encountered with programming the HHCs for address canvassing and NRFU, the dress rehearsal was suspended after the mailout/mailback phase, though the mailed-back forms were data captured and processed and a mock redistricting data file was issued in order to test those systems.

Data Capture

Census 2000 was the first largely computerized census, from capturing data to releasing the final results on the Internet. In 2010, three high-technology data capture centers processed more than 150 million census questionnaires using state-of-the-art optical character recognition (OCR) and optical mark recognition (OMR) technology that can recognize and decipher handwritten responses in pen or pencil. A contractor provided the data capture system and the staffing to operate the system at two of these sites—in Baltimore County, Maryland, and

Phoenix, Arizona. The third site was the NPC, the Census Bureau's permanent facility in Jeffersonville, Indiana. DACMO was responsible for managing the contractors running the data capture centers.

Major Census Operations

Except for the major changes noted in the introduction (no long form, enhanced address lists and maps, and HHC automation of address canvassing), the operational plans for the 2010 census differed in relatively minor ways from those of other recent decennial censuses. Operational integration teams focused on qualitative improvements to operations, in part by adding a few operations such as group quarters validation and enumeration at transitory locations. In addition, the CCM survey was redesigned to produce estimates of both net coverage and components of coverage error. Thus, 2010 will be the first census from which components of coverage error will be made available. The Census Bureau also decided to change the schedule of production of coverage estimates from recent censuses. For 1990 and 2000, estimates of net coverage had been made available in time to be considered for adjustment of redistricting data. For 2010 the bureau decided in 2003 that no statistical adjustment would be considered for redistricting data. The Census Bureau also decided to delay the production of coverage estimates to allow time for calculation of component error estimates.

Address List Compilation

The Geography Division is responsible for the development of the MAF that identifies all living quarters with a geographic location from the Census Bureau's TIGER database. TIGER links each living quarters to a spatial location and a specific geographic area. It provides the map products and geographic files for data collection.

Under the 2010 census Local Update of Census Addresses (LUCA) Program, the Geography Division sent participating state, local, and tribal government representatives the MAF listings and maps for areas under their jurisdiction to obtain information to correct or further update the MAF. The addresses the LUCA participants supplied and the existing address and street locations in MAF and TIGER were verified during the 2009 address canvassing operation. OMB managed an appeals process to resolve differences between the Census Bureau and localities regarding what should be included in the address list.

Questionnaire Development, Production, and Mailing

Development of the census questionnaires is generally managed at Census Bureau headquarters by the DMD, which coordinates decisions on the content of the questionnaires with OMB and other federal agencies. These decisions are based on information obtained from many stakeholders. Congress first reviewed the subjects for the 2010 census in 2007 and then the specific questions for the census forms in 2008.

The 2010 census short form was mailed to roughly 90 percent of the housing units and hand delivered to roughly 9 percent (the remaining 1 percent, located in remote areas, were enumerated in person). Production mailing of the appropriate census forms was managed by the DSPO and DACMO and conducted by multiple contractors and the NPC. Forms were available in English and five other languages (simplified Chinese, Korean, Spanish, Russian, and Vietnamese) when requested by calling the TQA phone lines. Bilingual English-Spanish questionnaires were delivered to approximately 13 million housing units located in areas with the highest proportions of Spanish-speaking households who did not speak English very well. In addition, questionnaire language guides were available in 60 languages, and a special mailing of postcards was sent to areas with high concentrations of households speaking Chinese, Korean, Russian, and Vietnamese, alerting them to the special TQA phone lines for assistance in their language.

For the first time, based on its research findings, the census included a replacement mailing. For housing units in areas with historically low mailback response rates, all housing units received a replacement mailing. For housing units in areas with historically high mailback response rates, no housing units received a replacement mailing. For those in the middle, the DSPO delivered a file of addresses only for nonresponding housing units to the printing contractor, and the replacement questionnaires were mailed over a five-day period in early April 2010.

Unaddressed "Be Counted" questionnaires were available in roughly 30,000 questionnaire assistance centers and about 10,000 other sites for those individuals who thought they might have been missed. TQA operators could also take responses over the telephone.

Advertising, Partnerships, and Other Census Promotion

The associate director for communications managed 2010 census promotional efforts. The efforts included paid advertising (in 28 languages), partnerships, and media public-relations programs. For only the second time in its history, the Census Bureau used a paid advertising campaign for a decennial census. The campaign included a national media campaign; a targeted advertising effort; and special advertising messages and campaigns, including digital (Internet) advertising. This program was coordinated by the Census 2010 Publicity Office under the associate director for communications. The census partnership program, managed by the Field Division, included over 200,000 partnership agreements with other federal agencies; state, local, and tribal governments; community organizations; and businesses. Over 3,000 partnership specialists and support staff worked in the RCCs to support this program, and the American Recovery and Reinvestment Act (ARRA) of 2009 supplied additional funding for both the advertising and partnership programs. The media and public-relations component consisted of media specialists assigned to the RCCs to cultivate local press contacts and respond to local media inquiries. These specialists took guidance from the Public Information Office, also under the associate director for communications.

Recruitment and Training

Recruitment and training of the hundreds of thousands of temporary employees for the 2010 census were managed by the LCOs through the Field Division, which provided guidance on recruitment methods, selection, and pay rates. Compensation depended on local prevailing wage rates. Because of the recession of 2008–2010, sufficient recruiting was possible without major advertising efforts. Training took place for all field operations in advance, starting with field operations supervisors, then crew leaders, and then enumerators.

Data Collection and Enumeration

The major enumeration activities for the 2010 census occurred between March and August 2010. Data processing activities supported enumeration by identifying areas where information was missing or incomplete. The following activities were managed by the DMD and carried out by the Field Division, the DSSD, and other divisions as indicated:

- **Mailout/mailback and other distribution of census questionnaires.** The U.S. Postal Service delivered census questionnaires to about 90 percent of all housing units. For 90 percent of the remaining households (9 percent of the total), a census worker left the questionnaire to be filled out and mailed back, while updating the list of addresses for the area. This procedure is known as Update/Leave (U/L). In the remaining areas, which were sparsely settled or remote, census workers collected information directly. Each address or location was listed, and census maps were updated with the location. This procedure is called Update/Enumerate (U/E).

- **Group quarters enumeration.** For living quarters identified as other than housing units (for example, nursing homes and jails) by the address canvassing and group quarters validation operations, enumerators were sent to gather personal information about all residents. Examples of the populations covered by this operation were people without housing, those living in campgrounds, prisoners, and college students in dormitories.

- **Telephone and Internet assistance.** The Census Bureau operated a toll-free TQA system, run by a commercial phone center, and provided assistance in completing census questionnaires in English, Spanish, Mandarin, Cantonese, Russian, Vietnamese, and Korean. Respondents also were able to access a census Web site for assistance in completing their questionnaires.

- **Nonresponse follow-up (NRFU).** Despite efforts to encourage everyone to provide information, some persons and households did not do so. Starting about four weeks after census day, census workers were sent to follow up at all addresses for which a completed questionnaire was not received. Census staff also visited housing units potentially classified in error during NRFU to determine the status of the address on census day.

- **Coverage follow-up (CFU).** The CFU operation obtained computer assisted interviews by telephone to resolve two types of potential miscounts: population-count discrepancy and large-household follow-up to obtain missing data for households with more than six persons. The census questionnaire also included two questions that were intended to identify potential missed individuals and potential duplicates. Based on research showing the likely yield of roster changes, several million additional phone calls were made to resolve many of the potential problems. For missing or incomplete responses to population or housing items, a content edit was made solely by computer through statistical imputation with no telephone or personal visit follow-up.

- **Unduplication of multiple responses.** The Census Bureau reviewed information when more than one questionnaire data set was captured for a census address, such as through a "Be Counted" form or the replacement mailing.

- **Other data collection.** Census 2010 had separate data collection efforts for special places such as outlying areas, remote areas, reservations, and hard-to-count areas. Separate data collection was also conducted for special populations such as overseas federal civilian and military employees; transients; and, through group quarters enumeration, those in special living quarters such as institutions and group homes and people with no usual residence. As with the basic data collection, most of these efforts were conducted through the LCOs (headquarters staff coordinated with federal agencies directly on the overseas counts).

- **Census Coverage Measurement (CCM).** This separate, independent survey was used to measure the differential coverage of the population in 2010. A sample of blocks was drawn by the DSSD. An independent address list was prepared for these blocks, and about 180,000 independent personal interviews were conducted. Coverage factors, computed to assess the census results by matching CCM survey results to the census, will be released in 2012. In addition to conducting a survey to measure census coverage, the Census Bureau also compiles alternative estimates using a technique referred to as demographic analysis (DA). DA is carried out by building estimates of the total U.S. population using vital statistics on births and deaths. Additional administrative records are used to produce estimates of in-migration to and out-migration from the United States. The DA "middle" population estimate of 308,475,000 was quite close to the census result of 308,745,538; estimates were made available for the black and non-black populations at the national level in late 2010.

Data Transmission

Using dedicated links and other secure lines, a contractor-supplied telecommunications network linked all census offices for 2010, including census headquarters in Suitland, Maryland, the 494 LCOs, the 12 ROs, the 12 RCCs, the Puerto

Rico area office, and the Census Computer Center in Bowie, Maryland. A second Census Bureau contractor established communications links among the three PDCCs, the commercial telephone centers, and the Bowie computer center to assist with transmission of information from scanned paper forms, TQA, and the CFU operation. The TMO, DSPO, and DACMO managed data transmission.

Research to Improve Future Censuses.

The key source of information for future censuses is the 2010 Census Program of Evaluations and Experiments (CPEX). In addition, the Census Bureau will be retaining all data from its systems for potential future research activities, including images of the questionnaires. The Census Bureau has established a National Academy of Sciences (NAS) panel to review the 2010 census and provide advice for improving the 2020 census.

Data Dissemination

The two most important products of the census are the state population counts for reapportionment of the House of Representatives and the population counts for blocks within each state for use in redistricting (that is, redrawing legislative districts). The Census Bureau director is required to deliver the former to the president by December 31 of the census year (December 31, 2010, for the 2010 census). The latter are required by Public Law 94-171 to be delivered to the states within one year after census day (by March 31, 2011, for the 2010 census). Both of these 2010 census products were delivered on time. Individual states have their own timing requirements for the completion of redistricting.

Census 2010 data are being disseminated by an updated version of the data retrieval system established for Census 2000 called the American FactFinder (AFF), which was developed under contract. This system enables data users to access prepackaged data products, data documentation, and online help as well as download data to build their own custom data products offline. AFF is also used to disseminate ACS estimates.

See also *Accuracy and Coverage Evaluation; Address list development; Advertising the census; Advisory committees; American Community Survey; Data dissemination and use; Enumeration: field procedures; Enumeration: group quarters; Staffing.*

DANIEL H. WEINBERG
JOHN H. THOMPSON

BIBLIOGRAPHY

U.S. Bureau of the Census. *2010 Census Operational Plan (Version 3.0).* Washington, D.C.: U.S. Department of Commerce, Economic and Statistics Administration, 2010.

Popular Culture and the Census

The decennial census and census taking have sparked popular conceptions with contradictory aspects. The public recognizes the census as part of the national political fabric. Depending on attitudes of the moment toward politics and the political system, cultural depictions of census practice include both positive and negative images, and they range from patriotic images of community to concerns about an overbearing state. These depictions also frequently employ humor, satire, and irony. The census is nevertheless a relatively rare and unobtrusive event, and thus the media, opinion makers, and cultural leaders, as well the general citizenry, frequently have trouble remembering each decade what the decennial census is all about. They thus have to be reminded to understand the enterprise at all. Together, these facets of the census process have made for a particularly rich legacy of images over the course of American history.

The U.S. government has taken a decennial census since 1790, initially as a mechanism to reapportion and redistrict seats in the U.S. House of Representatives and state and local and legislative districts every ten years. Early in the history of the republic, it became clear that patterns of population growth and change were dramatic and diverse. The decennial census became a major symbolic landmark for the nation, an event that focused public attention on the growth and westward expansion of the nation, looking backward to assess what had changed and forward to anticipate the future.

Evidence of such attention exists in the form of artifacts, paintings, cartoons, poetry, fiction, comedy routines, and political satire. The evidence took the form of text, images, sound recordings, radio, television, and video as the technologies of culture themselves developed. The nineteenth-century forms included artifacts, paintings and drawings, and text. The twentieth- and twenty-first-century forms added the new analog and digital electronic media.

Early Art: Ceramics, Paintings, and Cartoons

Cultural forms of reaction to the census began in the first decade of census taking in the 1790s. That year, the federal government published the census results in a simple, 56-page printed book of tabular results. Sometime in the 1790s, enterprising ceramicists in Britain saw the potential for sales in the bare list of numbers. They produced a Liverpool creamware pitcher, a popular ceramic of the day, which listed the population results for the states from the 1790 census on its side. Under the title "Prosperity to the United States," the artists turned the bare table into a patriotic testimonial to the new American states. One surviving pitcher is in the Smithsonian Institution's collection of ceramics.

By the mid-nineteenth century, painters and cartoonists had also taken up the subject of the census. Their focus was the encounter between census-taker and resident at the family threshold or home. Genre painter Francis Edmonds created *Taking the Census* in 1854. The painting is now on view in the Metropolitan Museum of Art in New York City. Edmonds portrayed a census-taker and his assistant visiting a family to take the 1850 count. The household of seven is arrayed around the hearth; the household head counts on his fingers to provide the information. The census-taker is well dressed; he stands to record the information and keeps his hat on. He does not mean to stay long. The family is a large one and symbolizes the prosperity of the mid-nineteenth century nation. Despite the rustic setting, symbols of prosperity (a clock) and patriotism (George Washington's portrait) adorn the mantel.

Cartoons and drawings appeared in the periodical press in the mid-nineteenth century, and these also depicted the enumerator interviewing a family at home. *The Great Tribulation* from the 1860 *Saturday Evening Post*, for example, captured a family's consternation at a boorish enumerator, presumably appointed due to his political connections through the spoils system that had become an object of criticism at the time. The caption noted intrusive questions about a respectable family that led the family members to blanch with disdain. In the second half of the nineteenth century, such images proliferated and were re-created as the census approached. They continue today in the spate of census cartoons that appear each decade.

Sound and Television

In the late nineteenth century, the advent of sound recording led to oral productions with the census as a theme. The census-taker surveying his neighborhood or community is usually the subject. Americans of the late nineteenth century were familiar with the poem "Casey at the Bat," first published in 1888 and reproduced in written and audio versions ever since. The Irish character "Michael Casey" was a well-known persona for turn-of-the-century actors who performed short routines of ethnic humor, poems, and stories, and recorded those routines on wax cylinders. Actor John Kaiser recorded "Casey Taking the Census" in 1905, in which the listener heard Michael Casey climb the stairs to encounter Mrs. Castoria Mulcahy. The recording explored the humor in census taking as the enumerator asked personal questions about Mrs. Mulcahy's situation and confronted her ignorance of the census and her suspicions of the whole enterprise. This genre tends to reappear each decade and was notably represented in the 2010 census round with the *Saturday Night Live* skit featuring Tina Fey as the interviewer and Betty White as the respondent at the door.

Poets and novelists have also used the census and the census-taker as symbols of larger themes. In April 1921 Robert Frost published "The Census-Taker" in *The New Republic*, in the collection *New Hampshire*. Frost described the northern New England of the early twentieth century as a world out of the mainstream, a world of depopulation and emptiness that had been abandoned and passed by. In Frost's poem, the census-taker encountered only vacant dwellings. Caleb Carr's best-selling murder mystery *The Alienist*, set in 1890s New York City, used an ominous census theme to evoke the disorder and danger of urban life. Even the controversies surrounding the census undercount became a subject for television drama. In 1999, *The West Wing* produced an episode that focused on the political controversies around sampling.

Artistic Representation from the Bureau

Census officials were slower than artists and the print media to employ art, music, or other forms of artistic representation to convey the results of the census or to encourage participation in the census. The first visual representations that appeared in the published census results were maps of population density, which began appearing in the 1860s. Initially engraved and sold as single sheets in black and white, by the 1870 census, such maps were published as a separate *Statistical Atlas* using color plates. They were visually considerably more effective in conveying the patterns of population growth and change than the earlier tables of text. The Census Office made other innovations in data visualization for public presentation. Census officials invented the concept of the "center of population" and mapped the data.

Advertising the coming census became a feature of census promotion in the early twentieth century. The director of the 1910 census, Edward Dana Durand, convinced President William Howard Taft to produce the first census proclamation to announce the goals of the count, assure respondents of the importance of cooperating, and call upon the patriotic duty of Americans to "stand up and be counted." The proclamation has continued as a tradition ever since, espousing unity within diversity, civic responsibility, and patriotism. The Census Bureau has produced posters, pens and pencils, coffee mugs, buttons, tote bags, and other popular items for later censuses. Advertising posters and photographic images are now a standard feature of census promotion. See the photo insert for some examples of census advertisements.

Electronic Age

With the emergence of the Internet in the 1990s, the distinctions among visual, textual, oral, and video depictions of census information collapsed. The census process is photographed and filmed, tweeted, and podcasted as it happens, both by the popular electronic and print media and the Census Bureau's own publicity office. The results are available in multiple forms of presentation. The Census Bureau "FactFinder" logo branded film and text explications of census information and methods in the 1970s and 1980s. Today the American Fact-Finder (AFF) is a Web-based data extraction system for population, housing, economic, and geographic data and technical background. The census Web site (www.census.gov/) changes constantly, both because the data are constantly updated and because census officials are adding to and experimenting with communication methods, including a running tabulation of estimated population growth called the "Population Clock" (see www.census.gov/main/www/popclock.html).

See also *Advertising the census; Center of population; Media attention to the census.*

. . . .   MARGO J. ANDERSON

BIBLIOGRAPHY

Anderson, Margo J. "The Census, Audiences, and Publics." *Social Science History* 32, no. 1 (2008): 1–18. doi:10.1215/01455532-2007-011.

Schulten, Susan. "The Cartography of Slavery and the Authority of Statistics." *Civil War History* 56, no. 1 (2010): 5–32. doi:10.1353/cwh.0.0141.

Population Estimates and Projections

The Census Bureau has a long history of producing population estimates and projections for various levels of geography. The term *population estimate* refers to the population at either the current time or some time in the past, while the term *population projection* refers to the population at a future date.

The Census Bureau produces population estimates annually for the nation, states, counties, and subcounty areas. The Census Bureau's population estimates begin with the latest decennial census, which is updated with vital statistics and estimates of international and domestic migration. These estimates are referred to as post-censal estimates. After each decennial census, the Census Bureau produces a set of intercensal estimates, which are based on two consecutive censuses. The Census Bureau also produces population projections at the national level.

History

The Census Bureau began producing national population estimates in the early 1900s, state population estimates in the 1940s, and estimates for counties and subcounty areas on a regular basis in the 1970s. Over the years the amount of demographic and geographic detail of the population estimates has increased, often due to mandates in federal legislation. The Census Bureau's production of estimates below the state level on a regular basis was in response to the State and Local Fiscal Assistance Act of 1972, which required updated population estimates for around 36,000 local governmental units for general revenue sharing. In the mid-1990s, the Census Bureau began producing school district level estimates of children ages 5–17 for use in allocating funds for programs to aid disadvantaged children under Title I of the Elementary and Secondary Education Act, now known as the No Child Left Behind Act.

The legal requirement for the Census Bureau to produce population estimates is given in Title 13 of the United States Code. Title 13, Section 181 states:

> During the intervals between each census of population required under section 141 of this title, the Secretary, to the extent feasible, shall annually produce and publish for each state, county, and local unit of general purpose government which has a population of fifty thousand or more, current data on total population and population characteristics and, to the extent feasible, shall biennially produce and publish for units of general purpose government current data on total population.

Currently, the Census Bureau produces population estimates annually that are disaggregated by age, sex, race, and Hispanic origin for the nation, states, and counties. These population estimates are for July 1 of each estimate's year. The Census Bureau also produces total population estimates for incorporated places, minor civil divisions, and school districts on an annual basis, along with estimates of school-age children for school districts. In addition to producing population estimates, the Census Bureau produces estimates of housing units at the state and county level. These housing unit estimates are used in the production of the population estimates for incorporated places and minor civil divisions.

The Census Bureau works closely with its state partners in the Federal-State Cooperative for Population Estimates (FSCPE). This cooperative was created in the late 1960s to help coordinate work between the Census Bureau and the states. The state agencies, designated by their respective governors, work in cooperation with the Census Bureau to produce population estimates. The FSCPE agencies supply vital statistics, information about group quarters such as college dorms or prisons, and data on housing units. Prior to release, the Census Bureau's population estimates are sent to the FSCPE agencies for review and comment. In addition, some FSCPE agencies produce their own population estimates and projections.

The FSCPE also works with the Census Bureau on research to evaluate population estimates methodology. In the mid-2000s, the Census Bureau and the FSCPE worked collaboratively on a research project to evaluate the housing unit methodology. This effort documented that for the majority of counties, the cohort component method used by the Census Bureau performed better than the housing unit method

(Devine et al., in press). Members of the FSCPE are also working with the Census Bureau to evaluate different methods for producing population estimates after the 2010 census.

In addition to its annual population estimates, the Census Bureau produces population projections for the United States by age in single years, sex, race, and Hispanic origin. Recently, the Census Bureau has produced national population projections every four years (in 1996, 2000, 2004, and 2008). The national projections typically have gone out to the year 2050. Historically, the Census Bureau produced population projections for the states but has not done so since Census 2000.

The Social Security Administration (SSA) also produces national population projections on an annual basis. SSA includes its population projections in the annual report of the Board of Trustees of the Federal Old-Age, Survivors and Disability Insurance (OASDI) Trust Funds. Each SSA report has a set of population projections.

The SSA typically projects the population for 75 years into the future. It updates its population base (the starting point for its projections) to the latest Census Bureau population estimates each year. The SSA projections are for the population in the Social Security universe and are disaggregated by age, sex, and marital status. They do not include race or Hispanic-origin detail. SSA includes in its projections (1) residents of the 50 states and the District of Columbia (corrected for estimated net undercount in the 2000 census); (2) civilian residents of Puerto Rico, the U.S. Virgin Islands, Guam, American Samoa, and the Commonwealth of Northern Mariana Islands; (3) federal civilian employees and persons in the U.S. Armed Forces abroad and their dependents; (4) noncitizens living abroad who are insured for Social Security benefits; and (5) all other U.S. citizens abroad.

The population projections from the two agencies differ in some respects. The Census Bureau projects population by age, sex, race, and Hispanic origin, while the SSA projects population by age, sex, and marital status. The assumptions about future fertility, mortality, and net international migration also differ between the two sets of projections. Historically, the Census Bureau has projected slightly higher fertility than SSA, slightly lower mortality, and increasing net in-migration. The net result is that the Census Bureau's projected population for 2050 is higher than SSA's projected population.

Uses

The Census Bureau's population estimates have many uses at the federal, state, and local governmental levels. One of the most important of these uses is as one factor in federal funding formulae to allocate over $400 billion each year.

The Census Bureau uses its population estimates by age, sex, race, and Hispanic origin as controls for its household surveys, such as the American Community Survey (ACS) and the Current Population Survey (CPS). These population controls are applied to the survey data at different levels of geography so that the survey data agree with the population estimates by demographic characteristics. The controls are used to account for undercoverage in the survey, as household surveys typically have lower coverage of certain groups than the decennial census.

The Census Bureau's population estimates are used as denominators for national and subnational statistics such as birth and death rates for the United States, states, and counties. Population estimates are used as the denominator for disease incidence (for example, the National Cancer Institute uses the estimates to determine the incidence of cancer by age, sex, and race). The population estimates are used by the U.S. Department of the Treasury to set state bonding authorities each year. Both the U.S. Senate and the Federal Election Commission (FEC) use annual population estimates to determine spending limits in political campaigns. Data on men turning age 18 each year are provided annually to the Selective Service System. At the local level, population estimates are used by planning agencies for the development and evaluation of programs such as day care, job training, transportation planning, and elder care.

Population projections also have a wide variety of uses. The Office of Management and Budget (OMB) and the Council of Economic Advisers use population projections in their budget forecasts. The U.S. Department of Labor's Bureau of Labor Statistics uses the Census Bureau's population projections in its projections of the country's labor force. SSA uses its population projections in its annual report to Congress on the actuarial (financial) status of the OASDI (Social Security) Trust Funds.

Methods for Estimates

The Census Bureau produces population estimates at the national, state, and county level by using the component of change method. At the national level, this method begins with the latest decennial census, adds births and an estimate of international in-migration, and subtracts deaths and emigration. For states and counties, the method is essentially the same but with the addition of an estimate of domestic migration. Currently, estimates for counties are added to the state level, and then both state and county estimates are considered in the national estimate.

The data for the components of change come from a variety of administrative data sources.

The National Center for Health Statistics (NCHS) and the FSCPE provide data on births and deaths at the county level. For the population under age 65, domestic migration is estimated using data from federal tax returns. Individuals are matched year to year on tax returns. People who have a different address in year two than in year one are considered movers, while people with the same address in both years are considered nonmigrants. These data are then used to model net migration at the county level. For the population age 65 and older, change in Medicare enrollment at the county level is used to model net domestic migration.

Data from the ACS and the Puerto Rico Community Survey (PRCS) are used to estimate net international migration at the national, state, and county level. To estimate foreign-born immigration, the question on residence one year ago in the ACS is used. The foreign-born who said they were living outside of the United States one year ago are considered immigrants. A residual method using Census 2000 and various years of the ACS is used to estimate foreign-born emigration. Emigration rates are calculated by surviving forward (that is, aging people by one year at a time and applying age-specific death rates) the foreign-born population in Census 2000 and comparing the size of that population to data from the ACS on the foreign-born who entered before 2000. These rates are generated for two groups: those who entered between 1990 and 1999 and those who entered prior to 1990. These rates are applied to the foreign-born population in consecutive years of the ACS who are at risk of emigrating (that is, the foreign-born in the ACS who lived in the United States in the prior year).

Net native emigration is estimated based on work done by Schachter that examined data from other countries' censuses on people who were either born in the United States or who were U.S. citizens. Schachter used data from 2 consecutive censuses in over 80 countries to develop an estimate of net migration of U.S. natives to these countries.

Movement between the United States and Puerto Rico is measured using both the ACS and the PRCS. People in the ACS who said they lived in Puerto Rico one year ago are considered immigrants to the United States, and people in the PRCS who said they lived in the United States one year ago are considered emigrants from the United States.

The age, sex, race, and Hispanic-origin detail in the population estimates is developed using a cohort component of change method. These detailed estimates are produced at the national, state, and county levels. The population estimates use the race categories mandated by the OMB's 1997 standards: "white"; "black or African American"; "American Indian and Alaska Native"; "Asian"; and "Native Hawaiian and Other Pacific Islander." The race categories used in the population estimates differ from those used in the 2000 census and the 2010 census in one important respect. Both Census 2000 and the 2010 census allowed respondents to select the category referred to as "some other race." When the 2000 and 2010 Census data were edited to produce the population estimates base, respondents who selected the "some other race" category alone were assigned to one of the OMB-mandated categories. For those respondents who selected the "some other race" category and one or more of the other race categories, the edits ignored the "some other race" selection. The 1997 OMB standards on collecting data on race also allow for people to select more than one race. Therefore, the population estimates are produced for five race-alone categories, five alone-and-in-combination categories, and the aggregate "two or more races" population.

Data on race on birth and death records from NCHS historically are provided in the four single-race categories specified by OMB's 1977 directive. These data need to be converted from the older race categories to the new race categories. This is done using race-bridging factors developed by NCHS. For births, the race-bridging factors are used to convert the single race of mothers and fathers to the 1997 OMB race categories. For a child who has parents of different races, race is assigned using data from Census 2000 on race reported for children with parents who are of different races (see "National Population Estimates," at www.census.gov/popest/topics/methodology/, and www.cdc.gov/nchs/nvss/bridged_race.htm).

The demographic detail for the domestic migration component comes from two sources: person-level data on federal tax returns provided by the Internal Revenue Service and the Census Bureau's Person Characteristics File (PCF). The PCF is derived from SSA's 100 percent file, other administrative records data, and Census 2000. For the international migration component, the demographic detail is derived from Census 2000 and the ACS.

The Census Bureau uses a distributive housing unit method to estimate the total population of incorporated places and minor civil divisions. The housing unit method uses estimates of housing units that have been updated over the decade with information from the Census Bureau's Building Permit Survey on the number of building permits, comments from the FSCPE members, and other data sources. An estimate of housing loss is also applied to the housing unit estimates. The updated housing units are combined with occupancy rates and persons per household decennial census to estimate a household population. An estimate of the number of people living in group quarters is added to this household population estimate, and then these subcounty population estimates are included in the county total population estimate.

Methods for Population Projections
Both the Census Bureau and SSA produce population projections at the national level using the cohort component method. The components of change (births, deaths, and net international migration) are projected for each birth cohort (persons born in a given year). For each year, the population is advanced one year of age using survival rates and levels of net international migration projected for the year. A new birth cohort is added to form the population under age 1 by applying age-specific fertility rates to the female population ages 15–49 and updating the new cohort for the effects of mortality and net international migration.

Historically, the Census Bureau produced multiple sets of projections with lower and upper bounds for mortality and fertility. In 2008, the Census Bureau released a set of projections with only one series of assumptions. In 2009, the Census Bureau released a supplemental set of projections that altered only the assumptions about net international migration. This set included four series: (1) one with high levels of net international migration; (2) one with low levels of net international migration; (3) a series in which net international migration was held constant; and (4) a series with zero net international migration from 2000 forward, which was produced for analytical purposes.

Evaluation
The Census Bureau evaluates its population estimates using decennial census data. For instance, the population estimates for 2010 that are based on Census 2000 are compared to the 2010 census counts for April 1. The initial comparisons of the 2010 census counts to the population estimates for 2010 indicate that the population estimates are very close to the census counts at the national level and for the majority of the states.

See also *Coverage evaluation; Demographic analysis; Income and poverty measures; Uses of the census and ACS: federal agencies; Vital registration and vital statistics.*

. . . . VICTORIA A. VELKOFF

BIBLIOGRAPHY
Board of Trustees, Federal Old-Age and Survivors Insurance and Federal Disability Insurance Trust Funds. *The 2010 Annual Report of the Board of Trustees of the Federal Old-Age and Survivors Insurance and Federal Disability Insurance Trust Funds.* U. S. Congress, House Document no. 111-137. Washington, D.C.: U.S. Government Printing Office, 2010. Available at www.ssa.gov/OACT/TR/2010/tr10.pdf.
Devine, J., J. Reese, J. G. Robinson, K. West, B. Ahmed, and S. Wetrogan. "A Summary of Findings from the Housing Unit–Based Estimates Research Team." U.S. Census Bureau, Population Division Working Paper, forthcoming.
Ingram D. D., J. D. Parker, N. Schenker, J. A. Weed, B. Hamilton, E. Arias, and J. H. Madans. *United States Census 2000 Population with Bridged Race Categories: Data Evaluation and Methods Research.* Vital and Health Statistics Series 2, no. 135. Hyattsville, Md.: National Center for Health Statistics, 2003. Available at www.cdc.gov/nchs/data/series/sr_02/sr02_135.pdf.
Office of Management and Budget. *Revisions to the Standards for the Classification of Federal Data on Race and Ethnicity: Federal Register Notice, October 30, 1997.* Available at www.whitehouse.gov/omb/fedreg_1997standards/.
Reamer, A. D. *Counting for Dollars: The Role of the Decennial Census in Geographic Distribution of Federal Funds.* Washington, D.C.: Brookings, Metropolitan Policy Program, 2010.
Schachter, J. "Estimating Native Emigration from the United States." Memorandum developed during contract work for the U.S. Census Bureau, December 24, 2008.
U.S. Census Bureau. *Directive No. 15: Race and Ethnic Standards for Federal Statistics and Administrative Reporting, May 12, 1977.* Available at http://wonder.cdc.gov/wonder/help/populations/bridged-race/Directive15.html.

Post-Enumeration Survey

The Census Bureau conducts a post-enumeration survey (PES) after a census in order to measure how well the census covered the population. The PES measures two types of enumeration errors: omissions and erroneous enumerations. The Census Bureau staff studies these gross errors to understand the causes of census coverage error and to improve census taking methods. To measure the overall accuracy of the census, the Census Bureau estimates the net coverage error, which describes the difference between the two types of gross errors.

History
The Census Bureau conducted its first PES after the 1950 census. An evaluation of the 1940 census had demonstrated the need for an assessment of census coverage. A match of draft registration records to the 1940 census count of adult males of draft age showed, surprisingly, that more males were registered for the draft than were enumerated in the census.

The Census Bureau also conducted a PES after the 1960, 1980, 1990, 2000 and 2010 censuses and a complete or partial PES after test censuses in preparation for the 1980, 1990, 2000, and 2010 censuses. The PES consists of two sample surveys: a sample of census enumerations (the E-sample) and an independent sample of the population (the P-sample). The E-sample measures erroneous enumerations, and the P-sample measures omissions. The erroneous enumerations include duplications, inclusions of people in the wrong area, and enumerations of people who are not living in the United States. The P-sample is independent of the census and selects blocks, clusters of blocks, or segments of blocks, including all the housing units in the selected areas. The PES requires that a list of those housing units be made because using the census address list would mean that the P-sample and the census were not independent.

The implementation and estimation methodology of the PES has evolved over the years. In 1950 the idea behind the PES was to perform a much higher-quality census interview with highly trained interviewers; therefore, the PES interview was assumed to yield the truth. The true population size was taken to equal the census count multiplied by the ratio of the number of people in the PES housing units divided by the number of people the census found in those housing units.

The 1950 P- and E-samples each had about 25,000 housing units and were designed to overlap as much as possible. Sample selection occurred in two stages. First, the United States was divided into primary sampling units, of which 270 were selected. Within the primary sampling units, groups of six to ten housing units, called *segments,* were selected. The E-samples consisted of all the census enumerations coded as residing in the selected segments.

Interviewers were instructed to interview an adult resident at each housing unit in their assigned segments. The interviewers' materials contained the results of the original census interviews in their segments, concealed on a folded page. The interviewers were to refer to the original results only for comparison purposes, after conducting the interview. The idea was that the comparison would improve the results and resolve any discrepancies.

The results of the 1950 PES were disappointing. The survey did not find as large an undercount as demographic techniques showed to be present. Evidently the interviewers often merely confirmed the original interview and did not find missed housing units or missed people. The same weaknesses appeared in the undercount estimates based on the 1960 PES. The design of the 1960 PES again aimed to ascertain the truth. The P- and E-samples were selected independently, but there was no attempt to make them overlap. The P-sample contained 25,000 dwellings and was an area sample of 2,500 segments. The selected segments were a subsample of the segments canvassed for the 1959 Survey of Change and Residential Finance (SCARF). The enumerators had information from the census and from the SCARF to aid in their reenumeration and their search for missed and erroneously included dwellings.

The E-sample was a sample of 15,000 dwellings from the list of those in the census. On average, the sample had 2 clusters of 3 dwellings from each of the 2,400 census enumeration districts contained in the 335 primary sample units chosen for the Current Population Survey (CPS), which measures the unemployment rate. The interviewers were given the addresses but not the names of the occupants listed in the census.

Dual-Systems Estimation

The Census Bureau did not conduct a PES of the 1970 census; however, improvements in methodology led the Census Bureau to conduct one after the 1980 census. The improvements came from United Nations (UN) sponsored developments, in which a dual-systems (or capture-recapture) estimation method was used to estimate population size in other countries. Dual-systems estimation required only that the PES be a second, independent enumeration of a sample of households rather than an improved enumeration good enough to be considered the truth.

Respondents to the 1980 PES were matched to the original enumeration on a case-by-case basis, and dual-systems estimation was used to estimate the total population. One complication arose over the issue of whether a person was considered correctly enumerated if he or she were counted at any address or only at one *correct* address. Another complication arose because some people moved between the time of the census and the PES interview.

Whether a person can be enumerated correctly at only one or multiple addresses is important because of the case-by-case matching. The matching operation has to know where to search for census enumerations. With *any-address matching,* the PES interviewer asks the respondent to list all the addresses where he or she may have been enumerated. If the matching operation finds the respondent at one of these addresses or close to one of these addresses, the person is considered correctly enumerated. With *unique-address matching,* the PES interviewer asks the respondent for a usual residence. In order to be enumerated correctly, the respondent has to be enumerated at that address. Unique-address matching is easier to implement because only one address has to be considered.

The complication of how to handle movers is addressed in three variations of the PES. In PES-A, the members of the P-sample are the residents of a sampled housing unit on census day. In PES-B, the members of the P-sample are the residents of the housing unit when the PES interview is conducted. A hybrid known as PES-C uses the number of movers into the sampled housing units (PES-B definition) to estimate the number of movers and the match rate for the people who have moved out (PES-A definition) to estimate the match rate for movers. All three variations have advantages and disadvantages. With PES-A, the movers have to be traced so that they can be interviewed, or the interviewers have to rely on neighbors. However, the matching is easier because the enumeration is at the sampled housing unit if the movers were enumerated. With PES-B, the movers are easy to find because they now live at the sampled housing unit, but they must remember their former addresses well enough for census staff to find them in the census records. PES-C attempts to incorporate the best of the other two variations, but the interviewers have to collect much more information than they do with PES-A or PES-B.

The 1980 PES used unique-address matching and the PES-B mover treatment. The matching operation was clerical and very time-consuming. The P- and E-samples for the 1980 PES were selected in completely different ways. The P-sample interviews were supplementary questions in the April and August waves of the CPS, which uses a two-stage design where primary sampling units about the size of counties are selected at the first stage and then segments of four housing units are selected within each selected primary sampling unit. The P-sample included approximately 124,000 housing units, with 62,000 from each wave. The E-sample consisted of 10 enumerations selected from each enumeration district in the United States, for a total sample size of about 110,000 households. Interviewers visited each household and verified that each person enumerated at the housing unit was a real person and that the address was each person's usual residence. The interviewers also verified that the geographic coding for the housing unit was correct. If the people who were enumerated in the census had moved, the interviewers inquired at other residences in the neighborhood and at the post office to determine who had lived at the address on census day.

Controversy

After the 1980 census, New York City, among others, sued, asking that the results of the 1980 PES be used to adjust the census for undercount. The Census Bureau took the position that the PES results were not of high enough quality to be used to adjust the census, and the courts did not order an adjustment.

Many people inside and outside the Census Bureau had concerns about the validity of the dual-systems estimates for the PES. A technical disadvantage was that they may be subject to correlation bias because people missed by the census also tend to be missed by the PES. Poststratification of the respondents by geography, sex, age, racial and ethnic groups, and population density reduces the bias by grouping together people with similar chances of being counted. However, the poststratification may not describe all the heterogeneity of enumeration probabilities. Some variations of the estimation methodology have been designed to reduce the correlation bias, but these have not been successfully implemented.

Another disadvantage of dual-systems estimation in a PES is that the matching between two independent lists, the PES and the census, requires a substantial amount of time. The matching requires that both the census enumeration files and the PES files be available. Furthermore, matching people who move between the time of the census and the PES is a complicated, time-consuming process.

After the 1980 census, the Census Bureau launched a research program that made substantial improvements in PES methodology by taking advantage of advances in computer technology and implementing design adaptations. The case-by-case clerical matching was replaced by computerized matching with clerical review and matching of the difficult cases. For the computerized matching algorithms to be used efficiently, the P- and E-samples had to come from the same blocks. This was the basis of the sample design for the 1990 PES.

The 1990 PES was designed specifically for census coverage evaluation of the population living in housing units and non-institutional group quarters and used unique-address matching and PES-B treatment of movers. The sample selection used a single-stage design in which the United States was stratified by geographic area, percent minority population, percent renters, and urban versus rural areas. A sample of blocks was then selected within each stratum. The sample consisted of about 5,300 block clusters and 172,000 housing units. The design of the stratification complemented the poststratification used in the estimation of population size for small areas.

In July 1990 interviewers conducted P-sample interviews in the sample blocks. The persons found in these interviews were matched to the census enumerations in these same blocks and one ring of surrounding blocks. A follow-up interview in November 1990 checked the status of anyone in the P-sample who did not have a matching census enumeration. Follow-up interviewers also investigated any E-sample enumerations in the sample block that did not have a matching P-sample person.

PES estimates of the 1990 census undercount, produced in 1991, were not used to adjust the census. The Census Bureau evaluated the 1991 estimates extensively and synthesized the evaluation results in the estimation of the total error in the estimates. In 1992 the PES estimates were revised and considered for use in the bureau's Population Estimates Program. After careful evaluation, however, the Census Bureau decided not to use the PES estimates in this program, although they were used to adjust the population estimates from major household surveys.

New Status

The PES gained new prominence in the preparations for Census 2000. The plan was to use the results of the 2000 PES, called the Accuracy and Coverage Evaluation (ACE) survey, to adjust the census numbers for net undercount for the redistricting of congressional seats and other purposes. To assess whether the ACE estimates were sufficiently reliable to use in an adjustment, the Census Bureau (1) reviewed ACE operational data to validate whether the implementation of the ACE was successful, (2) assessed the ACE estimates for consistency with historical patterns of undercount and independent demographic analysis benchmarks, and (3) reviewed measures of the quality of the ACE estimates that were available in early 2001. However, there was inconsistency between the ACE and demographic analysis estimates. The Census Bureau decided to recommend not adjusting the census numbers for redistricting in March 2001.

Subsequently, the Census Bureau considered adjusting Census 2000 with estimates from the ACE on two other occasions, but each time it decided not to adjust. In October 2001, the Census Bureau decided not to adjust Census 2000 for other purposes because newly available evaluation data indicated problems with the ACE detection of erroneous enumerations. After producing the ACE Revision II estimates in March 2003, the Census Bureau decided not to adjust the census base for the Population Estimates Program. The reasons for this decision included inconsistencies with demographic analysis for children ages 0–9 and problematic estimates for some small areas.

Despite not being used for census adjustment, the ACE evaluations and analyses for the decisions revealed surprises about Census 2000 and left a legacy that would influence census-taking and coverage evaluation methods for some time to come. The design of the ACE applied the basic concepts of a PES. The E- and P-samples used the same sample of block clusters, each of which could be one block or several smaller blocks grouped together. A sample of 11,303 block clusters was selected from all block clusters in the 50 states and the District of Columbia. In very large block clusters, a subsample was selected. The E-sample had 311,029 housing units, and the P-sample had 300,913 housing units—the largest PES sample size to date.

The ACE used unique-address matching. It also used PES-C mover treatment because the initial plans for Census 2000 called for sampling for follow-up of nonrespondents to the census mail questionnaires. Under this design, all the movers into the ACE sample blocks who had not been enumerated on a mail questionnaire might not have been selected for the nonresponse follow-up (NRFU) sample, but all the census mail nonrespondents in the ACE sample blocks and surrounding blocks could have been designated for NRFU, which would have made matching in the ACE blocks feasible. However, in 1999 the U.S. Supreme Court barred the use of statistical sampling to calculate the population for the purpose of reapportioning the House of Representatives. At that point, changing the ACE design to PES-B would have been difficult, if not impossible, so the PES-C was retained even though the reason for its selection no longer existed.

The ACE interviewers used laptop computers to collect data from respondents. The laptop had the advantage of containing the entire questionnaire and could automatically do branching when different answers required different subsequent questions. The interviewers transmitted the responses electronically to the ACE processing center, where a computer-assisted clerical operation matched the P-sample people to the census enumerations in the sample blocks, expanding the search to the surrounding blocks for a subsample of the enumerations where there was a possibility that the housing unit was geographically coded to the wrong block. The easier cases were matched by computer before the matchers received the data. The matchers used an automated system to view the census data and the P-sample data.

The ACE Revision II estimates were the first coverage error estimates for any U.S. census that found an overcount for the nation as a whole. Although the PES had found erroneous enumerations in previous censuses, the estimated net undercount was always positive, indicating that omissions were larger. Consequently, the design of census operations focused on avoiding omissions as much as possible with the belief that procedures for avoiding duplication were adequate.

A surprising revelation from ACE Revision II was that duplicate enumerations occurred in the census much more frequently than previously observed or suspected. Studies of duplication as part of the ACE Revision II program estimated 5.8 million duplicate enumerations in the Census 2000 count of 281 million. The duplicates occurred disproportionately among the population under age 30. Duplicate enumerations within a block cluster appear to have arisen from operational errors, such as a dwelling having two different addresses on the address list. A reinterview study, limited since it was a long time after census day, found that the causes of duplicate enumerations in different states or counties included moving situations, people visiting family/friends, people with vacation/seasonal homes, college students, prisoners, and children in shared custody situations. The technical innovation that allowed discovery of the duplicate enumerations was the scanning of census forms by optical character recognition (OCR) and optical mark recognition (OMR) technologies, which converted the names and other information on the census questionnaires into electronic format. This made possible a computerized match of census records for the entire nation.

Several evaluation studies indicated weaknesses in the ACE collection of census-day residence. Previously, the assumption for a PES had been that questionnaire probes about usual residence and moves asked by high-quality interviewers could obtain accurate information. However, a computerized search for P-sample people among the census enumerations outside the limited area where the ACE matching operation had searched provided evidence to the contrary. Reviews of the questionnaires found unreliable identification of moves, second homes, and stays in group quarters residences, concluding that how the questionnaires asked about the usual residence of a person was fundamentally flawed and would require intensive questionnaire redesign and testing to ameliorate.

For the first time, the ACE Revision II estimation used a poststratification that reflected one set of variables related to erroneous inclusions and a different set of factors related to omissions. However, the use of separate poststratification variables and the choice of the variables, particularly those concerning census operations for the E-sample (which were census proxy response and a variable for timing of the return of the census questionnaire), appeared to have been problematic for some of the smaller areas. Some small places, which are cities and towns, received estimates of extreme overcounts (greater than 10 percent).

For the first time, the Census Bureau decided to include a correction for correlation bias in the ACE Revision II estimator by using sex ratios from demographic analysis estimates. In the presence of overcounts, it is possible that the estimated net error without including correlation bias might not even be in the right direction. The simple model used for the correlation bias adjustment in the ACE Revision II estimates assumed that corrections needed to be made only for adult males and not for adult females or children.

The evidence of a large number of erroneous enumerations and omissions in Census 2000 in spite of the net coverage error being very close to zero led the Census Bureau to design a new methodology for the 2010 PES, which was called the 2010 Census Coverage Measurement (CCM) Program. The new methodology was designed to provide separate estimates of erroneous enumerations and omissions for the 2010 census, with a focus on providing information to aid in planning for the 2020 census.

See also *Accuracy and Coverage Evaluation; Capture-recapture methods; Census testing; Coverage evaluation; Demographic analysis; Errors in the census.*

. . . . MARY H. MULRY

BIBLIOGRAPHY

Chandrasekar, C., and W. E. Deming. "On a Method of Estimating Birth and Death Rates and the Extent of Registration." *Journal of the American Statistical Association* 44, no. 245 (1949): 101–115.

Fay, R. E., U.S. Bureau of the Census. *The Coverage of Population in the 1980 Census.* PHC 80-E4. Washington, D.C.: U.S. Department of Commerce, 1988.

Hogan, H. "The 1990 Post-Enumeration Survey: An Overview." *The American Statistician* 46, no. 4 (1992): 261–269. Available at www.amstat.org/sections/SRMS/proceedings/papers/1990_087.pdf.

Hogan, H. "The Accuracy and Coverage Evaluation: Theory and Design." *Survey Methodology* 29, no. 2 (2003): 129–138. Available at www.statcan.gc.ca/ads-annonces/12-001-x/6782-eng.pdf.

Marks, E. S., W. P. Mauldin, and H. Nisselson. "The Post-Enumeration Survey of the 1950 Census: A Case History in Survey Design." *Journal of the American Statistical Association* 48, no. 262 (1953): 220–243.

Marks, E. S., W. Seltzer, and K. J. Krótki. *Population Growth Estimation: A Handbook of Vital Statistics Measurement.* New York: The Population Council, 1974.

Marks, E. S., and J. Waksberg. "Evaluation of Coverage in the 1960 Census Through Case-by-Case Checking." In *Proceedings of the Social Statistics Section,* 62–70. Washington, D.C.: American Statistical Association, 1966.

Mulry, M. H. "Summary of Accuracy and Coverage Evaluation for the U.S. Census 2000." *Journal of Official Statistics* 23, no. 3 (2007): 345–370. Available at www.jos.nu/Articles/article.asp.

Mulry, M. H., and B. D. Spencer. "Accuracy of the 1990 Census and Undercount Adjustments." *Journal of the American Statistical Association* 88, no. 423 (1993): 1080–1091.

National Research Council. *The Bicentennial Census: New Directions for Methodology in 1990.* Panel on Decennial Census Methodology. Constance F. Citro and Michael L. Cohen, eds. Committee on National Statistics, Commission on Behavioral and Social Sciences and Education. Washington, D. C.: The National Academies Press, 1985.

Price, D. O. "A Check on Underenumeration in the 1940 Census." *American Sociological Review* 12, no. 1 (1947): 44–49.

U.S. Bureau of the Census. *The Post-Enumeration Survey: 1950; An Evaluation Study of the 1950 Censuses of Population and Housing.* Technical Paper no. 4. Suitland, Md.: U.S. Bureau of the Census, 1960.

Pre-Computer Tabulation Systems

The Census Bureau relied on hand tabulation for compilation and tabulation of census returns from the first census in 1790 until the introduction of machine tabulation late in 1872. The bureau continued to support experimentation and innovation with regard to tabulating census results well into the twentieth century and was among the first to recognize the usefulness of computers for data processing in the 1940s.

No clerical force was employed at the federal level for the compilation, verification, or correction of returns for the first three decennial censuses (1790–1810). The Act of March 1, 1790, which created the legislative framework for the censuses of 1790, 1800, 1810, 1820, and 1830, simply required that assistant marshals provide "accurate returns of all persons, except Indians not taxed" and that U.S. marshals would "transmit to the President of the United States the aggregate amount of each description of persons within their respective districts." Beginning in 1800, however, aggregate returns were turned over to the secretaries of states. The fourth census (1820) employed an unidentified number of clerks (total remuneration $925), whose specific tasks were also undisclosed.

New Tabulation Age

In several respects, the fifth decennial census (1830) represented the dawning of a new tabulating age. For the first time in decennial census taking history, uniform printed schedules were distributed by the secretary of state, Martin Van Buren, to the U.S. marshals for their assistants to use. Marshals were required to deliver one copy of each schedule filled out to the clerk of the district court and to the secretary of state, together with their compiled totals. Second, legislation passed on February 3, 1831, required the secretary of state

> to note all the clerical errors in the returns of the marshals and assistants, whether in the additions, classification of inhabitants, or otherwise, and cause said notes to be printed, with the aggregate returns of the marshals, for the use of Congress.

In an effort to comply with this directive, secretary of state Van Buren for the first time employed 43 temporary clerks to carry out this task.

The ambitious scope of the sixth decennial census's (1840) schedule, dictated by the 1830 and 1840 Census Acts, almost ensured that a clerical force would be required to assist with compilation and tabulation of census returns. As before, the secretary of state, John Forsyth, was required to note "all the clerical errors in the returns of the marshals and assistants, whether in the additions, classification of inhabitants, or otherwise, and that he should direct to be printed the corrected aggregate returns only." To this effort, the 1840 Census Act provided for a superintending clerk, a recording clerk, two assistant clerks and other such clerks as were necessary "to examine and correct the returns from the marshals and their assistants." The maximum size of the 1840 census office workforce was 28 employees.

By 1850 there was a strong general appreciation among census pundits of the necessity for improving census machinery. An act approved on March 3, 1849, established a Census Board composed of the secretary of state, the attorney general, and the postmaster general. The act also provided for the appointment by the board of a secretary—Joseph C. G. Kennedy was the first appointee, later assuming the title of superintendent of the census (1850–1853). Further legislation, passed on May 23, 1850, significantly altered the scope of the canvass, necessitating among other things a larger office workforce in Washington, D.C. Compilation and tabulation of the results of the seventh census were begun under Superintendent Kennedy and completed under Superintendent James D. B. DeBow (1853–1854). The maximum size of the 1850 Census Office workforce was 160. Clerks employed in the Census Office during the 1850 decennial census period held only temporary positions, and in the *Compendium of the Seventh Census* DeBow lamented the difficulties he faced in obtaining qualified personnel. In his introductory remarks in the *Compendium of the Seventh Census*, DeBow complained that some clerks had

> never compiled a table before, and are incapable of combining a column of figures correctly. Hundreds of thousands of pages of returns are placed in the hands of such persons to be digested. If any are qualified it is no merit of the system. In 1840 returns were given out by the job to whoever would take them. In 1850 such was the pressure of work, that almost anyone could at times have a desk. (18)

The eighth decennial census (1860) continued the practice of hiring a temporary clerical workforce to carry out the task of hand compilation and tabulation of the enumeration. An act approved on May 5, 1860, created a classical clerical workforce for the Census Office, including a superintendent and a chief clerk. The maximum office workforce reached 184 clerks.

Second Tabulation Age

The innovation of standardized printed schedules and provision of a clerical office workforce brought about the first tabulation age. Machine tabulation initiated the second tabulation age. The mechanization of tabulation had its beginnings in late 1872, when the Census Office experimented with a tallying machine invented by Charles W. Seaton, the chief clerk of the Census Office. Seaton was paid $15,000 by order of the act of June 10, 1872, in full compensation of all claims against the government for the machine's use in the ninth or any subsequent census. The Seaton machine, as it was known, was used extensively in tabulating the 1880 census. Census clerks used long paper tally sheets. Seaton's invention was simply a wooden box containing parallel rollers that unwound these sheets at the bottom and rewound them at the top. The machine condensed a long tally sheet to a workable surface for the clerk. Hundreds of clerks still did the actual tallying by hand, but the Seaton machine significantly sped up the tabulation process.

By the last quarter of the nineteenth century, the sheer scope of the decennial census and the broad demand for the statistics generated by the count challenged the Census Office to develop an efficient and accurate method of compilation and tabulation. In 1890 the electric tabulating machine was used for the first time. Herman Hollerith, a Census Office employee, developed the Hollerith Electric Tabulating Machine, which used punch cards, in the 1880s, and the machine was used in the eleventh decennial census.

The system that Hollerith developed consisted of individual cards, the keyboard punch, and a series of automatic machines that verified, sorted, counted, and tabulated census data. Information gathered for each individual at the enumeration was first transferred to small cards measuring 6 5/8 by 3 1/4 inches by means of a mechanical keypunch. The position of the hole on the card indicated the particular fact to be recorded. Once punched, the cards were run through a verification machine that threw out all inconsistencies and provided a count for subsequent checking purposes. Next, the cards were separated into classes or groups by an automatic sorting machine capable of handling several hundred cards per minute. The cards were then run through a machine that counted and tabulated them. The tabulating machine held a pin box that contained a needle, set on a fine spiral spring, for each possible hole in a card. The pin box was brought down over each card in turn; those needles meeting an unpunched surface were depressed, and those passing through the punched hole made an electrical contact below, which in turn registered on a dial. At the conclusion of each "run," the counters were read and the result recorded. According to the Census Office, in the hands of an experienced and capable clerk, the Hollerith Electric Tabulating Machines tabulated an average of 8,000–10,000 cards in a working day of six-and-a-half hours. In 1890 and 1900 the machines were run by hand.

During the twelfth census the Hollerith system was again used, with some refinements which sped up the tabulation process. Added to the machines used for the eleventh decennial tabulation were adding-machine attachments used for preparing the statistics of agriculture. Automatic feeders and an improved automatic sorting machine were also used "to great advantage." The automatic sorting machine employed in 1900 was a three-foot-square and five-foot-high frame, directly over a column of ten boxes. As with the tabulating machine, the cards in the 1900 sorter were fed downward one by one, before the pin box. The cards entered one of ten chutes determined by the electromagnet, which in turn led to the ten boxes. Before a run, a clerk worked out the combinations of the pins in the pin box. Dials on the outside of the machine recorded the number of cards as they passed through, thus allowing the clerks to note their progress and to keep a record of daily productivity. Publicity for the Census Office championed the efficiency of the new machines and calculated that if the tallies of age, sex, nativity, and occupation had been made by hand, it would have taken 100 clerks 7 years, 11 months, and 5 days to complete the work.

The Census Bureau, which was made permanent in 1902, used its first intercensal period to refine tabulating machinery and to tackle new problems created by the solution of electric tabulation—namely, preparing the cards for tabulation (a process called *editing*). A congressional appropriation of $40,000 in February 1905 and the subsequent organization of the bureau's own machine shop in July 1905 allowed the bureau to begin developing its own tabulation machinery and thus to bypass the costly rental fees it had incurred for the previous decennial census. By late 1907 the bureau's machine shop declared that its tabulating and keypunching machines were far superior to those of its predecessors and ready for use in the thirteenth decennial census.

The keypunching and tabulating machines developed by the Census Bureau were indeed different in a number of respects from their predecessors. Whereas the keypunching machine used in 1900 had only one key, that of 1910—which resembled a typewriter—had more than 250 keys corresponding to the various facts sought by the tabulation. The machine required an operating clerk to align the keys and the holes before punching, which theoretically allowed for the correction of errors before the actual punching began. The tabulating machines employed during the 1900 census recorded their counts on dials and the results had to be transcribed by a clerk, but the 1910 version automatically printed the results of the counts. Automatic rather than hand feeding of the cards into the tabulator also sped up the process. The bureau used 300 keypunching machines and 100 semi-automatic electric tabulating machines for the count of the thirteenth decennial census.

Declarations of the superiority of the updated keypunching machine proved to be premature. The bureau's attempts to correct the problems concurrent with the tabulation of the thirteenth census were unsuccessful, and the clerks were forced to use the old machines, thus slowing the entire process considerably. It is clear from the annual reports of the director of the census to the secretary of commerce, from 1920 to the 1930s, that the bureau focused considerable attention on the details of office work, particularly those of editing, keypunching, tabulating, and verifying the census returns, which in turn led to improvements in the speed and efficiency of the machine tabulation process. As the U.S. population continued to grow in complexity and diversity in the twentieth century, the Census Bureau remained committed to refinement and innovation with regard to all aspects of tabulating the census returns.

See also Decennial censuses: 1880 census; Decennial censuses: 1890 census; Decennial censuses: 1900 census; Decennial censuses: 1910 census; Decennial censuses: 1920 census; Decennial censuses: 1930 census; Decennial censuses: 1940 census.

. . . . DIANA L. MAGNUSON

BIBLIOGRAPHY

DeBow, J. D. B. *Statistical View of the United States . . .: Being a Compendium of the Seventh Census . . . .* Washington, D.C.: Robert Armstrong, 1853. Available at www2.census.gov/prod2/decennial/documents/1850c-01.pdf.

Merriam, William R. *American Census Taking from the First Census of the United States: Reprinted from The Century Magazine for April, 1903.* Washington, D.C.: Government Printing Office, 1904. Available at www.archive.org/details/cu31924013916030/.

Truesdell, Leon Edgar. *The Development of Punch Card Tabulation in the Bureau of the Census, 1890–1940.* Washington, D.C.: U.S. Government Printing Office, 1965.

U.S. Bureau of the Census. *The Story of the Census, 1790-1916.* Washington, D.C.: Government Printing Office, 1916.

Wright, Carroll D., and William C. Hunt. *The History and Growth of the United States Census.* Washington, D.C.: Government Printing Office, 1900.

Private Sector

The U.S. Decennial Census is a federal data collection program undertaken for federal purposes. However, businesses use census information to increase their efficiency and competitiveness, and private companies have developed census-based information products that are used widely in business applications.

History of Census Data Use in Business Decision Making

The use of census data in strategic and tactical decision making by U.S. businesses is widespread. This reflects the fact that demographic data are of great use to private enterprises seeking to be competitive and responsive to increasingly diverse consumer, community, and employee populations. Improved technology for accessing and processing census data has increased private sector utilization of census data over time.

Businesses have probably used U.S. census data for well over 100 years. In the nineteenth century, the census provided information on manufacturing, agriculture, mining, and fisheries, and companies likely used these data in production planning. For example, census data would help manufacturers of farm equipment know where farms were located. In the twentieth century, companies used demographic and socioeconomic data from the census to determine where to sell a growing line of products to a growing population of consumers.

Applications were limited, as census data were available only in printed publications provided by the Census Bureau, or in some cases by private publishers, which reported data on population, income, and sales for every county and hundreds of cities. Such publications were used to allocate sales and advertising dollars to sales territories, evaluate sales performance, and aid in decisions about where to open new stores.

The last 30 years of the twentieth century saw rapid change in how businesses accessed and used census data, driven by advances in computer technology. With the release of 1970 census data on computer tapes for public use, businesses could make large-scale use of the data, targeting areas and population segments with a precision not feasible when using data only available in print. By the 1990s, corporate technology systems, geographic information systems (GIS) software, and employee expertise allowed companies to receive, store, and analyze large data files from the Census Bureau, State Data Centers (SDCs), and the value-added data vendors described below. Merging census data with internal and industry data created powerful analytic and information foundations that helped companies create strategic goals and improved tactical plans and operations.

The Internet and personal computing provide the most recent platform for the expansion of business analytics and planning using census data. Business analysts are able to use powerful search engines to find economic, geographic, and demographic data. Information from a variety of sources, including local planning agencies, the Census Bureau's American FactFinder (AFF) Web site, and private sources, is readily available; results can be displayed on a thematic map or report and can be accessed anywhere using mobile technology such as smartphones and wireless Internet. GIS map products help business executives identify market potential with easy-to-read maps showing stores, competitors, and customer locations as layers over road networks, land features, and income thematic layers. Business analysts and leaders expect the fact-driven decisions made possible through accurate, broad-based data and GIS software.

How Businesses Use Census Data

Users of census data include companies in many industries such as consumer product manufacturing, retail, financial services, real estate, housing, transportation, travel and entertainment, and health care. Census data are used for many key functions: informing decisions on targeted sales and marketing, strategic planning, human resources planning and staffing, site location, merchandising, media and communications, logistics and distribution networks, and financial forecasting. Census data are used broadly for macro strategic planning and narrowly for near-term tactical planning.

The 2010 census will be an important benchmark to document regional, metropolitan, and sociodemographic trends during a decade of significant social and economic change. Examples of changes that are important for business are the growth of the Hispanic population, movement between cities and suburbs, changes in the workforce, and the aging of the population. The size and location of the Hispanic population are important for Spanish-language advertising and communications, merchandising, and product placement. Investing capital in locations close to a company's core customers is likely to generate strong returns; for example, a U.S. apparel chain could use census data to identify areas with large numbers of people who fit its core-customer profile, such as women in the 35–54 age group. Investing capital in locations where qualified potential employees live can reduce training expenses and thus create a competitive advantage, so companies might use census data on levels of education to decide where to open a distribution center or call center.

As the U.S. became more diverse—in race and ethnicity, income and education, housing, and types of households—business strategy shifted from a mass-market, one-size-fits-all model to targeted segmentation by community, neighborhood, Zip+4, and even household. The census is particularly well suited to targeting objectives because it provides consistent data nationwide and for very small areas. People tend to live in neighborhoods reflecting their life cycle stages: families with school-age children cluster in suburban areas, while young urbanites and retirees live near urban centers or in areas rich with amenities. Launching a product or service is more efficient and effective in areas where the target population is concentrated. Families with teenagers in high school and household incomes above $75,000 are the target audience for smartphones and college savings plans. A product test in an area with few such families would not be successful. Combining census data with company information about customers

further enhances business plans and sales goals. Young white nonhispanic children prefer different soft drinks than do seniors or Hispanic populations, and companies can use census data on the age or ethnicity of local populations to help them target product offerings in local stores or restaurants.

In addition to data from the decennial census, other census data are very important to business decision making, including those from the economic census; the annual Consumer Expenditure Survey; and the American Community Survey (ACS), which is part of the decennial program. The economic census provides annual and five-year data on sector activity, allowing the measurement of market share and evaluation of industry trends. Is a particular store channel growing at the expense of another? Is a certain merchandise line moving from brick-and-mortar stores to online sales? The Consumer Expenditure Survey measures consumer spending by key demographic and household attributes. How much do households spend on eating at home versus away from home? Is a change in consumer spending patterns temporary due to the recent recession, or is the new frugality a long-term trend? The ACS provides timely socioeconomic and demographic data for communities and neighborhoods and enables the development of enhanced small-area estimates every year. The first release of small-area five-year data became available in late 2010 and is expected to transform business's use of census data for strategic and tactical advantage.

Private Sector Disseminators

As early as 1929, *Sales and Marketing Management Magazine* was promoting the business use of census data by publishing its "Survey of Buying Power," which combined population, income, and sales data for counties and cities. But as described above, it was the release of the 1970 census on computer tapes that prompted the widespread use of the census in business applications. With machine-readable data, one could efficiently analyze large quantities of data for small areas, and many businesses were quick to recognize the benefits of applications such as those described above. However, few companies were equipped to process the massive census files, and the Census Bureau was not equipped to respond to the demand for its data. In response, a number of private companies purchased the census files, and—there being no copyright on census data—established themselves as value-added disseminators of the information.

In contrast to the Census Bureau's bulk dissemination, private suppliers provided quick and flexible access to the census—for a price. If a business needed income or home-ownership data for neighborhoods in a metropolitan market, or reports comparing the demographics of alternative trade areas, private suppliers were the best source. One could use data provided by private suppliers to define several areas and quickly identify their demographic characteristics or to identify areas with concentrations of target populations such as affluent families with children. Private suppliers also offered flexibility in area definition, providing data for "geometric" areas such as a one-mile radius around a store. Their products also provided census data aggregated to industry-relevant areas, such as current ZIP codes, media markets, and telecommunications service areas. The Census Bureau has since become a more user-friendly disseminator of its own data, but private suppliers still offer the greatest flexibility in retrieving data for custom geographic areas.

Data from private suppliers soon expanded beyond the repackaging of census data. Business applications require current data, so private suppliers now produce small-area estimates of basic population counts and characteristics based on sources such as U.S. Postal Service residential address counts and a variety of proprietary databases. Because businesses need content beyond that provided by the census, the suppliers estimate non-census indicators such as wealth and sales potential. Supplemental data on business and employment are added to identify commercial and workplace markets, and many businesses integrate their own data with those provided by the private suppliers.

Many private suppliers use census data to develop lifestyle cluster systems—that is, neighborhood types that are predictive of consumer behavior and provide a shorthand way of applying the census. Using neighborhood clusters, rather than detailed census tables, businesses can efficiently identify the characteristics of their customers, locate untapped concentrations of similar populations, and advertise to them through their preferred media.

Some private suppliers provide value-added geographic information. The census provides the basic framework of blocks, block groups, tracts, and associated spatial data, and the private suppliers turn this information into commercial products. Among these are boundaries for computer mapping, address coding systems that link addresses to geographic units or latitude/longitude coordinates, and cross-reference files used to build nonstandard areas (such as ZIP codes or cable television service areas) from small-area census geography.

Dissemination technology is an essential and always changing part of the data business. In the 1980s, mainframe computer dissemination products gave way to desktop systems that accessed data on compact disks. These systems have been refined over the years, and data suppliers worked with GIS providers to integrate state-of-the-art data and mapping technologies. Dissemination through the Internet has become common, allowing users online access to huge databases of census and proprietary data as well as mapping resources.

The Census Bureau also has begun Internet dissemination with products that have become more flexible and user-friendly. However, few businesses seek only census data, so private suppliers continue to provide a wide array of proprietary estimates and database products. They tailor these products to the applications of businesses in industries such as retail, financial services, health care, and telecommunications.

In fact, private suppliers have extended so far beyond the repackaging of census data that one can lose sight of how dependent they are on the census. But while many data products are several steps removed from the census, most still build on census data. Consumer and media usage surveys draw representative samples and weight responses based on census counts or on census-based estimates. Even the seemingly independent consumer databases—with millions of person and household records—estimate some attributes based on small-area census data and are coded to census geography. And the content of these databases is much less extensive than that provided by recent censuses.

Data content has become an important issue, as the 2010 census provides none of the long-form data from previous censuses that have been popular in business applications. Instead, data on income, education, mobility, language, and other characteristics are now provided by the ACS. The ACS presents private suppliers with challenges and opportunities. With the ACS providing annual updates to long-form content (free of charge on the Census Bureau's Web site), one might expect the demand for suppliers' products to diminish. However, a major impact is unlikely, as even ACS estimates reflect data collected from one to five years in the past. Add to that the mix of one-, three- and five-year data, the complicated interpretation of multi-year period estimates, and the continuing need for aggregation to custom areas, and there is ample opportunity to add value to ACS data. Once again, private suppliers can build products that make Census Bureau data more readily applicable to business purposes.

The private data business has never focussed on the repackaging and dissemination of census data. It is about providing businesses with valuable information and the necessary tools and knowledge to efficiently apply this information. The business sector produces impressive resources of its own, but the decennial census, now in tandem with the ACS, remains the statistical foundation of many business applications. Private suppliers, and the companies that use their value-added products, continue to benefit from the U.S. Decennial Census and related programs.

See also *Dissemination of data: electronic publications; Data dissemination and use.*

. . . . . JOAN GENTILI NAYMARK AND KEN HODGES
WITH CONTRIBUTIONS BY EDWARD J. SPAR

BIBLIOGRAPHY

Benson, Clea. "Not Enough Information." *CQ Weekly* (December 7, 2009): 2810–2816.

Brookings Institution. *State of Metropolitan America: On the Front Lines of Demographic Transformation.* Washington, D.C.: Brookings Institution, 2010. Available at www.brookings.edu/~/media/Files/Programs/Metro/state_of_metro_america/metro_america_report1.pdf.

Censky, Annalyn. "How to Cash In on the Census." *CNNMoney.com,* March 16, 2010. http://money.cnn.com/galleries/2010/news/1003/gallery.census/index.html.

The Economist. "America's Census and Business: A Count that Counts." January 7, 2010. www.economist.com/node/15213827/.

Exter, Tom. "What the 2010 Census Will Show." *Directions Magazine,* June 10, 2010. www.directionsmag.com/articles/what-the-2010-census-will-show/122354/.

Kintner, Hallie J., Thomas W. Merrick, Peter A. Morrison, and Paul R. Voss, eds. *Demographics: A Casebook for Business and Government.* Boulder, Colo.: Westview Press, 1994.

Merrick, Thomas W., and Stephen J. Tordella. "Demographics: People and Markets." *Population Bulletin* 43, no. 1 (1988): 2–46.

Pol, Louis G., and Richard K. Thomas. *Demography for Business Decision Making.* Westport, Conn.: Quorum Books, 1997.

Russell, Cheryl. "The Business of Demographics." *Population Bulletin* 39, no. 3 (1984): 1–40.

Seckler, Valerie. "Deciphering the Census Signs." *Women's Wear Daily,* March 31, 2010.

Thomas, Richard K., and Russell J. Kirchner. *Desktop Marketing: Lessons from America's Best.* Ithaca, N.Y.: American Demographic Books, 1991.

Weiss, Michael J. *The Clustering of America.* New York: Harper & Row, 1988.

PUMS (Public Use Microdata Samples)

Public Use Microdata Samples (PUMS) are computerized microdata files produced by the Census Bureau for population research. PUMS files allow analysts to define their own tabulations and conduct detailed, multivariate analyses of population and housing issues. The files provide analysts with greater freedom to extract information from census data than do Summary Tape Files (STFs), which contain extensive, but finite, pretabulated data.

Contents

PUMS files have been released for censuses from 1960 to 2000 and for American Community Survey (ACS) samples since 2000 and for the 2010 census short-form data. The information in the PUMS files consists of individual records for a sample of housing units, including the detailed characteristics of each unit and the people residing in it. For example, in 1990 PUMS files contained 500 occupational categories, ages by single years up to 90, and wages in dollars up to $140,000. To protect the confidentiality of respondents, the Census Bureau excluded or restricted information that could lead to the identification of a housing unit or an individual. Although the PUMS files contain essentially all of the information collected, as well as some variables that were created by the Census Bureau by recoding the original information, response ranges on some variables were limited to further protect respondent confidentiality.

Groups outside of the Census Bureau have created Integrated Public Use Microdata Series (IPUMS) files from records of census years from 1850 through 2000 and for the ACS since 2000. These files, created by a variety of individual researchers with funding from the National Institutes of Health and the National Science Foundation, are designed to facilitate the use of census data as a time series. They are available through the Minnesota Population Center (MPC). The IPUMS files are structured with a common format, impose consistent variable coding, and document changes in variables over time. More geographic detail is available in the pre-1940 samples because confidentiality restrictions on individual-level census responses expire after 72 years.

Each PUMS file contains all of the information collected from a subsample of the population. In contrast, the pretabulated data in STFs that the Census Bureau prepares from the census long form and now from the ACS are based on the full sample of the population surveyed. The PUMS samples were constructed by selecting housing units, including vacant units, as well as a sample of persons living in institutions and other group quarters.

The PUMS files were designed to be nationally representative. They contain statistical weights for each person and housing unit, which, when applied to the individual records, expand the sample to represent the total population. Tabulations from PUMS files produce estimates of population characteristics and are subject to sampling variability.

File Types

PUMS files may provide different types of samples. One example would be a 5 percent sample of housing units that includes estimates for states and geographic subdivisions of states. Another would be a 1 percent sample of housing units and estimates for Metropolitan Areas (MAs), including those that cross state boundaries. Although decennial PUMS files contain a small percentage of the total records, they are still large, containing millions of records.

Unlike in the STFs, geographic detail in the PUMS files is limited. Tabulations from the STFs are available for a variety of political and statistical geographies, including counties, places, census tracts, and block groups, whereas the identification of geographic units from the PUMS files is limited to areas of 100,000 persons or more. The lowest level of geography available currently in the PUMS files is the Public Use Microdata Area (PUMA). Each PUMA must have a population of at least 100,000 and consists of a whole county or a subcounty area, such as a Minor Civil Division (MCD) in New England, a place, or a group of tracts. Counties or subcounty areas with a population of less than 100,000 were combined to produce PUMAs of at least 100,000 population.

PUMS files contain two types of records, arranged hierarchically, for each housing unit included in the sample. The first type is a housing unit record; the second is a record for a person. Housing unit and person records contain different information. Person records follow a housing unit record, one for each inhabitant of the housing unit. Each of the records contains a serial number linking persons to the proper housing unit. Persons selected into the sample who are living in group quarters have a dummy housing unit record as a place holder in the file, maintaining the file hierarchy. Person records do not follow records for vacant housing units.

PUMS files are used by a variety of individuals and organizations, including federal, state, and local governments; academic researchers and students; the business sector, including marketing firms; and public service organizations. PUMS files are useful when information on small geographic areas is not required and when there is a need to study the relationships among census variables not presented in other Census Bureau products.

The Census Bureau makes PUMS files available for download. See, for example, the Census 2000 Gateway at www.census.gov/main/www/cen2000.html or the ACS site, www.census.gov/acs/www/ ("Data & Documentation" tab). Files are available for the nation as a whole and for states and the District of Columbia.

See also *Confidentiality; Content; Geography: Distribution of population; IPUMS (Integrated Public Use Microdata Series); Long form; Metropolitan areas; State data centers; Summary files.*

. . . . NANCY E. DUNTON
REVISED BY MARGO J. ANDERSON

BIBLIOGRAPHY

U.S. Bureau of the Census. *1990 Census of Population and Housing: Public Use Microdata Samples, United States; Technical Documentation.* D1-D90-PUMS-14-TECH. Washington, D.C.: U.S. Bureau of the Census, 1992. Available at www2.census.gov/prod2/decennial/documents/D1-D90-PUMS-14-TECH-01.pdf.

U.S. Census Bureau. *2000 Census of Population and Housing: Public Use Microdata Sample (PUMS), United States; Technical Documentation.* Washington, D.C.: U.S. Census Bureau, 2003. Available at www.census.gov/prod/cen2000/doc/pums.pdf.

Race: Questions and Classifications

Each census since the very first in 1790 has included a question on race. However, the content of the question, the terminology, and the number of categories have changed considerably due to research and political factors.

Race is a fluid concept whose meaning has changed over time and across societies and geographic boundaries. Social scientists of the late nineteenth and early twentieth centuries saw the concept as a scientific one, rooted in biological and genetic differences among peoples. Today, the Census Bureau's use of the term reflects self-identification, with an emphasis on race being a social construct that does not reflect any biological or genetic reference. Currently, the census's use of the term reflects common usage by the general public as evidenced by the actions of the legislative and judicial bodies of the country. Policy concerns and changing social attitudes, as well as changes in the racial makeup of the population, have contributed to how people have classified themselves and others, how they have been categorized racially in official statistics, and how the federal government has used these data.

The Constitution of the United States requires the collection of population data by race in the decennial census. Article 1, Section 2, contains the following language:

> Representatives and direct taxes shall be apportioned among the several States which may be included within this Union, according to their respective numbers, which shall be determined by adding to the whole number of free persons, including those bound to Service for a term of years, and excluding Indians not taxed, three-fifths of all other Persons. The actual Enumeration shall be made within three years after the first Meeting of the Congress of the United States, and within every subsequent Term of ten Years, in such Manner as they shall by Law direct.

This ambiguous language was used to classify the population of the United States into three distinct groups: "white," "black or African Americans," and "American Indians." "Other persons" was the euphemism for "slaves" in the text of the Constitution. "Indians not taxed" were those American Indians who owed allegiance to their tribes, not to the United States.

Early Classification

The 1790 census operationalized the language of the Constitution by asking for the name of the head of the family and the number of people in each household who were free white males age 16 and over, free white males under age 16, free white females, all other free persons (that is, free people of color), and slaves. Since 1790, the categories and the methods for collecting data on race have changed many times. The number of racial classification categories expanded from 3 in 1790 to 16 in 1990. The 1860 census was the first to identify American Indians separately; "Chinese" was added as a race category in 1870. By the 1930 census, the number of racial categories had expanded to ten—"white," "negro," "Indian," "Chinese," "Japanese," "Mexican," "Filipino," "Hindu," "Korean," and "other." The "Mexican" category met opposition from both Mexican Americans and the Mexican government and was not repeated in later censuses. The "Hindu" category was not repeated after 1940. The categories "Hawaiian," "part Hawaiian," "Aleut," and "Eskimo" were added in 1960. Asians and Pacific Islanders have been classified as racial groups, and the nativity question on the census, asked of all residents from 1850 to 1950, also identified residents born in the countries of Asia or the Pacific islands.

In earlier years, the census attempted to quantify the amount of black or American Indian blood among the inhabitants of the United States. Various definitions, such as "full-blooded" for American Indians and "black" or "mulatto" for people of African descent, were used in different censuses to categorize people. Individuals were considered American Indians if they were full-blooded, if they were enrolled by a tribe or registered at an Indian agency, or, in the 1890 census, if those who knew them considered them to be American Indians.

Prior to 1960, the observations of enumerators determined the designated race of respondents. Starting in 1960, Americans enumerated themselves on a mail questionnaire. As a result, the format of the question on race changed. The 1960 question asked, "Is this person White, Negro, American Indian, Japanese, Chinese, Filipino, Hawaiian, Part Hawaiian, Aleut, Eskimo (etc.)?"

For most of the nation's history, the United States was often considered a country of two major races: white and black. Until recently, whites comprised about 80 percent of the population. Blacks represented from 12 to 19 percent of the total population. The proportion of people in the "other race" category was very small and grew minimally, in part because citizenship laws restricted naturalization to whites and, until the 1960s, restrictive immigration quotas largely prevented nonwhites from coming to the United States.

Census 2000 and New Classifications

For 200 years, each inhabitant of the United States was classified in the decennial census in one and only one racial group, despite the presence of people of mixed racial ancestry who did not identify as being in a single racial category. The racial identity of such individuals in the decennial censuses has changed along with legal mandates and societal perceptions. In some years the census dealt with multiracial respondents by including mixed-race categories (for example, "mulatto" and "part Hawaiian") in the codes used for the race question. If there was no appropriate multiracial race category, over the years, the Census Bureau has identified these individuals by the race of the mother, the race of the father, or the first racial group mentioned by the respondent. People of mixed white and other racial parentage were generally classified according to the race of their nonwhite parent. People of mixed African American and American Indian ancestry were generally categorized as "negro" unless the American Indian features were clearly predominant or unless the individual was accepted in the community as an American Indian. In the 1950 census, the Census Bureau attempted to categorize as separate groups some triracial mixture of white, negro, and American Indian people living in certain compact communities in the eastern United States. These communities have existed for some time and were locally recognized by special names, such as Siouian or Croatan, Moor, and Tunica.

Along with greater self-reporting in the 1960 and later censuses came greater criticism of having to choose a single racial category. People of mixed race or their parents objected that it was unfair having to choose between the race of the mother and that of the father. For the question on race in the 1990 census, separate codes were assigned to a few predefined combinations reported in the "other race" response category (such as "white and black," "white and Indian," and "white and Japanese") to identify the size of such groups.

Much of the recent pressure for changing the race classification is a result of the growth in interracial unions and the number of children in such unions. The number of interracial couples grew from fewer than 0.5 million in 1960 to about 1.5 million in 1990, while the number of children in such marriages reached about 2 million in 1990. Although the multiracial issue is often thought of as involving primarily blacks and whites, children in such interracial unions have consistently represented only about 20 percent of all children in such interracial families. By contrast, in 1990 about 34 percent of all children in interracial families with at least one white partner were American Indian, and 45 percent were Asian.

The Office of Management and Budget (OMB) in the Executive Office of the President sets standards for statistical classifications. In response to legislative, programmatic, and administrative requirements set by the federal government, OMB in 1977 issued its *Directive No. 15: Race and Ethnic Standards for Federal Statistics and Administrative Reporting*. These standards specified four racial categories: "white," "black," "American Indian or Alaskan Native," and "Asian or Pacific Islander." OMB also specified two ethnic categories: "Hispanic origin" and "Not of Hispanic origin." According to the standards, people of Hispanic origin could be of any race. After the 1990 census, the standards came under criticism for no longer reflecting the increasing racial and ethnic diversity of the country. OMB solicited extensive public comment, undertook extensive consultation and public hearings, and issued revised standards—with five racial categories—in 1997. These new regulations defined the questions for Census 2000.

In Census 2000, respondents were asked to complete the following question on race for every household member: "What is this person's race? Mark [X] for one or more races to indicate what this person considers himself/herself to be." There are 15 response categories. Data from this question could be collapsed to comply with the five minimum racial categories—"white," "black or African American," "American Indian and Alaska Native," "Asian," "Native Hawaiian and Other Pacific Islander"—identified by OMB in 1997 (see Table 1). Since the standards stated that "respondents shall be offered the option of selecting one or more racial designations," the census question on race also permitted individual respondents to mark two or more race categories to indicate mixed racial parentage. Additionally, the Census Bureau obtained permission from OMB to include as a separate category "some other race."

Table 1. The Office of Management and Budget's Categories and Definitions of Racial Groups Used in Census 2000

CATEGORY	DEFINITION
American Indian or Alaska Native	A person having origins in any of the original peoples of North and South America (including Central America), and who maintains tribal affiliation or community attachment.
Asian	A person having origins in any of the original peoples of the Far East, Southeast Asia, or the Indian subcontinent including, for example, Cambodia, China, India, Japan, Korea, Malaysia, Pakistan, the Philippine Islands, Thailand, and Vietnam.
Black or African American	A person having origins in any of the black racial groups of Africa. Terms such as "Haitian" or "Negro" can be used in addition to "Black or African American."
Native Hawaiian or Other Pacific Islander	A person having origins in any of the original peoples of Hawaii, Guam, Samoa, or other Pacific Islands.
White	A person having origins in any of the original peoples of Europe, the Middle East, or North Africa.

2010 Census

The 2010 Census question asked all persons to report their races, with each respondent having the option of reporting two or more races. The Census Bureau did not provide a definition of race; evidence from census studies indicated that respondents would answer according to their own self-perceptions of race.

The 2010 race question, as in previous censuses, included a number of Asian and Pacific Islander national-origin groups. It had 12 specific categories—"white," "black, African Am., or Negro," "American Indian or Alaska Native," and nine Asian and Pacific Islander groups—as well as three residual categories, "other Asian," "other Pacific Islander," and "some other race." Three categories required write-in entries: people reporting as "American Indian or Alaska Native" were asked to report the name of their enrolled or principal tribe. Those reporting as "other Asian," "other Pacific Islander," or "some other race" were asked to write in their group or race separately.

Changes from Census 2000 to the 2010 Census

The major change from the Census 2000 question on race to the 2010 question on race was the wording of the question. The phrase "to indicate what this person considers himself/herself to be" in the instruction was deleted. Prior to Census 2000, the Census Bureau had conducted studies with different formats that allowed more than one race to be reported. The studies included panels with and without examples of detailed national-origin groups and American Indian or Alaska Native tribes, but they did not provide direct evidence about these examples' effects. Because there was no clear evidence to suggest that removing examples had an adverse effect on the reporting of race, the examples were dropped in an effort to make the Census 2000 questionnaire more user-friendly. Some constituents postulated that this action led to an increase in nonspecific reporting of Asian and Pacific Islander and American Indian and Alaska Native tribal groups.

Research during the decade focused on comparing results from a two-question format (the Hispanic-origin question, followed by the race question) with an experimental three-question format (a shortened Hispanic-origin question followed by a shortened race question, followed by a modified ancestry question). In the three-question format, the Hispanic-origin question included a "yes" and "no" response option, and the question on race included the five minimum race categories required by the OMB (see above) as well as "some other race." The modified ancestry question was intended to elicit detailed information on all race and ethnic groups. An introduction was added to the ancestry question to provide clarification of the intent of the question and to increase respondents' willingness to provide detailed information. The expectation was that the question would produce data that could be used for editing and imputation when the respondent left the question on race blank. Results of the studies led

the Census Bureau to abandon the idea of a shortened question on race and Hispanic origin and to resort to a question similar in design to the 2000 question on race. However, the research suggested that including examples in the "other Asian" and "other Pacific Islander" categories increased reporting of specific Asian and Pacific Islander national-origin groups.

The Census Bureau generally tested the race and Hispanic origin questions as a package because it has learned that a small change in one question may affect the other. Therefore, the instructions to the question on Hispanic origin for the 2010 census were changed to read "NOTE: Please answer BOTH Question 5 about Hispanic origin and Question 6 about race. For this census, Hispanic origins are not races."

The 2010 census question on race builds upon the success of the 2000 census, while maximizing self-response and producing detailed national-origin groups for the Asian and Pacific Islander race groups.

Data Tabulations

Many federal agencies, including the U.S. Departments of Commerce, Education, Labor, and Justice, use decennial census information on race. All levels of government use information on race to implement and evaluate federal statutes, such as the Equal Employment Opportunity Act, Civil Rights Act, Voting Rights Act (1965), Public Health Act, and Fair Housing Act, among others. Public and private organizations use race data to identify areas where groups may require special services and to plan and implement programs that address specific educational, housing, and health needs. The private sector uses data on race and ethnicity to identify areas with a high concentration of a targeted racial population, allowing businesses to develop marketing plans for the purpose of selling goods or providing services tailored to that population's needs.

Much like data from the 2000 Census, data on race from Census 2010 were tabulated using at least two different approaches. The "single-race tabulation approach" presented data for the six single races and for a "two or more races" category. Data for the specified Asian groups shown on the questionnaire were collapsed into the "Asian" race category, and data for the specified Pacific Islander groups were collapsed into the "Native Hawaiian and Other Pacific Islander" race category.

For selected data products, such as the Public Law 94-171 Redistricting File, data were shown for 57 possible combinations of more than one race. The 57 possible combinations comprised 15 categories of two races, 20 categories of three races, 15 categories of four races, 6 categories of five races, and 1 category of six races (see Table 2). Also shown on this file were the 6 single-race categories for a total of 63 categories.

For other purposes, a second approach showed data for the single-race groups alone or in combination with one or more of the five OMB groups and the "some other race" group used in the census:

Table 2. Combinations of Two or More Races: 57 Categories

TWO RACES	
White, and Black or African American White, and American Indian and Alaska Native White and Asian White, and Native Hawaiian and Other Pacific Islander White, and Some Other Race Black or African American, and American Indian and Alaska Native Black or African American, and Asian Black or African American, and Native Hawaiian and Other Pacific Islander	Native Hawaiian and Other Pacific Islander, and Some Other Race Black or African American, and Some Other Race American Indian and Alaska Native, and Asian American Indian and Alaska Native, and Native Hawaiian or Other Pacific Islander American Indian and Alaska Native, and Some Other Race Asian and Native Hawaiian, and Other Pacific Islander Asian and Some Other Race

THREE RACES	
White, Black or African American, and American Indian and Alaska Native White, Black or African American, and Asian White, Black or African American, and Native Hawaiian and Other Pacific Islander White, Black or African American, and Some Other Race White, American Indian and Alaska Native, and Asian White, American Indian and Alaska Native, and Native Hawaiian and Other Pacific Islander White, American Indian and Alaska Native, and Some Other Race White, Asian, and Native Hawaiian and Other Pacific Islander White, Asian, and Some Other Race White, Native Hawaiian and Other Pacific Islander, and Some Other Race Black or African American, American Indian and Alaska Native, and Asian Black or African American, American Indian and Alaska Native, and Native Hawaiian and Other Pacific Islander	Black or African American, American Indian and Alaska Native, and Some Other Race Black or African American, Asian, and Native Hawaiian and Other Pacific Islander Black or African American, Asian, and Some Other Race Black or African American, Native Hawaiian and Other Pacific Islander, and Some Other Race American Indian and Alaska Native, Asian, and Native Hawaiian and Other Pacific Islander American Indian and Alaska Native, Asian, and Some Other Race American Indian and Alaska Native, Native Hawaiian and Other Pacific Islander, and Some Other Race Asian, Native Hawaiian and Other Pacific Islander, and Some Other Race

FOUR RACES	
White, Black or African American, American Indian and Alaska Native, and Asian White, Black or African American, American Indian and Alaska Native, and Native Hawaiian and Other Pacific Islander White, Black or African American, American Indian and Alaska Native, and Some Other Race White, Black or African American, Asian and Native Hawaiian, and Other Pacific Islander White, Black or African American, Asian, and Some Other Race White, Black or African American, Native Hawaiian and Other Pacific Islander, and Some Other Race White, American Indian and Alaska Native, Asian and Native Hawaiian, and Other Pacific Islander White, American Indian and Alaska Native, Asian, and Some Other Race	White, American Indian and Alaska Native, Native Hawaiian and Other Pacific Islander, and Some Other Race White, Asian, Native Hawaiian and Other Pacific Islander, and Some Other Race Black or African American, American Indian and Alaska Native, Asian and Native Hawaiian, and Other Pacific Islander Black or African American, American Indian and Alaska Native, Asian, and Some Other Race Black or African America, American Indian and Alaska Native, Native Hawaiian and Other Pacific Islander, and Some Other Race Black or African American, Asian, Native Hawaiian and Other Pacific Islander, and Some Other Race American Indian and Alaska Native, Asian, Native Hawaiian and Other Pacific Islander, and Some Other Race

FIVE RACES	
White, Black or African American, American Indian and Alaska Native, Asian, and Native Hawaiian and Other Pacific Islander White, Black or African American, American Indian and Alaska Native, Asian, and Some Other Race White, Black or African American, American Indian and Alaska Native, Native Hawaiian and Other Pacific Islander, and Some Other Race	White, Black or African American, Asian, Native Hawaiian and Other Pacific Islander, and Some Other Race White, American Indian and Alaska Native, Asian, Native Hawaiian and Other Pacific Islander, and Some Other Race Black or African American, American Indian and Alaska Native, Asian, Native Hawaiian and Other Pacific Islander, and Some Other Race

SIX RACES
White, Black or African American, American Indian and Alaska Native, Asian, Native Hawaiian and Other Pacific Islander, and Some Other Race

- White alone or in combination with one or more other races
- Black or African American alone or in combination with one or more other races
- American Indian and Alaska Native alone or in combination with one or more other races
- Asian alone or in combination with one or more other races
- Native Hawaiian and Other Pacific Islander alone or in combination with one or more other races
- Some other race alone or in combination with one or more other races

This was a tally of responses and not respondents, so the total for the six categories exceeded the total population.

In selected data products, data for the Asian groups and the Native Hawaiian and Other Pacific Islander groups were shown separately on the questionnaire, along with data for selected American Indian and Alaska Native tribes. For the 2010 census, less data on race and other characteristics were released in the form of printed reports and more data were available through the American FactFinder (AFF), the Census Bureau's electronic data dissemination system.

After much testing and congressional objection, plans to drop the "some other race" response from the race question were abandoned. Extensive research focused on how to obtain better reporting of all groups in the question on race.

See also *African-origin population; Asian American population; American Indians and Alaska Natives; Hispanic/Latino ethnicity and identifiers; Native Hawaiian and other Pacific Islander (NHOPI) population; White or European-origin population; White population of the United States.*

. . . . CLAUDETTE BENNETT

BIBLIOGRAPHY

Bennett, Claudette, Nampeo McKenney, and Roderick Harrison. "Racial Classification Issues Concerning Children in Mixed-Race Households." Paper presented at the annual meeting of the Population Association of America, San Francisco, April 6–8, 1995.

———. "Reporting of One or More Races in the 1996 Race and Ethnic Targeted Test (RAETT): Implications for Census 2000." Paper presented at the annual meeting of the Population Association of America, Chicago, April 2–4, 1998.

National Research Council. *Spotlight on Heterogeneity: The Federal Standards for Racial and Ethnic Classification; Summary of a Workshop.* Barry Edmonston, Joshua Goldstein, and Juanita Tamayo Lott, eds. Committee on National Statistics, Commission on Behavioral and Social Sciences and Education. Washington, D.C.: The National Academies Press, 1996.

Office of Management and Budget. *Directive No. 15: Race and Ethnic Standards for Federal Statistics and Administrative Reporting, as adopted on May 12, 1977* (1977). Available at http://wonder.cdc.gov/wonder/help/populations/bridged-race/Directive15.html.

Office of Management and Budget. "Revisions to the Standards for the Classification of Federal Data on Race and Ethnicity." *Federal Register* 62, no. 210 (1997): 58782–58790. Available at www.whitehouse.gov/omb/fedreg_1997standards.

U.S. Bureau of the Census. *200 Years of U.S. Census Taking: Population and Housing Questions, 1790–1990.* Washington, D.C.: U.S. Government Printing Office, 1989. Available at http://www.census.gov/history/pdf/200years.pdf.

———. *Planning for Census 2000: Questions Planned for Census 2000; Federal Legislative and Program Uses.* Washington, D.C.: U.S. Government Printing Office, 1998.

———. *Twenty Censuses: Population and Housing Questions, 1790–1980.* Washington, D.C.: U.S. Government Printing Office, 1978. Available at www.census.gov/history/pdf/20censuses.pdf.

U.S. Commission on Civil Rights. *Racial Categorization in the 2010 Census: A Briefing before the United States Commission on Civil Rights Held in Washington, DC, April 7, 2006.* Washington D.C.: U.S. Commission on Civil Rights, 2009. Available at www.usccr.gov/pubs/RC2010Web_Version.pdf.

Related Data Sources

Many data sources in addition to the decennial census and the American Community Survey (ACS) provide information about the population. These sources include federal, state, and local administrative records; federally sponsored household surveys; population estimates and projections; small-area estimates of income and other characteristics; and other censuses. The decennial census is the largest and most costly of these data sources, followed by other censuses and the ACS.

Beginning with the census of 2010, the census provided basic demographic information every ten years for purposes of reapportionment and redistricting and to serve as the starting point for annual population estimates throughout the decade, while the ACS provided data on a wide range of topics for small as well as large geographic areas and population groups. Compared with the census long-form sample that previously collected data on characteristics of the population, the ACS estimates have the advantage that they are updated every year, although they must be cumulated over one, three, and five years to provide estimates of sufficient reliability for small geographic areas.

Related data sources offer their own benefits and limitations. The decennial census and ACS both contribute to and benefit from other data sources.

Administrative Records

Administrative records contain data collected for the purpose of operating a program or providing a service. Major federal administrative records on the population include Social Security Administration (SSA) records of wage earnings and benefits, Internal Revenue Service (IRS) individual income tax returns, and Medicare records of payments and services maintained by the U.S. Centers for Medicare and Medicaid Services (formerly the U.S. Health Care Financing Administration). Major state and local administrative records on the population include records for recipients of food stamps and cash welfare assistance, Medicaid records, unemployment insurance benefit records, state income tax records, and records of vital events (including births and deaths). Many state and local record systems receive federal funding and provide data for federal uses.

The Census Bureau uses administrative records, including IRS tax returns, Medicare records, and vital statistics, along with data from the previous census and the ACS to develop population estimates for the nation, states, and small geographic areas by age, sex, race, and ethnicity. The estimates for a census year developed through a similar process called demographic analysis (DA) are used, in turn, to evaluate the completeness of coverage of the population in that census. There has been exploratory research to determine if IRS tax returns and other administrative records could provide a much less expensive alternative to the census for obtaining the head count and basic characteristics. Research was conducted as part of the 2000 census to assess whether administrative records could provide information equivalent to the short form or could augment the census by providing information for households that do not mail back a census questionnaire; similar research is being conducted for the 2010 census. Administrative records are also used to evaluate the quality of reporting in the census and household surveys (for example, for wage income) and to produce income and other estimates for small areas between censuses.

The advantages of administrative records are that they can be used at low additional cost for such statistical purposes as developing population estimates and evaluating survey quality and that they are collected and recorded on a frequent basis. However, they typically have limited subject matter detail; the addresses in the records may be out-of-date or differ in other ways from people's actual places of residence. Also, their content, frequency of collection, and other features are subject to change to suit operational program needs rather than statistical information needs.

Household Surveys

The federal government sponsors a large number of continuing and one-time household surveys, many of which use the master address list from the previous census, supplemented by information on new construction, as the frame from which to draw samples for interviews. Other federally sponsored surveys use summarized census data for geographic areas to develop sample designs that appropriately represent different areas of the country and different population groups. Surveys that use the census master address list as a sampling frame are conducted by the Census Bureau because of the requirement in Title 13 of the United States Code for protecting the confidentiality of individually identifiable information obtained in the census.

Household sample surveys typically include a very small fraction of households in comparison to those included in the census, but they are usually conducted much more frequently than the census and obtain much greater detail on specific subjects. The ACS is an exception with regard to its large size—it samples 240,000 households each month (2.9 million households per year, recently increased to 3.4 million households per year), using a mail questionnaire similar to the 2000 census long form with computer assisted telephone and in-person follow-up. Over a five-year period, the ACS sample size is about two-thirds the size of the 2000 long-form sample.

Examples of other major federal household surveys are the following.

Current Population Survey (CPS)

This is a personal and telephone interview monthly survey of a sample of about 60,000 households. It is conducted to obtain data for calculating the official monthly unemployment rate and is supplemented in some months by special questionnaires such as the Annual Social and Economic (ASEC) Supplement, which includes 100,000 households interviewed from February through April of each year. Other supplements include volunteering (September, every year), educational enrollment (October every year), voting (November, in even years), and food insecurity (December, every year). The main (core) survey is sponsored by the U.S. Bureau of Labor Statistics (BLS).

National Health Interview Survey

This is a personal interview household survey conducted each week, with separate weekly samples cumulating to about 35,000 households for the year. The questionnaire includes a core set of health and demographic items and questions on current health topics, which change each year. It is sponsored by the National Center for Health Statistics (NCHS).

National Survey of College Graduates (NSCG, 2003 Panel)

This is a mail survey with telephone and personal interview follow-up of about 50,000 people who reported on the 2000 census long form that they had a bachelor's degree and who in their first interview in 2003 reported a science or engineering degree or occupation. These people are interviewed every two years. This survey is used with the National Survey of Recent College Graduates and the Survey of Doctorate Recipients to profile the nation's science and engineering workforce. It is sponsored by the National Science Foundation's National Center for Science and Engineering Statistics. A new NSCG sample was recently drawn from the ACS, using information not only on occupation but also on field of bachelor's degree. The latter is a new question for the ACS introduced in 2009.

Survey of Income and Program Participation (2008 Panel)

The Survey of Income and Program Participation (SIPP) is a personal and telephone survey that is currently following a sample of adults and children in about 45,000 households who were initially interviewed in fall 2008. Interviews are being conducted every 4 months for 48 months. The SIPP includes an extensive core questionnaire on demographic characteristics, work experience, earnings, program participation, and transfer income by month and asset income for the four-month period, as well as one or more modules on special topics such as child care, disability, net worth, and pension plans. It is sponsored by the Census Bureau. SIPP is undergoing a redesign to be implemented beginning in 2013; the redesigned SIPP will likely collect data annually and use event history calendar techniques to provide accurate month-by-month information.

Population Estimates and Projections

The Census Bureau has an extensive and long-standing program of population estimates and projections. These projections have many uses, including as controls for the ACS and other household surveys so that the survey estimates cover the population as completely as possible, as denominators for vital rates (for example, birth and death rates), and as the basis for allocating federal funds to states and localities. Currently, the bureau produces estimates of total population by age, sex, race, and Hispanic origin annually for the nation, states, and counties with a reference date of July 1. (Long-range population projections for the United States and states are issued periodically.) The bureau also produces estimates of total population every year for metropolitan areas, places, and, in selected states, county subdivisions. In the mid-1990s, the bureau began a program to produce annual estimates of total population and of people ages 5–17 for school districts.

Population estimates and projections are produced by using a variety of data sources. The estimates begin with the counts from the most recent census. Data sources that are used to update the census counts include birth and death records, information on immigrants, Medicare records, IRS tax return records (to estimate interarea migration), state school enrollment data, and other sources.

To produce substate population estimates, the Census Bureau works closely with state agencies that are members of the Federal-State Cooperative for Population Estimates (FSCPE), which was established in the late 1960s. State FSCPE agencies provide data to the Census Bureau (for example, vital statistics and information about group quarters and housing units) for producing estimates, and they review the estimates before they are released. State FSCPE agencies also frequently prepare their own population estimates and projections.

Small-Area Socioeconomic Estimates

In 1993, the Census Bureau began a program of Small-Area Income and Poverty Estimates (SAIPE). Previously, from 1971 to 1987, the bureau produced estimates of per capita income for governmental jurisdictions for use in allocating general revenue sharing funds.

Currently, the Census Bureau produces estimates every year for states and counties of median household income, people in poverty, children under age 5 in poverty (states only), children ages 5–17 in poverty, and people under age 18 in poverty. The bureau also produces annual estimates of children ages 5–17 in poverty for school districts.

The SAIPE estimates are currently produced using statistical models that incorporate data from such sources as the ACS, the 2000 census, population estimates, food stamp records, IRS tax return records, and U.S. Bureau of Economic Analysis (BEA) personal income estimates. BEA produces total and per capita personal income estimates quarterly for states and annually for counties. The income estimates are based on a large number of data sources from administrative records, censuses, and surveys; the per capita income estimates are the result of dividing the income estimates by the Census Bureau's census-based population estimates.

Beginning in 2005, the Census Bureau implemented a similar program of Small Area Health Insurance Estimates (SAHIE) with support from the Centers for Disease Control and Prevention. SAHIE estimates are provided by year for states and counties of people with and without health

insurance coverage by age (people under age 64, ages 18–64, ages 50–64 [states only], and ages 40–64); sex; income at or below 200 percent or 250 percent of the poverty threshold for all people; and income at or below 200 percent of poverty for people under age 18. In addition, SAHIE estimates are provided for states by race and ethnicity (white non Hispanic, black non Hispanic, and Hispanic).

Other Censuses

The federal government conducts periodic censuses of governments and economic entities. Such censuses were previously fielded in conjunction with the population census but are now conducted at different times. The U.S. Department of Agriculture conducts a census of agriculture every five years. The Census Bureau conducts a census of state and local governments and an economic census every five years. The scope of the economic census has expanded so that it now covers nearly all of the U.S. private economy, including manufacturing, minerals and mining, wholesale and retail trade, utilities, transportation, communication, construction, finance, insurance, and real estate.

See also *Agricultural censuses; American Community Survey: introduction; Confidentiality; Demographic analysis; Economic censuses; Federal administrative records; Federal household surveys; Income and poverty measures; Population estimates and projections.*

. . . . CONSTANCE F. CITRO

BIBLIOGRAPHY

National Research Council, *Reengineering the Survey of Income and Program Participation.* Panel on the Census Bureau's Reengineered Survey of Income and Program Participation. Constance F. Citro and John Karl Sholz, eds. Committee on National Statistics, Division of Behavioral and Social Sciences and Education. Washington, D.C.: The National Academies Press, 2009. Available at http://www.nap.edu/catalog.php?record_id=12715.

National Research Council. *Small-Area Income and Poverty Estimates: Priorities for 2000 and Beyond.* Panel on Estimates of Poverty for Small Geographic Areas. Constance F. Citro and Graham Kalton, eds. Committee on National Statistics, Division of Behavioral and Social Sciences and Education. Washington, D.C.: The National Academies Press, 2000. Available at http://www.nap.edu/catalog.php?record_id=9957.

National Research Council. *State and Local Government Statistics at a Crossroads.* Panel on Research and Development Priorities for the U.S. Census Bureau's State and Local Government Statistics Program. Committee on National Statistics, Division of Behavioral and Social Sciences and Education. Washington, D.C.: The National Academies Press, 2007. Available at http://www.nap.edu/catalog.php?record_id=12000.

National Research Council. *Using the American Community Survey for the National Science Foundation's Science and Engineering Workforce Statistics Program.* Panel on Assessing the Benefits of the American Community Survey for the NSF Division of Science Resources Statistics. Committee on National Statistics, Division of Behavioral and Social Sciences and Education. Washington, D.C.: The National Academies Press, 2008. Available at http://www.nap.edu/catalog.php?record_id=12244.

U.S. Bureau of Labor Statistics and U.S. Bureau of the Census. *Current Population Survey: Design and Methodology.* Technical Paper no. 63RV. Washington, D.C.: U.S. Bureau of Labor Statistics and U.S. Bureau of the Census, 2002. Available at www.bls.census.gov/cps/tp/tp63.htm.

Residence Rules

The goal of the decennial census is to count every resident once, only once, and in the right place according to a residence rule or set of rules or guidelines. A deceptively simple-sounding concept, residence rules are complex; they are inextricably linked to such core concepts as the basic unit of measurement and who should be counted in the census, and they are subject to interpretation from any number of (valid) perspectives.

The act of March 1, 1790, characterized as "contain[ing] about 1,600 words and not a single definition" (Clemence 1987, 18), set a long-term course regarding residence rules for every census that has followed, yet it left key details of that course unspecified. With its simple mandate that people be counted at their "usual place of abode" (1 Stat. 101, section 5), the act established the basic de jure or "usual residence" concept for the census. Left open to interpretation were both parts of the clause: What exactly constitutes a "place of abode," how should one's "usual" residence be determined if ties exist to multiple places? The act also defined the basic task as "caus[ing] the number of the inhabitants within [the U.S. marshals'] respective districts to be taken" (1 Stat. 101, section 1)—leaving open for future censuses the question of who is an "inhabitant" and thus should be included in census counts.

For many people, the identification of a single, usual residence is a simple matter, but for others, "usual" residence is much more ambiguous—and this was the case even in that first census. Groups of people such as college students, maritime crews, and owners of multiple homes were difficult to count from the outset. The concept was vexing even for the highest authorities of the inaugural census, in part because the seat of government itself was in flux during the 36 weeks of official conduct of the count, shifting from New York to Philadelphia. Hence, Thomas Jefferson—the first census director as secretary of state in 1790—was counted at his Monticello home, but he also signed a census schedule in a tavern in Philadelphia where the government was currently seated. President George Washington spent the vast majority of those weeks either traveling the nation or at the seat of government, but he was almost certainly counted as head of household at Mount Vernon.

Historical Evolution

Residence Rules

The 1850 census was a landmark for the evolution of residence rules in their current form. In that year, the instructions to U.S. marshals singled out two population groups whose enumeration in the census remains controversial. First, the instructions directed that "students in colleges, academies, or schools, when absent from the families to which they belong," should be counted where they "boarded or lodged" on the designated census date. Second, the crews of naval and maritime vessels should ideally be counted at their homes on land or, otherwise, at the particular port to which the boat is assigned.

In subsequent censuses, clarifications—or reversals—were made to these rules. For instance, the 1870 instructions (using language that remained in place for several censuses) advised that "seafaring men are to be reported at their land homes, no matter how long they may have been absent, if they are supposed to be still alive." Likewise, by 1880, the preference for counting students shifted from the college or school location to the parental home. This reverted in the 1950 census, in response to the the influx of returning World War II veterans attending college with GI Bill assistance, to the current (as of 2010) rule of counting college students at their school location.

The number of rules increased over time, as new censuses included rules meant to clarify or improve the handling of situations encountered in previous censuses or perceived as new challenges to accurate counting. For instance, the enumerator instructions for the 1880–1900 censuses were the first to explicitly mention how soldiers and civilians at the military forts and posts that dotted the growing country should be counted—even though those instructions wavered between counting them at the post or at the homes from which they were "absent." Similarly, the enumerator instructions for the 1900 census added a clause for "persons engaged in internal transportation" (for example, railroad workers) away from their homes for long stretches (they were to be counted at their family homes). The 1900 instructions also recognized the changing nature of the hotel industry—gradually shifting from the long-term "public house" model to today's short-term-stay model—by instructing enumerators not to count the "transient guests of a hotel" at the hotel "unless they are likely otherwise to be omitted from the enumeration."

By the 2000 census, the number of formal census residence rules had swelled to 31, along with a statement about how residence should be determined for people on different time cycles. For example, people on a weekly cycle in which they spent most weeknights at a place close to their work but maintained a permanent residence further away from work were to be counted at the work residence.

Unit of Measurement

As the formal residence rules evolved over the decades, so too did the related concept of the census unit of measurement, the unit relative to which the residence rules define an individual person's attachment. The same 1850 U.S. marshal instructions that produced the first formal residence rules were also the first to attempt a key definition: *family* became the basic unit of the census, although actual kinship was not part of the definition. "A widow living alone and separately providing for herself, or 200 individuals living together and provided for by a common head," or even the "resident inmates of a hotel [or] jail"—these cases "should each be numbered as one family." Gradually, *family* gave way to other terms as census planners grappled to define the activities—eating, living, staying, sleeping, or some combination thereof—that characterized the unit of interest. The 1890 census bluntly ruled sleeping to be the defining activity—"a person's home is where he sleeps." The term *dwelling-house* was used as the core definition ten years later in the 1900 census. Between 1940 and 1960, the current terms of *household* and *housing unit* came into census vogue, initially focusing on the physical attributes of such units (for example, kitchen facilities) and, later on, the number of persons that differentiated a conventional *household* from a group quarters location.

Inclusion in Census Totals

The concept of an "inhabitant" population total of the United States has changed relatively little for the bulk of the population over the decades, although it has sometimes come under challenge. The most important change was in the status of American Indians. From 1790 through 1860, "Indians not taxed" were excluded from the census by law because they were regarded as belonging to separate nations, but all subsequent censuses have included them. Otherwise, census-enabling legislation has never made distinctions among residents by citizenship or legal status; all persons residing within the boundaries of states, territories, and the District of Columbia are to be counted (although slaves from 1790 to 1860 were counted as only three-fifths of a person for purposes of reapportionment). Residence rules have always provided for inclusion of people from other countries living in the United States on census day, whether they were U.S. citizens, legal residents, or undocumented immigrants. The rules have excluded only visitors from other countries whose stay is temporary. Rules for inclusion of Americans overseas in the resident population, or the Americans overseas population, or neither population, have varied from census to census. So, too, have rules for including some components of the American overseas population (merchant seamen, military at sea or on land bases overseas, federal civilian employees overseas, and private U.S. citizens living abroad) in the counts for reapportionment.

Lawsuits were filed prior to the 1980–2010 censuses challenging the inclusion of undocumented immigrants in the census counts used for apportionment. The courts have typically decided these cases on narrow, technical grounds against those bringing suit, and these censuses have made major efforts to encourage undocumented immigrants to be counted.

Differing Residence Standards

Title 13 of the United States Code, which governs census taking today, does not prescribe a "usual residence" concept for the census, much less define it. This lack of specificity gives the Census Bureau maximum latitude to carry out its work, but it also means that the residence "rules" of the census remain largely up to interpretation. This became a more consequential issue following the switch to primary reliance on mail to conduct the census in 1970. Previously, the Census Bureau's task was to train enumerators on how to handle ambiguous residence situations. As of 1970, the task became one of trying to get millions of census respondents to grasp—and follow—the Census Bureau's residence concepts based only on the information included in the census questionnaire.

The inherent problem with the "usual residence" concept—and an enduring struggle faced by the Census Bureau in articulating that concept—is that there is no single right answer to the question of what defines *usual*. In everyday life, people experience myriad standards for defining and establishing residency in a legal sense—among them, for voter registration, taxation purposes, and qualifying for in-state college tuition—that can vary greatly by state or even municipality. Such standards may include elements of physical presence (for example, living at a place for 30 days before an election) or financial presence (for example, use of a utility bill to show residency to get a driver's license).

Significantly, definitions of residence in regulatory settings—and in the minds of the public—may also include elements of intent, such as intent to eventually return to a place even though one is temporarily somewhere else or intent to remain at a place even though one may have just moved in. The balance between intent and the length of a "temporary" absence or presence can be emotionally charged. Should people displaced from their homes by a natural disaster (such as 2005's Hurricanes Katrina and Rita) be considered residents of the place where they currently reside if they eventually hope and plan to return to those homes?

In one of the legal challenges to the 1990 census, the Commonwealth of Massachusetts disputed the Census Bureau's allocation of U.S. Department of Defense employees living overseas to the states shown as their home of record in personnel files. The U.S. Supreme Court sided with the Census Bureau's approach in *Franklin v. Massachusetts* (505 U.S. 788, 1992), but in a specific section joined by eight justices, the Court formalized a new term in the census residence lexicon. The court held that usual residence "can mean more than mere physical presence, and has been used broadly enough to include some element of allegiance or enduring tie to a place." The *enduring ties* metric has endured, consonant with the adage that "home is where the heart is"—suggesting that usual residence may be defined as much by family, kinship, friendship, or community affiliations to a place as by a strict majority-of-nights-stayed metric. In recent years, the enduring ties standard has played prominently into arguments that persons in correctional facilities would more fairly be counted at some home location rather than the prison or jail.

Precise definitions of usual residence are also complicated by changing social norms and living situations. Greater rates of cohabitation of couples—couples who live together but are unmarried—and cultural acceptance of cohabitation challenge traditional concepts of households. Indeed, the answer to the question of when moving in together truly becomes living together may depend on which partner in the couple is interviewed. The prevalence of divorce and joint physical custody arrangements for children of divorced couples creates technical and emotional conundrums in identifying a single place as a child's usual residence. Innovations in technology and transportation also continue to shape modern households and the definition of residence. Recreational vehicles make it possible for modern "nomads" to live on the road for months at a stretch, rapid air travel makes it possible for employers to deploy staff across the nation (or around the world) for extended periods, and cellular phones and e-mail further serve to untether people from a single physical address.

Residence Rules in 2010 and Beyond

A National Research Council panel was established in 2006 to review the existing residence rules for the decennial census and advise on directions for 2010. The panel argued that the rules for the 2000 census were more a set of *exceptions* to a concept of usual residence than an explication of one. It suggested that the Census Bureau adopt a core, small set of residence principles; embedded in the panel's statement of principles was a switch to a *plurality* definition of usual residence (where one lives or sleeps "more than any other place") instead of the bureau's more vague *majority* definition (lives or sleeps "most of the time"). The panel also urged the use of additional questions to elicit residence information, rather than relying on instruction blocks and allowing respondents to list an "any residence elsewhere" address location. For the 2010 census, the Census Bureau made very few of these suggested changes, though it did restructure its internal residence rule document into a single underlying rule and 13 broad "residence situation" categories.

The National Research Council panel also urged that research be conducted on the effects of the discrepancy between the residence concepts in the Census Bureau's two flagship products. While the decennial census uses its "usual residence" or de jure concept, the American Community Survey (ACS) uses something closer to a "current residence" or de facto concept—using intent to remain at a place for two months (or absence for more than two months) to define *residence*. The practical, quantitative consequence of the discrepancy in residence standards is unknown. It may be the case that the multi-year averaging of data in the ACS largely smooths out discrepancies, but it may also be the case that the different standard causes sharp differences for some areas or population subgroups (for example, towns with large seasonal "snowbird" or "sunbird" populations). This question awaits further research.

See also *Americans overseas; Enumeration: group quarters; Housing; Immigration.*

. . . . DANIEL L. CORK

BIBLIOGRAPHY

Clemence, T. E. "Place of Abode." In Council of Professional Associations on Federal Statistics, *Decennial Census Residence Rules: Proceedings of the December 15–16, 1986, Conference, Washington, DC.* Washington, D.C.: U.S. Census Bureau, 1987.

Council of Professional Associations on Federal Statistics. *Decennial Census Residence Rules: Proceedings of the December 15–16, 1986, Conference, Washington, DC.* Washington, D.C.: U.S. Census Bureau, 1987.

Gauthier, J. G., U.S. Census Bureau. *Measuring America: The Decennial Censuses from 1790 to 2000.* POL/02-MA(RV). Washington, D.C.: U.S. Census Bureau, 2002. Available at www.census.gov/prod/2002pubs/pol02marv-pt1.pdf.

National Research Council. *Once, Only Once, and in the Right Place: Residence Rules in the Decennial Census.* Panel on Residence Rules in the Decennial Census. Daniel L. Cork and Paul R. Voss, eds. Committee on National Statistics, Division of Behavioral and Social Sciences and Education. Washington, D.C.: The National Academies Press, 2006. Available at http://www.nap.edu/catalog.php?record_id=11727.

Rural Areas

The U.S. census does not ask respondents whether they live in a rural or urban area. Rather, since 2000 the Census Bureau has determined the extent of rural and urban populations only after people and housing units are enumerated and assigned to census blocks. Those blocks are then determined to be rural or urban on the basis of population density and proximity to a core urban area. In 2000, that core urban area was a census block group, while for the 2010 census it was changed to census tracts. To understand what *rural* means, one must first learn what *urban* means. The Census Bureau defines "rural" as comprising all territory, population, and housing units not classified as "urban."

Prior to 2000, in census data products from the 100 percent count, "rural" was further divided into "places of less than 2,500" and "not in places." That division distinguished those portions of the rural population living in densely settled, built-up areas from those living in more scattered, low-density locations. The urban area is now divided into Urbanized Areas (UAs) with a population greater than 50,000 and Urban Clusters (UCs) with a population of at least 2,500 but less than 50,000.

In data products based on the census long-form sample, another distinction recognizes the increasing reality that the occupational activity of farming is no longer tightly identified with rural residency. Rural population and housing units are subdivided into "rural farm" and "rural nonfarm" subcategories. In the 1990 census, "rural farm" comprised all rural housing units and people on farms, with *farms* defined as places from which $1,000 or more of agricultural products were sold in 1989. "Rural nonfarm" comprised the remaining rural housing units and people, or approximately 94 percent of the total rural population.

The "urban" and "rural" classifications cut across other hierarchies. For example, there generally is both urban and rural territory within geographic units ranging from census tracts to metropolitan and nonmetro politan areas.

In censuses prior to 1950, a somewhat different definition of the urban population was used that excluded many large, densely settled unincorporated areas. In 1950, formally recognizing patterns of increasingly decentralized settlement, the Census Bureau adopted the concept of the UA and delineated boundaries for many unincorporated places, which are today called census designated places (CDPs). The effect of this change was to include more territory as "urban" beginning in 1950. This definition of urban and rural territory has been maintained substantially unchanged, although modest exceptions have occurred in each of the succeeding censuses. For exact definitions, data users should consult the appendices that are included in virtually all census data products.

All recent censuses include tables showing various characteristics of rural territory and populations. The concept of *urbanization*, generally defined as the processes that result in a rising proportion of the total population living in

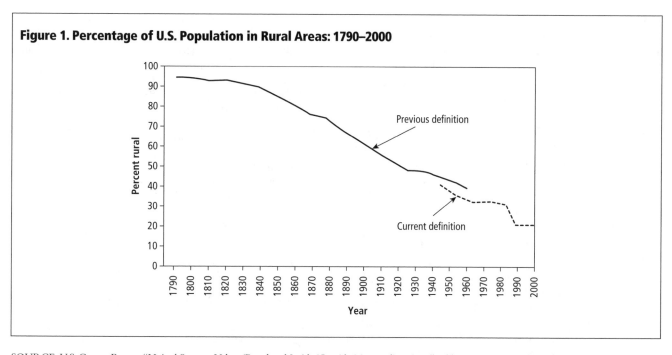

Figure 1. Percentage of U.S. Population in Rural Areas: 1790–2000

SOURCE: U.S. Census Bureau. "United States – Urban/Rural and Inside/Outside Metropolitan Area." Table GCT-PH1. Population, Housing Units, Areas, and Density: 2000. From Census 2000 Summary File 1 (SF1) available in American FactFinder.

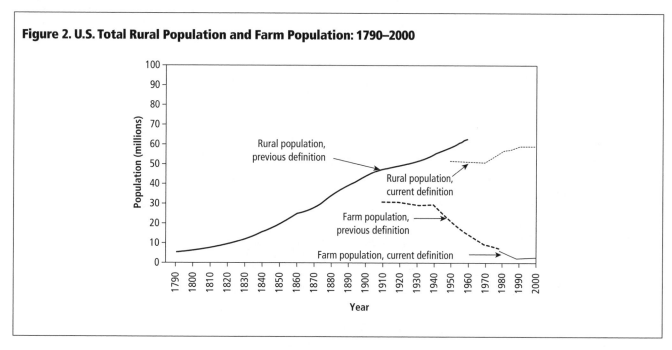

Figure 2. U.S. Total Rural Population and Farm Population: 1790–2000

SOURCE: U.S. Census Bureau. "United States – Urban/Rural and Inside/Outside Metropolitan Area." Table GCT-PH1. Population, Housing Units, Areas, and Density: 2000. From Census 2000 Summary File 1 (SF1) available in American FactFinder.

urban communities, is a common feature in such tables. Urbanization results both from an increase in the size of existing places and through additions of new places to the "urban" category. The obverse of these processes, resulting in a declining proportion of the population living in rural territory, is reflected in Figure 1. The U.S. population declined from 95 percent rural to 21 percent rural between the censuses of 1790 and 2000 (note that the censuses of 1950 and 1960 tabulated urban and rural population counts according to both the old definition and the new). By 1920, less than half the population lived in rural areas. The pace of steady decline in the proportion of the population classified as "rural" was interrupted only twice in 200 years. As noted by researcher Glenn V. Fuguitt, the decades of the 1930s and 1970s witnessed (for largely different reasons) substantial increases in the rural population.

Often overlooked in examining the widely recognized trend of a declining *proportion* of the population living in rural areas are two less well-known facts. First, the land area in the United States is overwhelmingly rural; the 2000 census classified more than 97 percent of the 3.54 million square miles in the country as rural. Second, the number of people living in rural areas—more than 59 million persons in 2000—has been growing rather steadily. Indeed, were it not for the change in the definition of rural territory introduced in the 1950 census, today's rural population would be at an all-time high (see Figure 2). However, the population living on farms (the definition of which has changed over time) is at an all-time low, at just under 3 million persons.

The decline of farming as the dominant rural activity, and twentieth-century changes in technology, communications, transportation, and standards of living, have mostly broken down the isolation and sense of solidarity that once characterized rural communities in America. As a consequence, many Americans who live in rural areas are able to lead lives not much different from those of their urban counterparts. Indeed, many of them work and routinely take part in the larger commercial and cultural life of America's urban cities.

The decennial census has served as a principal source of data over the decades to document in detail the characteristics of both urban and rural Americans, a role that will now be shared with the American Community Survey.

See also *Agricultural censuses; Decennial censuses: 1920 census; Metropolitan areas; Urban areas.*

PAUL R. VOSS
. . . . REVISED BY JEFF HARDCASTLE

BIBLIOGRAPHY

Fuguitt, Glenn V. "The Nonmetropolitan Population Turnaround." *Annual Review of Sociology* 11 (1985): 259–280. doi:10.1146/annurev.so.11 .080185.001355.

Fuguitt, Glenn V., David L. Brown, and Calvin L. Beale, with assistance from Max J. Pfeiffer. *Rural and Small Town America.* New York: Russell Sage Foundation, 1989.

Hathaway, Dale E., J. Allan Beegle, and W. Keith Bryant. *People of Rural America.* 1960 Census Monograph Series. Washington, D.C.: U.S. Government Printing Office, 1968.

U.S. Census Bureau. *United States—County by State, and for Puerto Rico.* Table GCT-PH1: Population, Housing Units, Area, and Density: 2000.

———. *United States—Urban/Rural and Inside/Outside Metropolitan Area.* Table GCT-P1: Urban/Rural and Metropolitan/Nonmetropolitan Population: 2000.

Sampling for Content

Every census from 1940 through 2000 obtained responses for some content items from samples of the population selected with known probability. The role of sampling in the 1940 census was limited, but by 1960 the majority of population and housing items were asked on a sample basis. The 2010 census did not include sample items because, beginning in 2005, the continuous American Community Survey (ACS) has obtained the sample content previously asked on the census.

The use of scientifically selected probability samples makes it possible to obtain accurate data at substantially less cost and burden on respondents compared to asking the entire population. Sampling adds error to the data, but the extent of this type of error (called sampling variability) can readily be assessed.

History

Prior to the 1930s and the demands for information to assess the Great Depression, the federal government made very little use of probability sampling. Surveys conducted before that time, such as Consumer Expenditure Surveys during World War I, generally selected samples with, at best, limited regard for the laws of probability. Consequently, the error properties of the data could not readily be determined.

Application of probability sampling to federal government statistics required theoretical and practical developments. Jerzy Neyman, beginning in the 1920s, pioneered the theory of using probability methods to sample "finite populations," such as U.S. households. (Neyman was a Polish statistician who came to the United States in 1938.) In the 1930s, federal agencies began serious exploration of ways to implement probability sampling for such purposes as obtaining statistics on unemployment, notably in a 2 percent survey of households on U.S. Postal Service routes as part of the 1937 Census of Unemployment.

It was a logical next step to use sampling in the census. Almost from the beginning, the census was a vehicle to obtain additional useful information beyond the minimum necessary for the constitutionally mandated head count for reapportionment and redistricting of seats in the U.S. House of Representatives. The 1930 census schedule included upwards of 40 items (and schedules in some previous censuses were

even longer), all of which were asked of the entire population. For 1940 there was pressure to add more questions on socioeconomic status and to include a new set of questions on the adequacy of housing. To accommodate these needs, the decision was made, for the first time, to ask six new questions of a 5 percent sample of the population instead of everyone.

The 1950 census extended the use of sampling for content and featured a fairly complex sample design. About two-fifths of the questions were asked on a sample basis. Sample sizes for population items were 20 percent and 3.3 percent. A matrix design was used for housing sample items—every 20 percent of households were asked one or two housing items in addition to the complete-count housing questions.

In 1960 about three-fourths of the population items and two-thirds of the housing items were asked on a sample basis. Sample sizes were 25 percent for population items and 25, 20, and 5 percent for housing items. The 1960 census first used separate "short" (complete-count) and "long" (sample) forms for each household. The Postal Service delivered unaddressed short forms containing the complete-count items to all housing units, whether occupied or vacant; the forms were to be filled out and held for an enumerator to pick up. At every fourth household in urban areas, the enumerator left one of two versions of a long form, containing additional sample items, for the household to fill out and mail back (in rural areas, enumerators obtained long-form answers on the spot).

The 1970 census employed a short form and two long forms. Because of the use of mailout/mailback techniques on a large scale, each long form included complete-count as well as sample population and housing items. Both versions of the long form included a common set of sample items that were asked of 20 percent of households. In addition, one version included sample questions asked of 15 percent of households, while the other version included questions asked of 5 percent of households.

The 1980 census used a short form and one long form, but different fractions of households received the long form in different types of places. The long-form sampling rate was 1 in 2 in governmental units, such as towns and townships estimated to have fewer than 2,500 people, and 1 in 6 in all other areas. The overall sampling rate was about 19 percent of households. In 1990 there was again a short form and one long form. Three sampling rates were used for the long form; these varied by estimated population size—1 in 2, 1 in 6, and 1 in 8—for an overall sampling rate of about 17 percent of households. In 2000 there were four long-form sampling rates—1 in 2, 1 in 4, 1 in 6, and 1 in 8—for an overall sampling rate similar to that of 1990. The 2010 census dropped the long form; it included only ten questions asked of every head of household on a single form.

The specific content on the long-form sample question-naires varied over time, but some items were asked repeatedly (see "Long form," Table 1, which lists population and hous-ing items by type of form in the 1960–2000 censuses). The 1990 and 2000 long forms were somewhat shorter than the 1980 long form. In 2000 all housing items that were previ-ously on the short form, except for the item on tenure (owner or renter), were moved to the long form; in previous censuses, 7 to 13 housing items were included on the short form along with 5 to 6 population items.

The ACS, which became operational in 2005, contained the content that was previously asked on the census long form (see *American Community Survey: content*). The sample design were similar to that of the 2000 long-form sample in that larger sampling rates are used for governmental units with small numbers of people and smaller sampling rates were used for census tracts in larger governmental units. The ACS cur-rently uses 5 initial sampling rates, which range from 1 in 10 to 1 in 63 on an annual basis, generating monthly samples of 240,000 housing units (including households and vacant units) and annual samples of 2.9 million housing units. (Residents of group quarters are also sampled.) Some housing units turn out to have been demolished or converted into other uses. The final housing unit sample size is also significantly reduced by a cost-saving procedure in which the ACS sends interviewers to a subsample of housing units that have not responded by mail and cannot be contacted by telephone. Consequently, about 2 million sample housing units provide data in the ACS each year and are used for 1-year estimates for geographic areas with at least 65,000 people; while 6 million sample housing units are cumulated for 3-year estimates for geographic areas with at least 20,000 people; and 10 million sample housing units are cumulated for 5-year estimates for all geographic areas, includ-ing small governmental units, census tracts, and block groups.

Even 5-year cumulations of ACS sample housing units fall short of the 17 million housing units in the 2000 census long-form sample. Beginning in June 2011, the ACS sample increased to 295,000 housing units each month or about 3.4 million per year, and it began implementation of a plan to modify the initial sampling rates to improve the estimates for smaller census tracts relative to larger census tracts. Assuming funding continues to be sufficient to maintain this increased initial sample size for the ACS, the effective sample size, after subsampling, will be about 11.5 million housing units cumu-lated over 5 years.

Processing and Quality

Data products from the 1960–2000 censuses that contained just the short-form items were produced from the entire set of census records (complete count). Data products from the 1960–2000 censuses that included the long-form-sample items (together with responses to short-form items for households in the sample) were produced in a second pass of only the sample records. The sample records were first weighted by the inverse of the sampling rate to equal the total population and then reweighted to achieve consistency between the complete count and sample-based estimates of short-form characteristics (for example, age). The reweighting technique is called *iterative proportional fitting*, or *raking ratio estimation*. It forced agreement on basic characteristics, which reduced the sampling variability of the long-form estimates and likely reduced any biases that might have occurred in the sample selection.

Data products from the complete count were provided for geographic areas as small as individual city blocks, while sample data products were provided for groups of blocks and larger areas. The reason was the sampling variability in the long-form estimates, which could make it difficult to compare very small geographic areas reliably. Thus, long-form estimates for areas smaller than about 10,000–15,000 people should be used with caution. Other kinds of error in the long-form data, such as item nonresponse and misreporting, occurred in the complete-count data as well. These sources of error were cor-rected in the census processing to the extent possible by rou-tines that edit the data for consistency and supply missing data values through imputation techniques.

See also *American Community Survey: data products; American Community Survey: methodology; American Community Survey: questionnaire content; Content determination; Editing, imputation, and weighting; Long form.*

. . . . CONSTANCE F. CITRO

BIBLIOGRAPHY

Anderson, Margo J. *The American Census: A Social History.* New Haven, Conn.: Yale University Press, 1988.

Duncan, Joseph W., and William C. Shelton. *Revolution in United States Government Statistics, 1926–1976.* Washington, D.C.: U.S. Department of Commerce, Office of Federal Statistical Policy and Standards, 1978.

National Research Council. *Using the American Community Survey: Benefits and Challenges.* Panel on the Functionality and Usability of Data from the American Community Survey. Constance F. Citro and Graham Kalton, eds. Committee on National Statistics, Division of Behavioral and Social Sciences and Education. Washington, D.C.: The National Academies Press, 2007. Available at http://www.nap.edu/catalog.php?record_id=11901.

Sampling in the Census

Scientific probability sampling techniques have contributed importantly to many aspects of census operations since the decision was made to ask some questions in the 1940 census on a sample basis. Sampling has been used in the census for content, coverage evaluation, coverage improvement follow-up surveys, quality control of field operations and processing, and testing and experimentation. Sampling was planned to be used in the 2000 census not only for such purposes as adding content and conducting experiments but also to help produce the census population totals for states for reapportionment of the U.S. Congress. However, a January 1999 U.S. Supreme Court decision stated that statistical sampling could not be used for the counts for reapportionment, so the plans to use sampling for this purpose were dropped. This article covers uses of sampling in the census with the exception of content, which is covered in the "Sampling for content" entry.

Sampling for Coverage Evaluation

Sample surveys have been used to evaluate the completeness of coverage of the population in every census since 1950. In the 1950, 1960, 1980, 1990, 2000, and 2010 censuses, a post-enumeration survey (PES) was conducted shortly after the census field enumeration, and the results were used to evaluate the census count. A PES was not conducted in 1970, but a match of census records with the Current Population Survey (CPS) provided similar information.

The methodology for designing and using the PES evolved to the point where PES results in 2000 were to be used to correct the official census counts through an Integrated Coverage Measurement (ICM) program. (The corrected population totals would be obtained by matching the PES with the census records and applying a statistical technique called dual-systems estimation.) However, the U.S. Supreme Court ruled that existing law precluded the use of survey sampling for the population counts for states to be delivered by December 31, 2000, for purposes of congressional reapportionment. Hence, the plan was to use the results of an Accuracy and Coverage Evaluation (ACE) survey to evaluate and possibly correct the detailed census counts released after that date for such purposes as drawing congressional and state legislative district boundaries and allocation of federal funds to state and local governments. Because of errors discovered in the ACE—principally that it did not detect many duplicate enumerations—the ACE results were not used to correct the 2000 census counts. There are no plans to use the 2010 Census Coverage Measurement (CCM) survey for correction purposes, but it will be used for evaluation of the 2010 census.

Sample-Based Programs for the Count

The 1970 census saw the first use of specific programs to improve population coverage by rechecking the address list and trying to find people who might have been missed in the regular enumeration. Two of these procedures were carried out on a sample basis. One of the sample-based procedures was the National Vacancy Check, in which a sample of addresses initially designated as vacant or nonresidential was revisited by enumerators. The second such procedure was the Post-Enumeration Post Office Check (PEPOC). In this operation, the Postal Service identified addresses in selected areas of 16 southern states that were missed in the enumeration, and Census Bureau staff revisited a sample of those addresses to determine whether there were people at those locations who should be included in the census. The results of both programs were used to impute additional people to the census count. For example, on the basis of the National Vacancy Check of a sample of units, 8.5 percent of all vacant

units were reclassified as occupied, and people were imputed to those units. The 1970 census is the only census in which statistical sampling procedures have been used to add people to the count.

Sampling for nonresponse follow-up (NRFU) was part of the Census Bureau's original plan for the 2000 census; it refers to a method of enumeration that employs a probability sample of nonresponding households to estimate the total population of nonresponding households (those who failed to return their census questionnaires). The advantage of this method is that enumerators are required to visit only some nonresponding households to obtain census data rather than visit all such households.

The Census Bureau wanted to reduce the costs and time of the 2000 census as compared to the 1990 census, and one of the largest cost elements of the 1990 census was the need to hire and train approximately 500,000 interviewers to visit in person each household that did not return a questionnaire in the mail. Enumerators visited approximately 35 percent of the entire mailback universe in 1990—including occupied and vacant households and addresses erroneously included on the mailing list—during the NRFU operation.

Accordingly, the Census Bureau's Census 2000 Plan, announced on February 28, 1996, included sampling for follow-up of nonresponding households. Such sampling was to be conducted at the census tract level. (A census tract is a neighborhood of approximately 4,000 people. Over 600,000 census tracts were associated with the 1990 census.) Following repeated attempts (for example, via multiple mailings to each address, advertising, outreach, and so on) to obtain responses from every household, a probability sample was to be selected from the collection of all nonresponding households in each tract. For tracts with an initial mail response rate of less than 85 percent, the sampling rate of the nonresponding households was to be large enough to have direct contact with 90 percent of all households in the tract. For tracts with at least an 85 percent response rate, the sampling rate of the nonresponding households was to be 1 in 3. In addition, the sampling rate for a recheck of vacant units was to be 30 percent. A statistical procedure called "nearest-neighbor hot deck" would then have been used to add people to the count to represent those addresses not contacted directly. The basic concept is that data for each of the noncontacted households would be obtained by substituting data from a nearby household selected from among the contacted households.

By combining sampling for NRFU and ICM to correct the count on the basis of a large PES in its original Census 2000 Plan, the Census Bureau intended to produce a "one-number census" in 2000. The expectation was that sampling for NRFU would reduce not only census costs but also the time to complete the enumeration, which, in turn, could make it possible to conduct a coverage evaluation survey in time to adjust the census counts by December 31, 2000. (A shorter time period could also perhaps improve the quality of the follow-up if fewer people were missed or counted twice due to moving.) Sampling for NRFU would introduce sampling error, which would be larger for smaller geographic areas, but that error could be measured.

The Census Bureau first formally tested the concept of a one-number census in its 1995 Census Test, which was conducted at three sites (Paterson, New Jersey; Oakland, California; and six parishes in northwest Louisiana). The second major test occurred during the Census 2000 dress rehearsal, conducted for the most part during 1998 at 3 sites (Sacramento, California; the city of Columbia, South Carolina, and 11 surrounding counties; and Menomonie County, Wisconsin, and the Menomonie Reservation).

In spite of the advantages of reduced costs and time and more careful control of the follow-up process, the use of sampling for obtaining the population count in the 2000 census, including the use of sampling for follow-up of nonresponding households, was not acceptable to everyone. Congress expressed concern about the constitutionality of sampling, the possibility that the use of statistical methods would allow the data to be manipulated for political advantage, and the magnitude of sampling error in very small geographical areas (for example, at the block level). Almost two months after the beginning of fiscal year 1998, President Bill Clinton signed a compromise bill that, among other things, permitted the U.S. House of Representatives to sue the Census Bureau with the understanding that the case on the constitutionality of sampling in the census would be on a fast-track schedule to the U.S. Supreme Court. Lawsuits were filed, and two lower courts' rulings were promptly appealed to the Supreme Court.

On January 25, 1999, in a 5–4 decision, the Court announced that Section 195 of the Census Act (Title 13, United States Code) "prohibits the proposed uses of statistical sampling in calculating the population [of the United States] for purposes of apportionment [of the U.S. House of Representatives]." The Court also noted that when Congress amended Section 195 of the Census Act in 1976, it "changed a provision that permitted the use of sampling for purposes other than apportionment into one that required that sampling be used for such purposes if 'feasible.'"

The Court's decision implied that use of sampling for follow-up of nonresponding households had to be eliminated from the Census 2000 plan and that there had to be follow-up of all nonresponding households. This decision was based on the wording of the Census Act and not on the U.S. Constitution. Hence, the constitutionality of sampling to help produce census counts remains unanswered. In its revised plan for the 2000 census, announced on February 24, 1999, the Census Bureau stated that, while it would follow up with all nonresponding households, it still planned to implement a PES of about 300,000 households instead of the originally planned 750,000 households. This was expected to provide an improved count that would be available for use for purposes other than apportionment, such as the distribution of federal funds and redistricting within the states. As it turned out, problems in the ACE survey precluded its use for these purposes.

Subsequent to the 2000 census, Utah brought a suit against the U.S. Department of Commerce in which it challenged the apportionment count, claiming that imputations of persons in households when the size of the household was not known constituted sampling and therefore was unlawful. On June 20, 2002, in a 5–4 decision, the Supreme Court ruled that whole-person imputation did not constitute sampling (*Utah v. Evans*, 536 U.S., 452, 2002).

Other Uses of Sampling

Censuses since 1940 have routinely used sampling for quality control of many aspects of census field and processing operations. The 1940 census first used sampling to verify the quality of work of coders and keypunchers. Each census since 1940 has used sampling to verify interviews conducted by an enumerator to uncover "curbstoning" (making up responses rather than interviewing the household) and other problems.

Censuses since 1940 have also used sampling to test questionnaires and operational procedures prior to taking the census and to try out procedures experimentally as part of the census that could improve future censuses. Examples include an experiment in the 1950 census to test the use of a household questionnaire instead of the traditional ledger-like "line" schedule on which enumerators recorded information for more than one household; experiments prior to the 1960 census of self-enumeration with mailed-out or mailed-back questionnaires; an experiment in the 1980 census of telephone follow-up of nonresponding households using telephone directories organized by address; and extensive tests of alternative questionnaire formats and mailing packages prior to the 2000 census to identify formats that would encourage a higher mailback response rate.

Finally, sampling has been used in some censuses for follow-up surveys that select respondents with particular characteristics in order to obtain more detailed information about them. For example, the National Science Foundation sponsored a survey of people who reported their census occupation as "scientist" or "engineer" following the 1960, 1970, 1980, 1990, and 2000 censuses. The next such National Science Foundation survey is using the American Community Survey (ACS) as the sampling frame. Sometimes, such follow-up surveys have been helpful in evaluating and improving the census itself, as when a disability survey after the 1970 census identified problems with the census information on disability.

See also *Accuracy and Coverage Evaluation; Capture-recapture methods; Census testing; Coverage evaluation; Coverage improvement procedures; Editing, imputation, and weighting; Long form; Post-enumeration survey; Sampling for content.*

. . . . CONSTANCE F. CITRO

BIBLIOGRAPHY

Anderson, Margo, J. *The American Census: A Social History*. New Haven, Conn.: Yale University Press, 1988.

Duncan, Joseph W., and William C. Shelton. *Revolution in United States Government Statistics, 1926–1976*. Washington, D.C.: U.S. Department of Commerce, Office of Federal Statistical Policy and Standards, 1976.

Killion, R. A. "Memorandum to J. H. Thompson: Decision to Increase Nonresponse Follow-up Sampling Rates for High Response Tracts." Census 2000 Decision Memorandum no. 34, U.S. Bureau of the Census, Washington, D.C., January 2, 1998.

———. "Memorandum to J. H. Thompson: Decision to Use Hot Deck for Nonresponse Follow-up and UAA Vacant Estimation and Decision on Late Returns." Census 2000 Decision Memorandum no. 41, U.S. Bureau of the Census, Washington, D.C., January 28, 1998.

———. *The 2000 Census: Counting Under Adversity*. Panel to Review the 2000 Census. Constance F. Citro, Daniel L. Cork, and Janet L. Norwood, eds. Committee on National Statistics, Commission on Behavioral and Social Sciences and Education. Washington, D.C.: The National Academies Press, 2004.

National Research Council. *The Bicentennial Census: New Directions for Methodology in 1990*. Panel on Decennial Census Methodology. Constance F. Citro and Michael L. Cohen, eds. Committee on National Statistics, Commission on Behavioral and Social Sciences and Education. Washington, D.C.: The National Academies Press, 1985.

———. *Envisioning the 2010 Census*. Panel on the Design of the 2010 Census Program of Evaluations and Experiments. Lawrence D. Brown, Michael L. Cohen, Daniel L. Cork, and Constance F. Citro, eds. Committee on National Statistics, Commission on Behavioral and Social Sciences and Education. Washington, D.C.: The National Academies Press, 2010.

———. *Measuring a Changing Nation: Modern Methods for the 2000 Census*. Panel on Alternative Census Methodologies. Michael L. Cohen, Andrew A. White, and Keith F. Rust, eds. Committee on National Statistics, Commission on Behavioral and Social Sciences and Education. Washington, D.C.: The National Academies Press, 1999.

———. *Modernizing the U.S. Census*. Panel on Census Requirements in the Year 2000 and Beyond. Barry Edmonston and Charles Schultze, eds. Committee on National Statistics, Commission on Behavioral and Social Sciences and Education. Washington, D.C.: The National Academies Press, 1995.

U.S. Bureau of the Census. "Assessment of Accuracy of Adjusted Versus Unadjusted 1990 Census Base for Use in Intercensal Estimates." Report of the Committee on Adjustment of Postcensal Estimates, August 7, 1992. Available at www.census.gov/dmd/www/pdf/Adjresearch.pdf.

Vacca, E., M. Mulry, and R. A. Killion. "The 1995 Census Test: A Compilation of Results and Decisions." 1995 Census Test Results Memorandum no. 46. U.S. Bureau of the Census, Washington, D.C., 1996.

Wright, Tommy. "Sampling and Census 2000: The Concepts." *American Scientist* 86, no. 3 (1998): 245–253. doi:10.1511/1998.3.245.

———. "A One-Number Census: Some Related History." *Science* 283 (1999): 491–492. doi:10.1126/science.283.5401.491.

Wright, Tommy, and Howard Hogan. "Census 2000: Evolution of the Revised Plan." *Chance* 12, no. 4 (1999): 11–19.

Staffing

A decennial census of housing and population is an enormous national data collection operation that requires planning and project management similar to that of an Olympic Games. It is a complex program that requires large numbers of temporary employees to carry out hundreds of interrelated tasks. During the 2000 census, in excess of 3.7 million applicants were tested to attain a projected peak staff of 864,000 employees. During the 2010 census, approximately 3.9 million applicants were tested to attain a projected peak staff of 1.2 million employees.

Recruitment and Training

All decennial census staff must be recruited, hired, and trained to carry out their jobs within a very short period of time. One of the key historical factors that allowed the Census Bureau to successfully recruit large numbers of people who could handle complex, interrelated decennial census tasks was

that the Census Bureau frequently was able to hire people who already had basic job skills. Supervisory experience was necessary for office or field supervisor positions. Temporary office clerks needed to know the basics of office clerical work. Field enumerators needed to be able to use a map to locate specific addresses. Enumerators also needed to have organizational skills to follow up efficiently on missing interviews, and they had to be able to face rejection when working with the public. All decennial census workers had to be able to use a variety of reference manuals and materials, and they had to be able to read and follow directions. The 2010 census plan incorporated substantial increases in the automation of training, field data collection, and office support operations; therefore, it was important that all managers/supervisors, field staff, and office staff commanded minimal automation skills.

In censuses before 1980, the Census Bureau often relied on people who were not actively seeking permanent employment. Many were attracted to temporary census jobs by the thought of earning extra money while helping with an important cause. Middle-aged women and female homemakers were the backbone of the decennial census staff (and even today, the decennial census enumerator staff is composed predominantly of women). This staff was supplemented with retirees, college students, and others who were usually unemployed at the time of recruitment.

Today a larger percentage of the total population is already in the labor force, and that percentage continues to increase. Lifestyles, goals, and ambitions of working-age people continue to change. The percentage of working-age women joining the permanent labor force continues to increase. Those who seek permanent employment find little attraction in a six-to-eight-week decennial census job. Furthermore, since 1960 the number of households in which both husband and wife are part of the labor force has increased significantly. The percentage participation in the labor force of married women with children under age six has increased even more dramatically. This pattern of higher numbers of women already in the permanent workforce means that fewer women are readily available to work on the decennial census.

The continuing increase in the cost of living is another factor that influences the availability of applicants who historically would have been part of the decennial census applicant pool. The elderly who live on Social Security or small retirement annuities and who need to supplement their income often prefer permanent part-time jobs over decennial census jobs that last only six to eight weeks. Permanent part-time work spreads earnings over the course of a year and generally produces a greater annual income supplement. Temporary census jobs provide an opportunity to earn some spending money, but they can be inadequate for those who need an ongoing supplement to their monthly income.

Thus, when the Census Bureau recruits for decennial census workers from the pool of applicants who historically have worked on the census, it must either compete for large numbers of people who are already employed, or it must seek retirees or attract the unemployed, who may be looking for

Table 1. Census Bureau Personnel Taking the Census, 1960–2010

	1960	1970	1980	1990	2000	2010
Number of local census offices	399	393	412	449	520	494
Peak field staff	187,500	223,038	458,523	510,000	512,826	585,729
Processing staff	2,000	2,600	5,400	11,000	NA*	NA*
Average enumerator pay per hour	$1.60	$2.56	$4.03	$7.50	$12.17	$17.36

NOTE: Hourly pay rates in 1970 and 1980 are estimated based on average pieces of work (households, "vacant" housing units, or nonexistent housing units) completed per hour; actual hourly pay rates are presented with no inflation adjustment.

* Not applicable because function was contracted out.

SOURCES: 1960–1990, National Research Council Panel on Census Requirements in the Year 2000 and Beyond, *Modernizing the U.S. Census* (Washington, D.C.: The National Academies Press, 1995); 2000, *Pre-Appointment Management System/Automated Decennial Administrative Management System (PAMS/ADAMS) Employees Paid Report* (Washington D.C.: U.S. Census Bureau, 2000); 2010, Decennial Applicant Personnel and Payroll System (DAPPS) Employees Paid Report (Washington D.C.: U.S. Census Bureau, 2010).

permanent work instead of a short-term job. During the 2010 census, an unusually high national unemployment rate of 9.3 percent made the recruitment of workers less difficult than during the 2000 census. In addition, the gender composition of the 2010 census local census office (LCO) workforce— 57 percent female and 43 percent male—included a lower percentage of females than in previous censuses.

Pay and Workload

In the 1980 census, workers averaged seven to eight hours per day on the clock. During the 1990 census, they averaged six hours per day, and in the 1995 census test, they averaged five hours per day. During the 2000 census, average worker hours per day decreased to four. Because an enumerator is paid portal to portal, and travel time from home to a given assignment area is the same whether the enumerator works one hour or eight, the time available for enumeration is proportionally less as the number of hours worked per day decreases. Part of the reason for the shorter work day is the relatively fewer hours each day that most respondents can be found at home, another trend that makes the enumeration job more difficult. Reduced census employee hours per day/week increases staffing requirements and training costs. These increasing staff requirements, compiled by the National Research Council, are displayed in Table 1.

In the 1970 and 1980 censuses, enumerators often quit because they were not paid in a timely manner. They were paid by the amount of work completed (by household, "vacant" housing unit, or nonexistent housing unit) once or twice during the entire enumeration period. Hourly pay rates and weekly pay periods were instituted for all enumerators for the 1990 census. The hourly rates in 1990, ranging from $5 to $10 for enumerators, were keyed to local economic variables for each of the 449 field offices used to conduct the census. Census 2000 plans continued the hourly pay methodology and expanded the 1990 program to implement locality-based pay. The 2000 program strengthened analysis of local economic variables and made available a wider range of pay rates. For Census 2000, the Census Bureau attempted to expand the labor pool from which it could recruit by negotiating with other federal and state agencies that manage retirement and income-transfer programs (that is, the Federal Civilian and Military Retirement program, the Public and Indian Housing program, and the Welfare to Work program) to reduce barriers and encourage beneficiaries of the various programs to work for the Census Bureau.

Evaluations of the 2000 census hourly pay structure, as used in the 2000 census dress rehearsal, showed that the Census Bureau was able to hire and retain an adequate staff of enumerators. Productivity during the dress rehearsal, conducted in 1998, was highest among part-time employees, employees who had previous work experience, and individuals who were not part of the active labor force (for example, retirees). The strength of the new pay structure, the effective assignment and supervision of work, and the administrative difficulty of implementing incentives led to a recommendation against using separate incentive payments for productivity in the 2000 census. For the 2010 census, the Census Bureau contracted with Westat Corporation to replicate the 2000 census pay rate methodology for the development of the 2010 census temporary staff pay rates. The 2010 census pay rates were highly effective in attracting applicants for 2010 census jobs. For the 2010 census, the total applicant goal was 3,800,000, and the total number of applicants was 3,872,400. The recruiting for early field operations was tremendously successful; as a result, the Census Bureau did not implement a planned 10 percent increase in LCO staff pay rates in calendar year 2010.

See also *Enumeration: field procedures; Organization and administration of the census.*

. . . . TIMOTHY J. DEVINE

BIBLIOGRAPHY

National Research Council. *Modernizing the U.S. Census.* Panel on Census Requirements in the Year 2000 and Beyond. Barry Edmonston and Charles Schultze, eds. Committee on National Statistics, Commission on Behavioral and Social Sciences and Education. Washington, D.C.:

The National Academies Press, 1995. Available at http://www.nap.edu/catalog.php?record_id=4805.

Neece, Lorraine, and Janice Pentercs. *1970, 1980, 1990 Decennial Census Cost Comparison*. Unpublished paper, 1993.

Stuart, John. *2000 Decennial Census Labor Force Issues: Escalating Enumeration Costs*. Unpublished paper, 1995.

U.S. Bureau of the Census. *Census 2000 Dress Rehearsal: Evaluation Summary*. Washington, D.C.: U.S. Government Printing Office, 1999. Available at www.census.gov/census2000/evaluations/pdf/finalrep.pdf.

———. *Census 2000 Operational Plan*. DMD/01-1419. Washington, D.C.: U.S. Government Printing Office, 2000. Available at www.census.gov/dmd/www/pdf/Operational2000.pdf.

———. *Decennial Applicant Personnel and Payroll System (DAPPS) Employees Paid Report*. Washington, D.C.: U.S. Government Printing Office, 2010.

———. *Pre-Appointment Management System/Automated Decennial Administrative Management System (PAMS/ADAMS) Employees Paid Report*. Washington, D.C.: U.S. Government Printing Office, 2000.

———. *Statistical Abstract of the United States 1998: The National Data Book*. 118th ed. Washington, D.C.: U.S. Government Printing Office, 1998.

U.S. Bureau of Labor Statistics. *Employment Status of the Civilian Noninstitutional Population, 1940 to Date*. Available at www.bls.gov/cps/cpsaat1.pdf.

State and Local Censuses

The federal government has taken a decennial census each decade since 1790, and, for the most part, state and local governments have relied on these census results for information about their populations. For much of the nineteenth century, however, many state governments also took periodic censuses, usually in years different from those of federal counts. Though census taking at the state level ceased about 1945 and is no longer a function of state government, its practices may be usefully compared to those of the federal effort. The state census data, both published and unpublished (in the surviving manuscript schedules), provide additional demographic, economic, and social information about the American population.

State censuses, which varied greatly in their scope, form, content, frequency, quality, and publication style, have been analyzed primarily by librarians and genealogists (for analyses prepared by two such specialists, see the bibliography at the end of this entry). Researchers interested in the quality and completeness of an individual state or local census, or in publications about it, should consult these experts and local or state archival sources.

Like the federal census, state censuses were political instruments before they were demographic ones. Most commonly, they were mandated in state constitutions to provide the basis for apportioning representatives in the state legislatures. In other cases, legislatures instituted censuses to serve state government functions, such as apportioning taxes or planning state economic policy. Territorial governments conducted censuses to demonstrate that the territories under their jurisdictions had sufficient populations to apply for statehood.

Only eight states have never taken a state or territorial census: Connecticut, Idaho, Kentucky, Montana, New Hampshire, Ohio, Pennsylvania, and Vermont. Between 1810 and 1945, 27 states took 160 separate censuses; between 1801 and 1907, 43 territorial censuses were taken. In two out of every three years

in the nineteenth century, a state or territory commissioned a census somewhere in the continental United States.

Variety of Methods

States and territories used a wide variety of administrative mechanisms to collect, tabulate, and publish census data. Usually tax assessors collected the data, and the secretary of state made a routine count of the population in a small number of categories in the field. These totals were sent to the state capitol building to be published in a page or two of a legislative journal. Sometimes, though, states created full-scale census offices. State officials appointed enumerators to take the census and supervised elaborate tabulations and publication of several volumes of data. Some state constitutions mandated periodic censuses that were never taken. Others directed states to take repeated censuses at short intervals—sometimes as short as four years.

The duration of data collection efforts—meaning the period from when states began to collect census data to when they stopped—also varied from state to state. For some states, such as New York, 100-year data series exist; for others, such as Maryland in 1776, single censuses exist that were never replicated.

Though diverse in practice and duration, state census taking conformed to definite patterns. Most obviously, the history of state censuses was tied to that of the states themselves: a census could not be taken unless a state or territory had been defined. Only 6 of the original 13 states took complete-count censuses after the nation's founding in 1787: Georgia, Massachusetts, New York, New Jersey, Rhode Island, and South Carolina. New York was the first to do so. Like the other original states, including Pennsylvania, Connecticut, and Vermont, New York first counted voters or taxables. New York took the first complete-count census in 1795 and repeated it in 1801 and 1807. Unlike the other census taking states, however, New York in 1814 began counting the total population. By 1825 it had instituted a regular decennial census in the fifth year of the decade, which continued through 1875. It took no census in 1885. The series resumed in 1892, returned to the fifth year of the decade in 1905, and ended in 1925. Georgia began to collect census data in 1810 but stopped with the Civil War. The other original states did not begin taking censuses until well after their admission to the Union. Massachusetts, which became a state in 1788, started counting its population in 1837, while South Carolina, also admitted to the Union in 1788, began taking censuses in 1868. Except for New York, none of the original 13 states built censuses into the fabric of their earliest political lives.

Census taking in the "western states"—including the old Northwest and South Central regions—followed a different pattern. Although only 6 (46 percent) of the original 13 states took censuses, 21 (60 percent) of the other 35 states in the continental United States took censuses at some time in their histories. Twenty-one states also took censuses while they were territories. Sixteen of them continued to take censuses after becoming states.

The most common type of state census included a simple population count, with minimal publication of the results.

States published one-half of the census results in documents of 30 pages or fewer and one-third of the results in documents of fewer than 10 pages. Once a state invested in census taking, it could become a fairly elaborate exercise that grew for several decades in size and complexity. In a quarter of the censuses, the states published works between 275 and 4,800 pages. Prior to 1870, the mean number of pages published in state census publications was 84; after 1870, it climbed to 560, though page counts varied widely.

Regional Patterns

Regional patterns among the state censuses reflected larger economic and political conditions. From the mid-nineteenth to the early twentieth centuries, the eastern industrial states of New York, New Jersey, Rhode Island, and Massachusetts used their censuses to monitor the growth of the industrial economy and to measure the proportions of natives and foreigners, workers and farmers. Midwestern states such as Michigan, Wisconsin, Iowa, and Kansas emphasized data on population, agriculture, and manufacturing. Kentucky, Tennessee, Ohio, and Indiana, which were admitted to the Union between 1792 and 1816, began collecting data on free male electors in the early nineteenth century and continued these counts into the early twentieth century, never developing full-scale state censuses.

States once part of Mexico or the Spanish or French colonial empires (for example, Texas, New Mexico, California, Arizona, and Louisiana) have censuses dating from their common history with those nations. Both Hawaii and Alaska took censuses in the nineteenth century, long before they joined the Union in 1959.

States stopped taking censuses when they recognized that they could save money by using the federal data, which were of sufficient size and quality for state and local government purposes, or by contracting with the Census Bureau for special surveys as needed. In the 1920s state and local governments appealed to the federal government to provide them with local tabulations. In recent years the Census Bureau has worked closely with state demographic services, and state demographic agencies have republished state and local data from the federal enumeration.

See also *Census tracts; State data centers.*

. . . . MARGO J. ANDERSON

BIBLIOGRAPHY
Dubester, Henry J. *State Censuses.* Millwood, N.Y.: KTO Microform, 1977.
———. *State Censuses: An Annotated Bibliography of Censuses of Population Taken after the Year 1790 by States and Territories of the United States.* New York: Burt Franklin, 1969. First printed in 1948 by U.S. Government Printing Office.
Lainhart, Ann S. *State Census Records.* Baltimore: Genealogical Publishing, 1992.

State and Local Governments: Legislatures

Census numbers ensure that our representative districts for the U.S. Congress, state legislatures, and city and town governments reflect accurate population totals. Once every ten years, Americans stand up to be counted as required by law. States always have used census data, but the relationship between the states and the Census Bureau and how states use census data dramatically changed in 1975. This new relationship, initiated after the passage of Public Law 94-171, which amended Article 1, Section 2, title 13, section 141 of the U.S. Constitution, forever changed the way in which states would use census data. The passage of the Civil Rights Act of 1964 and the Voting Rights Act (1965) also had a direct impact on the manner in which the decennial census was conducted and tabulated, increasing the interest in tabulations by race.

Former Redistricting Methods

By 1965 the courts had ruled that the use of racial criteria in drawing districts was constitutional. States, which were attempting to draw districts of equal population; courts, which were trying to enforce the Voting Rights Act; and the U.S. Department of Justice, which was trying to review plans for compliance with this new mandate simply did not have enough census data for small geographic areas to be able to perform these duties. As a result, there was keen interest in the tabulations by race for small geographic areas. The 1970 census tabulations were woefully inadequate for the purposes of redistricting, particularly with legal criteria establishing a "one person/one vote mandate." Various state legislators, under the leadership of the National Legislative Conference (part of the Council of State Governments and later the National Conference of State Legislatures), brought their concerns regarding the 1970 census tabulations to Congress. This led to Congress passing Public Law 94-171 in late 1975.

It is important to remember that the 1980 census was the last census taken before the automation of the geographic framework within the Topologically Integrated Geographic Encoding and Referencing (TIGER) system. Nevertheless, for the 1980 census, states provided precinct plans to the bureau in a variety of formats. In addition, five states that fell under the Section 5 provision of the Voting Rights Act (requiring preclearance of their newly drawn plans) contracted with the Census Bureau to obtain census tabulation blocks for the purpose of drawing lines that would result in equal distribution of populations. With the development of the TIGER database, the Census Bureau was able to develop a formula to automatically assign each piece of ground or water to create 1990 census block coverage. Nationwide block numbering in an automated database provided the small-area geography and data that states believed they needed in order to follow the law. The die was cast.

The 1980 census was the first census to follow Public Law 94-171, which requires the Census Bureau to submit to the secretary of commerce a plan identifying the geographic areas for which specific tabulations of population are desired. (The secretary deferred this obligation to the Census Bureau, which created the Census Redistricting Data Office in order to comply.) Not only were states provided with the opportunity to submit small-area geography required for legislative redistricting, but the bureau was also instructed by Congress to deliver the decennial census results within one year of census day beginning in 1980.

New Methods of Redistricting

With the passage of Public Law 94-171 in 1975 and its strict data distribution requirements, very quickly both the states and the Census Bureau realized that the antiquated manner in which geographic areas were collected, stored, and tabulated needed to be automated. The Census Bureau set forth a 20-year plan to develop the TIGER database, but states did not want to wait until Census 2000. Again the states went to Congress, and the bureau was instructed to move forward with the development of the TIGER database in time to meet the demands and products of the 1990 census. With the development of TIGER came nationwide block numbering. With nationwide block numbering and a program that permitted states to submit block boundary suggestions, the bureau was now meeting the needs of the state legislatures in their data tabulation and dissemination efforts.

Many states participated in the 1990, 2000, and 2010 Block Boundary Suggestion Project (BBSP). After analyzing the 1980 tabulation blocks provided under contracts, states found the BBSP useful, if not actually imperative. Through their analysis, states realized quickly that the Census Bureau was using the requirements for field enumeration when formulating census blocks. However, states needed more flexibility in the requirements in order to prepare their post-census redistricting plans.

Since that time, the Redistricting Data Program (RDP) has grown to be a full-fledged and multifaceted program containing five phases, all meant to serve the states and their data needs. After each decennial census, the redistricting data office works with the National Conference of State Legislatures to evaluate the Census Bureau's RDP to determine if any changes are needed for the next census and what should stay the same. This joint effort results in a report. The last evaluation, *Designing P.L. 94-171 Redistricting Data for the Year 2010 Census: The View from the States* is available in hard copy and online.

Every two years the bureau corresponds with states that have more than one congressional representative to confirm possible changes to their congressional and state legislative districts. The Census Bureau is retabulating the 2010 decennial redistricting data for the 113th Congress and newly drawn state legislative districts. These tabulations are not only interesting but can be used to demonstrate the success of drawing congressional districts with a very tight deviation, sometimes with a deviation of just one person. These data are very important if a state finds itself in court. In addition to the importance of race, ethnicity, and total population from the redistricting summary file, voting age (18 and over) is another variable used to determine voter strength in drawn districts. More information on the guidelines each state uses for redistricting is available through *Redistricting Law 2010*, published by the National Conference of State Legislatures.

With the advent of the American Community Survey's (ACS) five-year period estimates, data users are able to obtain sample estimates of demographic and socioeconomic characteristics for state legislative districts, census tracts, and block groups (state legislative district information will only be available in the ACS as five-year estimates). Data for current districts will be updated annually after 2010. This will be particularly important to data users looking for variables often studied during the redistricting process, such as citizenship. Many analysts look at the voting strength of a district to determine if it is truly a fairly drawn district. Thus, census data—from both the 2010 census enumeration and from the ACS sample—play important roles in this type of analysis. In addition to citizenship information, the ACS includes variables such as language spoken at home, English-language ability, income, and educational attainment, all of which provide potentially valuable information on the composition of districts.

The Public Law 94-171 Redistricting Files, which were released by the Census Bureau beginning in February 2011, ensure compliance with the Public Law 94-171 mandate to deliver the redistricting summary file no later than April 1 in the year following each decennial census. These five tables, composed of four population tallies and one housing unit tally that is new for 2010 (vacancy/occupied status), have been used to draw the plans. Moreover, the analysis will likely employ administrative data (that is, voter registration and voter return) and the 2010 TIGER/Line Shapefiles, which will provide the shapes and codes of the 2010 census tabulation blocks, block groups, and census tracts.

Prior to release of the 2010 decennial census data and the five-year ACS estimates, litigation in voting rights cases used the ACS as evidence either in favor of a plan or in an effort to strike a plan down. Census data will always be a powerful tool for use in the courts. States will use census data to defend their plans, and others will use both the ACS and decennial census data to argue against the passage of the same plan. Decisions are a matter of interpretation.

See also *Apportionment and districting; Congress and the census; Grassroots groups; Litigation and the census; State and local censuses.*

. . . . TIM STOREY AND CATHY MCCULLY

BIBLIOGRAPHY
National Conference of State Legislatures. *Redistricting Law 2010.* Washington, D.C.: National Conference of State Legislatures, 2009.
U.S. Census Bureau. American Community Survey: Geographic Areas Published. Available at www.census.gov/acs/www/data_documentation/areas_published/.
———. *Designing P.L. 94-171 Redistricting Data for the Year 2010 Census: The View from the States.* P.L. 94-171(RV). Washington, D.C.: U.S. Government Printing Office, 2004. Available at http://www.census.gov/rdo/pdf/DesignPL94-171.pdf.
———. "Strength in Numbers: Your Guide to Census 2010 Redistricting Data From the U.S. Census Bureau." Washington, D.C.: U.S. Census Bureau, 2010. Available at www.census.gov/rdo/pdf/StrengthInNumbers2010.pdf.

State and Local Governments: Uses of the Census and ACS.

See *Uses of the census and ACS: state and local governments.*

State Data Centers

State Data Centers (SDCs) serve as statistical clearinghouses for census and related economic and demographic information, technical assistance, research, and analysis. Dissemination of the results of the national census is a mammoth undertaking. After the release of the 1970 decennial census reports and computer files, it became evident to the Census Bureau that the systems for disseminating results were inadequate to meet the demand for data. This demand was largely driven by the need for local demographic, housing, and economic data for grant applications and business analysis. Because much of the census data were available only in computerized media, processing of the computer files required mainframe computer capabilities and specialized programming. Access to the data was costly and available only through organizations with significant resources and technical expertise. To alleviate this roadblock, the Census Bureau began a pilot project to explore the feasibility of establishing central, state-managed centers that would provide inexpensive and ready access to each state's data.

The project drew quick acceptance, and in 1978 the Census Bureau formalized the SDC program and began the process of establishing centers in each state. By 1982 all 50 states were voluntarily participating. Currently, the program includes the 50 states, the District of Columbia, Puerto Rico, Guam, the Northern Mariana Islands, and the U.S. Virgin Islands. In 1988 the bureau announced an expansion of the data center concept to emphasize the economic census and other economic programs. This expansion established 15 pilot sites for the new Business and Industry Data Center (BIDC) program. Currently, 23 states participate in the joint SDC/BIDC program. The BIDC program allowed for an expansion of the state network to include organizations providing services and outreach to the business community.

Program Objectives

The original goal of the network was to provide the public with efficient access to U.S. Census Bureau data, as well as geographic and reference products. With the advent of the American FactFinder (AFF) system for Census 2000, access to the Census Bureau's data, from virtually all of its programs, was vastly improved. While the SDC network continues to expand data access and use, its focus has shifted to more specialized value-added data products, analysis, and education. This is becoming an even more important core service as the American Community Survey (ACS) becomes the mainstream Census Bureau demographic data product. Services are provided to a wide range of data users, including state and local governments, businesses, the media, not-for-profit organizations, and the general public. Specific objectives of the network include the following:

- Providing an institutional structure for the dissemination and maintenance of census statistical products within each state
- Providing increased and comprehensive technical assistance in the access and use of census data
- Providing education and training to users through workshops, presentations, and publications
- Creating value-added products while moderating the cost of access to census data

- Actively participating in census planning and operations to improve procedures and products
- Increasing awareness of the importance of the decennial and economic censuses to the general public and businesses to improve response

These objectives have been largely met over the 30-year history of the program, and this nationwide network has become a model of federal-state cooperation.

Program Structure

The organizational structure of the program varies from state to state, but all states provide services to meet the core objectives. The lead agency in each state is appointed by the governor and signs a formal agreement with the Census Bureau, which outlines the duties and responsibilities of the state and the Census Bureau and the resources devoted to the program. The lead agency is typically an executive-level agency such as the state department of labor, planning, economic development, or budget, and it may involve the state library or a major university. The lead agency may designate one or more coordinating agencies to share administrative responsibilities or serve in an advisory capacity to the network. The lead agency also designates affiliate organizations, which generally serve a local, county, or regional area. Organizations such as county and regional planning agencies, public libraries, university centers, and councils of governments serve as affiliates. Affiliates participating through the BIDC program include trade organizations, chambers of commerce, small-business development centers, and other organizations serving business needs or member organizations. Nationwide the data center network includes more than 1,700 participating agencies. These agencies are represented by a steering committee of nine representatives, elected by the various state lead agencies.

Products and Services

The Census Bureau provides, without charge, copies of all printed reports, computer files in various media, and Internet access to all lead agencies. Coordinating and affiliate agencies also have access to a limited number of print and computerized products and services through the lead agency. With the continued expansion of electronic products over printed media, Internet access and expertise are requirements of participation. Statistical resources for other state and federal agencies such as the U.S. Bureau of Economic Analysis (BEA); the U.S. Bureau of Labor Statistics (BLS); and state departments of labor, health, and education are often available through the network.

Data centers provide a wide range of services to data consumers, including the following:

- *Technical assistance and consulting:* Information services range from providing a single statistic over the phone to creating customized data extracts from electronic data sources. Nationally, the data center program responds to more than a half million requests each year. More significantly, in an illustration of how data services have shifted to the Internet, hits on SDC Web sites number over 460 million per year, representing 68 million user sessions. Data centers also produce specialized value-added products in published and computerized media.

- *Training and outreach:* The network provides general information on the census and training in the use of geographic and data products, research techniques, and demographic analysis (DA). Increasing emphasis is on the uses and limitations of the ACS data, particularly for small-area analysis.

- *2010 census planning:* Data centers act as liaisons between state and local governments and the Census Bureau on planning and operations for the decennial census. Data centers provide detailed feedback to the Census Bureau on local operations, data content, and product development, and they conducted some 3,900 presentations in support of Census 2010 and the ACS. The data center program has been instrumental in reviewing and commenting on new versions of the AFF dissemination system, which is the Census Bureau's Internet site for release of all census data products and materials.

It is important to note that the federal government provides no direct financing to SDC participants. Likewise, affiliates and coordinating agencies provide services without direct funding from their respective state lead agencies; all support is in the form of in-kind products and services. As a result, SDC networks vary in the level of resources and staff devoted to the program. These factors can often limit the level of products and services provided but can also allow for substantial flexibility for states to determine how their data centers will operate. Core competencies were developed in an attempt to ensure that each state program provides an acceptable level of service. Responsibility for meeting the core competencies can now be shared among state network participants rather than being the sole responsibility of the lead agency.

Meeting the Challenge of Census 2010

The Census Bureau has changed significantly over the 30 years of the SDC program, and each state has had to incorporate those changes into its operations. Initially, the centers were "the place to go" for census data, support, and technical assistance. Data centers received the highest priority for release of products, and they added value to the computerized tape files by creating print products beyond the Census Bureau's standard series. The advent of CD-ROM technology and its use for release of 1990 census summary data gave data users direct access to information that previously required mainframe tape processing.

Census 2000 and the Internet brought another major shift in how data consumers acquire census information and in the services and products that data centers provide. The data centers' role has shifted from primary data processing to providing increased technical assistance and support. While users have detailed census summaries at their fingertips, it is increasingly important that they have access

to intermediaries who know about the census, how the data are gathered, what the limitations of the data are, how to use them, and most importantly, how not to use them. This is especially true with the ACS. A large contingent of census experts has been cultivated throughout the nation in the 30-year operation of the SDC program. After Census 2010, less of that expertise will be applied to processing data, and more will be applied to the development of value-added products, education of census data users, and analysis of how the nation is changing.

See also *Uses of the census and ACS: state and local governments.*

. . . . ROBERT SCARDAMALIA

BIBLIOGRAPHY

Lavin, Michael R. *Understanding the Census: A Guide for Marketers, Planners, Grant Writers and Other Data Users.* Kenmore, N.Y.: Epoch Books, 1996.

National Research Council. *Modernizing the U.S. Census.* Panel on Census Requirements in the Year 2000 and Beyond. Barry Edmonston and Charles Schultze, eds. Committee on National Statistics, Commission on Behavioral and Social Sciences and Education. Washington, D.C.: The National Academies Press, 1995.

National Research Council. *Using the American Community Survey: Benefits and Challenges.* Panel on the Functionality and Usability of Data from the American Community Survey. Constance F. Citro and Graham Kalton, eds. Committee on National Statistics, Division of Behavioral and Social Sciences and Education. Washington, D.C.: The National Academies Press, 2007.

U.S. Census Bureau. *State Data Center & Business and Industry Data Center Network 2008 Annual Report.* Washington, D.C.: U.S. Census Bureau, 2009. Available at www.census.gov/sdc/2008report.doc.

Statistical Policy

See *International statistical system and its governance; Federal statistical system oversight and policy: intersection of OMB and the decennial census*

Summary Files

Summary files (SFs) are computerized summaries of decennial census data. They include predefined data summaries (frequency counts or tabulations) for all geographic entities recognized or defined by the Census Bureau. For example, Table 1 shows Summary Table P5 on race and Hispanic origin for the United States from the 2010 census SF1, and the same table is included for all geographic areas on SF1.

The first SFs, on magnetic tape for use on mainframe computers, were developed for the 1960 census, primarily as tools for internal Census Bureau research and a few specialized organizations. With the 1970 census, SFs on magnetic tape became widely used standard products, which were often referred to as Summary Tape Files (STFs). The tabulations are predefined and include more detail than printed reports. The SFs for the 1980 and 1990 censuses were very similar to those for 1970, occupying fewer tapes each decade as technology became more sophisticated. In the early 1990s, after initial release on tape, the SFs were released on CD-ROM, ushering in the Census Bureau's transition to dissemination for personal

Table 1. Example of a Summary Table: Table P5 from 2010 SF1

NOTE: For information on confidentiality protection, nonsampling error, and definitions, see www.census.gov/prod/cen2010/doc/sf1.pdf.	United States
Total:	308,745,538
Not Hispanic or Latino:	258,267,944
White alone	196,817,552
Black or African American alone	37,685,848
American Indian and Alaska Native alone	2,247,098
Asian alone	14,465,124
Native Hawaiian and Other Pacific Islander alone	481,576
Some other race alone	604,265
Two or more races	5,966,481
Hispanic or Latino:	50,477,594
White alone	26,735,713
Black or African American alone	1,243,471
American Indian and Alaska Native alone	685,150
Asian alone	209,128
Native Hawaiian and Other Pacific Islander alone	58,437
Some other race alone	18,503,103
Two or more races	3,042,592

SOURCE: P5. Hispanic or Latino Origin by Race [17] - Universe: Total Population: Census 2010 Summary File 1 (SF 1)

computers. The SFs for the 2000 census were no longer tape files, but equivalent data summaries were distributed on CD-ROM and on the Internet.

Preparing Summary Files

To prepare most of the decennial census data products, the Census Bureau tallies by computer the basic records containing individual information. This procedure produces specified summary statistics for various types of areas about persons, families, households, and housing units. The tabulated data are recorded on the Census Bureau's internal-use SFs, which are used to generate the contents of printed reports and public SFs.

From 1960 through 2000, SFs were generally organized into two basic file sets, one for the data collected from the complete count of the population on the short form and one for the sample data collected on the long form. Within this framework, the files were organized to maximize the availability of data for any given geographic area while remaining within the legal limits that prevent disclosure of confidential information. For example, the smallest geographic level (city

blocks or larger rural areas of similar populations) was not available for the sample data.

There were four basic SFs for the 2000 census. SF1 included 286 tables from the complete population and housing counts presented for all geographic entities, including blocks. SF2 included 47 tables from the complete count with such detail as single years of age and with separate iterations for up to 249 race, ethnic, and Hispanic groups, but the smallest geographic area was the census tract. SF3 included 813 tables of sample population and housing characteristics for all geographic areas down to the block group. A special SF3 file (SF3B) included data for ZIP codes, a popular summary level that is not a traditional census geographic area. SF4 was by far the most detailed, with 323 tables of sample population and housing characteristics and separate presentations for as many as 336 population groups defined by race, American Indian or Alaska Native tribe, Hispanic-origin group, and ancestry. Census tracts were the smallest geographic areas included in SF4. For the 1970 and 1980 censuses, SF5 was an extremely detailed file for larger geographic areas with more than 100,000 data cells. By 1990 SF5 had been discontinued, as the focus had shifted to producing more specialized SFs.

SFs typically contain data for many geographic levels in a single "file." Summary-level codes are used to differentiate the geographic levels. The 2000 SF2 and SF4 also include record-type codes to distinguish among records for different racial or ethnic groups. Because of the inclusion of separate ethnic records for each geographic area, the structure of SF2 and SF4 was far more complex than the structure of SF1 and SF3.

On the SFs of past censuses, the data were stored as strings of digits, which were grouped into logical records. A printout of one of these files showed simply a mass of unlabeled characters. Specialized software was typically used to define and display the data, following location and definition information in the appropriate technical documentation of each file. When the first SFs from the 1970 census were released, the files required programmers to define and use them. A consortium of universities and other large-scale data users formed the Summary Tape Assistance, Research, and Training (START) community to share the costs of acquiring the files and of developing software and documentation for using the SFs. Under the START community's auspices and the leadership of John C. (Jack) Beresford, Data Use and Access Laboratories (DUALabs) developed the MOD-Series, a set of computer programs that defined the file structures and contents and produced formatted data reports. Using compressed data files and data dictionaries, the MOD-Series programs were highly innovative for their time. By the 1980s, other software entered the scene, including the Census Bureau's CENSPAC, but many of the larger users continued to use the MOD-Series. With the first CD-ROM SFs for the 1990 census, dBASE format files became an option, and software to display the summary tables was included with the data.

SFs for the 2000 census are available on DVD or online through American FactFinder (AFF), with many options for downloading, displaying, and processing the data. AFF has greatly expanded the concept of SFs to include profiles and quick tables, ranking tables, and geographic comparison tables. ASCII (American Standard Code for Information Interchange) files are still available for users who prefer to choose their own software. In addition to the basic SFs, special SFs are typically produced. Most important is the Public Law 94-171 Redistricting File, which is the very first summary of data to be released for each census. This file satisfies the legal requirement, established in 1975 by Public Law 94-171, that within a year of census day, the Census Bureau must send all state legislatures and governors the data they need to redefine districts for their state legislatures. These data also are usually used to delineate revised districts for the U.S. House of Representatives. The 2000 Public Law 94-171 Redistricting File included basic population counts for many geographic levels down to the block.

Other special SFs have included an Equal Employment Opportunity file (EEO file) and a County-to-County Migration file. The EEO file provided special detailed occupation tabulations by race and sex to determine compliance with federal EEO laws. The County-to-County Migration file provided data from the full sample to establish detailed patterns of migration that exist throughout the nation.

Sometimes a special SF can be requested and paid for by a user or group of users, provided that it does not violate the Census Bureau's confidentiality restrictions. The Census Bureau developed the 1990 Census Transportation Planning Package (CTPP) in conjunction with other federal and state agencies and nongovernmental organizations. Distributed by the departments of transportation of individual states and on CD-ROM by the federal Bureau of Transportation Statistics, the CTPP showed characteristics of workers presented by place of residence, cross-tabulated by place of work. The 1990 CTPP (and the product that followed in 2000) provided details on place of work for residents of different geographic areas and for workers at their county and census tract of work. One file even provided selected information on the characteristic of worker flows—that is, workers with specific origins and destinations.

2010 Census Summary Files

The 2010 census electronic SFs have been distributed on the Internet through AFF and on DVD. Because there was no long form in the 2010 census, there are only two major Summary Files, SF1 and SF2. In addition to tables for the total population, many of the tables are presented separately for detailed race and Hispanic or Latino categories and American Indian and Alaska Native tribes. SFs from the American Community Survey (ACS) are replacing SF3 and SF4, the old SFs based on the long form.

The geographic iterations on national files will include summary tabulations for the nation; regions; divisions; states; counties; county subdivisions; places; American Indian and Alaska Native (AIAN) areas; Metropolitan Areas (MAs) or Core Based Statistical Areas (CBSAs); Urbanized Areas (UAs); state parts of divided AIAN areas, MAs, and UAs; and congressional districts. Separate files for each state will include states; counties; county subdivisions; places; census tracts; state parts of divided AIAN areas, MAs, and UAs; block groups; congressional districts; Zip Code Tabulation Areas (ZCTAs); and blocks. Some of the more detailed tables will not be presented for block groups or blocks.

See also *American Community Survey: data products; Data dissemination and use; Dissemination of data: electronic products.*

. . . . DEIRDRE A. GAQUIN

BIBLIOGRAPHY

Kaplan, Charles P., and Thomas L. Van Valey. *Census '80: Continuing the Factfinder Tradition.* Washington, D.C.: U.S. Government Printing Office, 1980.

U.S. Bureau of the Census. *1990 Census of Population and Housing: Guide, Part A. Text.* 1990 CPH-R-1A. Washington, D.C.: U.S. Government Printing Office, 1992. Available at www.census.gov/prod/cen1990/cph-r/cph-r-1a.pdf.

U.S. Census Bureau, Census Product Catalog. www.census.gov/mp/www/cat/.

U.S. Census Bureau, Data Access Tools. www.census.gov/main/www/access.html.

Tabulation Geography

All census data analysis takes place in a geographic context. We look at the characteristics of people and housing in space—that is, in a defined geographic area. The size of the areas for which data are available range from as large as the United States as a whole to as small as a city block. Many different types of geographic areas lie in between.

The Census Bureau publishes its data at a wide variety of geographic levels. Some of these areas are political, some are statistical, and some are administrative. For many users and applications, the published geographic areas are sufficient. In other cases, users need to aggregate the published geography so that they can use data for user-defined geographic areas.

Political Geography

The term *political geography* refers to geographic areas that are defined in law and in which, usually, the government is run by elected officials. The most common political geographic areas are the states, counties, and county subdivisions.

States

These are the 50 states of the United States. Some other areas are state equivalents or are treated as such in the publication of census data. These include the District of Columbia, Puerto Rico, and the outlying territories.

Counties

Every state has counties (called parishes in Louisiana). The number of counties in the states varies widely, ranging from 254 in Texas to 3 in Delaware. In four states (Maryland, Missouri, Nevada, and Virginia), independent cities are treated as county equivalents. The District of Columbia and Guam are also each considered the equivalent of a county. Counties or county-equivalent areas completely cover the territory of each state. At the time of the 2010 census, there were 3,141 county areas in the United States.

County Subdivisions

About half the states have legally defined minor civil divisions (MCDs), which are recognized in census data publications as county subdivisions. (In the remaining 22 states, statistical areas called census county divisions [CCDs] are used for data presentation.) MCDs vary widely in their level of importance as functioning governments. For this reason, they are treated differently in census data publications in different states. The major groupings are New England towns, the Mid-Atlantic states, and the Upper Midwest.

- In the six New England states (Maine, New Hampshire, Vermont, Massachusetts, Rhode Island, and Connecticut), government was organized in towns prior to the Revolutionary War. In these states, towns deliver most of the governmental services, and counties are far less influential.
- In the Mid-Atlantic states of New York, New Jersey, and Pennsylvania, a variety of labels describe MCDs. These include town, township, borough, city, village, and district. Regardless of name, virtually all of them are functioning units of local government.
- The states of the Upper Midwest (Michigan, Minnesota, and Wisconsin) divide their counties into cities and townships (called towns in Wisconsin). Although the township was designed as a rural form of government, many townships have large populations (in excess of 25,000) and have developed into full-scale municipal governments. All are functioning units of government.

Towns, townships, and other similar areas are not incorporated, but the MCDs in the 12 states listed above are important units of government. For this reason, the Census Bureau now publishes data for them in the same way that data are published for incorporated areas of the same population size. Prior to 1980 these data were only published for the New England states.

Place

There are two categories of places: incorporated places and census designated places (CDPs). Incorporated places are legally recognized entities. Naming conventions vary by state; some of the terms commonly used are *city, village, borough,* and *town.* More than one term may be used in a given state; if so, there are legal differences between them. Places may or may not be independent of MCDs. For example, in Michigan, cities are incorporated places that are independent of townships, whereas a village is an incorporated place that remains part of its township. Places may cross MCD boundaries (if they are not independent of MCDs) or county boundaries. This leads to hierarchical presentation in electronic census products (see the example of hierarchy in Figure 1).

Some other types of areas may appear to be political geography but are not. These include various types of *political districts* (congressional, state representative, state senate, or county commissioner) and *election areas* such as wards and voting precincts. Although this geography is used for political purposes, the areas are not general governmental units providing a variety of services to their residents. Census data may be published for them by the Census Bureau (congressional districts) or by data service organizations at the state and local levels for incumbent officeholders and others wishing to link or analyze data for these areas.

Statistical Geography

The term *statistical geography* refers to geographic areas created expressly for aggregation and presentation of data. Statistical geography is entirely within the control of the Census Bureau or of the intermediaries who create these types of geographic areas for local use.

Census Tract

The best-known unit of statistical geography is the census tract. Census tracts were originally developed as a way to look at small areas within large cities. The census tract program was extended nationwide for publication of 2000 census data. Census tracts never cross county boundaries. In the strong MCD states (New England, Mid-Atlantic, and Upper Midwest), census tract boundaries often match the MCD lines as well.

Census tracts are important in and of themselves (that is, to view data for a small area), but they are equally important as building blocks for administrative and service geography. Because some tracts are small (fewer than 1,000 housing units) and because response rates to the census long form are low in some areas, the American Community Survey (ACS) data for a single census tract often carry high sampling errors. This makes the information unreliable. However, tracts are still very useful in the building-block approach to data analysis. The same was true for long-form data published for census tracts in the 2000 census and earlier. With added attention to the sampling error problems inherent in ACS data, the criteria for revising census tracts for the 2010 census included much stricter adherence to the elimination of tracts with small populations and housing unit counts.

Block Group

Block groups are subdivisions of census tracts defined as the blocks beginning with a single digit. Thus, tract 3062 may have block group 1, block group 2, and so on. Block groups are designed to have about 400 housing units and population of 1,000, but many vary significantly from that ideal. The problems with data quality outlined earlier for census tracts apply even more strongly to block groups. Thus, they should only rarely be used as individual areas. Their main function is to serve as building blocks to larger-area geography. Block group data from the ACS will be available on a more limited basis than data for census tracts and larger geographic areas.

Block

A census block is, strictly speaking, not statistical geography. It describes a physical area, bounded by visible features such as streets, railroads, and water. Occasionally, especially in rural areas, drainage ditches or power lines may be used to define blocks. Block data are often outdated before they are published. People and households move in and out, people die, and babies are born continually. Because most blocks have small population and housing unit counts, only 100 percent data, or short-form data, are tabulated for them. The housing data items are much more reliable and consistent than the population items. For 2000 and 2010, the only housing data available are the housing unit counts, occupancy/vacancy rates, and tenure (rent or own).

As with block groups, the primary use of block data is as building blocks to other geography, especially voting precincts. Block data have also served an important function as the source of housing unit counts for sampling frames used in local surveys.

Metropolitan Areas

Metropolitan areas (MAs) are groups of counties that are geographically contiguous and share common economic and social bonds. In New England, towns, rather than counties, are used as the building blocks of MAs. Responsibility for defining MAs lies with the federal Office of Management and Budget (OMB). MAs are intended for statistical use only. However, over the decades they have taken on nonstatistical uses that were not originally intended. These uses include many federal laws that reference them, as well as various private-sector applications.

Prior to the 2000 census, OMB undertook a substantial analysis of the MA concept, leading to a two-tier definition of areas: *metropolitan* areas and *micropolitan* areas. This two-tier model was implemented in 2003 after the census. MAs continued to be delineated for urban cores of 50,000 persons or more. Micropolitan areas were delineated for urban cores of between 10,000 and 50,000 persons.

Census County Divisions

CCDs are used in states where there are no MCDs or where the MCDs are weak or unknown to the public. A total of 22 states defined CCDs for the 2010 census. Like census tracts and some other programs, they are a cooperative effort between the state and the Census Bureau.

Administrative Geography

The term *administrative geography* refers to areas that exist to deliver services. They are often independent of standard political geographic areas, except that they are unlikely to cross state lines. The Census Bureau published data in 2000 for three types of administrative areas: school districts, voting districts, and ZIP codes.

School districts are independent geographic areas in 35 to 40 states. Elected school boards select school administrators. School districts are within the control of state governments. In 1980 and 1990 a special *School District Data Book*, created in cooperation with the National Center for Education Statistics (NCES), combined census data with administrative data for each school district. Later publication of data for these districts has continued to be a cooperative project with NCES.

Voting districts, called "voting precincts" in many states, are important geographic areas because voting data are tabulated by this geography. Linking census data with voting data is the core activity involved in redistricting, the process of redrawing congressional, state legislative, and other districts every ten years. The Census Bureau delivers voting district data under the mandate of Public Law 94-171, passed in 1975. The data file, called the Public Law 94-171 Redistricting File, is often referred to as "PL" for short. The law requires the file to be released, for every state, no later than April 1 of the year after the census. As such, it is the first data file to be released.

ZIP codes are often called the "universal geo-code" because they are almost always attached to administrative or local data files that include addresses. Thus, a wide variety of users want to use census data tabulated by ZIP code. It is important to remember that ZIP codes are administrative units created by the U.S. Postal Service for the purpose of delivering mail. They need not even refer to a defined spatial land area. Even when they do, the boundaries are often difficult to discern. For example, their boundaries may not be on streets. Some roads may be served by more than one post office and, therefore, have overlapping ZIP codes. The Census Bureau has created a special statistical area called a Zip Code Tabulation Area (ZCTA), which assigns each census block to a single ZIP code for purposes of data publication.

Although the Census Bureau has published only data for these three sets of geography, local data providers (often called "intermediaries") aggregate census tracts and/or block groups to produce and publish census data for local administrative or service geography. Examples in the public and nonprofit sectors include police precincts, health service areas, school-attendance areas (within a school district), territories of neighborhoods and community organizations, rural water districts, and catchment areas for delivery of mental health services.

The private sector uses aggregation techniques for similar purposes. Examples include sales territories and radio-listening and television-viewing areas. Another frequent data application in the private sector is tabulation of demographic or economic profiles for the population located in a circle defined by a radius centering on a site of interest. A standard report may show the data for a one-mile radius, a three-mile radius, and a five-mile radius. A geographic information system (GIS) determines the census block groups that meet the distance criteria and aggregates them for the profile.

Published Geographic Areas

Historic census printed reports usually present data for the same geographic areas in one table. For example, in typical decennial census reports, all counties in the state were located in one table, while places in the state were in another. In electronic products such as CD-ROMs, geographic areas are presented in hierarchical order, from the largest to the smallest (see the example of

---

Figure 1. Example of Tabulation Geography Hierarchy

State
  County A
    County subdivision 1 in county A
      Place within county subdivision 1 within county A
        Tract 101 within place
          Block group 1 in tract 101
          Block group 2
        Tract 102 in place
          Block group 1 in tract 102
          Block group 2 in tract 102
      Remainder of county subdivision 1
        Tract 102 in remainder
          Block group 3 in tract 102
    County subdivision 2
      (Iteration of records for place/remainder and tract repeated)
    County subdivision 3
      (Iteration of records for place/remainder and tract repeated)

---

hierarchy in Figure 1). In 2010 most census data were published via American FactFinder (AFF), an online system for accessing the data. Specific geographic areas are requested via a selection mechanism in the system.

See also *Census tracts; Dissemination of data: electronic products; Dissemination of data: printed publications; Geographic information systems (GIS); Metropolitan areas.*

. . . . PATRICIA C. BECKER

BIBLIOGRAPHY

U.S. Bureau of the Census. *A Guide to State and Local Census Geography*. 1990 CPH-I-18. Washington, D.C.: U.S. Government Printing Office, 1993.

U.S. Census Bureau. 2010 Census Redistricting Data [P.L. 94-171] Summary Files. www.census.gov/rdo/data/2010_census_redistricting_data_pl_94-171_summary_files.html.

———. American Community Survey: Geographic Areas Published. www.census.gov/acs/www/data_documentation/areas_published.

Three-Fifths Compromise

The Three-fifths compromise is the name given to the provision in the U.S. Constitution that mandated how members of the U.S. House of Representatives were to be apportioned among the states. The provision, in Article I, Section 2, based apportionment on a population count of the "whole Number of free Persons" and "three fifths of all other Persons"—that is, three fifths of the slaves. African and African ancestry slaves composed almost 20 percent of the population in the country at the time. The provision resulted from an intense debate among members of the 1787 Constitutional Convention about the guiding principle for allocating House members.

The Framers agreed that the sovereignty of the states derived from the "People of the United States." They therefore decided that state population sizes would determine how seats in the House would be allocated. They also built into the Constitution a requirement for a periodic population count, or census.

North versus South

As the Framers confronted the question of whether such a population count would include all people—including women, children, aliens, and slaves, all of whom had no political rights—they considered whether the formula for apportioning representatives should differentiate among the population's demographic or civil classes. While northern states with few slaves opposed including slaves in the population to be counted, southern states supported doing so, claiming that although slaves were not "people" with political rights, they nevertheless contributed to the political and economic welfare of the states in which they resided. Southerners further admitted that since the census would also be used to allocate direct taxes among the states, slaves could be counted as members of the taxable population.

The resulting compromise meant that the census counted both slaves and free persons. It "discounted" the size of a state's slave population to three-fifths of the total before adding it to the state's free population to produce the official apportionment population. The Framers chose the fraction after debating various ratios. As James Madison and Alexander Hamilton noted in *The Federalist Papers*, the "reasoning" behind the compromise "may appear to be a little strained in some points," but the three-fifths requirement proved "the least objectionable among the practicable rules."

Impact on the Census

From 1790 to 1860, therefore, the census questionnaire distinguished between the free and slave populations. Census reports listed the states' total and apportionment populations and generally included breakdowns for the slave and free populations of smaller geographic divisions and demographic groups. From the outset of the Republic, then, these requirements embedded a "race" or "color" classification in census questions, which yielded elaborate racial statistics. The compromise and the resulting census data provided fodder for antebellum debates about the future of slavery, known as the "peculiar institution." Racists proposed amending the Constitution to base House representation on the white population only. Opponents of slavery pointed to the compromise to rebut claims that the Constitution was silent on the legitimacy of slavery.

In 1865 the Thirteenth Amendment to the Constitution abolished slavery and the Three-fifths compromise, but it did not grant political rights to freed persons. After the Civil War, southern states reentering the Union expected to receive the full apportionment for their former slaves. These states were therefore slated to increase their relative weight in the House of Representatives and the Electoral College. Nonetheless, it was clear that southerners intended that whites would continue to dominate politics. The potential for the southern states' increased representation in the House and the Electoral College prompted Congress to pass further provisions—particularly the Fourteenth Amendment (Section 2), the Fifteenth Amendment, and these amendments' implementing legislation—to reconstruct the Union and to give freed persons the right to vote.

After the war, freed persons voted and participated in government, and postbellum censuses included questions on voter participation to monitor compliance with the newly enacted amendments. After the turn of the twentieth century, freed persons were effectively disenfranchised through seemingly color-blind provisions, such as those authorizing the white primary, the poll tax, and literacy tests. During the Second Reconstruction of the 1950s and 1960s, Congress revisited the issue and passed the Voting Rights Act (1965) to require racially unbiased political participation in the United States. Census statistics on race again became essential to answering the question of whether all people of the United States "counted" and were effectively participating in government.

See also *Civil War and the census.*

. . . .   MARGO J. ANDERSON

BIBLIOGRAPHY

Ohline, Howard A. "Republicanism and Slavery: Origins of the Three-Fifths Clause in the United States Constitution." *William and Mary Quarterly* 28, no. 4 (1971): 563–584.

U.S. Insular Areas

The United States currently has four insular areas. The U.S. Virgin Islands in the Caribbean near Puerto Rico constitute 134 square miles on 3 major islands: St. Croix, St. John, and St. Thomas. Guam is the southernmost of the Mariana Islands, south of Japan and east of the Philippines, and is 210 square miles. The rest of the Mariana Islands are the Northern Mariana Islands, an archipelago of more than 20 islands and 179 square miles, with Saipan being the largest island in size and population but with populations also living on Rota and Tinian. American Samoa, the only U.S. insular area in the Southern Hemisphere, is 77 square miles, with most of the population living on Tutuila but with populations also living on the 3 Manua Islands, Aunuu, and Swains Island.

The first insular area over which the United States gained jurisdiction was Guam, which Spain ceded to the United States in October 1898 under the Treaty of Paris, ratified in 1899. The United States acquired American Samoa, a group of seven islands, in accordance with a convention among the United States, Great Britain, and Germany, ratified in 1900. American Samoa annexed Swains Island in 1925. In 1917, the United States purchased the Virgin Islands, comprising 50 islands and cays, from Denmark. The United States administered the Northern Mariana Islands between 1947 and 1986 as a United Nations (UN) strategic trust by an agreement approved by the UN Security Council and the United States. The Northern Mariana Islands became a commonwealth in 1986.

Because characteristics of the insular areas differ, the presentation of census data for them is not uniform. The 1960

Table 1. Summary Population Statistics, United States and Insular Areas: 2000

CHARACTERISTIC	UNITED STATES	VIRGIN ISLANDS	GUAM	AMERICAN SAMOA	NORTHERN MARIANA ISLANDS
Population	281,421,906	108,612	154,805	57,291	69,221
Median age	35.3	33.4	27.4	21.3	28.7
Persons per household	2.59	2.64	3.89	6.05	3.66
Percent 5 years and over:					
Living in same house in 1995	54.1	61.8	53.0	75.0	37.8
Living outside area in 1995	2.9	10.5	17.4	13.4	37.6
Speaking only English at home	82.1	74.7	38.3	2.9	10.8
Percent 25 years and over:					
High school graduate	80.4	60.6	76.3	66.1	69.2
Bachelor's degree or higher	24.4	16.8	20.0	7.4	15.5
Percent 16 years and over:					
In the labor force	63.9	65.2	65.6	52.0	84.1
*Unemployed**	5.8	8.6	11.5	5.2	3.9
Median family income in 1999	$50,046	$28,553	$41,229	$18,357	$25,653

* as a percent of the civilian labor force

SOURCE: Adapted from U.S. Bureau of the Census, *Statistical Abstract of the United States, 2004–2005* (Washington, D.C.: U.S. Government Printing Office, 2005), tables 1305 and 1307.

Census of Population covered the U.S. Virgin Islands, Guam, and American Samoa. It excluded the Northern Mariana Islands because their census was conducted in April 1958 by the Office of the High Commissioner. The 1960 Census of Housing excluded American Samoa. From 1970 onward, the decennial censuses covered all four areas. In 2000 the population of Guam was 154,805; the U.S. Virgin Islands, 108,612; American Samoa, 57,291; and the Northern Mariana Islands, 69,221. A summary of comparisons from the 2000 census appears in Table 1.

The 1959, 1969, 1978, and 1987 Censuses of Agriculture covered American Samoa, Guam, and the U.S. Virgin Islands; the 1964, 1974, and 1982 censuses covered only Guam and the Virgin Islands, and the 1969, 1978, 1987, 1992, and 1997 censuses included the Northern Mariana Islands. The Census of Agriculture was conducted in American Samoa and the Northern Mariana Islands in 1990 along with the population and housing censuses. Subsequent agriculture censuses included all four areas.

Beginning in 1967, Congress authorized the economic censuses to be taken at five-year intervals for years ending in 2 and 7. Prior economic censuses were conducted in Guam and the U.S. Virgin Islands for 1958 and 1963. In 1972 the Census of Construction Industries was conducted for the first time in the U.S. Virgin Islands and Guam. From 1982 onward, the three areas were covered at five-year intervals. American Samoa joined the program with the 2002 Economic Census and continued in 2007. In 2007 the U.S. Virgin Islands had 2,583 business establishments, Guam had 3,143, the Northern Mariana Islands had 1,191, and American Samoa had 812.

For mid-year 2009, the Census Bureau estimated the population of Guam to be 178,000; the U.S. Virgin Islands, 110,000; American Samoa, 66,000; and, the Northern Mariana Islands, 51,000. The bureau bases its population estimates on births, deaths, and net migration.

The U.S. insular areas are unique in terms of social and economic data that have been collected in that they received a census long form in 2010 because they are not part of the American Community Survey (ACS). There are a number of reasons for this, including the absence of an address list from which to draw a sample, unique questionnaire content requirements, and the lack of permanent staff in these areas to carry out continuous data collection. Nonetheless, discussions are occurring about the future inclusion of the U.S. insular areas in the ACS program as a way of providing a socioeconomic picture of these places more than once a decade.

See also *Census of Puerto Rico.*

. . . .   MICHAEL J. LEVIN

BIBLIOGRAPHY

U.S. Census Bureau. *Statistical Abstract of the United States, 2004–2005.* Washington, D.C.: U.S. Government Printing Office, 2005. Available at www.census.gov/prod/2004pubs/04statab/pop.pdf.

———. *Statistical Abstract of the United States, 2010.* Washington, D.C.: U.S. Government Printing Office, 2009. Available at www.census.gov/prod/www/abs/statab2006_2010.html.

Waite, Preston J. "Decision Not to Conduct the American Community Survey in the Island Areas During 2010 Decennial Census Cycle." 2010 Census Decision Memorandum Series, no. 8, December 23, 2004.

Urban Areas

The census defines urban areas and territory in order to provide statistics on the population living in cities and towns, or in city-like conditions, as opposed to rural or noncity territory. Prior to 1850, the census provided separate populations for many cities and towns but did not summarize them as a group. From 1850 to 1870, limited data were presented on cities grouped by population size, but the term *urban* first appeared in the *Statistical Atlas* in 1874, when it was defined as comprising places with populations of at least 8,000.

From 1874 to 1930, the census used various cutoffs ranging from 8,000 down to 2,500 as the minimum size for defining an urban place. In 1940, data on the urban population based essentially on the 2,500 cutoff were presented for each census back to 1790, broken down by size of place. With minor revisions and the addition of data for 1950 determined on the same basis, this series for 1790–1950 has been published in each subsequent census. In 1950 the "urban" category was expanded to include qualified census designated places (CDPs) and all population within Urbanized Areas (UAs), and in 2000 it was augmented with the creation of Urban Clusters (UCs), as discussed below. However, these expansions could not be carried back to the early censuses.

While common usage in recent decades often has distinguished *urban* from *suburban*, U.S. Census Bureau usage generally has defined *urban* as part of a dichotomy, with *rural* describing all territory and population not designated as urban.

Defining Urban Territory

Before 1950 the "urban" category consisted only of incorporated municipalities recognized by their states (cities, towns, boroughs, villages, and so on), provided they met the established size cutoff. This approach assumed that nearly all population clusters having a city- or town-type character also had incorporated status, and it assumed that any urban development that overflowed city limits either would be quickly annexed or would achieve separate incorporation. These assumptions generally were correct until about 1900, although incomplete identification of incorporated municipalities produced significant gaps in the census list of urban places, especially prior to 1870.

A perennial problem with using municipalities as the basis for defining *urban* was that in New England, the basic municipal unit is the town, an entity that typically includes both one or more population clusters and extensive open country. After the census had tried various alternatives, the 1790–1950 urban series treated New England towns as urban only if they were judged to contain a cluster with a population of at least 2,500 and to have more than half of their population in clusters. The 1790–1950 series also treated certain densely settled townships in other states as urban, starting with the 1930 census.

By the time this solution was adopted, however, urban overflow beyond city boundaries had become a more serious problem for the "urban" definition. Such development existed on a small scale as early as 1790, notably around Philadelphia, but after about 1900, rapid population growth, improvements in public transportation, and increased automobile ownership produced extensive suburban expansion at the same time that annexations by large cities slowed. The result was the development of suburban areas that were not separately incorporated and that therefore were left out of the "urban" definition.

The 1950 census dealt with this problem by introducing the concept of the Urbanized Area (UA), providing a better separation of urban and rural population in the vicinity of the larger cities. A UA was defined to include each city of at least 50,000 and its more or less contiguous built-up suburbs, incorporated or not. The UA boundary did not divide incorporated cities or villages but included only the built-up parts of suburban townships and New England towns. All population within UA boundaries was defined as "urban."

Also introduced in 1950 was the systematic recognition of significant population clusters located outside UAs and lacking separate municipal status. These unincorporated places, known since 1980 as CDPs, were defined for clusters down to populations of 1,000, with those of at least 2,500 classified as "urban." Together, the recognition of the UAs and CDPs added a net 6.7 million to the urban population of 1950, increasing it from 59.6 to 64.0 percent of the national total.

The 1950 UA delimitations were based on pre-census fieldwork and a density of at least 500 housing units per square mile; in 1960 the density limit was lowered slightly to 1,000 persons per square mile. Although emphasizing built-up continuity, the UA definitions always have permitted some gaps of up to 1.5 miles under specified circumstances. Some cities of less than 50,000 had UAs defined for 1970, and starting in 1980 a UA was recognized for each area with a total population of 50,000, essentially irrespective of the size of its main municipality.

Beginning in 1970 the "extended city" concept has excluded from UAs and the "urban" category the sparsely settled portions of incorporated places whose boundaries include large areas of open country. Pickard used the 1970 census criteria to augment the UA database by defining UAs of at least 50,000 for 1920–1960.

Technical advances permitted interactive analysis of population density at the census block level in 1990 and automated UA delineation in 2000. This facilitated letting UA boundaries exclude thinly populated blocks even if they were within municipal boundaries. Expanding the practice adopted in 1950, UAs were allowed to jump across up to 2.5 miles of low-density territory to reach an outlying population concentration, with no additional jump allowed beyond the first one. Some partly urbanized areas below the 1,000 density limit could be included down to a minimum of 500 persons per square mile, and special rules allowed some UAs to extend across rivers and floodplains wider than 2.5 miles.

However, the major new development in 2000 was the recognition of UCs, which are identified by applying the delineation rules used for UAs to identify all clusters of at least 2,500 population, thus either including or disqualifying individual incorporated places and CDPs of that size. Application of the 2000 approach to 1990 data has shown that the net increment to the urban population was 7 million, raising the 1990 urban share of the population from 75.2 to 78.0 percent.

Delineations at the block level in 2000 had resulted in the sometimes confusing classification of tiny portions of many municipalities as "rural," but among changes adopted for 2010, a revised technique treats such portions as "urban" if they are within a generally densely populated census tract. Identification of commercial and industrial zones as "urban" even when their population density is low will be facilitated by use of newly available land-cover data. The central places of UAs and UCs will no longer be identified separately, largely because the UA central places list would be very similar to the Metropolitan Area (MA) central places list and there is no apparent need to maintain both lists.

Where UAs recognized separately in 2000 have grown together by 2010, generally they will still be recognized as separate UAs rather than merged, although their boundaries will be updated based on 2010 density and other criteria. However, UCs recognized in 2000 that qualify to be merged with UAs or with other UCs in 2010 will not retain separate recognition.

Growth of the Urban Population

According to the 1790–1950 historical urban series, the 1790 urban population was 201,655 or 5.1 percent of the national total. As defined for the 2000 census, the urban population was 222.4 million, or more than 1,000 times its 1790 size. The urban population first exceeded 10 percent of the national total in 1840, 25 percent in 1870, and 50 percent in 1920, and it was 79 percent in 2000.

The level of urbanization has varied greatly by region. The populations of the New England and Middle Atlantic census divisions were more than half urban by 1880, and they were joined by the East North Central and Pacific divisions in 1910. The West North Central, West South Central, and Mountain divisions first exceeded 50 percent urban in 1950; the South Atlantic in 1960; and finally the East South Central division in 1970. By 2000 the only states whose populations were less than half urban were Mississippi, West Virginia, Maine, and Vermont, the last of which was the least urban at 38.2 percent.

The UAs and UCs, defined by density and land use, contrast with the Metropolitan and Micropolitan Areas, which are defined as functional areas centered on UAs or UCs. Almost invariably, urban territory expands with each census, and its definition in terms of units as small as census blocks precludes same-area comparisons over time. Although in 2000 the urban and metropolitan population totals were quite similar, at 222 million and 226 million respectively, and 90 percent of the urban population was within MAs, the latter category also included 45 percent of the nation's rural population.

The Rationale for the Urban/Rural Classification

Census publications have offered little rationale for the choice of 2,500 or any other population cutoff. There always has been uncertainty about whether population clusters in roughly the 2,500–10,000 range should properly be seen as mainly like larger places, and hence "urban," or mainly like the countryside, and hence "rural." Similar questions have characterized efforts to define urban population in other countries, where the cutoffs adopted range from a few hundred up to 30,000. The United Nations (UN) has not recently tried to achieve international uniformity on the topic; however, the "urban" category is regularly summarized by population size category in census statistics, providing some data for those who wish to evaluate the impact of a different cutoff.

In 2000, as it had since 1950, the "urban" classification constituted a residence category reflecting population density. It corresponds quite closely to the population living at an urban density (1,000 or more per square mile) and in a cluster of at least 2,500 population.

In an era in which urban densities are dropping, many city workers commute from the country, and the social and cultural distinctions between city and country people are seen as fading away. It is therefore easy to overlook the extreme disparity in population density that continues to exist between urban and rural territory. The 79.0 percent of the nation's population classified as "urban" in 2000 lived on only 2.6 percent of the nation's land area. The mean population density of urban territory in 2000 was 2,404 per square mile, or 141 times that of all rural areas, which was 17 per square mile. Even in Connecticut, the state where the two measures were closest, urban density was more than 12 times rural density.

At the time the census first reflected the urban/rural dichotomy in the nineteenth century, few people questioned the major significance of the contrast between high-density urban and low-density rural living conditions. Today, although the density disparity remains great, its social and economic concomitants have changed substantially. But no alternative concept has acquired sufficient consensus to persuade the Census Bureau to replace the existing definition.

See also *Metropolitan areas.*

. . . . RICHARD L. FORSTALL

BIBLIOGRAPHY

Pickard, Jerome P. *Dimensions of Metropolitanism.* (Research Monograph no. 14; Appendices, Research Monograph 14A). Washington, D.C.: Urban Land Institute, 1967.

Truesdell, Leon E.. *The Development of the Urban-Rural Classification in the United States: 1874 to 1949.* Current Population Reports, Population Characteristics, Series P-23, no. 1. Washington, D.C.: U.S. Bureau of the Census, 1949.

U.S. Bureau of the Census. *2000 Census of Population and Housing, Population and Housing Unit Counts.* PHC-3-1, Parts I and II. Washington, D.C.: U.S. Government Printing Office, 2004, tables 4–10.

U.S. Office of Management and Budget. "Urban Area Criteria for the 2000 Census." Federal Register 76, no, 164 (2011): 53030-53043.

Walker, Francis A.. *Statistical Atlas of the United States Based on the Results of the Ninth Census 1870: With Contributions from Many Eminent Men of Science and Several Departments of the Government.* New York: J. Bien, 1874.

Uses of the Census and ACS: Federal Agencies

Agencies of the U.S. government use the data from each decennial census—and increasingly from the American Community Survey (ACS)—for a wide range of purposes. These include distribution of funds to states and localities; enforcement of civil rights laws; and program administration, planning, and evaluation. Federal statistical agencies, such as the U.S. Bureau of Labor Statistics (BLS) and the National Center for Health Statistics (NCHS), also use census and ACS data to support their programs throughout the decade. Some federal uses of census data involve the head count and such basic characteristics as age and sex, which are obtained for all households on the census short form; other uses involve additional characteristics (for example, income), which were obtained for a sample of households on the census long form through 2000 and are now obtained through the continuous ACS.

Many federal agency uses are mandated by law, either directly or indirectly, in that the census or the ACS is the only feasible data source to satisfy a mandate. A criterion for including an item in the census or the ACS is that it serves an important federal purpose. No item is included because it serves exclusively the interest of some other community (for example, business or academia), although many other organizations and individuals in addition to federal agencies use census and ACS data.

Government Allocation Programs

Each year, billions of dollars of federal funds (about $400 billion in fiscal year [FY] 2008) are allocated and distributed to state and local governments or are used to reimburse state expenditures by means of formulas that include census population counts, population estimates based on the previous census, or characteristics from the 2000 census or the ACS (for example, income). The largest program that is funded based on census data is Medicaid, which accounted for $247 billion in federal spending in FY 2009. Under Medicaid, the federal government reimburses a percentage of each state's expenditures for medical care services for low-income people, including elderly and disabled people and families with dependent children. The percentage of expenditures reimbursed for each state is determined by a formula that uses per capita income estimates from the U.S. Bureau of Economic Analysis (BEA). BEA develops personal income estimates for regions, states, and counties by using a wide range of administrative records; census-based population estimates; and data from the ACS, other censuses, and surveys.

Another large formula-allocation program is Title I of the Elementary and Secondary Education Act, which supports compensatory education programs to meet the needs of educationally disadvantaged children. Title I funds (more than $12 billion in FY 2010) are provided to school districts on the basis of annual estimates of poor school-age children. These estimates formerly derived from the most recent census long-form sample and were updated only once every ten years; currently, annual estimates are obtained from statistical models developed by the U.S. Census Bureau. These models incorporate poverty estimates from both the ACS and the 2000 census. Yet another formula-allocation program is the Community Development Block Grant (CDBG) program, which seeks to improve urban communities in terms of housing and economic opportunities for low-income people. This program allocates funds to states on the basis of the larger of two amounts computed under two formulas. Both formulas currently use data from the 2000 census and the census-based Population Estimates Program, including total population, poverty population, and overcrowded housing units in the first formula and total population, poverty population, and housing units built before 1940 in the second formula. The CDBG program also allocates funds directly to localities on the basis of formulas that use census data. Total allocations to states and localities amounted to over $4 billion in FY 2010.

Other Uses of Census Data

Census data are widely used for civil rights enforcement. The Voting Rights Act (1965) and subsequent amendments require the U.S. Department of Justice to review redistricting plans in certain states and localities to ensure that they do not abridge voting rights for African Americans or language minorities, the latter being defined as people of Spanish heritage, American Indians, Asian Americans, and Alaska Natives. This review requires small-area data on age, race, and ethnicity.

In addition, the 1975 and later amendments to the Voting Rights Act require the director of the Census Bureau to determine counties, cities, towns, and townships that must implement procedures for bilingual voting to protect the rights of language minorities. These determinations are currently made by using 2000 census long-form sample data on mother tongue, citizenship, educational attainment, and English-language ability together with age, race, and ethnicity data.

The U.S. Equal Employment Opportunity Commission has regularly used census long-form sample labor force data for ZIP codes and other geographic areas to analyze statistical evidence in class action charges of employment discrimination. As small-area data products become available on an annual basis from the ACS and the 2000 census data become increasingly outdated, the ACS will likely become the preferred data source for civil rights enforcement.

Federal agency uses of census data for program operations are numerous. For example, the U.S. Department of Homeland Security uses 2000 census data for cities and towns on place of birth, citizenship, year of entry, and other long-form characteristics for planning and evaluation and for preparing congressionally required reports. As another example, the U.S. Department of Transportation uses 2000 census long-form data on disability for traffic analysis zones (TAZs) to monitor

compliance with the Federal Transit Act and the Americans with Disabilities Act (1990). Increasingly, the ACS will become the preferred source for these and other uses of small-area population and housing characteristics.

The census and ACS likewise serve several important functions for statistics compiled by federal statistical agencies. Census-based estimates of the population by age, sex, race, and ethnicity are used as denominators for vital rates, such as the birth rates and death rates by age that are produced by NCHS. Census-based population estimates are also used to adjust the weighting factors for interviewed households in sample surveys like the ACS and the Current Population Survey (CPS) to more accurately reflect the distribution of the population. This procedure is necessary because household surveys invariably have higher net undercoverage of the population than does the census itself. In addition, population characteristics ascertained in the ACS will increasingly serve as the basis for specialized surveys, such as a survey of college graduates by the National Science Foundation that uses ACS data on educational attainment.

Census and ACS data have many other federal statistical agency uses. The BEA uses census and ACS data, along with administrative records, to develop regional, state, and county personal income estimates. In turn, BEA state estimates are used in several federal fund allocation and reimbursement programs such as Medicaid, the Child Care and Development Block Grant, the Home Improvement Partnership Program, and others. The U.S. Office of Management and Budget (OMB) has used decennial census data on place of work to define Metropolitan Statistical Areas (MSAs); OMB uses the data to determine the linkages between central cities and their surrounding contiguous territory. MSAs defined following the 2010 census will reflect ACS data on commuting. In turn, many federal agencies make use of MSAs, such as when determining eligibility for fund allocations.

See also *American Community Survey: questionnaire content; Apportionment and districting; Content determination; Federal statistical system oversight and policy: intersection of OMB and the decennial census; Income and poverty measures; Long form; Population estimates and projections.*

. . . . CONSTANCE F. CITRO

BIBLIOGRAPHY

National Research Council. *Using the American Community Survey: Benefits and Challenges.* Panel on the Functionality and Usability of Data from the American Community Survey. Constance F. Citro and Graham Kalton, eds. Committee on National Statistics, Division of Behavioral and Social Sciences and Education. Washington, D.C.: The National Academies Press, 2007. Available at http://www.nap.edu/catalog .php?record_id=11901.

Reamer, Andrew D. *Counting for Dollars: The Role of the Decennial Census in the Geographic Distribution of Federal Funds.* Washington, D.C.: Brookings, 2010. Available at www.brookings.edu/~/media/Files/rc/ reports/2010/0309_census_dollars/0309_census_report.pdf.

U.S. General Accounting Office. *Formula Grants: Effects of Adjusted Population Counts on Federal Funding to States.* GAO/HEHS-99-69. Washington, D.C.: U.S. Government Printing Office, 1999. Available at www.gao .gov/archive/1999/he99069.pdf.

Uses of the Census and ACS: State and Local Governments

State and local governments are major users of census data for a wide variety of purposes, making them major stakeholders in the decennial census process and all aspects of the American Community Survey (ACS). Census and ACS data are frequently a key part of demonstrating need on applications for funding at all levels of government. State and local governments prepare informational and comparative profiles about the size and characteristics of states' and communities' populations to attract new businesses, new residents, tourists, and students. Census data also form the basis for producing local population estimates and projections.

Allocation of Power and Money

The initial purpose of conducting the census was to provide the information needed to ensure that every state got its fair share of political power and paid its fair share of federal taxes. The U.S. Constitution provided a means of periodically changing the number of representatives that each state has in the House of Representatives and the direct taxes due from each state. (The reference to taxation was removed from the Constitution in 1913 by the Sixteenth Amendment.) Over the centuries since the Constitution was first ratified, legislation and court decisions have expanded the application of this fairness principle so that every resident is equally represented at all levels of government. The adjustments that ensure equal representation are done through reapportionment and redistricting of legislative bodies at all governmental levels every decade when new population figures are released by the U.S. Census Bureau. Similarly, members of many local boards, commissions, and service districts are elected to represent geographic areas that are redrawn to recognize population growth and diversity using data from the most current census.

According to the Census Bureau report *Federal Aid to States for Fiscal Year 2009*, the federal government distributed $552 billion to state and local governments that year. Distribution of federal funds is often based on complex formulae that are at least partially dependent on census data. In addition, in many cases, the allocation of dollars to jurisdictions within states by state governments is based on formulae that use either population data from the decennial census or employment, income, or related data from the ACS.

Many federal and state local assistance programs are targeted to specific types of communities, such as economically distressed areas. The enabling legislation for these programs often specifically states minimum eligibility requirements. Frequently, eligibility for these programs is determined for small areas, such as census tracts, based on selected census characteristics, such as poverty or unemployment rates that exceed some threshold. These data come almost exclusively from the decennial census or the ACS.

The allocation of money for a program is the first step in providing services to people. Just as important is placing a program into communities where it will provide the greatest benefits. One of the most wasteful acts of government is to direct services to the wrong geographic areas. For example, if a limited amount of money were available to educate a community about the dangers of lead paint to children, the local government would want to identify those areas where people were most at risk from lead paint. To do this, community leaders could look at local census data to identify large concentrations of homes built before a certain date that house large numbers of children.

Program Planning and Evaluation

A major function of state and local governments is to plan programs aimed at improving the quality of life for people in their jurisdictions. To do this, governments need to have a clear understanding of their communities. While they may have a general feel for a community's makeup and needs, they must have numbers to support these impressions. They get many of these numbers from the census.

While local governments are heavy users of census data in all of its variations, they also provide census data by answering written and telephone requests as well as by publishing agency newsletters, reports, and speeches. Some local agencies provide staff for information desks and provide access to census publications. Local governments are active in displaying, interpreting, and consulting on census data; providing comparisons with other communities; identifying and explaining population trends; and translating national census press releases into local terms. Over the past decade, much of this dissemination has taken place through Web sites created by local governments.

Local government staff may provide workshops and training to help policymakers, government officials, the press, and the public understand census data and use them appropriately. This assistance has become more important over the past decade with full implementation of the ACS and the large group of products that have become available annually as part of that program. Services may involve looking up census or ACS data on an organization's Web site or navigating the Census Bureau's Web site to obtain the latest ACS information to support a legislative analysis or business decision. Moreover, the release of one- three- and five-year period estimates from the ACS has required local government staff to re-educate data users on the differences between decennial census single point-in-time data and the multi-year period estimates from the ACS.

The contribution of state and local governments to the dissemination and use of census data has been substantial. In one study done by Gaines in the mid-1990s, 134 organizations (23 state government agencies, 80 local government organizations, and 31 university-based data providers) filled more than 22,000 census data requests from within their own organizations in a 1-year period, for an average of 170 requests per organization. Many times these requests came from people outside the organizations. Increasingly, the staffs of these organizations are answering highly technical questions about the data from the same people who used to call for simple numbers.

The demand for census data is so acute because they are the only comprehensive information available for local areas. Frequently, census data are used by community planners to determine the severity of a problem. For example, factors that may deter residents from utilizing government services, such as limited English ability or low educational attainment, must be identified. By looking at the census data on English-language ability, language spoken at home, and years of school completed, these barriers can be identified, quantified, and overcome. Furthermore, census data on the location of residents with such difficulties are an essential part of effective program targeting and resource allocation.

Along with planning new programs, government officials are responsible for evaluating existing programs. Often this is done with census data. Consider, for example, a community program aimed at reducing teen pregnancies. While the total number of teenagers who become pregnant over a number of years can be ascertained, these data do not tell the whole story. They must be evaluated relative to the number of teens in the community. That is, to determine whether the rate of teen pregnancies is dropping or rising, public health officials must chart any changes in the overall number of teens in the community. Thus, to determine what is really happening, data on pregnancies must be examined along with Census Bureau estimates of the population by sex and age.

Facility Planning

Census data are commonly used in decisions about the type and location of facilities the community needs. For example, a community might be experiencing growth in its population and in the number of jobs. Normally, this situation indicates a need either to build more roads or improve the community's mass transit system. However, community growth does not necessarily mean that a need for more roads or an improved mass transit system exists. Journey-to-work data from the ACS could reveal that the number of people traveling to work at any one time is well below the capacity of the highway system. If, however, the highways are close to capacity, some action is needed. The data also might show that people are commuting to unexpected locations, suggesting that different bus routes be designed. When information about the number of people commuting between two census tracts or traffic analysis zones (TAZs)—when they left home, how they traveled to work, and how long their commutes took—is combined with local knowledge about the transportation network, employment data, and local surveys of commuters, a clear picture of the community's transportation needs emerges.

In many cases, the data are used in an indirect manner that is invisible to the data user. For example, consider a growing community that is concerned about the need to provide additional classroom space for students in the school system. To determine whether more schools or classrooms are needed, the community's planners would look at projections and estimates of the community's population over time. While the planners might not realize this, the estimates and projections are ultimately based on decennial census population and housing data.

Disaster Planning

Another area where census data are commonly used is emergency or disaster planning. In this governmental function, one of the largest concerns is how people will be relocated during an emergency. Census data can help address two fundamental aspects of this problem.

First, the government can figure out how many people might need to be moved and from where by looking at population data for the smallest geographic units for which data are available in the areas that might be affected by a disaster. For example, by matching census population data with specific areas that might be flooded, emergency planners can easily determine the number of people who would need to be evacuated if a levee fails.

Second, the government can anticipate how to move these people by examining several characteristics of the community described by the data. In particular, the data will tell how many vehicles the residents have access to, the number of households without cars or trucks available to them, and who might need public transportation. Similarly, a community may need special transportation services for disabled residents.

Economic Development and Marketing

In an attempt to improve economic opportunities for people living in their jurisdictions, governments try to attract new businesses. While they frequently use a variety of incentives to do this and must have the types of facilities and infrastructure in place that a given business needs, they also must show that a community has the character for which a business is looking. A business might wonder if it can get the number of workers that it needs or whether the area is sparsely or densely populated. These questions can be answered based on data from the decennial census and the ACS.

States also can use Census Bureau data on government finances to show businesses the trends in total taxes for an area. Furthermore, a state can show a business that supporting industries already exist in the area. By using data from the economic census, County Business Patterns, and annual economic surveys, the cost of producing a certain amount of output in different geographic areas can be compared.

State and Local Governments as Stakeholders

The Census Bureau is responsible for conducting the decennial census, but state and local government employees often have extensive knowledge about local census data; changing population structures and trends; and characteristics of population changes stemming from births, deaths, and migration patterns. They also are aware of changing settlement patterns resulting from new subdivisions, special housing programs, shifts in land use and zoning, and changing physical and political features that affect census geography, such as new roads and updated city boundaries. Thus, the Census Bureau uses local knowledge and expertise in the many preparations for conducting a decennial census.

A majority of cooperative activities, and some of the most formalized, between the Census Bureau and local governments involve identifying or verifying local geographic features, such as streets, housing unit counts, and address information, prior to conducting the census. State and local governments also provide valuable input to the Census Bureau's questionnaire content determination process. Local officials help the Census Bureau identify areas within their communities that may be difficult to count. They describe and locate areas where their residents experience linguistic isolation or have limited English-language ability, where new immigrants reside, and where the homeless congregate. They pinpoint special facilities, nursing homes, institutions, and other group quarters. They also provide introductions to community leaders and gatekeepers who will help the census enumerator gain access to difficult-to-count areas. Some government agencies are asked to help with efforts to recruit the enormous temporary workforce needed to take the census. Sometimes, considerable local resources are utilized—an investment that many states and localities are willing to make because of the importance of an accurate census count.

See also *Apportionment and districting; Data dissemination and use; Local involvement in census taking; State and local governments: legislatures; Uses of the census and ACS: federal agencies.*

. . . . LEONARD M. GAINES, LINDA GAGE,
AND JOSEPH J. SALVO

BIBLIOGRAPHY

Bryant, Barbara Everitt, and William Dunn. *Moving Power and Money: The Politics of Census Taking.* Ithaca, N.Y.: New Strategist, 1995.

Gaines, Leonard M. "The Selection of Census Data in State Data Center/Business and Industry Data Center Organizations: A Gatekeeping-Based Model." PhD diss., Rensselaer Polytechnic Institute, 1997.

Lavin, Michael. *Understanding the Census: A Guide for Marketers, Planners, Grant Writers, and Other Data Users.* Kenmore, N.Y.: Epoch Books, 1996.

Myers, Dowell. *Analysis with Local Census Data: Portraits of Change.* San Diego, Calif.: Academic Press, 1992.

Paez, Adolfo. "U.S. Census Data Uses." *Government Publications Review* 20, no. 2 (1993): 163–182.

U.S. Census Bureau. *Federal Aid to States for Fiscal Year 2009.* Washington, D.C.: U.S. Government Printing Office, 2010. Available at www.census.gov/govs/cffr/.

U.S. General Accounting Office. *Formula Grants: Effects of Adjusted Population Counts on Federal Funding to States.* GAO/HEHS-99-69. Washington, D.C.: U.S. Government Printing Office, 1999. Available at www.gao.gov/archive/1999/he99069.pdf.

Uses of the Census and ACS: Transportation

In 1960 the U.S. Bureau of the Census first asked, "Where did you work last week?" on the decennial census long form. Since that time, the transportation community has recognized the importance of the data related to that question and has purchased a group of special tabulations every ten years.

The data package that the transportation community has developed is different from any other data released by the Census Bureau because it includes tabulations of workers at the workplace and tabulations of the flow of workers between home and work. The main reason for commissioning a custom tabulation is to acquire tables designed especially for transportation planning. In addition to workplace and flow tabulations, more two- and three-way tables are included that use the variables related to means of transportation (for example, car, subway, and bus) and the number of vehicles available to the household than are included in standard census products.

Another unique feature of the transportation special tabulations and data products is the geography for which the data are reported. With standard census products, the smallest areas are census tracts and block groups, which are designed for reporting residential population. However, for transportation planners, traffic analysis zones (TAZs) are the primary geographic units. These are approximately the same size as block groups but are defined with the travel behavior of the public in mind. They are used to support applications that make use of transportation-forecasting models.

The key variables that the transportation planner must take into account include the following:

- Linking home location to workplace location to create the flow between home and work (that is, the commute)
- Travel mode (6 modes in 1960, expanded to 12 in 1980)
- Vehicle occupancy (added in 1980)
- Travel time to work (added in 1980)
- Departure time (added in 1990)
- Carpool occupancy (added in 1990, reduced from 8 categories to 6 in 2000)
- Arrival time at work (added in 1990)

Taken together, these variables represent the journey-to-work data. A critical element of the journey-to-work data is that it allows the analyst to link sociodemographic characteristics—especially household income, vehicles available, persons and workers per household, and limited English-language ability—to the commute characteristics.

One final element that sets the transportation special tabulations apart from standard census data products is the population universe for which the data are reported. For example, several tables focus only on "workers in households." Unlike standard census tables, which tend to focus on "all workers," many of the travel-forecasting models require information specifically for the workers in households, excluding those living in group quarters.

Among the benefits of the decennial census long form was its very large sample for a single point in time, which allowed for reliable tabulations for small geographic areas. The consistent survey methods used by the Census Bureau allowed for comparisons across Metropolitan Areas (MAs) in national publications.

History of Special Tabulations

The first special tabulation purchased by the transportation community used the 1970 census long-form responses. It had 112 separate buyers, mostly Metropolitan Planning Organizations (MPOs), which contracted directly with the Bureau of the Census. By 1980 there were 152 purchasers, and in 1990 and 2000 the American Association of State Highway Transportation Officials (AASHTO) implemented a special "pooled-fund" program, which made the data available to all the state departments of transportation and MPOs across the country. While the individual agencies and organizations contracted for the data, the specifications for the data product were developed by an ad hoc committee with members from the Transportation Research Board (TRB) and the Federal Highway Administration. Furthermore, with the implementation of the American Community Survey (ACS) in 2005 and the AASHTO pooled-fund purchase, oversight has shifted to a formal oversight board with a paid manager. Table 1 outlines the history of special tabulation purchases.

Over the years, the names of the special tabulations have changed, but the basic concepts have remained the same. For 1970 and 1980, the special tabulations were known as the Urban Transportation Planning Package (UTPP), and for 1990 and 2000 they were called the Census Transportation Planning Package (CTPP). However, with the change to the ACS and the need to produce several different data products, the CTPP concept was broadened, and the name was changed to the Census Transportation Planning Products (CTPP) program.

Transportation Planning Applications

With almost a 50-year history of use of the census journey-to-work data, the transportation literature is filled with examples of its use. In a recent National Cooperative Highway Research Program report, *A Guidebook for Using American Community Survey Data for Transportation Planning*, the uses of census data are placed into the following five categories:

1. Descriptive analysis and policy planning
2. Trend analysis
3. Transportation market analysis
4. Survey development and survey weighting
5. Travel-demand modeling

The Census Transportation Planning Products of the Federal Highway Administration publishes articles on current research and analyses in *Status Report* (see box).

Table 1. Special Tabulation, 1970–2005+

	BUYERS/USERS	DIRECT COSTS (IN MILLIONS)	TABLES
1970	112	$0.6	43
1980	152	$2.0	82
1990	All states and MPOs	$2.5	120
2000		$3.0	203
2005+	AASHTO consolidated purchase	$5.8	multiple products

SOURCES: Ed Christopher, "The CTPP: Historical Perspective," Office of Planning, Environment, & Realty (HEP), Federal Highway Administration, U.S. Department of Transportation, 2002, www.trbcensus.com/articles/ctpphistory.pdf.

Ron McCready, "Census Transportation Planning Products (CTPP) Consolidated Purchase," *CTPP Status Report,* January 2008, www.fhwa.dot.gov/ctpp/sr0108.htm.

U.S. Department of Transportation, Census Transportation Planning Products, http://www.fhwa.dot.gov/planning/census_issues/ctpp/.

U.S. Department of Transportation, *Census Transportation Planning Products Program 2008–2012 Mid-Program Report* (Washington, D.C.: Census Transportation Planning Products, 2010), http://ctpp.transportation.org/Documents/CTPPMid-ProgReportFinal.pdf.

THE FEDERAL HIGHWAY ADMINISTRATION (FHWA) PLANNING OFFICE STATUS REPORT

Starting in 1998, the Federal Highway Administration (FHWA) Planning Office has produced the *Status Report*. This triannual publication includes articles on the latest census data developments in the transportation community. Articles on how the data are used include the following:

- "CTPP Data to Support Transit Ridership Forecasting" by Ken Cervenka (May 2010)
- "Model-Based Synthesis of Household Travel Survey Data" by Liang Long and Jane Lin (December 2009)
- "Vehicle Availability and Mode to Work by Race and Hispanic Origin, 2007" by Elaine Murakami (April 2009)
- "Analysis of Iterative Proportion Fitting in the Generation of Synthetic Populations" by Laura McWethy (April 2009)
- "Using Census Data to Analyze Limited English Proficiency (LEP) Populations for Transit Applications" by Mary Kay Christopher and Ed Christopher (May 2008)
- "Using CTPP 2000 Data for the Trans Texas 35 Corridor Model" by Jonathan Avner (August 2007)
- "Use of CTPP at the Eastgate MPO, Youngstown, Ohio" by Kathleen Rodi (September 2006)
- "Northeastern Illinois CTPP Journey to Work Flow Summaries" by Brad Thompson and Sid Weseman (September 2006)
- "Use of CTPP 2000 in FTA New Starts Analysis" by Eric Pihl (April 2006)
- "Use of CTPP Data for Commuter Rail Demand Analysis in Danbury, Connecticut" by Bruce Kaplan and Karla Karash (April 2006)
- "County to County Commute Flow in the Minneapolis-St Paul Region" by Bob Paddock (May 2003)

SOURCE: U.S. Department of Transportation, *CTPP (Census Transportation Planning Products) Status Report,* www.fhwa.dot.gov/ctpp/status.htm.

Descriptive Analysis and Policy Planning

Descriptive analysis is the most common use of the journey-to-work data to describe current conditions as they relate to policy goals. For example, reducing travel times in congested areas may be a goal, and average travel times for the commute trip may be used as part of the travel time measure. Similarly, new policies to promote livability and reduce greenhouse gas (GHG) emissions focus attention on nonmotorized travel modes. Patterns of suburban residences and employment centers impact total vehicle miles of travel (VMT) and GHG emissions. The availability of small-area data for transportation planning has allowed for their use at the individual neighborhood and community level.

In the past decade, following 9/11 and Hurricane Katrina, more attention has been paid to emergency preparedness and evacuation planning. Armed with data for both residence and workplace locations, analysts can create data summaries and profiles of the "daytime" population.

Trend Analysis

Trend data are generally well understood by policymakers, the public, and the media. Transportation planners need to monitor how a region's population has changed over time to better understand how the area's transportation system has evolved. While the literature is replete with demographic trend studies, the transportation planner is also concerned with commuter flows, travel time changes, and mode share shifts. Some of the trend analyses done for transportation utilizing these data include examining changes in auto ownership by race and Hispanic origin and the effects of those changes on travel mode choices; the effects of increased participation by women in the labor force; and the development of suburban employment centers and how this affects travel mode choice and VMT.

Transportation Market Analysis

Transportation market analyses are conducted for all transportation modes, including mass transit, ride sharing, and highways. Regarding transit service, market analysis is done for assessing the limited English proficient (LEP) population with regard to transit service. Also, Title VI analysis as it relates to environmental justice is done to ensure transportation plans are equitable; that is, transit service upgrades, whether they are small improvements to bus services or major transit investments, provide equitable, effective, and efficient service to all communities. In the recent past, the workplace data and vehicle occupancy data were combined to analyze the market penetration of carpooling to the work site for air-quality analysis purposes. National Cooperative Highway Research Program Report 588 documented other analysis, including the following:

- An Atlanta benefits-and-burdens study examined journey-to-work travel patterns (mode, travel time, origin/destination) by race/ethnic group and income and by matching characteristics of workers at residence locations with characteristics of workers at work locations. The study also examined vehicle availability by race/ethnic group, income, and geography.

- The Delaware Valley Regional Planning Commission used 1980 UTPP data and 1990 and 2000 CTPP data to assess the ridership potential for several possible transit improvements, including high-speed rail, express buses, and park-and-ride service, as well as local bus service.

- The Minnesota Department of Transportation, Pioneer Valley Planning Commission in Massachusetts, King County Department of Transportation in Washington State, and Denver Regional Transit District have all used population and workers-at-the-workplace densities to determine types and frequency of service needed.

- The Chicago Transit Authority has used decennial census data and CTPP zone data on minority status and income as primary inputs to quantitative analyses designed to ensure that transit service is fairly distributed and that any cuts in service (due to budget constraints) do not disproportionately affect low-income or minority populations.

- The Federal Transit Administration has encouraged the use of census and CTPP data in the ridership-forecasting validation phase to evaluate the merits of new transit projects.

Survey Development and Survey Weighting

Within the transportation-planning field, CTPP data are among the many data used to build a picture of travel. To build a more complete picture, larger MAs may conduct their own household travel surveys, generally on a 7- to 15-year cycle. A household travel survey often uses a diary to capture all trips taken by members of a household within a specified period—usually a 24-hour day—noting the travel modes used, the reasons for travel, the starting and ending locations, the times in which the trips were made, and a variety of demographic and household information. Because these surveys are very expensive (nearing $200 per completed household in 2010), the samples are often small (less than 1 percent of the households in an area) and have limited geographic detail.

When analysts develop a household travel survey, the CTPP and standard census tabulations come into play at three distinct points. First, standard census tabulations are used in the sample design. Typically, the household survey is stratified using a combination of household size, number of workers per household, and vehicles available. Second, after the survey is complete, the census/ACS data are used to weight the results. And third, census data are often used for survey validation. For example, the analyst can compare the travel mode usage logged in the household travel survey to the census/ACS results. Another check is to compare the home-to-work trip length distribution between the two sources.

Extreme care must be taken when comparing one survey to another, especially when comparing the results of a small household travel survey to the ACS. While the decennial census long form provided a greater degree of certainty due to smaller margins of error, and much more was known about its biases and use in these applications, little is known about how well the ACS and the travel surveys compare.

Travel-Demand Modeling

Within the transportation field, mathematical models are developed to assist policy-planning analysis and formulate long-range plans. A main purpose of the travel-demand model is to simulate current travel. Once this is done, the model is used to forecast travel demand and behavior 20 and 30 years into the future, given planned changes to transportation infrastructure and projected demographics and land use. Travel-demand models are used by almost all of the MPOs for a variety of purposes, such as air quality assessments as part of environmental impact analyses that are required by law.

While the models vary, they generally have three to five distinct steps in which standard census tabulations and CTPP data come into play. These include trip generation, where the volume of trips to and from TAZs is quantified. Information on commuting—travel time, frequency of commuting, and modal split (for example, car, bus, and subway)—is used to simulate flows of traffic along transportation networks. This analysis then permits the identification of traffic congestion points and other issues that can be brought to bear on decisions related to infrastructure planning and the implementation of policies to mitigate problems.

What Does the Future Hold?

With the replacement of the decennial long-form sample with the ACS, the transportation community has had to consider how the ACS affects the custom transportation tabulations. The community faces the following key issues:

- Period versus point-in-time estimates
- Reduced sample sizes increase the margins of error
- Impact of disclosure rules to protect an individual's confidentiality

Period versus Point-in-Time Estimates

Transportation models have been developed to use point-in-time values, such as gasoline prices and traffic counts on specific dates. Because the ACS small-area data represent a five-year period, analysts must attempt to reinterpret the five-year period into a usable point in time. Variables like fuel and housing prices have been volatile in the last five years, making a five-year estimate more problematic to interpret. When working with large geographic units, the one-year ACS data are more current, but extending them to the smaller areas does not make good statistical sense.

Reduced Sample Size Increases Margins of Error

The five-year ACS estimates will be based on a smaller sample than that of the census long form. As a consequence, standard errors in the ACS data are at least 1.5 times higher relative to those of the long-form data. This affects both the utility and reliability of the data for small areas, which are especially important for transportation data users, given their reliance on small-area estimates.

Impact of Disclosure Rules to Protect an Individual's Confidentiality

Starting with the 2000 transportation special tabulations, the Bureau of the Census applied new disclosure and confidentiality rules. All table data now needed to be rounded, and thresholds were applied to flow tables before the bureau would approve them for release. According to the threshold rule, all the flow tables needed at least three unweighted records for each origin-destination pair, or the table was suppressed. For example, there needed to be at least three people in the unweighted sample who traveled between TAZ X and TAZ Y for the data to be released. Given that TAZs are about the same size as block groups, this meant that many data cells were simply not provided. With the changeover to the ACS data collection methodology, the transportation community assumed that the disclosure rules would be less restrictive, but instead the rules became more restrictive.

One of the more restrictive rules affected the number of cross-tabulations that could be obtained with the variable means of transportation to work. In the initial CTPP design proposed by the transportation community, 17 variables in the ACS were supposed to be cross-tabulated with this variable, but the Census Bureau limited the number of cross-tabulations to just 5 variables because of disclosure rules. The Census Bureau's Disclosure Review Board ruled that these cross-tabulations could be used to string together unique sets of characteristics, which could potentially be matched to the sample of records in the Public Use Microdata Samples (PUMS). Even though the PUMS file does not identify geographic areas of under 100,000 persons, it was determined that a unique record for a small area from the CTPP could, through the use of PUMS attributes, be linked to a single person, thus triggering a confidentiality violation.

The transportation community protested but was unsuccessful in convincing the Census Bureau that these rules were too restrictive, and the rules have stayed in place. To remedy the situation, the transportation community took two major steps. The first was to significantly reduce the number of cross-tabulations using the means-of-transportation variables and to reduce the number of cells in these tables by collapsing the number of categories for the travel modes. Another was to commission a $550,000 research project to develop a data-masking (or synthesizing) routine to allow for the TAZ-level tables (which cover small areas) to be released. It is yet to be determined just how valuable the data will be, given the reduction in number of tables and creation of synthetic estimates.

Realizing that the future utility of the ACS data for transportation planning is uncertain, the transportation community is exploring different data sources for travel flows (origin-destination patterns). The Census Bureau's Longitudinal Employer-Household Dynamics (LEHD) data, public data that are derived from administrative records, are one option that is under careful evaluation. But the real promise is in emerging technologies. Two showing promise are data collection activities utilizing digital footprinting that use cell phones and Bluetooth tracking.

In conclusion, the benefits of the census long form and the ACS have been to tie demographic characteristics such as household income, vehicle ownership, age, race, and education to specific travel behavior and transportation characteristics for very small geographic areas. Other private sources may be able to provide excellent origin-destination data, but they lack the demographic characteristics of census/ACS data. Consequently the transportation community needs to evaluate the trade-offs among the different data sources that provide origin-destination information across time and space with some linkage to demographic characteristics.

See also *Long form.*

. . . . . ED J. CHRISTOPHER AND ELAINE MURAKAMI

BIBLIOGRAPHY
Beimborn, Edward A. "A Transportation Modeling Primer." (1995, updated 2006). Available at www4.uwm.edu/cuts/utp/models.pdf.
Bureau of Transportation Statistics, U.S. Department of Transportation. *Implications of Continuous Measurement for the Uses of Census Data in Transportation Planning.* Washington, D.C.: U.S Bureau of Transportation Statistics, 1996. Available at www.trbcensus.com/acs/implications.pdf.
Christopher, Ed. J. "The CTPP: Historical Perspective." Census Transportation Planning Products, Office of Planning, Environment, & Realty (HEP), Federal Highway Administration, U.S. Department of Transportation, 2002. Available at www.trbcensus.com/articles/ctpphistory.pdf.
Federal Highway Administration. *CTPP* [Census Transportation Planning Products] *Status Report.* www.fhwa.dot.gov/ctpp/status.htm (accessed July 2011).
Members and Friends of the Transportation Research Board's Travel Survey Methods Committee (ABJ40). *The On-Line Travel Survey Manual: A Dynamic Document for Transportation Professionals.* Available at www.travelsurveymanual.org/.
National Research Council. *Census Data and Urban Transportation Planning.* Transportation Research Board Special Report 145. Washington, D.C.: The National Academies Press, 1974.
———. *Census Data and Urban Transportation Planning in the 1980s.* Transportation Research Board. Naomi Kassabian, ed. Transportation Research Record 981. Washington, D.C.: The National Academies Press, 1984.
———. *Census Data in Urban Transportation Planning.* Transportation Research Board Special Report 121. Washington, D.C.: The National Academies Press, 1971.
———. *Decennial Census Data for Transportation Planning: Case Studies and Strategies for 2000; Proceedings of a Conference, Irvine, California, April 28–May 1, 1996 (Volume 1).* Transportation Research Board Conference Proceedings 13. Washington, D.C.: The National Academies Press, 1997.
———. *Decennial Census Data for Transportation Planning: Case Studies and Strategies for 2000; Proceedings of a Conference, Irvine, California, April 28–May 1, 1996 (Volume 2).* Transportation Research Board Conference Proceedings 13. Washington, D.C.: The National Academies Press, 1997.
———. *Decennial Census Data for Transportation Planning: Proceedings of a Conference, Irvine, California, March 13–16, 1994.* Transportation Research Board Conference Proceedings 4. Washington, D.C.: The National Academies Press, 1995.
———. *A Guidebook for Using American Community Survey Data for Transportation Planning.* Transportation Research Board. National Cooperative Highway Research Program Report 588. Washington, D.C.: Transportation Research Board, 2007. Available at http://onlinepubs.trb.org/onlinepubs/nchrp/nchrp_rpt_588.pdf.
———. *Proceedings of the National Conference on Decennial Census Data for Transportation Planning: Orlando, Florida, December 9–12, 1984.* Transportation Research Board Special Report 206. Washington, D.C.: The National Academies Press, 1985.
U.S. Department of Transportation, *Census Transportation Planning Products Program 2008–2012 Mid-Program Report* (Washington, D.C.: Census Transportation Planning Products, 2010), http://ctpp.transportation.org/Documents/CTPPMid-ProgReportFinal.pdf.
———. Census Transportation Planning Products, http://www.fhwa.dot.gov/planning/census_issues/ctpp/.

Veterans' Status

The U.S. Department of Veterans Affairs (VA) uses the information on veterans' status collected by the census, and, beginning in 2005, the American Community Survey (ACS), to calibrate its veteran population model. This information is also available to the general population in the microdata releases from the Census Bureau.

Today, individuals interested in veterans and veterans' issues take for granted the availability of veterans' population data by gender, age, and period of military service down to the county level. These estimates, anchored to the previous census and updated annually for separations from the service, as well as estimates of mortality and migration, are prepared by and available from the National Center for Veterans Analysis and Statistics, Office of Policy and Planning, U.S. Department of Veterans Affairs. However, this was not always the case.

History of the Veteran Status Question

The census of 1840 represented the first effort of the U.S. government to collect data on veterans. This information was used in updating the records of pensioners from the Revolutionary War. The next census to collect data on veterans was in 1890; data were collected on those who had served in the Union and Confederate Armies. While the censuses of 1910, 1930, 1940, and 1950 did include veteran status questions, the results were never published due to a relatively high nonresponse rate.

When plans were made for the census of 1960, it became apparent that with the increasing numbers of veterans and programs available only to those who had served during specific periods of service, more accurate data were needed. Beginning in 1960, and continuing in each succeeding census, the veteran status questions have been refined to reflect more accurately the definition of who is a veteran as well as to meet the data needs of an increasing number of programs and services available to veterans. In 1960 the veteran status question was asked only of males age 14 and over. Specifically, they were asked if they had served in the "Army, Navy, or other Armed Forces of the United States," and if so, to indicate whether that service had occurred during the "Korean War," "World War II," "World War I," or "any other time." Virtually the same question was used in 1970; the only change was the addition of the "Vietnam Conflict" to the list of periods of service.

The veteran status questions were changed dramatically for the 1980 census. First, the question was reworded to ask if the person was "a veteran of the active-duty military service in the Armed Forces of the United States." Specific mention of the Army and Navy was removed. In addition, those who had served only in the National Guard or Reserves were referred to the instruction guide. (Veteran status and associated benefits are available to those whose service was limited to the National Guard or Reserves, but only if they were called up to active duty.)

Second, the list of periods of service was changed. Specifically, the terms *Korean War* and *Vietnam Conflict* were relabeled as *Korean Conflict* and *Vietnam Era*. In addition, instead of having all peacetime service covered by the catch-all category "any other time," the period between the Korean Conflict and the Vietnam Era and the period after the Vietnam Era were specified, since veterans of those periods could be eligible for different benefits. The new list included the following:

- May 1975 or later
- Vietnam Era
- February 1995 to July 1964
- Korean Conflict
- World War II
- World War I
- Any other time

Lastly, and perhaps most importantly, the 1980 census was the first to ask the veteran status of both men and women. As a result, the census attempted the first accurate count of women veterans. Subsequent analysis as a result of the findings of the 1984 Survey of Female Veterans indicated that the census results may have overestimated the number of women veterans, particularly in World War II and peacetime periods prior to World War II. The overestimate may have resulted from the fact that organizations women served in were not granted veteran status by the federal government.

The veteran status questions were further refined for the 1990 census. Because it is difficult to distinguish between active-duty service and service in the Reserves or National Guard, the question was revised to allow respondents to address the issue actively (through questions) rather than passively (through responding to instructions). The new question asked: "Has this person ever been on active-duty military service in the Armed Forces of the United States or ever been in the United States military Reserves or the National Guard?" The answer list included the following:

- Yes, now on active duty
- Yes, on active duty in the past, but not now
- Yes, service in Reserves or National Guard only
- No

This query was followed by a question asking respondents to specify the periods in which their active-duty service occurred. This list was the same as that used in 1980 with the addition of a new peacetime category of "September 1980 or later." Also added was a question asking for the total number of years of active-duty military service with a space for the number of years to be entered. Those additions were in response to legislation effective September 1980, which requires 24 months of active-duty service before an individual is eligible for most veterans' benefits. This last question was further revised and simplified in 2000 by providing only two response categories: "Less than 2 years" and "2 years or more."

In 2000 the veteran status questions were included on the long form, which went to approximately one in six households. Shortly after the 2000 census, the Bureau of the Census replaced the long form with the ongoing American Community Survey (ACS). The veteran status questions are now included on the ACS. The current series is similar to the series included in the 2000 census. The first question asks if the "person ever served on active duty in the U.S. Armed Forces, military Reserves, or National Guard." As in the past, the term *active duty* is defined as not including training, but it does include activation, "for example, for the Persian Gulf War." In addition, the number of response categories has been increased to account for the ACS methodology and to include the military actions in Afghanistan and Iraq, where many Reserve and Guard units were activated. The response categories now include the following:

- Yes, now on active duty
- Yes, on active duty during the last 12 months, but not now
- Yes, on active duty in the past, but not during the last 12 months
- No, training for Reserves or National Guard only *(Skip to series on VA service-connected disability)*
- No, never served in the military *(Skip to next series)*

The specific periods of service have also been revised to add service since 2001 and remove World War I, the latter of which is now included in the period of service before December 1941. Respondents are asked to mark all of the following periods in which they served:

- September 2001 or later
- August 1990 to August 2001 (including Persian Gulf War)

- September 1980 to July 1990
- May 1975 to August 1980
- Vietnam Era (August 1964 to April 1975)
- March 1961 to July 1964
- February 1955 to February 1961
- Korean War (July 1950 to January 1955)
- January 1947 to June 1950
- World War II (December 1941 to December 1946)
- November 1941 or earlier

This series is followed by a question asking if the person has a VA service-connected disability rating and, if so, to specify the rating in one of the following categories:

- 0 percent
- 10 or 20 percent
- 30 or 40 percent
- 50 or 60 percent
- 70 percent or higher

Tabulating and Reporting the Number of Veterans

A note on how the VA tabulates and reports the veteran population is in order. For tabulation purposes, individual veterans are considered to have served in either wartime or peacetime. Veterans who have served in both are considered wartime veterans.

A peacetime veteran is reported in only one peacetime period. If veterans have served in more than one peacetime period, they are counted in the most recent. Veterans are counted in all wartime periods in which they served. Reports typically show all those who served in a particular wartime period (labeled "Total") as well as those who served only in that period (labeled "No Prior Wartime Service").

Estimates of the veteran population based on the previous census are published in a variety of sources, most notably the *Annual Report of the Secretary of Veterans Affairs*. They are also available upon request, at the county level by gender as well as by age or period of service, from the National Center for Veterans Analysis and Statistics. This office is responsible for preparing projections of the veteran population until at least the next census.

Beginning in the 1980s, the number of veterans began to decrease. Since that time, the 16 million World War II veterans have experienced high mortality. The latest (September 30, 2010) estimate of the surviving members of the greatest generation is approximately 2 million. This number is expected to decrease by over 85 percent during the next ten years. While our nation has participated in military combat since the end of Vietnam, the conflicts have not been associated with large-scale inductions. Even with the activation of Reserve and Guard units for U.S. involvement in Afghanistan and Iraq, the veteran population has continued to decline from 26.7 million counted in the 2000 census to an estimated 22.7 million as of September 30, 2010. Given a constant number of active-duty personnel for the foreseeable future, the veteran population is expected to decline by an additional 4 million over the next ten years.

Sources of Data on Veterans

The most detailed source of data on veterans' status and their associated socioeconomic characteristics is the microdata releases from the ACS. Annual updates on the estimated veteran population are made by the National Center for Veterans Analysis and Statistics. The Bureau of Labor Statistics (BLS) produces monthly estimates of veterans' unemployment, collected in the monthly Current Population Survey (CPS), though the user is cautioned to be mindful of the associated standard errors. The *Annual Social and Economic Supplement* (ASEC) to the CPS, collected February–April, contains additional questions on veterans' status and characteristics.

In addition, the VA Office of the Assistant Secretary for Policy and Planning (and its predecessors) has sponsored periodic surveys of the veteran population. Reports from these surveys are available to the public. General data on veterans' use of VA health services and benefits are available in the *Annual Report of the Secretary of Veterans Affairs.* Detailed data on veterans' use of VA health services are available at the VA Information Resources Center (Hines VA Hospital, P.O. Box 5000, Hines, IL 60141-5000), and detailed data on the use of veterans' benefits are available from the Office of the Undersecretary for Benefits, U.S. Department of Veterans Affairs (810 Vermont Avenue NW, Washington, D.C. 20420).

See also *Disability; Long Form.*

. . . . STEPHEN J. DIENSTFREY

BIBLIOGRAPHY

Cowper, D. C., L. R. Heltman, and S. J. Dienstfrey. *The Concept of Veteran Status in the U.S. Decennial Censuses: 1960–90.* Princeton, N.J.: Association of Public Data Users, 1994.

U.S. Bureau of the Census. *1970 Census of Population: Subject Reports; Veterans.* PC(2)-6E. Washington, D.C.: U.S. Government Printing Office, 1973. Available at http://www2.census.gov/prod2/decennial/documents/42045402v2p6d6e_TOC.pdf.

———. *1980 Census of Population (Volume 1, Chapter D: Detailed Population Characteristics).* PC(1)-D. Washington, D.C.: U.S. Government Printing Office, 1984. Available at www.census.gov/prod/www/abs/decennial/1980cenpopv1.html.

———. *1990 Census of Population: Social and Economic Characteristics, United States.* 1990 CP-2-1. Washington, D.C.: U.S. Government Printing Office, 1993. Available at www.census.gov/prod/cen1990/cp2/cp-2-1.pdf.

———. *U.S. Census of Population: 1960. Subject Reports: Veterans: Selected Social and Economic Data for Former Members of the Armed Forces.* PC(2)-8C. Washington, D.C.: U.S. Government Printing Office, 1964. Available at www2.census.gov/prod2/decennial/documents/41927948v2p8a-8c_ch09.pdf.

U.S. Department of Veterans Affairs, Office of Policy. *Veteran Population Model: VetPop 2007.* Washington, D.C.: U.S. Department of Veterans Affairs, 2008). Available at www1.va.gov/VETDATA/docs/Demographics/VetPop07-ES-final.pdf.

U.S. Department of Veterans Affairs, Veterans Benefits Administration. *The Veterans Benefits Administration: An Organizational History: 1776–1994.* Washington, D.C.: U.S. Department of Veterans Affairs, 1995.

Vital Registration and Vital Statistics

In 2007 a total of 4,316,233 live births and 2,423,712 deaths were reported in the United States. These figures were obtained through vital record registration systems maintained in the 50 states, New York City, and the District of Columbia. *Vital registration* is the recording of events occurring to individuals, such as births, deaths, marriages, and divorces, on a continuous basis as those events occur. *Vital statistics* are the numerical data compiled from those records and include information on characteristics of the individuals who experienced the events during a designated period, such as a year. A census, on the other hand, is based on enumeration or a count of a particular population and its characteristics at a point in time.

States register vital records of birth, death, marriage, and divorce under the legal authority of the individual states, but they use methods for registration and data collection that are comparable from state to state. All states then provide data from these records to the National Center for Health Statistics (NCHS) in the U.S. Department of Health and Human Services, which compiles the data into national vital statistics for the United States. However, this system for obtaining national vital statistics data was developed only in the twentieth century.

Since the U.S. Constitution does not provide for vital registration, this process evolved as a state function in the United States differently from the way it evolved in many other countries that have national systems for registering vital events. The first birth and death statistics published for the entire United States were based on information collected as part of the 1850 census. Although these reports were inaccurate and incomplete, collection of birth and death statistics continued with each decennial census through 1900, when the system was changed to collect vital statistics information through the legal registration of these events. Improvements were made over time in the completeness and quality of information collected through the vital registration process. Today, vital statistics data are collected nationally by the NCHS through a cooperative arrangement with all states, New York City, and the District of Columbia. NCHS also collects and publishes vital statistics data for five territories (Puerto Rico, U.S. Virgin Islands, Guam, American Samoa, and the Commonwealth of the Northern Marianas Islands).

Early Collection of Vital Statistics

Vital registration began in churches, particularly in England, when clergy began keeping records of christenings, burials, and marriages. In 1639 the Massachusetts Bay Colony required courts to keep records of legal events, including births, deaths, and marriages. Other colonies followed this model of recording vital events as legal statements of fact to ensure the rights of individuals. Often, records of deaths included information on age and cause of death, so these records were useful for studying patterns of disease when epidemics occurred. As the relationship between causes of death and bad sanitary conditions became apparent, the need for better and more accurate collection of vital-events data and a better registration system was recognized. In 1842 Massachusetts adopted the first state vital registration law that contained provisions for collection of specified types of information, including causes of death.

Perceiving the need for national data, officials in the Census Office established for the 1850 census added questions to that census to collect information on persons "Born within the year," "Married within the year," and "Disease, if died within the year." While it was known that people could sometimes not remember and report past events accurately, this system for collecting national vital statistics persisted until the early 1900s. Census counts of deaths for 1850, 1860, and 1870 are believed to be about 40 percent short of the actual number of deaths.

As the need for better public health information increased, physicians and others pushed for a more aggressive vital registration system to obtain the statistics necessary to monitor disease outbreaks. While a number of cities and a few states had vital registration systems, they used different forms and collection methods. In 1879 Congress created the National Board of Health to promote complete and uniform registration of vital events.

For the 1880 census, the concept of "registration area" was developed for accepting registration records from areas having death records in satisfactory detail. Two states, Massachusetts and New Jersey, and several large cities were able to meet the criteria to become part of the official registration area in 1880. Books of blank death certificates were provided to physicians to complete for each death they attended. The books were then collected by census-takers and were used to improve the accuracy of death reporting.

Due to differences in collection methods, forms used, and the manner of recording data, the 1880 Census Office had difficulty tabulating death records obtained for the 1880 count. Therefore, the Census Office wrote to all states and cities with a population over 5,000 recommending a standard form of death certificate to be used for the 1890 census. Also, in 1890 an attempt was made to monitor the probable registration completeness. Again for the 1900 census, intensive efforts were made to promote the use of a standard death certificate. By January 1900, 12 states had adopted the standard form, 6 other states and the District of Columbia had adopted it in part, and 71 large cities in other states had adopted the form in some manner. The 1900 census included figures on deaths from states and cities that were believed to have at least 90 percent of the deaths registered.

Improvement of Vital Statistics Data

In 1902 the Bureau of the Census was made a permanent full-time agency of the federal government. The act creating the bureau authorized the director to obtain, on an annual basis, copies of records filed in vital statistics offices of states and cities with adequate birth and death registration systems. At this point, the effort to obtain counts of deaths as part of the decennial census was abandoned, and the development of an annual system for collection of vital statistics from the registration of vital events was begun.

To have a uniform system for registration of vital events, the Census Bureau began to develop a model law for vital registration; drafted standard forms; prepared instructions for physicians and others completing vital records; formulated rules for statistical practice, including a system for mortality classification; and began establishing working relationships with state and local registrars. Promotional efforts helped states pass uniform legislation and become part of the death registration area. Starting in 1913, the Census Bureau began to locate agents in state health agencies to promote registration and to improve the quality of information about vital records.

The first annual report on mortality statistics, published by the bureau in 1906, presented data for the five years from 1900 to 1904 as if the data for each year constituted a separate annual report. The volume included details on deaths for the registration states and cities by month of death, age at death, sex, "color," and cause of death. In 1914 the bureau published the first table separating resident and nonresident deaths. Prior to that time, published data were presented only by place where the event had occurred.

In 1915 the birth registration area was formed, and the bureau began publishing annual statistical data on natality. The 1915 volume (published in 1917) contained data for 776,304 live births in the registration area, which contained 10 states and the District of Columbia. Tables included data on month of birth, sex, "color," parent nativity (that is, parents' country of birth) of white children, and deaths of children under one year of age.

Growth in the number of states included in the birth and death registration areas was slow. In 1924 the bureau established a committee to bring all states into the registration area by 1930. An effort was made to educate boards of health, physicians, and citizens about the need for these data for public health. Not until 1933 were all states included in the registration areas for births and deaths.

After 1933 the Census Bureau began working to improve data on the records for all states and to research new fields of vital statistics. In 1935 births and deaths were reported by place of residence of the mother or decedent; this procedure greatly improved the usefulness of the data. Under the leadership of Halbert L. Dunn, a physician and biometrician, the Division of Vital Statistics (DVS) within the bureau was greatly strengthened to include more professional staff. Other innovations included a monthly reporting system to provide provisional figures on births, publication of a series of special monographs, and the expansion of annual published volumes to include more extensive tabulations by socioeconomic group and more analytical and interpretative material. Emphasis was also placed on expanding field work to improve the completeness and accuracy of the information reported on the original certificates, coordinating activities between the federal and state offices to eliminate duplication of effort, and stimulating research within the DVS.

The DVS began the collection of national marriage and divorce data in 1940, following the pattern used for births and deaths. Transcripts of marriage and divorce records were collected from state vital statistics offices. Although national marriage data for 1939 and 1940 provided some detail other than numbers of occurrences, marriage records were available for only 30 states. Divorce data published for 1939 included only a dozen states. Efforts to collect marriage and divorce data were suspended during World War II, but in 1944 the bureau resumed publishing the number of occurrences by state.

In 1942 the president of the United States acknowledged problems with national vital statistics data and asked the Bureau of the Budget to conduct a study and make recommendations for improvement. In 1943 the concept of a cooperative vital statistics system of state vital record offices and a national federal office was proposed. The national office would provide financial and technical aid to assist state vital record offices in correcting defects to achieve standardization of vital record agencies, methods, and requirements. The plan also called for transferring the DVS from the Bureau of the Census to the Public Health Service as a separate organizational unit. The president accepted these recommendations, and in 1946 the vital statistics functions were transferred to the Public Health Service and the National Office of Vital Statistics was established.

In 1960 the National Office of Vital Statistics merged with the National Health Survey to become the NCHS. In the early 1970s, NCHS through the Cooperative Health Statistics System (later to become the Vital Statistics Cooperative Program [VSCP]) began to fund states in automating their vital statistics systems so that data in standard formats meeting national standards could be transferred electronically to NCHS, speeding the availability of data by reducing coding and data entry. Through this effort, detailed birth, death, fetal death, induced termination of pregnancy, and marriage and divorce data were transferred electronically to NCHS, although induced termination of pregnancy, marriage, and divorce data collection never achieved national coverage.

The National Death Index was instituted in 1979 and now contains over 60 million death records to help health and medical investigators with mortality ascertainment activities. During this same period, NCHS began sharing its automated mortality-coding systems with the states to improve the comparability of cause-of-death coding and the availability of multiple-cause-of-death information. Beginning in 1987, linked birth and infant death records were transferred electronically to NCHS to provide researchers with expanded data sets so they could better understand causes of infant death and plan intervention strategies.

In 1994 and 1995 the collection of detailed records from states of induced termination of pregnancy, marriage, and divorce was terminated. Now only counts of marriages and divorces are collected from states. However, since 1973, the National Survey of Family Growth (NSFG) has been housed within the DVS and collects data on marriage, divorce, and cohabitation as well as pregnancies and births, in a survey setting, partially compensating

for the loss of individual record data for abortions, marriages, and divorces. The NSFG, along with other outside surveys, is used to help provide a national view of fertility and family formation and dissolution.

Current Vital Statistics

Today the states and the NCHS continue to work together to develop standard forms, definitions, and procedures for data collection and uniform procedures for coding and processing data. With the advent of the Internet, the computer automation of vital-statistics systems at the state level has now moved to hospitals, certifying physicians, and funeral directors. The development of Web-based electronic birth and death registration systems offers the potential for greatly improved timeliness and quality of vital statistics. Also, the advent of the Internet has facilitated a host of data access systems, which allow users to analyze and map vital statistics outcomes easily at the local, state, and national levels (for example, DVS's VitalStats).

In addition to being used to monitor and assess public health, vital statistics are employed to measure a variety of and demographic social issues such as teenage pregnancy and out-of-wedlock births. Death records contain items on the decedent's place of residence, age, race, sex, education, occupation, marital status, and cause of death. Birth record information has expanded to include the mother's place of residence, age, race, Hispanic origin, marital status, education, and number of previous children as well as medical items about prenatal care and delivery. Birth records also contain birth weight and other medical information on the infant. For infants who die, birth and death records are linked so that researchers can study factors about the birth and the mother's medical and demographic information that may have a relationship to the infant's death.

The most recent revision (2003) of the birth certificate has highlighted the use of vital statistics data for tracking critical maternal and infant health issues. Data on preterm and low-birth-weight infants are being used to highlight persistent disparities in birth outcomes. New data on gestational diabetes and newborn admission to a neonatal intensive care unit (NICU), for example, are focusing attention on important risk factors and the use of high-level health services to manage the care of fragile infants. Because vital statistics data are available at the state and county level, public health authorities and policy makers can examine geographic disparities and focus their interventions more precisely.

At the Census Bureau, birth and death data are among the main components used in the Population Estimates Program to develop annual estimates of the total population and selected characteristics for the nation, states, counties, and places between censuses. NCHS compiles special counts of births and deaths by age, sex, race, and Hispanic origin for each county in the United States from the national database that contains data from all state vital record offices; the Census Bureau in turn uses NCHS's counts to prepare population estimates. These population estimates are then used as denominators in the calculation of vital statistics rates and as the basis for health and disease incidence rates, as well as for many other program and planning purposes.

Future Challenges

With the advent of the Internet and the widespread availability of computer power to health care professionals, researchers, and the public, vital statistics face a rapidly changing future with respect to data collection and access. The implementation of electronic death registration systems and the automation of cause-of-death coding have made it possible to release more timely information on causes of death, as well as to provide day-to-day and year-to-date surveillance of emerging causes of deaths and deaths of acute public health significance. However, as the public enjoys ever-expanding access to databases on the Internet that could potentially be linked to other data sources, it becomes critical to determine how confidentiality can be protected while, at the same time, important data are provided to researchers and policymakers.

With the advent of electronic health records, NCHS is developing national data transfer standards that will allow for the sharing of information between electronic vital registration systems and electronic health records. This effort has the potential to improve the timeliness and data quality of birth and death statistics and to provide the mechanism for collection of other health outcomes related to the vital event. However, it is unknown whether vendors of electronic health records systems will follow electronic health record standards to the extent that comparable data from medical records can be transferred to the vital registration systems. Also unknown is whether data providers will provide more complete and accurate information via electronic health records than by way of existing medical record systems (both manual and automated).

State vital registration laws and regulations will need to be modified to account for electronic registration of events as well as to meet growing concerns over the security of the systems and procedures for registering and issuing vital records. To meet these challenges, the Model State Vital Statistics Act and Regulations, last modified in 1992, are undergoing their most significant changes in 50 years, and the draft revision will be made available for state consideration in late 2011. Since some states have not significantly changed their vital registration laws for many decades, the extent to which state legislatures now see the need to modernize laws and regulations in a way that will improve vital registration and the National Vital Statistics System is not clear. Although the questions are many, the future for timely and high-quality vital statistics looks promising.

See also *Data capture; Data products: evolution; Family and household composition of the population; Federal administrative records; Population estimates and projections; Related data sources.*

CHARLES J. ROTHWELL WITH CONTRIBUTIONS BY
. . . . DOROTHY S. HARSHBARGER

BIBLIOGRAPHY

Centers for Disease Control and Prevention. VitalStats. www.cdc.gov/nchs/vitalstats.htm.

Hetzel, Alice M. *U.S. Vital Statistics System: Major Activities and Developments, 1950–95.* (PHS) 97-1003. Hyattsville, Md.: U.S. Department of Health and Human Services, National Center for Health Statistics, 1997. Available at www.cdc.gov/nchs/data/misc/usvss.pdf.

National Center for Health Statistics, Division of Vital Statistics. "History and Organization of the Vital Statistics System, Historical Development." In *Vital Statistics of the United States, 1950 (Volume 1),* 2–19. Washington, D.C.: Government Printing Office, 1953.

Rothwell, Charles J. "Reengineering Vital Registration and Statistics Systems for the United States." *Preventing Chronic Disease* 1, no. 4 (2004). Available at www.cdc.gov/pcd/issues/2004/oct/04_0074.htm.

U.S. Bureau of the Census. *Birth Statistics for the Registration Area of the United States, 1915, First Annual Report.* Washington, D.C.: U.S. Department of Commerce, 1917.

———. *Special Reports: Mortality Statistics, 1900 to 1904.* Washington, D.C.: Government Printing Office, 1906. Available at www.cdc.gov/nchs/data/vsushistorical/mortstatsh_1900-1904.pdf.

U.S. Department of Health and Human Services, Centers for Disease Control and Prevention. "Change in Marriage and Divorce Data Available from the National Center for Health Statistics." *Federal Register* 60, no. 241 (1995): 64437–64438. Available at www.gpo.gov/fdsys/pkg/FR-1995-12-15/pdf/95-30566.pdf.

Ventura, Stephanie J. "Vital Statistics from the National Center for Health Statistics." In *Data Needs for Measuring Family and Fertility Change After Welfare Reform,* Douglas J. Besharov, ed. College Park, Md.: Maryland School of Public Affairs Welfare Reform Academy, 2001. Available at www.welfareacademy.org/pubs/dataneeds/dataneeds-intro.pdf.

Voting Rights Act

See *African-origin population; Apportionment and districting; Race: questions and classifications.*

White or European Origin Population

Since the first census in 1790, a question assessing the race of individuals has been asked every decade. While the racial categories used by Census Bureau have changed over time, "white" has always been an included category.

European ethnicity, on the contrary, has been enumerated by the census in a variety of ways during the last 200 years. The earliest estimates of the ethnicity of the U.S. population were based upon an analysis of the surnames of individuals. The 1850 census was the first to include a question about the birthplaces of individuals; the 1880 census added a question about the birthplaces of individuals' parents.

For the next century, only the first two generations of European immigrants could be identified by the census. In 1980, the inclusion of an ancestry question meant that all of those identifying with a particular national-origin group would be counted. The 1990 census kept the ancestry question but, as was the case with the 1980 census, no longer kept the parental birthplace question.

The 2000 census followed the 1990 census with regard to the nativity and ancestry questions but put into effect a major change in racial categorization. While "white" was still a category, individuals were able to choose multiple racial identifications. For the first time since the earliest censuses, which counted "mulattoes" and "half-breeds," the census counted individuals who identified as partly white in that way.

The 2010 census followed the lead of the 2000 census with regard to the collection of race data; however, the ancestry question was no longer asked. The ancestry question continues to be asked on the American Community Survey (ACS), though, so estimates of the size of the European American population can be made for all but the smallest areas.

Direct Identifiers of Whites and European-Origin Groups

Before 1960 the census enumerator was responsible for recording a person's race; beginning with the 1960 census, individuals chose the racial category in which they were counted. The 1990 and 2000 censuses explicitly asked respondents which race they "consider themselves to be."

The relative size of the white population in the United States has remained fairly consistent throughout the last 200 years, although there has been a clear downward trend since mid-twentieth century. The 1790 census indicated that 80.7 percent of Americans were white. The percentage of the U.S. population that is white peaked at almost 90 percent in 1930 and 1940. According to the 1990 census, 83.9 percent of Americans were white. In the 2000 census, 75 percent of the U.S. population claimed to be white, a proportion that fell to 69 percent if one limits the tally to nonhispanic whites.

The identification of European-origin groups falls into three broad categories: surnames, nativity, and ancestry. *Surnames* in this case refers to the use of the surnames of individuals to impute their ethnic backgrounds. This was the method of the earliest census in 1790. The earliest estimates probably overestimated the number of those of English background, as names that were Anglicized upon immigration as well as names that had no other discernible ethnic origin were assigned to the "English" category. Subsequent re-estimates have found that roughly 60 percent of the U.S. white population was of English extraction, with the next largest groups being the Scottish, Irish, and Germans. The other nationalities calculated were Dutch, French, Swedish, and Spanish.

Nativity questions are queries about the birthplace and citizenship of respondents and, in some years, their parents. The first census year in which an individual's place of birth was recorded was 1850. In 1870, a question was introduced that established whether one's parents were foreign- or native-born, although not until 1880 did the specific parental-birthplace question appear on the census. The parental-birthplace question was dropped after the 1970 census.

From 1950 to 1980, respondents were explicitly instructed to record the place in which their mother resided when they were born (as opposed to the exact location at which they were born) as their birthplace, but this instruction was dropped in 1990. Before 1900, the birth country was recorded simply based on the responses of the individual who was surveyed. Beginning with the 1900 census, the birth country was recorded as "a region whose people have direct relation with other countries." In 1940, enumerators were instructed to record the birth country as it had existed in 1937, to introduce an element of comparability, despite shifting political boundaries that had not been an issue in earlier census counts.

Ancestry questions were initially included on the 1980 census. For the first time, the census captured the full extent of the self-identified European American population. Until this time, only those who were European immigrants themselves or the children of European immigrants were enumerated; the third generation (and beyond) was simply classified as "native-born whites."

In 1980 individuals could respond with as many ancestry groups as they wished. The 1990 census restricted responses to a maximum of two ancestral groups. Hence, one can know the number of "English-Germans" as opposed to those who identify solely as "English" or "German." The 1990 and 2000 questions include *ethnic origin* in the terms of the query, and both give examples of possible responses. Additionally, those whose ethnicity is Canadian, Arab, Australian, and so on, are often "whites," although they would not be counted as "European Americans."

The detailed instructions for the ancestry question note that a religious group should not be reported as an ancestry group. Hence, the number of Jewish Americans must be estimated via other means, and distinctions between, for example, Irish Catholics and Irish Protestants are not discernible with census data.

Factors Influencing the Variability of Racial and Ethnic Identification

While the racial identification of whites by the census is more straightforward than ethnic identification, some factors can influence the number of individuals who are officially counted as white. One of the chief factors is the composition of the other racial categories into which one may be assigned. There has been considerable variation throughout the years in these other categories; several of these labels have implications for whom the Census Bureau counts as white. The mixed-race categories, in particular, have some obvious overlap with the single-race category of "white." While "mulattoes" would typically have been counted as black if forced into a single-race category, some would perhaps be identified as white. "Half-breed" was included as an option on earlier censuses; this group contained those who were part American Indian and part another race. While a small overall percentage of the population, this group no doubt contained some who would be identified as white on later censuses without the "half-breed" category.

Significant changes started in the 2000 census with regard to the ambiguity of racial identification, as those who had previously identified with a single race now record all of the races with which they identified. Some respondents who had previously identified as white now assigned themselves to two or more racial groups; 2 percent of respondents checked "white" in combination with one or more other races in 2000. Since those who had previously identified as black or Asian or any other group could also check multiple races, it would be difficult to ascertain which of the respondents who checked "white" as one of the racial groups with which they identified have been recorded as such in previous censuses. It would also

be impossible to determine whether such individuals were considered as white or as another race by the people and institutions with which they have contact.

Another factor influencing the size of the tallied white population is the method by which the census is administered. Before 1960, census-takers assigned respondents to a racial category. From 1960 onwards, racial classification has been based upon the self-identification of individuals.

Perhaps the biggest factor in recent years that influences white racial identification in the census is the way in which "Hispanic" identity has been enumerated. While a separate question addressing the hispanicity of respondents has appeared on the census, "Hispanic" has never been an option for individuals answering the race question. Throughout the years, most Hispanics have been classified as white, although this has been influenced both by the design of the census and the shifting nature of Hispanic ethnic consciousness. In 1930 the Census Bureau included a category of "Mexican" in the race question, but it was not repeated in later years. The censuses of 1940 and 1950 explicitly instructed enumerators to classify Hispanics as white. An "other" race category was added in 1910; it is not clear how many Hispanics were counted as white or as "other race" between 1910 and 1940. Since the addition of a separate Hispanic question in 1980, a substantial number of Hispanics have identified as white.

Difficult as it may be to assemble accurate racial estimates from the census, the measurement of European ancestry has been subject to even greater variability throughout the history of the census. As mentioned, the initial attempt to glean ethnicity from the 1790 census counts relied upon an analysis of the ethnic origin of surnames. While this was a reasonable way to estimate the ancestry of the population, given the available data, it is likely that numerous individuals were misclassified. The Anglicization of names, name changes due to marriage, and the ambiguous ethnicity of names such as *Miller* or *Abraham* contribute to the unreliability of these estimates.

While the introduction of nativity questions to the census in 1850 was a great advance over the surname method of ascertaining ethnicity, there were nonetheless problems with the accuracy of responses to this question. Chief among these was the variability of the political boundaries; national entities such as Germany and Poland took many forms throughout the nineteenth and twentieth centuries. The responses of individuals to the country-of-birth question could depend upon their ages, political beliefs, and dates of immigration to the United States. While the census gave precise instructions for how to handle these issues in certain years, in other years the respondents or enumerators were free to answer the question with no guidance given. In a further effort to clarify the ethnic origins of the white population, from 1910 to 1940 the census asked foreign-born respondents to identify their mother tongues and/or the mother tongues of their fathers and mothers.

The ancestry question from the 1980 and 1990 censuses introduced different sources of inconsistency into the estimation of the ethnicity of Americans. For the first time, self-assessment and choice played a role in the assignment of ethnic identifiers. In the 1980 census, individuals could list as many ethnic-origin groups as they wished, although only the first two were tabulated by the census. The exceptions were 17 of the most common three-ethnicity combinations, such as English-German-Irish.

The chief difficulty in assessing the size of various European ethnic groups in the United States with this method is the variation in the specificity of the terminology used to describe one's ancestry. Some respondents refer to ethnic groups, while others refer only to the nation of origin. For example, some "Yugoslavian" respondents specified their membership in certain ethnic groups within Yugoslavia, while others did not. The same ambiguity holds true for the Swiss respondents.

The counts of specific groups may be flawed using this method. As mentioned, the numbers and characteristics of Jewish Americans are difficult to assess based upon census data, as no religious information is recorded, even if religion is indistinguishable from the ethnicity of the group. The "Scotch-Irish" group is another problematic group. "Scotch-Irish," a distinct ethnicity representing origins in Northern Ireland, is especially prevalent among those living in several South Atlantic states. However, the 1980 census recorded this group as being equivalent to those who had multiple Scotch and Irish ancestries. The 1990 census corrected this problem.

Conclusion

The U.S. Census has included questions identifying the race of white Americans since the first census in 1790. Factors such as the inclusion of a variable number of other racial categories as well as the instructions given to census enumerators have influenced the count of whites. The census (or, in recent years, the ACS) has directly measured European ancestry through either nativity or ancestry questions since 1850. This information is subject to greater subjectivity and variability than the race question.

See also *Foreign-born population of the United States; Hispanic population; White population of the United States.*

. . . . MONICA MCDERMOTT

BIBLIOGRAPHY

Alba, Richard D. *Ethnic Identity: The Transformation of White America.* New Haven, Conn.: Yale University Press, 1990.

Farley, Reynolds. *The New American Reality: Who We Are, How We Got Here, Where We Are Going.* New York: Russell Sage Foundation, 1996.

Hochschild, Jennifer L., and Brenna Marea Powell. "Racial Reorganization and the United States Census, 1850–1930: Mulattoes, Half-Breeds, Mixed Parentage, Hindoos, and the Mexican Race." *Studies in American Political Development* 22, no. 1 (2008): 59–96. doi:10.1017/S0898588X08000047.

Lieberson, Stanley, and Mary C. Waters. *From Many Strands: Ethnic and Racial Groups in Contemporary America.* New York: Russell Sage Foundation, 1988.

Perlmann, Joel, and Mary C. Waters, eds. *The New Race Question: How the Census Counts Multiracial Individuals.* New York: Russell Sage Foundation, 2002.

Ruggles, Steven, and Matthew Sobek, with assistance from Catherine A. Fitch, Patricia Kelly Hall, and Chad Ronnander. *Integrated Public Use Microdata Series: Version 2.0.* Minneapolis: Historical Census Projects, Department of History, University of Minnesota, 1997.

White Population of the United States

A question about the race of respondents has been included in the census since 1790. Additional information about the ethnicity, occupational, and educational characteristics of the white population has been added in subsequent censuses.

Size and Geographic Distribution

The relative size of the white population in the United States remained fairly constant from the first census in 1790 until the mid-twentieth century, when a marked drop-off began (see Figure 1). The first census enumerated 3,140,531 white persons, or 80.7 percent of the total population. The 2010 census counted 231,040,398 white persons; 75 percent of the population checked "white" alone or in combination (including those who also checked "Hispanic or Latino"), while 197,000,000 persons, or 63.7 percent of the population, were nonhispanic whites alone. The greatest percentage of whites in the population was counted in 1940, when 89.8 percent of the population was identified as white in the census. Figure 1 illustrates the long-term historical patterns and projections to 2050. The data from 1980 to 2050 are for nonhispanic whites.

The geographic concentration of the white population has always been skewed, due to the history of slavery and immigration in the United States. The nature of this distribution has exhibited little variation over the last 200 years relative to many other variables. The South has characteristically been the area with the lowest concentration of whites in terms of percentage of the population, especially if one considers hispanicity as an ethnicity rather than as a race. The entry of slaves into the South logically led to a greater percentage of African Americans in this area than in the rest of the country.

In the 1790 census, South Carolina and Virginia were both less than 60 percent white, while all of the New England states were over 97 percent white. By 1850 the geographic distribution had become more extreme; all of the New England states were now 99 percent white, while the slave states of Louisiana, Mississippi, and South Carolina were less than half white. Only 41.1 percent of South Carolina's population was white in 1850. Numerically, New York, Pennsylvania, and Ohio had the largest white populations in that year.

By 1900, both Louisiana and South Carolina were approximately 41 percent white. At the other end of the spectrum, 11 states were 99 percent white, including all of the New England states. Newly added states in the Midwest and West were also predominantly white; Wisconsin, Iowa, and Minnesota had the greatest percentage of whites (outside of New England) in 1900. The largest numbers of whites were in New York, Pennsylvania, and Illinois.

The 1950 census indicated the smallest percentages of whites in the Deep South, as had been the case historically. Mississippi now had the lowest percentage of whites (54.6 percent), although none of the southern states any longer had a minority-white population.

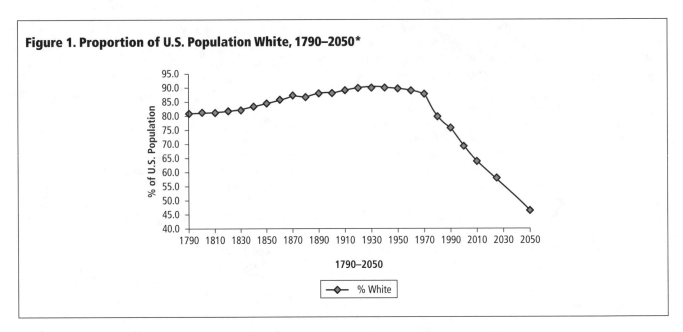

Figure 1. Proportion of U.S. Population White, 1790–2050*

1790–2050

— ◆ — % White

SOURCE: Historical Census Statistics on Population Totals by Race, 1790 to 1990, and by Hispanic Origin, 1970 to 1990, for the United States, Regions, Divisions, and States, www.census.gov/population/www/documentation/twps0056/twps0056.html; Elizabeth M. Greico and Rachel C. Cassidy, *Overview of Race and Hispanic Origin: 2000,* C2KBR/01-1 (Washington, D.C.: U.S. Census Bureau, 2001), available at www.census.gov/prod/2001pubs/c2kbr01-1.pdf ; U.S. Census Bureau, Projections of the Population by Sex, Race, and Hispanic Origin for the United States: 2010 to 2050, www.census.gov/population/www/projections/summarytables.html.

* Figures for 2025 and 2050 are projections. Figures for 1980–2050 are nonhispanic whites.

The 2000 census showed that the West had the lowest percentage of whites of any region, driven by Hawaii (24 percent white) and California (60 percent). These figures were even more exaggerated in 2010 if one considers only nonhispanic whites, in which case three states were minority white: Hawaii (23 percent), and New Mexico and California (40 percent). The Midwest is the region with the highest proportion of whites, although the states with the largest percentage of whites are Maine and Vermont (94 percent), and New Hampshire (93 percent). California, Texas, and New York have the largest white populations in terms of numbers.

Intermarriage rates can affect the overall size of the white population. Throughout most of the history of the United States, intermarriage rates have been quite low. However, recent censuses have witnessed nonnegligible intermarriage rates for whites: 3 percent in 1990 and 3.7 percent in 2000. If this trend continues, it can be expected to have an impact upon the overall size of the white population as these couples have children who may or may not identify as white.

Immigration and Ethnicity

The entire white population of the United States is constituted of immigrants and the descendants of immigrants. Throughout the nineteenth century, almost 90 percent of all immigrants to the United States were of European origin. The chief area from which white immigrants originated is Europe, although Canada, Australia, and parts of Central and South America have also contributed to the white population

of the United States. The numbers and sources of immigrants have a considerable impact upon the size of the white population. In the wake of decades of sizable immigration from Europe, the white population was at its highest level (almost 90 percent) in 1930 and 1940. However, recent shifts in the countries of origin of most immigrants have led to a decline in the proportion of the U.S. population that is white.

While the first census in 1790 did not directly ask about ethnicity or birthplace, census calculations based on the surnames of enumerated individuals found an overwhelming concentration of people of English extraction—more than 80 percent. Subsequent recalculations of the same data using different methods have found a more modest yet still sizable proportion of English Americans, over 60 percent. Only Pennsylvania, with a population that was one-third German, had fewer than half of its residents being of English extraction. New York and New Jersey both had sizable Dutch populations.

The introduction of the birthplace question in 1850 led to more precise estimates of the ethnic composition of the U.S. white population. In 1850, over 92 percent of the foreign-born population was from Europe; by the 2003 American Community Survey (ACS), that proportion had declined to 14.2 percent. Until the late nineteenth century, most immigrants were from northern and western Europe. Between 1880 and 1930, southern and eastern Europe came to lead immigration to the United States. Immigration from Europe has fallen off dramatically since the passage of the Immigration Act of 1965, which enabled Asian and Latin American countries to send more of their numbers to the United States. While 99.8 percent of the U.S. foreign-born population was white in 1850, this number had fallen to an all-time low of 46 percent by 2007.

The introduction of ancestry questions in the 1980 census gave the clearest picture yet of the ethnic distribution of the white population. In 1980, English and German predominated as the ancestries of the greatest number of Americans, with each ancestry being claimed by about one-quarter of the population. Irish Americans were also a sizable group, with 21 percent of the population claiming Irish ancestry. French, Italian, and Scottish ancestries were each claimed by more than 5 percent of the individuals counted. In the 1990 census, English slipped to being the third most popular ancestry group, with German and Irish being the first and second, respectively.

Demographic Characteristics

Native-born whites are the oldest of any group in America. With a median age of 37.7, the age distribution of whites is vastly different from that of native-born Hispanics or those who check multiple races (median age, 22.7). About 56 percent of white Americans age 18 or older live in husband–wife families; another 24 percent have never married. Native-born whites stand out as having low fertility rates. The birth rate for nonhispanic white women in 2008 was 11.4 per 1,000 (compared to 22.1 per thousand for Hispanic women). According to the 2006 Current Population Survey (CPS), 22.5 percent of nonhispanic white women between the ages of 40 and 44 had never had a child. This is the highest rate for any racial group and compares to rates of 16.4 percent for black women and 14.4 percent for Hispanic women.

Employment and Income

Whites have always had lower levels of unemployment than other races; this continues to be the case today. The unemployment rate for the U.S. white male population has hovered around 4 percent since 1960, with sharp spikes during the recessions of the mid-1970s, mid-1980s, late 1990s and late 2000s. The unemployment rate for white women has been closer to 6 percent, although the unemployment figures for 2009 (in the midst of a deep recession) indicated that white women had a lower rate (7.3 percent) than white men (9.4 percent). According to CPS data, white men work more hours per year than any group but Asian men. In 2009 the average white man worked five hours more per week than the average white woman.

The 2000 census indicated that 53.6 percent of all families living in poverty were white; whites as a whole had a poverty rate of 7.5 percent. According to the 2000 census, the per capita income for the population as a whole was $21,587 in 1999; for whites, the figure was $23,918.

Future Projections

The white population is expected to decline further as a proportion of the overall U.S. population. The Census Bureau projects that nonhispanic whites will be 46.3 percent of the population by 2050. Fertility rates, age distribution, and immigration rates contribute to the declining proportion of whites. Since the current white population has a low fertility rate and a high median age relative to other groups, and whites are a declining percentage of immigrants to this country, nonhispanic whites are projected to experience the greatest relative decline in numbers during the next 50 years. The decline is only in terms of proportion of the total population; the actual count of the U.S. white population is expected to steadily increase.

See also *Composition of the population; White or European-origin population.*

. . . .   MONICA MCDERMOTT

BIBLIOGRAPHY

Dye, Jane Lawler, U.S. Census Bureau. *Fertility of American Women: 2006.* P20-558. Washington, D.C.: U.S. Government Printing Office, 2008. Available at www.census.gov/prod/2008pubs/p20-558.pdf.

Farley, Reynolds. *The New American Reality: Who We Are, How We Got Here, Where We Are Going.* New York: Russell Sage Foundation, 1996.

Grieco, Elizabeth M., U.S. Census Bureau. *Race and Hispanic Origin of the Foreign-Born Population in the United States: 2007.* ACS-11. Washington, D.C.: U.S. Government Printing Office, 2010. Available at www.census.gov/prod/2010pubs/acs-11.pdf.

Grieco, Elizabeth M., and Rachel C. Cassidy. *Overview of Race and Hispanic Origin: 2000.* C2KBR/01-1. Washington, D.C.: U.S. Census Bureau, 2001. Available at www.census.gov/prod/2001pubs/c2kbr01-1.pdf.

Kivisto, Peter. *Americans All: Race and Ethnic Relations in Historical, Structural, and Comparative Perspectives.* Belmont, Calif.: Wadsworth, 1995.

Lieberson, Stanley, and Mary C. Waters. *From Many Strands: Ethnic and Racial Groups in Contemporary America.* New York: Russell Sage Foundation, 1988.

U.S. Census Bureau. Projections of the Population by Sex, Race, and Hispanic Origin for the United States: 2010 to 2050. Available at www.census.gov/population/www/projections/summarytables.html.

Women in the Decennial Census

Since it was first taken in 1790, the decennial census has included information on the sex distribution of the population—hence, on the situation of women. Censuses from 1790 to 1840 gathered information on the number of people in households by sex and by age. The original census recorded the number of people per household who were free (white males age 16 and over, white males under age 16, white females, and all other free people) and slaves. Although the age and racial categories changed, the census schedules for 1800–1840 contained similar household counts. In 1850 the census began recording the characteristics of individuals living in each household. Since then, data on sex have been collected separately from age or race, and the number and type of questions have expanded.

Because data are collected by sex, analyses can differentiate responses and determine, for example, the difference between personal income levels of women and men. Numerous social and economic characteristics of women can be examined, including age, race, Hispanic or Latino origin, educational level, occupation, income, family type, and poverty status. Responses to census questions can be compared across censuses to examine how women's characteristics have changed over time. Beginning in 1940, many of these detailed characteristics were collected for only a sample of the population. They were collected on a separate long form between 1960 and 2000. Because the 2010 census had no long form, most detailed analyses of women's characteristics will now come from the American Community Survey (ACS), the large sample survey that has replaced the long-form sample. In the 2010 census, respondents were asked to provide the sex, age, Hispanic origin, race, and relationship to the householder for every household member. For other characteristics, ACS questions were designed to maximize comparability to the data previously collected on the census long form.

Questions about fertility, for women only, have been on some censuses. Between 1890 and 1910, the census asked women how many children they had borne and how many were still living. Between 1940 and 1990, women were asked for the number of children ever born, but the 1940–1970 censuses limited this question to women who were or had ever been married. The ACS now asks women if they have given birth within the past year but not the total number of children. Age at first marriage and number of times married were also recorded during the middle decades of the twentieth century, but these were asked only of women in 1940.

Historical analyses of women's lives are restricted by three census enumeration procedures. First, for much of U.S. history, less information was collected about women than about men. For example, from 1790 to 1840, only the name of the household head was listed on the census form. Since women were considered dependents of men, as relatives or servants, women's names rarely appear in censuses before 1850. Similarly, in 1790 free white males were divided into two age cohorts of "under age 16" and "age 16 and over," but no age breakdowns were available for the free white female population. An individual-level question on occupation was asked of males from 1850 onward; for females, the question was first asked in 1860, and information on housekeeping duties (the most common occupation for women in the past) was not tabulated for wives, daughters, or other relations to the household head. Second, relationship to household head was not recorded for family members until 1880. Third, until 1980, women were never classified as heads of household in married-couple families if the husband was present. Although these limitations restrict certain analyses, they do not affect examination of women's lives from the 1980 census to the present.

Many federal agencies, including the U.S. Departments of Commerce, Education, Labor, and Justice, use decennial census information on women. Numerous federal statutes require the Census Bureau to collect information on sex in order to implement or evaluate social programs. Community planners at both the state and local levels also use census data, broken down by sex, to evaluate future needs for child care, education, and employment. At all levels of government, this information is used to enforce equal opportunity for women as specified by civil rights acts.

Overall, the decennial census is one of the most important sources of information on the situation of American women, both in the past and today. Since the sex distribution of the U.S. population is generally close to 50 percent male and 50 percent female, the analysis of sex distributions is of interest when the distribution diverges from the norm. Such divergence is found in analyses of the greater number of widows than widowers, of geographic areas where men outnumber women, or of occupations held by disproportionate numbers of women or men. Census, and now ACS, data are used to analyze changes in the labor force participation of women, especially mothers of young children, and increases in college education among women.

Finally, the changing status of women over the centuries can be seen in the administration of the census itself. The Census Office began to employ women as enumerators and clerks to process census data in the late nineteenth century. In 1989 Barbara Everitt Bryant became the first woman to be appointed director of the Census Bureau, and she was succeeded by Martha Farnsworth Riche as director from 1994 to 1998.

See also *American Community Survey: questionnaire content; Demographic analysis; Family and household composition of the population; Occupation and education.*

. . . .   DEIRDRE A. GAQUIN

BIBLIOGRAPHY

Bianchi, Suzanne M., and Daphne Spain. *American Women in Transition.* New York: Russell Sage Foundation, 1986.

Spain, Daphne, and Suzanne M. Bianchi. *Balancing Act: Motherhood, Marriage, and Employment among American Women.* New York: Russell Sage Foundation, 1996.

Spraggins, Reneé E. *We the People: Women and Men in the United States.* CENSR-20. Washington, D.C.: U.S. Government Printing Office, 2005. Available at www.census.gov/prod/2005pubs/censr-20.pdf.

U.S. Bureau of the Census. *Planning for Census 2000: Questions Planned for Census 2000; Federal Legislative and Program Uses.* Washington, D.C.: U.S. Government Printing Office, 1998.

———. *Twenty Censuses: Population and Housing Questions, 1790–1980.* Washington, D.C.: U.S. Government Printing Office, 1979. Available at www.census.gov/history/pdf/20censuses.pdf.

Wright, Carroll D. *The History and Growth of the United States Census.* Washington, D.C.: Government Printing Office, 1900.

APPENDIX

~

Census Leadership, 1850–2010

Superintendents of the Census Office, Department of Interior, (1850–1902)

Joseph Camp Griffith Kennedy	1850–1853, 1858–1865
James D. B. DeBow	1853–1855
Francis Amasa Walker	1869–1871, 1879–1881
Charles W. Seaton	1881–1885
Robert Porter	1889–1893
William Rush Merriam	1899–1902

Directors of the Bureau of the Census, (1902–2010)

Department of the Interior (1902–1903)

William Rush Merriam	1902–

Department of Commerce and Labor (1903–1913)

William Rush Merriam	–1903
Simon Newton Dexter North	1903–1909
Edward Dana Durand	1909–1913

Department of Commerce (March 1913 to date)

William Julius Harris	1913–1915
Sam Lyle Rogers	1915–1921
William Mott Steuart	1921–1933
William Lane Austin	1933–1941
Vergil Daniel Reed (acting)	Feb. 1941–May 1941
James Clyde Capt	1941–1949
Philip Morris Hauser (acting)	Aug. 1949–March 1950
Roy Victor Peel	1950–1953
Robert Wilbur Burgess	1953–1961
Albert Ross Eckler (acting)	March 1961–May 1961
Richard Montgomery Scammon	1961–1965
Albert Ross Eckler	1965–1969
George Hay Brown	Sept. 1969–1973
Vincent P. Barabba	1973–1976, 1979–1981
Robert L. Hagan (acting)	1976–1977, 1979
Manuel D. Plotkin	1977–1979
Daniel B. Levine (acting)	1979, 1981
Bruce K. Chapman	1981–1983
C. Louis Kincannon (acting)	1983, 1989
John C. Keane	1983–1989
Barbara Everitt Bryant	1989–1992
Harry Scarr (acting)	1993–1994
Martha Farnsworth Riche	1994–1998
James Holmes (acting)	1998
Kenneth Prewitt	1998–2001
William Barron (acting)	2001–2002
Charles Louis Kincannon	2002–2008
Steve H. Murdock	2008–2009
Robert Groves	2009–

U.S. Population and Area, 1790–2010

DATE	LAND AREA (IN SQUARE MILES)	POPULATION		POPULATION INCREASE FROM PREVIOUS CENSUS	
		TOTAL	PER SQUARE MILE	NUMBER	PERCENTAGE
Aug. 2,1790	864,746	3,929,625	4.5	—	—
Aug. 4,1800	864,746	5,308,483	6.1	1,378,858	35.1%
Aug. 6,1810	1,681,828	7,239,881	4.3	1,931,398	36.4%
Aug. 7,1820	1,749,462	9,638,453	5.5	2,398,572	33.1%
June 1,1830	1,749,462	12,866,020	7.4	3,227,567	33.5%
June 1,1840	1,749,462	17,069,453	9.8	4,203,433	32.7%
June 1,1850	2,940,042	23,191,876	7.9	6,122,423	35.9%
June 1,1860	2,969,640	31,443,321	10.6	8,251,445	35.6%
June 1,1870[a]	2,969,640	38,558,371	13.0	7,115,050	22.6%
June 1,1880	2,969,640	50,155,783	16.9	11,597,412	30.1%
June 1,1890	2,969,640	62,947,714	21.2	12,791,931	25.5%
June 1,1900	2,969,834	75,994,575	25.6	13,046,861	20.7%
Apr. 15,1910	2,969,565	91,972,266	31.0	15,977,691	21.0%
Jan. 1,1920	2,969,451	105,710,620	35.6	13,738,354	14.9%
Apr. 1,1930	2,977,128	122,775,046	41.2	17,064,426	16.1%
Apr. 1,1940	2,977,128	131,669,275	44.2	8,894,229	7.2%
Apr. 1,1950	2,974,726	150,697,361	50.7	19,028,086	14.5%
Apr. 1,1960	3,540,911	179,323,175	50.6	28,625,814	19.0%
Apr. 1,1970[b]	3,540,023	203,211,926	57.4	23,888,751	13.3%
Apr. 1,1980[c]	3,539,289	226,545,805	64.0	23,333,879	11.5%
Apr. 1,1990[d]	3,536,278	248,709,873	70.3	22,164,068	9.8%
Apr. 1,2000[e]	3,537,438	281,422,426	79.6	32,704,124	13.2%
Apr. 1,2010[f]	N/A	308,745,538	87.4	27,310,936	9.7%

NOTES:

a. Population later revised to include adjustment of 1,260,078 for underenumeration in the southern states. Revised census count is 39,818,449.

b. Figures corrected after the 1970 final reports were issued.

c. Total population has been revised since the 1980 census publications. Data by age, race, Hispanic origin, and sex have not been revised.

d. Includes count question resolution corrections processed through December 1997 and does not include adjustments for census coverage errors.

e. The revised April 1, 2000, census count includes count question resolution corrections processed through May 2002 and does not include adjustments for census coverage errors.

f. The Census Bureau in 2011 released population and population density figures from the 2010 census, but the table did not include an exact land area amount.

SOURCE: Michael R. Haines, "Population, Population Density, and Land Area: 1790–2000 [Original counts for census dates]," table Aa1-5, in *Historical Statistics of the United States, Earliest Times to the Present: Millennial Edition*, ed. Susan B. Carter, Scott Sigmund Gartner, Michael R. Haines, Alan L. Olmstead, Richard Sutch, and Gavin Wright (New York: Cambridge University Press, 2006). Available at http://dx.doi.org/10.1017/ISBN-9780511132971.Aa1-109; U.S. Census Bureau, Resident Population Data, http://2010.census.gov/2010census/data/apportionment-pop-text.php.

U.S. Center of Population, 1790–2010

Mean Center of Population for the United States: 1790 to 2010

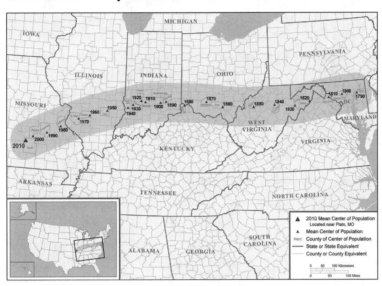

SOURCE: "Mean Center of Population for the United States: 1790 to 2010" U.S. Census Bureau, http://2010.census.gov/news/pdf/centerpop_mean2010_1.pdf

Table: Mean Center of Population of the United States: 1790–2010

CENSUS YEAR	NORTH LATITUDE	WEST LONGITUDE	APPROXIMATE LOCATION OF MEAN CENTER
United States			
2010	37.517534	92.173096	Texas County, MO, 2.7 miles northeast of Plato
2000	37.69699	91.80957	Phelps County, MO, 2.8 miles east of Edgar Springs
1990	37.87222	91.21528	Crawford County, MO, 9.7 miles southeast of Steelville.
1980	38.13694	90.57389	Jefferson County, MO, 1/4 mile west of DeSoto.
1970	38.46306	89.70611	St. Clair County, IL, 5 miles east-southeast of Mascoutah.
1960	38.59944	89.20972	Clinton County, IL, 6-1/2 miles northwest of Centralia.
1950	38.80417	88.36889	Clay County, IL, 3 miles northeast of Louisville.
Conterminous United States			
1950	38.83917	88.15917	Richland County, IL, 8 miles north-northwest of Olney.
1940	38.94833	87.37639	Sullivan County, IN, 2 miles southeast by east of Carlisle.
1930	39.06250	87.13500	Greene County, IN, 3 miles northeast of Linton.
1920	39.17250	86.72083	Owen County, IN, 8 miles south-southeast of Spencer.
1910	39.17000	86.53889	Monroe County, IN, in the city of Bloomington.
1900	39.16000	85.81500	Bartholomew County, IN, 6 miles southeast of Columbus.

CENSUS YEAR	NORTH LATITUDE	WEST LONGITUDE	APPROXIMATE LOCATION OF MEAN CENTER
1890	39.19889	85.54806	Decatur County, IN, 20 miles east of Columbus.
1880	39.06889	84.66111	Boone County, KY, 8 miles west by south of Cincinnati, OH.
1870	39.20000	83.59500	Highland County, OH, 48 miles east by north of Cincinnati.
1860	39.00667	82.81333	Pike County, OH, 20 miles south by east of Chillcothe.
1850	38.98333	81.31667	Wirt County, WV, 23 miles southeast of Parkersburg. [a]
1840	39.03333	80.30000	Upshur County, WV, 16 miles south of Clarksburg. Upshur County was formed from parts of Barbour, Lewis, and Randolph Counties in 1851. [a]
1830	38.96500	79.28167	Grant County, WV, 19 miles west-southwest of Morefiled. Grant County was formed from part of Hardy County in 1866. [a]
1820	39.09500	78.55000	Hardy County, WV, 16 miles east of Moorefield. [a]
1810	39.19167	77.62000	Loudoun County, VA, 40 miles northwest by west of Washington, DC.
1800	39.26833	76.94167	Howard County, MD, 18 miles west of Baltimore. Howard County was formed from part of Anne Arundel County in 1851.
1790	39.27500	76.18667	Kent County, MD, 23 miles east of Baltimore.

NOTES: Before 1960, calculations exclude Alaska and Hawaii. The *mean center of population* is that point at which an imaginary, flat, weightless, and rigid map of the United States would balance if weights of identical value were placed on it so that each weight represented the location of one person on the date of the census. The map and table illustrate the population's westward migration since 1790.

NA = not available.

[1] West Virginia was set off from Virginia on December 31, 1862, and was admitted as a state on June 19, 1863.

SOURCE: U.S. Census Bureau, Geography Division, "Centers of Population Computation for the United States 1950 - 2010," March 2011, http://2010.census.gov/news/pdf/cop2010_documentation1.pdf.

Congressional Apportionment, 1789–2010

State	YEAR OF CENSUS[a]																						
	(1789)[b]	1790	1800	1810	1820	1830	1840	1850	1860	1870	1880	1890	1900	1910	1930[c]	1940	1950	1960	1970	1980	1990	2000	2010
AL				1[d]	3	5	7	7	6	8	8	9	9	10	9	9	9	8	7	7	7	7	7
AK																	1[d]	1	1	1	1	1	1
AZ														1[d]	1	2	2	3	4	5	6	8	9
AR						1[d]	1	2	3	4	5	6	7	7	7	7	6	4	4	4	4	4	4
CA								2	3	4	6	7	8	11	20	23	30	38	43	45	52	53	53
CO										1[d]	1	2	3	4	4	4	4	4	5	6	6	7	7
CT	5	7	7	7	6	6	4	4	4	4	4	4	5	5	6	6	6	6	6	6	6	5	5
DE	1	1	1	2	1	1	1	1	1	1	1	1	1	1	1	1	1	1	1	1	1	1	1
FL							1[d]	1	1	2	2	2	3	4	5	6	8	12	15	19	23	25	27
GA	3	2	4	6	7	9	8	8	7	9	10	11	11	12	10	10	10	10	10	10	11	13	14
HI																	1[d]	2	2	2	2	2	2
ID											1[d]	1	1	2	2	2	2	2	2	2	2	2	2
IL				1[d]	1	3	7	9	14	19	20	22	25	27	27	26	25	24	24	22	20	19	18
IN				1[d]	3	7	10	11	11	13	13	13	13	13	12	11	11	11	11	10	10	9	9
IA							2[d]	2	6	9	11	11	11	11	9	8	8	7	6	6	5	5	4
KS									1[d]	3	7	8	8	8	7	6	6	5	5	5	4	4	4
KY		2	6	10	12	13	10	10	9	10	11	11	11	11	9	9	8	7	7	7	6	6	6
LA				1[d]	3	3	4	4	5	6	6	6	7	8	8	8	8	8	8	8	7	7	6
ME				7[d]	7	8	8	7	5	5	4	4	4	4	3	3	3	2	2	2	2	2	2
MD	6	8	9	9	9	8	6	6	5	6	6	6	6	6	6	6	7	8	8	8	8	8	8
MA	8	14	17	13[e]	13	12	10	11	10	11	12	13	14	16	15	14	14	12	12	11	10	10	9
MI						1[d]	3	4	6	9	11	12	12	13	17	17	18	19	19	18	16	15	14
MN								2[d]	2	3	5	7	9	10	9	9	9	8	8	8	8	8	8
MS				1[d]	1	2	4	5	5	6	7	7	8	8	7	7	6	5	5	5	5	4	4
MO					1[d]	2	5	7	9	13	14	15	16	16	13	13	11	10	10	9	9	9	8
MT											1[d]	1	1	2	2	2	2	2	2	2	1	1	1
NE									1[d]	1	3	6	6	6	5	4	4	3	3	3	3	3	3
NV									1[d]	1	1	1	1	1	1	1	1	1	1	2	2	3	4
NH	3	4	5	6	6	5	4	3	3	3	2	2	2	2	2	2	2	2	2	2	2	2	2
NJ	4	5	6	6	6	6	5	5	5	7	7	8	10	12	14	14	14	15	15	14	13	13	12
NM														1[d]	1	2	2	2	2	3	3	3	3
NY	6	10	17	27	34	40	34	33	31	33	34	34	37	43	45	45	43	41	39	34	31	29	27
NC	5	10	12	13	13	13	9	8	7	8	9	9	10	10	11	12	12	11	11	11	12	13	13
ND											1[d]	1	2	3	2	2	2	2	1	1	1	1	1
OH			1[d]	6	14	19	21	21	19	20	21	21	21	22	24	23	23	24	23	21	19	18	16
OK													5[d]	8	9	8	6	6	6	6	6	5	5
OR								1[d]	1	1	1	2	2	3	3	4	4	4	4	5	5	5	5
PA	8	13	18	23	26	28	24	25	24	27	28	30	32	36	34	33	30	27	25	23	21	19	18
RI	1	2	2	2	2	2	2	2	2	2	2	2	2	3	2	2	2	2	2	2	2	2	2
SC	5	6	8	9	9	9	7	6	4	5	7	7	7	7	6	6	6	6	6	6	6	6	7
SD											2[d]	2	2	3	2	2	2	2	2	1	1	1	1
TN		1[d]	3	6	9	13	11	10	8	10	10	10	10	10	9	10	9	9	8	9	9	9	9
TX							2[d]	2	4	6	11	13	16	18	21	21	22	23	24	27	30	32	36
UT												1[d]	1	2	2	2	2	2	2	3	3	3	4
VT		2	4	6	5	5	4	3	3	3	2	2	2	2	1	1	1	1	1	1	1	1	1
VA	10	19	22	23	22	21	15	13	11	9	10	10	10	10	9	9	10	10	10	10	11	11	11
WA											1[d]	2	3	5	6	6	7	7	7	8	9	9	10
WV									3[d]	3	4	4	5	6	6	6	6	5	4	4	3	3	3
WI							2[d]	3	6	8	9	10	11	11	10	10	10	10	9	9	9	8	8
WY											1[d]	1	1	1	1	1	1	1	1	1	1	1	1
Total	65	106	142	186	213	242	232	237	243	293	332	357	391	435	435	435	437[f]	435	435	435	435	435	435

SOURCES: Biographical Directory of the American Congress; U.S. Census Bureau, "Apportionment Data," http://2010.census.gov/2010census/data/apportionment-data-text.php.

a. Apportionment effective with congressional election two years after census.

b. Original apportionment made in Constitution, pending first census.

c. No apportionment was made in 1920.

d. These figures are not based on any census but indicate the provisional representation accorded newly admitted states by Congress, pending the next census.

e. Twenty members were assigned to Massachusetts, but seven of these were credited to Maine when that area became a state.

f. Normally 435 but temporarily increased 2 seats by Congress when Alaska and Hawaii became states.

Percentage of the House of Representatives for Each State after Each Apportionment

STATES	CENSUS APPORTIONMENT 1790	1800	1810	1820	1830	1840	1850	1860	1870	1880	1890	1900	1910	1930	1940	1950	1960	1970	1980	1990	2000	2010
AL				1.4	2.1	3.1	3.0	2.5	2.7	2.5	2.5	2.3	2.3	2.1	2.1	2.1	1.8	1.6	1.6	1.6	1.6	1.6
AK																	0.2	0.2	0.2	0.2	0.2	0.2
AZ														0.2	0.5	0.5	0.7	0.9	1.1	1.4	1.8	2.1
AR						0.4	0.9	1.2	1.4	1.5	1.7	1.8	1.6	1.6	1.6	1.4	0.9	0.9	0.9	0.9	0.9	0.9
CA							0.9	1.2	1.4	1.8	2.0	2.1	2.5	4.6	5.3	6.9	8.7	9.9	10.3	12.0	12.2	12.2
CO										0.3	0.6	0.8	0.9	0.9	0.9	0.9	0.9	1.1	1.4	1.4	1.6	1.6
CT	6.7	5.0	3.9	2.8	2.5	1.8	1.7	1.7	1.4	1.2	1.1	1.3	1.2	1.4	1.4	1.4	1.4	1.4	1.4	1.4	1.1	1.1
DE	1.0	0.7	1.1	0.5	0.4	0.4	0.4	0.4	0.3	0.3	0.3	0.3	0.2	0.2	0.2	0.2	0.2	0.2	0.2	0.2	0.2	0.2
FL							0.4	0.4	0.7	0.6	0.6	0.8	0.9	1.1	1.4	1.8	2.8	3.4	4.4	5.3	5.7	6.2
GA	1.9	2.8	3.3	3.3	3.8	3.6	3.4	2.9	3.1	3.1	3.1	2.8	2.8	2.3	2.3	2.3	2.3	2.3	2.3	2.5	3.0	3.2
HI																	0.5	0.5	0.5	0.5	0.5	0.5
ID											0.3	0.3	0.5	0.5	0.5	0.5	0.5	0.5	0.5	0.5	0.5	0.5
IL				0.5	1.3	3.1	3.8	5.8	6.5	6.2	6.2	6.5	6.2	6.2	6.0	5.7	5.5	5.5	5.1	4.6	4.4	4.1
IN				1.4	2.9	4.5	4.7	4.6	4.5	4.0	3.7	3.4	3.0	2.8	2.5	2.5	2.5	2.5	2.3	2.3	2.1	2.1
IA							0.9	2.5	3.1	3.4	3.1	2.8	2.5	2.1	1.8	1.8	1.6	1.4	1.4	1.1	1.1	0.9
KS								0.4	1.0	2.2	2.2	2.1	1.8	1.6	1.4	1.4	1.1	1.1	1.1	0.9	0.9	0.9
KY	1.9	4.3	5.5	5.6	5.4	4.5	4.3	3.7	3.4	3.4	3.1	2.8	2.5	2.1	2.1	1.8	1.6	1.6	1.6	1.4	1.4	1.4
LA				1.4	1.3	1.8	1.7	2.1	2.1	1.8	1.7	1.8	1.8	1.8	1.8	1.8	1.8	1.8	1.8	1.6	1.6	1.4
ME				3.3	3.3	3.1	2.6	2.1	1.7	1.2	1.1	1.0	0.9	0.7	0.7	0.7	0.5	0.5	0.5	0.5	0.5	0.5
MD	7.6	6.4	5.0	4.2	3.3	2.7	2.6	2.1	2.1	1.8	1.7	1.6	1.4	1.4	1.4	1.6	1.8	1.8	1.8	1.8	1.8	1.8
MA	13.3	12.1	11.0	6.1	5.0	4.5	4.7	4.1	3.8	3.7	3.7	3.6	3.7	3.4	3.2	3.2	2.8	2.8	2.5	2.3	2.3	2.1
MI						1.3	1.7	2.5	3.1	3.4	3.4	3.1	3.0	3.9	3.9	4.1	4.4	4.4	4.1	3.7	3.4	3.2
MN								0.8	1.0	1.5	2.0	2.3	2.3	2.1	2.1	2.1	1.8	1.8	1.8	1.8	1.8	1.8
MS				0.5	0.8	1.8	2.1	2.1	2.1	2.2	2.0	2.1	1.8	1.6	1.6	1.4	1.1	1.1	1.1	1.1	0.9	0.9
MO				0.5	0.8	2.2	3.0	3.7	4.5	4.3	4.2	4.1	3.7	3.0	3.0	2.5	2.3	2.3	2.1	2.1	2.1	1.8
MT											0.3	0.3	0.5	0.5	0.5	0.5	0.5	0.5	0.5	0.2	0.2	0.2
NE									0.3	0.9	1.7	1.6	1.4	1.1	0.9	0.9	0.7	0.7	0.7	0.7	0.7	0.7
NV									0.3	0.3	0.3	0.3	0.2	0.2	0.2	0.2	0.2	0.2	0.5	0.5	0.7	0.9
NH	3.8	3.5	3.3	2.8	2.1	1.8	1.3	1.2	1.0	0.6	0.6	0.5	0.5	0.5	0.5	0.5	0.5	0.5	0.5	0.5	0.5	0.5
NJ	4.8	4.3	3.3	2.8	2.5	2.2	2.1	2.1	2.4	2.2	2.2	2.6	2.8	3.2	3.2	3.2	3.4	3.4	3.2	3.0	3.0	2.8

Continued

Percentage of the House of Representatives for Each State after Each Apportionment

STATES	1790	1800	1810	1820	1830	1840	1850	1860	1870	1880	1890	1900	1910	1930	1940	1950	1960	1970	1980	1990	2000	2010
NM														0.2	0.5	0.5	0.5	0.5	0.7	0.7	0.7	0.7
NY	9.5	12.1	14.9	16.0	16.7	15.2	14.1	12.9	11.3	10.5	9.6	9.6	9.9	10.3	10.3	9.9	9.4	9.0	7.8	7.1	6.7	6.2
NC	9.5	8.5	7.2	6.1	5.4	4.0	3.4	2.9	2.7	2.8	2.5	2.6	2.3	2.5	2.8	2.8	2.5	2.5	2.5	2.8	3.0	3.0
ND											0.3	0.5	0.7	0.5	0.5	0.5	0.5	0.2	0.2	0.2	0.2	0.2
OH			3.3	6.6	7.9	9.4	9.0	7.9	6.8	6.5	5.9	5.4	5.1	5.5	5.3	5.3	5.5	5.3	4.8	4.4	4.1	3.7
OK													1.8	2.1	1.8	1.4	1.4	1.4	1.4	1.4	1.1	1.1
OR								0.4	0.3	0.3	0.6	0.5	0.7	0.7	0.9	0.9	0.9	0.9	1.1	1.1	1.1	1.1
PA	12.4	12.8	12.7	12.2	11.7	10.8	10.7	10.0	9.2	8.6	8.4	8.3	8.3	7.8	7.6	6.9	6.2	5.7	5.3	4.8	4.4	4.1
RI	1.9	1.4	1.1	0.9	0.8	0.9	0.9	0.8	0.7	0.6	0.6	0.5	0.7	0.5	0.5	0.5	0.5	0.5	0.5	0.5	0.5	0.5
SC	5.7	5.7	5.0	4.2	3.8	3.1	2.6	1.7	1.7	2.2	2.0	1.8	1.6	1.4	1.4	1.4	1.4	1.4	1.4	1.4	1.4	1.6
SD											0.6	0.5	0.7	0.5	0.5	0.5	0.5	0.5	0.2	0.2	0.2	0.2
TN		2.1	3.3	4.2	5.4	4.9	4.3	3.3	3.4	3.1	2.8	2.6	2.3	2.1	2.3	2.1	2.1	1.8	2.1	2.1	2.1	2.1
TX							0.9	1.7	2.1	3.4	3.7	4.1	4.2	4.8	4.8	5.1	5.3	5.5	6.2	6.9	7.4	8.3
UT												0.3	0.5	0.5	0.5	0.5	0.5	0.5	0.7	0.7	0.7	0.9
VT	1.9	2.8	3.3	2.3	2.1	1.8	1.3	1.2	1.0	0.6	0.6	0.5	0.5	0.2	0.2	0.2	0.2	0.2	0.2	0.2	0.2	0.2
VA	18.1	15.6	12.7	10.3	8.8	6.7	5.6	4.6	3.1	3.1	2.8	2.6	2.3	2.1	2.1	2.3	2.3	2.3	2.3	2.5	2.5	2.5
WA											0.6	0.8	1.2	1.4	1.4	1.6	1.6	1.6	1.8	2.1	2.1	2.3
WV									1.0	1.2	1.1	1.3	1.4	1.4	1.4	1.4	1.1	0.9	0.9	0.7	0.7	0.7
WI							1.3	2.5	2.7	2.8	2.8	2.8	2.5	2.3	2.3	2.3	2.3	2.1	2.1	2.1	1.8	1.8
WY											0.3	0.3	0.2	0.2	0.2	0.2	0.2	0.2	0.2	0.2	0.2	0.2
States at peak %	9	1	2	1	4	2	1	1	2	2	3	3	5	1	0	0	1	0	2	0	2	6
States at lowest %	1	0	1	5	1	2	4	4	2	1	2	2	1	11	0	0	1	2	1	3	1	3
Total	10	1	3	6	5	4	5	5	4	3	5	5	6	12	0	0	2	2	3	3	3	9

Peak Representation · Lowest Representation

NOTE: Percentages do not include provisional representatives not based on census (e.g., divisor of 1950 is 435, not 437, because Hawaii and Alaska are not included in the calculation. If multiple years have the same apparent peak or lowest value, further decimal places are used to break the tie. If the values are identical, the first such year is used. Because the percentage has been constant for Hawaii and Alaska, there is no peak or lowest.

Methods of Congressional Apportionment

All methods of apportionment require determining the population total and setting the size of the U.S. House of Representatives, which currently has 435 members. The Constitution requires all states to receive at least one seat; therefore, 385 seats must be apportioned after each of the 50 states receives 1. Each method must set a rule for treating fractions or remainders. What should be done if a state deserves 3.6, 4.2, or 43.7 representatives? Each of the four methods explained below provides an answer.

Thomas Jefferson's method. Find a number, a divisor, that will produce quotients for all the states that sum to the required total for the body. Disregard any fractions.

Alexander Hamilton's method. Calculate the proportion of each state's population of the total population to find its "quota" of seats. Give each state its quota in whole numbers, disregarding the fractions. If the allocation does not sum to the total, give the states with the largest remainders additional seats until all the seats have been allocated.

Daniel Webster's method. Find a number, a divisor, that will produce quotients for all the states that sum to the required total for the body when fractions greater than 0.5 are rounded up and fractions less than 0.5 are rounded down.

Joseph Hill's method. Find a number, a divisor, that will produce quotients for all the states that will minimize the relative difference in constituency size (the size of population per representative) between any two states. In practice, Hill's method rounds a fraction up as it exceeds the geometric mean of the two integers (for example, the geometric mean of 1 and 2 is 1.41, compared with the arithmetic mean of 1.5).

See also Apportionment and districting.

Notes: For some years (for example, 1850–1900 and 1930), the same apportionment would have resulted from two different methods. Congress did not reapportion itself after the 1920 census. There are other possible apportionment methods.

Chronology of the States of the Union

STATE	DATE ADMITTED TO UNION	STATE	DATE ADMITTED TO UNION
1. Delaware	Dec. 7, 1787	26. Michigan	Jan. 26, 1837
2. Pennsylvania	Dec. 12, 1787	27. Florida	Mar. 3, 1845
3. New Jersey	Dec. 18, 1787	28. Texas	Dec. 29, 1845
4. Georgia	Jan. 2, 1788	29. Iowa	Dec. 28, 1846
5. Connecticut	Jan. 9, 1788	30. Wisconsin	May 29, 1848
6. Massachusetts	Feb. 6, 1788	31. California	Sept. 9, 1850
7. Maryland	Apr. 28, 1788	32. Minnesota	May 11, 1858
8. South Carolina	May 23, 1788	33. Oregon	Feb. 14, 1859
9. New Hampshire	June 21, 1788	34. Kansas	Jan. 29, 1861
10. Virginia	June 25, 1788	35. West Virginia	June 20, 1863
11. New York	July 26, 1788	36. Nevada	Oct. 31, 1864
12. North Carolina	Nov. 21, 1789	37. Nebraska	Mar. 1, 1867
13. Rhode Island	May 29, 1790	38. Colorado	Aug. 1, 1876
14. Vermont	Mar. 4, 1791	39. North Dakota	Nov. 2, 1889
15. Kentucky	June 1, 1792	40. South Dakota	Nov. 2, 1889
16. Tennessee	June 1, 1796	41. Montana	Nov. 8, 1889
17. Ohio	Mar. 1, 1803	42. Washington	Nov. 11, 1889
18. Louisiana	Apr. 30, 1812	43. Idaho	July 3, 1890
19. Indiana	Dec. 11, 1816	44. Wyoming	July 10, 1890
20. Mississippi	Dec. 10, 1817	45. Utah	Jan. 4, 1896
21. Illinois	Dec. 3, 1818	46. Oklahoma	Nov. 16, 1907
22. Alabama	Dec. 14, 1819	47. New Mexico	Jan. 6, 1912
23. Maine	Mar. 15, 1820	48. Arizona	Feb. 14, 1912
24. Missouri	Aug. 10, 1821	49. Alaska	Jan. 3, 1959
25. Arkansas	June 15, 1836	50. Hawaii	Aug. 29, 1959

SOURCE: *Encyclopedia of American History: Bicentennial Edition* (New York: Harper & Row, 1976), 616.

Growth and Cost of the Decennial Census, 1790–2010

YEAR	POPULATION (MILLIONS)	NUMBER OF ENUMERATORS[a]	MAXMUM SIZE OF OFFICE FORCE	TOTAL PAGES IN PUBLISHED REPORTS	CENSUS COST (THOUSANDS OF NOMINAL $)	COST PER CAPITA (NOMINAL $)	INFLATION FACTOR (1982–84 = 100)	INFLATION-ADJUSTED CENSUS COST IN THOUSANDS (2010 $)	INFLATION-ADJUSTED CENSUS COST PER CAPITA (2010 $)
1790	3.9	650[b]	c	56	44	$0.01	8.86	1,083	$0.28
1800	5.3	900[b]	c	74	66	$0.01	12.17	1,183	$0.22
1810	7.2	1,100[b]	c	469	178	$0.02	11.92	3,256	$0.45
1820	9.6	1,188	d	288	208	$0.02	11.36	3,993	$0.42
1830	12.9	1,519	43	214	378	$0.03	8.94	9,220	$0.71
1840	17.1	2,167	28	1,465	833	$0.05	8.38	21,676	$1.27
1850	23.2	3,231	160	2,165	1,423	$0.06	7.57	40,991	$1.77
1860	31.4	4,417	184	3,189	1,969	$0.06	8.06	53,270	$1.70
1870	39.8[e]	6,530	438	3,473	3,421	$0.09	12.65	58,971	$1.48
1880	50.2	31,382	1,495	21,458	5,790	$0.12	9.91	127,403	$2.54
1890	62.9	46,804	3,143	26,408	11,547	$0.18	8.82	285,481	$4.54
1900	76.0	52,871	3,447	10,925	11,854	$0.16	8.14	317,553	$4.18
1910	92.0	70,286	3,738[f]	11,456	15,968	$0.17	9.21	378,065	$4.11
1920	105.7	87,234	6,301[f]	14,550	25,117	$0.24	20.04	273,304	$2.59
1930	122.8	87,756	6,825[f]	35,700	40,156	$0.33	16.70	524,336	$4.27
1940	131.7	123,069	9,987[f]	58,400	67,527	$0.51	14.03	1,049,532	$7.97
1950	151.3	142,962	9,233	61,700	91,462	$0.60	24.08	828,248	$5.47
1960	179.3	159,321	2,960	103,000	127,934	$0.71	29.62	941,840	$5.25
1970	203.3	166,406	4,571	200,000	247653[g]	$1.22	38.84	1,390,402	$6.84
1980	226.5	457,523	9,481	300,000	1,078,488	$4.76	82.38	2,854,760	$12.60
1990	248.7	510,000	17,763	500,000[h]	2,492,830	$10.02	130.70	4,159,040	$16.72
2000	281.4	~865,000	NA	NA	4,500,000	$15.99	172.20	5,698,432	$20.25
2010	308.7	~635,000	NA	NA	13,000,000	$42.11	218.06	13,000,000	$42.11

[a] Designated as assistants to the marshals, 1790–1870.

[b] Estimated; records destroyed by fire.

[c] None employed.

[d] Amount expended for clerk hire: $925.

[e] Revised to include adjustments for underenumeration in southern states; unrevised number is 38,558,371.

[f] Includes all employees in years 1910–1940. Most of the 700 to 900 in the permanent force were probably actually engaged in decennial operations at the peak period.

[g] At July 1969 pay rates; covers some additional expenditures for tests of new procedures introduced in 1970.

[h] By 1990 the emergence of electronic forms of publication—for example, electronic tape, microfiche, CD-ROM, and Internet publications—made print pages published a weak indicator of census data distributed.

Sources: Adapted from A. Ross Eckler, *The Bureau of the Census* (New York: Praeger, 1972), 24; Barry Edmonston and Charles Schultze, eds., "Census Cost Increases and their Causes," in *Modernizing the U.S. Census* (Washington, D.C.: U.S. Government Printing Office, 1995), 44–58; U.S. Census Bureau, *Measuring America: The Decennial Censuses From 1790 to 2000* (Washington, D.C.: U.S. Government Printing Office, 2002), appendix A, A-1, http://www.census.gov/prod/www/abs/ma.html; U.S. Government Accountability Office, "2010 Census: Preliminary Lessons Learned Highlight the Need for Fundamental Reforms," GAO-11-496T, April 6, 2011, http://www.gao.gov/products/GAO-11-496T; Lawrence H. Officer, "The Annual Consumer Price Index for the United States, 1774–2010," MeasuringWorth, 2011, http://www.measuringworth.com/uscpi/.

Census 2010 Questionnaire: Short Form

Following are sample pages from the short questionnaire used in the 2000 census and the American Community Survey form from the same year. The editors have reprinted three representative pages from the short form (pages 1, 2, and 5) and ten representative pages from the ACS. The omitted pages merely repeat the same questions for additional persons. Whereas the short form asks respondents only for basic demographic and housing information, the long form requests this basic information as well as other data on housing, education, veteran status, and employment, among other topics. A full archive of ACS questionnaires, including those for Group Quarters and Puerto Rico, is available at http://www.census.gov/acs/www/methodology/questionnaire_archive/

The short form of the 2010 census is available at http://2010.census.gov/2010census/about/interactive-form.php

---

United States Census 2010

U.S. DEPARTMENT OF COMMERCE
Economics and Statistics Administration
U.S. CENSUS BUREAU

This is the official form for all the people at this address.
It is quick and easy, and your answers are protected by law.

Use a blue or black pen.

Start here

The Census must count every person living in the United States on April 1, 2010.

Before you answer Question 1, count the people living in this house, apartment, or mobile home using our guidelines.

- Count all people, including babies, who live and sleep here most of the time.

The Census Bureau also conducts counts in institutions and other places, so:

- Do not count anyone living away either at college or in the Armed Forces.
- Do not count anyone in a nursing home, jail, prison, detention facility, etc., on April 1, 2010.
- Leave these people off your form, even if they will return to live here after they leave college, the nursing home, the military, jail, etc. Otherwise, they may be counted twice.

The Census must also include people without a permanent place to stay, so:

- If someone who has no permanent place to stay is staying here on April 1, 2010, count that person. Otherwise, he or she may be missed in the census.

1. **How many people were living or staying in this house, apartment, or mobile home on April 1, 2010?**

   Number of people = ☐

2. **Were there any <u>additional</u> people staying here April 1, 2010 that you <u>did not include</u> in Question 1?**
   Mark ☒ all that apply.

   ☐ Children, such as newborn babies or foster children
   ☐ Relatives, such as adult children, cousins, or in-laws
   ☐ Nonrelatives, such as roommates or live-in baby sitters
   ☐ People staying here temporarily
   ☐ No additional people

3. **Is this house, apartment, or mobile home —**
   Mark ☒ ONE box.

   ☐ Owned by you or someone in this household with a mortgage or loan? *Include home equity loans.*
   ☐ Owned by you or someone in this household free and clear (without a mortgage or loan)?
   ☐ Rented?
   ☐ Occupied without payment of rent?

4. **What is your telephone number?** *We may call if we don't understand an answer.*
   Area Code + Number
   ☐☐☐ - ☐☐☐ - ☐☐☐☐

OMB No. 0607-0919-C: Approval Expires 12/31/2011.

Form **D-61** (1-15-2009)

5. **Please provide information for each person living here. Start with a person living here who owns or rents this house, apartment, or mobile home. If the owner or renter lives somewhere else, start with any adult living here. This will be Person 1.**
   What is Person 1's name? *Print name below.*

   Last Name
   First Name ____ MI ☐

6. **What is Person 1's sex?** *Mark ☒ ONE box.*
   ☐ Male ☐ Female

7. **What is Person 1's age and what is Person 1's date of birth?**
   Please report babies as age 0 when the child is less than 1 year old. Print numbers in boxes.

   Age on April 1, 2010 ☐☐☐   Month ☐☐ / Day ☐☐   Year of birth ☐☐☐☐

→ **NOTE: Please answer BOTH Question 8 about Hispanic origin and Question 9 about race. For this census, Hispanic origins are not races.**

8. **Is Person 1 of Hispanic, Latino, or Spanish origin?**

   ☐ **No,** not of Hispanic, Latino, or Spanish origin
   ☐ Yes, Mexican, Mexican Am., Chicano
   ☐ Yes, Puerto Rican
   ☐ Yes, Cuban
   ☐ Yes, another Hispanic, Latino, or Spanish origin — *Print origin, for example, Argentinean, Colombian, Dominican, Nicaraguan, Salvadoran, Spaniard, and so on.*

9. **What is Person 1's race?** *Mark ☒ one or more boxes.*

   ☐ White
   ☐ Black, African Am., or Negro
   ☐ American Indian or Alaska Native — *Print name of enrolled or principal tribe.*

   ☐ Asian Indian ☐ Japanese ☐ Native Hawaiian
   ☐ Chinese ☐ Korean ☐ Guamanian or Chamorro
   ☐ Filipino ☐ Vietnamese ☐ Samoan
   ☐ Other Asian — *Print race, for example, Hmong, Laotian, Thai, Pakistani, Cambodian, and so on.* ☐ Other Pacific Islander — *Print race, for example, Fijian, Tongan, and so on.*

   ☐ Some other race — *Print race.*

10. **Does Person 1 sometimes live or stay somewhere else?**
    ☐ No ☐ Yes — *Mark ☒ all that apply.*

    ☐ In college housing ☐ For child custody
    ☐ In the military ☐ In jail or prison
    ☐ At a seasonal or second residence ☐ In a nursing home
     ☐ For another reason

→ **If more people were counted in Question 1, continue with Person 2.**

U S C E N S U S B U R E A U

1. Print name of `Person 2`

Last Name

First Name ___ MI

2. How is this person related to Person 1? *Mark* **X** *ONE box.*

☐ Husband or wife
☐ Biological son or daughter
☐ Adopted son or daughter
☐ Stepson or stepdaughter
☐ Brother or sister
☐ Father or mother
☐ Grandchild

☐ Parent-in-law
☐ Son-in-law or daughter-in-law
☐ Other relative
☐ Roomer or boarder
☐ Housemate or roommate
☐ Unmarried partner
☐ Other nonrelative

3. What is this person's sex? *Mark* **X** *ONE box.*

☐ Male   ☐ Female

4. What is this person's age and what is this person's date of birth?
Please report babies as age 0 when the child is less than 1 year old.
Print numbers in boxes.

Age on April 1, 2010   Month   Day   Year of birth

→ **NOTE:** Please answer BOTH Question 5 about Hispanic origin and Question 6 about race. For this census, Hispanic origins are not races.

5. Is this person of Hispanic, Latino, or Spanish origin?

☐ **No,** not of Hispanic, Latino, or Spanish origin
☐ Yes, Mexican, Mexican Am., Chicano
☐ Yes, Puerto Rican
☐ Yes, Cuban
☐ Yes, another Hispanic, Latino, or Spanish origin — *Print origin, for example, Argentinean, Colombian, Dominican, Nicaraguan, Salvadoran, Spaniard, and so on.* ↘

6. What is this person's race? *Mark* **X** *one or more boxes.*

☐ White
☐ Black, African Am., or Negro
☐ American Indian or Alaska Native — *Print name of enrolled or principal tribe.* ↘

☐ Asian Indian   ☐ Japanese   ☐ Native Hawaiian
☐ Chinese   ☐ Korean   ☐ Guamanian or Chamorro
☐ Filipino   ☐ Vietnamese   ☐ Samoan
☐ Other Asian — *Print race, for example, Hmong, Laotian, Thai, Pakistani, Cambodian, and so on.* ↘   ☐ Other Pacific Islander — *Print race, for example, Fijian, Tongan, and so on.* ↘

☐ Some other race — *Print race.* ↘

7. Does this person sometimes live or stay somewhere else?

☐ No   ☐ Yes — *Mark* **X** *all that apply.*

☐ In college housing   ☐ For child custody
☐ In the military   ☐ In jail or prison
☐ At a seasonal or second residence   ☐ In a nursing home
                              ☐ For another reason

→ **If more people were counted in Question 1 on the front page, continue with Person 3.**

---

1. Print name of `Person 3`

Last Name

First Name ___ MI

2. How is this person related to Person 1? *Mark* **X** *ONE box.*

☐ Husband or wife
☐ Biological son or daughter
☐ Adopted son or daughter
☐ Stepson or stepdaughter
☐ Brother or sister
☐ Father or mother
☐ Grandchild

☐ Parent-in-law
☐ Son-in-law or daughter-in-law
☐ Other relative
☐ Roomer or boarder
☐ Housemate or roommate
☐ Unmarried partner
☐ Other nonrelative

3. What is this person's sex? *Mark* **X** *ONE box.*

☐ Male   ☐ Female

4. What is this person's age and what is this person's date of birth?
Please report babies as age 0 when the child is less than 1 year old.
Print numbers in boxes.

Age on April 1, 2010   Month   Day   Year of birth

→ **NOTE:** Please answer BOTH Question 5 about Hispanic origin and Question 6 about race. For this census, Hispanic origins are not races.

5. Is this person of Hispanic, Latino, or Spanish origin?

☐ **No,** not of Hispanic, Latino, or Spanish origin
☐ Yes, Mexican, Mexican Am., Chicano
☐ Yes, Puerto Rican
☐ Yes, Cuban
☐ Yes, another Hispanic, Latino, or Spanish origin — *Print origin, for example, Argentinean, Colombian, Dominican, Nicaraguan, Salvadoran, Spaniard, and so on.* ↘

6. What is this person's race? *Mark* **X** *one or more boxes.*

☐ White
☐ Black, African Am., or Negro
☐ American Indian or Alaska Native — *Print name of enrolled or principal tribe.* ↘

☐ Asian Indian   ☐ Japanese   ☐ Native Hawaiian
☐ Chinese   ☐ Korean   ☐ Guamanian or Chamorro
☐ Filipino   ☐ Vietnamese   ☐ Samoan
☐ Other Asian — *Print race, for example, Hmong, Laotian, Thai, Pakistani, Cambodian, and so on.* ↘   ☐ Other Pacific Islander — *Print race, for example, Fijian, Tongan, and so on.* ↘

☐ Some other race — *Print race.* ↘

7. Does this person sometimes live or stay somewhere else?

☐ No   ☐ Yes — *Mark* **X** *all that apply.*

☐ In college housing   ☐ For child custody
☐ In the military   ☐ In jail or prison
☐ At a seasonal or second residence   ☐ In a nursing home
                              ☐ For another reason

→ **If more people were counted in Question 1 on the front page, continue with Person 4.**

Use this section to complete information for the rest of the people you counted in Question 1 on the front page. *We may call for additional information about them.*

Person 7

Last Name

First Name

MI

Sex
☐ Male
☐ Female

Age on April 1, 2010

Date of Birth
Month   Day   Year

Related to Person 1?
☐ Yes
☐ No

Person 8

Last Name

First Name

MI

Sex
☐ Male
☐ Female

Age on April 1, 2010

Date of Birth
Month   Day   Year

Related to Person 1?
☐ Yes
☐ No

Person 9

Last Name

First Name

MI

Sex
☐ Male
☐ Female

Age on April 1, 2010

Date of Birth
Month   Day   Year

Related to Person 1?
☐ Yes
☐ No

Person 10

Last Name

First Name

MI

Sex
☐ Male
☐ Female

Age on April 1, 2010

Date of Birth
Month   Day   Year

Related to Person 1?
☐ Yes
☐ No

Person 11

Last Name

First Name

MI

Sex
☐ Male
☐ Female

Age on April 1, 2010

Date of Birth
Month   Day   Year

Related to Person 1?
☐ Yes
☐ No

Person 12

Last Name

First Name

MI

Sex
☐ Male
☐ Female

Age on April 1, 2010

Date of Birth
Month   Day   Year

Related to Person 1?
☐ Yes
☐ No

Thank you for completing your official 2010 Census form.

FOR OFFICIAL USE ONLY

JIC1   JIC2

American Community Survey (ACS) 2010 Questionnaire Form

13190012

U.S. DEPARTMENT OF COMMERCE
Economics and Statistics Administration
U.S. CENSUS BUREAU

THE **American Community Survey**

This booklet shows the content of the American Community Survey questionnaire.

Please complete this form and return it as soon as possible after receiving it in the mail.

This form asks for information about the people who are living or staying at the address on the mailing label and about the house, apartment, or mobile home located at the address on the mailing label.

 If you need help or have questions about completing this form, please call **1-800-354-7271.** The telephone call is free.

Telephone Device for the Deaf (TDD):
Call 1–800–582–8330. The telephone call is free.

¿NECESITA AYUDA? Si usted habla español y necesita ayuda para completar su cuestionario, llame sin cargo alguno al **1-877-833-5625.** Usted también puede pedir un cuestionario en español o completar su entrevista por teléfono con un entrevistador que habla español.

For more information about the American Community Survey, visit our web site at: http://www.census.gov/acs/www/

Start Here

➡ **Please print today's date.**
Month Day Year

➡ **Please print the name and telephone number of the person who is filling out this form.** We may contact you if there is a question.
Last Name

First Name   MI

Area Code + Number

➡ **How many people are living or staying at this address?**
• **INCLUDE** everyone who is living or staying here for more than 2 months.
• **INCLUDE** yourself if you are living here for more than 2 months.
• **INCLUDE** anyone else staying here who does not have another place to stay, even if they are here for 2 months or less.
• **DO NOT INCLUDE** anyone who is living somewhere else for more than 2 months, such as a college student living away or someone in the Armed Forces on deployment.
Number of people

➡ **Fill out pages 2, 3, and 4 for everyone, including yourself, who is living or staying at this address for more than 2 months. Then complete the rest of the form.**

U S C E N S U S B U R E A U

FORM **ACS-1(INFO)(2010)KFI**
(05-14-2009)

OMB No. 0607-0810

INFORMATIONAL COPY

13190020

Person 1

(Person 1 is the person living or staying here in whose name this house or apartment is owned, being bought, or rented. If there is no such person, start with the name of any adult living or staying here.)

1 What is Person 1's name?
Last Name *(Please print)*   First Name   MI

2 How is this person related to Person 1?
[X] Person 1

3 What is Person 1's sex? *Mark (X) ONE box.*
[ ] Male   [ ] Female

4 What is Person 1's age and what is Person 1's date of birth?
Please report babies as age 0 when the child is less than 1 year old.
Print numbers in boxes.
Age (in years)   Month   Day   Year of birth

→ **NOTE: Please answer BOTH Question 5 about Hispanic origin and Question 6 about race. For this survey, Hispanic origins are not races.**

5 Is Person 1 of Hispanic, Latino, or Spanish origin?
[ ] **No,** not of Hispanic, Latino, or Spanish origin
[ ] Yes, Mexican, Mexican Am., Chicano
[ ] Yes, Puerto Rican
[ ] Yes, Cuban
[ ] Yes, another Hispanic, Latino, or Spanish origin – *Print origin, for example, Argentinean, Colombian, Dominican, Nicaraguan, Salvadoran, Spaniard, and so on.* ↗

6 What is Person 1's race? *Mark (X) one or more boxes.*
[ ] White
[ ] Black, African Am., or Negro
[ ] American Indian or Alaska Native — *Print name of enrolled or principal tribe.* ↗

[ ] Asian Indian   [ ] Japanese   [ ] Native Hawaiian
[ ] Chinese   [ ] Korean   [ ] Guamanian or Chamorro
[ ] Filipino   [ ] Vietnamese   [ ] Samoan
[ ] Other Asian – *Print race, for example, Hmong, Laotian, Thai, Pakistani, Cambodian, and so on.* ↗   [ ] Other Pacific Islander – *Print race, for example, Fijian, Tongan, and so on.* ↗

[ ] Some other race – *Print race.* ↗

Person 2

1 What is Person 2's name?
Last Name *(Please print)*   First Name   MI

2 How is this person related to Person 1? *Mark (X) ONE box.*
[ ] Husband or wife   [ ] Son-in-law or daughter-in-law
[ ] Biological son or daughter   [ ] Other relative
[ ] Adopted son or daughter   [ ] Roomer or boarder
[ ] Stepson or stepdaughter   [ ] Housemate or roommate
[ ] Brother or sister   [ ] Unmarried partner
[ ] Father or mother   [ ] Foster child
[ ] Grandchild   [ ] Other nonrelative
[ ] Parent-in-law

3 What is Person 2's sex? *Mark (X) ONE box.*
[ ] Male   [ ] Female

4 What is Person 2's age and what is Person 2's date of birth?
Please report babies as age 0 when the child is less than 1 year old.
Print numbers in boxes.
Age (in years)   Month   Day   Year of birth

→ **NOTE: Please answer BOTH Question 5 about Hispanic origin and Question 6 about race. For this survey, Hispanic origins are not races.**

5 Is Person 2 of Hispanic, Latino, or Spanish origin?
[ ] **No,** not of Hispanic, Latino, or Spanish origin
[ ] Yes, Mexican, Mexican Am., Chicano
[ ] Yes, Puerto Rican
[ ] Yes, Cuban
[ ] Yes, another Hispanic, Latino, or Spanish origin – *Print origin, for example, Argentinean, Colombian, Dominican, Nicaraguan, Salvadoran, Spaniard, and so on.* ↗

6 What is Person 2's race? *Mark (X) one or more boxes.*
[ ] White
[ ] Black, African Am., or Negro
[ ] American Indian or Alaska Native — *Print name of enrolled or principal tribe.* ↗

[ ] Asian Indian   [ ] Japanese   [ ] Native Hawaiian
[ ] Chinese   [ ] Korean   [ ] Guamanian or Chamorro
[ ] Filipino   [ ] Vietnamese   [ ] Samoan
[ ] Other Asian – *Print race, for example, Hmong, Laotian, Thai, Pakistani, Cambodian, and so on.* ↗   [ ] Other Pacific Islander – *Print race, for example, Fijian, Tongan, and so on.* ↗

[ ] Some other race – *Print race.* ↗

13190046

Person 5

1 **What is Person 5's name?**
Last Name *(Please print)*   First Name   MI

2 **How is this person related to Person 1?** *Mark (X) ONE box.*

☐ Husband or wife   ☐ Son-in-law or daughter-in-law
☐ Biological son or daughter   ☐ Other relative
☐ Adopted son or daughter   ☐ Roomer or boarder
☐ Stepson or stepdaughter   ☐ Housemate or roommate
☐ Brother or sister   ☐ Unmarried partner
☐ Father or mother   ☐ Foster child
☐ Grandchild   ☐ Other nonrelative
☐ Parent-in-law

3 **What is Person 5's sex?** *Mark (X) ONE box.*

☐ Male   ☐ Female

4 **What is Person 5's age and what is Person 5's date of birth?**
Please report babies as age 0 when the child is less than 1 year old.
Print numbers in boxes.

Age (in years)   Month   Day   Year of birth

→ **NOTE: Please answer BOTH Question 5 about Hispanic origin and
Question 6 about race. For this survey, Hispanic origins are not races.**

5 **Is Person 5 of Hispanic, Latino, or Spanish origin?**

☐ **No,** not of Hispanic, Latino, or Spanish origin
☐ Yes, Mexican, Mexican Am., Chicano
☐ Yes, Puerto Rican
☐ Yes, Cuban
☐ Yes, another Hispanic, Latino, or Spanish origin – *Print origin, for example,
Argentinean, Colombian, Dominican, Nicaraguan, Salvadoran, Spaniard,
and so on.* ↗

6 **What is Person 5's race?** *Mark (X) one or more boxes.*

☐ White
☐ Black, African Am., or Negro
☐ American Indian or Alaska Native — *Print name of enrolled or principal tribe.* ↗

☐ Asian Indian   ☐ Japanese   ☐ Native Hawaiian
☐ Chinese   ☐ Korean   ☐ Guamanian or Chamorro
☐ Filipino   ☐ Vietnamese   ☐ Samoan
☐ Other Asian – *Print race,*   ☐ Other Pacific Islander –
for example, Hmong,   *Print race, for example,*
Laotian, Thai, Pakistani,   *Fijian, Tongan, and*
Cambodian, and so on. ↗   *so on.* ↗

☐ Some other race – *Print race.* ↗

→ **If there are more than five people living or staying here,
print their names in the spaces for Person 6 through Person 12.**
We may call you for more information about them. ↗

Person 6
Last Name *(Please print)*   First Name   MI

Sex ☐ Male   ☐ Female   **Age (in years)**

Person 7
Last Name *(Please print)*   First Name   MI

Sex ☐ Male   ☐ Female   **Age (in years)**

Person 8
Last Name *(Please print)*   First Name   MI

Sex ☐ Male   ☐ Female   **Age (in years)**

Person 9
Last Name *(Please print)*   First Name   MI

Sex ☐ Male   ☐ Female   **Age (in years)**

Person 10
Last Name *(Please print)*   First Name   MI

Sex ☐ Male   ☐ Female   **Age (in years)**

Person 11
Last Name *(Please print)*   First Name   MI

Sex ☐ Male   ☐ Female   **Age (in years)**

Person 12
Last Name *(Please print)*   First Name   MI

Sex ☐ Male   ☐ Female   **Age (in years)**

4

13190053

Housing

→ **Please answer the following questions about the house, apartment, or mobile home at the address on the mailing label.**

1 Which best describes this building?
Include all apartments, flats, etc., even if vacant.

- ☐ A mobile home
- ☐ A one-family house detached from any other house
- ☐ A one-family house attached to one or more houses
- ☐ A building with 2 apartments
- ☐ A building with 3 or 4 apartments
- ☐ A building with 5 to 9 apartments
- ☐ A building with 10 to 19 apartments
- ☐ A building with 20 to 49 apartments
- ☐ A building with 50 or more apartments
- ☐ Boat, RV, van, etc.

2 About when was this building first built?

- ☐ 2000 or later – *Specify year*

  [____]

- ☐ 1990 to 1999
- ☐ 1980 to 1989
- ☐ 1970 to 1979
- ☐ 1960 to 1969
- ☐ 1950 to 1959
- ☐ 1940 to 1949
- ☐ 1939 or earlier

3 When did PERSON 1 (listed on page 2) move into this house, apartment, or mobile home?

Month   Year

[____] [_____]

A *Answer questions 4 – 6 if this is a HOUSE OR A MOBILE HOME; otherwise, SKIP to question 7a.*

4 How many acres is this house or mobile home on?

- ☐ Less than 1 acre → *SKIP to question 6*
- ☐ 1 to 9.9 acres
- ☐ 10 or more acres

5 IN THE PAST 12 MONTHS, what were the actual sales of all agricultural products from this property?

- ☐ None
- ☐ $1 to $999
- ☐ $1,000 to $2,499
- ☐ $2,500 to $4,999
- ☐ $5,000 to $9,999
- ☐ $10,000 or more

6 Is there a business (such as a store or barber shop) or a medical office on this property?

- ☑ Yes
- ☐ No

7 a. How many separate rooms are in this house, apartment, or mobile home?
Rooms must be separated by built-in archways or walls that extend out at least 6 inches and go from floor to ceiling.

- *INCLUDE bedrooms, kitchens, etc.*
- *EXCLUDE bathrooms, porches, balconies, foyers, halls, or unfinished basements.*

Number of rooms

[____]

b. How many of these rooms are bedrooms?
Count as bedrooms those rooms you would list if this house, apartment, or mobile home were for sale or rent. If this is an efficiency/studio apartment, print "0".

Number of bedrooms

[____]

---

8 Does this house, apartment, or mobile home have –

	Yes	No
a. hot and cold running water?	☐	☐
b. a flush toilet?	☐	☐
c. a bathtub or shower?	☐	☐
d. a sink with a faucet?	☐	☐
e. a stove or range?	☐	☐
f. a refrigerator?	☐	☐
g. telephone service from which you can both make and receive calls? *Include cell phones.*	☐	☐

9 How many automobiles, vans, and trucks of one-ton capacity or less are kept at home for use by members of this household?

- ☐ None
- ☐ 1
- ☐ 2
- ☐ 3
- ☐ 4
- ☐ 5
- ☐ 6 or more

10 Which FUEL is used MOST for heating this house, apartment, or mobile home?

- ☐ Gas: from underground pipes serving the neighborhood
- ☐ Gas: bottled, tank, or LP
- ☐ Electricity
- ☐ Fuel oil, kerosene, etc.
- ☐ Coal or coke
- ☐ Wood
- ☐ Solar energy
- ☐ Other fuel
- ☐ No fuel used

13190061

Housing (continued)

11 a. LAST MONTH, what was the cost of electricity for this house, apartment, or mobile home?

Last month's cost – *Dollars*

$ ___ .00

OR
- [ ] Included in rent or condominium fee
- [ ] No charge or electricity not used

b. LAST MONTH, what was the cost of gas for this house, apartment, or mobile home?

Last month's cost – *Dollars*

$ ___ .00

OR
- [ ] Included in rent or condominium fee
- [ ] Included in electricity payment entered above
- [ ] No charge or gas not used

c. IN THE PAST 12 MONTHS, what was the cost of water and sewer for this house, apartment, or mobile home? *If you have lived here less than 12 months, estimate the cost.*

Past 12 months' cost – *Dollars*

$ ___ .00

OR
- [ ] Included in rent or condominium fee
- [ ] No charge

d. IN THE PAST 12 MONTHS, what was the cost of oil, coal, kerosene, wood, etc., for this house, apartment, or mobile home? *If you have lived here less than 12 months, estimate the cost.*

Past 12 months' cost – *Dollars*

$ ___ .00

OR
- [ ] Included in rent or condominium fee
- [ ] No charge or these fuels not used

12 IN THE PAST 12 MONTHS, did anyone in this household receive Food Stamps or a Food Stamp benefit card? *Include government benefits from the Supplemental Nutrition Assistance Program (SNAP). Do NOT include WIC or the National School Lunch Program.*
- [ ] Yes
- [ ] No

13 Is this house, apartment, or mobile home part of a condominium?
- [ ] Yes → **What is the monthly condominium fee?** *For renters, answer only if you pay the condominium fee in addition to your rent; otherwise, mark the "None" box.*

  Monthly amount – *Dollars*

  $ ___ .00

  OR
  - [ ] None
- [ ] No

14 Is this house, apartment, or mobile home – *Mark (X) ONE box.*
- [ ] Owned by you or someone in this household with a mortgage or loan? *Include home equity loans.*
- [ ] Owned by you or someone in this household free and clear (without a mortgage or loan)?
- [ ] Rented?
- [ ] Occupied without payment of rent? → *SKIP to* **C**

B *Answer questions 15a and b if this house, apartment, or mobile home is RENTED. Otherwise, SKIP to question 16.*

15 a. What is the monthly rent for this house, apartment, or mobile home?

Monthly amount – *Dollars*

$ ___ .00

b. Does the monthly rent include any meals?
- [ ] Yes
- [ ] No

C *Answer questions 16 – 20 if you or someone else in this household OWNS or IS BUYING this house, apartment, or mobile home. Otherwise, SKIP to* **E** *on the next page.*

16 About how much do you think this house and lot, apartment, or mobile home (and lot, if owned) would sell for if it were for sale?

Amount – *Dollars*

$ ___ .00

17 What are the annual real estate taxes on THIS property?

Annual amount – *Dollars*

$ ___ .00

OR
- [ ] None

18 What is the annual payment for fire, hazard, and flood insurance on THIS property?

Annual amount – *Dollars*

$ ___ .00

OR
- [ ] None

6

13190079

Housing (continued)

19 a. Do you or any member of this household have a mortgage, deed of trust, contract to purchase, or similar debt on THIS property?

☐ Yes, mortgage, deed of trust, or similar debt

☐ Yes, contract to purchase

☐ No → *SKIP to question 20a*

b. How much is the regular monthly mortgage payment on THIS property? *Include payment only on FIRST mortgage or contract to purchase.*

Monthly amount – *Dollars*

$ _____ .00

OR

☐ No regular payment required → *SKIP to question 20a*

c. Does the regular monthly mortgage payment include payments for real estate taxes on THIS property?

☐ Yes, taxes included in mortgage payment

☐ No, taxes paid separately or taxes not required

d. Does the regular monthly mortgage payment include payments for fire, hazard, or flood insurance on THIS property?

☐ Yes, insurance included in mortgage payment

☐ No, insurance paid separately or no insurance

20 a. Do you or any member of this household have a second mortgage or a home equity loan on THIS property?

☐ Yes, home equity loan

☐ Yes, second mortgage

☐ Yes, second mortgage and home equity loan

☐ No → *SKIP to* **D**

b. How much is the regular monthly payment on all second or junior mortgages and all home equity loans on THIS property?

Monthly amount – *Dollars*

$ _____ .00

OR

☐ No regular payment required

D *Answer question 21 if this is a MOBILE HOME. Otherwise, SKIP to* **E** *.*

21 What are the total annual costs for personal property taxes, site rent, registration fees, and license fees on THIS mobile home and its site? *Exclude real estate taxes.*

Annual costs – *Dollars*

$ _____ .00

E *Answer questions about PERSON 1 on the next page if you listed at least one person on page 2. Otherwise, SKIP to page 28 for the mailing instructions.*

13190087

Person 1

→ **Please copy the name of Person 1 from page 2, then continue answering questions below.**

Last Name

First Name   MI

7 Where was this person born?

☐ In the United States – *Print name of state.*

☐ Outside the United States – *Print name of foreign country, or Puerto Rico, Guam, etc.*

8 Is this person a citizen of the United States?

☐ Yes, born in the United States → *SKIP to 10a*

☐ Yes, born in Puerto Rico, Guam, the U.S. Virgin Islands, or Northern Marianas

☐ Yes, born abroad of U.S. citizen parent or parents

☐ Yes, U.S. citizen by naturalization – *Print year of naturalization* ⌐

☐ No, not a U.S. citizen

9 When did this person come to live in the United States? *Print numbers in boxes.*

Year

10 a. At any time IN THE LAST 3 MONTHS, has this person attended school or college? *Include only nursery or preschool, kindergarten, elementary school, home school, and schooling which leads to a high school diploma or a college degree.*

☐ No, has not attended in the last 3 months → *SKIP to question 11*

☐ Yes, public school, public college

☐ Yes, private school, private college, home school

b. What grade or level was this person attending? *Mark (X) ONE box.*

☐ Nursery school, preschool

☐ Kindergarten

☐ Grade 1 through 12 – *Specify grade 1 – 12* ⌐

☐ College undergraduate years (freshman to senior)

☐ Graduate or professional school beyond a bachelor's degree *(for example: MA or PhD program, or medical or law school)*

11 What is the highest degree or level of school this person has COMPLETED? *Mark (X) ONE box. If currently enrolled, mark the previous grade or highest degree received.*

NO SCHOOLING COMPLETED

☐ No schooling completed

NURSERY OR PRESCHOOL THROUGH GRADE 12

☐ Nursery school

☐ Kindergarten

☐ Grade 1 through 11 – *Specify grade 1 – 11* ⌐

☐ 12th grade – **NO DIPLOMA**

HIGH SCHOOL GRADUATE

☐ Regular high school diploma

☐ GED or alternative credential

COLLEGE OR SOME COLLEGE

☐ Some college credit, but less than 1 year of college credit

☐ 1 or more years of college credit, no degree

☐ Associate's degree *(for example: AA, AS)*

☐ Bachelor's degree *(for example: BA, BS)*

AFTER BACHELOR'S DEGREE

☐ Master's degree *(for example: MA, MS, MEng, MEd, MSW, MBA)*

☐ Professional degree beyond a bachelor's degree *(for example: MD, DDS, DVM, LLB, JD)*

☐ Doctorate degree *(for example: PhD, EdD)*

F *Answer question 12 if this person has a bachelor's degree or higher. Otherwise, SKIP to question 13.*

12 This question focuses on this person's BACHELOR'S DEGREE. Please print below the specific major(s) of any BACHELOR'S DEGREES this person has received. *(For example: chemical engineering, elementary teacher education, organizational psychology)*

13 What is this person's ancestry or ethnic origin?

(For example: Italian, Jamaican, African Am., Cambodian, Cape Verdean, Norwegian, Dominican, French Canadian, Haitian, Korean, Lebanese, Polish, Nigerian, Mexican, Taiwanese, Ukrainian, and so on.)

14 a. Does this person speak a language other than English at home?

☐ Yes

☐ No → *SKIP to question 15a*

b. What is this language?

For example: Korean, Italian, Spanish, Vietnamese

c. How well does this person speak English?

☐ Very well

☐ Well

☐ Not well

☐ Not at all

15 a. Did this person live in this house or apartment 1 year ago?

☐ Person is under 1 year old → *SKIP to question 16*

☐ Yes, this house → *SKIP to question 16*

☐ No, outside the United States and Puerto Rico – *Print name of foreign country, or U.S. Virgin Islands, Guam, etc., below; then SKIP to question 16*

☐ No, different house in the United States or Puerto Rico

b. Where did this person live 1 year ago?

Address (Number and street name)

Name of city, town, or post office

Name of U.S. county or municipio in Puerto Rico

Name of U.S. state or Puerto Rico   ZIP Code

8

13190095

Person 1 (continued)

16 Is this person CURRENTLY covered by any of the following types of health insurance or health coverage plans? *Mark "Yes" or "No" for EACH type of coverage in items a – h.*

	Yes	No
a. Insurance through a current or former employer or union (of this person or another family member)	☐	☐
b. Insurance purchased directly from an insurance company (by this person or another family member)	☐	☐
c. Medicare, for people 65 and older, or people with certain disabilities	☐	☐
d. Medicaid, Medical Assistance, or any kind of government-assistance plan for those with low incomes or a disability	☐	☐
e. TRICARE or other military health care	☐	☐
f. VA (including those who have ever used or enrolled for VA health care)	☐	☐
g. Indian Health Service	☐	☐
h. Any other type of health insurance or health coverage plan – *Specify* ⤵	☐	☐

[   ]

17

a. Is this person deaf or does he/she have serious difficulty hearing?

☐ Yes
☐ No

b. Is this person blind or does he/she have serious difficulty seeing even when wearing glasses?

☐ Yes
☐ No

G *Answer question 18a – c if this person is 5 years old or over. Otherwise, SKIP to the questions for Person 2 on page 12.*

18

a. Because of a physical, mental, or emotional condition, does this person have serious difficulty concentrating, remembering, or making decisions?

☐ Yes
☐ No

b. Does this person have serious difficulty walking or climbing stairs?

☐ Yes
☐ No

c. Does this person have difficulty dressing or bathing?

☐ Yes
☐ No

H *Answer question 19 if this person is 15 years old or over. Otherwise, SKIP to the questions for Person 2 on page 12.*

19 Because of a physical, mental, or emotional condition, does this person have difficulty doing errands alone such as visiting a doctor's office or shopping?

☐ Yes
☐ No

20 What is this person's marital status?

☐ Now married
☐ Widowed
☐ Divorced
☐ Separated
☐ Never married → *SKIP to* **I**

21 In the PAST 12 MONTHS did this person get –

	Yes	No
a. Married?	☐	☐
b. Widowed?	☐	☐
c. Divorced?	☐	☐

22 How many times has this person been married?

☐ Once
☐ Two times
☐ Three or more times

23 In what year did this person last get married?

Year [   ]

I *Answer question 24 if this person is female and 15 – 50 years old. Otherwise, SKIP to question 25a.*

24 Has this person given birth to any children in the past 12 months?

☐ Yes
☐ No

25

a. Does this person have any of his/her own grandchildren under the age of 18 living in this house or apartment?

☐ Yes
☐ No → *SKIP to question 26*

b. Is this grandparent currently responsible for most of the basic needs of any grandchild(ren) under the age of 18 who live(s) in this house or apartment?

☐ Yes
☐ No → *SKIP to question 26*

---

c. How long has this grandparent been responsible for the(se) grandchild(ren)? *If the grandparent is financially responsible for more than one grandchild, answer the question for the grandchild for whom the grandparent has been responsible for the longest period of time.*

☐ Less than 6 months
☐ 6 to 11 months
☐ 1 or 2 years
☐ 3 or 4 years
☐ 5 or more years

26 Has this person ever served on active duty in the U.S. Armed Forces, military Reserves, or National Guard? *Active duty does not include training for the Reserves or National Guard, but DOES include activation, for example, for the Persian Gulf War.*

☐ Yes, now on active duty
☐ Yes, on active duty during the last 12 months, but not now
☐ Yes, on active duty in the past, but not during the last 12 months
☐ No, training for Reserves or National Guard only → *SKIP to question 28a*
☐ No, never served in the military → *SKIP to question 29a*

27 When did this person serve on active duty in the U.S. Armed Forces? *Mark (X) a box for EACH period in which this person served, even if just for part of the period.*

☐ September 2001 or later
☐ August 1990 to August 2001 (including Persian Gulf War)
☐ September 1980 to July 1990
☐ May 1975 to August 1980
☐ Vietnam era (August 1964 to April 1975)
☐ March 1961 to July 1964
☐ February 1955 to February 1961
☐ Korean War (July 1950 to January 1955)
☐ January 1947 to June 1950
☐ World War II (December 1941 to December 1946)
☐ November 1941 or earlier

28

a. Does this person have a VA service-connected disability rating?

☐ Yes (such as 0%, 10%, 20%, ... , 100%)
☐ No → *SKIP to question 29a*

b. What is this person's service-connected disability rating?

☐ 0 percent
☐ 10 or 20 percent
☐ 30 or 40 percent
☐ 50 or 60 percent
☐ 70 percent or higher

9

13190103

Person 1 (continued)

29 **a. LAST WEEK, did this person work for pay at a job (or business)?**

- ☐ Yes → *SKIP to question 30*
- ☐ No – Did not work (or retired)

b. LAST WEEK, did this person do ANY work for pay, even for as little as one hour?

- ☐ Yes
- ☐ No → *SKIP to question 35a*

30 **At what location did this person work LAST WEEK?** *If this person worked at more than one location, print where he or she worked most last week.*

a. Address (Number and street name)

[   ]

If the exact address is not known, give a description of the location such as the building name or the nearest street or intersection.

b. Name of city, town, or post office

[   ]

c. Is the work location inside the limits of that city or town?

- ☐ Yes
- ☐ No, outside the city/town limits

d. Name of county

[   ]

e. Name of U.S. state or foreign country

[   ]

f. ZIP Code

[   ]

31 **How did this person usually get to work LAST WEEK?** *If this person usually used more than one method of transportation during the trip, mark (X) the box of the one used for most of the distance.*

☐ Car, truck, or van	☐ Motorcycle
☐ Bus or trolley bus	☐ Bicycle
☐ Streetcar or trolley car	☐ Walked
☐ Subway or elevated	☐ Worked at home → *SKIP to question 39a*
☐ Railroad	
☐ Ferryboat	☐ Other method
☐ Taxicab	

J *Answer question 32 if you marked "Car, truck, or van" in question 31. Otherwise, SKIP to question 33.*

32 **How many people, including this person, usually rode to work in the car, truck, or van LAST WEEK?**

Person(s)

[   ]

33 **What time did this person usually leave home to go to work LAST WEEK?**

Hour   Minute

[   ] : [   ]   ☐ a.m.
                   ☐ p.m.

34 **How many minutes did it usually take this person to get from home to work LAST WEEK?**

Minutes

[   ]

K *Answer questions 35 – 38 if this person did NOT work last week. Otherwise, SKIP to question 39a.*

35 **a. LAST WEEK, was this person on layoff from a job?**

- ☑ Yes → *SKIP to question 35c*
- ☐ No

b. LAST WEEK, was this person TEMPORARILY absent from a job or business?

- ☐ Yes, on vacation, temporary illness, maternity leave, other family/personal reasons, bad weather, etc. → *SKIP to question 38*
- ☐ No → *SKIP to question 36*

c. Has this person been informed that he or she will be recalled to work within the next 6 months OR been given a date to return to work?

- ☐ Yes → *SKIP to question 37*
- ☐ No

36 **During the LAST 4 WEEKS, has this person been ACTIVELY looking for work?**

- ☐ Yes
- ☐ No → *SKIP to question 38*

37 **LAST WEEK, could this person have started a job if offered one, or returned to work if recalled?**

- ☐ Yes, could have gone to work
- ☐ No, because of own temporary illness
- ☐ No, because of all other reasons (in school, etc.)

38 **When did this person last work, even for a few days?**

- ☐ Within the past 12 months
- ☑ 1 to 5 years ago → *SKIP to* **L**
- ☐ Over 5 years ago or never worked → *SKIP to question 47*

39 **a. During the PAST 12 MONTHS (52 weeks), did this person work 50 or more weeks? Count paid time off as work.**

- ☐ Yes → *SKIP to question 40*
- ☐ No

b. How many weeks DID this person work, even for a few hours, including paid vacation, paid sick leave, and military service?

- ☐ 50 to 52 weeks
- ☐ 48 to 49 weeks
- ☐ 40 to 47 weeks
- ☐ 27 to 39 weeks
- ☐ 14 to 26 weeks
- ☐ 13 weeks or less

40 **During the PAST 12 MONTHS, in the WEEKS WORKED, how many hours did this person usually work each WEEK?**

Usual hours worked each WEEK

[   ]

10

13190111

Person 1 (continued)

L Answer questions 41 – 46 if this person worked in the past 5 years. Otherwise, SKIP to question 47.

41 – 46 CURRENT OR MOST RECENT JOB ACTIVITY. *Describe clearly this person's chief job activity or business last week. If this person had more than one job, describe the one at which this person worked the most hours. If this person had no job or business last week, give information for his/her last job or business.*

41 Was this person –
Mark (X) ONE box.

☐ an employee of a PRIVATE FOR-PROFIT company or business, or of an individual, for wages, salary, or commissions?

☐ an employee of a PRIVATE NOT-FOR-PROFIT, tax-exempt, or charitable organization?

☐ a local GOVERNMENT employee (city, county, etc.)?

☐ a state GOVERNMENT employee?

☐ a Federal GOVERNMENT employee?

☐ SELF-EMPLOYED in own NOT INCORPORATED business, professional practice, or farm?

☐ SELF-EMPLOYED in own INCORPORATED business, professional practice, or farm?

☐ working WITHOUT PAY in family business or farm?

42 For whom did this person work?

If now on active duty in the Armed Forces, mark (X) this box → ☐ and print the branch of the Armed Forces.

Name of company, business, or other employer

[_____]

43 What kind of business or industry was this?
Describe the activity at the location where employed. (For example: hospital, newspaper publishing, mail order house, auto engine manufacturing, bank)

[_____]

44 Is this mainly – *Mark (X) ONE box.*

☐ manufacturing?
☐ wholesale trade?
☐ retail trade?
☐ other (agriculture, construction, service, government, etc.)?

45 What kind of work was this person doing?
(For example: registered nurse, personnel manager, supervisor of order department, secretary, accountant)

[_____]

46 What were this person's most important activities or duties? *(For example: patient care, directing hiring policies, supervising order clerks, typing and filing, reconciling financial records)*

[_____]

47 INCOME IN THE PAST 12 MONTHS

Mark (X) the "Yes" box for each type of income this person received, and give your best estimate of the TOTAL AMOUNT during the PAST 12 MONTHS. (NOTE: The "past 12 months" is the period from today's date one year ago up through today.)

Mark (X) the "No" box to show types of income NOT received.

If net income was a loss, mark the "Loss" box to the right of the dollar amount.

For income received jointly, report the appropriate share for each person – or, if that's not possible, report the whole amount for only one person and mark the "No" box for the other person.

a. Wages, salary, commissions, bonuses, or tips from all jobs. *Report amount before deductions for taxes, bonds, dues, or other items.*

☐ Yes → $ [_____].00
☐ No   TOTAL AMOUNT for past 12 months

b. Self-employment income from own nonfarm businesses or farm businesses, including proprietorships and partnerships. *Report NET income after business expenses.*

☐ Yes → $ [_____].00 ☐ Loss
☐ No   TOTAL AMOUNT for past 12 months

c. Interest, dividends, net rental income, royalty income, or income from estates and trusts. *Report even small amounts credited to an account.*

☐ Yes → $ [_____].00 ☐ Loss
☐ No   TOTAL AMOUNT for past 12 months

d. Social Security or Railroad Retirement.

☐ Yes → $ [_____].00
☐ No   TOTAL AMOUNT for past 12 months

e. Supplemental Security Income (SSI).

☐ Yes → $ [_____].00
☐ No   TOTAL AMOUNT for past 12 months

f. Any public assistance or welfare payments from the state or local welfare office.

☐ Yes → $ [_____].00
☐ No   TOTAL AMOUNT for past 12 months

g. Retirement, survivor, or disability pensions. *Do NOT include Social Security.*

☐ Yes → $ [_____].00
☐ No   TOTAL AMOUNT for past 12 months

h. Any other sources of income received regularly such as Veterans' (VA) payments, unemployment compensation, child support or alimony. *Do NOT include lump sum payments such as money from an inheritance or the sale of a home.*

☐ Yes → $ [_____].00
☐ No   TOTAL AMOUNT for past 12 months

48 What was this person's total income during the PAST 12 MONTHS? *Add entries in questions 47a to 47h; subtract any losses. If net income was a loss, enter the amount and mark (X) the "Loss" box next to the dollar amount.*

☐ None OR $ [_____].00 ☐ Loss
    TOTAL AMOUNT for past 12 months

→ **Continue with the questions for Person 2 on the next page. If only 1 person is listed on page 2, SKIP to page 28 for mailing instructions.**

Standards for the Classification of Federal Data on Race and Ethnicity

The Office of Management and Budget (OMB) sets standards for statistical classifications. In 1977 OMB issued "Race and Ethnic Standards for Federal Statistics and Administrative Reporting," which specified four racial categories: "White," "Black," "American Indian and Alaskan Native," and "Asian and Pacific Islander." It also specified two ethnic categories: "Hispanic Origin" and "Not of Hispanic Origin." According to the standards, people of Hispanic origin could be of any race.

After the 1990 census, the standards were criticized for no longer reflecting the increasing racial and ethnic diversity of the country. After soliciting extensive public comment, OMB in 1997 issued revised standards (popularly known as Statistical Directive 15). The text of the revised standards, which defined the questions for the 2000 census, appears below.

Standards for Maintaining, Collecting, and Presenting Federal Data on Race and Ethnicity

This classification provides a minimum standard for maintaining, collecting, and presenting data on race and ethnicity for all Federal reporting purposes. The categories in this classification are social-political constructs and should not be interpreted as being scientific or anthropological in nature. They are not to be used as determinants of eligibility for participation in any Federal program. The standards have been developed to provide a common language for uniformity and comparability in the collection and use of data on race and ethnicity by Federal agencies.

The standards have five categories for data on race: American Indian or Alaska Native, Asian, Black or African American, Native Hawaiian or Other Pacific Islander, and White. There are two categories for data on ethnicity: "Hispanic or Latino," and "Not Hispanic or Latino."

1. Categories and Definitions

The minimum categories for data on race and ethnicity for Federal statistics, program administrative reporting, and civil rights compliance reporting are defined as follows:

—*American Indian or Alaska Native.* A person having origins in any of the original peoples of North and South America (including Central America), and who maintains tribal affiliation or community attachment.

—*Asian.* A person having origins in any of the original peoples of the Far East, Southeast Asia, or the Indian subcontinent, including, for example, Cambodia, China, India, Japan, Korea, Malaysia, Pakistan, the Philippine Islands, Thailand, and Vietnam.

—*Black or African American.* A person having origins in any of the black racial groups of Africa. Terms such as "Haitian" or "Negro" can be used in addition to "Black or African American."

—*Hispanic or Latino.* A person of Cuban, Mexican, Puerto Rican, South or Central American, or other Spanish culture or origin, regardless of race. The term "Spanish origin" can be used in addition to "Hispanic or Latino."

—*Native Hawaiian or Other Pacific Islander.* A person having origins in any of the original peoples of Hawaii, Guam, Samoa, or other Pacific Islands.

—*White.* A person having origins in any of the original peoples of Europe, the Middle East, or North Africa.

Respondents shall be offered the option of selecting one or more racial designations. Recommended forms for the instruction accompanying the multiple response question are "Mark one or more" and "Select one or more."

2. Data Formats

The standards provide two formats that may be used for data on race and ethnicity. Self-reporting or self-identification using two separate questions is the preferred method for collecting data on race and ethnicity. In situations where self-reporting is not practicable or feasible, the combined format may be used.

In no case shall the provisions of the standards be construed to limit the collection of data to the categories described above. The collection of greater detail is encouraged; however, any collection that uses more detail shall be organized in such a way that the additional categories can be aggregated into these minimum categories for data on race and ethnicity. With respect to tabulation, the procedures used by Federal agencies shall result in the production of as much detailed information on race and ethnicity as possible. However, Federal agencies shall not present data on detailed categories if doing so would compromise data quality or confidentiality standards.

a. Two-question format

To provide flexibility and ensure data quality, separate questions shall be used wherever feasible for reporting race and ethnicity. When race and ethnicity are collected separately, ethnicity shall be collected first. If race and ethnicity are collected separately, the minimum designations are:

Race:
    —*American Indian or Alaska Native*
    —*Asian*
    —*Black or African American*
    —*Native Hawaiian or Other Pacific Islander*
    —*White*
Ethnicity:
    —*Hispanic or Latino*
    —*Not Hispanic or Latino*

When data on race and ethnicity are collected separately, provision shall be made to report the number of respondents in each racial category who are Hispanic or Latino.

When aggregate data are presented, data producers shall provide the number of respondents who marked (or selected) only one category, separately for each of the five racial categories. In addition to these numbers, data producers are strongly encouraged to provide the detailed distributions, including all possible combinations, of multiple responses to the race question. If data on multiple responses are collapsed, at a minimum the total number of respondents reporting "more than one race" shall be made available.

b. Combined format

The combined format may be used, if necessary, for observer-collected data on race and ethnicity. Both race (including multiple responses) and ethnicity shall be collected when appropriate and feasible, although the selection of one category in the combined format is acceptable. If a combined format is used, there are six minimum categories:

—*American Indian or Alaska Native*
—*Asian*
—*Black or African American*
—*Hispanic or Latino*
—*Native Hawaiian or Other Pacific Islander*
—*White*

When aggregate data are presented, data producers shall provide the number of respondents who marked (or selected) only one category, separately for each of the six categories. In addition to these numbers, data producers are strongly encouraged to provide the detailed distributions, including all possible combinations, of multiple responses. In cases where data on multiple responses are collapsed, the total number of respondents reporting "Hispanic or Latino and one or more races" and the total number of respondents reporting "more than one race" (regardless of ethnicity) shall be provided.

3. Use of the Standards for Record Keeping and Reporting

The minimum standard categories shall be used for reporting as follows:

a. Statistical reporting

These standards shall be used at a minimum for all federally sponsored statistical data collections that include data on race and/or ethnicity, except when the collection involves a sample of such size that the data on the smaller categories would be unreliable, or when the collection effort focuses on a specific racial or ethnic group. Any other variation will have to be specifically authorized by the Office of Management and Budget (OMB) through the information collection clearance process. In those cases where the data collection is not subject to the information collection clearance process, a direct request for a variance shall be made to OMB.

b. General program administrative and grant reporting

These standards shall be used for all Federal administrative reporting or record keeping requirements that include data on race and ethnicity. Agencies that cannot follow these standards must request a variance from OMB. Variances will be considered if the agency can demonstrate that it is not reasonable for the primary reporter to determine racial or ethnic background in terms of the specified categories, that determination of racial or ethnic background is not critical to the administration of the program in question, or that the specific program is directed to only one or a limited number of racial or ethnic groups.

c. Civil rights and other compliance reporting

These standards shall be used by all Federal agencies in either the separate or combined format for civil rights and other compliance reporting from the public and private sectors and all levels of government. Any variation requiring less detailed data or data which cannot be aggregated into the basic categories must be specifically approved by OMB for executive agencies. More detailed reporting which can be aggregated to the basic categories may be used at the agencies' discretion.

4. Presentation of Data on Race and Ethnicity

Displays of statistical, administrative, and compliance data on race and ethnicity shall use the categories listed above. The term "nonwhite" is not acceptable for use in the presentation of Federal Government data. It shall not be used in any publication or in the text of any report.

In cases where the standard categories are considered inappropriate for presentation of data on particular programs or for particular regional areas, the sponsoring agency may use:

a. The designations "Black or African American and Other Races" or "All Other Races" as collective descriptions of minority races when the most summary distinction between the majority and minority races is appropriate;
b. The designations "White," "Black or African American," and "All Other Races" when the distinction among the majority race, the principal minority race, and other races is appropriate; or
c. The designation of a particular minority race or races, and the inclusion of "Whites" with "All Other Races" when such a collective description is appropriate.

In displaying detailed information that represents a combination of race and ethnicity, the description of the data being displayed shall clearly indicate that both bases of classification are being used.

When the primary focus of a report is on two or more specific identifiable groups in the population, one or more of which is racial or ethnic, it is acceptable to display data for each of the particular groups separately and to describe data relating to the remainder of the population by an appropriate collective description.

5. Effective Date

The provisions of these standards are effective immediately for all new and revised record keeping or reporting requirements that include racial and/or ethnic information. All existing record keeping or reporting requirements shall be made consistent with these standards at the time they are submitted for extension, or not later than January 1, 2003.

Census data and background information on census questions and methods are increasingly available on the Web sites of national statistical agencies. To assist in the search for useful information, the editors have compiled the following list of sites on the census. The list was current at the time of the book's publication in July 2000. The editors attempted to choose sites that showed some degree of stability, but site addresses may change or sites may disappear altogether. The list is divided into four sections: (1) Census Information, (2) Census Bureau Sites, (3) Congressional Sites, and (4) Other Useful Sites.

SOURCE: "Revisions to the Standards for the Classification of Federal Data on Race and Ethnicity," *Federal Register* 62, no. 210 (October 30, 1997): 58782–58790.

Census on the Web

There are many avenues for finding census data and information about census procedures and data uses on the Internet. The sites below provide an entrée into these sites, starting with the Census Bureau's home page. Following the Census Bureau's sites are selected sites for other federal statistical agencies, other data portals that offer census data and services, and international sites.

U.S. Census Bureau

http://www.census.gov/

The U.S. Census Bureau home page is the starting point for finding data and information about the census.

http://factfinder2.census.gov/ (formerly http://factfinder.census.gov/)

American FactFinder is the starting point for retrieving data tabulations from the census and the American Community Survey.

http://www.census.gov/acs/www/

This starting point for working with the American Community Survey (ACS) directs the user to all aspects of the ACS, including information for respondents, the user's guide, and recent results.

http://www.census.gov/cps/

This starting point for working with the Current Population Survey directs the user to all aspects of the CPS, including information for respondents, the user's guide, and recent results.

http://www.census.gov/geo/www/reference.html

Find here resources for understanding Census Bureau geography.

http://dataferrett.census.gov/

DataFerrett is a data analysis and extraction tool with recoding capabilities to customize federal, state, and local data to suit individual analysis requirements.

http://www.census.gov/main/www/glossary.html

Census Bureau definitions and explanations of terms are available on the main glossary page.

http://www.census.gov/compendia/statab/

This site provides access to the *Statistical Abstract of the United States.*

http://www.census.gov/sdc/

The State Data Center Program is a liaison between state and local governments to disseminate census data to the public.

The main Census Bureau History pages are at http://www.census.gov/history/. A particularly rich collection of historical census publications in PDF format, including the published census volumes, is available at http://www.census.gov/prod/www/abs/decennial/index.html.

Other U.S. Government Sites with Data on the American Population

Appendix D of National Research Council, *Principles and Practices for a Federal Statistical Agency*, 4th ed, Constance F. Citro, Margaret E. Martin, and Miron L. Straf, eds., Committee on National Statistics (Washington, D.C.: The National Academies Press, 2009), http://www.nap.edu/catalog.php?record_id=12564, provides links to the statistical agencies of the federal government. The Committee on National Statistics' (CNSTAT) Web site is http://www7.nationalacademies.org/cnstat/.

Historical Data Sites

United States Historical Census Data Browser, which provides tabulated data from published census volumes, is available at http://mapserver.lib.virginia.edu/. Microdata from the population censuses from 1850 to 1880 and from 1900 to the present are available for download and tabulation at the Minnesota Population Center site, http://usa.ipums.org/usa/.

National and International Statistical Services around the World

The Census Bureau's listing of international statistical agencies is at http://www.census.gov/aboutus/stat_int.html.

Statistics Canada can be found at http://www.statcan.gc.ca/.

Mexico's central statistical agency, Instituto National de Estadística y Geografía, is at http://www.inegi.org.mx//default.aspx.

The United Nations Statistics Division is at http://unstats.un.org/unsd/default.htm.

The international Integrated Public Use Microdata Series is available at https://international.ipums.org/international/.

Glossary

Following is a selection of terms that arise frequently in discussions about the census. Far from comprehensive, this glossary nevertheless covers many of the concepts, statutes, processes, and phrases that may be unfamiliar to readers. For further detail, see U.S. Census Bureau, Definitions and Explanations of Terms, http://www.census.gov/main/www/glossary.html.

Accuracy and Coverage Evaluation (ACE). A coverage measurement method that was used to determine the number of people and housing units missed or counted more than once in Census 2000.

Address canvassing. The operation of a census employee to canvass (travel in a systematic way) assigned census blocks, looking for every place where people live, stay, or could live or stay.

Address Control File (ACF). The 1990 residential address list used to label questionnaires, control the mail response check-in operation, and determine the nonresponse follow-up workload. See also *Master Address File (MAF); Nonresponse follow-up.*

Address List Improvement Act of 1994 (P.L. 103-430). Permits local governments to receive and review the address list used to mail questionnaires before the census (first applied in the 2000 census Local Update of Census Addresses (LUCA) program, provided that reviewers sign an agreement not to disclose any information and to use the list solely for the purpose of making the census more accurate. It also allows for the transfer of address information between the U.S. Postal Service and the Census Bureau for decennial census purposes.

Address register area. A small geographic area, usually a block group or part of a block group, established by the Census Bureau as a basic unit for data collection by a single enumerator during the 1990 decennial census. Conceptually equivalent to a 1980 or earlier decennial census enumeration district.

Address register. A book used by enumerators in a census that contains the street address and related information for every housing unit and special place listed or enumerated during the census. Now called an assignment area. See also *Special place.*

Administrative geography. Areas that exist to deliver services. They are often independent of standard political geographic areas, except that they are unlikely to cross state lines. The Census Bureau published data in recent censuses for three types of administrative areas: school districts, voting districts, and zip codes.

Administrative records. Records collected and maintained by federal, state, and local agencies for the purpose of program implementation, monitoring, and administration. Examples at the federal level include tax returns, demographic and earnings records of the Social Security Administration, and immigrant information from the Office of Immigration Statistics in the U.S. Department of Homeland Security. At the state and local level, records are kept on births, deaths, marriages, and divorces (much of this for reporting to higher governmental entities), as well as on driver's licenses, on participation in programs for health and welfare, and on the size and characteristics of the housing stock. These data are useful because they can be used to check the quality of the decennial census, as a supplement to the census, or as a means of constructing population estimates and projections.

Advance census report. An unaddressed short-form census questionnaire with respondent instructions delivered by the U.S. Postal Service to housing units in sparsely populated areas. The respondent completes the questionnaire and retains it for pickup by an enumerator.

Advisory committee. A committee of members of the public who meet occasionally to give advice to the Census Bureau. The members may come from stakeholder groups, professional organizations, or state and local government. Examples include the Commerce Secretary's 2000 Census Advisory Committee and the American Statistical Association/American Economic Association Census Advisory Committee.

Age heaping. The tendency of people to report their age in censuses and surveys in round numbers, particularly numbers ending in 0 or 5.

American FactFinder (AFF). The Census Bureau's electronic system for access and dissemination of data on the Internet. The system offers prepackaged data products and the ability to build user-selected tables and maps. (http://factfinder.census.gov/)

Apportionment. The process of dividing up the 435 memberships, or seats, in the House of Representatives among the fifty states.

"Be Counted" program. Program to provide a means for people who believed they were not counted to be included in the enumeration. The Census Bureau placed unaddressed census questionnaires ("Be Counted" questionnaires) at selected sites that were easily accessible to and frequented by large numbers of people. The questionnaires also were distributed by the Questionnaire Assistance Centers and in response to requests received through Telephone Questionnaire Assistance.

Block group. A combination of census blocks that is a subdivision of a census tract or block numbering area (BNA). A block group consists of all blocks whose numbers begin with the same digit in a given census tract or BNA. The block group is the lowest level of geography for which the Census Bureau has tabulated sample data. All areas had block groups beginning with the 1990 census.

Block numbering area. An area delineated by state officials or the Census Bureau for the purpose of grouping and numbering decennial census blocks in counties or statistically equivalent entities in which census tracts have not been established. Thus, a BNA is equivalent to a census tract in the Census Bureau's geographic hierarchy.

Census 2000 Supplementary Survey (C2SS). Operational test conducted as part of the 2000 census. It used the American Community Survey questionnaire to collect demographic, social, economic, and housing data from a national sample. The survey was used to test the operational feasibility of converting from the long-form sample to the American Community Survey.

Census block. The smallest entity for which the Census Bureau collects and tabulates decennial census information; bounded on all sides by visible and nonvisible features shown on Census Bureau maps. Occasionally, especially in rural areas, drainage ditches or power lines may be used to define blocks. Because most blocks have small population and housing unit counts, only 100-percent data, or short-form data, are tabulated for them. See also *Short form*.

Census briefs. Short documents providing findings from the census, current demographic surveys, and the economic census. They contain colorful charts to illustrate major points.

Census day. Since 1930, April 1 of years ending in zero.

Census designated place. A statistical area defined for a census as a densely settled concentration of population that is not incorporated but that resembles an incorporated place in that it can be identified with a name. See also *Incorporated place*.

Census feature class code. An alphanumeric code that uniquely identifies the basic characteristics of a map feature in the Census Bureau's TIGER file. See also *TIGER (Topologically Integrated Geographic Encoding and Referencing System)*.

Census in Schools. Census Bureau program to distribute instructional materials about the decennial census to school administrators, teachers, and children.

Census tract. Small, relatively permanent statistical subdivision of a county or equivalent entity that is updated by local participants prior to each decennial census as part of the Census Bureau's Participant Statistical Areas Program (or by the Census Bureau in situations where no local participant existed or where state, local, or tribal governments declined to participate). The primary purpose of census tracts is to provide a stable set of geographic units for the presentation of statistical data. Census tracts generally have a population size between 1,200 and 8,000 people, with an optimum size of 4,000 people. See also *Metropolitan Area*.

Census Transportation Planning Package (CTPP). Aggregate data on the number and characteristics of workers obtained from the long-form sample and presented for the full hierarchy of census geography down to the traffic analysis zone (TAZ) level (a TAZ is usually one or more blocks, block groups, or census tracts) and organized as summary files. Files from the CTPP in 2000 (and in earlier censuses back to 1970) were created through a cooperative effort that included federal, state, and local transportation agencies. While data for 1990 and 2000 are available for all areas of the nation, earlier data were available only for selected areas, based on contractual agreements with local groups of transportation officials. These files are unique in that they provide users with data on workers (as opposed to residents) for small areas and, as such, are used extensively by local planning organizations. CTPP products are being produced from the American Community Survey one-year, three-year, and five-year estimates.

Computer assisted interviewing (CAI). A group of methods for using computers to assist with data collection. CAI surveys can be either interviewer-administered (conducted in person using a laptop computer or by telephone using a shared computer) or self-administered (conducted using surveys disseminated to respondents by telephone, by the Internet, or on a computer disk).

Count Question Resolution (CQR). Census Bureau process whereby state, local, and tribal government officials may ask the Census Bureau to verify the accuracy of the legal boundaries used for the census, the geographic allocation of living quarters and their residents in relation to those boundaries, and the accuracy of the count of people recorded by the Census Bureau for specific living quarters.

Coverage evaluation. Statistical studies conducted to evaluate the level and sources of coverage error in censuses and surveys.

Current Population Survey. Monthly sample survey of the U.S. population that provides employment and unemployment figures as well as current data about other social and economic characteristics of the population. Collected for the Bureau of Labor Statistics by the Census Bureau.

Data capture. The process by which survey responses are transferred from written questionnaires to an electronic format for tabulation. Currently done by optical scanning; from 1960 to 1990, by FOSDIC; from 1890 to 1950, using punch cards. See also *FOSDIC*.

DataFerrett. Census Bureau data analysis and extraction tool with recoding capabilities to customize federal, state, and local data to suit user requirements. FERRETT stands for Federated Electronic Research, Review, Extraction, and Tabulation Tool. (http://dataferrett.census.gov/)

Delivery Sequence File. U.S. Postal Service (USPS) computer file containing all mailing addresses serviced by the USPS. The USPS continuously updates the DSF as its letter carriers identify addresses for new delivery points and changes in the status of existing addresses. The Census Bureau uses the DSF as a source for maintaining and updating its Master Address File.

Disclosure Review Board. Internal Census Bureau committee that sets the confidentiality rules for all data product releases. A checklist approach is used to ensure that potential risks to the confidentiality of the data are considered and addressed before any data are released.

Enumeration district. A geographic area, often used as a work unit or unit of measure, into which counties are divided for the purpose of taking a census. Enumeration districts (also referred to as enumeration areas) were replaced with address register areas as the data collection units in the 1990 census and with block groups for data tabulation. See also *Address register; Block group*.

Enumerator. A census field operations employee. A person who collects information by interviewing.

Erroneous enumeration. A person counted incorrectly in the census, for example, because the person is counted more than once or because the person is counted at the wrong location, according to census residence rules. A college student living in a dormitory away from home on April 1 would be an erroneous enumeration if the student was listed on the questionnaire as a resident of the parental home. See also *Omission; Overcount; Undercount.*

Federal Depository Library Program. A cooperative venture between the U.S. Government Printing Office (GPO) and America's library community, the purpose of which is to make government information readily accessible to the general public at no cost to the user. Under the provisions of the program, the GPO provides participating libraries with publications and databases at no charge; in exchange, the libraries agree to provide the public with access to these materials.

Follow-up. A secondary census or survey operation, predominantly in data collection, carried out to successfully complete an initial operation. It is most often a telephone or personal visit interview to obtain missing data or clarify original responses.

FOSDIC (Film Optical Sensing Device for Input to Computers). From 1960 to 1990, census questionnaires were microfilmed. The answers were read from the microfilmed questionnaires using FOSDIC and converted to electronic codes in computer tape format.

Geographic center of area of the United States. The point at which the surface of the United States would balance if it were a plane of uniform weight per unit of area. In early 2000 that point fell in Butte County, South Dakota, as it has since the 1960 census, after Alaska and Hawaii became states. The geographic center of the coterminous United States (forty-eight states and the District of Columbia) is in Smith County, Kansas.

Geographic information systems (GIS). Electronic systems designed to capture, store, manipulate, analyze, manage, and present geographically referenced data, merging the tools of cartography, statistical analysis, and database technology.

Geographic tabulation unit base. A geographic record containing a unique combination of geographic codes. It is the smallest unique area required for tabulation purposes above the block group level. See also *Block group.*

Gross error. The sum of the erroneous enumerations and the omissions in the census. See also *Erroneous enumeration; Omission; Overcount; Undercount.*

Group quarters. A place where people live that is not a housing unit. There are two types of group quarters: institutional (for example, nursing homes, mental hospitals, and correctional institutions) and noninstitutional (for example, college dormitories, ships, hotels, group homes, and shelters).

Handheld computer (HHC). A small electronic device used by Census Bureau field staff to conduct address listing in the 2010 census.

Hard-to-count areas. An area designated by the Census Bureau for which the environment or population may present difficulties for enumeration.

Housing unit. A house; apartment; mobile home or trailer; group of rooms or single room occupied as a separate living quarters or, if vacant, intended for occupancy as a separate living quarters. The definition of separate living quarters for the 2000 and 2010 censuses was that the occupants live separately from any other individuals in the building and have direct access from outside the building or through a common hall. Additional criteria, such as the presence of a kitchen or cooking equipment for the exclusive use of the occupants, were used to define a housing unit in previous censuses.

Impute. To assign answers to questions with missing responses on the basis of information from other respondents. Sometimes people are added to the census count by imputation.

Incorporated place. Legally recognized entities. Naming conventions vary by state; some of the terms commonly used are *city, village, borough,* and *town.* More than one term may be used in a given state.

Integrated coverage measurement. A coverage measurement technique that combines estimates of missed persons with enumeration results before producing a single set of official census results.

Integrated Public Use Microdata Series (IPUMS). A coherent individual-level national database that describes the characteristics of the American population in census years spanning the period from 1850 through 2000 and each year of the ACS. It combines nationally representative probability samples produced by the Census Bureau for the period since 1940 with new high-precision historical samples produced at the University of Minnesota and elsewhere. See also *Public Use Microdata Sample (PUMS).*

List/enumerate. A method of enumeration in which enumerators canvass a geographic area, list each residential address, and collect a questionnaire from or enumerate the household.

List/leave. A method of enumeration in which enumerators list each residential address and at the same time deliver the census forms for return by mail.

Local census office (LCO). A temporary office established for decennial census data collection purposes. These offices manage address listing field work, conduct local recruiting, and visit living quarters that have not returned questionnaires in the mail.

Local Update of Census Addresses (LUCA). A product of the Address List Improvement Act of 1994, this program was established to elicit review and feedback from representatives of local and tribal governments on the bureau-compiled address list for the 2000 census. It was used again for the 2010 census.

Long form. The decennial census questionnaire containing 100-percent (short form) and sample questions, used for the censuses from 1960 to 2000. Sent to a sample of addresses in the census, long forms typically contain the short-form person and housing items that all households are asked to provide, together with additional items that only the households in the long-form sample are asked to provide. Whereas short-form items are generally limited to basic demographic and housing questions, long-form items cover such topics as income, employment, veteran status, transportation to work, education, and others. These data are currently collected on the American Community Survey.

Mailout/mailback. Descriptive of the enumeration method in which the U.S. Postal Service delivers decennial census questionnaires to specific addresses and the respondents mail them back to the district office or processing office for processing. Mailout/mailback is the primary method of data collection for U.S. censuses today.

Master Address File (MAF). The Census Bureau's permanent list of addresses for individual living quarters, which is linked to the TIGER database. The MAF is updated by the Census Bureau on a regular basis using information from the U.S. Postal Service and other sources. While the MAF serves as the source of addresses for the decennial census, a sample of addresses is taken from the MAF each year as the basis for the American Community Survey (ACS). See also *TIGER (Topologically Integrated Geographic Encoding and Referencing System)*.

Median center of population. The intersection of two median lines: one a north-south line (a meridian of longitude) chosen so that half the population lives east of it and half west, and the other an east-west line (a parallel of latitude) selected so that half the population lives north of it and half south. The median center of population for the 2010 census was near Petersburg, Indiana.

Metropolitan Area (MA). A collective term established by the U.S. Office of Management and Budget (OMB) to refer to Metropolitan Statistical Areas, consolidated Metropolitan Areas, New England county Metropolitan Areas, and primary Metropolitan Statistical Areas. The OMB designates MAs based on the concept of functional integration between core and periphery areas, using data on commuting. In most areas of the nation (for example, outside of New England), MAs are composed of whole counties.

Metropolitan Statistical Area (MSA). Office of Management and Budget–designated statistical area associated with at least one urbanized area that has a population of at least 50,000. The Metropolitan Statistical Area comprises the central county or counties containing the core, plus adjacent outlying counties having a high degree of social and economic integration with the central county or counties as measured through commuting.

Microdata. Information contained in the individual unit records for each member of the population or establishment covered by a census or survey.

Micropolitan Statistical Area. Office of Management and Budget–designated statistical area associated with at least one urban cluster that has a population of at least 10,000 but less than 50,000. The Micropolitan Statistical Area comprises the central county or counties containing the core, plus adjacent outlying counties having a high degree of social and economic integration with the central county or counties as measured through commuting.

Multi-year estimates. Estimates of survey results created by combining data from more than one year of data collection to produce the estimate. The American Community Survey provides estimates for three-year and five-year periods.

National Content Test. Mail survey of a large sample of housing units conducted several years before the census. A national content test is used to test alternative question wording and the feasibility of including proposed new or modified questions.

Nonresponse follow-up. A decennial census operation in which enumerators visit addresses from which no questionnaires have been returned by mail.

Nonsampling error. An error that occurs during the measuring or data collection process. Nonsampling errors can yield biased results when most of the errors distort the results in the same direction.

Numident file. Also known as the SSA Numident file, the Numident contains data collected from applications for Social Security numbers and replacement cards as well as applications to change the name associated with a previously issued number. Data recorded on the Numident include the Social Security number, date of birth, sex, race, Hispanic origin, country of birth, and all names associated with that number.

Omission. A person missed in the census. See also *Erroneous enumeration; Overcount; Undercount*.

Optical character recognition (OCR). Technology that uses an optical scanner and computer software to "read" human handwriting and convert it into electronic form.

Optical mark recognition (OMR). Technology that uses an optical scanner and computer software to scan a page, recognize the presence of marks in predesignated areas, and assign a value to the mark depending on its specific location and intensity on a page.

Overcount. The total number of people counted more than once or otherwise enumerated erroneously in the census. See also *Erroneous enumeration; Omission; Undercount*.

Paper-based operations control system (PBOCS). Census Bureau system for managing the workflow and staff for paper operations and the related quality activities. It was used by regional census centers, local census offices, and headquarters during the 2010 enumeration.

P.L. 94-171. The public law that requires the Census Bureau to provide the decennial census data required for congressional redistricting to the states by April of the year following the year of the census enumeration.

Political geography. Geographic areas that are defined in law and in which, usually, the government is run by elected officials. The most common political geographic areas are states, counties, and county subdivisions.

Post-enumeration survey (PES). A coverage measurement survey that is conducted several months after the April census date and is designed to identify the number of people missed, counted twice, or counted at the wrong location. From the results of the survey, the Census Bureau calculates corrected population counts for the nation and geographic areas.

Poststratum/poststrata. Data cohort(s) or grouping(s) of people for use in census evaluation studies, particularly to measure undercount, for example, all white, non-Hispanic male renters ages 18–22 in a rural area or all white, Hispanic male renters ages 18–22 in a rural area.

Public Use Microdata Area (PUMA). Geographic entity for which the Census Bureau issues census and American Community Survey tabulations that is included as an identifying code on individual records in Public Use Microdata Samples. PUMAs have a minimum census population of 100,000 and cannot cross a state line. PUMAs are aggregated into "super-PUMAs," which must have a minimum census population of 400,000.

Public Use Microdata Samples (PUMS). Computerized files containing a sample of individual census long-form or American Community Survey records showing most population and housing characteristics. See also *Integrated Public Use Microdata Series (IPUMS)*.

Redistricting. The process of redrawing congressional, state legislative, and local political boundaries every ten years using population counts provided to the states by the Census Bureau.

Research Data Center (RDC) program. National network of research sites administered by the U.S. Census Bureau's Center for Economics Studies (CES) that permits authorized researchers to access confidential census microdata for research. The objective of the RDC is to increase the utility and quality of the Census Bureau data products by conducting, facilitating, and supporting microdata research.

Response rate. The percentage of housing units for which the Census Bureau received completed questionnaires for an area. The numerator includes responses from the following sources: mailed-in questionnaires (including responses from mailout/mailback, update/leave, and urban update/leave areas and the "Be Counted" program), responses collected from Telephone Questionnaire Assistance, and Internet responses. The denominator represents the total number of housing unit identification numbers (a code assigned to each unique address) from the mailout/mailback, update/leave, and urban update/leave universes.

Return rate. The total number of households returning a questionnaire by mail divided by the number of occupied housing units that received a questionnaire by mail or from a census enumerator (the only units that can return a questionnaire). This measure cannot be derived until the enumeration is completed and the final number of occupied housing units is determined.

Schedule. Also called forms or returns, schedules are the questionnaires, listing individuals by name, that are filled out by census takers.

Service-based enumeration (SBE). Data collection method to count people at facilities that primarily serve people without conventional housing. These facilities include emergency or transitional shelters, soup kitchens, and regularly scheduled mobile food van stops. In addition, service-based enumeration counts people at targeted nonsheltered outdoor locations where people might have been living in March (before census day, April 1) without paying to stay there and who did not usually receive services at soup kitchens, shelters, or mobile food vans. These facilities and locations need special procedures separate from the group quarters enumeration.

Shelter and Street Night. An enumeration conducted before Census Day in which enumerators visit shelters, missions, and any other areas where emergency housing has been set up to enumerate each resident. Enumerators also visit pre-identified street locations to enumerate those people living on the street.

Short form. The decennial census questionnaire requesting basic demographic and housing information. See also *Long form*.

Simplified questionnaire test. A test conducted in 1992 to determine the effects of form length, respondent-friendly construction, and a request for the respondent's Social Security number on mail responses.

Source and Accuracy Statement. Published by the Census Bureau with each survey, this statement documents the level of sampling error and its impact on survey-based estimates. Typically, estimates are provided with a variety of statistics that indicate the estimates' degree of uncertainty, such as confidence intervals or standard errors, and are suppressed from publication if deemed unreliable based on these measures.

Special census. A federal census conducted at the request and cost of a local government to obtain population figures between decennial censuses.

Special place. A place where people live or stay that is different from the usual private house, apartment, or mobile home and that requires different decennial census procedures. Examples are hospitals, prisons, hotels, motels, orphanages, nursing homes, dormitories, marinas, military installations, and large rooming or boarding houses. See also *Group quarters*.

State Data Center. A state agency or university research center that acquires Census Bureau data products through a special cooperative agreement and disseminates these data to clientele through a network of statewide affiliate agencies and organizations.

State economic area. A single county or group of counties within a state that have similar economic and social characteristics as determined by various governmental agencies.

Statistical Administrative Records System (StARS). U.S. Census Bureau research project designed to build annual databases of personal and address data using administrative records from various government agencies for use for statistical purposes by the Census Bureau only. StARS will be used to evaluate the 2010 census.

Statistical geography. Geographic areas, such as census tracts, created expressly for aggregation and presentation of data.

Summary Tape Files. Tabulations of decennial census complete count and sample population and housing data presented as aggregates for a hierarchy of geographic areas ranging in size from census blocks to totals for the nation and regions. Summary Tape Files are also produced from the American Community Survey (block groups are the lowest level of tabulation provided).

Survey of Income and Program Participation (SIPP). A continuing longitudinal survey that obtains detailed information about sources and amounts of income, participation in public and private transfer programs, asset holdings, and related topics. The survey follows members of originally sampled households over time with interviews every four months; a new sample (panel) is introduced periodically. Since the beginning of SIPP in 1983, the number of interviews and the sample size for each panel have varied, as has the frequency with which a new sample is introduced.

TIGER (Topologically Integrated Geographic Encoding and Referencing) system. A computer database that contains all census-required map features and attributes for the United States and its possessions, plus the specifications, procedures, computer programs, and related input materials required to build and use it.

Title 13 of the United States Code. Originally enacted in 1954, the law under which the Census Bureau operates. It also protects the confidentiality of census information and establishes penalties for disclosing this information.

Top-coding/bottom-coding. The practice of limiting the publication of detail by combining responses from the top or the bottom of a distribution. A top-code for a variable is an upper limit on all published values of that variable. Any value greater than this upper limit is replaced by the upper limit or is not published on the microdata file at all. A bottom-code is a lower limit on all published values for a variable. The practice is often used to prevent disclosure of information on individual respondents. Income is often top-coded to prevent the identification of high earners in a data set.

Undercount. The total number of people missed in the census. The difference between the overcount and the undercount is the net undercount. See also *Erroneous enumeration; Omission; Overcount; Undercount.*

UNIVAC (UNIVersal Automatic Calculator). The first nondefense computer, UNIVAC was developed by the Census Bureau in conjunction with the National Bureau of Standards (now the National Institute of Standards and Technology) and the Eckert-Mauchly Computer Corporation in the late 1940s. The first UNIVAC was delivered to the Census Bureau's Data Tabulation Office in Philadelphia on March 31, 1951. Initially, UNIVAC sped up the tabulation process and increased the capacity for more elaborate data tabulations.

Update/Enumerate (U/E). A method of data collection conducted in communities with special enumeration needs and where many housing units may not have house-number-and-street-name mailing addresses. Enumerators canvass assignment areas to update residential addresses, including adding living quarters not included on the address listing pages, update Census Bureau maps, and complete a questionnaire for each housing unit.

Update/Leave. A method of enumeration in which the enumerators deliver decennial census forms for return by mail and at the same time update the census mailing list.

Urbanized Area. An area identified by the Census Bureau that contains a central place surrounded by a closely settled incorporated and unincorporated area. An urbanized area has a combined population of at least 50,000.

ZIP Code Tabulation Area (ZCTA). A statistical entity developed by the Census Bureau to approximate the delivery area for a U.S. Postal Service five-digit ZIP code, based on the residential mailing addresses in the Census Bureau's Master Address File. ZCTAs are aggregations of census blocks that have the same predominant ZIP code associated with their addresses.

INDEX

Bold topic and page numbers indicate primary treatment of a subject. Figures, maps, and tables are indicated by f, m, and t following page numbers.